PHL

D1582611

THE
PAUL HAMLYN
LIBRARY

DONATED BY
THE PAUL HAMLYN
FOUNDATION
TO THE
BRITISH MUSEUM

opened December 2000

THE FLAG FEN BASIN

*Archaeology and environment of a
Fenland landscape*

Dedication

To the memory of two departed friends,
Jenny Coombs and Robert Kiln

THE FLAG FEN BASIN

*Archaeology and environment of a
Fenland landscape*

Francis Pryor

with major contributions by
J C Barrett, S D Bridgeford, D G Buckley, D G Coombs, C Evans,
C A I French, P Halstead, J Neve, J P Northover, M Robinson,
R G Scaife, and M Taylor

and principal illustrations by
J Coombs, D Hopkins, and C J Irons

ENGLISH HERITAGE

2001

ARCHAEOLOGICAL REPORTS

Copyright © English Heritage 2001

Published by English Heritage at the National Monuments Record Centre,
Great Western Village, Kemble Drive, Swindon SN2 2GZ

ISBN 1 85074 753 9
Product Code XA 20013

A CIP catalogue record for this book is available from
the British Library

All rights reserved
No part of this publication may be reproduced or transmitted in any form
or by any means, electronic or mechanical, including photocopying, recording
or any information storage and retrieval system, without permission in writing
from the publisher.

Text edited by Mike Ponsford
Design and layout: Val Kinsler, 100% Proof
Edited and brought to press by David M Jones and Andrew McLaren, Publications, English Heritage
Indexed by Susanne Atkin

Printed by Snoeck-Ducaju & Zoon, Ghent

936.2651 PRY

Contents

Figures vii
Tables xiii
Contributors xv
Acknowledgements xvi
Summary xviii
Résumé xx
Zusammenfassung xxii

1   Introduction: The Flag Fen Basin
A summary of the principal archaeological features . 1
The distribution of archaeological subsites
        and trenches 3
Flag Fen Basin in its Fenland setting 3
The scope and purpose of the report 6
A brief guide to the report 7
Grid references 7
A summary of published research 7
Continuing research: the Northey Landfall Project 10
Changing interpretations: the role of ritual 10
Conservation and preservation 11

2   Recent research in south Fengate
by Christopher Evans and Francis Pryor
The Depot site 18
Soil micromorphological analysis
        by C A I French and H Lewis 20
Principal results 22
The dating of the Storey's Bar Road fields
        reconsidered *by C Evans and J Pollard* 25
Discussion 26
The 1997 excavations 27
Third Drove excavations: Site O 30
Off-terrace investigations 32
The Boongate Roundabout 32
The Tower works 33
Third Drove excavations: Site Q 50

3   Recent research in central and north Fengate
The Global Doors site 37
The Paving Factory Site 37
The 1990 excavations at Cat's Water 38
Soil micromorphological analysis *by C A I French* . 39
The 1997 excavations 47

4   The Power Station excavations, 1989
The site in its setting 52
The circumstances of the excavations 52
Areas excavated and site grids 52
Soil micromorphology *by C A I French* 53
The excavations 58

5   Excavation and survey at Northey, 1982–94
Geographical setting 74
Previous work in the region 74
Neolithic and Bronze Age 75
Discussion 80

6   Excavations at Flag Fen 1982–95
Trial trenches and other exposures 81
Methods and techniques 93
A note on levels 93
Post-depositional effects 94
The subdivisions of Area 6 95
The posts of the alignment 95
Area 6: level-by-level analysis 96
Level 1 97
Level 2 112
Level 3 121
Level 4 131
Levels 5 and 6 140
Area 6: excavation of the post rows 152
Discussion 157

7   The wood *by Maisie Taylor*
The waterlogged wood: sampling and
        taphonomy 167
The Flag Fen wood assemblage 171
The Power Station wood assemblage 186
The waterlogged wood: woodworking 202
Joints 203
The waterlogged wood: artefacts 212

8   Tree-ring studies *by Janet Neve with Cathy Groves*
The Flag Fen and Power Station dendrochronology
        by Cathy Groves 229
Dendrochronology of the Flag Fen Basin
        by Janet Neve 232

**9   Prehistoric pottery from the Power Station
and Flag Fen** *by J C Barrett*
The problem 249
The assemblage 249

10 Metalwork
by David Coombs
Catalogue 255
Discussion: Iron Age 292
Analysis of the metalwork
        by B M Rohl and J P Northover 298
Metallographic examination of a socketed ferrous
        axehead from the Power Station
        by Vanessa Fell and Chris Salter 309
Late Bronze Age Swords and Spears from the Power
        Station and Flag Fen *by S D Bridgeford* 309

11 Finds of flint, stone, and shale
Flint 318
Stone 321
A note on the petrology of the Power Station
        stone axe fragments *by D F Williams* 321
Shale 322
The saddle querns from Flag Fen
        by D G Buckley and C J Ingle 322

Report on the examination of four Bronze Age
   quernstones from Flag Fen
      by A P Middleton and S G E Bowman 328

**12 Non-human and human mammalian bone
remains from the Flag Fen platform and Power
Station post alignment**
by Paul Halstead, Ellen Cameron, and Stephen Forbes
Methods of analysis 330
Formation of the assemblage: recovery, attrition
   and discard 343
The nature of the animals discarded 348
Conclusion 349

13 Flag Fen: the vegetation and environment
by Robert G Scaife
Aims and methodology 351
Pollen analytical methodology 351
Plant macrofossil analyses 352
The pollen data 352
Flag Fen: the changing environs 378
The Flag Fen Basin development:
   a summary 380
Terrestrial vegetation of the environment around
   Flag Fen: a summary 381

**14 Soils and sediments: the Flag Fen environs
survey**
by C A I French
Description 382
Interpretation 382
Conclusions 383

15 Late Bronze Age Coleoptera from Flag Fen
by Mark Robinson
Results 384

16 Radiocarbon and absolute chronology
by Alex Bayliss and Francis Pryor
Radiocarbon analysis 390

**17 The development of the prehistoric land-
scape in the Flag Fen Basin** *by C A I French*
Third millennium BC 400
Earlier second millennium BC 400
The later second millennium BC 401
The first millennium BC 402
The Roman and later periods 403
Conclusions 404

**18 Discussion, part 1: patterns of settlement
and land-use**
Definitions 405
The nature of prehistoric landscape change 405
Landscape 1: the earlier Neolithic 406
Landscape 2: the later Neolithic 407
Landscape 3: the Bronze Age 408
Landscape 4: the earliest Iron Age 413
Landscape 5: Middle Iron Age to Roman 413

19 Discussion, part 2: the Flag Fen timber structures
Dates and phasing 421

**Appendix 1 Detailed soil micromorphological
descriptions of samples from the Depot and
Cat's Water sites, Fengate** *by C A I French* 437
**Appendix 2 Detailed soil micromorphological
descriptions of samples from the Power Station
site** *by C A I French* 445
**Appendix 3 Concordance list of published and
archive trench designations** 448
**Appendix 4 Thin section descriptions of the
quernstone samples**
by A P Middleton and S G E Bowman 449
**Appendix 5 Detailed soil micromorphological
descriptions of the Flag fen environs**
by C A I French 450

Bibliography 451

Index 464

Figures

Fig 1.1   Location map of Flag Fen. 1
Fig 1.2   Flag Fen in its Fenland settings 2
Fig 1.3   Map of the Flag Fen region showing later
           prehistoric topography in outline 3
Fig 1.4   Map showing the location of principal
           Neolithic and Bronze Age features 4
Fig 1.5   Map showing location of areas
           excavated 1968–97 5
Fig 1.6   Map of Fengate showing the location of
           excavations that have taken place since
           the ROM/DoE project of 1971–8 8
Fig 1.7   Schematic section from Fengate to
           the Flag Fen timber platform 9
Fig 1.8   Flag Fen excavations 1982–93 and plan
           of visitor centre, lake, and pond. 12
Fig 1.9   Inserting the polythene membrane
           through the bund 13
Fig 1.10   Schematic section to show how water
           is retained within the Flag Fen mere. . . . 13
Fig 1.11   The artificial mere shortly after its
           initial flooding. 14
Fig 1.12   Visitor centre foundations, stage 1. 15
Fig 1.13   Visitor centre foundations, stage 2. 15
Fig 1.14   Visitor centre foundations, stage 3. 15
Fig 1.15   Visitor centre foundations, stage 4. 15
Fig 1.16   Visitor centre foundations, stage 5. 15
Fig 1.17   Visitor centre foundations, stage 6. 16
Fig 1.18   Visitor centre foundations, stage 7. 16
Fig 2.1   Aerial view of the Depot site from
           the south-east 17
Fig 2.2   The Depot site (1992): cropmark plan . . 18
Fig 2.3   The Depot site (1992): trench
           location plan 19
Fig 2.4   The Depot site (1992): general plan
           of Neolithic and Bronze Age features . . . 20
Fig 2.5   The Depot site (1992): plan of the
           Late Bronze Age/Early Iron Age
           settlement compound 21
Fig 2.6   The Depot site (1992): general plan of
           Iron Age and Roman features. 22
Fig 2.7   The Depot site (1992): the west end
           of Trench 3 23
Fig 2.8   The Depot site (1992): view looking
           north across Trench 4 24
Fig 2.9   The Depot site (1997) plan of
           trial trench. 28
Fig 2.10   Sites O and Q: location of trenches
           (after Cuttler 1998) 30
Fig 2.11   Site O: rim sherd of Collared Urn
           and perforated clay weight from the
           small pit F120. 31
Fig 2.12   Site O, Area 1: pit F120 31
Fig 2.13   Boongate Roundabout excavations
           (1995). 33
Fig 2.14   The Tower Works site: subsoil contours
           and trench location plan 34

Fig 2.15   The Tower Works site: possible
           post-built structure in Trench E 35
Fig 3.1   Map showing location of Global
           Doors (1993) and Paving Factory
           (1994) sites 37
Fig 3.2   Plan and sections of the Bronze Age
           linear ditch found at the Global
           Doors site (1993) 38
Fig 3.3   Cat's Water excavation (1974–90):
           general plan. 39
Fig 3.4   Cat's Water excavation (1990): plan
           of features in Area 1. 40
Fig 3.5   Cat's Water excavation (1990):
           Area 1, ditch 3 (F122), section 2. 43
Fig 3.6   Cat's Water excavation (1990):
           Area 1, ditch 3 (F121) section 5 43
Fig 3.7   Cat's Water excavation (1990):
           Area 1, ditch 4 (F121), section 10 43
Fig 3.8   Cat's Water excavation (1990): plan
           of features in Area 2. 44
Fig 3.9   Cat's Water excavation (1990): plan
           of features in the south part of Area 2 . . 45
Fig 3.10   Cat's Water excavation (1990): Area 2,
           general view of ring-ditch, looking west . 46
Fig 3.11   Cat's Water excavation (1990):
           Area 2, ring-ditch, section 6. 46
Fig 3.12   Cat's Water excavations (1997):
           trench location plan 48
Fig 3.13   Cat's Water excavations (1997): plan
           of features comprising Structure 1. 49
Fig 4.1   Power Station excavations (1989):
           general plan. . . . . between pages 52–3
Fig 4.2   Power Station excavations (1989):
           section through the Fen Causeway 53
Fig 4.3   Power Station excavations (1989):
           western portion of Area 1. 54
Fig 4.4   Power Station excavations (1989):
           central portion of Area 1. 55
Fig 4.5   Power Station excavations (1989):
           eastern portion of Area 1 56
Fig 4.6   Power Station excavations (1989):
           ditch 8, section 1 60
Fig 4.7   Power Station excavations (1989):
           ditch 8, section 4 61
Fig 4.8   Power Station excavations (1989):
           ditch 8, section 5 61
Fig 4.9   Power Station excavations (1989): the
           ditch F12, section 20. 62
Fig 4.10   Power Station excavations (1989): Area
           1, trench B. Plan of wood in level 1 . . . 63
Fig 4.11   Power Station excavations (1989): Area
           1, trench B. Plan of wood in level 2 . . . 64
Fig 4.12   Power Station excavations (1989): Area
           1, trench B. Plan of wood in level 1 . . . 65
Fig 4.13   Power Station excavations (1989): Area
           1, trench B. Plan of wood in level 2 . . . 66

Fig 4.14 Power Station excavations (1989): first exposure of posts in trench G 67

Fig 4.15 Power Station excavations (1989): Area 1, trench A. Plan of wood in level 1 . . . . between pages 66–7

Fig 4.16 Power Station excavations (1989): Area 1, plan of wood in level 1, trench D 68

Fig 4.17 Power Station excavations (1989): general view of wood in level 1, trench D 69

Fig 4.18 Power Station excavations (1989): brushwood filling an earlier shallow ditch 69

Fig 4.19 Power Station excavations (1989): close-up of brushwood filling an earlier ditch 70

Fig 4.20 Power Station excavations (1989): sketch plan of dog bones around post . . . 70

Fig 4.21 Power Station excavations (1989): view of dog bones around post, looking south . . 70

Fig 4.22 Power Station excavations (1989): outline sections of the large pit F87 71

Fig 4.23 Power Station excavations (1989): plan showing features around pit F87 . . . . between pages 72–3

Fig 4.24 Power Station excavations (1989): profiles of small pits associated with F87 73

Fig 5.1 Northey: map showing course of the Fen Causeway Roman road 74

Fig 5.2 Northey: cropmarks of probable Iron Age date 75

Fig 5.3 Northey: cropmarks east of Northey Road 76

Fig 5.4 Northey: cropmarks east of Northey Road 77

Fig 5.5 Northey: cropmarks of probable Bronze Age and Neolithic date 78

Fig 5.6 Northey: plan of Trial Trench 1 with section through possible barrow ditch . . . 79

Fig 5.7 Northey: plan of Trial Trench 2 with sections through the droveway ditches . . 79

Fig 6.1 Flag Fen excavations (1982–93): location of trenches 82

Fig 6.2 Flag Fen, Area 1: plan of wood exposed prior to construction of the water main 83

Fig 6.3 Flag Fen, Area 2: plan of wood in Levels 1 (above) and 2/3 (below) 83

Fig 6.4 Flag Fen, Area 2: general view of wood in Level 1, looking north 84

Fig 6.5 Flag Fen, Area 3: trial trench to select area for new visitor centre 84

Fig 6.6 Flag Fen, Area 4: security trench around island in lake: plan of posts 85

Fig 6.7 Flag Fen, Area 4: general view of post tops (possibly Rows 3 or 4) 86

Fig 6.8 Flag Fen, Area 4: close-up of post tops . 86

Fig 6.9 Flag Fen (1982): the Mustdyke dykeside exposure . . . . between pages 86–7

Fig 6.10 Flag Fen, Area 5: plan of wood in Levels 1 and 2 87

Fig 6.11 Flag Fen, Area 5: general view of wood in Level 1 87

Fig 6.12 Flag Fen, Area 5: plan of wood in Levels 3 and 5 88

Fig 6.13 Flag Fen, Area 7: plan of first exposure of wood in trench immediately east of the Mustdyke 89

Fig 6.14 Flag Fen, Area 8: highest level of wood exposed in excavations of 1993 90

Fig 6.15 Flag Fen, Area 6A, techniques of excavation: general view of excavations within temporary shelter, 1986 season 91

Fig 6.16 Flag Fen, Area 6, techniques of excavation: exposing timbers of Level 1 . 92

Fig 6.17 Flag Fen, Area 6, techniques of excavation: working above the wood using planks supported on trapped blocks 93

Fig 6.18 Flag Fen, Area 6B, techniques of excavation: general view of excavations within permanent shelter, 1987 season. A tour is in progress 94

Fig 6.19 Flag Fen: plan of numbered uprights in Area 6 . . . . between pages 96–7

Fig 6.20 Flag Fen, Areas 6A, 6B, and 6D: general plan of wood exposed in Level 1 . . . . between pages 96–7

Fig 6.21 Flag Fen, Area 6A, Level 1 . . . . between pages 96–7

Fig 6.22 Flag Fen, Area 6A, Levels 1 and 2, south-east end of trench 97

Fig 6.23 Flag Fen, Area 6B, Level 1: general plan 98

Fig 6.24 Flag Fen, Area 6B, Level 1: photomontage of south-west part of the excavations 99

Fig 6.25 Flag Fen, Area 6B, Level 1: view, looking east, of planks between posts of Rows 3 and 2 100

Fig 6.26 Flag Fen, Area 6B, Level 1: view looking east along the posts of Row 3, showing two possible walkways 101

Fig 6.27 Flag Fen, Area 6B, Level 1: plan of numbered wood in north-east quadrant 102

Fig 6.28 Flag Fen, Area 6B, Level 1: plan of numbered wood in south-east quadrant 103

Fig 6.29 Flag Fen, Area 6B, Level 1: vertical view of wood in south-east quadrant 104

Fig 6.30 Flag Fen, Area 6B, Level 1: plan of numbered wood in south-west quadrant . . . 105

Fig 6.31 Flag Fen, Area 6B, Level 1: low oblique view of wood in south-west quadrant . . 106

Fig 6.32 Flag Fen, Area 6B, Level 1: vertical view of wood in south-west quadrant 106

Fig 6.33 Flag Fen, Area 6B, Level 1: posts of Row 2 107

Fig 6.34 Flag Fen, Area 6B, Level 1: general view of the posts of Row 3 107

Fig 6.35 Flag Fen, Area 6B, Level 1: vertical view of the posts of Row 3 107

Fig 6.36 Flag Fen, Area 6B, Level 1: plan of numbered wood in north-west quadrant . . . 108

Fig 6.37 Flag Fen, Area 6D, Level 1: general plan 109

Fig 6.38 Flag Fen, Area 6D, Level 2: general plan, prior to lifting 110

Fig 6.39 Flag Fen, Area 6D, Level 1: close-up of large oak planks in east part of the excavations within the poolside area . . . 111

Fig 6.40 Flag Fen, Areas 6A and 6B: general plan of wood exposed in Level 2 . . . . between pages 112–13

Fig 6.41 Flag Fen, Area 6A, Level 2: general plan of wood, with principal pieces numbered . . . . between pages 112–13

Fig 6.42 Flag Fen, Area 6B, Level 2: general plan 113

Fig 6.43 Flag Fen, Area 6B, Level 2: photomontage 114

Fig 6.44 Flag Fen, Area 6B, Level 2: excavation in progress 115

Fig 6.45 Flag Fen, Area 6B, Level 2: view across the excavation, looking west 115

Fig 6.46 Flag Fen, Area 6B, Level 2: view east along post Row 3 116

Fig 6.47 Flag Fen, Area 6B, Level 2: plan of numbered wood in north-east quadrant 117

Fig 6.48 Flag Fen, Area 6B, Level 2: plan of numbered wood in south-east quadrant 118

Fig 6.49 Flag Fen, Area 6B, Level 2: plan of numbered wood in south-west quadrant . . . 119

Fig 6.50 Flag Fen, Area 6B, Level 2: plan of numbered wood in north-west quadrant . . . 120

Fig 6.51 Flag Fen, Area 6B, Level 2: wood in the north-west quadrant 121

Fig 6.52 Flag Fen, Areas 6A and 6B: general plan of wood exposed in Level 3 . . . . between pages 120–1

Fig 6.53 Flag Fen, Area 6A, Level 3: general plan of wood, with principal pieces numbered . . . . between pages 120–1

Fig 6.54 Flag Fen, Area 6A: general view of wood exposed in Level 3, looking south 122

Fig 6.55 Flag Fen, Area 6B, Level 3: general plan 123

Fig 6.56 Flag Fen, Area 6B, Level 3: photomontage of timbers south of Row 3 124

Fig 6.57 Flag Fen, Area 6B, Level 3: view along possible walkway between the posts of Rows 3 and 4 125

Fig 6.58 Flag Fen, Area 6B, Level 3: view looking west between Rows 2 and 3 125

Fig 6.59 Flag Fen, Area 6B, Level 3: general view looking north 126

Fig 6.60 Flag Fen, Area 6B, Level 3: plan of numbered wood in north-east quadrant 127

Fig 6.61 Flag Fen, Area 6B, Level 3: plan of numbered wood in south-east quadrant 128

Fig 6.62 Flag Fen, Area 6B, Level 3: plan of numbered wood in south-west quadrant . . . 129

Fig 6.63 Flag Fen, Area 6B, Level 3: plan of numbered wood in north-west quadrant . . . 130

Fig 6.64 Flag Fen, Areas 6A and 6B: general plan of wood exposed in level 4 131

Fig 6.65 Flag Fen, Area 6A, Level 4: general plan of wood, with principal pieces numbered . 132

Fig 6.66 Flag Fen, Area 6B, Level 4: general plan 133

Fig 6.67 Flag Fen, Area 6B, Level 4: photomontage of excavated wood 134

Fig 6.68 Flag Fen, Area 6B, Level 4: plan of numbered wood in north-east quadrant 136

Fig 6.69 Flag Fen, Area 6B, Level 4: plan of numbered wood in south-east quadrant 137

Fig 6.70 Flag Fen, Area 6B, Level 4: plan of numbered wood in south-west quadrant . . . 138

Fig 6.71 Flag Fen, Area 6B, Level 4: close-up of wood in south-west quadrant 139

Fig 6.72 Flag Fen, Area 6B, Level 4: view along posts of Rows 1 and 2, looking north-west 140

Fig 6.73 Flag Fen, Area 6B, Level 4: plan of numbered wood in north-west quadrant . . . 141

Fig 6.74 Flag Fen, Areas 6A and 6B: general plan of wood exposed in Levels 5 and 6 . . . 142

Fig 6.75 Flag Fen, Area 6A, Levels 5 and 6: general plan of wood, with principal pieces numbered 143

Fig 6.76 Flag Fen, Area 6A, Levels 6 and 7: general plan of wood at the northern end of the trench 144

Fig 6.77 Flag Fen, Area 6B, Levels 5 and 6: general plan 145

Fig 6.78 Flag Fen, Area 6B, Level 5: photomontage of excavated wood 146

Fig 6.79 Flag Fen, Area 6B, Levels 5 and 6: general view of north half of excavation 147

Fig 6.80 Flag Fen, Area 6B, Level 5: view along post Rows 3 and 4 147

Fig 6.81 Flag Fen, Area 6B, Levels 5 and 6: plan of numbered wood in north-east quadrant 148

Fig 6.82 Flag Fen, Area 6B, Level 5: close-up of articulated timbers (B2644 and B2883) 149

Fig 6.83 Flag Fen, Area 6B, Levels 5 and 6: plan of numbered wood in south-east quadrant 150

Fig 6.84 Flag Fen, Area 6B, Levels 5 and 6: plan of numbered wood in south-west quadrant 151

Fig 6.85 Flag Fen, Area 6B, Level 6: view of wattle wall or revetment around posts of Row 1 152

Fig 6.86 Flag Fen, Area 6B, Level 6: wattle wall or revetment around posts Row 1 as finally excavated 152

Fig 6.87 Flag Fen, Area 6B: distribution plan of wattle walls/revetments 153

Fig 6.88 Flag Fen, Area 6B, Level 6: vertical view showing parts of two querns partially obscured by overlying timbers 154

Fig 6.89 Flag Fen, Area 6B, Level 6: close-up of two querns *in situ* below the timbers of Level 6 154

Fig 6.90 Flag Fen, Area 6B, Level 6: plan showing position of three querns and lowest level of wattle revetment around Row 1 155

Fig 6.91 Flag Fen, Area 6B, Level 6: close-up of flesh-hook socket *in situ* 155

Fig 6.92 Flag Fen, Area 6B, Level 6: haft (B2737) for socketed axe *in situ* 155

Fig 6.93 Flag Fen, Area 6B, Levels 5 and 6: plan of numbered wood in north-west quadrant 156

Fig 6.94 Flag Fen, Area 6B: work in progress in the final stages of the excavation, during removal of the posts 157

Fig 6.95 Flag Fen, Area 6B, Level 6: posts of Row 3 immediately prior to removal . . . 157

Fig 6.96 Flag Fen: section along western face of Area 6B, showing excavated levels and sand and grave walkway 'floors' between the posts of Rows 2–4 . . . . between pages 158–9

Fig 6.97 Flag Fen, Areas 6A and B: plan of posts, showing wood species 159

Fig 6.98 Flag Fen, Areas 6A ad 6B, Level 1: distribution of oak timbers . . . . between pages 160–1

Fig 6.99 Flag Fen, Areas 6A and 6B, Level 2: distribution of oak timbers . . . . between pages 160–1

Fig 6.100 Flag Fen, Areas 6A and 6B, Level 3: distribution of oak timbers . . . . between pages 160–1

Fig 6.101 Flag Fen, Areas 6A and 6B, Level 4: distribution of oak timbers 161

Fig 6.102 Flag Fen, Areas 6A and 6B, Level 5: distribution of oak timbers 161

Fig 7.1 Progressive drying out of oak and alder over a six-week period 169

Fig 7.2 Flag Fen, Area 6A: roundwood lengths and diameters 171

Fig 7.3 Diagram showing position and orientation of woodchip categories 172

Fig 7.4 Flag Fen, Area 6A: timber lengths and original diameters 173

Fig 7.5 Flag Fen, Area 6A: lengths of woodchips by class 174

Fig 7.6 Flag Fen, Area 6A: all woodchips by length 175

Fig 7.7 Flag Fen, Area 6A: breadth of woodchips by class 178

Fig 7.8 Flag Fen, Area 6A: all woodchips by breadth 179

Fig 7.9 Flag Fen, Area 6A: thickness of woodchips by class 180

Fig 7.10 Flag Fen, Area 6A: all woodchips by thickness 182

Fig 7.11 Flag Fen, Area 6A: breadth: length ratios of woodchips by class 183

Fig 7.12 Flag Fen, Area 6A: all woodchips, breadth:length ratios 184

Fig 7.13 Comparative breadth:length ratios of woodchips from the enclosure ditch at Etton 185

Fig 7.14 Power Station: roundwood lengths and diameters 185

Fig 7.15 Power Station: timber lengths and original diameters 186

Fig 7.16 Power Station: length of woodchips by class 190

Fig 7.17 Power Station: all woodchips by length 190

Fig 7.18 Power Station: breadth of woodchips by class 191

Fig 7.19 Power Station: all woodchips by breadth 192

Fig 7.20 Power Station: thickness of woodchips by class 192

Fig 7.21 Power Station: all woodchips by thickness 193

Fig 7.22 Power Station: breadth:length ratios of woodchips by class 193

Fig 7.23 Power Station: all woodchips, breadth:length ratios 193

Fig 7.24 Blade-width frequencies of toolmarks from upper deposits at Flag Fen, Areas 6A and 6B 198

Fig 7.25 Blade-width frequencies of toolmarks from lower deposits at Flag Fen, Areas 6A and 6B 199

Fig 7.26 Blade-width frequencies of toolmarks from upper and lower deposits at Flag Fen, Areas 6A and 6B 199

Fig 7.27 Blade-width frequencies of flat and low flanged axes from Lincolnshire 200

Fig 7.28 Blade-width frequencies of flanged axes and palstaves from Lincolnshire 200

Fig 7.29 Blade-width frequencies of socketed axes from Lincolnshire 201

Fig 7.30 Measurements used to calculate the blade-curvature index 201

Fig 7.31 Beaver tooth marks on modern maple wood from Canada and Bronze Age wood from Flag Fen Area 6B 202

Fig 7.32 Ways of splitting wood using the natural tendencies of the timber 203

Fig 7.33 Posts with joints 204

Fig 7.34 Hewn surface of timber B2356 from Area 6B and the same timber showing direction of hewing 205

Fig 7.35 Unused upright from Area 6B, timber B1421 205

Fig 7.36 Mortises cut through roundwood 206
Fig 7.37 Mortises cut through planks 207
Fig 7.38 Mortises cut through heavy timber 207
Fig 7.39 Mortises cut through roundwood or
          partly reduced roundwood 208
Fig 7.40 Timbers with slots 209
Fig 7.41 Lap and housing joints 209
Fig 7.42 Lap joints on roundwood 210
Fig 7.43 Housing joints 210
Fig 7.44 The lower portions of two possible alder
          rafters from Flag Fen, Area 6B 211
Fig 7.45 Plank ends with joints or partial joints . 211
Fig 7.46 Ends of larger, half-split, and reduced
          roundwood timbers, with joints 212
Fig 7.47 Sundry small pieces and fragments,
          with evidence for joints 212
Fig 7.48 The wheel fragment from Flag Fen,
          Area 6C, and reconstruction 214–15
Fig 7.49 Flag Fen Area 6C, part of tripartite
          wheel *in situ* 216
Fig 7.50 Part of a Late Bronze Age tripartite
          wheel from Cottenham, Cambs 216
Fig 7.51 Possible roughout for hub from Flag
          Fen, Area 6B 216
Fig 7.52 Part of oak axle and peg from Flag Fen,
          Area 6B 217
Fig 7.53 Possible roughout for axle, Flag Fen,
          Area 6B 218
Fig 7.54 Part of possible flail from Flag Fen,
          Area 6B 219
Fig 7.55 Close-up of the end notch and hole
          of the possible yoke or flail from
          Flag Fen, Area 6B 219
Fig 7.56 Fragments of oak axe hafts from the
          Power Station, Area 1 220
Fig 7.57 Complete haft for socketed axe from
          Flag Fen, Area 6B 221
Fig 7.58 Wooden hammer from Flag Fen,
          Area 6B 222
Fig 7.59 Wooden hammer from Flag Fen,
          Area 6B 223
Fig 7.60 Sketch showing the position in the
          tree of axe hafts 223
Fig 7.61 Sketch showing the position in the
          tree of hammer B3249 223
Fig 7.62 Cross sections of shafts, handles,
          and a scabbard 224
Fig 7.63 Projections of ray patterns in axe
          sockets 224
Fig 7.64 Part of handle, Flag Fen, Area 6D 225
Fig 7.65 Flag Fen, Area 6A, willow scoop 227
Fig 7.66 Flag Fen, Area 6A, hollowed log
          vessel in oak 228
Fig 7.67 Wooden needle or bodkin from
          Flag Fen, Area 6B 228

Toolmark figures
Fig T1   Flag Fen, Area 6A (A series) corpus
          of toolmarks (A0–A4600) 194

Fig T2   Flag Fen, Area 6A (A series) corpus
          of toolmarks (A4601–A7420) 194
Fig T3   Flag Fen, Area 6A (A series) corpus
          of toolmarks (A7421–A8300) 194
Fig T4   Flag Fen, Area 6A (A series) corpus
          of toolmarks (A8301–A8800 and
          addendum) 195
Fig T5   Flag Fen, Area 6B (B series) corpus
          of toolmarks (B0–B1010) 195
Fig T6   Flag Fen, Area 6B (B series) corpus
          of toolmarks (B1011–B1730) 195
Fig T7   Flag Fen, Area 6B (B series) corpus
          of toolmarks (B1731–B2250) 195
Fig T8   Flag Fen, Area 6B (B series) corpus
          of toolmarks (B2251–B2670) 196
Fig T9   Flag Fen, Area 6B (B series) corpus
          of toolmarks (B2671–B2935) 196
Fig T10   Flag Fen, Area 6B (B series) corpus
          of toolmarks (B2936–B3300) 196
Fig T11   Flag Fen, Area 6B (B series) corpus
          of toolmarks (B3301–B3630) 196
Fig T12   Flag Fen, Area 6B (B series) corpus
          of toolmarks (addendum) 197
Fig T13   Power Station (Y series) corpus of
          toolmarks Y0–1395 197

Fig 8.1   Bar diagram showing tree-ring sequences
          from Row 1, Row 5, and unknown rows
          from the Power Station 230
Fig 8.2   Bar diagram showing tree-ring
          sequences from the central rows
          at the Power Station 230
Fig 8.3   Bar diagram showing tree-ring sequences
          from the unknown rows at Flag Fen . . . 231
Fig 8.4   Bar diagram showing tree-ring sequences
          from Rows 2–5 from Flag Fen 231
Fig 8.5   Bar diagram showing tree-ring sequences
          from samples with sapwood present from
          both Flag Fen and the Power Station . . 232
Fig 8.6   Bar diagram showing tree-ring sequences
          sorted by both row (1, 5, unknown)
          and area from the Power Station 232
Fig 8.7   Bar diagram showing ring sequences
          sorted by both row (central) and area
          from the Power Station 233
Fig 8.8   Distribution of tree-ring samples from
          the Power Station 237
Fig 8.9   Distribution of tree-ring samples from
          Flag Fen, Area 6 240
Fig 9.1   Late Neolithic, Beaker, and Early
          Bronze Age pottery 250
Fig 9.2   Pottery from Flag Fen, Area 6 251
Fig 9.3   Pottery from the Power Station 252
Fig 9.4   Distribution of recorded pottery finds
          from the Power Station 254
Fig 10.1 Dirks and rapiers from the
          Power Station 256
Fig 10.2 Late Bronze Age swords from the
          Power Station 257

Fig 10.3   Rivets, pommels, chapes, and small
            items from the Power Station 259
Fig 10.4   Ferrules and spearheads from the
            Power Station and Flag Fen 262
Fig 10.5   Daggers, knives, and other objects from
            the Power Station and Flag Fen 264
Fig 10.6   Socketed axe, razors, awls, buttons, and
            other objects from the Power Station . . 266
Fig 10.7   Beads, bracelets, and smaller objects in
            tin and copper alloy from the Power
            Station 270
Fig 10.8   Iron Age brooches, and objects in lead,
            tin, and copper alloy from the Power
            Station and Flag Fen 273
Fig 10.9   Pins of Bronze and Iron Age date from
            the Power Station and Flag Fen 275
Fig 10.10   Rings and miscellaneous objects of
            probable Bronze Age date and iron
            objects and a shoe buckle from the
            Power Station 279
Fig 10.11   Miscellaneous objects, mainly of Iron
            Age date, from the Power Station 281
Fig 10.12   Distribution of early metalwork at
            the Power Station site 295
Fig 10.13   Distribution of Late Bronze Age
            weaponry at the Power Station site 296
Fig 10.14   Distribution of knives, razors, socketed
            gouge, socketed axe, and tanged
            daggers at the Power Station site 296
Fig 10.15   Distribution of pointed rivets and
            two socketed spikes at the Power
            Station site 297
Fig 10.16   Distribution of lead and white metal
            objects at the Power Station site 297
Fig 10.17   Distribution of bronze rings at the
            Power Station site 298
Fig 10.18   Distribution of bronze pins and pin
            fragments at the Power Station site 298
Fig 10.19   Distribution of tanged awls at the
            Power Station site 299
Fig 10.20   Distribution of Iron Age and later
            metalwork at the Power Station site . . . 299
Fig 10.21   Lead isotope analysis: Taunton/Penard
            Phases 304
Fig 10.22   Lead isotope analysis: Wilburton Phase . 306
Fig 10.23   Lead isotope analysis:
            Ewart Park Phase 306
Fig 10.24   Phosphorus distribution map of
            sample from iron socketed axehead 309
Fig 10.25   Late Bronze Age swords and spearheads
            from the Power Station and Flag Fen . . 311
Fig 10.26   Details of sword 6 312
Fig 10.27   Details of sword 4 313
Fig 10.28   Details of sword 5 313
Fig 10.29   Details of sword 7 314
Fig 10.30   Details of spearhead 47 314
Fig 10.31   Details of spearhead 46 315
Fig 10.32   Details of spearhead 49 316
Fig 10.33   Details of spearhead 51 316

Fig 11.1   Flints from Cat's Water (1990) and
            the Power Station (1989) 319
Fig 11.2   Histogram showing breadth:length
            ratios of all flint flakes from the
            Power Station 320
Fig 11.3   Northey (1994): selected flints from
            Trial Trench I 321
Fig 11.4   Polished stone axe fragments from
            the Power Station 321
Fig 11.5   Polished shale bracelets 322
Fig 11.6   Quern from Flag Fen Area 6B
            (Other Find 24) 323
Fig 11.7   Quern from Flag Fen Area 6B
            (Other Find 26) 324
Fig 11.8   Quern from Flag Fen Area 6B
            (Other Find 27) 325
Fig 11.9   Quern from Flag Fen Area 6B
            (Other Find 28) 325
Fig 13.1   Pollen diagram of the mere section 353
Fig 13.2   Pollen diagram of Northey, section 4 . . 358
Fig 13.3   Pollen diagram of the platform section . 363
Fig 13.4   Pollen diagram of the Fengate B section 363
Fig 13.5   Pollen diagram of taxa from Level 1
            of Flag Fen platform 370
Fig 15.1   Species groups of Coleoptera from
            Flag Fen 384
Fig 16.1   Probability distributions of dates
            from isolated features in the Fengate
            landscape 391
Fig 16.2   Probability distributions of dates from the
            sequence around the post alignment . . . 391
Fig 16.3   Probability distributions of dates from
            the Neolithic activity on the Storey's
            Bar Road site 391
Fig 16.4   Probability distributions of dates from
            the central Bronze Age field system . . . 391
Fig 16.5   Summary of the chronological sequence
            of the principal phases and events 397
Fig 16.6   Probability distributions of the main
            dates from the Flag Fen Basin 399
Fig 16.7   Probability distributions of dates from
            the dated tree-ring sequence at
            Flag Fen 399
Fig 18.1   Map showing location and orientation
            of the earlier Neolithic and Bronze
            Age landscapes 406
Fig 18.2   Map showing principal features of the
            Bronze Age landscape in the vicinity of
            the post alignment 409
Fig 18.3   Plan of the Newark Road 'community
            stockyards' 415
Fig 18.4   General plan of the Storey's Bar Road
            (Bronze Age) farm stockyards 417
Fig 18.5   Hypothetical reconstruction of the
            drafting gate arrangements, Storey's Bar
            Road (Bronze Age) farm stockyards . . . 418
Fig 18.6   Cropmarks of a later Bronze Age to
            Iron Age field system at West Deeping
            in the Welland valley 419

Fig 19.1 The Flag Fen post alignment, Area 6: isometric reconstruction of Phase 1 422

Fig 19.2 The Flag Fen post alignment, Area 6: isometric reconstruction of Phase 3 (early and middle stages) 424

Fig 19.3 The Flag Fen post alignment, Area 6: isometric reconstruction of Phase 3 (late and final stages) 425

Fig 19.4 La Tène, Switzerland: general plan showing the location of timbers and other finds . . . . between pages 434–5

Tables

1.1 Archaeological projects conducted in the Flag Fen Basin discussed in the text 6

2.1 Summary and chronology of pedogenesis and land-use 19

3.1 Summary of the soil horizons present at the Cat's Water site 39

4.1 Summary of soil, sediment, and palynological results 57

7.1 Principal categories of wood and timber from Area 6A 169

7.2 Flag Fen, Area 6A: roundwood dimensions 170

7.3 Flag Fen, Area 6A: roundwood debris dimensions 170

7.4 Flag Fen, Area 6A: timber dimensions 170

7.5 Flag Fen, Area 6A: timber debris dimensions 173

7.6 Flag Fen, Area 6A (all levels): dimensions of slab or sapwood removal chips (in mm) 173

7.7 Flag Fen, Area 6A (all levels): dimensions of tangentially aligned woodchips (in mm) 176

7.8 Flag Fen, Area 6A (all levels: dimensions of radially aligned woodchips (in mm) 176

7.9 Flag Fen, Area 6A (all levels): dimensions of woodchips off roundwood (in mm) 176

7.10 Flag Fen, Area 6A (all levels): dimensions of cross-grain woodchips (in mm) 177

7.11 Flag Fen, Area 6A (all levels: dimensions of unclassifiable woodchips (in mm) 177

7.12 Flag Fen, Area 6A (all levels): dimensions of all woodchips (in mm) 177

7.13 Summary of woodchips from Area 6A, by category 179

7.14 Comparative dimensions of slabs or sapwood removal chips from the enclosure ditch at Etton (in mm) 181

7.15 Comparative dimensions of tangentially aligned woodchips from the enclosure ditch at Etton (in mm) 181

7.16 Comparative dimensions of radially aligned woodchips from the enclosure ditch at Etton (in mm) 181

7.17 Comparative dimensions of woodchips off roundwood from the enclosure ditch at Etton (in mm) 184

7.18 Principal categories of wood and timber from the Power Station 186

7.19 Power Station site: roundwood dimensions (in mm) 187

7.20 Power Station site: timber dimensions (in mm) 187

7.21 Power Station site: timber debris dimensions (in mm) 188

7.22 Power Station site: dimensions of tangentially aligned woodchips (in mm) 188

7.23 Power Station site: dimensions of radially aligned woodchips (in mm) 188

7.24 Power Station site: dimensions of woodchips off roundwood (in mm) 189

7.25 Power Station site: dimensions of cross-grain woodchips (in mm) 189

7.26 Power Station site: dimensions of all measured woodchips (in mm) 189

7.27 Summary of woodchips from the Power Station, by category 191

7.28 Comparison of blade widths: Flag Fen toolmarks and selected Bronze Age axe types 197

7.29 Comparison of blade curvature indices: Flag Fen toolmarks and selected Bronze Age axe types 198

8.1 Summary of same-tree groups identified. Sample numbers prefixed 'Y' are from the Power Station; samples prefixed 'A' or 'B' are from Flag Fen 229

8.2 Details of the tree-ring dates for the Power Station site 234

8.3 Details of the tree-ring dates for Flag Fen . . 238

8.4 t value matrix of timbers within single tree mean B0061M 243

8.5 Ring-width data of the site master curve for the Flag Fen Basin, 1406–937 BC 244

8.6 Results of comparisons of the Power Station (FG137T), Flag Fen (FF88T) and combined Flag Fen Basin (FFB225T) masters and reference chronologies spanning the Bronze Age 245

8.7 t value matrix showing the general level of cross-matching between the Power Station and Flag Fen 247

9.1 Comparison of sherd numbers in each fabric between the Power Station and Flag Fen, Area 6 253

9.2 Sherd groups indicative of single vessels as recovered from Flag Fen, Area 6 253

10.1 List of metalwork finds from Flag Fen and the Power Station 284

10.2 Non-ferrous metal analyses from Flag Fen and the Power Station 302

10.3 Lead isotope data for metalwork from Flag Fen and the Power Station 305

10.4 ICP-MS analysis of tin objects from Flag Fen and Hauterive-Champréveyres 307

10.5 Minor and trace element composition of axehead 269 309

11.1 Summary of flints from Cat's Water excavations (1990), by category 318

11.2 Summary of flints from the Power Station, by category 318

11.3 Quantities and dimensions of flints from the Power Station: complete utilised flakes . 320

11.4 Quantities and dimensions of flints from the Power Station: complete waste flakes . . . 320

11.5 Quantities and dimensions of flints from the power Station: breadth:length ratios 320

12.1 Catalogue of identified mammalian bone from the platform site 332

12.2 Catalogue of identified mammalian bone from the post alignment site 336

12.3 Minimum numbers of body parts and individuals from the platform site 344

12.4 Minimum numbers of body parts and individuals from the post alignment site 345

12.5 Numbers of identified mammalian specimens with traces of knawing and butchery from the platform site 345

12.6 Numbers of identified mammalian specimens with traces of knawing and butchery from the post alignment site 345

12.7 Age at death of cattle at the platform site (MNI) 346

12.8 Age at death of cattle at the post alignment site (MNI) 346

12.9 Age at death of sheep at the platform site (MNI) 346

12.10 Age at death of sheep at the post alignment site (MNI) 347

12.11 Stature of dogs from the platform site 347

12.12 Stature of dogs from the post alignment site 347

13.1 Suggested correlation of pollen assemblage zones and summary of environmental change 378

15.1 Coleoptera from Flag Fen (depth in mm) . . 385

15.2 Species groups of Flag Fen Coleoptera 388

15.3 Host plants of the phytophagous Coleoptera 388

16.1 Summary table of radiocarbon dates 392

16.2 Estimated date ranges for the events defined in the model 398

16.3 Wiggle matching UB-3422 to UB-3427 . . . 398

17.1 Summary of the main landscape history events in the Flag Fen Basin 404

Contributors

J C Barrett
Department of Archaeology and
Prehistory
University of Sheffield
Northgate House
West Street
Sheffield S1 4ET

Dr Alex Bayliss
English Heritage
23 Savile Row
London W1S 2ET

Dr S G E Bowman
Department of Scientific Research
The British Museum
Great Russell Street
London WC1B 3DG

Sue Bridgeford
Department of Archaeology and
Prehistory
University of Sheffield
Northgate House
West Street
Sheffield S1 4ET

D G Buckley
Heritage Conservation Group
Essex County Council Planning
Division
County Hall
Chelmsford CM1 1HQ

Ellen Cameron
c/o Department of Archaeology and
Prehistory
University of Sheffield
Northgate House
West Street
Sheffield S1 4ET

Professor T C Champion
Department of Archaeology
University of Southampton
Highfield
Southampton SO17 1BJ

Dr D G Coombs
Department of Archaeology
University of Manchester
Manchester M13 9PL

Christopher Evans
Cambridge Archaeological Unit
Department of Archaeology
University of Cambridge
Downing Street
Cambridge CB2 3DZ

Vanessa Fell
The Ashmolean Museum
Beaumont Street
Oxford OX1 2PH

Stephen Forbes
c/o Department of Archaeology and
Prehistory
University of Sheffield
Northgate House
West Street
Sheffield S1 4ET

Dr Charles French
Department of Archaeology
University of Cambridge
Downing Street
Cambridge CB2 3DZ

Cathy Groves
Sheffield Dendrochronology Laboratory
Archaeology Research School
University of Sheffield
West Court
2 Mappin Street
Sheffield S1 4DT

Dr Paul Halstead
Department of Archaeology and
Prehistory
University of Sheffield
Northgate House
West Street
Sheffield S1 4ET

Dr Caroline Ingle
Heritage Conservation Group
Essex County Council Planning
Division
County Hall
Chelmsford CM1 1HQ

Dr Helen Lewis
Department of Archaeology
University of Cambridge
Downing Street
Cambridge CB2 3DZ

A P Middleton
Department of Scientific Research
The British Museum
Great Russell Street
London WC1B 3DG

Janet Neve
c/o Fenland Archaeological Trust
Flag Fen Excavations
Fourth Drove
Fengate
Peterborough PE1 5UR

Dr Peter Northover
Department of Materials
University of Oxford
Begbroke Business and Science Park
Sandy Lane
Yarnton
Oxford OX5 1PF

Dr Francis Pryor
Fenland Archaeological Trust
Flag Fen Excavations
Fourth Drove
Fengate
Peterborough PE1 5UR

Dr Mark Robinson
University Museum
Parks Road
Oxford OX1 3PW

Dr B M Rohl
C/o Research Laboratory for
Archaeology
6 Keble Road
Oxford OX1 3QJ

Dr Robert G Scaife
Department of Geography
University of Southampton
Highfield
Southampton SO17 1BJ

Chris Salter
Department of Materials
University of Oxford
Begbroke Business and Science Park
Sandy Lane
Yarnton
Oxford OX5 1PF

Maisie Taylor
Fenland Archaeological Trust
Flag Fen Excavations
Fourth Drove
Fengate
Peterborough PE1 5UR

Dr D F Williams
Department of Archaeology
University of Southampton
Highfield
Southampton SO17 1BJ

Acknowledgements

The discovery of the site at Flag Fen in November 1982 set in motion a train of events that none of the participants could have anticipated. At the time, the team was working on two other English Heritage projects, one in the Fens (the Dyke Survey), the other at Etton, in the lower Welland valley. We fondly believed that we had finished with Fengate, but it was not to be. I am therefore particularly grateful to the members of the team of 1982 who steeled themselves to return to an area we thought we had left for good. Those key team members were Bob Bourne, David Crowther, Charles French, Kasia Gdaniec, David Gurney, Bob Middleton, and Maisie Taylor.

It would be impossible to thank everyone who has helped with the Flag Fen project, but certain names stand out. Dr Geoffrey Wainwright, until recently Chief Archaeologist for English Heritage, has been our strongest and most loyal supporter, although he did not believe all our hypotheses (but I will allow that he was proved correct on the post alignment, which I had thought was a rectangular building). Richard Bradley was delighted that the focus of the site changed from domestic to ritual at the time he was writing his seminal text, *The Passage of Arms*, and he has always been a source of provocative ideas. Mike Parker-Pearson, who was our English Heritage inspector when the site was discovered, has kept a refreshingly anarchic eye on us ever since. Our friends and colleagues in the English Heritage Fenland Project have been splendid allies, most especially David Hall, Tom Lane, and John Coles. Mike Corfield, of the Ancient Monuments Laboratory, has been of great assistance in setting-up the Preservation Hall and in providing us with practical assistance and helpful advice.

Non-contributors to the present report who have been particularly helpful to the project include Bob Bewley, Ben Booth, Richard Darrah, Ian Kinnes, Paul Middleton, Stuart Needham, Rog Palmer, Steve Upex, and Philip Walker. Chris and Anne Chippindale produced the splendid Special Section on Flag Fen in *Antiquity* (1992) and have been regular visitors, friends, and supporters. Brian Fagan has also been a special friend of the project and has helped spread the word across North America through his many fine publications. I wish I had thought of his title, *The Time Detectives* — writing popular archaeology is a very difficult art, but no-one writes so well or with such authority. Paul Jordan, David Mitchell, and David Collison produced lively and accurate television films about the project.

Chapters 2 and 3 of the report are devoted to commercial excavations in the Flag Fen Basin, and I would like to acknowledge the special help I have received from Chris Evans of the Cambridge University Archaeological Unit. Other project managers and site directors have been very helpful, especially Richard Cuttler (Birmingham University Field Archaeology Unit), Dave Gibson (Cambridge University Archaeological Unit), and Nansi Rosenberg (John Samuels Archaeological Consultants). Simon Kaner and Louise Austen were caring and cooperative curators when Fengate was in Cambridgeshire's jurisdiction; now that the City of Peterborough is a unitary authority, I have enjoyed excellent cooperation and support from Ben Robinson, who helped me track down certain elusive barrows.

The writing of Chapter 19 was greatly aided by a study tour that Maisie and I made to the Jura, the Swiss Lakes, and southern Bavaria, generously funded by a travel grant from the British Academy.

The wood report (Chapter 7) has been a major undertaking and Maisie Taylor wishes to thank Toby Fox for his help as research assistant; Rob Sands for sight of his PhD thesis and for many useful discussions; Frank Rowley, who measured and calculated curvature indices for the Lincolnshire axes, and Linda Ireson for collating the Flag Fen toolmark data.

Janet Neve (Chapter 9) offers special thanks to Jennifer Hillam and Cathy Groves of the Sheffield Dendrochronology Laboratory for help, advice, and comments on the text; to Ian Tyers for the computer software and for his time spent making it work smoothly; to Ernie Pepper of Peterborough Regional College, who translated previously measured data from BBC to Atari format, and to Mike Baillie and David Brown at the Palaeoecology Centre, Queen's University, Belfast, for their help, particularly with dating.

The authors of the querns report in Chapter 11 (Dave Buckley and Caroline Ingle) wish to acknowledge the assistance of Nigel Brown for reading the text and providing useful comments.

The authors of Chapter 16 (Alex Bayliss and Francis Pryor) would like to thank Cathy Groves of the University of Sheffield and Gerry McCormac of Queen's University, Belfast, for their helpful contributions on the interpretation of the dendrochronology and wiggle-matching.

The initial preparation of this report took place during the transitional period between the traditional way of writing reports and the modern world of *Management of Archaeological Projects*, 2nd edition (English Heritage 1992), and the evolution from MS-DOS to Windows. These changes have caused problems and delays and I would like to thank those contributors who have waited so patiently for their reports to appear in print. I trust that they think that their wait has been worthwhile. Here, I must also say a very special word of thanks to Dave Coombs, who managed to produce a first-rate report during an extended period of enormous personal distress. Jenny is greatly missed.

The production of a large report is always difficult and I could not have finished it without the willing assistance of Dave Hopkins, artist/draughtsman at Archaeological Project Services of Heckington, Lincs, and the members of the Publications Department at English Heritage, especially Dr David M Jones. Toby Fox and Martin Redding were splendid research assistants and helped to sort out several knotty problems. Derek Rootes produced most of the photomontage plans.

Finally, Flag Fen is still open to the public, despite the extraordinary lack of interest shown by the new unitary authority of Peterborough. I am therefore particularly grateful to Sir Jocelyn Stevens GCVO, former Chairman of English Heritage, for his personal and corporate support for our work. The two other principal contributors to the Flag Fen Preservation Hall were Hawker Siddeley Power Engineering Ltd and Eastern Electricity Ltd. IVO Generation Services Ltd gave Fenland Archaeological Trust the computer with which the many files of this report were compiled and edited. Anglian Water Services Ltd, who own most of the archaeological site of Flag Fen, have proved to be a sympathetic, practical, and financially supportive landlord.

Our close neighbours at the Peterborough Power Station have helped in many ways on a daily basis. We owe very special thanks, therefore, to our friends in the world of business and commerce — Robin Gourlay, Pekka Osterlund, Rex Perkins, Bob Price, Richard Rigg, Garner Roberts, Bill Watson, and Paul Woodcock. The late Derek Williams, City and County Councillor, loved Flag Fen, sheep, and sheepdogs; it is thanks to him and the City and County Councils of 1989 that we now possess our fine visitor centre and museum.

His Royal Highness the Duke of Gloucester GCVO has taken an active interest in Flag Fen and its survival. In 1986 he kindly agreed to become the royal patron of Fenland Archaeological Trust, the charitable organisation that was set up to manage the affairs of Flag Fen. The late Robert Kiln, who was equally at home in archaeology and business, purchased the land on which the Preservation Hall now stands through the R J Kiln Trust. He was also an active member of Fenland Archaeological Trust. Finally, Peter Boizot, owner of Peterborough United Football Club and philanthropist of the City, has supported Flag Fen in a manner appropriate to the site's local, national and international importance. We are most fortunate to have him as our friend and patron.

Summary

The Flag Fen Basin is an area of low-lying land on the western margins of the Fens of eastern England on the outskirts of the city of Peterborough, formerly in Cambridgeshire. The area has been the subject of near-continuous archaeological research since about 1900. In 1968, when central government designated Peterborough a New Town, commercial development rapidly gathered pace. Most of the archaeological research described in this report took place in response to new building projects in the last three decades of the century.

During the Fengate Project of 1971–8, a ditched field system of Bronze Age date was recorded on the dry land of Fengate, on the western side of the Flag Fen Basin; subsequent research at Northey, on the eastern side of the basin, has revealed a similar field system. The fields of Northey and Fengate were defined by ditches and banks, on which hedges were probably planted. The fields were grouped into larger holdings by parallel-ditched droveways that ran, at right angles, down to the wetland edge.

The Fengate field system was first laid out in the Early Bronze Age and went out of use in the early first millennium BC. The Northey field system has yet to be investigated in detail. New evidence suggests that the Fengate fields were laid out in two phases. The central and northern elements were set out perhaps four or five centuries before the southern element. The latter continued in use for a similar period, after the abandonment of the rest of the system. The Bronze Age fields were laid out for the management of large numbers of livestock, principally sheep and cattle. Animals were grazed on the rich wetland pastures of Flag Fen in the drier months of the year and returned to the flood-free grazing around the fen edge to over-winter.

At Newark Road and Fourth Drove, the heart of the Fengate Bronze Age field system was laid out in a complex pattern of droveways, yards, and paddocks, centred around a major droveway. It is interpreted as a communal 'marketplace' for the exchange of livestock and for regular social gatherings. The droveway through these 'community stockyards' continued east until it encountered the edge of the regularly flooded land at the Power Station site, where the line of the drove was continued by five parallel rows of posts. These ran across the gradually encroaching wetland of Flag Fen to Northey, some 1200m to the east.

The five rows of posts are collectively termed the 'post alignment'. Dendrochronology shows them to have been in use for some 400 years, between approximately 1300 and 900 BC. Some 200m west of the Northey landfall, the post alignment crossed a contemporary large artificial platform constructed of timber. Although the nature, use, and development of the platform is not yet understood, it was undoubtedly closely linked physically and functionally with the post alignment.

Since conditions of preservation were excellent in the wetter parts of Flag Fen, it was possible to study woodworking in some detail. The earliest timbers were generally of alder and other wetland species, but oak was also used in later phases. Woodchips and other debris suggest that most of the woodworking was of large timbers and that there was little processing of coppice, except in the lower levels. Examination of the toolmarks indicates that socketed axes were used almost exclusively. A number of wooden artefacts and reused pieces were found. These included part of a tripartite wheel, an axle, and a scoop.

Study of the animal bone and pottery showed two distinct assemblages at the Power Station and Flag Fen sites. The former was dominated by domestic material, which might have derived from settlement on the fen edge nearby. There was also a significant ritual component at both sites, but principally at Flag Fen; ritual finds included complete ceramic vessels and the remains of several dogs.

A large assemblage of metalwork clearly demonstrated the importance of ritual at both sites. Some 275 items of prehistoric metalwork were found at Flag Fen and along the southern part of the post alignment at the Power Station. The metalwork, mainly of bronze and tin, included weaponry, ornaments, and several Continental imports. There was evidence that many of the items had been deliberately smashed or broken before being placed in the water. A significant proportion of the assemblage could be dated to the Iron Age and must have been placed in the waters at the alignment, long after the posts had been abandoned.

The posts of the alignment at Flag Fen were accompanied by five levels of horizontal wood, which served as a reinforcement, foundation, and, in places, as a path with associated narrow tracks. The posts served a number of purposes: as a guide for travellers along the tracks, as a near-solid wall, and as a palisade, constructed in the manner of a *chevaux-de-frise*. There was also evidence for transverse timber and wattle partitions, which divided the alignment into segments 5–6m in length.

It is suggested that these segments had an important ritual role. The partitions were further emphasised by the placing of offerings, or boundary deposits of valuable items, such as unused quernstones. Segments within the post alignment might have served a role similar to the segments of a causewayed enclosure ditch. Taking the nearby site of Etton as an example, it is suggested that the segments might have been used for ritual purposes by people of different kin groups. It is also suggested that the private or kin-group rites at Flag Fen took place at times of the year when the main community stockyards at the western end of the post alignment were the scene of regular social gatherings.

The report also includes a detailed summary of recent commercial excavations at Fengate.

There is new evidence for an earlier Neolithic organised landscape. This was laid out as a wide band or strip aligned on a newly discovered embayment on the fen edge. After the abandonment of the Bronze Age fields, settlement moved above the 5m contour: excavation at the Tower Works site has shown a connection between the well known Late Bronze Age–Early Iron Age pits, first revealed in the early decades of the present century, and the final use of the Fengate Bronze Age fields. The earliest Iron Age settlement at the Tower Works site includes evidence for nucleated settlement and at least one rectangular building.

The reassessment of the Fengate landscape brought about by recent commercial development has had a profound effect on our understanding of the area, and especially the Iron Age and early Roman periods. The well known Cat's Water settlement, for example, can now be placed within a landscape context based on solid palaeoenvironmental evidence. Recent commercial excavation has also thrown new light on the significance of the 'natural' fen margin at the very edge of habitable land. In modern commercial excavations, soil micromorphology and palynology have also been employed to clarify our picture of the changing environment since earlier Neolithic times. With research ongoing, few regions in Britain, or elsewhere, can or will offer such an integrated picture of later prehistoric settlement, land-use, and ritual.

Résumé

Le bassin de Flag Fen consiste en une étendue de basses terres en bordure ouest des Fens ou marécages de l'est de l'Angleterre dans les environs de la ville de Peterborough, qui faisait auparavant partie du comté de Cambridgeshire. La région a été l'objet de recherches archéologiques quasi-continues depuis environ 1900. En 1968, quand le gouvernement central a accordé à Peterborough le statut de ville nouvelle, le développement économique a rapidement pris son essor. La plupart des recherches archéologiques décrites dans ce rapport ont eu lieu en réponse à de nouveaux projets de chantiers de construction au cours des trois dernières décennies du siècle.

Pendant la campagne de Fengate de 1971-8, on a identifié un système de champs avec fossés datant de l'âge du bronze a été identifié sur les terres sèches de Fengate, du côté ouest du bassin de Flag Fen; des recherches postérieures à Northey, du côté est du bassin, ont révélé un système de champs similaire. Les champs de Northey et de Fengate étaient délimités par des fossés et des talus, sur lesquels étaient probablement plantées des haies. Les champs se trouvaient groupés en parcelles plus conséquentes par des chemins, bordés de fossés parallèles, qui descendaient à angle droit jusqu'en bordure des marécages.

Le système de champs de Fengate fit sa première apparition au début de l'âge du bronze et cessa d'être utilisé au début du premier millénaire avant J.-C. Le système de champs de Northey n'a pas encore été étudié en détail. De nouveaux témoignages donnent à penser que les champs de Fengate ont été tracés en deux étapes. Les éléments situés au centre et au nord ont été délimités peut-être quatre ou cinq siècles avant la partie située au sud. Cette dernière continuera à être en usage pendant une période équivalente après l'abandon du reste du système.

La configuration des champs de l'âge du bronze les destinaient à l'élevage d'un grand nombre d'animaux, en particulier des moutons et des bovins. Les animaux pâturaient les riches terres marécageuses de Flag Fen pendant les mois les plus secs de l'année et retournaient vers les pâturages non-inondables en bordure des marécages pour y passer l'hiver. A Newark Road et Fourth Drove, le coeur du système de champs de l'âge du bronze consistait en un quadrillage complexe de chemins, cours et enclos, dont le centre était un important chemin de passage pour le bétail. On pense qu'il s'agissait d'une 'place du marché' commune qui servait pour les échanges de bétail et des rassemblements à caractère social. Le chemin qui traversait ces 'parcs à bestiaux communautaires' continuait vers l'est jusqu'à ce qu'il rejoigne le bord des terres régulièrement inondées sur le site de la centrale, là, le chemin se prolongeait par cinq rangées de poteaux parallèles. Celles-ci, traversant les marécages de Flag Fen qui gagnaient peu à peu du terrain, continuaient jusqu'à Northey, à environ 1200m à l'est.

On a donné comme nom collectif à ces 5 rangées de poteaux: 'l'alignement de poteaux'. La dendrochronologie montre qu'elles ont été en usage pendant environ 400 ans, entre approximativement 1300 et 900 avant J.-C. A quelques 200m à l'ouest de la dépression de Northey, l'alignement de poteaux traversait une grande plateforme artificielle en bois datant de la même époque. Bien qu'on n'ait pas encore compris la nature, l'usage et l'évolution de cette platforme, elle était sans aucun doute étroitement liée, matériellement aussi bien que par sa fonction, à l'alignement de poteaux.

Puisque les conditions de conservation étaient excellentes dans les parties les plus humides de Flag Fen, on a pu étudier en détail le travail du bois. Les essences les plus anciennes étaient en général l'aune et d'autres espèces typiques des terrains marécageux, mais le chêne a aussi été utilisé au cours des phases plus tardives. Des copeaux et autres débris donnent à penser qu'on fabriquait surtout le gros bois et qu'on travaillait peu le taillis; sauf aux niveaux les plus bas. Un examen des marques faites par les outils indique qu'on utilisait presque exclusivement des haches à cavité. On a trouvé un certain nombre d'objets manufacturés en bois et des morceaux réutilisés. Ceux-ci comprenaient un morceaude roue tripartite, un essieu et une écope-. L'étude des os d'animaux et de la poterie a montré deux assemblages distincts sur les sites de la centrale et de Flag Fen. Le premier était dominé par des matériaux d'origine domestique, qui pouvaient avoir leur origine dans une occupation en bordure du marécage proche. On a également trouvé sur les deux sites, mais en particulier à Flag Fen, un nombre significatif de trouvailles d'ordre rituel; les vestiges rituels comprenaient des vases en céramique complets et les restes de plusieurs chiens.

Une importante collection d'objets en métal démontrait clairement l'importance du rituel sur les deux sites. On a trouvé quelques 275 objetsen métal préhistoriques à Flag Fen et le long de la partie sud de l'alignement de poteaux au niveau de la centrale. Les objets en métal, surtout en bronze et en étain comprenaient des armes, des ornements et plusieurs importations du continent. Des témoignages confirmèrent que beaucoup de ces articles avait été délibérément brisés ou cassés avant d'être placés dans l'eau. Une proportion non négligeable de l'assemblage datait de l'âge du fer et avait dû être placée dans l'eau au niveau de l'alignement, longtemps après que les poteaux aient été abandonnés.

A Flag Fen les poteaux de l'alignement s'accompagnaient de cinq couches de bois placées horizontalement, elles servaient de renfort, de fondation et, à certains endroits de sentier en association avec d'étroites pistes. Les poteaux remplissaient diverses fonctions, ils servaient à guider les voyageurs le long des pistes, ils formaient un mur presque compact et une palissade, construite à la manière des 'chevaux de frise'. On a trouvé aussi des preuves de l'existence de séparations transversales en bois et clayonnage qui divisaient l'alignement en segments de 5–6m de longueur.

On émet l'idée que ces segments jouaient un important rôle rituel. Le rôle des partitions était encore accentué par le placement d'offrandes, ou le dépôt de bornage d'objets de valeur, tels que des meules non utilisées. Il se peut que certains segments à l'intérieur de l'alignement de poteaux aient joué le même rôle que les segments de fossés des enclos à chaussée empierrée. Si on utilise comme exemple le site d'Etton, situé à proximité, on peut penser que les segments ont peut-être été utilisés dans un but rituel par des individus appartenant à divers groupes familiaux. On suggère aussi que les rites privés ou concernant ces groupes familiaux se déroulaient à Flag Fen à des moments de l'année où les principaux enclos à bétail communaux à l'extrémité ouest de l'alignement de poteaux étaient le théâtre de rassemblements sociaux réguliers.

Ce rapport comprend également un résumé détaillé des récentes fouilles commerciales à Fengate. Il apporte de nouvelles preuves de l'existence d'un paysage organisé néolithique plus ancien. Il s'organisait en une large bande ou ruban aligné sur une baie nouvellement découverte en bordure de la zone marécageuse. Après l'abandon des champs de l'âge du bronze, l'occupation se déplaça au-dessus de la ligne de contour des 5 mètres: des fouilles sur le site de Tower Works ont fait apparaître un lien entre les fossés de la fin de l'âge du bronze et du début de l'âge du fer que nous connaissons bien, puisqu'ils ont été révélés pour la première fois dans les premières décennies du siècle actuel, et l'usage final des champs de l'âge du bronze de Fengate. La plus ancienne occupation de l'âge du fer sur le site de Tower Works comprend des témoignages d'occupation en noyau et au moins un bâtiment rectangulaire.

La réévaluation du paysage de Fengate amenée par le récent développement commercial a eu un profond effet sur notre compréhension de la région, et en particulier sur les périodes de l'âge du fer et du début de l'époque romaine. La célèbre occupation connue sous le nom de Cat's Water, par exemple, peut maintenant être replacée dans son contexte paysager qui repose sur de solides preuves paléo-environnementales. De récentes fouilles commerciales ont également jeté une lumière nouvelle sur la signification de la marge marécageuse 'naturelle' tout au bord de la zone habitable. Au cours des fouilles commerciales récentes on a aussi employé les techniques de micromorphologie du sol et d'analyse des pollens afin d'éclairer notre vision de cet environnement changeant depuis les premiers temps néolithiques. Avec la poursuite des recherches, peu de régions en Grande-Bretagne ou ailleurs, peuvent ou vont offrir une image aussi intégrale d'une occupation de la fin de la préhistoire, de son utilisation de la terre et de ses rituels.

Traduction: Annie Pritchard

Zusammenfassung

Das Flag Fen Becken ist ein Gebiet von niegrig liegendem Land an den westlichen Grenzen der Niederungen von Ostengland (Fens of Eastern England) and den Randgebieten der City of Peterborough, vormals in Cambridgeshire. Das Gebiet war nahe zu ständig das Subjekt archeologischer Untersuchungen seit circa 1900. In 1968, wenn Peterborough von der zentralen Regierung als eine Neue Stadt designiert wurde, gewann die kommerzielle Entwicklung schnell an Geschwindigkeit. Der größte Teil der archeologischen Untersuchungen beschrieben in dieser Studie, vollzog sich als Antwort zu Neubauprojekten in den letzten dreißig Jahren des Jahrhunderts.

Während des Fengate — Projektes von 1971–8 ist ein Feldgrabensystem des Bronzezeit im Trockenland von Fengate verzeichnet worden an der Westseite des Flag Fen Beckens. Folgende Untersuchungen in Northey, auf der Ostseite des Beckens, haben ein ähnliches Feldsystem hervorgebracht. Die Felder von Northey und Fengate sind definiert durch Graben und Wälle, auf denen wahrscheinlich Hecken angepflanzt wurden. Diese Felder sind gruppiert in größeren Besitzschaften bei parallel begrabten Treibwegen, welche in rechten Winkeln nach unten zu den Naßlandrändern verlaufen.

Das Fengate Feldsystem wurde erstmals in der Bronzezeit ausgelegt und wurde seit dem frühen ersten Jahrtausend BC nicht mehr benutzt. Das Northey Feldsystem ist noch nicht im Detail untersucht worden. Neueste Ergebnisse deuten auf eine Auslegung des Feldsystem in zwei Phasen hin. Die zentralen und nördlichen Elemente wurden vier bis fünf Jahrhunderte vor dem südlichen Element ausgelegt. Das letztere war für eine ähnliche Periode nach dem Gebrauch des Rest des Systems in Benutzung.

Die Bronzezeitfelder waren für das Mangement einen sehr großen Viehbestandes ausgelegt, prinzipiell für Schafe und Rinder. Die Tiere graßten auf reichen Naßlandweiden der Flag Fen in den trockeneren Monaten und kehrten zu den flutenfreien Weiden am Niederungsrand zum Überwintern zurück. Bei Newark Road und Fourth Drove, das Herz des Fengate Bronzezeitfeldsystems war ausgelegt in einem komplexen Werk von Treibwegen, Höfen, Stallungen zentriert um einen Haupttreibweg. Dieser ist interpretiert als ein „Marktplatz" für den Austausch von Viehbestand und für reguläre soziale Zusammenkünfte. Der Treibweg durch diese Gemeinschaftsviehhöfe verläuft östlich bis zum regelmäßig überfluteten Land an dem Kraftwerk wo die Linie des Treibweges von fünf Reihen von Pfosten weitergeführt wurde. Diese verliefen über das allmählich vordringende Naßland von Flag Fen zu Northey, um 1200m nach Osten.

Diese fünf Pfostenreihen werden allgemein als „Pfostenausrichtung" bezeichnet. Dendrokronologie zeigt, daß sie für ungefähr 400 Jahre benutzt wurden, zwischen 1300 und 900 BC. 200m westlich vom Northey Landfall die Pfostenausrichtung kreuzt ein zeitgenössige künstliche hölzerne Plattform von Balken gebaut. Die Bedeutung dieser Plattform ist zum heutigen Zeitpunkt noch nicht geklärt, ist jedoch zweifellos physikalisch und funktionell mit der Pfostenausrichtung verbunden.

Da die Bedingungen für den Erhalt hervorragend in den nässeren Gebieten der Flag Fen waren, ist es möglich die Holzarbeiten im Detail zu studieren. Die frühen Bauhölzer waren normalerweise Erle und andere Naßlandspezien, aber auch Eiche wurde in den letzten Phasen benutzt. Holzsplitter und andere Überreste beweisen, daß in der Regel große Holzbalken wurden daß das Prozessieren von Wäldern nur in den unteren Ebenen ausgeführt wurde. Untersuchungen der Werkzeugmäler deuten auf eine fast exklusive Nutzung von gefassten Äxen hin. Eine Anzahl von hölzernen Artefakten und wieder verwendeten Teilen wurden gefunden. Diese beinhalteten dreiseitiges Rad, eine Achse und eine Schaufel.

Studien der Tierknochen und Töpferarbeiten zeigen zwei unterschiedliche Montagestätten am Kraftwerk und an der Flag Fen Seite. Die erste war von dominiert bei häuslichen Material, welches vielleicht von Siedlungen am Rand der Niederung in der Nähe. An beiden Standorten war ein beträchtlicher Anteil von Ritualen, prinzipiell bei Flag Fen, rituelle Funde umfassten komplette Töpfereigefässe und die Überreste von mehreren Hunden.

Eine große Anhäufung von Metallarbeiten demonstriert die Wichtigkeit von Ritualen an beiden Standorten. Um die 275 Stücke von prähistorischen Metallarbeiten wurden bei Flag Fen und im südlichen Teil der Pfostenausrichtung bei dem Kraftwerk gefunden. Die Metallarbeiten, hauptsächlich Bronze und Blech, umfassten Waffen, Ornamente und mehrere kontinentale Importe. Es gibt Beweise, daß viele der Teile absichtlich vor dem das Wasser zerstört und zerbrochen wurden. Eine beträchtliche Anzahl der Anhäufung stammt aus der Eisenzeit und muß in der Ausrichtung ins Wasser vor der Aufgabe der Pfosten plaziert wurden.

Die Pfosten der Ausrichtung bei Flag Fen waren von fünf Schichten von horizontalen Hölzern, welche als Verstärkung, Fundament benutzt wurden und in Stellen als Pfad enge Wege verbanden. Die Pfosten hatten verschiedene Funktionen: als Wegweiser für Reisende auf den verschiedenen Wegen, als eine fast vollständige Wand und Palisade, gebaut in einer Art *chevaux-de-fris*. Es gibt außerdem Beweise für quer liegende Holz- und Flechtwerkteilungen, welche die Ausrichtung in Segmente von 5–6m Länge aufteilte.

Es wird angenommen, daß diese Segmente eine wichtige rituelle Funktion besaßen. Die Bedeutung der Teilungen wird durch die Plazierung von Gaben, begrenzende Lagerungen von Wertgegenständen, z.B. unbenutzte Mahlsteine. Segmente innerhalb der Pfostenausrichtung haben wahrscheinlich eine ähnliche Bedeutung haben wie die Segmente des Dammes und des Einfriedungsgrabens. Den nahen Standort von Etton als Beispiel verwendend, wird angenommen, daß die Segmente von Gruppen verschiedener Verwandschaftsbeziehungen für rituelle Zwecke benutzt wurden. Es wird außerdem angenommen, daß die Rituale der verschiedenen privaten oder Familiengruppen in einer Zeit unternommen wurden in welcher die Hauptgemeinschaftsviehhöfe die Szene von regulären sozialen Zusammentreffen waren.

Die Studie beinhaltet außerdem eine detailierte Zusammenfassung der letzten kommerziellen Ausgrabungen bei Fengate. Dort gibt es Beweise für eine frühere neolithische Aufteilung der Landschaft. Diese war als ein weites Band oder Streifen ausgelegt auf einer kürzlich gefundenen Einbuchtung am Niederungsrand. Nach der Aufgabe der Bronzezeitfelder die Besiedlung zog sich über die 5m Kontur hinaus: Ausgrabungen and dem Tower Works Standort haben eine Verbindung aufgezeigt zwischen den Gruben der gut bekannten späteren Bronzezeit und der frühen Eisenzeit, erstmals ersichtlich gemacht in den frühen Jahrzehnten des 20.Jahrhunderts und die letzte Benutzung der Fengate Bronzezeitfelder. Die früheste Eisenzeitansiedlung an den Tower Works Standorten umfaßt Beweise der Kernsiedlungen und mindestens eines rechteckiges Gebäudes.

Die Wiederbeurteilung der Fengate Landschaft herbeigeführt durch die letzten kommerziellen Entwicklungen hatte einen tiefgreifenden Effekt auf unser Verständnis dieses Gebietes, im spezifischen der Eisenzeit und frühen römischen Perioden. Die gut bekannte Cat's Water Siedlung kann nun in einen landschaftlichen Zusammenhang plaziert werden, basierend auf soliden paläoumweltlichen Beweisen. Letzte kommerzielle Ausgrabungen haben außerdem neues Licht auf die Bedeutung des „natürlichen" Niederungsrandes an der eigentlichen Kante des bewohnbaren Landes. In modernen kommerziellen Ausgrabungen, Boden-Mikromorphologie und – Palynologie wurden auch eingesetzt um unser Bild von der sich wandelnen Umwelt seit frühen neolitischen Zeiten klarer zu machen. Mit fortwährenden Untersuchungen, wenige Regionen in Großbritannien, oder woanders, können oder werden solch ein integriertes Bild von späteren prähistorischen Siedlungen, landnutzend und rituell, bieten.

Übersetzung: Norman Behrend

1 Introduction: The Flag Fen Basin

A summary of the principal archaeological features

Fengate and Flag Fen lie on the south-eastern limits of the city of Peterborough (Fig 1.1) in the former county of Cambridgeshire, centred on OS NGR TL 227989. Peterborough is positioned approximately in the middle of the western margins of the Fens (Fig 1.2). Prior to largescale drainage in the seventeenth century and later, the Fens were Britain's largest wetland (Godwin 1978).

The Flag Fen basin considered here comprises three archaeological landscapes: Fengate (now an industrial suburb of Peterborough), Flag Fen, and Northey (a small hamlet). The countryside of the basin is very low-lying and, before being drained, was characterised by large areas of freshwater or slightly brackish wetland surrounded by a drier, flood-free, fen-edge plain (Fig 1.3). In the Peterborough area, this plain was composed of river Nene first-terrace gravels (Horton *et al* 1974) and owes its archaeological importance to a series of prehistoric and Roman landscapes around the periphery of the wetter fen.

A large 'island' of Jurassic clay, capped with gravel, lay about a kilometre east of the Fengate fen edge and was separated from it by part of the drained wetland known today as Flag Fen. This 'island' is nowadays largely covered by the town of Whittlesey and its outlying suburbs, Coates and Eastrea (Fig 1.1). A north-easterly peninsula of the Whittlesey 'island' almost extends to the Peterborough 'mainland' at Flag Fen. This peninsula, now known as Northey, is today cut off from the rest of Whittlesey 'island' by the canalised, artificial course of the river Nene (Fig 1.3).

For present purposes, the archaeological features at Flag Fen comprise two main elements: an alignment of wooden posts about a kilometre in length and a wooden platform of very approximately 1.4ha in extent (Fig 1.4). The post alignment runs from the gently sloping dryland landscape of Fengate, south-eastwards to the slightly steeper dry land of Northey 'island'.

The post alignment meets the platform (of which it is an integral part) closer to Northey than Fengate (Fig 1.4). The main period of construction and use of both platform and post alignment was the Late Bronze Age, but there was also significant, and associated, activity before and after that period.

The post alignment connects the landscapes of the basin. At the western landfall the posts coincide with a major boundary droveway formed by ditches 8 and 9 of the Fengate Bronze Age system (Fig 1.4; Pryor 1980). At the eastern end, it is not known precisely where the posts terminate upon reaching drier land, but recent research has revealed cropmarks of similar ditched droveways that are aligned (more-or-less) on the post alignment (Fig 1.4).

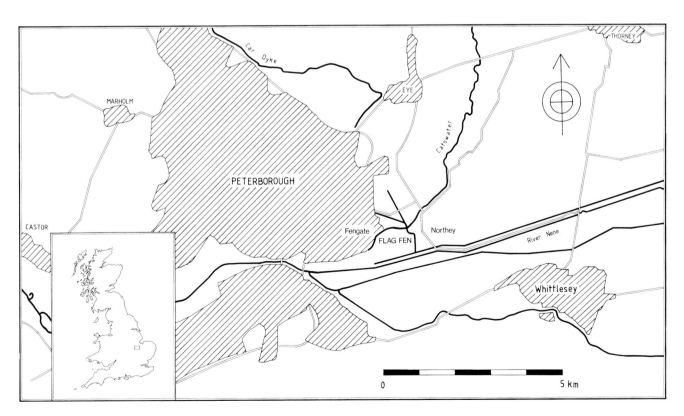

Fig 1.1 Location map of Flag Fen

1

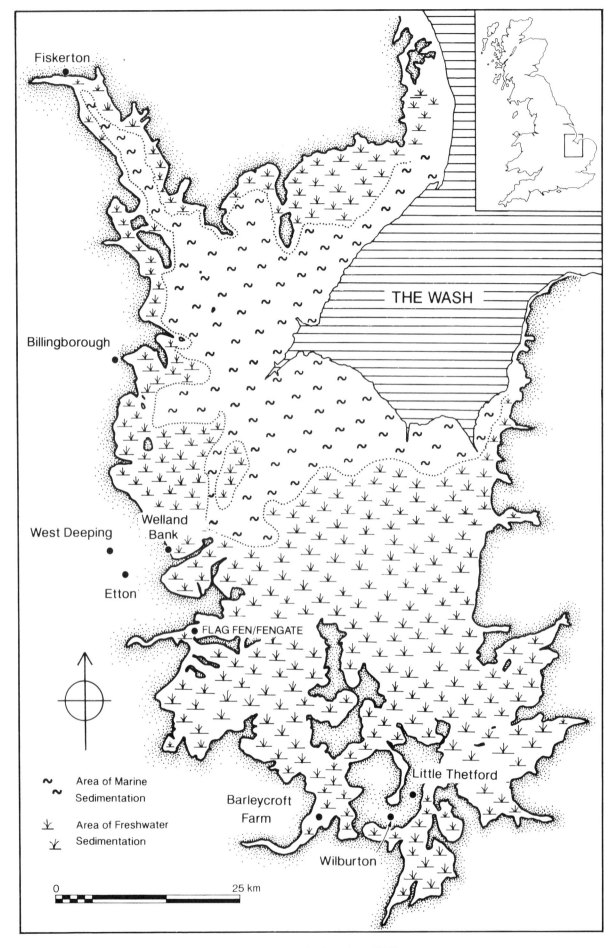

Fig 1.2 Flag Fen in its Fenland setting, c *700–600 BC (based on Waller 1994, 76)*

The succession of ancient landscapes at Fengate are reviewed in Chapter 18. They can be summarised as follows:

Landscape 1: the earlier Neolithic
Landscape 2: the later Neolithic
Landscape 3: the Bronze Age
Landscape 4: the earliest Iron Age
Landscape 5: Middle Iron Age to Roman

The distribution of archaeological subsites and trenches

All significant archaeological trenches excavated in the Flag Fen Basin between 1968 and 1997 are shown in Figures 1.5 and 1.6 and Table 1.1. The small trenches of the Flag Fen wetland are shown in an inset in Figure 1.5. They are covered in greater detail in Chapter 6 (Fig 6.1).

The area has been subject to archaeological investigation for many years and by a growing number of organisations. In the interests of brevity and consistency a standard terminology will be used (Table 1.1). It should be noted that the position of trenches within Sites O and Q has been omitted for reasons of client confidentiality.

Flag Fen Basin in its Fenland setting

The Fens once formed Britain's largest wetland, comprising approximately one million acres. Apart from one or two nature reserves, they are now entirely drained.

Wetland deposits formed in a shallow natural depression around the Wash as a direct result of the post-Glacial rise in sea levels (Louwe-Kooijmans 1980; Shennan 1982).

Towards the coast the surface deposits are of marine origin and mainly comprise silts and finer silty clays. Further inland, these deposits are more variable and range from freshwater peats to alluvial spreads. These superficial deposits still cover, obscure, and protect significant areas of prehistoric remains. The nature of the subsoil will often determine the quality and quantity of archaeological preservation. The Flag Fen Basin is fortunate in this respect, as the underlying first-terrace gravel is capped by a thin layer of clay into which the posts of the Bronze Age alignment and platform were driven (Fig 1.7). This layer of clay has helped to maintain a high local groundwater table. In the southern Fens, on the other hand, sandy subsoils (for example, in the region around Mildenhall in Suffolk) have proved less resistant to drainage and intensive agriculture. In these areas, Neolithic and even Mesolithic sites are under constant threat of desiccation and erosion (eg Hall and Coles 1994, fig 5). The Fens are of unique archaeological importance and have recently been the subject of a major English Heritage survey (Hall and Coles op cit).

The Fenland Survey and its companion palaeoenvironmental programme have drawn attention to the diversity of the many micro-regions that characterised

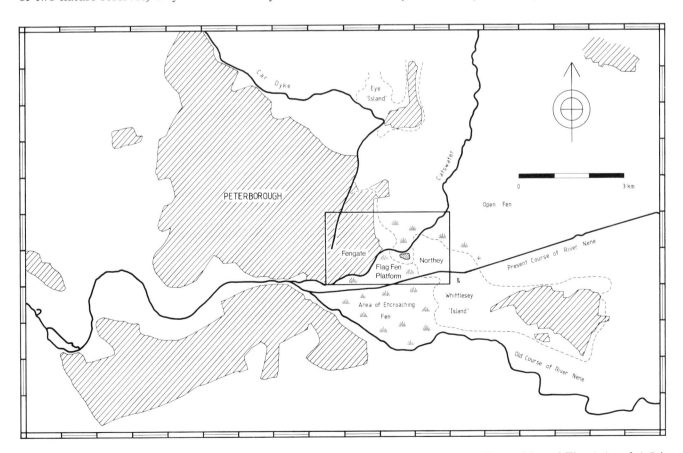

Fig 1.3 Map of the Flag Fen region, showing later prehistoric topography in outline. The position of Figs 1.4 and 1.5 is shown in inset

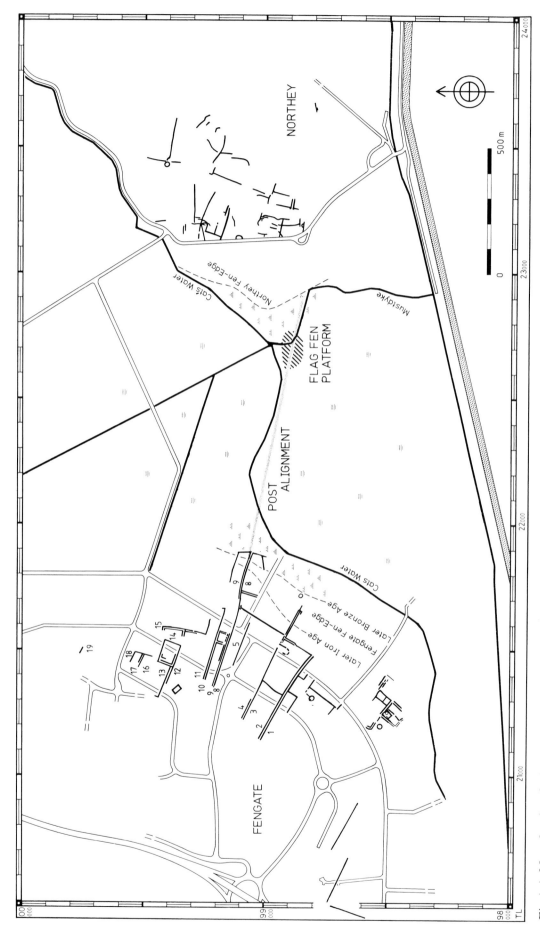

Fig 1.4 Map showing the location of principal Neolithic and Bronze Age features

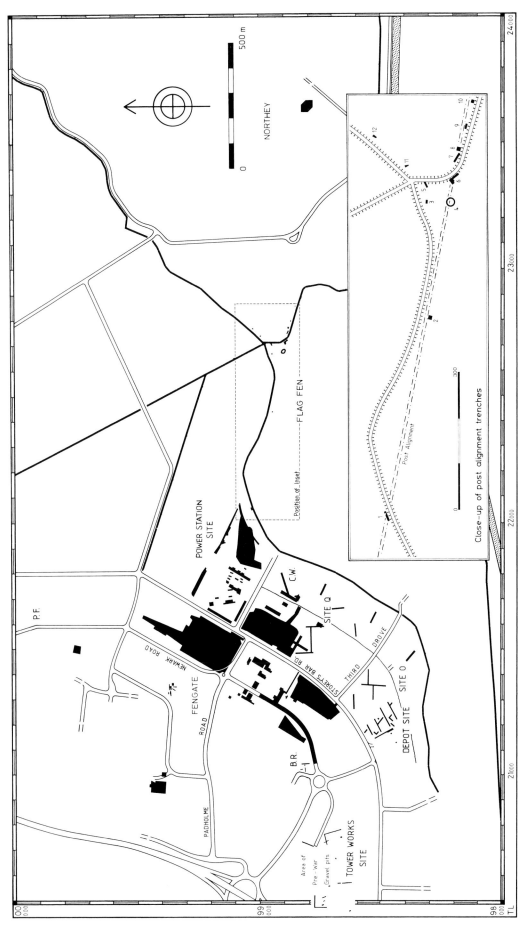

Fig 1.5 Map showing location of areas excavated 1968–97. BR = Boongate Roundabout site; CW = Cat's Water sites

Table 1.1 Archaeological projects conducted in the Flag Fen Basin discussed in the text

full description	*short description*	*main references*
Pre-war researches of G Wyman Abbott and others in the Fengate gravel pits	Gravel Pits sites	Abbott 1910; Leeds 1922; Hawkes and Fell 1945
Nene Valley Research Committee excavations, 1968 (Director: C Mahany)	Site 11	Pryor 1993
Royal Ontario Museum/Department of the Environment, Fengate Project, 1974–8	ROM/DoE	Pryor 1974; 1978; 1978; 1980; 1984a
Fenland Archaeological Trust/English Heritage Flag Fen Fen excavations, 1982–95	Flag Fen	this volume
Fenland Archaeological Trust/English Heritage, Power Station excavations, 1989	Power Station	this volume
Fenland Archaeological Trust, Cat's Water Excavations, 1990	Cat's Water (1990)	this volume
Cambridge University Archaeological Unit, Ex-Murden's Depot evaluation excavations, 1992	Depot Site (1992)	Evans 1992
Fenland Archaeological Trust, 1997	Depot Site (1997)	Pryor 1997a
Fenland Archaeological Trust, Global Doors factory watching brief/excavations, 1993	Global Doors	this volume
Fenland Archaeological Trust, Newark Road paving factory watching brief/excavations, 1994	Paving Factory	this volume
Birmingham University Field Archaeology Unit, Boongate roundabout evaluation excavations, 1995	Boongate Roundabout	Cuttler 1995
Cambridge University Archaeological Unit, Recycling Facility, evaluation excavations, 1996	Third Drove	Gdaniec 1998
Cambridge University Archaeological Unit, Excavations at the Coop site, 1997	Cat's Water (1997)	Gibson 1998
Cambridge University Archaeological Unit, Tower Works, Fengate evaluation excavations, 1997	Tower Works	Lucas 1997a and b
Birmingham University Field Archaeology Unit, evaluation excavations south of Third Drove (Site Q) and north of Third Drove (Site O), both 1998	Site Q / Site O	Cuttler 1998

the ancient Fens (Waller 1994a). This recent major publication describes the general archaeological and topographical landscape of the Fens more than adequately and need not be repeated here. Suffice it to say that the present study is the investigation of just one Fenland microregion, located close to the confluence of the river Nene and the Fenland basin: as was the case elsewhere in the Fenland, wetness gradually increased in the Flag Fen Basin in the second and first millennia BC.

The scope and purpose of the report

This volume discusses excavation and survey undertaken in and around Flag Fen since the publication of the first major report (Pryor *et al* 1986). A review of recent research at a number of sites in Fengate (to the west) and Northey (to the east) of the main site will be included.

In an ideal world, a major monograph ought to provide a final statement about a given body of research. In the Flag Fen area, however, significant new discoveries are regularly being made in the course of implementing *Planning Policy Guidance Note 16* (PPG16) projects; many of these have significantly affected our original interpretations of the various sites' roles. For example, the Northey field or paddock system (Chapter 5) represents a major new element in the landscape, but it was only revealed by aerial photography as late as August 1994. The Fengate Tower Works site (Chapter 3) has led to a radical reappraisal of the earlier discoveries of G Wyman Abbott (1910). Inevitably, therefore, this volume must be treated as yet another interim statement, albeit a detailed one.

It is perhaps surprising that the pace of research in the region has not slowed appreciably, following completion of the major excavation project by English Heritage of 1982–92 (Pryor and Taylor 1992; Pryor *et al* 1992). The bulk of the present report will be devoted to that project, but a number of commercial contract excavations, which have made a significant contribution to our understanding of the region's prehistoric past, will also be considered in Chapters 2 and 3.

Research at Flag Fen subsequent to the English Heritage project has been funded from three sources: the generosity of the landowners (Anglian Water Services Ltd); visitor-generated income, and university training excavations (Pryor 1989). Taken together, these funds amounted to approximately one-sixth of the budget previously provided by English Heritage.

Fieldwork and post-excavation research in 1993 and 1994 have perforce been limited in scope, but the more significant results have merited inclusion in this report. It is essential that archaeological research at Flag Fen continues, even on a reduced scale, since waterlogged archaeological features in the area are constantly under threat through land drainage.

A brief guide to the report

The present chapter will summarise the principal discoveries of the ROM/DoE project of 1971–8, which is essential to a proper understanding of Flag Fen and its landscape. Chapters 2 and 3 are summary syntheses of smaller excavations carried out after the main ROM/DoE project.

Chapter 4 is devoted to the Power Station excavations of 1989. This work took place prior to the implementation of PPG16 (DoE 1990) and includes some salvage excavation. Chapter 5 is devoted to the eastern landfall of the post alignment at Northey 'island'. It includes recent aerial photographic evidence and a short account of the trial trenches opened in 1994.

Chapter 6 is concerned with the excavation of the Flag Fen post alignment and the timber platform. The excavations described took place mainly between the discovery of the site in 1982 and 1992. the last season of large-scale work.

Chapters 7–15 deal with the finds or specialists' reports. These are followed by more general reviews, starting with a reconsideration of the dating evidence (Chapter 16), followed by a discussion of the palaeoenvironment of the Flag Fen Basin, and, finally, two general chapters of synthesis (Chapters 18 and 19).

Grid references

North in all plans is Ordnance Survey Grid North. Intra-site grid references use the OS system, but with the initial letters (usually TL) and first digits of the easting and northing removed. Thus the full OS NGR TL 2128198752 would appear as site grid 1281 8752.

A summary of published research

It is to be hoped that, after three decades of post-war research into the ancient landscape of the Peterborough fen margins, the publication of this report will represent a significant milestone. Thirty years of near-continuous research was preceded by seventy-five years of intermittent, but highly significant discoveries, most of which were made in the hand-dug gravel pits of Fengate.

The finds of G Wyman Abbott

Much of the earlier material from Fengate was collected by the noted local antiquarian and solicitor, George Wyman Abbott. For over twenty years, Abbott made regular visits to gravel pits in the region, where he obtained pottery and other finds directly from the workmen.

The small privately owned gravel pits of Fengate were mainly situated to the south-west of the present research area, on land that was generally above the 5m contour. It is apparent from Abbott's notes and records, now held in the University Museum of Archaeology and Ethnology, Downing Street, Cambridge, that the area of the pre-war gravel pits (Figs 1.5 and 1.6) included a number of discrete sites, but until very recently it has not proved possible to differentiate between them. A recent desk-based study (Lucas 1997a) has successfully disentangled many of the complexities of the Gravel Pits sites, to reveal a number of more closely defined areas of occupation. The desk-based survey and the subsequent Tower Works excavations (Lucas 1997b) have resolved many of the more serious problems. The current position is further discussed in Chapter 3.

Abbott's well known paper of 1910 was cowritten with R A Smith. Smith's discussion of Neolithic ceramics in the light of the Fengate discoveries led to the widespread use and adoption of the term 'Peterborough' to describe the heavily decorated vessels of the later Neolithic tradition. Abbott's next collaboration was with another noted archaeologist, E T Leeds, who lived within sight of Fengate at the nearby Fenland 'island' of Eye. Leeds' paper (1922) was mainly concerned with Beaker pottery found at Fengate and other local gravel pits. Some, but not all, the material examined by Smith and Leeds is in Peterborough Museum.

Since the present report is largely concerned with the Bronze Age, it is appropriate to recall the unusual 'little skin bag' cremations found by Abbott in the old Fengate gravel workings. The excavator's notebooks, quoted by Hawkes and Fell (1945), describe an oval ring-ditch that enclosed 20 inhumation burials of the Early Bronze Age; within the area occupied by the inhumations were 130 cremations in 'little skin bags', one of which was accompanied by a bucket urn. This extraordinary site also contained a 'crematorium'. The whereabouts of this material is not known, but it would seem that the cemetery would best belong to a Middle Bronze Age and East Midlands variant of the broader Deverel-Rimbury tradition.

Hawkes and Fell considered that the cremations were probably of Iron Age date, but the Iron Age pottery came not from the surface but from pits. Further, much of it would today be considered of 'post-Deverel-Rimbury' or Late Bronze Age/Early Iron Age type. The neatest explanation is that the cremations belonged to a compact cremation cemetery of Deverel-Rimbury type,

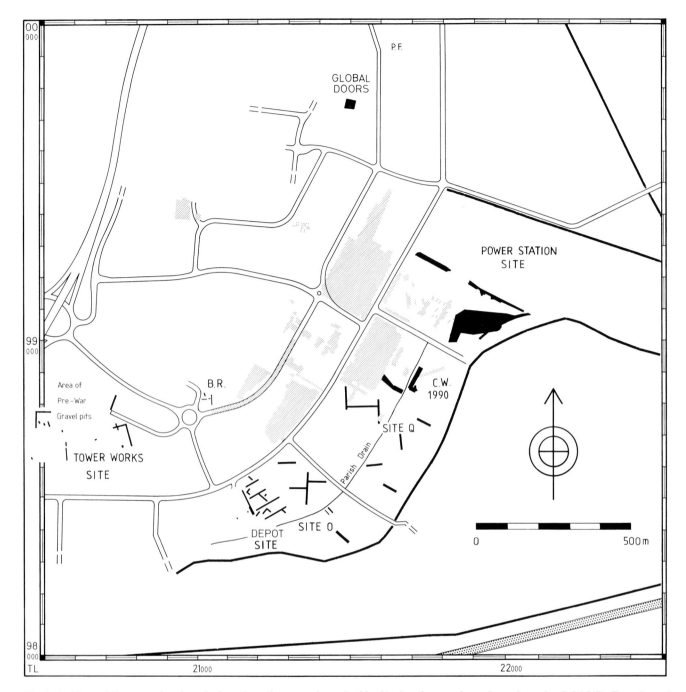

Fig 1.6 Map of Fengate showing the location of excavations (in black) that have taken place since the ROM/DoE project of 1971–8 (hatched)

comparable, for example, with Simons Ground, Dorset; it is not unusual to find Deverel-Rimbury cremations within or around Early Bronze Age barrows and ring-ditches (White 1982). A recent local parallel for the use of organic containers for human remains has been found at Deeping St Nicholas, Lincs (French 1994, 108).

The third major study to use material recovered by Abbott was that by Isobel Smith (1956). The actual pottery studied by Smith, or a proportion of it, today resides in the study collections of University College, London (Institute of Archaeology). It has often been remarked that Late Neolithic Fengate Ware, first defined by Smith in her thesis of 1956, has not been

found at the type-site in any quantity, subsequent, that is, to Abbott's earlier work.

The largest assemblage of Fengate Ware has been excavated at Etton, a few miles north of Peterborough, from surprisingly early contexts (Pryor 1998a). At Etton, the Fengate pottery was not recovered on the main body of Maxey 'island' to the north, despite large-scale excavation, but confined to within the causewayed enclosure (Pryor and French 1985). It is just possible, therefore, that the original pits that produced Fengate Ware could have been part of a monument similar to that at Etton. There are further slight hints that another causewayed enclosure lies beneath the peaty alluvium of Flag Fen, close by the Power Station.

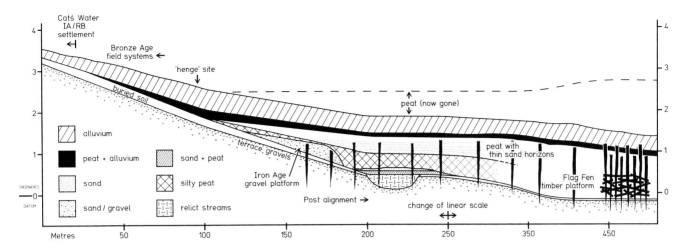

Fig 1.7 Schematic section from Fengate to the Flag Fen timber platform. Note the change in the linear scale at 250m

The fourth use of Abbott's data was that of Clare I Fell, whose study of the later Bronze and Iron Age pottery from Fengate pit groups (Hawkes and Fell 1945) formed the basis of Cunliffe's Fengate–Cromer group of the fifth to the third century BC (Cunliffe 1991, 566).

The ROM/DoE Fengate project, 1971–8

In the later 1960s, central government designated Peterborough as a new town, whose population was set to grow from 80,000 to 180,000. When Fengate was selected as an area for industrial development, the Royal Commission for Historical Monuments (England) undertook a special survey of the antiquities in the areas threatened by development (RCHM 1969). This report, which used many aerial photographs by Professor St Joseph (from the Cambridge Collection), showed that, although the archaeological remains at Fengate were still largely intact, they were under immediate threat of destruction by the construction of the new town's eastern industrial area.

Following publication of the Royal Commission's report, the erstwhile Nene Valley Research Committee (a research committee of the Council for British Archaeology) urgently set about organising a Fengate rescue project. At first, work was piecemeal, but of a high standard, despite the urgency of the threat. Fengate Site 11, a Neolithic mortuary enclosure and Beaker settlement, was excavated by Christine Mahany in 1969, the first year of the NVRC rescue project (Mahany 1969; Pryor 1988; 1993).

An editorial appeal by Andrew Selkirk in *Current Archaeology*, which drew attention to the plight of archaeological sites in the path of Peterborough New Town, was seen by the present author, then a curatorial assistant in the Royal Ontario Museum, Toronto. With the backing of the museum's Chief Archaeologist, Dr A D Tushingham, and the Nene Valley Research Committee's Chairman, the late Professor W F Grimes, a combined rescue and research programme

for Fengate was drawn up. This led to a long-term, collaborative venture, jointly funded by the (then) Inspectorate of Ancient Monuments, Department of the Environment, and the Royal Ontario Museum. The ROM/DoE Fengate project took place between 1971 and 1978. The results are published in four volumes (Pryor 1974; 1978; 1980 and 1984a). The finds are housed in Peterborough Museum.

Perhaps the most significant result of this project was the discovery of an organised landscape, dating broadly to the second millennium BC, based upon ditched rectilinear fields and droveways. The land divisions were laid out along, and at right angles to, the contemporary fen edge (Fig 1.4; Pryor 1980, 178–89). In terms of this report, this Bronze Age landscape was first laid out early in the period and stayed in use for about a millennium.

The development of research objectives

The approach to research has been as detailed as practical constraints would allow. Special emphasis has been placed on the spatial distribution of a variety of data, ranging from phosphate concentrations to potsherds. There have, of course, been a number of false starts. At the completion of the ROM/DoE project, for example, it was felt that the general picture of developing culture in the area was quite well understood. Then, in 1982, the Dyke Survey (French and Pryor 1993, 68–76) revealed that the Borough Fen ring-fort was Iron Age and not medieval. Later that year the Flag Fen platform and post alignment was discovered (Pryor 1991, 74–83). Both discoveries have had a profound effect on views of later prehistoric life in the area and have led to several reassessments of the significance of the results of the original ROM/DoE project (eg Pryor 1996).

Until 1982, research had been oriented towards domestic and agrarian aspects of ancient life and what might be termed 'culture:land relations'. After that date, the focus of research broadened in that the relationship of ancient communities to their changing environment was seen to be only part of the picture. Far greater emphasis is now placed upon the role of ritual and the changing state of intercommunal social and political relations than was previously the case.

The Flag Fen Basin is now seen as an important element within the broader palimpsest of landscapes that together comprised the prehistoric fenland. Nevertheless, at least two important question remain to be answered: were the developments in the Flag Fen Basin unique and are there other Flag Fens? These topics will be discussed in Chapter 19.

Two reasons have been mentioned as to why the focus of research changed after 1982. The third factor was the excavation of the nearby causewayed enclosure at Etton (Pryor 1998a). From the outset, it was apparent that this site contained an important ritual or symbolic component. Etton and Flag Fen were excavated simultaneously in the summers of 1983 to 1987. Although they were separated by over two millennia, it was impossible to ignore certain broad similarities: the placing of objects in shallow water; the destruction of fine items; the careful delineation of space, and the repeated symbolic manipulation of certain artefact types including weapons, pottery, and querns.

It is not suggested that there was a direct link between sites so widely separated in time. Having said this, both sites fulfilled certain common social and farming needs and there must also have been a degree of 'parallel evolution': the simultaneous excavation of two sites that at first were thought to be dissimilar undoubtedly emphasised their perceived similarities. This observation might help to explain the genesis (and bias) of some of the hypotheses suggested in this report.

As the scope of research broadened after 1983, the methods of excavation were modified in an attempt to obtain ever greater detail. This approach was undoubtedly a result of the excavation of the Etton enclosure ditch, where the structured deposits placed in the ditch bottom and within various recuts were examined with minute care: the key to understanding the original motives behind a site's use in antiquity has been shown to lie in the detailed pattern of its archaeological deposits at both Etton and Flag Fen.

The English Heritage Fenland Project was based upon a series of parish-by-parish surveys. Fieldwalking and the study of existing aerial photographs were combined to produce a series of period plans. The archaeological evidence was then superimposed upon reconstructed contemporary topographic maps. The project, which covered an enormous area, has produced some very important results. These have provided invaluable contextual information for the present study (Hall and Coles 1994; Waller 1994a).

A main aim of the various Flag Fen, Fengate, and Northey projects has been the recognition and identification of deeply buried archaeological remains. This work has mainly been based on the dyke survey (French and Pryor 1993), but special emphasis has been placed on repeated aerial survey, undertaken by the Nene Valley Research Committee's aerial archaeologist, Dr S J Upex. Although most seasons reveal something new, either as a soil mark or cropmark, the results of the 1994 survey were unusually rewarding. They will be described in Chapter 5.

Continuing research: the Northey Landfall Project

Fenland Archaeological Trust is a participant in the Millennium Commission's Green Wheel cycleway project. The aim of this project, organised by Peterborough Environment City Trust, is to construct a cycleway 'ring-road' around the city that will feature a number of visitor centres on the route, among which is Flag Fen. The cycleway will pass along the edge of Northey 'island', at the point where the post alignment is projected to reach dry land. The principal research aim can be stated simply: how does the Northey landfall compare with the Fengate one? In preliminary investigations (March 1998), a bronze ring, closely comparable to examples from the Power Station (cf below, Fig 10.10, 234), was found near the surface of the buried palaeosol.

The Northey Landfall Project will necessitate predetermination archaeological investigation, in line with PPG16, but, given the area's known archaeological importance, a number of additional surveys and subsidiary excavations are scheduled to take place in 1999. These works will include a major geophysical survey of the post alignment's Northey landfall (undertaken on behalf of *Time Team*), together with metal-detecting, trial trenching, and environmental sampling. All available aerial photographs will be reassessed and plotted by Rog Palmer. The results of the Northey Landfall Project will be published separately (it is hoped, should the results warrant it, in a forthcoming monograph on Northey and Flag Fen).

Changing interpretations: the role of ritual

Although the ROM/DoE project provided extensive evidence for settlement and land-use, aside from a single ring-ditch (Pryor 1978, 33–8) and a few burials (listed in Pryor 1984a, 258), the project produced few features that could be associated with ritual or ceremonial. These findings were in broad agreement with Abbott's research, which only revealed a single non-settlement site, a group of Bronze Age cremations (Hawkes and Fell 1945). Research carried out after 1978 has, however, substantially redressed the balance in favour of ritual, in terms both of new sites and new interpretation.

In the Cat's Water excavations of 1990 (Chapter 3), a hitherto unknown hengiform monument was disinterred. In addition, further research into Mahany's Site

11 and the Padholme Road 'house' (Pryor 1974) has indicated that both were probably funerary structures. A third Neolithic mortuary structure was found at Cat's Water in 1997 (Chapter 3). The Flag Fen post alignment and platform also probably served a mainly ritual purpose (Chapter 18). The new interpretation of the post alignment largely came about as a result of the Power Station excavations of 1989 (Chapter 4).

Conservation and preservation

This section considers the archaeological burial environment, and the efforts made to keep large areas of waterlogged deposits wet, a process intended to counteract the effects of a retreating groundwater table.

Desiccation and the archaeological buried environment

The principal known threat to the organic deposits at Flag Fen is probably desiccation. Since the 1950s, their environment has been characterised by a falling groundwater table, largely brought about by artificial drainage. The medieval Mustdyke (Halliday 1986), a large drain that cuts through the post alignment, is the main surface water flood relief channel for the Eastern Industrial Area of Peterborough (Fig 1.4). The water level in this dyke is kept as high as possible, thanks to the cooperation of the Environment Agency, but, even so, in summer months it is found to be regularly at least a metre below the highest Bronze Age horizontal timbers. In winter, it might briefly rise close to the level of the lowest horizontal timbers. The Mustdyke undoubtedly exerts a 'draw-down' effect on the local groundwater table.

In addition to dewatering, the site is also affected by other factors, the most obvious of which is sewage sludge. Sludge is currently spread over some 200 acres immediately south and west of the Mustdyke. The effects of sludge and other (mainly agricultural effluents) are presently being monitored by two independent projects: the first, the Waterlogged Anoxic Archaeological Burial Environments (WANABE) Project, is funded by English Heritage and based at Durham University; the second is funded jointly by English Heritage, Anglian Water Services Ltd, and the University of Surrey. The latter is more site-specific and is concerned with the microbiological activity associated with sewage and sludge in archaeological contexts.

The first results of the WANABE Project have recently been published by the Ancient Monuments Laboratory (Caple and Dungworth 1998). This report includes interim results of a ten-day programme of monitoring at Flag Fen (ibid, appendix 1). The monitoring of the chemical and physical condition of waterlogged deposits (in which measurements were taken automatically at ten-minute intervals) showed that the

archaeological deposits were moderately reducing and neutral. Further reports will appear through the Ancient Monuments Laboratory.

The artificial lakes as 'water conditioners'

Despite fears expressed in discussion, recent research has shown that water seeping from the large lake at the visitor centre is not oxygenated, despite the fact that it is pumped from the Mustdyke nearby. Caple and Dungworth (ibid, paragraph 5.5) have discussed this phenomenon and it should be noted that the area in which their monitoring took place still receives a steady flow of seepage from the nearby lake. They report:

> The site was discovered as a result of operations to improve the drainage in the area, which has seen a progressive decline in the water table. The cleaning of the drainage ditches, Mustdyke and Cat's Water, allowed the discovery of Flag Fen but this now poses a threat to the site, as the platform lies above the new water table. This has been countered by the excavation of lakes adjacent to the site. The water level in the lakes is maintained by pumping water up from the drainage ditches, which then slowly filters through the platform back to the drainage ditches. Pumped water usually has high levels of dissolved oxygen, which would encourage the breakdown of organic materials, but the use of the lake to allow the pumped water to stagnate should alleviate this problem. The monitoring...took place within one of the areas currently being excavated and at the same level as well preserved timbers within the platform. The redox values obtained were in the region of −300 mV.

Construction of the artificial lakes

The construction of the Flag Fen mere in July 1987 was the first successful attempt in England to preserve an archaeological site threatened by destruction through dewatering. Of the two lakes constructed in 1987 and 1988, the former (Fig 1.8, LAKE) seems to have been wholly successful, but the latter (Fig 1.8, POND) has exhibited problems of seepage and requires regular topping up. Both lakes were constructed at low capital cost, using materials that were readily obtainable from builders merchants.

Many visitors to Flag Fen have expressed an interest in the constructional details of the lakes and the lightweight semi-floating foundations of the new visitor centre, which is located in the main artificial mere. This building actually sits on top of the post alignment, its weight so effectively spread by the special foundation arrangements that it appears to cause the Bronze Age timbers no harm.

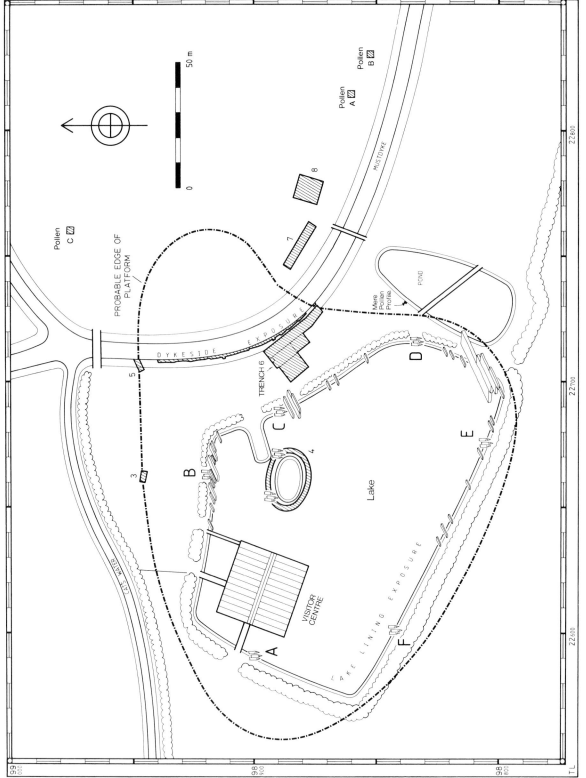

Fig 1.8 Flag Fen excavations 1983–93 and plan of visitor centre, lake, and pond. Excavated areas hatched

Fig 1.9 Inserting the polythene membrane through the bund to form the main artificial mere, July 1987

The main lake at Flag Fen has a circumference of some 400m and encloses an area just short of a hectare (about two acres). Water is held within the mere by a polythene membrane. In plan (Fig 1.8) it is notable for having no sharp corners, which might have presented practical difficulties when inserting the polythene membrane. The polythene used is builders' DPM (damp-proof membrane) of 1000-gauge thickness (0.250mm), which was obtained in rolls 20 × 3.5m. Longer rolls would have been better, but the extra weight might have caused handling problems.

A bulldozer fitted with extra wide, low ground-pressure, 'bog crawler' tracks was used to push the top-soil into a bund, or bank, approximately 1m high. This bank was sufficiently wide and consolidated to carry a tracked hydraulic excavator (Fig 1.9). The machine excavated a metre-wide trench through the bund down to the underlying clay, some 2–3m below the bund surface (Fig 1.10). The plastic sheet was lowered into the trench and held in place using long poles. The trench was then backfilled along approximately half its length. The next sheet of polythene overlapped the first sheet on the inside (lakeside) such that water pressure held the two together. It was originally planned to fix the sheets together with adhesive tape, but this proved to be practically impossible, due to rainfall and mud. Accordingly a generous overlap of at least a metre was allowed. It took one day to construct the bund and approximately four days to insert the membrane. Another day was spent landscaping and making good. The total cost of machine hire and materials was approximately £2500. Using a pump kindly provided by the (then) Anglian Water Authority, the mere was

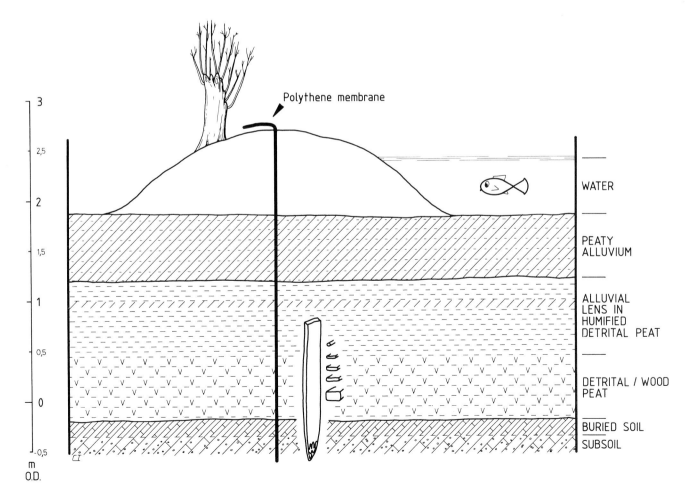

Fig 1.10 Schematic section to show how water is retained within the Flag Fen mere

Fig 1.11 The artificial mere shortly after its initial flooding

filled with water. The average water depth is approximately 300mm (Fig 1.11). Marginal plants, including *Typha angustifolia* and *Iris pseudacorus*, were introduced to eliminate sludge pollution and to encourage the establishment of a naturally balanced floral and faunal community.

The second lake, or pond, was very much smaller than the first. Its corners were necessarily tighter (Fig 1.8) and it was also constructed in the late season of a particularly dry summer, which caused the underlying clay to crack — two probable reasons why this lake requires more topping up than the large mere. By the summer of 1994, however, the rate of topping up had slowed down, doubtless due to the natural blocking of leaks.

Coles (1995) has suggested that schemes that involve polythene were inadvisable for two reasons. First, it was suggested that burrowing animals would bore through the membrane. The Flag Fen lakes, which in winter are populated by rats from the sludge settling fields, have so far not experienced any problem from burrowing animals. If this were to happen, the damage could easily be repaired from the surface with an adhesive polythene patch, as used by farmers to repair wrapped silage bales and readily available from agricultural stockists.

Coles' second objection concerns the longevity of polythene. Before constructing the Flag Fen membrane, the manufacturers (Visqueen Ltd) were consulted. They reported that, provided it was kept away from ultraviolet light (sunlight), the material's life in use was not known. It is, however, widely used in the building industry, where a life expectancy of 60 years is quite usual. If the polythene has to be eventually replaced, the costs, as above, are minimal. In the meantime, despite Coles' notes of caution, something substantial has been done to arrest or delay deterioration. In the light of experience at the Flag Fen, polythene offers a low-cost solution that most archaeological organisations could afford. Butyl rubber (a material approved by Coles by implication) costs in round terms more than ten times as much as polythene but, like polythene, it is also susceptible to damage by ultraviolet light over time.

Construction of the visitor centre lightweight foundations

An architect's drawing of the foundations of the visitor centre has already been published and contains details and specifications of the various materials used (Pryor 1992a, fig 4). The purpose of this brief account is to

Fig 1.12 Visitor centre foundations, stage 1: organic mud is scraped off the drained mere bed

Fig 1.15 Visitor centre foundations, stage 4: the underlying geotextile is wrapped around the styrofoam and weighted down

Fig 1.13 Visitor centre foundations, stage 2: styrofoam blocks are unloaded

Fig 1.16 Visitor centre foundations, stage 5: a revetment bund of Oxford clay is heaped against the edge of the styrofoam 'raft'

explain how the foundations were positioned without harming the extremely fragile archaeological remains that lay about a metre below the surface.

All the work was carried out either from platforms, or by machines fitted with wide, low-ground-pressure crawler tracks. The foundations were designed by Dr Ron West of the consulting engineers, Posford Duvivier, and work was carried out by the staff of Fenland Archaeological Trust under Posford Duvivier's supervision.

Fig 1.14 Visitor centre foundations, stage 3: styrofoam boards are laid on a bed of geotextile covered with a thin layer of sand

Fig 1.17 Visitor centre foundations, stage 6: formers and mesh reinforcement are put in position prior to the pouring of a single-piece concrete slab

Fig 1.18 Visitor centre foundations, stage 7: the building is erected on the concrete slab

After lowering the water level in the lake by about a metre, the ground was allowed to dry. A thin skim of lakebed organic mud was then removed from the site of the proposed building, which was then levelled (Fig 1.12). The lightweight foundations were formed of a styrofoam platform measuring approximately 20 × 14m and 660mm thick. Styrofoam boards were delivered in bundles of four, each bundle measuring 8 × 4 × 2ft (2.43 × 1.22 × 0.6m; Fig 1.13). The bundles were laid by hand on a geotextile sheet on the dried lakebed, which had been covered with a thin layer of washed sand. The geotextile retained the sand and provided a mud-free working surface (Fig 1.14). Laying the slabs took ten hours and special care was taken to chose a still, windless day. Once the styrofoam

slabs had been laid in place, the geotextile was folded around the outside, parcel fashion, and the whole weighted down with scaffolding planks. This arrangement was sufficient to prevent breezes from penetrating the lightweight platform overnight (Fig 1.15).

On the following day, a stiff, blue clay bund was placed around the platform and carefully pressed into position (Fig 1.16). This bund effectively protected the styrofoam raft from all but gale-force winds. Formers and reinforcing mesh for a single-piece concrete slab were then positioned above a damp-proof membrane that covered the entire styrofoam platform (Fig 1.17). After the concrete had been poured and allowed six weeks to cure, work could begin on the building itself (Fig 1.18).

2 Recent research in south Fengate

by Christopher Evans and Francis Pryor

Chapters 2 and 3 are devoted to summary descriptions of pre-determination contract excavations carried out in Fengate after the implementation of PPG16 (DoE 1990). These sometimes limited and fragmented excavations will be presented by area, to provide some sense of landscape coherence. This chapter will consider work carried out south-east of Third Drove. Chapter 3 will describe fieldwork further north, mainly on the fen edge adjacent to the original ROM/DoE Cat's Water subsite.

The important technique of micromorphological analysis of soils was not readily available when the ROM/DoE excavations took place. It has therefore been decided to present the micromorphology reports in

Fig 2.1 Aerial view of the Depot site (mid foreground) from the south-east. The Neolithic/Bronze Age ring-ditch, early Iron Age 'settlement compound' and later Iron Age ditch 17 (defining the fen edge) are particularly clear. The 1973 Storey's Bar Road excavations are still visible (upper right). Photographed July 1977. Reproduced by kind permission of the Cambridge University Committee for Aerial Photography

greater detail than would normally be the case in an overview. This is also appropriate, given the survival of palaeosols, which were particularly well preserved close to the fen edge. Soil micromorphology aside, each report will be presented in three parts. After a brief introduction, the principal results will be described and a final section will consider the project's wider implications. The Cambridge University Archaeological Unit's excavations at the Depot site in 1992 led directly to an important reassessment of the accepted dating of the Bronze Age field boundary ditches at Storey's Bar Road. A summary by Evans and Pollard of the main points of that reassessment appears at the beginning of the discussion of the Depot (1992) excavations.

The pace of commercial development in and around Peterborough increased in 1995, with consequent problems of curation. In response, English Heritage commissioned a review of the region's archaeological potential which was produced, for limited circulation, mainly amongst curators, contractors, and clients (Pryor 1997b). The production of the curatorial review was timed to coincide with the emergence of Peterborough as a unitary authority (in April 1998), with its own archaeological development control procedures. The curatorial guide has proved to have been very useful, not only during the difficult process of transferring curatorial control from one authority to another, but in making routine and often rapid pre-determination assessments in an area of great archaeological potential and complexity.

The excavations discussed below have produced some remarkable and surprising results. A few stand out, such as the ditches with associated banks and 'cultural strata' (eg floors or surfaces) found to survive at the Cambridge University Archaeological Unit's Depot site (1992). Similarly, the Third Drove evaluation programme of 1998 revealed further evidence of Bronze Age settlement within the ditched field system. The Tower Works project exposed an important later Bronze Age settlement which included a substantial possible rectilinear building, Bronze Age gravel pits, and ditches of the known Bronze Age field system. Work at Cat's Water in 1997 revealed yet another Neolithic mortuary structure aligned on the same orientation as the two known from previous work in the area, suggesting others remain to be found. Such discoveries are a reminder that the full picture, even in so intensively studied an area, is still only partially visible.

The Depot site

The Cambridge University Archaeological Unit was commissioned to undertake field evaluation of a site *c* 1.5ha in extent, within the Fengate Industrial Estate at OS NGR TL 212985 (Fig 1.6; Evans 1992). The work was carried out in anticipation of the construction of a city council works depot and took place in September 1992. The area investigated was on the south-western side of the Bronze Age field system close to the edge of the fen. The ground surface sloped more than a metre from north to south (4.20m to 3.00m OD).

Before fieldwork began, Rog Palmer was commissioned to rectify and analyse the aerial photographic evidence for the area; this included air photos not available to the ROM/DoE project (Figs 2.1 and 2.2).

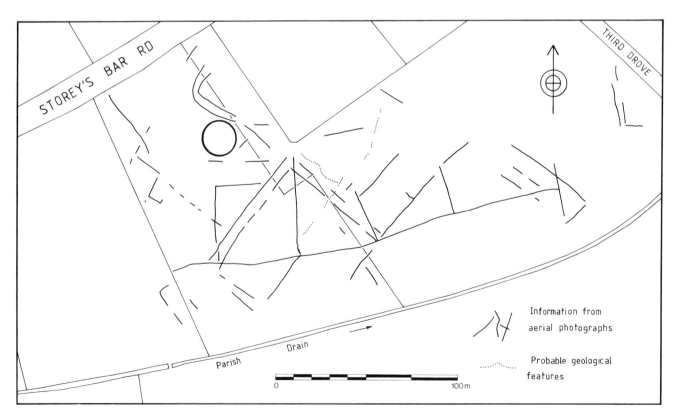

Fig 2.2 The Depot site (1992): cropmark plan (after Evans 1992)

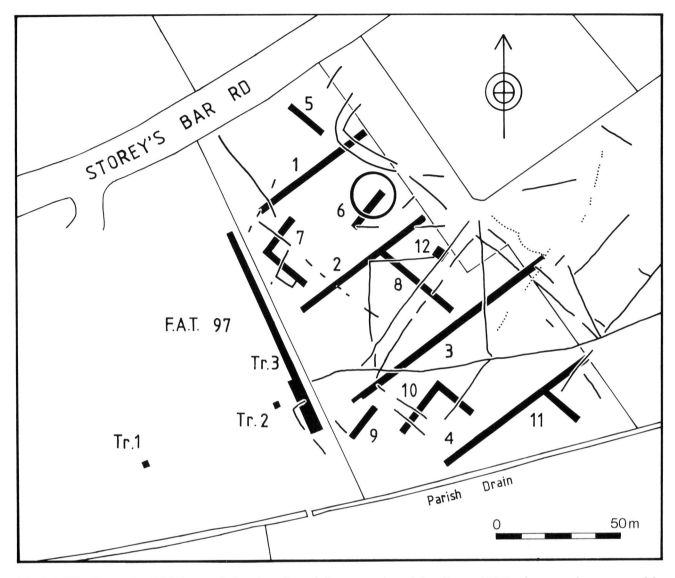

Fig 2.3 The Depot site (1992): trench location plan of the excavations (after Evans 1992); three trenches excavated by Fenland Archaeological Trust in 1997 (Tr 1–3) are also plotted

Eleven trial trenches, each 2m wide, and a 'test station', 5m square, were excavated, covering approximately 950m²; together these trenches provided a 6.5% sample of the development area (Fig 2.3).

Stratigraphic survival proved to be exceptional in the lower-lying, or south-eastern, half of the site, where upcast banks and other surfaces survived seemingly intact. Features of several periods were recorded. A ring-ditch of later Neolithic or Early Bronze Age date pre-dates ditches of Bronze Age fields (Fig 2.4). While the Depot fields clearly formed part of the wider Fengate Bronze Age system, they were laid out in a more obvious coaxial pattern, in roughly square 'blocks'. They may also have been short-lived. One round building was found associated with these fields, although a rectilinear palisaded enclosure containing another round house probably dates to the Bronze/Iron Age transition (Fig 2.5). Finally, a 'late' (Iron Age/ Roman) series of ditched fields, on a different alignment to the Bronze Age system, was found at the edge of the fen (Fig 2.6). Iron Age settlement features,

Table 2.1 Summary and chronology of pedogenesis and land-use

date	landscape development
pre-Early Bronze Age	Brown earth/argillic brown earth
Early Bronze Age	Ring-ditch/(barrow) construction (Profiles A and B)
Bronze Age	Droveway construction (Profiles D and E; ?tillage in Profiles F and H)
earlier Iron Age	Turf stripping?/turf construction/ burnt stone spread (Profiles F and H); some alluvial clay/silt deposition
Roman	Ditch/bank construction (Profile G); some alluvial clay/silt
late Roman and post-Roman	Disturbance/alluviation — severe truncation and reworking of the A horizon

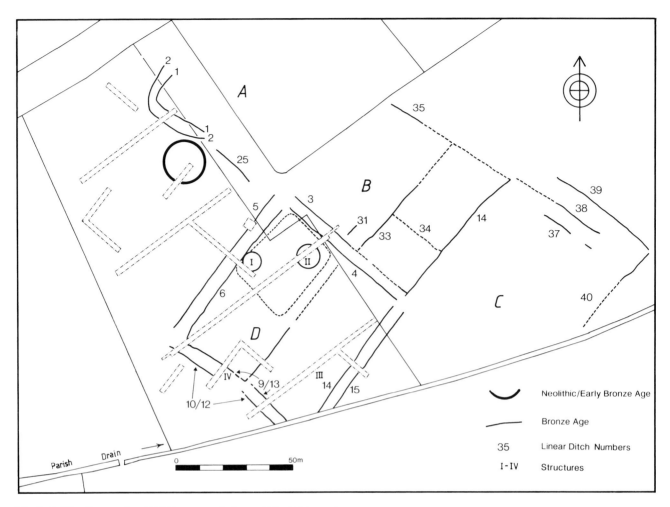

Fig 2.4 The Depot site (1992): general plan of Neolithic and Bronze Age features (after Evans 1992)

including a possible turf-built structure or clamp, were also found in this south-eastern area (see Table 2.1).

Soil micromorphological analysis
by C A I French and H Lewis

Soil micromorphological analyses were undertaken of samples from eight buried soil profiles. The Depot site provided an ideal opportunity to examine the buried landscape contemporary with the Bronze Age and Iron Age field systems revealed by assessment excavation. Since during the ROM/DoE excavations of 1971–8, soil micromorphological techniques were not normally available, the opportunity to conduct extensive analyses at this site, which is in a similar zone of the fen-edge landscape to that at the Newark Road and Cat's Water subsites, was all the more important. Moreover, the palaeosols at the Depot site had been protected from later disturbance by earthworks and/or the subsequent deposition of about 300–600mm of silty clay alluvium.

The eight profiles examined are arranged in chronological order. Full details are lodged with the site archive in the unit's offices, Cambridge. Detailed soil micromorphological descriptions are given in Appendixes 1, 2, and 5.

The Late Neolithic/Early Bronze Age ring-ditch (Features 1 and 2)

Profile A: Trench 6 (south side), immediately outside ring-ditch (Feature 2), to the south-west

0–340mm	alluvium
340–620mm	(disturbed?) buried soil/ploughsoil (Profile A1)
620–760mm	intact relict soil (Profile A2)
760–780mm	stone line
>780mm	subsoil

Profile B: Trench 6, inside 'barrow mound' (Feature 1), at edge of ring-ditch

0–350mm	alluvium
350–600mm	buried soil in or under barrow (Profiles B1 and B2)
600–630mm	stone line
>630mm	subsoil

Profile C: Trench 2, *c* 10m east of barrow ditch — undisturbed

0–340mm	alluvium
340–600mm	buried soil (Profiles C1 and C2)
>600mm	subsoil

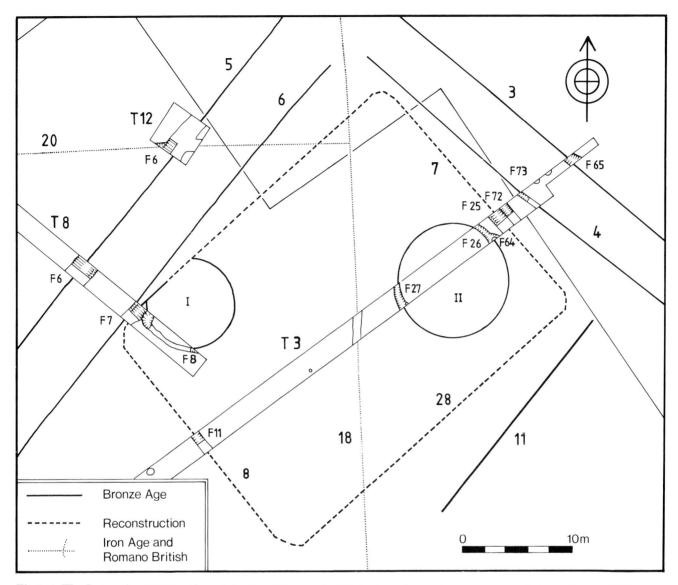

Fig 2.5 The Depot site (1992): plan of the Late Bronze Age/Early Iron Age settlement compound (after Evans 1992)

The Bronze Age droveways (Features 6 and 7 and 30 and 31)

Profile D: Trench 8, between east–west running droveway ditches (Features 6 and 7)

0–380mm	alluvium
380–640mm	soil, truncated beneath bank (Profiles D1 and D2)
>640mm	subsoil

Profile E: Trench 3, between north–south running droveway ditches (Features 30 and 31)

0–320mm	alluvium
320–700mm	buried soil truncated under bank (Profiles E1 and E2)
>700mm	subsoil

The Iron Age burnt stone spread (Features 14 and 20)

Profile F: Trench 4, sealed beneath Iron Age burnt stone layer (Feature 14; Profiles F1/A, F1/B, F2/A, and F2/B)

Profile H: Trench 4, taken down vertical truncation of possible turf wall line (Feature 20; Profiles H1 and H2)

The Roman ditch/bank (Feature 29)

Profile G: Trench 3, under bank associated with Roman ditch (Profiles G1 and G2)

Discussion

The profiles appear to represent the lower horizons of a moderately well to poorly developed brown earth. The upper horizons of this soil (*c* 100–150mm) were truncated in most areas, and/or reworked through possible earlier turf stripping and tillage, and through subsequent alluvial aggradation processes.

Strong clay enrichment/illuviation obviously occurred after cairn, droveway, and barrow construction, as none of the B horizons underneath these features show enrichment of this sort. This is consistent with the generally accepted interpretation that the

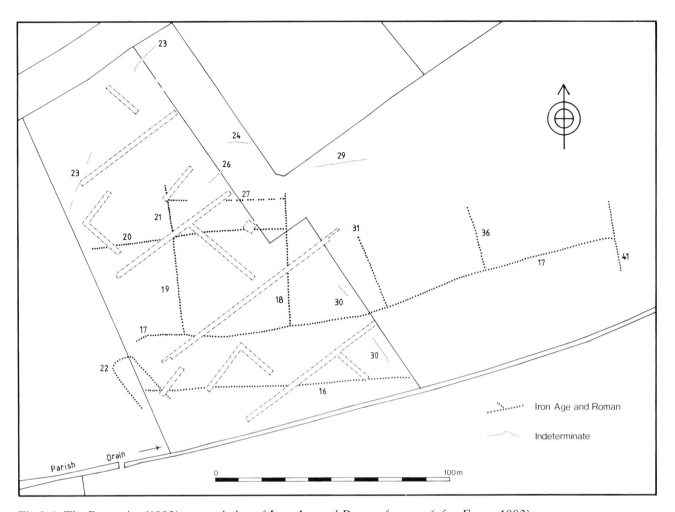

Fig 2.6 The Depot site (1992): general plan of Iron Age and Roman features (after Evans 1992)

influence of the seasonal aggradation of alluvial fine material increased substantially in this location only in later periods. The disturbance associated with the construction of the Bronze/Iron Age features should have caused some fines release and movement, but this influence is difficult to determine due to the impact of contemporaneous minor/later major alluvial aggradation.

The lower part of G, the profile associated with a Roman bank, shows increased clay translocation. This suggests that some clay input/movement events occurred before and/or during the Roman period, but that the major alluvial activity on the site is post-Roman. There is some evidence that soil disturbance through tillage occurred on the lower part of the site before the Iron Age. Whether or not there was cultivation in this area during the Iron Age and Roman periods is unknown. Favourable conditions for pastoral activities would also seem to have existed, at least before the Iron Age, as indicated by turf development. The nature of land use related to the Bronze Age field system is unclear from the micromorphological evidence alone, and it will be interesting to compare these results to those of phosphate analysis conducted on the site.

Finally, the buried soil was probably subjected to seasonal wetting and drying associated with a fluctuating groundwater table and occasional flooding throughout much of its history. A horizon development

shows that it was not waterlogged, however, until later flooding events in Roman and post-Roman times, even in the lowest parts of the site.

Principal results

The ring-ditch and Neolithic activity

Trench 6 was positioned to cut a small ring-ditch (*c* 20m external diameter), visible on aerial photographs in the north-east quarter of the site (Figs 2.1 and 2.3). The location of the trench in relationship to the cropmark plot, however, fell slightly further south than intended. Rather than running west from its centre, the trench cut obliquely across its southern sector.

The defining ring-ditch was 3m wide and 1.1m deep (from the top of the gravel), with a broad, if irregular, U-shaped profile. Its primary fills consisted of inter-lensed dark yellow-black sands and gravel, evidently derived from weathering of its sides. This was sealed by secondary deposits of mid to dark grey and light brown sandy loams. Along the inner edge of the upper profile was a wedge of quite pure light yellow sandy gravel. The uppermost fill had been truncated and it was apparent that the outer edge had been recut. This secondary profile was 2.15m wide and 0.65m deep, and of broadly splayed U shape. Its base corresponded with a shelf in the outer profile.

Despite evidence for recutting, the area enclosed by the ring-ditch did not prove complex. A possible post-setting trench was found to run parallel with and 2.2m inside the line of the ring-ditch. This consisted of a linear slot 0.35m wide and 0.1m deep, in which were found subcircular postholes: the southern, 0.4m in diameter and 0.15m deep; the northern, 0.35–0.4m across and 0.12m deep. Given its size and the frequency of gravel in its upper profile, there can be little doubt that the ring-ditch was the quarry source for an upcast earthwork of some sort and that the postsetting trench may have held a timber revetment.

Only a few small fragments of bone (from tertiary contexts) were found in the ring-ditch proper, while no finds were retrieved from the interior. The rarity of finds makes the dating of the monument difficult, but this in itself is remarkable, in that it suggests that there was only minimal background activity in the immediate vicinity prior to its construction. It may be supposed that the ring-ditch was probably of later Neolithic or Early Bronze Age date.

After much deliberation, it was concluded that there was no evidence to suggest that the buried soil or turf within its interior had been stripped away in the course of construction, as had happened, for example, at Maxey (Pryor and French 1985, 237); nor was there evidence of ancient or modern plough damage. It was therefore concluded that the mound was either very small or, more probably, that it was an embanked ring-ditch — in effect a hengiform, but lacking an entranceway. It should be recalled that the evidence for a mound was also slight in the case of the Storey's Bar Road ring-ditch and barrow (Pryor 1978, 53). The gravel fill within the upper part of the ditch probably represented an episode of backfilling or levelling, prior to the recutting of the ditch. Given the history of later land-use in this area (discussed below), it is likely that any remaining upcast had been ploughed out during the later Iron Age or, more probably, in early Roman times.

The vast majority of the site's worked flint assemblage would appear to be of post-Neolithic date. The only noteworthy earlier pieces were a number of Neolithic blades (including one serrated) recovered from the buried soil in Trench 8, and a fine macehead from Trench 3, also from the buried soil. The latter piece, probably ground down from a larger macehead or axe, is probably of Late Neolithic/Early Bronze Age date. While very small, and given the rarity of such objects, it is nonetheless a significant 'symbol of power'.

Bronze Age: the ditch system

It was assumed, given what was already known of the archaeology of Fengate, that the rectilinear cropmarks were of Bronze Age date. None of the finds or stratigraphic evidence contradicts this dating, but little positive evidence was recovered to confirm it.

The layout of the ditch system is illustrated in Figure 2.4. The ditches varied considerably in size (Fig 2.5), and were sometimes accompanied by banks or remnants of banks. Figure 2.7 shows two Bronze Age ditches (8 and 9) with a sealed, preserved bank.

Fig 2.7 The Depot site (1992): the west end of Trench 3 (looking north) showing Bronze Age double ditches 8 and 9 (bottom left and centre); note the sealed gravel bank to ditch 9. Ditch 17 of the Iron Age 'late' field system is visible, upper right

Bronze Age: evidence for settlement — Structures I and II and the settlement compound

Trench 8 was extended to determine the size of a round structure (I) found at the southern end of the trench (Fig 2.5). This structure was defined by a possible shallow eaves-drip gully (0.6m wide and 0.2m deep), about 7m in diameter. The buried soil within the interior had been truncated by *c* 0.1m and there was evidence for two postholes. It can only be concluded that this was a small round building. Since densities of associated finds were extremely low, it is questionable, however, whether it could be interpreted as a house. Almost no finds were recovered from the excavated portions of the gully and its interior 'floor' area. On the other hand, five pieces of bone and six sherds (plus crumbs) of Bronze Age pottery were found within the adjacent, metre-long excavated segment of Ditch 6. This is a relatively high artefact density for settlement features associated with the Bronze Age field system at Fengate (cf Pryor 1980, 174).

The settlement compound revealed in Trenches 3 and 8 is so far without parallel at Fengate (Fig 2.5). The eaves-drip gully (width 0.7–0.8m, depth 0.4m) of a round building (Structure II) *c* 10m in diameter was exposed in Trench 3 (F26 and 27). The filling of F26 was rich in charcoal which probably derived from a sunken pit-oven (F64) which had been dug into the eastern side of this gully, adjacent to the southern side of the trench. Set 0.15m above the floor of either a pit, or more likely a recut of the gully itself (perhaps associated with an entranceway), was a fired clay oven plate, *c* 40mm thick. Fragments of this were scattered throughout the filling. No postholes were found within the interior of the building, although one, perhaps part of an eaves support, was found on the edge of F27.

It is suggested that Structure II was associated with the compound, which was defined by the steep-sided post bedding trench comprising ditches 7, 8, and 28. The compound, which measured 34 × 26m, was aligned somewhat askew to the orientation of the main Bronze Age ditched fields. The evidence suggests that Structure II and the settlement compound were laid out shortly after the fields had gone out of use, but remained visible as earthworks, perhaps into the Bronze Age/Iron Age transition period.

Iron Age: the occupation spread — Structure III and the 'late' field system

Evidence for Iron Age settlement was found in Trench 4, which was located at a point where the underlying terrace gravel dropped away westwards towards the fen edge — a natural depression followed by the Parish Drain (Fig 2.8). The lower-lying deposits in Trench 4 were therefore wet, if not actually waterlogged. Occupation features included a shallow clay-lined pit (1m in diameter with a flat base, 0.3m deep) which produced sherds of Middle Iron Age 'scored ware', and a spread of occupation debris that extended for 2.2m east of the pit. The midden-like debris included large cobbles (many burnt), pieces of fired clay, Iron Age potsherds, and fragments of bone in a dark, mottled, sandy silt, 0.08–0.12m thick. Perhaps surprisingly, the assemblage did not include saltern briquetage.

Directly to the east of the occupation spread, the buried palaeosol had been truncated. Away from the zone of truncation, which was approximately 30m across, the palaeosol was about 50mm thick. Within the zone it was either absent or consisted of a very thin residue. The cause of the truncation was probably anthropogenic as there was little evidence for water scour in the area (Charles French personal communication).

Fig 2.8 The Depot site (1992): view looking north across Trench 4, showing burnt stones and other debris of the Iron Age 'occupation spread'

Since ard marks were observed below the alluvium, ploughing must have been a factor, but it could not have been the sole cause of the erosion.

Structure III was located in Trench 4 (Fig 2.4) and was undoubtedly closely associated with the Iron Age occupation spread. The main feature of this structure was a straight wall-line, oriented north–south. It consisted of a charcoal stain (0.18m wide), the possible remains of a timber base-plate, with traces of vertical posts (0.15m diameter) set on either side. This lay within the upper portion of a trough (0.48m wide and 0.15m deep), filled with dark grey sand-silts. This feature is perhaps best seen as a burnt wall-line, but no return was found at either end. Immediately west of the wall-line was an area of compacted cobbles, 3m wide, which is probably best interpreted as a floor or hardstanding. Just east of the possible floor were three postholes that may also have been part of the structure. Two suggestions are proposed: Structure III may not have been a building, but a construction that served an industrial function, such as a firing clamp for burning turf removed from the nearby truncation zone; more plausibly, the structure was always semi-subterranean and was partially terraced into the truncated east face of the buried soil. If this is accepted, it could originally have been a rectangular, turf-built house or outbuilding. In which case, the buried soil may have been truncated both to provide building material (turf) and improve drainage in the adjacent area.

Although Fengate is well known for its Bronze Age fields, so far little has been learned about any subsequent system of ancient land management. The ROM/DoE Cat's Water excavations provided evidence for Iron Age and Roman stockyards, droveway, and settlement, but no actual fields or paddocks were revealed (Pryor 1984a). The 'late' (Iron Age/Roman) fields described below are therefore of some importance.

The 'late' fields are laid out on a very different alignment to the earlier, Bronze Age, system (Figs 2.5 and 2.6). The later alignment appears to follow the edge of the fen, as defined in general terms by the Parish Drain, quite closely. The system would appear to have depended upon three principal ditches (16, 17, and 20) which ran east–west along the fen margin. The longest (17) was excavated in 1998, in Trench 4 of the adjacent Third Drove site (Site O; see below), where it was shown to have origins in the Middle Iron Age.

Ditch 20 could be traced for 82m. Generally it measured 1.15m in width, but was as wide as 1.3m, due to off-centre recutting; its depth in Trench 12 was *c* 0.55m. In Trench 7 it was both wider (1.5m) and deeper (0.7m), with a more V-shaped profile. Ditch 17 (205m long) was U-shaped, *c* 1.9m wide and 0.8m deep; Ditch 16 was U-shaped (0.5–0.8m wide and 0.30–0.50m deep); it also showed evidence of recutting.

There were five main north–south ditches (19/21, 18, 31, 36, and 41), which were broadly similar in shape and size to those just described. There was evidence that banks accompanied ditches 16, 20, and 21.

Precise dating of the system is difficult, but there can be little doubt that it commenced within the Middle/Late Iron Age and continued in use into Roman times. Ditch 15 was clearly cut by the clay-lined pit, described above, which yielded sherds of Middle Iron Age 'scored ware'. Turning to the system's later use, a backfilled recut of ditch 20 in Trench 7 could be firmly dated to the later first or early second century AD. The only evidence for a *terminus ante quem* was provided by ditch 16 in Trench 9, which was clearly cut by a later Roman enclosure ditch (22). Some elements of the system, for example, ditches 17–19/21, may have continued in use as late as the third century AD.

Roman

A scatter of small pits or postholes indicated probable Romano-British settlement in the area. The only substantial feature was a small rectilinear ditched enclosure at the south-west corner of the site, which produced pottery of the third century AD. The purpose of this low-lying enclosure is uncertain.

The dating of the Storey's Bar Road fields reconsidered
by C Evans and J Pollard

The dating of the Storey's Bar Road sequence, as published (Pryor 1978), hinges upon the interrelationship between the ring-ditch/barrow and the ditches of the field system. No central burial was recovered within the former and the logic of the site turns upon the fact that the effort required to construct the monument (ie the digging of the ditch circuit) was disproportionate if all that was intended was the deposit on the surface of the Collared Urn cremation found within its interior (Pryor 1978, 60). The Grooved Ware enclosed settlement then became associated with the ring-ditch, the focus of a contemporary field system. Subsequently, in the earlier Bronze Age, the ring-ditch circuit was recut in its entirety, a barrow constructed in its interior, and, still later, the field system (which continued in use well into the second millennium) was extended across its eastern edge. This is, arguably, an unduly complex sequence.

When the site was excavated in the earlier 1970s, the now ubiquitous ring-ditch monuments were not common. At the time, few Neolithic settlements had been excavated and expectations of discovering unambiguously domestic structural evidence within the lowlands of southern English river valleys were high (eg McInnes 1971): the idea of an enclosed occupation apparently manifest in the Fengate ring-ditch fitted the mood of the day.

Within the Storey's Bar Road report, Bradley contributed a reinterpretation of the Playden site in search of parallels for enclosed ring-ditch settlements (Bradley 1978). Since that time, however, Playden has itself been reevaluated as a hengiform monument with a primary ritual function (Cleal 1982) and, over the last twenty years, comparable ring-ditched settlements have not been forthcoming. Given this, and in the light of the Depot site excavations, it seems appropriate to reconsider the Storey's Bar Road (SBR) sequence, as this has major ramifications for dating the origins of the Fengate field system. No radiocarbon determinations were obtained from the two key components of the complex, the ring-ditch and the field system itself. Their dating relies solely upon the artefactual evidence and claimed patterns of relationship with the numerous Grooved Ware-associated pits scattered across the site. Late Neolithic ceramics and lithics were present in quantity from all parts of SBR Area I, and later (Bronze Age) material virtually absent. Possible Beaker sherds came from the upper fill of the ring-ditch, in which Collared Urn was also present, and a barbed-and-tanged arrowhead was recovered from a small pit or posthole in the southern part of the area (feature B10). Such homogeneity in the finds assemblage no doubt provided support for an argument of chronological unity in the complex.

Despite the virtual absence of Bronze Age material, there are good reasons for placing the ring-ditch and field system in the early to mid second millennium BC, several centuries later than the date originally envisaged. Attention will first be turned to the ring-ditch, which was considered the focus for the Grooved Ware settlement. The ceramic assemblage from this feature is clearly mixed with a large residual component. This includes fragments of plain bowl, Grooved Ware and Bronze Age urn. The dating is clinched by a sherd of Collared Urn from the primary silts (layer 3) of the ring-ditch on its east side. This must be either contemporary with the construction of the monument, or provide a *terminus post quem* for it.

Although it was argued that the ditch had been recut after the Neolithic occupation had ceased (in order to provide material for a mound), the published sections show no such sequence. Indeed, there is every reason to assume that once constructed the monument had been left to decay naturally. A cremation associated with a similar undecorated Collared Urn on the inner edge of the ring-ditch has a radiocarbon determination of cal BC 2040–1430 (HAR-400; 3410±120 BP), within the conventional earlier Bronze Age range (Longworth 1984). If an Early Bronze Age date is accepted for the digging of the ring-ditch, it must be assumed that the Grooved Ware and flint from its fills, most of which came from the upper layers 1 and 2, are residual. As Pryor argued, deturfing for the construction of the barrow mound (1978, 60; or alternatively a ring-ditch embankment) probably resulted in the redeposition of earlier Grooved Ware finds into the area of the ditched interior, much of which later weathered into the ditch: the illustrated Neolithic sherds from the ring-ditch, and more significantly those from the ditches of the field system, are small and apparently weathered (ibid, fig 37, 21–38), unlike those from pits with firm third millennium cal BC radiocarbon dates (eg B16; ibid, fig 39, 13–19).

Two stratigraphic relationships exist between the field system and other structural components. The southern extension of ditch W24 cuts into the base of the tertiary silt of the ring-ditch, an unequivocal relationship, given the minor scale of the field system. It seems unlikely that the system could have been maintained for the 500 years necessary for a Grooved Ware-attributed ditch to have been extended across the upper fills of a Collared Urn-associated ring-ditch/barrow. The date of the Collared Urn cremation within the monument probably provides a truer attribution for the field system, one in keeping with the Depot system.

Only one feature with a firm primary Grooved Ware assemblage (Pit B50) to demonstrate the early date of the field system was recorded as cutting the ditches. Yet there was clearly ambiguity in this relationship (it was not visible in the published section; Pryor 1978, fig 33), and the supporting argument for the primacy of the ditch is circular (ibid, 21).

Although small and largely derived from a single pit context, the composition of the faunal assemblage is another argument that can be brought to bear. Sharing the same basic three-way ditched drove pattern, the Storey's Bar Road field system is considered ancestral to the main body of the Fengate system. As has been argued (Pryor 1996), it is reasonable to presume a continuity of stock usage, given shared principles of field layout. Yet, the faunal remains from Storey's Bar Road are dominated by cattle and pig, typical of Grooved Ware-associated animal bone assemblages (67.9% and 24.1% respectively, with low sheep at 8%; Harman 1978, 181). These data contrast with other portions of the Fengate Bronze Age system (eg Newark Rd: 18% sheep and only 4.9% pig; Biddick 1980, 225). In other words, if the basic layout of the field system primarily related to sheep management, then its design was probably inappropriate for a Grooved Ware 'economy'. If the animal bone from Grooved Ware contexts is therefore to be disassociated from the Storey's Bar Road field system, there is no reason why the relationship of the remainder of the early assemblage is not also residual.

In conclusion, the grounds for 'deconstructing' the Storey's Bar Road sequence can be summarised as follows:

1   The fact that one of the field ditches extends across the fills of the ring-ditch/barrow must reflect its true relationship with the field system. The latter postdates the monument, with the Bronze Age dates from the Collared Urn cremation and Well W17 probably bracketing the (maximum) lifetime of the fields.
2   Disassociating the Grooved Ware remains from the field system, there is no reason why such a complicated mechanism as the recutting of the entire ring-ditch/barrow circuit need be evoked to explain the

presence of earlier Bronze Age material in primary contexts, with later Neolithic material predominant within the ditch's upper fills. The Bronze Age finds must date the monument's construction, the Grooved Ware material deriving from an open settlement in the immediate vicinity.

Discussion

The ring-ditch

The discovery of a southern ring-ditch in Fengate provides yet another ritual or non-domestic element in the landscape. The present ring-ditch and two other ritual monuments from Fengate (the Cat's Water 1990 henge and the Storey's Bar Road ring-ditch/barrow) are regularly spaced within the later, Bronze Age, field system and may have been used as sights to guide its initial laying-out. Certainly it would appear that ditches 1, 2, and 25 of the Depot Bronze Age system bend to respect the ring-ditch (Fig 2.4). This would indicate that the monument was either physically visible or was still respected as a place of importance.

Bronze Age

The Depot field system differs from the central Bronze Age system in that it is more truly coaxial. The main Fengate system consists of a series of major paired ditches which ran down to the fen edge. The land between them was irregularly subdivided into rectangular plots. At the Depot site long boundaries run both north-east–south-west (ditches 11/33 and 14) and north-west–south-east (ditches 35/38, 1/3, and 2/4). Ditches and double ditches appeared to divide the system into four blocks each of approximately 70m^2 each (Fig 2.4) as follows:

Block A: north and west side: ditches 1 and 2 (cropmark ditch 25 south-western continuation of 2); south side: projection of ditches 5 and 6; east side: projection of ditch 35.
Block B: north side: projection of ditches 5 and 6; west side: ditch 3; south side: ditch 14; east side: ditch 35 (block internally divided by ditches 31, 33, and 34).
Block C: north side: ditch 14; west side: projection of ditches 3 and 4; east side: ditches 37–9; south side: ditch 40.
Block D: north side: ditches 5 and 6; west side: ditches 9/13 and 10/12; east side: ditches 3 and 4; south side: ditches 14 and 15.

The double ditches of the Depot system do not resemble the ditched droveways of the main Fengate system. With the exception of ditches 1 and 2, the corner angles are too sharp to drive animals around without difficulty. They are probably best explained either as sources of gravel for banks or raised paths, or as side-ditches for hedge lines.

Evidence from the ditches of the Depot system suggests that the fields there were not as long-lived as the main Fengate Bronze Age system. Most display relatively little evidence of recutting. Their profiles were not broad, irregular Us (the type of pattern produced through successive cleaning out), but approximately regular, if broad, V-shaped profiles. Perhaps this portion of the system was more short-lived than in the north-east (Newark Road, Fourth Drove, and Cat's Water) where proximity to Flag Fen may have resulted in more intense maintenance.

Whatever the case, evidence for long-term renewal was not generally apparent at the Depot.

Given that the eaves-drip gully of Structure I had drained into ditch 6, there can be little doubt of its date and association with the Bronze Age system. This small round building is typical of those previously found at Fengate (eg Pryor 1980, 53–61). The larger building, Structure II, is more problematic. While no pottery was recovered from the fill of its eaves-drip gully, a few large sherds of Iron Age date were found within the buried soil in the vicinity. Although these may have derived from other features in the area, the scale of Structure II would be more typical of Iron Age round buildings in the Fengate area than Bronze Age examples.

The alignment of the Depot Bronze Age field system is close to that of the Storey's Bar Road subsite. The relatively small scale of ditches on both sites is also very similar. It would appear most probable, therefore, that the two formed part of one and the same system. If that is indeed the case, it becomes necessary to re-examine the dating of Storey's Bar Road, which was thought to have its origins in the later Neolithic period (Pryor 1978, 65). By contrast, the Depot fields can be shown to be both Bronze Age and relatively short-lived.

Iron Age and Roman

There is no evidence of major settlement during either of these periods. Occupation features were found in the southern quarter of the site for both periods, while Roman settlement features also extend along its western margin. The location of these later features would seem to relate directly to the proximity to the fen. The continued maintenance of ditches from the Iron Age well into Roman times represents a remarkable degree of continuity in land-use. Only a very small portion of this later field system was investigated (Fig 2.6). Ditches 16, 17, and 20 all seem to extend westwards into the area investigated in 1997, beyond the limits of the site. Unfortunately, however, it was not possible to precisely tie together the elements common to both sites.

Given its scale and situation within the local landscape, it is reasonable to presume that the Iron Age ditch system directly relates to the Cat's Water settlement, some 400m to the north-east. Perhaps the

Depot 'late' ditches marked divisions within winter-flooded meadows. The status of contemporary domestic or settlement features around the site's southern margins is, however, less certain. Do these remains represent a discrete small community, perhaps specialising in wetland edge-specific activities (such as reed gathering, fishing, and fowling), or was it a seasonal 'out-station' of the Cat's Water settlement?

The 1997 excavations

A second evaluation excavation at the Depot site was carried out by Fenland Archaeological Trust in February 1997 (Pryor 1997a). The site was located at OS NGR TL 21069850, immediately south-west of the area of the 1992 excavations (Fig 2.3, FAT 97: Tr 3). In a single trial trench, the large number of archaeological features attested to Neolithic, Bronze Age, earlier Iron Age, later Iron Age, and Roman settlement and land-use (Fig 2.9).

Although individual features could not be directly related to the 1992 project, it was possible to draw general parallels between the two sites. The most unusual discovery was a possible roadway (with two side ditches) of probable early Iron Age date. In view of the large amount of information in the trench, it was decided to take the opportunity to protect the archaeological features as far as possible beneath a large lightweight commercial building: the concrete floors of the two warehouses planned for the site were placed on top of the undisturbed alluvium and separated from it by a geotextile membrane.

Principal results

The single trial trench (Fig 2.9) was cut through about 250–300mm of alluvium. This revealed a palaeosol, somewhat thinner than usual (100mm), which may have been truncated by erosion prior to alluviation. An extraordinary abundance of archaeological pits, ditches, gullies, and postholes was recorded. It is worthwhile briefly listing the features (from north to south) in order to illustrate the richness of the site:

Feature 16: a V-shaped linear ditch, whose entire filling was sealed by gravel upcast from the adjacent Iron Age ring-gully (F27). There were no finds, but both filling and colour are reminiscent of the usual Fengate Bronze Age field ditches. This is supported by its relationship to the Iron Age gully. Feature 16 runs at right angles to F15 and most probably forms part of the same field/paddock system.

Feature 27: a ring-gully for a round building. The filling contained a sherd of wheel-thrown Late Iron Age pottery. The exposed surface of the filling also revealed a deposit of wood ash and finely comminuted charcoal which had not been fired *in situ*. Unusually the ring-gully was accompanied by a low external bank of gravel which sealed F16.

Features 24, 25, 26, and 31: a distribution of four small pits or postholes that clearly curved to respect the adjacent late Iron Age ring-gully. Parallels for such an arrangement are hard to find. Perhaps the pits/postholes were the remains of external buttress posts required to shore up the walls in the building's later years?

Feature 10: a Late Iron Age/Early Roman linear ditch. The basal filling contained eight sherds of an almost complete Late Iron Age or early Romano-British cordoned bowl.

Feature 11: large pit or butt-end of large ditch, possibly associated with small pits/postholes immediately adjacent (see below, F19, 20, and 22). Late Iron Age or early Roman.

Features 14, 20, and 22: three small pits/postholes possibly associated with the larger pit, Feature 11 (above). Only one (20) produced pottery, which was of Late Iron Age or early Romano-British type.

Features 17 and 18: two small pits with thin (<10mm) clay lining and scraps of shell-tempered pottery; possibly Iron Age.

Feature 32 and 33: two parallel linear ditches with similar fillings, but no datable artefacts. A later Iron Age date seems unlikely, as the superficial alluvium did not dip into the tertiary filling of either ditch. On the other hand, the alignment of the ditches does not respect that of the Bronze Age system. Is an Early Iron Age (?early first millennium BC) date indicated? The buried soil between the two ditches was harder and well compacted, slightly more gravel-rich, and was heavily stained with iron/manganese. In his report French considered this a possible made-up road/trackway surface (French 1997). The two side-ditches would have provided drainage and a source of gravel for the possible trackway surface.

Feature 28: a linear ditch with similar filling to the two parallel ditches just described (F32 and 33). The superficial alluvium did not dip into the tertiary filling, nor were there indications of a bank/track surface. The ditch clearly cut through the filling of the probable Bronze Age linear ditch, F15. Possibly early Iron Age?

Feature 15: a shallow linear ditch running at right angles to Feature 10 (see above). Cut by ?early Iron Age ditch, Feature 28 (above). There were no finds, but the pale filling and stratigraphic relationship to Feature 28 suggest a Bronze Age date.

Features 8 and 7: two backfilled pits (with a high gravel content and secondary and tertiary fillings absent). Pit 7 produced a large, fresh, blade-like utilised flake in dark high quality flint. The pits were steep-sided and possibly dug to receive the backfill within them. Such features are a common feature of Neolithic sites in the region (cf Pit Y4, Storey's Bar Road subsite; Pryor 1978, fig 20). Pit 8 produced no datable finds, but was otherwise very similar to Pit 7. A Middle/later Neolithic date is indicated.

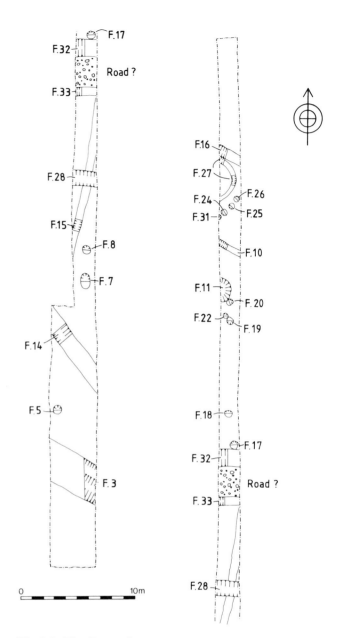

Fig 2.9 The Depot site (1997): plan of trial trench showing principal archaeological features (after Pryor 1997a)

Feature 14: a shallow linear ditch of probable Roman date. Alluvium dipped into the filling and two weathered sherds of Nene Valley Colour-Coated Ware were found on the feature surface during machining. The ditch does not appear on air photographs. Its alignment can not be fitted into the plan of ditches revealed in the adjacent Depot (1992) excavations.

Feature 5: a small pit. ?Roman

Feature 3: a large linear ditch of two, possibly three phases. Alluvium dipped into the upper fillings which produced sherds of later Romano-British pottery. The lower primary filling was of two phases. The first was Iron Age (possibly Middle Iron Age), which was partially cut out by a later Iron Age/Early Roman recut. Later Roman material accumulated in the tertiary filling of this recut. This feature might possibly be an extension of ditch 22 (Late Iron Age/early Roman) of the adjacent Depot (1992) site (Fig 2.6).

Discussion

Few trial trenches could have produced such a diverse collection of archaeological features. The excavations of 1992 and 1997 have clearly demonstrated that the southern parts of Fengate are of the greatest archaeological importance. The discussion is arranged by period and attention is drawn to the possible Early Iron Age roadway.

Neolithic

The presence of the two pits (F7 and 8), which resemble the so-called 'small filled pits' of the Etton causewayed enclosure or Hurst Fen, might argue for the presence of a settlement or ritual site of some significance (Pryor forthcoming; Clark *et al* 1960). It is arguable whether they might be associated with the nearby Depot (1992) ring-ditch or the Storey's Bar Road Grooved Ware settlement (Evans 1992; Pryor 1978).

Bronze Age

Two linear ditches running at right angles (F15 and 16) almost certainly form part of the Bronze Age field/enclosure system revealed in the Depot excavations of 1992. Their presence was unexpected, however, as they do not appear on aerial photographs and their alignment was not picked up in any of the (1992) trenches (experience has shown that the boundary ditches of rectilinear fields frequently turn at right angles directly beyond a trial trench!). Fortunately, their alignment conforms precisely to the Depot 1992 Bronze Age enclosure pattern. As is almost invariably the case when Fengate Bronze Age ditches are investigated by trial trenching, there were no finds. The tertiary, upper, infilling of the northerly ditch (16) was sealed by a lens of gravel upcast from the later Iron Age ring-gully (27) alongside.

Earlier Iron Age

Since features of this period were not expected, evidence for this (controversial) dating is both slight and indirect, as there were no finds. The features concerned are the linear ditches, F28, 32, and 33. While the three ditches are oriented very approximately on the Depot (1992) later Iron Age/Early Roman alignment, such closely spaced and parallel ditches are not found in the later Iron Age/Early Roman phase of that site, where the fields or paddocks seem to have been laid out in a rather spare manner and were without droveways or other subsidiary features. The capping alluvium did not dip into the tertiary filling of these ditches, which was the case not only in later Iron Age/Early Roman ditches elsewhere in the trench, but also in the 1992 and in the ROM/DoE Cat's Water excavations of the 1970s Fengate project (Pryor 1984a, pl 11, in which the alluvium shows as darker ditches).

This would suggest that the ditches in question were completely filled by the onset of alluviation in the later Iron Age.

The alluviation provides an approximate *terminus ante quem*. A *terminus post quem* is provided by the Bronze Age linear ditch, F15, which was quite clearly cut by the ditch F28. Similarly, although their intersection was close to the trench side, it was just possible to see that ditch 33 might also have cut the same Bronze Age feature. Taken together, the available evidence would indicate a date in the earlier Iron Age, or at the Bronze/Iron Age transition. The buried soil between ditches F32 and F33 was very hard and gravel-rich and may have formed a road/trackway surface, or a very shallow bank. Undated and although apparently oriented north–south, a similar and possibly related metalled 'way' was found to have sealed the buried soil in the western end of Trench 3 in the 1993 Depot excavations (Evans 1992).

Features of this period have not been revealed before in this area of Fengate. In the ROM/DoE campaign, the only earlier Iron Age settlement was at Vicarage Farm, well to the north-west (Pryor 1974 and 1984). Many artefacts of this period including early La Tène fibula brooches, swan's neck- and ring-headed pins and a looped iron socketed axe of probable La Tène C type (Fig 10.20) were found in the Power Station excavations. These items must surely have been placed among the posts by people living in the locality. The Tower Works site (discussed below) provides an obvious candidate for such a settlement. Located in the middle of the old 'Gravel Pits Settlement Area' (Fig 1.5), the three ditches and probable roadway of the present site are pointing in the general direction of the 'Gravel Pits Settlement Area'. It is possible, therefore, that this road or track could have provided a dry route along the edge of the wetland between the settlement area to the south-west and the Flag Fen ritual focus to the north-east. The early first millennium was a period of rapidly increasing wetness in the area when such a roadway may have been a necessity. A similar fen-margin roadway of possible Bronze Age date has recently been excavated at Welland Bank, just north of Peterborough (Pryor 1998b, 109–23 and 1998c).

Later Iron Age/Early Roman

Features of this period form by far the majority and provide solid evidence for *in situ* domestic settlement. The linear ditches on the lower-lying land (F3 and F14) probably formed part of the rural landscape (enclosures to do with livestock-handling and pasture partitioning) but the features on the higher land at the northern end of the trench are wholly domestic and include the eaves-drip gully of a small round house. The large quantities of pottery and animal bone recovered suggest a permanent, if not necessarily long-lived settlement, probably similar in nature to that at Cat's Water to the north (Pryor 1984a).

Roman

Evidence for late occupation is admittedly limited. Although alluviation may have begun in the later Iron Age, it reached something of a climax in the third century AD, after which regular flooding continued for several centuries. The pottery from the most low-lying and southerly linear ditch (F3) is from the upper (secondary/tertiary) fills and can be dated to the third century AD, just prior to the onset of serious flooding. A broadly similar picture was obtained at Cat's Water (Pryor 1984a, 227–30). Perhaps the later Romano-British settlement along the Fengate fen margins may have been episodic or temporary, more a 'presence' than permanent settlement.

Third Drove excavations: Site O

A team from Birmingham University Field Archaeology Unit, under the direction of Richard Cuttler, undertook evaluation work over an area of 6.47ha, centred on OS NGR TL 21209825 (Fig 1.6; Cuttler 1998). This project was undertaken in March and April 1998, in anticipation of development on either side of Third Drove. The site is located at the edge of the fen. An approximate boundary between the

wetter and drier ground is provided by the Parish Drain (Fig 2.10). Twelve trial trenches were placed to assess archaeological and palaeoenvironmental preservation. The seven located north-east of Third Drove (Site Q) will be dealt with in the following chapter; here, only the results from the five excavated in the field to the south-west (Site O) will be considered. An abundance of Neolithic, Bronze, and Iron Age settlement features and further Bronze Age field ditches were revealed in these trenches; four were on the 'dry' terrace gravels adjoining the 1992 Depot site (1–4) and a fifth was cut in the deeper deposits south of the Parish Drain (Fig 2.10).

Principal results

A buried soil sealed beneath the alluvium survived over the entire area. Trench 1 revealed at least eight small pits and a scatter of postholes. These were most probably settlement features as three of the pits produced Late Bronze Age pottery.

The features in Trench 2 were more varied. Towards its eastern end, postholes sealed by a layer of silt, which produced Late Neolithic or Early Bronze Age pottery, most probably formed part of a single structure. At its western end was a group of small pits,

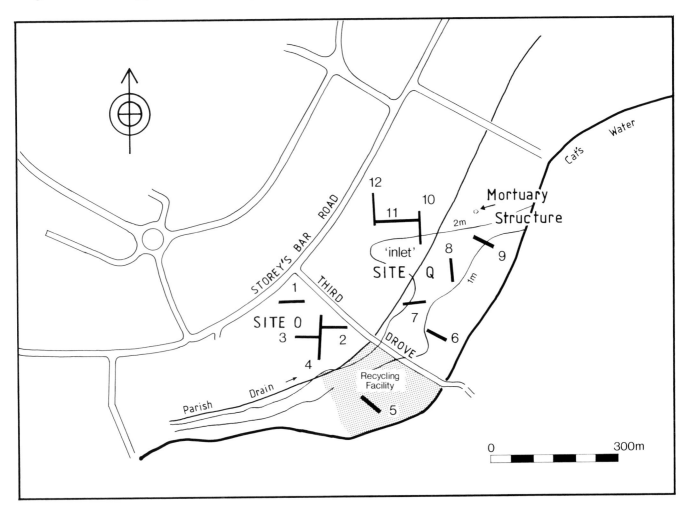

Fig 2.10 Sites O and Q: location of trenches (after Cuttler 1998)

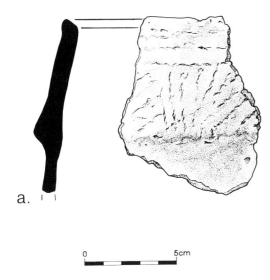

Fig 2.12 Site O, Area 1: the small pit F120 (photograph by Birmingham University Field Archaeology Unit)

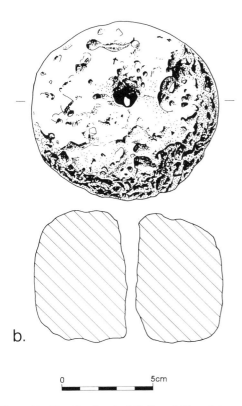

Fig 2.11 Site O: sherd of Collared Urn (a) and perforated clay weight (b) from the small pit F120 (drawing courtesy of Birmingham University Field Archaeology Unit)

more bun-like than cylindrical. Its upper and lower end surfaces are pitted and abraded, which might suggest use, or secondary reuse, as a net sinker. The association of Collared Urn sherds with an axially-perforated clay weight, possibly a loomweight, is of considerable importance, as it potentially represents an early example in Britain of cloth manufacture (Timothy Champion personal communication; Champion 1975). The cord-impressed decoration of the Collared Urn is closely similar to an example found in the buried soil at the Power Station site (below Fig 9.1, 5) and from a filled pit at Newark Road (Pryor 1980, fig 58, 21). Although all three sherds were found in non-funerary contexts, whether these were simple domestic contexts is perhaps another question. A sample of about 70% of features was excavated. Together these features provide evidence for an earlier Bronze Age settlement of some size and importance.

At the eastern end of Trench 3 were excavated at least three linear ditches on the same north-west–south-east alignment as the ditches of the larger Bronze Age field system. These appeared to correspond directly with the eastern side of Evans' Block C (above, this chapter: the dating of the Storey's Bar Road fields reconsidered). Two of these ditches could have formed the sides of a droveway leading down to the edge of the fen; the other was accompanied by a low bank. It seems reasonable to suppose that the settlement found at the west end of the trench may be associated (and contemporary with) the ditches at the east end. The Bronze Age field/droveway ditches were found in Trenches 3 and 4, which they traversed at an angle. Finally, Trench 4 revealed many features and a complex succession of deposits.

Briefly, phase 1 in Trench 4 was Late Neolithic to Middle Bronze Age in date and consisted of pits, postholes, and the possible droveway ditches just described. The evaluation trench provided some evidence that it might eventually prove possible to subdivide this phase using stratigraphy (something not yet achieved for this early period at Fengate).

postholes, and a linear ditch, most of which probably pre-dated the Late Bronze Age on stratigraphic grounds.

The western end of Trench 3 revealed two gullies and a group of five pits and postholes and pits, one of which (F120) produced a large, unabraded rim sherd of Collared Urn, fired clay daub, and a perforated clay weight (Figs 2.11a and b and 2.12). The weight is

To the second phase (Early to Middle Iron Age) belonged pits (some clay-lined), many fire-cracked cobbles, and some macrobotanical evidence for crop processing. Further pits, more burnt stones, and yet more evidence for crop processing or straw burning were assigned to the third phase, plus a large, recut ditch and accompanying bank, which ran parallel to the edge of the fen. This ditch is clearly visible on air photographs and formed part of the Depot 'late' (Middle Iron Age/Romano-British) system, where it was designated ditch 17.

Phase 4 of Trench 4 was the latest, but not necessarily the final phase. It consisted of shallow scoops beneath the alluvium and a large depression resembling a shallow pool, all sealed beneath the alluvium. This phase probably dated to the later Iron Age and perhaps into the Roman period.

Discussion

Neolithic/Bronze Age

An important and unexpected discovery was the scatter of pits, postholes, and related features in Trenches 1–4. Finds indicate that these features can be dated, in round figures, to the duration of the second millennium BC. In fact, they may be a contemporary and later development of the Grooved Ware settlement of the Storey's Bar Road subsite nearby (Pryor 1978). The discovery of pottery and non-linear features suggests that elements of this settlement could have lasted until Late Bronze Age times. If so, this reflects an unusual degree of settlement longevity (later Neolithic to Late Bronze Age). It should also be noted here that at least one large pit, containing fresh sherds of Grooved Ware and a possible aurochs skull, was recently (February 1999) found on the east side of Storey's Bar Road, during evaluation ahead of a small development at TK Packaging Ltd (not planned or illustrated here, but located about 150m south-west of the fen-edge 'inlet' shown in Figure 2.10). The excavations at Site O and at TK Packaging Ltd have more than doubled the known extent of the original Storey's Bar Road Grooved Ware settlement(s).

Bronze Age

Three Bronze Age ditches and indications of at least one bank were found in Trenches 3 and 4. These ditches may have formed a droveway, in turn a part of the larger Bronze Age field system. It is also possible that the pits and postholes of a settlement could have been associated with the early use of the droveway. A similar, although less well preserved, association between non-linear features (which produced Collared Urn sherds) and ditched droveways was observed at the Newark Road subsite (eg Pryor 1980, fig 59).

Iron Age

The main body of new information concerns the low-lying settlement within Trench 4. This complex of Middle and Late Iron Age features clearly formed part of the same settlement as the Depot Site. The significant point to note is that it was an intact, stratified, undisturbed Iron Age settlement with known boundaries. To find stratification on lowland domestic Iron Age sites is rare, even in the Fens (eg Evans and Serjeantson 1988). Although the Parish Drain will have adversely affected waterlogged deposits in its vicinity, the presence of clay-rich fills in deeper features suggests that organic material may confidently be anticipated (French and Taylor 1985). Evidence from the Depot excavations of 1992 and Trench 4 of Site Q would suggest that the Iron Age levels in this area have not been significantly disturbed by Romano-British activity, as was often the case at Cat's Water (Pryor 1984a).

Off-terrace investigations

A trench was cut in the deeper peat and alluvium deposits in the field south of the Parish Drain, as part of the Birmingham University Field Archaeology Unit's 1998 programme (Fig 2.10, trench 5; Cuttler 1998). This area had previously been subject to a test pit and auger survey, following which, in 1996 two trenches were excavated adjacent to the drain, under the direction of Kasia Gdaniec (OS NGR TL 21429848; Gdaniec 1998). The trenches straddled the southern edge of the terrace, where the ground sloped from north-west–south-east. Over the 20m length of the two trenches, the top of the buried soil dropped from 1.97 to 1.58m OD and the natural gravels sloped from 1.74 to 1.34m OD.

Approximately 17 features of possible or probable anthropogenic origin were cut into the terrace gravel in both trenches. There were also a number of natural stream channels. The archaeological features consisted of irregular scoop-like pits with splayed sides and flattish bases. One could possibly have been a small ditch. It was clear that many of the features had been disturbed by trampling and by root action, possibly in antiquity. Finds included flint flakes, bone fragments, and a single small sherd of Bronze Age pottery.

Although limited, these exposures provided evidence for Bronze Age settlement close to the fen edge. Pollen was well preserved and included cereals (wheat and barley) and weeds of waste ground. As there was also evidence for grassland, a mixed agricultural economy is suggested. Pollen analysis indicated that the cereal pollen may have derived from the settlement area associated with the archaeological features (Scaife 1998a).

The Boongate Roundabout

In March 1994, a team from Birmingham University Field Archaeology Unit under the direction of Richard Cuttler (1995) carried out a small evaluation on a site located immediately south-east of the ROM/DoE Storey's Bar Road subsite (OS NGR TL 210988; Fig 1.6, BR). Although of limited scale, it revealed evidence for a buried soil and a probable Neolithic settlement. The results serve to 'bridge' the sites on Storey's Bar Road and Third Drove (Site O).

Four trenches were excavated (Fig 2.13). Due to curatorial problems, this was a 'retrospective' evaluation in that recently laid hardcore foundations had to be removed in order to access the archaeological deposits. As part of the initial construction, part of the ploughsoil and upper alluvium had been removed. Beneath the latter was a layer of dark orange sand-silt 250–330mm thick (probably a palaeosol), which sealed the archaeological features beneath.

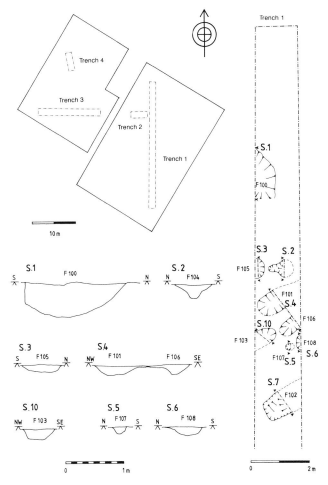

Fig 2.13 Boongate Roundabout excavation (1995): upper — trench location plan; lower — probable Neolithic features in Trench 1 (after Cuttler 1995)

Trench 1 produced several archaeological features filled with a pale and homogeneous sand-silt closely comparable with the buried soil directly above (Richard Cuttler personal communication). Experience at Fengate has shown that features containing such a filling frequently pre-date the Bronze Age. A good example was the Neolithic 'house' of the Padholme Road subsite (Pryor 1974, 6–14). Similar 'early' archaeological features in Trench 1 included F100–101 and F103–8 (Fig 2.13). The few finds

included a serrated backed blade (with lustre) from F100 and a flake from F103. An abraded fragment of pottery from F103 is undoubtedly pre-Iron Age, but it is impossible to be more precise.

Despite the practical difficulties of carrying out this excavation so late in the development, it was nonetheless possible to come to some significant conclusions. As well as confirming that a palaeosol was present and that preservation was good, the cluster of postholes and small pits provide evidence for a probable Neolithic settlement. Moreover, if the very pale filling of the features and the single backed blade can be taken at face value, the settlement might prove to be earlier rather than later in the period. If the Boongate features were part of an earlier Neolithic settlement site, however, was the putative settlement located in an extension of the aligned earlier Neolithic landscape (represented by the Padholme Road 'house', the Cat's Water 1997 mortuary structure, and other features; Pryor 1988), or was it part of another, altogether separate, landscape? This problem will be considered further in the discussion of the earlier Neolithic landscape in Chapter 18.

The Tower Works

In January and February 1997, the Cambridge University Archaeological Unit evaluated a site 7.6ha in extent in the southern part of Fengate (OS NGR TL 206987; Fig 1.6). The excavation was the first modern project to investigate the area of pre-war Gravel Pits (Lucas 1977a and b). It revealed that preservation was excellent, even close to the actual gravel pits. Buried soils were encountered, including an organics-rich 'dark earth' dated to the earlier first millennium BC. The main archaeological features were all of Late Bronze Age/Early Iron Age date and included pits, field ditches, and an unusual post-built rectangular building aligned on the orientation of the known Bronze Age field system.

As almost all the area investigated was covered with hardstanding, the original surface had been removed for hardcore and concrete rafts. Preserved beneath alluvium, a truncated buried soil had survived in all the trenches which had not been affected by gravel quarrying in the early decades of the century.

Principal results

The geology consisted of Nene first-terrace gravels overlying Jurassic Cornbrash limestone. In most cases, the natural substratum reached in the evaluation trenches was an orange gravelly sand which capped the cleaner gravels to a depth of *c* 0.2m and was reached at *c* 5m OD in the north to *c* 4m OD in the south. At the highest point of the site, the underlying cornbrash was reached at 4.4m OD, some 0.7m below the top of the natural sands and gravels. Presently, the ground surface of the site lies between about 6m OD at the north and 5m OD at the south. There is, however, a fairly sharp break of slope just below the 5m contour, which coincides approximately with the boundary between the northern and southern parts of the site. The break of slope is also visible in the subsoil contours (Fig 2.14) Archaeological remains were found in three areas: in the north-west (Trenches B, G, H, and J), where features were mainly of Late Bronze Age/Early Iron Age date; in the south-west (Trench D), where features were post-medieval and Roman, and in the south-east, where they were Late Bronze Age/Early Iron Age and Roman. The Roman features consisted of linear ditches that may have been associated with the double-ditched Romano-British droveway excavated in 1973 (Pryor 1984a, fig 11, ditches P12 and P13). Only the prehistoric features will be discussed in detail here. Modern quarrying was identified across the entire northern part of the site (all of Trenches A and C, parts of B, E, and K, and all of Test Pits 1 and 2)

Late Bronze Age/Early Iron Age

It should be stressed that there was evidence for very dense settlement. More than 600 sherds of later

Bronze Age date (some 4kg; Hill 1997) and some 400 animal bones were recovered from the evaluation.

Pits: The earliest features on the site consisted of a group of intercutting pits in Trench B, which extended east at least as far as Trench J. They had been backfilled with redeposited natural gravel and their sides were almost all vertical, with sharp, angular corners. No complete pit was seen in Trench B but they were presumed to be rectangular or square. The absence of weathering on the edges, and the almost horizontal layering of the fills, suggest rapid, intentional backfilling. Some settling of an organically-rich 'dark earth' occurred in the uppermost profiles of these features.

A buried soil, which sealed the pits, was exceptionally dark in the middle of Trench B and throughout Trench J, but had become much paler in the southern end of Trench B and in Trenches G and H. In trenches B and J, it also contained a large quantity of artefacts, especially pottery, which typically consisted of large, unabraded sherds. The dark, organic nature of this soil is almost certainly the product of occupation or middening. It is estimated to have covered a minimum

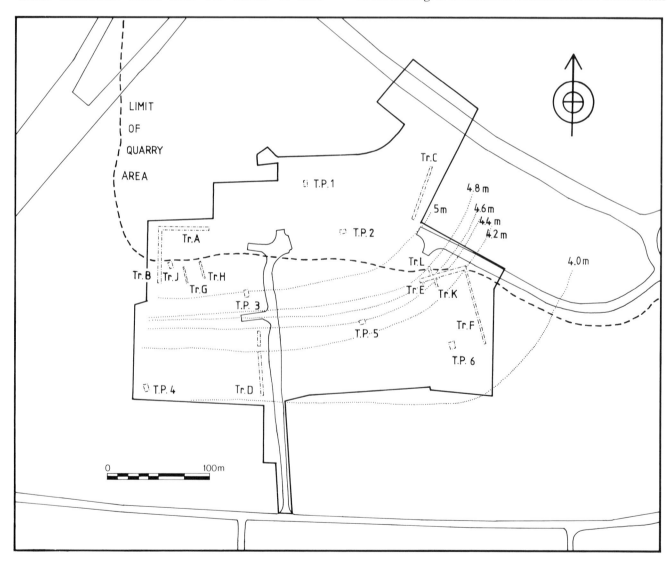

Fig 2.14 The Tower Works site: subsoil contours and trench location plan (after Lucas 1997)

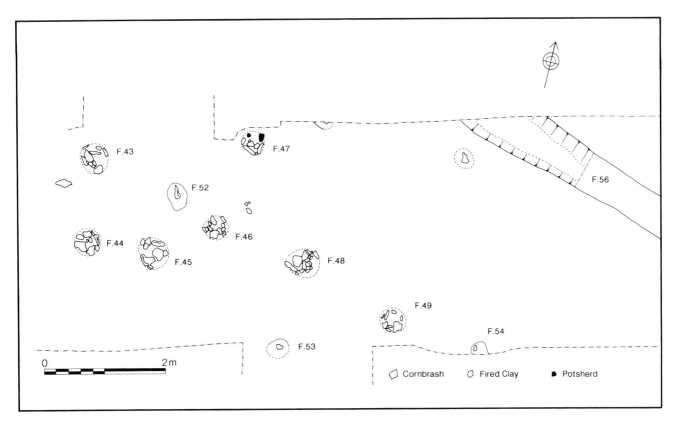

Fig 2.15 The Tower Works site: possible post-built structure in Trench E (after Lucas 1997)

area of about 200m², probably extended north (where it has been quarried away) and east (beneath a cinema car park). This 'dark earth' also seemed to reflect the extent of the underlying pits. It rested directly on them and an earlier land surface. This, in turn, had possibly been deturfed or somehow truncated. Between this layer and the pits was a slightly paler buried soil. In Trench B, postholes were cut through it. A gravel surface had been laid on the soil in Trench J.

Ditches: Possible field boundary ditches, similar in shape and filling to those excavated in the ROM/DoE project, were found in Trenches G, H, and F. Their orientation (but not their known extent) has been plotted on the general plan (Fig 1.4). These features occurred in areas where the buried soil was very much paler than the 'dark earth' found around the areas of settlement.

The rectilinear structure: A ditch and group of stone-lined postholes were found in Trenches E, F, K, and L; these features were tentatively attributed to this phase on the basis of pottery and their alignment on securely dated ditches in Trenches G and H (Fig 2.15). They all appeared to have been cut through the lower levels of a buried soil and were sealed by a later Roman and post-Roman buried ploughsoil.

The postholes were arranged in two rows running east-north-east–west-south-west, with a single outlier (F47). To the north-east of the postholes, a ditch (F56) ran parallel to the main row. F56 was U-shaped with gently sloping sides and a flat base. It was 0.8m wide and 0.15–0.2m deep, and filled with sandy silt

and occasional gravel pebbles; the filling also contained abraded pottery and bone. This ditch may well have been associated with the postholes, as it did not continue into Trench F nearby. It must either have returned west or terminated.

The ten postholes of the possible structure (F43–9, F52–4) were cleaned and recorded, but were not excavated. All consisted of essentially the same components — they were cut through the lower buried soil to a depth of at least 0.2m and had been lined with upright fragments of cornbrash, irregular-shaped 'bricks' of fired clay, and occasional large fragments of pottery. In two cases (F47, F48), it was possible that the feature had held two posts of about 0.1–0.15m diameter, but most seem to have held just one timber of about 0.2m diameter. The associated (lower) buried soil, which was about 0.1m thick, was composed of fairly compact, dark silty loam with occasional gravel pebbles.

The postholes lay below an upper buried soil, about 0.2m thick. This was very dark and resembled 'dark earth'. Two metre-square test pits were excavated through this buried soil to assess the density of finds. This averaged 5 sherds per test pit. The dark nature of the soil and the density of finds suggest concentrated activity, such as middening or occupation. The fact that this buried soil was so dark above the stonelined postholes suggests that it owes its colour and composition to prehistoric rather than to later activity (eg Roman). The full extent of the upper buried soil is uncertain, but is known to have covered about 1650m².

Discussion

Later Bronze Age/Early Iron Age pits

The excavations demonstrated two foci of prehistoric occupation: a western area (Trenches B, J, G, and H) and an eastern area (Trenches E, F, K, and L). The tightly clustered intercutting pits of the western area were interpreted as backfilled gravel quarry pits. The use to which such gravel was put is illustrated by the metalled layer in Trench J which almost certainly appears to be an original 'laid' ground surface, later used as a dump for refuse.

Bronze Age field ditches

The alignment of these ditches corresponds with that of F56 and the associated post structure in Trench E. The ditches are clearly part of the larger field system and align with the main Bronze Age droveways and field system along the fen edge (Fig 1.4). It is, however, curious that this alignment seems to ignore local topography. The medieval roads, First, Second, and Third Drove, are laid out at right-angles to the fen edge and give the impression of radiating away from the low rise in the terrace, on which Tower Works is located. The prehistoric ditches cut across the direction of slope, in conformity with the main system to the north-east. This might suggest that the fields in the south-west were laid out later than those closer to the Flag Fen post alignment, in the Newark Road, Fourth Drove, and Cat's Water subsites of the ROM/DoE project, or at least that the system had its origins in the south-east. A suggested shorter chronology for the fields in the southern part of the system would accord well with what we now know about the dating of fields in the Depot and Storey's Bar Road sites.

The rectilinear structure

The settlement in the eastern part of the site was also demarcated by an organically enriched, buried soil which lay over the possible post-built structure and the associated ditch, F56. The relation of this ditch and the pattern of the postholes remains ambiguous; the coalignment of the ditch, however, and a central line of postholes (F43–F54) suggest that they may be part of a rectangular structure, at least 12m long. The postholes would have supported the main frame of a longhouse, the ditch forming part of an enclosure or eaves-drip gully associated with the building. Such buildings, though rare in Britain, are not unknown. At least two rectangular Late Bronze Age/Early Iron Age buildings were found at the Welland Bank quarry, some five miles north of Peterborough (Pryor 1998c); another has been found at Barleycroft Farm, in the lower Ouse valley (Evans and Knight 1997; Fig 1.2). All three sites were associated with ditched fields. In addition, like Tower Works, Welland Bank also featured a large expanse of 'dark earth' around its settlement. The relationship of the Tower Works settlement to the ditched field system will be considered in Chapter 18.

Tower Works and the collections of G Wyman Abbott

It is appropriate to compare the large quantity of pottery recovered from the Tower Works site with the assemblage gathered by Abbott. The material from Tower Works is, however, notable for its lack of finer and decorated vessels which characterise the Abbott collection (Hawkes and Fell 1945). This disparity may reflect chronology. It is possible, taking this view, that the Tower Works group (if 'group' is the right word) might belong within the Later Bronze Age, say 900–700 BC, rather than the Early Iron Age (Hill 1997, 37). Cunliffe (1991, 566) places the Fengate Gravel Pits material within the fifth to third century BC. A somewhat earlier date for the Tower Works material would certainly accord better with the known dating of other features associated with the ditched fields of Fengate.

3 Recent research in central and north Fengate

This chapter will be concerned with the results of developer-funded investigations north and west of Third Drove. It begins with brief descriptions of two outlier excavations within the northern extent of the Bronze Age field system and continues with sites nearer the Cat's Water.

The Global Doors site

In 1993 Fenland Archaeological Trust undertook a recording brief on the Global Doors site, located immediately west of Newark Road, some 300m north-west of the Newark Road subsite investigated in the ROM/DoE campaign (OS NGR TL 21409978; Fig 1.6). The site had been partially disturbed by the construction of a dyke along its west boundary (Fig 3.1) and there were tips of hardcore and rubble along the dykeside. An inspection of available aerial photographs showed that the site was under pasture or made ground and nothing of archaeological interest was found. An area approximately 30 × 28m was stripped (Fig 3.2). Although the ground was disturbed in many places, it was apparent that the buried soil that covered most of the nearby Newark Road subsite was still largely intact

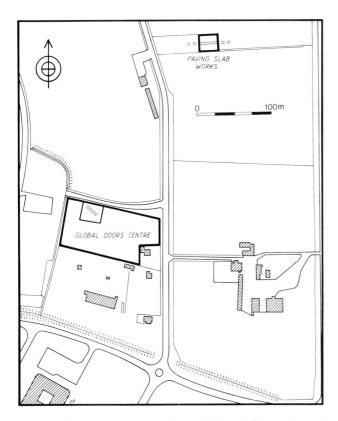

Fig 3.1 Map showing location of Global Doors (1993) and Paving Factory (1994) sites. The approximate orientation of probable Bronze Age field boundary ditches is shown at each site

and survived to a thickness of about 250mm. This suggests that preservation of archaeological deposits in this general area will, in the future, be good. It had been believed that the area was too high to allow sufficient levels of protective alluvium to have accumulated.

The only visible archaeological feature in the machine-cut trench was a straight linear ditch that traversed the excavated area diagonally (Fig 3.2). The ends were in disturbed ground. No recuts, butt ends, or entranceway gaps were visible on the cleaned surface. The ditch ran almost straight for 28.5m, but there were slight changes of course at either end: to the north-east the ditch veered slightly north and to the south-east it veered slightly to the south.

In the least disturbed area, towards the centre of the exposure, two sections were excavated by hand. These revealed a single uniform layer of sand-silt with gravel pebbles (10YR 5/4). In texture and colour this filling was reminiscent of the Newark Road Bronze Age field ditches. The open U shape was also typical, as was the ditch's size and profile (Fig 3.2). The only finds were two very small sherds of handmade pottery. Both were found in primary contexts, close to the ditch bottom. The pottery was soft and poorly fired, with a reduced (black) core, entirely typical of pottery found in ditches of the Bronze Age system. That alluvium was absent from the ditch filling would further support a pre-Iron Age attribution for the use and construction of this feature.

The Paving Factory Site

In the year following the Global Doors work, a watching brief was undertaken on a factory development on the east side of Newark Road, some 250m north-east of the former site, at OS NGR TL 21459995 (Figs 1.6 and 3.1). As in this instance the developer did not require a heavily reinforced factory floor, it was decided to leave the subsoil in place. Only the topsoil was removed. No archaeological features were visible in the exposed underlying alluvium. The walls of the building required strip footings and these were inspected after the excavation.

One feature was clearly visible. It was an open U-shape, slightly larger than the 1993 ditch, but with a very similar filling. Unfortunately, it was considered unsafe to enter the unshored trench. The feature's appearance in section (ie its colour, consistency, and profile) was very reminiscent of Bronze Age field boundary ditches excavated on the nearby Newark Road subsite (Pryor 1980, 23–130).

The ditch could be observed at either end of the factory site, but it was only possible to obtain an approximate idea of orientation and alignment, indicated by a dashed double line in Figure 3.1.

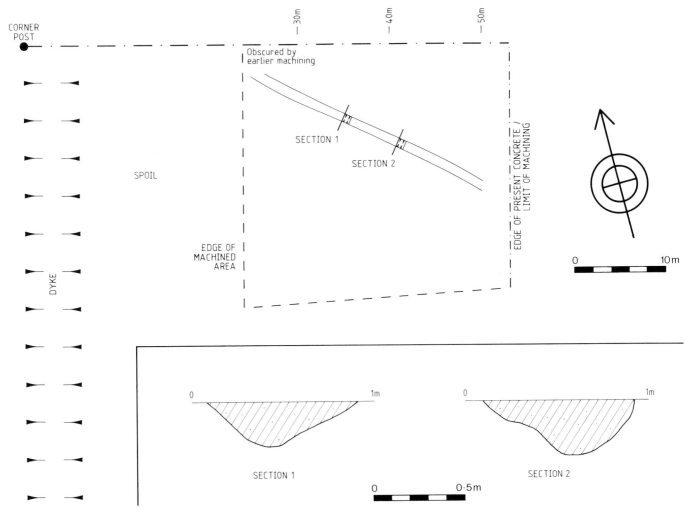

Fig 3.2 Plan and sections of the Bronze Age linear ditch found at the Global Doors site (1993)

Without being absolutely certain, it might have run parallel to the Global Doors ditch. Since the upper filling of the ditch did not contain alluvium, this would indicate that the ground surface above the ditch was level when the alluvium began to form in Iron Age times. Such a condition would favour a date well before the Iron Age for the feature's abandonment.

Discussion

The evidence from these two small sites would suggest that the Fengate Bronze Age ditches extended well to the north of the Newark Road subsite. Both sites also produced unexpected but good evidence for the survival of an extensive palaeosol. Much of the land around the large Perkins Diesel Engines factory (and especially the extensive old sports ground that lies immediately north of Global Doors) has been down to grass and has not been ploughed in modern times. This, combined with the presence of a known palaeosol, would suggest that some of the best preserved archaeological sites in Fengate still remain to be discovered. It is probable, moreover, that being relatively high and well drained, this area might reveal extensive evidence for Bronze Age settlement.

The 1990 excavations at Cat's Water

In the 1990 excavations at Cat's Water, a small Class I henge monument enclosing at least one 'mini-henge' was found. The proximity of the henge close to the fen margins might have provided a focus on that parts of the subsequent Bronze Age field system were aligned. Further elements of the Bronze Age field system were also traced eastwards, towards the fen edge. The excavations were carried out by Fenland Archaeological Trust under the site direction of Dermot Bond. The area of development lay within the ROM/DoE Cat's Water subsite. It also extended east, however, across the Parish Drain, and onto land that had only been subject to limited trial trenching during the ROM/DoE project (Fig 1.6). Aerial photographs had not revealed any cropmarks, but this was probably due both to the presence of alluvium directly below the ploughsoil and to the fact that the area had been under permanent pasture for many years.

Two areas were excavated (Fig 3.3). Area 1 was positioned to follow Bronze Age ditches 3 and 4 towards the fen edge. The original (1976) excavation was still open and although heavily overgrown, it was

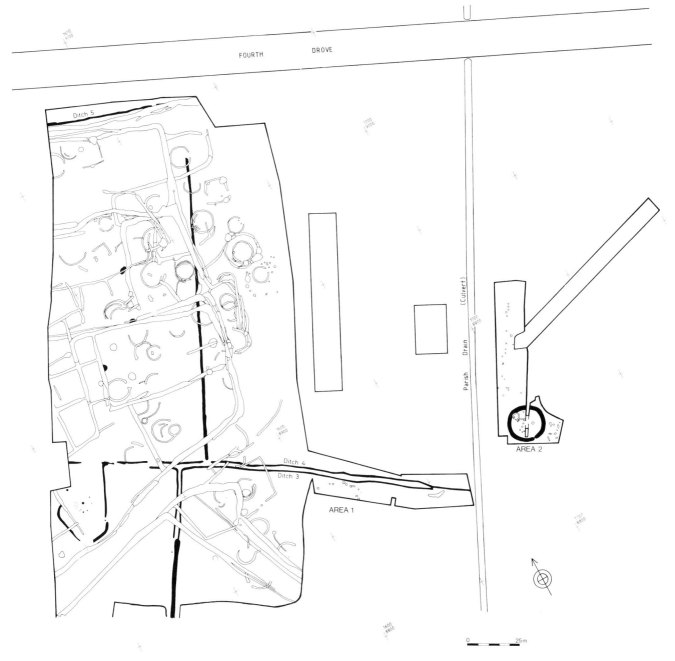

Fig 3.3 Cat's Water excavation (1974–90): general plan. Later Neolithic and Bronze Age features are shown in black

just possible to locate the two ditches and to follow their course eastwards. Area 2 was opened speculatively to assess what might be present in a part of the site that was seemingly devoid of archaeological features.

Soil micromorphological analysis

by C A I French

Of the four buried soil profiles examined, three were taken from north-west to south-east across the fen edge (Fig 3.4). Profile 3 was situated adjacent to and on the southern edge of the area excavated in 1975–8. The buried soil was here overlain by 350mm of alluvial topsoil. Profile 1 was situated about 75m to the south of Profile 3 (at grid 992 1008) and was overlain by

Table 3.1 Summary of the soil horizons present at the Cat's Water site

profile		main fabric	subsidiary fabrics
3:	upper half	Eb/upper B	lower A
	lower half	B(t)	–
1:	upper half	Eb	lower A
	middle	Eb	–
	lower half	upper B	lower A
2:	upper half	alluviated A	lower A/Eb
	middle quarter	Eb	lower A
	lower quarter	B(t)	–

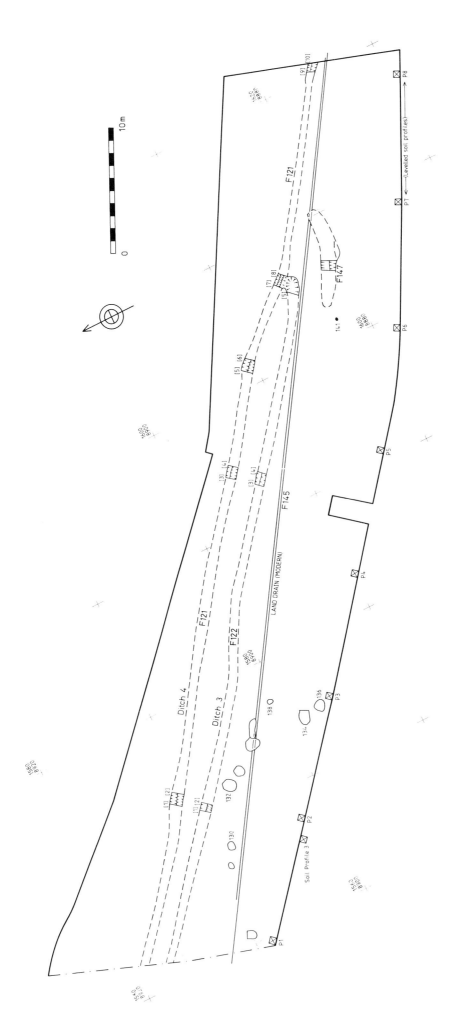

10 m

0

Ditch 4

Ditch 3

F121

F122

F121

F145

LAND DRAIN (MODERN)

F121

F147

[9]
[10]

[7] [8]
[5]

[5] [6]

[3] [4]

[3] [4]

[1] [2]

[1] [2]

138

132

136

134

130

14.1

Soil Profile 3

P1

P2

P3

P4

P5

P6

P7

P8

(Levelled soil profiles)

1620
8880

1580
8900

1600
8880

1600
8900

1580
8940

1580
8300

1540
8320

Fig 3.4 Cat's Water excavation (1990): plan of features in Area 1

150mm of peat and 500mm of peaty alluvium. Profile 2 was situated in the centre of the Bronze Age ring-ditch to the south of Profile 1 (at grid 1000 995) and was overlain by about 180mm of peat and about 320mm of peaty alluvium. The buried soil survived to a thickness varying between 150 and 300mm.

Profile 4 was situated at what appeared to be a compacted 'floor or yard' surface (at grid 1013 1030). This surface, which was composed of compacted soil, sand, and gravel over several square metres, apparently sealed an organic buried soil.

Detailed soil micromorphological descriptions are given in Appendix 2. A summary of the soil horizons represented in each profile examined is given in Table 3.1. The composition and characteristics of the three buried soil profiles (1–3) provided complementary results:

Profile 3: A depth of soil *c* 150mm thick was sealed beneath a mixture of desiccated peat and alluvium. The upper and lower halves of the surviving soil profile are composed of a homogeneous sandy loam. It is dominated by the medium and very fine sand fractions, with lesser amounts of silt and clay. It is relatively porous and contains very little organic matter. The absence of textural pedofeatures and organic matter in the upper half of the profile suggests that this is eluvial or Eb horizon material or the upper part of the B horizon of a brown earth.

About half of the groundmass of the upper half of the profile is composed of a second fabric. It is characterised by amorphous zones of random/reticulate striated groundmass, which is composed mainly of non-laminated dusty clay. This is indicative of the slaking or movement and redeposition of fines down the profile as a result of saturation associated with freshwater flooding and alluviation. It is suggested that these alluvially derived zones of the upper half of the profile are lower A horizon material.

There are two main types of clay coating present in the lower half of the buried soil, occasional laminated limpid clay and many non-laminated dusty clay coatings. The strong birefringence and distinct laminations indicate successive episodes of the illuviation of pure clay that can only occur under stable wooded conditions (Bullock and Murphy 1979). Thus the lower half of this soil is representative of the Bt or argillic horizon of an argillic brown earth (Avery 1980).

As only the lower A and Bt horizon of this brown earth survive, the overlying A horizon is absent. It is probable that the soil has suffered some later soil truncation, and/or the upper A horizon has become incorporated within the overlying alluvium. Certainly the presence of lower A horizon material in a partially heterogeneous mixture with the underlying Eb/B horizons is suggestive of considerable soil disturbance prior to burial.

This sample location was just inland and to the north of the furthest landward extent of the peat. This soil therefore enjoyed a long history of development.

Burial by alluvium began to occur in the later Roman period. Evidence for this took the form of alluvial infill of third-century AD ditches of the adjacent Cat's Water site (French 1992b). Nevertheless, analysis of this soil profile suggests that this soil was subject to continued additions of silty clay alluvium for some time prior to burial by alluvium.

Profile 1: the buried soil is composed of three main fabrics in a heterogeneous mixture. Fabric 1 is a sandy (clay) loam with even proportions of medium, fine and very fine quartz, silt, and clay. This poorly sorted fabric contains minor amounts of organic matter and much amorphous sesquioxide impregnation. Textural pedofeatures are abundant, and include occasional non-laminated limpid clay and abundant non-laminated dusty clay coatings in the groundmass. The former limpid clay coatings indicate the former presence of stable wooded conditions, while the latter coatings are indicative of soil disturbance and/or alluvial intercalation of fines. Considered together, this fabric probably represents the upper B horizon of an argillic brown earth.

Fabric 2 is a clay loam that is dominated by silt and clay. It contains some organic matter (more than in fabric 1) and small zones of amorphous sesquioxide impregnation. The dominant feature of this fabric is the presence of very abundant non-laminated dusty clay throughout the fabric. The amount of intercalation with silty clay is indicative of the incorporation of alluvially derived fines as would occur in a lower A horizon.

Fabric 3 is a loamy sand that is dominated by very fine quartz sand (35%) and the coarser sand fractions (45%). It contains minor amounts of organic matter and non-laminated dusty clay. This very depleted material is probably indicative of an eluvial or Eb horizon of an argillic brown earth.

The buried soil is made up of the following horizons and soil fabrics (from the base to the top):

upper half: mainly Eb (75%) horizon in heterogeneous mixture with upper B (20%) and lower A (5%) horizon material
upper part of lower half: Eb horizon material
lower half: upper B horizon (90%) in heterogeneous mixture with lower A (10%) material

In general, there is an absence of organic matter and evidence of faunal mixing. This suggests that the upper half of the A horizon has either been truncated or it has been incorporated within the overlying peat.

The mixture of fabrics throughout the profile indicates considerable soil disturbance. As the deposition of the overlying peat is unlikely to have caused this disturbance, it is possible that this soil was ploughed in later prehistory. Indeed, the abundance of non-laminated dusty clay as intercalations throughout the groundmass might be associated with slaking as a result of the mechanical disturbance of the soil. On the other hand, these dusty coatings are not sufficiently 'dirty' to suggest prolonged ploughing. It is more probable that these intercalations are associated with freshwater flooding and the seasonal addition of alluvial fines to the soil profile (as observed in profiles 4–6 at the adjacent Fengate Power Station site). In one case, the actual sequence of deposition of the textural pedofeatures was clear. First, there were non-laminated coatings of light yellow dusty clay in the void space around a grain. This was followed by the deposition of organic and sesquioxide stained, yellowish brown, non-laminated silty clay. Thirdly, there was the deposition of yellow, non-laminated dusty clay acting to completely infill the void space. These features probably represent first, soil disturbance, second, possible ploughing, and third, alluviation.

Profile 2: the thin buried soil within the centre of the ring ditch/hengiform site exhibits three horizons. The upper horizon is composed of an homogeneous silty clay with very small amounts of a sandy loam fabric (similar to the main fabric in the underlying middle horizon). It is dominated by dense, limpid and non-laminated dusty (impure) clay, although the groundmass as a whole is very open and porous (up to 50%). These characteristics suggest that this is an upper A horizon that has been subject to the addition of considerable quantities of freshwater-eroded and -carried silts and clays, or alluvium, prior to the overlying period of peat development.

The middle horizon is composed of a heterogeneous mixture of two fabrics. The dominant fabric is a sandy loam, with very little organic matter, 30% amorphous sesquioxide impregnation, and many non-laminated dusty clay coatings in the groundmass and voids. This fabric is essentially similar to fabric 1 in Profile 1, and is suggestive of the Eb horizon material of a brown earth.

This fabric also contains a few eroded aggregates of silt and birefringent limpid clay, which indicate that this soil was also receiving alluvial material. In turn, this is indicative of the erosion of other (argillic) soils upstream and upslope.

The second and more minor fabric in the upper horizon is a sandy clay loam, which is dominated by silt and non-laminated dusty clay. This fabric is very similar to fabric 2 of Profile 1. Thus this is an alluvially derived lower A horizon fabric that has been mixed into the underlying soil fabric by a combination of water action and mechanical disturbance.

The lower horizon exhibits a sandy loam fabric. The absence of organic matter and the abundance of illuvial material suggests that this soil might be grading downwards to a poorly developed Bt horizon.

Profile 4: the soil beneath the possible 'floor' or 'yard' surface exhibits a dense, homogeneous loamy sand with a massive microstructure. It is dominated by equal proportions of medium, fine and very fine quartz sand. It contains very little organic matter and very rare non-laminated dusty clay coatings. In the field, this amorphous feature appeared as a compacted sand and gravel surface. It was overlain by <100mm of soil and sealed a very organic soil layer. In terms of soil characteristics, the soil material might be upper B or lower A horizon material. Nevertheless, the sealing effect of the surface might have prevented some further soil development.

Discussion

This area of the fen edge once supported an argillic brown earth, rather poorly developed but once associated with some woodland cover. Well before the later Neolithic period, the land was ostensibly cleared: the soil suggests that it suffered some disturbance, perhaps by some minor agricultural activity. Then the soil became subject to the addition of alluvially derived silt and clay fines, which was accompanied by the mass movement of soil within the soil profile. At this point in time, a flood meadow environment became established, probably in the later Bronze Age. Peat growth followed as base water levels rose in the fen basin to the east, thus burying the Bronze Age landscape. Alluvial influences probably continued off and on during the period of peat growth, but alluvial aggradation gained the upper hand from the later Roman period onwards.

Corroborative evidence of the presence of former woodland in the Fengate area is provided by the palynological analysis (Chapter 13). There are also occasional limpid coatings present in the buried soil. These coatings are generally associated with weathering and clay translocation in forest soils under disturbed broadleaved woodland (Fedoroff and Goldberg 1982). The apparently poorly developed argillic or Bt horizon in the buried soil at Fengate might be partly due to postdepositional effects and losses, that is, the Bt fabric has suffered damage and depletion as a result of tree clearance and tree-throw, and subsequent leaching of the soil (Macphail *et al* 1987).

Although there is a mixture of soil fabrics in all three profiles, there is no unequivocal evidence to suggest that this soil has been cultivated. The heterogeneous mixture of lower A and Eb soil horizons at first suggests mechanical soil disturbance associated with ploughing. The intrusive lower A fabric is, however, more probably the result of saturation of the soil and very localised 'colluviation' or mass movement down-profile.

In addition, the dusty clay coatings seldom contain abundant very fine organic matter, which would be expected if these coatings were 'agricutans'. Nevertheless, there are a few examples in Profile 1 in which the non-laminated dusty or silty clay coatings is very 'dirty', or contain much fine amorphous organic matter. These few examples suggest the possibility of some minor arable activity in this part of the fen edge prior to peat formation.

In conclusion, the following sequence of events is evident in the surviving buried soil at the Cat's Water site:

1 The development of an argillic brown earth prior to the Bronze Age. Although it was not particularly well developed, it implies the former presence of woodland in this part of the fen edge.

2 Deforestation and soil disturbance occurred prior to the laying out of the Bronze Age field system.

3 Once the soil was open, presumably as pasture, it received eroded soil material from elsewhere. This comprised alluvially derived silt and clay, as well as eroded fragments of other soils. These features indicate that the soil was periodically flooded with fresh water, and it is probable that a flood meadow environment pertained during this period or the later Bronze Age.

4 As base levels rose in the fen to the east, this fen-edge soil became buried by subsequent peat development, probably in the later Bronze Age/Iron Age.

5 During the later Roman period and subsequently, there was renewed freshwater flooding. With it came large amounts of silty clay alluvium, which was derived from the clearance and probably cultivation of upland heavier soils further up the Nene valley to the west.

Principal results

Area 1

Bronze Age linear ditches 3 and 4 (Fig 1.4), located in the overgrown ROM/DoE (1976) trench, were followed as far eastwards as possible. A sufficiently large area on either side was cleared to detect any north–south ditches that might be associated with them (Fig 3.3). The gap or possible droveway between the ditches remained more or less constant (about 2–3m) as they extended eastwards from the original excavation for a distance of some 55m. At this point, the southerly ditch (3) terminated. Ditch 4, however, continued eastwards for a further 17m, where it left the excavation and the area of development.

Fig 3.5 Cat's Water excavation (1990): Area 1, ditch 3 (F122), section 2. Metre scale

Ditches 3 and 4 were shallow and their filling a homogeneous sand-silt with occasional gravel pebbles. Although their infilling showed no signs of recutting, both ditches were marked by a low ridge along their gravel bottoms, suggesting that each had been recut slightly off-centre at least once (Figs 3.4 and 3.5). It was often difficult to determine the edge of the ditches with any precision. This suggests that the area around them

Fig 3.6 Cat's Water excavation (1990): Area 1, ditch 3 (F121) section 5. The courses of ditches 3 and 4 have been marked on the site surface (view looking north-west). Metre scale

Fig 3.7 Cat's Water excavation (1990): Area 1, ditch 4 (F121), section 10 at east edge of excavation, showing complete modern soil profile. Metre scale

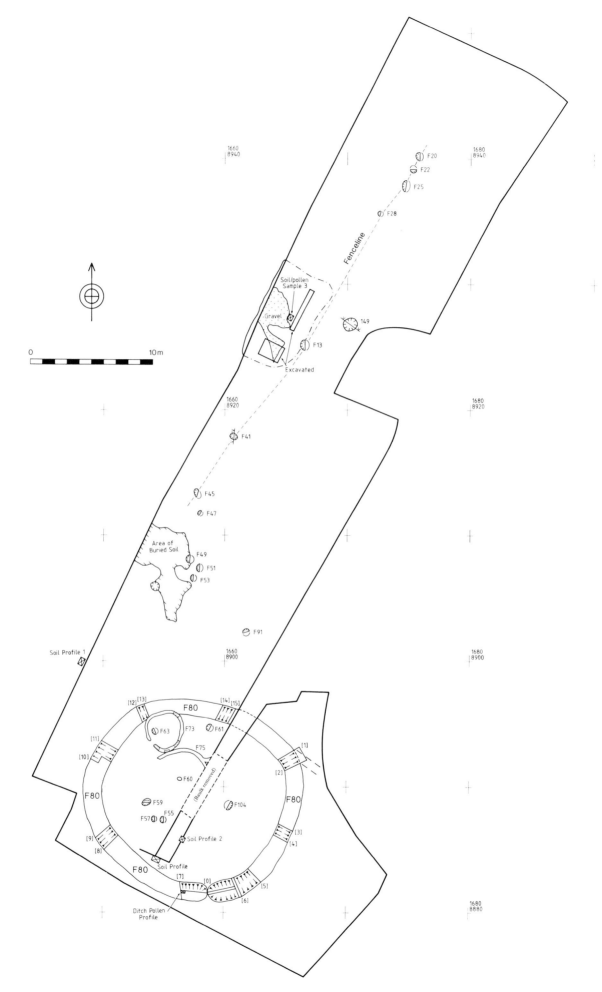

Fig 3.8 Cat's Water excavation (1990): plan of features in Area 2

had been disturbed in antiquity, perhaps by the trampling of livestock. Alternatively, the disturbance could be entirely natural, due to cryoturbation in late glacial times. Section 5, ditch 4, illustrates this disturbance well. Here, a pit-like patch of silt was located on the possible droveway south of the section line (Fig 3.6).

Ditch 4 left the excavations at the eastern edge of Area 1. At this point the topsoil was thicker than elsewhere, due to the presence of a large drainage dyke, immediately to the east. It was hoped that the upcast from the dyke would have preserved evidence for a bank alongside the ditch, but despite a most careful inspection of the section, this was not visible (Fig 3.7).

Area 2

This area produced a variety of features, including a group of non-linear ones that contained no finds. They extended from north-north-east to south-south-west and probably represent the remains of a fenceline. The features, which were sharply defined, included many charcoal flecks in their fillings. They were shallow

(100–200mm), but it should be recalled that the C horizon gravel surface, where they were first identified, probably lay about 200–300mm below the original A and B soil horizons (Pryor 1980, fig 128, layer 3). If they were postholes or stakeholes, the timbers would have penetrated half a metre, more than enough to support a fence.

The features of the probable fenceline are (Fig 3.8): F20, F22, F25, F26, F13, F41, and F45. Other features in the vicinity might represent realignments of, or repairs to, the fence. When viewed in the field, the seven postholes made a most striking row.

By far the most significant and unexpected discovery was F80, a penannular ditch with a single, very narrow, entranceway to the south (Fig 3.9). The ditch was of open U-shaped profile and the filling was a homogeneous sand-silt with occasional gravel pebbles.

The filling of the ditch consisted of two distinct layers of similar composition. The higher layer was, however, darker and contained fewer pebbles. The lower layer represented the primary and secondary infilling of the ditch. The higher layer had formed slowly over a greater length of time and probably represents the tertiary processes of natural infilling.

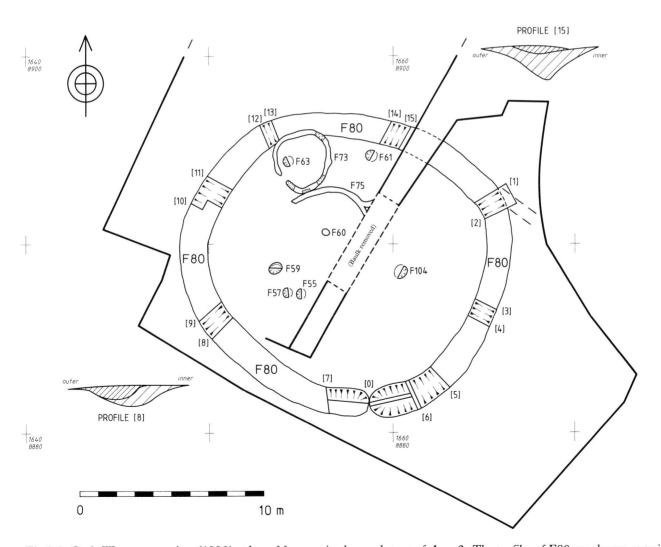

Fig 3.9 Cat's Water excavation (1990): plan of features in the south part of Area 2. The profiles of F80 are drawn at twice the plan scale

The ditch was regular in outline at the surface, measuring approximately 1.3m to 1.9m in width and from 0.4m to 0.9m in depth. In plan, the ditch appeared more oval than circular, with a pronounced flattening along the northern side, more or less opposite the entranceway (Fig 3.9). In the field, the penannular ditch appeared perfectly circular (Fig 3.10). Its internal diameter ranged from 14.2m (northwest–south-east) to 14m (north-east–south-west).

Fig 3.10 Cat's Water excavation (1990): Area 2, general view of ring-ditch, looking west

Fig 3.11 Cat's Water excavation (1990): Area 2, ring-ditch section 6 (for location of section line see Fig 3.9)

The entranceway, as excavated, was closed, but if an allowance is made for weathering, an original width of no more than about a metre is indicated. The natural subsoil in the immediate vicinity was quite sandy and would have weathered readily. The natural erosion of an already narrow entranceway is good evidence that the ditch was never actually backfilled.

There was no conclusive direct evidence for a bank, as the ditch infilling was generally homogeneous (Fig 3.11). The upcast from the ditch must, however, have been placed somewhere. The tertiary filling of profile 8 is towards the outer edge of the ditch, perhaps suggesting that the filling of the inner edge accumulated

more quickly, due to the slippage of bank material. A more convincing argument, this time for an external bank, is provided by the small penannular ditch F73. The date of this feature is uncertain, but as its filling did not contain alluvium, this would indicate a date earlier than the Middle/Late Iron Age. If the larger penannular ditch was accompanied by an internal bank, then it might be expected that the smaller ditch would either respect it and be placed to one side, or would be very much larger on the side that did not cut into the bank — but it was both regular in plan and even in depth. If this smaller penannular ditch was associated with the main ditch in some way, this evidence clinches the matter and suggests that a bank probably ran around the outside of the monument.

Within the area enclosed by the main penannular ditch (F80) were a series of shallow possible pits or postholes and another curving gully, F75 (Fig 3.9). The pit/postholes might have been natural features. Similarly, the larger diameter gully (F75) could be natural, were it not for the fact that it appears to carefully respect the smaller penannular gully, F73. The latter was clearly defined in the ground and its regular shape showed plainly that it was manmade. In profile it was only 50mm deep and of open U shape. Like the larger ditch (F80), it was slightly flattened in plan, with an internal diameter of approximately 2.7m. The width of the gap was a mere 200mm.

The ditch of F73 had been cut into the weathered edge of the large penannular ditch and its positioning clearly respected the larger feature. Stratigraphically, therefore, F73 postdates F80.

The form of the penannular ditch aside, the only dating evidence came from a small pit or posthole, F91, some 6m north of F80. This feature produced a small rimsherd of unusual form, but carrying decoration reminiscent of Mildenhall or Peterborough styles (Fig 9.1, 1).

Discussion

Inspection of the general plan (Fig 3.3) leaves little doubt that further west, beneath the features of the ROM/DoE Iron Age settlement, ditches 3 and 4 defined the sides of a droveway (itself part of a coherently laid-out system), which gave access to four paddocks in the vicinity of a small enclosed roundhouse settlement (Pryor 1980, fig 94). To the east, on the other hand, the arrangement of the ditches makes less immediate sense.

The two ditches ran sufficiently parallel across Area 1 to suggest that they lined a droveway. In this first phase the drove probably ended close to the spot where ditch 3 abutted ditch 4. Ditch 4 might originally have ended at the point where its course took a pronounced southerly bend at section 5/6 (Fig 3.4). Unfortunately the section at this point showed no evidence for a termination. This is not surprising, however, given the homogeneity of the ditch filling and the fact that it had been regularly affected by fluctuating groundwater levels.

The pronounced bend in ditch 4 east of section 5/6 suggests that the easterly extension of ditch 4 might be later than the droveway and suggests that the drove had gone out of use as a means of leading stock to the fen-edge grazing. Its use as a property boundary continued nonetheless to be significant. In later chapters it will be seen that the boundary role of many Fengate droves was probably of equal importance to their 'main' function as routes along which livestock were driven.

The fact that neither ditch 3 nor ditch 4 yielded any finds was not unexpected. The ditches of the Fengate Bronze Age field system were notoriously devoid of finds, which is why so large a proportion, by volume, of the various ditches had to be excavated by hand. In the case of the Cat's Water 1990 excavations, resources only allowed a few small sections to be excavated. Enough ditch filling was sifted, however, to suggest that there was no permanent settlement in the immediate vicinity (compare eg Pryor 1980, fig 51).

The fence posts of Area 2 looked more convincing in the field than on paper, but there is a clear linear tendency (Figs 3.3 and 3.8). It is also quite apparent that the posited fenceline of Area 2 ran at right angles to ditches 3 and 4. The posts of the possible fenceline also passed close to the penannular ditch, as if respecting it. This leads to the suggestion that the penannular ditch was used as a marker for laying out this particular part of the enclosure system.

The hengiform monument

It is tentatively suggested from the evidence that the large penannular ditch was once accompanied by an external bank. Since it also had a single entranceway, it would belong to Atkinson's Class I henge monuments (Atkinson 1951). Finds consisted of a handful of fresh flints, which are probably (and tentatively) of Neolithic date (see Chapter 11). The shape of the penannular ditch is entirely consistent with local usage, where many of the known henge monuments are small (Pryor and French 1985). Further, its position so close to the encroaching fen edge and the absence of alluvium in the tertiary filling of the ditch would effectively rule out an Iron Age date. Nor were there any indications of door, porch, or wall posts. Taken together with the absence of domestic refuse, this surely suggests that the site served a non-domestic role.

The narrowness of the entranceway is also in keeping with local Neolithic ritual practice, as witnessed by the constricted example into the structure beneath the Maxey oval barrow (Pryor and French 1985, fig 14). Indeed, the narrowness of the access itself indicates ritual use: a constricted entrance allowed admission to the interior, but, at the same time, excluded the uninitiated from the sacred area (eg Thomas 1991, fig 6.3). Without stratified material for dating evidence it is impossible to be precise, but a Late Neolithic date would best fit this monument. Such a date would accord with the Neolithic pottery found in the nearby small pit or posthole, F91 (Fig 9.1, 1).

The most intriguing features in Area 2 were perhaps the two small gullies, Features 73 and 75. As it is difficult to say much about the rather fragmentary larger gully (F75), discussion will be confined to the smaller and more complete feature, F73. By any standards F73 is a rather small penannular gully, with a diameter of under 3m. The simplest explanation is that it represents the drip trench of a thatched circular stackstand, a class of site frequently encountered in the Netherlands (Buurman 1979). Similar stackstands were found at Maxey in Iron Age and Roman times (Pryor and French 1985, structures 11 and 24). Recent excavations at West Deeping, near Maxey, have also produced them (Fig 1.2; Jonathan Hunn personal communication). Generally speaking, however, prehistoric stackstands lacked an entranceway and frequently had a large central post against which the hay or straw was stacked. This post also served to hold the thatched lid or roof in place (Buurman 1979).

If feature 73 was an Iron Age stackstand, the gully would have been expected to contain alluvium, which it did not, and to be located on higher, drier land within the large Cat's Water settlement, a few metres to the west. On the contrary, it was firmly placed within the hengiform monument and, moreover, it would appear to have respected the main penannular ditch, F80. It is, therefore, perhaps best explained, however improbably, as a late and tiny henge or hengiform monument.

Very small henges are known from Maxey and in one case they appeared to be 'nested' rather in the manner suggested in the present instance. The smallest henge of the group known as Site 69 at Maxey had an internal diameter of 4m — somewhat larger than Fengate, but nonetheless comparable (Simpson 1981, fig 3). Henges less than 14m in diameter are classed by Harding and Lee (1987, 68) as 'mini-henges'; if this is one, F73 must be one of the smallest of this group in Britain and perhaps more aptly termed a 'micro-henge'.

The 1997 excavations

The 1997 Cat's Water excavations were centred on OS NGR TL 21609880. The 3.8ha site was located immediately south-east of the ROM/DoE Cat's Water site and was adjacent to the 1990 project (Fig 1.6). The excavation took place in June and July 1997 and was conducted by the Cambridge University Archaeological Unit (Gibson 1998; Gibson and Pollard forthcoming). The two main discoveries were a subrectangular Neolithic post-built ritual or mortuary structure and pits containing Grooved Ware, which were located close by the henge monument excavated in 1990.

Principal results

Eight trenches were opened (Fig 3.12). The natural gravel substratum fell from 2.74m OD at the west end of Trench 2 to at 1.91m OD at the east end of Trench 6. Trenches 1–3 and 8 revealed a thin scatter of

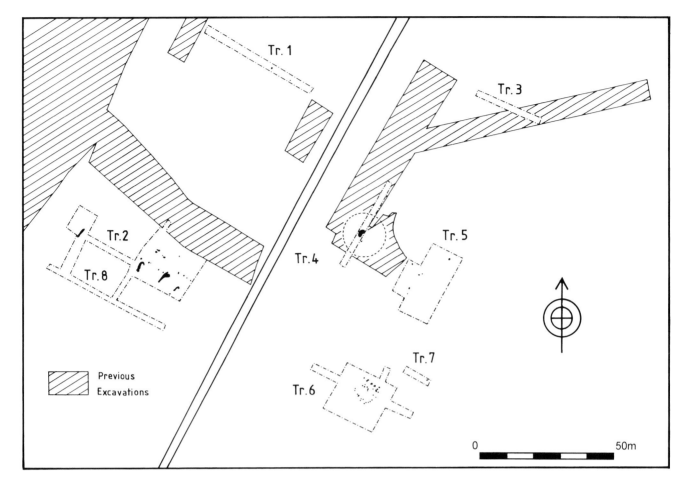

Fig 3.12 Cat's Water excavations (1997): trench location plan (after Gibson 1998)

convincing archaeological features, confirming the hypothesis that the Cat's Water Iron Age settlement did not continue eastwards towards the fen (Pryor 1984a, 213).

In Trench 4 was found a single small pit that contained probable Neolithic pottery and flints. Four pits were found in Trench 5, two of which produced Neolithic finds, including sherds of Grooved Ware; Trench 7 revealed a small pit of possible Neolithic date.

Three postholes discovered during the initial evaluation in Trench 6 indicated the possible presence of an early post-built structure. When the trench was subsequently extended, 32 postholes were exposed beneath a thin palaeosol. The postholes were of two types, distinguishable by size. They formed a rectangular structure, measuring 8 × 5m, which was aligned north-west–south-east. The north, east, and south walls were similar, comprising six, five, and six postholes respectively (Fig 3.13). The west wall differed markedly in having only three postholes. The postholes on the north side were slightly larger in diameter than the other three walls. The dating evidence for this structure depends on a Neolithic plainware bowl recovered from F1006. The postholes were relatively substantial, ranging in depth from 0.07m (F1069) to 0.38m (F1006). Most possessed steep or vertical sides and bases ranging from flat to pointed.

The position of the plainware bowl in F1006 and possible traces of post removal in F1055 and F1059 suggest that some if not all of the posts were intentionally removed rather than being left to rot *in situ*. The lack of iron-pan, which would have formed by water fluctuating between the gravel and the post, supports the idea that the posts were removed (Charles French personal communication).

Two outlying postholes adjacent to the north side were perhaps related to the original structure, possibly forming a porch or annexe (Fig 3.13, F1073 and F1060). On a slightly differing alignment immediately to the north of the structure was a further series of pits or more substantial postholes (F1040–49). These were larger in both diameter and depth and dated by finds later than the original structure: F1042 contained fragments of a Mortlake vessel; F1043 contained sherds of Fengate Ware.

The stylistic range of pottery from the structure and adjacent pits presents a chronological problem (see Pollard 1998a). The plain bowl from F1006 is evidently Early Neolithic. Claims that such pottery continued in use into the third or even second millennium BC (eg Green 1976) result from a lack of awareness of the problems of residuality. The fresh condition of this vessel demonstrates that it must have been deposited immediately following breakage. Dates for

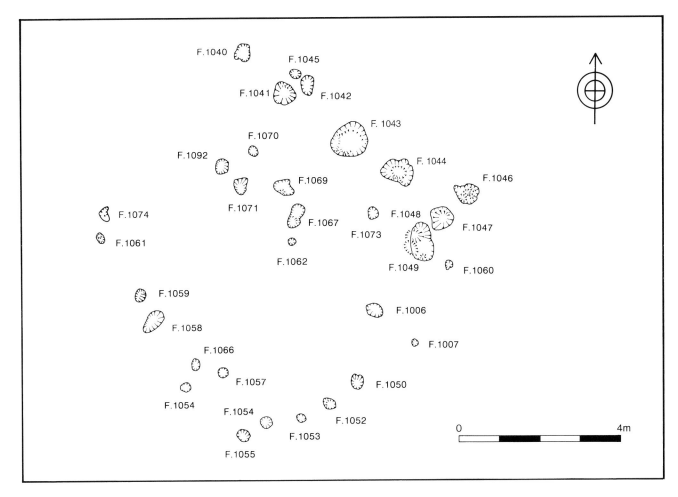

Fig 3.13 Cat's Water excavations (1997): plan of features comprising Structure 1, Trench 6 (after Gibson 1998)

Peterborough Ware (of which the bowl from F1042 is a good example) span a wide range (Gibson and Kinnes 1997), although the main period of use probably lay at the transition from the fourth to the third millennium BC. Given the typological succession from Ebbsfleet to Mortlake to Fengate, the sherds from F1043 would be later still, although current dating evidence suggests a degree of overlap with Mortlake Ware (Gibson and Kinnes 1997, 67). To summarise, the ceramics from this apparently discrete group of features might span several centuries.

Discussion

The pits and postholes within Trench 6 undoubtedly formed part of a built structure. Little evidence for domestic settlement was found in the immediate vicinity, which might otherwise have been expected, given the excellent conditions for preservation. The nature of much domestic Neolithic settlement in lowland Britain is becoming increasingly clear. Thomas has suggested (1991, 15) that settlement features might have consisted of informal patterns of pits, scoops, and postholes, rather than more formally arranged patterns involving clearly defined and spatially discrete houses. The Storey's Bar Road Grooved Ware settlement (Pryor 1974; Evans and Pollard, above, Chapter 2) and the

scatter of Neolithic features at the Boongate Roundabout (Chapter 2) are good examples of such occupation sites.

While the structure is probably best explained in terms of a tradition of mortuary or ritual architecture, a seemingly domestic parallel has recently been excavated from a Grooved Ware settlement at Over, Cambs (Pollard 1998b). The selection of particular vessels — in the present case the plainware bowl in the primary phase and the Peterborough Ware sherds in the adjacent pits or postholes — is reminiscent of the selection of the atypical assemblage found at the Padholme Road structure and has been reinterpreted as a mortuary structure (Pryor 1991, 51). It is also aligned north-east–south-west, on the same orientation as the Padholme Road mortuary structure and the rectangular enclosure of Site 11.

The absence of animal bone might not reflect conditions of preservation alone, as the preservation of Neolithic bone was perfectly adequate (if not good), at the nearby Cat's Water subsite (Pryor 1984a, 19). The carbonised plant remains from the structure produced but one possible grain of free threshing wheat. The lack of evidence for cereals in a domestic context, however, might also be due to the site's low-lying and wet location (Pryor 1988, 68).

Four small Neolithic pits were found in Trench 5. One produced Grooved Ware, the style of pottery most commonly associated with henge monuments

(Wainwright and Longworth 1971, 235–306). Since artefactual evidence for dating was not found in features associated with the henge excavated in 1990, the recovery of Grooved Ware from pits so close to the monument in 1997 must be considered significant.

Third Drove excavations: Site Q

The Birmingham University Field Archaeology Unit excavated seven trenches at Site Q, north-east of Third Drove, during their 1998 evaluation programme (Fig 2.10, trenches 6–12; Cuttler 1998). These trenches revealed an undulating fen edge, with a significant 'inlet' close to the Neolithic mortuary structure described in the previous section.

Principal results

Trench 6 revealed a succession of peaty and alluvial deposits similar to those of Trench 5, south-east of Third Drove, but there were no features of archaeological interest. The remaining trenches (7–9) revealed evidence for a buried 'inlet', whose significance will be considered in the discussion below.

Preservation across Site Q was generally poorer than in the field south-east of Third Drove; there was less alluvial cover and the buried soil showed evidence of truncation. Trenches 11 and 12 produced no evidence that the Grooved Ware settlement of Storey's Bar Road extended into the Cat's Water subsite. Bronze Age ditches were, however, found in Trenches 11 and 12. Trench 12 passed through the southerly extension to the ROM/DoE Cat's Water open-area excavation (Area XI) and revealed the unexcavated Bronze Age ditch (F862) within it (Pryor 1984a, 21). The junction of Trenches 11 and 12 revealed a large ditch of probable Bronze Age date, which ran at right angles to the ROM/DoE F862, best interpreted as an easterly extension of either ditch 1 or ditch 2 of the ROM/DoE system (Fig 1.4).

Discussion

Earlier Neolithic

An important linear distribution of earlier Neolithic sites would appear to terminate immediately south of the Cat's Water subsite, at the 1997 mortuary structure. Other elements included a second mortuary structure, a multiple burial and a ditched mortuary enclosure (Pryor 1993, fig 100). It is difficult to name a comparable group of earlier Neolithic sites elsewhere in England. It would now seem probable that these sites were oriented on the 'inlet' discussed above.

Bronze Age

Trenches 11 and 12 provided evidence that ditches 1 and 2 of the Fengate system might also be aligned on the 'inlet' north of the Fenlake Business Centre. It is

possible that waterlogged material directly relating to the droveway will be found in low-lying deposits there. These trenches also satisfactorily proved that the Cat's Water Iron Age settlement did not extend far beyond the original open-area excavations (Pryor 1984a).

The nature of the fen edge

Prior to the Power Station excavations of 1989, the edge of what French (1992b) has described as 'the area of encroaching fen', had not been closely examined. At the Power Station site the gradient of the fen edge was very gradual indeed, falling only 1m in about 100m. The area cleared was too small to be able to characterise the nature of the fen margin with any precision, but it seemed to be gently sloping and even — quite distinct from the Northey side of the Flag Fen Basin, which was steeper and more irregular, with clearly defined 'bays' or 'inlets'. A relict, Pleistocene, stream channel skirted the edge of the terrace gravel at the Power Station, where there was evidence to suggest that this stream still flowed in Bronze Age times, perhaps during the wetter months of winter.

The trenches south-east of the Parish Drain have clearly defined the nature of the underlying Neolithic and Bronze Age fen edge. They show it to be very much more irregular than the Power Station excavations had suggested. In places, the slope of the gravel subsoil was quite steep, especially in Trench 9 and towards the southern end of Trench 10. The edge of the gravel subsoil was shelving somewhat more steeply at the north end of this area, close to the Cat's Water 1997 excavations.

Perhaps the most striking feature of the buried land surface was the 'inlet' roughly defined by the 2m contour (Fig 2.10). This 'inlet' might have been produced by a stream that was actively flowing in later prehistory, but this seems unlikely. Instead it might be supposed that it was eroded by a succession of Pleistocene or early Flandrian watercourses, of which the peaty palaeochannels found in Trench 8 are examples.

The undulating and varied fen edge in this area would have provided an environment of great potential in the Neolithic period, with excellent opportunities for fishing and wildfowling. In Holland a similar undulating environment in the Rhine/Meuse estuary was shown to be very rich in evidence for Neolithic and earliest Bronze Age settlement (Louwe-Kooijmans 1974). It is, therefore, of considerable interest that the earlier Neolithic mortuary structure (Gibson 1998) was found at the very edge of this embayment.

The area east of the Parish Drain and south of Third Drove contrasts with that to the north. The edge slopes more steeply, but it is also well defined and more regular. Trench 5 indicated that there were no buried 'islands' in this area. A clearly defined edge to the wetland was important to the arable and livestock farmers of the Bronze and Iron Ages. They further formalised the boundary with a substantial linear ditch (Fig 2.6, ditch 17).

In sum, it is becoming evident that the diverse and varied nature of the fen edge at Fengate might have been an attraction in its own right. Recent research has also indicated that the varying character of the fen edge through space and time might have been in part responsible for the different types of archaeological site encountered. There is, of course, the danger of being environmentally deterministic. What is suggested is that ancient communities were attracted to the area by different landforms, but also by other, purely cultural factors, too. The landforms did not of themselves determine who settled in the area, or when, but microtopography would appear to have played a major part in the various decision-making processes of prehistoric settlers in the area.

4 The Power Station excavations, 1989

The site in its setting

Peterborough Power Station is located on the northern part of the ROM/DoE Fourth Drove subsite (Pryor 1980, fig 3) and on land to the north and east of it (Fig 1.6). Some of the lowest-lying land in Fengate, the surface of the gravel terrace subsoil is at approximately 1.75m OD at the west-north-west end of the main area excavation and below 1.2m OD towards the east-south-east end, where it dips below superficial deposits of peaty alluvium (Fig 4.1, Area I). Throughout the ROM/DoE project these fields were kept for hay and grazing. Until recent times they were regularly flooded in winter. The land has never been deep ploughed and most of the three or four land drains encountered during archaeological earthmoving operations were completely blocked. They were of two-inch (50mm) internal diameter and probably laid by hand in the 1920s (the late George Tebbs of Flag Fen Farm personal communication). Drainage was improved by the enlargement of the Mustdyke in 1973 and the construction of a small balancing pond or reservoir immediately to the north-east of the power station. The Mustdyke was again enlarged and deepened in 1982 (when the timbers of the post alignment were first revealed). Today the power station sits on ground raised up with crushed limestone. In 1990, all the silts and peaty soils that once covered the fields beneath the power station were removed in bulk to landfill sites — and with them any archaeological residues.

The circumstances of the excavation

Although the power station was constructed prior to the publication of PPG16 (DoE 1990), the developers took a very responsible attitude to their archaeological obligations by commissioning an environmental impact assessment from the consulting engineers Ove Arup Ltd. This document drew attention to the area's archaeological importance and cited the four Fengate reports as supporting evidence. A map was prepared that collated most of the known archaeological information. These data were obtained from published sources and from consultation with the county archaeologist in Cambridge. The power station project had reached an advanced stage by the time the author's attention was drawn to it by Peterborough City Council's Planning Department. Archaeological comments on the proposal were requested, particularly the County Archaeologist's assertion that the threatened area's archaeological needs would be satisfied by a watching brief. The author contested this assessment of the area's potential and as a result, one member of the developing consortium (Hawker Siddeley Power Engineering Ltd) generously agreed to fund an exploratory excavation. After the discovery of the post alignment and its associated metalwork, English Heritage provided a substantial grant to fund a major rescue campaign.

The initial discussions took place in January 1989 and excavations began as soon as the danger of air frosts was past. The first trenches (Areas 3 and 4) were excavated by the author, but it soon became apparent that members of Fenland Archaeological Trust were already heavily committed to post-excavation research and to excavation at Flag Fen and elsewhere.

Subsequently, small teams from the County Council Archaeological Unit and Lincoln City Unit were contracted to undertake the initial work, under the site direction of Tim Malim. At the end of August, upon the completion of Mr Malim's contract, site direction was again taken up by the author and the Flag Fen team. The contracted teams excavated the droveway ditches and the trenches within Area 1. The Flag Fen team mapped the post alignment, supervised the metal-detecting, and carried out the main lifting and recording of the post alignment.

Areas excavated and site grids

The land chosen for the power station was known to be archaeologically important, because at least three ditches of the ROM/DoE Bronze Age system ran towards it from the Fourth Drove subsite immediately to the north-west (Pryor 1980, fig 78). Posts of likely Bronze Age date were also found immediately to the south-east, next to the Cat's Water, during the laying of a water main in 1987 (Fig 1.5, inset — area 1).

Areas 3 and 4 were excavated, in the late winter of 1989, under the author's direction. Mr Malim's team worked on Area 2 and the original, central portion of Area 1 (Fig 4.1). The Flag Fen team organised the enlargement of Area 1.

Area 4 was positioned diagonally to the orientation of the Bronze Age field system in the hope that it would pick up ditches running both east–west and north–south. In the event it found neither. Area 3 was orientated similarly and for the same reasons, but after removal of topsoil, it quickly became apparent that the subsoil of terrace gravel was too low-lying to detect field boundary ditches. The only archaeological feature of any note was the gravel makeup and surface of the Fen Causeway Roman road (Fig 4.2).

Area 2 was positioned to locate and to provide a transect across the post alignment, which at the time was believed to be a simple causeway leading to the Flag Fen platform. The central part of Area 2 was excavated to follow the posts to their landfall. The area was subsequently enlarged, both as a result of the

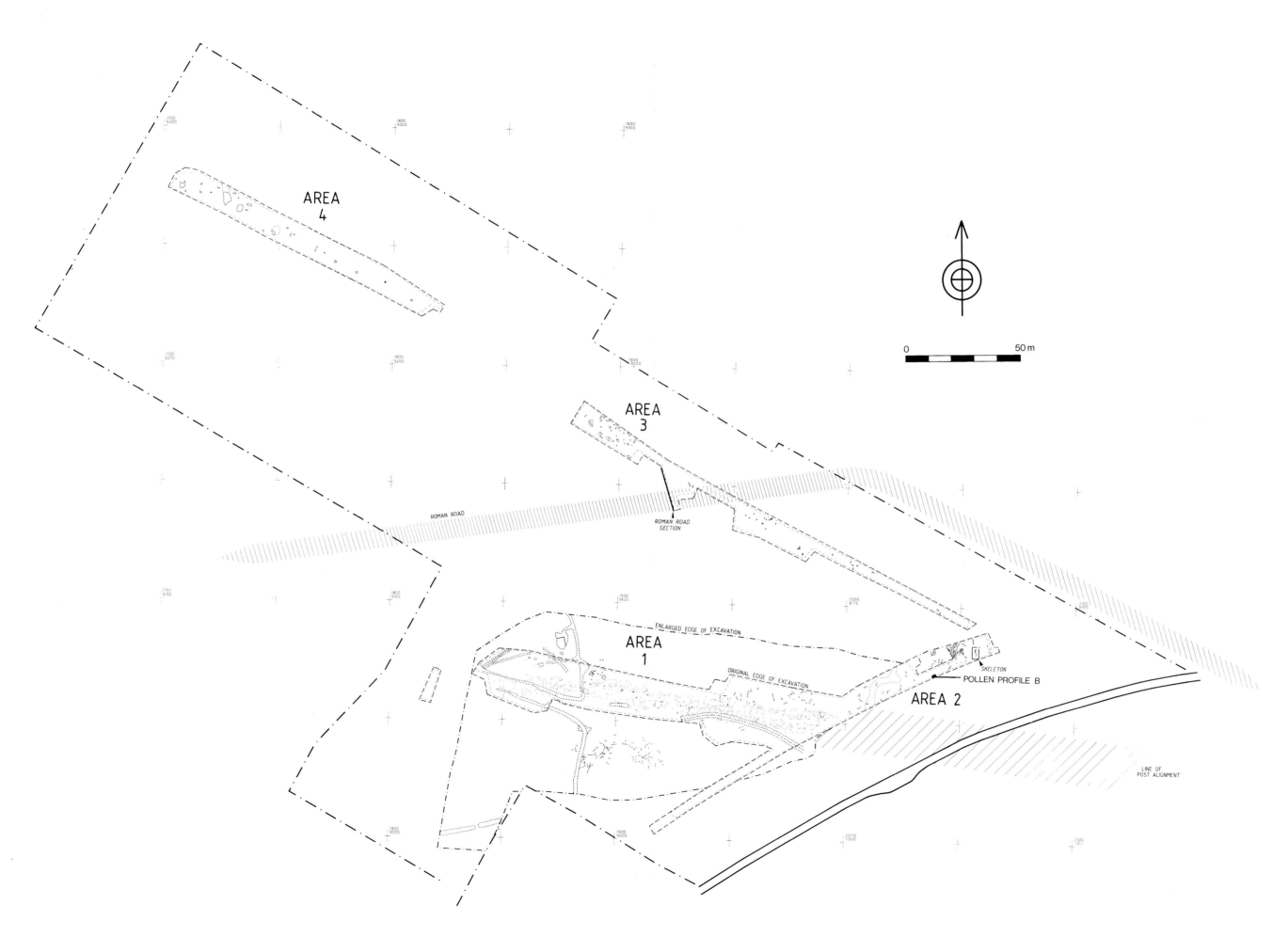

AREA
4

AREA
3

ROMAN ROAD

ROMAN ROAD
SECTION

0   50 m

ENLARGED EDGE OF EXCAVATION

AREA
1

ORIGINAL EDGE OF EXCAVATION

SKELETON

POLLEN PROFILE B

AREA 2

LINE OF
POST ALIGNMENT

Fig 4.1 Power Station excavations (1989): general plan. Note that the original outline of Area 1 is shown within its enlargement

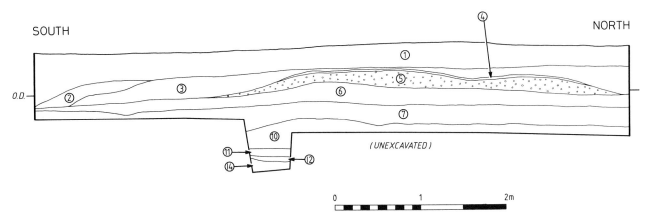

SOUTH

NORTH

O.D.

(UNEXCAVATED)

0   1   2m

Fig 4.2 Power Station excavations (1989): section through the Fen Causeway Roman road, Area 3. For location see Fig 4.1. Key to layers: 1, topsoil/alluvium; 2, made ground (recent/modern?); 3, alluvial silts; 4, road surface; 5, road makeup; 6, later Iron Age silty peat; 7, 10, first/second millennium BC silts; 11, buried soil; 12, 14 bedded first-terrace Nene Gravels

metal-detector survey and to plot the course of the droveway formed by ditches 8 and 9 of the Bronze Age system as it approached the wetland edge.

Within Area 1, which was very large, a series of hand-cut trenches (A–H) was opened to examine the old land surface in and around the posts of the alignment (for locations see plans in Figs 4.3–4.5). Not all the trenches produced significant results, and only the more significant trench plans will be discussed.

To avoid damaging the posts, it was decided not to machine down to the level of the old land surface in their vicinity. Sapwood and bark was poorly preserved on the Power Station site, but where it was present it was often to be found directly above the posts' long pencil-like sharpened points. These points penetrated deep into the terrace gravel subsoil, but the sharpening marks made by axes were often still just visible within and above the buried soil that lay directly on the gravel (Fig 4.2). The sharpening had itself removed bark and sapwood and so it was decided to leave a covering of some 200–300mm of silt above the buried soil in order to protect the posts and to retain moisture. Given the extreme heat and dryness of the summer, this proved to be a wise precaution.

Soil micromorphology
by C A I French

The deposits of archaeological interest at the Power Station lay beneath 1–1.5m of water-derived material, principally consisting of silty alluvium and humified peats (Fig 1.7).

These upper layers were mainly laid down in the first millennium BC and later. The underlying subsoil consists of Pleistocene terrace gravels upon which there is a buried palaeosol. The archaeological material occurred in or on the palaeosol, but features such as pits or ditches were cut through it to penetrate the terrace gravels below (Fig 4.2). Six soil profiles were examined from the excavation:

1   The 'reddened area' in the uppermost alluvium, Trench II;

2   The sand bank on the western side of the post alignment, Trench I;

3   The sand bank on the eastern side of the post alignment, Trench I;

4   The basal peat and buried soil, sample column 3, Trench II;

5   The basal peat and buried soil, sample column 2, Trench I;

6   The buried soil, sample column 1, Trench I.

The results will be discussed in three groups: the buried soil; the two sand banks; and the 'reddened area'.

The thin sections were prepared and described according to Murphy (1986) and Bullock *et al* (1985). The results and interpretations are described below and the individual descriptions are given in Appendix 2.

Results and interpretation

The buried soil

Sample profiles 4 and 5 were similar and will, therefore, be described together. Two main fabrics were evident. The upper two-thirds of the surviving soil (fabric 1) is a calcitic sand/silt, with dense, amorphous calcite comprising up to 60% of the fabric. This fabric also contained considerable amounts of organic matter including fragments of wood, plant tissue, and peat. The mixture of soil, amorphous calcite, and organic matter suggests that this is the upper surface of an *in situ* soil. The deposition and accumulation of amorphous calcite is probably the result of base-rich freshwater flooding on a seasonal basis, the calcium precipitating as calcite crystals when the floodwaters receded. The high organic matter content might result from a combination of *in situ* accumulation and minor peat growth, as well as the incorporation of organic material carried in floodwaters.

The underlying soil fabric 2 is a sandy loam that is slightly more porous than fabric 1. It also contains a considerable amount of organic matter in the form of

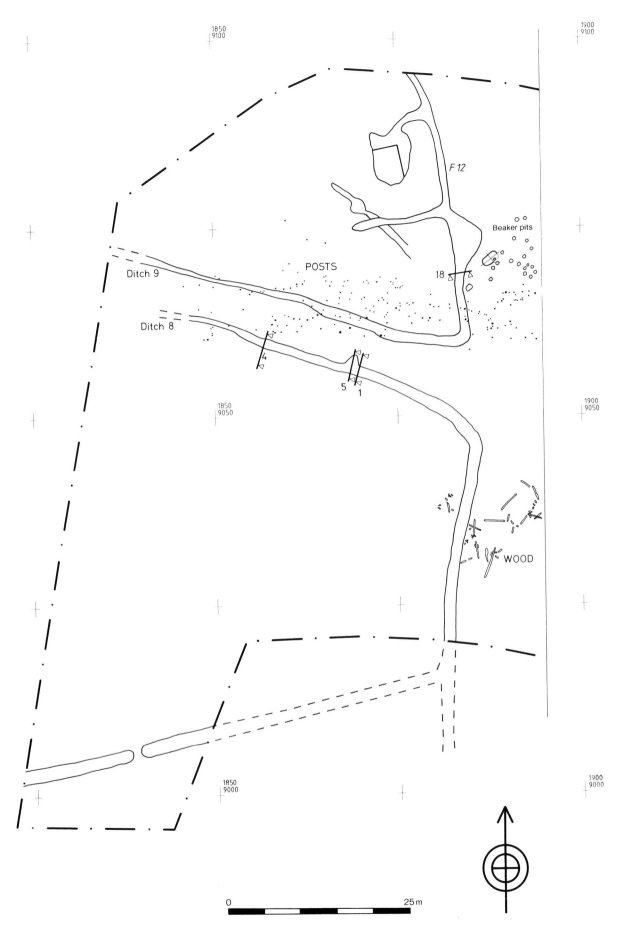

Fig 4.3 Power Station excavations (1989): western portion of Area 1 showing second-millennium ditches, post alignment, outlying scatter of wood, and Beaker period pits

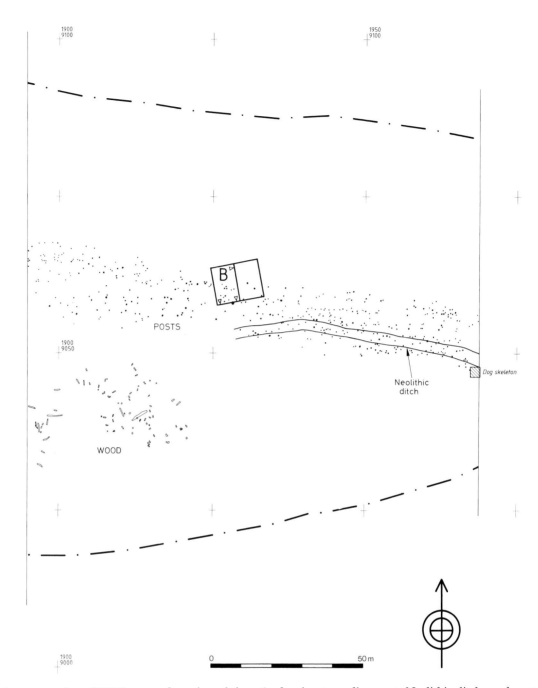

Fig 4.4 Power Station excavations (1989): central portion of Area 1, showing post alignment, Neolithic ditch, and scatter of wood. The dog skeleton is shown in detail in Figure 4.20

frequent plant tissue fragments. These characteristics are suggestive of an Ah or turf horizon. Consequently, fabric 1 probably represents the first aggradation of freshwater-borne sediments on the existing surface of the turf. This probably occurred in a water-meadow type of environment. There is also abundant non-laminated dusty clay in the groundmass, which is probably indicative of the intercalation of silty clay. This material is probably derived from fine sediments (or alluvium) carried in floodwaters that settled out of suspension in a still-water environment and became incorporated in the upper horizon of the underlying soil. The small quantities of limpid clay and laminated dusty clay present might also have derived from eroded

soil material carried in floodwater, which then became incorporated in the turf horizon through faunal soil mixing.

There are several more minor indications of the role of flooding of this soil. First, much of the plant root/stem material has been replaced by sesquioxides and/or ferruginised, which are indicative of much alternate wetting and drying. Second, a few crystals of lenticular gypsum occur in the void space. This is precipitated as a result of the over-saturation of the soil solution.

The buried soil in sample column 6 did not exhibit the calcitic fabric 1 of sample columns 4 and 5 (above), but displayed two distinct fabrics in two separate horizons.

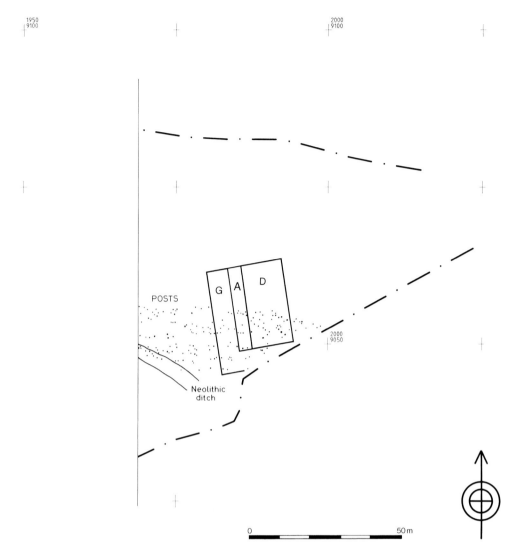

Fig 4.5 Power Station excavations (1989): eastern portion of Area 1, showing location of post alignment (passing out of excavation north-east of Neolithic ditch)

The upper fabric 1 or upper horizon is a very organic sandy loam to loam. It contained frequent fragments of peat, plant tissue, and wood, as well as much intercalated silty clay. The latter suggests the incorporation and addition of alluvium associated with freshwater flooding. Small quantities of limpid clay and sub-rounded aggregates of an organic silt fabric were also incorporated in this soil horizon, and are suggestive of soil erosion and redeposition by water action. This horizon probably represents the upper A or turf horizon.

The lower fabric (2) or lower horizon is predominantly composed of medium and fine quartz sand. This clean sand contains very little organic matter and exhibits almost no other characteristics. It therefore probably represents the transition zone to the subsoil or B/C horizon.

Thus, sample profiles 4, 5, and 6 exhibit general similarities and suggest the same sequence of development. A poorly developed brown earth survives as a thin (<100mm thick) turf horizon. It rests on a sandy subsoil, and is overlain by a thin (<70mm) alluvially derived horizon dominated by amorphous calcite and

organic matter. This sequence occurred in a water-meadow environment, in a fen-edge/terrace zone that was already cleared and established as grassland.

The sand banks

Two linear bands of white sand *c* <100mm thick and <1.5m in width were visible immediately to either side of the post alignment or causeway. In thin section, both of these sand banks (sample profiles 2 and 3) were composed predominantly of porous, poorly sorted, medium sand, and contained frequent plant tissue and wood fragments. Other very minor components include aggregates of eroded soils, rare fragments of illuvial clay and silty clay, small zones and infills of amorphous phosphatic-iron compounds, angular fragments of shell, and a zone of calcite crystals. The predominance of one size fraction, medium sand, and its poorly sorted nature suggests that this is eroded and redeposited material derived from elsewhere by water action. Given that the subsoil in the immediate vicinity is a sandy gravel river terrace, the position of these sand banks is at right angles to the natural contour and to an underlying relict stream. The sand banks apparently formed to either side of a vertical obstacle and might represent the accumulation of bed scour of a seasonal stream that followed the natural contour of the fen edge. Independent sedimentological analysis of these same sand banks by Passmore and Macklin has suggested a similar origin for these deposits (*see* Discussion of the soil micromorphology, below).

The 'reddened area' in the upper alluvium

Although the sediment sampled was apparently atypical, therefore noteworthy, and demanded explanation, its analysis has served to describe the various constituents of the upper alluvial horizon at Fengate.

There are three poorly sorted and much intermixed fabrics present in the upper alluvium. Fabric 1 predominates (85% of groundmass) and is composed of a relatively dense silty clay with up to 50% of the fabric impregnated with amorphous sesquioxides. The clay fraction is composed entirely of non-laminated limpid clay. This is essentially an alluvial fabric.

Fabric 2 (*c* 10%) is a silt loam with a relatively high clay content that occurs as large aggregates within fabric 1. As this soil material is more typical of the lower B horizon of a brown forest soil, the aggregates of this soil must have eroded from elsewhere and were deposited along with the alluvial fines (fabric 1). Fabric 3 (*c* 5%) is an organic silt loam with a high clay content. It too, probably derives from a brown forest soil, although probably from the A horizon.

Fabrics 2 and 3 are undoubtedly fragments of soil eroded from elsewhere. Their clay content exhibits many to abundant non-laminated limpid clay coatings, which are indicative of stable woodland cover (Bullock and Murphy 1979), and many to abundant non-laminated dusty clay coatings, which indicate soil disturbance (Courty and Fedoroff 1982). Thus, these soil pedofeatures represent a soil that had first developed under forested conditions and was then subject to tree clearance, probably associated with human activity. These eroded soils might have derived from the immediate vicinity on the higher part of the adjacent terrace, and/or further upstream in the lower Nene valley, and have been transported downstream in seasonal floodwaters and deposited along with the alluvium (eg fabric 1).

The dense, relatively non-organic nature of fabric 1 suggests that this silty clay alluvium accumulated in quiet water conditions with little vegetation growth. The reddening of about 50% of the matrix is the result of amorphous sesquioxide impregnation due to alternate wetting and drying conditions. The matrix has also been later fire-reddened, possibly by an overlying peat fire.

Discussion of the soil micromorphology

The micromorphological analysis of the buried soils and selected sediments and the sedimentological analysis (Passmore and Macklin in preparation) exhibit a remarkable degree of similar and complementary results. The results of these analyses are summarised in Table 4.1. The micromorphological analysis of the

Table 4.1 Summary of soil, sediment, and palynological results

stratigraphy (top)	description/events	date
peat (Unit 4)	desiccated, deflated detrital peat, now largely absent as a result of drainage since seventeenth century AD	medieval
alluvium (Unit 3)	silty clay, seasonally flooded ?water meadow environment; contains eroded soils from inland	Roman/post-Roman
peaty sandy silt (Unit 2)	widespread peat growth with wet fen carr environment; influx of more weathered sediments suggests intermittent alluvial influence	Iron Age
peaty sandy silt with thin peat lenses (Unit 1.3)	slightly coarser, less organic and higher minerogenic content than below, inwash of coarser alluvial sediments, interrupted by periods of local environmental stability	Iron Age (Late) Bronze Age
silty peat (Unit 1.2)	peat growth and shallow water	Late Bronze Age
linear sand banks (Unit 1.2)	coarse minerogenic sands, mainly medium quartz; deposition by water against post alignment as a result of locally migrating river channel	900–800 BC
coarse minerogenic sands (Unit 1.1)	alluvial origin in base-rich water meadow	pre-900 BC
buried soil (Unit 1.0) (base)	sandy loam to loam with well established turf; subject to deposition of fine alluvial sediments and eroded soil material	pre-900 BC

pre-fen buried soil at three locations has suggested the presence of an established turf. It was subject to the addition of alluvially derived and borne fine sediments, presumably deposited as a result of seasonal flooding with fresh water. Indeed, the upper part of the buried soil is composed of a sand/silt. These coarse minerogenic sands are believed to be alluvial in origin (Unit 1.1). These sands were probably accumulating prior to 900–800 BC when the Power Station post alignment was constructed on this part of the fen edge.

The sand that accumulated to either side of the post alignment lies directly on the upper surface of the coarse sands (Unit 1.1). It is overlain by fine-grained peaty sediments or a silty peat (Unit 1.2). These sands might represent either a marshy, low-energy depositional environment, which is possibly related to base level rises in the fen to the east and/or a facies change associated with a locally migrating river channel.

There are four arguments in support of the latter possibility. First, the sand 'banks' are linear and have accumulated against both long sides of the post alignment just as would occur in a coastline situation. Second, the sand itself is dominated by one size fraction only, medium-sized quartz sand, which is strongly suggestive of sorting and deposition as a result of water action (Morgan 1979). Third, the geological borehole survey of the site has revealed the presence of a substantial pre-Flandrian relict river channel following the line of the present contour (A Collings of Ove Arup personal communication). This relict channel exactly underlies the postulated later Bronze Age channel. Fourth, the siting of the timber causeway at a right angle to the fen-edge contour and postulated stream/river channel, plus the deposition of significant metalwork to either side of the post alignment just off the dryland edge, also tend to back up this theory of the presence of a former water course following the natural contour from south-west to north-east along this part of the fen edge.

The alluvial and sand phases are overlain by slightly coarser, less organic sediments with a higher minerogenic content, or a peaty sandy silt (Unit 1.3). It is suggested that these represent an inwash of coarser sediments, punctuated by periods of local environmental stability, essentially alternate alluvial phases and peat growth phases, respectively. Throughout the later first millennium BC, these sediments aggraded and were finally overwhelmed by peat growth, which forms unit 2. It is this main period of peat growth that was responsible for burying the Flag Fen platform and the Fengate post alignment.

Unit 3 or silty clays dominated the upper one-third of the profile. These alluvial sediments contain soil material derived from eroded topsoils. This supposition is confirmed by the micromorphological analysis, which revealed the presence of silty clay alluvium, ie lower B and A horizon material derived from the erosion of argillic or brown forest earth soils from

upstream/upland areas to the west. The inclusion of these various sediments indicates much deforestation and/or cultivation of well developed soils further inland during the post-Roman period, as documented elsewhere in lowland river valleys in England (eg Jones 1981; Lambrick and Robinson 1979).

General conclusions

1   The pre-fen soil in the shallow basin of what was to become peat fen in the later Bronze Age was a poorly developed and shallow brown earth with established turf.

2   Within the later Bronze Age, this soil became subject to seasonal flooding with base-rich fresh water. This was responsible for the aggradation of silt and clay fines, amorphous calcite and organic debris. It is envisaged that this took place in a water-meadow environment. As a corollary, this area would have been available for grazing as seasonal pasture, particularly in the late spring, summer and early autumn months.

3   At about the same period a post alignment was constructed at a right angle to the contour and fen edge, which ran from the dryland terrace of Fengate across the fen basin to the Flag Fen wooden platform. It is suggested that this post alignment crossed a small stream course that followed an earlier relict river course along the natural contour at the dryland edge. Two linear sand banks built up as natural bars against the barrier created by the post alignment.

4   As the base levels rose in the fen to the east, peat growth began to encroach on this part of the fen/terrace edge. This probably occurred very late in the Bronze Age and early in the Iron Age.

5   The post-Roman alluvium was dominated by derived and redeposited fine sediment associated with freshwater flooding. Fragments of dryland soils eroded from elsewhere are also incorporated in this alluvium. The erosion from which the alluvial material is derived is undoubtedly associated with the deforestation and/or cultivation by man of 'heavier' (ie more clayey) land upstream and upslope to the west.

The excavations

The Power Station site was characterised by accumulations of alluvial material that had slowly built up, burying archaeological deposits *in situ*. In practical terms, this meant that more recent contexts had to be entirely removed before the earlier levels below could be examined. To reflect this, and to explain why certain deposits were truncated by the removal of others above them, the excavations will be described in reverse chronological order, starting with the most recent.

The Fen Causeway Roman road

The Fen Causeway traversed the north-east part of the Power Station subsite and was visible on the surface as a gravel spread and a low agger (Fig 4.1). It is known that the field had been regularly ploughed in the present century, but it had never been deep ploughed (ie subsoiled using a ripper tine). This shallow ploughing had undoubtedly caused damage to the road surface and might help to account for the undulations in section (Fig 4.2). The thin, cemented layer (Fig 4.2, layer 4) that appeared to cap the road and form a hard load-bearing surface is probably best interpreted as a post-depositional phenomenon. This 'false surface' was probably brought about by fluctuating groundwater leading to the precipitation of iron salts, manganese, and so on.

The Fen Causeway was constructed of dumped gravel placed directly on the peat, without a layer of brushwood to spread the load (Kenny 1933; Phillips 1970, map sheet K; Silvester 1991, 95–115). As at the Newark Road subsite, some 400m east-south-east, the road was built of dumped aggregates (Pryor 1980, fig 86).

Iron Age

The low-lying Power Station subsite would have become increasingly wet during the Iron Age and this undoubtedly accounts for the dearth of archaeological features encountered. A gravel platform probably dates to this period, which is otherwise notable for the discovery of a single human skeleton and a scatter of domestic debris (probably from the Cat's Water settlement some 200m to the east-south-east). Some significant Iron Age metalwork finds were, however, revealed in the metal-detector survey, which is discussed below and in Chapter 10.

The gravel platform

The gravel platform was a difficult feature to understand in the field, as it was composed of seemingly natural (ie clean) terrace gravel, which capped the tertiary filling of the Bronze Age ditch 4 beneath. The posts of the alignment at first appeared to have been driven through the layer of gravel, which would have been almost impossible stratigraphically. It was not until several weeks into the excavation that, in one or two places, gravel was found to overlie and seal the tops of those posts that had rotted off at a lower level in antiquity.

The vertical occurrence of the Iron Age sand and gravel is shown in Fig 1.7 and its horizontal spread is mapped in Fig 4.3. It was observed in section to form the highest, capping layer, of ditch 8 (Figs 4.6–4.8, layer 9). It should be noted, however, that the top of the gravel layer shown in these sections had been truncated by earthmoving operations, when layer 9 was believed to be a natural deposit. Some 10–20mm of gravel might have been removed in this way.

The dating of the sand and gravel spread depends upon a number of factors. First, stratigraphy shows that the Bronze Age droveway ditch 3 had been almost completely filled to the top when the gravel was deposited, probably by natural agencies. Posts of the alignment were driven into the same infilled ditch from the end of the Middle Bronze Age. Second, the spread of gravel capped these posts where they had rotted off, at a low level. This would suggest that they still protruded just above the ground surface as low stumps. It can be demonstrated, again stratigraphically, that the gravel spread pre-dates the Roman Fen Causeway, as it was sealed by layer 6 (later Iron Age silty peat), which in turn lay directly below the Roman road (Figs 1.7 and 4.2).

The most likely use for a dumped deposit of gravel on the very edge of the regularly flooded land would be as a hardstanding, pier, or platform. A solid, well drained platform at the post alignment's landfall would certainly have been required in the Iron Age, by which time water levels were continuing to rise. The many contemporary metalwork finds from the Power Station site and from Flag Fen proper, some 600m to the east, demonstrate that the location of the post alignment was still a site of regular ritual activity into the second century BC and possibly later.

The human skeleton

A badly decayed human skeleton was found in the silts of Area 2, some 40m north of the post alignment (for location see Fig 4.1). The skeleton was found during earthmoving operations and took the form of a white calcareous stain in the darker silts. It was only clearly visible when freshly exposed, but there was no doubt as to what it was — the skull was particularly indicative. The body was orientated north-east–south-west, head to the north. It was difficult to be certain, but the body was either fully extended or slightly flexed with arms probably at the sides. The head faced north-north-west, but it was not possible to decide whether the body rested on its back or front. From its size, the body was that of a youth or adult. The skeletal stains were located some 200mm above the base of the silts, in contexts that were significantly higher than the level at which the main spread of ancient metalwork had been deposited or had sunk to. Its position in the silts suggested that it had found its way into (or been placed in) the water in Iron Age times.

The metal-detector survey

A thin covering of silty alluvium lay over most of Area 1, east of Bronze Age ditches 8 and 9, at the west end of the excavation. This deposit had been left in place, as we have seen, to prevent posts of the alignment from drying out, but it also served to conceal the presence of lower-lying finds and features.

The only readily available means of artefact recovery that could penetrate this thin protective covering was the metal detector. It was realised that this would produce a limited and probably biased picture of the overall distribution of finds, but at least one category of artefact could be recovered with some degree of completeness.

Members of the Soke Metal Detector Club were invited to carry out a survey and their first find was a nearly complete bronze Wilburton sword. Encouraged, the members of the club began to reveal large quantities of metalwork around the posts. Each item was excavated and recorded by a member of the excavation staff. By June it was clear that more metalwork finds must lie outside the limited area cleared to that date. Accordingly, Area 1 was greatly expanded down to the level of the lower alluvium. A very thorough metal-detector survey took place while this large-scale earthmoving operation was underway. It is therefore certain that the collection of metal finds is fairly complete, although, as was recognised at the time, a proportion had undoubtedly been removed with the overburden.

When the survey began, the area to be searched was parcelled up into some 15 areas, each of which was searched by a member of the club. After 15–20 minutes, or when satisfied that the area assigned had been satisfactorily covered, members moved to another area. At the end of the second day, each area had been searched by every member of the club and the rate of recovery, which had begun with an artefact every few minutes, had been reduced to a trickle.

After the initial survey of the original, restricted, or 'core' area of Area 1, the subsequent earthmoving campaign of its expansion phase was checked by two experienced members of the club who would carefully search the area stripped each day. This usually took two or three hours. It was essential to ensure that the newly machined land was cleared of metalwork before nightfall, as it was known that illegal metal-detector users would sometimes search the site after dark, despite the fact that the police had been informed and patrolled Fourth Drove regularly.

Bronze Age

The vast majority of features revealed in Area 1 were of Bronze Age date. The discussion will begin with a consideration of the droveway ditches and their associated features. The posts and other timbers of the post alignment will then be considered.

The droveway ditches and associated features

It has been seen that the ditched fields of the Bronze Age system were laid out at right angles to the fen (Fig 1.4) and were partitioned at regular intervals by double-ditched droveways, which ran from the higher ground to the wetland edge. The Power Station

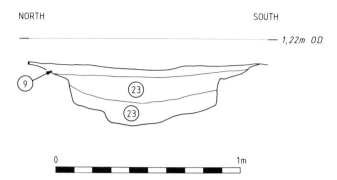

Fig 4.6 Power Station excavations (1989): ditch 8, section 1 (for location see Fig 4.3). Key to layers: 9, cemented gravels; 23, sand-silt above clay-loam

excavations have provided the only opportunity so far to examine how these droveways behaved on reaching the wetland edge.

The most extensively and intensively examined droveway of the Bronze Age system was (perhaps fortunately) the one that ran into the Power Station site. The drove formed by ditches 8 and 9 was examined closely in the ROM/DoE Newark Road and Fourth Drove excavations (Pryor 1980, 23–157). After examination of the general layout of the Bronze Age system, it was concluded that the main droves formed boundaries or subdivisions in the landscape, perhaps between individual land holdings (Pryor 1980, 171, and Pryor 1990).

The droveway formed by ditches 8 and 9 was exposed in Area 1 of the Power Station subsite for the last 50m of its length. The surface width of the droveway was about 4m. The southerly ditch 8 turned sharply south, at or very near the wetland edge, passing out of the excavation 50m further south. Another ditch, probably of the Bronze Age system, was encountered in an extension to the excavation to the south-west (Fig 4.3). This ditch ran west-south-west–east-south-east. Its possible course has been shown by a dashed line in Figure 4.3. The narrow entranceway through the ditch is undoubtedly an ancient feature, but there was insufficient time to examine it further.

Droveway ditches 8 and 9 were cut into the gravel subsoil and were on average 0.5–1m deep, with an open, somewhat irregular, stepped U profile, similar to (if shallower than) those of the Fourth Drove and Newark Road subsites (Fig 4.3). Three sections through ditch 8 are shown in Figures 4.6–4.8. Section 1 (Fig 4.6) is typical and contains two layers, a lower primary and secondary deposit and a higher, tertiary fill. In at least one place, the infilling of the ditch had been disturbed in antiquity (Fig 4.7) and the deposits intermixed. The ditch was sealed beneath the Iron Age gravel platform (layer 9), which had sunk into the top of the filling.

This would suggest that the disturbance shown in Figure 4.7 took place in the Bronze Age. Only one feature, a well-like pit (F27) could be shown to be broadly contemporary with ditch 8 on stratigraphic

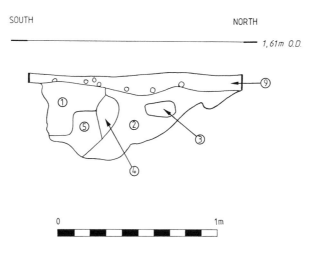

Fig 4.7 Power Station excavations (1989): ditch 8, section 4 (for location see Fig 4.3). Key to layers: 1, sandy clay; 2, mottled silty clay; 3, blue clay; 4, clay-silt with gravel; 5, dark sandy clay; 9, cemented gravels

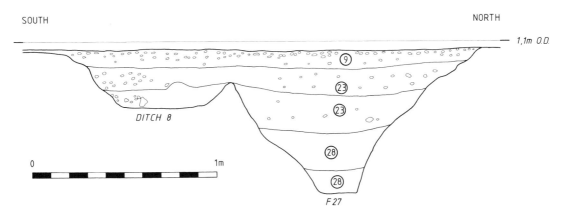

Fig 4.8 Power Station excavations (1989): ditch 8, section 5 (including pit F27; for location see Fig 4.3). Key to layers: 9, sand and gravel; 23 sand-silt above clay-loam; 28 clay-silt above clay

grounds (Fig 4.8). It was considerably deeper than the ditch and could have served as a drainage sump or waterhole. It is peculiar, however, that it was positioned in the droveway rather than in the field or paddock to the south. Its location might provide another indication that the Bronze Age droveway ditches in this low-lying part of Fengate might have fallen out of use early on.

The excavation of the northerly droveway ditch (9) presented practical difficulties as its filling was penetrated by the tips of numerous posts (Fig 4.3). It too was sealed beneath the makeup of the Iron Age platform. Initially, some narrow sections were cut through the ditch, but as it soon became apparent that these would rapidly dry out the entire deposit, it was decided, in the interests of dendrochronological sampling, not to excavate ditch 9 until the last of the posts had been lifted. In the event, the very dry season meant that this operation had to be postponed until later September, when time ran short and a machine had to be used (Pryor 1992a). It was impossible for practical

reasons to lift so many timbers without causing serious disturbance to the underlying Bronze Age ditch. As a result of these problems, no sections were obtained through ditch 9 in the Power Station excavations, although numerous sections have been cut in the Fourth Drove and Newark Road subsites nearby.

Ditch 9 turned sharply north some 50m into Area 1. With ditch 8 to the south it formed a flared, funnel-like end to the droveway (Fig 4.3). North of the post alignment, ditch 9 was known as F12, as it was not apparent that the two ditches were parts of the same feature until all the posts had been removed. Feature 12 had been dug through undulating and very wet clay gravels that had plainly been the cause of local drainage difficulties. A number of pits and ditch-like features had been excavated around the ditches. Time did not allow a thorough examination of these features, but many contained sherds of Iron Age pottery in their fillings. Some could best be described as waterholes or shallow ponds and might have owed their amorphous shapes to animal trample.

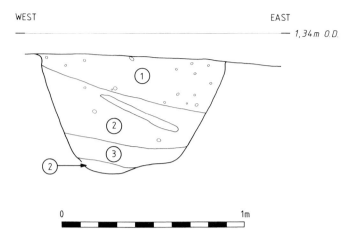

Fig 4.9 Power Station excavations (1989): ditch, F12, section 18 (for location see Fig 4.3). Key to layers: 1, dark clay-silt; 2, mixed sand-silt, gravel and wood fragments; 3, redeposited gravel with sand-silt

Ditch F12 is described by the excavators as being backfilled (Fig 4.9). The repetition of layers could hardly have been achieved any other way. Water action might also have played its part in the backfilling process.

The post alignment

The term 'post alignment' was chosen to describe a band of posts 10m in width that ran from the Power Station site, through Flag Fen to Northey 'island' to the east. The term 'alignment' has been selected because it has no functional implications. Discussion of the various functions or roles the post alignment awaits the final discussion (Chapter 19). Here it is sufficient to note that the posts began their course across Flag Fen at approximately the point where the Bronze Age droveway (formed by ditches 8 and 9) ended at the edge of the regularly flooded land.

The most westerly posts of the post alignment were found some 15m into Area 1, at site grid 1846 9068 (Fig 4.3). The posts ran down the centre of the excavation in an east-south-east direction (Fig 4.4) and continued beyond the area cleared (Fig 4.5). The width of the alignment varied slightly from 7m (west) to 10m. The total length of the alignment exposed within Area 1 was 147m.

The vast majority of the posts were of oak. They had long, pencil-like, sharpened tips and had been firmly driven through the buried soil and into the underlying terrace gravels (Fig 1.7). As a matter of record, all individually numbered timbers found during the power station excavations were assigned to the Y series of numbers. These numbers, which were assigned in the field, are used in their respective reports by Maisie Taylor and Janet Neve (Chapters 7 and 8). The post alignment in the Power Station excavations contained many fewer posts than in Flag Fen some 850m to the east-south-east. This doubtless reflects the fact that the water was shallower here and

that firm ground could be reached much closer to the surface. Even so, the number of posts revealed at the relatively high level at which the mechanical stripping stopped — some 1200 in all — is remarkable. As will be seen shortly, hand excavation revealed many additional posts. Without being too precise, the number of posts that survived in Area 1, at all levels, was closer to 2000.

The excavation had to take place within strict time constraints. Since much time had been spent in the hand-excavated trenches, it was clear by September that, despite the dry ground conditions, a start would have to be made on lifting the main mass of posts.

Before the decision was made to use a mechanical excavator, a few posts were removed by hand. The main advantage of hand excavation is that a split post's orientation could be recorded. It also goes without saying that it is more gentle. Many of the posts had been driven deep into the underlying gravel subsoil where they were often cemented into place by deposits of iron-pan and manganese. On average, two posts per day could be removed in this manner by a two-person team, but there was slightly less than a month in which to remove about 1000.

The decision to remove all the exposed posts by machine was made with some reluctance and after close consultation with the two specialists concerned, Maisie Taylor and Janet Neve.

It was agreed that the hand-excavated areas had produced enough accurate information on the orientation of the posts and that a broad dendrochronological survey of the entire length of the alignment would throw much-needed light on its construction and function. Moreover, as the Power Station posts were smaller than those at Flag Fen, Janet Neve doubted whether the hand-excavated areas alone had produced sufficient long-lived samples to allow the two sites to be correlated dendrochronologically. The alignment posts were excavated with a 4WD Kubota 1.5 tonne mini-digger, fitted with a 300mm toothed bucket.

The hand-excavated trenches

A series of six (A–H) hand-excavated trenches was opened. Each trench was excavated to the top of the underlying terrace gravel in spits of c 100mm that followed the undulations of the different layers; in other words, the spits (or levels, to use the term preferred here) were stratigraphic. Features of particular interest were observed in trenches A, B, D, and G. Information on the remainder is housed in the archive. The four selected trenches will be described from west to east along the course of the post alignment.

Trench B (Figs 4.10–4.13)

Trench B was located on the north side of the post alignment at grid E1925 (Fig 4.4). It was excavated in two halves.

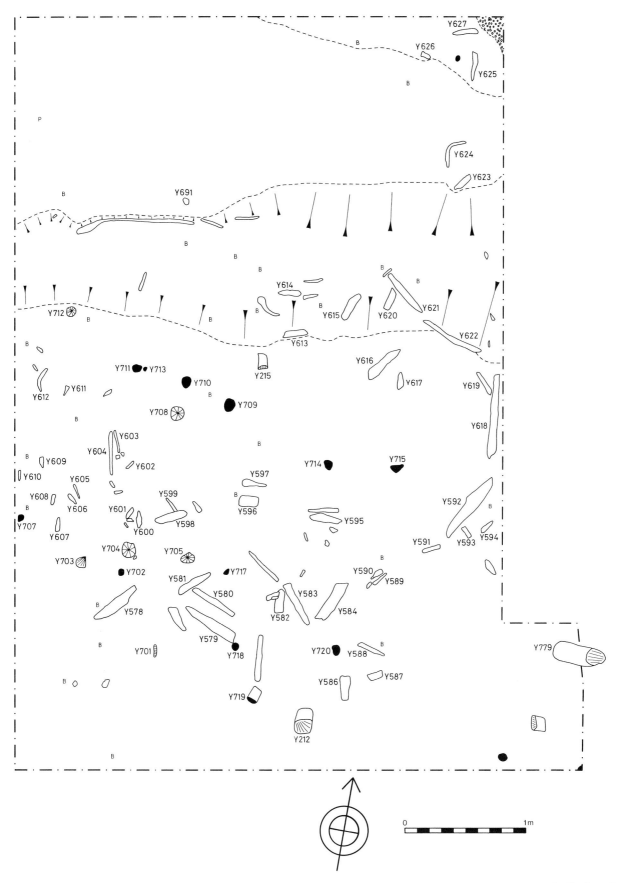

Fig 4.10 Power Station excavations (1989): Area 1, trench B. Plan of wood in level 1, west half of trench (for location see Fig 4.4)

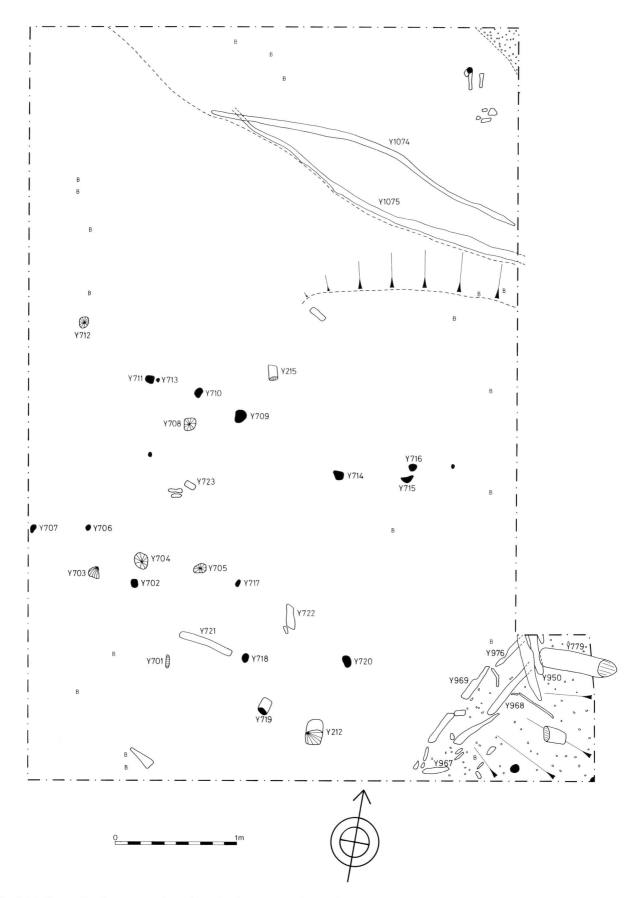

Fig 4.11 Power Station excavations (1989). Area 1, trench B. Plan of wood in level 2, west half of trench (for location see Fig 4.4). Note fragment of possible revetment wall, lower right

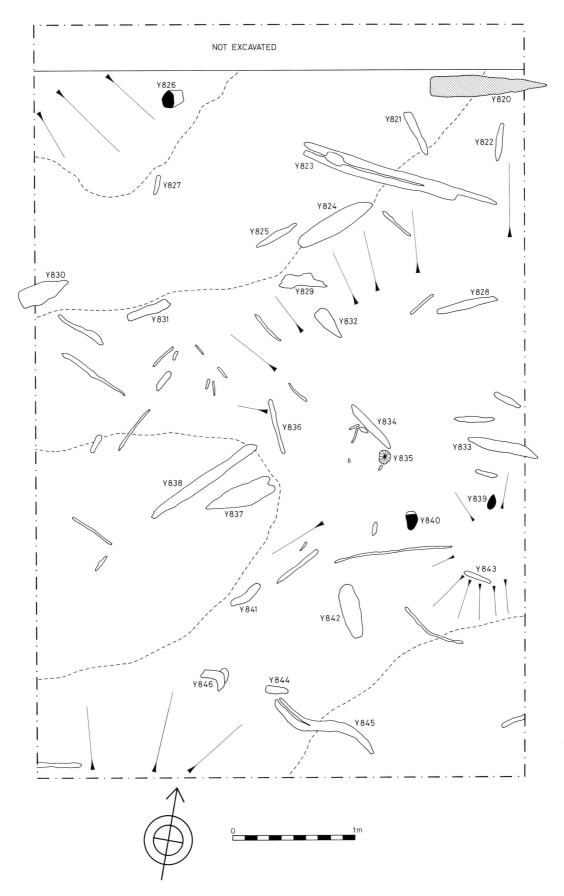

NOT EXCAVATED

Fig 4.12 Power Station excavations (1989): Area 1, trench B. Plan of wood in level 1, east half of trench (for location see Fig 4.4). The upright removed in antiquity (Y820) is hatched

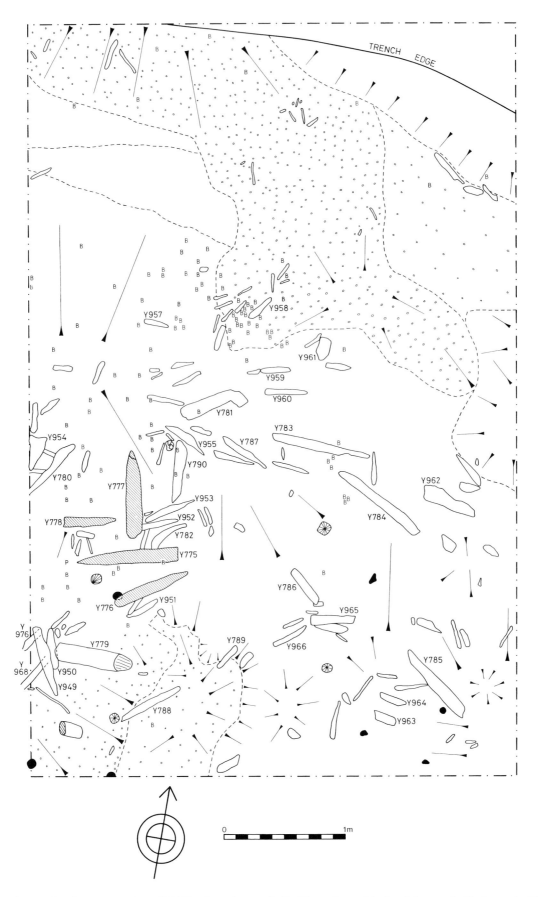

Fig 4.13 Power Station excavations (1989): Area 1, trench B. Plan of wood in level 2, east half of trench (for location see Fig 4.4). Uprights removed in antiquity (Y775–778) are hatched

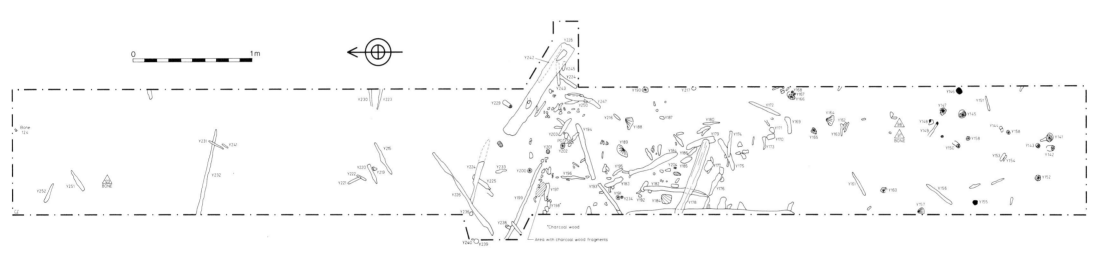

Fig 4.15 Power Station excavations (1989): Area 1, trench A. Plan of wood in level 1 (for location see Fig 4.5)

4: THE POWER STATION EXCAVATIONS, 1989 67

In the western half, level 1 revealed little of real interest other than a series of posts and a few scattered horizontal timbers, mainly of oak (Fig 4.10). Along the north side of the posts was a shallow depression, possibly a naturally eroded feature. Level 2 was of more interest. The depression petered out to a shallow escarpment and several new posts were found (Fig 4.11), some quite close to posts already revealed in level 1. The main feature was a double row of horizontal wood in the south-east corner of the excavation (Y967–9 and 976). This wood was found where terrace gravel had been used to backfill a shallow, natural depression. At the centre of this parallel-sided arrangement was a large post (Y779), which leaned at an angle (probably due to post-depositional disturbance). This recalls the 'cavity walls' or revetments of rows 1, 2, and 5 of the main Flag Fen site (Chapter 6; Pryor *et al* 1986, figs 7–8). The principal difference between this 'cavity wall' and those of the main site was its orientation at right angles to the main axis of the post alignment. If it was a wall, it might have acted as a barrier to those travelling along the alignment.

In the eastern half of Trench B, more horizontal timbers than before were exposed in level 1. These included at least one split oak plank with a rectangular mortise hole (Fig 4.12, Y823). Timber Y820, found in the north-east corner of the trench, was undoubtedly the tip of an upright that had rotted off at the top and been pulled from the ground in antiquity. It was found at too low a level to be later. Large quantities of wood were found in level 2, including the north-east end of the 'cavity wall' found in the western part of the trench (Fig 4.13). At the north-east end of the 'wall' was a group of four posts that had also rotted off at the top and been pulled from the ground in antiquity. These are the only examples yet found at Fengate or Flag Fen where it can be shown that posts of the alignment had been removed from the ground in prehistoric times. No postholes were found in the immediate vicinity, suggesting that the posts had been removed from elsewhere, brought to this particular location, and used like the other horizontal timbers to provide firm ground underfoot. It should be noted here that, with a single possible exception, the posts removed from the stream infilling of trench D (described below) were far smaller than those just discussed.

Trenches G and A (Figs 4.14–4.15)

Trench G was the most westerly of the group A, G, and D, which were close to the eastern boundary of the site (Fig 4.5). It was the first hand-excavated area to be opened and revealed irregular rows of posts and a few horizontal timbers, none of which were in a good state of preservation (Figs 4.14–4.15). The area was selected for hand excavation because it was located in a low-lying part of the site where the potential for preservation appeared excellent. It was decided to extend the trench eastwards, in the hope that preservation

Fig 4.14 Power Station excavations (1989): first exposure of posts in trench G, looking north-west (for location see Fig 4.5)

would improve. The timbers in this trench (A) were indeed better preserved (although they were by no means as good as trench B) and included a double-mortised split oak plank (Y226), which had been pegged in place by a peg in its north-west mortise hole. The distance, centre to centre, between the two mortise holes was 500mm. This timber provided the first good evidence that at least some of the horizontal timbers of the Power Station subsite were *in situ*. The area of horizontal wood was concentrated around the northern side of the post alignment.

Trench D (Figs 4.16–4.19)

Trench D was situated immediately east of trench A and was excavated at the height of the summer's heat in difficult circumstances. Preservation was much better than in the contiguous trenches to the west. Finds included a group of three double-mortised split oak planks (Figs 4.16–4.17). This group of planks was found close to the double-mortised plank in trench A (Fig 4.15); the horizontal timbers were also confined to the northern part of the post alignment. The two timbers to the north-west (Fig 4.16, A) consisted of a lower double-mortised plank and the damaged remains of another lying on top of it. The distance centre to centre between the mortise holes of the lower plank was 1010mm. The fragmentary plank was harder to measure, but a similar measurement appears probable. The second timber to the north-east (Fig 4.16, B) was very much longer and the distance between its two mortises was greater (2250mm).

The third group, to the south (Fig 4.16, C), again consisted of two timbers, one complete and one fragmentary. The lower, more complete, plank had an enlarged mortise to the south-west. The distance between the two innermost mortises was 1000mm and less between the fragmentary mortises of the higher plank (about 750mm). Finally, a single plank (Fig 4.16, D) to the south-west of C appeared to have

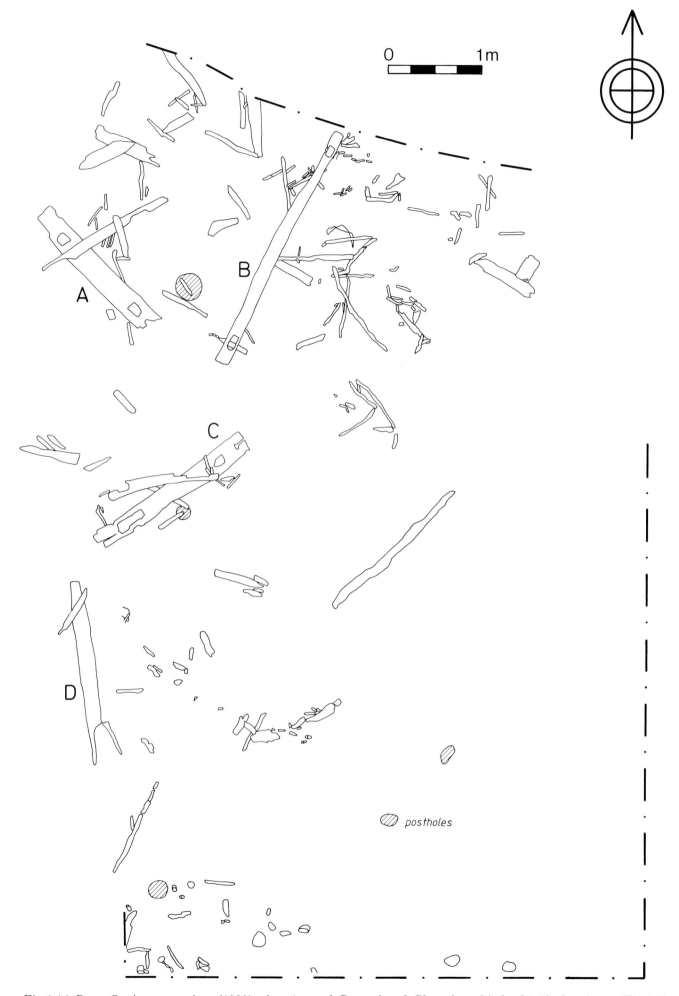

Fig 4.16 Power Station excavations (1989): Area 1, trench D, north end. Plan of wood in level 1 (for location see Fig 4.5)

0   1m

A

B

C

D

posttholes

Fig 4.17 Power Station excavations (1989): Area 1, trench D, north end. General view of wood in level 1, looking south (for location see Fig 4.16)

a single enlarged mortise at the southern end. The spacing of the mortise holes in the various double-mortised planks found in trenches A and D exhibited a very wide variety. This would indicate that they did not represent the disturbed remains of a single corduroy-style pegged trackway, as these generally consist of planks where the mortise (or peg) holes were evenly spaced (eg Raftery 1990, fig 10). To arrange the

pegs in any other way would present obvious hazards to anyone travelling along the trackway. Even allowing for minor variations, there are at least three groups of mortise spacings: 500mm (trench A), *c* 750–1000mm (A, C), and 2250mm (B). This might suggest, perhaps improbably, that as many as three trackways were represented. Alternatively, the timbers could have been reused from other structures.

In levels 2 and 3, at the south end of trench D, a shallow (300mm deep) ditch or stream course was revealed. Many posts had been driven through this infilled feature, but the clear impressions of six post-holes (marked by their darker filling) showed that posts had been removed in antiquity, doubtless to allow water to pass along the course of the earlier stream in wetter (Iron Age?) times, and perhaps when the post alignment had gone out of use as a path or trackway (Fig 4.18).

Even though the stream channel had filled in naturally, the top of the filling must have provided a muddy obstacle to anyone passing along the post alignment. Efforts had clearly been made to consolidate its surface with quantities of small roundwood, some of which had clearly been placed in position in rough bundles (Fig 4.19). The treatment of the relict stream channel illustrates well the dilemma that faced the constructors of the post alignment — people wanted to pass along it, yet water had to pass through it.

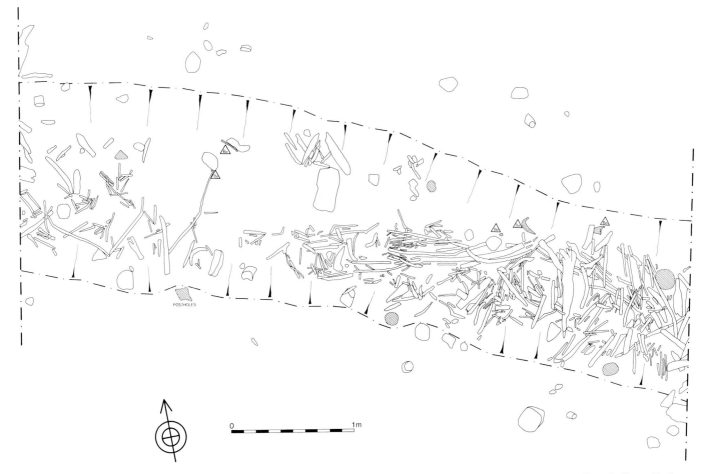

POSTHOLES

0   1m

Fig 4.18 Power Station excavations (1989): Area 1, trench D, south end. Brushwood filling an earlier shallow ditch (for location see Fig 4.5)

Fig 4.19 Power Station excavations (1989): Area 1, trench D, south end. Close-up of brushwood filling an earlier ditch. For location see Fig 4.18

Two bundles of wattle-sized roundwood were found in a ditch in the Cat's Water Iron Age settlement (Pryor 1984a, pls 16–17). This feature was a small enclosure ditch associated with a roundhouse. At the time, the wattle bundles were interpreted as a 'brush drain' (essentially a land drain) put in a ditch that was subject to regular silting up. Until recent times, bundles of wattle were placed in ditches in Holland to form simple bridges or temporary fords for the use of livestock (Roel Brandt personal communication). Given the new evidence from the Power Station site, the bridge/ford interpretation of the Cat's Water wattle bundles would appear more probable than the original 'brush drain' hypothesis.

The dog skeleton (Figs 4.20–4.21)

The animal bone assemblage included a number of dog bones from several individuals, but (with one exception) none was found *in situ* (see Chapter 13). Although the bones of the exception had been subject to some post-depositional disturbance, doubtless caused by prehistoric water action and later drying out, many of the animal's principal skeletal elements were in place. The bones lay close to a large oak post, probably part of Row 1, at the southern margin of the post alignment (Fig 4.4).

The bones lay directly on top of the buried soil (Fig 4.20). This would indicate a Bronze Age rather than Iron Age date. The head and most of the body lay south and east of a large post. This post appeared during excavation to have been driven into the ground in such a way as to pull two of the long bones of a back leg down into the ground. One of the vertical leg bones can be see clearly in Fig 4.21. It is possible that the effect was produced post-depositionally — the oak wood had shrunk and the bone had fallen into the void produced. Alternatively, the post was driven into the ground and in the process had pulled the articulated leg bones into the subsoil with it. The animal was presumably dead when the post was driven home. It seems improbable, however, that the association of the

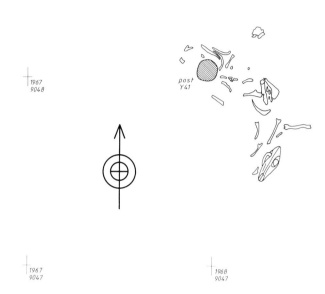

Fig 4.20 Power Station excavations (1989): Area 1, trench D. Sketch plan of dog bones around post (for location, see Fig 4.4)

Fig 4.21 Power Station excavations (1989): Area 1, trench D, looking south. View of dog bones around post. Note bones of back leg dipping into post socket (see also Fig 4.20)

dog with the post was down to coincidence alone. If the phenomenon was not entirely post-depositional, a ritual connection is surely indicated.

Beaker period features (Figs 4.22–4)

A group of ten small pits containing Beaker or possible Beaker period pottery, charcoal, a few flints, and bone was located immediately east of ditch 9, at the point where it veered sharply northwards at the wetland edge

The large pit lay on the landward edge of the group of ten small pits (Fig 4.23). There was no obvious pattern to the arrangement of these pits, but one or two observations are possible. Seven pits appeared to have been arranged in pairs (F97/8, F94/5, F94/3, F104/5). Another group of three lay close by F87, and one of these had been cut into its upper filling. Two small pits or stakeholes lay immediately south of the edge of the large pit and were positioned so very close to it that they were probably contemporary with it. All the pits were steep-sided, generally flat bottomed, and filled with a uniform deposit of charcoal-stained sand-silt with occasional burnt and fire-cracked stones (Fig 4.24).

Small sherds of Beaker-like pottery were found in the filling of F87 and the outlying pits. Many of the sherds were too small to identify of themselves, but they were similar enough to the few decorated and diagnostic pieces of Beaker pottery.

If this group of features represents the remains of a settlement, it is remarkable that there was no trace of a building. It would also be unlikely for a settlement to be established on ground so close to regularly flooded land, when there was ample naturally drained land immediately to the west. Indeed, a Beaker period roundhouse was recorded in the 1969 Site 11 excavations, some distance 'inland' to the west (Pryor 1993, fig 95).

The small pits grouped around F87 would normally be regarded as contemporary with it, were it not for the fact that one of the pits was cut into its uppermost filling. The dark, charcoal-rich filling was similar in all features, as was the Beaker pottery found within them. The steep angle of sides of F87 and the absence of any naturally derived rapid silting suggests that it had been filled in deliberately, as had the small pits. Backfilling is confirmed by the sections, where it can be seen that the various layers are irregular and do not show the usual division into primary, secondary, and tertiary deposits of naturally infilled features (Fig 4.22). It is possible that a single small pit could have been cut into F87 as the large pit was filled in at approximately the same time. The stepped profile of F87 suggests progressive enlargement or deepening, which makes it possible that each episode of digging was followed by one of backfilling, rather in the manner of a causewayed enclosure ditch.

The stepped side of F87 (Fig 4.22) suggests three, possibly four, episodes of enlargement. This pattern might be echoed in the pits, three of which were grouped close to F87 and three or perhaps four pairs of pits to the north-east. Burnt stones occur at the top and the bottom of the large pit's filling, which again suggests episodic use.

That the small pits were not postholes can be stated with some confidence, as there were no traces whatsoever of post 'ghosts', nor was there any evidence for post packing. Had posts rotted off in situ, as happened to the shallowest and most westerly posts of the alignment, then the void left by the rotted post would later

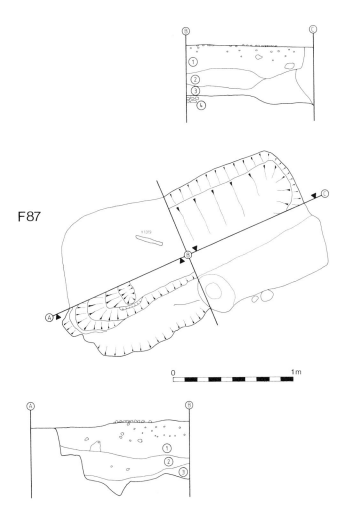

F87

Fig 4.22 Power Station excavations (1989): Area 1, trench D. Outline sections of the large pit F87. Key to layers: 1, dark clay-silt with burnt stones and charcoal; 2, charcoal-stained clay-silt, fewer stones; 3, dark clay-silt with flecks of burnt matrix; 4, natural terrace gravels capped with burnt stones

(Fig 4.3). They were cut into the gravel subsoil, had vertical or bell-shaped sides, and were most probably filled in very shortly after their initial excavation. They were mainly concentrated to the east of a large, contemporary pit (F87).

Feature 87 was rectilinear in plan and measured 2.82 × 1m. On excavation, three of its sides proved to be vertical or undercut, but that to the south-west was sharply stepped, as if progressively deepened by means of a central, axial, gully. The surface of the pit was marked by a dumped deposit of charcoal and fire-cracked stones, but the filling of the pit around this deposit showed no signs of heat. All the layers of infilling (Fig 4.22) were rich in comminuted charcoal. There was no evidence for rapid silting in the form of side wall collapse. The natural base of the pit was reddened around a deposit of fire-cracked stones, suggesting that this had been the site of an *in situ* fire. Presumably this fire had been lit at a time of year when the groundwater table was low.

have been filled with charcoal-free silty alluvium. The filling of the Beaker pits was, however, even and homogeneous and almost certainly derived from deliberate infilling.

The function of these enigmatic features is harder to define. Their location at the extreme edge of the wetland and at the mouth of an important droveway suggests that, in common with other Beaker period features at Fengate, they performed a boundary role (Pryor 1992b, 519). Fires were lit, but there is no sign of, for example, saltern briquetage. Taken together, the evidence indicates that these features were non-utilitarian and that their function involved episodic but recurrent activity. Since they most probably served a marking or boundary role, their occurrence so close to the western landfall of the post alignment is unlikely to be the result of coincidence alone.

Neolithic ditch

As the posts of the alignment were removed mechanically, the ground beneath was hardly in a suitable state for the recognition of buried subsoil features. Very careful earthmoving was required to remove loose soil, together with the lowest levels of lower silts, and the surface of the buried soil. This delicate operation took four days to perform in the area where the posts of the alignment had once stood. On completion, a wide and very shallow ditch was clearly revealed, which appeared to be of at least two phases (4.4–4.5; represented by the three dashed lines in Fig 4.1).

As the two phases were parallel, they most probably represent individual episodes of ditch maintenance, which were probably broadly contemporary. The original profile of the ditch was a very shallow, open U. Similar shallow features, including pits (eg Pryor 1984a, fig 90) and ditches (eg Pryor 1984a, fig M83, section 54) were found in very wet contexts in the Cat's Water Iron Age settlement. It would appear, therefore, that the extreme shallowness of these features simply reflected the high groundwater table.

Only some 20–50mm of infilling remained in the ditch, which must have been full (and probably obliterated by water action) when the first posts were driven through it. It is reasonable to suppose that the homogeneous sand-silt and occasional gravel pebbles that filled both phases of the ditch were naturally derived. Two sherds of plain handmade pottery (possibly of Peterborough Ware) were found in the ditch.

Discussion

The Power Station excavations of 1989 were important to an understanding of the relationship between wetland and dryland landscapes. Too often wetland sites are considered in a contextual vacuum and in isolation from the flood-free land where people actually lived and farmed.

The first general point concerns the alignment of the various features encountered. The two ditches (8 and 9) of the Bronze Age droveway ran down to the fen edge and then veered sharply away, leaving the droveway open towards the fen. This confirms beyond any doubt its function as a droveway. It is presumed that the fen to the east was open and unfenced and would have been used for hay and summer grazing. This tends to confirm earlier interpretations of the Fengate economy (eg Pryor 1980). A droveway of the broadly contemporary field system at Borough Fen, immediately north of Peterborough, which is visible as a cropmark, can be seen to behave in precisely the same way when it too met the edge of the floodplain (Pryor 1998b, fig 56, upper).

Immediately north-east of the mouth of the droveway was a group of possible Beaker period features of uncertain use. The location at the extreme edge of the fen and the evidence for the setting of fires might suggest that they once formed part of a saltern, were it not for the absence of briquetage and brackish or estuarine species within the pollen sequence (Chapter 13). There is some evidence to suggest that there were three or four episodes of Beaker activity. In the Etton report, it has been suggested that repeated visits to a significant place might have played a part in fixing a certain spot in peoples' minds, for ritual or other purposes (Pryor 1998a). Here it might have been thought necessary to mark its northern edge at the spot where the droveway ended. This northern side of the droveway was the aspect that faced outwards, across the open tracts of fen.

The very shallow Neolithic ditch (Figs 4.4–4.5) is a feature of some significance: it might have formed part of a precursor to the Bronze Age system, as it was roughly aligned on what was later to become a significant part it. Although it can not be regarded as part of that system, it could provide a *terminus post quem* for the main elements of the fully developed Bronze Age field system. The ditch does, however, provide some evidence that the Late Neolithic landscape that preceded the main Bronze Age ditched fields might not have been quite as open as currently thought.

The land at the end of the droveway had been an important boundary or marker for at least a millennium before the first posts of the alignment were driven into the ground (Chapter 16). It would also appear that the boundary was important both inside and outside the Bronze Age field system: within it, the droveway was a focus of the central element of the system (the three elements: north, central, and south are described in Chapter 18), but it also marked out distinct landholdings and provided the main axis of a proposed communal stockyard (Pryor 1980 and 1996; see also Chapter 18). In the open grazing of the fen, it might have marked the inner edge of land that was held in common by the communities living in Fengate and Northey. In the open fen, to the north of the boundary formed by the drove and the post alignment, different rules might have applied.

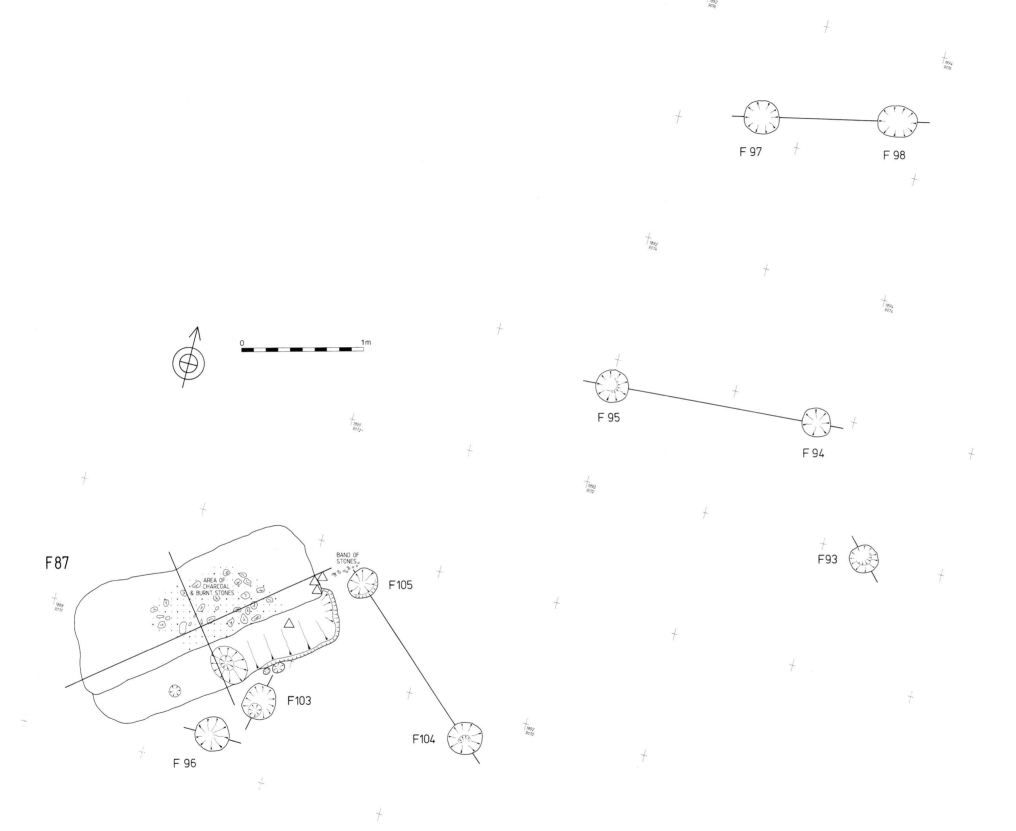

F 97   F 98

F 95

F 94

F 93

F 87

AREA OF
CHARCOAL
& BURNT STONES

BAND OF
STONES

F 105

F103

F104

F 96

Fig 4.23 Power Station excavations (1989): Area 1, trench D. Plan showing the arrangement of smaller features around the large pit F87 (for location see Fig 4.3)

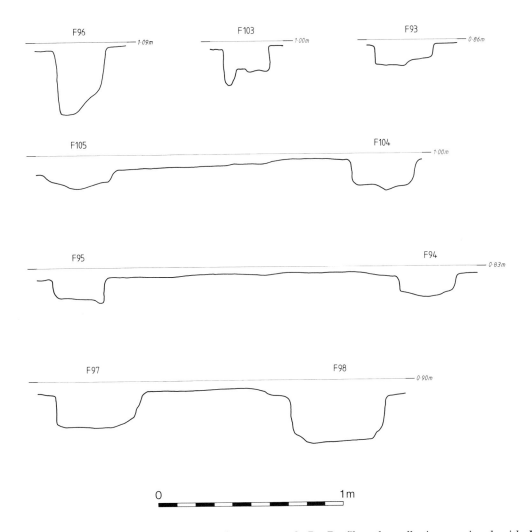

Fig 4.24 Power Station excavations (1989): Area 1, trench D. Profiles of small pits associated with F87 (for section locations see Fig 4.23)

The Iron Age gravel platform was not recognised as such for several weeks. Its presence coincided with an area of relict stream channels that skirted around the edge of the terrace gravel (Pryor 1992a, fig 8) and merged with the latter very gradually. It was not until some sharp showers of rain washed gravel away and revealed posts of the alignment beneath that its true significance was revealed. While its Iron Age date seems assured, its actual age is less so.

The gravel makeup of the platform appears to have been laid in a single episode. The platform coincided quite precisely with the post alignment, but fanned out to north and south at the junction with the terrace gravel. The best explanation for the platform is that it provided hardstanding, which could have been used by people to disembark from boats and so on. The gravel ended quite abruptly at the eastern end and there was no sign of significant accumulations of gravel further

along the post alignment. This would argue against the suggestion that the entire post alignment had been used as footings for a dumped gravel road or causeway in Iron Age times.

The presence of a substantial Iron Age feature should occasion no surprise, given the quantity and quality of Iron Age material that was found at both the Power Station subsite and further out in Flag Fen itself.

The poorly preserved human skeleton of a youth or adult was one of the few archaeological discoveries made north of the post alignment. It lay in Iron Age silts, in an extended or slightly crouched posture. An Iron Age body found in such circumstances is bound to be regarded as a sacrificial or ritual offering, rather than belonging to the victim of an accident such as drowning. In this instance there was no unequivocal evidence either way.

5 Excavation and survey at Northey, 1982–94

In this chapter, the archaeological landscape of the eastern landfall of the Flag Fen post alignment is considered, commencing with a brief review of the area in its setting. The main theme of the chapter is an account of the principal archaeological features. These include Neolithic and Bronze Age barrows and fields, Iron Age enclosures, a possible temple, and the Roman Fen Causeway (Fig 5.1). The chapter concludes with a short discussion.

Geographical setting

The modern hamlet of Northey lies in the parish of Thorney. Today, Northey is separated by the canalised course of the river Nene from the rest of the natural 'island' of Whittlesey, which lies some 4km to the south-east. The 'island' consists of Oxford Clay capped with Pleistocene gravels (Horton *et al* 1974). In antiquity, the river Nene would have entered the Fenland basin south of Whittlesey 'island', which was connected to the higher land of Fletton and Peterborough by a narrow 'isthmus' at modern King's Dyke and Stanground (Hall and Coles 1994, fig 24; Hall 1987, fig 43).

Previous work in the region

Northey lies outside the Designated Area of Peterborough New Town and therefore was not included within the Royal Commission volume (RCHM 1968). In many respects this was unfortunate, as the true cultural context for the prehistoric sites in eastern Peterborough was not just Fengate — the entire Flag Fen Basin, including the eastern dryland at Northey, must also be taken into account.

The importance of Northey was realised in April 1977 when, during a chance walk through the gravel quarry, then in operation, parallel droveway ditches identical in every respect to those currently being excavated at Fengate were observed. A rapid salvage excavation was immediately mounted. The two parallel ditches produced flintwork, Bronze Age pottery, and convincing evidence for salt extraction. A report on the site and its salterns was published by David Gurney who was then a member of the ROM/DoE Fengate team (Gurney 1980). The 1977 Northey excavation appears in the Fenland Survey report as Thorney Site 46 (Hall 1987, fig 30 and microfiche gazetteer).

In 1982 and subsequent seasons, the English Heritage South-West Fen Dyke survey carried out

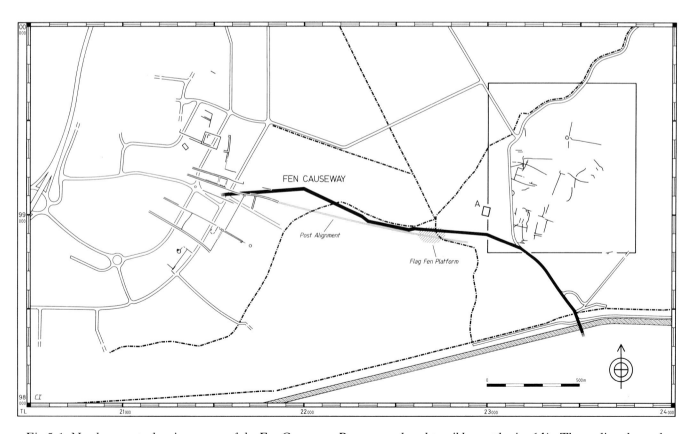

Fig 5.1 Northey: map showing course of the Fen Causeway Roman road and possible temple site (A). The outline shows the position of cropmarks planned (Figs 5.3 and 5.4)

Fig 5.2 Northey: cropmarks of probable Iron Age date. A, linear features; B, quarry pit; C and D, enclosures (for location see Fig 1.4)

detailed examinations of drainage dykes in the region. These produced evidence for extensive pre-Roman buried palaeosols and numerous archaeological features, including Bronze Age ditches thought to be the remains of Fengate Bronze Age-style fields or paddocks (French and Pryor 1993, dykes 8–19).

The Fenland Survey covered the same area at approximately the same time (Hall 1987). Aerial photographs showed two distinct rectilinear enclosures (Fig 5.2, C and D) close to Northey Road; these were considered to be of Roman or possibly Iron Age date

(Hall 1987, fig 33, extreme lower left). The survey also revealed a negative (ie parch) rectilinear soil mark in the field south and west of the Northey Road (Fig 5.1, A); it was tentatively considered to be a temple, possibly of Iron Age date (Hall 1987, pl x and fig 32, site 44).

Neolithic and Bronze Age

A series of oblique colour aerial photographs was taken by S J Upex, Nene Valley Research Committee aerial archaeologist, in July 1994. It had been a dry

Fig 5.3 Northey: cropmarks east of Northey Road. Photograph by S J Upex, Nene Valley Research Committee

late spring and early summer and the marks were unusually clear in the ripening winter wheat. The first view (Fig 5.3) shows the field to the east of Northey Road, with the old gravel workings of the 1977 excavations upper right. The smaller, wartime, gravel pit is visible at the top of the picture, slightly left of centre. The near-vertical view shows the more faint, pre-Iron Age cropmarks with greater clarity (Fig 5.4).

Interpretation of the cropmarks is complicated by the presence of periglacial and other features. For example, an apparent concentration of pits (Fig 5.3, top left) were, upon investigation, found to be natural solution features; many of the linear features might eventually be shown to be of periglacial origin. There are nonetheless many features of undoubted archaeological significance. These have been plotted using the agricultural sprayer wheelings (at 13m intervals) as a guide. The accuracy of the plot was confirmed by two trial trenches, which will be discussed briefly below.

The plot of cropmarks of possible Neolithic or Bronze Age date revealed a probable barrow, due north of the small wartime gravel workings (Fig 5.5, A). The mound showed clearly as a pale negative cropmark and there were indications of a surrounding ditch. Radiating from the barrow were three linear ditches to north, east, and south. To the west, although the cover of peaty alluvium was too thick to be certain, there were very slight indications of a fourth ditch, also aligned on a cardinal point of the compass. The three linear ditches were plainly aligned on the barrow and stopped short of it. Another north–south linear ditch could just be seen east of Halfpenny Toll House and east–west ditches to the south of it. Some of the linear features north of the second barrow/ring-ditch at B might prove to be of natural origin, but others undoubtedly form part of the arrangement already described. The same might be said of the linear features south and east of the old gravel pit.

The ring-ditch lies in part below the bank of Northey Road (Fig 5.5, B). On the ground there are slight indications of a barrow mound within the ring-ditch. It is of note that this barrow appears to be sited in an area devoid of field/paddock boundary ditches. The south end of the field contains many linear ditches, most of which closely resemble those of the Bronze Age system at Fengate. These ditches include a distinct droveway, which was investigated in Trial Trench 2. Close examination of the photographs showed possible ring-gullies and pits, but these are too slight to allow a reliable record to be made.

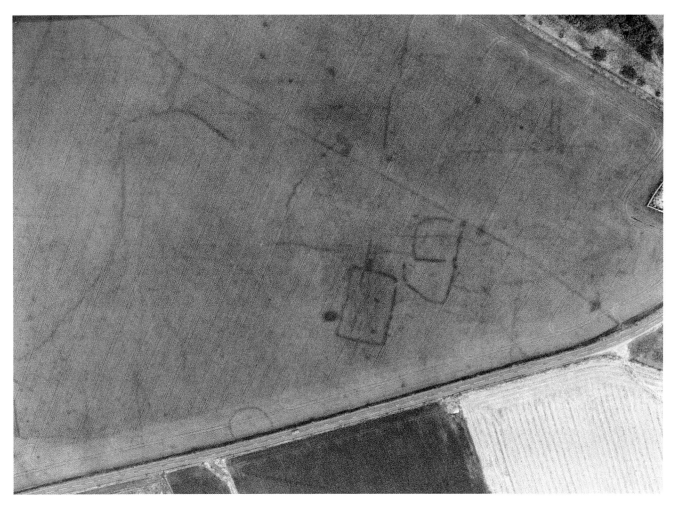

Fig 5.4 Northey: cropmarks east of Northey Road. Photograph by S J Upex, Nene Valley Research Committee

A surface survey of the field revealed very little, probably because the soil includes a substantial alluvial component. Unfortunately, the field was not ploughed in 1994/5, as it was given over to Set Aside. Recovery conditions were therefore very poor. Since the farmers have never pan-busted nor deep ploughed the field, however, preservation is likely to be very good below the surface. This proved to be the case in the two trial trenches.

Trial Trench 1

This trench was excavated to investigate the possible barrow (Figs 5.5, A and 5.6). A steep-sided ditch was encountered. This had been cut through the palaeosol (layer 5) while a bank (layer 3) had been thrown up along its eastern side. Two distinct layers showed in the ditch filling, probably representing rapid primary and slower secondary silting. The presence of gravel pebbles in the primary filling (layer 6) might possibly suggest deliberate backfilling, but this would need to be proven by soil micromorphology. The entire trench was sealed beneath approximately half a metre of peaty alluvium.

The area enclosed by the ditch was more difficult to interpret. Buried soil was present and there were signs of a gravel mound (layer 4). There was also much

evidence for burning *in situ*. Removal of the mound material close to the section through the ditch revealed a small pit filled with sand-silt similar to the buried soil, plus quantities of charcoal, broken animal bone, and burnt stones. This steep-sided feature resembled the 'small filled pits' encountered at Etton (Pryor 1998a).

The few flints found in the secondary filling of the ditch (layer 2) are generally of Neolithic type and are discussed in Chapter 12.

Trial Trench 2

Trial Trench 2 was positioned in the south-west part of the field to investigate two ditches of a possible Bronze Age droveway (Figs 5.5 and 5.7). The parallel ditches of the drove turned sharply north and south, about 15m west of the trial trench; at the corners of this sharp turn were pit-like enlargements. Although not at the fen edge, the general arrangement of these parallel ditches strongly resembled the Bronze Age droveway at the Power Station, thereby supporting the argument that this was another example and not a hedge setting.

The trial trench revealed a buried palaeosol about 0.15m thick. This is somewhat thinner than might otherwise be expected and would indicate some truncation.

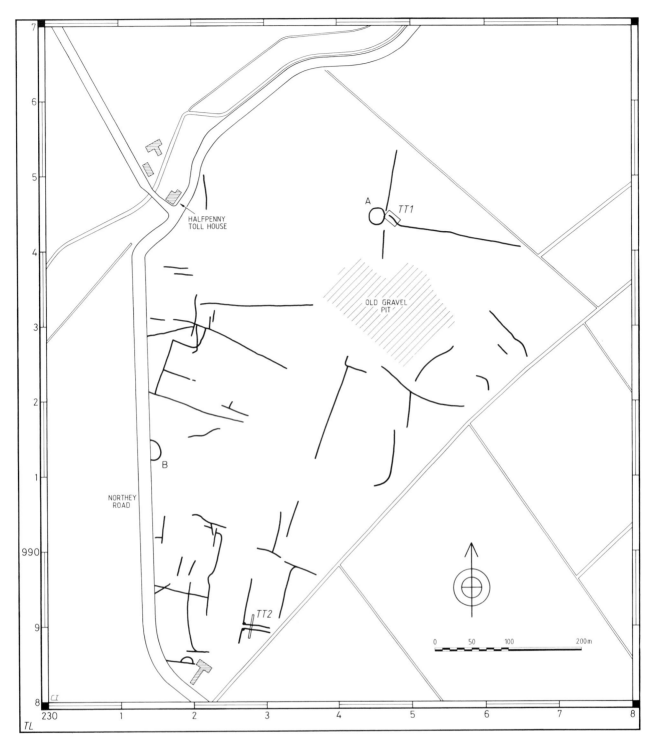

Fig 5.5 Northey: cropmarks of probable Bronze Age and Neolithic date. The positions of Trial Trenches 1 and 2 are shown. A, possible Neolithic barrow; B, ring-ditch (for location see Fig 1.4)

The north-east part of the trench had been disturbed by a modern land drain and so was extended to the south-east, where an undisturbed length of ditch was revealed. The distance between the two ditches was approximately 3m and there were very slight indications for two external banks. The filling of both ditches was identical — sand-silt with scattered gravel pebbles. The filling blended imperceptibly into the buried soil above and would seem to have accumulated naturally through processes of erosion. There was no stratigraphic evidence for recutting, although the

open profile of the ditches indicated that maintenance must have taken place. The possible droveway surface had not been consolidated with sand or gravel.

Iron Age and Roman

Cropmarks

Two enclosures were visible on aerial photographs close to Northey Road. Their substantial ditches probably penetrated to the water table, which might help to

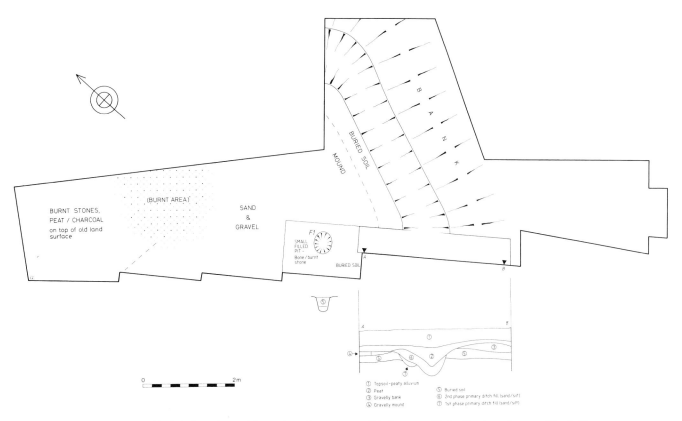

Fig 5.6 Northey: plan of Trial Trench 1 with section through possible barrow ditch (for location see Fig 5.5)

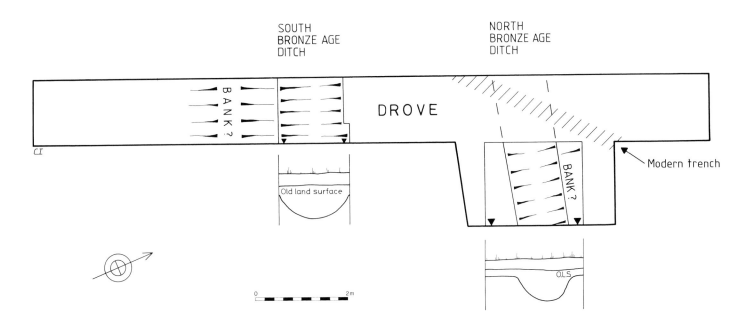

Fig 5.7 Northey: plan of Trial Trench 2 with sections through the droveway ditches (for location see Fig 5.5)

account for their dark cropmarks (Fig 5.2, C and D). Neither enclosure appeared to respect the earlier, probable, Bronze Age ditches around them and they are both, therefore, likely to be of Iron Age or Roman date; Hall (1987) favoured the latter, the present author the former. Only excavation would resolve the matter. North of enclosure C, a large cropmark at B probably represents a quarry pit dug to provide gravel for nearby yard surfaces. Waterlogged material can

confidently be expected from this feature. Around the two enclosures are numerous smaller pits, which are probably 'sock' (ie groundwater) wells; some of these might belong with the earlier Bronze Age field system and most will prove to be waterlogged.

The linear ditches were probably manmade in the vicinity of the two enclosures, especially those to the south. The only doubtful ditches are those at A (Fig 5.2). Although they form an apparent droveway, the ground south-east of Halfpenny Toll is very low-lying (2–3m OD) and it is hard to imagine how Iron Age droveways could have been constructed in this area. From this evidence, they might prove to be of natural origin. Only excavation can resolve the problem.

Undoubtedly the most visually striking feature is the small rectilinear soil mark north of the bend in the Fen Causeway and west of Northey Road (Fig 5.1, A). Hall very tentatively considers it a possible Iron Age temple (1987 fig 32); the present author thinks that it might have been associated with the Fen Causeway in some way and was perhaps a roadside inn or stopping place.

The Fen Causeway

The Fen Causeway or Fen Road was the only major Roman route across the Fens (Margary 1973, Road 25). It ran from Peterborough via Whittlesey and March to Denver, where it joins the Norfolk system. It originated at *Durobrivae* (Wild 1974), but its precise route through Peterborough is not known. Excavation at Fengate in the 1970s revealed no trace of it in the fields of the Padholme Road subsite and it seems probable that it lies beneath Padholme Road itself. The course of the Fen Causeway immediately east of Peterborough was first revealed in the Royal Geographical Society survey (Phillips 1970, pl vi). Subsequent aerial survey by Dr S J Upex of the Nene Valley Research Committee (Pryor 1991, fig 99) and Cambridge University (Hall 1987, pl x) has revealed the course of the road from Fengate to Northey across Flag Fen (Fig 5.1).

Discussion

Dr Upex's new aerial photograhs illustrate the great importance of visiting and revisiting key areas, even when cropmarks are thought to be fully understood.

They reveal a well preserved Bronze Age landscape, sealed beneath alluvium and running down to wet fen, to the north, west, and south. Following the recent excavations, the edge of the Bronze Age wetland at Northey, as mapped by the Fenland Project (Hall 1987, fig 30), must now be moved 'downhill' by some considerable distance.

The dating of the various features has to be tentative. Setting aside the meagre finds from Trial Trench 1 (which indicate a late third or second millennium BC date for the barrow) the droveway ditches of Trial Trench 2 produced no datable finds. This was entirely expected. The Fengate Bronze Age ditches were notoriously 'clean' in this respect, thereby illustrating the absurdity of attempting to date such features with samples as low as 2%. This unhappily is an accepted curatorial practice currently. The filling of the shallow ditches was very pale in colour.

At Fengate, ditches of the south element of the Bronze Age system were generally slighter than those further north and it has been suggested that they might be somewhat later. This might also apply at Northey. A Middle Bronze Age date for the droveway in Trench 2 might fit the evidence best.

The droveway and associated ditches revealed in Trial Trench 2 and from the air share the same orientation as the post alignment, but are located some 120m further north. This provides grounds for expecting the Northey landfall of the post alignment to end at a main droveway, like the Fengate landfall at the Power Station subsite, a kilometre to the west. The post-Bronze Age features immediately east of Northey Road (Fig 5.2) appear as very dark cropmarks and there is a high probability that they continue below the modern water table. Their fillings could well provide important palaeoenvironmental samples from dryland contexts, which could be compared with pollen and other sequences obtained at Flag Fen.

6 Excavations at Flag Fen, 1982–95

The discovery of Flag Fen in November 1982 has been described in some detail in a number of recent publications (eg Pryor *et al* 1986 and Pryor 1991). There is no need to repeat those accounts, other than to note that the discovery took place during an English Heritage-funded survey of freshly cleaned-out drainage dykes (French and Pryor 1993).

A main purpose of the dyke survey was to locate archaeological sites and associated palaeoenvironmental deposits before they appeared as surface scatters whose context and true significance would have been largely destroyed by ploughing and drainage. This survey, while useful in many respects, did not provide an uncontaminated source of palaeoenvironmental information that could be associated more directly with the archaeological deposits of Flag Fen. Accordingly, in 1993 a survey was undertaken specifically to examine palaeoenvironmental deposits in the immediate environs of the site. The results of that survey are discussed by French in Chapter 14. This chapter will describe the excavation of waterlogged deposits at Flag Fen. The first report (Pryor *et al* op cit) was a detailed discussion of levels 1 and 2 of what in this report has been termed Area 6A. For the sake of completeness, the wood from levels 1 and 2 in Area 6A has been represented alongside that found in subsequent excavations in Areas 6B and 6D, but the detailed descriptions of the first report have not been repeated.

The excavations are described in two parts. The first considers all the trial trenches and other exposures of wood associated with the platform and post alignment, apart from the trenches of the main research excavations that have been combined and relabelled as Area 6 (Fig 6.1). Excavations within Area 6 form the main subject matter of this chapter and will be described in the second part. The chapter concludes with a discussion. Appendix 3 contains a concordance of publication and archive trench designations.

Trial trenches and other exposures

The description that follows will consider each of the trenches excavated at Flag Fen since 1982, working from west to east. The trenches are located in Figures 1.5 (inset) and 6.1.

Area 1

This trench was opened in 1987 following the discovery of wooden posts in a narrow slit trench excavated by Fenland Archaeological Trust for a 32mm water main from Fourth Drove to a temporary visitor centre immediately west of the main mere (Fig 6.2).

The trench measured 1.5 × 9m. Preservation was poor, largely due to the presence of a drainage ditch (the Cat's Water) immediately to the south. It was not possible to measure the width of the alignment accurately but it was, however, possible to discern two distinct rows of oak posts (Fig 6.2): W13, W10, W11, W15–18, W23–5 and W1–7, W9, and W19). An irregular (probably disturbed) scatter of horizontal wood lay amid and around the southern row. Despite the poor preservation, it was possible to determine that most of this horizontal wood was of non-oak species (Pryor 1991, fig 82). Several small pegs were found *in situ* (eg Fig 6.2, W3, W4, and W8). They might well have been used to fasten larger planks in place. A large non-archaeological trench was opened 3–4m north-east of Area 1. This trench was to carry the main gas supply to the power station but archaeologists from the Trust were unable to inspect it when it was open. Archaeologists working on behalf of the gas company reported that no archaeological material had been disturbed by this work. After backfilling, however, the smashed remains of a large tangentially split oak plank were seen protruding from the compressed backfill. From its preservation and general appearance, this was without doubt an ancient timber.

In July 1990, a small machine-dug sondage or trial trench was excavated in the Anglian Water Services sludge-spreading area, some 200m east of Area 1 (Pryor 1992a, fig 6, TT1990A). This trench was excavated and backfilled in an afternoon to assess whether the post alignment was present and still waterlogged. The work showed that it was both present and dry. The posts were large and of oak. There was also at least one layer of horizontal timber, which was much better preserved than in Area 1 to the west.

Area 2

Area 2 was opened in 1987 following the discovery of large oak posts in Area 1 (Fig 1.5). It was immediately evident that preservation was very much better than in Area 1 and it was decided to restrict the size of the trench to minimise any damage that might be caused by disturbance and consequent dewatering.

Excavation in Area 2 exposed large split oak posts and a quantity of horizontal timbers, including two substantial split oak planks, Z56 and Z111 (Fig 6.3). The plank Z56 had been cut away in antiquity to accommodate an upright (Z57), which had subsequently collapsed (Fig 6.4). The plank Z111 was cut square at each end and was pierced by a large rectangular mortise hole, which in turn was pierced by another timber, Z119. The latter served to peg the plank in place; two other pegs had been driven in alongside the

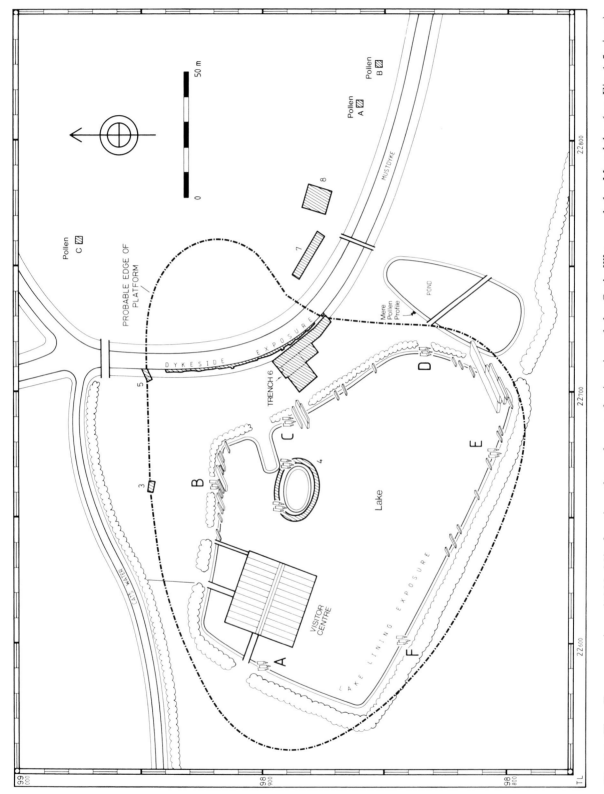

Fig 6.1 Flag Fen excavations (1982–93): location of trenches at the junction of the Cat's Water and the Mustdyke (see Fig 1.5, inset). The location of timber revealed in the lake lining exposure is indicated schematically

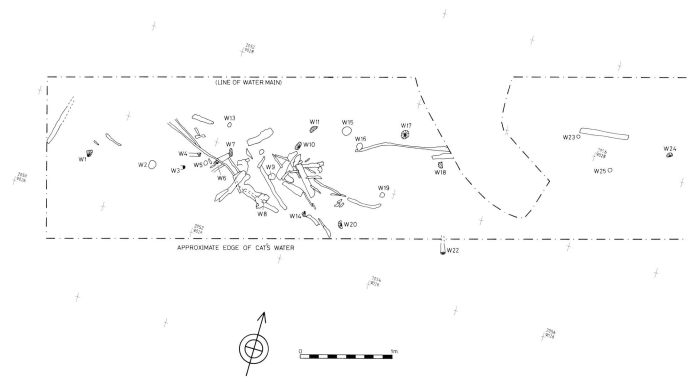

Fig 6.2 Flag Fen, Area 1: plan of wood exposed in excavations prior to the construction of the water main (for location see Fig 1.5, inset)

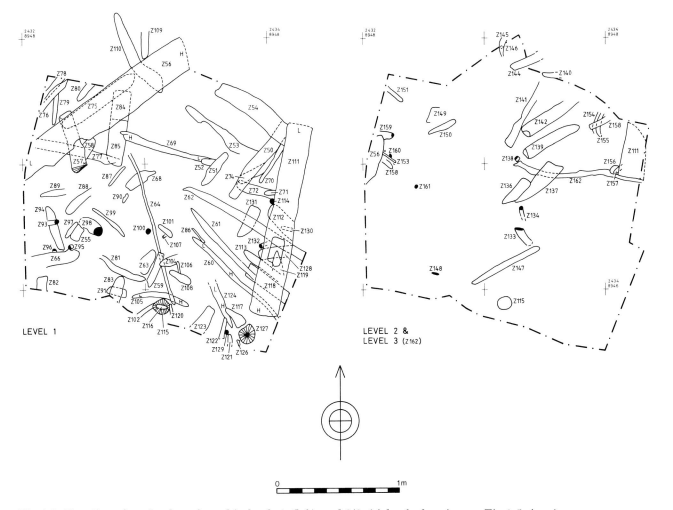

Fig 6.3 Flag Fen, Area 2: plan of wood in levels 1 (left) and 2/3 (right; for location see Fig 1.5, inset)

Fig 6.4 Flag Fen, Area 2: general view of wood in level 1, looking north

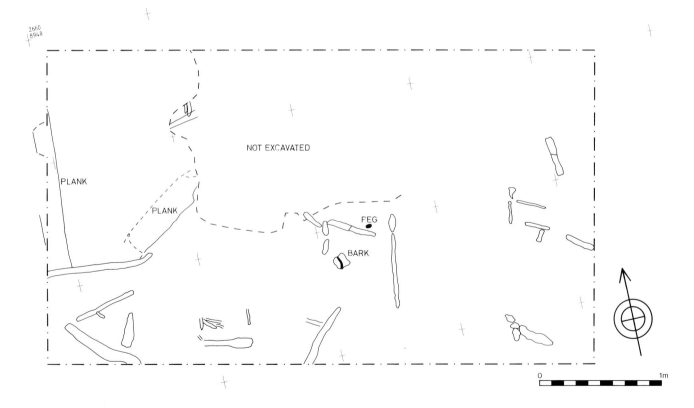

Fig 6.5 Flag Fen, Area 3: trial trench to select area for new visitor centre (for location see Fig 6.1). Plan of superficial wood exposed (but not lifted or excavated)

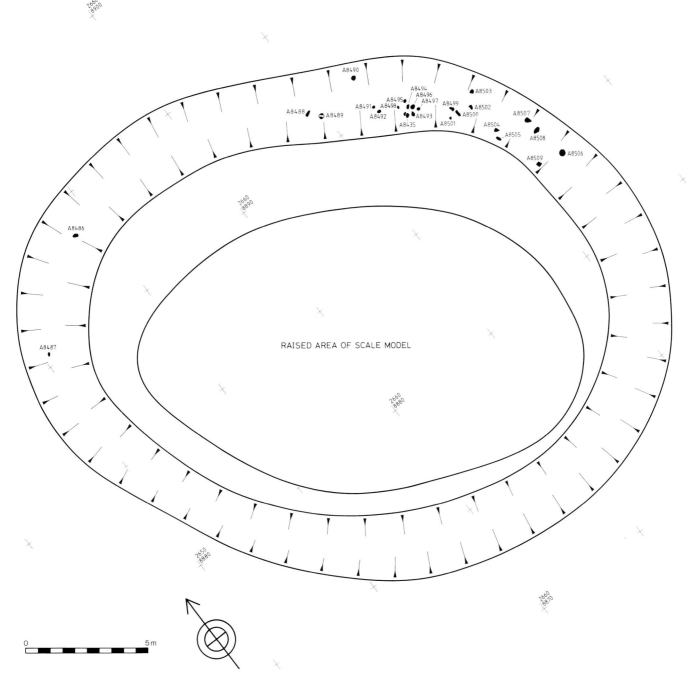

Fig 6.6 Flag Fen, Area 4: security trench around island in lake — plan of posts (for location see Fig 6.1)

plank's west edge (Z114 and Z132). The level at which the planks occurred was also marked by a thin, discontinuous spread of sand and fine gravel. The gravel, which very occasionally included larger stones, was too coarse to have been waterborne and was probably spread to provide a secure foothold on the wet planks. Similar thick deposits of sand and fine gravel were found between the posts of Rows 2 and 3 in Area 6.

Area 3

Area 3 was excavated in 1987 to assess the archaeological potential of land where a new visitor centre might be located without causing archaeological damage (Fig 6.1).

It was excavated in late autumn during a time of early air frosts; accordingly it was decided to reveal the barest minimum of wood to minimise archaeological damage (Fig 6.5). The trench was large (4 × 5m) and was located some 48m north of the post alignment. The excavations indicated quantities of wood, including one large plank along the western edge of the trench and another, slightly smaller, nearby. Apart from a single small peg near the centre of the trench, there were no uprights protruding above the level of the horizontal timbers. A surveyor's 'arrow' was used to probe for further timber elsewhere in the trench. Almost the entire area was found to contain hard, resistant wood, most probably oak planking.

In these circumstances, it was decided to cover the bottom of the trench with polythene sheeting prior to backfilling. Experience had shown that this prevented drying out while the backfill consolidated. No wood was lifted or disturbed.

Area 4

It would be misleading to describe Area 4 as an archaeological trench (Fig 6.1). It was dug in June 1987 to provide soil to top a small artificial island that would model the approximate extent of the timber platform when the large artificial lake or mere was flooded (Chapter 1). The oval trench (Fig 6.6) was about half a metre deep and the appearance of post tops at so high a level came as a surprise. The first posts were exposed around the north-east part of the trench This group was closely clustered (Fig 6.7) and rows were not immediately apparent. Only the very tops of the posts were exposed (Fig 6.8). Excavation continued at a higher level, but even so two further posts were revealed (A8486–7) in the north-west segment of the trench.

As already noted, the level at which the tops of posts appeared was remarkably high in the area of the artificial lake. This might be explained by the practice, abandoned after 1986, of constructing shallow lagoons into which sewage sludge was pumped. The sludge

Fig 6.8 Flag Fen, Area 4: close-up of post tops

remained in the lagoons for the summer months, during which time the liquid component evaporated. The construction of the lagoons required the raising of low earth bunds, which acted as coffer dams. If the same land was regularly bulldozed to provide soil for the bunds, it is possible that over time the surface would be gradually lowered.

The dykeside exposure

The first timbers to be discovered at Flag Fen were revealed on the south-west side of the Mustdyke about 90m south of its junction with the Cat's Water drain (Fig 6.1). After the initial discovery it was decided that the side of the dyke should be cut back in order to reveal the full extent of the timbers' spread. This cutting took some three weeks to perform and approximately 73m of timbers were exposed along the gentle curve of the dyke (Fig 6.9). The straight-line distance of the exposure was approximately 63m.

Working on the slope of the dykeside in the frosty conditions of December was very difficult. In compensation, the water level had been lowered to allow engineering work to take place and preservation was remarkably good. The archaeological effects of deepening and enlarging the dyke had yet to be felt. The posts were concentrated in a single area some 8m wide, which was located 8.25m north of the southern limit of the exposure. The thickest concentration of horizontal timbers was about 20m north of the post alignment. In this area were a number of substantial oak planks, including two mortised pieces, one of which had been pegged in place through its mortise (Pryor *et al* 1986, pl 20b).

At the time, it was believed that the dykeside exposure had revealed the full extent of the timbers. At either end of the exposure, however, the peat was dry, crumbly, and well humified.

In these areas, it was difficult to cut back the edge enough to reveal the timbers without causing unacceptable damage to the dykeside. In both instances,

Fig 6.7 Flag Fen, Area 4: general view of post tops (possibly Rows 3 or 4). The excavator in the background is forming the bund around the mere

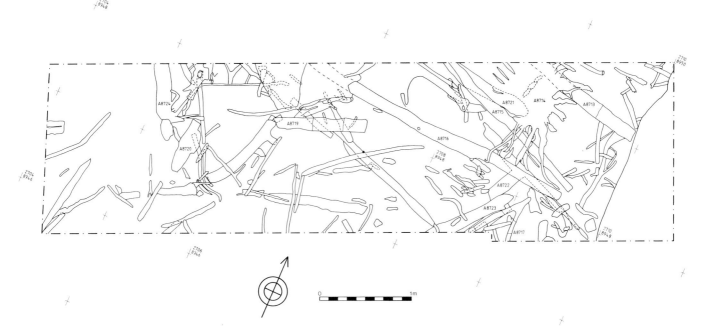

Fig 6.10 Flag Fen, Area 5: plan of wood in levels 1 and 2. Note that timbers A8713, 8715, 8716, and so on form the north-west revetment to the platform (for location see Fig 6.1)

the dykeside exposure had missed the evidence for a possible revetment around the platform edge.

Area 5

In 1988, this area was positioned to reveal any timbers that might be disturbed by the construction of a dyke-side walkway (Fig 6.1). The walkway was constructed near the water level in the Mustdyke, using the 'step' left by the original dykeside exposure of 1982. Access to this walkway was by means of a ramp, which was to be located just north of the timber spread as revealed in the dykeside exposure. In the event, however, the northerly end of the timber exposed in the dykeside proved to be false, since quantities of timber were exposed in the new trench, including a series of

Fig 6.11 Flag Fen, Area 5: general view of wood in level 1, looking west, with revetment timbers in the foreground

trimmed alder logs that probably once formed a revetment along the platform's north side (Fig 6.10, A8713, A8715, A8716, and A8721, plus unnumbered timbers). The logs are best interpreted as foundations for a perimeter walkway (Figs 6.9 and 6.11).

The logs of the revetment foundations were laid roughly parallel to the platform's perimeter. Some of the timbers were substantial and all had had their side branches removed (Fig 6.10). Below the upper level of timber (level 1), there was little additional material beneath the possible revetment (level 2), apart from three short parallel split oak planks that might have acted as bearers for disturbed revetment timbers, and another, southerly large log that might also have formed part of the revetment (Fig 6.12). At this lower level (3) it was notable that there was a greater concentration of wood and timber to the west of the revetment, ie towards the interior of the platform. Again, most of this wood was either woodworking debris or had been trimmed of its side shoots. There was no brushwood.

The near-complete absence of walkway timbers above the edge revetment in this area can in part be explained by recent dykeside collapse. An alternative explanation is that damage was caused by storms some time in antiquity. It will be seen below that the northerly side of the post alignment in Area 8 was undoubtedly damaged in this way.

The lake lining exposure

In Chapter 1, the construction of the lake and its lining was described in some detail. While the work was going on, a close watch was kept for ancient timbers. It was not possible, however, to examine any of the timbers

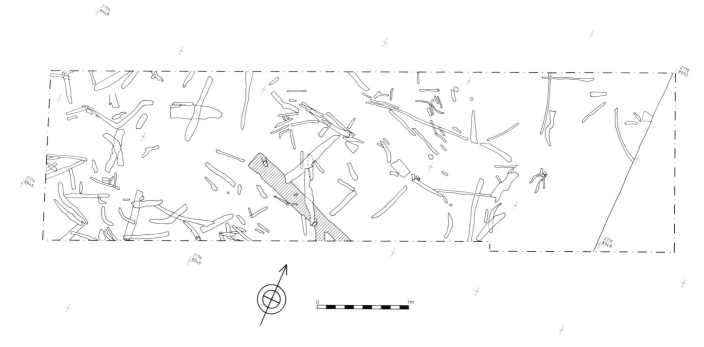

Fig 6.12 Flag Fen, Area 5: plan of wood in levels 3 and 5 (for location see Fig 6.1)

in situ at the bottom of the trench because of the danger of collapse. Several brought to the surface by the machine were examined as part of the dendrochronological study (Chapter 8). Careful notes were kept of the position and occurrence of timber and the results are presented in schematic form in Fig 6.1.

Wood was found around the entire circuit of the lake, but particularly heavy concentrations of horizontal timbers are represented by schematic planks — the larger the plank the heavier the concentration of timber (Fig 6.1). Posts were encountered at six separate locations (Fig 6.1, A–F). The most dense concentrations of posts were at A and C, on the post alignment, but another significant concentration was also observed at B, to the north. The concentrations at D, E, and F all contained more than one post, but due to the wetness and depth of the peat around the south side of the lake, it was difficult to be more precise.

Area 7

This large trench (25 × 5m) was excavated in 1990 to examine the preservation of the post alignment on the east side of the Mustdyke (Fig 6.1). Four rows of posts could clearly be seen and these probably coincided with Rows 2–4 of the main excavation (Fig 6.13). The posts of Row 1 usually appeared at a slightly lower level than the others, probably because they were often of alder, rather than oak, and were the earliest posts to be sunk. They would have rotted-off when the groundwater table was significantly lower.

The trench was opened during an extremely hot summer, and so it was decided not to expose more wood than was absolutely necessary. Accordingly, a small area of horizontal timber was exposed north-west

of Row 5. Excavation revealed a small fragment of copper alloy bracelet, probably of Wilburton type, close to the posts (David Coombs personal communication). There were also large quantities of oak woodchips, which had been dusted liberally with sand and fine gravel. By August, as the conditions had become far too hot to continue, the trench was sealed with polythene sheeting and backfilled. To minimise damage, it has not been reopened.

Area 8

Area 8 was first excavated in the summer of 1993, after it was learned that Hawker Siddeley Power Engineering Ltd and Eastern Group plc had together agreed to fund a permanent display of Bronze Age timbers preserved *in situ*. It was decided to place the new facility on the east side of the Mustdyke, but sufficiently far away from the dyke to avoid any possible contamination by pollution (a continuing problem, given the scale of industrial development in Fengate, upstream).

Area 8 was the trench that was eventually to be covered by the new Preservation Hall (which opened in May 1995 and encloses an area 10m square). Excavation in 1993 confirmed that timbers were in fact present and a preliminary plan of them was drawn. That plan (Level 1) was checked and edited on completion of the construction work and appears here as Fig 6.14. It is a great tribute to Kiers, the constructors of the Preservation Hall, that no damage was caused to the fragile remains in the trench, which were protected by a temporary scaffolding floor. Subsequently many of the less well preserved wood fragments were removed; the current display therefore consists of a

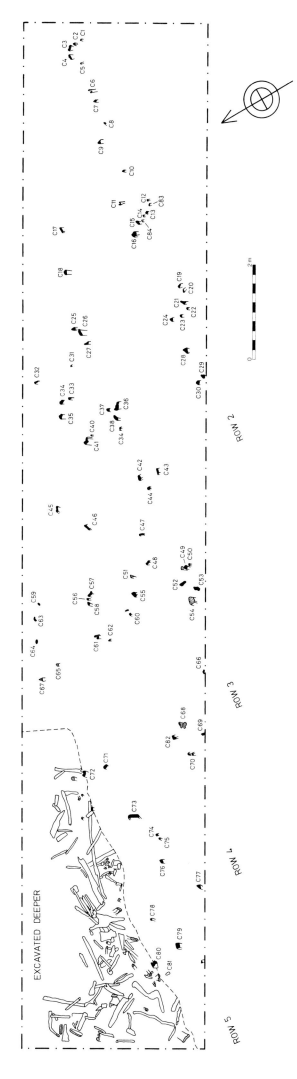

Fig 6.13 Flag Fen, Area 7: plan of first exposure of wood in trench immediately east of the Mustdyke. Note that horizontal timber was only encountered in the north-east corner, where a small area was excavated c 300mm deeper than the rest of the trench (for location see Fig 6.1)

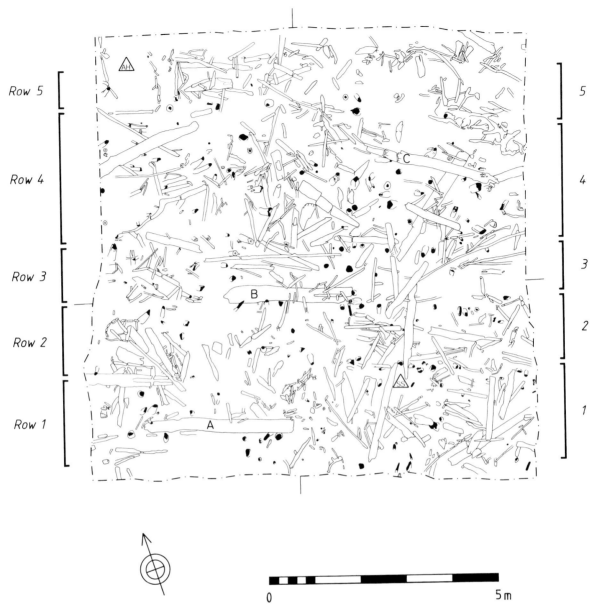

Fig 6.14 Flag Fen, Area 8: highest level of wood exposed in the excavations of 1993, prior to construction of the Preservation Hall. The designation of Rows 1–5 is provisional

mixture of timbers from Levels 1 and 2. The only change of any significance between levels 1 and 2 was the removal of most of the wood north of Row 5. When this material was removed, the lower parts of a wattle 'cavity wall' or revetment were revealed around the posts of row 5, at either end of the excavation. Although the rows of posts were generally quite clearly defined, Row 2 appeared to branch near the centre of the excavation and with Row 1, to veer southwards. Row 3 contained the greatest number of posts. Row 4 was far less well defined and consisted more of a scatter of posts than a distinct row. Row 5, on the other hand was narrow and generally straight. It should be added at this point that no timbers have been disturbed or sampled, as this would have harmed the display, and indeed its preservation. Consequently, and without dendrochronological information, it is impossible to be precise about the identification of the various rows.

While it is also very hard to identify the species of horizontal timber (where endgrain is not always visible) without taking samples, macroscopic inspection suggests that the vast majority of uprights and horizontal timbers were of oak.

White sand and fine gravel with larger gravel pebbles was found on the surface of the horizontal timbers between Rows 1 and 2; it was also found around the posts of Row 3. It was not, however, found around the posts of Rows 4 and 5. As the spread of sand and gravel in Area 6 nearby was mainly between Rows 2 and 3, it is possible that Row 1 has been misidentified as such. This problem will only be resolved by further excavation outside the Preservation Hall.

A bronze leaf-shaped socketed spearhead of Late Bronze Age type (Fig 6.14, SS and Fig 10.4, 51) was found by metal detector below the timbers of Level 2, just south of Row 2, some 2m into the excavation from the east side. A pick or hook of red deer antler, closely resembling that from Newark Road, Fengate (Pryor 1980, fig 76), was found in the north-west corner of the excavation, just outside (north of) Row 5 (Fig 6.14, AH). Louwe-Kooijmans has found similar antler hooks with Beaker period fishing assemblages and considers they could have been used to raise traps from the water (Louwe-Kooijmans 1974, fig 106). Certainly such a hypothesis would accord well with the findspot of the Flag Fen example.

Three large horizontal timbers lie in prominent positions in the preserved excavation (Fig 6.14, A–C). All are of oak. A is a radial quarter split and knotty trunk, axed square at each end and pegged in place; B is a tangentially split plank and C is a (reused?) round-wood timber. Timber B has parallel-sided (and presumably broken) slots or projections of uncertain purpose at each end. B and C are also pegged into position. These three larger-than-average timbers are positioned diagonally within the excavation and span a strip of soft peaty ground, possibly the remains of a relict stream channel. Immediately south of timber A, excavations in 1994 revealed a large number of small pegs that might have secured another large timber, which has subsequently been lost.

During excavation, it was very apparent that the timbers around Row 5 were more disrupted than those to the south. This was doubtless a reflection of the fact that that Row 5 was probably erected relatively late, at a time when water levels had risen substantially. The posts of Row 5 would also have taken the full brunt of winter gales blowing in from the open fen to the north-east.

Areas 9 and 10

Two trenches were excavated mechanically in 1993 to take pollen samples and to investigate the preservation of deposits closer to the Northey 'island' landfall (Fig 1.5, inset). Neither trench impinged upon the post alignment. The wood in Trench 9 was very poorly preserved, doubtless because of dewatering caused by the nearby Mustdyke. No wood was found in Trench 10 and the peat had almost completely vanished. Buried prehistoric soils were, however, present in both trenches.

Areas 11 and 12

Two additional small trenches were excavated mechanically in the same year at Areas 9 and 10 to provide pollen samples (Fig 1.5, inset). Neither produced evidence for human activity in the form of woodworking or timber. Both revealed significant accumulations of lake marl above the terrace gravels, which might help to explain why the post alignment made its Northey landfall further south. At this stage, the size of the lake remains unknown, but the depth of the marl indicates a body of water of some size.

Area 6: methods and areas excavated

Area 6 was the main excavation at Flag Fen. The site was selected since, from examination of the dykeside exposure, the timbers there were known to be in good condition. It was also evident that, because of the recently enlarged dyke that ran alongside them to the north-east, the waterlogged wood was in imminent danger of drying out.

Wetland archaeology has a reputation for being labour intensive and expensive. At Flag Fen efforts have been made to keep down costs by selecting simple techniques that rely more on ingenuity than sophisticated technology. It was known that English Heritage funding would have to cease after 1992 and there seemed little point in attempting to develop expensive state-of-the-art procedures, eg computer mapping, electronic distance measurement, and so on, when future budgets would be insufficient to cover even the insurance costs of the equipment.

The following account begins with a brief discussion of the excavation and recording techniques employed at Flag Fen. It is followed by a short historical description of the subdivisions (A–D) of Area 6.

A note on grid references in the detailed descriptions

Because of the large quantities of timber found in Area 6 it has not always been possible to number every significant piece illustrated, especially in instances of repetition, eg uprights that might appear in six separate level plans. Even if an individual piece has been numbered it might not always be easy to find in the sometimes cluttered plans. The grid reference will therefore be to the square in which the number of the specified piece appears. Grid references are in the form: easting followed by northing and are based on the Ordnance Survey National Grid (as noted in Chapter 1).

Fig 6.15 Flag Fen, Area 6A, techniques of excavation: general view of excavations within temporary shelter, 1986 season

Fig 6.16 Flag Fen, Area 6, techniques of excavation: exposing timbers of level 1. Note the level ground surface behind the figure

Methods and techniques — general excavation procedures

The development of excavation techniques at Flag Fen is a story of increasing technical simplification. The main practical problem was caused by the fact that within a given trench the archaeological remains had no edges. Put another way, the excavators could only approach the preserved wood from above. Under this option, two-level scaffolds were initially constructed to enable the excavators to lie, or hang, above the timbers they were working on (Fig 6.15; see also Pryor *et al* 1986, pls 7a, 9b, and 10b).

The early scaffolds worked well until the time came to move them either sideways (eg to work round a large post) or vertically. At this juncture, it was difficult to work with heavy steel tubes without damaging the ancient timbers. On two occasions, indeed, the scaffolding collapsed when individual fittings slipped; the damage, although localised, was considerable and affected more than just one level of timber. The unsightly scaffolds also obtruded into photomontage plans (eg Pryor *et al* 1986, pls 1 and 2) and were unpopular with visitors. In 1987, it was decided to abandon scaffolds entirely and to work from improvised platforms made from lighter, less ungainly materials. When working on the highest level, one way around the problem was to leave intact a few millimetres of the overlying peaty alluvium, which was then carefully levelled and left in place. This material furnished an excellent excavation platform, provided that its surface was kept dry (Fig 6.16). When working on lower levels, the improvised platforms consisted of a network of planks and offcuts of timber supported on blocks, which, in turn, rested on pieces of old carpet or pads of silt (Fig 6.17). The planks could be tacked or clamped in place if necessary. A light, rigid aluminium bridge was positioned over the excavations to give tour guides and supervisors a general view of work in progress (Fig 6.18).

Until 1989 plans (drawn at 1:10) were prepared from a photomontage (Areas 6A and 6B). This worked quite well, but after a number of seasons it was found to be too mechanistic: important relationships and other patterns were missed because a photograph, and not the actual wood, was being used as the primary source of information.

Great pains were taken to ensure that the overhead camera was located at precisely the same position to give continuity between levels, but it was impossible to ensure that the lens was at precisely the same angle from one year to the next. In addition, wind would sometimes move the supporting structure. These and other factors account for the variation that can be seen between plans of the same quadrant made at different levels. The horizontal wood was rarely affected, but the vertical posts can appear to lean in different directions at various levels; this effect is most evident at Levels 4 and 5 where the posts were at their tallest.

Fig 6.17 Flag Fen, Area 6, techniques of excavation: working above the wood using planks supported on wrapped blocks

In an attempt to avoid some of these interpretative and practical problems, following the season of 1989, a conventional planning frame is used to prepare the first draft of the plan, but vertical photographs are also taken as an important additional source of information. The photomontage plans provide a record of the site at a specific time, whereas the level-by-level plans are successions of information pertaining to specific levels.

All the wood in Area 6A was numbered and entered into the computer database. In Areas 6B–6D a more selective approach was adopted. Each timber was measured *in situ* and the decision whether to assign an individual wood number was made on the spot. Once numbered, the dimensions entered the wood database and the piece was further examined by Maisie Taylor (whose procedures are described in greater detail in Chapter 7).

A note on levels

The various subdivisions of Area 6 were excavated by levels. It is difficult to describe what constituted a level, other than to say that each was approximately 100mm thick. Sometimes, but only rarely, it was possible to work to a 'real' or stratigraphic level that defined itself, such as a sand-sprinkled surface. In most instances, however, the excavators let the wood define its own level by not chasing an individual timber below more than a single crossing timber. It could be said that the levels defined themselves, therefore, but too much importance should not be assigned to them as self-contained stratigraphic units. They should best be seen, perhaps, as a combination of 'conventional' stratigraphic contexts and arbitrary spits.

By and large, most non-vertical timbers lay *in situ* horizontally, which undoubtedly supports the idea that, as the waters around them rose, the platform and the walkway around the post alignment were built up in a succession of layers. Angled timbers that ran

Fig 6.18 Flag Fen, Area 6B, techniques of excavation: general view of excavations within permanent shelter, 1987 season. A tour is in progress (guide — Colin Richards)

from Level 1, at the top, to Level 6, at the bottom, are unknown. At most, such timbers would run between two levels. In almost every instance, timbers that appeared on plans of successive levels were either of particular importance or were of unusually large diameter. For example, many of the larger diameter logs in Level 4 also appeared in Level 5, where they were more clearly defined. Important timbers, such as large planks or pieces with complex or unusual joints, were usually lifted in the level below that in which they first appeared. This was a practical measure: many of the large planks required the insertion of support from beneath and this in turn required an adequate working easement all the way around.

Post-depositional effects

Preservation was remarkable, but it is nonetheless important to attempt to quantify the extent to which the timbers found *in situ* represented a true picture of what might originally have been placed in the ground.

There were certain clear indications that post-depositional effects had not been too severe: timbers, both vertical and horizontal, still butted hard up against each other and the sharpened tips of posts had not shrunk from the sides of their holes. Similarly, timbers that had been pegged in place through a mortise still touched or fitted snugly around their pegs. It would appear that the main shrinkage or compression, which was most probably due to drying out, took place radially in the case of roundwood, or transversely in the case of split timber. In effect these timbers had become 'squashed', and in the case of smaller roundwood the squashing was accompanied by considerable sideways splay. The compression noted here was very much worse in the higher than in the lower levels and roundwood was affected more than split timber.

The very highest level was more affected by compression than others. Some pieces of roundwood from Level 1 had been almost flattened and small pegs, which in antiquity were probably driven in flush with the ground surface, protruded above that surface by some 0.1–0.2m (eg Fig 6.15). This would indicate the extent of compression suffered by the highest and driest deposits. It was unusual to find seriously compressed roundwood below Level 1. It has already been noted that the north-facing posts and timbers of Area 8, closer to the Northey landfall, were eroded and displaced by storms and wave action. This type of mechanical damage did not appear to have happened in Area 6. It probably reflects the fact that at this point the timbers were still protected by the makeup of the surrounding timber platform. In addition to qualitative observation of the wood in the field, it has also been possible to quantify taphonomic effects in the statistical study of the wood (Chapter 7).

The subdivisions of Area 6

Problems with conjoining plans

The various subdivisions of Area 6 are shown in Figure 6.1. It took upwards of five years to complete the excavation within the individual subareas of Area 6. There was a gap of four years between the opening of Areas 6A and 6B. At the conclusion of each season, all major timbers that had to be cut off at the baulk between the subareas were identified with Dymo labels, securely pinned in place with at least two stainless steel pins. The baulk itself was then sealed under polythene sheeting. Failure to do this was known to result in massive erosion. Unfortunately, these measures provided an ideal winter dormitory for rats, water voles, and other burrowing creatures that inhabited the dykeside. The colder the winter, the greater the population of uninvited guests. Straw insulation was found to make matters worse. At the start of every season only a few labels survived the winter and the baulk inevitably suffered extensive animal burrowing. These erosional processes explain the narrow void between the plan of Areas 6A and 6B; they also explain the difficulties that were encountered when attempting to marry together once-complete timbers, unless they were of exceptional size. The greatest problems were experienced when attempting to tie up the successive plans of Areas 6A and 6B. Fewer problems were encountered with Areas 6B and 6D, largely because the erection of a storm-proof shelter in 1987 allowed the excavation to be regularly patrolled for vermin.

Area 6A

Following the initial trial trenches and auger surveys carried in 1983 (Pryor *et al* 1986, 4–6), Area 6A was the first open area of any size to be excavated, beginning in the spring of 1984. The first report included plans and photomontage reproductions of Levels 1–4 inclusive (Pryor *et al* 1986, figs 4–5, pls 1–3). These plans, slightly modified to accord with the levels defined in subsequent excavations, are reproduced in the present report. New work is recorded for the first time in the southern part of Area 6A; Levels 5–7 are also reported for the first time. Excavation in Area 6A was completed in 1986.

Area 6B

This area was initially opened in 1985 and a plan of the uprights and the very uppermost parts of Level 1 appeared in the first report (Pryor *et al* 1986, fig 4, lower half of plan). It soon became apparent that it would not be practical to excavate the enlarged area until Area 6A had been completed. The enlargement was, therefore, sealed under polythene and reburied. Work in 6B was resumed in 1987, after the purchase of the storm-proof shelter. Access for the general public also had to be provided; this, together with the shape of the new building and the arrangement of the access gangway, dictated the layout of Area 6B. Area 6B was completed in 1992 and the shelter was moved to cover Area 6D in the spring of 1993.

Area 6C

This small area to the south-east of Area 6B has been excavated intermittently between 1989 and the present. It was initially excavated because the peats had begun to dry out, as the ground involved then formed a promontory. It also proved difficult to erect a satisfactory wind-proof shelter alongside the large shelter, especially in winter when winds blowing along the dyke deflected off the large shelter in turbulent eddies. These would lift packing and protective material off the ground. Several temporary shelters were removed in this way. In many respects, Area 6C has not been a success: it is too small to see general patterns and it is physically cut off from the main excavations. It would have been wiser in retrospect to have concentrated on providing a tough impermeable membrane to prevent drying out along its north-east and north-west faces. This has been done elsewhere (alongside Area 6D) and has proved most successful.

Area 6D

Work began in Area 6D in the late spring of 1993. At the time of writing, all the timbers of Level 1 and some of those of Level 2 have been lifted. It has not been possible for practical reasons, however, to publish detailed numbered plans of timbers lifted in 1994. Unnumbered plans of Levels 1 and 2 are reproduced, therefore, in the detailed level-by-level descriptions that follows.

The posts of the alignment

The posts of the alignment were the only substantial uprights encountered in Area 6 (Fig 6.19). Many small pegs were found in all levels, but there was no evidence to suggest that they ever protruded above the surfaces of the horizontal timbers. These surfaces were probably the ones that people actually walked upon. The posts were arranged in five rows and as the majority in each row was driven into the upper 200–300mm of the terrace gravel underlying the site, the posts provide a constant reference point from one level of horizontal wood to the next. A few additional posts were revealed as the excavations continued, but a comparison of the post density in Level 1 (Fig 6. 20) with that of Level 5 and 6 (Fig 6.73 below) shows a very small proportionate increase in numbers. What has increased in the lower level is the apparent length of the posts, which simply reflects the fact that six levels of horizontal wood have been removed.

With the exception of the alder posts of Row 1, which were on average a few tens of millimetres shorter that the mainly oak posts of Rows 2–5, most of the post tops were revealed some 200–300mm above the timbers of Level 1. Most of the post tops had a wrinkled, gnarled appearance, which suggested that they had rotted off at that level in antiquity and that the weakened tissues had subsequently been compressed. Very few had been cut off, and the few that had been were cut at the level of the horizontal timbers. None had been cut off higher up. In some cases posts were cut off to allow access along a walkway. These instances will be described below. The dating of the five rows of posts will be considered in Chapter 8. The post rows were numbered 1–5, working from south to north (Fig 6.20). In order to place them in their stratigraphic contexts, details of the excavation of the posts will be given after the level-by-level description, which follows directly. First, however, it is necessary to provide brief notes on the general character of the rows.

Row 1

Row 1 was unlike any of the others. It was composed almost entirely of alder (the exception being a single post of poplar or willow). Neither alder nor poplar/willow could be dendrochronologically dated, but alder in particular was found to occur more frequently among horizontal timber in earlier or lower levels. For this reason it has been assumed that the posts of Row 1 in Area 6 were earlier than the other four rows. The individual posts of this row were widely separated and did not appear to have been replaced. There were no tight clusters or groups, as frequently happened within other rows. Perhaps most significantly, Row 1 was breached by a gap or entranceway of considerable width (5.2m) in Area 6D. This is the only substantial gap in any of the post rows found to date and probably marked an area of special significance — dubbed here the 'poolside area'. This area will be considered in greater detail below.

Row 2

Row 2 was almost entirely composed of oak posts, which were more closely spaced than in Row 1.

There was a possible gap or entranceway that coincided with the large gap in Row 1, immediately to the south. The posts of Row 2 appeared to run more parallel to Row 3 than to Row 1 and it is, therefore, possible that the two rows bounded a walkway that ran between them.

Row 3

Row 3 was the central row and by far the densest and most tightly confined of the five rows. There were no possible gaps or entranceways through it. It was mainly composed of oak, but there were significant numbers of non-oak species too.

Row 4

It might be a misnomer to describe Row 4 as a row. There were indications in Level 1 of a short walkway between the posts of Rows 3 and 4 in the west part of Area 6B, but in the west part of Area 6B and in 6A the posts (presumably of Row 4) spread across the intervening space to Row 3. From a strictly archaeological point of view, their straggling, random layout has more in common with a linear *chevaux de frise* than with a post row. As with Row 3, the majority of posts in Row 4 were of oak.

One further point should be made. The posts of Row 4 often leant at varying angles, but always towards the north. This was visible throughout Area 6, and in Area 8. This could be seen as a post-depositional effect, were it not for the fact that the most severe winter storms come from the north. Yet although the prevailing wind is from the south-west, none of the posts to the south of Row 4 appeared to have been affected in the same way. The conclusion is hard to avoid that the posts of Row 4 were deliberately driven in at an angle.

Row 5

When viewed in plan, Row 5 formed a sharp northerly edge to the straggling posts of Row 4, but, unlike that row (with one exception), Row 5 is entirely composed of oak. Although only a short length was exposed (6.5m), the posts were evenly spaced and aligned in a straight line. A similar pattern was observed in Area 8.

Area 6: level-by-level analysis

This analysis considers a wealth of material. Special efforts have been made to structure the data in a manner that allows detail to be appreciated within a recognisable wider context. This has not always been straightforward. Within each level the deposits are considered by Area. Area 6B is divided into four quadrants: north-east, south-east, south-west, and north-west.

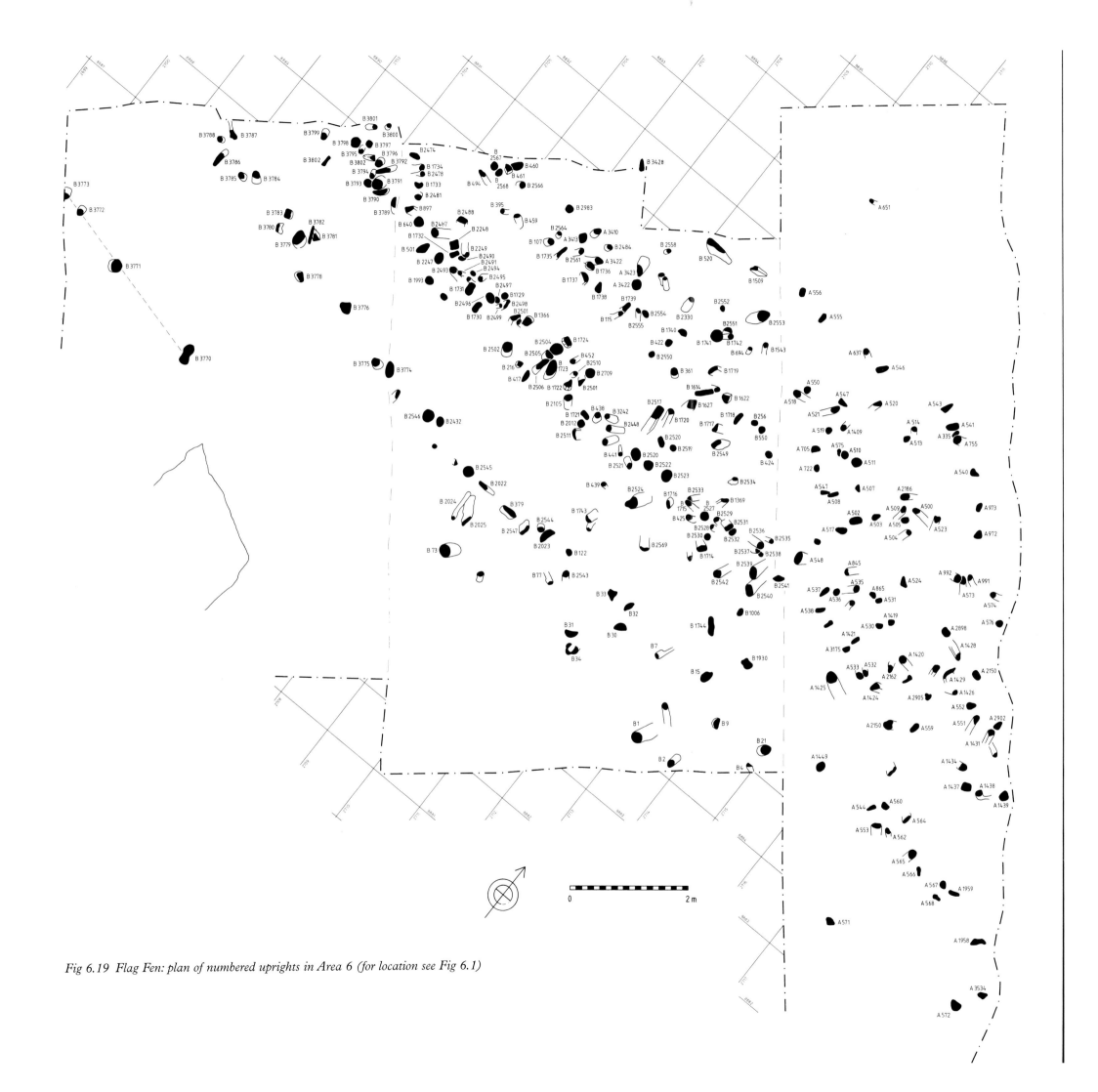

Fig 6.19 Flag Fen: plan of numbered uprights in Area 6 (for location see Fig 6.1)

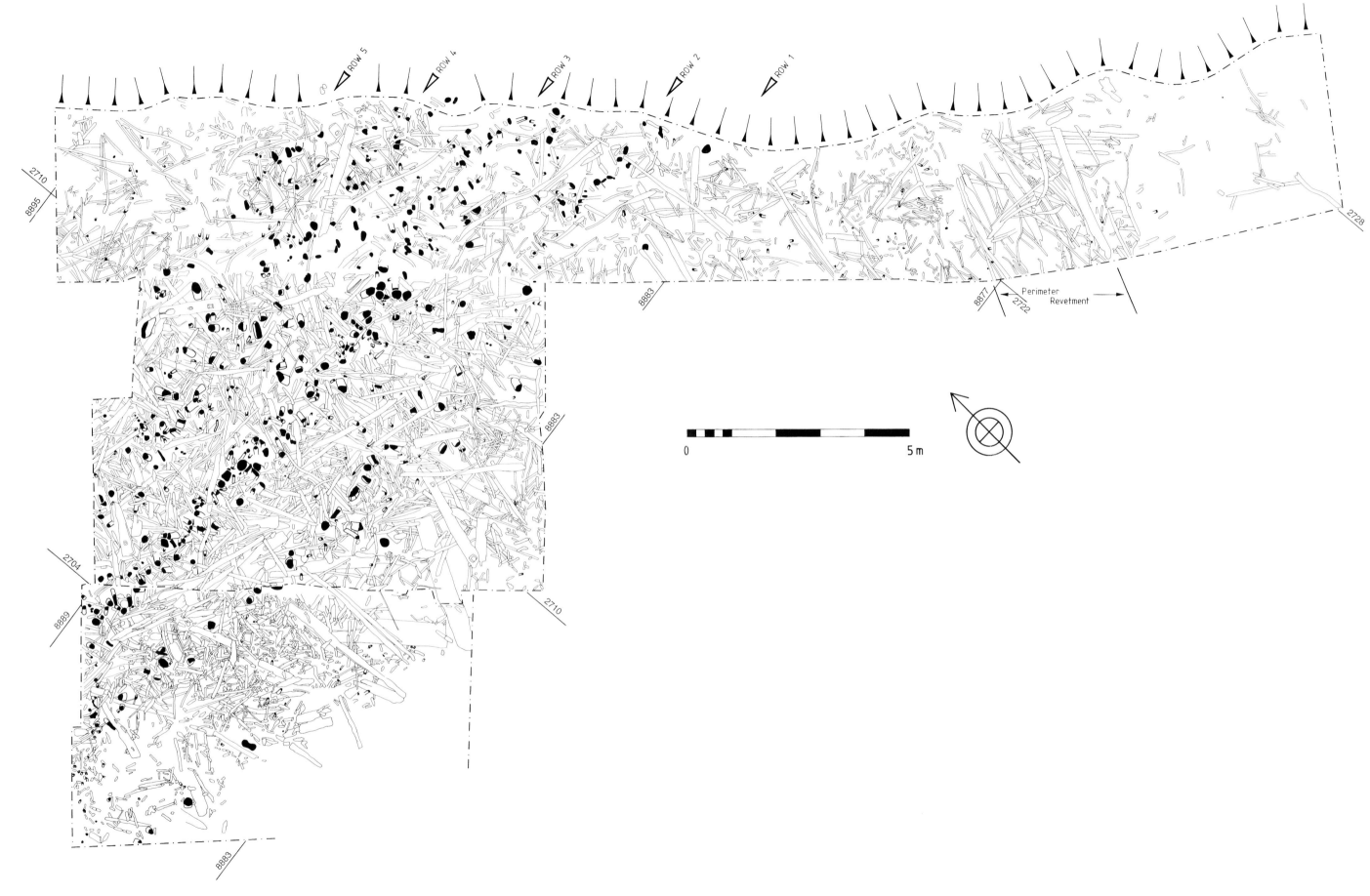

ROW 5 ROW 4 ROW 3 ROW 2 ROW 1

2710
8895

2728

8883

8877
2722
Perimeter
Revetment

8883

2704

8889

2710

8883

0   5 m

Fig 6.20 Flag Fen, Areas 6A, 6B, and 6D. General plan of wood exposed in Level 1 (for location see Fig 6.1)

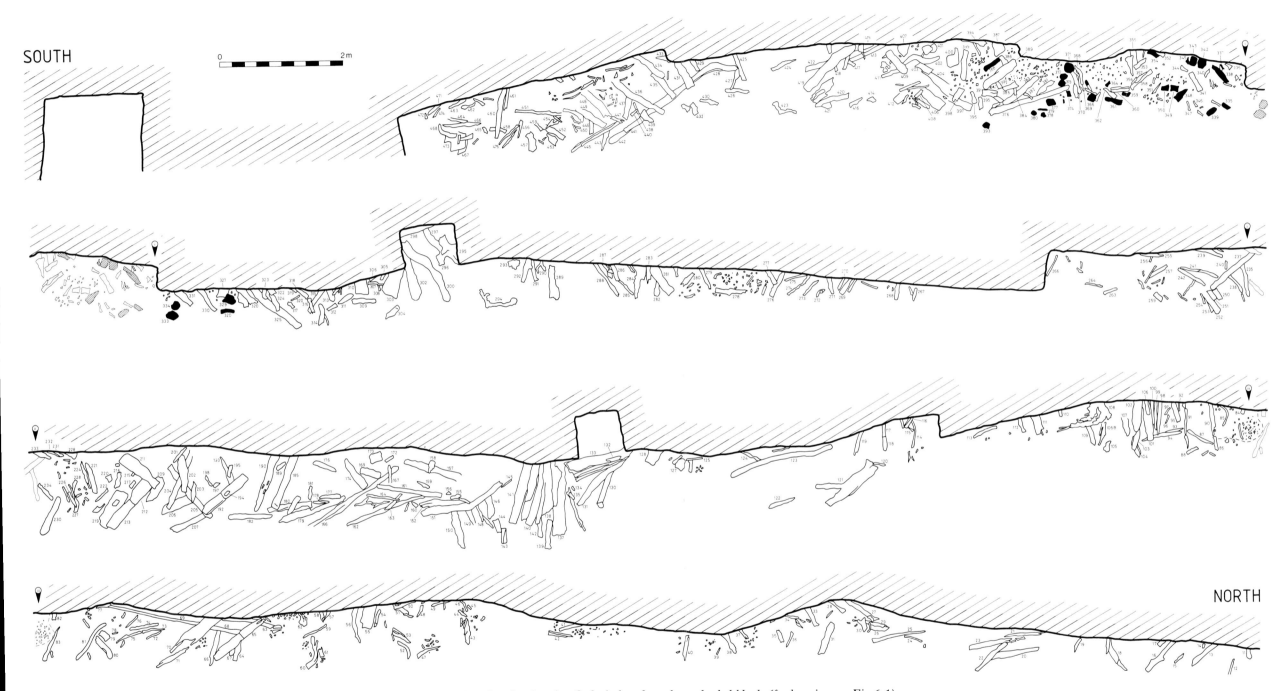

SOUTH

NORTH

Fig 6.9 Flag Fen (1982): the Mustdyke dykeside exposure; wood numbers were assigned to the A series. Oak timbers have been shaded black (for location see Fig 6.1)

Level 1

Area 6A

This area was affected more than any other by the drying-out that followed the deepening of the Mustdyke in 1982. These effects were most severe in the uppermost levels.

The post alignment

There were two principal points of interest at this level (Fig 6.21). The first was the two long roundwood poles that lay along the axis of the alignment, one north of Row 2, the other between Rows 3 and 4. These were not fixed to the ground by pegs, as was the case with foundation timbers, and were considered in the first report to be collapsed roof or superstructure timbers (Pryor *et al* 1986, pl 7b); the rejection of the building hypothesis makes that explanation impossible. At present their original role remains unclear.

The second point of interest was not identified in the first report. Close inspection of the plan (Fig 6.21) revealed a number of smaller timbers and possible wattles that ran to the north of Row 5 and on either side of it. When compared with plans of Levels 2 and 4 (Figs 6.40 and 6.44 below), it is possible that this wattlework might have been a remnant of a revetment along the north side of the post alignment. The possible revetment along Row 5 closely resembled another possible revetment along Row 5 exposed in Area 8 (Fig 6.14).

Level 1 revealed much sand and fine gravel around the horizontal timbers between Rows 2 and 3, although greater quantities were to be found in Level 2.

The perimeter revetment

This feature has already been discussed in the first report and a photomontage has been published (Pryor *et al* 1986, pl 1). Although some of the planks were substantial, especially A4614 (Fig 6.22), the structure

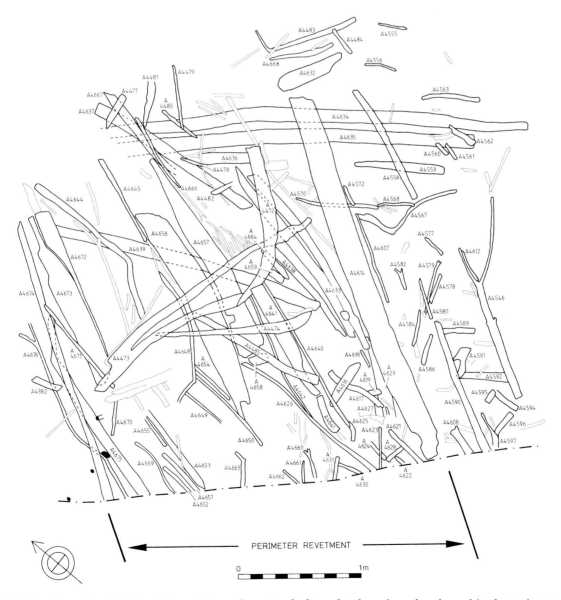

Fig 6.22 Flag Fen, Area 6A, Levels 1 and 2, south-east end of trench: plan of numbered wood in the perimeter revetment

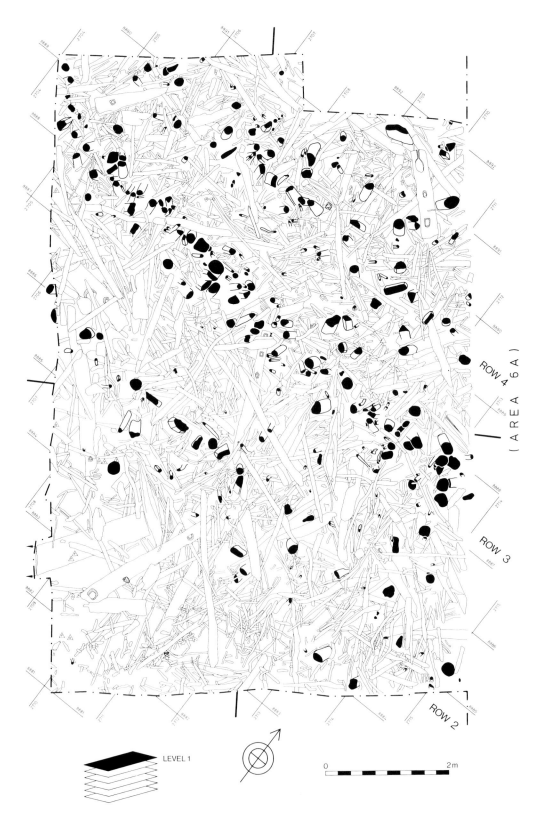

ROW 4 (AREA 6A)

ROW 3

ROW 2

LEVEL 1

0   2m

Fig 6.23 Flag Fen, Area 6B, Level 1: general plan (for location see Fig 6.20)

itself was of shallow construction. Five of the main Level 1 planks were of split oak (Fig 6.22: A4633, A4641, A4657, and A4673). The revetment measured approximately 2.7m wide. A few bearers were laid transversely to the main planks: three were visible in Level 1 (Fig 6.20, A4634–5 and A4639); another was encountered in Level 2 (Fig 6.40: A4397).

The edge of the revetment showed some signs of damage, perhaps caused by wind or wave action. For example, the two bearers A4634 and A4635 protruded about 1.6m beyond the large plank A4614. There were also three roundwood timbers (A4558, A4546, and A4590) that might once have been part of an outer wall or log-pile revetment, and were later largely removed.

Fig 6.24 Flag Fen, Area 6B, Level 1: photomontage of south-west part of the excavations

Beyond these timbers there was an abrupt void where very little wood was present. The few scraps at the extreme south-east edge of the excavation were most probably natural driftwood (Fig 6.21). Given this slight evidence for erosional damage, it is perhaps worth noting that the revetment showed very little evidence for the pegging down of timbers; nor were there any signs that gravel or stones had been used, as was frequently the case in, for example, the crannogs of Scotland (Morrison 1985, fig 3.7). This would indicate that the revetment was located in a position where storm damage was not anticipated.

Area 6B

Area 6B had been the largest open-area exposure of wood at Flag Fen, prior to the opening of Area 8; it measured 6.6 × 9.9m (Fig 6.22). Preservation of Level 1 in Area 6B was very much better than in Area 6A, which was closer to the dykeside (Fig 6.23; cf Pryor *et al* 1986, pl 2). Like Area 6A alongside it, Area 6B was characterised by large timbers, including a number of substantial split oak planks. Many of these carried mortise holes and might have been reused (Fig 6.23).

Another element was a few long roundwood logs or large poles, which lay on top of the main mass of timbers. This feature had also been noted in Area 6A (above). These logs might be clearly seen in the photomontage (Fig 6.24) and in general views of the excavations (Figs 6.25–6). As already noted, their original purpose is hard to explain: they might have fallen from the post row superstructure, or perhaps served as markers at the very end of the final phase of use of the post alignment.

Area 6B: north-east and south-east quadrants

These quadrants are detailed in Figures 6.27 and 6.28. The white sand and fine gravel noted in Area 6A continued south-west into Area 6D. It was thickest between the posts of Rows 2 and 3 where a number of thinly split oak planks were laid on the ground as a walkway between the uprights (Fig 6.25). These planks included B125, B270, B18, B126, and B160 (Fig 6.27: grid 2712 8885). The northern side of Row 3 also included a walkway, but it was slightly narrower and less formally floored with planking. This walkway had also been spread with sand and gravel, but in smaller quantities.

Fig 6.25 Flag Fen, Area 6B, Level 1: view, looking east, of planks between posts of Rows 2 (right) and 3 (left)

It ran parallel to and immediately north of grid northing 8888 (Fig 6.27). To the north, the posts of Row 4 formed a more irregular edge to the walkway than the posts of Row 2, to the south. In a few cases, 'stray' posts of Row 4 impinged significantly upon the walkway (see eg Fig 6.26 and Fig 6.27, at grid 2711 889).

The walkways on either side of the central Row 3 were blocked off or restricted in two areas, close to the north-east edge of the excavations. The posts blocking the walkway formed by Rows 3 and 4 (Fig 6.27: grid 2710 8888) were both larger and more closely spaced than those that restricted the more southerly walkway of Rows 2 and 3 (Fig 6.28, grid 2713 8885). The two sets of 'blocking' posts can be seen most clearly at Level 3, by which time the height of the uprights relative to the horizontals had become greater. The Level 3 general view (Fig 6.45 below) is particularly clear — the peg immediately beyond the scale in the foreground shows the original surface of the Level 1 walkway. In this view the narrow, but densely packed post row is Row 3. In the background, the blocking posts can be seen. Those of the Rows 3–4 walkway lean to the north, as do the other posts of Row 4. In the distance can be seen the two central blocking posts of the

Rows 2–3 walkway; all the other blocking posts of the Rows 2–3 walkway were cut off at ground level in antiquity. Only posts B15 and B21 were left intact and these were positioned axially, ie one behind another, in the very centre of the walkway. Here, they would have provided a check or impediment (but not a barrier) to access along the walkway. The blocking posts to the north of Row 3, on the other hand, were very much more substantial. The 'walkway' of Rows 3–4 was narrower and far less robustly constructed than that of Rows 2–3. There were fewer planks and greater use had been made of small roundwood (Fig 6.29).

Area 6B: south-west quadrant

The south-west quadrant at Level 1 (Fig 6.30) contained a rather enigmatic deposit of timber immediately to the south of Row 1. It consisted of a zone of seemingly unused large oak timbers (Figs 6.30–32). The big timbers were largely confined within and to the south of the gap between posts B73 (grid 2708 8884) and B31 (grid 2711 8884) of Row 1. A small, near-complete, fineware dimple-based Late Bronze Age jar (below, Fig 9.2, 7) had been placed alongside B73,

Fig 6.26 Flag Fen, Area 6B, Level 1: view looking east along the posts of Row 3, showing two possible walkways between Row 3 and Rows 2 (right) and 4 (left)

Fig 6.27 Flag Fen, Area 6B, Level 1: plan of numbered wood in north-east quadrant (for location see Fig 6.23)

Fig 6.28 Flag Fen, Area 6B, Level 1: plan of numbered wood in south-east quadrant (for location see Fig 6.23)

a large post at Level 1. In Levels 4 and 5, this post was thought to form part of a transverse segment boundary. To the south, a massive, tangentially split oak plank B63 (grid 2705 8883), ran out of Area 6B to the south-west. It was dressed square at its north-east end. Its other end (in Area 6D) was V-shaped and lopsided, characteristic of the felled end of a tree trunk, seen in axial section. Two Late Bronze Age (post-Deverel Rimbury) plain coarseware potsherds were found below the plank when it was lifted.

Next to the squared butt of B56 was another large split oak timber, B61 (grid 2709 8884) This had a long, pencil-like sharpened point, but, as there was no clay or gravel adhering to it, this suggests it had never been driven into the ground (Fig 6.33). A large, double-mortised plank (B51: grid 2709 8882) had been placed south of B53, directly upon B61 and another oak tenoned plank, B52 to the south-west (grid 2710 8882). Two other planks (B45 and B47) also formed part of the deposit. Plank B45 lay above B51 and B47.

Fig 6.29 Flag Fen, Area 6B, Level 1: vertical view of wood in south-east quadrant. The prominent mortised piece is wood B154 (for location see Fig 6.23)

All six oak timbers were in direct contact with each other and were almost certainly contemporary. Janet Neve has shown that timbers B63 and B61 were probably split from the same tree (below, Table 8.3).

Since the vast majority of large timbers were found in Level 1, they can therefore be dated to the latest phase at Flag Fen. The posts of Row 1 were, however, probably driven into the ground some 3–4 centuries earlier (Chapter 16). By the time the later timbers were deposited, the earlier posts must have been rotten stumps protruding just 300mm above the new surface that was then being built up. It is notable that the earlier posts, which must have been completely waterlogged by this stage, were not kicked over or removed. On the contrary, the later timbers appear to have been placed in the ground, together with the small ceramic vessel, in a manner that respected the earlier posts.

Area 6B: north-west quadrant

The central line of posts, Row 3, formed a most remarkable and dense physical barrier (Figs 6.34 and 6.38). On average, there were some 12 posts to the metre. Without discounting post-depositional effects, it was notable to what extent the posts of Row 3 had remained vertical. There was certainly no tendency to lean in a particular direction, like, for example, the

posts of Row 1, which leaned to the south, or those of Row 4, which leaned to the north. The close packing of the posts in Row 3 is well illustrated in a vertical view (Fig 6.35).

A feature of Row 3 not shared by other post rows was the inclusion of angled horizontal timbers that breached or traversed the row (Fig 6.36). Examples in this quadrant included B91 (grid 2705 8888), B108 (grid 2706 8887), B114 (grid 2707 8888), and B358–9 (grid 2709 8887). There is no evidence that any of these timbers had collapsed, nor had they been pegged into position so as to underpin timbers (many examples of this practice will be seen in Level 3 and below). It appears rather that they provided very restricted access through an otherwise almost solid barrier.

Area 6D: the 'poolside area'

Where part of Area 6D was devoid of timbers, the peaty silts contained numerous fragments of water snail shells (Charles French personal communication). This area is interpreted as an ancient pool or area of open water, named the 'poolside area'. The timbers of the post alignment close by it were remarkable in a number of respects (Figs 6.37–9). The posts of Row 1 were breached by a gap some 5.2m wide, most of which fell within Area 6D (Fig 6.19).

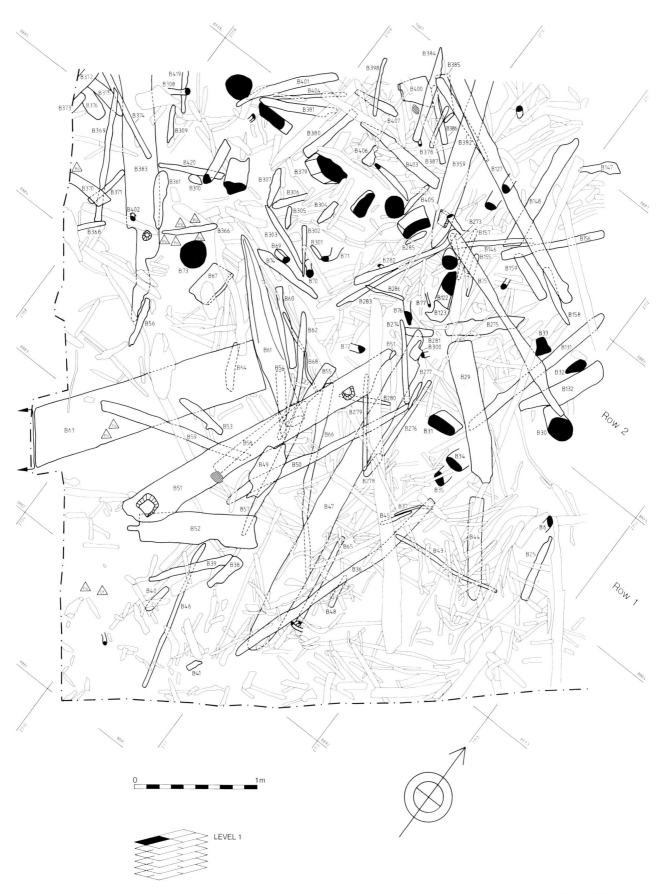

Fig 6.30 Flag Fen, Area 6B, Level 1: plan of numbered wood in south-west quadrant (for location see Fig 6.23)

Fig 6.31 Flag Fen, Area 6B, Level 1: low oblique view of wood in south-west quadrant. The mortised piece in the foreground is B51 (for location see Fig 6.23)

Fig 6.32 Flag Fen, Area 6B, Level 1: vertical view of wood in south-west quadrant. The double-mortised piece is B51 (for location see Fig 6.23)

Fig 6.33 Flag Fen, Area 6B, Level 1: posts of Row 2. The mortised upright is wood B379. The large pointed timber between B379 and the Row 1 post in the foreground is the unused upright, B63

Fig 6.34 Flag Fen, Area 6B, Level 1: general view of the posts of Row 3, looking west. Note the posts of Rows 1 and 2 in the background

Fig 6.35 Flag Fen, Area 6B, Level 1: vertical view of the posts of Row 3. The posts of Row 4 are to the lower left

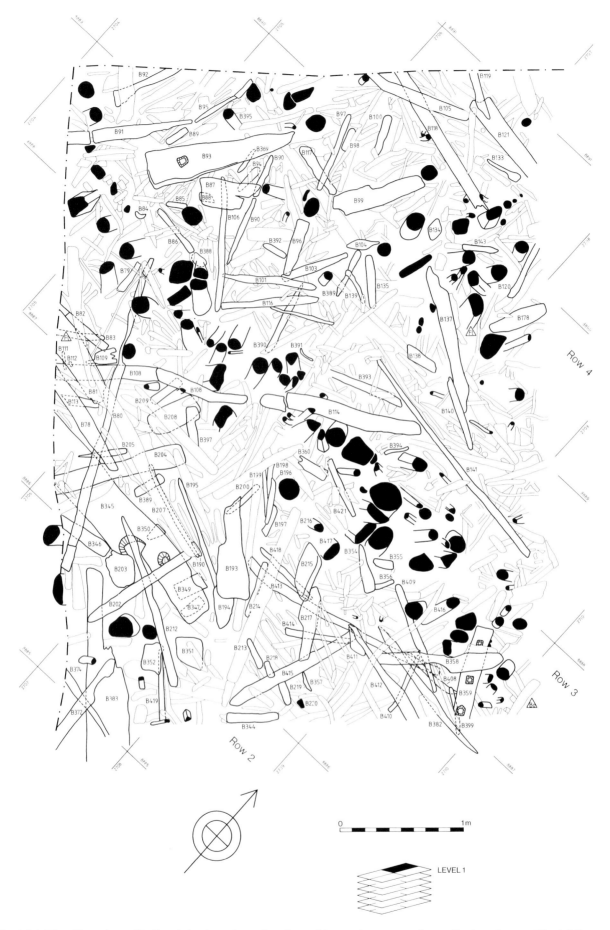

Fig 6.36 Flag Fen, Area 6B, Level 1: plan of numbered wood in north-west quadrant (for location see Fig 6.23)

B63

ROW 2

ROW 3

ROW 1

△ S = SCABBARD △ 29

▦ = LINE of POSSIBLE PORTAL

0   2m

Fig 6.37 Flag Fen, Area 6D, Level 1: general plan (for location see Fig 6.20)

Fig 6.38 Flag Fen, Area 6D, Level 2: general plan, prior to lifting (for location see Fig 6.20)

The gap coincided with a kink or step in the alignment of Row 1: in Area 6B the posts of Rows 1 and 2 were about 1.1m apart; in Area 6D they were 2.5m apart.

The large oak plank (B63) from the zone of big timbers in Area 6B (Fig 6.30), was found in Area 6D at its south-east corner (Fig 6.37). Immediately next to it was found another plank of comparable size and quality, yet to be assigned a number (Fig 6.37, XX). The two planks might prove to have been split from the same oak butt. Two large oak timbers lay above plank XX, and there were others close by. Plank XX was fully exposed in Level 2 (Fig 6.38) and was found to be dressed square at each end and to possess a small square mortise hole close to its north-west end. Additional large oak timbers were exposed in the area between plank XX and the nearest post of Row 1.

The posts of Row 1 were all of alder and were widely spaced. The post that marked the edge of the gap was, however, unusually large (Fig 6.19: post B3770, and Fig 6.39). Two other unusually large alder posts, found in Rows 2 and 3 at right-angles to Row 1, were aligned almost exactly on B3770 (Fig 6.19: posts B3779 and B3793).

The three posts together could have formed the uprights of an entranceway or portal structure (Fig 6.37). If this was a portal, it formed a boundary between the relatively small roundwood and woodchip makeup of the surfaces between Rows 1, 2, and 3 and the altogether different zone of big timbers. This change can clearly be seen in the plans of Levels 1 and 2 (Figs 6.37–8). It will be suggested below that the portal formed part of a major transverse or segment boundary, of which other elements only became visible in Levels 4 and 5.

Approximately a metre east of the hypothetical portal between Rows 1 and 2, many dog bones were recovered; these bones clearly occurred in a group, but did not appear to have been articulated *in situ*. A copper-alloy decorated La Tène II scabbard plate of an iron short sword (Fig 10.11, 273) was found close to the possible portal (Fig 6.37). The scabbard plate had been deliberately damaged. At least two fragments lay in peaty muds perhaps 50–100mm above the timbers of Level 1 (Coombs and Pryor 1994). As with the dog bones of Levels 1 and 2, the presence of the scabbard plate is difficult to account for in other than ritual contexts.

A striking feature of Area 6D was the absence of timber south of Row 1. A test pit within Area 6D was excavated in 1993 to investigate this phenomenon. The pit revealed a few stray timbers and a single post (probably of willow). The soil matrix was fine grained and probably water sorted. There were also numerous fragments of snail shells of aquatic species (Charles French personal communication). As this area was probably an open pool, the zone of large timbers might represent efforts to consolidate the more than usually spongey ground close to it. The spread of dog bones found

Fig 6.39 Flag Fen, Area 6D, Level 1: close-up of large oak planks in east part of the excavations, within the 'poolside area'

within the timbers of Levels 1 and 2 extended into the muds of the pool's sides, adjacent to the post alignment.

One final point, mentioned briefly above, deserves further discussion. The possible portal posts of Rows 2 and 3 were in alder, a species that was not otherwise encountered in Row 2, and was by no means common in Row 3. This might suggest that the structure was early in the Flag Fen sequence. Alternatively, the use of alder for such structures might have been significant for its own sake; perhaps a structure first built in alder was subsequently maintained in that wood, despite the widespread availability of oak in the later periods. Immediately east of the portal post in Row 2 was a gap of a metre, with another slightly narrower one beyond. No corresponding gap was found in the closely packed posts of Row 3.

The surface of the 'walkway' between the posts of Rows 2 and 3 in Level 1 was significantly higher than elsewhere. It was also spread with quantities of sand and fine gravel. Sand and gravel was also spread around the timbers within the portal, but was concentrated around the two gaps in the posts of Row 2 — as if it had been 'walked' through on the feet of people entering the poolside area from the main walkway. At both levels, the ground surface between the posts of Rows 1 and 2 was soft, peaty, and inadequately made up with wood or timber. It was as if that area had been abandoned in favour of the main walkway between Rows 2 and 3. This might have continued in use, perhaps intermittently, well into the Iron Age (if the sword scabbard plate can be regarded as evidence).

In summary, it is suggested that the poolside area was of ritual importance. In the latest phases it was entered via a walkway between Rows 2 and 3. Visitors passed through an alder portal, which spanned Rows 1 to 3 and turned towards the poolside through two gaps in the posts of Row 2. The soft ground around the edge of the pool was consolidated with very large oak timbers. Evidence for ritual is provided by the discovery of numerous dog bones and the damaged plate of a La Tène sword scabbard. These, however, are manifestations of Iron Age or very late late Bronze Age activity. The origins of the poolside ritual area must lie in the possible portal and the large gap between the posts of Row 1, both of Middle Bronze Age date.

Level 2

The horizontal wood of Level 2 was more tightly packed together than that of Level 1 (Fig 6.40). It also included fewer large oak timbers. In all the subareas of Area 6, the timbers of Level 2 were remarkably well preserved and had clearly not been subjected to some of the post-depositional erosion (and possibly redeposition) that had affected wood in Level 1. The presence of much sand and fine gravel, almost entirely confined to the walkway between the posts of Rows 2 and 3, also indicated that this level had escaped significant post-depositional erosion.

Area 6A

The principal new feature of Level 2 in Area 6A was only fully appreciated as a result of opening Areas 6C and 6D, several seasons after its original excavation. The feature in question was a narrow wood-free zone to the south of Row 1, which was orientated approximately north-east–south-west (Fig 6.41). This wood-free zone was not the result of later activity as several timbers intruded into it and had not been truncated. A similar wood-free zone was found along the south-east and south-west sides of Area 6C; it continued into Area 6D via the south corner of Area 6B (Fig 6.42), where it widened out into the pool, south of the post alignment.

The full width of the wood-free zone in Areas 6C and 6D could not be ascertained, but it was wider in Area 6C than in 6A. The narrower channel of Area 6A might have drained into the larger pool. A point of some interest is the width of the wood-free zone in Area 6A. In Level 2 it was approximately 1.5m wide, but in the level below (Fig 6.53 below) it had become very much more substantial and better defined. Its width in Level 3 was about 2.0m.

At the southern end of Area 6A the edge of the platform was less sharply defined than in Level 1 and it had also spread some 2m further south-east. It is possible, however, that this spread represents a natural accumulation of driftwood, as it was less tightly packed than wood elsewhere on the platform and was characteristically composed of small roundwood. One large oak plank was found below two others in Level 1, which ran parallel to it. This lower oak plank was also part of the edge revetment.

A wattle 'cavity wall' was found in Row 5 on either side of the large mortised oak plank considered in the first report to be a threshold or doorway (Pryor *et al* 1986, fig 6). It is probable that this wattlework formed a revetment along the post alignment's north side. The 'threshold' would have provided restricted access from the north side of the alignment into the narrow walkway between Rows 4 and 5.

Area 6B

The horizontal wood of Area 6B, Level 2 was generally smaller and more tightly-packed than that of Level 1 (compare Fig 6.42 with 6.23). Much of it was pegged into position with small pegs, often made from pieces split from larger oak timbers. The southern corner of the excavation was notably less densely packed than the rest of Area 6B. Since the peaty matrix in this area included a large number of water snail shells (Charles French personal communication), this most probably formed a continuation of the pool in Area 6D, discussed above. Large split oak planks were less frequently found than in Level 1. Level 2 was instead characterised by many straight roundwood logs, often (but not invariably) of oak (Fig 6.43). Removal of the Level 1 timbers revealed a number of smaller posts within and around the main posts of Rows 3 and 4 (Fig 6.44). Quantities of sand and fine gravel between the posts of Rows 2 and 3 strongly suggested that this area had been used as a walkway. There was also a narrower walkway between Rows 3 and 4. At a point where the two rows almost touched, a plank had been laid between them to allow access both through and across (Fig 6.45). This plank (B1596) lay at the very base of Level 2; it is illustrated with timbers of Level 3 in Figure 6.60 (grid 2709 8888).

The alignment of the longer, larger logs, which mostly lay at the base of Level 2 or within Level 3, was usually parallel with, or at right angles to the post rows. This arrangement had an informal box-like structure. It can be seen quite clearly in the photomontage (Fig 6.43), but it is also visible in a low oblique view taken along Row 3 (Fig 6.46). In the latter view, the box-like arrangement of logs can be seen to start at lower left; the long log runs away from the camera towards a large upright in Row 4. It is pegged at the far end. Another log then runs right at right angles through the posts of Row 3 to join yet another log, which runs away from the camera at the base of the Row 2 posts.

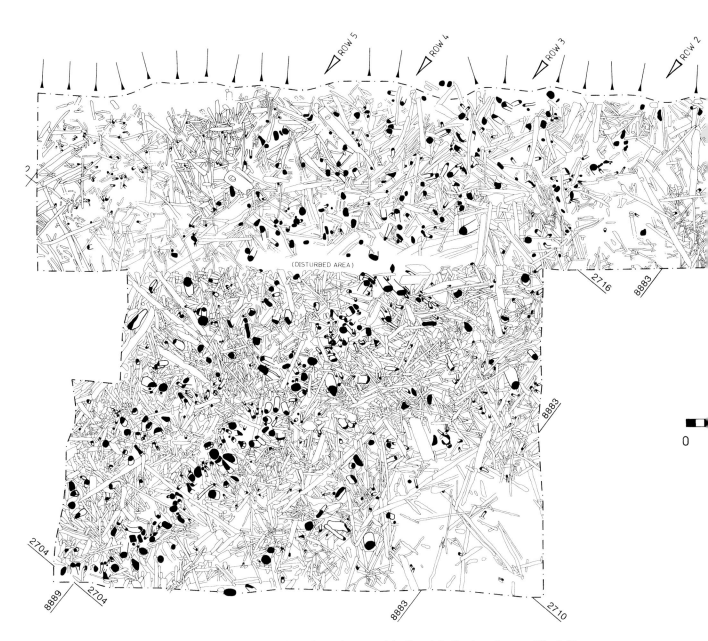

ROW 5

ROW 4

ROW 3

RCW 2

2

2716

8883

8883

2704

8889

2704

8883

2710

(DISTURBED AREA)

0

Fig 6.40 Flag Fen, Areas 6A and 6B: general plan of wood exposed in Level 2 (for location see Fig 6.1)

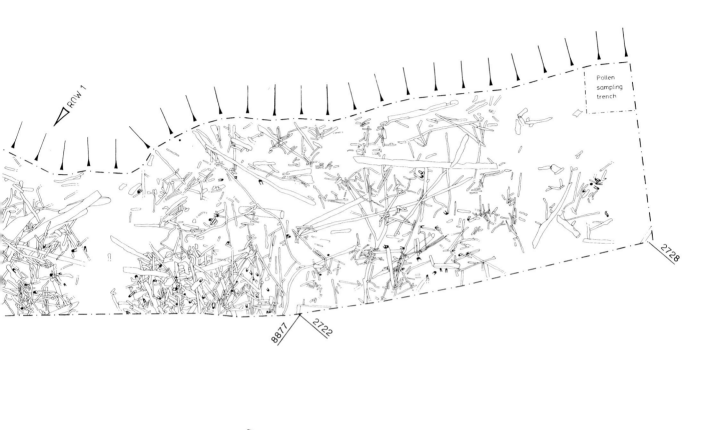

ROW 1

Pollen
sampling
trench

2728

8877   2722

5m

Area 6B: the north-east quadrant

This quadrant contained a dense spread of wood (Fig 6.47). The split oak posts of Row 5 (eg B520: grid 2709 8891) were accompanied by one or possibly two parallel oak planks, of which one (B480: grid 2708 8891) was almost fully exposed. It was pegged in place at its east end. At least two other oak posts were present directly outside the excavated trench on line with (and to the east of) the large split upright, B520. The end of another oak plank, B652 (grid 2707 8891) immediately north of the east end of B480, suggests perhaps that the two planks were perhaps the remains of a sill plate beneath a 'cavity wall' revetment

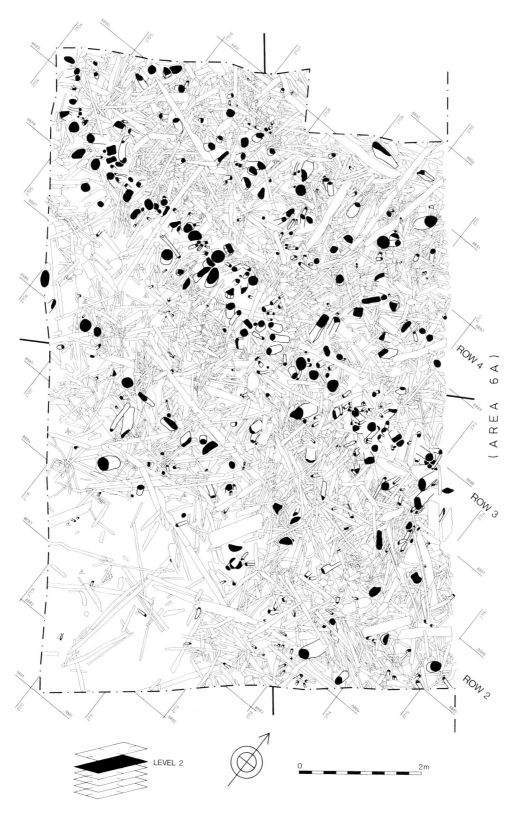

LEVEL 2

0   2m

Fig 6.42 Flag Fen, Area 6B, Level 2: general plan (for location see Fig 6.40)

114

Fig 6.43 Flag Fen, Area 6B, Level 2: photomontage. The southern portion had not been excavated at this stage

Fig 6.44 Flag Fen, Area 6B, level 2: excavation in progress with the posts of Row 4 (foreground) and Row 3

Fig 6.45 Flag Fen, Area 6B, Level 2: view across the excavation, looking west, showing post Rows 2–4 (from left to right)

Fig 6.46 Flag Fen, Area 6B, Level 2: view east along post Row 3 (centre right at scale)

(Pryor *et al* 1986, fig 8). Alternatively, the plank and post arrangement might have acted as some sort of revetment in its own right, without the need for any further superstructure.

The underlying support timbers beneath the dispersed posts of row 4 appeared to tie together the posts of Rows 4 and 5 (eg B524: grid 2709 8891 and B530: grid 2710 8890). As in Area 8 (above), the posts of Row 4 were sharply bounded to the north by Row 5. These possible 'cross-ties' between the two rows suggest that Rows 4 and 5 might be broadly contemporary. Although the main orientation of the horizontal timbers was either at right angles to or parallel with the post rows, a few timbers in the south half of the quadrant were orientated north-east–south-west, ie diagonal to the post rows. This orientation was dominant in the south-east quadrant.

The south corner of the quadrant contained the closest concentration of posts of Row 3. Between Rows 3 and 4 a large number of small pieces of wood, woodchips, and so on, might have formed a walkway or hardstanding; this wood was embedded in a matrix composed largely of peat with quantities of sand and fine gravel. Four large split oak posts in grid square 2710 8888 narrowed the gap between Rows 3 and 4. An oak plank was just visible in plan below the smaller wood of the walkway. This timber (B1596) lay at the interface of Levels 2 and 3 and is shown in Figures 6.45 and 6.60 (below) at grid 2709 8888 (Level 3). An oak log (B750: grid 2710 8888), perhaps a reinforcement or support, appeared to have been jammed between a group of smaller posts in Row 3.

Area 6B: the south-east quadrant

The extraordinarily close network of wood in this quadrant was among the most complex to excavate and record at Flag Fen (Fig 6.48). At the north end of the quadrant were the posts of Row 3. To the south were Rows 2 and 1 (B1 and B2: grid 2713 8884). Running due north from B1 was an irregular line of posts at right angles to the main post rows. This was continued in the north-east quadrant by two groups of small stakes or pegs that ran between Rows 3 and 4 (Fig

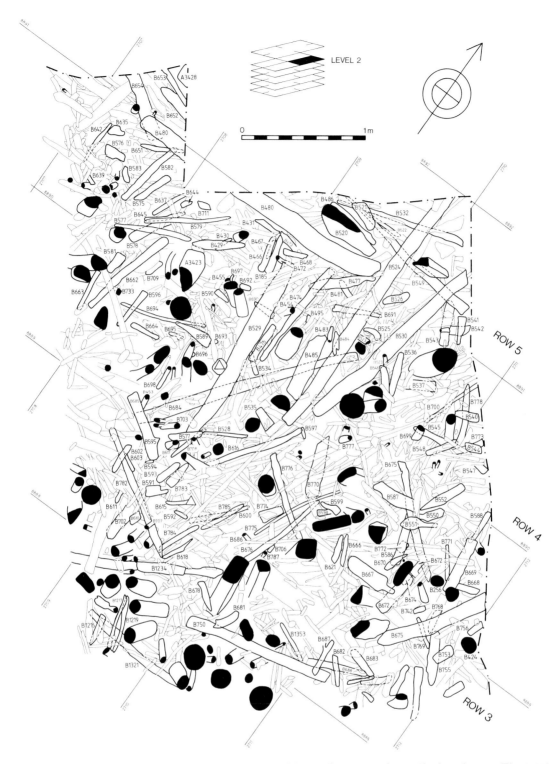

Fig 6.47 Flag Fen, Area 6B, Level 2: plan of numbered wood in north-east quadrant (for location see Fig 6.42)

6.47: grids 2709 8888 and 2708 8889). These two groups were separated by a narrow gap or pathway that included a number of flat split oak timber offcuts (eg B591–4). These posts or pegs might have formed part of a cross-wall or screen, but they did not appear to have been joined by wattle or any other form of reinforcement, either at this level or below. A similar, but slighter and shorter row of small pegs was found to run parallel to (but south of) the group just described in Level 5, between Rows 1 and 2 (Fig 6.80 below,

B2190, B2214, and B3139: grid 2712 8884). These stakes might have provided anchorage for an earlier version of the later cross-wall.

As was noted in the discussion of the north-east quadrant, the dominant orientation of larger horizontal timbers in this quadrant was north-east–south-west, ie diagonal to the axis of the main post rows. Two groups of timbers were orientated in this fashion. The longer and larger ran the width of the walkway between Rows 3 and 2. They abutted and were sometimes

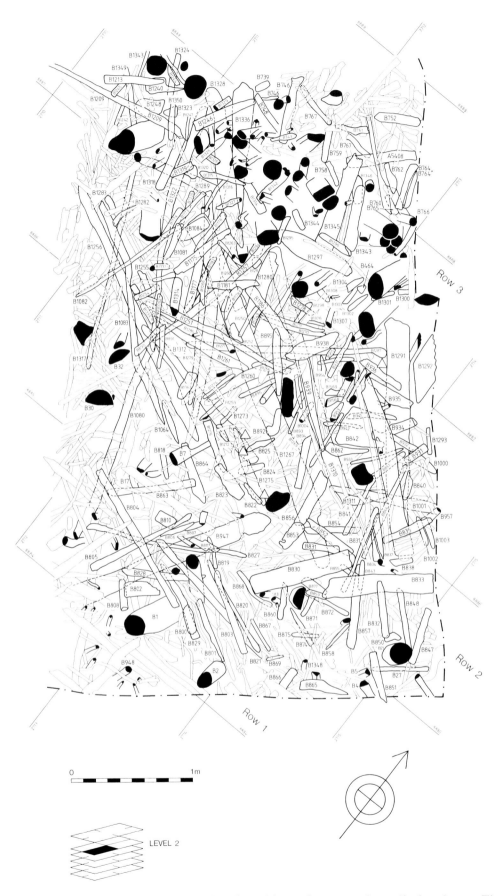

Fig 6.48 Flag Fen, Area 6B, Level 2: plan of numbered wood in south-east quadrant (for location see Fig 6.42)

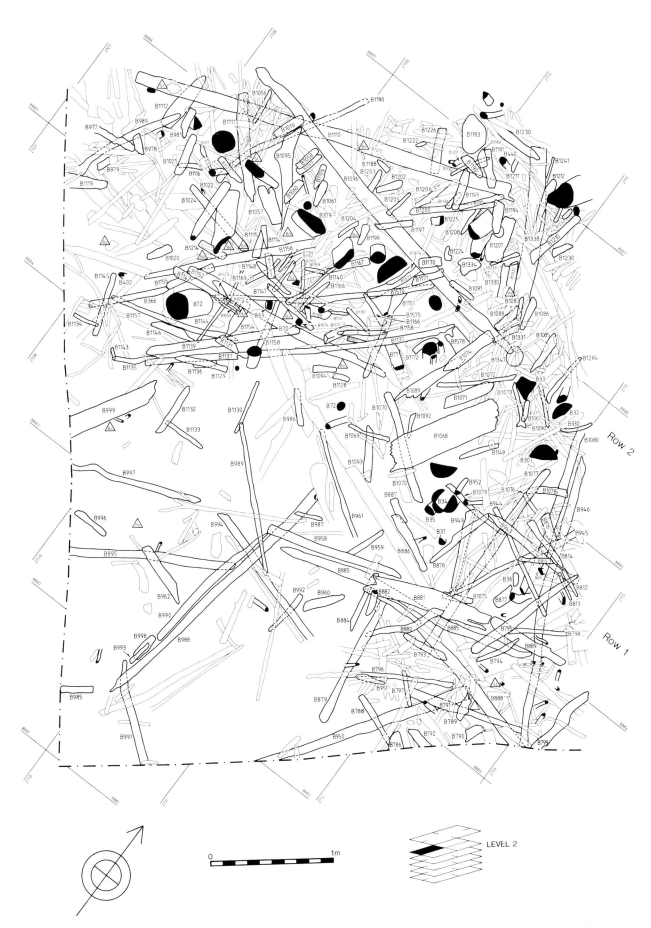

Fig 6.49 Flag Fen, Area 6B, Level 2: plan of numbered wood in south-west quadrant (for location see Fig 6.42)

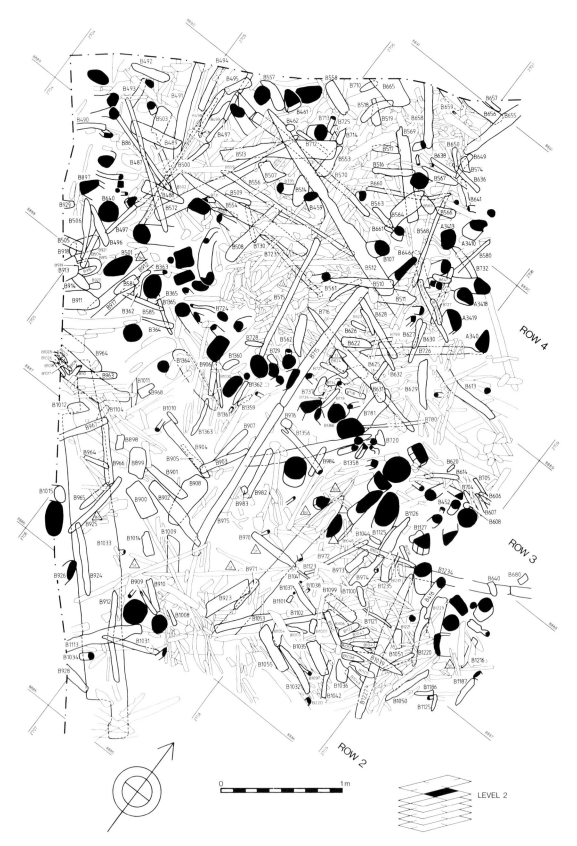

Fig 6.50 Flag Fen, Area 6B, Level 2: plan of numbered wood in north-west quadrant (for location see Fig 6.42)

pegged against the posts of both rows at either end. This must indicate that both rows were broadly contemporary. One plank (B1267: grid 2713 8885) measured 3.15m in length. The second diagonal arrangement of wood was found at a slightly higher

level within Level 2. The wood (mainly roundwood) was shorter and smaller than that just described and had been placed between the posts of Rows 1 and 2. In this instance, the horizontal wood had not been integrated within the uprights with such care, and it is

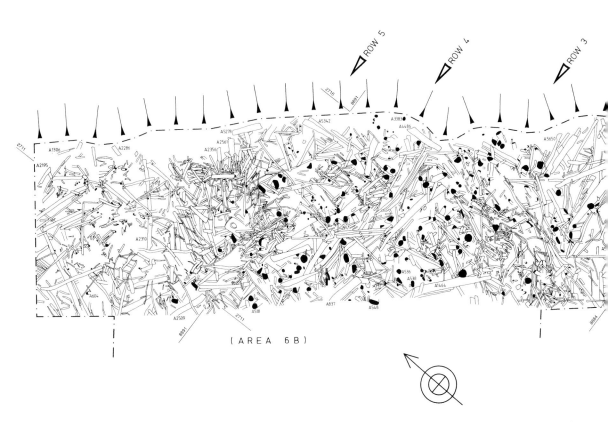

ROW 5

ROW 4

ROW 3

(AREA 6B)

Fig 6.53 Flag Fen, Area 6A, Level 3: general plan of wood, with principal pieces numbered (for location see

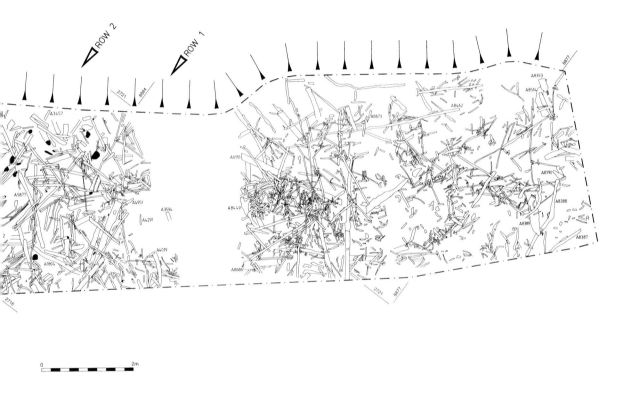

ROW 2

ROW 1

A3457

A5877

A4951

A4291

A3594

A1804

A4019

2716

A6110

A8449

A8686

A8673

A8462

A8393

A8514

A8390

A8388

A8389

A8387

2721

8877

2721

8994

2721

8877

0   2m

Fig 6.52)

probable that this deposit represents secondary consolidation of the surface at a time when the posts of Row 1 had rotted off.

Area 6B: the south-west quadrant

The south corner of the quadrant contained far less wood than elsewhere (Fig 6.49). The matrix contained many water snail shells (Charles French personal communication). The long, straight timbers of Level 2 in this area were probably laid down to provide a firm base or foundation for the much larger timbers of Level 1. Many had been pegged in place, eg (from west–east) B999 (grid 2708 8883), B886 (grid 2711 8884), B988 (grid 2710 8882), B885 (grid 2710 8883), B879 (grid 2711 8882), and B950 (grid 2711 8882).

Two unusually long timbers had also been pegged in place immediately north of Row 2: timbers B1096 (grid 2709 8886) and B1110 (grid 2708 8886) were both approximately 3.15m long. They probably acted as bearers for the planks of the Level 1 walkway above them and also formed part of the box-like structure discussed above (Level 2, Area 6B).

Area 6B: the north-west quadrant

The walkways on either side of Row 3 were very evident at this level (Fig 6.50), because the small wood (mainly chips) of the walkway surface, or surfaces, could be seen to form a thin skin, which overlay and conformed to the contours of the larger roundwood bearers directly below. The small wood (which does not appear on the plan) also filled voids between the bearers (for example, directly north of Row 3 in grid 2705 8888). One bearer was particularly noteworthy (B715: grid 2707 8888). It passed through the posts of Row 3 transversely and had been placed hard alongside a thin radially split oak post; it was pinned next to the post by a stout roundwood stake. Other, somewhat smaller bearers had been positioned parallel to B715 between Rows 2 and 3, at intervals of approximately 1m (numbered timbers include B912–7: grid 2705 8887; B968: grid 2705 8887; B1227: grid 2709 8886). Between Rows 3 and 4 the pattern was more complex: again, there were transverse bearers (eg B572: grid 2705 8888; B508: grid 2706 8888), but below them was another layer of bearers, this time running axially along the post rows (eg B554: grid 2705 8889; B716: grid 2707 8888; B613: grid 2704 8889).

During excavation it was clear that the timbers between Rows 2 and 3 had been subjected to much wear. There were quantities of sand and fine gravel and the many short, flat oak planks (eg B899–902, B908–9, and B1014: grids 2705 8886–8887) had worn upper surfaces Their undersides frequently showed the surface cracks and crazing associated with wet rot. The deposit continued into Level 3 (see south-west quadrant below; Fig 6.62).

Fig 6.51 Flag Fen, Area 6B, Level 2: wood in the north-west quadrant. The hook-shaped plank in the foreground is wood B1033 (for location see Fig 6.50)

A timber deserving special attention formed part of the heavily worn trampled deposit just mentioned and also had a heavily worn upper surface. Timber B1033 (grid 2706 8886) was a large oak plank that featured rectilinear 'hooks' at each end (Fig 6.51). This was probably a reused piece that was closely positioned between two posts of Row 2 and pegged down by B1034 (grid 2705 8885).

Level 3

Taken as a whole, the timbers from Level 3, especially around the south part of the post alignment, were individually larger than in the upper two levels (Fig 6.52). It was also noticeable that many of the more substantial timbers had been aligned on the axis of the post alignment and that a high proportion were positioned close to (and usually contiguous with) two or more posts of the various rows.

Area 6A

At this level the timber-free zone of Level 2 had become larger and more sharply defined (Fig 6.53). To the east of the relict stream or watercourse the spread of horizontal wood and timber now extended to the very edge of the excavation, but not significantly beyond it (hand-cut trial trenches confirmed this). Unlike other parts of Area 6, the wood in this area was generally quite small, but there were few pieces that could be described as brushwood or driftwood with any certainty. Most of the wood was straight and had been trimmed. Furthermore, the longer pieces were aligned in a regular pattern, orientated north-east–south-west or south-east–north-west. There was a notable concentration of smaller wood on a made-up base of larger pieces immediately south-east of the relict watercourse. This perhaps functioned as a hard-standing by the water's edge.

Turning to the north end of Area 6A, the area north of the post alignment was built up with an informal lattice of roundwood. Close to Row 5, however, there was a marked change as the wood became smaller and far more closely packed. This was also the only place where sand was found outside the post alignment. In the first report this dense spread of wood was interpreted as an entranceway structure outside a supposed doorway. As a general statement this still holds good, but the doorway would have given access to the post alignment, not a building (Pryor *et al* 1986, 8). A wattle 'cavity wall' was found along the posts of Row 2. This was probably a revetment to the south side of the Rows 2–3 walkway (Fig 6.26; Pryor *et al* 1986, fig 8). The area within the post alignment was characterised by large timbers that were laid along the axis of the post row, but sometimes they were positioned at an angle to the post rows (Fig 6.54).

Fig 6.54 Flag Fen, Area 6A: general view of wood exposed in Level 3, looking south. The posts in the foreground belong to Row 2

Area 6B

At Level 3, the timbers of Area 6B (Figs 6.55 and 6.56) are best considered in four general categories. Undoubtedly, the most striking of these visually was the slightly raised narrow walkway between the posts of Rows 3 and 4 (Fig 6.57). South of Row 3 there was a wider pathway between Rows 3 and 2 (Fig 6.58), which was probably built in two sections (Fig 6.59). The west section was of small, closely packed wood. That to the east was of longer, larger timbers. The horizontal wood south of Row 2 was less densely packed, but there was a much-trampled area of hardstanding (which continued from Level 2 above) immediately north of Row 1, at the extreme east edge of the excavation. North of Row 4, close to the point where it ran into Area 6A, the spread of horizontal wood was much denser than that south of Row 1. At Level 3, the palisade or *chevaux de frise*-like arrangement of the posts in Row 4 became very much more apparent than at higher levels (Fig 6.57).

Area 6B: the north-east quadrant

The non-linear arrangement of posts in Row 4 was very evident by Level 3, where the width of the row was defined by two long split oak planks (Fig 6.60). To the north, plank B1523 (grid 2709 8890) undoubtedly served as a revetment, as it was pegged in place by no less than 13 pegs or stakes; two of these had been driven through mortise holes at either end of the plank. Two metres to the south-east, plank B1596 (grid 2709 8888) was also pegged in place, but only by four pegs. It also abutted two posts, one in Row 3 and one in Row 4 and probably served as a narrow walkway between the northern, revetted edge of Row 4 and Row 5. Unlike the revetment plank, all of whose pegs protruded above the plank, the pegs that fixed B1596 in place were driven in flush with its surface. The wood in this area was small and there were traces of sand. The hypothetical walkway would have been just wide enough for one person. The extreme north-east corner of the excavation revealed the entire width of this narrow walkway, as far north as the upright B3428. North of Row 5 there were indications of an outer wattle-like revetment (eg Fig 6.60: B1503–4, B1497, and A4139: grid 2709 8891).

Excavation down to Level 3 revealed a number of new pegs that secured horizontal timbers in place within the uprights of Row 4. Some long, relatively thin poles that might perhaps be seen as lacing rather than simple strengthening revetments, were particularly noteworthy. One example (3.5m long) was B1565 (grid 2710 8889), which ran diagonally across most of Row 4 and was held in position by at least 11 pegs. Another, shorter example (2.1m long), B1569 (grid 2709 8889), crossed the row more transversely, but as it 'laced' together four posts, it only required pegging at one spot (peg B444: grid 2710 8889).

The walkway between Rows 3 and 4 was systematically supported by five parallel and evenly spaced horizontal 'sails' (to use the term appropriate to hurdles) or bearers (from east–west: B1617, B1586, B1616, B1575, B1564: grids 2710 8889 to 2710 8888). Some of these had been pushed between posts, or had been pegged in position.

The lacing together and revetting of the widely spaced posts of Row 4 was in sharp contrast to the closely packed posts of Row 3, which will be reviewed in the following section.

Area 6B: the south-east quadrant

The posts of Row 3 continued into the south-east quadrant from the north-east quadrant (Fig 6.61). As in the north-east, the posts of Row 3 were closely packed and do not seem to have required any revetment or lacing together at this level. They most probably acquired their stability through being packed together so closely. A probable revetment timber

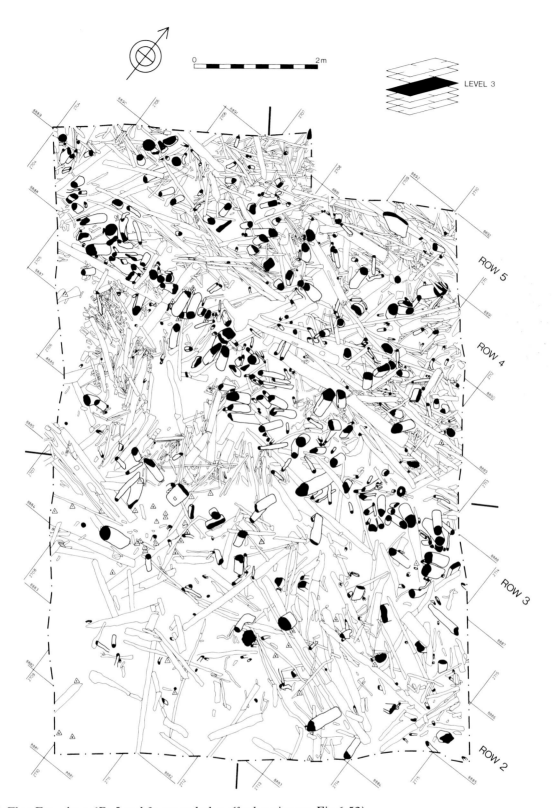

LEVEL 3

ROW 5

ROW 4

ROW 3

ROW 2

Fig 6.55 Flag Fen, Area 6B, Level 3: general plan (for location see Fig 6.52)

was B1633, which was placed hard against a large leaning upright and pegged against it by four pegs (grid 2712 8887). Directly below B1633 was a complete Deverel-Rimbury pottery jar, decorated with finger-tipped impressions (below Fig 9.2, 6). The vessel lay on its side and had undoubtedly been deliberately placed below the pegged-down timber B1633.

Immediately north of Row 3 and at the east edge of the excavation (grid 2712 8888) was a group of small, flat pieces of wood (B1609 and so on) that were a continuation of the walkway between Rows 3 and 4, as revealed in the north-east quadrant (Fig 6.60).

The larger, more spaced-out timbers south of Row 3 (eg B1777 or B1758: grid 2713 8885) probably formed the foundations of the walkway of diagonal pieces in Level 2.

124

Fig 6.56 Flag Fen, Area 6B, Level 3: photomontage of timbers south of Row 3

Fig 6.57 Flag Fen, Area 6B, Level 3: view along possible walkway between the posts of Rows 3 (left) and 4 (right), looking west

This finds some support in the frequent occurrence of pegs that were seen to hold in place the various timbers, both large and small.

One unusual arrangement of timber merits further description. Two oak timbers (B1788 and B1784: grid 2712 8884) had been positioned between a southerly post of Row 2 and a post of Row 1. One timber (B1784) had probably been reused, as it featured a large slot of sufficient size to accommodate a door, for example. It is possible that the two timbers allowed access from Row 1 to Row 2 at a large gap between the posts of Row 1. The north-east end of B1784 gave onto another timber, (B1788: grid 2711 8885) which passed through a gap in Row 2, thereby giving access to the walkway between Rows 2 and 3. At wetter times of the year there can be little doubt that the exceptionally low-lying area immediately south of Row 1 would have been difficult to cross with any ease.

Area 6B: the south-west quadrant

The extreme south corner of Area 6B was very wet at this level, but no serious attempt had been made to consolidate or cover it with wood in antiquity (Fig 6.62). This is in contrast to the levels above and (perhaps strangely) below. A few pegs remained from Level 2, but the scatter of timber of Level 3 was largely unsecured.

Fig 6.58 Flag Fen, Area 6B, Level 3: view looking west between Rows 2 (left) and 3 (right)

It should be noted, however, that the wood was not naturally derived driftwood, as there are no side branches or twiggy pieces. Some of the longer pieces (eg B1974: grid 2710 8883 or B1973: grid 2711 8883) were probably positioned as bearers to carry the timbers of Levels 1 and 2.

It would appear that the 3m-gap in Row 1, centred on the grid point 2710 8884, coincided with a particularly soft spot, and that foot traffic was routed around it by way of the pathway between Rows 2 and 3.

Fig 6.59 Flag Fen, Area 6B, Level 3: general view looking north, with the posts of Row 1 in the foreground

Immediately west of the gap, however, the walkway between Rows 1 and 2 resumed. It was constructed of reused oak timbers that were carefully placed on the ground to form a planked walkway 0.5m in width. The upper surfaces of the parallel timbers (which were overlain by similar timbers in Level 2, above) had clear signs of wear and abrasion (Maisie Taylor personal communication) and there were quantities of sand and fine gravel. The undersides of all timbers showed evidence of having had wet rot in antiquity. The north-east corner of the quadrant included smaller pieces of closely laid wattle-like wood that formed part of the walkway surface between Rows 2 and 3. This will be described below, under the north-west quadrant.

A thin line of wattle-like roundwood ran across the gap in Row 1 referred to above (grid 2710 8884). Two courses of wattle were visible in Level 3 (B2208, B2194, and B1825). They had been pegged in position and at this level appeared to form an early attempt to consolidate the wet area that was ultimately to be 'bridged' by the very large timbers of Level 1 (Fig 6.30). The wattle was not woven in the manner of a hurdle. It had instead been laid between the posts and pegged down to form a revetment to contain the outward spread of material placed beneath the timbers between Rows 1 and 2. The full extent of this wattle revetment was revealed in Levels 4 and 5.

Area 6B: the north-west quadrant

Four contrasting (or possible) walkways were revealed in this quadrant at Level 3 (Fig 6.63). The posts of Row 3 ran diagonally across the quadrant, along grid northing 8888. The dispersed posts of Row 4 occupied a zone about 1m wide. North of Row 4 was a possible narrow walkway between it and Row 5; the pegs of this walkway were level with its surface. The underlying timbers of the walkway between Rows 3 and 4 were exposed at the north-east corner of the quadrant. These large timbers (eg B1397, B1411, and B1412: grid 2705 8889) had been located within the posts of the two rows to provide stability. Parts of the walkway surfacing were preserved at a slightly higher level at grid 2707 8889.

The tightly packed posts of Row 3 were not generally supported by horizontal timbers, with the apparent exception of the large roundwood timber B1421 (grid 2707 8887). Its north end featured two ear-like projections and it lay transversely across the row. Its south end was found to have a long pencil-like sharpened point like other uprights at Flag Fen. As the tip was clean and had never been driven into the ground, B1421 is best interpreted as an unused upright.

The smaller pieces of wood comprising the lower levels of the walkway surface between Rows 2 and 3 were still visible in Level 3 (in Level 2 the wearing

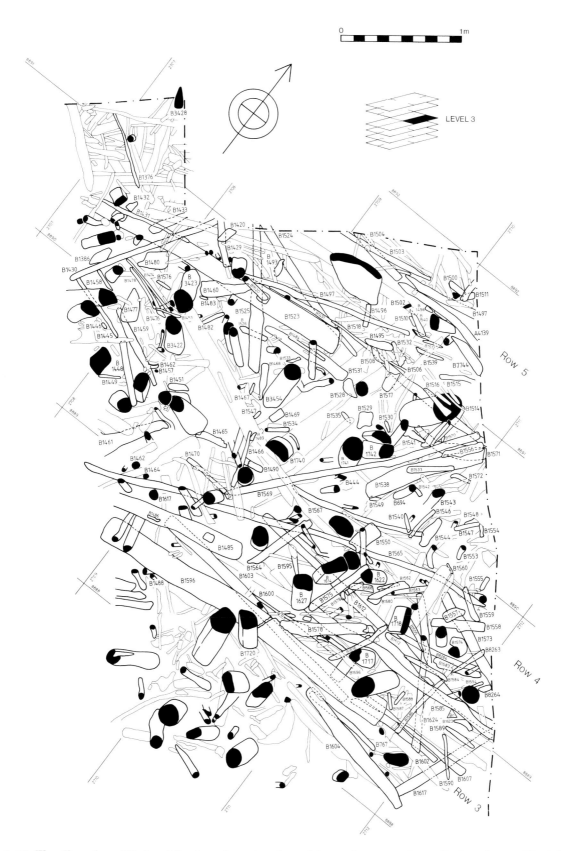

Fig 6.60 Flag Fen, Area 6B, Level 3: plan of numbered wood in north-east quadrant (for location see Fig 6.55)

Fig 6.61 Flag Fen, Area 6B, Level 3: plan of numbered wood in south-east quadrant (for location see Fig 6.55)

Fig 6.62 Flag Fen, Area 6B, Level 3: plan of numbered wood in south-west quadrant (for location see Fig 6.55)

Fig 6.63 Flag Fen, Area 6B, Level 3: plan of numbered wood in north-west quadrant (for location see Fig 6.55)

surface consisted largely of short, flat oak planks). Cross-ties within and between the posts of Row 2 helped secure the foundations of the Row 2/3 walkway in place. These cross-ties were at the same level as the presumed earlier walkway or pathway of reused planks between Rows 2 and 1 (Fig 6.62, B2059: grid 2707 8884 and so on).

Level 4

Level 4 was the first exposure of the large timbers, mainly alder logs, which comprised the foundation layers of the post alignment's horizontal component (Fig 6.64). Although large timbers occurred in Area 6A (Fig 6.65), they were mainly found in Area 6B (Fig 6.66). It was also at this depth that the differentiation between levels began to break down. Many of the larger timbers were considerably thicker than the hitherto consistent width of 100mm between the levels. The photomontage plan gives an impression of the size of the logs (Fig 6.67).

The main concentration of large logs was south of Row 3. For convenience, the term 'log layer' adopted in the field will be used here. In general terms Level 4 is characterised as the log layer, plus material level with it, whereas Level 5 was the log layer, plus the uppermost

level of material lying beneath it, where present. This distinction, which is admittedly unsatisfactory, is best seen by comparing the overall plans of Area 6B, Levels 4 and 5 (Fig 6.66 and below, Fig 6.77).

In Level 4 the general character of the wood became more apparent. North and south of the post alignment, especially in Area 6A, there seemed to be a haphazard spread of trimmed roundwood and a lack of timbers. Within the post alignment, the area south of Row 3 featured the distinctive log layer, which was less formal than a corduroy road surface (eg Raftery 1992, fig 4.3), but which had undoubtedly been laid with a broadly similar purpose in mind. North of Row 3 the large horizontal timbers were more rare, but they were generally longer and usually ran axially along the post rows. In this area it was the mass of posts that dominated the plans.

Evidence for possible partitioning in Levels 4 and 5

The potential evidence for partitioning reviewed here is tentative, but given the hundreds of posts and numerous long horizontal timbers, it would be a poor scholar who could not discern some form of coherent pattern in so promising a source. Having said this,

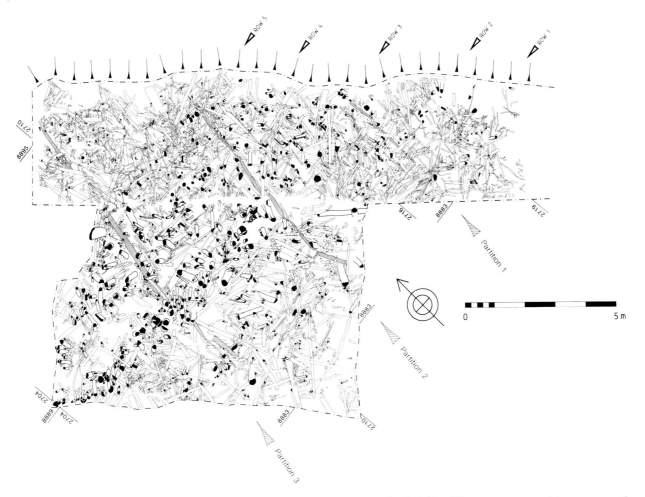

Fig 6.64 Flag Fen, Areas 6A and 6B: general plan of wood exposed in level 4. Possible transverse partitions are numbered 1–4 (for location see Fig 6.1)

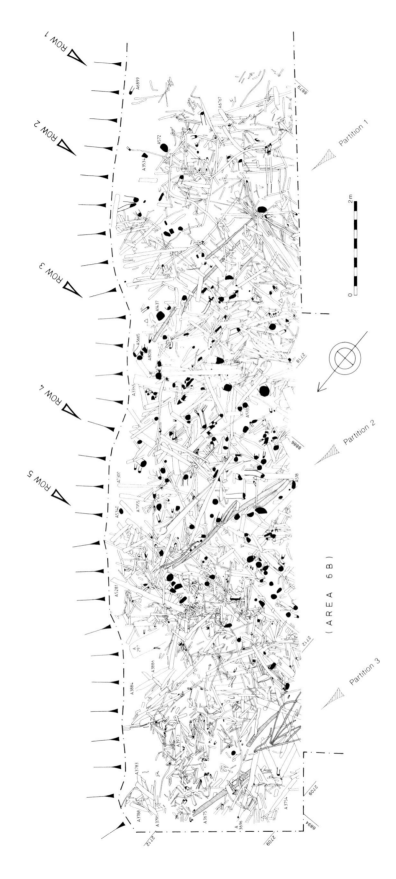

Fig 6.65 Flag Fen, Area 6A, Level 4: general plan of wood, with principal pieces numbered. Possible transverse partition timbers have been shaded (for location see Fig 6.64)

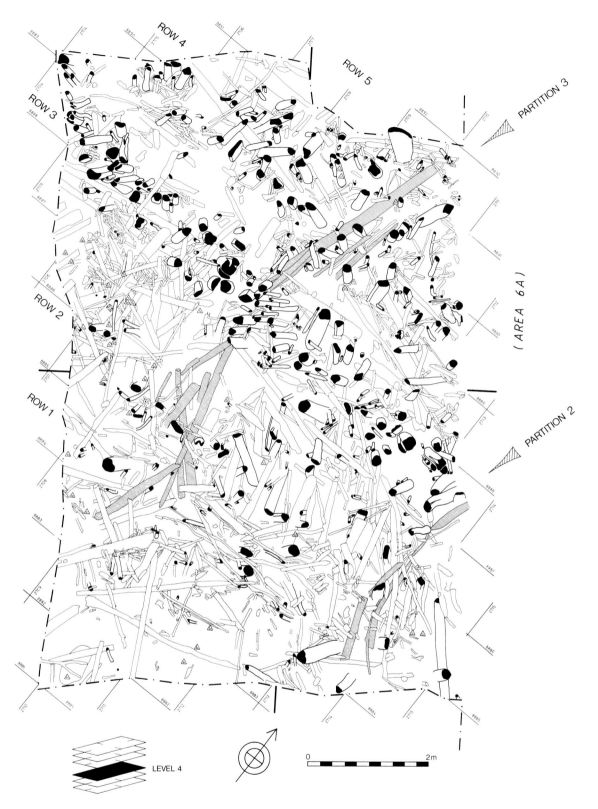

Fig 6.66 Flag Fen, Area 6B, Level 4: general plan. Possible transverse partition timbers have been shaded (for location see Fig 6.64)

the pattern of partitioning identified seems to be internally consistent and quite regularly laid out. Furthermore, as will be seen, it is not based on the size and arrangement of timbers alone.

Partitioning was first suggested by a series of evenly spaced and extra large posts in the earliest row, Row 1. These posts generally lined up quite well with other

alder posts in Row 3, across the axis of the alignment, to form a box-like or cellular structure (below, Fig 6.97). It was also notable that, around the larger posts, the transverse horizontal timbers were of variable size and were not always confined to a narrow zone between two rows. In places they formed parallel arrangements reminiscent of the so-called 'cavity wall'

Fig 6.67 Flag Fen, Area 6B, Level 4: photomontage of excavated wood

revetments encountered elsewhere (eg partition 3, Fig 6.66; it is more clearly visible in the plan of Levels 5 and 6, Fig 6.75).

The possible partitions occurred at approximate 5m intervals. They ran at right angles to the post alignment axis and, where they were visible in their entirety, they crossed all five post rows. They have been numbered from east to west. Structural details of the possible partitions are given below, in the descriptions of the subareas.

The possible partitions were usually marked by extra-large posts in Rows 1–5, or by groups of short transverse lines of posts within the posts of Rows 2–5. Both can clearly be seen in Level 4, partition 3 (Fig 6.64). The massive split oak post (B520) of Row 5 marked the north end of partition 3 in Area 6B. Partition 3 was aligned on the only post (A651) that stood outside the post alignment, by some 2m, on the north side.

Evidence for the possible partitions will be reviewed in the discussion at the conclusion of this chapter. Their role will be considered in Chapter 19. Timbers of the possible partitions have been shaded on all the relevant plans of Levels 4 and 5. They will be discussed in detail in the appropriate section below.

Area 6A

It was decided not to attempt to excavate the scatter of wood on the southern side of the relict watercourse revealed in Level 3. While excavating Level 3 it had been apparent that Level 4 in this area would consist of a thin, scrappy spread of wood. In the event, however, the decision not to excavate was overridden by the winter storms of 1986, which lifted the plastic sheeting and allowed frosts to destroy what wind did not dry out. Fortunately, the other covers of Area 6A remained in place. Inspection of the damaged wood, combined with some exploratory salvage excavation revealed that little of any value had been lost. Excavation, it should be noted, also proved that the discontinuous, but apparently wood-free areas along the dykeside (Fig 6.65), were the result of drying out and erosion by water flowing along the dyke. A certain amount of damage was also caused during the excavation of the initial dykeside exposure in 1982 (Fig 6.9).

The main point to note in the plan (Fig 6.65) is the difference between horizontal wood within and without the post alignment, Rows 2–5. In the areas outside the post alignment, the wood had been laid in a seemingly haphazard, lattice-like pattern. There were numerous long, thin, straight pieces, suggestive of thick coppice rods or poles. Within the post alignment the horizontal timbers were larger and arranged more formally.

Turning to the possible partitions, the horizontal transverse timbers of partition 1 (Fig 6.65) were of no more than average thickness, but the posts in Rows 1 and 3 were far larger than average (eg A1437) and

included a tight group in Row 3 (A5665, A8036, and so on). The horizontals of partition 2 were larger and the partition posts of Rows 3 and 4 were also substantial; there were traces of a possible wattle wall that ran parallel to partition 2 at its north end around Row 5 and possibly beyond. Partition 3 might possibly have extended north of Row 5 via an area of possible disturbed wattle and the large north–south timber A3675. Partition 3 might have been aligned on A651 (shown on the plan of Levels 6 and 7, Fig 6.75), one of only two substantial posts that were found outside the confines of the alignment itself (the other lay south of the alignment in Area 6D).

Area 6B

The most striking aspect of Level 4 in Area 6B was undoubtedly the informal corduroy-like arrangement of trimmed alder logs between Rows 2 and 3 (Fig 6.66). This transverse log layer provided the foundation for the walkway timbers of Levels 1 and 2, which were laid on the more axially arranged 'bearers' of Level 3. The pattern of foundation timbers was different, being more random or haphazard west of partition 3. The soft wet area south of Row 1 contained a number of quite widely spaced, but very long timbers, which, again, were probably foundation supports. There was little timber between the dense concentration of outward-leaning posts of Rows 3 and 4, largely because of lack of space for them (Fig 6.67); the point where partition 3 crossed this gap was the only exception to this. The timbers within the dispersed posts of Row 4 in general ran axially to the row and appeared to have been jammed within the space available, doubtless to act as supports. An unusual discovery was a complete, very lightly used saddle quern at the extreme south corner of the excavation (Other Find 24). This quern might have been an outlier of the group found in Level 5 (below).

Area 6B: the north-east quadrant

The plan of this quadrant at this level is devoted to the posts of Rows 3–5 (Fig 6.68). Row 5 was represented by the large split oak timber in grid 2709 8891. Immediately north of it were two parallel timbers (B2328, B7630), which abutted it and were pegged into position by some six pegs. The builders were unable to drive this large timber to any great depth into the underlying gravel and clay and it became loose during excavation. Some of the smaller, adjacent pieces of wood (eg B2300) might have been ancient attempts to fix it more securely in position. There were few horizontal timbers of any size within Row 4, apart from the large plank B2318 (grid 2709 8890) and the smaller timbers to the east (B2396, B1741, and so on: grid 2709 8889). It is suggested that these were timbers, all of which were secured in place by numerous pegs, were timbers of partition 3.

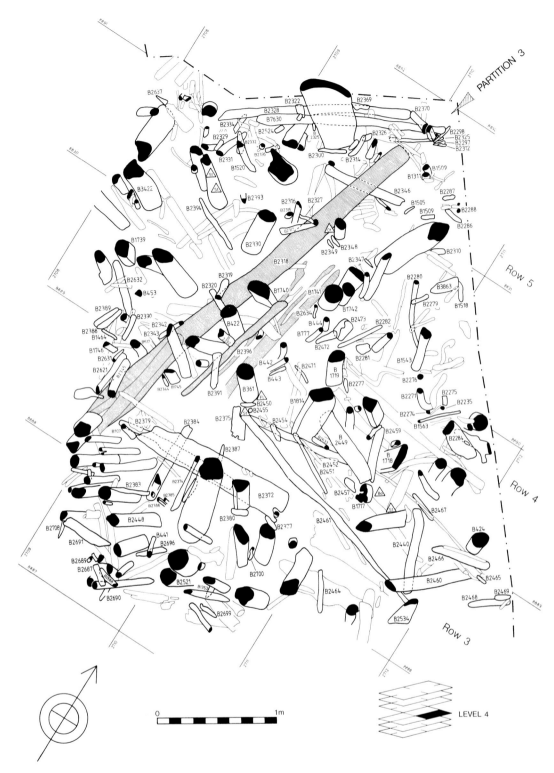

Fig 6.68 Flag Fen, Area 6B, Level 4: plan of numbered wood in north-east quadrant. Possible transverse partition timbers have been shaded (for location see Fig 6.66)

The posts of Rows 3 and 4 were separated by a few horizontal timbers (B2372, B2461: grid 2710 8888), which represented the foundations or lowest courses of the narrow walkway encountered in Levels 2 and 3. B2372 had been pegged down securely at each end. At the east end it had been pegged through a broken mortise hole.

Area 6B: the south-east quadrant

Post Row 3 continued from the north-east quadrant. There was very little space within it for horizontal timbers, apart, that is, for those of possible partition 2 (Fig 6.69). In this quadrant, the partition was notable for the size of the three transversely aligned uprights in Rows 1, 2 and 3, which helped to define it (timbers B1:

Fig 6.69 Flag Fen, Area 6B, Level 4: plan of numbered wood in south-east quadrant. Possible transverse partition timbers have been shaded (for location see Fig 6.66)

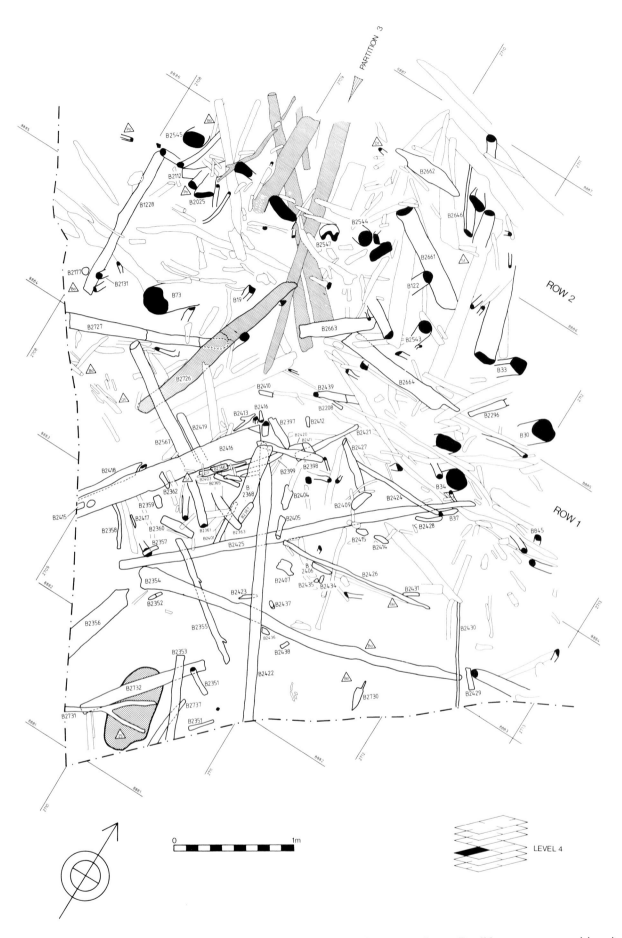

Fig 6.70 Flag Fen, Area 6B, Level 4: plan of numbered wood in south-west quadrant. Possible transverse partition timbers have been shaded (for location see Fig 6.66)

grid 2713 8884, B15: grid 2713 8885, and B2540: grid 2713 8887). As with partition 3 in the north-east quadrant (Fig 6.68: grid 2709 8888), the posts associated with partition 2 effectively blocked, or severely constricted, the already narrow walkway between Rows 3 and 4 (grid 2713 8888).

Part of the log layer between Rows 2 and 3, an important feature of Level 4, was visible in this quadrant (large timbers in grids 2711 8815 to 2712 8815). The logs appeared to have been jammed between uprights, but they could just as readily have been fixed in position by uprights driven in at the time; an experiment would rapidly establish which technique was the most effective. East of the possible partition, the log layer gave way to smaller timbers.

South of Row 2 (ie south of grid line 8885 northing) the timbers of the space between Rows 1 and 2 were harder to define, perhaps because they had been compressed by the heavier timbers of previous levels. At the south-west corner of the quadrant, however, immediately south and east of B30 (grid 2711 8885), there was evidence for an informal wattle revetment or barrier, which ran along the south side of Row 2, parallel to another, similar wattle barrier in Row 1 (not visible in this quadrant). The two barriers are best seen in the next (south-west) quadrant and in the photomontage plan (Fig 6.67).

Area 6B: the south-west quadrant

At this level, the spread of timber was thinner than elsewhere in Area 6B (Fig 6.70). The south half of this quadrant (approximately south of grid 8884 northing) was wetter than the rest of Area 6B, both during excavation and in antiquity. The wet area was overlain by an irregular, lattice-like arrangement of very long, straight and trimmed timbers (Fig 6.71). These included B2416 (grid 2709 8883), B2425 (grid 2710 8882), B2356 (grid 2709 8882), and B2422 (grid

Fig 6.71 Flag Fen, Area 6B, Level 4: close-up of wood in south-west quadrant (for location see Fig 6.70)

2711 8882). These timbers were doubtless intended to spread the load of the overlying timbers. The wetness might also help to explain why the posts of Rows 1 and 2 almost converged in this area. Row 1 shifted north to skirt around the wet patch of ground. Post B34, Row 1 (grid 2711 8884), for instance, was located just 0.8m south-west of post B30, Row 2. The northward diversion of Row 1 is clearly seen in Figure 6.72.

The edge of the wet area appears to have been revetted by two woven wattle walls around the posts and pegs of Row 1 (on either side of post B34: grid 2711 8884) and south of Row 2 (B30: grid 2711 8885). The two parallel wattle revetments can be clearly seen in the photomontage (Fig 6.67). They run diagonally directly above the two lower right-hand scales, for just over 2m. The Row 1 wattle revetment was more clearly revealed in Level 5. A complete, lightly used saddle quern (Other Find 24) was found, right side up, in the south corner of the quadrant (grid 2710 8881). A simple domestic or structural explanation for the stone seems inadequate. It must have sunk rapidly in the soft peaty matrix and was found resting on the organic muds that overlay the basal clays. If it had been used to provide a solid base for horizontal timbers, other evidence might be expected — such as other hardcore or a superstructure of some sort. As it was, the wood that lay directly above the quern was flimsy and of little consequence.

Although probably less wet, the soft area extended beyond grid 8885 northing. Soft ground might account for the numerous large, flat timbers, which appeared to spread out, finger fashion from the south end of partition 3. This can be clearly seen on the photomontage (Fig 6.67). Soft ground, too, probably explains the need for the log layer in Levels 4 and 5 between Rows 2 and 3. Five logs of this deposit are visible east of the partition (eg B2661: grid 2710 8885). The log layer is particularly clear in the photomontage (Fig 6.67).

Area 6B: the north-west quadrant

The wet conditions underfoot, already touched upon in the discussion of the south-west quadrant, probably also explain the very dense buildup of wood between Rows 2 and 3 around grid 2706 8886 (Fig 6.73: B2674 and so forth). This might have represented compressed walkway material. Beneath can be seen a layer of larger support timbers. The area also produced a number of animal bones and potsherds.

Two large alder logs were positioned on either side of five southerly posts of Row 3, centred on grid 2706 8887. The two logs were pegged tightly against the uprights between them and other horizontal timbers rested upon them, ladder fashion. The ladder-like arrangement is clearly visible in the plan (Fig 6.73). The photomontage (Fig 6.67) was made some time after the plan and it illustrates the lower deposits within Level 4. The two parallel alder logs are clearly visible, lower left.

Fig 6.72 Flag Fen, Area 6B, Level 4: view along posts of Rows 1 and 2, looking north-west (for location see Fig 6.66)

The area between Rows 3 and 4 (centred on grid 8889 northing) contained remarkably little horizontal wood. Perhaps due to the many posts around it, this zone had been raised slightly above the level of the surrounding area. It might have provided a dry walkway without the need for additional logs or planks. The deposits here contained quantities of sand and fine gravel, some of which had undoubtedly been washed down from higher levels. The 'blank' between Rows 3 and 4 in this level is in sharp contrast to the situation revealed in Level 3 (Fig 6.63).

The posts of Row 4 had been strengthened by a large, trimmed alder log (B2572: grid 2707 8889), which had been laid along the centre of the row, at a slight angle to the main axis. Other logs of the same size and alignment were found lower down in Level 4 of Row 4, in the north-east quadrant. They can be seen, together with B2572, in the photomontage (Fig 6.67). The contrast between the longer, slender axial poles of Rows 3 and 4 and the shorter, larger diameter logs of the log layer between the pathway of Rows 2–3 should be noted. This pattern is most unlikely to have been a result of chronology and might instead reflect different patterns of (anticipated) use or traffic-flow.

Levels 5 and 6

By the time the lowest two levels, 5 and 6, had been reached, it had become hard to draw secure stratigraphic distinctions between the levels. Level 6 is therefore best seen as a response to very wet conditions where the subsoil (for whatever reason) required an extra layer of consolidation and, almost certainly, has no chronological significance.

The principal discoveries of Levels 5 and 6 included the full definition of the basal log layer between Rows 2 and 3, the discovery of three saddle querns at the south end of partition 3, and the exposure of wattlework revetments along Row 1 and the southern edge of Row 4 (Fig 6.74).

Area 6A

The distribution pattern of horizontal wood in this level was in three quite distinct zones (Fig 6.75). North of Row 2, the wood was generally a thin scatter, especially towards the dykeside to the east; this was probably in response to a slight hummock in the underlying subsoil. Wood within the post alignment was scrappy and there were very few substantial timbers.

Fig 6.73 Flag Fen, Area 6B, Level 4: plan of numbered wood in north-west quadrant. Possible transverse partition timbers have been shaded (for location see Fig 6.66)

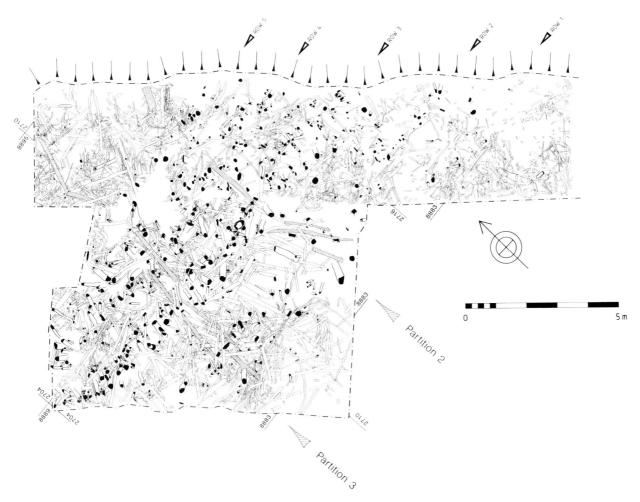

Fig 6.74 Flag Fen, Areas 6A and 6B: general plan of wood exposed in Levels 5 and 6. Possible transverse partition timbers have been shaded (for location see Fig 6.1)

The only area that showed signs of systematic buildup was the space between Rows 2 and 3, at the junction with Area 6B. Again, this was probably a response to wetter ground conditions.

North of Row 5, as the solid ground fell gently away, this was reflected in the foundation timbers. Indeed, before the area could be cleared of all wood, it was necessary to excavate a further two levels (Levels 6 and a possible Level 7; Fig 6.76).

Even at these low levels the evidence for partitions was still quite strong, except for partition 1; most horizontal wood in this area was scrappy and it would appear that the initial marking out had been confined within Level 4.

The horizontal timbers that marked partition 2 were very substantial, but passed north (rather than south as in Level 4) of the posts in Rows 3–5. The north end of the possible partition was marked by a concentration of smaller wood. Partition 3 was composed of largely the same timbers as in Level 4 (Fig 6.65), but they were more fully exposed in Levels 5 and 6 (Fig 6.75). By Level 7, entirely new partition timbers had been revealed (Fig 6.76). These timbers lay on the south side of the posts that had formed the south edge of the partition in Levels 4 and 5. This slight southwards shift (of less than 1m) accorded well with the alignment of partition 3 in Area 6B (Fig 6.77).

Area 6B

A number of remarkable finds were made at, or close to, the south edge of the post alignment, in the south-west quadrant of Area 6B. This distribution is of some interest, in that it echoes the distribution of metalwork found at the Power Station site, some 800m to the west. The plan (Fig 6.77) and photomontage (Fig 6.78) clearly show that partition 3 was an important transverse structure. Its southern end, in Rows 1 and 2, was built upon a thick mass of long, straight timbers, which provided a solid base on soft ground. It is interesting to note that the northern end of partition 3 in Area 6A, Level 7 (Fig 6.77), resembled that to the south, with its finger-like arrangement of large horizontal timbers to spread the load. The large parallel timbers, which took partition 3 through the posts of Rows 3 and 4, lay directly below those of Level 4. It is difficult to see what practical purpose such an arrangement might have served. The horizontal timbers of partition 3 ran along the north side of the posts that marked the partition in Rows 2 and 3 (Fig 6.79).

The area between Rows 3 and 4, which had remained largely devoid of horizontal timber in the previous level, was thickly spread with smaller roundwood in the lowest two levels (Fig 6.80). Two parallel walls or revetments, fashioned from stout, pole-like wattle,

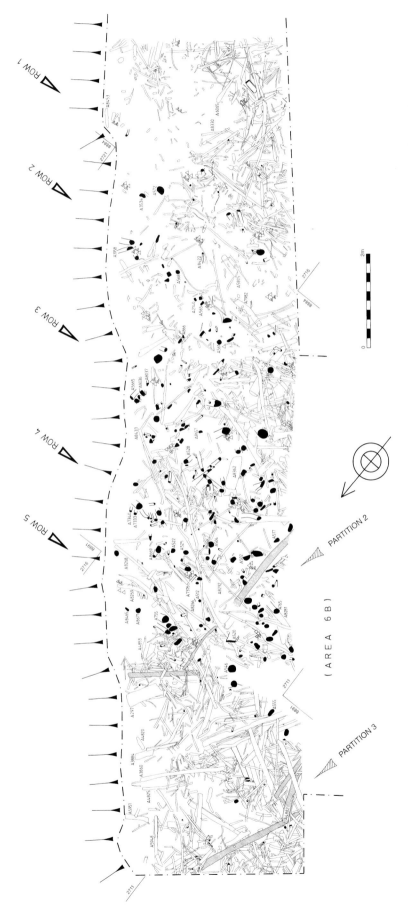

Fig 6.75 Flag Fen, Area 6A, Levels 5 and 6: general plan of wood, with principal pieces numbered (for location see Fig 6.74)

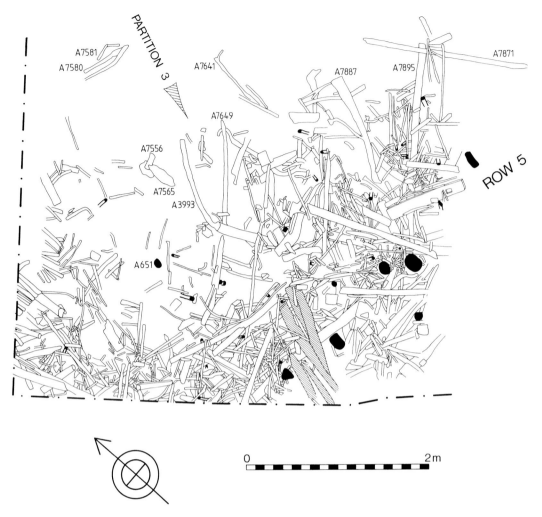

Fig 6.76 Flag Fen, Area 6A, Levels 6 and 7: general plan of wood at the northern end of the trench with principal pieces not visible in levels 5–6 numbered (for location see Fig 6.75)

were clearly visible in this area, towards the north-west corner of the excavation (Fig 6.80).

Practical difficulties began to be experienced in the lowest levels. By Level 5 the posts stood so tall (Fig 6.80) that, when they were draped with polythene sheeting, they formed, in effect, a tent. This meant that it became almost impossible to sheet the horizontal timbers below them closely enough to retain moisture overnight. At the same time, run-off from the roof of the shelter and from the land around the excavation began ponding within the trench. In order to relieve the latter problem, it was decided to improve the outfall from the excavation to the Mustdyke by way of a small cutting in the north-east corner. This required the removal of several posts and stakes in Row 5. Little could be done about the tent effect, other than excavating as fast as possible and using saturated sponges in the worst-affected areas.

Thanks to an extraordinary last-minute effort by the excavation team, it proved possible to remove the posts late in the same season in which the horizontal timbers of Levels 5 and 6 were lifted. The posts were by now so fully exposed that they would not have survived the winter intact, if left *in situ*.

Area 6B: the north-east quadrant

In the lowest two levels, horizontal timbers in the north-east quadrant were mainly confined to the area around the posts (Fig 6.81). Articulated timbers were rarely encountered at Flag Fen, but one of the few examples was found at the north-east edge of the excavation on the boundary between the north-east and north-west segments. The two timbers in question were B2644 (not on plan) and B2883: grid 2706 8891 (Fig 6.82). At first, the two timbers appeared to form part of a reused assembly, perhaps from a building, but when excavated, it could be seen that the roundwood B2644 had been forced through the rectilinear mortise hole in B2883 to make an *ad hoc* cruciform construction. This structure was probably intended to spread the load when people used the narrow walkway between the northern posts of Rows 4 and 5. The articulated timbers are visible in the photomontage directly below the 'step' at the left-hand edge (Fig 6.78). The roundwood timber (B2644) lay directly above the copper alloy tongue chape (Other Find 41). As the chape could not have found its way below the timber by natural means, it must have been placed there before the cruciform construction was lowered into the wet ground.

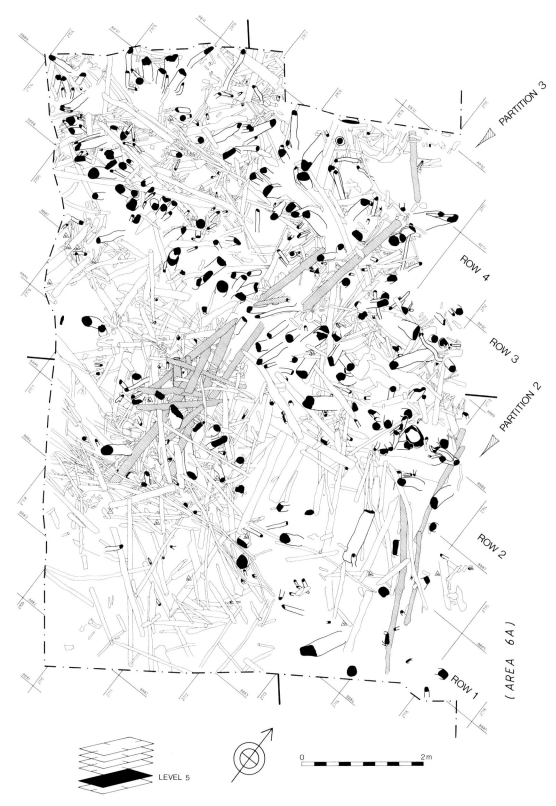

Fig 6.77 Flag Fen, Area 6B, Levels 5 and 6: general plan. Possible transverse partition timbers have been shaded (for location see Fig 6.74)

The drainage difficulties discussed in the previous section led to the removal of the large split oak upright of Row 5, B520 (grid 2709 8891), together with other smaller posts and pegs in the area. B520 is marked on Figure 6.19 and its position by a plywood plank in the photomontage (Fig 6.78). Partition 3 was represented

by two parallel alder logs B2806 (grid 2709 8888) and B2745 (grid 2710 8890), which lay directly beneath the partition timbers of Layer 4. North of these two alder logs was another, B2738 (grid 2709 8891), aligned north-east–south-west. Whether or not this was part of the possible partition, it might also have

Fig 6.78 Flag Fen, Area 6B, Level 5: photomontage of excavated wood

Fig 6.79 Flag Fen, Area 6B, Levels 5 and 6: general view of north half of excavation

Fig 6.80 Flag Fen, Area 6B, Level 5: view along post Rows 3 (right) and 4 (left)

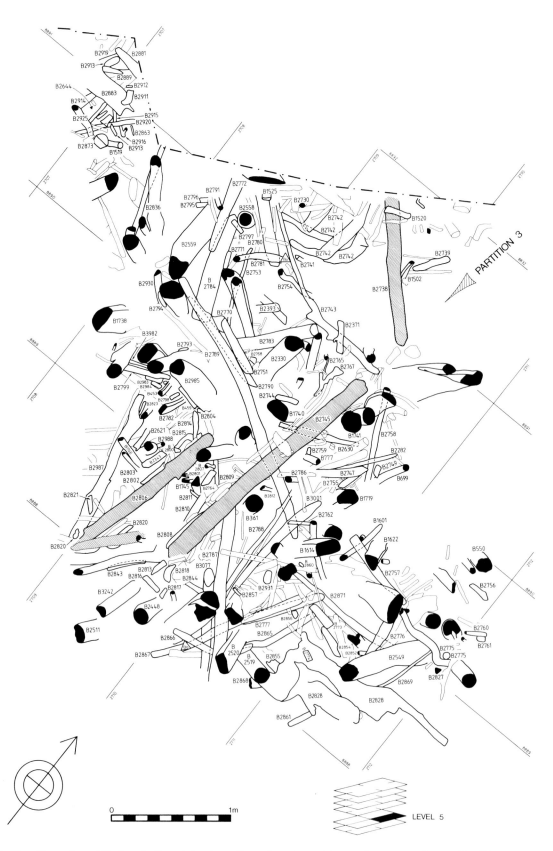

Fig 6.81 Flag Fen, Area 6B, Levels 5 and 6: plan of numbered wood in north-east quadrant. Possible transverse partition timbers have been shaded (for location see Fig 6.77)

served to underpin the timbers of Rows 4 and 5, like B2772 (grid 2708 8891) some 1.5m to the west. B2738 ran up against the (removed) large upright B520 and lay directly beneath the partition timbers of Level 4. It was pegged in position by B1502 (grid 2709 8891).

The posts of Row 4 were secured and supported by substantial diagonal and longitudinal timbers. This arrangement contrasted with the short transverse timbers, which were fitted between the posts of Rows 3 and 4 and provided foundations for the narrow walkway in the levels above. Where the Rows 3–4 walkway passed out of the quadrant to the east (at grid 2711 8888), the clearly defined transverse timbers gave way to ill-defined, but large, pieces of decayed roundwood or thick reused planks. This mass of wood was assigned a single number, B2828. It had been used to consolidate a small wet patch where the density of posts on either side would have made it difficult to accommodate transverse timbers.

Fig 6.82 Flag Fen, Area 6B, Level 5: close-up of articulated timbers B2644 and B2883 at north side of excavation between north-east and north-west quadrants (best seen in Fig 6.77)

Area 6B: the south-east quadrant

The principal interest in this quadrant was the log layer of rough, corduroy-like arrangement between Rows 2 and 3 (Fig 6.83). These logs formed the basal foundations for the walkway (mainly of Levels 1–3) between Rows 2 and 3. The logs lay between partitions 2 and 3 and included the following: B3049 and B3050 (grid 2710 8886), B3088 and B3033 (grid 2711 8886), B3066, B1288, and B3125 (grid 2712 8886). The south side of Row 3 was also bounded by logs, which were orientated along the alignment axis, lay above the transverse logs, and would have defined the north side of the walkway. The timbers of partition 2 passed across the Rows 2–3 walkway to north and south.

The partition timbers included B2205 (grid 2713 8884), B3124 (grid 2713 8885), B3129, and B3163 (grid 2713 8885), B3153 (grid 2713 8887), and B2850 (grid 2713 8888). Only the southernmost timber (B2205) had already appeared in Level 4. Sherds of pottery and animal bones were found in the vicinity of the partition within grid squares 2712 8884, 2712 8885, and 2714 8885.

Area 6B: the south-west quadrant

A large quantity of trimmed and straight timber, aligned approximately east-north-east–west-south-west and concentrated in the north corner of the quadrant, probably formed partition 3 (Fig 6.84). This timber was aligned on the large Row 1 post, B73 (grid 2708 8884).

The wattle wall or revetment ran immediately south of Row 1; it survived four to five courses high at its east end (Fig 6.85). At its west end, it fanned out to the south of the large Row 1 post, B73 (grid 2708 8884). The components of the wattle wall (from east to west) included B3570 (grid 2712 8884), B3571, and B3570 (grid 2711 8884), B3572, and B3611 (grid 2709 8884), B3662 (grid 2707 8884), and, at the west edge of the excavation centred on grid 8884 northing (from north-west–south-east), B3626, B3618, B3615, B3462, B3628, B3614, and B3456. As none of the small roundwood or wattles had been pegged down, it is possible that the fanning out at the west end was either caused accidentally during its use or a post-depositional effect. This spread of material was probably a result of collapse, a suggestion finds support in a pair of pegs (grid 2708 8884) located directly east of the large post B73. Almost identical pairs of pegs secured the wattle in place at intervals of about 0.75m, due east of B73.

The fan of possible collapsed wattles suggest that the original height of the wall or revetment was some 7–10 courses and in the order of 300–500mm (Fig 6.86). The general distribution of wattle walls or revetments in Area 6 is shown in Figure 6.87.

A group of three saddle querns (Other Finds 26–8) were found at the base of Level 6 directly below and touching the lowest timbers (Figs 6.88 and 6.89). They were arranged in a group south-east of the large Row 1 post B73, centred on grid 2709 8884 (Fig 6.90). Another quern (Other Find 24) was found in Level 4 (above) at grid 2710 8881, some 2m to the south (Fig 6.70). As it is thought that the difference in level might not be significant, the four stones can be reasonably seen as a group.

One of the larger timbers that supported the wattle wall or revetment of Row 1 also concealed a copper-alloy flesh hook (Fig 6.91). As with the chape from the north-east quadrant (above), this careful positioning suggests deliberate deposition. When the saddle quern encountered in Level 4 was lifted, a complete socketed axe haft of oak (B2737) was found below and south of

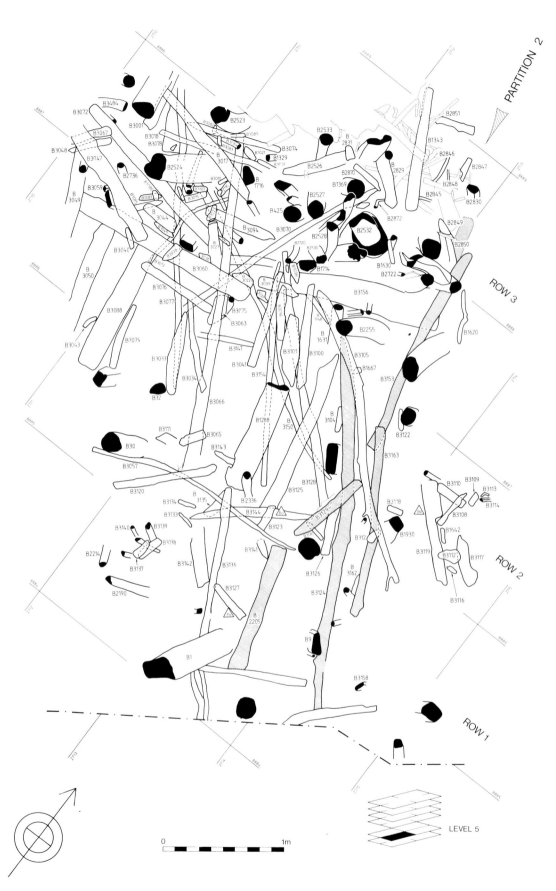

Fig 6.83 Flag Fen, Area 6B, Levels 5 and 6: plan of numbered wood in south-east quadrant. Possible transverse partition timbers have been shaded (for location see Fig 6.77)

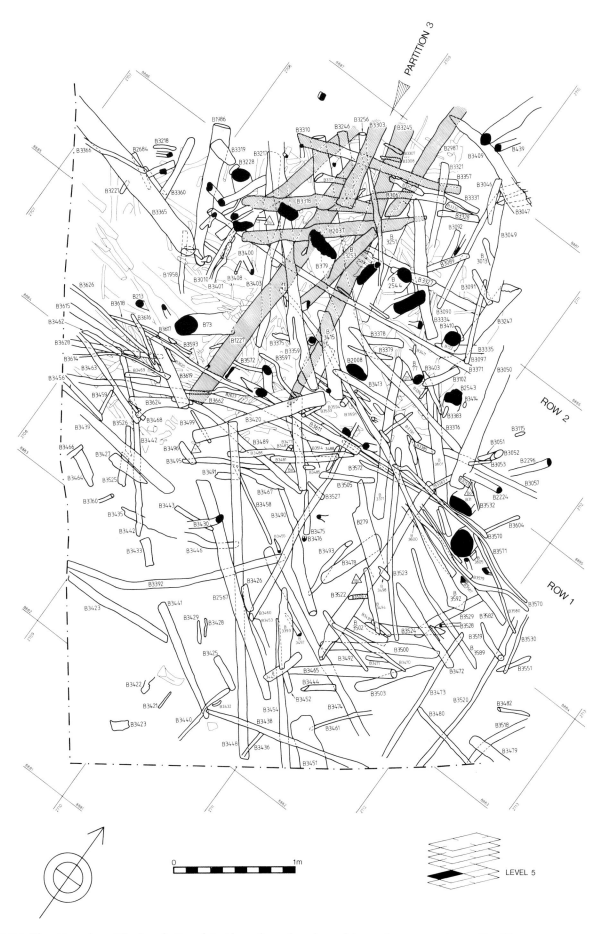

Fig 6.84 Flag Fen, Area 6B, Levels 5 and 6: plan of numbered wood in south-west quadrant. Possible transverse partition timbers have been shaded (for location see Fig 6.77)

Fig 6.85 Flag Fen, Area 6B, Level 6: view of wattle wall or revetment (parallel and to right of string line) around posts of Row 1. Note the two quernstones at centre top

Fig 6.86 Flag Fen, Area 6B, Level 6: wattle revetment/ wall of post Row 1 as finally excavated. Note the two querns, upper left

the quern at the extreme southern edge of the excavation at grid 2710 8881 (Fig 6.92). It is possible that the hooked axe haft had been used to prop the quern upright or on its edge, perhaps as part of depositional rites (cf Etton, Pryor 1998).

North of the wattle revetment of Row 1, the southern timbers of partition 3, first revealed in Level 4, were seen to dip southwards towards the slightly lower-lying, wetter area. It should be noted that the longest timber of the possible partition, B1277, lay beneath the wattle revetment of Row 1 (Fig 6.83). On stratigraphic grounds this would indicate that the partition was at least as old as Row 1, which can be dated dendrochronologically to *c* 1300 BC.

Area 6B: the north-west quadrant

The contrast between areas of posts and possible walkways is very evident in the plan of this quadrant (Fig 6.93). The posts of Row 4 can be seen to stand alone, with very few foundation timbers. Along the south side, the narrow walkway between Rows 3 and 4 was underpinned or revetted by stout wattles both to the north (by B2908: grid 2704 8889), B2940, B2905:

grid 2705 8889), B2949, and B2950: grid 2707 8889) and to the south (by B2965: grid 2705 8888 and B2966: grid 2705 8888).

The posts of Row 3 were reinforced by another layer of substantial, long timbers below the parallel ladder-like arrangement described in Level 4. Examples include B2965 (grid 2705 8888), B2980 (grid 2705 8890), and B2961 (grid 2705 8887). The latter timber measured at least 2.5m in length and had been broken in antiquity.

North-west of partition 3, the lowest level of the walkway between Rows 2 and 3 was composed of smaller, shorter logs than in the log layer proper to the east. There was, however, more evidence for the use of pegs in the former area (eg B3202, B3215, and so on, along grid 8887 northing).

Area 6: excavation of the post rows

The final stage of excavation in Area 6 was the removal of the posts. Efforts were made to record tip depths and these data are available in the computer archive. As the tips of the posts in most instances had become encrusted with solid manganese and iron-pan deposits,

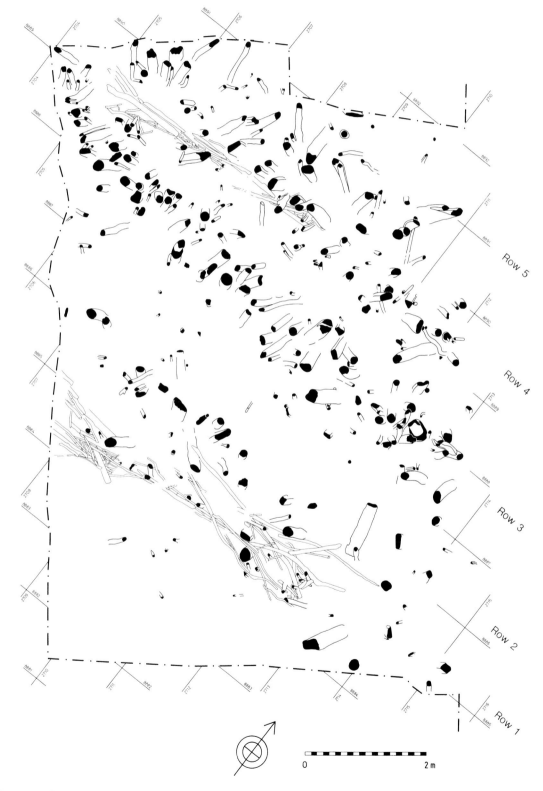

Fig 6.87 Flag Fen, Area 6B: distribution plan of wattle walls/revetments

Fig 6.88 Flag Fen, Area 6B, Level 6: vertical view showing parts of two querns partially obscured by overlying timbers (centre, lower right)

Fig 6.89 Flag Fen, Area 6B, Level 6: close-up of two querns in situ *below the timbers of Level 6*

removing them from the ground was extremely difficult (Fig 6.94). Trial and error showed that, after removing the lowest horizontal wood and searching the ground between and around the posts with a metal detector, the best technique was to work sideways, at a quarry face about half a metre in depth. The most solid encrustations of pan could then be shattered at the edge by using a cold chisel and heavy hammer (if necessary). Surprisingly, it was discovered that the wood was unaffected by the vibration and only suffered in rare cases of direct impact.

Post-depositional effects

In general, the condition of the posts was good and axe marks could clearly be seen once the clay and encrustation had been removed. It was noticeable, however, that many of the smaller posts (ie those below 100mm diameter or breadth) had buckled some 300mm above the basal clay and gravels (Fig 6.95). This buckling does not seem to have been the result of heavyhandedness in antiquity, as the tips showed no apparent signs of impact damage and had not splayed or splintered. The location of the lowest sharp bend in many posts was at the transition from the finely grained organic muds (the stratigraphic equivalent of the palaeosol found elsewhere at Fengate and Northey) to the overlying alluvial deposits.

It is possible that at certain periods and seasons the groundwater might have dropped to this depth during the course of its natural fluctuation. The organic mud

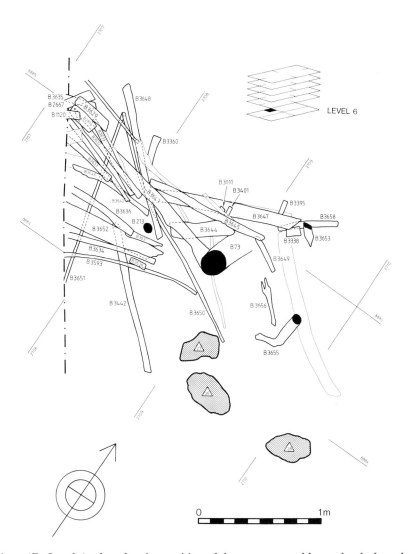

Fig 6.90 Flag Fen, Area 6B, Level 6: plan showing position of three querns and lowest level of wattle revetment around Row 1

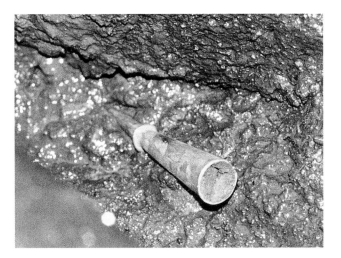

Fig 6.91 Flag Fen, Area 6B, Level 6: close-up of flesh-hook socket in situ

Fig 6.92 Flag Fen, Area 6B, Level 6: haft (B2737) for socketed axe in situ *close to south edge of excavation*

and the overlying alluvial deposits are of different composition and texture and probably possessed different water retention capabilities. Any wood that passed through them would inevitably have been subject to stress. Factors such as these might help to account for

the sharp, splinterless breakages, which could not have occurred in wood that had retained any significant elasticity (Maisie Taylor personal communication). It is probable, therefore, that the buckling took place at some time after deposition.

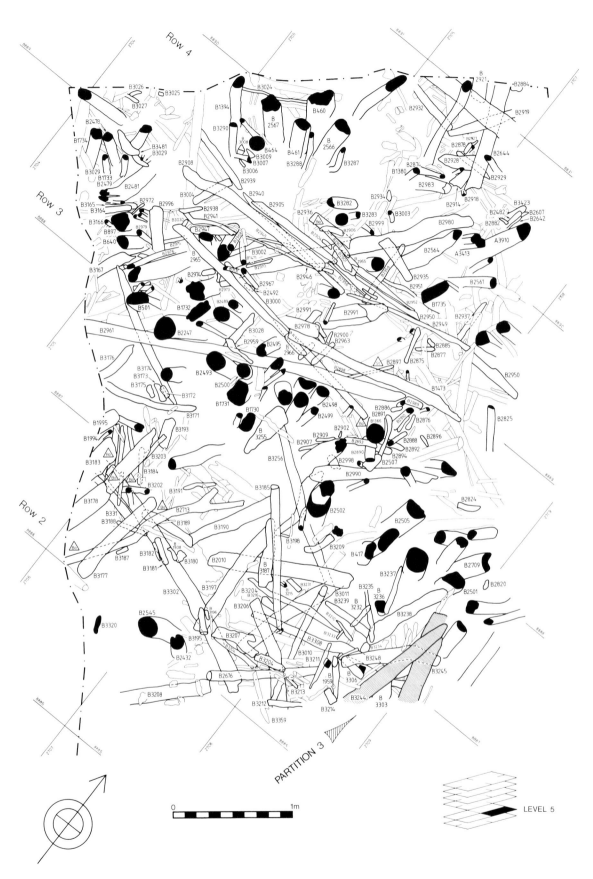

Fig 6.93 Flag Fen, Area 6B, Levels 5 and 6: plan of numbered wood in north-west quadrant. Possible transverse partition timbers have been shaded (for location see Fig 6.77)

Fig 6.94 Flag Fen, Area 6B: work in progress in the final stages of the excavation, during removal of the posts (1993 season)

Fig 6.95 Flag Fen, Area 6B, Level 6: posts of Row 3 immediately prior to removal. The tips are lodged in the basal clay that caps the terrace gravels. The water table has been artificially raised

The vertical section

Once all the posts had been removed, it became possible to draw the long, western, section of Area 6B in its entirety (Fig 6.96). The low-lying and wet peats at the extreme south corner could not be removed as there was a possibility that this would undermine the corner post of the excavation shelter. Apart from the shelly detrital peats of the southern corner, the matrix was very homogeneous and there were no macroscopically visible layers, erosion channels, or other disconformities. The entire sequence would belong within Dr French's zone of 'detrital peats and thin sand horizons', which lie below the peaty alluvium of later Iron Age and Roman times (Fig 1.7). These higher deposits were removed mechanically in order to provide a flat surface upon which the excavation shelter could be positioned.

At the conclusion of the excavation, it was decided to make an accurate record of the position of all timbers in the western baulk, prior to sealing them within

a waterproof membrane and reburial. These measures were an attempt to retain water within the next area to be excavated, Area 6D. In the section, deposits of sand and fine gravel, which had been placed on the walkway surfaces, are shown between the posts of Rows 3 and 4.

Discussion

This discussion will review the evidence for the composition, phasing, and extent of the post alignment, platform, and associated features. In Chapter 19 the site's social, regional, and wider contexts will be considered.

So far, the evidence from stratigraphy and horizontal relationships has been reviewed. Inevitably, most of the data were derived from the long-term research excavations of Area 6, as these provided a sufficiently open area to view the general layout of the timbers. They also revealed at least five separate layers of construction, use, and collapse. Following analysis of the results of the main excavations, attention will be briefly turned to the size and extent of the post alignment east of Fengate. The platform has yet to be excavated as fully as the post alignment and it is difficult to attempt more than a few provisional remarks on its construction, extent, and role. The chapter will conclude with an account of the structural and stratigraphic relationship between the post alignment and the platform.

The post alignment: layout and structure

The morphology of the post alignment

The post alignment has been examined in two trenches within the wet fen proper, using small open-area excavations. Both Areas 6 and 8 (Fig 6.1) revealed a similar layout of 5 post rows and indications of wattle revetments. Elsewhere, for example at the Power Station or in Area 1, the size and layout of the post alignment suggests only a broadly similar arrangement. In both these areas, since the posts were less clearly arranged in rows, it was hard to discern a pattern in the horizontal wood.

It has been suggested that the alder posts of Row 1 are among the earliest in the sequence revealed in Area 6. By the same token, it is also suggested that the alder posts included within Row 3, which seem to form rough pairs with those of Row 1, were also early (Fig 6.97). The oak posts of Rows 2–5 have been shown by dendrochronology to have been the result of near-continuous repair, rebuilding, enlargement, and maintenance carried out between and within the twelfth to tenth century BC (Chapters 8 and 16). As yet, there is no evidence to suggest that the post alignment came about in a haphazard or unplanned fashion by, for example, the amalgamation of a series of disparate trackways. The artefactual evidence supplies, moreover, a broadly similar date range, essentially from the late Middle Bronze Age to the later Iron Age, both at the Power Station and in Area 6 of Flag Fen. These general considerations suggest that the post alignment was indeed a single, integral monument and it is reasonable therefore to seek evidence that might provide clues on how it was laid out, constructed, and used.

The present discussion is only concerned with the post alignment's use and maintenance as a timber structure, which dendrochronology (at the Power Station and Flag Fen) suggests was between the mid thirteenth and the latter part of the tenth century BC (Chapter 8, Discussion). The nature of the subsequent (mainly Iron Age) ritual presence within and around the abandoned post alignment, will be considered in Chapter 19.

Initially, the analysis will be confined to the three subareas of Area 6: Areas 6A, 6B, and 6D. Later, parallels will be sought from elsewhere at Flag Fen. The five post rows (the first evidence that presented itself in the field) will be the starting point of the discussion.

The five post rows

The five rows were numbered from south to north. Species identifications of individual posts are given in Figure 6.97. Each row had distinctive features of its own, here summarised.

Row 1 was possibly the earliest and was composed exclusively of alder posts, which were widely, but evenly spaced. It was somewhat less straight than Row 2 and was broken by a wide gap between Areas 6B and 6D. On either side of the gap the posts were differently aligned. Those to the east were placed 2m further north than those to the west of the gap.

Row 2 was almost exclusively of oak. It was narrow and well defined, but the post spacings were much closer than Row 1. It was broken by a narrow gap that was positioned level with the west side of the gap in Row 1.

Row 3, the central row, was mainly composed of oak, but there were also substantial quantities of alder, ash, willow, poplar, and other less common woods such as *Acer campestre* (field maple) and Pomoideae (apple, pear, or hawthorn). The posts were very closely packed together and confined to a narrow band that resembled a wall in its final stages.

The posts of Row 4 were far less tightly packed than the other rows. It is perhaps best described as a linear zone of timbers that in plan resembles the haphazard arrangement in the stones of a hillfort's *chevaux de frise*. This row was mainly composed of oak, but with a significant component of ash and alder.

Row 5 resembled Row 2 in many respects and might originally have served a similar function. It was straight and tightly confined. It was also composed almost exclusively of oak. Although not interrupted by a significant gap in the line of posts, there was a restricted entranceway onto the platform to the north. This was marked by a spread of white sand and gravel beyond the confines of the post alignment and by a large split oak plank, which had been pegged into

position. This entranceway, which was identified in Levels 1 and 2, was described in the first report as a 'threshold' (Pryor *et al* 1986, fig 12).

The posts of the five rows were observed to lean, or to be angled, in a consistent manner (Fig 6.45 and 6.46): Row 1 leant to the south, sometimes quite sharply; the posts of Row 2 were generally vertical; the crowded posts of Row 3 were either vertical or were angled gently south; those of Row 4 leant mainly to the north, while the posts of Row 5 were generally vertical. The noticeable sharp contrast between Rows 3 and 4 can not be explained by post-depositional factors alone (Fig 6.57).

The spacing of the post rows

While attention has inevitably been focused on the rows of posts, the spaces between them were also significant. The width of the space between Rows 1 and 2 varied markedly on either side of the gap in Row 1. To the east it was approximately 1.5m, whereas to the west it was nearer 3m. The space between Rows 2 and 3 was 1.5m wide, whereas that between Rows 3 and 4 was narrow and, in places (for example Area 6A), seemingly discontinuous. Nowhere was it wider than about 1–0.5m. The space between Rows 4 and 5 was almost identical to that just described, either very narrow or non-existent.

Wattle walls and revetments

In the first report the wattle walls or revetments were considered to be the walls of a building, as they were confined to what were then thought to be the two outer walls (Rows 2 and 5; Pryor *et al* 1986, fig 6). The more widely spaced, outwardly leaning posts of Row 1 were thought to have been eave supports. No walls were found around the posts of Rows 3 and 4 (the north and south aisle posts of the hypothetical building).

A broadly similar pattern has been observed subsequently in Area 6B (Fig 6.87), with possible wall revetment footings in Rows 1 (Fig 6.85), 2 (Fig 6.70), and 5 (Fig 6.60). That around Row 1 in Level 5 was so well preserved that it was possible to estimate its original height (300–500mm).

Two rather crude, unwoven, wall-like structures of wattle were found on either side of the space between Rows 3 and 4 in Level 4 (Fig 6.93). The 'wattles' in this instance were more pole-like than those employed elsewhere at Flag Fen. These structures could have been used to underpin the edges of the overlying narrow walkway.

Now that the hypothesis for a building has been abandoned, it would seem reasonable to interpret the various wattle walls or wall footings as support and revetment for both vertical and horizontal timbers. Woven wattle is sufficiently tough and resilient to retain farm livestock. When tightly woven it can provide a very strong, yet flexible barrier that would have been well suited to the task (Pryor 1991, fig 43).

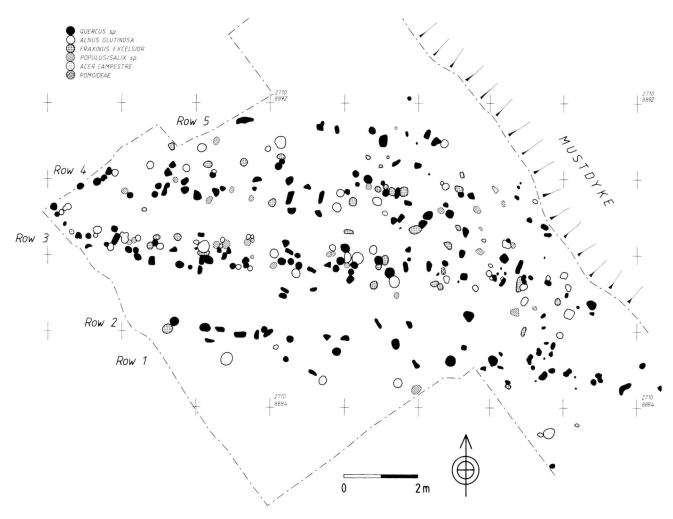

Fig 6.97 Flag Fen, Areas 6A and 6B: plan of posts showing wood species

The horizontal timbers

General plans of the timbers, with oak shown in black, have been prepared for each level of Area 6 (Figs 6.98–102). These clearly show a general decline in the quantities of oak from the initial high concentrations seen in Levels 1 and 2 (which were broadly similar) to those in Level 5, where oak was almost absent.

The uppermost timbers of Level 1 (Fig 6.97) were long trimmed logs with bark intact, which lay on the surface, unsecured by pegs. Below these, and also in Level 1, were numerous woodchips (often of oak) and a number of oak planks, some of which were very large. In Level 2 (Fig 6.98), the oak timbers were smaller in size, but the overall quantity of oak was, if anything, greater. This level showed much evidence for wear and trample along the pathway between Rows 2 and 3.

By Level 3 (Fig 6.100), oak was mainly confined to planks and larger timbers that ran axially, or at very oblique angles, along the alignment in a narrow zone between rows 3 and 4, and on either side of Row 2. Both sets of oak planks probably formed walkways and both showed much evidence for wear on their upper surfaces. The undersides frequently exhibited evidence for wet rot.

By Level 4 (Fig 6.101), the few oak planks were confined to the north side of the central row and to the outermost rows, 1 and 5. There was also a major change at this level in the overall size and alignment of the wood encountered: horizontal timbers were rarely found within Row 3; in Row 4 they were more dispersed, very long, often slender, and (with the exception of the possible partitions to be discussed below) often ran axially. The so-called 'log layer' of trimmed alder logs was first seen at this level. These logs had been laid in a rough corduroy pattern between the posts of Rows 2 and 3. Smaller timbers were laid transversely between Rows 2 and 3, to east and west of the large alder logs.

The lowest Level, 5 (Fig 6.102), was also characterised by large timbers. Oak was almost entirely confined to a few planks around the possible partition 3. The greatest concentration of large timbers was south of Row 3. North of Row 3, horizontal timbers ran axially or diagonally, except for the two partitions 2 and 3. Wet areas north of Row 5 (in Area 6A) and south of Row 1 (in Area 6B) had been consolidated with long timbers arranged at random or in a rough lattice-like pattern.

In summary, Level 1 represented some possible collapsed superstructure (the uppermost axial logs) and the highest buildup of flooring, which mainly comprised large oak planks and smaller infilling material. Level 2 largely consisted of accumulations of flooring material. Level 3 contained the uppermost foundation material, which bridged over the many gaps between the larger timbers of the level below and the smaller infill flooring in smaller timber of Level 2. It also included plank-built pathways between the posts of Rows 3 and 4 and around the posts of Row 2. Apart from a few planks of the Rows 3–4 walkway, the lowest two levels were composed of foundation or makeup timbers.

Finally, it should be stressed that the vast majority of wood seems to have been cut, trimmed, or selected for use. It would appear that the branching and often sinuous wood, so characteristic of the crown of a tree, had been rejected in favour of straighter pieces. Nor did any of the five levels include significant quantities of brushwood or driftwood.

Pathways, walkways, and areas of trample

A distinction has been drawn between the various narrow plank-built walkways and the wider pathway between Rows 2 and 3. The pathway could have accommodated two people walking side by side; the walkways, on the other hand, were for single-file traffic, reminiscent perhaps of a ship's gangways.

Current excavation in Area 6D has clearly demonstrated that the area between the posts of Rows 2 and 3 in Levels 1 and 2 was a slightly raised pathway. It consisted of numerous woodchips, short planks, and offcuts held in a peaty matrix of sand and fine gravel. The surface was worn and many of the woodchips were broken and crushed; the surface of the pathway was raised some 200mm above the surrounding wood. This was perhaps the most apparent length of 'short plank, chip, and sand' pathway so far identified in Area 6. It is also the most recent. The same type of pathway between Rows 2 and 3 was also identified in Levels 1 and 2 in Area 6A (where it was once interpreted as a building's floor) and in Area 6B.

A narrow plank and sand walkway was found in Levels 1 and 2 between Rows 4 and 5 in Area 6A and at the north-east corner of Area 6B. Another, perhaps even narrower, example was found between the posts of Rows 3 and 4 in Levels 1 and 2 in Areas 6A and 6B.

At the bottom of Level 2, and throughout Level 3, a succession of larger oak planks and fine sand was found close to the western edge of Area 6B (Fig 6.61: grid 2707 8885). These timbers had been heavily worn and the undersides of the planks showed signs of ancient wet rot. This walkway was probably a precursor of the wider pathway of Levels 1 and 2. It did not, however, continue further east in that form. Instead, it gave way to a less formal 'plank and long timber' style

of walkway, which might originally have connected with the 'plank and long timber' walkway that ran along the north side of Row 2, also in Level 3.

The best example of a 'plank and long timber' style of walkway is that in the narrow gap between the posts of Rows 3 and 4 in Levels 3 and 4 (Fig 6.100). The planks were mainly of oak. In Area 6B, the walkway was bounded on either side by the large pole-like wattle revetments of Level 3.

Evidence for transverse partitions

Evidence was found for possible transverse partitions in Levels 4 and 5 of Area 6. Once recognised at these low levels, further evidence was also found higher in the sequence. For ease of reference, the segments of post alignment between the various partitions are defined by the partition numbers.

The evidence for the existence of possible transverse partitions was diverse and has already been considered in some detail. Here the earlier discussion will be drawn together, but further evidence, unrelated to the layout and deposition of the timbers, will also be included. Row 1 included a number of unusually large posts, which stood out from the others on account of their size. These posts were found at intervals of approximately 5m. Running north from the posts in Row 1 were horizontal timbers that, unlike other horizontals, consistently passed through the post rows. The crossing points in Rows 3 and 4 were marked by groups of posts, which clustered at the possible partitions.

When the plans of Levels 4 and 5 were viewed at a small scale, it became clear that the arrangement of the lower foundation timbers respected the possible partitions in a general manner. In Level 4 (Fig 6.64), for example, the horizontal timbers within the post alignment in segment 1–2 differed from those in segment 2–4; in the former, there were many more horizontal timbers and the neat arrangement of posts in Row 3 appeared to break down. The log layer between Rows 2 and 3 stopped at partition 2, to be replaced by very much smaller timbers in segment 1–2. This would suggest that the partitioning was not just an initial arrangement, perhaps to facilitate the organisation of the alignment's construction, but rather an arrangement of longer term significance.

In Level 5 the log layer could also be seen to stop abruptly at partition 2, which was marked by a concentration of poles. The main southwards spread of timber into the wet area at the southern end of Area 6B took place in segment 2–3, and the large logs of the log layer failed to continue into segment 3–4. The wattle revetment of Row 1 began at post B73, the southern marker of partition 3.

Is there enough evidence for an additional partition, 4? Although excavations within Area 6D are still at too high a level to allow definitive proof of its existence, the three large alder posts in Rows 1, 2, and 3

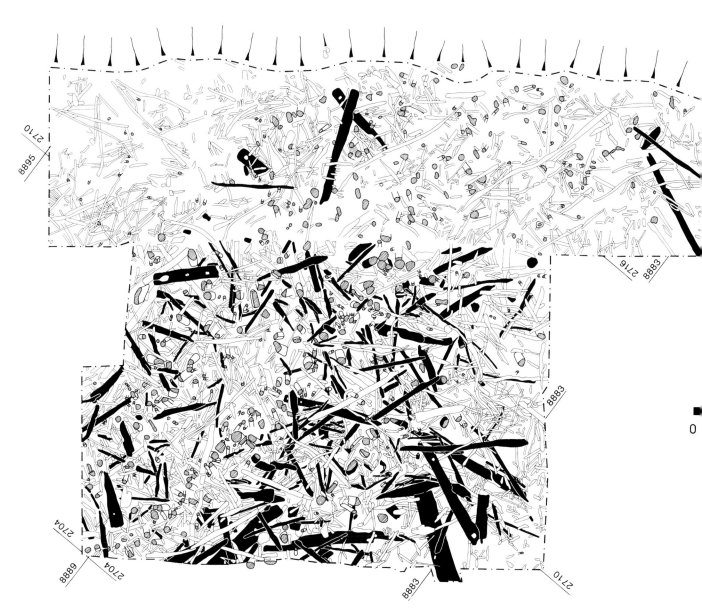

Fig 6.98 Flag Fen, Areas 6A and 6B, Level 1: distribution of oak timbers (in black); for location see Fig 6.1

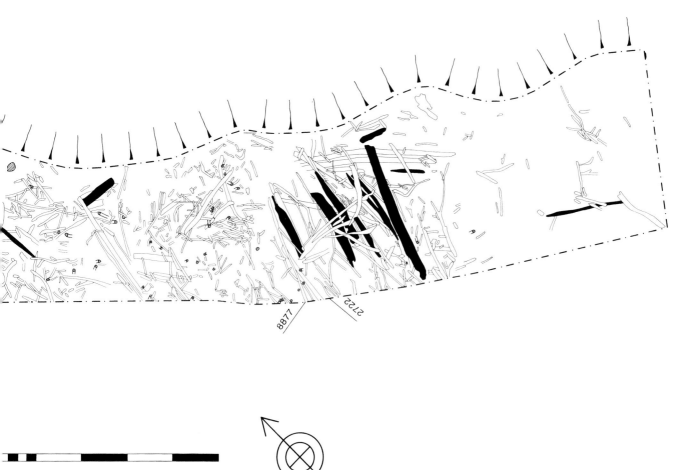

8877

2722

5m

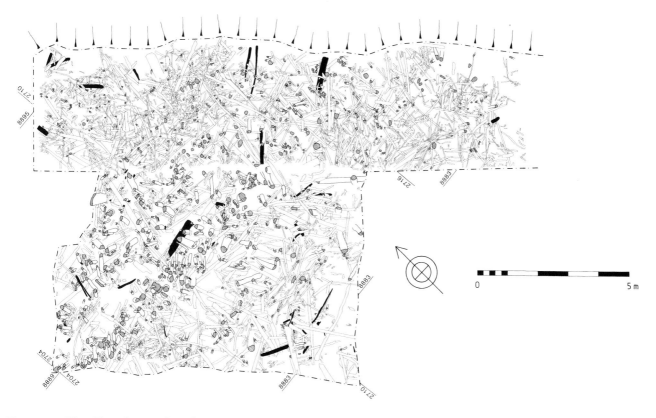

Fig 6.101 Flag Fen, Areas 6A and 6B, Level 4: distribution of oak timbers (in black); for location see Fig 6.1

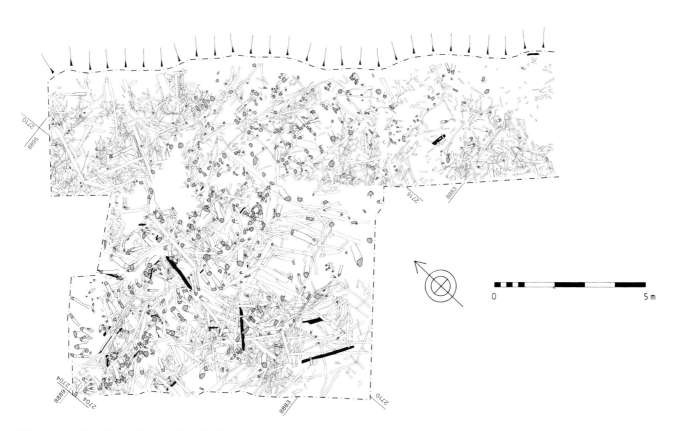

Fig 6.102 Flag Fen, Areas 6A and 6B, Level 5: distribution of oak timbers (in black); for location see Fig 6.1

(which might possibly have supported a portal) occur some 6m west of partition 3. Future excavation will reveal whether there were transverse horizontal timbers between the three alder posts in Levels 4 or 5. Perhaps the strongest argument in favour of partition 4 is that segment 3–4 was clearly defined by the gap in post Row 1, the gap being the segment. East and west of that segment the posts were similarly and regularly spaced. There was also a significant change in the alignment of Row 1 on either side of segment 3–4.

In Level 5, the partitioning was marked by a possible boundary deposit of three saddle querns (Fig 6.90), which were placed close to the southern boundary post of partition 3 (B73). It might be significant that all three querns were placed within the same segment (2–3). Post B73 was also the scene of another, but later, possible boundary deposit. A small Late Bronze Age fineware jar with a dimpled base had been placed close to the large post in Level 1. The vessel was complete, apart from a small chip at the rim. On stratigraphic grounds this deposit had to belong to the latest replacement of the horizontal timbers, around 900 BC. The very latest of the possible partition boundary deposits consisted of several fragments of a finely decorated sword scabbard plate (Other Find 29), which had been placed between Rows 1 and 2 (Area 6D) directly against partition 4. The scabbard plate is decorated with a stylised dragon pair, which can be dated to around 150 BC. If the scabbard is indeed a deliberate ritual deposit intended to mark a partition (and it is the second part of that proposition that is contentious) it would appear that the segmentation of the post alignment continued for perhaps 700–800 years after the final maintenance of the timber structure.

The wood-free zones of Area 6

All the subareas (A–D) of Area 6 contained wood-free zones that were most probably patches of open water, either contemporary with the post alignment and platform, or earlier. So far, the site has not produced evidence for later stream channels that cut into the Bronze Age timbers. The excavations of Area 8 revealed indirect evidence for an earlier stream channel or watercourse bridged in separate places by three large horizontal timbers. From the research viewpoint, it is unfortunate that these timbers will not be removed as they now lie within the Preservation Hall. It is nonetheless probable that a wood-free zone will eventually be revealed below them.

The main wood-free zones of Area 6 interconnected with each other, but were characterised by different stratigraphic sequences. The narrow wood-free zone of Area 6A was entirely covered by wood in Level 1 and was not revealed until Level 2; by Level 3 it was wider and very much better defined. In Level 4 its northern edge appeared to mark the platform's

southern boundary. In Areas 6C and 6D the wood and timber of Level 1 did not cover the wood-free zone. The evidence would suggest that the wood-free zones were areas of open water, perhaps old stream courses that had ceased to flow actively (Charles French personal communication). By a late stage in the site's development (in Level 1?) the narrower, shallower channels had silted up sufficiently to allow their surfaces to be consolidated or even bridged over with wood. This hypothesis finds support in the progressive narrowing of the wood-free zone of Area 6A, in Levels 1 to 3.

The larger wood-free zone of Area 6D was treated somewhat differently. Instead of attempting to bridge it over or cover it, efforts were made to consolidate the sides. These efforts were particularly clear in Area 6B where the southern corner of the excavation just impinged upon the wood-free zone that was revealed more fully to the west, in Area 6D (the 'pool'). In the lowest levels, the southern corner of Area 6B was characterised by many straight timbers (eg Fig 6.23), including some in oak (which was unusual in Levels 5 and 6). The 'cavity wall' of Row 1 in Levels 5 and 6 might be part of these revetment works (Fig 6.87). Finally, the deposition of the three querns might represent both a practical and a symbolic attempt to shore up the edge of the open pool immediately prior to the construction of the post alignment and platform. On the other hand, they might have served, as we have seen (above, Levels 5 and 6, Area 6A), to mark the position of partition 3.

The 'poolside area' of Area 6D

Segment 3–4 was marked by a gap in Row 1. A possible portal has been suggested to account for the three large alder posts that occurred in a transverse row across the alignment in Rows 1, 2, and 3 (Fig 6.37). Rows 4 and 5 were not exposed in Area 6D. In addition to the possible portal, a fine La Tène sword scabbard plate (Other Find 29) was found high in Level 1, between Rows 1 and 2 and immediately east of the portal. A concentration of dog bones was found in Level 2, below the scabbard plate and east of it. These bones spread from the area between Rows 1 and 2 southwards into the pool or open water immediately south of Row 1. The pool was edged on its north side by a series of substantial oak planks, which included two massive tangentially split oak examples. Janet Neve's dendrochronological study (Chapter 8) has shown that one of these (B63) had been split from the same tree as other timbers in Area 6B, which would suggest that it had not been reused, but had been made to be placed on the ground.

The seemingly profligate use of very high quality timber, the pool itself, the possible portal, the deliberate destruction of a fine sword scabbard plate, and the deposition of dog bones all suggest that the poolside area was one of special ritual importance.

Constructional sequence

The fundamental structural sequence seems to be reasonably clear and is summarised below. Phase 1 was the period of initial activity, dated dendrochronologically at the Power Station to the mid thirteenth century BC. Phase 2 was a period lasting about a century and a half, during which the monument was probably in use (in other words, there is no evidence for abandonment), but maintenance and construction work was minimal. Construction was resumed at the turn of the twelfth century/first quarter of the eleventh century BC (Phase 3). This phase of construction and renewal lasted until the final repairs in the second half of the tenth century BC. Unfortunately, the tree-ring evidence does not throw much light on the succession of the various post rows. The sequence suggested below is, therefore, based on structural and stratigraphic considerations.

There are other problems. The constructional sequence is difficult to demonstrate stratigraphically because most horizontal timbers (and particularly the alder logs, which are characteristic of the lowest levels) would undoubtedly have sunk well into (if not actually through) the soft alluvial peats, until they came to rest against another timber or reached the organic muds that capped the underlying clays and gravels. Such sinkage has made difficult the definition of the various constructional phases.

The plans of the five excavated levels show that there were very few horizontal timbers that passed through the posts of Row 3 from side to side, other than those of the possible partitions, and even they were broken at Row 3. Row 3 is therefore treated as a major stratigraphic and physical division. It also contained a substantial number of posts in alder, which argues in favour of an early date for its initial laying-out (Fig 6.97). Row 1 can be shown to be early by dendrochronology (Chapter 9). From Level 3 and upwards (ie from the onset of Phase 3), the stratigraphy becomes more clear cut, as the layers of wood and timber built up. Below that, there is always a possibility that significant levels of buildup have been lost by decay or erosion.

The principal stages of the constructional sequence of the post alignment in Area 6 of Flag Fen can be summarised as follows:

Phase 1A (Level 5)

The overall alignment of post Rows 1 and 3 is determined. Transverse partitions are set out and are marked by rituals including the deposition of querns at partition 3.

Phase 1B (Level 5)

The first posts of Rows 1 and 3 are driven in. Transverse partitions are marked by horizontal timbers and large posts in Row 1. A mistake is made in positioning the posts of Row 1 at partition 4. Possible portal constructed at partition 4.

Phase 1C (Level 5)

Long foundation timbers are laid between the posts of Rows 1–3.

Phase 1D (Levels 4 and 5)

Long foundation timbers are reinforced by the addition of large logs of the log layer between Rows 1 and 3; these also provide support for the posts of Row 3. A 'plank and long timber' walkway is constructed along the north side of Row 1.

Phase 2

A period of use and stability with no major constructional work.

Phase 3 (Levels 3 and 4)

Unfortunately the tree-ring study is unable to provide clues as to the order in which various events took place, so what follows is a best guess that uses stratigraphic evidence, on the one hand, and is not at variance with the dendrochronological evidence, on the other. The first four events might well prove to have been contemporary, or might have taken place in a different order. The events that followed were more probably sequential:

Row 1 is abandoned. The first posts of Rows 2 and 4 are driven in and a 'plank and long timber' walkway between Rows 3 and 4 is constructed.
Transverse partitions are extended to include post rows north of Row 3.
Basal horizontal timbers are laid linking Row 3 to Row 4 and beyond.
Posts of Row 5 are driven in and wattle revetment is constructed.
A narrow 'short plank, chip, and sand' walkway is constructed between Rows 4 and 5.
Later in this phase the southern 'plank and long timber' walkway along Rows 1 and 2 is abandoned to rising water.
A new, wider 'short plank, chip, and sand' pathway is constructed between Rows 2 and 3.
A wattle revetment is added to Row 2.
The narrow walkway between Rows 3 and 4 continues in use throughout this phase.
Towards the end of the phase, horizontal oak timbers are introduced to bind together and shore up the many accumulated posts of Row 4.
The narrow walkway between Rows 3 and 4 probably goes out of use.
Row 3 is by now an impenetrable wall.

Large oak planks are used to raise the ground level of the Rows 2–3 pathway and the edge of the 'poolside area'.

Finally a pathway between posts of Rows 2–3 is raised above large oak planks by the addition of oak wood-chips and other smaller material. This level was found to have been eroded elsewhere in Area 6 and only survives in Area 6D.

Phase 4

Once maintenance of the timbers had ceased, the post alignment was visited episodically, mainly for ritual purposes.

The post alignment: pattern and purpose

The discovery in 1993 of a fine Iron Age scabbard plate decorated with Celtic art (below, Fig 10.11, 273) is sufficient excuse to borrow Sir Cyril Fox's well-known title for this discussion, but it is also very apt: the pattern and purpose of the extraordinary timber structure at Flag Fen were always closely linked. From the outset, moreover, it appears to have been purpose-built and there seems little doubt that a major part of that purpose was ritual and perhaps of much older origin. Like Neolithic long barrows two millennia earlier, the Flag Fen post alignment was internally divided, both axially and transversely. The segments were separated by transverse partitions at intervals of approximately 5m. The two axial halves of the alignment were separated by the densely packed posts of the central Row 3.

The north part of the alignment included post Rows 3–5. In essence this part consisted of a wall, barrier, boundary, or palisade. Its north side was marked at its maximum extent in Phase 3 by the strictly linear posts of Row 5, which were revetted close to the waterline by a double (or cavity) wattle wall. There was a narrow walkway behind (ie south of) the posts of Row 5. Row 5 was breached by a narrowly restricted entranceway, which gave onto a slightly raised, or built up, area on the platform to the north of the alignment.

The posts of Row 4 formed a haphazard but broadly linear band of posts, resembling a *chevaux de frise*. In Levels 4 and 5 the posts were supported by long axial or diagonal horizontal timbers that tied the posts of Row 4 into those of Row 5. Others tied them to the posts of Row 3 and provided support for the narrow plank-built walkway that ran between Rows 4 and 3.

Row 3 was in use for the entire life of the monument. By its later stages (3 and 4) it formed an almost solid wall composed of tightly packed posts in a linear band no more than a metre wide.

The southern axial half of the structure included the posts of Rows 1–3. This part can be broadly characterised as given over to a main pathway, associated walkways, and ritual areas, such as the 'poolside area'

of segment 3–4. This pattern of use would accord well with the southerly distribution of metalwork recorded at the Power Station.

The first walkway was probably along Row 1, where it skirted around a particularly wet spot in Areas 6B and 6D. This walkway was revetted by low wattle walls along Rows 1 and 2. As water levels rose, these early walkways were abandoned in favour of a wide, well finished pathway laid on a bed of long timbers. They, in turn, rested on the large alder logs of the log layer of Levels 4 and 5, between the posts of Rows 2 and 3. The pathway between Rows 2 and 3 was built up in at least three episodes during Phase 3, of which the penultimate (in Level 1) involved the use of some very large oak planks. Massive oak planks were also used to provide hardstanding around the edge of the ritually important poolside area in segment 3–4.

In its final years, perhaps even as late as the earliest Iron Age, it is possible that the northern, or palisade part of the alignment had been allowed to decay — all that remained was a slightly raised walkway between the rotted off stumps of the posts of Rows 2–3.

The largest gap in any post row was in Row 1, on the southern side of the alignment. The southern side faced onto the large embayment. This extended south and west from the narrow strait, which the post alignment traversed. So far as is known, the southerly embayment was surrounded by the fields and pastures belonging to the communities who constructed and used the Flag Fen alignment. This enclosed and controlled embayment might well have been considered 'safe', when compared with the open expanses of developing fen to the north and east. This contrast between the 'friendly' landscape of the south and the 'hostile' landscape of the north is marked by the narrowly restricted gap in the north-facing Row 5. This gap, which was marked by a large 'threshold plank', resembled more a door than a gateway (Fig 6.52; Pryor *et al* 1986, fig 6, doorway).

It is an oversimplification, however, to characterise the two axial halves of the alignment as palisade versus pathway/ritual. There were, for example, at least two walkways on the northerly, defensive or palisade side of Row 3, and there were ritual depositions among the posts of Rows 3 and 4 (such as the broken chape, below Fig 10.3, 42, from Area 6B, Level 4). Which said, rituals that involved any number of people could not readily have taken place among a forest of posts, nor could a walkway have provided a spectacular or daunting structure to impress a friend or discourage a foe. The alignment must surely be seen as a whole. It meant many things to many people: an impressive construction that symbolised a community's success and self-esteem; a suitable place to start the final journey to the next world, and it might also have served a defensive or boundary role. Many other explanations are possible, but, on present evidence, it is doubtful whether it would have served the single practical purpose of traversing a piece of boggy ground. These, however, are themes that will be pursued further in Chapter 19.

The post alignment: extent

The post alignment's course across Flag Fen has been demonstrated in a number of trial trenches and other excavations. Immediately east of the Power Station the complete width of the post alignment was exposed in Area 1 (Fig 1.5, inset). The next properly excavated and recorded exposure of a small part of the post alignment was Area 2, some 400m east of Area 1. This trench also revealed well preserved horizontal oak planks. In 1990, a less formal trench was, however, rapidly excavated midway between Areas 1 and 2, in order to assess groundwater conditions. This trench located two large oak posts and several split oak timbers (Pryor 1992a, fig 6: TT1990A).

Insertion of the polythene membrane around the edge of the lake revealed posts of the alignment at two points (Fig 6.1, A and C). The tops of posts were also found in Area 4, within the lake (Fig 6.6). The alignment passed from the lake, through the main excavations of Area 6 and the dykeside exposure of 1982 across the Mustdyke (where its presence was recorded by drainage engineers in 1976). On the east side of the dyke its full extent was revealed in Areas 7 and 8. No attempts have yet been made to trace its course between Area 8 and the dry land of Northey, but recent landscape works, hedge planting and so on, have shown that at least some posts are present immediately below the base of the topsoil.

The lake lining exposure revealed posts outside the alignment at four separate locations (Fig 6.1, B, D–F). The concentration of posts at B was particularly dense and well defined. These outlying groups of posts could not be explained as separate post alignments in their own right, as they were too insubstantial. No further exposures of posts have been observed, moreover, in either the Cat's Water or Mustdyke during recent machine cleaning of these dykes. The simplest explanation for the outlying posts is that they represent lateral extensions of the proposed transverse partitions between segments of the post alignment. The distances are too great to allow any precision, but post group D aligns well with the position of a hypothetical partition 1; similarly, group B would align quite convincingly on a hypothetical partition 11. Post groups E and F are too distant from Area 6 to test this valid, but unproven hypothesis.

The platform: construction and extent

The Flag Fen timber platform is an enigmatic construction. Indeed, it might not have been a solid platform at all, but rather a series of consolidated areas interspersed with watercourses and pools. There does, however, seem to have been a clearly defined and revetted perimeter walkway. This is of considerable importance as it would have bounded and defined the space occupied by the platform. If the platform served a mainly ritual role, moreover, the clear definition of its limits would have been essential. The need to define a special space within a wider area (in this case a wetland) that was not otherwise bounded, finds parallels in regions distant from the Fens (Bradley et al 1994).

The perimeter revetment resembled the main walkway of the post alignment (that between Rows 2 and 4) in important respects. It had roundwood foundations and, where preserved (ie in Area 6A, Level 1), it had a well laid plank surface. The exposure of the perimeter revetment in Area 5 (Fig 6.10) revealed parallel logs that probably formed the revetment's foundations. Unfortunately, higher levels were not preserved in this area due to a combination of drying out (with consequent slippage of the dykeside) and of storm damage in antiquity. One plank (A8719) set back from the dyke was, however, found lying above the logs. This plank could well have belonged to a disrupted walkway surface. Planks were found in the small trial trench, Area 5, and these, too, could have formed part of the perimeter walkway.

The original dykeside exposure of 1982 is still the only opportunity yet to examine a complete cross-section of the platform (Fig 6.9). The spread of timber, wood, and debris continued for some 72m. The thickest buildup of horizontal timbers was found about 14m north of the post alignment, the area illustrated in the first report (Pryor et al 1986, pl 4b).

The nature of the platform is hard to establish from so little evidence. Within Area 6 there were pools and areas of open water. If water played an important part in contemporary ritual practices, indeed, it would not be illogical to expect a 'little Venice' of pools, creeks, and relict streams, where rites could take place in privacy and safety, and be witnessed by an audience. The main distinction between these wet places and those of the open fen to the north-east was their enclosure within the perimeter walkway revetment and their proximity to the post alignment.

The relationship of the platform and post alignment

The dendrochronological analysis has demonstrated that horizontal timbers close to the post alignment came from the same trees as certain posts in the main rows. The felling of an oak plank (A4614) from the perimeter revetment walkway of Area 6A was dated dendrochronologically to 1002–957 BC. This demonstrates beyond doubt that the platform and the post alignment were contemporary.

A possible clue to the relationship between the platform and the post alignment might be provided by the identification of possible transverse partitioning. Perhaps walkways along some or all of the partitions would have linked the post alignment to outlying parts of the platform. Certainly the planks of partition 3, for example, would have provided an accessible, if narrow, access through the otherwise impenetrable wall of Row 3 posts.

An inkling as to how the platform might have been organised is provided by the two gaps in the outer post rows, 1 and 5: that in Row 5 was narrow and restricted, whereas that in Row 1 occupied all of segment 3–4. This might suggest that the activities that took place on the platform north of the alignment had to do with actual or symbolic hostility. The platform south of the alignment was safer territory, both actually and symbolically, where a very different range of activities could have taken place. This might help to explain why the platform was so very much larger south of the alignment. It might also help to explain why the only group of posts, or possible partition wall, found north of the alignment (Fig 6.1, B) was much bigger than any of the groups to the south (Fig 6.1, D–F).

7 The wood

by Maisie Taylor

The prehistoric wood from Flag Fen and the Power Station site will be considered in this chapter. It is arranged in five main sections: the wood itself; a statistical analysis of timber and by-products; a discussion of toolmarks and the type of tools that might have been used; a consideration of the reduction of timber and the evidence for joints, and short descriptions of artefacts and artefact fragments.

The waterlogged wood: sampling and taphonomy

Sampling and recording

When the first wood was excavated at Flag Fen, it was not possible to put the site into a functional category that might suggest an appropriate method of analysis. It was therefore decided that, in the first instance, all wood would be planned, numbered, and retained for further study. Once a complete cross-section of the wood deposits had been recorded and retrieved it would be possible to design a sampling strategy. The original sequence of numbers was prefixed 'A' and the 'A series' accounted for nearly 9000 pieces of wood from all levels. The A series coincided with the excavation of Area 6A. It is the A series material that has been used for the statistical characterisation of the wood from Flag Fen. In later excavations (Areas 6B–D) similar excavation methods to those used in Area 6A have continued, but a simpler method of sampling has been introduced.

As each level was exposed, the individual pieces were clearly defined while *in situ*. After the cleaned level had been photographed and planned, as much wood as possible was lifted. Where necessary, the plan was amended as the wood was lifted. Subsequent to the A Series, numbers were only allocated to some of the pieces, usually the worked wood. A provisional record was made of the numbered wood with its provenance details, which included a spot height (OD), measurements, description, and, if necessary, a sketch. Much of the wood was not numbered, however, but sampled and recorded by metre square and spot height. By the time Area 6B had been completed, the sampling of each metre square had begun to produce repetitive data. As a result, this practice has recently been dropped in favour of spot sampling to monitor the 'background noise' of the platform makeup.

Taphonomy: wear, rot, and breakage

The examination of ancient wear and rot on wood at Flag Fen has proved invaluable for interpreting the site, which does not have conventional occupation horizons.

Some material shows signs of exposure on the surface for an extended period before burial, indicated by wet rot, fungus, and insect attack. Wet rot occurs where, for example, wood becomes partly waterlogged when lying face down on a wet surface. Waterlogged wood sometimes shows signs of ancient wet rot on the underside (French and Taylor 1985). This can be used as an indicator of the level of the water table at the time of burial. The penetration of wood by fungus in ancient times is detectable in the laboratory (Boddy and Ainsworth 1984, 96). It can also be detected on site by simple visual examination, as in 1989, when a well preserved bracket fungus was retrieved from the excavation of Area 6B. The fungus was within what later turned out to be a wattlework structure.

Virtually no evidence for the woodworm beetle was discovered among the Coleoptera (Chapter 16), but occasional examples of insect damage have been observed on the waterlogged wood. In 1993, as part of a practical project, a Cambridge undergraduate, Charles Watkinson, took photographs and samples of insect-damaged wood and showed them to two experienced entomologists for identification (Dr George McGavin, Assistant Curator of Entomology at the University Museum and Dr Martin Speight, Forest Entomologist for the Department of Zoology at the University of Oxford).

The entomologists identified eight small exit holes in a worked surface on B2784 as of *Anobiidae*, probably woodworm. It was also suggested that, as the holes were not distorted and as woodworm does not commonly exit through bark, the beetle attack had been made on the worked surface. The main conclusion drawn from this evidence is that, for at least a year or two after it was worked, B2784 had not been waterlogged. The general rarity of woodworm might suggest that timber was felled specifically to be used at Flag Fen. It will become apparent from other evidence (eg tree-ring studies, Chapter 8) that this was often the case. There must always, however, have been other, perhaps less formal, sources of procurement, such as wood felled by beavers, reused structural timber, and wood from timber stacks nearby. These, however, can be seen as the exceptions that prove the rule, in that most of the wood used at Flag Fen was cut down and divided up close to where it was going to be used.

Ancient wear, rot, and breakage can only be reliably detected when the quality of preservation is first-rate. Subsequent damage and deterioration might mask the original condition of the wood. It is therefore important to understand the effects that post-depositional events can have on waterlogged wood. When excavated, the quality of wood might be the result of a number of factors, the starting point being the original quality of the material. Different species and wood from various parts of a tree might react differently to the same conditions. The speed with which the material was covered or the length of time that it remained uncovered before becoming waterlogged are two important factors that would have affected the quality of subsequent preservation.

The effects of plant roots on waterlogged material can be severe. Some cereals and reeds have very penetrating roots, although tree and shrub roots can also cause a great deal of damage. There is some evidence that the penetration of roots might speed up deterioration for reasons other than simple physical damage. Root holes might bring oxygen to deep levels, for example, and some roots contain substances that can be used as a source of food by damaging organisms such as fungi (Boddy and Ainsworth 1984, 96). At Flag Fen, damage from plant roots was generally restricted to the area immediately alongside the Mustdyke. Here, reed roots were a problem, even penetrating oak heartwood. This added greatly to the problems of lifting. In certain cases softer material (eg sapwood) can be destroyed completely. A less obvious problem can occur after the wood is lifted, wrapped, and stored. If a viable reed root is contained inside the wrapping, it might start to grow again, causing extensive damage.

The rate at which wood is excavated will have a bearing on its condition. If wood is disturbed before it is excavated, allowing the access of light and air, it will deteriorate rapidly while still technically buried. The structure of the wood will also have been much altered and weakened by waterlogging. This will usually mean that the aerobic decay, which begins as soon as air is available, will be very rapid. Fluctuations in the water table can produce similar effects. Decay, microbial activity, and physical collapse will begin whenever the water table drops below the waterlogged level. Deterioration will continue until the water table rises again, but the damage that has been done is irreversible. This was a problem with wood not only close to the Mustdyke at Flag Fen, but also over much of the area of the Power Station site, situated as it was on the very edge of the zone of waterlogging.

If (as is usual) there are minerals in the ground water or matrix in which waterlogged material is buried, there is a chance that they might be deposited in the wood in the form of mineral salts. These salts might crystallise inside the woody structure causing damage, or they might be reduced by the bacteria that are naturally present in certain peats, including those at Flag Fen. There is little problem with the crystallisation of the mineral salts in the wood at Flag Fen, as long as it is stored under water. In mineral soils, organic material can become cemented into the matrix by iron-pan. This forms where the ground water, rich in minerals, can move with relative freedom through a free-draining matrix, such as gravel. Once this movement has been slowed down by the presence of organic material,

these minerals can be transferred from the groundwater into the softer material. This was one of the biggest problems encountered on the Power Station site. The worked points of many posts could not be cleaned of sand and gravel, which had been cemented onto the wood by iron salts.

Change of land use might begin the process of deterioration in waterlogged deposits. Deep ploughing can allow air in, causing oxidation, as well as bacterial and fungal action on the material that was so recently waterlogged. The wood from the Power Station site was in a very fragile state when excavated. Drying out was already well advanced in most parts of the site, which made interpretation of some of the material very difficult — much of the fine detail was lost. Deep ploughing or drainage would have accelerated the process of disintegration, already well under way. Animals can accelerate damage to organic deposits. Burrowing animals will speed up the process of aeration and soft, recently waterlogged organic material can easily be gnawed and pushed out of the way. In the early days at Flag Fen, rats were a serious problem on the dykeside. In recent years, rabbits burrowing into archaeological deposits has become a potentially more troublesome problem.

The effects of drying out on different species of wood

Different species of tree and wood from different parts of the plant might react differently to the same burial conditions. The most obvious example is in oak, where the heartwood might survive in waterlogged conditions, retaining a good deal of its strength and flexibility. The sapwood of mature timber and young stems and branches are much softer and deteriorate rapidly once excavated. One of the reasons for this is the high proportion of cellulose in the younger wood. Another factor might be that the living sapwood conducts food materials around the tree and will adapt to conducting the water into the wood when it becomes waterlogged. The cellulose becomes softened in waterlogged conditions and in young wood there might be no secondary cell walls to take the strain. As waterlogged sapwood dries out, it might collapse rapidly without the support of water in the cells.

The heartwood of oak, in particular, might retain some elasticity even though waterlogged for hundreds of years. It might still distort and begin to disintegrate when it dries out, but it can sometimes retain some of its original strength. If wood remains waterlogged for long enough, it is bound to lose its elasticity. Eventually even substantial timbers will snap under their own weight (Fig 6.95). Some species contain varying amounts of resins, oils, and acids, which might affect the quality of preservation. Oak is one of the woods that contain a number of substances, notably tannic acid. Waterlogged mature oak heartwood changes its character and rarely

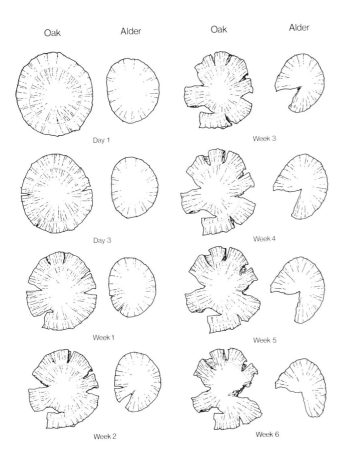

Oak Alder Oak Alder

Day 1 Week 3

Day 3 Week 4

Week 1 Week 5

Week 2 Week 6

Fig 7.1 Progressive drying out of oak and alder over a six-week period. At Day 1 the diameter of the oak was c 200mm and the alder c 150mm

becomes soft or spongy. Instead, after an extended period of burial in waterlogged conditions, it usually becomes much harder.

It was felt necessary to replicate the effects of drying out on the two principal species of waterlogged wood encountered at Flag Fen. Pieces of waterlogged Bronze Age oak (diameter *c* 200mm) and alder (diameter *c* 150mm) roundwood (these sizes were commonly encountered in excavation) were stored in cool, shady conditions and photographed at regular intervals over a six-week period (Fig 7.1). The sapwood of the oak began to shrink and split within days. After a week, the splitting penetrated the heartwood, which then opened up radially and around the rings. The worst and most rapid damage took place in weeks two and three. The alder log showed only very slight radial cracking in the first week. At the end of the second week, one radial crack had penetrated to the pith of the wood. This split then developed until the wood had almost completely exfoliated.

The two different patterns of drying out were noticed in upper levels at Flag Fen. Ash wood had deteriorated in a similar way to oak, but the distortion along the rings was greater. Hazel, and willow/poplar, which are diffuse porous woods, behaved in much the same way as alder. The rapidity of the changes was remarkable and followed earlier observations of Neolithic wood from Etton (French and Taylor 1985).

The speed of the changes has serious implications for storage — unless air is completely excluded and the wood is kept very moist, surface changes will be the inevitable result.

The statistical analysis

The statistical analysis of wood from Flag Fen and the Power Station site follows the procedures established in the Etton report (Taylor 1998). Further, special attention has been paid to the comparability of wood measurements at the two sites. The assemblages represent different types of woodworking, using stone tools, on the one hand, and bronze, on the other. If these major technological differences can be demonstrated and quantified using the metrical data presented below, the approach has some validity. It would then be appropriate to develop it in future research.

The statistical analyses are based on those commonly used in flint studies. Flint knapping and woodworking are reductive technologies that involve the controlled and directed use of force. In archaeological terms each technology has its own idiosyncrasies. The hammerstone and the axe each produce distinctively shaped products and by-products, which in turn can be measured. The source materials also have features in common: wood has bark and sapwood, whereas flint has cortex. On the other hand, flint can be weighed, but waterlogged wood cannot, as the weight will vary according to the water absorbed at the time of weighing. As to the tools used to reduce the source material, these can vary considerably, but wood has the advantage over flint in that it might preserve clear toolmarks. For these various reasons, it is considered appropriate to use a statistical approach of proven archaeological worth to study woodworking and its by-products.

Comparative figures from Etton

The archaeological study of woodworking and woodworking by-products is still at a comparatively early stage and much has been learned since the Etton data were first analysed in 1985–7. This is particularly true of certain by-products, such as timber debris and woodchips. In the light of subsequent experience,

Table 7.1 Principal categories of wood and timber from Area 6A

	number	*%*
natural roundwood	317	5.55
root	58	1.02
roundwood	3214	56.32
roundwood debris	72	1.26
timber	331	5.80
timber debris	101	1.77
debris	1614	28.28
total	5707	100.00

Table 7.2 Flag Fen Area 6A: roundwood dimensions (in mm)

length	0–200	200–400	400–600	600–800	800–1000	1000–1200	1200–1400	1400–1600	1600–1800	1800–2000	2000–2200	2200–2400	2400–2600	2600–2800	2800>	total
	1013	1126	434	234	116	58	52	51	22	17	14	7	6	2	11	3163
	32.03%	35.60%	13.72%	7.40%	3.67%	1.83%	1.64%	1.61%	0.70%	0.54%	0.44%	0.22%	0.19%	0.06%	0.35%	100%

diameter	0–20	20–40	40–60	60–80	80–100	100–120	120–140	140–160	160–180	180–200	200–220	220–240	240–260	260–280	280>	total
	48	100	45	14	14	6	3	6	3	2	1	2	1	1	1	247
	19.43%	40.49%	18.22%	5.67%	5.67%	2.43%	1.21%	2.43%	1.21%	0.81%	0.40%	0.81%	0.40%	0.40%	0.40%	100%

Table 7.3 Flag Fen Area 6A (all levels): roundwood debris dimensions (in mm)

length	0–200	200–400	400–600	total
	32	23	12	67
	47.76%	34.33%	17.91%	100%

original diameter	0–20	20–40	40–60	60–80	80–100	10–120	120–140	140–160	160–180	180–200	200–220	220–240	240–260	260–280	total
	–	21	15	8	6	–	–	1	–	–	–	–	–	2	53
		39.62%	28.30%	15.09%	11.32%			1.89%						3.77%	100%

Table 7.4 Flag Fen Area 6A: timber dimensions (in mm)

length	0–200	200–400	400–600	600–800	800–1000	1000–1200	1200–1400	1400–1600	1600–1800	1800–2000	2000–2200	2200–2400	2400–2600	2600–2800	2800>	total
	42	69	54	48	24	27	17	16	9	8	1	–	4	1	5	325
	12.92%	21.23%	16.62%	14.77%	7.38%	8.31%	5.23%	4.92%	2.77%	2.46%	0.31%		1.23%	0.31%	1.54%	100%

original diameter	0–20	20–40	40–60	60–80	80–100	100–120	120–140	140–160	160–180	180–200	200–220	220–240	240–260	260–280	280>	total
	2	7	10	5	22	14	15	11	9	8	4	3	2	4	3	119
	1.68%	5.88%	8.40%	4.20%	18.49%	11.76%	12.61%	9.24%	7.56%	6.72%	3.36%	2.52%	1.68%	3.36%	2.52%	100%

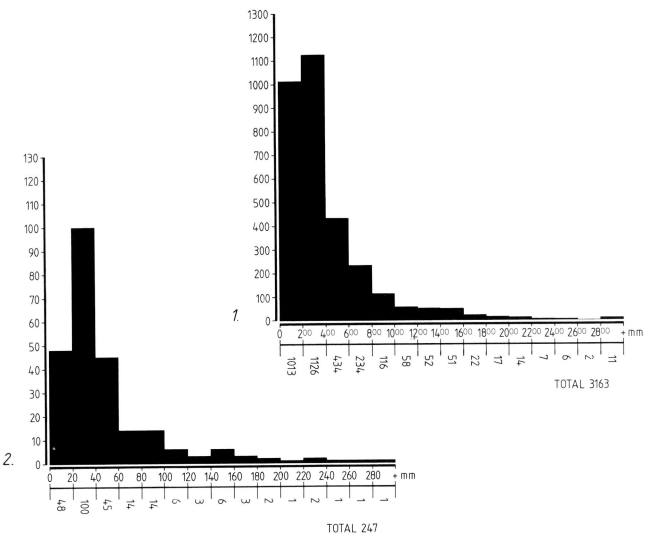

Fig 7.2 Flag Fen, Area 6A: roundwood, lengths (1) and diameters (2). Measurements in mm

it was decided to reexamine the entire Etton database, to ensure that the figures used to express various categories of data were comparable with Flag Fen. The conclusions in the Etton report remain entirely unaffected by the reworking of the data offered here, which has mainly to do with detail. Since Etton and Flag Fen will probably be used as type-sites for the study of woodworking for some time, it is essential that the two should compare closely in actuality and not merely on paper.

The Flag Fen wood assemblage

The sample

The excavation of Area 6A involved the numbering and recording of some 9000 pieces of wood. No subsampling or discarding took place, however, until the recording of dimensions and other observations had been completed. The assemblage might therefore be regarded as broadly representative of the wood that was deposited in antiquity. The data were computerised using the Fenland Archaeological Trust's

Maxarc database software (Booth *et al* 1984). Maxarc has subsequently been replaced by a more widely available, Access-based, system.

The principal categories of wood

Wood or wood fragments of less than 10mm diameter/width were generally not lifted or recorded. All non-woody material, such as reed rhizomes, was also discarded. It was possible to classify approximately 63.41% of the wood entered in the database. This, the classifiable component, will be treated as 'the assemblage', in the discussion that follows. Table 7.1 lists the principal categories of wood and timber that could be positively identified. Each will be discussed in turn after a short note on comparability with the earlier Neolithic wood assemblage from Etton.

Although strenuous efforts were made to ensure that the two assemblages were truly comparable, some problems were nonetheless difficult to resolve. At Etton, for example, roundwood was treated as a by-product. This was because the main woodworking tasks at that site were to do with coppice products.

It was therefore considered probable that the round-wood (mainly straight rods) that had been left in the enclosure ditch had either been rejected for use or was surplus to requirements. At Flag Fen, the situation was very different. Most of the roundwood seems to have been used as foundations or makeup to build up the surface either of the platform or the walkways between the rows of the alignment. Far from being a by-product of some other process, the Flag Fen roundwood was brought to the site to fulfil a very specific purpose. In the discussion that follows, the clear cut distinction between the implements and by-products of flint analysis and the products and by-products of the Etton wood report (Taylor 1998, 133) has been abandoned in favour of a more descriptive terminology that carries fewer functional implications. The dilemma posed by the seemingly straightforward distinction between implements and by-products provides a timely warning that, although they are both reductive technologies, the working of wood and of flint might have been approached with different cultural attitudes in antiquity.

Natural roundwood can also be described as branchwood. It was rarely straight and was usually knobbly, with side shoots. It formed only a small part (5.55%) of the identifiable assemblage (Table 7.1). Similarly, roots (1.02%) were of negligible importance. When encountered, roots belonged either to trees that had been felled (and had later resprouted) prior to the construction of the platform and post alignment, or they were parts of trees that had grown on the top of the horizontal timber, some time after the monument's last period of maintenance. Naturally occurring wood (natural roundwood and root) comprised 6.57% of the assemblage.

The equivalent categories at Etton formed a far larger proportion of the entire assemblage (25.78%). This would support the suggestion that the Flag Fen assemblage represents a selection of wood that was brought to the site for use there. The site might even have been cleared prior to the monument's construction. At Etton on the other hand, the wood in the ditch represents the accumulated detritus, deliberate deposition, and debris of abandonment of an outdoor 'workshop' where wood was processed for use elsewhere.

Roundwood was numerically, at 56.32%, the most important category of wood found at Flag Fen (Table 7.1). It is prone to post-depositional compaction, which causes radial distortion and only 246 (or 7.65%) of the 3214 pieces escaped these effects (Table 7.2; Fig 7.2). As undistorted roundwood was found in all levels, the sample, although slightly smaller than the ideal, is probably representative of the whole.

Wood is less prone to shrinking along its length (Kaye and Cole-Hamilton 1993) and this dimension is therefore of considerable analytical importance. That is why the entire roundwood assemblage was measured, although pieces that passed out of the excavated area were not included in the statistics. The Flag Fen roundwood was consistently very much longer than

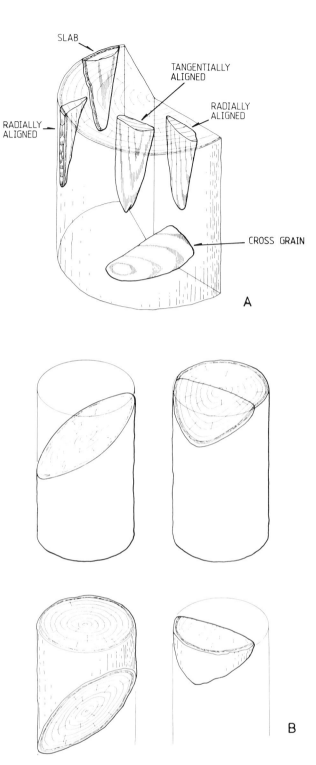

Fig 7.3 Diagram showing position and orientation of woodchip categories (after Taylor 1998)

that from Etton, where just over 71% of pieces were less than 250mm long; at Flag Fen the proportion of similarly sized roundwood is approximately half that. The Flag Fen roundwood statistics have a far gentler fall-off curve as length increases: at Etton 92.98% of the roundwood was less than half a metre in length; at Flag Fen the figure was about 74.49%. The Etton assemblage had just 15 pieces (1.00%) that were longer than a metre, whereas at Flag Fen the figure was 240 pieces (7.59%). A comparison of the undistorted

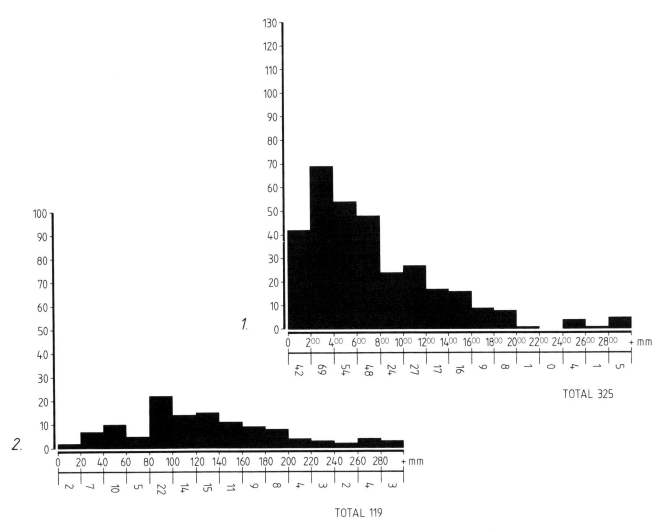

Fig 7.4 Flag Fen, Area 6A: timber, lengths (1) and original diameters (2). Measurements in mm

Table 7.5 Flag Fen Area 6A: timber debris dimensions (in mm)

length 0–200	200–400	400–600	600–800	800–1000	1000–1200	1200–1400	1400–1600	1600–1800	total
9	35	31	16	3	1	–	2	2	99
9.09%	35.35%	31.31%	16.16%	3.03%	1.01%		2.02%	2.02%	100%

Table 7.6 Flag Fen Area 6A (all levels): dimensions of slabs or sapwood removal chips (in mm)

length 0–50	50–100	100–150	150–200	200–250	250–300	300–350	350–400	400–500	500–600	600>	total
–	10	23	19	20	20	6	4	6	2	5	115
	8.70%	20.00%	16.52%	17.39%	17.39%	5.22%	3.48%	5.22%	1.74%	4.35%	100%

breadth 0–10	10–20	20–30	30–40	40–50	50–60	60–70	70–80	80–90	90–100	100>	total
–	–	3	13	21	16	17	22	11	3	9	115
		2.61%	11.30%	18.26%	13.91%	14.78%	19.13%	9.57%	2.61%	7.83%	100%

thickness 0–5	5–10	10–15	15–20	20–25	25–30	30–35	35–40	40–45	45–50	50>	total
2	21	15	32	19	10	7	1	2	2	4	115
1.74%	18.26%	13.04%	27.83%	16.52%	8.70%	6.09%	0.87%	1.74%	1.74%	3.48%	100%

174

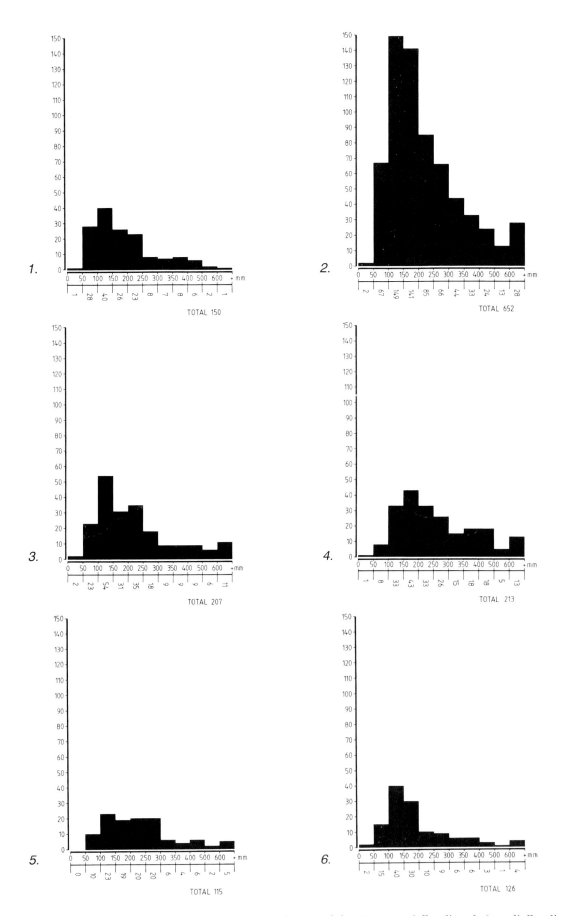

Fig 7.5 Flag Fen, Area 6A: length (mm) of woodchips by class: 1, slabs; 2, tangentially aligned; 3, radially aligned; 4, off roundwood; 5, cross-grain; 6, unclassifiable

diameters is even more revealing: at Etton no less than 66.41% were less than 20mm, whereas the Flag Fen figure is only 19.43%.

The foregoing dimensions suggest that the Flag Fen roundwood assemblage was of poles and larger pieces, whereas that at Etton was of rods or wattle (Taylor 1998). An important point to note is that, although the Flag Fen assemblage includes a numerically significant proportion of wattle-sized pieces, their depositional circumstances suggested that they were not intended to be used for the manufacture of wattlework items, other perhaps than for the construction of a few wattle revetments. The Etton assemblage on the other hand, contained wattle-sized pieces alone: there was almost no larger (ie structural), element present. Roundwood debris essentially consists of offcuts, where the bark of the wood is visible in a band wider than approximately 20mm; this distinguishes it from woodchips off round-wood, which is discussed in greater detail below (Fig 7.3, lower left). The proportion of roundwood debris was small (1.26%), but its presence showed that wood-working was taking place *in situ* (Table 7.3). Timber (Table 7.4) and timber debris (Table 7.5) formed a significant component (7.57%) of the assemblage (Table 7.1). At Etton it was of negligible importance (two pieces, or 0.04% of the assemblage). The histogram of timber lengths (Fig 7.4) shows that the timber was proportionately very much longer than the roundwood. Its original diameters (where these could be reliably estimated) were also much more substantial, which indicates, of course, that large roundwood, mainly of the range 80–200mm, was selected for conversion into timber.

The figure for debris includes woodchips and detached bark (Table 7.3). Woodchips accounted for 1463 pieces, or 90.64% of the debris total. There were 151 pieces of detached bark (2.64% of the total assemblage). The woodchips proved to be particularly well suited to statistical analyses, which are described below.

Woodchips: description

The categories of woodchip discussed here were first defined in the Etton report (Taylor 1998). Aside from unclassifiable pieces, five categories of woodchip have been defined:

Slabs (or bark/sapwood trimming woodchips)
Tangentially aligned woodchips
Radially aligned woodchips
Woodchips off roundwood
Cross-grain woodchips

The way in which woodchips related to the original wood has been illustrated schematically (Fig 7.3).

The following brief description is taken from the Etton report (Taylor 1998). Woodchips that resulted from the removal of bark and/or sapwood were known as 'slabs'.

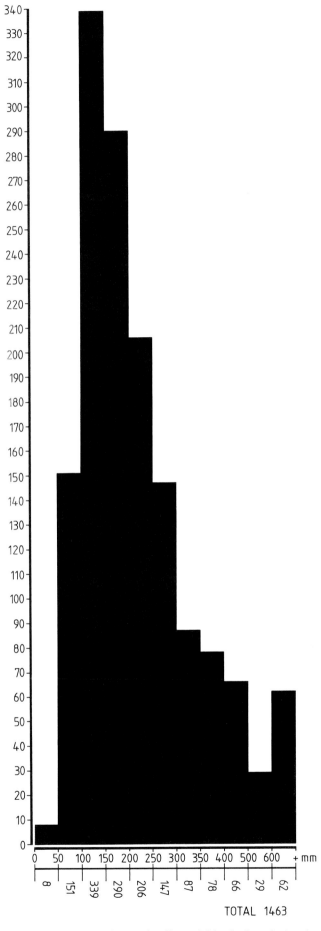

Fig 7.6 Flag Fen, Area 6A: all woodchips by length (mm)

Table 7.7 Flag Fen Area 6A (all levels): dimensions of tangentially aligned woodchips (in mm)

length

0–50	50–100	100–150	150–200	200–250	350–300	300–350	350–400	400–500	500–600	600>	total
2	23	54	31	35	18	9	9	9	6	11	207
0.97%	11.11%	26.09%	14.97%	16.91%	8.70%	4.35%	4.35%	4.35%	2.90%	5.31%	100%

breadth

0–10	10–20	20–30	30–40	40–50	50–60	60–70	70–80	80–90	90–100	100>	total
1	3	20	41	50	30	25	20	8	5	4	207
0.48%	1.45%	9.66%	19.81%	24.15%	14.49%	12.08%	9.66%	3.86%	2.42%	1.93%	100%

thickness

0–5	5–10	10–15	15–20	20–25	25–30	30–35	35–40	40–45	45–50	50>	total
9	32	41	44	22	25	12	10	4	3	5	207
4.35%	15.46%	19.81%	21.26%	10.63%	12.08%	5.80%	4.83%	1.93%	1.45%	2.42%	100%

breadth:length ratio

0–0.5	0.5–1.0	1.0–1.5	1.5–2.0	2.0–2.5	2.5–3.0	3.0–3.5	3.5–4.0	4.0>	total
12	58	53	41	22	8	5	5	3	207
5.80%	28.02%	25.60%	19.81%	10.63%	3.86%	2.42%	2.42%	1.45%	100%

Table 7.8 Flag Fen Area 6A (all levels): dimensions of radially aligned woodchips (in mm)

length

0–50	50–100	100–150	150–200	200–250	350–300	300–350	350–400	400–500	500–600	600>	total
2	67	149	141	85	66	44	33	24	13	28	652
0.31%	10.28%	22.85%	21.63%	13.04%	10.12%	6.75%	5.06%	3.68%	1.99%	4.29%	100%

breadth

0–10	10–20	20–30	30–40	40–50	50–60	60–70	70–80	80–90	90–100	100>	total
–	7	64	128	159	111	69	43	35	18	18	652
	1.07%	9.82%	19.63%	24.39%	17.02%	10.58%	6.60%	5.37%	2.76%	2.76%	100%

thickness

0–5	5–10	10–15	15–20	20–25	25–30	30–35	35–40	40–45	45–50	50>	total
40	110	111	153	71	58	41	24	10	17	17	652
6.13%	16.87%	17.02%	23.47%	10.89%	8.90%	6.29%	3.68%	1.53%	2.61%	2.61%	100%

breadth:length ratio

0–0.5	0.5–1.0	1.0–1.5	1.5–2.0	2.0–2.5	2.5–3.0	3.0–3.5	3.5–4.0	4.0>	total
47	170	189	124	51	33	20	10	83	652
7.21%	26.07%	28.99%	19.02%	7.82%	5.06%	3.07%	1.53%	1.23%	100%

Table 7.9 Flag Fen Area 6A (all levels): dimensions of woodchips off roundwood (in mm)

length

0–50	50–100	100–150	150–200	200–250	350–300	300–350	350–400	400–500	500–600	600>	total
1	8	33	43	33	26	15	18	18	5	13	213
0.47%	3.76%	15.49%	20.19%	15.49%	12.21%	7.04%	8.45%	8.45%	2.35%	6.10%	100%

breadth

0–10	10–20	20–30	30–40	40–50	50–60	60–70	70–80	80–90	90–100	100>	total
–	2	21	33	38	31	36	15	15	13	9	213
	0.94%	9.86%	15.49%	17.84%	14.55%	16.90%	7.04%	7.04%	6.10%	4.23%	100%

thickness

0–5	5–10	10–15	15–20	20–25	25–30	30–35	35–40	40–45	45–50	50>	total
–	4	22	31	33	29	25	19	14	9	27	213
	1.88%	10.33%	14.55%	15.49%	13.62%	11.74%	8.92%	6.57%	4.23%	12.68%	100%

breadth:length ratio

0–0.5	0.5–1.0	1.0–1.5	1.5–2.0	2.0–2.5	2.5–3.0	3.0–3.5	3.5–4.0	4.0>	total
22	68	54	41	12	7	4	1	4	213
10.33%	31.92%	25.35%	19.25%	5.63%	3.29%	1.88%	0.47%	1.88	100%

Table 7.10 Flag Fen Area 6A (all levels): dimensions of cross-grain woodchips (in mm)

length											
0–50	50–100	100–150	150–200	200–250	350–300	300–350	350–400	400–500	500–600	600>	total
1	28	40	26	23	8	7	8	6	2	1	150
0.67%	18.67%	26.67%	17.33%	15.33%	5.33%	4.67%	5.33%	4.00%	1.33%	0.67%	100%

breadth											
0–10	10–20	20–30	30–40	40–50	50–60	60–70	70–80	80–90	90–100	100>	total
–	2	28	28	41	18	13	7	10	–	3	150
	1.33%	18.67%	18.67%	27.33%	12.00%	8.67%	4.67%	6.67%		2.00%	100%

thickness											
0–5	5–10	10–15	15–20	20–25	25–30	30–35	35–40	40–45	45–50	50>	total
11	29	29	23	20	11	13	8	2	2	2	150
7.33%	19.33%	19.33%	15.33%	13.33%	7.33%	8.67%	5.33%	1.33%	1.33%	1.33%	100%

breadth:length ratio										
0–0.5	0.5–1.0	1.0–1.5	1.5–2.0	2.0–2.5	2.5–3.0	3.0–3.5	3.5–4.0	4.0>		total
7	38	35	30	25	9	3	3	–		150
4.67%	25.33%	23.33%	20.00%	16.67%	6.00%	2.00%	2.00%			100%

Table 7.11 Flag Fen Area 6A (all levels): dimensions of unclassifiable woodchips (in mm)

length											
0–50	50–100	100–150	150–200	200–250	350–300	300–350	350–400	400–500	500–600	600>	total
2	15	40	30	10	9	6	6	3	1	4	126
1.59%	11.90%	31.75%	23.81%	7.94%	7.14%	4.76%	4.76%	2.38%	0.79%	3.17%	100%

breadth											
0–10	10–20	20–30	30–40	40–50	50–60	60–70	70–80	80–90	90–100	100>	total
1	4	12	38	30	18	11	2	3	2	5	126
0.79%	3.17%	9.52%	30.16%	23.81%	14.29%	8.73%	1.59%	2.38%	1.59%	3.97%	100%

thickness											
0–5	5–10	10–15	15–20	20–25	25–30	30–35	35–40	40–45	45–50	50>	total
5	26	27	27	18	8	7	4	2	–	2	126
3.97%	20.63%	21.43%	21.43%	14.29%	6.35%	5.56%	3.17%	1.59%		1.59%	100%

breadth:length ratio										
0–0.5	0.5–1.0	1.0–1.5	1.5–2.0	2.0–2.5	2.5–3.0	3.0–3.5	3.5–4.0	4.0>		total
9	28	37	20	16	8	3	5	–		207
7.14%	22.22%	29.37%	15.87%	12.70%	6.35%	2.38%	3.97%			100%

Table 7.12 Flag Fen Area 6A (all levels): dimensions of all woodchips (in mm)

length											
0–50	50–100	100–150	150–200	200–250	350–300	300–350	350–400	400–500	500–600	600>	total
8	151	339	290	206	147	87	78	66	29	62	1463
0.55%	10.32%	23.17%	19.82%	14.08%	10.05%	5.95%	5.33%	4.51%	1.98%	4.24%	100%

breadth											
0–10	10–20	20–30	30–40	40–50	50–60	60–70	70–80	80–90	90–100	100>	total
2	18	148	281	339	224	171	109	82	41	48	1463
0.14%	1.23%	10.12%	19.21%	23.17%	15.31%	11.69%	7.45%	5.60%	2.80%	3.28%	100%

thickness											
0–5	5–10	10–15	15–20	20–25	25–30	30–35	35–40	40–45	45–50	50>	total
7	222	245	310	183	141	105	66	34	33	57	1463
4.58%	15.17%	16.75%	21.19%	12.51%	9.64%	7.18%	4.51%	2.32%	2.26%	3.90%	100%

breadth:length ratio										
0–0.5	0.5–1.0	1.0–1.5	1.5–2.0	2.0–2.5	2.5–3.0	3.0–3.5	3.5–4.0	4.0>		total
98	381	404	287	141	74	38	24	16		1463
6.70%	26.04%	27.61%	19.62%	9.64%	5.06%	2.60%	1.64%	1.09%		100%

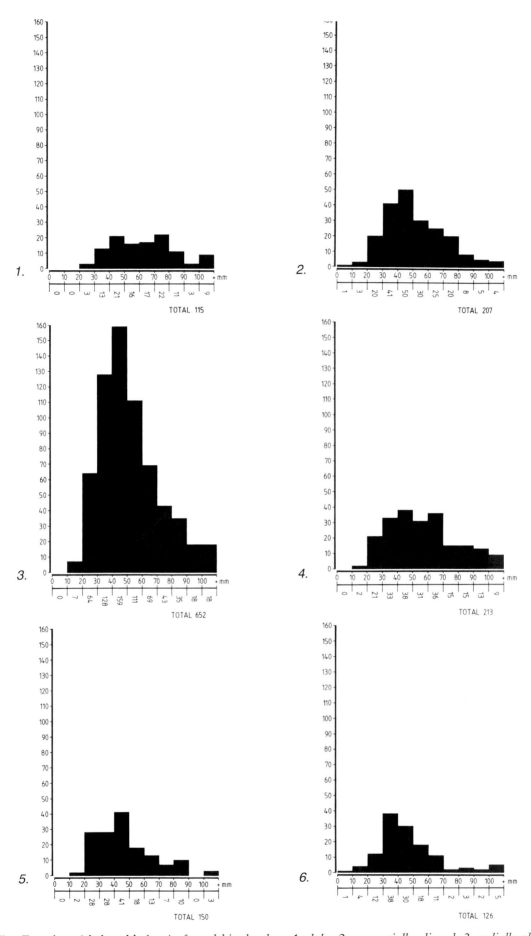

Fig 7.7 Flag Fen, Area 6A: breadth (mm) of woodchips by class: 1, slabs; 2, tangentially aligned; 3, radially aligned; 4, off roundwood; 5, cross-grain; 6, unclassifiable

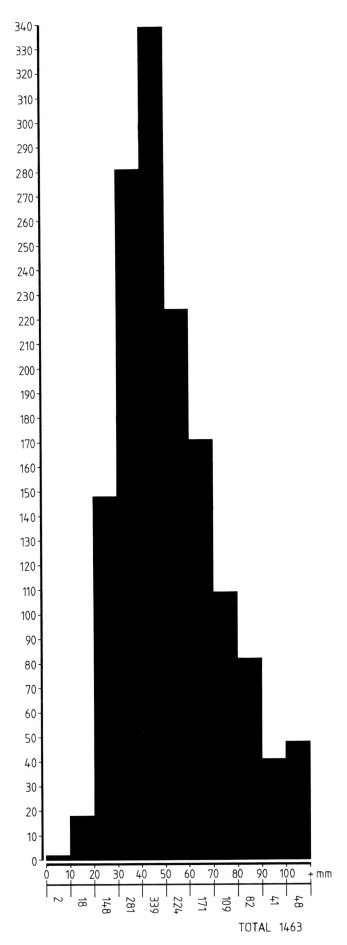

Fig 7.8 Flag Fen, Area 6A: all woodchips by breadth

TOTAL 1463

They were probably the most distinctive of all wood-chips. Sometimes woodchips were produced by the sharpening of roundwood. They included a very small amount of heartwood in addition to the sapwood and bark. These would be classified as roundwood wood-chips. Woodchips would only be classed as slabs if they were relatively thin, and followed the grain exactly, so that there was no heartwood attached to them. The term derives from the description applied to the bark/sapwood removal waste produced by the modern timber industry (BS 565:1972). Tangential woodchips have their worked surfaces clearly running tangentially to the growth rings, whereas radial woodchips cut across them (often at right angles) in the radial plane. Cross-grain woodchips were not encountered at Etton, probably because it was not a timberworking site. Cross-grain woodchips were readily identified in the field, once their diagnostic features had been pointed out. As a category they were very variable.

For ease of comparison, histograms of woodchip dimensions are given in the following order: length, breadth, thickness, and breadth: length ratio (Figs 7.5–12). Data used to compile the histograms are presented by woodchip category (Tables 7.6–12, pp 173, 176–7). Flag Fen produced a large assemblage of woodchips, which are categorised and quantified in Table 7.13.

Table 7.13 Summary of woodchips from Area 6A, by category

	number	%
slabs	115	7.86
tangentially aligned	207	14.15
radially aligned	652	44.57
off roundwood	213	14.56
cross-grain	150	10.25
unclassified	126	8.61
total	1463	100.00

Slabs

Slabs or bark/sapwood removal chips were tangentially (or circumferentially) aligned and shared a broadly similar set of statistics to tangentially aligned woodchips (Table 7.6; Fig 7.4, 1). There were no marked peaks in any of the distributions; the main departure from the norm was a tendency for slabs to be broader than other woodchip types. It is still not clear precisely how slabs were removed, but this tendency towards broader chips suggests a specific technique. Perhaps the bark and sapwood were notched at intervals to encourage the woodchips to 'run' further along the grain, or, once started, the woodchips were levered off rather than chopped.

Tangentially aligned woodchips

As was noted above, the measurements for tangentially aligned woodchips resemble those for slabs, especially as regards length (Table 7.7; Fig 7.5, 2).

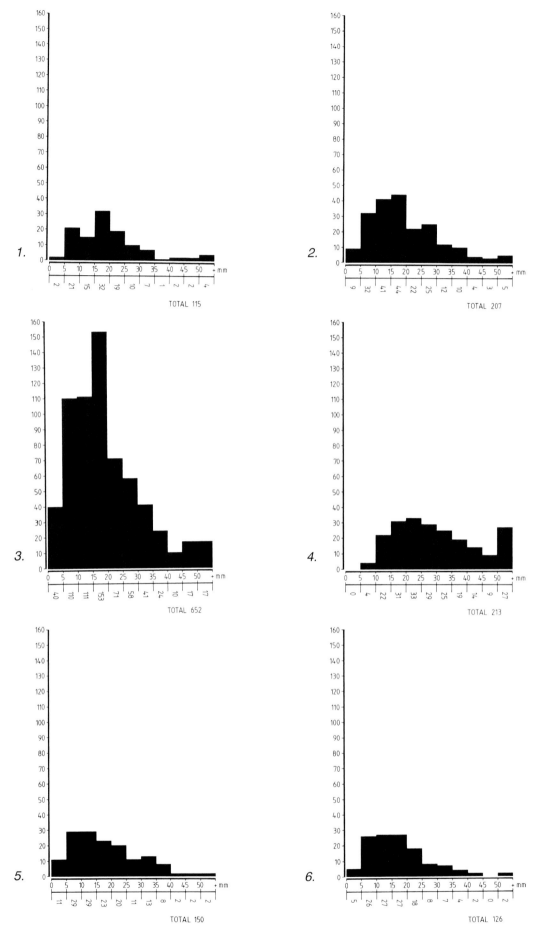

Fig 7.9 Flag Fen, Area 6A: thickness (mm) of woodchips by class: 1, slabs; 2, tangentially aligned; 3, radially aligned; 4, off roundwood; 5, cross-grain; 6, unclassifiable

Table 7.14 Comparative dimensions of slabs or sapwood removal chips from the enclosure ditch at Etton (in mm)

length											
0–50	50–100	100–150	150–200	200–250	350–300	300–350	350–400	400–500	500–600	600>	total
45	106	53	22	14	8	2	1	4	–	3	258
17.44%	41.09%	20.54%	8.53%	5.43%	3.10%	0.78%	0.39%	1.55%		1.16%	100%

breadth											
0–10	10–20	20–30	30–40	40–50	50–60	60–70	70–80	80–90	90–100	100>	total
1	29	67	73	44	15	12	8	5	2	2	258
0.39%	11.24%	25.97%	28.29%	17.05%	5.81%	4.65%	3.10%	1.94%	0.78%	0.78%	100%

thickness											
0–5	5–10	10–15	15–20	20–25	25–30	30–35	35–40	40–45	45–50	50>	total
19	88	69	41	17	10	8	2	1	1	2	258
7.36%	34.11%	26.74%	15.89%	6.59%	3.88%	3.10%	0.78%	0.39%	0.39%	0.78%	100%

breadth:length ratio									
0–0.5	0.5–1.0	1.0–1.5	1.5–2.0	2.0–2.5	2.5–3.0	3.0–3.5	3.5–4.0	4.0>	total
5	19	52	56	48	28	20	20	10	258
1.94%	1.94%	20.16%	21.71%	18.60%	10.85%	7.75%	7.75%	3.88%	100%

Table 7.15 Comparative dimensions of tangentially aligned woodchips from the enclosure ditch at Etton (in mm)

length											
0–50	50–100	100–150	150–200	200–250	350–300	300–350	350–400	400–500	500–600	600>	total
12	59	48	37	10	2	2	4	2	–	–	176
6.82%	33.52%	27.27%	21.02%	5.68%	1.14%	1.14%	2.27%	1.14%			100%

breadth											
0–10	10–20	20–30	30–40	40–50	50–60	60–70	70–80	80–90	90–100	100>	total
2	22	60	45	20	11	6	5	2	2	1	176
1.14%	12.50%	34.09%	25.57%	11.36%	6.25%	3.41%	2.84%	1.14%	1.14%	0.57%	100%

thickness											
0–5	5–10	10–15	15–20	20–25	25–30	30–35	35–40	40–45	45–50	50>	total
7	41	51	37	26	8	1	2	1	2	–	176
3.98%	23.30%	28.98%	21.02%	14.77%	4.55%	0.57%	1.14%	0.57%	1.14%		100%

breadth:length ratio									
0–0.5	0.5–1.0	1.0–1.5	1.5–2.0	2.0–2.5	2.5–3.0	3.0–3.5	3.5–4.0	4.0>	total
8	35	44	46	24	7	4	4	4	176
4.55%	19.89%	25.00%	26.14%	13.64%	3.98%	2.27%	2.27%	2.27%	100%

Table 7.16 Comparative dimensions of radially aligned woodchips from the enclosure ditch at Etton (in mm)

length											
0–50	50–100	100–150	150–200	200–250	350–300	300–350	350–400	400–500	500–600	600>	total
23	5	55	21	14	4	4	2	–	2	1	211
10.90%	40.28%	26.07%	9.95%	6.64%	1.90%	1.90%	0.95%		0.95%	0.47%	100%

breadth											
0–10	10–20	20–30	30–40	40–50	50–60	60–70	70–80	80–90	90–100	100>	total
8	45	65	36	28	12	7	2	5	1	2	211
3.79%	21.33%	30.81%	17.06%	13.27%	5.69%	3.32%	0.95%	2.37%	0.47%	0.95%	100%

thickness											
0–5	5–10	10–15	15–20	20–25	25–30	30–35	35–40	40–45	45–50	50>	total
19	60	54	34	14	13	3	6	5	–	3	211
9.00%	28.44%	25.59%	16.11%	6.64%	6.16%	1.42%	2.84%	2.37%		1.42%	100%

breadth:length ratio									
0–0.5	0.5–1.0	1.0–1.5	1.5–2.0	2.0–2.5	2.5–3.0	3.0–3.5	3.5–4.0	4.0>	total
10	33	56	54	29	9	12	6	2	211
4.74%	15.64%	26.54%	25.59%	13.74%	4.27%	5.69%	2.84%	0.95%	100%

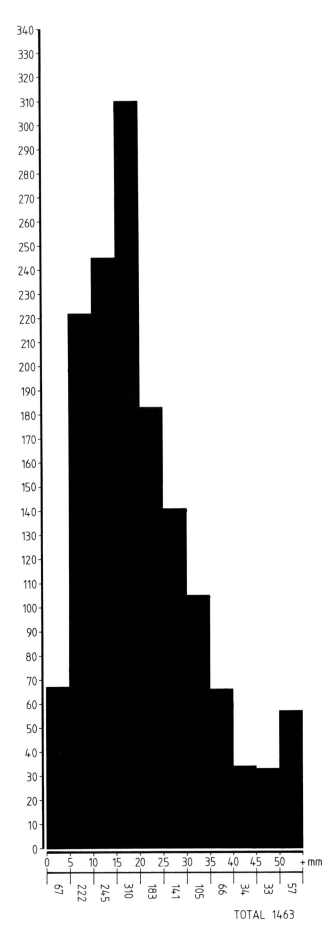

Fig 7.10 Flag Fen, Area 6A: all woodchips by thickness (mm)

Tangentially aligned chips were often removed from the heartwood or the inner sapwood, which would be harder than the outer rings. This could be another factor explaining why tangentially aligned woodchips were thinner and narrower than slabs.

Radially aligned woodchips

Radially aligned woodchips formed the largest category of woodchips (Table 7.8; Fig 7.5, 3). All distributions are characterised by pronounced peaks. The breadth/length ratios are strongly biased in favour of 'blade-like' (ie long and narrow) woodchips. This would suggest that the majority of radially aligned woodchips were the result of using oblique blows.

Woodchips off roundwood

The measurements of this category are undoubtedly affected by the size and shape of the roundwood itself (Table 7.9; Fig 7.5, 4). This might help to explain why the length curve shows such a gradual fall off and why so many of these woodchips were very thick.

Cross-grain woodchips

Cross-grain woodchips were removed from larger timbers by transverse, or near right-angled blows (Table 7.10; Fig 7.5, 5). They are characteristically short, of average width (when compared with other categories), and notably thin. Their breadth: length ratio shows a more pronounced tendency towards the short and squat than any other category.

Unclassifiable woodchips

The various measurements might suggest that the majority of unclassifiable woodchips were from roundwood (Table 7.11; Fig 7.5, 6).

Woodchips: discussion

The composition of the Flag Fen woodchip assemblage is given in Table 7.13 and a histogram of breadth: length ratios of the entire assemblage appears as Figure 7.12. The discovery of numerous bronze implements, including a socketed axe (Chapter 10), would suggest that the woodchip assemblage at Flag Fen was made by bronze axes, whereas that from Etton was made by polished stone and flint axes. The principal point of difference, typologically speaking, is that cross-grain woodchips are present at Flag Fen, but not at Etton. This could be entirely attributed to the fact that Etton was a site where coppice products were worked. In modern terms, the woodworking had less to do with carpentry and more to do with woodland crafts and bodging. There was evidence, however, that at least some timberworking took place. This evidence consisted of the northern gateway, which was known to have

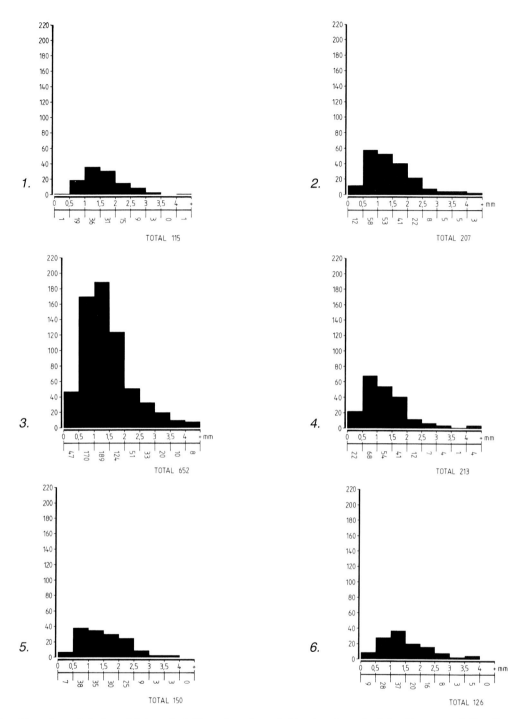

Fig 7.11 Flag Fen, Area 6A: breadth:length (×5) ratios of woodchips by class: 1, slabs; 2, tangentially aligned; 3, radially aligned; 4, off roundwood; 5, cross-grain; 6, unclassifiable

been made from squared-up timbers, the presence of thick, detached bark, and at least one oak plank. The presence of sapwood removal chips at Etton also suggests that timbers larger than wattles were being worked. Despite this, there were no cross-grain wood-chips in the assemblage from the enclosure ditch.

It might well be possible to detach cross-grain woodchips with a polished stone axe, but that is not to say that it commonly took place. The cross-grain chip is removed by a steep, or right-angled blow that would cause a considerable impact shock. Such a blow might well detach a flake from a stone axe's edge and experi-

ments have shown that there is less danger of breakage when working along the grain (Olausson 1982). If the axes were also valuable items in their own right, there might have been a strong disincentive to perform such tasks. As a testable hypothesis, it is suggested here that the presence of cross-grain woodchips as a significant category might, in the absence of other evidence, be an indication that metal axes were being used.

Tables and histograms of measurements and of breadth:length ratios have been prepared for the four principal categories of woodchips found at Etton Tables 7.14–17; Fig 7.13). The curves of the slab, tangential,

Table 7.17 Comparative dimensions of woodchips off roundwood from the enclosure ditch at Etton (in mm)

length

0–50	50–100	100–150	150–200	200–250	350–300	300–350	350–400	400–500	500–600	600>	total
2	17	17	18	6	11	5	2	1	3	1	83
2.41%	20.48%	20.48%	21.69%	7.23%	13.25%	6.02%	2.41%	1.20%	3.61%	1.20%	100%

breadth

0–10	10–20	20–30	30–40	40–50	50–60	60–70	70–80	80–90	90–100	100>	total
–	16	30	15	9	5	2	2	3	1	–	83
19.28%	36.14%	18.07%	10.84%	6.02%	2.41%	2.41%	3.61%	1.20%		100%	

thickness

0–5	5–10	10–15	15–20	20–25	25–30	30–35	35–40	40–45	45–50	50>	total
1	14	24	10	10	9	5	4	1	2	3	83
1.20%	16.87%	28.92%	12.05%	12.05%	10.84%	6.02%	4.82%	1.20%	2.41%	3.61%	100%

breadth:length ratio

0–0.5	0.5–1.0	1.0–1.5	1.5–2.0	2.0–2.5	2.5–3.0	3.0–3.5	3.5–4.0	4.0>			total
10	38	19	10	3	–	–	2	1			83
12.05%	45.78%	22.89%	12.05%	3.61%			2.41%	1.20%			100%

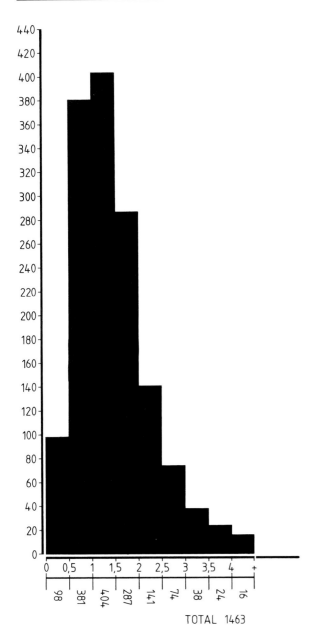

TOTAL 1463

Fig 7.12 Flag Fen, Area 6A: all woodchips, breadth:length ratios (×5)

and chips-off-roundwood woodchips conform quite well to their Flag Fen equivalents. The radially aligned chips from Etton, however, formed a far smaller proportion of the assemblage than at Flag Fen, with less pronounced peaks. In general, the Etton distributions favoured the shorter, squatter end of the graph and there were fewer sharp steps than at Flag Fen.

Taking the two woodchip assemblages as a whole, the first point to note is that both are of a good size for cross-comparison. As regards length, the Etton assemblage shows a more even shape, without the pronounced peak found at Flag Fen (Fig 7.6). In general terms, the Etton curve is arranged one cell shorter than that for Flag Fen, but both follow approximately the same fall-off curve. The 'tail' of greatest length at Flag Fen is, however, greater.

The figures for breadth show a greater disparity. The Etton assemblage covers approximately the same range, but has a far less pronounced peak and a tendency towards greater width. The tendency for Etton figures to be less peaked and to have a more gradual fall-off curve than Flag Fen is also seen in the thickness histograms for the two assemblages. Finally, the breadth/length ratios continue the process seen in the three dimensions: the Etton figures are less peaked and show a preference for shorter, squatter chips than the more markedly long and narrow (blade-like) distribution at Flag Fen. The rapid fall off of the Flag Fen distribution contrasts with the gentle curve of Etton.

The Etton statistics show fewer sharp changes, either between the woodchip categories themselves, or within individual graphs. The reason for this will require further research, but it suggests that stone axes were used in fewer distinctively different ways. Metal axes can be hammered, they can be used to hew or shave and they are particularly effective when used obliquely, in the manner of a billhook. Stone axes on the other hand require a steeper angle of attack if they

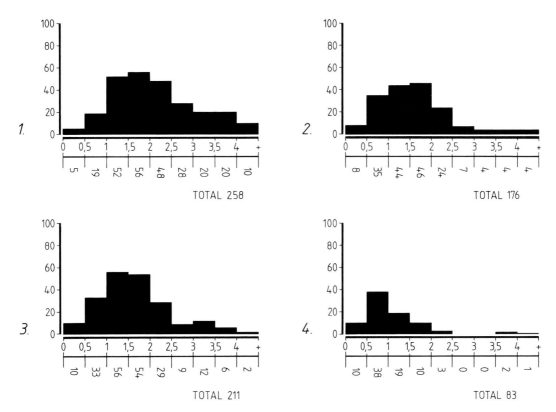

Fig 7.13 Comparative breadth:length ratios of woodchips from the enclosure ditch at Etton: 1, slabs; 2, tangentially aligned; 3, radially aligned; 4, off roundwood

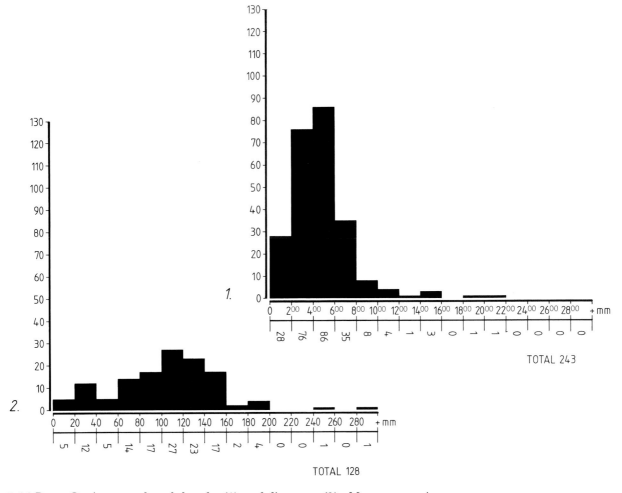

Fig 7.14 Power Station: roundwood, lengths (1) and diameters (2). Measurements in mm

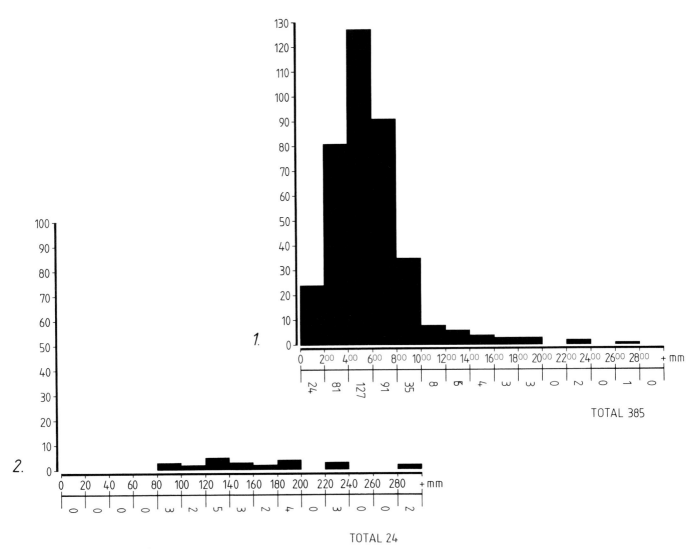

Fig 7.15 Power Station: timber, lengths (1) and original diameters (2). Measurements in mm

are not to glance off the work; similarly they are not well suited to a very steep angle of attack. They are best used to chop. An interesting insight into different techniques required for using stone and metal axes came out in the experiments done in the 1950s in Draved Wood in Denmark (Jorgensen 1985). A method of felling trees that involved chopping and cleaving was used. The experimenters found this technique more efficient for stone axes than the conventional chopping method. In short, it is suggested that the greater variability observed within and between the Flag Fen woodchip categories is a significant distinguishing criterion for metal axes.

The Power Station wood assemblage

The Power Station wood assemblage was undoubtedly affected by post-depositional factors. The waterlogged peaty deposits had largely gone. All that was left was a partially dried-out cover of silty alluvium. Some horizontal wood and timber was preserved, but nowhere were there quantities to compare with Flag Fen.

A large proportion of the wood was also timber. This reflects the fact that the posts of the alignment survived very much better than the horizontal wood.

The principal categories of wood

The list of categories of wood found at the Power Station site (Table 7.18) probably reflects the sample bias.

Table 7.18 Principal categories of wood and timber from the Power Station

	number	%
natural roundwood	2	0.19
root	1	0.09
roundwood	250	23.65
roundwood debris	6	0.57
timber	393	37.18
timber debris	44	4.16
debris	361	34.15
total	1057	100.00

Table 7.19 Power Station site: roundwood dimensions (in mm)

length	0–200	200–400	400–600	600–800	800–1000	1000–1200	1200–1400	1400–1600	1600–1800	1800–2000	2000–2200	2200–2400	2400–2600	2600–2800	2800>	total
	28	76	86	35	8	4	1	3	–	1	1	–	–	–	–	243
	11.52%	31.28%	35.39%	14.40%	3.29%	1.65%	0.41%	1.23%		0.41%	0.41%					100%

original diameter	0–20	20–40	40–60	60–80	80–100	100–120	120–140	140–160	160–180	180–200	200–220	220–240	240–260	260–280	280>	total
	5	12	5	14	17	27	23	17	2	4	–	–	1	1	–	128
	3.91%	9.38%	3.91%	10.94%	13.28%	21.09%	17.97%	13.28%	1.56%	3.13%			0.78%	0.78%		100%

Table 7.20 Power Station site: timber dimensions (in mm)

length	0–200	200–400	400–600	600–800	800–1000	1000–1200	1200–1400	1400–1600	1600–1800	1800–2000	2000–2200	2200–2400	2400–2600	2600–2800	2800>	total
	24	81	127	91	35	8	6	4	3	3	–	2	–	1	–	385
	6.23%	21.04%	32.99%	23.64%	9.09%	2.08%	1.56%	1.04%	0.78%	0.52%		0.26%		0.26%		100%

original diameter	0–20	20–40	40–60	60–80	80–100	100–120	120–140	140–160	160–180	180–200	200–220	220–240	240–260	260–280	280>	total
	–	–	–	–	3	2	5	3	2	4	–	3	–	–	2	24
					12.50%	8.33%	20.83%	12.50%	8.33%	16.67%		12.50%			8.33%	100%

Table 7.21 Power Station site: timber debris dimensions (in mm)

length 0–200	200–400	400–600	600–800	800–1000	1000–120	1200–1400	total
5	20	15	4	–	–	1	45
11.11%	44.44%	33.33%	8.89%			2.22%	100%

Table 7.22 Power Station site: dimensions of tangentially aligned woodchips (in mm)

length 0–50	50–100	100–150	150–200	200–250	350–300	300–350	350–400	400–500	500–600	600>	total
1	2	10	13	14	8	13	6	8	8	6	89
1.12%	2.25%	11.24%	14.61%	15.73%	8.99%	14.61%	6.74%	8.99%	8.99%	6.74%	100%

breadth 0–10	10–20	20–30	30–40	40–50	50–60	60–70	70–80	80–90	90–100	100>	total
–	–	2	10	14	30	14	11	4	2	2	89
		2.25%	11.24%	15.73%	33.71%	15.73%	12.36%	4.49%	2.25%	2.25%	100%

thickness 0–5	5–10	10–15	15–20	20–25	25–30	30–35	35–40	40–45	45–50	50>	total
–	1	4	16	13	17	6	13	5	8	6	89
	1.12%	4.49%	17.98%	14.61%	19.10%	6.74%	14.61%	5.62%	8.99%	6.74%	100%

breadth:length ratio 0–0.5	0.5–1.0	1.0–1.5	1.5–2.0	2.0–2.5	2.5–3.0	3.0–3.5	3.5–4.0	4.0>	total
9	31	31	9	4	1	3	1	–	89
10.11%	34.83%	34.83%	10.11%	4.49%	1.12%	3.37%	1.12%		100%

Table 7.23 Power Station site: dimensions of radially aligned woodchips (in mm)

length 0–50	50–100	100–150	150–200	200–250	350–300	300–350	350–400	400–500	500–600	600>	total
–	15	25	33	26	16	14	18	14	12	8	181
	8.29%	13.81%	18.23%	14.36%	8.84%	7.73%	9.94%	7.73%	6.63%	4.42%	100%

breadth 0–10	10–20	20–30	30–40	40–50	50–60	60–70	70–80	80–90	90–100	100>	total
–	1	10	28	40	46	21	15	9	3	8	181
	0.55%	5.52%	15.47%	22.10%	25.41%	11.60%	8.29%	4.97%	1.66%	4.42%	100%

thickness 0–5	5–10	10–15	15–20	20–25	25–30	30–35	35–40	40–45	45–50	50>	total
–	6	11	24	23	30	16	23	8	14	26	181
	3.31%	6.08%	13.26%	12.71%	16.57%	8.84%	12.71%	4.42%	7.73%	14.36	100%

breadth:length ratio 0–0.5	0.5–1.0	1.0–1.5	1.5–2.0	2.0–2.5	2.5–3.0	3.0–3.5	3.5–4.0	4.0>	total
12	65	40	32	23	7	1	–	1	181
6.63%	35.91%	22.10%	17.68%	12.71%	3.87%	0.55%		0.55%	100%

Table 7.24 Power Station site: dimensions of woodchips off roundwood (in mm)

length

0–50	50–100	100–150	150–200	200–250	350–300	300–350	350–400	400–500	500–600	600>	total
–	1	4	4	7	3	2	2	2	1	–	26
	3.85%	15.38%	15.38%	26.92%	11.54%	7.69%	7.69%	7.69%	3.85%		100%

breadth

0–10	10–20	20–30	30–40	40–50	50–60	60–70	70–80	80–90	90–100	100>	total
–	–	1	2	2	7	4	3	6	1	–	26
		3.85%	7.69%	7.69%	26.92%	15.38%	11.54%	23.08%	3.85%		100%

thickness

0–5	5–10	10–15	15–20	20–25	25–30	30–35	35–40	40–45	45–50	50>	total
–	–	–	2	–	4	1	5	1	4	9	26
			7.69%		15.38%	3.85%	19.23%	3.85%	15.38%	34.62%	100%

breadth:length ratio

0–0.5	0.5–1.0	1.0–1.5	1.5–2.0	2.0–2.5	2.5–3.0	3.0–3.5	3.5–4.0	4.0>	total
–	7	6	11	1	–	–	–	1	26
	26.92%	23.08%	42.31%	3.85%				3.85%	100%

Table 7.25 Power Station site: dimensions of cross-grain woodchips (in mm)

length

0–50	50–100	100–150	150–200	200–250	250–300	300–350	350–400	400–500	500–600	600>	total
–	3	5	8	7	6	4	5	4	1	–	43
	6.98%	11.63%	18.60%	16.28%	13.95%	9.30%	11.63%	9.30%	2.33%		100%

breadth

0–10	10–20	20–30	30–40	40–50	50–60	60–70	70–80	80–90	90–100	100>	total
–	–	3	10	14	6	5	4	1	–	–	43
		6.98%	23.26%	32.56%	13.95%	11.63%	9.30%	2.33%			100%

thickness

0–5	5–10	10–15	15–20	20–25	25–30	30–35	35–40	40–45	45–50	50>	total
–	–	2	7	7	7	3	4	3	7	3	43
		4.65%	16.28%	16.28%	16.28%	6.98%	9.30%	6.98%	16.28%	6.98	100%

breadth:length ratio

0–0.5	0.5–1.0	1.0–1.5	1.5–2.0	2.0–2.5	2.5–3.0	3.0–3.5	3.5–4.0	4.0>	total
4	20	6	7	2	2	1	1	–	43
9.30%	46.51%	13.95%	16.28%	4.65%	4.65%	2.33%	2.33%		100%

Table 7.26 Power Station site: dimensions of all measured woodchips (in mm)

length

0–50	50–100	100–150	150–200	200–250	350–300	300–350	350–400	400–500	500–600	600>	total
1	21	44	58	54	33	33	31	28	21	15	339
0.29%	6.19%	12.98%	17.11%	15.93%	9.73%	9.73%	9.14%	8.26%	6.19%	4.42%	100%

breadth

0–10	10–20	20–30	30–40	40–50	50–60	60–70	70–80	80–90	90–100	100>	total
–	1	16	50	70	89	44	33	20	6	10	339
	0.29%	4.72%	14.75%	20.65%	26.25%	12.98%	9.73%	5.90%	1.77%	2.95%	100%

thickness

0–5	5–10	10–15	15–20	20–25	25–30	30–35	35–40	40–45	45–50	50>	total
–	7	17	49	43	58	26	45	17	33	44	339
	2.06%	5.01%	14.45%	12.68%	17.11%	7.67%	13.27%	5.01%	9.73%	12.98	100%

breadth:length ratio

0–0.5	0.5–1.0	1.0–1.5	1.5–2.0	2.0–2.5	2.5–3.0	3.0–3.5	3.5–4.0	4.0>	total
25	123	83	59	30	10	5	2	2	339
7.37%	36.28%	24.48%	17.40%	8.85%	2.95%	1.47%	0.59%	0.59%	100%

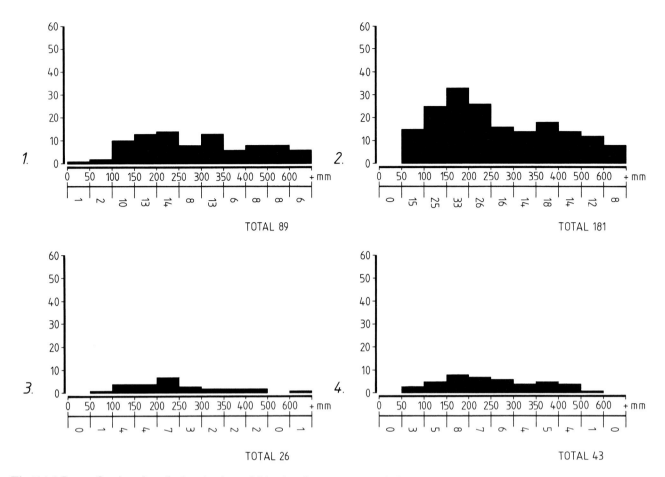

Fig 7.16 Power Station: length (mm) of woodchips by class: 1, tangentially aligned; 2, radially aligned; 3, off roundwood; 4, cross-grain

The predominance of timber is a feature that has already been referred to, but the relatively high proportion of debris (34.15%) must indicate that, as at Flag Fen, woodworking was taking place *in situ*.

The roundwood found at the Power Station (Fig 7.14; Table 7.19) was generally of smaller diameter than that at Flag Fen and it was notably shorter.

Timber, as has been noted, was largely in the form of posts. As in the case of roundwood, the majority of timbers was shorter than at Flag Fen and there was a sharp fall off after 1000mm (Fig 7.15; Table 7.20). By contrast, the original diameters were larger. This undoubtedly reflects the fact that most of the timbers were posts. As the presence of timber debris is significant, the small sample's bias towards the larger end of the scale was probably caused by post-depositional factors (Table 7.21). These will be discussed more fully in the following section.

Woodchips

The woodchip statistics (Tables 7.22–27) from the Power Station present a remarkable contrast with Flag Fen. The absence of slabs is most notable, as is the flattened appearance of all the histograms (Figs 7.16–23). It is suggested that these effects are most probably the result of post-depositional factors. A simple observation is relevant in this instance. Unless fully

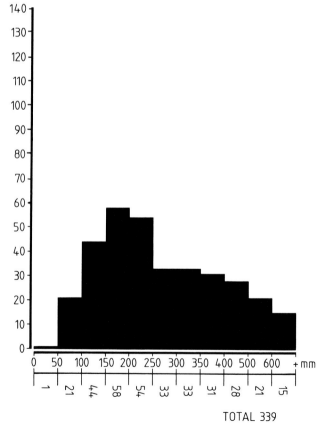

Fig 7.17 Power Station: all woodchips by length (mm)

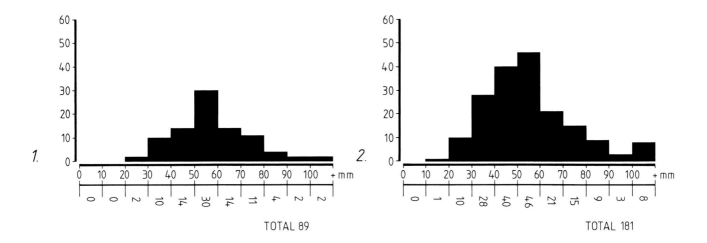

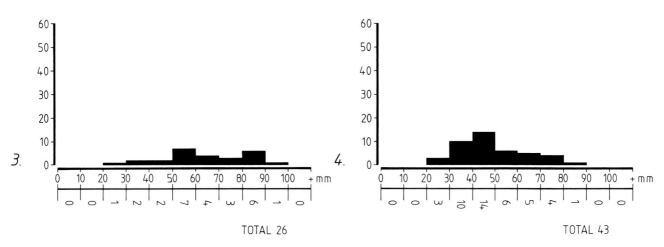

Fig 7.18 Power Station: breadth (mm) of woodchips by class: 1, tangentially aligned; 2, radially aligned; 3, off roundwood; 4, cross-grain

waterlogged, wood will float, and small pieces of wood, such as chips, are readily removed by flowing water. Similarly, a shallow, fluctuating water environment of higher energy than that at Flag Fen would also encourage the aerobic deterioration of wood, such as sapwood (which still retained nutrients that could be of use to organisms such as fungi). This might help to account for the absence of sapwood removal chips (or slabs).

Inspection of the various graphs and tables shows a strong skewing in favour of size, ie longer lengths, greater widths and thicknesses. As might be expected, this bias is particularly evident in the figures for woodchip thickness, which show a marked preference for thicker pieces (Fig 7.21). This should be compared with the Flag Fen figures (Fig 7.10).

Discussion

At first glance, the category by category composition of the Power Station wood assemblage was what might be expected of a site where woodworking was taking place. On closer inspection, however, it is evident that

certain key elements were either absent or are grossly underrepresented. The flatness of the metrical data histograms is particularly significant. These factors, together with what is known about the Power Station water environment, strongly suggest that the data have been skewed by post-depositional factors. These factors could be predicted on the basis of the sedimentary history of the site, but it is most instructive to see their effects illustrated so clearly by statistics.

Table 7.27 Summary of woodchips from the Power Station, by category

	number	%
slabs	1	0.29
tangentially aligned	89	25.80
radially aligned	181	52.46
off roundwood	26	7.54
cross-grain	43	12.46
unclassifiable	5	1.45
total	345	100.00

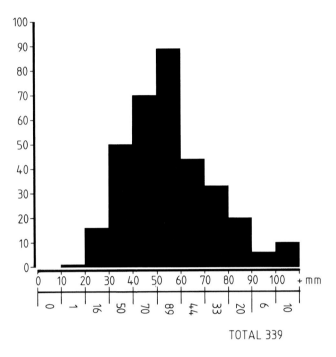

Independent corroboration of the post-depositional distortion hypothesis is provided by the dendrochronological study, which reported very poor preservation of sapwood on the Power Station posts (Chapter 8). This would be entirely consistent with the disappearance of sapwood removal woodchips whose absence is otherwise inexplicable.

Fenland sites, unlike the rainwater-fed bog sites of western Britain, are prone to disturbance by fast-flowing water. It would now appear that there is an archaeological means of identifying such processes, especially on sites where woodchips occur in any number. In future, metrical data of this sort could be used as an indicator of otherwise unsuspected distorting taphonomic factors. It will be enlightening to compare the data from Flag Fen and Etton with Fenland Project excavations, such as Market Deeping in the lower Welland valley, where woodchips were abundant amidst the 'general carpentry detritus' (Lane 1992, 46). As it is of Iron Age date, the latter site is of added importance and could provide data on the important third step in the development of prehistoric woodworking, from bronze to iron.

Fig 7.19 Power Station: all woodchips by breadth (mm)

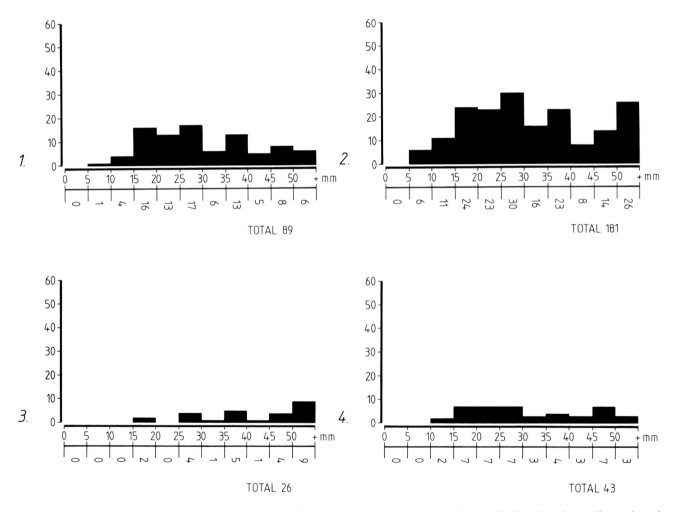

Fig 7.20 Power Station: thickness (mm) of woodchips by class: 1, tangentially aligned; 2, radially aligned; 3, off roundwood; 4, cross-grain

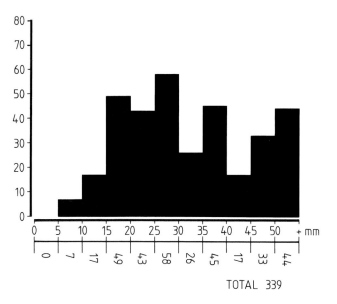

Fig 7.21 Power Station: all woodchips by thickness (mm)

Fig 7.23 Power Station: all woodchips, breadth:length (×5) ratios

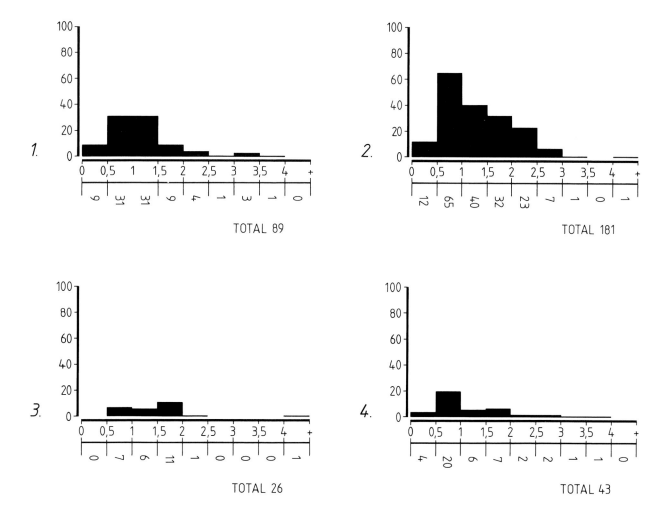

Fig 7.22 Power Station: breadth:length (×5) ratios of woodchips by class: 1, tangentially aligned; 2, radially aligned; 3, off roundwood; 4, cross-grain

Toolmarks

Definitions and method of recording

The corpus of complete toolmarks from Flag Fen and the Power Station is presented here as Figures T1–T13; these are drawings taken directly off the piece, where it could be seen that the edge of the cutting tool had bitten into the wood, leaving a profile. A tool mark is not to be confused with a tool facet, which is the scar left by the cutting tool after it has passed through the wood. Tool facets occur more frequently, but are less reliable indicators of tool type and can vary according to the angle and direction of the cutting tool.

The corpus includes some incomplete toolmarks, where there was sufficient information to allow the original shape of the tool to be gauged. Partial toolmarks have not been included, but a complete record might be found in the site archive.

A special debt of thanks is owed to Dr Rob Sands (Edinburgh University) for his close collaboration. At the time of writing, Sands is currently working on the toolmarks from Oakbank Crannog and efforts have been made to ensure that the datasets from Oakbank and Flag Fen are comparable. Sands has been able to construct a database of dimensions and profiles of North British bronze axes, on the basis of the published corpus (Schmidt and Burgess 1981).

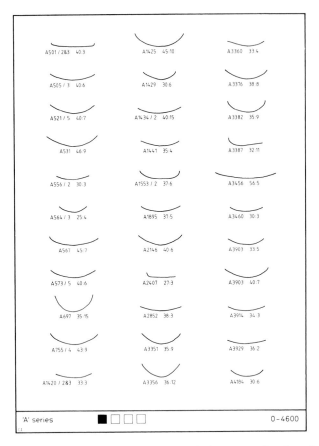

Fig T1 Flag Fen, Area 6A (A series) corpus of toolmarks (A0–A4600)

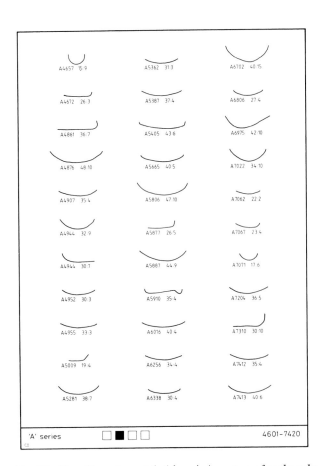

Fig T2 Flag Fen, Area 6A (A series) corpus of toolmarks (A4601–A7420)

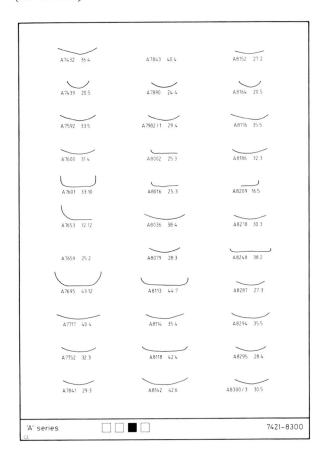

Fig T3 Flag Fen, Area 6A (A series) corpus of toolmarks (A7421–A8300)

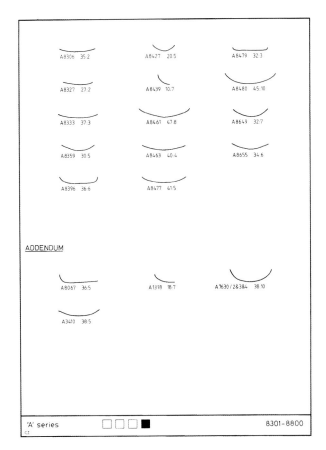

Fig T4 Flag Fen, Area 6A (A series) corpus of toolmarks (A8301–A8800 and addendum)

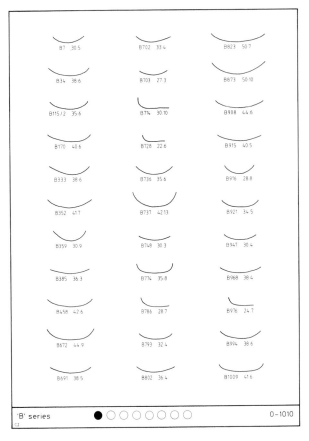

Fig T5 Flag Fen, Area 6B (B series) corpus of toolmarks (B0–B1010)

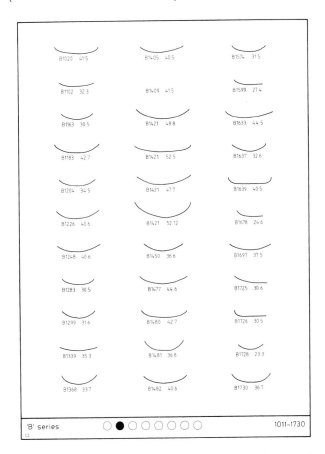

Fig T6 Flag Fen, Area 6B (B series) corpus of toolmarks (B1011–B1730)

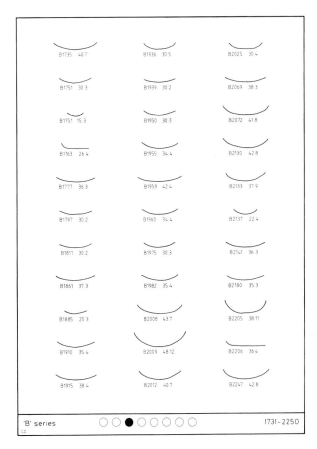

Fig T7 Flag Fen, Area 6B (B series) corpus of toolmarks (B1731–B2250)

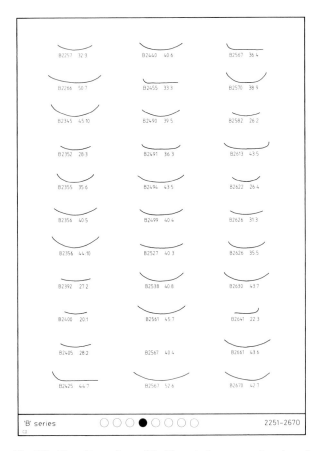

Fig T8 Flag Fen, Area 6B (B series) corpus of toolmarks (B2251–B2670)

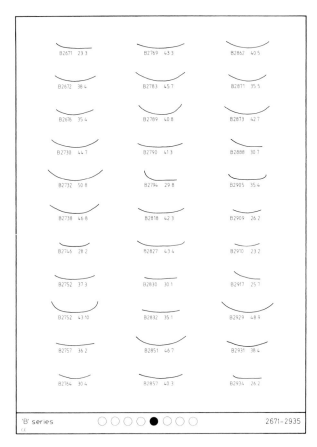

Fig T9 Flag Fen, Area 6B (B series) corpus of toolmarks (B2671–B2935)

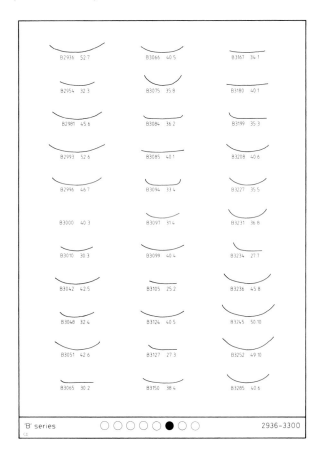

Fig T10 Flag Fen, Area 6B (B series) corpus of toolmarks (B2936–B3300)

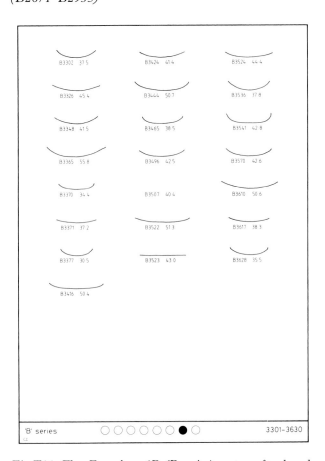

Fig T11 Flag Fen, Area 6B (B series) corpus of toolmarks (B3301–B3630)

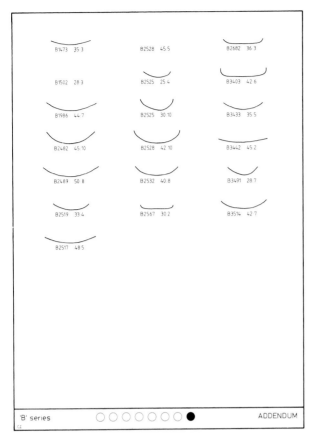

Fig T12 Flag Fen, Area 6B (B series) corpus of toolmarks (addendum)

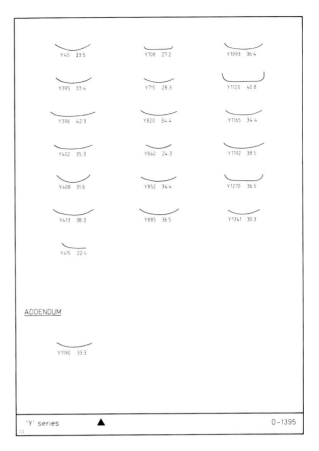

Fig T13 Power Station (Y series) corpus of toolmarks (Y0–1395)

Unfortunately no such body of work exists for the Southern British material. For the purposes of the present study, axe dimensions have therefore been taken from Davey's (1973) corpus of Lincolnshire Bronze Age metalwork. The study is in two parts — a discussion of blade widths, followed by blade curvature indices.

Blade widths

For the purposes of the present study, toolmarks were only taken from horizontal timbers at Flag Fen, since posts could not be reliably phased. The deposits in

Areas 6A and 6B were divided into two halves, an upper (from 0.89m to 0.3m OD) and a lower (0.29m to 0m OD). The blade widths were measured and statistics calculated (Table 7.28). The figures clearly demonstrate that the same type of tool was used throughout the life of the monument.

There is no statistically significant difference between blade widths in the two halves, nor in the combined assemblage.

A comparison of blade widths between Flag Fen and measured axe blades shows that the Flag Fen marks were narrower than actual axe blades (Table 7.29).

Table 7.28 Comparison of blade widths: Flag Fen toolmarks and selected Bronze Age axe types

toolmark	average blade width (mm)	standard deviation of blade width	minimum blade width (mm)	maximum blade width (mm)	number of axes in calculation	sources
Flag Fen (all deposits)	38.06	6.83	15	55	168	
Flag Fen (upper half)	38.06	6.12	15	52	83	
Flag Fen (lower half)	33.06	7.50	15	55	85	
axe type						
Wilburton	42.67	5.25	38	50	3	Sands 1994
south-eastern	43.00	7.11	24	52	30	Sands 1994
Yorkshire	46.59	4.59	32	58	211	Sands 1994
socketed	47.44	4.73	27	63	170	Davey 1973
all flanged and palstaves	55.71	12.49	24	87	70	Davey 1973
flat and low flanged	60.60	13.22	36	78	20	Davey 1973

Table 7.29 Blade curvature indices: comparison of Flag Fen toolmarks with selected Bronze Age axe types

toolmark	average curvature index (%)	standard deviation of curvature index	minimum curvature index (%)	maximum curvature index (%)	number of axes in calculation	sources
Flag Fen (all deposits)	14.83	7.03	0.00	60.00	168	
Flag Fen (upper half)	16.18	7.86	2.94	60.00	83	
Flag Fen (lower half)	13.52	5.87	0.00	30.30	85	
axe type						
flat and low flanged	24.90	9.28	7.69	47.06	20	Davey 1973
all flanged and palstaves	24.79	7.57	10.00	45.45	70	Davey 1973
socketed axes	19.18	7.34	0.00	35.29	170	Davey 1973
Wilburton	17.81	6.35	11.25	26.40	3	Sands 1994
south-eastern	17.04	6.52	4.41	35.87	23	Sands 1994
Yorkshire	14.54	6.53	1.30	34.09	163	Sands 1994

The closest fit was with socketed axes of three specific types, and from Lincolnshire in general. The disparity between marks and actual blades might, in part, reflect the fact that seemingly complete marks in wood might not represent an entire blade width; in other words, only the central part of the blade might have bitten into the timber (for this study, skewed marks were rejected as incomplete).

Toolmarks in ancient wood are also more likely to become compressed through time, as the wood itself shrinks.

Blade-width frequencies showed a very similar pattern in the three Flag Fen groups (Figs 7.24–6). As expected, this pattern reinforced the results of the statistical analysis. Histograms of the published blades from Lincolnshire showed two contrasting patterns. The earliest two groups (flat/low flanged axes and flanged axes/palstaves) had consistently broader blades, combined with a more diffuse distribution of measurements (Figs 7.27–8). The shape of the socketed axe curve, however, closely followed that of the Flag Fen toolmarks, even though the range of values was

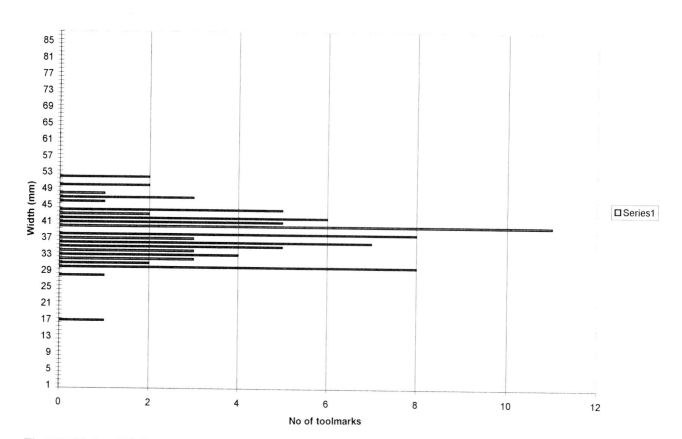

Fig 7.24 Blade-width frequencies of toolmarks from upper deposits at Flag Fen, Areas 6A and 6B (0.89–0.3m OD)

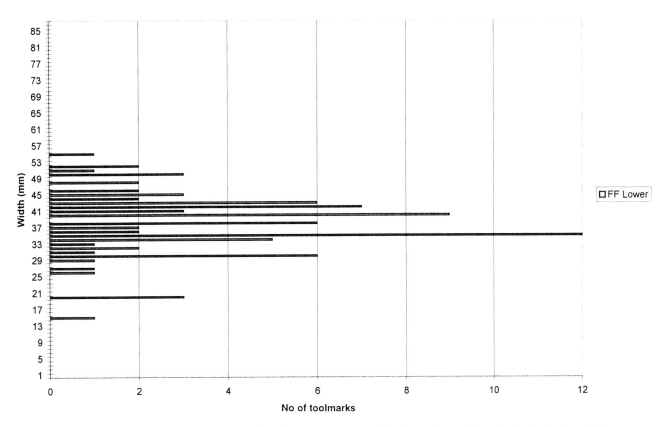

Fig 7.25 Blade-width frequencies of toolmarks from lower deposits at Flag Fen, Areas 6A and 6B (0.29–0m OD)

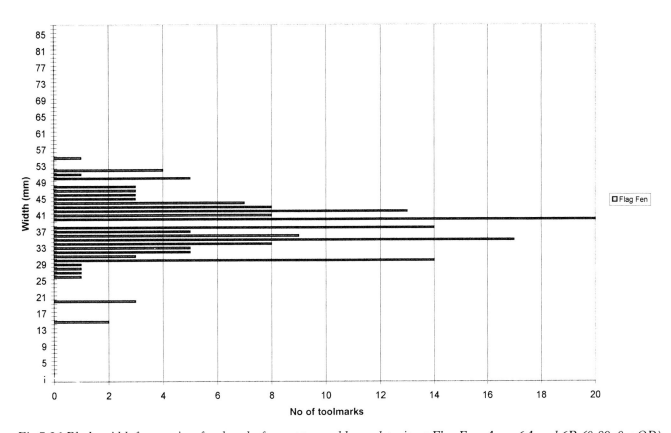

Fig 7.26 Blade-width frequencies of toolmarks from upper and lower deposits at Flag Fen, Areas 6A and 6B (0.89–0m OD)

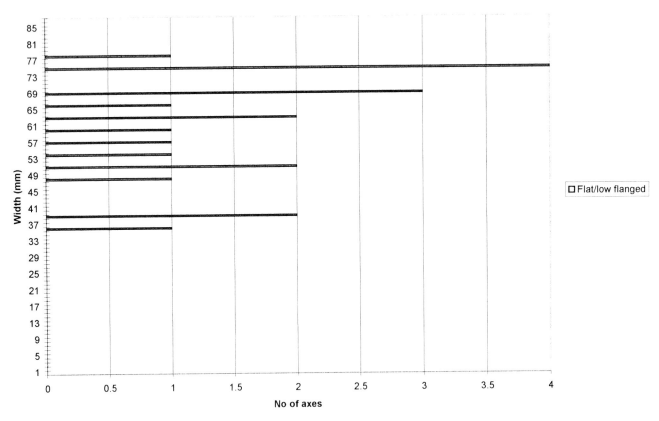

Fig 7.27 Blade-width frequencies of flat and low flanged axes from Lincolnshire (after Davey 1973)

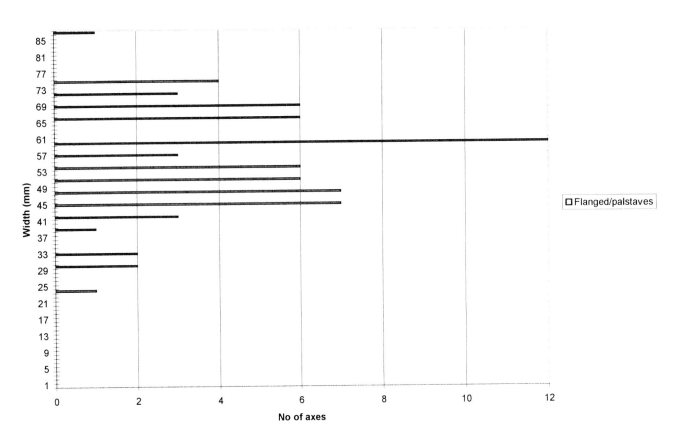

Fig 7.28 Blade-width frequencies of flanged axes and palstaves from Lincolnshire (after Davey 1973)

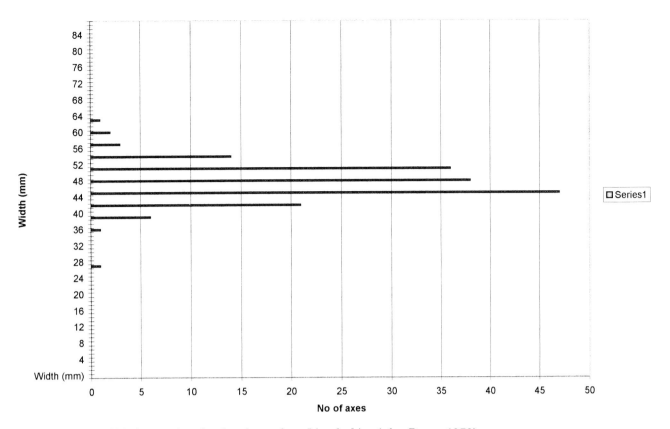

Fig 7.29 Blade-width frequencies of socketed axes from Lincolnshire (after Davey 1973)

consistently some 10mm higher (Fig 7.29). This might suggest that the difference might largely be explained in terms of post-depositional distortion.

Blade-curvature indices

An index of blade curvature was calculated for each blade or tool mark, in which the depth of curvature was expressed as a percentage of the complete blade width (Fig 7.30). An analysis of blade-curvature indices of the Flag Fen assemblage again shows the same general homogeneity, but toolmarks from deposits of the lower half show less curvature than might otherwise be expected. It is difficult to explain this.

Comparative figures for blade curvature follow those for width. Earlier forms are generally more curved, and the best match with Flag Fen is again provided by socketed axes; the match with socketed axes of Yorkshire type is close and the sizes of the two assemblages (163 axes and 168 toolmarks) are also closely comparable.

Discussion of tool types and toolmarks

The figures described above strongly indicate that the sole axe type used at Flag Fen was the socketed axe. This is perhaps surprising, given that the site was first occupied towards the end of the Middle Bronze Age. This might indicate that implements with broader blades were principally used for tasks more fitted to a

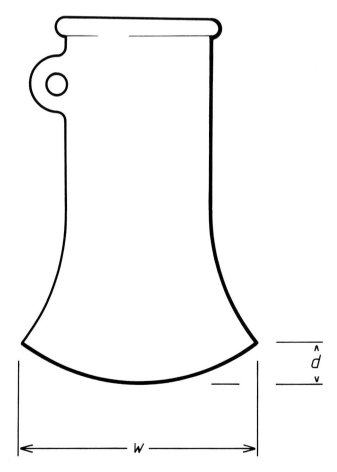

Fig 7.30 Measurements used to calculate the blade-curvature index

modern billhook, such as coppicing and hedging. It might also suggest that the fashion for different types or styles of axes changed rapidly. As Sands (1994 and 1997) has shown, the study of toolmarks offers another form of independent relative dating that might prove useful in those cases of waterlogged sites where dendrochronology is impossible and where reliably associated artefacts are rare or absent.

The waterlogged wood: woodworking

Natural woodworking: beavers

The beaver was probably quite common in Britain throughout prehistory, and in some areas it survived into medieval times. Among a number of objects accompanying an Anglo-Saxon burial excavated in the nineteenth century at Burwell, near Cambridge, was a beaver tooth set in bronze (Fox 1923, 262). Beaver bones have been found in various contexts dating from the postglacial period onwards. The following short note, written over a hundred years ago, is probably a good summary of what we know:

> The remains of the beaver are tolerably abundant in the Fens. The animal became extinct in England in the 12th and 13th century, but it still survives in the Rhône and in the rivers of Lithuania and Scandinavia. So far as my observation goes the beaver did not build dams in the Fens, owing, in all probability, to the abundance of still water. The late J K Lord, himself an experienced trapper, informed me that in North America the beaver only constructs dams in running streams, and chooses still water where possible to save the trouble of architecture (Miller and Skertchly 1878, 348).

The European beaver (*Castor fiber*) and Canadian beaver (*Castor canadensis*) are very similar in their habitat and habits. Neither necessarily build dams and lodges, and it is recorded that in some areas beavers live in burrows in the banks of slow-moving rivers (Corbet and Ovenden 1980). The most important factors, as far as the beavers are concerned, are the presence of slow-moving water and of broad-leaved trees, their food plants. The environment of the Fengate/Northey embayment would have presented a suitable habitat and supported many of the beaver's food plants. These would have included the favoured tree species of poplar, maple, willow, and alder. It has been pointed out that the activities of beavers in building lodges and dams can affect water levels extensively and other aspects of the local environment (Coles and Orme 1982, 67–72).

Beaver-modified wood from Flag Fen

The tooth marks of beavers are quite distinctive and are readily distinguished from toolmarks (Fig 7.31). Beaver-chewed wood from the Flag Fen platform has been compared with modern wood modified by Canadian beavers (kindly supplied by Charles French). In total, eight pieces of beaver-modified wood have been found at Flag Fen, and all were from low levels (0.04–0.29m OD).

In every case the wood was alder (*Alnus glutinosa*), a favourite food for beavers. One piece (B2257) was quite large (compressed diameter 80–95mm) and over 2m long. Originally cut from a coppice stool with an axe, the stem had been chewed half through by beaver. It is quite possible that the stem was chewed by the beaver while still growing and was then removed from the stool with the other poles when the coppice was cut. All the other pieces of 'beavered' wood were much smaller in length and diameter. Most of these pieces have distorted diameters, perhaps because they come from low in the platform. The estimated undistorted

0   40mm

Fig 7.31 Beaver tooth marks on modern maple wood from Canada (left), and Bronze Age wood (B2257) from Flag Fen Area 6B (right)

diameters range from 20 to 50mm. Only one other piece, B3462, had been worked by both humans and beavers. One end had been trimmed by an axe from one direction and the other end had been gnawed by a beaver. This pole also had side stems, which had been removed by an axe. Piece B3006 was not very well preserved but one end and one side shoot was almost certainly trimmed by beaver.

The relatively small diameter of the wood chewed by beavers at Flag Fen suggests that it was food rather than constructional wood. Beavers cut down and chew much more wood than they can actually eat. Some wood is dragged under water to store for winter food, but quantities of wood debris lie around in areas 'grazed' by beavers. The fact that the beaver wood was found low down in the platform makeup suggests that beavers were active in the vicinity before construction began, and that they were possibly driven away by human activity. Once alder was being systematically coppiced to produce poles, the attention of beavers would have been unwelcome.

Reduction of timber

The most common method used to reduce the large timbers excavated at Flag Fen was splitting (Fig 7.32). There was no direct evidence in the form of wedge 'scars' on any of the surfaces, but experimental work at

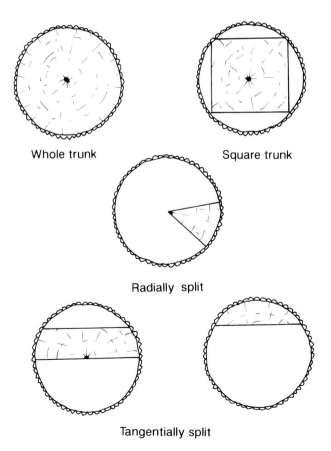

Whole trunk   Square trunk

Radially split

Tangentially split

Fig 7.32 Ways of splitting wood using the natural tendencies of the timber

Flag Fen suggests that splitting green wood with seasoned wood wedges need not leave visible marks (Pryor 1991, 77–81).

Worked timbers are illustrated in a series of outline drawings (Figs 7.33, 7.36–43, 7.45–7). Sections by each outline show the alignment of medullary rays. Both oak and ash were split radially, although ash was usually split only into in halves or quarters. Oak was often finely reduced, sometimes to very thin planks (Fig 7.37, 18). Ash timbers were often split cleanly in half. It was rare to find other species split, or when they were split it was usually crude. Only the largest butts (trunks) of oak were split tangentially (eg Fig 7.37, 16; Fig 7.38, 20). There was seldom any direct evidence for further dressing of the timber, although it could often be deduced. A rare example of hewn wood (B2356) showed the skill of the woodworker (Fig 7.34). This particular timber had been worked in the wettest part of the site and was then left *in situ*. Not only was the timber preserved in the finest condition, but the woodchips generated during its working were found with it. On detailed examination of this piece, it was possible to see that the hewing had probably been carried out with an axe and not with an adze. The way in which wood had been systematically removed in one direction was quite clear. A smaller piece of hewn wood (B2626), excavated nearby and at the same level, was less well preserved but produced useful data. Both pieces came from trees that were originally of similar diameter (180mm) and had been split in half. Both retained some of their bark. Timber B2356 still showed the signs of felling at one end. B2626 had been roughly trimmed at one end.

Joints

In the catalogue entries, toolmarks are expressed in the form w:d, where w represents blade width and d the depth of curvature (Fig 7.30).

Joints associated with posts

Posts that were still earthfast had lost their upper parts, but in several, mortise joints had survived in their lower sections (Fig 7.33). There were a few pieces that appeared to have been the broken or cut upper parts of posts. There were also three pieces that, although found lying at or near the horizontal, were probably originally made to be posts.

Catalogue of illustrated posts with joints (Fig 7.33)

1 B667: wood species: oak (*Quercus* sp); joints: single tenon (105 × 140 × 45mm); dimensions: length, 400mm; oval, 160 × 140mm; context: Area 6B, Level 2 (0.83m OD), grid 2710 8888; notes: felled post.
2 B1421: wood species: alder (*Alnus glutinosa*); joints: 'eared' housing joints (85mm and 80mm); blind mortise (120 × 120mm); mortise in tip (70 × 70mm); dimensions: length, 4020mm; oval, 220 × 185mm;

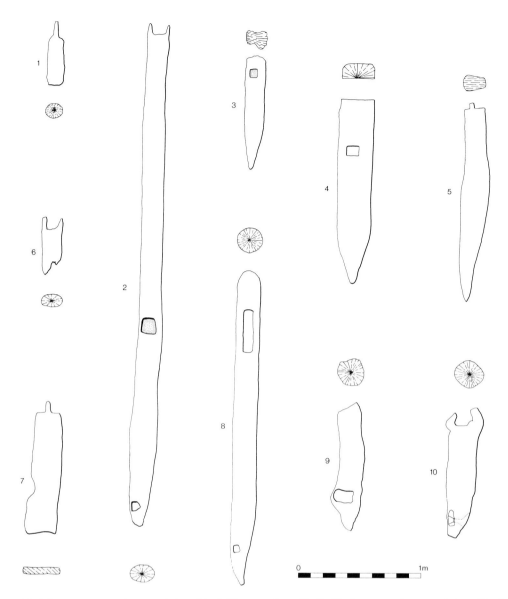

Fig 7.33 Posts with joints: upper section surviving (1, 6, 7); complete (2, 5, 8); lower section surviving (3, 4, 9, 10)

context: Area 6B, Level 4 (0.41m OD), grid 2708 8889; notes (Fig 7.35): toolmarks, on tip (48:8), on unfinished mortise (52:5), and (47:7) on complete mortise (52:12).

3   B1721: wood species: oak (*Quercus* sp); joints: blind mortise (52 × 55 × 32mm); dimensions: length, 900mm; width, 195mm; thickness, 160mm; context: Area 6B, Level 4 (1.06–0.46m OD), grid 2709 8887.

4   B379: wood species: oak (*Quercus* sp); joints: mortise (110 × 100 × 95mm); dimensions: length, 1650mm; width, 290mm; thickness, 130mm; context: Area 6B, (1.02–0.39m OD), grid 2709 8885.

5   B61: wood species: oak (*Quercus* sp); joints: single tenon (134 × 70 × 60mm); dimensions: length, 1715mm; width, 200–295mm; thickness, 130–160mm; context: Area 6B, Level 1 (0.66–0.46m OD), grid 2709 8884.

6   B499: wood species: alder (*Alnus glutinosa*); joints: 'eared' housing joint (100mm and 90mm); dimensions: length, 482mm; oval, 105 × 70mm; context: Area 6B, Level 2 (0.57–0.53m OD), grid 2705 8889.

7   B52: wood species: oak (*Quercus* sp); joints: single tenon (170 × 55mm); dimensions: length, 1235mm; width, 270mm; thickness, 50mm; context: Area 6B, Level 1 (0.47m OD), grid 2710 8882.

8   B4176: wood species: possibly alder (*Alnus glutinosa*); joints: slot (357 × 80mm); mortise (65 × 46mm); dimensions: length, 2510mm; oval, 200 × 141mm; context: Area 6D, Level 5 (0.50–0.31m OD), grid 2703 8884.

9   A1425: wood species: poplar/willow (*Populus/Salix* sp); joints: mortise in tip (155 × 95mm); dimensions: length, 970mm; diameter, 200mm; context: Area 6A (0.67m OD), grid 2716 8886.

10   B2247: wood species: alder (*Alnus glutinosa*); joints: mortise in tip (125 × 60mm). Dimensions: length, 1460mm; diameter, 220mm; context: Area 6B, Level 3 (0.76–0.87m OD), grid 2706 8888; notes: toolmarks (42:8).

Mortises

There were enough unfinished mortises to be able to describe with some certainty the method of their fabrication, which was invariably the same. The best example for illustration was the complete upright (Fig 7.33, 2) that was found among horizontal timbers of the platform.

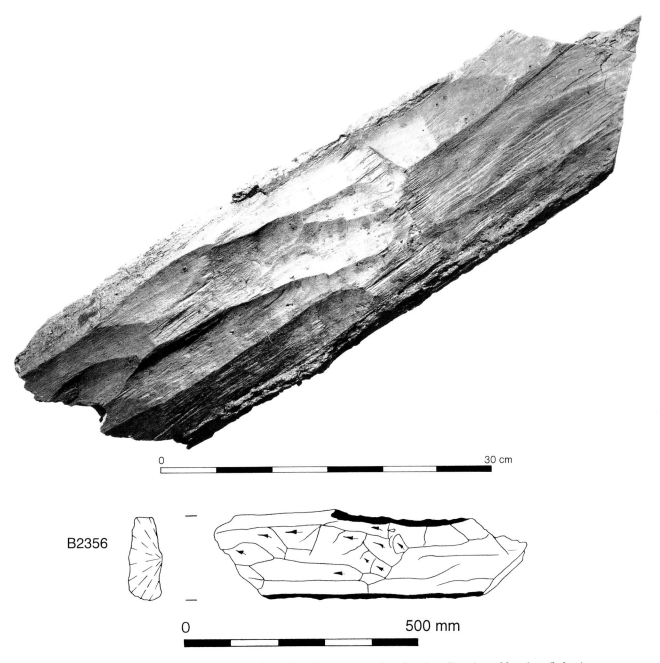

B2356

0   30 cm

0   500 mm

Fig 7.34 Hewn surface of timber B2356 from Area 6B. The same timber showing direction of hewing (below)

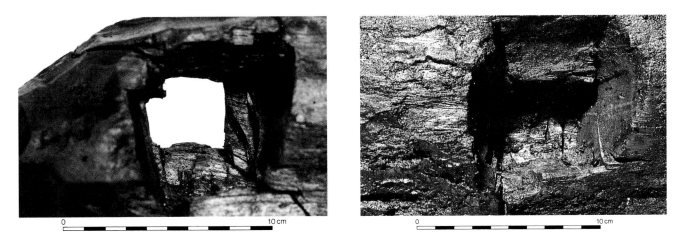

0   10 cm   0   10 cm

Fig 7.35 Unused upright from Area 6B, timber B1421: unfinished mortises at tip (left) and part-way up (right). For outline of whole timber see Figure 7.33, 2

The timber was lying at a slight angle. The lower part was so well preserved that it was possible to see in some detail how the two mortises had been cut. Both mortises were cut with an axe, chopping across the grain and gouging out the wood between the cuts (Fig 7.35). The direction and angle of chopping was quite clear, as were the profiles of the axes used. The mortises were cut from both sides and have a slightly waisted profile. The mortise near the tip, which was completely cut through, shows from the profile that an axe with a slightly flat blade had been used to do most of the work, although there were one or two clear marks of a second axe with a more curved blade. This blade was so similar in profile to the blade that was used to sharpen the tip, that they were almost certainly the same tool. Yet a third axe with a very curved blade was used to cut the unfinished mortise in the tip.

Mortises in various shapes and sizes were found on the timber from the platform, and, less commonly, on the timber from the Power Station (Figs 7.36–9). Mortises, both complete (holes) and blind (recesses), were very common in Bronze Age carpentry and, except for the tiniest examples (on artefacts eg B1751 and B3130, described below), those at Flag Fen were invariably cut with axes. Mortises were of various sizes and cut through different types of timber, presumably to perform different functions.

Catalogue of illustrated mortises

11 B3245: wood species: unidentified; joints: mortise (55 × 40mm); dimensions: length, 3300mm; width, 155–196mm; original diameter, 155mm; context: Area 6B, Level 6 (0.34–0.24m OD), grid 2709 8884; notes: hewn on both sides; toolmarks (50:10).

12 B3143: wood species: unidentified; joints: mortise (87 × 82mm); dimensions: length, 2870mm; width, 260mm; thickness, 170mm; context: Area 6B, Level 6 (0.13m OD), grid 2712 8885.

13 B3507: wood species: unidentified; joints: mortise (165 × 70mm); dimensions: length, 1170mm; diameter, 190mm; context: Area 6B; Level 6 (0.06m–0.05m OD), grid 2709 8883; notes: toolmarks (40:4).

14 B2318: wood species: oak (*Quercus* sp); joints: ?'eared' housing joint/broken mortise (190 × 80mm); dimensions: length, 3450mm; width, 210mm; thickness, 45mm; context: Area 6B; Level 4 (0.32m OD), grid 2709 8888.

15 A1805: wood species: oak (*Quercus* sp); joints: mortise (97 × 77mm); dimensions: length, 2255mm; width, 150–180mm; thickness, 10–65mm; context: Area 6A, Level 2 (0.45–0.42m OD), grid 2718 8883.

16 B47: wood species: oak (*Quercus* sp); joints: mortise (95 × 70mm); broken mortise (160 × 60mm); dimensions: length, 2820mm; width, 220mm; thickness, 40mm; context: Area 6A, Level 1 (0.58–0.41m OD), grid 2710 8883.

17 B1523: wood species: oak (*Quercus* sp); joints: two mortises (96 × 88mm and 106 × 65mm); dimensions: length, 2905mm; width, 192mm; thickness, 23–48mm; context: Area 6B, Level 3 (0.51–0.41m OD), grid 2708 8890; notes: pegs B1519 and B1520 passed through the mortise holes.

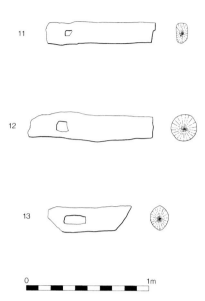

Fig 7.36 Mortises cut through roundwood

18 B2416: wood species: unidentified; joints: mortise (120 × 85mm); half mortise (100 × 75mm); dimensions: length, 1860mm; width, 150–245mm; thickness, 40mm; context: Area 6B, Level 4 (0.24–0.15m OD), grid 2709 8883.

19 A3511: wood species: oak (*Quercus* sp); joints: mortise (130 × 90mm); dimensions: length, 1390mm; width, 168–235mm; thickness, 25–70mm; context: Area 6A, Level 2 (0.35–0.25m OD), grid 2718 8883.

20 B169: wood species: oak (*Quercus* sp); joints: two oval mortises (243 × 130mm and 100 × 54mm); one square mortise (136 × 93mm); dimensions: length, 1440mm; width, 250mm; thickness, 70mm; context: Area 6B, Level 1 (0.62–0.53m OD), grid 2710 8890.

21 A2173: wood species: oak (*Quercus* sp); joints: mortise (110 × 85mm); half mortise (110 × 95mm); dimensions: length, 740mm; width, 320mm; thickness, 60mm; context: Area 6A, Level 2 (0.52–0.42m OD), grid 2714 8891; notes: same as A1161.

22 B51: wood species: oak (*Quercus* sp); joints: two mortises (110 × 110mm and 92 × 90mm); dimensions: length, 2530mm; width, 217–300mm; thickness, 90mm; context: Area 6B, Level 1 (0.60–0.48m OD), grid 2710 8883.

23 B359: wood species: oak (*Quercus* sp); joints: three mortises (85 × 45mm, 70 × 50mm, and 100 × 80mm); one unfinished mortise (60 × 35mm); dimensions: length, 2120mm; width, 190mm; thickness, 85mm; context: Area 6B, Level 1 (0.54m OD), grid 2709 8886; notes: toolmarks on unfinished mortise (30:10).

24 B4171: wood species: unidentified; joints: mortise (100 × 85mm); broken mortise (115 × 110mm); dimensions: length, 2054mm; width, 120mm; thickness, 60mm; context: Area 6D, Level 5 (0.42–0.33m OD), grid 2701 8886.

25 B1485: wood species: oak (*Quercus* sp); joints: mortise (78 × 69mm); dimensions: length, 1662mm; width, 107–60mm; thickness, 97mm; original diameter: 160mm; context: Area 6B, Level 4 (0.46m OD), grid 2709 8888.

26 A3566: wood species: willow (*Salix* sp); joints: mortise (95 × 50mm); dimensions: length, 1830mm; width, 170mm; thickness, 75mm; context: Area 6A, Level 3 (0.40m OD), grid 2719 8882.

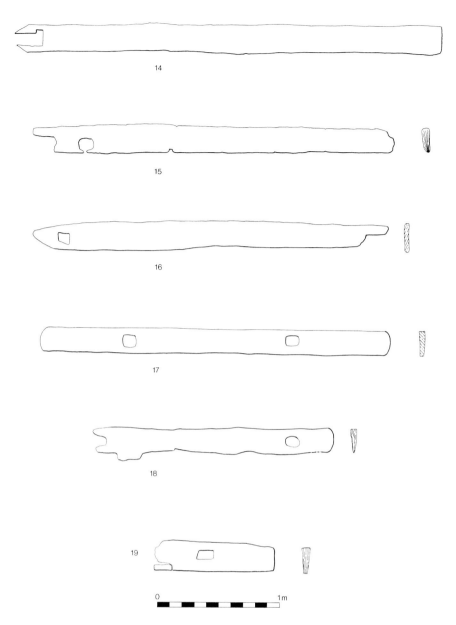

Fig 7.37 Mortises cut through planks

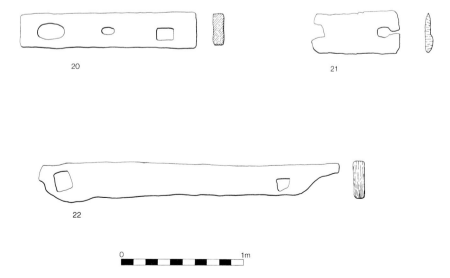

Fig 7.38 Mortises cut through heavy timber

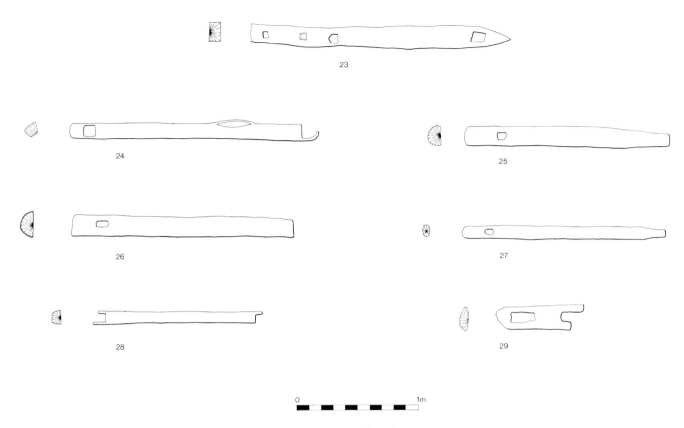

Fig 7.39 Mortises cut through roundwood or partly reduced roundwood

27 B450: wood species: unidentified; joints: mortise (70 × 35mm); dimensions: length, 1650mm; oval, 100 × 80mm; context: Area 6B, Level 1 (0.71m OD), grid 2709 8888.

28 A862: wood species: oak (*Quercus* sp); joints: two broken mortises (90 × 67 × 55mm and 45 × 75mm); dimensions: length, 1350mm; width, 100mm; thickness, 65mm; context: Area 6A, Level 2 (0.45–0.37m OD), grid 2715 8887.

29 A6175: wood species: oak (*Quercus* sp); joints: mortise (190 × 80mm); broken mortise (180 × 80mm); dimensions: length, 725mm; width, 187mm; thickness, 70mm; context: Area 6A, Level 2 (0.32m OD), grid 2721 8878.

Note: other mortises not illustrated in Figs 7.36–9 include:

Mortises cut through roundwood or partly reduced roundwood: Fig 7.40, 30, 31; Fig 7.41, 32.
Timbers with blind (recessed) mortises: Fig 7.33, 2, 3; Fig 7.42, 39.
Posts with mortises: Fig 7.33, 2, 4, 8–10.
Broken mortises: Fig 7.45, 49–53.
Other broken mortises: Fig 7.33, 6; Fig 7.46, 7.55–7.

Slots

Slots were essentially elongated mortises and were cut in the same way (ie with axes from two sides; Fig 7.40). There were two slotted timbers from the platform. Both were of very similar fabrication. A possible post (Fig 7.33, 8), found lying horizontally, had an elongated mortise cut through it. As it was considerably longer than any other mortise, it could be classified as a slot

Catalogue of illustrated slots

30 B2059: wood species: oak (*Quercus* sp); joints: two mortises (140 × 90mm and 70 × 70mm); one slot (680 × 85mm); dimensions: length, 3070mm; width, 170–200mm; thickness, 48–83mm; context: Area 6B, Level 3 (0.31m OD), grid 2708 8884.

31 B1784: wood species: unidentified; joints: mortise (50–105 × 75mm); slot (755 × 80mm); dimensions: length, 3300mm; width, 160mm; thickness, 60mm; context: Area 6B, Level 3 (0.44m OD), grid 2714 8884; notes: worn on upper surface.

Tenons

Strictly speaking, as a tenon should be the same size as (and exactly fit) the mortise, there were no tenons in the timber from the Flag Fen or the Power Station (Corkhill 1979, 575). As the 'tenons' were much more slender than the mortises, they are more correctly described as locating pegs. The single 'tenons' were intended to locate a mortise hole; double 'tenons' or 'ears' were a form of housing joint, designed to take a cross member.

Tenons illustrated with other types of joint include: single tenons on posts (Fig 7.33, 1,5, and 7); tenons on heavy timber (Fig 7.38, 22); on lighter timber (Fig 7.45, 52); on planks (Fig 7.47, 59); double, on posts (Fig 7.33, 2, 6).

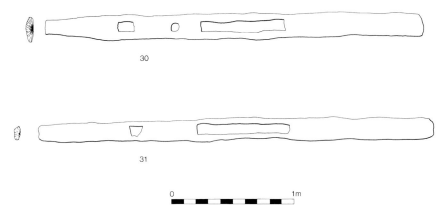

Fig 7.40 Timbers with slots

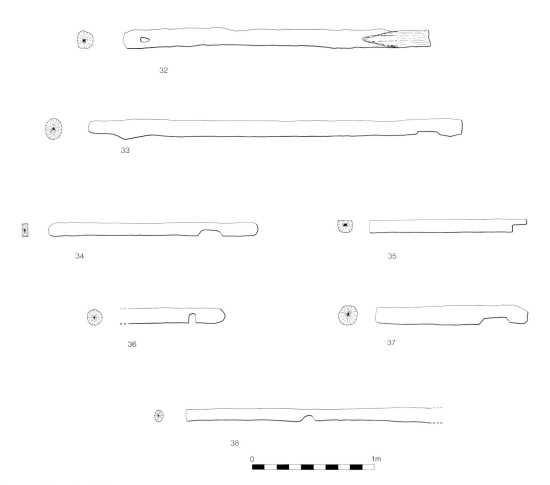

Fig 7.41 Lap and housing joints

Lap joints

The most sophisticated and carefully cut lap joints were both on one timber (Fig 7. 41, 33) from Area 6B, which was incomplete (it continued into the baulk). Most other lap joints were slighter and cruder (eg Fig 7.41, 32). Lap joints were mainly found on large roundwood, presumably because of the problems of overlapping or joining wood with round sections to make a stable structure (Figs 7.41–2). Other lap joints include: Fig 7.42, 41; Fig 7.47, 60–64, 66–8.

Catalogue of illustrated lap joints

32 B2635: wood species: unidentified; joints: mortise (72 × 35mm); lap joint (275 × 30mm); dimensions: length, 2500mm; oval, 165 × 140mm; context: Area 6B, Level 4 (0.50–0.24m OD), grid 2704 8887; notes: hewn, one end chamfered; mortise is angled.

33 B947: wood species: unidentified; joints: housing joint (165 × 20mm); dimensions: length, 3050mm; diameter, 120mm; context: Area 6B, Level 2 (0.55–0.29m OD), grid 2713 8884; notes: toolmarks (30:4).

34 B1152: wood species: alder (*Alnus glutinosa*); joints: housing joint (182 × 47mm); dimensions: length,

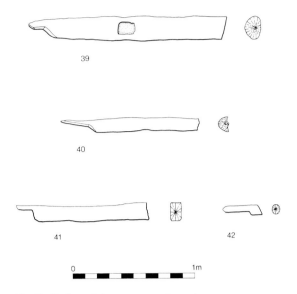

Fig 7.42 Lap joints on roundwood

1700mm; width, 95mm; thickness, 76mm; context: Area 6B, Level 2 (0.51–0.42m OD), grid 2709 8884.

35 B4167: wood species: possibly alder (*Alnus glutinosa*); joints: lap joint (115 × 55mm); dimensions: length, 1305mm; width, 105mm; thickness, 138mm; context: Area 6D, Level 5 (0.35m OD), grid 2704 8887; notes: hewn on underside.

36 A4003: wood species: alder (*Alnus glutinosa*); joints: housing joint (70 × 50mm); dimensions: length, 720mm; oval, 140 × 90mm; context: Area 6A, Level 2 (0.46–0.43m OD), grid 2718 8882.

37 B1986: wood species: unidentified; joints: housing joint (190 × 50mm); dimensions: length, 2514mm; oval, 160 × 122mm; context: Area 6A, Level 3 (0.31–0.25m OD), grid 2707 8886; notes: toolmarks (44:7).

38 B1603: wood species: unidentified; joints: housing joint (110 × 45mm); dimensions: length, 2010mm; oval; 120 × 90mm; context: Area 6B, Level 3 (0.51–0.25m OD), grid 2711 8888; notes: post B686 smashed into this piece.

39 B3088: wood species: unidentified; joints: blind mortise (140 × 95mm); lap joint (115 × 90mm); dimensions: length, 1645mm; width, 125–184mm; original diameter, 184mm; context: Area 6B, Level 6 (0.35–0.09m OD), grid 2711 8885; notes: underside hewn flat; white sand in blind mortise; toolmarks (38:4).

40 B3524: wood species: unidentified; joints: lap joint (215 × 70mm); dimensions: length, 1140mm; width, 115mm; thickness, 75mm; original diameter, 115mm; context: Area 6B, Level 6 (0.04–0.15m OD), grid 2711 8883; notes: toolmarks (44:4).

41 B2664: wood species: unidentified; joints: lap joint (140 × 90mm); dimensions: length, 1137mm; width, 150mm; thickness, 90mm; context: Area 6B, Level 4 (0.38–0.24m OD), grid 2710 8884; notes: hewn square.

42 B1541: wood species: unidentified; joints: lap joint (165 × 30mm); dimensions: length, 260mm; oval, 95 × 85mm; context: Area 6B, Level 2 (0.47m OD), grid 2710 8889.

Housing joints

Catalogue of illustrated housing joints (Fig 7.43)

43 B1033: wood species: oak (*Quercus* sp); joints: two housing joints (220 × 170mm and 250 × 390mm); dimensions: length, 2870mm; width, 360–410mm; thickness, 100mm; context: Area 6B, Level 2 (0.40–0.31m OD), grid 2706 8887.

44 B345: wood species: oak (*Quercus* sp); joints: mortise (100 × 100mm); housing joint (200 × 170mm); dimensions: length, 1800mm; width, 400–155mm; thickness, 70mm; context: Area 6B, Level 1 (0.56m OD), grid 2706 8886.

45 B1999: wood species: unidentified; joints: two housing joints (140–245 × 95mm and 85 × 80mm); dimensions: length, 860mm; width, 170mm; thickness, 80mm; context: Area 6B, Level 3 (0.35–0.20m OD), grid 2707 8886.

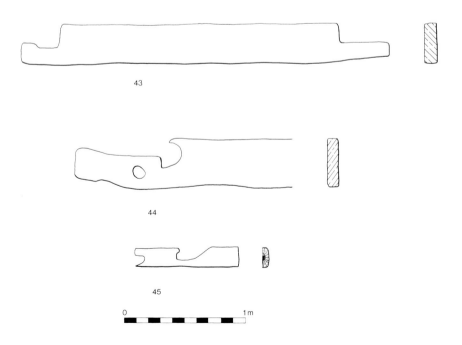

Fig 7.43 Housing joints

Dovetails

The only examples of dovetail joints found at Flag Fen were on the wheel (Fig 7.48).

Possible rafters

Two alder timbers from Area 6B were thought to be possible rafters, on the grounds of their length and their distinctively chamfered ends (Fig 7.44). The chamfers were cut at an angle of 40°. Only the lower portions were photographed. The original lengths of the two timbers were 2230mm (B2422) and 2563mm (B2567).

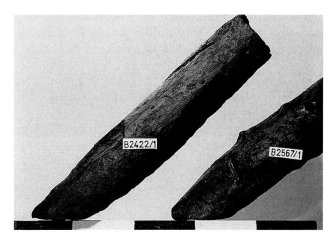

Fig 7.44 The lower portions of two possible alder rafters from Flag Fen, Area 6B. Note the chamfered lower ends

Joints on small and broken material

Catalogue of plank-end fragments (Fig 7.45)

46 B154: wood species: oak (*Quercus* sp); joints: mortise (90 × 70mm); dimensions: length, 1330mm; width, 150–205mm; thickness, 28mm; context: Area 6B, Level 1 (0.54m OD), grid 2713 8885.

47 B393: wood species: oak (*Quercus* sp); joints: mortise (90 × 65mm); dimensions: length, 670mm; width, 70mm; thickness, 30mm; context: Area 6B, Level 1 (0.61m OD), grid 2707 8888.

48 B4200: wood species: unidentified; joints: mortise (75 × 65mm); dimensions: length, 390mm+; width, 180mm; thickness, 68mm; context: Area 6D, Level 5 (0.44m OD), grid 2708 8881.

49 B842: wood species: oak (*Quercus* sp); joints: broken mortise (115 × 70mm); dimensions: length, 430mm; width, 315mm; thickness, 5–65mm; context: Area 6B, Level 2 (0.54m OD), grid 2713 8886.

50 B1292: wood species: oak (*Quercus* sp); joints: broken mortise (130 × 80mm); dimensions: length, 720mm; width, 125–190mm; thickness, 54–70mm; context: Area 6B, Level 2 (0.61–0.49m OD), grid 2713 8887; notes: same as A5437.

51 B974: wood species: oak (*Quercus* sp); joints: broken mortise (74 × 90mm); single tenon (170 × 59mm); dimensions: length, 340mm; width, 59–135mm; thickness, 40–63mm; context: Area 6B, Level 2

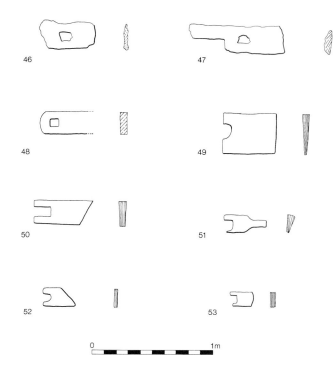

Fig 7.45 Plank ends with joints or partial joints

(0.63m OD), grid 2708 8887; notes: possible top of upright.

52 B1306: wood species: oak (*Quercus* sp); joints: broken mortise (60 × 60mm); dimensions: length, 250mm; width, 144mm; thickness, 30mm; context: Area 6B, Level 2 (0.51–0.46m OD), grid 2713 8886; notes: peg B1307 held this piece in place.

53 A2838: wood species: oak (*Quercus* sp); joints: broken mortise (80 × 65 × 53mm); dimensions: length, 208mm; width, 115mm; thickness, 50mm; context: Area 6A, Level 2 (0.45m OD), grid 2713 8889; notes: peg A3346 passed through the mortise.

Fragments of larger, half-split and reduced roundwood timbers, with joints (Fig 7.46)

54 B499: wood species: alder (*Alnus glutinosa*); joints: broken mortise (100 × 105mm); dimensions: length, 482mm; oval, 105 × 70mm; context: Area 6B, Level 2 (0.57–0.53m OD), grid 2705 8889.

55 A8342: wood species: oak (*Quercus* sp); joints: broken mortise (45 × 80mm); dimensions: length, 900mm; width, 25–140mm; thickness, 83mm; context: Area 6A, Level 5 (0.21–0.03m OD), grid 2714 8891.

56 B1550: wood species: oak (*Quercus* sp); joints: broken mortise (25 × 70mm); dimensions: length, 285mm; width, 120–130mm; thickness, 70mm; context: Area 6B, Level 3 (0.47–0.40m OD), grid 2710 8889.

57 B296: wood species: oak (*Quercus* sp); joints: broken mortise (50 × 105mm); dimensions: length, 360mm; width, 160mm; thickness, 35–80mm; context: Area 6B, Level 1 (0.62–0.51m OD), grid 2713 8887.

Catalogue of sundry small pieces and fragments (Fig 7.47)

58 B493: wood species: oak (*Quercus* sp); joints: complex multifaceted joint (110mm reducing to 50mm in width;

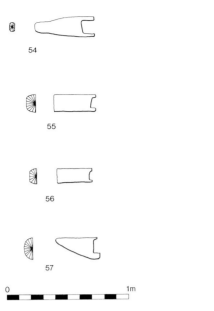

Fig 7.46 Ends of larger, half split and reduced roundwood timbers, with joints

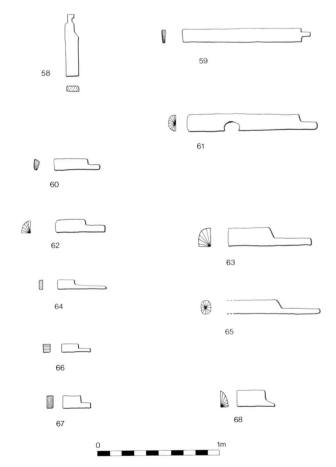

Fig 7.47 Sundry small pieces and fragments, with evidence for joints

possible housing joint 50 × 20mm); dimensions: length, 490mm; width, 110mm; thickness, 45mm; context: Area 6B, Level 2 (0.60m OD), grid 2704 8888.

59 B512: wood species: oak (*Quercus* sp); joints: single tenon (80 × 50mm); dimensions: length, 2100mm;

width, 135mm; thickness, 35mm; context: Area 6B, Level 2 (0.58–0.54m OD), grid 2706 8889.

60 B1358: wood species: oak (*Quercus* sp); joints: lap joint (95 × 45mm); dimensions: length, 1270mm; width, 90mm; thickness, 65mm; context: Area 6B, Level 2 (0.87–0.41m OD), grid 2707 8888.

61 A4833: wood species: ash (*Fraxinus excelsior*); joints: two broken mortises (120 × 60mm and 130 × 80mm); dimensions: length, 1060mm; width, 140mm; thickness, 50mm; context: Area 6A, Level 5 (0.35–0.29m OD), grid 2714 8891.

62 B1417: wood species: oak (*Quercus* sp); joints: lap joint (153 × 45mm); dimensions: length, 410mm; width, 93mm; thickness, 78mm; context: Area 6B, Level 3 (0.35m OD), grid 2705 8890.

63 A5341: wood species: unidentified; joints: lap joint (320 × 90mm); dimensions: length, 690mm; width, 146mm; thickness, 98mm; context: Area 6A, Level 3 (0.28m OD), grid 2716 8891.

64 B1243: wood species: oak (*Quercus* sp); joints: lap joint (170 × 40mm); dimensions: length, 400mm; width, 80mm; thickness, 35mm; context: Area 6B, Level 2 (0.51m OD), grid 2710 8887.

65 A3860: wood species: alder (*Alnus glutinosa*); joints: lap joint (320 × 80mm); dimensions: length, 1840mm; width, 105mm; thickness, 75mm; context: Area 6A, Level 4 (0.21–0.18m OD), grid 2712 8893.

66 B3421: wood species: unidentified; joints: lap joint (100 × 35mm); dimensions: length, 234mm; width, 65mm; thickness, 65mm; context: Area 6B, Level 6 (0.11m OD), grid 2710 8881; notes: hewn square.

67 B591: wood species: oak (*Quercus* sp); joints: lap joint (90 × 55mm); dimensions: length, 230mm; width, 40–100mm; thickness, 50mm; context: Area 6B, Level 2 (0.90m OD), grid 2709 8888.

68 B1240: wood species: oak (*Quercus* sp); joints: worn lap joint (70 × 80mm); dimensions: length, 310mm; width, 125mm; thickness, 60mm; context: Area 6B, Level 2 (0.61m OD), grid 2710 8887.

Tree nails and pegs

There was no evidence for pegging of any joints. Bronze Age woodworkers were quite capable of making fine dowels and cutting small holes (see below, discussion of hafts and handles), but so far none have been found, either together or associated with joints. There was also no evidence (ie fibres or their impressions) that lashing was used to bind joints together.

The waterlogged wood: artefacts

The term 'artefact' is used in the sense of portable artefacts to describe manufactured objects other than structural timbers and their fixings. The artefacts described below are arranged by method of manufacture, as follows: the wheel and associated items; yokes, hafts, and hammers; handles, shafts, and miscellaneous items. Each discussion is prefaced with a short summary in note form giving dimensions, wood identification, and contextual details. The diameter of compressed roundwood is given in the form: large/small.

Wheels and associated items

The wheel

Components of the wheel (Figs 7.48 and 7.49) comprise:

1 One outer segment; a plank (B3833) in alder (*Alnus glutinosa*); dimensions:length, 810mm; width, 345mm; thickness, 35mm.

2 Two braces (B3834 and B3835) in oak (*Quercus* sp). The dimensions are discussed with the dovetail slot, below.

3 Two dowels in ash (*Fraxinus excelsior*); dimensions: length surviving, 52mm; diameter, 27 × 24mm (approx); context: Area 6C, Level 5 (0.35m OD), grid 2715 8884. One segment of a tripartite wheel with broken braces and dowels still in place was found in 1994 in Area 6C, Level 5 (Fig 7.49). The plank from which the wheel segment was carved was 810mm long, and between 34 and 39mm thick. As the segment was an outer third of the original wheel, this would have meant that the wheel was approximately 800mm in diameter.

The use of alder for the wheel might reflect the local availability of the wood. The tripartite wheels from Doogarymore, Co Roscommon, were made of alder (Lucas 1972). Alder is quite a light wood, but it does not split easily and is resistant to rotting in wet conditions. It should be noted that there was a considerable difference in the thickness of the planks of the Flag Fen and the Doogarymore wheels. Although they were of similar diameter, the Doogarymore wheel was between 70 and 100mm thick, compared with 34–39mm for the Flag Fen segment.

Both braces were still in their slots when the wheel was excavated. The slots were carefully cut dovetails and the braces were a close fit. Both braces were in very poor condition. They were made of oak sapwood, with the bark still attached, which probably explains their condition. The wood was taken from quite a young tree, to judge by the thickness of the bark, which was only a few millimetres. In one place, where the growth rings could be clearly seen, there were nine. It is possible to think of a number of reasons why oak sapwood might have been used for the braces. Although oak sapwood is not considered durable, it is just as strong as heartwood when green and is easily worked (Desch 1977). There might have been problems when the wood seasoned and distorted, but the design of this wheel would have made replacement of the braces fairly simple. The dovetails would also have acted as 'splints' to restrain excessive warping.

The dovetail slots were tapered and narrowest towards the rim of the wheel (52mm tapering to 40mm). They were also shallower towards the rim, starting at 21mm and rising to 15 and 17mm. The dovetail was very evenly cut and the bottom of the slot was dead flat. The tapering and change of depth was clearly intentional, presumably to help secure the braces when they were forced into the slots.

One of the dowels was loose in its hole, allowing it to be removed and examined more closely. In section, it was a carefully cut oval, 52mm long. Ash would have been chosen for these dowels for its shock-absorbing properties.

Solid wheels could have a square hole with a fixed axle, where the axle and wheel revolve together. An alternative design has the wheel turning on the axle. Where the wheel turns on the axle, the wheel has to have a reinforced centre. In some wheels this takes the form of a carved boss in the central plank; in others a nave is carved separately and inserted into a hole in the centre (Piggott 1983, figs 4 and 5) illustrate the various types of prehistoric disc wheels).

Wheels with lunate openings, such as that from Flag Fen, have been found with inserted naves (Piggott 1983 fig 5, 5) and a likely roughout for this kind of nave was found at Flag Fen (see below, B3610). A Late Bronze Age tripartite wheel with lunate openings and external bracings, very similar to the one from Flag Fen, was excavated from a waterlogged fortified island in the Federsee in Wurttemberg. It was complete with inserted nave and axle in place. The photograph of this wheel shows how the Flag Fen wheel was probably mounted. A reconstruction of the wheel and the other parts from the excavation is quite convincing (Piggott 1983 fig 59). The Federsee wheel has been used as the basis for a reconstruction drawing showing how the wheel and other components of the vehicle found at Flag Fen could have been assembled (Fig 7.48). Both the axle (see below, B1751) and the wheel are quite slight when compared with other tripartite wheels.

Diameters of prehistoric slab wheels vary from little more than 0.5m to approximately 1m across. The Flag Fen wheel was probably about 800mm in diameter. The plank of the wheel was only 35 to 39mm thick and the diameter of the axle was between 50 and 55mm. This does not suggest a cart for carrying loads, but more a relatively lightweight vehicle for carrying people. The evidence for wheeled vehicles in Britain during the Bronze Age is very slight, and from England virtually non-existent. A fragment of a tripartite wheel was found a few months earlier than the Flag Fen example, during excavations at Cottenham (Evans 1993b). This wheel appears to be very similar, except that it is made of ash (*Fraxinus excelsior*) and is possibly a little larger in diameter (Fig 7.50). The method of construction is very similar, as the planks are dowelled together and braced externally. Carbon dates suggest that the wheel is Early Iron Age in date (Chris Evans personal communication).

During earlier excavations at Fengate, a piece of a slab wheel was excavated but not recognised at the time. At the Cat's Water site, an Early Iron Age stake was found with a dovetail joint cut into it (Taylor 1984, 175–6, fig 124). In 1984, a dovetail joint of such an early date was unique and the original purpose of the reused stake was obscure. It is now apparent that the

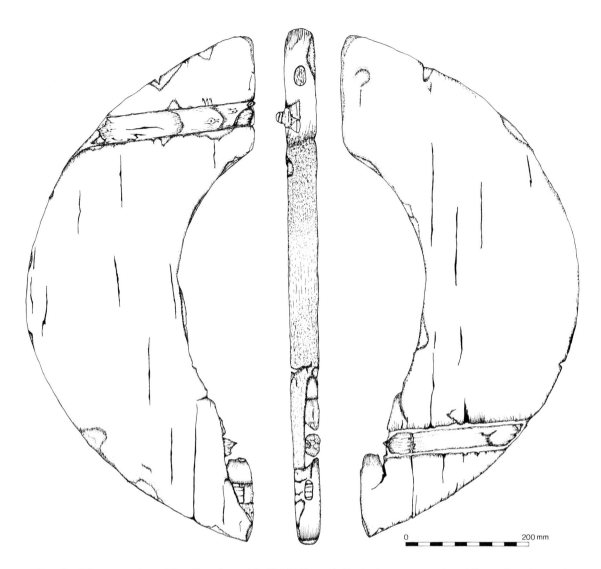

Fig 7.48 The wheel fragment from Flag Fen Area 6C (B3833) and (facing) reconstruction (dimensions in mm)

stake was made from a piece split off one plank of a tripartite wheel. Since the marks in the joint were all fresh, it seems likely that the plank had split during construction or soon afterwards. The stake was recorded as radially split. In fact, the original plank must have been tangentially split out of the trunk and the stake then split radially off the plank. A tangential split would be the most efficient way to manufacture a relatively thin and even plank of large enough size. Now that the stake has been recognised as part of a wheel, there are several additional points to note. The wheel from which the stake was derived was at least as large as the one excavated at Flag Fen, although a precise estimate of size is not possible. It should also be noted that there is no sign of any dowels adjacent to the dovetail on the stake, although there is more than enough space. This would suggest either that the wheel was made without dowels or (more probably) that the stake originated from nearer the centre of the plank.

Indirect evidence for a wheeled vehicle was provided in 1997 in excavations at Welland Bank Quarry, near Market Deeping, Lincs, some 8km north of Fengate

(Francis Pryor personal communication). Here, several sets of ruts belonging to a two-wheeled vehicle, or vehicles, were found in Late Bronze Age or earliest Iron Age contexts. The distance between the two wheels was consistently 1100mm and the width of the ruts was approximately 50mm. These marks could well have been made by a light trap or cart of the type suggested above for Flag Fen.

Possible roughout for hub

Wood B3610 (Fig 7.51): wood species: not identified; dimensions: length, 425mm; diameter (compressed), 195–85mm; size of holes, 65 × 65 × 35mm (deep) and 90 × 90 × 40mm (deep); context: Area 6B, Level 5 (0.11m OD), grid 2709 8884.

A section of a small tree trunk, completely cleaned of bark but otherwise barely shaped. Both ends have been cut square and holes have been started at each end, centrally. It is suggested that this might be an early stage in roughing out a nave to be used with a similar type of wheel and axle to those discussed above.

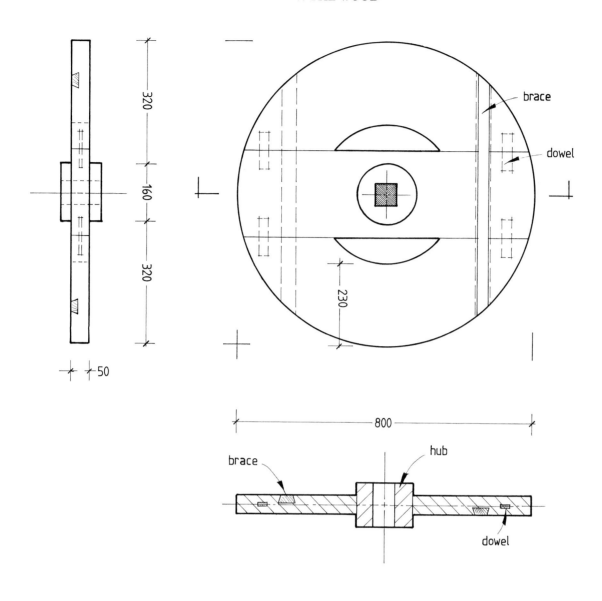

brace

dowel

320

160

320

50

230

800

brace

hub

dowel

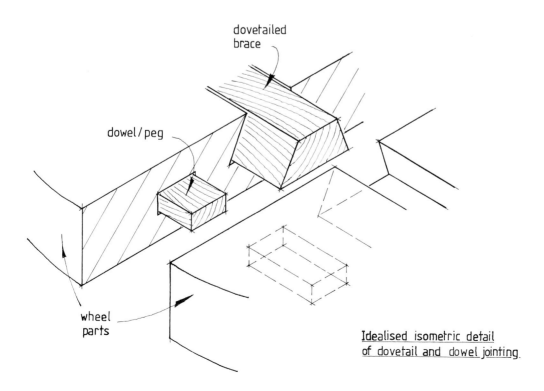

dovetailed
brace

dowel/peg

wheel
parts

Idealised isometric detail
of dovetail and dowel jointing

Axle

Wood B1751 (Fig 7.52): wood species: oak (*Quercus* sp); dimensions: length of dowel, 360mm; diameter of dowel section, 50–55mm; length of square section, 145mm; width and thickness of square section, 75 × 85mm (tapering); length and breadth of mortise hole, 25 × 21mm; context: Area 6B, Level 2, grid 2709 8889.

The object is incomplete, having sheared in antiquity at the point where the section changes from round to square. It was subsequently roughly modified to make it slightly more pointed and then hammered into the ground as a peg. In form, the object is a dowel (Corkhill 1979, 154). It was carefully made and well finished. The diameter varies little over its length and the square section was carefully trimmed, using an axe with a blade at least 30mm wide. The edges were then rounded.

The square hole has very sharp corners on the outside, but is not uniform in shape along its whole length. It has been cut from both sides, indicated by a slight ridge in the middle and a cut mark in the side of the hole.

Fig 7.49 Flag Fen Area 6C, part of tripartite wheel (B3833) in situ

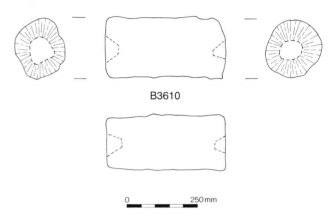

B3610

0   250 mm

Fig 7.51 Possible roughout for hub from Flag Fen, Area 6B (B3610)

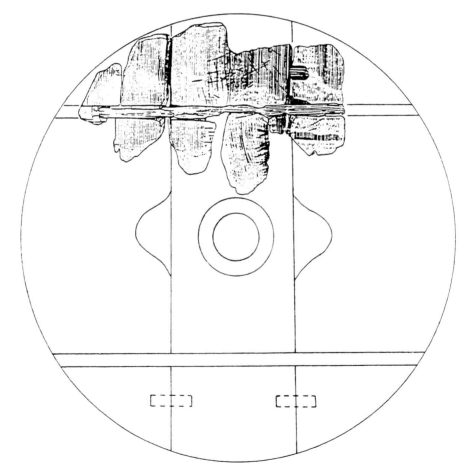

Fig 7.50 Part of a Late Bronze Age tripartite wheel from Cottenham, Cambs (from Evans 1993b: NB — no scale given in source)

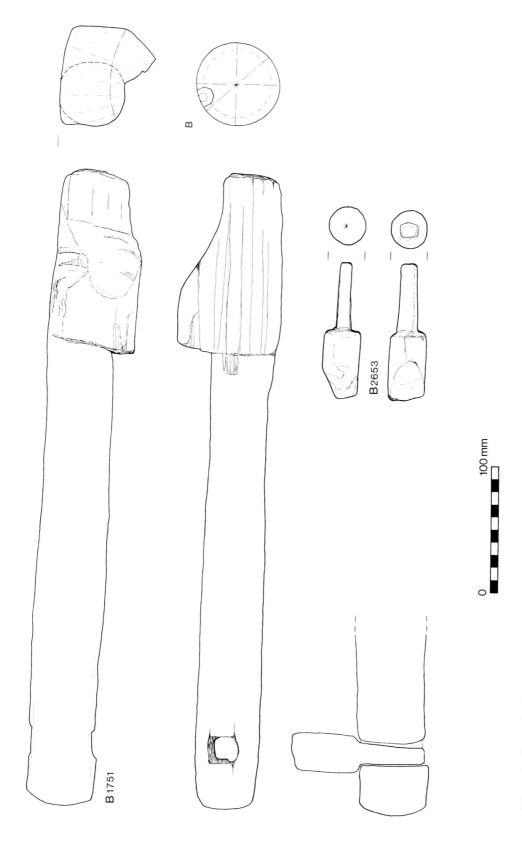

Fig 7.52 Part of oak axle and peg from Flag Fen, Area 6B

There is also slight, but distinct facetting on one of the inner faces, which gives a maximum tool width of just 20mm. There are flimsy, ragged pieces of wood in the corners, which suggests that the tool could not cut the square shape so cleanly within the dowel hole. These traces of wood inside the hole and the survival of the slight facetting suggest that it was not heavily used subsequently. The hole has been slightly buckled, probably by the blows to the end when it was used as a peg.

Since the axle is made from the outer part of an oak tree, a considerable proportion of the wood is sapwood (Fig 7.52, B). With such a small section surviving, it is difficult to calculate the original size of the tree, but it is likely to have been in the region of 300mm in diameter, split radially into eighths. The maximum number of growth rings appears to be 15, suggesting fairly rapid growth.

Peg

Wood B2653 (Fig 7.52): wood species: not identified (in conservation); dimensions: length, 110mm; original diameter, 32mm; length of square section, 55mm; width and thickness of square section, 15 × 11mm; context: Area 6B, Level 5 (0.10m OD), grid 2705 8890 The peg was shaped out of a piece of roundwood. One end was left unshaped, but trimmed obliquely. The other end had been trimmed down and carefully shaped to a square section. Slight axe marks show where the wood was squared up at the transition from round to square.

This peg would fit the square hole in the axle (B1751), leaving space for a wedge. There is no evidence that the peg was ever used, as the edges of the square section were quite sharp when it was first excavated. The problem with using this peg as a lynch pin is that it would not project beyond the end of the hole. Although it might have been secured with a wedge, this would not be an ideal fixing. A small peg was found near the wheel at Doogarymore (Lucas 1972). Since this was even less suitable for a lynch pin, the author suggested that it was for securing the nave within the hole in the wheel. This might explain the function of the Flag Fen peg.

Possible roughout for an axle

Wood B1970 (Fig 7.53); wood species: oak (*Quercus* sp); dimensions: length, 480mm; width, 80mm; thickness, 70mm; context: Area 6B, Level 3 (0.31m OD), grid 2709 8883 This piece was shaped out of roundwood, one end carefully rounded, the other more roughly shaped, retaining some sapwood. One end was trimmed almost square; the other was roughly trimmed from two directions and retains toolmarks.

Yokes and flails

Yoke

Wood A2405 (Pryor *et al* 1986, fig 11); wood species: probably oak; dimensions: length, 655mm; max width, 90mm, min, 55mm; max thickness, 40mm, min, 30mm; context: Area 6A, Level 2 (0.42m OD), grid 2713 8892

This piece was published in the first report (Pryor *et al* 1986). It was radially split and trimmed to a rounded shape with a hole at each end. The form is quite common in Ireland (Wood-Martin 1886, pl xvi).

Possible flail

Wood B3130 (Figs 7.54–5); wood species: oak (*Quercus* sp); dimensions: length, 395mm; width, 48mm; thickness, 45mm; notch width, 15mm, depth, 10–13mm; hole, max diameter 15mm; context: Area 6B, Level 5 (0.14m OD), grid 2713 8885.

Dowel made from split oak, including heartwood and sapwood, with notch and hole in one end. The other end has rotted off in antiquity. The notch has been cut by a series of parallel blows with a relatively straight-bladed axe, although there are not enough toolmarks to define a specific tool shape. The hole is slightly oval, slightly funnel shaped, and slightly crooked. It has not been drilled but cut, probably from both sides, but more heavily from one side, using a gouge similar in shape to one already seen in toolmarks from the site. Multiple threshing flails in the collections of

0   30 cm

Fig 7.53 Possible roughout for axle, Flag Fen, Area 6B (B1970)

the Museum of Rural Life at Gressenhall have components very similar to this dowel, but as these date to the nineteenth century AD, it would be manifestly unsafe to draw direct parallels with the Bronze Age.

The situation has been complicated by a similar piece (B3517) excavated later (1995) at Flag Fen. More of the second piece survives and appears to be part of a yoke. It is, however, very straight for a yoke, which would make it quite different from those known in Scotland and elsewhere. Further research is needed (and underway).

Axe hafts and a hammer

One-piece axe haft

Wood Y930 (Fig 7.56, upper); wood species: oak (*Quercus* sp); dimensions: length of handle (broken and incomplete), 96mm; width and thickness of handle (at the break), 50 × 40mm; length of foreshaft, 230mm; diameter, 40mm, tapering; context: Power Station Area 1, old land surface, 0.66m OD, grid 1929 9023

This is a one-piece haft for a socketed axe, shaped from a fork or branch. The haft was in very soft condition and, because it was in one of the areas where waterlogged material was not expected, it was badly

damaged in the act of discovery. Luckily, enough survived for comparisons to be made with the complete one-piece haft found later at Flag Fen. The handle was trimmed radially and shaped roughly oval. The foreshaft remains in the round and at first appeared to be a smaller side branch. On more detailed examination, it would seem that it has been heavily trimmed down from a piece of much larger diameter.

Two-piece axe haft

Wood Y1143 (Fig 7.56, lower); wood species: oak (*Quercus* sp); dimensions: length of handle (broken and incomplete), 48mm and 177mm; width and thickness, 62 × 40mm, tapering; context: Power Station Area 1, old land surface, 0.66m OD, grid 1929 9023.

Handle part of two-piece axe haft, found in association with socketed axe (Fig 10.6, 60). The axe retains part of the foreshaft in its socket. The foreshaft was trimmed down from a half log. The haft had been badly damaged in antiquity and was in several pieces before it was deposited in the ground. The haft was so fragmentary and soft that a replica was made almost immediately before the wood could deteriorate further, with the loss of constructional details. The replica haft (with a replica axehead), was subsequently used to fell trees and for experimental purposes.

0   30 cm

Fig 7.54 Part of possible flail from Flag Fen, Area 6B (B3130)

0   10 cm

Fig 7.55 Close-up of the end notch and hole of the possible flail from Flag Fen, Area 6B (B3130)

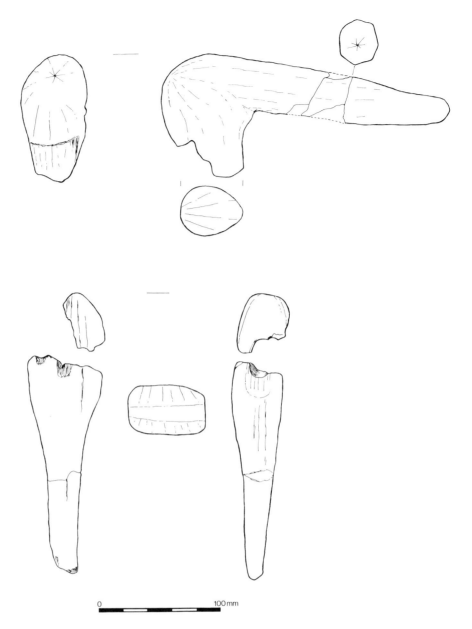

Fig 7.56 Fragments of oak axe hafts (Y930 and Y1143) from the Power Station, Area 1

Another two-piece axe haft was recently found near Shepperton and is now housed in Chertsey Museum, Surrey. This haft is quite different from the Flag Fen example. In the Shepperton haft, the hole is in the foreshaft and the shaft fits into that hole. The Shepperton wood has been identified as oak in the foreshaft and ash in the shaft. The foreshaft appears to have been shaped from a radially split piece of wood. The haft, which is oval, appears to have been shaped from roundwood. These provisional observations were made after examining the axe in poor light through the glass of its case, since no other access was permitted at the time.

It is interesting to speculate whether the Shepperton axe was hafted for a different purpose. Even if the wood was ash, the use of shaped round-wood for the haft, plus the small section of the haft, makes it hard to believe that the axe would have stood up well to heavy or sustained use.

One-piece axe haft

Wood B2737 (Fig 7.57; the axe haft is also shown *in situ* in Fig 6.92); wood species: oak (*Quercus* sp); dimensions: handle, length, 757mm, diameter, 30–36mm; head, length, 443mm, width, 36–47mm, shaped to oval section 28 × 24mm; notches 170mm and 165mm from tip; notches 8mm and 14mm deep; context: Area 6B, Level 5/6 (0.03m OD), grid 2710 8881

This is a complete one-piece haft, trimmed out of roundwood, in an excellent state of preservation. There are both similarities and differences in the method of construction of this axe haft when compared with Y930 (above). The haft has been made out of a fork or branch and the foreshaft trimmed down from the round. The foreshaft was originally of a much greater diameter than the handle and has been trimmed down considerably. Although the axe haft as a whole gives the impression that it had not been used

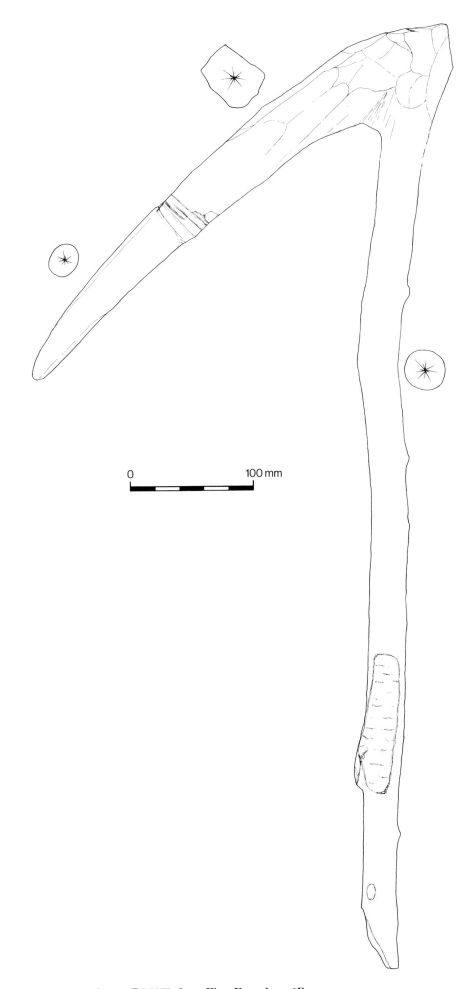

Fig 7.57 Complete haft for socketed axe (B2737) from Flag Fen, Area 6B

0   100 mm

much (the toolmarks in the slots on the foreshaft and the facets on the head are all very sharp), the tip of the foreshaft does appear to have been forced into a socket. The tip is smooth, rounded, and slightly compressed for the last 50mm or so.

The rough notches were a most unusual feature and, as they penetrate almost halfway through the haft, could have served no useful purpose. There are two possible explanations. The notches were precisely opposite each other and could have formed the beginnings of a reworking to give a haft with a shorter reach. Alternatively, they could be seen as a deliberate effort to render the haft unserviceable prior to its deposition.

Hammer

Wood B3249 (Figs 7.58 and 7.59); wood species: not identified (in conservation); dimensions: handle, length (incomplete), 340mm; diameter, 31mm; head, length, 200mm, width, 20–67mm; context: Area 6B, Level 5 (0.20m OD), grid 2711 8886.

The hammer was made in much the same way as the one-piece axe hafts, except that the head was much heavier and the face of the hammer has been bruised and crumpled with use. The handle of the hammer is roundwood, with sapwood and bark over part of the surface. The head was shaped from a larger trunk than the axe hafts, but uses the strength derived from the natural shape in the same way.

Hammers or mallets occur throughout prehistory. The earliest one in Britain, from Meare Heath in Somerset, dates to about 3000 BC (Coles and Hibbert 1972). This example was also carved from one piece, although it is shaped more like a modern mallet. The roundwood handle originally grew at right-angles to the roundwood head. The Flag Fen hammer is shaped to make use of the natural grain of the wood for maximum strength. Later mallets, such as the ones from Glastonbury (Bulleid and Gray 1911, fig 88) or The Breiddin (Britnell and Earwood 1991, 168–9) were made in the modern manner, with a hole in the head for a separate shaft.

The two one-piece axe hafts and the hammer are all taken from slightly different parts of the tree (Figs 7.60 and 7.61). Although these forms are not well known in England, they occur widely on the continent,

0   5 cm

Fig 7.58 Wooden hammer (B3249) from Flag Fen, Area 6B

especially in Germany and Switzerland (eg Schlichtherle and Wahlster 1986, fig 129).

Although three axe hafts were found at Flag Fen, only one axe was found with wood in the socket. The pattern of rings and rays of this fragment clearly indicated that the foreshaft was shaped from a half split log (Fig 7.62, 7). If the other axe hafts had been broken in their sockets they would have left a very different pattern. In both the one-piece axe hafts, the centre portion of the wood from which they were formed would have been left in the socket (eg Fig 7.63, A and B). In the two-piece axe haft from Shepperton, a similar piece to the Flag Fen two-piece haft would have been left but with subtle differences (Fig 7.63, C). The foreshaft would not have included the centre of the tree, the grain instead aligned with the rays of the wood running from top to bottom of the socket. In the Flag Fen axe the rays were running from one side to the other. The alignment of the foreshaft in the Shepperton axe haft would have meant that the hole in the foreshaft was cut along the rays. This could have led to the foreshaft splitting when the axe was used. It is hard to see whether this particular two-piece haft was very practical.

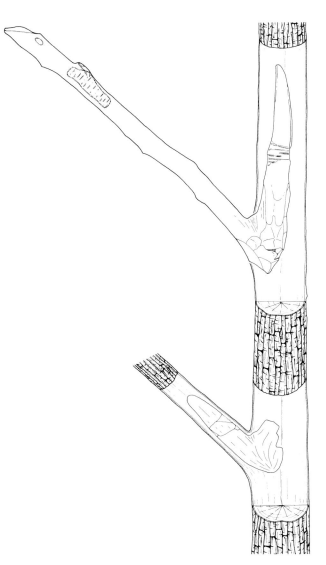

Fig 7.60 Sketch showing the position in the tree of axe hafts B2737 (top) and Y930 (bottom)

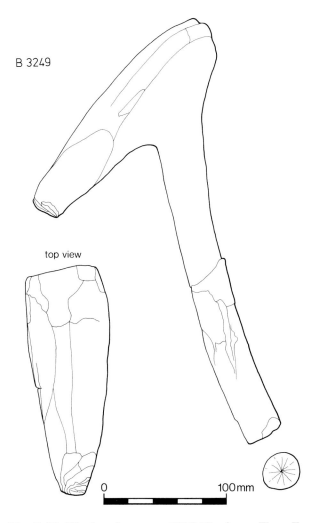

B 3249

top view

0   100mm

Fig 7.59 Wooden hammer (B3249) from Flag Fen, Area 6B

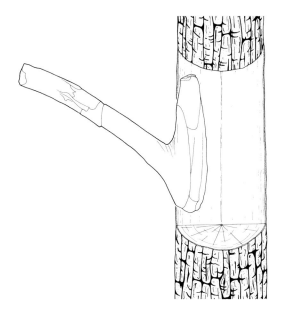

Fig 7.61 Sketch showing the position in the tree of hammer B3249

Given the profound understanding that Bronze Age woodworkers had of the structure of wood and the use of grain, it seems unlikely that the construction of the Shepperton axe haft was a mistake. A more likely explanation is that the haft was not constructed for hard use, but for its appearance.

Handles and shafts

Antler hilt fixings for tanged dagger

Wood unnumbered (not illustrated); wood species: not possible to identify; dimensions: not recorded; context: Power Station Area 1, old land surface (scoop in?), grid 1966 9015. A tanged dagger was found during the Power Station metal-detector survey with its antler handle lying on top of the blade (Fig 10.5, 54 and 54a). When first excavated the socket of the antler handle still contained two thin pieces of tangentially split lath, which were presumably wedges to hold the handle firmly in place. When examined under a magnifying glass, each wedge showed three growth rings. It was not possible to identify the species but both pieces were definitely diffuse porous, which means that they could

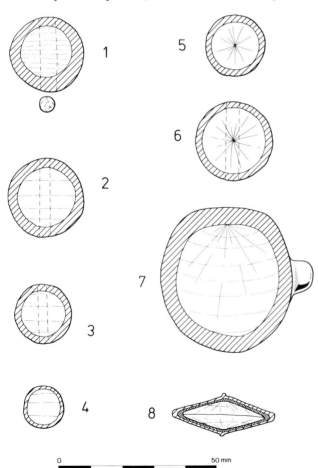

Fig 7.62 *Cross sections of shafts, handles, and a scabbard: 1–2 spear shafts; 3–4 ferrule shafts; 5 gouge handle; 6 flesh-hook handle; 7 socketed axe foreshaft; 8 sword scabbard (chape). Numbers 1, 3–5, and 7 from the Power Station; 2, 6, 8 from Flag Fen*

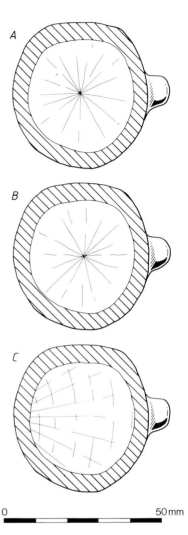

Fig 7.63 *Projections of ray patterns in axe sockets (not to scale). A, single-piece axe haft from the Power Station (Y930); B, single-piece axe haft from Flag Fen (B2737); C, two-piece axe haft from Shepperton*

not have been oak or ash. The most common diffuse porous woods at Flag Fen were alder, willow, poplar, and hazel. Wood other than oak was rarely found on the Power Station site. The wedges were sketched in the field, but did not survive the conservation process at The British Museum.

Gouge handle

Wood Y1400 (Fig 7.62, 5); wood species: Pomoideae/*Prunus* sp; context: Power Station Area 1, old land surface, grid 1874 9043

The handle of the socketed gouge (Fig 10.5, 57) was a simple piece of roundwood, 15mm in diameter, tapered to a point and jammed into the socket. This unsophisticated method of making a handle for a gouge would have produced a perfectly serviceable handle. In use, the handle would have been forced into the socket with very little sideways stress and roundwood would have been quite strong enough. Earwood illustrates two gouges of later date from Glastonbury, with handles made in exactly the same way

(Earwood 1993, fig 127). The choice of wood for the handle is excellent, as *Prunus* sp and Pomoideae wood are both durable and hard and do not split readily. The handle was used for radiocarbon sample OxA-5960.

Flesh-hook handle

Wood unnumbered (Fig 7.62, 6); wood species: not identifiable; context: Area 6B, Level 6 (0.20m OD), grid 2710 8885

Some of the wood of the handle of the flesh hook (Fig 10.5, 58) remained in the socket when it was first found. The handle of the flesh hook, like that of the gouge, was made out of shaped roundwood, approximately 20mm in diameter. The use of shaped roundwood, rather than the more robust dowels of spears, hints at the way that the flesh hook was probably used — any force applied straight, either through pushing or pulling. If the flesh hook had been used with strong sideways pressure, a less flexible dowel handle would have been required. Although it was possible to see that it was roundwood and very fine grained, the wood in the socket was not sufficiently substantial for species identification.

Handle

Wood B3660 (Fig 7.64); wood species: not identified (in conservation); dimensions: length (incomplete), 128mm; diameter, 30–33mm; context: Area 6D relict stream bed, *c* 0.50m OD.

The end of a handle excavated from a relict stream or watercourse near the post alignment might indicate what the missing parts of the gouge or flesh-hook handles might have looked like (both are described above). The handle was made of roundwood but was carefully facetted and smoothed and the butt end had been facetted or rounded, making a very neat finish.

The diameter of the handle was larger than both the gouge and the flesh-hook sockets, but it could have

been reduced to fit them. Close examination of the photographs of the Glastonbury gouges suggests that the handles were thinned, or even stepped, to make a good fit with the sockets. If this kind of shaping is projected onto the Flag Fen handle, it would have been more likely to have fitted the flesh hook than the gouge.

Spear shaft

Wood B2475 (Fig 7.62, 2); wood species: ash (*Fraxinus excelsior*); context: Area 6B, Level 4 (0.05m OD), grid 2711 8885

The tip of a shaft was found in the socket of a pegged, leaf-shaped socketed spearhead (Fig 10.4, 49). The shaft was split down from the round and shaped to a dowel of 18mm diameter. There were four growth rings in the shaft, which was held in the socket by the corroded remains of a bronze rivet, which passed through the wood at right angles to the rings.

Spear shaft

Wood Y1401 (Fig 7.62, 1); wood species: ash (*Fraxinus excelsior*); context: Power Station, Area 1, old land surface, grid 1900 9030

The shaft of a socketed spearhead (Fig 10.4, 47; Fig 7.60, 1) split down and shaped to 15mm diameter (ten rings). The shaft was held in its socket by a wooden dowel peg (Y1402), of 4mm diameter, which passed through the wood at right angles to the rings. An example of a bronze spearhead with part of the shaft and a wooden peg was found at the West Furze Lake Dwelling in Holderness (Smith 1911, 603).

Ferrule shaft

Wood no Y1403 (Fig 7.62, 3); wood species: ash (*Fraxinus excelsior*); context: Power Station, Area 1, old land surface, grid 1903 9052

B 3660

0   100 mm

Fig 7.64 Part of handle, Flag Fen, Area 6D

The ash shaft found within the shorter ferrule (Fig 10.4, 45) was split down from roundwood and shaped to 14mm diameter. There were four growth rings in the shaft, which was held in the socket of the ferrule with a copper-alloy rivet that passed through the wood at right angles to the rings.

Ferrule shaft

Wood Y1404 (Fig 7.62, 4); wood species: ash (*Fraxinus excelsior*); context: Power Station, Area 1, old land surface, grid 1972 9002

This ash shaft was found within the long tubular ferrule (Fig 10.4, 44). It shaft was split out of round-wood and shaped to 10mm diameter. There were three growth rings present.

The shafts assessed

Two spears and two ferrules from Flag Fen and the Power Station had substantial remains of shafts in their sockets. They were all dowel, split out of fairly large ash roundwood. It was not possible to determine the diameters of the original trunks from the slight curvature of the rings exposed in the end. Shaft Y1401 came from a tree that was extremely slow grown, with very narrow rings. The two copper-alloy rivets and the wooden peg were all driven through the shafts exactly at right angles to the growth rings. This would be the strongest way of pegging them.

A survey of known spear shafts in 1978 listed more than 18 spear shaft fragments with species identification (Green 1978). Of these, nearly half were *Fraxinus excelsior* (ash). An addendum to the paper lists a further 17 spear shafts and two ferrules from the Museum of London. Fifteen of these 19 species identifications are ash. Ash is certainly an intelligent choice of wood for a spear shaft. It can be coppiced to produce the thicker straight poles, which can readily be reduced to dowel. A young ash pole would not make a good haft because it has a large pith and much sap-wood, which reduce strength and reliability (Edlin 1973, 28). Ash wood is as strong as oak, but is much harder (Desch 1973, 109). The shock-absorbing characteristics and flexibility of ash mean that it has been used for hafts and handles until modern times.

One final point remains to be considered. Was there any evidence that the shafts in question had been broken before deposition? None of the wood was found to project beyond the sockets, which might indicate that preservation conditions (caused by corrosion products and so on) within the socket were better than outside. This might indeed apply at the Power Station, where preservation conditions were poorer, but at Flag Fen this can not be argued. If complete shafts had been present, they would have survived. Small fragments of wood were visible in the socket of the pegged socketed spearhead from Flag Fen Area 8 (Fig 10.4, 51; Fig 10.26, lower left). That from Area 6B (Fig 10.4, 49)

only retained the tip of its shaft and its pegs. Although it is impossible to determine whether the shafts had been broken-out (ie there were no obvious signs of shearing or splintering), this apparent lack of evidence was almost certainly a post-depositional or survival effect. Given the peaty matrix and the softness of the wood in the sockets, it was not possible to define or recognise such features. Taken together, the evidence possibly suggests that the shafts of at least some of the spears were removed before the metal heads were placed in the ground.

Miscellaneous artefacts

Scoop

Wood A8458 (Fig 7.65); wood species: willow (*Salix* sp); dimensions: length, 285mm; max breadth, 97mm; context: Area 6A, Level 5 (0.16m OD), grid 2719 8890

The scoop was shaped from a half-split willow log with a diameter of at least 200mm. The bowl of the scoop was shaped across the grain and so well finished that no clues survive as to the method of fabrication.

The leading edge seems to be slightly worn and has a rounded profile compared to the sides, which are square. The bowl is shaped to run smoothly into the handle, which is quite chunky. Although the handle is damaged, it is possible to see remnants of the shaped, rounded end, which indicates that almost the complete length has survived. The short, sturdy handle, the slightly flattened curve of the bowl, and the wear on the end all favour the suggestion that it was a scoop for dry goods, butter, and so forth, rather than a ladle.

Spoons and ladles are common wooden artefacts from all periods (see, for example, Coles and Coles 1989, 21, 69, and 76). A number of similar ladles were found at Glastonbury (Bulleid and Gray 1917, fig 100) and Caldicot (Earwood 1993, 31).

Hollowed log vessel

Wood A7945 (Fig 7.66); wood species: oak (*Quercus* sp); dimensions: height of wall, 80mm; original diameter of log, 248mm; thickness of base, 23mm; thickness of wall, 19mm; context: Area 6A, Level 6 (0.22m OD), grid 2709 8893

The vessel was formed from an oak log with a diameter of more than 248mm. There was no sign of sapwood, which might have been trimmed or simply worn off. The base of the container was rounded, presumably by wear, and no traces of fabrication remained, either inside or out. The vessel was broken in antiquity when it split radially. Only this single fragment was found, despite careful excavation of the area. It should also be noted that it was in poor condition when found, deep within the waterlogged deposits. This must surely indicate that it was already broken and in poor condition when it was lost or buried.

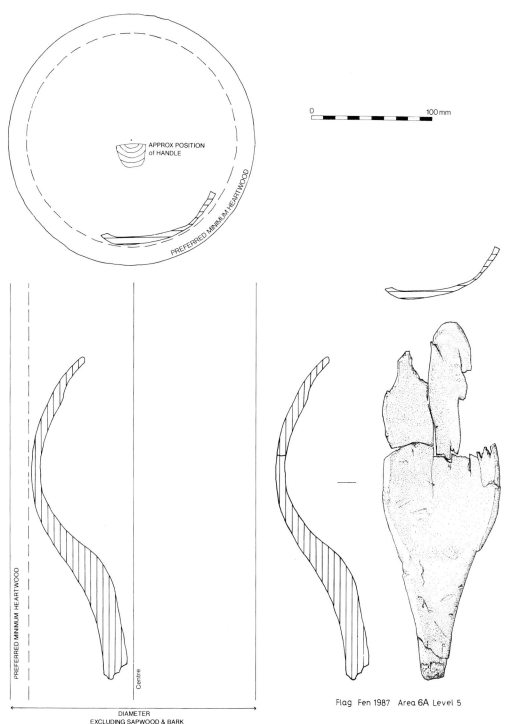

0   100 mm

APPROX POSITION
of HANDLE

PREFERRED MINIMUM HEARTWOOD

PREFERRED MINIMUM HEARTWOOD

Centre

DIAMETER
EXCLUDING SAPWOOD & BARK

Flag Fen 1987 Area 6A Level 5

Fig 7.65 Flag Fen, Area 6A, willow scoop

The fragment was in a relatively poor and worn condition, but it would probably have been possible to detect any signs of lathe turning had they been there. The inner and outer surfaces of the vessel were completely smooth with no ridges, lines or grooves to suggest that it had been turned. Since even the plainest turned vessels from Glastonbury had decorative grooves and lines (Earwood 1988, fig 87), the Flag Fen vessel was presumably hand carved from the solid.

Stave fragments of Bronze Age date have been found and there are a number of vessels hollowed from logs, but with separate bases, like the Stuntney bucket (Clark and Godwin 1940). A one-piece, flat-bottomed vessel appears to be very unusual. It is possible that the vessel was originally not much deeper than the fragment that has survived. Earwood has pointed out that it is not easy to carve deep vessels from a single piece of wood (Earwood 1993, 54).

Shears 'shoe' box

Wood Y1405 (Fig 10.11, 276a); wood species: ash (*Fraxinus excelsior*); dimensions: length, 294mm; width, 64mm; thickness, 35mm; context: Power Station Area 1, from spoil heap of pre-alluvial buried soil at grid 1900 9040.

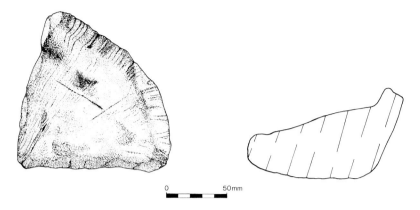

Fig 7.66 Flag Fen, Area 6A, hollowed log vessel in oak

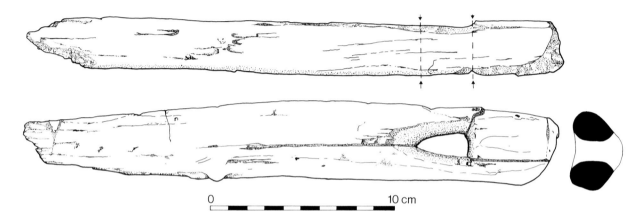

Fig 7.67 Wooden needle or bodkin from Flag Fen, Area 6B

The box for the shears was carved from an ash log approximately 100mm in diameter. The wood is slow grown, with very narrow rings. It is not particularly straight-grained wood and also contains a number of small knots. The circular hole in the floor of the box (9mm diameter) is a knot hole, the knot having fallen out in antiquity.

The purpose of the box would have been to keep the shears sprung shut, to conserve the spring. The slot in the bottom of the box would have been for a whetstone. The traces of iron at either end suggest a fastener or a mechanism for stopping the shears from falling out.

There are other Bronze and Iron Age examples of purpose-built or fitted boxes, especially from Ireland. These were not made to hold shears specifically, but to protect valuable objects. Some were carefully shaped to ensure that the object was held securely — a good example is the alder box and lid that were shaped to fit a gold fibula from Killymoon (Earwood 1993, 41). The shears box from the Power Station site was made and shaped with particular care. In the nineteenth century almost identical boxes for shears were known as 'shoes'.

Wooden needle or bodkin

Wood B2875 (Fig 7.67); wood species: not identified (in conservation); dimensions: length, 292mm; width, 48mm; thickness, 22mm; context: Area 6B, Level 5 (0.07m OD), grid 2707 8888.

This object was fashioned from roundwood, half split and carefully trimmed, with a triangular hole. The tip was slightly damaged. The triangular hole was made with the two longer sides well chamfered and the shorter side rounded, but not actually chamfered. The hole was fairly well worn.

Wooden needles or bodkins have been used by a number of craftsman, particularly thatchers. The wear on the tip could well have been caused by pushing through dry reeds or straw.

Tongue chape

Wood B2476 and B2477 (Fig 7.62, 8; Fig 10.38); wood species: too thin to identify; context: Area 6B, Level 5 (0.15m OD), grid 2709 8883

The wood remains in the chape consisted of two tangentially split laths, split out of relatively immature wood and used in the scabbard back to back, ie sapwood to sapwood. This might be because the sapwood was softer and more flexible. Although the chape was completely waterlogged when excavated, and there was no chance that the wood had begun to dry out, there were gaps between the wood and the metal of the chape. This might be due to the loss of the material that once bound the scabbard (?leather). On the other hand, it might have been done intentionally, to allow the wood to expand into the gap when the sword was in the scabbard.

8 Tree-ring studies
by Janet Neve with Cathy Groves

The majority of this chapter is devoted to Janet Neve's original research into the dendrochronology of the Flag Fen Basin. That work was mainly carried out in the late 1980s and early 1990s (Neve 1999). In the intervening period, however, new information has been made available that enables the original report to be seen in a new light. It has also proved possible to answer two specific questions that could not have been answered previously.

This reassessment of Janet Neve's original work is by Cathy Groves.

The Flag Fen and Power Station dendrochronology — recent research
by Cathy Groves

Since the original analysis and interpretation of the dendrochronological results was undertaken by Janet Neve, information concerning the association of each timber with a particular post alignment has become available for about 65% of the dated timbers. Five post alignments were identified in the main excavation at Flag Fen. It was thought that these were also all present at the Power Station site, although the central three rows (2–4) can not be reliably distinguished from one another. Thus Row 1 at Flag Fen is equivalent to Row 1 at the Power Station and Row 5 at Flag Fen is equivalent to Row 5 at the Power Station. A rapid reinterpretation of the dendrochronological results was requested, taking this new information into account. Two specific aims were identified:

1 to provide estimates for the felling dates for each row/alignment at both Flag Fen and the Power Station
2 to determine whether there is a chronological construction sequence along the length of the Power Station alignment. Time constraints imposed by strict publication deadlines prevented any major reworking of the data.

Thus the reassessment of the interpretation was undertaken on those samples dated by Janet Neve. It is known that the majority of the timbers are posts rather than planks, but, without returning to the archive, it was not possible to identify the individuals. Consequently, the reassessment does not take this factor into account. The majority of the dated timbers are either radial or tangential splits, but without additional information it is not possible to determine whether or not some samples are the inner sections of much larger trees.

In order to aid the attempted reassessment of the results, new sets of bar diagrams were produced. The samples were sorted into groups according to their site and row location or, where detailed information was not available, just site (Figs 8.1–4). The 'same-tree' sample groups were checked and the results summarised, incorporating both site and row information (Table 8.1).

Table 8.1 Summary of the 'same-tree' groups identified. Sample numbers prefixed 'Y' are from the Power Station; samples prefixed 'A' or 'B' are from Flag Fen

samples	row	samples	row
Y0188	unknown	Y1031	5
Y1060	central	Y1049	5
		Y1050	5
Y0064	5	A0546	5
Y0205	unknown	A3370	unknown
Y0347	unknown	A4658	unknown
Y0398	central	B3666	unknown
		B1732	3
Y1192	central	A8560	unknown
Y1198	unknown	B0178	unknown
		B0180	unknown
		Y0184	central
Y0010	1	B0058	unknown
Y0012	central	B2024	2
Y0120	1	B0061	unknown
Y0123	central	B0063	unknown
		B0190	unknown
		B1721	3
Y0113	central	B0284	unknown
Y0998	5	B1744	unknown
Y1050	5	B0486	unknown
Y1305	central	B1719	4
		B1720	3
Y0086	5	B3659	unknown
Y1342	5	Y0410	central
Y0101	5		
Y0106	5		

Interpretation

Overall, the results show that there was probably a period of major construction activity in the first half of the thirteenth century BC, followed by a lull, though not necessarily a complete cessation of activity. Construction activity appears to have increased again at the turn of the twelfth century BC, to have carried on throughout the eleventh century BC, and into the early part of the tenth century BC. Activity then tails off during the tenth century and appears to have stopped around the turn of the tenth century.

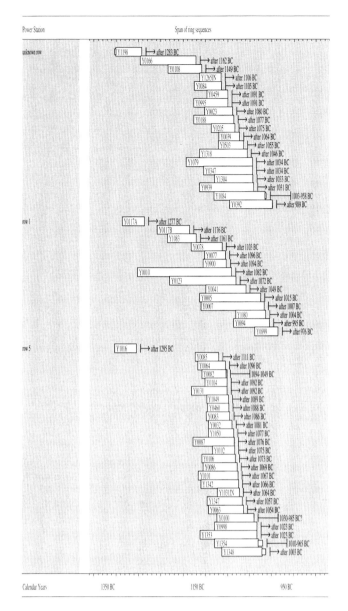

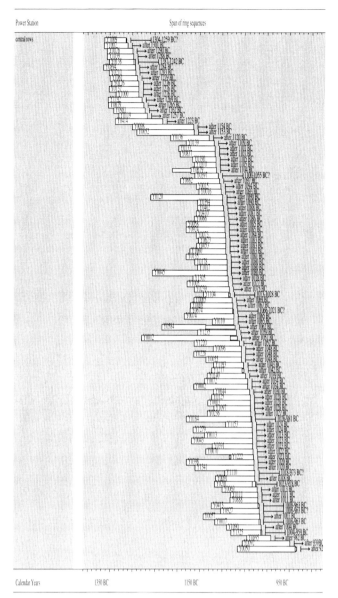

Fig 8.1 Bar diagram showing the relative positions of the dated tree-ring sequences from Row 1, Row 5, and unknown rows from the Power Station and their associated felling dates

Fig 8.2 Bar diagram showing the relative positions of the dated tree-ring sequences from the central rows fom the Power Station and their associated felling dates

In order to enable comparison between the dendrochronological dating evidence and that from radiocarbon dates derived from various materials associated with the utilisation of the structures, a 'minimum usage' period has been derived from the dendrochronological results for each site. It must be stressed that this is not a dendrochronological felling date range, but an estimate of the shortest possible period over which the structures were in use. The Power Station structure could have come into use as late as 1254 BC and have gone out of use at the earliest in 924 BC. The Flag Fen structure could have come into use as late as 1094 BC and gone out of use at the earliest in 955 BC.

The overall intra- and inter-site crossmatching of the dated assemblage, along with the 'same-tree' group information clearly shows that a coherent single area woodland is under exploitation throughout the three-century

period of fluctuating constructional activity. By combining information from the dendrochronological analysis with that of the woodland characterisation studies, it might be possible to determine whether there is any change in age structure of the total oak wood assemblage through time. This might provide information concerning exploitation patterns.

The same-tree groups show links between different rows on each site, between rows and unassigned samples, and, in two instances, between Flag Fen and the Power Station. The high percentage of samples with no trace of sapwood and thus only a *terminus post quem* for felling makes it difficult to address either of the two aims stated above in any detail. In an attempt to address the first of these aims (at least broadly), a further bar diagram (Fig 8.5) was produced showing the 41 samples for which it was possible to produce either a felling date range or a precise felling date.

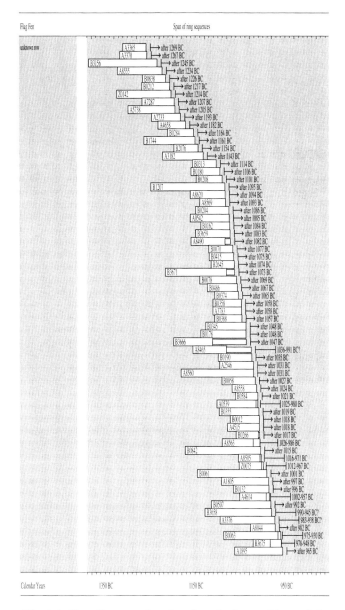

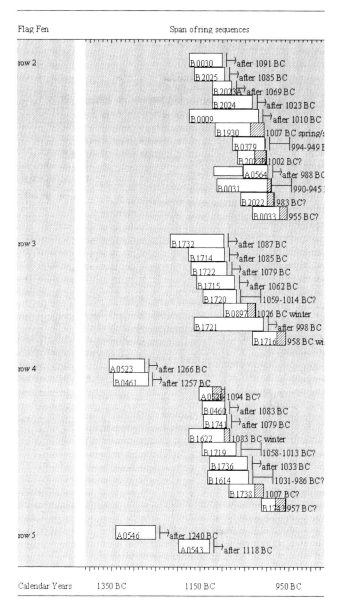

Fig 8.3 Bar diagram showing the relative positions of the dated tree-ring sequences from the unknown rows fom Flag Fen and their associated felling dates

Fig 8.4 Bar diagram showing the relative positions of the dated tree-ring sequences from Rows 2–5 from Flag Fen and their associated felling dates

This emphasises the range of felling dates found throughout the post alignments. It clearly demonstrates that the dendrochronological results can not identify any positive links or clear differences in date, either between rows or the two sites. The constructional history appears complex and, potentially, virtually random as far as repairs are concerned. For dendrochronology to provide detailed constructional information on such potentially complex structures, a far higher percentage of samples with bark edge, and hence felling dates precise to the calendar year, are required.

In an attempt to address the second aim, further bar diagrams were produced with the Power Station samples grouped by row and also by the area from which they were obtained (Figs 8.6–7). No obvious differences are apparent from the dendrochronological results, but this might again be due to the few precise felling dates obtained. Consequently, it is not possible

to either confirm or refute the hypothesis that there is a chronological development sequence along the length of the exposed alignment at the Power Station.

Conclusion

The analysis has successfully provided broad chronological information for the construction of the post alignments. It indicates major periods of construction in the mid thirteenth century, throughout the eleventh century, and early tenth century BC. Due to the low number of samples for which precise felling dates could be obtained, however, it has not been possible to produce the more detailed chronological information originally hoped for.

The Flag Fen/Power Station complex has produced a robust and extremely valuable dendrochronological dataset. It is the largest assemblage yet dated from the

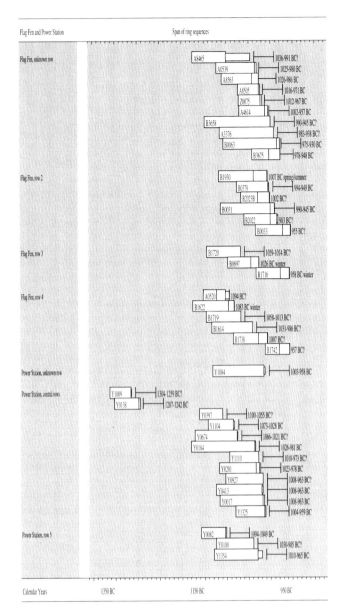

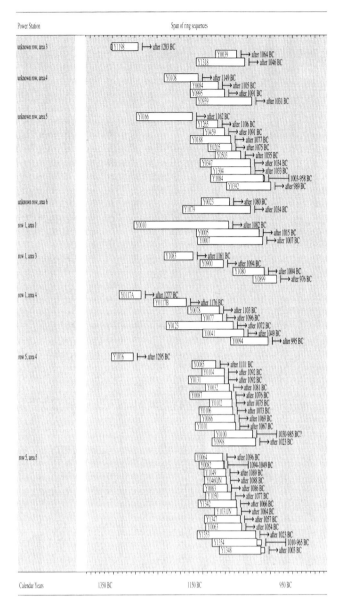

Fig 8.5 Bar diagram showing the relative positions of the dated tree-ring sequences and their associated felling dates for samples with sapwood present from both Flag Fen and the Power Station

Fig 8.6 Bar diagram showing the relative positions of the dated tree-ring sequences sorted by both row (1, 5, unknown) and area (see Fig 8.8) from the Power Station

Bronze Age and spans a period in England from which data coverage is scarce, both geographically and chronologically. The chronology produced has already proven valuable in assisting the dating of other Bronze Age timbers from southern England, such as Harters Hill, Somerset (Jennifer Hillam personal communication), Greylake, Somerset (Robert Howard personal communication), and Rookhall, Essex (Jennifer Hillam personal communication).

Dendrochronology of the Flag Fen Basin

by Janet Neve

The Fengate/Northey landscape, located on the southeast limits of the city of Peterborough, Cambridgeshire, has been under archaeological investigation by

Fenland Archaeological Trust since 1983. The Director of Archaeology, Dr Francis Pryor, and some other members of staff had also taken part in work at Fengate during the 1970s. The archaeological remains are principally prehistoric, ranging from the Neolithic to Iron Age and Roman. Although there are three main elements to this landscape, the dendrochronological work is concerned with the archaeological investigation of the Flag Fen Basin. This is situated between the dry, or flood-free, Fengate landscape on the west and the flood-free landscape of Northey 'island' on the eastern side.

Two elements in the Flag Fen Basin are the focus of this study: a kilometre-long timber post alignment, which has been interpreted as a boundary or defensive palisade; and a manmade wooden platform or 'island' covering approximately 1.4ha (3.5 acres). The posts run across the basin from the Fengate fen edge to the

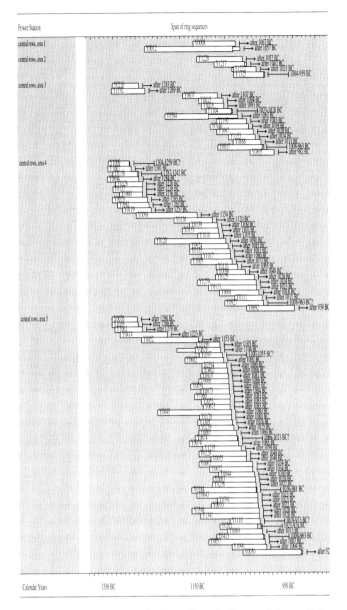

Fig 8.7 Bar diagram showing the relative positions of the dated tree-ring sequences sorted by both row (central) and area (see Fig 8.8) from the Power Station

edge of Northey 'island'. The platform is on the line of the post alignment, but lies closer to Northey than Fengate (Fig 1.4). Research indicates that the platform and post alignment are dated to the later Bronze Age, but there was also activity before and after this date (Pryor *et al* 1986 and Pryor 1992). During the initial investigations of 1983 and 1984, it was apparent that there was potential for dendrochronology. This was initially to comprise a major element in the PhD research of Nigel Holman at the University of Cambridge. Subsequently, the direction of his research moved away from Flag Fen. When the trust became aware of the situation it was decided to undertake the study in-house under the supervision of the Sheffield Dendrochronology Laboratory, which is funded by English heritage. Any samples obtained by Nigel Holman and thought to be suitable for the present study were remeasured. It was sometimes possible to

replace samples in bad condition, as many of the timbers had been resampled at a later date and these had remained at Flag Fen.

The tree-ring analysis was undertaken with the following aims:

1   To construct a master chronology for the Flag Fen Basin that would provide (if possible) a dated framework for the site. This might also have wider uses such as assisting in the dating of other sites and providing more data for English Oak chronologies in general.
2   To correlate phases of development within the post alignment, the platform, and its revetment.
3   To try and establish whether the post alignment was originally built full length or extended westwards towards the ditched droveway (Fig 1.4, Ditches 8 and 9) as conditions became wetter.
4   To establish if the five rows of posts (most clearly visible on the platform) represent sequential phases of development or if they were in use all the time.
5   To look for any periods of abandonment that might be reflected in the tree rings, ie no felling activity.
6   To determine the presence or absence of one or more major felling phases in the post alignment and to establish if there is any correlation with similar phases within the platform.
7   To establish, if possible, how the site went out of use, ie did maintenance peter out slowly or was there a final episode of reconstruction followed by abandonment.

This report covers the excavations on the post alignment at the Fengate fen edge (referred to as the Power Station site) and on the timber platform, both on the line of and away from the post alignment (referred to as Flag Fen).

The areas and samples

The details and the locations of all the samples from the Power Station and Flag Fen have been recorded, but are not presented in this report. The details of the dated samples are presented in Tables 8.2 and 8.3. The complete record is archived at Flag Fen.

Power Station

Excavation took place between April and October 1989 ahead of the construction of a gas-fired power station on the Fengate fen edge. The area chosen by Peterborough Power Ltd was known to be archaeologically important as at least three second-millennium ditches were known to run into it from the Fourth Drove subsite immediately north-west (Pryor 1980). Posts of probable Bronze Age date had also been found immediately south-east in 1987 (Fig 1.5). The machine cleaning down to the old land surface revealed *c* 1200 vertical posts, mainly oak, covering an area 7–10m wide and more than 150m in length.

Table 8.2 Details of the tree-ring dates for the Power Station. A sapwood estimate of 10–55 rings is used to calculate the felling date ranges in the absence of bark edge (Hillam *et al* 1987)
+ = unmeasured rings; h/s = heartwood/sapwood transition; B = bark edge

area/sample	group	total rings	date span (BC)	sapwood	comment	felled (BC)
Y0002	5	120	1163–1044		1034+	
Y0003	5	95	1132–1038		?ring 11	1028+
Y0005	1	139	1163–1025		same tree Y0007	1007+
Y0007	1	144	1160–1017		same tree Y0005	1007+
Y0008	1	94	1170–1077			1067+
Y0010	1	211	1302–1092		same tree Y0012	1072+
Y0012	1	198	1279–1082		same tree Y0010	1072+
Y0015	3	55	1158–1104			1094+
Y0016	3	50	1152–1103			1093+
Y0017	3	102	1116–1015	3		1008–963
Y0023	6	63	1152–1090			1080+
Y0032	4	53	1143–1091			1081+
Y0039	3	47	1120–1074			1064+
Y0041	4	91	1149–1059			1049+
Y0043	5	136	1168–1033		same tree Y0125	1023+
Y0044	5	80	1119–1040			1030+
Y0045	5	166	1255–1090		?ring 148/9 = 1	1080+
Y0050	5	130+	1066–937		3 heartwood rings	924+
Y0052	5	128	1290–1163			1153+
Y0053	5	65	1157–1093		same tree Y1235	1059+
Y0055	5	79	1136–1058			1048+
Y0057	5	126	1142–1017		same tree Y0072	1007+
Y0058	5	86	1180–1095		same tree Y0074	1065+
Y0063	5	80	1143–1064			1054+
Y0064	5	62	1167–1106			1096+
Y0065	5	85	1163–1079			1069+
Y0066	5	67	1162–1096			1086+
Y0069	5	78	1100–1023			1013+
Y0070	5	105	1136–1032			1022+
Y0072	5	96	1139–1044		same tree Y0057	1007+
Y0073	5	65	1158–1094			1084+
Y0074	5	110	1184–1075		same tree Y0058	1065+
Y0076	5	57	1356–1300			1290+
Y0077	4	47	1152–1106			1096+
Y0078	4	70	1182–1113			1103+
Y0079	4	79	1353–1275			1265+
Y0082	5	57	1158–1102	2		1094–1049
Y0083	5	53	1148–1096			1086+
Y0084	4	61	1175–1115			1105+
Y0085	4	53	1173–1121			1111+
Y0086	4	77	1155–1079			1069+
Y0087	4	93	1178–1086			1076+
Y0091	4	88	1115–1028			1018+
Y0092	4	107	1055–949			939+
Y0094	4	83	1087–1005			995+
Y0096	4	63	1120–1058			1048+
Y0098	4	137	1300–1164		?rings 17 & 114	1154+
Y0100	4	85	1124–1040	?h/s		1030–985
Y0101	4	90	1166–1077		same tree Y0106	1067+
Y0102	4	50	1134–1085			1075+
Y0104	4	50	1151–1102			1092+
Y0106	4	76	1158–1083		same tree Y0101	1067+
Y0108	4	76+	1234–1159		dense band after 76	1149+
Y0110	4	48	1122–1075			1065+
Y0111	4	61	1081–1021			1011+
Y0113	4	107	1139–1033		same tree Y0998	1023+
Y0117A	4	50	1336–1287		to dense band	1176+
Y0117B	4	73	1258–1186		after dense band	1176+
Y0119	4	65	1331–1267			1257+

Table 8.2 *(cont'd)*

area/sample	group	total rings	date span (BC)	sapwood	comment	felled (BC)
Y0120	4	160	1259–1100		same tree Y0123	1072+
Y0123	4	149	1230–1082		same tree Y0120	1072+
Y0125	4	86	1123–1038		same tree Y0043	1023+
Y0126	4	61	1346–1286			1276+
Y0131	4	80	1181–1102			1092+
Y0133	4	81	1197–1117			1107+
Y0135	4	90	1180–1091			1081+
Y0136	4	86+	1215–1130		to dense band	1120+
Y0137	4	67	1352–1286			1276+
Y0138	4	59	1352–1294	3		1287–1242
Y0139	4	62	1180–1119			1109+
Y0140	3	85	1133–1049			1039+
Y0166	5	125	1296–1172			1162+
Y0178	5	72	1161–1090			1080+
Y0184	5	145	1179–1035	1		1026–981
Y0188	5	90	1176–1087		same tree Y1060	1077+
Y0190	5	52	1166–1115			1105+
Y0201	5	92	1117–1026	7		1023–978
Y0205	5	53	1137–1085			1075+
Y0210	3	60	1352–1293			1283+
Y0228	5	106	1163–1058			1048+
Y0236	5	97	1133–1037			1027+
Y0239	5	78	1162–1085			1075+
Y0347	5	111	1154–1044		same tree Y0398	1020+
Y0391	5	90	1122–1033			023+
Y0392	5	98	1096–999			989+
Y0394	5	56	1155–1100			1090+
Y0397	5	52	1161–1110	?h/s		1100–1055
Y0398	5	150	1179–1030		same tree Y0347	1020+
Y0402	5	58	1155–1098			1088+
Y0410	5	62	1158–1097			1087+
Y0413	5	105+	1124–1020		2 heartwood to h/s	1008–963
Y0414	5	106	1338–1233			1223+
Y0459	5	47	1147–1101			1091+
Y0460	5	48	1145–1098			1088+
Y0503	5	57	1121–1065			1055+
Y0584	3	98+	1234–1137		65 heartwood rings	1062+
Y0673	5	61	1153–1093			1083+
Y0674	5	95	1171–1077			1067+
Y0679	5	57	1170–1114		last 20 difficult	1104+
Y0682	5	87	1193–1107			1097+
Y0837	3	78	1194–1117			1107+
Y0888	3	62	1082–1021			1011+
Y0894	4	71	1364–1294			1284+
Y0895	3	55	1045–992			982+
Y0899	3	53	1038–986			976+
Y0900	3	52	1155–1104			1094+
Y0924	4	86	1180–1095			1085+
Y0927	4	86	1103–1018	?h/s		1008–963
Y0939	4	123	1163–1041			1031+
Y0981	4	71	1342–1272			1262+
Y0995	4	76	1176–1101			1091+
Y0998	4	97	1129–1033		same tree Y0113	1023+
Y1000	4	52	1337–1286			1276+
Y1005	4	92	1178–1087		?rings 21–5	1077+
Y1007	4	53	1363–1311		same tree Y1009	1301+
Y1009	4	48	1362–1315		same tree Y1007	1301+
Y1010	4	48	1162–1115			1105+
Y1016	4	49	1353–1305			1295+
Y1017	4	66	1155–1090			1080+
Y1031	5	50	1123–1074			1064+

Table 8.2 *(cont'd)*

area/sample	group	total rings	date span (BC)	sapwood	comment	felled (BC)
Y1039	5	59	1356–1298			1288+
Y1049	5	49	1147–1099		same as Y1050/1305	1077+
Y1050	5	57	1143–1087		same as Y1049/1305	1077+
Y1060	5	80	1172–1093		same tree Y0188	1077+
Y1061	5	62	1350–1289			1279+
Y1079A	6	98	1193–1096		to break	1034+
Y1079B	6	64	1107–1044		after break	1034+
Y1080	3	69	1082–1014			1004+
Y1083	3	65	1235–1171			1161+
Y1084	5	117+	1131–1015		2 heartwood to h/s	1003–958
Y1090	5	77	1090–1014		outer edge decayed	1004+
Y1097	3	81	1118–1038			1028+
Y1104	3	57+	1142–1086		3 heartwood to h/s	1073–1028
Y1110	5	67	1094–1028	?h/s		1018–973
Y1153	3	59	1092–1034			1024+
Y1192	3	76	1354–1279		same tree Y1198	1269+
Y1193	3	67	1119–1053			1043+
Y1198	3	59	1351–1293		same tree Y1192	1269+
Y1217	2	68+	1123–1058		4 heartwood rings	1042+
Y1220	2	101	1162–106			1052+
Y1222	2	51	1081–1031			1021+
Y1235	5	86	1154–1069		same tree Y0053	1059+
Y1265	5	48	1163–1116			1106+
Y1279	4	131	1164–1034			1024+
Y1304	5	88	1130–1043			1033+
Y1305	5	78	1165–1088		same as Y1049/50	1077+
Y1318	3	108	1163–1056			1046+
Y1325	2	69	1080–1012			1002+
Y1341	5	131	1160–1030			1020+
Y1342	5	85	1160–1076			1066+
Y1347	5	80	1146–1067			1057+
Y1348	5	93+	1113–1021		8 heartwood	1003+
Y1353	5	130	1162–1033			1023+
Y1354	5	100+	1129–1030		10 heartwood to h/s	1010–965

They ran from the gravel of the Bronze Age fen edge straight out towards the Flag Fen platform to the east. Subsequent work has revealed that these posts form a continuous band, beyond the limits of the 1989 Power Station trenches and the Flag Fen platform. A small number of horizontal timbers were also revealed.

Due to the size of the area, it was decided to hand dig a dozen or so trenches in and around the posts. An initial assessment of the posts was made as they were uncovered. Those that looked most suitable for tree-ring analysis were identified. It was decided that the samples that were outside the areas of the hand-dug trenches would be removed immediately by hand. The work was, however, carried out during a very hot, dry summer. The conditions, coupled with the physical problems of removing the samples in this way, led to the abandonment of the system. Also, many posts that had at first appeared to be unsuitable from the slight surface evidence, later turned out to be suitable. In a few cases the reverse was also true. As a result, it was decided to remove all the posts outside the hand-dug trenches with a machine. A Kubota mini-digger

was employed to remove systematically *c* 1100 posts that were soaked, wrapped, and filed on a rolling system. About 250 horizontal pieces of wood were also sampled. All wood samples from the Power Station have an identification number prefixed with the letter Y.

As the area excavated was so large, it has been decided to divide the area covered by the post alignment into five groups, each covering approximately 30m of its length. These have been numbered from the western landfall of the post alignment (Group 1), to the eastern extent of the trench (Group 5). Group 6 is a small group of samples that were excavated to the north of the post alignment. For the location of the Groups, see Figure 8.8.

Group 1

This area was the western extent of the post alignment and most of the posts were shown by the machine cleaning to be sitting in the gravel at the fen edge. The extremely dry conditions in the well-drained gravel

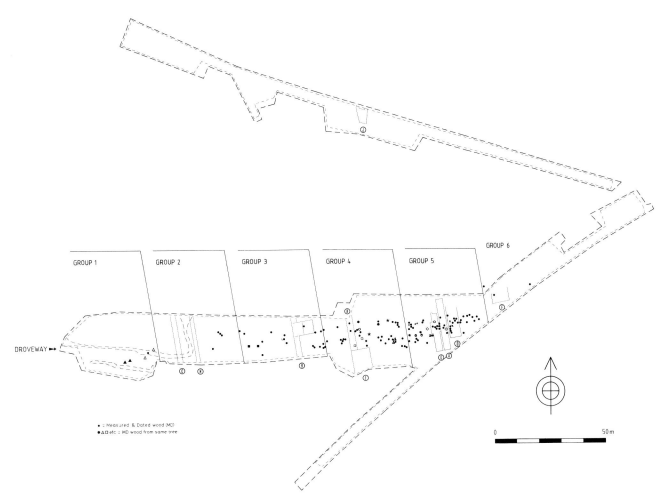

Fig 8.8 Distribution of tree-ring samples from the Power Station

meant that most of the posts were much too dry to obtain basic information such as dimensions and species. It was felt that time would be better spent trying to obtain more information from the few larger and better preserved samples. This was the only area in which all the samples were removed by hand. This was not only because they were removed first, but also because it was believed that by careful digging, information regarding the conditions in that area when the posts were placed there would also be revealed. This information is included in the Discussion section below. Seven of the posts removed from this area were examined. Sample Y0012 was placed in the ditch fill of feature F12, but the rest were dug into the gravel.

Group 2

A total of 12 samples were examined from this area, which was immediately east of Group 1. All were vertical posts. Sample Y0753 was obtained from the hand-dug trench, C. The field notes record Slot C as being very dry. The other hand-dug trench in this area, H, did not appear to contain any wood. The remaining 11 posts were all removed by machine from the area east of Trench C.

Group 3

A total of 65 samples were examined from this area. Fourteen samples were obtained from the hand-dug trench, B. Of these, Y0212, Y0835, and Y0839 were vertical posts, and Y0837 and Y0949 were believed to be 'uprooted' posts. The remaining nine samples from Slot B were all horizontal pieces. Y1312 was a large plank located approximately 23m south of the south (lower) edge of the post alignment. Y1318 was a vertical post that was uncovered approximately the same distance south of the posts, but 5m or so further east. It was believed to have been displaced by the machining. The remaining 49 samples were all vertical posts, which were removed by machine.

Group 4

In total, 105 samples were examined from this area. Ten samples, all from vertical posts, were obtained from the hand-dug trench, K. Only one horizontal plank was sampled, Y0032. This was located on the upper or northern limit of the post alignment. The only other sample to be removed by hand was Y0041, on the southern edge. This post was associated with the skeleton of a dog, and the evidence seems to indicate that the post had been driven through it. The remaining 93 samples were all removed by machine.

Table 8.3 Details of the tree-ring dates for Flag Fen. A sapwood estimate of 10–55 rings is used to calculate the felling date ranges in the absence of bark edge (Hillam *et al* 1987)

+ = unmeasured rings; h/s = heartwood/sapwood transition; B = bark edge

area/sample	group	total rings	date span (BC)	sapwood	comment	felled (BC)
A0520	6A	50+	1152–1103	19	9 sapwood to bark	1094
A0523	6A	82	1357–1276			1266+
A0539	6A	92	1122–1031	4		1025–980
A0542	6A	87	1181–1095		?ring 59	1085+
A0543	6A	70	1197–1128			1118+
A0546	6A	92	1341–1250		same tree A3370	1240+
A0564	6A	57	1054–998		after dense band	988+
A1085	6A	106	1112–1007			997+
A1895	6A	108	1082–975			965+
A2546	6A	76	1116–1041			1031+
A2733	6A	64	1266–1203			1193+
A3182	6A	90	1242–1153		?ring 70	1143+
A3365	6A	52	1330–1279			1269+
A3370	6A	61	1337–1277		same tree A0546	1240+
A3376	6A	123	1115–993	?h/s		983–938
A3783	6A	64	1131–1068		?ring 4	1058+
A4515	6A	71	1098–1028			1018+
A4614	6A	67	1071–1005	7	?ring 40	995+
A4658	6A	61	1252–1192		same trees B1732/B3666	1087+
A5738	6A	104	1318–1215			1205+
A7287	6A	71	1287–1217			1207+
A8044	6A	56	1047–992			982+
A8465	6A	75+	1175–1101		55 rings to ?h/s	1036–991
A8490	4	76+	1179–1104		12 heartwood rings	1082+
A8505	4	51	1074–1024	2		1016–971
A8555	LLE	99	1342–1244			1234+
A8558	LLE	55	1088–1034			1024+
A8560	LLE	161	1201–1041		same tree B0180	1031+
A8563	LLE	85	1110–1026	15	?close to bark	before 986
A8569	LLE	58	1160–1103			1093+
A8620	LLE	78	1181–1104			1094+
B0009	6B	155	1174–1020			1010+
B0012	6B	65	1092–1028			1018+
B0030	6B	75+	1175–1101		dense band after 75	1091+
B0031	6B	123	1113–991	9		990–945
B0033	6B	79	1033–955	17+B	?spring felled	955
B0058	6B	75	1111–1037		same tree B2024	1023+
B0061	6B	155	1165–1011		same trees B0063/B0190/B1721	975–930
B0063	6B	129	1107–979	6	same trees B0061/B0190/B1721	975–930
B0070	6B	54	1140–1087			1077+
B0078	6B	82	1160–1079			1069+
B0132	6B	80	1085–1006			996+
B0162	6B	65	1158–1094			1084+
B0178	6B	101	1158–1058			1048+
B0180	6B	64	1179–1116		same tree A8560	1031+
B0190	6B	75	1119–1045		same trees B0061/B0063/B1721	975–930
B0204	6B	74	1169–1096			1086+
B0208	6B	58	1168–1111			1101+
B0212	6B	62	1288–1227			1217+
B0266	6B	50	1079–1030			1020+
B0284	6B	58	1231–1174			1164+
B0313	6B	53	1176–1124			1114+
B0345	6B	90	1147–1058			1048+
B0355	6B	89	1117–1029			1019+
B0358	6B	64+	1131–1068		outer rings decayed	1058+
B0374	6B	53	1127–1075			1065+

Table 8.3 *(cont'd)*

area/sample	group	total rings	date span (BC)	sapwood	comment	felled (BC)
B0379	6B	73	1077–1005	h/s		995–950
B0388	6B	61	1127–1067			1057+
B0415	6B	55	1139–1085			1075+
B0460	6B	53	1145–1093			1083+
B0461	6B	80	1346–1267			1257+
B0486	6B	67	1143–1077		same trees B1719/20	1058–1013
B0507	6B	133	1134–1002			992+
B0584	6B	51	1081–1031			1021+
B0838	6B	51	1286–1236			1226+
B0842	6B	168	1192–1025			1015+
B0897	6B	72	1097–1026	18 + B	winter felled	1026/5
B1207	6B	164	1268–1105			1095+
B1614	6B	93	1133–1041	?h/s		1031–986
B1622	6B	93	1175–1083	13 + B	winter felled	1083/2
B1714	6B	82+	1176–1095		dense band after 82	1085+
B1715	6B	87	1158–1072		?rings 65–70	1062+
B1716	6B	75	1032–958	20 + B	winter felled	958/7
B1719	6B	78	1145–1068	?h/s	same as B0486/1720	1058–1013
B1720	6B	76	1144–1069	?h/s	same as B0486/1719	1058–1013
B1721	6B	157	1164–1008		same trees B0061/B0063/ B0190	975–930
B1722	6B	82	1170–1089			1079+
B1732	6B	121+	1217–1097		same tree A4658/B3666. Dense rings	1087+
B1736	6B	86	1128–1043			1033+
B1738	6B	79	1085–1007	20 + ?B		1007
B1741	6B	54	1142–1089			1079+
B1742	6B	56	1012–957	23 + ?B		957
B1744	6B	113	1283–1171			1161+
B1930	6B	111	1117–1007	31 + B	summer felled	1007
B2022	6B	75+	1060–986	14	2/3 sapwood to bark	986–3
B2023A	6B	45	1035–991		to dense band	1002
B2023B	6B	66	1067–1002	26 + ?B	after dense band	1002
B2024	6B	91	1123–1033		same tree B0058	1023+
B2025	6B	70	1164–1095		?ring 44	1085+
B2076	6C	54	1217–1164			1164
B2645	6B	52	1135–1084			1074+
B3658	6D	149	1148–1000	?h/s		990–945
B3659	6D	77	1169–1093			1083+
B3666	6C	87+	1218–1132		same trees A4658/B1732 Dense after18 heartwood rings	1087+
B3671	6C	136+	1236–1101			1073+
B3675	6C	64	1041–978	25		before 948
Z0075	2	54	1072–1019	3		1012–967
Z0142	2	121	1344–1224			1214+

Group 5

The largest number of samples was examined from the most easterly area of the post alignment within the excavation trench. This is probably due to the slightly better preservation as the gravel dipped further below the old land surface and the number of hand-dug trenches that provided more samples than any other area. These were Trenches G, A, and D. A total of 151 samples was obtained, 94 of these coming from the hand-dug trenches.

Samples were obtained from 24 vertical posts in Trench G. Three horizontals, Y0673, Y0725, and Y1271 were also examined. A total of 38 samples were obtained from Trench A, of which 22 were from vertical posts and 16 from horizontals. From Trench D, 18 vertical posts were examined and 11 horizontal pieces. A sample was also examined from a large horizontal plank, Y0027, which lay approximately 2m north of the post alignment. The vertical posts Y002 and Y003 were removed by hand at a very early stage in the excavations. The remaining 54 samples were all vertical posts, which were removed by machine.

Group 6

Five other samples were also examined, all of which came from the area north of the posts.

One sample, Y0812, was examined from Trench J, an area of roundwood that Maisie Taylor believes might have provided evidence of animal trampling. This trench was located in major Trench 3. Sample Y1392 was a thin split plank located approximately 15m north of the posts. Three other horizontal planks in this area were also sampled (Fig 8.1). Y0023, *c* 8m north of the posts had a mortise through which a peg had been driven. Y0205 was a large radially split plank and Y1079 was a tangentially split plank located approximately 15m to the north of the alignment.

Flag Fen

The samples from the platform and post alignment have been grouped under the system that will be used in writing the final report, which should make for easier integration of the information. The divisions are based on the system of trial trenches and full-scale excavation trenches. These are numbered sequentially from the westernmost trial trench close to the Power Station excavations (1) to the areas east of the Mustdyke, which have traced the course of the post alignment towards its eastern landfall on Northey 'island' (7 and 8). For details of the location of the areas see Figure 8.9.

A number of the areas excavated have not provided any samples for dendrochronological analysis: Area 1 was extremely dry and samples were only taken for radiocarbon dating; Area 3 was planned and backfilled without being sampled; Area 5 contained no suitable oak samples; Areas 7 and 8 are outside the scope of the present study, but might provide valuable material for future work.

Area 2

This was a small trench, little over 2 × 2m, which was located west of the Flag Fen car park approximately 300m from the main areas of excavation (Areas 6A–D). The wood was in an extremely dry condition, which was not helped by excavation or storage. Four samples, all from horizontal timbers, were analysed. Three of these came from the upper layer, Level 1 (Z0075, Z0118, and Z0131), and one from the lower Level 2 (Z0142).

Area 4

An oval trench was dug during the construction of a scale model, before the flooding of the mere in 1987 (see Fig 6.1). This revealed the upper portions of 25 vertical oak posts. Again, the wood was very dry, but a sample was taken from each of the posts. Unfortunately, most of the samples deteriorated in storage, but eight were examined.

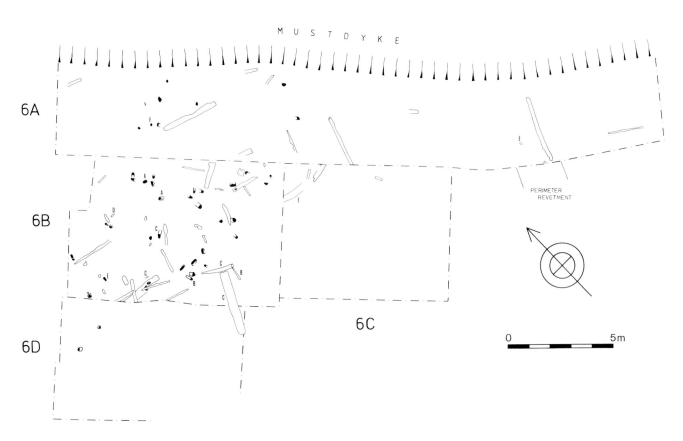

Fig 8.9 Distribution of tree-ring samples from Flag Fen, Area 6

Lake lining exposure

These samples were obtained in 1987 during the construction of the lake. It was decided to insert a polythene 'skirt' round the lake in order to give better water retention. This involved the digging of a narrow trench around the perimeter, approximately 4m deep and 0.45–0.6m wide. This work almost immediately revealed the presence of wood. Under very difficult conditions, sketch plans showing the approximate locations of samples and their numbers were made. One hundred and twenty-nine samples were taken. In some places, vertical posts could be seen in the section and these areas were plotted. It was impossible, however, to deduce whether samples were from vertical or horizontal timbers. The condition of the samples varied greatly, presumably as some came from much higher levels than others. Fifteen samples were examined.

Area 6A

This was the first area of the platform to be excavated. This took place between 1984 and 1987. The wood, even on excavation, was in very poor condition. This was probably due to the position of the trench on the edge of the Mustdyke. Samples were taken from this area in 1985 by Nigel Holman (see above), but as the present study only began in 1990, the long period in storage did not help their condition. Even with careful monitoring, the condition of some samples deteriorated so quickly that it was impossible to take thin sections for species identification or carry out ring counts. Sixty-two samples were examined, however. Twenty-six of these were from the platform (horizontals). Three of these samples, A2546, A3684, and A8276, were classified by Maisie Taylor as woodchips, although they were quite large. The remaining 36 samples were all taken from vertical posts.

Area 6B

This area was located approximately 5m from the dykeside, adjacent to the previously dug Area 6A (Fig 8.9). The samples taken from this area were in markedly better condition. This was probably due not only to the position of the trench further back from the Mustdyke, but also to improved techniques, a better shelter, higher groundwater content caused by seepage from the mere, and an improved watering system. All of these appeared to decrease the rate of deterioration in the ground.

A total of 239 samples were examined from this area. Of these, 69 were vertical posts. The remaining 170 were horizontal pieces from the makeup of the platform. Sample B0061, although lying horizontally, appeared to be a complete, though unused, vertical post.

Area 6C

This area lay adjacent to Area 6A and to the south of Area 6B. It has produced very few suitable samples, but five horizontal timbers, B2076, B3666, B3668, B3671, and B3675, were examined.

Area 6D

Located adjacent to Area 6B. Two samples, B3658 and B3659, were taken from this area during the summer of 1993.

Method

Selection of samples

This task was probably more difficult than on most sites, due to the number of samples and the fact that this study began after much of the wood had been examined and placed in storage. Due to the large amounts of wood and the shortage of staff, it was not possible to physically unwrap each sample, assess it and, if rejected, rewrap it. Wherever possible, eg in the case of many of the area 6B verticals, samples were assessed in the ground and potentially suitable ones were selected and removed, generally by sawing out a section. Where this was not possible, a variety of sources were used to help find potentially suitable samples. Plans and field records were consulted, as were Maisie Taylor's wood data. The presence of a comprehensive computer record for each numbered sample from the sites meant that pieces in very poor condition were not recorded in the tree-ring data. In the early stages of the tree-ring work, samples with small numbers of rings were also handed back, as there was no way under the system operating at that time of recording basic data in a useful way (see below).

The samples selected for analysis were prepared following the method given by Hillam (1985a). Samples were deep frozen for 48 hours and then their cross-section planed while still frozen, using a Surform. The upper surface was then allowed to thaw before the ring widths were measured.

Any samples that were unsuitable for measuring were rejected before measurement. During the early part of this work (1990–91), the samples were generally returned to the system and species identification carried out, in order to complete its data file. This was due to the fact that the computer programs in use had no facility to store large amounts of small-ring data, which would be in any way useful. During work in 1993, English Heritage agreed to upgrade the computer hardware and software. This meant that samples subsequently rejected could be recorded and a note made of the number of rings, average growth rate, and dimensions. Unsuitable samples are generally regarded as ones with fewer than 50 rings as the growth patterns might not be unique (Hillam *et al* 1987). Samples with 40–49 rings, however, were on the whole measured, unless the ring sequence was unclear. In some cases, this was because the sample had sapwood or bark edge, which might have helped to provide precise felling information. Such short ring sequences must therefore be checked with great care.

Analysis

The growth rings of suitable samples was measured to an accuracy of 0.01mm on a travelling stage, built by engineering students at Peterborough Regional College. Until mid 1993, the stage was connected to a BBC B+ microcomputer, which used a suite of tree-ring programs written by Dr J R Pilcher of The Queen's University, Belfast (Belfast Tree-Ring Programs).

This equipment was all provided by Fenland Archaeological Trust. Since that date, the stage has been connected to an Atari microcomputer using programs written by Ian Tyers (personal communication 1993). The funds for this were provided by English Heritage. All previously measured data have subsequently been transferred onto the Atari. Although this has been very time consuming, data are far more easily manipulated with the new system. In addition, any problems or queries are more quickly dealt with, as the system is compatible with that used by Sheffield Dendrochronology Laboratory, funded by English Heritage.

The measured sequences were plotted by hand on transparent semi-logarithmic graph paper. The graphs were then compared to check for visual similarities in annual ring patterns. This process was aided by the use of the crossmatching routines on the computer. The BBC used only Cros73 software (Baillie and Pilcher 1973), whereas the Atari also has Cross84 (Munro 1984). These routines give an objective measure of the degree of correlation between ring patterns. This is expressed as a t value (the Student's t-Test). A t value of 3.5 or above generally indicates a possible position of match, but the visual match between the graphs must also be acceptable (Baillie 1982, 82–5). All t values given in this report are based on Cros73.

By crossmatching ring sequences and combining the matched patterns, a site or area master curve is produced. Any newly measured or previously unmatched samples are then tested directly against the master. If they show good agreement with both the master and individual timbers within it, they too can be incorporated into the master. Generally, individual oak samples that match with a t value of over c 10 are likely to have originated from the same tree. This will not identify all same-tree timbers as samples known to have come from the same tree have given t values of less than 10. If two or more samples appear to have come from the same tree, a mean curve is made for those samples to produce a curve for the tree. This should mean that each curve in the master represents an individual tree and the master is not biased by several individual curves from the same tree.

Tree-rings are affected not only by the general climatic conditions, but also by the local conditions of the area in which the trees were growing. Anomalies resulting from the local growing conditions of individual trees are reduced by combining the ring widths of the trees together. In this way the common climatic signal is enhanced. Therefore a master curve has a better chance of obtaining an absolute date against a reference chronology than individual timbers.

Tree-ring dating can, naturally, only date the tree-rings present in the sample. Precise dates for the felling of trees can only be given if the sample possesses its bark or the bark edge. If only the early wood is present, the timber was probably felled during the late spring–early summer. If the ring appears to be complete, ie has both early wood and late wood, the tree was probably felled out of the growing season and is said to be winter felled. If there is sapwood but no bark edge, the felling estimate can be calculated by using the sapwood estimate of 10–55 rings (Hillam *et al* 1987). Where there is no sapwood, the addition of 10 rings (ie the minimum number of expected sapwood rings missing) to the heartwood will give a *terminus post quem* for felling, although the actual felling date could be much later. It must also be remembered that such dates do not give a date for the use of the timber. While it is highly unlikely that the timber used at Flag Fen was seasoned, Maisie Taylor has identified samples that she believes to have been reused in the make-up of the platform. Such information needs to be taken into account when interpreting the results.

Results

The details of all the dated samples are presented in Tables 8.2 and 8.3. A total of 355 samples were considered suitable for measurement. Of these, 250 have been dated. The ring-width data from the individual samples are stored at Flag Fen and Sheffield.

Power Station

Group 1: all seven timbers were found to be suitable. Two pairs of samples, Y0005 and Y0007, and Y0010 and Y0012, gave excellent visual matches against each other, which were confirmed by t values of 12.1 and 10.9 respectively. As it was probable that each pair was derived from the same tree, they were combined into single-tree means Y0005M and Y0010M. Together with sample Y0008, they combined to form a 286-year mean.

Group 2: seven of the twelve samples were rejected. Sample Y1325 had retained a small amount of sapwood. Four of the five measured samples crossmatched to produce a 151-year mean.

Group 3: of the 65 samples, 32 were rejected. Samples Y1192 and Y1198 gave an excellent visual match, which was confirmed by a t value of 14.8. They were combined to form the single-tree mean Y1192M.

This tree crossmatched with sample Y0210 to produce a 76-year mean. Nineteen of the remaining measured samples crossmatched to produce a 250-year mean. The two means did not crossmatch.

Group 4: 43 of the 105 samples were rejected. Excellent matches were found between samples Y0101 and Y0106 ($t=12$), Y0113 and Y0998 ($t=10.3$), Y0120 and Y0123 ($t=13$), and Y1007 and Y1009 ($t=12$). Each pair combined to form the single tree means Y0101M, Y0113M, Y0120M, and Y1007M. Forty-seven trees crossmatched to form a 416-year master. Four of these samples, Y0100, Y0138, Y0927, and Y1000, had some evidence of sapwood. Sample Y0125 was subsequently found to give an excellent visual match with Y0043 (Group 5). The *t* value of 9.9 was fractionally below the accepted figure for samples likely to have originated from the same tree. It was felt, however, that on the basis of the visual match and cross-sections of the samples it was probable that they were indeed from the same tree (Y0043M).

Group 5: 62 of the 151 samples were rejected. Ten of the remaining samples had sapwood. Several good matches were found between the samples Y0053 and Y1235 ($t=12.4$), Y0057 and Y0072 ($t=11.9$), Y0074 and Y0058 ($t=10.7$), Y0188 and Y1060 ($t=10.9$), Y0398 and Y0347 ($t=14.8$), and Y1305, Y1049, and Y1050. Sixty-three trees crossmatched to form a mean of 420 years. The samples Y1338 and Y1121 gave an excellent visual and statistical match ($t=14.2$) but could not be conclusively dated.

Group 6: two of the samples were rejected. The remaining three samples were measured and crossmatched to form a mean of 150 years.

Flag Fen

Area 2: two of the four samples from Area 2 were rejected before measurement. Sample Z0131 had too few rings and sample Z0118 had bands of rings that were too narrow to be accurately measured. The two measured samples had 54 and 121 rings, with the smaller of the two samples, Z0075 having some sapwood. The samples did not crossmatch, but were later dated against this master.

Area 4: six of the eight samples from this area were rejected as they did not contain a sufficient number of rings. One of the samples, A8505, retained some sapwood. The samples did not crossmatch but were later dated against the master.

Lake lining exposure: six of the 15 samples were rejected as they had too few rings. The remaining nine samples were measured and had between 41 and 161 rings. Two samples, A8554 and A8563, retained some sapwood. Six of the timbers crossmatched to form a 185-year mean. One of these samples, A8560, was later found to match the Area 6B sample B0180 both visually and statistically ($t=13.9$). Their data were combined to form the single tree mean A8560M. Two of the other samples, A8555 and A8552, did not match each other or the area master, but were later dated.

Area 6A: of the 62 samples examined, 28 were rejected as they had too few rings. The remaining 34 samples had between 43 and 123 rings. Only five (A0520, A0533, A0539, A3376, and A4614) retained any sapwood. Sample A0564 had a very narrow band and was only measured from the outer edge of this band to the outer edge of the sample.

The timbers A0546 and A3370, both vertical posts, gave an excellent visual match and produced a *t* value of 14. This would suggest that the timbers were probably part of the same tree. They were combined to produce a single ring pattern, A0546M. Twenty-four samples, including the mean A0546M, crossmatched to produce a 382-year mean. Thirteen of these samples were from horizontal timbers, the rest from vertical posts.

Area 6B: of the 239 samples examined from Area 6B, 143 were rejected. This rather high figure is the result of comprehensive sampling of the horizontal timbers of the platform. This is only a reflection of the number of samples rejected since mid 1993, however, as before this there was no facility to record the basic data in a useful form (see Method, above). The remaining 96 samples were measured. Only 32 samples had retained any sapwood, and of these B0033, B1622, B1716, B1930, and B2023 had bark or bark edge. A number of these samples had fewer than 50 rings, eg B0216, B1119, and B2522. Sample B0842 had most rings, with 168. B2023 had a band of unmeasurable rings in which the boundaries were not clear. Two sets of measurements were made: one before the band (B2023A) and one after to the probable bark edge (B2023B).

The samples were measured in small groups in no particular order. Any samples showing good visual and statistical matches were combined into an area mean before any more samples were dealt with. Unmatched samples were also checked against each other and against the mean as work progressed.

Four timbers, B0061, B0063, B0190, and the vertical B1721 produced excellent visual and statistical matches among themselves (see *t* value matrix, Table 8.4). It seems likely that all derived from the same tree and so all four were combined together into a single mean, B0061M4. Three vertical posts, B0486, B1719, and B1720 also produced consistently high *t* values and excellent visual matches. These were also combined into a single mean, B1719M3. Another excellent match was found between the vertical posts B2024 and B0058.

Table 8.4 *t* value matrix of timbers within single tree mean B0061M

	B0190	B0063	B0061	B1721	–
B0190		*	10.2	13.9	12.1
B0063		–	*	12.9	13.6
B0061		–	–	*	16.8
B1721		–	–	–	*

Table 8.5 Ring-width data of the site master curve for the Flag Fen basin 1406–937 BC (ring widths are in 0.01mm; the right-hand column shows the number of trees per year)

Year																				
1406 BC				479	384	202	312	73	148					1	1	1	1	1	1	
1400 BC	158	167	106	130	306	234	256	412	327	328	1	1	1	1	1	1	1	1	1	1
	88	78	99	54	123	143	230	198	126	78	1	1	1	1	1	1	1	1	1	1
	155	209	261	210	135	75	94	120	110	105	1	1	1	1	1	1	1	1	1	1
	213	179	163	77	105	150	168	126	179	212	1	1	1	1	1	1	2	3	3	3
	170	270	148	208	224	295	275	279	250	305	3	3	3	4	6	6	7	9	12	12
1350 BC	287	241	190	200	285	274	296	214	197	203	13	13	13	13	15	15	16	16	18	19
	264	251	173	261	255	183	224	211	180	143	19	19	20	21	21	21	21	21	21	22
	188	239	114	160	224	221	200	161	198	233	23	23	23	23	23	23	23	23	23	23
	221	164	145	160	156	152	124	105	134	134	23	23	24	24	24	24	24	24	24	24
	163	198	159	115	129	165	101	131	141	148	23	23	23	23	23	23	22	22	23	23
1300 BC	118	104	117	134	171	117	164	183	163	147	24	23	23	22	23	23	23	21	20	20
	119	152	170	158	121	94	103	125	142	105	21	21	21	22	23	20	20	21	21	21
	129	102	130	125	150	185	168	130	124	115	21	21	19	19	19	18	17	17	17	16
	155	143	148	130	105	106	107	98	116	108	16	16	17	17	16	16	16	16	16	16
	140	147	145	112	132	97	117	98	124	153	16	17	18	18	18	19	18	18	19	19
1250 BC	159	126	105	125	129	114	140	116	124	133	19	18	18	18	18	18	18	17	18	18
	112	103	189	158	147	163	155	110	148	108	18	18	18	18	19	19	21	21	20	21
	123	150	148	95	132	173	164	141	123	134	21	21	21	21	20	20	20	19	19	19
	129	132	171	125	124	144	139	123	103	111	19	19	19	20	19	20	19	19	19	19
	126	146	159	154	104	98	130	124	160	143	19	19	19	19	19	19	19	19	18	19
1200 BC	133	106	88	172	139	122	157	160	135	170	19	19	19	21	21	21	22	24	25	25
	187	162	143	128	129	157	145	169	185	184	25	25	25	25	25	24	25	25	26	29
	157	163	175	154	181	164	182	191	168	135	35	35	37	37	41	45	46	46	46	46
	158	119	185	198	193	188	191	204	192	137	47	49	51	52	54	56	58	63	67	69
	188	202	222	189	168	182	202	173	127	128	73	73	79	80	80	85	85	86	89	90
1150 BC	153	154	169	161	166	151	159	162	142	157	90	91	93	95	96	99	99	101	104	104
	148	146	159	152	184	186	161	164	177	167	105	107	107	108	109	110	112	115	116	119
	131	113	120	102	107	118	161	129	141	150	120	120	121	122	122	122	124	126	129	130
	113	103	152	148	161	150	150	130	123	110	131	113	113	136	136	137	134	135	135	135
	147	126	116	104	136	163	144	136	155	121	135	134	134	134	133	131	130	127	124	121
1100 BC	97	102	128	122	143	119	103	120	111	101	117	116	117	116	115	112	109	107	106	106
	119	107	110	145	130	117	128	129	152	131	105	101	100	101	97	97	93	92	94	95
	123	131	132	99	131	142	141	121	113	119	96	97	94	95	92	91	89	87	88	88
	100	109	145	145	116	105	125	111	109	123	88	88	87	85	84	84	83	82	82	81
	125	125	141	157	133	117	129	130	123	142	82	82	81	76	76	75	76	76	75	75
1050 BC	155	126	101	150	150	157	154	137	136	144	75	75	74	75	75	76	76	74	72	73
	150	167	121	133	122	143	153	174	164	178	69	67	68	66	65	65	64	62	58	57
	130	116	135	145	177	159	213	122	120	131	54	50	49	45	45	42	41	40	39	39
	141	120	124	157	173	154	192	120	93	92	36	34	33	32	30	30	28	26	27	26
	98	101	120	123	122	150	133	154	127	124	26	26	26	26	23	22	19	19	19	17
1000 BC	92	90	135	97	76	72	99	112	100	79	17	16	15	14	14	14	14	14	13	11
	129	118	100	128	145	112	104	137	98	87	10	10	10	10	10	8	8	8	8	8
	117	96	122	106	126	110	78	70	104	136	8	8	7	6	6	6	5	5	5	5
	118	103	102	139	158	124	97	143	137	88	5	5	5	5	5	5	5	5	5	5
	123	110	114	167	130	127	90	75	68	74	5	5	5	4	3	3	2	2	2	2
950 BC	83	79	115	47	61	63	59	48	60	66	2	2	1	1	1	1	1	1	1	1
	55	42	57	53							1	1	1	1						

This was confirmed by a *t* value of 15. These were combined into a single-tree mean B2024M. The ring widths of 59 trees were combined to form a 451-year master curve. Three samples, B1724, B1739, and B1740 showed good visual matches between them, confirmed by high *t* values. They could not, however, be conclusively dated.

Area 6C: all five timbers were found to be suitable, having between 50 and 136 rings. Two of the samples, B3666 and B3671, crossmatched to form a 136-year master. Sample B3675 did not match but was later dated against the Flag Fen master. This sample had 25 sapwood rings.

Area 6D: both samples were measured. Although they did not match each other they subsequently dated against the Flag Fen master.

Dating

The primary aim of the dendrochronological study at Flag Fen was to produce a long, well replicated site master, which might match the available reference chronologies, and so produce absolute dates for the site. All the work between 1990 and early 1992 was done with this aim in mind. Samples with as many annual growth rings as possible were selected from the Flag Fen platform and post alignment and from the Power Station for this purpose, ie samples with as many annual growth rings as possible. At this stage, matching area or group means were combined to form site masters.

Separate master curves were assembled for the Power Station (FG) and Flag Fen (FF).

These chronologies crossmatched very well. On the advice of Ian Tyers, they were kept separate so that data could be cross-checked. By 1992 a 397-year combined Power Station/Flag Fen master had been created. This was then compared with reference chronologies, an exercise that was carried out at the Sheffield Dendrochronology Laboratory and the Palaeoecology Centre, The Queen's University, Belfast. The data were compared with the Irish BLC7000 chronology (Brown *et al* 1986), and a significant match (*t* =5.27) was produced when the site chronology spanned the period 1363–967 BC. This potential was confirmed by the agreement with the South German chronology A200 Standard (*t* =7.4; Becker *et al* 1991, 647). These results meant that the dating of the combined Power Station/Flag Fen

Table 8.6 Results of comparisons of the Power Station (FG137T), Flag Fen (FF88T), and combined Flag Fen Basin (FFB225T) masters and reference chronologies spanning the Bronze Age

	FG137T	FF88T	FFB225T
A200 Standard, S. Germany	8.43	6.07	6.33
BLC7000, N. Ireland	6.27	4.12	4.58

chronology (1992 version) to the spread 1363–967 BC could be accepted with confidence (Neve 1992, 473). Following further work in 1993–4, the site masters have been extended and now cover the periods 1364–937 BC (Power Station) and 1406–955 BC (Flag Fen). The combined master for the Flag Fen Basin therefore covers the period 1406–937 BC (Table 8.5). The comparisons of all three 1994 masters with these reference chronologies are shown in Table 8.6.

Interpretation of the tree-ring dates

Details of all the dated samples are given in Table 8.2 and 8.3. The lack of sapwood means that few precise felling dates can be given, but some broad phases have been identified.

For the purposes of interpretation and discussion, the Power Station and Flag Fen have each been examined as whole areas. The exception to this is the lake lining exposure at Flag Fen, as little is known about the samples, eg whether horizontal or vertical, their size, or their levels.

Power Station

Only five of the 140 dated timbers from vertical posts retained any sapwood. Ten others finished at heartwood/sapwood transition or had unmeasurable rings ending at heartwood/sapwood transition.

The first sapwood ring of Y0138 dates to 1296 BC. Using the sapwood estimate discussed above (see Method), the tree was, therefore, felled after 1287 BC, but probably before 1242 BC. This sample comes from within a group of 17 timbers from 15 trees, which have *termini post quem* for felling varying from after 1301 BC to after 1257 BC.

Timber Y0082 retained two sapwood rings and was therefore felled sometime before 1094 and 1049 BC. Sample Y0201 was felled after 1023 but probably before 978 BC, Y0017 was probably felled sometime between 1008 and 963 BC, and Y1325 between 1004 and 959 BC. These timbers are part of a very long phase of continuous or possible periodic activity on the post alignment spanning more than a century.

There is a possible middle phase consisting of six posts with *termini post quem* for felling ranging from after 1176 BC to after 1149 BC.

There is evidence that after the main (third) phase of activity, the post alignment was subject to only periodic repair. The latest dated post has a *terminus post quem* for felling of after 927 BC.

Of the 12 dated horizontal timbers only one, Y0184, retained any sapwood. It was probably felled after 1026 BC but before 981 BC.

Flag Fen

The dated samples seem to indicate that there was activity on the platform and post alignment at Flag Fen from the late thirteenth to the early tenth century BC, the main phase of activity occurring between the late twelfth and early tenth century BC.

Thirteen of the dated vertical posts retained sapwood. Of these three had bark edge and a further seven had possible bark edge. Another six samples finished at heartwood/sapwood transition or at the point of possible transition. The felling ranges for the latter, along with all the other dated samples, are contained in Table 8.3.

Sample A0520 appeared to have complete sapwood, although the last nine rings were damaged and unmeasurable. The outer ring appeared to be complete and thus indicated felling during the winter of 1094–1093 BC.

The posts B1622 and B1930 both retained their bark. The former was felled in the winter of 1083–1082 BC, the latter in the summer of 1007 BC. Sample B0897 also retained complete sapwood and was felled in the winter of 1026–1025 BC.

Sapwood was present on A0539 and A8505, giving a felling range of after 1025 but not later than 980 BC for A0539, and after 1016 but not later than 971 BC for A8505. Samples B1738 and B2023B retained complete sapwood, B1738 giving a felling date of 1007 BC (the same as B1930) and B2023B a date of 1002 BC.

Three posts, B0031, B2022, and B3658, all have their final heartwood ring dating to 1000 BC. The sapwood of B2022 was complete, although the outer edge was damaged. This made it difficult to determine precisely how many unmeasured rings were present, but there were certainly no more than 2–3 to the bark edge. Consequently, this gives a felling date range of 986–983 BC. The felling range for the other two samples is after 990 but not later than 945 BC.

Samples B1742, B1716, and B0033 all retained complete sapwood, although only B1716 had bark present. B1742 was felled in 957 BC, B1716 winter felled in 958–957 BC, and B0033 summer felled in 955 BC.

In contrast, only five of the dated horizontal samples retained sapwood or evidence of the heartwood/sapwood transition. Sample Z0075 (Area 2), for example, has a range of after 1012, but not later than 967 BC. The plank A4614, which was identified as being part of the revetment of the timber platform, retained some sapwood and was therefore felled within the range 1002–957 BC. Sapwood was also found on B3675, giving a felling range of after 978 but before 948 BC.

Sample B0063 retained six sapwood rings, giving a felling date range of after 975 but not later than 930 BC. Three other samples, the horizontals B0061 and B0190, and the vertical B1721, are all thought to have derived from the same tree. Therefore, all are likely to have the same felling-date range.

The timbers

The vast majority of samples from both areas of the site had been radially or tangentially split. The proportion of samples that were quartered, halved, or whole trunks varies between the dated, undated, and unmeasured groups.

Over 66% of the dated samples from the Power Station were either 1/8 radial split or less, or tangentially split. At Flag Fen this figure is over 80%. The undated samples follow a similar pattern although at Flag Fen there is an equal number of roundwood samples. There is a higher proportion of roundwood than tangentially split timbers among the unmeasured samples from both areas although 1/8 radial or less is still the most common type. At the Power Station there are also significant numbers of half-split samples.

It is not possible to give an accurate assessment of the size and age of the parent trees as there is little evidence of sapwood or pith on the majority of the samples. The trees used must have ranged from less than 20 to over 200 years old when felled. Less than 18% of the measured samples contained more than 100 rings. The average number of rings per dated sample is 82. Allowing for an unknown number of pith and sapwood rings, it would seem likely that a large proportion of the samples were derived from trees c 100 years old or more when felled.

Although the average growth rate ranges from less than 0.5 to more than 8.5mm per year, the majority of samples have an average growth rate of 1–2 mm per year. The dated samples have an average ring width of 1.44mm per year. This implies that many of the trees must have grown under conditions that were limiting, possibly as dense woodland, which would result in slow growth. This, combined with the estimate that many of the trees could have been c 100 years old or more when felled, would seem to indicate that established woodland was being exploited.

Discussion

Tree ring dates have been obtained for 68% of the measured samples from the Power Station and Flag Fen. This high figure is probably due to the exploitation of the local woodland (see above). The early results of the pollen analysis undertaken by Rob Scaife would seem to indicate the presence of oak woodland in the area (Scaife 1992).

Although 225 trees have been dated, it has not been possible to provide a precise dating framework for the site, due to the scarcity of sapwood. Only ten dated samples had bark or possible bark edge. The importance of sapwood and bark edge has been clearly demonstrated at Fiskerton, Lincs (Hillam 1985b). While more evidence of sapwood and heartwood/sapwood transition survived at Flag Fen, only 60 (54% of the total number of samples submitted with sapwood) from both sites were suitable for measurement. Of those measured only 53% were dated. Unfortunately, sapwood is not so robust as heartwood and is less likely to survive in poor conditions. This was especially true at the Power Station and in Area 6A at Flag Fen.

Some references to the presence of sapwood have been found in the field notes, especially at the Power Station. Unfortunately, most of what had survived excavation had not survived storage.

The high quality crossmatching between the Power Station and Flag Fen masters, and sometimes among the individuals from within both masters, would seem to indicate that the timbers were being obtained for both areas from the same woodland. During the production of the site masters, each site was used as a cross-check against the other. Occasionally, samples were found that actually appeared to give better matches with the individuals of the opposing master than they did against the master for their own area (eg B1714). Sample A8560 from the lake lining exposure was found to cross-match with *t* values of over 10 with B0180 (Area 6B) and Y0002 and Y1084 (Power Station). Although these three samples did not give such high *t* values against each other, it is probable that they all originated from the same tree (Cathy Groves personal communication). An example of the general crossmatching between the two areas is shown in the form of a block matrix (Table 8.7).

Although it is not often possible to source the timber using dendrochronology, the best matches for the master curves have been against reference chronologies for gravel grown oaks. This accords well with Rob Scaife's pollen analysis. It is possible that some of the wood could have been felled from the gravels of Northey, at the eastern landfall of the post alignment. It is unlikely that timber felled at Northey would have been taken all the way to the Fengate end of the alignment, but as Flag Fen is more central, timber from both sides might have been used. This might be an explanation for the occasionally better matches between Flag Fen samples and the Power Station material.

Although it is not possible to produce a precise framework for the site, some observations can be made due to the large amounts of dated material. It is, however, important to note that, while oak represents over 95% of the wood excavated at the Power Station, the proportion of oak at Flag Fen is nearer 55%. This must be taken into account when interpreting these results. The separate master curves for the Power Station and Flag Fen broadly cover the same period. There are, however, very few samples from Flag Fen that appear to fit in with the early phases 1 and 2 identified at the Power Station. Both areas exhibit the same increase in activity during phase 3. This phase, in which the activity could be continuous or periodic, seems, however, to be longer at Flag Fen. By the late tenth century BC the Power Station posts seem to show evidence of less frequent repair or replacement.

The early phase 1 identified at the Power Station consists of 17 timbers from 15 trees with *termini post quem* for felling ranging from after 1301 BC to after 1257 BC. Two vertical posts from Flag Fen, A0523 and B0461, might be part of this group.

The second phase of posts identified at the Power Station could not easily be distinguished at Flag Fen. One timber, B1744, falls within the range of this group.

The great majority of vertical posts were felled (and presumably used more or less immediately) during a very long phase of possibly continuous or periodic activity spanning over a century at the Power Station and a century and a half at Flag Fen. While the phases cover broadly the same period, it is notable that there is still much activity within the post alignment and on the platform at Flag Fen during the late to mid tenth century BC. This is when the Power Station posts appear to require less frequent repair. Only 12 horizontal timbers were dated from the Power Station. Of these, 11 would appear to fall within phase 3 and only one (Y0184) had retained any evidence of sapwood.

All phases are represented in the horizontal wood at Flag Fen. Only one sample, A3365 with a *terminus post quem* for felling of after 1269 BC, is comparable with the Power Station phase 1. Most of the samples had *termini post quem* for felling within the range covered by phase 3. Unfortunately, as all these samples were split and few had retained any sapwood, an unknown number of outer rings might have been lost. The timber A4614 was one of the revetment planks excavated just to the south of the posts in Area 6A (Pryor *et al* 1986). The retained sapwood gives a possible date range for construction of the revetment in the last half of the tenth century BC (see Table 8.3).

The lack of sapwood and bark edge prevents the production of precise felling dates for all but a handful of the vertical posts. At the Power Station, the size of the area excavated and the number of samples subsequently dated might well have revealed important details regarding the development of the post alignment, had the sapwood survived. More sapwood survived at Flag Fen, but the relatively small areas excavated and the high proportion of species other than oak has meant that little additional information has been yielded by its presence.

Examination of the distribution of phase 1 posts at the Power Station shows that all but one of the posts dated (Y1016) are located towards the southern side of the post alignment. As a group, the average annual ring width was slightly higher than the average for the site

Table 8.7 *t* value matrix showing the general level of cross-matching between the Power Station and Flag Fen (values of less than 3.5 are not listed)

	Y1097	Y0003	Y0236	Y0184	Y1153	Y1279	Y0391	Y0043M
B1736	3.7	–	–	–	–	4.2	4.2	–
B1614	3.5	4.8	–	5.7	–	5.6	5.5	4.1
A2546	3.5	5.5	–	–	6.8	3.8	4.0	3.9
A8560M	–	–	4.4	10.9	–	4.6	–	8.6
A0539	–	–	–	4.4	–	4.7	–	3.5
A8558	–	–	–	–	–	3.8	–	3.9
B2024M	4.4	5.2	–	4.7	5.1	4.5	5.1	–

as a whole. Two-thirds of the samples were ¼ radial split or less, the highest proportion being ½ split. Their curves also show a high level of agreement with many *t* values of over 7. It would seem possible that all these 'early' posts derived from a small areas of not-too-dense woodland quite close to the site, ie the nearest supply of timber was exploited first.

If this hypothesis is used at Flag Fen, the scarcity of dated early posts could perhaps be explained by the fact that the nearest supply of timber was not oak. Large amounts of alder have been identified in the lowest levels of the platform. While it appears not to have been felled and left *in situ*, this might well have been growing nearby (Taylor 1992, 479–80). If the early levels of the platform had been constructed using this local supply, the earliest posts could have been derived from the same source. The most southerly row of posts, Row 1, appears to have been constructed entirely of widely spaced alder posts. It is possible that these posts could be part of the earliest phase of post alignment construction. This could prove difficult to determine dendrochronologically, due to the unsuitability of alder for tree-ring dating, but might be an aspect that could benefit from the use of radiocarbon dating.

At Flag Fen a group of three posts, B0031, B2022, and B3658, all have their final heartwood ring dating to the same year (see Results and Table 8.3). It is therefore possible that they were all felled in the same year and are broadly contemporary.

The platform and post alignment seem to have been in use from the late thirteenth century to the early tenth century BC. There are periods at the Power Station in which there appears to be little or no felling activity, eg between phases 1 and 2 and between 2 and 3. At Flag Fen such periods of inactivity can not be positively identified. This is due to the small number of vertical posts that are broadly contemporary with the early Power Station phases and the presence of horizontal wood (see Fig 8.4).

Unfortunately, none of the horizontal samples of this period retained any sapwood. By examination of the cross-sections of the samples, however, and assessing their original position within the trunk, it would seem unlikely that they had lost up to 100 rings or that they have been converted from the inner portions of much larger trees. It is therefore improbable that these 'earlier' samples are simply inner portions of phase 3 timbers (ie it is unlikely to be of a single phase). Also, much of the wood, both horizontal and vertical, is not oak and must be considered as undatable by dendrochronology. It is possible that much of the activity within this period is confined to the use of non-oak species.

Although there is little horizontal wood at the Power Station, both areas are only small parts of the same site. The apparent lack of activity might merely reflect a shift in the focus of that activity. It is possible that there were short periods of abandonment, or simply lack of repairs, between the early eleventh and mid tenth century BC, but they can not be identified without the presence of sapwood.

After the late tenth century BC, the posts of the Power Station post alignment would appear to have been subject only to periodic replacement or renewal. The latest post, Y0050, has a *terminus post quem* for felling of after 924 BC. At Flag Fen, there appears to be much more activity on the post alignment during the last half of the tenth century BC, ending at 955 BC with the driving in of post B0033. There are horizontal samples that might be contemporary with these posts, eg A1895. The evidence from the Power Station and the amount of other species of wood at Flag Fen would seem to indicate that the site went out of use slowly. Unfortunately, the lack of any local reference chronologies has meant that undated material can not be tested in any other way than against the site masters and the other unmatched samples. It is therefore possible that some of these samples are of later (or even earlier) date. This can not be tested, however, unless additional chronologies become available for the region.

Conclusion

The analysis of 661 horizontal and vertical timbers from the Power Station and the Flag Fen platform resulted in the production of a dated chronology for the Flag Fen Basin spanning the period 1406–937 BC. This should prove useful in future dendrochronological studies in this region It might also be of use in dating other Bronze Age sequences in lowland Britain that have shown no correlation with the bog oak chronologies of northern England.

It has not been possible to produce a detailed dating framework for the site due to the lack of sapwood, although felling dates for timbers from both areas have been identified from the thirteenth to the late tenth century BC. The results from the Power Station seem to indicate three phases of activity, which might be continuous or might be periodic. Although the results from Flag Fen are broadly similar, the earlier phases 1 and 2 can not be clearly identified. The high percentage of measured samples that produced dates and the high quality of some of the crossmatching is probably indicative of the exploitation of local woodland that was possibly quite dense and fairly well established.

9 Prehistoric pottery from the Power Station and Flag Fen

by John C Barrett

The problem

The excavation of the post alignment and platform raise some specific questions of interpretation. These concern: the constructional histories of the timber-works; the depositional histories of the artefacts, animal and human remains, and the environmental history within which these activities took place. Such 'site-specific' questions have also to be placed in the context of the larger landscape, ie the study of a particular artefact category derived from the Power Station and Flag Fen excavations. This study should be concerned with the specific and changing conditions under which humans occupied this part of the landscape, their various activities which resulted in the deposition of the material, and the different taphonomic processes which have created the material record being studied today. Analytically, these questions could be approached in quite traditional terms — establishing the chronological range of the material, its stratigraphic distribution, and the state of the artefacts upon recovery. Nonetheless, such analysis must move beyond the simple description of the assemblage to an understanding of the means of its creation.

Isolated from the wider context, the pottery assemblage from both the Power Station site and the Flag Fen platform is small in its own right and there is little to surprise us. Unlike the metalwork, no unusual forms are to be found among this material. When examined in the context of human activity, however, it gains a greater significance. The report therefore begins by establishing the approach towards that objective.

The nature of the timber structures at both the Power Station and Flag Fen, and their environmental context is discussed elsewhere. For our purposes, it should be remembered that the timbers and platform were built as a cordon running eastwards from the dry land out over a wet reed swamp, which had developed as the result of progressive inundation. The timbers cut off an embayed area to the south, into which fresh water streams emptied from the open fenland to the north. The water levels will have changed seasonally, perhaps occasionally flooding the platform, and, over time, peat encroached upon the structure.

The timbers were erected in the second half of the second millennium BC and represent a substantial modification of the environment. This was itself slowly changing with the flooding of the ancient water meadows which fringed the enclosed dry land around the bay.

The alignment maintained the west–east axis of the dry landscape, at the point where it met dry land; the processes of enclosure originated at least as early as the late Neolithic. Settlement on the dry land might have shifted as the waters encroached. At certain times, settlement might have moved further away from the areas excavated around the timbers. The timber structures do not appear to have been maintained beyond the end of the Bronze Age. In summary, the context for the depositional history of all the portable material is an increasingly wet fen, upon which a timber platform was built and linked to the dry land, probably to both the west and east, by a complex avenue of timbers that might have supported a walkway. The context is important because all the portable material was carried there and abandoned during an intermittent occupation of a changeable surface of soft peat, reed swamp, and freshwater pools. Such a surface is obviously ideal for the burial and preservation of the most superficial of discarded material, the kind of surface debris rarely encountered on dry land. The debris represented seemingly resulted from activities spatially removed from the more routine activities associated with dry-land settlement. The depositional context is therefore complex, which might be reflected in the pottery assemblage and the types of human activity. The problems raised by the methods by which the material was recovered should also be addressed. These are discussed in detail elsewhere, making clear that different levels of control were exercised in the excavation of the Flag Fen platform and the Power Station site. In the case of the latter, much effort appears to have been directed at the recovery of the timbers and, through the use of metal detectors, metal artefacts. These priorities will have undoubtedly skewed the known distribution of the pottery finds. It is also noticeable that the small-sized sherds well represented on the Flag Fen platform are poorly represented on the Power Station site.

The assemblage

The assemblage will be treated in three parts. A short consideration of fabrics will be followed by a catalogue of the illustrated pottery. The entire assemblage will then be described according to fabric and vessel form (full descriptions are contained in the site archive). The discussion of vessel forms is a description of the vessels from which the sherd material derived, along with the description of a few complete vessels.

Fabrics

Seven fabric groups have been identified:

1 Large shell inclusions in a hard fabric
2 Shell inclusions and numerous voids in a soft fabric
3 Dense small shell inclusions
4 Dense inclusions of sub-angular quartz grains

5   Crushed burnt flint inclusions with some additional sand and grog

6   A soft laminated fabric with numerous large voids

7   A hard fabric with numerous small voids

Three main groups of inclusions are thus identified, shell, sub-angular quartz sand, and flint.

Fabrics 6 and 7 might either have also contained shell, which has been lost due to soil conditions, or some vegetable material burnt out in firing. A great deal of the variation noticeable within each fabric group, including surface variation of the sherds, is also likely to reflect post-depositional chemical and mechanical erosion.

Catalogue of illustrated pottery (Figs 9.1–3)

1   Decorated rimsherd, later Neolithic. Fabric 3. Cat's Water 1990, F91 (small pit or posthole)

2   Decorated rimsherd, Beaker. Fabric 6. From backfilled pit F87, layer 1. Power Station, FNG 89, Pot 136

3   Decorated rimsherd, probably Early Bronze Age. Fabric 5. From hollow within buried soil grid 1905 9043, Power Station, FNG 89, Pot 3

4   Decorated rimsherd, Early Bronze Age. Fabric 6. From hollow or shallow ditch within or below buried soil, grid 1899 9043, Power Station, FNG 89, Pot 37

5   Two decorated rimsherds of Collared Urn. Fabric 5. From base of buried soil, grid 1944 9024, Power Station, FNG 89, Pot 152. Compare with Fig 2.11

6   Complete coarseware jar. Fabric 6. Flag Fen Area 6B, Level 3 (directly below timber B1633), grid 2712 8887, FF89, Pot 299

7   Complete fineware cup. Fabric 5. Flag Fen Area 6B, Level 1 (0.42m OD), grid 2708 8884, FF87, Pot 279

8   Rimsherds of plain bowl/jar. Fabric 5. Flag Fen Area 6B, Level 3, grid 2711 8888, FF88, Pot 294

9   Rim and upper body of concave jar. Fabric 5. Flag Fen Area 6A, below Level 5, grid 2718 8886, FF87, Pot 288

10 Rim, shoulder, and upper body of shouldered jar. Fabric 5. Flag Fen Area 6B, Level 1 (directly below timber B63), 0.36m OD, grid 2709 8882, FF87, Pot 285

11 Rim and body of plain bowl. Fabric 5. Flag Fen Area 6B, Level 2, 0.33m OD, grid 2709 8883, FF88, Pot 285

12 Rim and upper body of plain bowl/jar. Fabric 4. Flag Fen Area 6B, Level 4/5, grid 270 /8885, FF91, Pot 336

13 Rim and upper body of plain bowl/jar. Fabric 5. Flag Fen Area 6B, Level 4/5, 0.18–0.08m OD, grid 2707 8885, FF91, Pot 334

14 Rimsherd of plain bowl/jar. Fabric 4. Flag Fen Area 6A, Level 5, 0.22m OD, grid 2718 8885, FF87, Pot 334

15 Rim and upper body of decorated shouldered jar. Fabric 5. Flag Fen Area 6B, Level 1 (no grid), FF90, Pot 308

16 Rim and upper body of plain bowl. Fabric 3. Power Station Area 1, buried soil, grid 1983 9008, FNG 89, Pot 135

17 Rim and body of plain bowl. Fabric 4. Power Station Area 1, Trench G, buried soil, grid 1980 9150, FNG 89, Pot 82

18 Rim and body of plain bowl. Fabric 4. Power Station Area 1, Trench D, buried soil, grid 1992 9013, FNG 89, Pot 70

19 Rim and neck of shouldered jar. Fabric 5. Power Station Area 1, buried soil, grid 1954 9034, FNG 89, Pot 113

20 Rim, neck and shoulder of shouldered jar. Fabric 4. Power Station Area 1, buried soil, grid 1856 9030, FNG 89, Pot 134

21 Rim, neck, and shoulder of shouldered jar. Fabric 6. Power Station Area 1, buried soil, grid 1911 9046, FNG 89, Pot 99

22 Rim and upper body of concave bowl/jar. Fabric 7. Power Station Area 1, in silts and peats directly above buried soil, grid 1928 9035, FNG 89, Pot 2

23 Rim and body of shouldered jar. Vertical scoring on body. Fabric 4. Power Station Area 1, buried soil, grid 1855 9026, FNG 89, Pot 148

24 Complete profile of shouldered jar. Vertical scoring on body. Fabric 6. Power Station Area 1, buried soil, grid 1982 9036, FNG 89, Pot 101

The assemblage described

Many of the sherds are small in size, although there is a higher proportion of larger sherds represented from the Flag Fen platform; only 91 ceramic finds are recorded from the Power Station site and 312 from the Flag Fen platform. The nature of these sherd assemblages will be discussed more fully below.

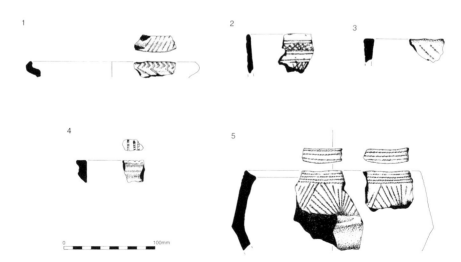

Fig 9.1 Late Neolithic, Beaker, and Early Bronze Age pottery sherds from Cat's Water (1990), 1, and the Power Station, 2–5

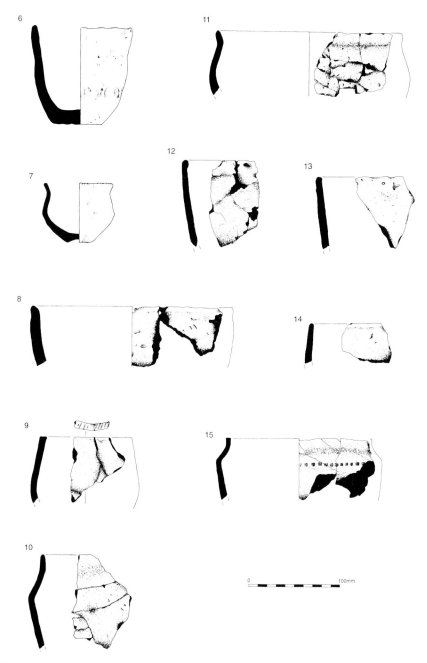

Fig 9.2 Middle to Late Bronze Age and Early Iron Age pottery vessels and sherds from Flag Fen, Area 6

Our understanding of the original vessel assemblages from which this material derived is limited by the relatively small size of both assemblages. Nonetheless, the fabrics, the forms of the vessels reconstructed from some of the sherds (some of which are illustrated in Figures 9.2 and 9.3), and comparisons between these variables and other local assemblages, allow this material to be placed within the relatively well established sequence of ceramic development between the Late Neolithic and the Iron Age.

The various Late Neolithic and Iron Age ceramic assemblages which have been recovered from the immediate vicinity of the fen edge (Pryor 1978, 1980, and 1984a) do not indicate that a strict sequence of different fabrics was in use over time. The fabrics of the late Neolithic include the use of grog, 'grits',

some sand and shell, as well as indications of vegetable material as additives to the clay (Pryor 1978, 69–79). In the material from the Bronze Age ditch systems, shell appears to occur more commonly, along with sherds marked by numerous voids, and the use of grog and flint as fillers (Williams 1980, 87–8). The Cat's Water Iron Age settlement produced pottery of essentially two fabric groups. One used shell, the other sub-angular quartz grains, although some grog was present among the sand. Some of the shell had dissolved to leave voids in the body of the fabric (Williams 1980 and Pryor 1984a). Shell is therefore widely used over a long period of time, sand appears more as a feature of the late assemblages, and flint occurs intermittently in the Late Neolithic and Early Bronze Age.

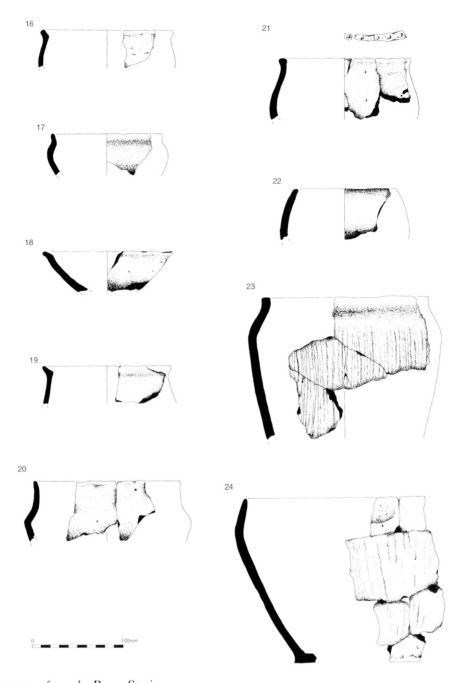

Fig 9.3 Iron Age pottery from the Power Station

When compared with the local assemblages, the range of fabrics recovered from the two sites therefore indicates that a very long history of deposition is likely to be represented by the pottery finds, probably extending from the Neolithic through to the Iron Age. This can be confirmed by an examination of the vessel forms represented. It will then be necessary to examine the way the depositional processes changed through time and the way these practices related to the history of the timber structures. For ease of reference, the sequence will be divided between a Late Neolithic and Early Bronze Age (late third to early second millennium), a Middle to Late Bronze Age (late second to early first millennium), and an Iron Age (late first millennium). This threefold division conforms broadly with the periods of the Bronze Age ditched fields, the timber structures published here, and the settlement complex at Cat's Water (Pryor 1984a).

Late Neolithic to Early Bronze Age

As already indicated, a simple chronological division between fabric groups is not possible. The earlier fabric groups from the Power Station appear particularly diverse. The earlier fabrics are likely to be represented by those with shell or vegetable fillers, although shell is used again in Iron Age fabrics. It is, however, unlikely that some of the eroded sherds of fabrics 6 and 7 represent earlier Neolithic material, given the context of their discovery (see below) and there is nothing diagnostic of this date

Table 9.1 Comparison of sherd numbers in each fabric between the Power Station and Flag Fen, Area 6

fabric	Power Station	Flag Fen
1	15	2
2	15	32
3	35	5
4	15	20
5	11	179
6	–	31
7	–	43

Table 9.2 Sherd groups indicative of single vessels as recovered from Flag Fen, Area 6

pot group/vessel	context	fabric	number of sherds
2	Area 2, Level 2	5	49
3	Area 3, Level 2	5	4
4	Area 2, Level 4	6	9
5	Area 2, Level 4	6	32
6	Area 3, Level 3	2	13
7	Area 2, Level 3	5	116
–	'Level 2'	7	11

from either site. The earliest diagnostic forms include Beaker and Early Bronze Age sherds (Fig 9.1, 2–5). All this material is in shell fabrics and finds comparison among the material from Storey's Bar Road (Pryor 1978, figs 37–42). The quantity of this diagnostic material is limited, all of it coming from the Power Station site.

Middle to Late Bronze Age

In general, material of this date is poorly represented among the recently excavated fen-edge sites, although late Bronze/Early Iron Age material is represented in the large collection of material recovered from the Fengate gravel pits (Hawkes and Fell 1945) and the smaller assemblage from Vicarage Farm (Pryor 1974, figs 14–15). Other finds from the area are restricted to a small scatter of material, some from isolated pits. Superficially, the indications are that the dryland settlement had shifted its focus to the west, at the time the timber structures were being constructed. This process continued after abandonment of the timber structures (see also the Tower Works site, Chapter 3). Material of this date is connected with the Power Station and Flag Fen timber structures, the forms spanning the bucket-shaped vessels typical of the Middle Bronze Age (Fig 9.2, 6) through to the plain jars, finer cups (Fig 9.2, 7), bowls, and jars (Fig 9.2, 8–9, 12–14) of the Late Bronze Age. Flint-gritted fabrics (Fabric 5) are well represented among the diagnostic sherds of this date.

Iron Age

A number of sherds are representative of Iron Age vessels. These are bowls (Fig 9.3, 16–18) and shouldered jars (Fig 9.3, 19–21 and 23–4), mostly undecorated, although the chronological range of the latter might be extensive with finger impressed decoration of the opening decades of the Iron Age (Fig 9.2, 15) and the later use of vertical score marks on the body of the vessel (Fig 9.3, 24). All this material is directly comparable to many of the vessel forms recovered from the Cat's Water settlement (Pryor 1984a, figs 102–4) and at Padholme Road (Pryor 1974, figs 20–22). A further comparison between the two assemblages is that both occur in shell and sand fabrics (Fabrics 14).

Deposition

Given the long history of ceramic deposition represented by the material from the Power Station and Flag Fen, a period which clearly began before the construction of the timber structures and continued after their possible inundation, it must be assumed that a number of different depositional processes have been at work. Of the two assemblages, that from the Power Station is the more difficult to analyse, being simply a spread of material recovered during the clearance of the peaty alluvium around the timber rows and in excavating the metalwork. The material recovered from the platform, on the other hand, has a far greater stratigraphic integrity.

The two site assemblages also differ in terms of their composition, represented most simply by a comparison of the numbers of sherds assigned to each fabric (Table 9.1). Taken at face value, however, this comparison is misleading, for a substantial amount of the material from the Flag Fen platform can be assigned to a small group of single vessels which were deposited as substantial fragments. These were then further reduced to sherds, either by trample or by compression from the overlying deposits. Four such deposits come from the 'floor' levels of the platform (two each from Levels 3 and 4) and three from the overlying Level 2. Details of these deposits are given in Table 9.2. From this it can be seen that 13 of the 32 sherds in Fabric 2 appear to come from a single vessel, 169 of the 179 sherds in Fabric 5 appear to come from three vessels, all 31 sherds of Fabric 6 come from two vessels, and 11 out of 43 sherds in Fabric 7 appear to come from one vessel. In addition to these sherd groups, a single complete cup in Fabric 5 was found (Fig 9.2, 7). It should be noted that fabrics 1, 3, and 4 are not represented by these single-vessel deposits.

Thus, of the 312 sherds recorded from the platform, 224 seem to derive from large portions of only seven or eight vessels. No real distinction in depositional process can be drawn between the deposits in Levels 3 and 4 and those in Level 2. Most of the pottery comes from Levels 3 and 2.

The pottery assemblage from the Flag Fen platform is dominated by ceramic forms whose chronological range could extend from Middle Bronze Age to earliest

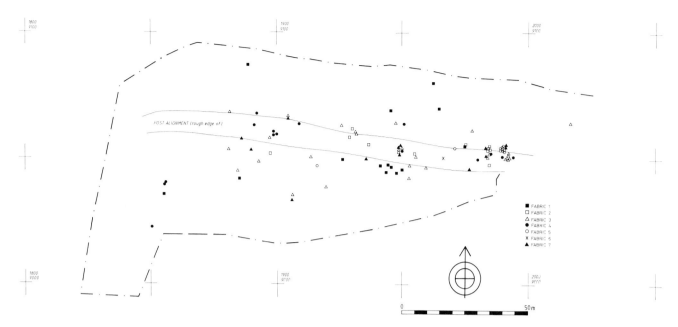

Fig 9.4 Distribution of recorded pottery finds from the Power Station

Iron Age (that is from the twelfth to the eighth century BC). Later material is, however, also represented on the platform site; Roman sherds are recorded from Level 1 and the very real possibility of the downward movement of material is indicated by the single occurrence of a saltglazed sherd recorded at Level 3.

The contrast between the platform and the material deposited around the timber piles on the Power Station site appears to be one of both chronology and of depositional processes. Neither fabrics 6 or 7 are represented in the area of the piles. Fabrics 5 and 2 are relatively minor components in an assemblage where the dominant fabric is fabric 3. This hard fabric with fine shell filler appears to be Iron Age. The fabrics which are represented by the deposition of large vessel fragments on the platform, and seem to date to the Mid to Late Bronze Age, are but a residual component among the material from the Power Station site.

The depositional history of the Power Station assemblage also seems to vary. The earliest finds include Beaker sherds from an infilled pit (F87), part of a group of features (Fig 4.23) which had been dug at the end of the Bronze Age droveway formed by ditches 8 and 9. The distribution of some of the remaining material is given in Figure 9.4. This record appears incomplete and we have already noted that the distribution of the pottery is likely to have been skewed by the excavation procedures. At best, therefore, this distribution can only be treated at the simplest of levels. It shows the deposition of sherd material, with the occasional complete or near-complete vessel, on the surface of the buried soil in Area 1, on the line or to the south of the timber piles. This depositional activity certainly took place at the time the timbers and platform were constructed and remained in use, but continued well after and into the Iron Age.

Conclusion

The intermittent occupation of the platform at Flag Fen involved the use of a small number of vessels (jars and cups), some of which were abandoned on site. The date of the material on purely typological grounds would normally be assigned to the earliest part of the first millennium BC (Barrett 1980). This falls at the end of the date range provided by the dendrochronology of the timber structure itself. A small amount of activity on the peat surface, which inundated the timbers, is indicated by some later sherd material. Towards the dry land, and along the line of the timber piles, only a small amount of residual material of Middle or Late Bronze Age date is known, although this does include the deposition of a single complete Middle Bronze Age vessel (Fig 9.2, 1) within the timbers of Area 6B, Level 3. This vessel was found beneath a log (B1633) which had been pegged into position above it, and is almost certainly, therefore, *in situ*. The greater proportion of material from the Power Station would appear to be Iron Age in date.

It would therefore appear that, with the exception of the single complete Middle Bronze Age jar, the activities involved in depositing a great deal of the metalwork were unconnected with the deposition of pottery. The distributions of the two groups of material do not overlap nor is the main weight of Late Bronze Age metalwork reflected in the pottery chronology. The distribution of the pottery and the animal bone residues also fail to provide a close match. The general impression given by the pottery is that the peat surface could be occupied, at least at certain times during the Iron Age, when the timber structures appear to have been buried. That occupation might be connected with the fen-margin settlement at Cat's Water. Whether it involved the construction of hardstandings on the peat, which have since been lost, is unknown.

10 Metalwork

by David Coombs

This chapter will consider metalwork found at the Power Station and at Flag Fen. The catalogue, which follows directly, includes results of metal analyses carried out by Peter Northover. This is followed by discussions of the Late Bronze Age and Iron Age objects. The chapter continues with a report on metal analyses by B M Rohl and Peter Northover and concludes with two shorter reports, a metallographic examination of the socketed ferrous axehead by Vanessa Fell and Chris Salter and a discussion of eight Late Bronze Age weapons by Sue Bridgeford.

Catalogue

The catalogue describes all metalwork found at Flag Fen and the Power Station, with the exception of a few undated scraps and amorphous fragments. Full contextual details are given in Table 10.1. Unless otherwise indicated, the context for all objects is the Power Station, Area 1, buried soil. Some of these were recovered from the spoil heap, as noted in the relevant entries.

Fig 10.1

1 Complete rapier, bent with a sharp blade; some slight damage to the edges. Bronze colour in places, the rest has a green- or rust-coloured patina with corrosion products. Two rivet notches. The blade has prominent raised rounded central portion.
Width at end: 28.9mm; width at shoulders: 39.7mm

Analysis:

Fe	Co	Ni	Cu	Zn	As	Sb	Sn	Ag	Bi	Pb	Au	S
0.14	0.02	0.36	87.74	0.00	0.09	0.11	10.54	0.04	0.00	0.40	0.01	0.64

Metal analysis suggests Middle Bronze Age/Late Bronze Age I (Taunton/Penard Phase).

2 Bronze dirk or rapier in two pieces. The blade is bronze coloured with heavy corrosion products at the break. Traces of wear show on the blade edge at the break The blade is also bent just below the break. Trapezoidal-shaped hilt plate; this half is bronze coloured in places with heavy green patina and corrosion products. The hilt plate has a central nick in the top and two rivets with expanded heads. Both of the rivet holes are snagged. On one face, part of the outline of an omega-shaped hilt plate can be seen. Blade of oval cross-section.
Length: 257mm: width at shoulders: 34.55mm; length of rivet 1: 11.5mm; rivet 2: 12.5mm; diameter of rivet head 1: 6.5–5.6mm; rivet head 2: 7.2–5.8mm

Analysis:

Fe	Co	Ni	Cu	Zn	As	Sb	Sn	Ag	Bi	Pb	Au	S
0.03	0.02	0.38	87.44	0.00	0.39	0.11	11.54	0.02	0.01	0.05	0.00	0.01

Metal analysis suggests Middle Bronze Age/Late Bronze Age I (Taunton/Penard Phase).

3 Small bronze dirk, fairly complete with sharp edges, though the tip is now rounded. Green/rust patina with bronze showing through in places. Two rivet notches and central depression in the hilt. Blade bent and asymmetrical.
Length: 131.74mm; width of hilt: 29.55mm

Analysis:

Fe	Co	Ni	Cu	Zn	As	Sb	Sn	Ag	Bi	Pb	Au	S
0.04	0.01	0.07	89.20	0.01	0.00	0.01	10.31	0.02	0.05	0.00	0.27	0.02

Metal analysis suggests Middle Bronze Age/Late Bronze Age I (Taunton/Penard Phase).

Fig 10.2

4 Bronze sword of Wilburton type. Fairly complete, but with damage along the edge. The damage begins at the bottom of the ricasso. The edge seems to be bent over in one direction. Bronze coloured in places, but with green patina for the most part. The tang is slightly asymmetrical and bulges to one side. There are slots in the tang and shoulders. Some of the metal partly fills one of the slots in the tang (or is it bad casting and the metal was never cleaned out?). Curved ricasso. Flattened oval cross-section to the blade. Section seems to be more bulbous on one side than the other.
Weight: 755g; length: 572mm; hilt length: 96mm; blade length: 476mm; maximum width shoulders: 50mm; maximum width blade: 42mm; centre of gravity: 178mm below shoulders; turning moment: 13439cm gm about shoulders

Analysis:

Fe	Co	Ni	Cu	Zn	As	Sb	Sn	Ag	Bi	Pb	Au	S
0.00	0.02	0.21	61.60	0.01	0.00	0.99	9.49	0.35	0.02	27.00	0.12	0.18

Metal analysis suggests Late Bronze Age II (Wilburton Phase).

5 Ewart Park type sword. The hilt has snapped at the tang and the point is missing. Large areas are bronze coloured, there are also areas of green patina and corrosion products. The blade has an oval-shaped cross-section, still quite sharp in places. The sharpening grooves are clearly visible. The tang is flattish with single rivet holes. The slight depression on one side of the tang might represent the place of a second rivet hole never punched through. There is a peculiar circular blob of green patina in the rivet-hole line. Only a slightly curving ricasso. There are slightly drooping ears to the ricasso. The tang has probably been deliberately broken.
Weight: 440g; length: >475mm; hilt length: 101mm; blade length: >374mm; maximum width shoulders: 46mm; maximum width blade: 35mm; centre of gravity: >129mm below shoulders; turning moment: >5676cm gm about shoulders

Analysis:

Fe	Co	Ni	Cu	Zn	As	Sb	Sn	Ag	Bi	Pb	Au	S
0.00	0.00	0.12	84.40	0.00	0.92	0.23	11.39	0.11	0.03	2.67	0.10	0.02

Metal analysis suggests Late Bronze Age III (Ewart Park/Carp's Tongue Phase).

6 Bronze Ewart Park sword. The sword is now bent and broken and in two pieces. It is in a rather badly corroded state with a pitted blade and tang. In colour it is green, red,

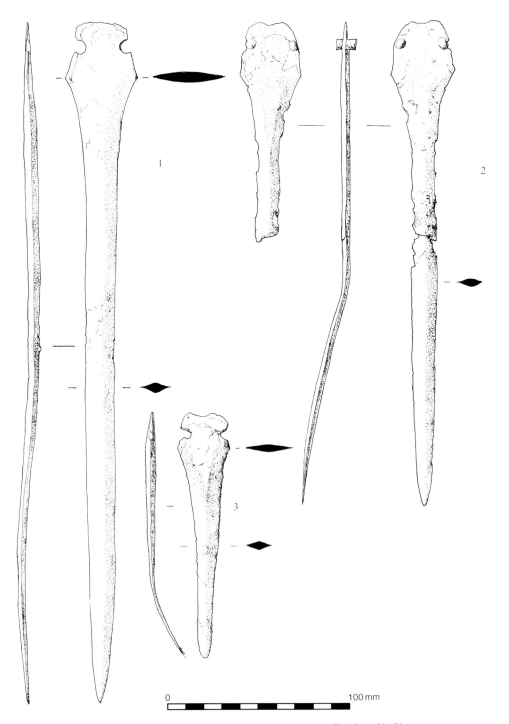

Fig 10.1 Dirks and rapiers from the Power Station (1–3)

and black in places. The point is still sharp, but the blade edges are badly damaged. In section, the blade is a flattened oval in shape, but towards the tip becomes a flattened lozenge. The tang is very narrow with well developed flanges. Two rivets remain in the tang and four in the shoulders. At first glance they appear to be set in individual rivet holes but are in fact set into rivet slots. There is no doubt that rivet slots were marked out in the mould and in places can be clearly seen in the casting. In some of the slots, however, there is also a solid metal filling that holds the rivets in place (were these slots not cleaned of waste metal and the rivet holes simply punched through them?). There is a curved ricasso and the sharpening grooves can be seen on the blade. The rivets are very thin, some of them are slightly bent over, and the heads are not expanded.

Weight: 660g; length: 619mm; hilt length: 100mm; blade length: 519mm; maximum width shoulders: 55mm; maximum width blade: >46mm; centre of gravity: 193mm below shoulders; turning moment: 12738cm gm about shoulders; diameter of rivets: 3.4mm, 3.4mm, 3.1mm, 3.2mm, 3.9mm, and 4.4mm

Analysis:
(At centre)

Fe	Co	Ni	Cu	Zn	As	Sb	Sn	Ag	Bi	Pb	Au	S
0.00	0.07	0.24	80.38	0.00	0.67	0.67	10.15	0.14	0.00	7.64	0.00	0.03

(Rivet)

Fe	Co	Ni	Cu	Zn	As	Sb	Sn	Ag	Bi	Pb	Au	S
0.00	0.02	0.10	64.29	0.02	0.37	0.32	5.96	0.09	0.03	28.72	0.07	0.01

Metal analysis suggests Late Bronze Age II (Wilburton Phase).

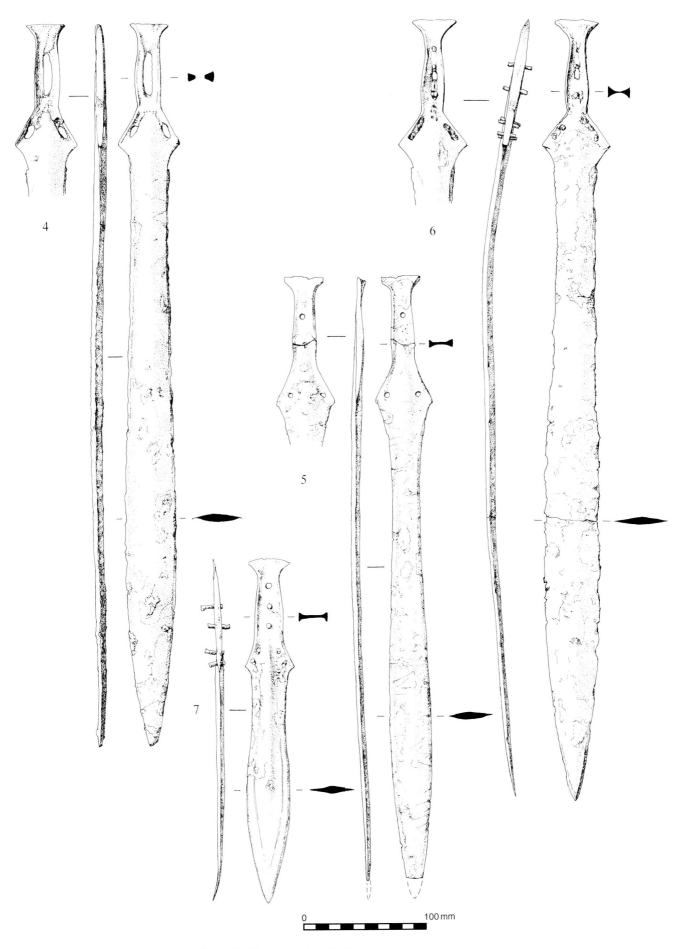

Fig 10.2 Late Bronze Age swords from the Power Station (4–7)

7   Miniature leaf-shaped sword. Large areas are bronze coloured, with small areas of patina and corrosion products. Four rivets still remain in the hilt and one is missing. Edges and tip of the blade are still very sharp. The tip is bent and so is the hilt. The tang has three rivet holes and developed shoulders. The tang widens towards the junction with the shoulders, which are narrow. There is a curved ricasso but the blade does not widen below it. There is quite a central swelling beginning between the upper two rivets on the shoulders and continuing onto the blade. The leaf blade is outlined by incised lines, beginning at the lower shoulder rivet holes. The upper part of the line has parallel horizontal short strokes punched into the grooves. The line becomes uneven towards the tip. The rivets have expanded ends. There are sharpening grooves.
Weight: 175g; length: 72mm; hilt length: 87mm; blade length: 185mm; maximum width shoulders: 40mm; maximum width blade: 35mm; centre of gravity: 45mm below shoulders; turning moment: 788cm gm about shoulders.
Length of rivets: 3.8mm, 3.8mm, 3.1mm, 3.6mm, 3.4mm, and 4.0mm

Analysis:

Fe	Co	Ni	Cu	Zn	As	Sb	Sn	Ag	Bi	Pb	Au	S
0.01	0.02	0.13	86.30	0.00	0.25	0.08	12.05	0.02	0.03	0.92	0.08	0.09

Metal analysis suggests Middle Bronze Age II/Late Bronze Age I (Taunton/Penard Phase).

Fig 10.3

8   Pointed rivet, complete, the point still sharp. Green patina, rough surface. Point has circular cross-section, subrectangular-sectioned shank.
Length: 3.97mm; diameter of centre: 7.46mm; diameter of shank: 5.88 × 6.36mm

9   Bronze pointed rivet. Dark green/black patina.
Length: 20.82mm; width at centre: 9.08mm; width of shank: 5.76mm

Analysis:

Fe	Co	Ni	Cu	Zn	As	Sb	Sn	Ag	Bi	Pb	Au	S
0.01	0.00	0.12	86.99	0.01	0.37	0.30	7.26	0.06	0.01	4.73	0.00	0.15

Metal analysis suggests Late Bronze Age III (Ewart Park/Carp's Tongue Phase).

10   Bronze pointed rivet. Dark green/rust patina. Circular shank expands into a pointed section with a distinct shoulder. The point is still sharp.
Length: 22.46mm; width at centre: 9.84mm; width of shank: 6.04mm

Analysis:

Fe	Co	Ni	Cu	Zn	As	Sb	Sn	Ag	Bi	Pb	Au	S
0.00	0.00	0.32	80.88	0.01	0.27	0.68	2.56	0.34	0.01	4.93	0.00	0.01

Metal analysis suggests Late Bronze Age II (Wilburton Phase).

11   Bronze pointed rivet. The point is slightly bent and the tip rounded. Grey/brown patina, with a rough surface. The shank is subrectangular in section. There is a slightly expanded end to the shank.
Length: 23.90mm; width at centre: 10.48mm; shank: 5.20 × 4.70mm

Analysis:

Fe	Co	Ni	Cu	Zn	As	Sb	Sn	Ag	Bi	Pb	Au	S
0.00	0.01	0.31	78.90	0.00	0.57	0.63	12.90	0.34	0.00	6.30	0.00	0.03

Metal analysis suggests Late Bronze Age II (Wilburton Phase).

12   Bronze pointed rivet. Dark green patina with traces of rust. Shank tends to be more rectangular than other examples.
Length: 30.74mm; width at centre: 7.93mm; shank: 4.60 and 5.07mm

Analysis:

Fe	Co	Ni	Cu	Zn	As	Sb	Sn	Ag	Bi	Pb	Au	S
0.01	0.01	0.11	90.40	0.00	0.78	0.29	6.99	0.08	0.03	1.23	0.04	0.03

Metal analysis suggests Late Bronze Age III (Ewart Park/Carp's Tongue Phase).

13   Bronze pointed rivet with tip of the spike missing. Green/black patina, with a very rough surface. The shank has a circular cross-section with traces of hammer marks.
Length: 23.89mm; width at centre: 10.8mm; diameter of shank: 4.92mm

Analysis:

Fe	Co	Ni	Cu	Zn	As	Sb	Sn	Ag	Bi	Pb	Au	S
0.03	0.02	0.11	89.53	0.01	0.14	0.26	6.60	0.08	0.00	3.13	0.00	0.09

Metal analysis suggests Late Bronze Age III (Ewart Park/Carp's Tongue Phase).

14   Bronze pointed rivet. The point is still sharp. Green/brown patina with a rough surface. The shank is slightly expanded at the end. Shank is hexagonal in cross-section.
Length: 24.31mm; width at centre: 9.99mm; width at the end of the shank: 4.99mm; length of point: 16.86mm

Analysis:

Fe	Co	Ni	Cu	Zn	As	Sb	Sn	Ag	Bi	Pb	Au	S
0.02	0.00	0.33	8.24	0.01	0.24	0.78	3.46	0.35	0.01	6.46	0.01	0.11

Metal analysis suggests Late Bronze Age II (Wilburton Phase).

15   Bronze pointed rivet. Dark green/light green patina, rough in places.
Length: 18.67mm; width at centre: 9.18mm; width of shank: 6.35mm

Analysis:

Fe	Co	Ni	Cu	Zn	As	Sb	Sn	Ag	Bi	Pb	Au	S
0.01	0.00	0.10	89.43	0.00	0.23	0.16	6.74	0.09	0.00	3.15	0.05	0.04

Metal analysis suggests Late Bronze Age III (Ewart Park/Carp's Tongue Phase).

16. Bronze pointed end from a rivet. The point is bent and most of the shank broken off. Dark green patina, part of surface rough.
Length: 14.56mm; shank: 3.91mm

17. Spike from possible pointed rivet, still sharp. Green/dark brown patina. Circular cross-section. Broken where it meets the rectangular shank.
Length: 25.97mm; diameter of shank: 7.68mm
Metal analysis suggests Late Bronze Age III (Ewart Park/Carp's Tongue Phase).

18. Bronze spike, possibly from a pointed rivet broken at one end (spoil heap).
Length: 24.1mm; diameter at break: 7.1mm

19. Bronze point. Green patina, rough surface. Point still sharp. Broken. Possibly fragment of a helmet rivet.
Length: 13.8mm; diameter: 4.8mm

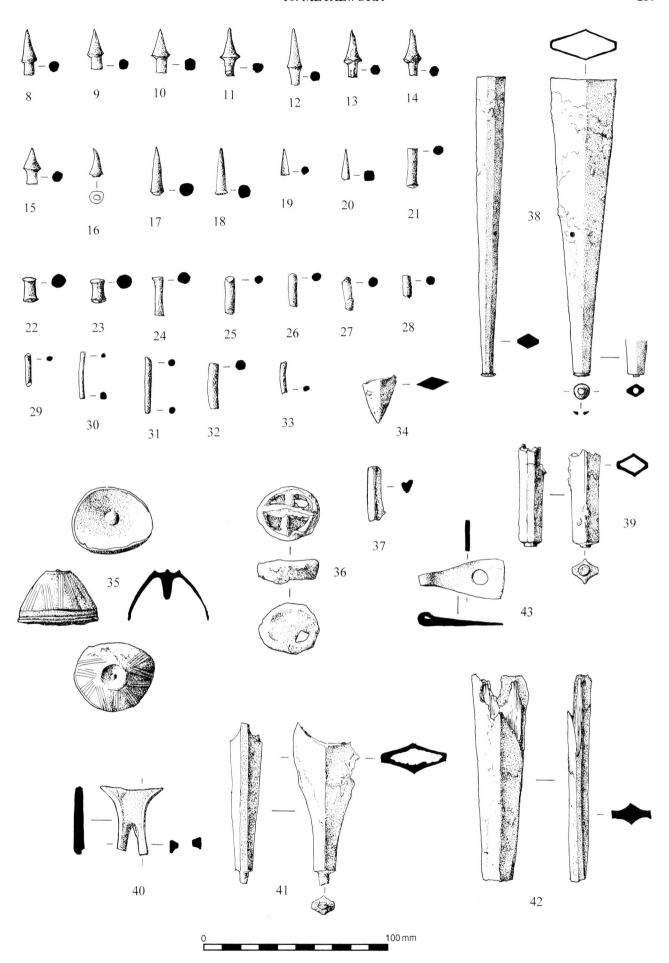

Fig 10.3 Rivets, pommels, chapes, and small items from the Power Station (8–43)

20. Bronze point, rectangular cross-section. Shank is broken off and point is still sharp. Green patina, rectangular cross-sectioned shank.
    Length: 16.90mm; diameter of shank: 4.20 × 4.93mm; diameter of point 5.10 × 5.17mm

21. Bronze rivet with slightly expanded head. Green/rust/black patina.
    Length: 21.13mm; width at ends: 7.92, 6.3mm; width of shank: 5.90mm

22. Bronze rivet with domed and expanded heads. Green patina with patches of bronze.
    Length: 13.72mm; diameter of ends: 7.52mm and 8.33mm; diameter of shank: 6.07mm

Analysis:

Fe	Co	Ni	Cu	Zn	As	Sb	Sn	Ag	Bi	Pb	Au	S
0.02	0.04	0.22	85.64	0.01	0.57	0.06	3.17	0.02	0.00	0.11	0.00	0.14

Metal analysis suggests Middle Bronze Age II/Late Bronze Age I (Taunton/Penard Phase).

23. Bronze rivet with expanded ends. Green/brown patina. Domed extremities to the rivet.
    Length: 13.48mm; diameter of ends: 8.96mm; 8.74mm; diameter of middle: 6.74mm

24. Bronze rivet. Bronze coloured with patched of green patina. Smooth in places. Expanded ends, one more than the other. Faceted body.
    Length: 21.1mm; diameter: 6.9 × 6.1mm

25. Bronze rivet, rough surface. Green/rust patina. Ends are cut at an angle.
    Length: 19.75mm; width at ends: 5.52mm, 5.47mm

26. Bronze rivet. Dark green patina with a rough surface.
    Maximum length: 16.74mm; diameter: 4.82mm

27. Bronze rivet, green/rust patina. Corrosion products have obscured details of the ends.
    Length: 18.11mm; width at ends: 6.43, 7.14mm; width of shank: 4.91mm

28. Cylindrical bronze rivet. Dark green patina with a rough surface.
    Maximum length: 16.74mm; diameter: 4.82mm

29. Bronze rivet, circular cross-section, slight hammering along the edges. Green/brown patina.
    Length: 17.09mm; diameter: 3.97mm

30. Bronze rivet. Bronze coloured with green patina, rough in small areas. Subrectangular cross-section. Narrower at the ends, which are almost circular.
    Length: 25.11mm; centre: 3.26 × 3.57mm

Analysis:

Fe	Co	Ni	Cu	Zn	As	Sb	Sn	Ag	Bi	Pb	Au	S
0.01	0.03	0.26	84.49	0.00	0.42	0.95	8.53	0.23	0.04	4.94	0.08	0.03

Metal analysis suggests Late Bronze Age II (Wilburton Phase)

31. Bronze peg, possibly a rivet. Green/rust coloured patina. Rough surface in places.
    Length: 29.71mm; diameter: 4mm

Analysis:

Fe	Co	Ni	Cu	Zn	As	Sb	Sn	Ag	Bi	Pb	Au	S
0.00	0.05	0.13	79.58	0.01	0.51	0.28	12.77	0.10	0.00	6.50	0.03	0.05

Metal analysis suggests Late Bronze Age III (Ewart Park/Carp's Tongue)

32. Bronze rivet. Green/rust patina with a rough surface. Has slight curve to it. Complete.
    Length: 24.4mm; diameter: 6.13mm

33. Small bronze shank, possibly a rivet. Dark green patina, rough surface in places.
    Length: 16.69mm; width: 3.78mm

34. Bronze tip from a sword blade. Green/dark brown patina. The tip, which is slightly bent, is still sharp and the edges appear undamaged. Sharpening grooves are still visible. Blade diamond shaped in cross-section.
    Maximum surviving length: 27.26mm; width at break: 19.89mm; maximum thickness: 6.12mm

Analysis:

Fe	Co	Ni	Cu	Zn	As	Sb	Sn	Ag	Bi	Pb	Au	S
0.02	0.02	0.09	90.44	0.01	0.05	0.01	9.20	0.01	0.01	0.06	0.00	0.04

Metal analysis suggests Middle Bronze Age II/Late Bronze Age I (Taunton/Penard Phase).

35. Pommel piece or terminal of cup shape. Bronze in colour with patches of light green/dark and rust-coloured patina. As the object is bent, it is difficult to determine whether it is oval or circular in shape, but probably oval. The object forms a terminal piece or a pommel. The top is dished and has a small central perforation. Decoration is executed in ribbed lines and is based on an arrow-shaped design with four vertical strips and three angled ones on either side. There are two horizontal grooves around the base. Internally there is a vertical projecting tang. The decoration is obscured in places and has been almost rubbed off.
    Diameter of cap: 44.13 × 34.73mm; height: 27.35mm

Analysis:

Fe	Co	Ni	Cu	Zn	As	Sb	Sn	Ag	Bi	Pb	Au	S
0.02	0.01	0.13	83.82	0.01	0.00	0.17	7.57	0.10	0.03	8.00	0.08	0.04

Metal analysis suggests Late Bronze Age III (Ewart Park/Carp's Tongue Phase).

36. Rough cast tin object. Oval-shaped cap-like object with central spine running down the long side and what appears to be two small rivets at right angles to it. There is a hole in one surface, presumably a casting defect. Tin-alloy pommel.
    Maximum dimensions: 34.02 × 28.37mm; thickness: 14.22mm

Analysis:

Fe	Co	Ni	Cu	Zn	As	Sb	Sn	Ag	Bi	Pb	Au	S
					99.00							

37. Fragment of sword hilt from slotted hilted sword. Bronze in places and with green patina
    Length: 29.22mm; thickness: 8.11mm

38. Tongue chape, complete with straight or very slightly concave opening. Corrosion products on the surface. Surface is multicoloured — green, reddish purple, and dark green. Single rivet hole in either face. Small projections at the base with separate washer. Wood in the socket (Fig 7.62, 8).

Length: 162.5mm; width at the top: 34.34mm; width at bottom: 8.83mm; thickness at top: 15.34mm; thickness at bottom: 6.75mm; thickness of metal: 1.08mm; diameter of washer (external): 8.78mm; diameter of washer (internal): 3.59mm

Analysis:

Fe	Co	Ni	Cu	Zn	As	Sb	Sn	Ag	Bi	Pb	Au	S
0.01	0.01	0.39	85.38	0.00	0.98	1.31	7.07	0.65	0.04	4.14	0.00	0.02

Metal analysis suggests Late Bronze Age II (Wilburton Phase).
Context: Flag Fen, Area 6B, Level 5

39. Tip from copper alloy lozenge-sectioned chape. Green/dark brown patina with lumps of corrosion products in places. Small circular projection on the tip.
Maximum surviving length: 51.62mm; width at top: 17.95mm; width at bottom: 14.55mm
Metal analysis suggests Late Bronze Age II (Wilburton Phase).

40. Fragment of sword hilt, from slotted hilt. Broken across the slot. Bronze coloured with patches of green patina. Slight flanges with pointed ears.
Width across the ears: 35.16mm; width at break: 17.17mm; thickness: 6.22mm

Analysis:

Fe	Co	Ni	Cu	Zn	As	Sb	Sn	Ag	Bi	Pb	Au	S
0.00	0.03	0.17	85.26	0.00	0.36	0.54	11.65	0.12	0.04	1.83	0.00	0.01

Metal analysis suggests Late Bronze Age II (Wilburton Phase).

41. Lozenge-sectioned tongue chape. Green/purple/black/brown patina. Patches of corrosion products in places. Broken at one of the top edges. Single rivet hole in one face only and a projection at the base.
Length: 85.86mm; width at mouth: 15.79mm; width at bottom: 12.07mm

Analysis:

Fe	Co	Ni	Cu	Zn	As	Sb	Sn	Ag	Bi	Pb	Au	S
0.00	0.03	0.15	79.50	0.02	0.27	0.49	6.88	0.16	0.02	12.35	0.00	0.15

Metal analysis suggests Late Bronze Age III (Ewart Park/Carp's Tongue Phase).

42. Bronze lozenge-sectioned chape broken at both ends. Traces of the wooden scabbard in the socket (Fig 7.62, 8).
Maximum surviving length: 110mm; width at top: 29mm; width at bottom: 16mm
Context: Flag Fen Area 6B, Level 4.

43. Bronze shield tab. Green/brown patina. Has a well made hole through the flat face and ill-formed hole at right angles to the main plane. There is no trace of wear in the small hole.
Length: 47.9mm; width at top: 7mm, bottom 19.6mm; thickness at top: 7.8mm, bottom 1.7mm

Analysis:

Fe	Co	Ni	Cu	Zn	As	Sb	Sn	Ag	Bi	Pb	Au	S
0.02	0.02	0.09	91.58	0.01	0.11	0.06	7.86	0.08	0.00	0.07	0.00	0.11

Metal analysis suggests Middle Bronze Age II/Late Bronze Age I Taunton/Penard Phase).

Fig 10.4

44. Bronze ferrule, found in two pieces. Green/brown patina with a rough surface. It has a rounded tip and no rivet holes. There is still wood in the socket (Fig 7.62, 4).
Diameter (external): 16.34mm; diameter (internal): 11.47mm; diameter of tip: 10.71mm; length: 332mm

Analysis:

Fe	Co	Ni	Cu	Zn	As	Sb	Sn	Ag	Bi	Pb	Au	S
0.02	0.01	0.06	91.97	0.00	0.05	0.07	4.66	0.04	0.01	3.06	0.00	0.12

Metal analysis suggests Late Bronze Age III (Ewart Park/Carp's Tongue Phase).

45. Bronze pointed tubular ferrule. Green/brown patina. The object is complete and there are traces of wood in the socket and wooden pegs are still in position (Fig 7.62, 3). Parts of the surface are rough. Wood from the socket produced a ^{14}C date of 2965±45 BP (OxA-5959).
Length: 104.16mm; diameter (external) at mouth: 17.44 × 18.19mm; diameter (internal) at mouth: 14.79 × 14.89mm

Analysis:

Fe	Co	Ni	Cu	Zn	As	Sb	Sn	Ag	Bi	Pb	Au	S
0.12	0.02	0.1	86.42	0.00	0.44	0.03	12.52	0.02	0.08	0.0	0.00	0.15

Metal analysis suggests Middle Bronze Age II/Late Bronze Age I (Taunton/Penard Phase).

46. Bronze spearhead. Has a green patina and rough surface. Bronze in small areas. Leaf shaped with two peg holes. The tip is still sharp but the blade edges have nicks. Traces of sharpening groove. Casting porous in places. Wooden shaft and pegs intact.
Weight: 97g; length: 157mm; blade length: 105mm; socket length: 52mm; maximum width blade: 38mm (70m from tip); socket diameter: 27.00mm (at end); socket diameter: 20.4mm (at blade join); socket wall thickness: 1.8–2.6mm

Analysis:

Fe	Co	Ni	Cu	Zn	As	Sb	Sn	Ag	Bi	Pb	Au	S
0.01	0.03	0.23	68.66	0.02	0.56	0.60	6.52	0.22	0.00	23.04	0.03	0.08

Metal analysis suggests Late Bronze Age III (Wilburton Phase).

47. Bronze socketed leaf-shaped spearhead. Dark green/light green/rust coloured patina. Traces of the wooden haft still remain in the socket and there is also a wooden peg. Slight damage to the point and along the edge.
Weight: 92g; length: 134mm; blade length: 79mm; socket length: 55mm; maximum width blade: 37mm (62mm from tip); socket diameter: 22.8mm (at end); socket diameter: 16.6 × 15.0mm (at blade join); socket wall thickness: 2.4–2.9mm

Analysis:

Fe	Co	Ni	Cu	Zn	As	Sb	Sn	Ag	Bi	Pb	Au	S
0.03	0.00	0.10	82.86	0.00	0.15	0.24	9.23	0.00	8.00	7.33	0.00	0.00

Metal analysis suggests Late Bronze Age III (Ewart Park/Carp's Tongue Phase).

48. Bronze basal-looped spearhead. Bronze/green/black/rust patina. Slightly bent towards the tip, which is still sharp. There is damage to the blade edges, which are still sharp. The casting webs were never removed and the loops still retain the waste metal. Remains of the wooden haft in the socket. There is a prominent raised central rib.
Length: 106.89mm; length of blade: 64.75mm; width of blade: 20.89mm; diameter of socket interior: 11.25mm; exterior: 14.60mm

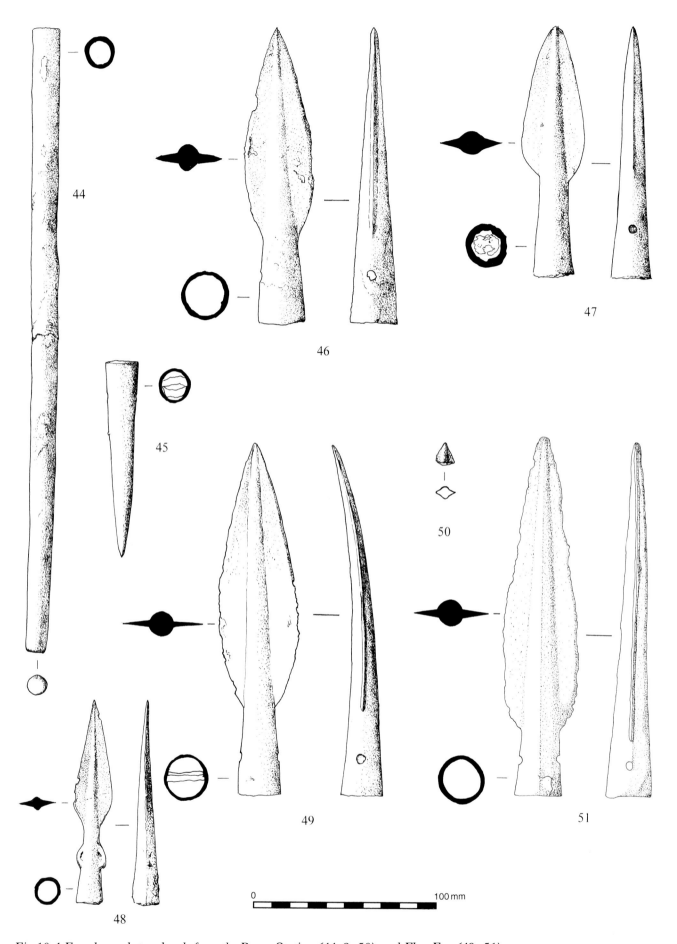

Fig 10.4 Ferrules and spearheads from the Power Station (44–8, 50) and Flag Fen (49, 51)

Analysis:

Fe	Co	Ni	Cu	Zn	As	Sb	Sn	Ag	Bi	Pb	Au	S
0.10	0.00	0.06	83.78	0.03	0.05	0.00	15.37	0.00	0.05	0.02	0.03	0.03

Metal analysis suggests Middle Bronze Age II/Late Bronze Age I (Taunton/Penard Phase).

49. Bronze leaf-shaped, pegged spearhead, bent. Blade edge is chipped especially towards the socket. The tip is fairly sharp. Slight traces of sharpening lines. Green patina with traces of red and black staining. Wood in socket and with wooden pegs.
    Weight: 135g; length: 188mm; blade length: 139mm; socket length: 49mm; maximum blade width: 45mm (100mm from tip); socket diameter: 24.4mm × 23.8mm (at end); socket diameter: 18.6 × 16.8mm (at blade join); socket wall thickness: 1.00mm–1.6mm

Analysis:

Fe	Co	Ni	Cu	Zn	As	Sb	Sn	Ag	Bi	Pb	Au	S
0.01	0.03	0.12	86.78	0.00	0.12	0.04	12.56	0.01	0.03	0.06	0.00	0.22

Metal analysis suggests Middle Bronze Age II/Late Bronze Age I (Taunton/Penard Phase).
Context: Flag Fen Area 6B, Level 4.

50. Tip from a bronze spearhead with raised central rib. Brown/green patina.
    Length: 12.69mm; width at break: 10.5mm; thickness at break: 5.75mm

51. Spearhead with leaf-shaped blade with rounded midrib and a slight ridge parallel to the edges. The socket has two peg holes. Remains of wood in the socket.
    Weight: 132g; length: 189mm; blade length: 156mm; socket length: 33mm; maximum width blade: >42mm (approx 118mm from tip); socket diameter: 26.2mm (at end); socket diameter: 22.4 × 21.8mm (at blade join); socket wall thickness: 1.8–2.8mm
    Context: Flag Fen Area 8, Level 2.

Fig 10.5

52. Badly broken knife or dagger, with the blade tip and the end of the tang missing. The tang tends towards a trilobate form with three rivet holes in a triangular configuration that still contains three rivets. The blade, which tends towards leaf shaped, is of lozenge cross-section.
    Maximum length: 194mm; width at shoulders: 31mm; blade width: 25mm

Analysis:

Fe	Co	Ni	Cu	Zn	As	Sb	Sn	Ag	Bi	Pb	Au	S
0.74	0.02	0.07	43.12	0.01	0.77	0.05	27.51	0.04	0.01	0.17	0.00	0.52

Metal analysis suggests Late Bronze Age IV (Llyn Fawr Phase).
Context: Flag Fen Area 6A, Level 5.

53. Knife/Dagger. Complete except for a missing tip. Bronze coloured in places, black in others. The flat tang is slightly bent to one side with a central vertical rib on either face. The possible line of the hilt can be seen in the patina on one face. The leaf blade has a rather flattened central portion. Sharpening grooves can be seen. The leaf blade has well defined shoulders.
    Width at end: 16.8mm; width at shoulders: 34mm

Analysis:

Fe	Co	Ni	Cu	Zn	As	Sb	Sn	Ag	Bi	Pb	Au	S
0.00	0.01	0.03	83.32	0.00	0.00	0.09	7.01	0.05	0.03	10.43	0.00	0.04

Metal analysis suggests Late Bronze Age III (Ewart Park/Carp's Tongue Phase).

54. Bronze dagger. Bronze shows through on both faces towards the tip, the rest is green/brown patina with corrosion products. The blade is bent and its edge is damaged in places. It has a rectangular tang, which has incurved edges and very slight flanges. There is a single rivet notch at the terminal. Oval cross-section to the blade and a convex end to the tang. The dagger was found with its antler handle (54a) and wooden fixings (Chapter 7). Length: 202mm; width at shoulders: 37.3mm; width at end of tang: 23.5mm

Analysis:

Fe	Co	Ni	Cu	Zn	As	Sb	Sn	Ag	Bi	Pb	Au	S
0.01	0.00	0.12	87.98	0.01	0.22	0.26	8.50	0.11	0.00	2.66	0.00	0.12

Metal analysis suggests Late Bronze Age III (Ewart Park/Carp's Tongue Phase).

55. Bronze dagger. A large area of it is bronze with patches of patina and corrosion products. The tip is still sharp but the blade edges are damaged. It has a rounded hilt plate, broken at the sides. Two clear rivet notches can be seen. The blade is of a rounded lozenge section.
    Length: 115.96mm; width at shoulder: 28.65mm

Analysis:

Fe	Co	Ni	Cu	Zn	As	Sb	Sn	Ag	Bi	Pb	Au	S
0.01	0.07	0.14	89.07	0.00	0.32	0.05	9.65	0.03	0.02	0.19	0.00	0.45

Metal analysis suggests Middle Bronze Age II/Late Bronze Age I (Taunton/Penard Phase).

56. Small, thick, flat bronze tanged knife with broken tang and point. Bronze/green/brown patina with some corrosion products. The edges still feel quite sharp. Remains of a rivet hole at break.
    Maximum length: 92.63mm; width at shoulders: 25.72mm

Analysis:

Fe	Co	Ni	Cu	Zn	As	Sb	Sn	Ag	Bi	Pb	Au	S
0.03	0.03	0.56	84.06	0.00	0.05	0.08	14.60	0.00	0.00	0.10	0.05	0.47

Metal analysis suggests Middle Bronze Age II/Late Bronze Age I (Taunton/Penard Phase).

57. Bronze gouge, complete. Bronze showing through towards the cutting edge. Green/dark brown patina with the surface heavily pitted in paces. There is a small hole in the groove. It has a slight trumpet-shaped mouth. The edge is still sharp and casting webs can be seen in the inside of the socket. Wood still in socket.
    Length: 79.5mm; width of cutting edge: 16.2mm; diameter of socket exterior: 18.9mm; diameter of socket interior: 15.2mm

Analysis:

Fe	Co	Ni	Cu	Zn	As	Sb	Sn	Ag	Bi	Pb	Au	S
0.08	0.01	0.07	91.37	0.02	0.05	0.09	7.04	0.07	0.00	1.22	0.00	0.02

Metal analysis suggests Late Bronze Age III (Ewart Park/Carp's Tongue Phase).
Wood from the socket produced a radiocarbon date of cal BC 1630±1420 (OxA-5960; 3230–45 BP).
Context: Power Station, Area 1, southern droveway ditch (8), upper primary filling.

58. Bronze flesh hook consisting of a single solid curved prong of triangular cross-section and a hollow socket with two rivet holes. There is a well defined collar

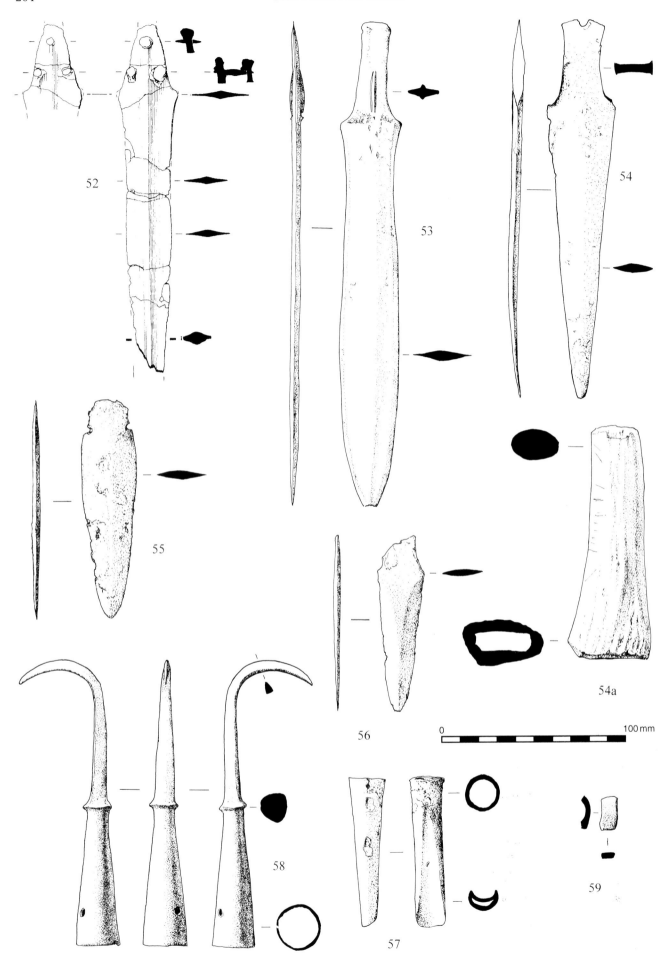

Fig 10.5 Daggers, knives, and other objects from the Power Station (53–7, 59) and Flag Fen (52, 58)

separating the prong from the socket. The tip of the prong is still very sharp and gives the impression that it had hardly being used. When discovered the object was a gleaming bronze colour. The flesh hook was found below a revetment timber of the earliest post row (1) and a date of 1300 BC or very slightly earlier is most probable (wood in socket; Fig 7.62, 6).
Length of socket: 73mm; diameter of socket: 25 × 25mm

Analysis:

Fe	Co	Ni	Cu	Zn	As	Sb	Sn	Ag	Bi	Pb	Au	S
0.01	0.04	0.12	86.47	0.01	0.40	0.03	12.70	0.02	0.03	0.13	0.00	0.02

Metal analysis places this object within Late Bronze Age I (Penard Phase).
Context: Flag Fen Area 6B, Level 6.

59. Small fragment of cast bronze, broken at both ends. Green patina. Probably a loop from a socketed axe.
Length: 17.66mm; thickness: 3.96mm; ends: 9.52mm, 9.28mm

Fig 10.6

60. Bronze socketed axe, green patina. Sides gradually expand to an expanded cutting edge, which is still sharp. There are four raised vertical ribs on one face and six on the other. Wood in the socket produced a radiocarbon date of cal BC 1000±810 (OxA-5976; 2740–45 BP).
Length: 112mm; width of blade: 53mm; mouth: 43 × 44mm

61. Fragment of copper alloy object classified as a razor, now in two pieces. Brown/green/red brown patina. There is a keyhole slot in the oval blade, which has part of the tang still surviving.
Maximum surviving length: 43.96mm; thickness: 0.72mm.

62. Bronze razor, green patina, smooth, with polished tang. Broken at the end. The central hole is present and it presumably had a slot. The edges of the blade are damaged. There is a well defined notch surviving on one edge, where the tang joins the blade.
Length: 74.01mm; width of blade: 24.05mm; thickness of blade: 1.91mm

63. Tanged bifid bronze razor. Green patina with patches of bronze showing through, smooth in places, in others rough. Edges damaged and chipped. On one face there are three converging ribs placed centrally above the tang. At the top of the blade is a slot leading to a perforation. Converging sides.
Maximum length: 83mm; maximum width: 36mm

Analysis:

Fe	Co	Ni	Cu	Zn	As	Sb	Sn	Ag	Bi	Pb	Au	S
0.06	0.01	0.25	88.78	0.00	0.50	0.47	8.13	0.31	0.01	1.41	0.01	0.04

Metal analysis suggests Late Bronze Age III (Ewart Park/Carp's Tongue Phase).

64. Complete bronze awl. Dark green/brown patina. In places it is rough with corrosion products. The point is still sharp. Unlike other awls, this one has a rectangular cross-section throughout apart from near the tip where it goes into a rounded section. The other end is a rounded chisel shape. It does not have the central swelling that can be seen on the other awls.

Length: 85.11mm; width at centre: 4.93mm; width at chisel end: 3.70mm

Analysis:

Fe	Co	Ni	Cu	Zn	As	Sb	Sn	Ag	Bi	Pb	Au	S
0.04	0.03	0.34	87.57	0.00	0.48	0.07	11.11	0.00	0.00	0.10	0.00	0.26

Metal analysis suggests Middle Bronze Age II/Late Bronze Age I Taunton/Penard Phase).

65. Bronze awl. One half is of rectangular section and terminates in a sharp chisel-like end. On one face it is rough and has light green patina. The other half is more circular, but has a series of facets running along the long sides. The point is still very sharp. Overall colour is dark bronze.
Length: 54.66mm; width at centre: 5.60mm; width of chisel edge: 4.29mm

Analysis:

Fe	Co	Ni	Cu	Zn	As	Sb	Sn	Ag	Bi	Pb	Au	S
0.01	0.01	0.19	86.25	0.01	0.42	0.61	9.65	0.34	0.03	1.21	0.01	0.02

Metal analysis suggests Late Bronze Age II (Wilburton Phase).

66. Bronze awl. Traces of green patina, but mostly dark brown. Pointed tip missing. For the most part is of rectangular cross-section with sharp, slightly damaged chisel-like end.
Length: 53.22mm; width at centre: 5.39mm

Analysis:

Fe	Co	Ni	Cu	Zn	As	Sb	Sn	Ag	Bi	Pb	Au	S
0.02	0.01	0.09	87.94	0.01	0.56	0.19	9.60	0.15	0.05	1.14	0.01	0.20

Metal analysis suggests Late Bronze Age III (Ewart Park/Carp's Tongue Phase).

67. Bronze awl. For the most part it is bronze coloured, although one face has heavy green patina. The tip is rounded rather than sharp. There is a clear distinction between the two halves.
Length: 52.7mm; width at shoulders: 5.14mm

Analysis:

Fe	Co	Ni	Cu	Zn	As	Sb	Sn	Ag	Bi	Pb	Au	S
0.00	0.02	0.14	87.52	0.00	0.85	0.36	7.68	0.21	0.06	3.15	0.0	0.02

Metal analysis suggests Late Bronze Age III (Ewart Park/Carp's Tongue Phase).

68. Bronze awl. Half is of rectangular section thinning out to a chisel end, the other merges to a circular section and pointed end. The rectangular-sectioned part has dark green patina, the other half is bronze coloured and smooth. The point is still sharp.
Length: 51.07mm; width at centre: 4.79mm

69. Bronze awl. Green/dark brown patina, rough surface. Pointed end smooth, rough surface on the rectangular-sectioned half. Pointed end is still sharp, the other end is chisel shaped.
Length: 43.60mm; width at centre: 4.83mm; width of chisel end: 3.03mm

Analysis:

Fe	Co	Ni	Cu	Zn	As	Sb	Sn	Ag	Bi	Pb	Au	S
0.01	0.03	0.07	87.46	0.00	0.11	0.19	10.42	0.20	0.00	1.22	0.12	0.07

Metal analysis suggests Late Bronze Age III (Ewart Park/Carp's Tongue Phase).

70. Bronze awl, which appears to be complete, although the point is rounded. One half is of rectangular cross-section with a chisel-like end, the other is rectangular with

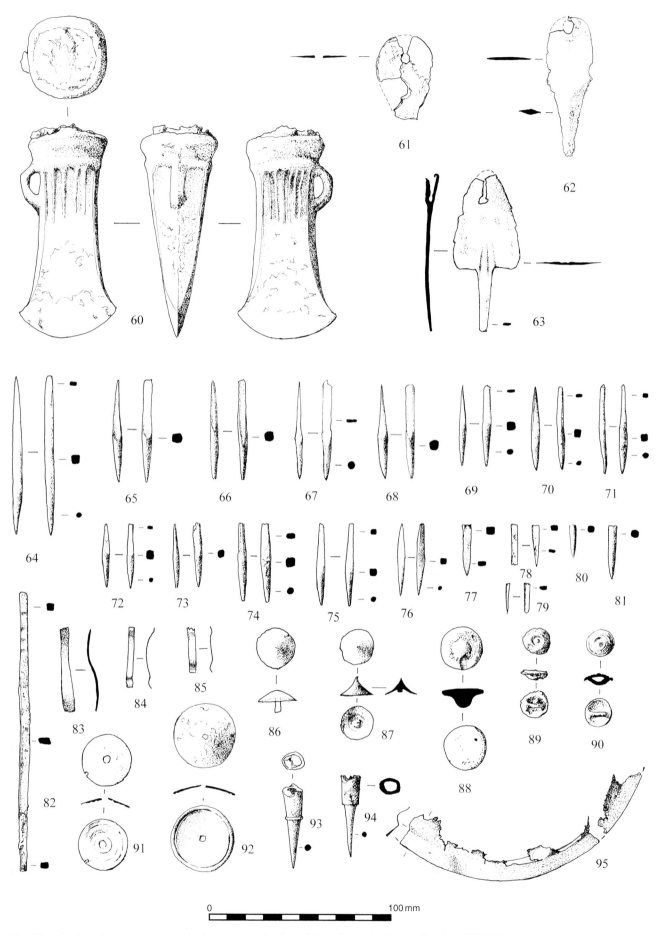

Fig 10.6 Socketed axe, razors, awls, buttons, and other objects from the Power Station (60–95)

a tip of circular cross-section. Green patina with slight traces of bronze.
Length: 44.47mm; width of chisel end: 2.94mm; width at centre: 3.45mm

Analysis:

Fe	Co	Ni	Cu	Zn	As	Sb	Sn	Ag	Bi	Pb	Au	S
0.02	0.01	0.22	86.27	0.01	0.10	0.46	9.99	0.23	0.05	2.56	0.08	0.03

Metal analysis suggests Late Bronze Age III (Ewart Park/Carp's Tongue Phase).

71. Bronze awl, green/brown patina with a badly corroded surface. Point is blunt. One half of rectangular cross-section, the other circular.
Length: 47.65mm; thickness at centre: 4.69mm; thickness at end: 2.74mm

Analysis:

Fe	Co	Ni	Cu	Zn	As	Sb	Sn	Ag	Bi	Pb	Au	S
0.01	0.00	0.33	86.08	0.00	0.55	1.01	6.58	0.44	0.04	4.80	0.08	0.08

Metal analysis suggests Late Bronze Age II (Wilburton Phase).

72. Bronze awl, broken at one end. The pointed end is complete and still sharp. Green patina with traces of darker patina. Broken at the end with a rectangular cross-section (from spoil heap).
Length: 34.80mm; width at centre: 4.53mm

Analysis:

Fe	Co	Ni	Cu	Zn	As	Sb	Sn	Ag	Bi	Pb	Au	S
0.00	0.04	0.32	85.55	0.00	0.58	1.04	8.39	?	0.04	3.74	0.00	0.06

Metal analysis suggests Late Bronze Age II (Wilburton Phase).

73. Bronze awl, broken at both ends. Green/brown patina. Half of rectangular cross-section, half rounded, with flat sides.
Length: 33.90mm; width at centre: 3.60mm

Analysis:

Fe	Co	Ni	Cu	Zn	As	Sb	Sn	Ag	Bi	Pb	Au	S
0.00	0.01	0.24	79.78	0.00	0.42	0.63	11.11	0.39	0.02	7.38	0.00	0.02

Metal analysis suggests Late Bronze Age II (Wilburton Phase).

74. Bronze awl broken at both ends. Green/rust coloured patina. Part of the surface is bubbly. Rectangular section in one half, circular in the other.
Length: 41.32mm; thickness at centre: 6.06mm

75. Bronze awl with one end broken. The other is a rounded point. Dark green patina with a rough surface. One half is of rectangular cross-section, the other circular. There is a swelling at the centre (from spoil heap).
Length: 44.13mm; width at centre: 4.96mm; width at broken end: 3.18mm

76. Bronze awl. Half of the object is of rectangular section, the other circular. The rectangular section is bronze with green patina, rough in places, the circular section is bronze and smooth. The pointed end is still quite sharp, the other end is chisel-like.
Length: 39.71mm; width at centre: 3.76mm

77. Bronze point, green patina. Largely rough surface but smooth on one face towards the tip. The tip is still sharp, slightly bent. Rectangular cross-section. Probably broken. Possibly the broken half of an awl.

Hammered and reworked into a point?
Length: 27.5mm; section: 5.1 × 4.6mm

Analysis:

Fe	Co	Ni	Cu	Zn	As	Sb	Sn	Ag	Bi	Pb	Au	S
0.00	0.01	0.12	90.31	0.00	0.11	0.19	8.04	0.09	0.04	1.06	0.01	0.04

Metal analysis suggests Late Bronze Age III (Ewart Park/Carp's Tongue Phase).

78. End of a bronze awl. Green patina and rough in places. Rectangular cross-section. The end terminates in three small prongs. Probably made deliberately rather than a casting flaw.
Length: 22.49mm; section: 3.47 × 3.78mm

79. Tang from awl. Green patina, rough surface in places. Rectangular section.
Length: 16.30mm; width of chisel end: 2.98mm

80. Pointed tip from a bronze awl, still sharp. Broken where the round cross-section merges into the rectangular. Green patina with a rough surface.
Length: 18.5mm; diameter of broken end: 3.60 × 3.48mm

81. Bronze point of an awl, broken at one end but still fairly sharp at the point, slightly bent. Circular cross-section. Green patina.
Length: 28.86mm; width at break: 4.98mm

82. Bronze rod, probably complete. Rectangular in cross-section and shape. Green/brown patina with patches of corrosion products.
Length: 148.16mm; section: 5.76 × 4.08mm

Analysis:

Fe	Co	Ni	Cu	Zn	As	Sb	Sn	Ag	Bi	Pb	Au	S
0.47	0.04	0.06	86.29	0.00	0.62	0.05	11.22	0.02	0.00	1.03	0.00	0.02

Metal analysis suggests Iron Age.

83. Bronze strip, broken at both ends. One end is wider than the other. Strip is bent. green/black patina.
Length: 45.24mm; width at ends: 6.30mm and 5.02mm; thickness: 0.90mm

84. Bronze strip, broken at both ends. Green patina, rough surface, with bronze showing through in places. Bent, the kink at the end is reminiscent of 227.
Length: 32.24mm; width: 3.70mm; thickness: 0.91mm

85. Fragment of thin bronze strip, broken at both ends. Green patina. The kink at the top is reminiscent of the top of a pair of bronze tweezers.
Length: 24.58mm; width: 4.01mm; thickness: 0.39mm

86. Bronze circular domed stud with central shank. Green/brown patina, rough surface. Shank is slightly expanded on the end.
Diameter of head: 21.39mm; thickness of the head: 1.78mm; length of shank + head: 11.63mm; diameter of shank: 3.76mm

87. Pointed bronze stud. Green patina and rough surface. The point is slightly bent. The shank on the reverse is missing, leaving only a stump.
Diameter: 18.8mm; height: 8.8mm; diameter of stump: 4.4mm; thickness of dome: 1.18mm

Analysis:

Fe	Co	Ni	Cu	Zn	As	Sb	Sn	Ag	Bi	Pb	Au	S
0.02	0.02	0.16	88.60	0.01	0.19	0.31	9.07	0.14	0.03	1.42	0.00	0.03

Metal analysis suggests Late Bronze Age III (Ewart Park/Carp's Tongue Phase).

88. Bronze disc. Green/black/rust patina with bronze in places. One surface is flat and smooth, the other is pitted. One surface has a central, rather rough projection, with crudely executed hole (which does not pass through) at right angles to it. A slight channel from the hole gives the appearance that the object had been cast onto a shank, which has become detached; alternatively, this represents the scar where the core had been.
Diameter of head: 23.70mm; thickness of head: 3.17mm

89. Small bronze button with flattened loop on the underside. Green patina with a rough surface. The shape of the button head tends towards oval. The button head has a small raised knob at its centre within a slight recess surrounded by a raised rib.
Diameter of button: 15.91 × 14.51mm; thickness: 1.54mm

90. Circular copper alloy button with semicircular loop on the reverse and green patina. In the centre of the upper face is a small raised knob set in a depression and surrounded by five concentric circular raised ribs, some of which are obscured in places.
Diameter of disc: 15.49mm; thickness: 1.36mm; thickness of loop: 2.60mm

91. Bronze circular disc with central perforation, concave shape. Under surface it is largely bronze coloured with patches of green patina. This surface is rough. Inner ?surface has some bronze colour but is largely heavy green patina. This surface also has holes in it. The inner surface is decorated with three concentric circular grooves around the perforation. The perforation is not perfectly circular and has jagged edges. The hole has not been cleaned out properly.
Diameter: 27.3mm; diameter of hole: 3.4mm; thickness: 0.9mm

92. Dished circular bronze disc with central rectangular perforation. The concave surface is rough, with patches of bronze colour and dark green–bluey green patina. Convex surface has an incised line (or is it cast?) just inside the edge and following the outline.
Diameter: 34.82mm; thickness: 1.05mm

Analysis:

Fe	Co	Ni	Cu	Zn	As	Sb	Sn	Ag	Bi	Pb	Au	S
0.22	0.04	0.07	88.47	0.02	0.42	0.01	9.71	0.03	0.03	0.79	0.02	0.14

Metal analysis suggests Iron Age.

93. Socketed spike. Green/brown patina, rough surface in places. Socket is broken and bent. Spike complete and still sharp and of circular cross-section. Distinct horizontal rib at junction of spike and socket.
Length: 46.59mm; length of spike: 27.63mm

Analysis:

Fe	Co	Ni	Cu	Zn	As	Sb	Sn	Ag	Bi	Pb	Au	S
0.01	0.01	0.15	89.31	0.00	0.05	0.37	8.11	0.16	0.00	1.80	0.00	0.11

Metal analysis suggests Late Bronze Age III (Ewart Park/Carp's Tongue Phase).

94. Socketed spike. Green patina with rough surface in places on the socket. Consists of a circular socket, broken and slightly flattened, and a solid spike of circular cross-section. The spike is slightly bent.
Length: 44.63mm; length of spike: 27.55mm

Analysis:

Fe	Co	Ni	Cu	Zn	As	Sb	Sn	Ag	Bi	Pb	Au	S
0.02	0.01	0.12	89.32	0.01	0.35	0.28	6.86	0.14	0.01	2.62	0.00	0.26

Metal analysis suggests Late Bronze Age III (Ewart Park/Carp's Tongue Phase).

95. Fragment of possible bronze bowl or helmet, out-turned rim or brim. Bent and broken. Bronze colour apart from small patches of green patina. Bent and broken.
Thickness of edge: 0.90mm; thickness of rest: 0.47mm

Analyses:

Fe	Co	Ni	Cu	Zn	As	Sb	Sn	Ag	Bi	Pb	Au	S
0.12	0.01	0.02	86.6	10.02	0.48	0.05	12.08	0.01	0.02	0.43	0.00	0.16
0.10	0.02	0.03	86.08	0.02	0.17	0.05	12.66	0.02	0.05	0.76	0.01	0.03

Metal analysis suggests Middle Bronze Age II/Late Bronze Age I (Taunton/Penard Phase).

Fig 10.7

96. Fragment of bronze, bronze coloured in places, green patina elsewhere. Possibly the edge of a socketed object. Shows a slight shoulder.
Length: 36.53mm; width: 8.60mm; thickness: 2.67mm

97. Bronze rod. Green/rust patina, rough surface, and rectangular cross-section.
Length: 25.00mm; width: 3.00mm; thickness: 2.00mm

98. Slightly curved strip of bronze with two small holes and the remains of two broken ones. Bronze coloured with small patches of green patina.
Length: 11.62mm; width: 4.79mm; thickness; 0.97mm

99. Small fragment of metal, one edge curved, the other slightly curved. Looks as if the curved edge is diverging in the corner. One face is decorated with two rows of minute punched dots. The other face has groups of horizontal rows of dots.
Length: 14.20mm; width: 4.16mm; thickness: 0.94mm

100. Half moon-shaped piece of tin alloy. Two flaps have been folded over on themselves with a swelling along the crease. It was possibly meant to be bent over a thin wire. Dark brown patina. When scratched on the edge it has a silvery colour.
Dimensions: 20.05 × 15.46mm; thickness: 1.68mm; thickness at crease: 3.41mm

Analysis:

Fe	Co	Ni	Cu	Zn	As	Sb	Sn	Ag	Bi	Pb	Au	S
0.01	0.01	0.03	0.33	0.00	0.00	0.00	99.32	0.00	0.00	0.27	0.04	0.00

Metal analysis suggests Late Bronze Age I/Late Bronze Age II (Penard/Wilburton Phases)

101. Bronze object, which appears to be complete: a tubular-shaped piece of metal of semicircular cross-section. Mostly bronze in colour with small areas of green patina. Largely smooth apart from a rough patch of green patina. The upper surface has three grooves at right angles to the long edge.
Length: 13.86mm; width: 8.24mm; thickness: 1.40mm

102. Small decorative piece of bronze, in the form of a segmented strip. Possibly broken at both ends; bronze coloured on one side, green patina on the other.
Length: 9.96mm; width: 4.31mm; thickness: 3.12mm

Analysis:

Fe	Co	Ni	Cu	Zn	As	Sb	Sn	Ag	Bi	Pb	Au	S
0.16	0.05	0.05	89.14	0.01	0.54	0.00	9.86	0.02	0.01	0.03	0.03	0.09

Metal analysis suggests Iron Age

103. Roughly rectangular (or truncated pyramidal) tin object with lobate corners and central perforation. Dark green/brown patina with a rough surface. The object is broken. Broken at the upper edge around the perforation.
Diameter: 16.03 × 13.88mm; depth of hole: 5.33mm; thickness: 8.43mm

Analysis:

Fe	Co	Ni	Cu	Zn	As	Sb	Sn	Ag	Bi	Pb	Au	S
0.04	0.02	0.00	0.20	0.00	0.00	0.00	99.35	0.00	0.00	0.34	0.00	0.04

Metal analysis suggests Late Bronze Age I/Late Bronze Age II (Penard/Wilburton Phases)

104. Small metal fragment with jagged edges. Black/rust coloured patina. Possibly bronze.
Length: 16.53mm; width: 4.86mm

105. Small piece of bronze, broken on three of its four edges. Dark brown patina. There is a slight curve to the extant edge. The cross-section is curved.
Length: 12.75mm; width: 6.57mm; thickness: 1.24mm

106. Amorphous scrap of bronze, dark green patina and rough surface.

107. Small rectangular piece of bronze strip. It could be part of 229. Broken at both ends. Green patina.
Length: 9.45mm; widths: 4.99mm and 4.63mm; thickness: 0.64mm

108. Fragment of bronze strip folded over, green patina, rough surface.
Dimensions: 15.8 × 8.8mm

109. Two fragments of bronze from the same object. It probably formed part of an openwork disc. Bronze on the decorated surface, green patina on the reverse. The decoration is rather crude with punched dots radiating from a circle with a central punched dot.
Thickness: 0.068mm

Analysis:

Fe	Co	Ni	Cu	Zn	As	Sb	Sn	Ag	Bi	Pb	Au	S
0.30	0.03	0.03	85.47	0.09	0.23	0.02	13.36	0.02	0.03	0.00	0.05	0.36

Metal analysis suggests Iron Age.

110. Small cylindrical object (lead?) with slightly dished ends (from spoil heap).
Dimensions: 6.89 × 5.63mm

111. Bronze rectangular object, bronze coloured, patches of green patina and corrosion products. Slightly bent. Two holes.
Dimensions: 17.05 × 11.14mm

112. Fragment of bronze, broken at both ends and one edge. Green patina with two areas of corrosion products. One edge is sharply angled.
Length: 21.11mm; width: 8.81mm; thickness: 0.75mm

113. Bronze fragment, broken around all its edges. Green patina. Shows a curved section. The convex face is smooth, the concave one rough. Cross-section of unequal thickness.
Length: 19.1mm; width: 10.5 × 6.4mm; thickness: 3mm and 1mm

114. Small fragment of metal (bronze?) with a rough surface. The piece is folded over on itself, broken on its edges. Green patina.
Dimensions: 7.46 × 11.10mm

115. Bronze object, broken at both ends. Green/brown patina. The metal is folded over on itself. Towards one end is a small rectangular perforation. Possibly the bow of a fibula?
Length: 23.98mm; width of expansion: 10.84mm; width at ends: 4.17 and 7.49mm; thickness: 1.54mm

116. Piece of metal, vaguely rectangular in shape. Black/rust-coloured patina. Iron?
Length: 22.78mm; width: 13.96mm

117. Piece of metal, vaguely rectangular in shape. Black/rust-coloured patina. Iron?
Length: 22.78mm; width: 13.96mm

118. Fragment of large copper-alloy ring of U-shaped cross-section. Green/black patina, rough surface. Material (clay?) still adhering to the inside. Remains of a possible oval-shaped hole along the outer edge. Binding strip?
Width: 9.03mm; thickness of metal: 1.66mm

Analysis:

Fe	Co	Ni	Cu	Zn	As	Sb	Sn	Ag	Bi	Pb	Au	S
0.02	0.00	0.02	76.85	0.00	0.00	0.04	17.00	0.01	0.03	5.96	0.01	0.06

Metal analysis suggests Late Iron Age/Romano-British.

119. Fragment of bronze with rough surfaces. Green/brown patina. Has one curved edge.
Length: 22.39mm; width: 6.34mm

120. Very small gold ring, slightly bent out of shape. Seems to be made up of three gold wires joined together. The three strands have been twisted and set with the central one standing slightly proud of the rest. The upper surface of the central one has been polished smooth. Remains of the twists can be seen in the sides. In one small area the strands appear to have been hammered flat.
Diameter (external): 11.94 × 11.17mm; diameter (internal): 9.67 × 9.38mm; thickness: 1.70mm

121. Flat strip of bronze coiled into a ring with overlapping ends. The ends are tapered. Green/brown patina with a rough surface.
Diameter (external): 22.61 × 20.30mm to 18.31 × 18.43mm; thickness: 1.14mm; width: 3.05mm

122. Fragment of cast ?bronze, green patina. Broken at both ends and bent. It bears the impression of twisted wire.
Diameter: 1.67mm

123. Circular bead in white metal. Biconical in section with four projections, one broken (from spoil heap).
Dimensions: 21.37 × 21.33mm; diameter of ring: 14.5 × 14.9mm; diameter (internal): 9.3 × 8.9mm; thickness: 6.1mm

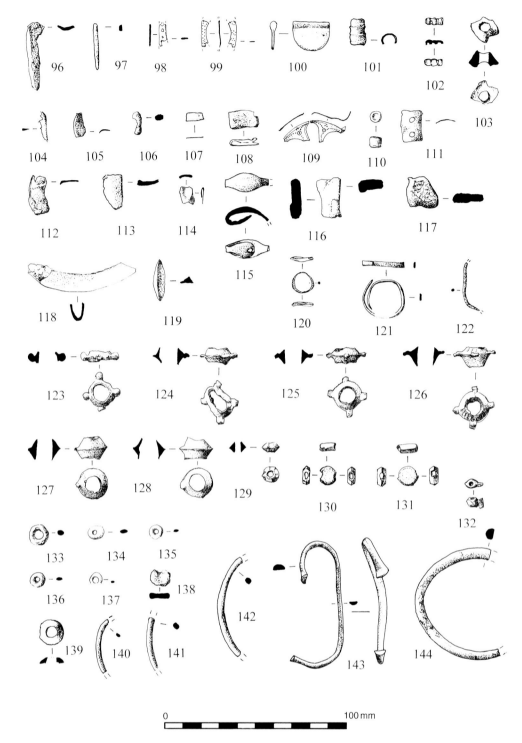

Fig 10.7 Beads, bracelets, and smaller objects in tin and copper alloy from the Power Station (96–144)

124. Circular tin bead with four projections. Bent out of
     shape.
     Maximum width: 8.2mm

Analysis:

Fe	Co	Ni	Cu	Zn	As	Sb	Sn	Ag	Bi	Pb	Au	S
0.01	0.01	0.00	0.09	0.01	0.00	0.00	99.83	0.00	0.02	0.01	0.00	0.01

125. Circular tin bead. Biconical in section with pronounced
     thin rib running around the edge in the centre. Four
     small equidistant projections. No traces of wear. Black
     patina.
     Dimensions across projections: 22.3 × 22.1mm; width:
     8.6mm; thickness: 3.2mm

Analysis:

Fe	Co	Ni	Cu	Zn	As	Sb	Sn	Ag	Bi	Pb	Au	S
0.03	0.00	0.00	0.20	0.01	0.55	0.00	99.16	0.00	0.00	0.03	0.00	0.01

126. Biconical tin bead, shiny black in colour. There are
     four projections but the raised rib and projections
     are not placed centrally on the section. Tapering
     hole.
     Diameter across the projections: 23.04 × 22.8mm;
     holes: 9.5 × 10.4mm; thickness: 3.9mm; width: 9.7mm

Analysis:

Fe	Co	Ni	Cu	Zn	As	Sb	Sn	Ag	Bi	Pb	Au	S
0.04	0.01	0.03	0.11	0.00	0.86	0.00	98.92	0.00	0.00	0.00	0.02	0.02

127. Biconical tin bead, shiny black in colour. No projections or traces of wear. Rough around the edges. Tapering hole. No visible signs that projections were ever present. Remains of a flash.
Diameter (external): 16.06mm; hole: 10.4 × 10.4mm to 9 × 9.2mm; width: 11.8mm; thickness 4.5mm

Analysis:

Fe	Co	Ni	Cu	Zn	As	Sb	Sn	Ag	Bi	Pb	Au	S
0.03	0.01	0.02	0.21	0.01	0.41	0.00	99.21	0.00	0.02	0.04	0.01	0.01

128. Biconical tin bead. There is one place on the perimeter where the projections might have been taken off. Hole tapers slightly. No real trace of wear.
Dimensions: 15.9 × 17.8mm; hole: 8.9 × 9.2mm to 10.8 × 10.1mm; width: 10.1mm; thickness: 4mm

Analysis:

Fe	Co	Ni	Cu	Zn	As	Sb	Sn	Ag	Bi	Pb	Au	S
0.01	0.01	0.01	0.16	0.03	0.00	0.00	99.70	0.00	0.05	0.02	0.00	0.00

129. Small biconical tin bead.
Diameter: 9.4mm; diameter of hole: 3.2mm; width: 5.3mm; thickness: 3.1mm

130. Bun-shaped bead with perforation in white metal. Damaged around one of the perforations.
Dimensions: 10.06 × 8.15mm; thickness: 4.9mm; oval perforation: 2.8 × 1.9mm

131. Object in white metal. Solid disc with casting flanges present. Oval perforation.
Dimensions: 10.74 × 11.6mm; thickness: 4.8mm; diameter of hole: 2.8 × 2.1mm

132. Tin object consisting of a cylinder with a perforation and a small projecting tab bent back upon itself.
Length: 9.2mm; width: 5.3mm

133. Small bronze ring. Green patina, rough surface.
Diameter (external): 11.44mm; diameter (internal): 4.62mm

134. Flattened disc bead in white metal (from spoil heap).
Dimensions: 9.7 × 7.6mm; thickness: 2.6mm

135. Flat disc tin bead, rough metal.
Dimensions: 7.8 × 8.1mm; diameter of hole: 2.2mm; thickness: 2.2mm

136. Flat ring in white metal. Asymmetrical and of flattened oval section.
Diameter: 7.9 × 8.2mm; diameter of hole: 2.5mm; thickness: 2.6mm

137. Small, oval-shaped piece of metal in white metal, with hole off-centre.
Dimensions: 6.99 × 6.58mm; diameter of hole: 2.98mm

138. Small fragment of metal, rough surface. Rust/green patina.
Dimensions: 10.90 × 9.06mm

139. Bronze ring. Green patina with a rough surface. More like a washer than anything else. Flat on one side, slightly curved on the other, with a central perforation.
Diameter: external: 13.43 × 12.74mm; diameter: internal 5.62mm; thickness: 2.73mm

140. Fragment of bronze bar, broken at both ends and bent. Green/brown patina, D-shaped section, thicker at one end than the other. Perhaps a bracelet fragment.
Length: 29.19mm; width: 4.06mm and 3.17mm

141. Fragment of curved bronze rod, thicker at one end than the other. Oval-shaped cross-section. Light green/dark green/rust-coloured patina. The surface is rough.
Length: 28.38mm; width at ends: 3.72, 2.89mm

142. Bronze bracelet fragment. Green/brown patina, rough surface. Flattened oval cross-section.
Width: 3.91mm; thickness 3.30mm

143. Bronze bracelet, complete but bent out of shape. Green patina. D-shaped cross-section with slightly expanded terminals.
Diameter of terminals: 7.44 and 6.33mm; thickness: 2.22mm; width: 4.02mm

Analysis:

Fe	Co	Ni	Cu	Zn	As	Sb	Sn	Ag	Bi	Pb	Au	S
0.08	0.13	0.13	82.17	0.00	0.92	0.18	11.37	0.08	0.09	5.89	0.00	0.08

Metal analysis suggests Late Bronze Age III (Ewart Park/Carp's Tongue Phase).

144. Bronze ring or bracelet in three pieces. One fragment is bronze coloured and smooth, the other two have bronze/green/black patina and are rough in places. The pieces have a D-shaped cross-section, with a flat underside. The pieces are of varying widths.
Narrowest width: 3.13mm; greatest width: 6.13mm

Analysis:

Fe	Co	Ni	Cu	Zn	As	Sb	Sn	Ag	Bi	Pb	Au	S
0.05	0.00	0.00	86.37	0.00	0.51	0.01	12.93	0.04	0.01	0.04	0.00	0.03

Metal analysis suggests Middle Bronze Age II/Late Bronze Age I (Taunton/Penard Phase).

Fig 10.8

145. Bronze fibula with faint ribbing on the bow. Part of the pin is still in place and the foot is badly corroded, with part of it missing. It can be identified as an Iron Age fibula of Langton type (Wheeler 1932, 71–4).
Length: 72mm; width of bow: 28mm
Context: Flag Fen Area 6B, Level 1

146. Bronze plate brooch. Bronze coloured in places with green/brown patina and an irregularly pitted surface. One end is larger than the other. On the reverse side is a central depression surrounded by a circle of dot-and-ring motifs. The same motifs, some faded or covered by corrosion products, follow the outlines of the ends of the brooch. The attachments for the pin (which is missing) are quite thick. On the upper side, the brooch has a flange running the entire edge. There is a central depression surrounded by two raised ribs (the depth suggests that it was meant to hold enamel or some other material). There are cup-shaped terminals to the extremities of the half-moon ends of the brooch.
Length: 76.84mm; width at ends: 41.57mm; 38.06mm; width at centre: 29.01mm; thickness: 5.22mm

Analysis:

Fe	Co	Ni	Cu	Zn	As	Sb	Sn	Ag	Bi	Pb	Au	S
0.28	0.02	0.01	87.89	0.00	0.28	0.03	10.20	0.02	0.04	0.20	0.01	0.05

Metal analysis suggests Late Iron Age/Romano-British.

147. Composite fibula of bronze and iron. The iron part is much corroded and bow shaped. Attached to it at right angles is a barrel-shaped piece of solid bronze. The ends are slightly constricted and there are parallel grooves running over half of one side. The other side is plain. There is an oblong perforation through the bronze piece in the centre.
Length: 31.9mm; length of bronze piece 18.3mm; diameter of bronze piece 5.4mm; diameter of hole: 2.5mm

148. Lead disc, bent at one edge. Grey in places where the lead shows through, brown skin on the rest.
Dimensions: 28.51 × 29.78mm; thickness: 4.33mm

149. Lead disc. Grey in colour.
Dimensions: 25.98 × 25.38mm; thickness: 5.38mm

150. Bronze arched fibula. Mostly bronze in colour with small areas of green patina and corrosion products. Fairly complete. The foot of the catchplate terminates in a circular disc with small central perforation. There is a small fantail projection that connects it to the bow (though not joined). The spring has four coils wound around a bar. On the top of the bow there is a deep recess following the arch of the bow, which has an inlay of tin, but only a small part survives.
Length: 47.9mm; width of spring: 14.58mm

Analysis:
(Bow)

Fe	Co	Ni	Cu	Zn	As	Sb	Sn	Ag	Bi	Pb	Au	S
0.04	0.02	0.02	89.78	0.00	0.22	0.01	9.69	0.02	0.02	0.15	0.00	0.02

(Inlay)

Fe	Co	Ni	Cu	Zn	As	Sb	Sn	Ag	Bi	Pb	Au	S
0.04	0.00	0.02	3.20	0.00	0.46	0.00	96.07	0.00	0.02	0.05	0.07	0.05

Metal analysis suggests Iron Age.

151. Small flattened cylindrical shaped piece of lead. Grey in colour.
Dimensions: 22.08 × 20.79mm; thickness: 14.95mm

152. Rectangular lump of lead with all faces slightly concave. Grey in colour.
Dimensions: 23.60 × 24.56mm; thickness: 12.19mm

153. Shield-shaped strapend with the metal folded over on itself. The profile at the fold is crenellated. One face is decorated with two horizontal lines of four round pellets, the rest obscured. On the other face are the lines of a faint herringbone pattern. The decoration is roughly executed. Dark green, smooth patina. Where scratched, it is a silvery colour. Could be tin or lead alloy.
Dimensions: 18.19mm × 17.49mm; thickness: 4.52mm

154. Model tin wheel. Now with black patina. There is a small central circle with four spokes linking it to an outer circle. The central area is dished. Casting flashes are still visible. The outer edge is decorated on both sides with small diagonal grooves. Cross-section of the outer circle is of diamond shape. The spokes and central circle have a flattened-oval cross-section.
Diameter of outer wheel: 23.14 × 24mm; diameter of centre: 9 × 8.5mm; diameter of hole: 3.5mm; width of edge: 3mm; thickness: 2.6mm

Analysis:

Fe	Co	Ni	Cu	Zn	As	Sb	Sn	Ag	Bi	Pb	Au	S
0.58	0.01	0.02	0.06	0.03	0.49	0.00	98.62	0.00	0.01	0.04	0.06	0.10

155. Lead roll.
Length: 18.34mm; maximum width: 10.07mm

156. Lead roll
Length: 14mm; maximum width: 11.13mm

157. Lead roll
Length: 32.8mm; maximum width: 11.8mm

158. Hollow pewter bag-shaped strapend. There are two small holes in three sides towards the top. Below one of the holes, internally, there is a small projection. Both faces are decorated in the same way. The decoration consists of two horizontal raised ribs at the top with two inverted Vs at either corner, a row of three dot-and-ring ornaments and two groups of inverted Vs. Casting web along the outer edge is clearly visible. The metal is slightly raised around the holes. Dark green/brown patina, smooth surface.
Length: 22.34mm; depth: 12.92mm; width: 5.36mm

Analysis:

Fe	Co	Ni	Cu	Zn	As	Sb	Sn	Ag	Bi	Pb	Au	S
0.00	0.01	0.00	0.23	0.00	0.00	0.00	57.09	0.00	0.01	42.64	0.02	0.00

159. Tin object, bent. It is of an oval shape with central cross. The arms of the cross have a triangular-shaped cross-section. The reverse of the object is flat. All around the outside edge are small teeth. There are two opposed projections at the ends of the arms of the cross. These are rectangular in shape. It appears to be complete.
Dimensions: 18.04 × 17.72mm

Analysis:

Fe	Co	Ni	Cu	Zn	As	Sb	Sn	Ag	Bi	Pb	Au	S
0.03	0.02	0.01	0.00	0.01	0.00	0.00	99.86	0.00	0.01	0.01	0.01	0.02

160. Lead roll
Length: 15.52mm; maximum width: 13.14mm

161. Lead roll
Length: 15.86mm; maximum width: 11.74mm

162. Lead roll
Length: 13.94mm; maximum width: 13.54mm

163. Bar of tin, of flattened oval section, broken at both ends. Dirty grey patina. There are some deep grooves in it at right angles to the long axis, these do not go all the way around and might be accidental.
Length: 21.5mm; width: 5.63mm

164. Trapezoidal tab in tin; silvery on one surface, tarnished on the other. Casting flashes not cleaned off from around the edges. Broken on the shortest side. Herringbone pattern on both faces, the central line prominent, the angled lines faint. Cast piece. Stress from the bend can be seen.
Maximum length: 18.65mm; width: 18.55 and 6mm; thickness: 1.28mm

Analysis:

Fe	Co	Ni	Cu	Zn	As	Sb	Sn	Ag	Bi	Pb	Au	S
0.00	0.01	0.01	1.73	0.00	1.97	0.00	96.07	0.00	0.07	0.13	0.00	0.00

165. Fragment of thin bronze, with no complete edges. Green/brown patina, shiny on one side.
Diameter: 15.8 × 14mm; thickness: 0.95mm

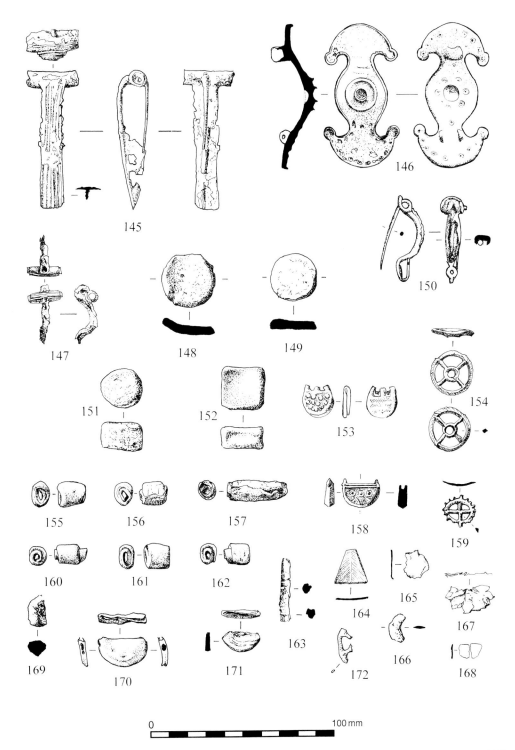

Fig 10.8 Iron Age brooches and objects in lead, tin, and copper alloy from the Power Station (146–72) and Flag Fen (145)

166. Curved fragment of white metal, crescent shaped with black patina and rough surface.
Length: 15.5mm; width: 6.9mm; thickness: 1.9mm

167. Fragment of thin foil, of crumpled white metal.
Thickness: 0.44mm

168. Two small fragments of grey-coloured tin that conjoin.
Dimensions: 12.42 × 7.25mm; thickness: 0.99mm

169. Metallic object, amorphous in shape. Rough surface, generally grey in colour. Silvery when scratched.
Length: 17.41mm; width: 9.78mm; thickness: 8.21mm

170. Could be part of the same object as 171. Flattened hollow disc in white metal, broken along the edge. It has two perforations on either side. Above the perforations the metal is recessed.
Dimensions: 27 × 15mm

171. Broken object in white metal. Hollow circular object, flattened.
Dimensions: 21 × 16mm

172. Fragment of tin object. Possibly part of a tin wheel with two spokes surviving, broken and bent.
Length: 18.9mm; width: 2.45mm; thickness: 1.9mm

Analysis:

Fe	Co	Ni	Cu	Zn	As	Sb	Sn	Ag	Bi	Pb	Au	S
0.02	0.00	0.00	0.80	0.00	0.14	0.00	74.29	0.00	0.01	24.72	0.01	0.00

Fig 10.9

173. Bronze pin with a flattened spherical head with midline horizontal groove. Tip missing and shank bent.
Diameter of head: 8mm; maximum surviving length: 105mm

Analysis:

Fe	Co	Ni	Cu	Zn	As	Sb	Sn	Ag	Bi	Pb	Au	S
2.43	0.03	0.09	48.37	0.01	0.42	0.05	20.17	0.05	0.05	0.35	0.06	0.57

Metal analysis suggests Middle Bronze Age II/Late Bronze Age I (Taunton/Penard Phases)
Context: Flag Fen Area 6B, Level 3

174. Pin with disc head. The shank is bent but the point is still sharp. Light green and dark green patina. Raised around the edge on the upper and lower face of the disc.
Diameter of the head: 11.99mm; thickness: of the head 4.50mm; length: 106.29mm; thickness of shaft: 3.35mm

Analysis:

Fe	Co	Ni	Cu	Zn	As	Sb	Sn	Ag	Bi	Pb	Au	S
0.00	0.03	0.28	82.84	0.00	1.44	0.72	8.08	0.25	0.02	6.21	0.02	0.09

Metal analysis suggests Late Bronze Age II (Wilburton Phase).

175. Bronze pin with small disc head (or nail headed). Dark green/black patina. Surface very rough. Most of the shank is missing. The top edge is slightly raised around the edge giving a dished appearance.
Length: 16.88mm; diameter of head: 10.78mm; diameter of shank: 3.06mm

176. Small disc-headed pin with the tip of the shank missing. Green patina. There is a distinct oblique cut into the shank near the head.
Diameter of head: 9.4mm

177. Bronze nail-headed pin, most of the shank is missing. Green patina with patches of rust.
Diameter of head: 8.12mm; diameter of shank: 2.30mm; length: 13.73mm

178. Small bronze pin head with most of the shank missing. Dark brown patina. Circular head with a central boss in a small depression.
Length: 12.43mm; diameter of head: 8.30mm; diameter of shank at break: 1.47mm

179. Bronze pin with the tip of the shank missing. Dull bronze in colour. The circular head has a central boss and the edge of the pin is slightly raised. The central boss stands proud above the top of the pin. The sides of the pin have two parallel grooves at the top and the bottom, leaving the centre in relief.
Length: 70.75mm; diameter of head: 8.98mm; thickness of the head: 2.57mm; thickness of shank at break: 2.28mm

Analysis:

Fe	Co	Ni	Cu	Zn	As	Sb	Sn	Ag	Bi	Pb	Au	S
0.01	0.04	0.22	85.68	0.00	0.62	1.19	9.46	0.43	0.08	2.29	0.0	0.02

Metal analysis suggests Late Bronze Age II (Wilburton Phase).

180. Bronze pin, tip of shank broken off, green/rust-coloured patina. Shank is bent below the head. Shank expands to a head. The head is a slightly concave circular dish with a raised small central boss.
Length: 47.83mm; head: 14.97mm; thickness of shank at break: 3.28mm

Analysis:

Fe	Co	Ni	Cu	Zn	As	Sb	Sn	Ag	Bi	Pb	Au	S
0.01	0.01	0.18	86.93	0.00	0.42	0.72	10.27	0.28	0.01	1.57	0.01	0.08

Metal analysis suggests Late Bronze Age II (Wilburton Phase).

181. Copper alloy ball-headed pin with broken shank. Bronze patina, but with bronze colour showing through in places on the shank and head.
Diameter of head: 13.95mm; diameter of shank: 5.35mm
Context: Flag Fen, Area 6B, Level 2.

182. Bronze pin. Bronze/green patina, surface is rough in places. The pin is knob headed with projecting horizontal ribs below. Below the head are faint traces of horizontal lines and below these are groups of parallel sloping lines giving the impression of a twisted stem.
Diameter of head: 6.68mm

Analysis:

Fe	Co	Ni	Cu	Zn	As	Sb	Sn	Ag	Bi	Pb	Au	S
0.05	0.05	0.32	86.48	0.01	0.49	0.95	9.27	0.41	0.02	1.90	0.02	0.02

Metal analysis suggests Late Bronze Age II (Wilburton Phase).

183. Bronze stud? Circular head and shank. Parts of the upper surface of the head are bronze with small patches of green patina The rest is green/rust-coloured patina. The upper surface of the head has small raised dot at the centre and a raised rib around the edge. The shank, which does not appear to have been broken, is tapering.
Diameter of head: 13.1mm; thickness of head: 1.8mm; length: 11.1mm; diameter of shank: 5.2 and 3.1mm

184. Nail-headed pin with the point missing. Dark green patina, corrosion products in places.
Width of head: 7.24mm; width of shank: 2.04mm; length: 26.49mm

185. Bronze nail-headed pin. The tip of the shank is broken. Metal is very rough. Light green/dark green/brown patina.
Length: 37.09mm; diameter of head: 5.84mm; diameter of shank: 2.37mm

186. Copper-alloy pin head with the shank missing. Green patina with bronze colour showing through in places. Turban-headed? pin. On the top is a central projection surrounded by multiple circular grooves on the outer edge of the head.
Maximum surviving length: 8.95mm; diameter of the head: 12.26mm

187. Head and part of the shank from a bronze ball-headed pin.
Diameter of head: 15mm; maximum surviving length: 43mm; width of shank: 5mm

Analysis:

Fe	Co	Ni	Cu	Zn	As	Sb	Sn	Ag	Bi	Pb	Au	S
0.62	0.01	0.03	86.85	0.00	0.21	0.01	12.73	0.02	0.00	0.14	0.00	0.04

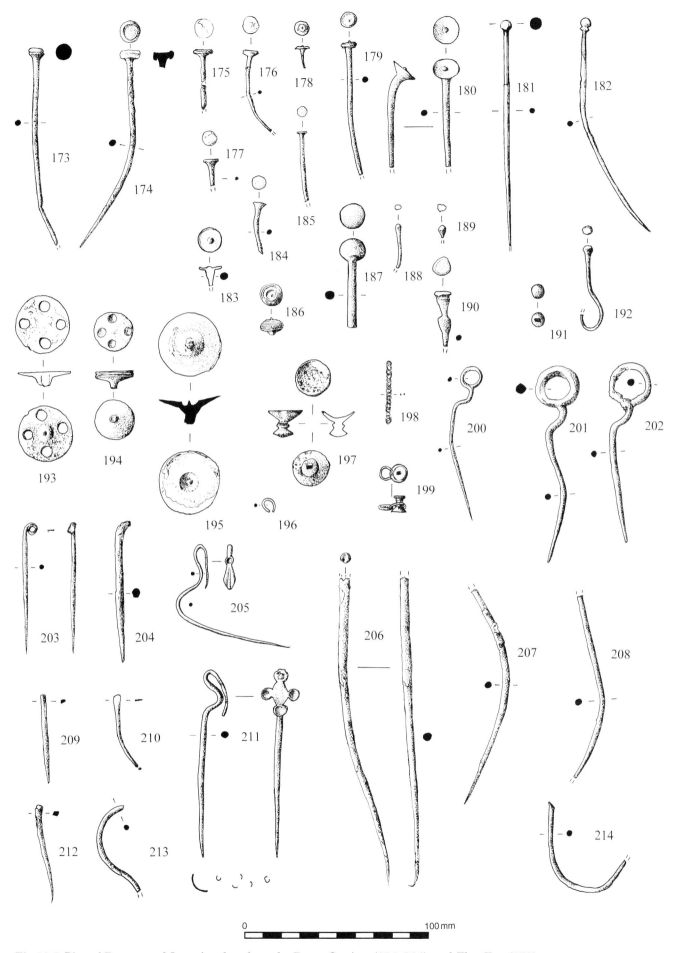

Fig 10.9 Pins of Bronze and Iron Age date from the Power Station (174–214) and Flag Fen (173)

Metal analysis suggests that the object belongs to Middle Bronze Age II/Late Bronze Age I (Taunton/Penard Phase).

188. Bronze pin, head swollen, rounded. Bent shank with part missing. Green patina, surface is rough.
Diameter of head: 3.81mm; diameter of shank: 2.08mm; length: 23.46mm

189. Very small blob of metal with green patina. Possibly a pin head but doubtful (from spoil heap).
Dimensions: 6.91 × 4.84mm

190. Bronze object, broken at one end at the shank. Circular nail head with swelling below it. The shank swells out again further down, then tapers again (from spoil heap)
Length: 30mm; diameter of head: 11.8mm

191. Bronze sphere, dirty brown in colour. Rectangular hole on the underside. Inside the hole is a very thin web of metal dividing the hole internally into two halves. Casting never cleaned out.
Diameter: 8.21mm; height: 7.30mm; hole: 3.47 × 2.08mm

192. Bronze pin, shank bent into a hook shape with tip missing. Green patina. The head is in the form of a small knob with a flat top.
Diameter of knob: 5.31mm

193. Bronze circular disc. Bronze/green/rust patina. Flat on one surface, the other has a central projection with a small central circular hole. The disc is perforated by four holes.
Diameter of disc: 29.26mm; thickness: 2.83mm at centre; at edge 1.77mm
Analysis:

Fe	Co	Ni	Cu	Zn	As	Sb	Sn	Ag	Bi	Pb	Au	S
0.01	0.07	0.11	91.72	0.01	0.16	0.05	5.63	0.04	0.03	2.20	0.02	0.06

Metal analysis suggests Late Bronze Age III (Ewart Park/Carp's Tongue Phase).

194. Possible pin head with the shank totally missing. Green/black patina with traces of bronze. The head consists of a circular disc. The upper face has four circular depressions.
Diameter: 20.75mm; thickness: 3.60mm; diameter of remains of shank: 4.13mm
Analysis:

Fe	Co	Ni	Cu	Zn	As	Sb	Sn	Ag	Bi	Pb	Au	S
0.06	0.02	0.09	79.02	0.00	1.23	0.20	15.86	0.04	0.05	3.31	0.00	0.12

Metal analysis suggests Late Bronze Age III (Ewart Park/Carp's Tongue Phase).

195. Possible head of pin. Only a short stub of the shank remains. Circular disc with central depression. In the middle of the depression is a short vertical point. Green patina, bronze showing around the edges. Bubbly surface in places.
Diameter: 33.38mm; diameter of shank: 6.79mm
Analysis:

Fe	Co	Ni	Cu	Zn	As	Sb	Sn	Ag	Bi	Pb	Au	S
0.28	0.01	0.09	83.56	0.00	0.29	0.03	11.21	0.04	0.03	4.27	0.00	0.19

Metal analysis suggests Late Bronze Age III (Ewart Park/Carp's Tongue Phase)

196. Broken link of fine bronze chain. Probably goes with 197 and 198 (note: object 196 is 1:1).

197. Head, dish shaped, below which are two swellings on a decorative pedestal. Underneath is a hole of rectangular section. Only slight areas of green patination. The rest is bright bronze in colour.
Diameter of head; 19.52mm; length: 12.47mm

198. Four major lengths of fine bronze chain. Made from bending small pieces of bronze. Links c 2.56mm across.

199. Bronze object. Green patina. It consists of a disc-shaped top on a pedestal with expanded base. There is a rectangular perforation through it. The pedestal has three horizontal ribs around it. Two links of a chain are still attached.
Length: 8.2mm; diameter: (top) 9 × 9.5mm, (bottom) 8mm; diameter: (top) 4 × 1.5mm, (bottom) 2.8 × 1.7mm

200. Bronze swan's-neck ring-headed pin, complete. The shank is bent; bronze coloured with patches of dark green patina. Made of bronze wire that has been bent round to form the ring head. The point is still sharp.
Diameter of ring head: 11.83mm exterior; diameter of ring head: 7.33mm interior
Analysis:

Fe	Co	Ni	Cu	Zn	As	Sb	Sn	Ag	Bi	Pb	Au	S
0.22	0.04	0.07	88.47	0.02	0.42	0.01	9.71	0.03	0.03	0.79	0.02	0.14

Metal analysis suggests Iron Age.

201. Swan's-neck ring-headed pin, with bent shank. Bronze-coloured small area on the ring head and a small area on the shank, the rest is dark green/light green/rust-coloured patina. The circular shank and head are chamfered.
Diameter of head: (external) 23.02mm, (internal) 13.01 × 11.54mm
Analysis:

Fe	Co	Ni	Cu	Zn	As	Sb	Sn	Ag	Bi	Pb	Au	S
0.13	0.01	0.05	89.56	0.00	0.05	0.02	9.80	0.03	0.05	0.24	0.00	0.04

Metal analysis suggests Iron Age

202. Complete bronze swan's-neck ring-headed pin. Shank bronze coloured, the top of the shank and ring head have corrosion products and green patina. The bronze has been bent over (ie not cast) to form the ring.
Length: 95.22mm; diameter of ring: (external) 24.18mm, (internal) 16.64mm; diameter of shank: 3.33mm
Analysis:

Fe	Co	Ni	Cu	Zn	As	Sb	Sn	Ag	Bi	Pb	Au	S
0.00	0.09	0.10	89.29	0.01	0.15	0.03	6.00	0.07	0.00	4.19	0.00	0.06

Metal analysis suggests Iron Age.

203. Complete bronze roll-headed pin, the shank is still sharp. Dark green/brown patina. Circular-sectioned shank with the end flattened and rolled over.
Length: 69.68mm
Analysis:

Fe	Co	Ni	Cu	Zn	As	Sb	Sn	Ag	Bi	Pb	Au	S
0.11	0.01	0.16	79.78	0.00	0.00	0.39	10.12	0.21	0.01	9.15	0.00	0.16

Metal analysis suggests Late Bronze Age III (Ewart Park/Carp's Tongue Phase).

204. Iron shank, broken at both ends and curving at thicker end. Difficult to know if bend was accidental or deliberate. Badly corroded, black/rust coloured.
Maximum length: 75.45mm; thickest part of the shank: 4.92mm

205. Bronze pin. Complete, the tip of the shank is still sharp. Circular shank (bent), but the head of the pin appears to be on the end of the swan's neck. The head is quite elaborate, consisting of a small cup surmounting a flattened-lozenge bronze tab with two incised vertical lines. Bronze coloured with dark green patina.
Length of head: 16.66mm; maximum width: 6.13mm

Analysis:

Fe	Co	Ni	Cu	Zn	As	Sb	Sn	Ag	Bi	Pb	Au	S
0.38	0.03	0.16	88.87	0.00	0.27	0.04	9.26	0.08	0.02	0.54	0.01	0.33

Metal analysis suggests Late Bronze Age IV (Llyn Fawr Phase).

206. Large shank from a pin with extremely sharp point, copper alloy. The lower two-thirds is bronze-coloured, the upper third has a black patina. At the top is a slight lenticular-shaped depression running across the shank.
Maximum diameter of shank: 5.37mm

Analysis:

Fe	Co	Ni	Cu	Zn	As	Sb	Sn	A	Bi	Pb	Au	S
0.02	0.03	0.16	88.96	0.01	0.44	0.03	10.16	0.00	0.05	0.08	0.00	0.06

Metal analysis suggests Middle Bronze Age II/Late Bronze Age I (Taunton/Penard Phase).

207. Copper-alloy pin shank, bent. The point is still very sharp. Green patina with corrosion products in places.
Maximum thickness: 3.78mm

208. Pin shank, broken at both ends with the edges of the break rounded. Dark green almost black patina with patches of lighter green and bronze in areas.
Diameter: 3.45mm

209. Fragment of bronze pin shank. Dark green and black patina. Surface is rough. The point is still quite sharp. Cross-section is rectangular, apart from the point, which is circular.
Length: 47.35mm; diameter: 3.73mm

210. Bronze shank with end flattened. Tip broken. Green patina.
Length: 39.65mm; diameter of shank: 3.73mm

211. Complete bronze pin. Green/black patina and bronze in places. Swan's neck at head of the pin terminating in an elaborate design. The head of the pin is a central oval shape surrounded by four cups, two of which are damaged with holes in them. Some small broken links of a chain are also associated, plus part of a larger loop.
Length: 100.03mm; dimensions of head: 25.91 × 19.76mm

Analysis:
(Inlays)

Fe	Co	Ni	Cu	Zn	As	Sb	Sn	Ag	Bi	Pb	Au	S
0.12	0.05	0.11	92.91	0.00	0.15	0.12	6.05	0.07	0.01	0.27	0.06	0.08

(Chain link)

Fe	Co	Ni	Cu	Zn	As	Sb	Sn	Ag	Bi	Pb	Au	S
0.30	0.03	0.02	74.00	0.01	0.11	0.00	24.56	0.00	0.00	0.45	0.01	0.50

Metal analysis suggests Late Bronze Age IV (Llyn Fawr Phase).

212. Tip from a bronze pin shank. Point is still sharp, green patina with a rough surface.
Length: 52.48mm; width: 3.81mm

213. Fragment of bronze shank. Bronze coloured with small patches of green patina. Circular cross-section
Width: 2.31mm; thickness: 2.41mm

214. Almost certainly a pin shank, broken at both ends. Green/dark brown patina. Bent and with a circular cross-section. The shank is thicker at one end than the other. Rough surface in places.
Thickness at each end: 3.49 and 2.59mm

Fig 10.10

215. Small bronze ring, cross-section of a flattened oval shape. Dark green patina.
Diameter (external): 10.8mm; diameter (internal): 6.51mm; thickness: 2.1mm

216. Small copper-alloy ring, dark green/black patina and corrosion products. Flattish oval cross-section.
Diameter (external): 13.79mm; diameter (internal): 11.14mm; thickness: 2.65mm

217. Misshapen bronze ring. Dark green patina. It is oval shaped and of unequal thickness, somewhat flattened and knobbly on one side, rounded on the other. A failed casting?
Diameter (external): 16.11 × 15.54mm; diameter (internal): 9.08 × 6.99mm

218. Small bronze ring, green patina, rough surface.
Diameter (external): 14.94mm; diameter (internal): 9.78mm

219. Small bronze ring. Oval rather than circular in shape and of circular cross-section. Light and dark green patina with small areas of bronze showing.
Diameter (external): 15.77 × 14.05mm
Thickness: 2.54mm

220. Bronze ring, slightly chamfered internal. Unequal thickness. Dark green patina.
Diameter (external): 17.36mm; diameter (internal): 11.93mm

221. Bronze ring. Green/black/rust patina. Slightly oval in shape.
Diameter (external): 21.34 × 20.04mm; diameter (internal): 15.77 × 14.90mm; thickness: 2.34mm

222. Bronze ring, green/rust patina with a rough surface. Diamond-shaped cross-section.
Maximum diameter (external): 25.09mm; maximum diameter (internal): 16.81mm

223. A bronze ring. This with 224 give the impression of being a pair. Dark green patina with some corrosion products. D-shaped cross-section.
Diameter (external): 20.38mm; diameter (internal): 10.69mm; thickness: 5.41mm

224. Dark green/black patina, bronze shows through in places. D-shaped cross-section.

Diameter: (external) 20.44mm, (internal) 12.05mm; thickness: 5.16mm

Analysis:

Fe	Co	Ni	Cu	Zn	As	Sb	Sn	Ag	Bi	Pb	Au	S
0.02	0.01	0.14	87.42	0.01	0.01	0.27	9.46	0.14	0.02	2.48	0.00	0.03

Metal analysis suggests Late Bronze Age III (Ewart Park/Carp's Tongue Phase).

225. Bronze penannular ring. Green patina, rough surface. It is slightly flattened and towards oval in shape. The two ends have been pressed close to each other.
Diameter (external): 25.07 × 22.29mm; diameter (internal): 18.31 × 16.40mm; thickness: 8.21mm

226. Bronze ring, rust-coloured patina with small patches of green patina. Circular cross-section.
Diameter (external): 26.24mm; diameter (internal): 19.70mm; thickness: 3.05mm

227. Bronze ring of unequal thickness and width, circular cross-section. Various shades of green patina and rough surface.
Diameter (external): 24.2mm; diameter (internal): 18.70mm; thickness: 3.2mm

228. Bronze ring, green patina, rough surface. Tending towards a lozenge-shaped cross-section but more rounded on the outer edge, sharper on inner one.
Diameter (external): 30mm; inner diameter: 17.8mm; thickness: 4.8mm

229. Bronze ring, dark green/light green/rust-coloured patina. Circular cross-section.
Diameter (external): 26.75mm; diameter (internal): 19.95mm

Analysis:

Fe	Co	Ni	Cu	Zn	As	Sb	Sn	Ag	Bi	Pb	Au	S
0.00	0.01	0.13	84.70	0.00	0.13	0.24	8.69	0.12	0.02	6.15	0.00	0.01

Metal analysis suggests Late Bronze Age III (Ewart Park/Carp's Tongue Phase).

230. Fragment of curved metal rod, possibly part of a ring, but rendered asymmetrical by breaking. Flattened-oval cross-section, thicker at one end. Metal rough, green patina.
Length: 28.75mm; thickness: 4.38mm; width: 3.29mm

231. Bronze ring, green/brown corrosion products on the surface. Of uneven thickness and chamfered internally
Diameter (external): 25.39 × 24.63mm; diameter (internal): 17.15 × 17.50mm

232. Bronze ring, dark green/brown patina with a rough surface. Circular cross-section, chamfered internally.
Diameter (external): 32.10mm; diameter (internal): 23.84mm

233. Bronze ring with a rough surface. Green/purple patina. In section it has a rounded outer edge and a sharp inner edge.
Diameter (external): 37.95mm; diameter (internal): 30mm; thickness: 4.36mm

234. Bronze ring. Green/brown patina. Tending towards circular cross-section. Width irregular.
Diameter (external): 44.07mm;diameter (internal): 34.1mm; maximum thickness: 5.42mm

235. Bronze penannular ring. Green patina with bronze in places and a rough surface. Slightly bent out of shape, it gives an oval appearance. Plain and with unexpanded ends.
Diameter (external): 28.93 × 25.90mm; diameter (internal): 24 × 21.5mm; thickness: 2.16mm

236 Fragment of a bronze ring. Dark green/light green patina with a rough surface and corrosion products. The ring is broken and is thinner at one end than the other. Oval cross-section.
Diameter at the ends: 3.3 × 4.6mm and 3.2 × 3.3mm

237. Copper-alloy ring, green/brown patina with a cross-section tending towards diamond shaped. The surface is rough.
Diameter (external): 43.92mm; diameter (internal): 35.35mm; thickness: 5.70mm

238. Fragment of bronze ring about half of which survives. Green patina and rough surface in places. Lozenge-shaped cross-section with the outer edge larger that the rest. Thickness: 5mm

239. Bronze ring. Light green/dark green patina, bronze in places. Smooth surface internally. Has raised central rib running around the exterior. Casting seam is visible on the interior.
Diameter (external): 29.28mm; diameter (internal): 221.82mm; thickness: 5.04mm

Analysis:

Fe	Co	Ni	Cu	Zn	As	Sb	Sn	Ag	Bi	Pb	Au	S
0.00	0.01	0.10	85.95	0.00	0.46	0.32	10.64	0.13	0.02	2.24	0.00	0.13

Metal analysis suggests Late Bronze Age III (Ewart Park/Carp's Tongue Phase).

240. Ring with green/dark brown patina with a rough surface. Diamond-shaped cross-section with a sharp-edged ridge running around the centre of the outer edge (from spoil heap).
Diameter (external): 24.30; diameter (internal): 16mm; thickness: 4.45mm

241. Bronze ring. Bronze in places, also with rust-coloured patina. D-shaped cross-section. Most of the object is smooth, especially in the interior. The outer edge has two grooves going all the way around.
Diameter (external): 29 × 27mm; diameter (internal): 20 × 20mm

Analysis:

Fe	Co	Ni	Cu	Zn	As	Sb	Sn	Ag	Bi	Pb	Au	S
0.09	0.01	0.05	83.38	0.01	0.05	0.06	16.29	0.00	0.02	0.03	0.00	0.04

Metal analysis suggests Middle Bronze Age II/Late Bronze Age I (Taunton/Penard Phase).

242. Bronze spiral ring. Brown colour throughout with small traces of green patina. It is formed from a bronze strip that has been wound around a circular core. Too big for a finger or toe ring and too small for a bracelet.
Diameter (external): 32.21mm; diameter (internal): 27.76mm; thickness: 2.51mm

Analysis:

Fe	Co	Ni	Cu	Zn	As	Sb	Sn	Ag	Bi	Pb	Au	S
0.30	0.01	0.04	88.48	0.02	0.56	0.12	9.92	0.17	0.02	0.39	0.01	0.08

Metal analysis suggests Iron Age.

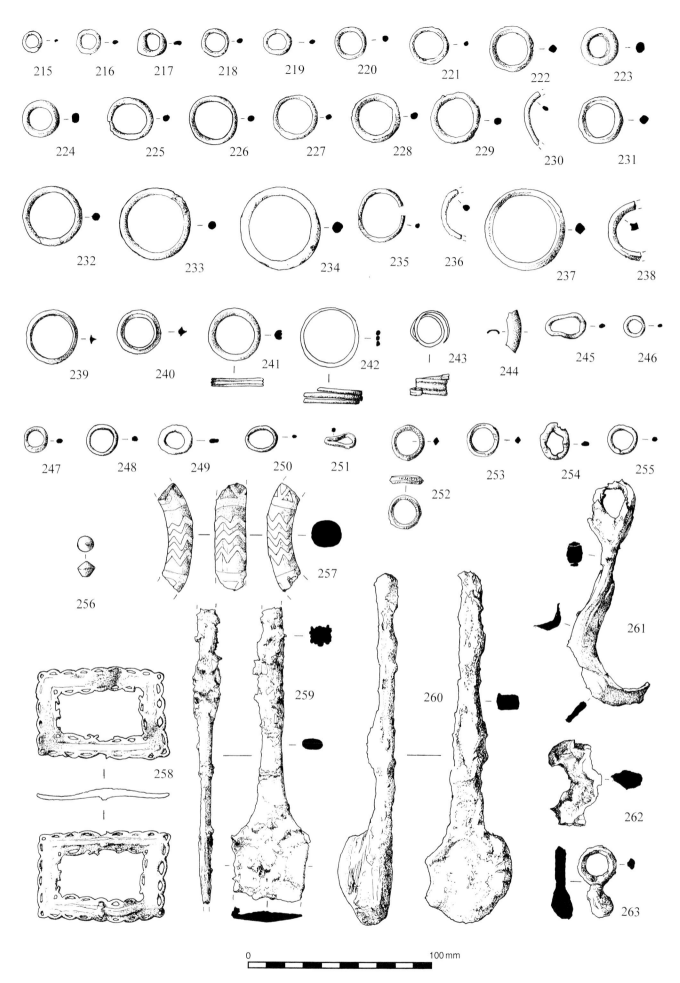

215 216 217 218 219 220 221 222 223

224 225 226 227 228 229 230 231

232 233 234 235 236 237 238

239 240 241 242 243 244 245 246

247 248 249 250 251 252 253 254 255

256 257 259 260 261

258 262 263

0   100 mm

Fig 10.10 Rings and miscellaneous objects of probable Bronze Age date (215–57) and Iron Age swords (259, 260), iron objects (261–3), and a modern shoe buckle (258), all from the Power Station

243. Bronze coiled ring made from a strip, wide at the centre and tapering to the edges. Bronze coloured in places, also green patina. Two grooved lines on the outer surface follow the outline and merge into one line near the terminals. The grooves have punched dots in them. Thickness: 9.06mm; width of terminals: 2.76mm, 2.59mm

Analysis:

Fe	Co	Ni	Cu	Zn	As	Sb	Sn	Ag	Bi	Pb	Au	S
0.11	0.11	0.03	86.25	0.02	0.10	0.09	12.42	0.02	0.00	0.83	0.00	0.02

Metal analysis suggests Iron Age.

244. Small fragment of a copper alloy ring of semicircular cross-section. Green/black patina. Width: 7.39mm; thickness: 1.18mm

245. Bent ring in white metal, rough surface.

246. Small tin ring with flattened-oval cross-section. The surface is pitted. Diameter (external): 11.9mm; diameter (internal): 1.31mm; thickness: 1.80mm

247. White metal ring with dark brown patina. Flattened-oval section of unequal thickness. Diameter (external): 14.03mm; diameter (internal): 8.15mm; thickness: 2.56mm

Analysis:

Fe	Co	Ni	Cu	Zn	As	Sb	Sn	Ag	Bi	Pb	Au	S
0.06	0.00	0.01	0.07	0.00	0.38	0.00	99.25	0.00	0.00	0.03	0.04	0.04

248. Slightly oval tin ring, black patina. Diameter (external): 18 × 16mm; diameter (internal): 12 × 12mm; thickness: c 2mm

249. Flat ring in white metal. Oval shape with an oval perforation. Surface of the metal is pitted. Diameter (external): 19.04 × 15.4mm; diameter (internal): 9.87 × 7.5mm; thickness: 2.5mm

250. Tin oval-shaped ring. Could have been bent out of shape. Rough surface and black patina. Diameter (external): 17.72 × 14.1mm; diameter (internal): 13.44 × 9.8mm; thickness: 1.8mm

251. Tin fragment, squashed ring. Dimensions: 17.63 × 8.64mm; thickness: 1.98mm

252. Tin ring with brown patina. The ring has a diamond-shaped cross-section and is decorated inside and out by two rows of short punch marks of various shapes. Diameter (external): 18.41mm; diameter (internal): 12.05mm; thickness: 4.13mm

Analysis:

Fe	Co	Ni	Cu	Zn	As	Sb	Sn	Ag	Bi	Pb	Au	S
0.06	0.01	0.00	0.44	0.06	0.00	0.00	99.35	0.00	0.01	0.03	0.03	0.01

253. Tin ring (with traces of iron and copper–X-ray fluorescence) Silvery appearance and black in places. Smooth, almost polished, in places. Has a diamond-shaped cross-section with short punched line decoration (internally and externally). Partly covered by corrosion products. Diameter (external): 18.21mm; diameter (internal): 12.22mm; thickness: 4.08mm

Analysis:

Fe	Co	Ni	Cu	Zn	As	Sb	Sn	Ag	Bi	Pb	Au	S
0.01	0.00	0.01	0.03	0.04	0.13	0.00	99.67	0.00	0.05	0.05	0.02	0.00

254. Flattened tin ring. Semicircular cross-section. Unequal thickness and width. Broken in one place. Diameter (external): 19.8mm; diameter (internal) 12.8mm; thickness 2.9mm

Analysis:

Fe	Co	Ni	Cu	Zn	As	Sb	Sn	Ag	Bi	Pb	Au	S
							99.00					

255. Tin ring of flattened oval section and a rough surface. Diameter (external): 16.5 × 16.02mm; diameter (internal): 9.7 × 10.43mm; thickness: 2.5mm

256. Small ?pyramidal-shaped pin head, shank missing. Green patina. Diameter: 9.61mm; height: 8.18mm

257. Fragment of a shale bracelet with a zigzag design executed in white metal (tin/lead?) inlay.

258. Pewter shoe buckle, bent and broken with an original central bar on the reverse. This is now missing although the ends are still visible. Tracery pattern internally and externally. Rectangular in shape. Modern (spoil heap). Dimensions: 71.89 × 46.59mm

259. Hilt of iron La Tène sword, badly corroded. Concretions adhering to the tang. The hilt has well defined shoulders. The tang is of rectangular cross-section. Width at shoulders: 42.67mm; width of blade at break: 38.20mm; length: 154mm; length of tang: 111.79mm

260. Iron hilt from a sword. It consists of the tang, shoulders, and a small portion of the blade. The tang is of rectangular cross-section and expands from the end to the shoulders. Below the shoulders a crescentic-shaped ricasso notch can be seen on one side. Traces of an omega-shaped hilt line can be seen in the corrosion products. The corrosion products obscure much of the detail of this sword. Maximum surviving length: 186mm; length of tang: 144mm

261. Iron hook, very corroded and with a flaking surface. There is a ring on one end. The hook piece is of concave cross-section. Diameter of ring (external): 23.9mm; diameter of ring (internal): 12.4 × 14.3mm; length: 120.8mm

262. Iron ring still covered in iron oxide concretions.

263. Iron ring-shaped object now in two pieces. Although heavily covered in corrosion products it can be seen that the ring is chamfered (faceted?) to produce a diamond cross-section. The piece was originally adhering to an amorphous lump of iron. Diameter (external): 22.79mm; diameter (internal): 11.03mm

Fig. 10.11

264. Iron ring, badly corroded with prominent lumps of corrosion. Circular cross-section. External thickness: 7.37mm

265. Bronze or iron object that has been subjected to heat. Surface is very rough, black, and very dark green in colour. Broken. Now consists of part of one horn and a

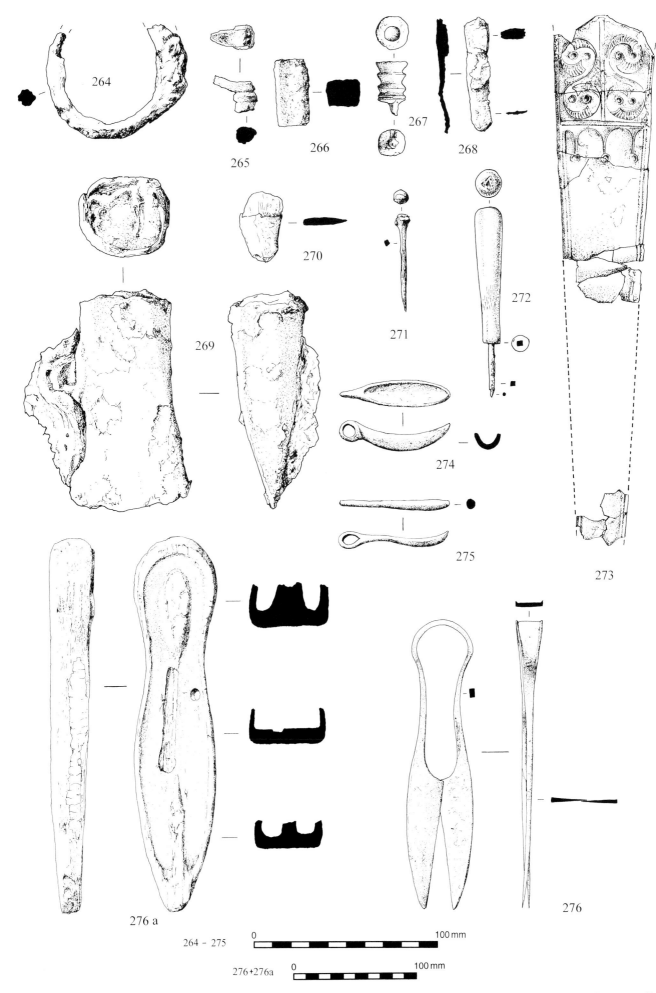

264

265

266

267

268

269

270

271

272

273

274

275

276 a

264 – 275

276+276a

0   100 mm

0   100 mm

276

Fig 10.11 Miscellaneous objects, mainly of Iron Age date, from the Power Station (264–72, 274–76a) and copper-alloy scabbard mount from Flag Fen (273)

short stem with an expanded portion at the top of the stem. Underneath there appears to be a small circular depression.

266. Iron rod of sub-rectangular section, dark patina with a rough surface.
Dimensions:37.4 × 16 × 19.8mm

267. Ribbed solid cylinder of iron with a broken tang. On the top of the cylinder is a central, small depression lined with a copper alloy.
Maximum surviving length: 28.17mm; diameter of top of cylinder: 17.47mm; diameter of bottom of cylinder: 14.41mm

268. Iron strip, badly rusted and corroded, the surface flaking off. Not identifiable.
Length: 60.43mm; width: 12.45mm; thickness: 6.12mm

269. Looped socketed axe in iron. Much iron corrosion.
Length: 116mm; blade width: 66mm;diameter (external): 50 × 42mm

270. Hollow iron object, fragile and corroded, broken at both ends and rust coloured. The extant edges taper. Metal has been folded over. Thinner at one edge than the other.

271. Iron nail with the point still sharp. Rectangular shank with an oval-shaped head. Head part obscured by corrosion products.
Length: 51.6mm; diameter of head: 8.3 × 9.02mm

272. Bone-handled awl. The awl is of iron and has a rectangular cross-section with stepped circular tip. Bone handle probably polished with wear. Small hole in the end of the handle suggests it was lathe turned.
Length: 102mm; length of handle: 73.22mm; length of point: 28.82mm; diameter of handle:14.2mm (top), 10.6mm (bottom); diameter of point: 3.5 × 3.3mm

273. Copper-alloy scabbard mount for short sword. Conserved, but still in a very fragile and broken state (Coombs and Pryor 1994). The larger part of it consist of a mouth portion with smaller fragments of the body. For the most part it has a dark green, shiny patina, but where this has flaked off, a light green powdery surface shows. Enough survives of the top edge to show that it had slight concave shoulders of a type well represented in the Iron Age. The side edges are clearly converging and, with the extant pieces of the body, it can be reconstructed as of triangular shape, maximum length *c* 473mm and 1mm thick.
The mount is elaborately decorated with shallow incised lines. The upper panel is divided into two areas by two vertical lines with two horizontal lines forming its bottom edge. The side border is defined by single lines. Below the two horizontal lines the edges of the mount are outlined in double lines.
On the upper panel, on either side of the vertical division, are two panels of fold over symmetrical decoration, consisting of S-shaped scroll designs, ultimately derived from dragon pairs. Within the roundels are faint indications of rocked tracer hatching. Each of the roundels has two small depressions outlined by raised lines.

Below this pattern the decoration consists of arcading, terminating in small circles.
Dimensions of large fragment: maximum length: 154mm; maximum width: 55mm; thickness: 1mm
Context: Flag Fen Area 6D, Level 1

274. Bronze boat-shaped mortar. Loop on the end (from spoil heap). Goes with 275.
Dimensions: 61.2 × 14.3mm

275. Bronze pestle. Reflects the shape of the mortar but shallower. Ring on end (from spoil heap).
Length: 60.6mm; width: 5.5mm

Analysis:

Fe	Co	Ni	Cu	Zn	As	Sb	Sn	Ag	Bi	Pb	Au	S
0.07	0.01	0.21	97.98	0.00	0.00	0.16	1.35	0.07	0.06	0.07	0.00	0.02

Metal analysis suggests Late Iron Age/Romano-British.

276. Bronze shears, complete and with little sign of wear (found on spoil heap). Made from one piece of metal, the blades are still sharp and the object is still usable. They are of a uniform green patina. The shears were found with their wooden box or shoe, which had been carved to fit the shears.

276a. The slot at the bottom of the box would have accommodated the whetstone. The shears would have been held in place by a retaining pin. The fabrication of the box is described by Maisie Taylor in Chapter 7.
Maximum length: 227mm; length of cutting edges: 101mm

Analysis:

Fe	Co	Ni	Cu	Zn	As	Sb	Sn	Ag	Bi	Pb	Au	S
0.11	0.10	0.06	90.61	0.01	0.19	0.01	9.65	0.02	0.02	0.20	0.04	0.00

Metal analysis suggests Iron Age.

Not illustrated
Several lumps of iron, including fragments of sword blade encased in concretions, were also found in the buried soil at the Power Station.

Discussion: Bronze Age

Objects associated with warfare: swords, chapes, spearheads, ferrules, and shield tab

The weaponry from Flag Fen and the Power Station belongs to the Middle and Late Bronze Ages and includes types well known in Europe. In their definitive study of dirks and rapiers, Burgess and Gerloff (1981) adopted the 'purely arbitrary figure of 30cm to divide dirks from rapiers on the basis that those shorter than this can generally have been used for stabbing'. On this basis object 2 (Fig 10.1) would be described as a dirk. As the authors stated, however, this was a purely arbitrary figure. The blade of flat mid section would seem to place it within the general category of their Group IV weapons.

As the weapon is damaged, any attempt to find close parallels would be useless and difficult. Group IV weapons comprise more that half the British and Irish rapier finds. Within the group, Gerloff and Burgess were able to distinguish an earlier group from a later one.

The latter have smaller butts than the earlier ones, while the rivet holes or notches tend to be set lower down in the butt, at the sides rather than in the corners. This they termed the Appleby tradition. The dating should be Penard Phase (Late Bronze Age I). The metal analysis places it in the Taunton/Penard Phase (Middle Bronze Age III/Late Bronze Age I).

The well developed trapezoidal hilt on the rapier (Fig 10.1, 1), with notches placed lower down, would seem to exclude this weapon from Burgess and Gerloff 's Group II and the lack of the triple arris cross-section would also exclude it from Group III. Its general home would appear to be somewhere within Group IV weapons, though it lacks the typical flattened centre to the cross-section. The metal analysis places it in the Taunton/Penard Phase.

The short weapon (Fig 10.1, 3), is either a rapier that has been cut down and refashioned or a very small complete weapon. The flattened centre to the blade is barely visible, due to the corrosion products. With such a cross-section, it can be placed in the Group IV category, with its various subclasses of notched rapiers. The metal analysis places it in the Taunton/Penard Phase. In Great Britain and Ireland, the late rapiers are found overwhelmingly in rivers and wet places.

Swords

From a detailed analysis of the swords, Bridgeford classified the Wilburton sword (Fig 10.2, 4) as belonging to the 'G' Variant of Burgess and Colquhoun (1988, pl 36, 224–9; pl 37, 230–3). These swords appear to lie at the end of the typological development of Wilburton swords, as shown by their presence in the Isleham hoard, Cambridgeshire (Britton 1960), and the Blackmoor hoard, Hampshire (Colquhoun 1979). The latter is accompanied by a series of radiocarbon dates that place it late in the sequence of Wilburton type hoards (cal BC 1030–900: OxA-5186; 2840±40 BP/cal BC 1260–830: OxA-5184; 2830±65 BP/cal BC 1040–820: OxA-5185; 2770±50 BP). Unlike other Wilburton sword variants, 'G' type has a widespread distribution.

The other two swords (Fig 10.2, 5, and 6) are of Ewart Park type, the commonest Late Bronze Age type and dated to Late Bronze Age III (Burgess and Colquhoun, 1988). This sword type has a widespread distribution (see Bridgeford below).

Bridgeford notes below that the miniature sword (Fig 10.2, 7), seems to be composed of a Ewart Park hilt, with an incised blade more reminiscent of other types of swords (Wilburton and Saint Nazaire types). The weapon was cast as a miniature sword and was not refashioned from a broken weapon. A number of weapons from Spain are much smaller than the norm, although none is as short as the Power Station weapon (Cameselle 1988, lam. XVI, 3; XXII, 1; Ruiz-Gálvez-Priego, 1984 fig 14, 1–4). There appears to be nothing comparable with this sword in the sword series from the British Isles (Eogan 1965; Burgess and Colquhoun 1988).

Pommel

The tin sword pommel (Fig 10.3, 36) is directly comparable to one from the Tosson, Simonside hoard (Burgess and Colquhoun 1988, pl 175, 6 and 7), found with two swords and a second lead pommel (the swords are Northern Step 1 of the Ewart Park series of Burgess and Colquhoun). There is also a similar lead pommel from Runnymede Bridge, Surrey (Needham and Hook 1988). Although pommels are extremely rare, their general form can be gauged from the pommel ends on solid hilted swords and unclassified Caledonian ones (Burgess and Colquhoun 1988 pl 3, 17–19).

Swords, especially those of the Wilburton type, are accompanied by tongue chapes. These objects are very much a feature of the Atlantic Late Bronze Age, being found especially in France, and occasionally in Spain and the Low Countries (Briard 1965; Coombs 1988). Flag Fen produced two chapes, one complete (Fig 10.3, 38), the other broken at both ends (Fig 10.3, 42). The Power Station also produced the end of a chape (Fig 10.3, 39) and a fairly complete example (Fig 10.3, 41). In 1972 three main types of tongue chape were identified (Burgess et al 1972):

A   Long tongue chapes, ranging in length from 255 to 380mm. They are found on both sides of the Channel during Late Bronze Age II (Eogan 1964, 288–93; Briard 1965, 177–9; Burgess 1968a, 9–17, 36–7).

B   Short tongue chapes of Stogursey type. These have a more squat appearance than A and are only 120–80mm in length. They first appear in late Wilburton hoards but are more characteristic of the following phase.

C   Diminutive type, average length 50–80mm. Some of these have a baggy appearance with a deeply concave mouth and markedly ogival sides. B and C are similar and differ only in size. The example from the Power Station (41) is very similar to that from the Broadness, Kent, find, from the River Thames (Burgess et al 1972, fig 14.44). The complete example from Flag Fen (38) belongs to type A, despite its length (160mm). The straight mouth opening is more common on French examples than English ones. The broken example from Flag Fen (42) would also seem to belong here.

Cambridgeshire, with the two large hoards from Wilburton and Isleham (which contain many examples of such chapes), appears to have been one of the main centres for their manufacture, although the only moulds known are from Dainton, Devon (Needham 1980), and Fimber, Yorkshire (Burgess 1968b, fig 21, a–g).

A number of tongue chapes have been found in rivers, especially the Thames. The end of a chape was found at the waterlogged site of Caldicot, Gwent (Briggs 1991, fig 8).

Table 10.1 List of metalwork finds from Flag Fen and the Power Station

Abbreviations: FF, Flag Fen; PS, Power Station; BS, buried soil; SH, spoil heap

this report no	archive prefix code	archive no	site	area	context	grid	this report no	archive prefix code	archive no	site	area	context	grid
1	met no	137	PS	1	BS	1902 9033	59	met no	264	PS	1	BS	1835 9045
2	met no	84	PS	1	BS	1883 9032	60	met no	93	PS	1	BS	1929 9033
3	met no	228	PS	1	BS	1938 9842	61	met no	13	PS	1	BS	1900 9046
4	met no	147	PS	1	BS	1871 9028	62	met no	23	PS	1	BS	1864 9064
5	met no	203	PS	1	BS	1868 9022	63	met no	105	PS	1	BS	1896 9029
5	met no	204	PS	1	BS	1968 9023	64	met no	278	PS	1	BS	1962 9013
6	met no	1	PS	1	BS	1974 9014	65	met no	209	PS	1	BS	1859 9024
7	met no	281	PS	1	BS	1882 9014	66	met no	190	PS	1	BS	1858 9033
8	met no	223	PS	1	BS	1855 9027	67	met no	87	PS	1	BS	1935 9019
9	met no	170	PS	1	BS	not noted	68	met no	172	PS	1	BS	not noted
10	met no	167	PS	1	BS	1863 9038	69	met no	224	PS	1	BS	1855 9028
11	met no	280	PS	1	BS	1976 9020	70	met no	213	PS	1	BS	1892 9029
12	met no	188	PS	1	BS	1850 9037	71	met no	262	PS	1	BS	1838 9028
13	met no	275	PS	1	BS	1976 9021	72	met no	258	PS	1	SH	1837 9016
14	met no	296	PS	1	BS	1976 9021	73	met no	210	PS	1	BS	1858 9024
15	met no	168	PS	1	BS	1362 9028	74	met no	211	PS	1	BS	1869 9030
16	met no	186	PS	1	BS	1850 9034	75	no met no	–	PS	1	SH	not noted
17	met no	218	PS	1	BS	1859 9022	76	met no	166	PS	1	BS	1864 9029
18	no met no	–	PS	1	SH	not noted	77	met no	109	PS	1	BS	1879 9030
19	met no	114	PS	1	BS	1872 9037	78	met no	279	PS	1	BS	1970 9023
20	met no	221	PS	1	BS	1851 9022	79	met no	225	PS	1	BS	1850 9029
21	met no	157	PS	1	BS	1869 9029	80	met no	44	PS	1	BS	1954 9023
22	met no	140	PS	1	BS	1903 9031	81	met no	276	PS	1	BS	1964 9011
23	met no	290	PS	1	BS	1900 9036	82	met no	284	PS	1	BS	1960 9075
24	met no	110	PS	1	BS	1873 9029	83	met no	217	PS	1	BS	1860 9020
25	met no	163	PS	1	BS	1865 9033	84	met no	229	PS	1	BS	1860 9033
26	no met no	–	PS	1	SH	not noted	85	met no	227	PS	1	BS	1846 9026
27	met no	158	PS	1	BS	1870 9028	86	met no	291	PS	1	BS	1900 9036
28	met no	148	PS	1	BS	1875 9028	87	met no	85	PS	1	BS	1883 9032
29	met no	232	PS	1	BS	1872 9020	88	met no	206	PS	1	BS	1863 9022
30	met no	230	PS	1	BS	1864 9025	89	met no	297	PS	1	BS	1884 9015
31	met no	216	PS	1	BS	1858 9026	90	met no	7	PS	1	BS	1023 9034
32	met no	86	PS	1	BS	1881 9026	91	met no	96	PS	1	BS	1917 9026
33	met no	185	PS	1	BS	1853 9032	92	met no	131	PS	1	BS	1847 9046
34	met no	9	PS	1	BS	1901 9046	93	met no	219	PS	1	BS	1857 9021
35	met no	128	PS	1	BS	1855 9042	94	met no	212	PS	1	BS	1949 9029
36	met no	160	PS	1	BS	1862 9022	95	met no	127	PS	1	BS	1858 9038
37	met no	164	PS	1	BS	1864 9033	96	met no	175	PS	1	BS	not noted
38	other	21	FF	6B	Level 5	2706 8890	97	met no	236	PS	1	BS	1845 9025
39	met no	11	PS	1	BS	1907 9044	98	met no	173	PS	1	BS	not noted
40	met no	162	PS	1	BS	1865 9033	99	met no	173	PS	1	BS	not noted
41	met no	14	PS	1	BS	1907 9038	100	met no	283	PS	1	BS	1959 9020
42	other	20	FF	6B	Level 4	2709 8883	101	met no	249	PS	1	BS	1842 9065
43	met no	117	PS	1	BS	1865 9042	102	met no	171	PS	1	BS	not noted
44	met no	293	PS	1	BS	1972 9002	103	met no	39	PS	1	BS	1900 9040
45	met no	24	PS	1	BS	1903 9052	104	met no	156	PS	1	BS	1916 9036
46	met no	274	PS	1	BS	1960 9022	105	met no	287	PS	1	BS	1853 9073
47	met no	138	PS	1	BS	1900 9030	106	met no	89	PS	1	BS	1937 9015
48	met no	205	PS	1	BS	1878 9020	107	met no	233	PS	1	BS	1857 9022
49	other	19	FF	6B	Level 4	2711 8885	108	met no	103	PS	1	BS	1893 9022
50	met no	57	PS	1	BS	1936 9011	109	met no	255	PS	1	BS	1832 9013
51	other	32	FF	8	Level 2	2779 8872	109	met no	261	PS	1	BS	1833 9009
52	other	5	FF	6A	Level 5	2714 8887	110	no met no	–	PS	1	SH	not noted
53	met no	98	PS	1	BS	1927 9020	111	met no	144	PS	1	BS	1897 9031
54	met no	32	PS	1	BS	1952 9013	112	met no	272	PS	1	BS	1852 9017
55	met no	277	PS	1	BS	1966 9015	113	met no	107	PS	1	BS	1889 9030
56	met no	145	PS	1	BS	1888 9034	114	met no	149	PS	1	BS	1875 9027
57	met no	33	PS	1	ditch	1874 9043	115	met no	194	PS	1	BS	1948 9031
58	other	25	FF	6B	Level 6	2719 8885	116	met no	155	PS	1	BS	1915 9031

Table 10.1 *(cont'd)*

this report no	archive prefix code	archive no	site	area	context	grid	this report no	archive prefix code	archive no	site	area	context	grid
117	met no	125	PS	1	BS	1863 9038	176	met no	90	PS	1	BS	1937 9017
118	met no	10	PS	1	BS	1908 9043	177	met no	174	PS	1	BS	not noted
119	met no	154	PS	1	BS	1926 9031	178	met no	267	PS	1	BS	1836 9029
120	met no	244	PS	1	BS	1894 9061	179	met no	271	PS	1	BS	1852 9015
121	met no	295	PS	1	BS	1940 9023	180	met no	257	PS	1	BS	1835 9013
122	met no	19	PS	1	BS	1877 9047	181	other	7	FF	6B	Level 2	2707 8888
123	no met no	–	PS	1	SH	not noted	182	met no	18	PS	1	BS	1886 9048
124	met no	197	PS	1	BS	1914 9013	183	met no	115	PS	1	BS	1868 9036
125	met no	200	PS	1	BS	1920 9010	184	met no	165	PS	1	BS	1864 9031
126	met no	195	PS	1	BS	1916 9011	185	met no	161	PS	1	BS	1867 9029
127	met no	196	PS	1	BS	1916 9013	186	met no	12	PS	1	BS	1905 9043
128	met no	198	PS	1	BS	1914 9013	187	met no	121	PS	1	BS	1889 9051
129	met no	95	PS	1	BS	1912 9023	188	met no	222	PS	1	BS	1853 9025
130	met no	129	PS	1	BS	1853 9039	189	no met no	–	PS	1	SH	not noted
131	met no	153	PS	1	BS	1929 9033	190	no met no	–	PS	1	SH	not noted
132	met no	101	PS	1	BS	1908 9023	191	met no	286	PS	1	BS	1857 9075
133	met no	187	PS	1	BS	1851 9035	192	met no	234	PS	1	BS	1854 9020
134	no met no	–	PS	1	SH	not noted	193	met no	199	PS	1	BS	1903 9017
135	met no	111	PS	1	BS	1873 9030	194	met no	214	PS	1	BS	1836 9027
136	met no	151	PS	1	BS	1882 9028	195	met no	215	PS	1	BS	1855 9020
137	met no	235	PS	1	BS	1856 9027	196	met no	184	PS	1	BS	1899 9025
138	met no	169	PS	1	BS	not noted	197	met no	184	PS	1	BS	1883 9049
139	met no	91	PS	1	BS	1947 9016	198	met no	184	PS	1	BS	1883 9049
140	met no	226	PS	1	BS	1847 9028	199	met no	102	PS	1	BS	1897 9022
141	met no	159	PS	1	BS	1863 9022	200	met no	135	PS	1	BS	1935 9020
142	met no	259	PS	1	BS	1834 9015	201	met no	130	PS	1	BS	1847 9045
143	met no	231	PS	1	BS	1856 9024	202	met no	177	PS	1	BS	not noted
144	met no	20	PS	1	BS	1866 9048	203	met no	292	PS	1	BS	1900 9031
145	other	6	FF	6B	Level 1	not noted	204	met no	139	PS	1	BS	1923 9027
146	met no	17	PS	1	BS	1883 9049	205	met no	146	PS	1	BS	1882 9036
147	met no	100	PS	1	BS	1910 9020	206	met no	16	PS	1	BS	1882 9050
148	met no	240	PS	1	BS	1844 9059	207	met no	116	PS	1	BS	1867 9037
149	met no	241	PS	1	BS	1849 9058	208	met no	123	PS	1	BS	1860 9044
150	met no	21	PS	1	BS	1863 9046	209	met no	180	PS	1	BS	not noted
151	met no	239	PS	1	BS	1863 9011	210	met no	191	PS	1	BS	1849 9032
152	met no	260	PS	1	BS	1837 9028	211	met no	237	PS	1	BS	1944 9120
153	met no	36	PS	1	BS	1958 9013	212	met no	183	PS	1	BS	1883 9049
154	met no	94	PS	1	BS	1920 9023	213	met no	268	PS	1	BS	1857 9013
155	met no	47	PS	1	BS	1950 9010	214	met no	288	PS	1	BS	1889 9032
156	met no	47	PS	1	BS	1950 9010	215	met no	29	PS	1	BS	1948 9018
157	met no	40	PS	1	BS	1900 9040	216	met no	30	PS	1	BS	1939 9028
158	met no	26	PS	1	BS	1994 9056	217	met no	294	PS	1	BS	1962 9001
159	met no	181	PS	1	BS	not noted	218	met no	193	PS	1	BS	1923 9052
160	met no	47	PS	1	BS	1950 9010	219	met no	126	PS	1	BS	1889 9036
161	met no	47	PS	1	BS	1950 9010	220	met no	143	PS	1	BS	1896 9030
162	met no	47	PS	1	BS	1950 9010	221	met no	201	PS	1	BS	1897 9071
163	met no	25	PS	1	BS	1885 9045	222	met no	150	PS	1	BS	1879 9033
164	met no	142	PS	1	BS	1898 9029	223	met no	27	PS	1	BS	1907 9049
165	met no	54	PS	1	BS	1898 9165	224	met no	27	PS	1	BS	1907 9049
166	met no	108	PS	1	BS	1882 9033	225	met no	252	PS	1	BS	1849 9059
167	met no	238	PS	1	BS	1891 9056	226	met no	285	PS	1	BS	1857 9069
168	met no	202	PS	1	BS	1897 9064	227	met no	83	PS	1	BS	1892 9058
169	met no	254	PS	1	BS	1843 9022	228	met no	104	PS	1	BS	1897 9029
170	met no	113	PS	1	BS	1873 9038	229	met no	134	PS	1	BS	1895 9030
171	met no	124	PS	1	BS	1863 9037	230	met no	178	PS	1	BS	not noted
172	met no	289	PS	1	BS	1903 9025	231	met no	141	PS	1	BS	1899 9031
173	other	18	FF	6B	Level 3	2714 8885	232	met no	282	PS	1	BS	1893 9020
174	met no	122	PS	1	BS	1861 9039	233	met no	43	PS	1	BS	1954 9023
175	met no	189	PS	1	BS	1950 9024	234	met no	81	PS	1	BS	1903 9030

Table 10.1 *(cont'd)*

this report no	archive prefix code	archive no	site	area	context	grid
235	met no	60	PS	1	BS	1890 9035
236	met no	34	PS	1	BS	not noted
237	met no	5	PS	1	BS	1944 9022
238	met no	99	PS	1	BS	1928 9015
239	met no	207	PS	1	BS	1863 9024
240	no met no	–	PS	1	SH	not noted
241	met no	248	PS	1	BS	1848 9068
242	met no	256	PS	1	BS	1838 9023
243	met no	247	PS	1	BS	1840 9068
244	met no	59	PS	1	BS	1932 9027
245	met no	182	PS	1	BS	not noted
246	met no	192	PS	1	BS	1924 9053
247	met no	4	PS	1	BS	1944 9022
248	met no	92	PS	1	BS	1921 9023
249	met no	176	PS	1	BS	not noted
250	met no	88	PS	1	BS	1935 9018
251	met no	208	PS	1	BS	1860 9025
252	met no	3	PS	1	BS	1947 9015
253	met no	28	PS	1	BS	1946 9017
254	met no	179	PS	1	BS	not noted
255	met no	97	PS	1	BS	1872 9024
256	met no	273	PS	1	BS	1842 9010
257	met no	106	PS	1	BS	1895 9029
258	met no	48	PS	1	SH	not noted
259	met no	118	PS	1	BS	1878 9041
260	met no	50	PS	1	BS	1955 9016
261	met no	38	PS	1	BS	1900 9040
262	met no	119	PS	1	BS	1874 9041
263	met no	136	PS	1	BS	1926 9023
264	met no	35	PS	1	BS	1998 9021
265	met no	266	PS	1	BS	1839 9002
266	met no	120	PS	1	BS	1882 9033
267	met no	6	PS	1	BS	1922 9033
268	met no	265	PS	1	BS	1835 9035
269	met no	52	PS	1	BS	1953 9019
270	met no	82	PS	1	BS	1885 9060
271	met no	41	PS	1	BS	1900 9040
272	met no	152	PS	1	BS	1919 9032
273	other	29	FF	6D	Level 1	2704 8885
274	no met no	–	PS	1	SH	not noted
275	no met no	–	PS	1	SH	not noted
276	met no	37	PS	1	SH	1900 9040

Spearheads

There are six plain leaf-shaped spearheads from the Power Station and Flag Fen, and one side-looped example. Side-loop spearheads have been studied in some detail by Rowlands (1976) who divided them into two main types, although he agreed that 'the features defining these two groups are not fully adhered to by all specimens'. This makes very difficult the assignment of the example from the Power Station (Fig 10.4, 48) to a particular class. The side loops are semi-circular, which according to Rowlands belongs to his

Group 2, and it lacks the protective loop plates of his Group 1. There are no definite associations of side-loop spearheads with Late Bronze Age material.

On association, Group 2 spearheads are found in Smith's (1959) Ornament Horizon hoards of the later phase of the Middle Bronze Age. Rowlands mentions the high lead content, typical of Late Bronze Age artefacts, in the spearheads from Fyfield, Berkshire, and Methwold, Norfolk, and cites these as supporting a Late Bronze Age survival. From Tormarton, Gloucestershire, there are two Group 2 spearhead points embedded in the pelvis and lumbar vertebrae of a skeleton. Radiocarbon dating of the tibia from the skeleton gave a date of cal BC 1410–900 BM-542; 2927±90 BP). There is also the tip of a possible Group 2 spearhead from Barrow Peck, Berwick St John, Barrow G10a, found with a cremation that gave radiocarbon dates of cal BC 1420–820 (BM-2023 R; 2900±110 BP and BM-1920 R; 2890±110 BP; O'Connor in Barrett *et al* 1991, 234).

Plain leaf-shaped spearheads with lanceolate outline were reintroduced into the British Bronze Age repertoire during the Penard Phase (Late Bronze Age I) and continued to be produced until the end of the Bronze Age. Metal analysis of two of the spearheads (Fig 10.4, 46 and 47) would place them in the Wilburton Phase (Late Bronze Age III). There is also the tip of a spearhead of unidentified type (Fig 10.4, 50).

Accompanying spearheads, especially in the Wilburton Phase, are tubular ferrules. The pointed ferrule (Fig 10.4, 45) from the Power Station belongs to the earliest form known in Britain and Ireland and is seen in the Late Bronze Age I hoards from Ffynhonnau, Brecon (Savory 1958, fig 13), and Ambleside, Cumbria (Needham 1982). Both of these hoards belong to the Penard Phase. The possible conical ferrule in the Langdon Bay find, Kent (O'Connor 1988), could also on association belong to the same period. Butler (1963) recognised the Continental affinities, equivalent to Montelius III–IV in Northern Europe, of the then known British pieces.

Needham's distribution map (1982) clearly shows the concentration in the Thames Valley of conical ferrules in Britain. The Power Station conical ferrule is the shortest definite complete ferrule in this country (though there are some with shorter estimated lengths). The wood in the socket gave a radiocarbon date range of cal BC 1390–1030 (OxA-5959; 2965±45 BP; Table 16.1).

In the Wilburton Phase (Late Bronze Age II) the ferrules became longer and cylindrical, with flat, rounded, or slightly expanded ends. They also form part of the contemporary assemblages in France (Briard 1965; Coffyn 1971) and are an integral part of the weapon complex of Atlantic Europe (Coombs 1975 and 1988).

The second ferrule (Fig 10.4, 44) is an example of the long type (length 332mm), so typical of the Wilburton Phase hoards. In the succeeding

Ewart Park/Carp's Tongue Phase (Late Bronze Age III) ferrules expand their distribution to the north and west of the country and are often shorter.

Shield tab

As shields only occur singly or in association with other shields in the British Isles, they are notoriously difficult to date. The shield tab (Fig 10.3, 43) originally fitted onto the back of a shield for suspension (Coles 1962, fig 4; Needham 1979, fig 2; Raftery 1982, figs 3 and 4). The present example is of the triangular form, which occurs on a number of different shield types in Europe. It should be noted that they are present on the early Nipperweise form (Needham 1979, fig 2). The precise dating of the Nipperweise type in England and on the Continent still remains problematic.

The context of shield finds in England is overwhelmingly rivers, fens, and bogs. Three complete shields are known from Cambridgeshire, one from Langwood Fen and two from Coveney Fen, found together (Coles 1962). The facts that shields, when found, are nearly always complete, that they or fragments never occur in hoards, and their watery contexts would suggest that they have an importance over and above the purely functional. Furthermore, experiments by Coles (1973, pl 16) have shown that bronze shields would not have withstood blows from weapons and are more likely to have been ceremonial.

Knives and daggers

Flag Fen and the Power Station site have produced five tanged knives/daggers. Tanged knives/daggers are not commonly found in the hoards of the British Late Bronze Age, in which socketed forms are far more common. Of the tanged forms found at the Power Station, the most easily recognisable Late Bronze Age type is one with a raised vertical rib on the tang (Fig 10.5, 53).

These knives formed the subject of a paper by Burgess (1982) and had been studied earlier by Hodges (1956). Burgess' map clearly shows a widespread distribution of such knives, largely found in hoards, stretching from the south to the north of England and also occurring in Ireland. There are also rare examples in the north of France, in the Dreuil hoard and in the oppidum of Saint Pierre en Chastre (Blanchet 1984, fig 146, 4 and 5; fig 158, 32).

Probably the earliest association is in the Isleham hoard, Cambridgeshire, where there are eight examples associated with Wilburton Phase material (Late Bronze Age II). Such knives are also known in the Broadward Complex hoards (Burgess *et al* 1972). Remaining associations point to a date within the Ewart Park/Carp's Tongue Phase (Late Bronze Age III). The notches seen below the tang on one knife (Fig 10.5, 55) can also be seen on some knives with narrow tangs in the Isleham hoard, Cambridgeshire.

The knife/dagger with slightly flanged tang, rivet notch on the top of the tang and antler handle (Fig 10.5, 54) is difficult to parallel. The triangular blade is a rare form for a Late Bronze Age knife/dagger. Flanged tangs are not completely unknown on Late Bronze Age knife/daggers, however. Some are reutilised sword blades. Rivetted tangs (Fig 10.5, 52) are also not unknown (eg Yattendon Court hoard, Berkshire (Burgess *et al* 1972, fig 18, 54), and Reach Fen hoard, Cambridgeshire.

The hilt form and three-rivet arrangement on the knife dagger from Flag Fen (Fig 10.5, 52) is unknown in the British Late Bronze Age. The trilobate form of the hilt and the three rivet holes are rather reminiscent of a class of dagger dated to the final phase of the Bronze Age or the earliest phase of the Iron Age in France (Blanchet 1984, 392–3, fig 213, 1.2; see also the example from Luce Bay, Ipswich (Rowlands 1976, pl 35). The metal analysis of the piece from Flag Fen suggests a date within Hallstatt C/D (earliest phases of the Iron Age).

Tools

Socketed axe

The ribbed socketed axe with parallel sides and back to front mouth section (Fig 10.6, 60) is perhaps best paralleled among the Sompting axes (Roseberry Topping Variant) of Schmidt and Burgess (1981, pl 103, 1615–30 and pl 104, 1631–42). One of the main concentrations of Sompting axes is in East Anglia and Cambridgeshire (Burgess 1969). The Roseberry Topping Variant occurs in a number of Ewart Park/Carp's Tongue hoards (Carleton Rode, Norfolk; Eaton, Norwich, Norfolk; Reach Fen, Feltwell, and Meldreth, Cambridgeshire). Burgess and Schmidt claim that 'there is some indication that Roseberry Topping axes developed before Sompting axes and they might even represent a preliminary stage in the evolution of the exaggerated Sompting form'. They should at least be contemporary in part with the Sompting form, which dates, on associations, to Hallstatt C/Llyn Fawr Phase/Late Bronze Age IV.

Awls

Since tools are comparatively rare finds at the Power Station and Flag Fen, it is surprising to find so many bronze awls represented among the finds (Fig 10.6, 64–81). Bronze double-pointed awls make their appearance associated with Beakers in this country (eg Kirkaldy, Fife; Clarke 1970, 1014) and occur in the Wessex graves of the Early Bronze Age (eg Wimborne St Giles and Preshute, Manton; Gerloff 1975, nos 69 and 241). These early awls tend to be double pointed, with central rectangular or circular thickening. From Down Farm, Gussage St Michael, Dorset, came an awl found in a cremation pit, east of a pond barrow.

The cremation was dated to cal BC 2320–1690 (BM-2189R; 3620±110 BP). From the same site came a single pointed awl accompanying a cremation, a Collared Urn, and two bone awls. The cremation has a radiocarbon date of cal BC 2280–1520 (BM-2190R; 3530±130 BP; Barrett et al 1991, 233).

Bronze awls have a number of Middle Bronze Age associations (eg Monkswood, Bishopsland, and Glentrool hoards). For the Later Bronze Age there are only a few associations. The example in the Thorndon hoard, Suffolk, is very similar to the Power Station example. Similar examples also occur in the material from Saint Pierre en Chastre, à Vieux Moulin, Oise (Blanchet 1984, fig 147). Here, some 16 objects are variously described as awls or points. The dating of this material belongs to Bronze Final II (equivalent to the Wilburton Phase in England, Late Bronze Age II). The site at Potterne, Wiltshire, contains eight awls similar to the Power Station examples (Andrew Lawson personal communication). Although double-ended awls are known from the beginnings of metallurgy, it would appear that awls with one end pointed and the other chisel-like belong to the Late Bronze Age. None of the pointed ends are really sharp. Metal analysis suggests that the Power Station awls belong to the Wilburton/Ewart Park Phase.

Socketed gouge

The socketed gouge from the Power Station site was found in the upper primary filling of the southern Bronze Age droveway ditch (Fig 10.5, 57). Eogan (1966) considered the origin of the socketed gouge in Europe, with a brief note on their dating. He concluded that socketed gouges were not known in Europe before the late second millennium BC, and that they made their first appearance on the Continent in the Caucasus, although tanged gouges had been known in that area from the end of the third millennium. In Transylvania, socketed gouges were firmly established by Hallstatt A1. In Europe north of the Alps, they are known in a Hallstatt B context from the Larnaud hoard, Jura. In Brittany, they appear in hoards of the Saint Brieuc des Iffs complex (Late Bronze Age II).

Burley (1955–6) divided the tool type into two, Class I, with a plain mouth, and Class II, with moulding around the mouth. These basic classes can be further sub-divided into Class I, with plain mouth and narrow blade, Class II, with a with deep collar around the mouth and a narrow blade, Class IIb, with ribs or incised lines around the mouth, and Class III, small squat type with wide, rather splayed cutting edge, with or without moulding, and never with ribs. In Britain, socketed gouges are found in hoards associated with the Wilburton Complex. These could, however, have been deposited late in the complex (Isleham, Cambridgeshire, Isle of Harty hoard, Kent, and Blackmoor, Hampshire). All of these gouges are of Class IIb type.

The socketed gouge from the Power Station belongs within Class I. Wood found in the socket gave a radiocarbon date range of cal BC1630–1420 (OxA-5960; 3230±45 BP; Table 16.1), which is unexpectedly early for a socketed gouge and would make it one of the earliest, if not the earliest examples in Europe. This early date accords well, however, with the stratigraphic contexts, which must pre-date Row 1, the earliest row of the post alignment, which was constructed in the first half of the thirteenth century BC.

Flesh hook

A single so-called 'flesh hook' was found at Flag Fen among the lowest level of timbers (Fig 10.5, 58). The use of the words 'flesh hook' highlights one of the major problems in Bronze Age descriptive terminology: the assignment of a functional term to an object whose real function is impossible to determine. Razors are another example. In describing the complex object from Dunaverny, Macalister (1949, 220) described it as a 'steelyard' and stated that this suggestion had been made in 1833 by a writer signing himself 'TA' in the Dublin *Penny Journal* of 22 June. Evans (1881) mentioned the same piece, but thought it later than the Bronze Age and simply called it a 'bronze rod'. It is arguable when the term 'flesh hook' was first applied to this class of artefact. The second edition of the British Museum Guide to the Antiquities of the Bronze Age (1920), in again describing Dunaverny, states that 'The implement illustrated here is probably a flesh hook, used ceremoniously like that of the priests in Eli's time'. In 1929, the hook from Little Thetford, Norfolk, was described as a flesh hook, as was the one from Lurgy, Ireland (Armstrong 1924).

In the British Museum Guide to the Later Prehistoric Antiquities of the British Isles (1953), the Little Thetford and Dunaverny pieces were illustrated and described as goads, and this possibility was also taken up by Ann Ross (1967). The term 'flesh hook' has found wide acceptance in the Continental literature — *crochet à viande, Fleishhaken, gancho para trinchar la carne*.

These objects have been discussed in some detail in two articles in particular (Jockenhövel, 1974; Gomez de Soto and Pautreau 1988). Jockenhövel was concerned with flesh hooks from the British Isles and the latter authors, although largely concerned with the elaborate example from Thorigné (Deaux Sèvres), also illustrated other European examples from France and Spain, together with Urnfield examples.

A number of forms of flesh hook can be distinguished. The simplest is a bent and curved rod of bronze, although it is difficult to see how these were actually hafted. They seem more akin to the hooks used in the *rôtisseries* of Atlantic Europe (Mohen 1977a). At the other end of the scale are the very complex double hooks. In terms of chronology the more complex ones appear to be late in the Bronze Age, with Carp's Tongue/Ewart Park associations.

The example from Flag Fen, with its single hook in line with the socket, finds its closest parallel with the hook in the Feltwell Fen hoard, Norfolk, which was found inside a class A1 cauldron (Gerloff 1986). There is also a hook, minus its socket, of the same triangular cross-section as the Flag Fen and Feltwell examples from Eriswell, Suffolk (Briscoe and Furness 1955). This was found, some months later, 3m north of a hoard of bronze weapons and a tangle of sheet bronze. The weapons in the first hoard would date it to the Penard Phase — 1200–1000 BC (Needham 1982). Without opening up the crumpled mass of sheet bronze, it is impossible to identify it. It does, however, have rivet holes, and it was originally described as 'the mounting of a vessel or other container'. The broken tip of a hook from the Marden hoard, Kent, is another possible parallel from the British Isles.

On the Continent, the Hio hoard, Pontvedra, Spain, contains three socketed single hooks, all broken (Coffyn 1985, pl LX, 10–12). One of these has a well defined collar between the socket and the hook. The associations within this hoard would point to a Carp's Tongue date for its deposition.

The dendrochronological date-by-association for the Flag Fen example would seem to be crucial, in that its close parallel at Feltwell Fen was found with a Class A1 cauldron. Hopefully, the flesh hook from there is also to be radiocarbon dated by its shaft fragment. Gerloff (1986) has suggested that the Class A1 cauldrons should be dated to the Penard Phase, based on the metal analysis of the Colchester and Feltwell Fen cauldrons. There is also the possibility that the example from Eriswell might have been associated with a bronze vessel. In the Hio hoard, there are also associations with fragments of riveted bronze sheet, almost certainly from a cauldron (Coffyn 1985, pl LXI, 7–17) and in the Prairie de Mauves hoard, Nantes, France, with a definite cauldron fragment (Briard *et al* 1966). Finally, there are a number of so-called flesh hook terminals associated with cauldron fragments in the Isleham hoard, Cambridgeshire (Britton 1960).

If the hooks were used with the cauldrons then they might be seen as part of the increasing body of evidence for ritual feasting in the Late Bronze Age in Atlantic Europe (Gomez de Soto 1993). Further evidence for feasting might also be provided by the *rôtisseries* of Atlantic Europe, which can now be dated as early as 1000 BC, following the discovery of one in the tomb at Amathus, Cyprus (Gomez de Soto 1991).

Razors

Three razors were found at the Power Station (Fig 10.6, 61–3). Razor 63 belongs to Jockenhövel's (1980) Feltwell type. These, apart from four examples found on the Continent, are all confined to the British Isles, where there are a large number of associated finds (Jockenhövel 1980, Taf 50). On association they belong in the Ewart Park/Carp's Tongue Phase (Late Bronze Age III). Blades of similar shape, but with separate handles, are known from the Wilburton Phase and are present in the Isleham hoard, Cambridgeshire, Ugley hoard, Essex, and the Boutigny hoard, France (Mohen 1977b, 335); all are of the same (Late Bronze Age III) date.

Not enough of razor 61 survives to be certain of its typology, but keyhole slots, as in this example, are known on a number of razor forms (Jockenhövel 1980, Feltwell and Henon types). Finally, the third possible razor (62) has no good parallels; it could well be a small knife.

Dress and display — pins and bracelets

Pins, along with other small and often broken items of a personal nature, while not being common in hoards of the Late Bronze Age in England (when compared to the Continent), occasionally turn up, however, on settlement sites of the period. The assemblages from Flag Fen and the Power Station contain comparatively large number of pins of the Late Bronze Age and Early Iron Ages. Some of the pin types are more easily placed in recognisable families than others. A large number are represented by undiagnostic shanks alone.

The roll-headed pin (Fig 10.9, 203) is a recognised type within the Bronze Age pin repertoire, although its wide occurrence in time and space makes it of little use for dating. In England it occurs in a number of non-hoard contexts, on sites ranging from settlements to caves and ritual deposits. Examples include Ivinghoe Beacon, Buckinghamshire (hillfort), Highdown Hill, Sussex (hillfort), Potterne, Wiltshire (midden deposit), Petters Sports Field, Runnymede, Surrey (enclosure ditch), cave sites at Heathury Burn, Durham and Symonds Yat, Herefordshire, and three from the Thames at Syon Reach, Brentford. All of these contexts would suggest a Late Bronze Age date.

The pin type seems to have been especially common in France, with at least 41 examples known from Fort Harrouard hillfort alone (Mohen and Bailloud 1987) and from the oppidum at Vieux Moulin, Saint Pierre en Chastre (Blanchet 1984, fig 150,13). The type is also known from Late Bronze Age Atlantic France (Gomez de Soto 1980, fig 64A, 5 and 6, fig 64B, 4, and fig 68,9).

The globular-headed pin with a rib below the head (Fig 10.9, 182) is close to the French '*épingle à petite tête globuleuse, avec nervure en dessus*'. This form is known in the north of France from Berry au Bac, 'Le Chemin de la Pêcherie' (Aisne) in Bronze Final IIb contexts; from Vieux Moulin,Oise, in the oppidum of Saint Pierre en Chastre of the same period, and at Catenoy (Oise) in Le Camp du César, where it is dated to Bronze Final IIIa. The example from Saint Pierre en Chastre is also decorated below the rib (Blanchet 1984, fig 149, 5) as is the example from the forest of Compiègne (Blanchet 1984, fig 175). Plain examples are also known from France (Blanchet 1984, fig 149, 5 and fig 175, 7and 8).

Although a fairly simple shape, knob-headed pins
(Fig 10.9, 187) appear to be rare in Bronze Age con-
texts. There is an example in the hoard from Fenny
Bentley, Derbyshire (Smith 1920, 37), where it is asso-
ciated with a hollow-bladed spearhead, which might
suggest a Late Bronze Age II date (Wilburton
Complex). The metal analysis also suggests a Late
Bronze Age II date. The type is also known in Late
Bronze Age III contexts in Northern France at Saint
Pierre en Chastre, Oise (Blanchet 1984, fig 149, 11).

There are a small number of pins that can be
described as nail and disc headed, although no doubt
these general descriptions cover a number of subtly different types. Such pins are known over a wide area of
Europe. It is obvious from the contexts of nail-headed
pins in Continental Europe that they have a long
chronology. The pins described as disc headed have a
variety of forms and thickness. Some have a slightly
raised edge to the disc. This feature is seen on other
pins from England in Late Bronze Age contexts, at
Potterne, Wiltshire, and the Isleham hoard,
Cambridgeshire. Two pins from the Power Station (Fig
10.9, 178 and 179) have a small central wart at the
centre of the disc. These central knobs are known from
a wide range of pins in Europe.

The ribbed, turban-headed pin with central knob
(Fig 10.9, 186) is reminiscent of the pin from the for-
est of Compiègne, which is of Late Bronze Age date
(Blanchet 1984, fig 175,3).

The cup-headed pin (Fig 10.9, 180) can be compared to a series of pins from Ireland, where there is
also an example with a central wart (Eogan 1974, fig
11, 1–8). Dished-headed pins, although considered
distinct from the Irish series by Eogan (O'Connor,
1980, 201), are known from the Heathery Burn cave,
Durham, Sion Reach, Brentford, and Brigg,
Lincolnshire. One of the pins from Thwing, Yorkshire,
has a slight, hollowed dished head (T Manby personal
communication). If it is indeed related to the Irish
series, pin 180 has a Late Bronze Age date. On metal
analysis it can be placed in Late Bronze Age II
(Wilburton Complex).

Bracelets, never very popular in Britain during Late
Bronze Age II, became commoner in Late Bronze Age
III, though never as popular as in Continental Europe.
The Power Station bracelet (Fig 10.7, 143), with oval
cross-section and slightly expanded terminals, is dated
on metal analysis to Late Bronze Age III (Ewart
Park/Carp's Tongue Phase). In general form it belongs
to the family of Covesea bracelets discussed by Benton
(1930–31, 182–4), Proudfoot (1955, 15–20 and
34–6), Hawkes and Clarke (1963, 242–6), and Coles
(1959–60, 39–41, 89–90), summarised by O'Connor
(1980). To quote O'Connor's conclusions 'Covesea
bracelets probably contain elements from Irish gold
bracelets and late Urnfield bronze bracelets via
Northern France and Southern England'. There is a
danger, however, of labelling any bracelet with expanded terminals as a Covesea type. Such simple bracelets

with slightly expanded terminals appear to be common
on the Continent (Vénat hoard, Charente, France
(Coffyn et al 1981, pl 33, 34 and pl 37, 32–5).

Miscellaneous

Socketed spike/punch

Two socketed spike/punches were found at the Power
Station (Fig 10.6, 93 and 94). Metal analyses indicate a
date within the Ewart Park Phase (Late Bronze Age III).
Such objects are not common in Bronze Age contexts
and their exact function remains unknown. A complete
socketed spike/punch was found in a small Late Bronze
Age hoard from Pigeons Cave, Great Ormes Head,
Caernarvonshire, associated with two gold lock rings
and a late palstave (Savory 1980, fig 40, 307.4) and in
the Ripoll hoard, Gerona, Spain (Monteaguado 1977,
Taf. 155.9). Both these are larger than the Power
Station examples and differ in detail. All four, however,
consist of a solid spike/punch and a socket.

Pointed conical rivets

There are eight complete pointed conical rivets, and
four spikes (possibly fragments of pointed rivets) from
the Power Station (Fig 10.3, 8–16). These objects are
extremely rare in the British Late Bronze Age. Four
similar rivets from the Nottingham Hill hoard,
Gloucestershire (Hall and Gingell 1974), have an average length of 2.6mm (the average length of the Power
Station rivets is 2.4mm). A lead conical pointed rivet
(length 2.4mm) was found at Runnymede Bridge,
Surrey (Needham and Hook 1988, fig 2.5) and similar
rivets are known from the Iron Age hoard from
Ringstead, Norfolk (Clarke 1951, 220, pl XIX, d–e).
Pointed rivets are known especially on Bronze Age
crested helmets, mainly from Italy and Central Europe
(Hencken 1971). Pointed rivets are also known in the
French hoard from Larnaud and Vénat (Hencken
1971), Saint Brieuc des Iffs (Briard 1972, XX), and
the deposit from Ria de Huelva, Spain, where they
were associated with fragments of a crested helmet
(Ruiz-Gálvez Priego 1995, pl 18, 21–3; pl 19, 1–14).
There are no examples of Late Bronze Age helmets
from Britain, despite proven expertise in beaten bronze
work, as seen, for example, on buckets, cauldrons,
shields, and horns. Hencken doubts whether the possible helmet fragment from Brentford, Middlesex
(Hencken 1971, fig 150d) is really from a helmet. The
contexts of the Nottingham Hill and Runnymede
Bridge finds would put pointed rivets into the Ewart
Park/Carp's Tongue Phase (Late Bronze Age III).

Studs and buttons

The assemblage contains a number of examples of
bronze studs and buttons with loop (Fig 10.6, 89–90)
and shank attachments (Fig 10.6, 86–7). Such objects

are often classified as 'horse gear' in the literature. In England, the Isleham hoard, Cambridgeshire, contains a number of examples of domed- and conical-headed buttons and studs with bar and shank attachments (Late Bronze Age II), and the Late Bronze Age III hoards from Llangwyllog, Anglesey, Reach Fen, Cambridgeshire, and Kensington, London, contain similar objects to 89 and 90 (O'Connor, 1980, 150 and 198–9).

Vessel/helmet fragment

A fragment of sheet bronze, perhaps from a vessel or helmet, was found at the Power Station (Fig 10.6, 95). So little of this object actually survives that it is impossible to be sure what it came from. If from a helmet, it is the first example of a Bronze Age helmet from this country. Equally rare are bronze vessels, apart from the cauldrons and buckets. There are cruciform handle attachments for a bowl in the Welby hoard, Leicestershire (Powell 1948), and fragmentary bronze sheet, possibly from a vessel, in the Adabrock hoard (Coles 1959–60). The Watford hoard, Hertfordshire, produced an elaborate sheet copper vessel, possibly with East Mediterranean connections (Coombs 1979, figs 11.7 and 11.8). Small cast bronze vessels also occur at the Welby hoard, Leicestershire (Powell 1948), and various sites in Scotland, including Ardoe (Aberdeenshire), Balmashanner (Angus), Glenalanar (Aberdeenshire), and the recently discovered hoard from Carrymuchloch, Perthshire (Trevor Cowie personal communication).

Rings

The metal-detector survey at the Power Station produced a large number of rings (Fig 10.10, 215–55). Rings of varying cross-section and internal diameter are known from a variety of Bronze Age contexts. Some hoards contain a number of examples (eg Blackmoor Hoard, Hampshire; Colquhoun 1979, fig 4.4, 70–88). It seems futile to speculate on the myriad uses to which these rings could have been put, ranging from the purely ornamental to the functional (eg chain mail). The majority of the rings from the Power Station have an internal diameter of 15–20mm.

Four rings (237–40) tend towards lozenge cross-sections, recalling the Blackmoor Hoard (Colquhoun 1979, fig 4.4, 74). The ring 240 has two grooves around its outer edge and has been assigned to the Middle Bronze Age Taunton Phase on metal analysis.

Possible tweezers

Two strips of metal that could have been part of tweezers (Fig 10.6, 84 and 85) were found at the Power Station. Tweezers in bone are known from Early Bronze Age Wessex graves (Gerloff 1975) and also in bronze from contemporary sites in Northern and Central Europe. In Britain, scant hoard associations suggest tweezers belong to Late Bronze Age III. Like pins and personal ornaments, tweezers are commoner on settlement sites than in hoards or as single finds (O'Connor 1980, 91, 221).

Objects in tin and lead

Needham and Hook (1988) have noted that 'the general dearth of metallic lead in British Bronze Age contexts is surprising as there can be little doubt that by the Late Bronze Age lead and lead-based alloys were readily available'. The extensive alloying of copper with lead, the finding of lead axes and other tools, and lead traces on the inside of bronze moulds clearly attest to the use of lead in the Late Bronze Age. There are only ten definite, recognisable lead objects from the British Isles and some of these are in a lead/tin alloy. The Power Station and Flag Fen produced a number of lead objects (the lead pommel has been described above).

The lead half cube (Fig 10.8, 152) is paralleled in the Runnymede Bridge finds (Needham and Hook 1988, fig 2.1), where the dimensions are 30.5mm square, maximum thickness 13.5mm, and weight 112.3g. The other parallel comes from the West Caistor hoard, Norfolk (Lawson 1979, fig 9.2, e). It measures 48 × 46mm, is 16mm thick, and weighs 148g. Again, this is a plano-convex block. Such squared lead objects probably formed part of a weight system, like lead discs (Fig 10.8, 148–9 and 151). The cited parallels can be dated to the Ewart Park/Carp's Tongue Phase. There are also two purse-like objects in white metal, possibly of lead.(Fig 10.8, 170 and 171).

Needham and Hook (op cit) list even fewer definite tin objects, the only examples cited being from the Early Bronze Age grave at Sutton Vernay, Wiltshire, and in the Late Bronze Age hoard from Llangwyllog, Anglesey (Lynch 1970, 207).

The Power Station site produced a number of objects that, when analysed, proved to be of tin or a tin/copper alloy. There were also a number of objects, however, not analysed, which had been made from white metal, and also possibly of tin or a tin alloy. The main categories of object are rings, beads of various sorts, tabs, thin foil, and a bar. The most interesting of all are a complete model tin wheel (Fig 10.8, 154), a fragment from another (Fig 10.8, 172), and a cog-like object (Fig 10.8, 159). These three objects all have parallels in a distinctive class of tin object found in Switzerland and the north of Italy, which date to the Late Bronze Age (Primas 1984, figs 2, 4, and 9). The wheel as a symbolic object is well known from Iron Age Europe and has been discussed in detail by Green (1984). Metal and ceramic wheel models are known from Western Europe in the Late Bronze Age (Chevillot and Gomez de Soto 1979).

The two tabs (Fig 10.8, 153 and 158) could be strapends of unknown date, although 158 is of pewter, which suggests a later date, nor is the decoration typical of the Late Bronze Age.

Discussion: Iron Age

Apart from the obvious objects that, on typology, can be assigned to the Iron Age, there are also a number of objects made of iron, which could belong to the period. Because of their non-specific attributes, however, they can not be definitely claimed as Iron Age. Of the certain Iron Age objects, weapons and ornaments comprise the overwhelming majority.

Warfare — swords and scabbard mount

The two tanged iron sword hilts (Fig 10.10, 259 and 260) are impossible to date precisely within the British Iron Age sequence. The two swords and fragments of their blades were found next to each other (Fig 10.16). On one of the hilts (260) it is possible to see the outline of the top of the scabbard mount in the corrosion products. The scabbard mount would have belonged to Stead's (1991) campanulate type. The high arch would possibly suggest a third-century-BC date. Dr Stead has kindly commented on drawings of the hilts:

> It would appear that the blade of 259 has a median ridge, which is quite common on La Tène I swords but not later types. The hilt tang of 260 seems to be very long (154mm), whereas most La Tène 1 swords seem to have tangs of 120–40mm. The mark of the bottom of the hilt end (or top of the scabbard) is not very helpful because it can be matched on Jope's dagger and on La Tène I, II and even III swords/scabbards. There is a reasonably good parallel for the semi-circular mark and the length of the hilt from Rudston, grave 146 (Stead 1991, fig 50). The possibility ought to be considered that they are Jope's (1961) daggers. The main argument against this is the length of tang on 260, although not many daggers have complete tangs. The blade widths are about average for La Tène swords.

A reconstruction of the scabbard mount (Fig 10.11, 273) suggests that it would have accompanied a short sword, but certainly not the two iron swords found at the Power Station. Short swords are known from the British Iron Age, for example from the river Witham, but they generally have anthropoid hilts (Fitzpatrick 1996). The elaborate engraved design on the scabbard mount can perhaps best be described as opposed Ss, rather than opposed dragons, although they might be a devolved form of the latter (Stead 1984a; Megaw and Megaw 1990).

The arrangement on the upper panel is of a type described by Duval (1975) as the simplest of the compositions found on Iron Age sword scabbards. Elaborate opposed Ss can also be seen on the scabbard from Hunsbury, Northamptonshire, which is somewhat reminiscent of the *lyre zoomorphes* design seen on the scabbards from Rungis, Val de Marne (Ginoux 1994, fig 6.1), which are dated to the mid third century BC, and from Liter, Veszprem (Megaw and Megaw 1990, fig 6.1). The arcading below the main design on the scabbard mount is rare on La Tène metalwork, although it appears to belong to a general class of decorative elements seen on early La Tène art (Jacobsthal 1944, pls 261–2) and on pottery, especially Glastonbury ware (Bulleid and Gray 1917). There is a scabbard mouth guard from Normanton le Heath, Leicestershire (Fitzpatrick 1994, fig 25.1), which has openwork arcading, and engraved arcading is also seen on a scabbard from Bussy-le-Château, 'la Croix-Meunière' (Ginoux 1994, fig 2.4), dated to La Tène Ia. Fold-over symmetry is also seen on many mirror designs (Fox 1958, 84–98).

The decorated cup-shaped object (Fig 10.3, 35) might be a sword pommel, but is quite unlike any known Bronze Age or Iron Age examples.

Labour and crafts — tools

Tools are almost entirely absent from the repertoire of Iron Age objects deposited at Flag Fen and the Power Station. The only recognisable objects belonging to this category are the iron socketed axe (Fig 10.11, 269) and the bronze shears (Fig 10.11, 276). The latter might be regarded as having a use and importance over and above that of a purely functional tool (below).

Iron socketed axes were the subject of a paper by Rainbow (1928), which was updated by Manning and Saunders (1972). Prior to 1972, at least 21 iron socketed axes were known from the British Isles, of which 16 were of the looped variety. Although the Power Station axe is very corroded, it would appear to have a symmetrical cutting edge, whereas the majority of British examples are asymmetrical. Its symmetrical cutting edge finds parallels with axes from Traprain Law, East Lothian (Manning and Saunders 1972, fig 4. 11), and Culbin Sands, Morayshire (Manning and Saunders 1972, fig 4.12).

Dating and chronology of these axes presents a problem, due to the lack of datable or secure contexts (Manning and Saunders 1972). The Traprain Law example might be as early as the seventh century BC, but this cannot be proved. On balance, it seems that the socketed axe was in use throughout the whole of the pre-Roman Iron Age. Not until the Roman period was it completely superseded by the shafthole axe, although this form had begun to appear before the Roman Conquest. Iron socketed axes have also been found in late Hallstatt and La Tène graves in Europe (see the discussion and distribution map in Krausse 1996, Abb 212, 299–306).

The bronze shears and their accompanying wooden box are unique within the British Isles. Although iron shears are known from both the Iron Age and the Roman periods, bronze shears are rare. Forbes, quoted in Ryder (1983, 96), claimed that bronze was not sufficiently elastic for shears, although he admitted that small shears made of bronze were known from Roman times. There are bronze shears from Co Kerry, Ireland (Anon 1976) and Loch Erribel, Sutherland (MacGregor 1976). Groningen Museum possesses a pair of bronze shears from a Dutch terp, which are only 75mm long. A pair of Iron Age bronze shears was noted in Mainz Town Museum.

The metal analysis of the Power Station shears suggests that they are of Iron Age date. The fact that the shears are in bronze and that they have their own specially made box would suggest that they had an original importance over and above that of mere farming implements. The shape of the shears is exactly the same as those implements used for sheep shearing over the centuries. Ryder (1983) claimed that a blade and handle measuring 3 inches (75mm) long are probably the smallest size that could be used to shear sheep. He also claimed that 'the greater tensile strength of iron compared with bronze enabled shears to be made that were large enough to clip sheep'.

The need to shear Iron Age sheep has also to be reliably established. Maisie Taylor notes that primitive breeds of the broad type likely to be encountered in later prehistoric times, such as the Shetland, do not retain their fleeces very well. In May and June the fleece naturally detaches and an animal could be plucked, or 'rooed', of its fleece very readily. Experience has shown that rooing is both faster and more efficient than shearing by hand. A complete fleece could be removed in 10 to 15 minutes. The resultant wool is of very high quality and lacks the 'double cut' ends of many hand-shorn fleeces. Double cuts make spinning, especially spindle spinning, more difficult and the yarn weaker. If the shears were indeed intended for use with animals, then they would make good dagging shears for the removal of soiled wool from around the animal's rear. Modern dagging shears are smaller than fleece-shearing shears and closely resemble the Iron Age examples under discussion. It does, however, seem intrinsically improbable that anyone should wish to make a ritual deposition of as mundane an item as dagging shears. Dagging shears take punishment during their use, and bronze, as Ryder has noted, is a less resilient metal than iron.

If shears in Iron Age and Roman times were merely to clip sheep, the number of occurrences of shears accompanying the warrior and rich burials of the Iron Age and Roman periods is striking. These include St Peter Port, Guernsey (Burns et al 1996, fig 60, 3/4a, 3/4b, and 3c); Hertford Heath, Hertfordshire (Hussen 1983); Dobova, Slovenia, tomb 10 (Lejars, 1994, 50.2); Intobio, Italy (Lejars 1994, 54.1), and Wederath-Belginum, Germany (Haffner 1989). The Guernsey shears had a decorated sheepskin case with the fleece on the inside. The spring had a leather strap passed through it and was wrapped in a coarse woven textile. The Wederath-Belginum cemetery also contained a number of rich Roman graves with shears.

Iron Age warrior graves in Denmark also occasionally contain shears (described as scissors in Hedeager 1992). None of these graves contained any other agricultural implements, which invites a number of questions to be put. Would the shears or scissors be regarded as the necessary accompanying objects of a warrior or person of status? Are they symbols of power, representing the wealth from flocks of sheep? Can the clipped moustaches of the bog body from Lindow Moss, Cheshire, also of Iron Age date, provide a clue (Stead et al 1986)? Can they be regarded as just another part of the toilet sets found in the Yorkshire Iron Age burials (Stead 1991)?

Dress and display — pins, fibulae, rings, and cosmetic set

Certain of the items deposited are associated with adornment of the human body, whether in the form of fasteners for clothing, or as implements for the preparation of cosmetics. A number of bronze pins can be placed within the Iron Age.

Three ring-headed pins were found at the Power Station (Fig 10.9, 200–202). These pins are common during the British Iron Age, in bronze and iron, although little study has been made of them since that by Dunning in 1934 (see also a summary by O'Connor 1980). O'Connor claims that the form seems to be an insular type and could be a typological development from the swan's-neck pin. The supposedly Late Bronze Age associations at Hagbourne Hill, Berkshire, and Thundersbarrow, Sussex, are obviously very questionable. Many of the classic Iron Age sites in Britain have produced examples of such pins, eg Maiden Castle, Dorset (Wheeler 1943, fig 87, 1–7); Mount Batten, Dorset (Cunliffe 1988, fig 34, 81); Harlyn Bay, Dorset (Whimster 1977, fig 30.6), and, in iron, Yorkshire burials (Stead 1991, fig 67. 1–3). Two pins (Fig 10.9, 205 and 211) could well be imports from Ireland. Pin 211 is very close to an example from Co Waterford (Raftery 1983, fig 139), and both have the swan's-neck shank seen on the ring-headed pins from England and Ireland (Raftery 1994, fig 80). Both of these pins have been dated on metal analysis to Hallstatt C–D. The pin 211 was associated with a small length of fine chain. There is another ornament associated with a length of fine chain (Fig 10.9, 197). This appears to have been a separate decorative head attached to a rectangular shank. Another decorative head, while having the same method of attachment, appears to have had a larger chain (Fig 10.9, 199). Chains are not generally found in the Late Bronze Age, which suggests that the pin with a length of chain claimed to be associated in the Thorndon/Exning hoard, Suffolk, must surely be a dubious association with Late Bronze Age metalwork.

One of the type fossils of the Iron Age, the fibula, is represented by three examples at Flag Fen and the Power Station, two of which are recognisable types. The fibula from Flag Fen (Fig 10.8, 145) is of the

Langton Down type, first identified by Wheeler (1932, 71–4). In Gaul such fibulae belong to the mid first century BC to the mid first century AD (Hattatt 1982, 80–82; Hattatt 1985, 35–7).

The fibula with tin inlay on the bow (Fig 10.8, 150) appears to be an example of Hull's Wessex Type 1Ba (Hull and Hawkes 1987, 95–103, pls 28–9); also illustrated is another fibula with groove on the bow to take inlay from Preston Candover, Hampshire (Hull and Hawkes 1987, pl 30, 2079, Type 1Bb). The Balksbury example of Wessex Type 1Ba is dated to the fourth century BC (Wainwright and Davies 1995, fig 39, 1).

The other fibula from the Power Station (Fig 10.8, 147) is more difficult to place and certainly has no counterpart in the Hull and Hawkes corpus (op cit). A general parallel can be seen in the Type K crossbar head brooches of Hawkes and Hull, which in Britain only occur at Mount Batten, Plymouth, and Harlyn Bay, Cornwall (Hawkes and Hull 1987, 49–52, pl 20). The suggested date is fifth century BC, at least.

The brooch (Fig 10.8, 146) is an example of the rare plate brooches known from the Iron Age. There are two examples, although not of the same design, in graves from Wetwang Slack, Yorkshire. Grave 155 contained a female burial, which gave a calibrated radiocarbon date of cal BC 380–60 cal AD (2110±80 BP). Grave 274, from the same cemetery, was also a female burial. It is possible that a third example is known from the Arras cemetery, Yorkshire (Hull and Hawkes 1987, 154–5, pl 43, 7902 and pl 44, 7893). Another example comes from Meare, Somerset. These brooches have recently been studied by Dent (1996). All of the brooches are tripartite plate brooches with hinged pins and inlay ornament, which was coral in one of the Yorkshire examples. The pelta design on the brooch from the Power Station is reminiscent of that on the brooch from Wetwang Slack, burial 274. Dent (1996) observes that the Power Station piece still retains a recess beneath the bow and that this could be a skeuomorph of hollows seen on the bows of Hull and Hawkes Group L brooches (1987, 63–7, pl 21–2), which are Late Hallstatt in date. The brooches seemed to have formed high status grave goods and might have been broken before deposition both in the graves, and in the waters at the Power Station. Plate brooches of this sort should date to Early and Middle La Tène.

From seeing a photograph of the small, complex gold ring (Fig 10.7, 120), Eluère has suggested two possible parallels, one in a tumulus from Le Chaffais, Doub, France, found with an Early Iron Age Mindelheim sword, three lignite bracelets, and many sherds (Eluère in press). The second parallel comes from tomb 13 in the Hallstatt cemetery, Austria (Eluère et al 1988, fig 1; Eluère 1989, fig 2). A date in the final phases of the Bronze Age or the earliest Iron Age has also been suggested by Dr Alicia Perea (personal communication). There are two coiled bronze rings from the Power Station, which on metal analysis and typology could belong to the Iron Age (Fig 10.10, 242 and 243).

The decorated coiled finger ring (243) is like one from Meare, Somerset (Coles 1987, fig 3.12, E62). The plain coiled ring (242) is of a type known in bronze and iron from a number of Iron Age sites: Balksbury, Hampshire (Wainwright and Davies 1995, fig 41, 8.12); Danebury, Hampshire (Cunliffe 1984, fig 7.25); and Maiden Castle, Dorset (Sharples 1991, fig 82, 3.4).

The two small fragments of decorated bronze (Fig 10.7, 109) could be from an openwork disc. If so, then they could be Iron Age, but as they are too fragmentary to be certain, they have been dated to the Iron Age by metal analysis. A complete openwork roundel has been found at Danebury, Hampshire (Cunliffe and Poole 1991, fig 7.5.1.94 and fig 7.8).

Cosmetic sets (Fig 10.11, 274 and 275) have been discussed in detail by Jackson (1985 and 1993) and the following discussion owes much to notes kindly provided by him. The set from the Power Station brings the total number of sets known from Britain to seven, although a large number of separate components are also known. The components of the Power Station set are among the simplest and plainest known. Although no two cosmetic sets are identical, the closest parallels for the Power Station mortar are unpublished examples from Undley, near Lackenheath (Suffolk), Brandon (Suffolk), and Middleton, Norfolk. Of the published examples Stonea, Cambridgeshire, and Colchester, Essex, come closest (Jackson 1985, fig 6, 25 and 36). Dating is still somewhat of a problem. Jackson claimed that no example can be dated earlier than AD 40–60, although they probably begin earlier. Fitzpatrick (in Thorpe et al 1994) quotes Stead and Rigby (1989) in saying that the set from King Harry Lane, Hertfordshire, is potentially, rather than certainly, of pre-Roman date. In discussing the recent find of an end-looped pestle from Normanton le Heath, Leicestershire (Thorpe et al 1994), Fitzpatrick noted that 'the Normanton le Heath find further suggests a late Iron Age origin for these sets without conclusively demonstrating one'. The Power Station set was found in the north-east corner of the site (Fig 10.16 below).

Miscellaneous

The fragment of U-sectioned binding strip (Fig 10.7, 118) belongs to the Late Iron Age–Early Roman period on metal analysis. In the Iron Age, such bronze bindings are known on a variety of objects, eg shields and a possible wooden lid from the Yorkshire burials (Stead 1991, figs 47 and 49). There are a number of curved and straight fragments of U-sectioned bindings from Danebury, Hampshire (Cunliffe and Poole 1991, fig 7.5.1.104).

On metal analysis, the bronze bar (Fig 10.6, 82), the bronze disc (Fig 10.6, 92), and the small decorated bronze strip (Fig 10.7, 102) have been assigned to the Iron Age. The lead rolls (Fig 10.8, 155–7, 160–62) can be compared to examples from Meare Village East,

Somerset (Coles 1987, 134–5), where they are described as net sinkers. The Power Station examples are small and might perhaps have been used as sinkers for fishing lines.

A series of objects can only be assigned to the Iron Age by virtue of the fact that they are made of iron. These are either functional objects, such as the iron awl with a bone handle (Fig 10.11, 272), the hook (Fig 10.10, 261), and various rings (Fig 10.10, 263 and Fig 10.11, 264) or incomplete or broken (eg Fig 10.10, 262 and Fig 10.11, 268).

The two decorated strap ends (Fig 10.8, 153 and 158) are impossible to parallel in the Bronze and Iron Ages. The fixing arrangement can be seen on a strap end from Balksbury, Hampshire (Wainwright and Davies 1995, Fig 40, 21). This has repoussé decoration and is dated to the later Roman period.

Ritual and the deposition of Iron Age metalwork

If it is accepted that Iron Age metalwork, like that in the Bronze Age, could have been deliberately deposited, then it is worth comparing the Flag Fen assemblage with other recognised Iron Age ritual sites. In Britain, these mainly consist of watery deposits, wells, shafts, and shrines (Wait 1985). Special deposits of material are also found, however, on numerous military and domestic sites. Wait (op cit) and Fitzpatrick (1984) give good summaries of watery deposits in the Iron Age. It is clear that in the Iron Age, the Bronze Age practice continued of making a large number of deposits in rivers, especially the Thames. Overwhelmingly, the bias is towards weaponry, tools occurring

only rarely. The emphasis on martial artefacts is also seen in other rivers. From shafts and wells come a great range of material. The metal objects include weapons, body armour, iron tools, especially those of blacksmiths and carpenters, jewellery, and coins. From the shrines, brooches and coins are the most frequent finds, but miniature bronze weapons, full-size iron ones, and horse and chariot fittings also occur (Wait op cit).

A similar situation prevails on the Continent, where rivers play a prominent role. Wet sites such as La Tène, and Nidau, Switzerland (Müller 1991, 526–9), contain large numbers of weapons, but also tools and fibulae. The dominance of weaponry, often deliberately broken, is also in evidence at Gournay (Bruneaux and Rapin 1988; Lejars 1994).

The distribution of prehistoric metalwork at the Power Station

The distribution of metalwork from the Power Station is presented in a series of schematic plans (Figs 10.12–20). Certain general trends emerge. First, a large proportion of the assemblage was found at the very edge of the dryland. The approximate boundary of the dryland would have been determined by the northerly and southerly extensions of the two droveway ditches, which probably served to mark out the edge of regularly flooded land. Very few items indeed were found on the northern side of the post alignment. The vast majority of these were on dry land. Early objects were confined to drier ground (Fig 10.12), but later (mainly Iron Age) objects appear to reverse this trend (Fig 10.20). It should also be noted that by the Iron

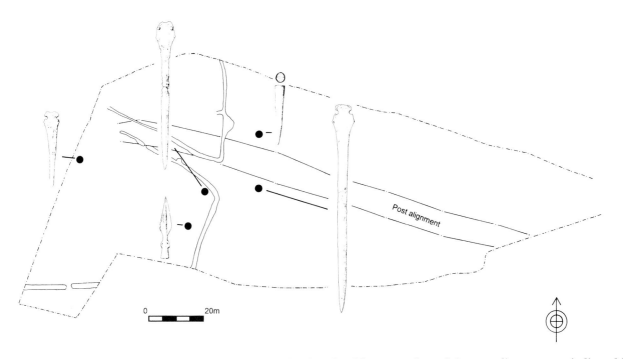

Fig 10.12 Distribution of early metalwork at the Power Station site. The outer edges of the post alignment are indicated by long broken lines

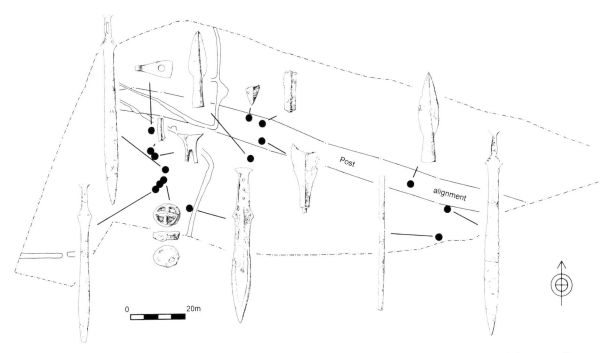

Fig 10.13 Distribution of Late Bronze Age weaponry at the Power Station site. The outer edges of the post alignment are indicated by long broken lines

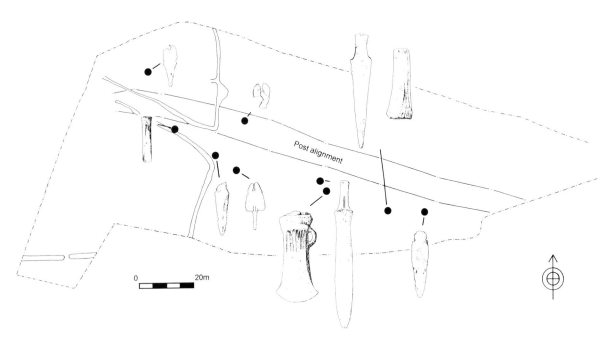

Fig 10.14 Distribution of knives, razors, socketed gouge, socketed axe, and tanged daggers at the Power Station site. The outer edges of the post alignment are indicated by long broken lines

Age the wet/dry interface would probably have moved 'inland' by several metres, perhaps thereby exaggerating the apparent tendency of Iron Age material to be deposited either in water or on wetter ground (Fig 1.4; Charles French personal communication). Although Bronze Age leaf-shaped swords tend to be concentrated on the drier ground, this is by no means a general rule (Fig 10.13). Other categories of tools or weapons do not show complementary distributions, with the notable exception of pointed (?helmet) rivets, which

occurred in two tight clusters (Fig 10.15). It is possible that the two groups of rivets represent two distinct events, in which two possible helmets were ritually taken apart or destroyed. It is perhaps noteworthy that many of the smaller objects seem to have been deposited some distance away from the post alignment (Figs 10.16 and 10.17). The occurrence of the three small lead cushion-shaped objects at the extreme western boundary of the excavation is of some interest, if these were indeed miniature anvils or backing blocks used

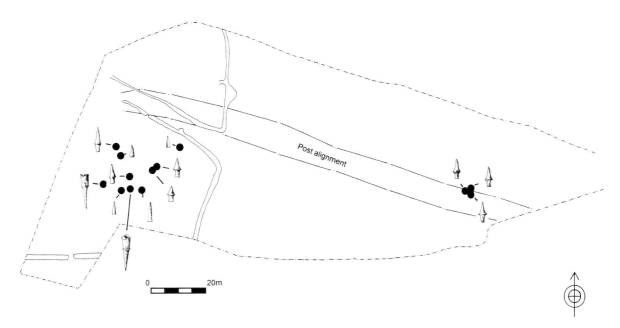

Fig 10.15 Distribution of pointed rivets and two socketed spikes at the Power Station site. The outer edges of the post alignment are indicated by long broken lines

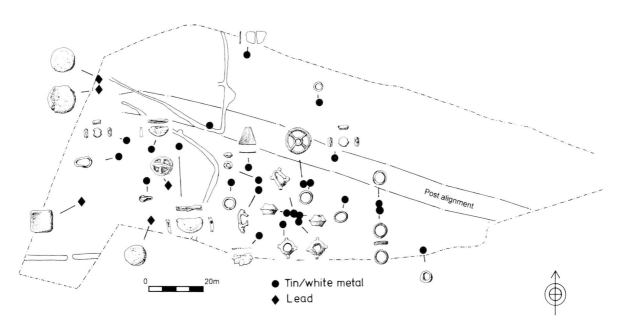

Fig 10.16 Distribution of lead and white metal objects at the Power Station site. The outer edges of the post alignment are indicated by long broken lines

when executing detailed decoration on sheet metal-work. A dryland distribution would certainly accord with *in situ* metalworking.

The distribution of pins shows a strong preference for drier ground. This might indicate a different type or pattern of ritual that might not necessarily have involved water at all (Fig 10.18).

Whether the clothes that normally would have accompanied the pins were also torn and damaged is, of course, uncertain; but dry cloth floats, which might help to account for this otherwise striking landward distribution.

The distribution of tanged awls shows two distinct clusters of finds, one wet, the other dry (Fig 10.19). It is tempting to suggest that again two types of ritual are represented; perhaps the completion of training or apprenticeship (dry ground) and the final deposition of a craftsman's equipment on death (wet ground).

Finally, the distribution of Iron Age finds (Fig 10.20) shows, as we have already noted, a mainly 'wet' distribution. The occurrence together of the two iron swords fragments is therefore of some note. The bronze shears (Fig 10.11, 276) were found on the spoil heap and their original location has been lost.

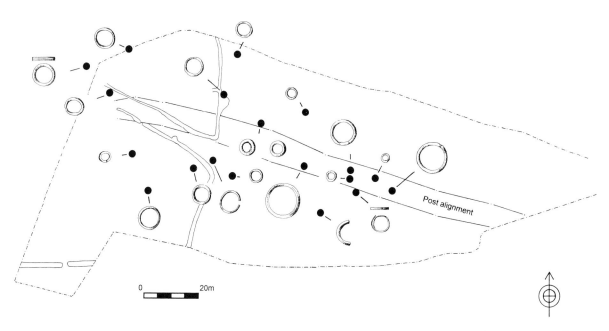

Fig 10.17 Distribution of bronze rings at the Power Station site. The outer edges of the post alignment are indicated by long broken lines

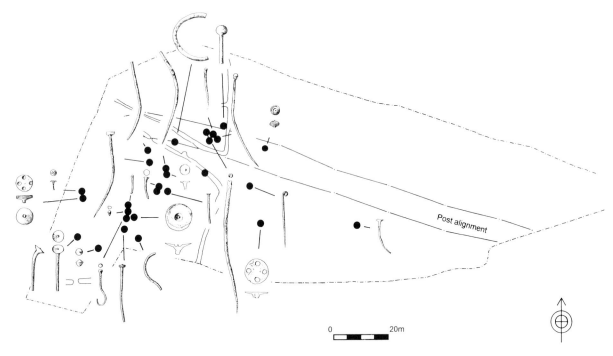

Fig 10.18 Distribution of bronze pins and pin fragments at the Power Station site. The outer edges of the post alignment are indicated by long broken lines

Apart from a spread along the wetland/dryland edge, the material is quite closely confined to the post alignment and does not spread out far on either side. This might well reflect the fact that, by Iron Age times, the posts had rotted away and would only have been visible in dry seasons.

Analysis of the metalwork
by B M Rohl and J P Northover

The first part of this paper is by J P Northover, the second (a discussion of the lead isotope analysis) by B M Rohl. The discussion of tin and tin alloy objects in the second part is by J P Northover.

The assemblage

The two later Bronze Age sites associated with Flag Fen, the Flag Fen platform, and the Fengate Power Station post alignment, have both produced important collections of metalwork. Seven copper-alloy objects were found during the excavation of Flag Fen. The rest were recovered from the area surrounding the post alignment. Of these, the majority were found to the

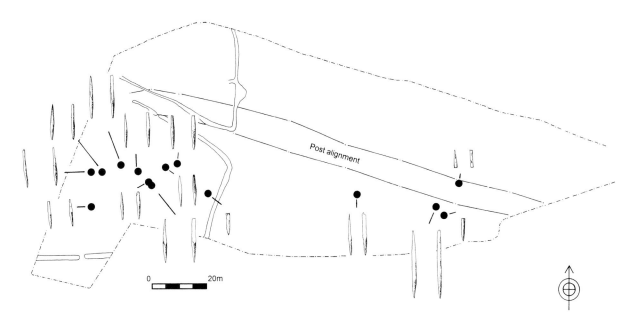

Fig 10.19 Distribution of tanged awls at the Power Station site. The outer edges of the post alignment are indicated by long broken lines

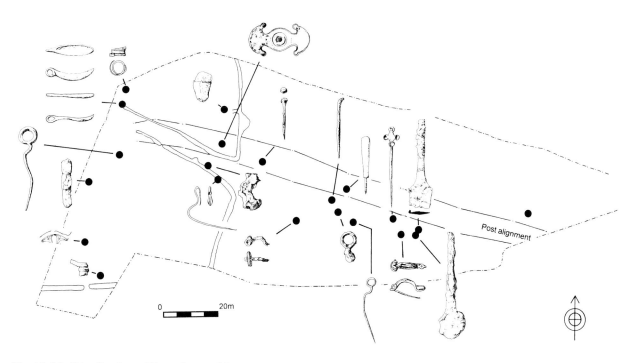

Fig 10.20 Distribution of Iron Age and later metalwork at the Power Station site. The outer edges of the post alignment are indicated by long broken lines

south of the Power Station with a degree of clustering of different classes of material within the area. Archaeological aspects of the metalwork have been reviewed in some detail by Coombs (1992), prior to his definitive discussion of the entire assemblage in the preceding section of this chapter.

The chronological spread of the material runs from the twelfth and eleventh centuries BC to *c* 300 BC. The small number of later pieces is partly attributable to the nearby presence of a Roman road. The great majority of the finds date to the later Bronze Age, say from the eleventh to the eighth century BC.

Coombs noted that, within this period, a number of types had a rather long production life and were difficult to date precisely. Subsequently, a primary object of the programme of metal analysis described in this paper was to use well-established correlations between composition, typology, and chronology to provide better dating for some of the material (cf Northover 1980, 1982, and 1983; Rychner and Kläntschi 1995). The other objectives were to look at the alloys used for types not well represented in existing analytical databases, notably the pins, and to investigate the composition of all the small 'white metal' finds. In the following discussion a conventional periodisation of the Bronze Age and Iron Age will be used:

Penard   twelfth–eleventh century BC
(Late Bronze Age I)
Wilburton   mid eleventh–mid tenth
(Late Bronze Age II)   century BC
Ewart Park   mid tenth–eighth
(Late Bronze Age III)   century BC
Llyn Fawr   seventh century BC
(Late Bronze Age IV–Hallstatt)
Hallstatt D   sixth–mid fifth century BC
(Early Iron Age)
La Tène   mid fifth century BC–
(Middle–Late Iron Age) Roman Conquest

Analysis of data

Since the analysis of Bronze Age metalwork became established in Britain in the 1950s, it has become clear that certain key changes in alloy composition occurred at specific horizons. For the material considered here, the two most important are the adoption of leaded bronze alloys at the start of the Wilburton period of the Late Bronze Age, now dated to the eleventh century BC (Brown and Blin-Stoyle 1959; Northover 1982) and the general abandonment of leaded bronze for much of the La Tène Iron Age (Northover 1991). Within this broad framework, there were regular changes in the details of alloy content, which depended on local choice, the availability of the necessary resources, and the degree of dependency on secondary, scrap supplies. At the same time, there were regular changes in the location and type of copper resources exploited, with consequent changes in impurity patterns. These have now been charted through the Bronze Age and into the Iron Age (Northover 1980 and 1991). Important changes occur at the Penard/Wilburton transition and at the beginning of the La Tène period.

The first is marked by a change from an As/Ni to As/Sb/Ni/Ag impurity patterns with a large increase in their concentrations, usually above 0.50% for As, Sb. The second is associated with the appearance of a copper type with As, Co, and Ni as the principal impurities, with $Co \geq Ni$. Iron contents up to 0.5% or more are common in this group. All these phenomena are recognisable in the Flag Fen analyses and were used to sort the analyses into a pattern that could be compared with the typological record.

In all, 115 samples were taken. Full analyses are presented for 113 and qualitative identifications for the remaining two. Of the 115, 18 samples, including the two analysed qualitatively, were from tin, and two from tin-lead alloy objects. The remaining 95 analyses were then sorted in descending order of antimony content and a cut off placed at 0.50% antimony. Twenty analyses fell into this category, of which the majority could

realistically be associated with the Wilburton period. These included typical Wilburton swords and chapes and one of the French variant. One analysis with only 0.32% antimony was added to this group, as this was a rivet from a Wilburton sword. It is possible that other similar analyses should be placed with the Wilburton objects, but there is no strong typological support for this. The next step was to identify other Late Bronze Age material, initially on the basis of lead content. The 74 remaining analyses were therefore sorted in descending order of lead content and a bar placed at 1%. This recognises the fact that not all Late Bronze Age objects had lead deliberately added to the melt at the time of casting. Some material, especially sheet, was left lead-free, while scrap would almost always have at least a residual lead content. From the resulting group, it was then necessary to remove a small number of objects that typologically belonged to the Iron Age and Roman periods. This left 34 objects that could be broadly assigned to the Ewart Park period; some might actually belong to the succeeding Llyn Fawr period, but can not be separated either typologically or metallurgically.

From the remaining 40 analysed objects, three could be identified as very late Iron Age or Roman, leaving 37 objects still to be assigned to a period, either to Penard or to the Iron Age. Two further reductions of the data could be made on the basis of composition. Examples with Co>Ni, which would almost certainly be Iron Age in date, were selected first, followed by those with Ni>0.3%, which previous experience suggested would almost certainly be early in the Penard period, or even date to the very end of the preceding Taunton period. These assumptions were vindicated by the correct selection of obvious Iron Age types such as the La Tène I fibula and a spiral ring on the basis of cobalt content, and the assignment of two Group IV rapiers to late Taunton/early Penard (cf Burgess and Gerloff 1981). The final division of analyses combining typology and composition placed 22 objects in the Penard period, four in the latest Bronze Age/earliest Iron Age, contemporary with Hallstatt C–D in Continental Europe, and eleven in the La Tène Iron Age. To these last should be added the tin inlay of the La Tène I fibula from among the tin analyses.

With this classification completed, the changes in use and deposition of bronze, period-by-period during the lifetime of the Flag Fen and Power Station sites, can now be reviewed.

Penard

Over half the 22 Penard and possible late Taunton objects that were analysed were from weapons or weapon accessories (eg the shield tab 43 and conical ferrule 45). This includes such well defined Middle Bronze Age types as the dirks and rapiers (Fig 10.1) and the side looped spearhead (48), but also includes parts of swords, weapons that were first introduced at this time.

Although the short sword (7) is problematic, as it has a rather Ewart Park-style hilt, other features are earlier and the sword is undoubtedly made from unleaded bronze. As short swords are known from the Wilburton period, this weapon should perhaps be placed at the end of Penard and overlapping with Wilburton. Also included here are pieces of sheet tentatively identified as parts from a helmet or helmets (95), but these are objects otherwise unknown in Britain. Another important prestige item is a flesh hook (58), similar to one found with the cauldron from Feltwell, Norfolk (Gerloff 1986). Other Penard pieces are ornamental pins and a ring and only one or two possible tools.

Wilburton

Characteristic of the Wilburton period are long tongue chapes and leaf-shaped swords with flanged, slotted hilts. Two examples came from the Power Station (4 and 6). From Flag Fen comes a chape with the plain section and straight mouth that define the French equivalent of the British long-tongue chape (38). The only other weapon is a spearhead. Tools are more apparent, with a number of short awls, engraving tools, and so on, similar to those from a contemporary settlement from near Compiègne in France (Blanchet 1984). Pins with Wilburton compositions tend to be knob headed or nail headed, with one disc-headed pin analysed. Three of the enigmatic conical rivets (nos 8–15) were analysed. These were initially identified as possible helmet parts, as Continental bronze helmets have such rivets. With the possible exception of the Power Station sheet metal fragments, however, helmets are unknown in Britain, apart from which, these rivets have not been closed. The conical rivets that appear much later on Llyn Fawr period cauldrons are much smaller. It seems preferable to assume that these were used to decorate other materials, such as wood or leather harness, wagons, or even personal ornaments.

Ewart Park

As discussed earlier, the antimony and arsenic contents of Ewart Park metalwork are lower than in Wilburton. Among several causes are the effects of recycling, the effects of incorporating purer ingot copper, and changes in the composition of imported scrap. On the east coast of England, these changes occurred more slowly than in the south, where the influence of scrap from the Carp's Tongue complex of Atlantic Europe was greater (the group is named after the appearance of their characteristic sword blade). There might also have been a contribution from British primary resources, but for the moment there are no data. Carp's Tongue scrap tends to have low Sb contents, with As>>Sb. There are several items in the Ewart Park list (Table 10.2) of this composition, primarily the disc-headed pins (174, 175, and so on), which have good north French parallels.

The Ewart Park material contains an even lower proportion of weapons and weapon-related material than the Wilburton group. These are a Ewart Park sword (5) and short tongue chape (41), a plain spearhead (46), spear ferrule (44), and tanged knives (55, 56) that could double as daggers. Continuity with Wilburton times is shown by the conical rivets and an even larger variety of tools. Given that the short tongue chape and spear ferrule would almost certainly be early Ewart Park in date, it is suggested that the use and deposition of metalwork at Flag Fen reached a peak in late Wilburton/early Ewart Park. In calendar years this is the tenth century BC, perhaps extending into the ninth, a dating that correlates well with the dendrochronology for the site.

Llyn Fawr/Early Iron Age

Some items in the Ewart Park list might, of course, belong here, but they can not be easily identified. Specific to the period are the swan's-neck pins (201, 202) and the chain associated with one of them (211). Coombs (above) has very tentatively assigned a three-riveted dagger (52) to the late Ewart Park or Llyn Fawr periods. Unfortunately, this is so corroded that a realistic analysis was not possible.

La Tène

Besides iron swords and an axe not discussed here, some definitive types, such as a La Tène I fibula, belong to the La Tène Iron Age. The fibula is remarkable in that its bow has a hollow back, inlaid with tin. It is possible that others exist, their inlays, now corroded, misidentified as coral. Also placed in this category, by virtue of their composition, are the shears and their wooden box (276). Ring-headed pins, spiral rings, and ribbed beads are all possible La Tène ornaments.

Roman

The three items analysed were a plate brooch, a medicine mortar, and a piece of U-shaped binding. The leaded bronze of the last item places it at earliest in the very latest Iron Age. The medicine mortar is also of interest in that the alloy contains only 1.5% tin, the same low tin content as others analysed (Northover unpublished).

Lead isotope analysis

It was possible to include 41 of the 115 analysed objects from Flag Fen in part of an extensive programme of lead isotope analysis of British Bronze Age metalwork. Material from the Penard, Wilburton, and Ewart Park periods was included, as well as two Iron Age objects. The data are listed in Table 10.3.

Table 10.2 Non-ferrous metal analyses from Flag Fen and the Power Station

sample	cat no	object	Fe	Co	Ni	Cu	Zn	As	Sb	Sn	Ag	Bi	Pb	Au	S
tin ornaments															
FF4	FNG181	tin wheel	0.03	0.02	0.01	0.00	0.01	0.00	0.00	99.86	0.00	0.01	0.01	0.01	0.02
FF91	FNG197	tin bead	0.01	0.01	0.00	0.09	0.01	0.00	0.00	99.83	0.00	0.02	0.01	0.00	0.01
FF83	FNG198	tin bead	0.01	0.01	0.01	0.16	0.03	0.00	0.00	99.70	0.00	0.05	0.02	0.00	0.00
FF1	FNG028	tin ring	0.01	0.00	0.01	0.03	0.04	0.13	0.00	99.67	0.00	0.05	0.05	0.02	0.00
FF89	FNG014	tin bead	0.04	0.02	0.03	0.39	0.04	0.00	0.00	99.44	0.00	0.00	0.00	0.04	0.01
FF2	FNG003	tin ring	0.06	0.01	0.00	0.44	0.06	0.00	0.00	99.35	0.00	0.01	0.03	0.03	0.01
FF87	FNG039	tin bead	0.04	0.02	0.00	0.20	0.00	0.00	0.00	99.35	0.00	0.00	0.34	0.00	0.04
FF84	FNG283	semi-circular tab	0.01	0.01	0.03	0.33	0.00	0.00	0.00	99.32	0.00	0.00	0.27	0.04	0.00
FF6	FNG004	white metal ornament	0.06	0.00	0.01	0.07	0.00	0.38	0.00	99.25	0.00	0.00	0.03	0.04	0.04
FF88	FNG196	tin bead	0.03	0.01	0.02	0.21	0.01	0.41	0.00	99.21	0.00	0.02	0.04	0.01	0.01
FF82	FNG200	tin object with knobs	0.03	0.00	0.00	0.20	0.01	0.55	0.00	99.16	0.00	0.00	0.03	0.00	0.01
FF17	FNG195	white metal ornament	0.01	0.00	0.01	0.38	0.00	0.14	0.00	99.14	0.00	0.01	0.02	0.00	0.31
FF24	FNG179	tin ring								99.00					
FF37	FNG180	tin alloy ornament								99.00					
FF90	FNG195	white metal ornament	0.04	0.01	0.03	0.11	0.00	0.86	0.00	98.92	0.00	0.00	0.00	0.02	0.02
FF37	FNG094	tin wheel	0.58	0.01	0.02	0.06	0.03	0.49	0.00	98.62	0.00	0.01	0.04	0.06	0.10
FF29	FNG142	white metal ornament	0.00	0.01	0.01	1.73	0.00	1.97	0.00	96.07	0.00	0.07	0.13	0.00	0.00
tin (Iron Age)															
FF6	FNG031	brooch inlay	0.04	0.00	0.02	3.20	0.00	0.46	0.00	96.07	0.00	0.02	0.05	0.07	0.05
tin-lead alloys															
FF86	FNG289	tin-lead wheel fragment	0.02	0.00	0.00	0.80	0.00	0.14	0.00	74.29	0.00	0.01	24.72	0.01	0.00
FF85	FNG026	pewter strapend	0.00	0.01	0.00	0.23	0.00	0.00	0.00	57.09	0.00	0.01	42.64	0.02	0.00
?Late Taunton/Early Penard															
FF55	FNG278	engraving tool	0.04	0.03	0.54	87.57	0.00	0.48	0.07	11.11	0.00	0.00	0.10	0.00	0.26
FF96	FNG137	rapier, Group IV	0.04	0.02	0.35	87.74	0.00	<0.20	0.11	10.54	0.05	0.00	0.40	0.01	0.64
FF54	FNG084	rapier hilt, Group IV	0.03	0.02	0.38	87.44	0.00	0.39	0.11	11.54	0.02	0.01	0.05	0.00	0.01
FF63	FNG145	small knife blade	0.03	0.03	0.58	84.06	0.00	<0.20	0.08	14.60	0.00	0.00	0.10	0.05	0.47
Penard															
FF64	FNG020	bracelet, penannular	0.05	0.00	0.00	86.37	0.00	0.51	0.01	12.93	0.04	0.01	0.04	0.00	0.03
FF18	FNG024	conical ferrule	0.12	0.02	0.14	86.42	0.00	0.44	0.03	12.52	0.02	0.08	0.07	0.00	0.15
FF71	FF	flesh hook	0.01	0.04	0.12	86.47	0.01	0.40	0.03	12.70	0.02	0.03	0.13	0.00	0.02
FF75	FNG132	?helmet fragment	0.12	0.01	0.02	86.61	0.02	0.48	0.05	12.08	0.01	0.02	0.43	0.00	0.16
FF116	FNG127	?helmet fragment	0.10	0.02	0.03	86.08	0.02	0.17	0.05	12.66	0.02	0.05	0.76	0.01	0.03
FF34	FNG121	knob-headed pin, large knob	0.62	0.01	0.03	86.85	0.00	0.21	0.01	12.73	0.02	0.00	0.14	0.00	0.04
FF73	FF018	nail-headed pin, corroded	2.43	0.03	0.09	48.37	0.01	0.42	0.05	20.17	0.05	0.05	0.35	0.06	0.57
FF94	FNG194	pin, head, S, leaf	0.19	0.01	0.02	90.18	0.00	0.68	0.02	8.51	0.00	0.07	0.30	0.00	0.03
FF93	FNG016	pin, shaft	0.02	0.03	0.16	88.96	0.01	0.44	0.03	10.16	0.00	0.05	0.08	0.00	0.06
FF27	FNG248	ring	0.09	0.01	0.05	83.38	0.01	<0.20	0.06	16.29	0.00	0.02	0.03	0.00	0.04
FF49	FNG117	shield tab	0.02	0.02	0.09	91.58	0.01	<0.20	0.06	7.86	0.08	0.00	0.91	0.00	0.11
FF52	FNG281	short sword	0.01	0.02	0.13	86.30	0.00	0.25	0.08	12.05	0.02	0.03	0.92	0.08	0.09
FF21	FNG205	side-looped spearhead	0.10	0.00	0.06	83.78	0.03	<0.20	0.00	15.37	0.00	0.05	0.02	0.03	0.03
FF53	FNG228	small notch-butt dirk	0.04	0.01	0.07	89.20	0.01	<0.20	0.01	10.31	0.02	0.05	0.00	0.27	0.02
FF69	FF019	spearhead	0.01	0.03	0.12	88.78	0.00	<0.20	0.04	12.56	0.01	0.03	0.06	0.00	0.22
FF7	FNG277	sword/knife blade	0.01	0.07	0.14	89.07	0.00	0.32	0.05	9.65	0.03	0.02	0.19	0.00	0.45
FF20	FNG009	sword point	0.02	0.02	0.09	90.44	0.01	<0.20	0.01	9.20	0.01	0.01	0.06	0.00	0.04
FF47	FNG140	sword rivet	0.02	0.04	0.22	85.64	0.01	0.57	0.06	13.17	0.02	0.00	0.11	0.00	0.14
Wilburton (Pb >1%; Sb >0.50%)															
FF14	FNG209	awl	0.01	0.01	0.19	86.25	0.01	0.42	0.61	9.65	0.34	0.03	1.21	0.01	0.02
FF72	FF021	chape, French	0.01	0.01	0.39	85.38	0.00	0.98	0.13	7.07	0.65	0.04	4.14	0.00	0.02
FF108	FNG011	chape, long tongue, British	0.03	0.03	0.09	80.18	0.02	1.43	1.52	9.04	0.56	0.06	6.57	0.06	0.41
FF43	FNG167	conical rivet	0.00	0.00	0.32	80.38	0.01	0.27	0.68	12.56	0.34	0.01	4.93	0.00	0.01
FF114	FNG296	conical rivet	0.02	0.00	0.33	78.24	0.01	0.24	0.78	13.46	0.35	0.01	6.46	0.01	0.11
FF42	FNG280	conical rivet	0.00	0.01	0.31	78.90	0.00	0.57	0.63	12.90	0.34	0.00	6.30	0.00	0.03
FF58	FNG258	engraving tool	0.00	0.04	0.32	85.55	0.00	0.58	1.04	8.39	0.25	0.04	3.74	0.00	0.06
FF12	FNG258	engraving tool	0.05	0.03	0.25	84.80	0.02	0.59	0.77	6.56	0.25	0.20	5.16	0.00	0.04

Table 10.2 *(cont'd)*

sample	cat no	object	Fe	Co	Ni	Cu	Zn	As	Sb	Sn	Ag	Bi	Pb	Au	S
Wilburton (Pb >1%; Sb >0.50%)															
FF95	FNG018	knob-headed pin	0.05	0.05	0.32	86.48	0.01	0.49	0.95	9.27	0.41	0.02	1.90	0.02	0.02
FF74	FF007	knob-headed pin	0.13	0.05	0.25	80.87	0.00	0.55	0.71	9.74	0.25	0.02	7.43	0.00	0.03
FF94	FNG122	nail-headed pin	0.00	0.03	0.28	82.84	0.00	1.44	0.72	8.08	0.25	0.02	6.21	0.02	0.09
FF36	FNG257	nail-headed pin	0.01	0.01	0.18	86.39	0.00	0.42	0.72	10.27	0.28	0.01	1.57	0.01	0.08
FF35	FNG271	pin, disc head	0.01	0.04	0.22	85.68	0.00	0.62	1.19	9.46	0.43	0.08	2.29	0.00	0.02
FF22	FNG274	plain pegged spearhead	0.01	0.03	0.23	68.66	0.02	0.56	0.60	6.52	0.22	0.00	23.04	0.03	0.08
FF46	FNG230	short rectangular rod	0.01	0.03	0.26	84.49	0.00	0.42	0.95	8.53	0.23	0.04	4.94	0.08	0.03
FF67	FNG210	small tool	0.00	0.01	0.24	79.78	0.00	0.42	0.63	11.11	0.39	0.02	7.38	0.00	0.02
FF68	FNG262	small tool	0.01	0.00	0.33	86.08	0.00	0.55	1.01	6.58	0.44	0.04	4.80	0.08	0.08
FF79	FNG147	Wilburton sword, centre	0.00	0.02	0.21	61.60	0.01	<0.20	0.99	9.49	0.35	0.02	27.00	0.12	0.18
FF81	FNG001	Wilburton sword, centre	0.00	0.07	0.24	80.38	0.00	0.67	0.67	10.15	0.14	0.00	7.64	0.00	0.03
FF56	FNG162	Wilburton sword, hilt	0.00	0.03	0.17	85.26	0.00	0.36	0.54	11.65	0.12	0.04	1.83	0.00	0.01
FF80	FNG001	Wilburton sword, rivet	0.00	0.02	0.10	64.29	0.02	0.37	0.32	5.96	0.09	0.03	28.72	0.07	0.01
Ewart Park (Pb >1%; Sb <0.5%)															
FF13	FNG213	awl	0.02	0.01	0.22	86.27	0.01	<0.20	0.46	9.99	0.23	0.05	2.56	0.08	0.03
FF15	FNG190	awl	0.02	0.01	0.09	87.94	0.01	0.56	0.19	9.60	0.15	0.05	1.14	0.01	0.20
FF107	FNG275	conical rivet	0.03	0.02	0.11	89.53	0.01	<0.20	0.26	6.60	0.08	0.00	3.13	0.00	0.09
FF115	FNG188	conical rivet	0.01	0.01	0.11	90.40	0.00	0.78	0.29	8.69	0.08	0.03	1.22	0.04	0.03
FF76	FNG170	conical rivet	0.01	0.00	0.12	86.99	0.01	0.37	0.30	7.26	0.06	0.01	4.73	0.00	0.15
FF30	FNG214	disc pin head	0.06	0.02	0.09	79.02	0.00	1.23	0.20	15.86	0.04	0.05	3.31	0.00	0.12
FF31	FNG199	disc pin head, 4 holes	0.01	0.07	0.11	91.72	0.01	0.16	0.05	5.63	0.04	0.03	2.20	0.02	0.06
FF77	FNG128	domed object, ?pommel	0.02	0.01	0.13	83.82	0.01	<0.20	0.17	7.57	0.10	0.03	8.00	0.08	0.04
FF51	FNG098	double-edged tanged knife	0.00	0.01	0.03	82.32	0.00	<0.20	0.09	7.01	0.05	0.03	10.43	0.00	0.04
FF78	FNG203	Ewart Park sword	0.00	0.00	0.12	84.40	0.00	0.92	0.23	11.39	0.11	0.03	2.67	0.10	0.02
FF26	FNG231	expanded terminal bracelet	0.08	0.13	0.13	82.17	0.00	0.92	0.18	11.37	0.08	0.09	5.89	0.00	0.08
FF107	FNG033	gouge	0.08	0.01	0.07	91.37	0.02	<0.20	0.09	7.04	0.07	0.00	1.22	0.00	0.02
FF61	FNG215	large disc pin head	0.28	0.01	0.09	83.56	0.00	0.29	0.03	11.21	0.04	0.03	4.27	0.00	0.19
FF45	FNG168	long conical rivet	0.01	0.00	0.10	89.43	0.00	0.23	0.18	6.74	0.09	0.00	3.15	0.05	0.04
FF41	FNG218	long conical rivet, fragment	0.00	0.03	0.12	77.71	0.00	<0.20	0.21	8.23	0.03	0.05	13.44	0.00	0.13
FF23	FNG138	plain pegged spearhead	0.03	0.00	0.10	82.86	0.00	<0.20	0.24	9.23	0.08	0.00	7.33	0.00	0.08
FF9	FNG105	razor, bifid, 3-rib	0.06	0.01	0.25	88.78	0.00	0.50	0.47	8.13	0.31	0.03	1.41	0.01	0.04
FF110	FNG207	ridged ring	0.00	0.01	0.10	85.95	0.00	0.46	0.32	10.64	0.13	0.02	2.24	0.00	0.13
FF26	FNG134	ring	0.00	0.01	0.13	84.70	0.00	<0.20	0.24	8.69	0.12	0.02	6.15	0.00	0.01
FF62	FNG292	roll-headed pin	0.11	0.01	0.16	79.78	0.00	<0.20	0.39	10.12	0.21	0.01	9.15	0.00	0.16
FF44	FNG216	round rod	0.00	0.05	0.13	79.58	0.01	0.51	0.28	12.77	0.10	0.00	6.50	0.03	0.05
FF48	FNG014	short tongue chape	0.00	0.03	0.15	79.50	0.02	0.27	0.49	6.88	0.16	0.02	12.35	0.00	0.15
FF66	FNG258	small awl	0.00	0.03	0.23	85.90	0.01	<0.20	0.42	6.63	0.13	0.05	6.38	0.22	0.00
FF60	FNG085	small disc-headed pin	0.02	0.02	0.16	88.60	0.01	<0.20	0.31	9.07	0.14	0.03	1.42	0.00	0.03
FF59	FNG087	small flat-bladed tool	0.00	0.02	0.14	87.52	0.00	0.85	0.36	7.68	0.21	0.06	3.15	0.00	0.02
FF101	FNG027	small thick-sectioned ring	0.02	0.01	0.14	87.42	0.01	<0.20	0.27	9.46	0.14	0.02	2.48	0.00	0.03
FF102	FNG224	small tool	0.01	0.03	0.17	87.48	0.00	<0.20	0.19	12.42	0.20	0.00	1.22	0.12	0.07
FF104	FNG172	small tool	0.03	0.01	0.17	88.89	0.00	0.23	0.44	8.26	0.20	0.02	1.48	0.02	0.25
FF113	FNG212	socketed punch	0.00	0.01	0.13	86.92	0.00	<0.20	0.37	10.78	0.14	0.00	1.52	0.03	0.07
FF38	FNG219	socketed punch	0.01	0.01	0.15	89.31	0.00	<0.20	0.37	8.11	0.16	0.00	1.80	0.00	0.11
FF57	FNG219	socketed punch	0.02	0.01	0.12	89.32	0.01	0.35	0.28	6.86	0.14	0.01	2.62	0.00	0.26
FF19	FNG293	spear ferrule	0.02	0.01	0.06	91.97	0.00	<0.20	0.07	4.66	0.04	0.01	3.06	0.00	0.12
FF50	FNG032	tanged knife with handle	0.01	0.00	0.12	87.98	0.01	0.22	0.26	8.50	0.11	0.00	2.66	0.00	0.12
FF103	FNG109	tang or tool point	0.00	0.01	0.12	90.31	0.00	<0.20	0.19	8.04	0.09	0.04	1.06	0.01	0.04
Hallstatt C-D (LBA III–EIA)															
FF70	FNG005	three-rivet dagger, corroded	0.74	0.02	0.07	43.12	0.01	0.77	0.05	27.51	0.04	0.01	0.17	0.00	52.00
FF109	FNG237	chain link (with pin)	0.30	0.03	0.02	74.00	0.01	<0.20	0.00	24.56	0.00	0.00	0.45	0.01	0.50
FF97	FNG146	swan's-neck pin, leaf head	0.38	0.03	0.16	88.87	0.00	0.27	0.04	9.26	0.08	0.02	0.54	0.01	0.33
FF111	FNG237	swan's-neck pin, inlays	0.12	0.05	0.11	92.91	0.00	<0.20	0.12	6.05	0.07	0.01	0.27	0.06	0.08

Table 10.2 *(cont'd)*

sample	cat no	object	Fe	Co	Ni	Cu	Zn	As	Sb	Sn	Ag	Bi	Pb	Au	S
La Tène Iron Age															
FF5	FNG031	La Tène I brooch, bow	0.04	0.02	0.02	89.78	0.00	0.22	0.01	9.69	0.02	0.02	0.15	0.00	0.02
FF111	FNG284	bar	0.47	0.04	0.06	86.29	0.00	0.62	0.05	11.22	0.02	0.00	1.03	0.00	0.02
FF32	FNG177	ring-headed pin	0.00	0.09	0.10	89.29	0.01	<0.20	0.03	6.00	0.07	0.00	4.19	0.00	0.06
FF33	FNG130	ring-headed pin	0.13	0.01	0.05	89.56	0.00	<0.20	0.02	9.80	0.03	0.05	0.24	0.00	0.04
FF40	FNG256	large spiral ring	0.30	0.01	0.04	88.48	0.02	0.56	0.12	9.92	0.17	0.02	0.39	0.01	0.08
FF112	FNG261	sheet ornament	0.30	0.03	0.03	85.47	0.09	0.23	0.02	13.36	0.02	0.03	0.00	0.05	0.36
FF92	FNG135	ring-headed pin	0.22	0.04	0.07	88.47	0.02	0.42	0.01	9.71	0.03	0.03	0.79	0.02	0.14
FF99	FNG171	ribbed bead	0.16	0.05	0.05	89.14	0.01	0.54	0.00	9.86	0.02	0.01	0.03	0.03	0.09
FF80	FNG037	shears	0.11	0.10	0.06	90.61	0.01	0.19	0.01	9.65	0.02	0.02	0.20	0.04	0.00
FF39	FNG247	spiral ring	0.11	0.11	0.03	86.25	0.02	<0.20	0.09	12.42	0.02	0.00	0.83	0.00	0.02
Late Iron Age/Roman															
FF105	FNG010	U-section binding, junction	*0.02*	*0.00*	*0.02*	*76.85*	*0.00*	*<0.20*	*0.04*	*17.00*	*0.01*	*0.03*	*5.96*	*0.01*	*0.06*
FF100	FNG246	medicine mortar	0.07	0.01	0.21	97.98	0.00	<0.20	0.16	1.35	0.07	0.06	0.07	0.00	0.02
FF28	FNG017	Roman brooch, plate	0.28	0.02	0.01	87.89	0.00	0.28	0.03	10.20	0.02	0.04	0.20	0.01	0.05

Note: figures in *italics* (Penard FF73, Hallstatt FF70 and FF109, Late Iron Age/Roman FF105) indicate analysis of corroded material

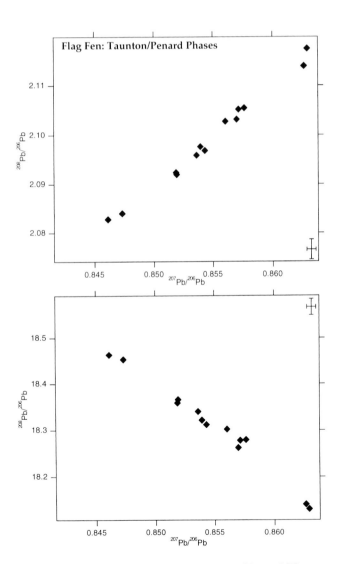

Fig 10.21 Lead isotope analysis: Taunton/Penard Phases

Bronze Age

The lead isotope ratios for the late Taunton/Penard objects are shown in Figure 10.21. The lead isotope ratios of other Taunton and Penard material from quite a large spread (Rohl in preparation) and the analyses of the bronzes from Flag Fen are consistent with this variation. It is believed that, at this time, much of the metal used in southern and eastern England was imported scrap, as exemplified by the finds from the Langdon Bay, Dover, shipwreck (Northover 1983). The lead isotope data from that site also fits the pattern. It is perhaps pertinent to make reference to the extreme values at both ends of the plots in Figure 10.21. These are (for $^{208}Pb/^{206}Pb$ >2.11) for the shield tab and a knob-headed pin. The shield tab very probably comes from an imported Nipperwiese shield (Needham 1979). The knob-headed pin could also be imported. The other extreme (for $^{208}Pb/^{206}Pb$ >2.09) is represented by a typical notch butt dirk and a ring.

The lead isotope analyses for the Wilburton objects are shown in Figure 10.22. A majority of the metalwork from the Wilburton Phase is leaded bronze (taken as Pb >1%); 53 Wilburton period metal objects from England and Wales have been analysed for their lead isotope composition (Northover and Gale 1983; Rohl 1995; Rohl and Needham 1998). Of these, 47 were leaded bronzes. The shaded area in Figure 10.22 is based on these analyses. Compared with Figure 10.21 there is a definite shift to lower $^{208}Pb/^{206}Pb$ values. There is a strong possibility that the lead came from a single source, or a small group of geologically very similar sources.

Mixing through recycling seems to have been done with alloys falling outside this tight grouping (Northover 1982), some local and some certainly imported.

Table 10.3 Lead isotope data for metalwork from Flag Fen and the Power Station

sample	cat no	object	$^{208}Pb/^{206}Pb$	$^{207}Pb/^{206}Pb$	$^{206}Pb/^{204}Pb$
tin ornaments					
439	FNG179	tin ring	2.09631	0.85373	18.292
437	FNG180	tin alloy ornament	2.08286	0.84784	18.427
tin (Iron Age)					
459	FNG031	brooch inlay	2.08122	0.84447	18.525
?Late Taunton/Early Penard					
426	FNG137	rapier, Group IV	2.09754	0.85361	18.340
423	FNG084	rapier hilt, Group IV	2.10305	0.85704	18.262
428	FNG145	small knife blade	2.09190	0.85192	18.366
Penard					
420	FF	flesh hook	2.09218	0.85190	18.359
425	FNG121	knob-headed pin, large knob	2.11748	0.86294	18.130
430	FNG248	ring	2.08274	0.84614	18.462
424	FNG117	shield tab	2.11396	0.86270	18.140
432	FNG281	short sword	2.10265	0.85608	18.302
429	FNG228	small notch-butt dirk	2.08394	0.84729	18.452
421	FF019	spearhead	2.10543	0.85769	18.278
431	FNG277	sword/knife blade	2.10514	0.85719	18.277
421	FNG009	sword point	2.09758	0.85397	18.322
427	FNG140	sword rivet	2.09677	0.85433	18.311
Wilburton (Pb >1%; Sb >0.50%)					
435	FF021	chape, French	2.09830	0.85440	18.290
442	FNG280	conical rivet	2.08699	0.84951	18.414
441	FNG274	plain pegged spearhead	2.08528	0.84932	18.389
440	FNG210	small tool	2.08831	0.84995	18.410
436	FNG147	Wilburton sword, centre	2.08584	0.84936	18.396
433	FNG001	Wilburton sword, centre	2.08964	0.84956	18.405
438	FNG162	Wilburton sword, hilt	2.08604	0.84923	18.408
434	FNG001	Wilburton sword, rivet	2.08759	0.84964	18.417
Ewart Park (Pb >1%; Sb <0.5%)					
451	FNG190	awl	2.08559	0.84928	18.399
455	FNG214	disc pin head	2.09089	0.84998	18.401
452	FNG199	disc pin head, four holes	2.09395	0.85223	18.344
448	FNG128	domed object, ?pommel	2.09620	0.85194	18.394
447	FNG098	double-edged tanged knife	2.08829	0.84974	18.420
454	FNG203	?helmet fragment	2.08599	0.84864	18.432
458	FNG231	expanded terminal bracelet	2.08458	0.84902	18.395
446	FNG033	gouge	2.08227	0.84754	18.430
456	FNG215	large disc pin head	2.08786	0.84760	18.488
450	FNG138	plain pegged spearhead	2.08807	0.84985	18.418
449	FNG134	ring	2.08612	0.84911	18.395
444	FNG014	short tongue chape	2.08781	0.84981	18.412
457	FNG219	socketed punch	2.08678	0.84902	18.428
443	FNG293	spear ferrule	2.08554	0.84950	18.386
445	FNG032	tanged knife with handle	2.08702	0.84968	18.399
La Tène Iron Age					
460	FNG037	shears	2.07689	0.84243	18.562

With a single exception, all the bronzes of the Wilburton Phase measured from Flag Fen are leaded and their lead isotope ratios are consistent with the established pattern. The exception is the French-style tongue chape, a certain import. Also plotted are the lead isotope compositions from two tin ornaments that probably date to this period.

The lead isotope data for the Ewart Park period are shown in Figure 10.23. A dotted outline marks the area occupied by the Wilburton grouping in Figure 10.22. The data from other Ewart Park material from sites in England and Wales are shaded. It is seen that the majority of the ratios also fall inside the Wilburton grouping, perhaps not surprising, given the suspected continuity.

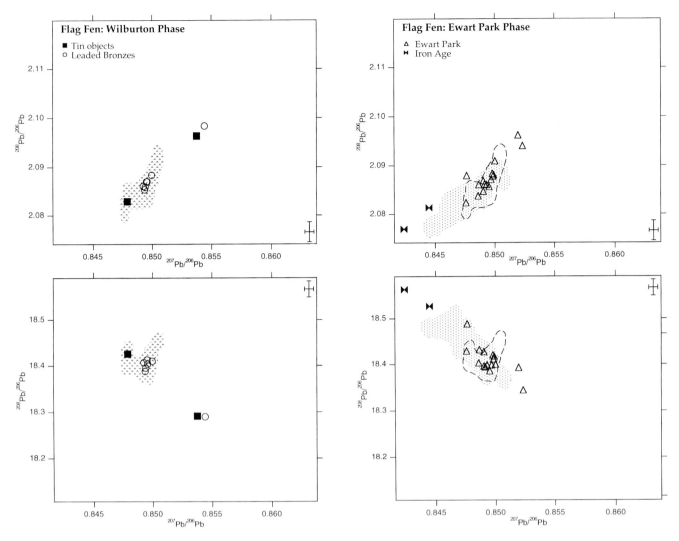

Fig 10.22 Lead isotope analysis: Wilburton Phase

Fig 10.23 Lead isotope analysis: Ewart Park Phase

Wilburton material would have been recycled and the same lead source could have remained in production. The extreme value $^{208}Pb/^{206}Pb$ values (>2.092) here are a peculiar domed object, which might be a pommel (Coombs 1992, fig 8.18) and a disc-headed pin, already alluded to as a possible Carp's Tongue import.

Iron Age

Two Iron Age objects were included in Figure 10.23. The material is from the brooch inlay, which contains both tin and the bronze it was bonded to, and the shears. The shift in resources implied by a shift in impurity pattern is confirmed.

Tin and tin alloy objects

Eighteen tin and two tin-alloy objects were recorded, by far the largest group from any British Bronze Age site. More recently, another tin object, a grooved strip, has appeared on a contemporary waterlogged site at Caldicot Castle, Gwent (Northover 1997). Before these finds were made, objects of metallic tin of Bronze

Age date were extremely scarce in the British Isles. From Ireland there were three rings of the 'Late Bronze Age' from Lough Gara and a neck ring from Kilsallagh (Coghlan and Case 1957). From England, Butler (1963) cites some tin beads from Sutton Verney, Wiltshire, now lost. In Wales, there is the tin object (possibly a damaged or miscast ornament) in the Llangwyllog, Anglesey, hoard (Lynch 1991).

This hoard can be dated to the Ewart Park period of the Late Bronze Age (late tenth to late eighth century BC) and is probably later rather than earlier within this period. Among the objects from Flag Fen and Fengate are found wheel-shaped (154, 159, and 172) and purse-shaped (153, 158, and 170–10) ornaments or votive objects, rings (eg 252), and objects that can tentatively be identified as beads (123–8). The wheel-shaped objects are unique in Britain but have very close parallels in Switzerland. Perhaps the closest is from Zürich Wallishofen-Haumesser, ZH (Primas 1984, Abb 4: 3, 5; 1985, fig 1: 3, 5), Estavayer-le-Lac, FR (Primas 1984, Abb. 4: 3, 5; 1985, fig 1: 3, 5), and Hauterive-Champréveyres, NE (Rychner-Faraggi 1993, pl 52.41). The objects catalogued by Primas from

Table 10.4 ICP-MS analysis of tin objects from Flag Fen (FF) and Hauterive-Champréveyres (HR)

sample no		Sn blnk	tin G	tin H	tin I	tin J	tin K	tin L	tin M	tin N	tin O
			FF 4-lobed bead (6)	FF 4-lobed bead (3)	FF biconic bead (4)	HR 18132 wheel	HR 6679 pendant	HR 19284 1/8	HR 19284 1/8	HR 19249 52/49	HR 19249 52/49
dilution factor		28954.178	17123.287	24220.023	18850.141	18264.840	18993.352	17969.451	38095.234	20387.359	
element	isotope	ppm	ppm	ppm	ppm	ppm	ppm	ppm	ppm	ppm	ppm
chromium	Cr 52	0.008	BBL	BBL	BBL	BBL	BBL	BBL	BBL	BBL	BBL
manganese	Mn 55	0.001	3.446	BBL	22.358	BBL	BBL	BBL	BBL	BBL	BBL
iron	Fe 57	0.099	76.575	BBL	2077.006	231.762	BBL	BBL	BBL	BBL	BBL
cobalt	Co 59	0.000	12.491	11.024	10.859	12.325	11.965	10.521	11.783	11.358	12.261
nickel	Ni 60	0.001	72.417	62.031	49.397	71.794	70.287	64.349	75.116	65.403	73.401
copper	Cu 63	0.002	188.091	18.490	22.107	10.803	BBL	BBL	BBL	104.616	BBL
zinc	Zn 64	0.006	BBL	BBL	5.852	1.424	BBL	BBL	8.469	BBL	BBL
arsenic	As 75	0.040	BBL	BBL	BBL	BBL	BBL	BBL	BBL	BBL	BBL
silver	Ag 107	0.001	BBL	BBL	BBL	BBL	BBL	BBL	BBL	BBL	BBL
indium	In 115	0.000	342.159	173.689	275.316	189.470	200.719	198.885	177.194	327.960	237.953
antimony	Sb 123	0.000	138.111	116.645	87.444	125.437	142.758	113.412	124.621	192.601	212.155
tungsten	W 184	0.001	BBL	BBL	BBL	BBL	BBL	BBL	BBL	BBL	BBL
iridium	Ir 191	0.000	BBL	BBL	BBL	BBL	BBL	BBL	BBL	BBL	BBL
gold	Au 197	0.001	BBL	BBL	BBL	BBL	BBL	BBL	BBL	BBL	BBL
lead	Pb 206	0.000	35.312	26.318	18.038	1382.341	13274.105	26.750	23.203	14047.421	12813.523
thorium	Th 232	0.000	BBL	BBL	BBL	BBL	BBL	BBL	BBL	BBL	BBL
uranium	U 238	0.000	BBL	BBL	BBL	BBL	BBL	BBL	BBL	BBL	BBL

Switzerland are not well stratified, coming from nine-teenth-century recoveries and excavations at Swiss lake settlements, especially around the lakes of Zürich, Zug, Neuchâtel, and Genf. Now that tin objects have been recovered from modern excavations, however, the repertoire has been widened, while their contexts indicate that they must date to the later Bronze Age, ie from the end of the eleventh century onwards. One object in Primas' catalogue is stratified, a U-shaped tin pendant from Zürich Gross-Hafner, and can be dated to c 1000 BC. Recent excavations at Auvernier and Hauterive, both adjacent to Neuchâtel North-East, have increased the range of tin objects from Switzerland while confirming their Late Bronze Age dating (Rychner 1987; Rychner and Rychner-Faraggi 1993). These include pieces of wire and strip, which provide something of a parallel for the Caldicot strip, but no piece with grooved decoration has so far been identified.

The dating of the Continental parallels makes the tin objects contemporary with the peak in activity at Flag Fen, from the late eleventh century BC through the tenth century. The problem they present is one of origin. Undoubtedly there are Continental imports at Flag Fen, such as the French-style chape, but it could be said that they are not to be expected at a site so peripheral to the continental mainland. Further, research has revealed no parallels geographically closer than the north-west Swiss ones. In which case, is this central European tin, British tin formed by people with detailed knowledge of Swiss practice, or has British tin been to Switzerland and back again? The parallels, especially for the wheel-shaped objects, are so close that a common origin must be assumed. In considering these, the four wheel-shaped ornaments with curved spokes from Meare Lake Village, Somerset should also be remembered (Gray and Bulleid 1953, 232, pl XLVI, Y2-4/6). Although found in ostensibly La Tène contexts, at least two, from the foundation of Mound 9 and under the clay of Mound 22, suggest that they might be residual from Late Bronze Age activity on the site. They obviously require further study, and the analysis of tin should now be taken as seriously as that of other Bronze Age metals. The provenancing of tin is a difficult matter, however, whether in terms of stable isotopes or of trace elements. To take the question for the Flag Fen tin ornaments a little further, trace element analyses were made by inductively coupled plasma mass spectrometry of three tin objects from Flag Fen and compared with related items from Hauterive Champréveyres (ICP-MS; the authors are grateful to S M M Young (Harvard University) for these analyses; Table 10.4; Northover and Gillies 1999). The difficulty with trace element analysis of tin is that tin metal can be made very pure by using early smelting technology. The most prominent impurity is usually iron; iron has an extremely low solid solubility in tin and forms intermetallic compounds called 'hardhead'. Other transition metal elements, such as manganese segregate to these inclusions. The overall concentration of iron in

these tin objects can be very low and also very variable. The approach taken was to look at ratios of transition metal concentrations to iron. The results were not conclusive but tended to show that tin at Flag Fen had had a rather different history than at Hauterive-Champréveyres. One interpretation could be that, with its lower iron (and therefore intermetallic) contents the Swiss material had been remelted more often, perhaps by reforming tin objects from elsewhere.

A note on analytical methods

Electron probe microanalysis

All objects were sampled by drilling with a bit 1mm in diameter; the samples were hot-mounted in copper-filled acrylic resin, ground, and polished. Analysis was by electron probe microanalysis with wavelength dispersive spectrometry; operating conditions were an accelerating voltage of 25kV, a beam current of 30nA and an X-ray take-off angle of 62°. Thirteen elements were analysed as detailed in Table 10.2; pure element and mineral standards were used with a count time of 10s per element. Detection limits were 100–200ppm (0.01–0.02%) for most elements, with the exception of 300ppm for gold and 0.2% for arsenic.

This last is because of the compromises made to avoid the well known interference between the strongest lines in the lead and arsenic spectra, the lead La and arsenic Ka lines, while making the analysis in a single pass. It was possible to use the relatively strong lead Ma line, but for arsenic the weak Kj3 line had to be used — hence the degradation in performance. More sensitive approaches to the analysis of arsenic exist but they were not thought necessary here. Three areas, each $50 \times 30\mu m$ were analysed on each sample; the mean compositions from each sample, normalised to 100% are set out in Table 10.2.

Lead isotope analysis

A subsample of the drillings used for microprobe analysis was taken for lead isotope analysis. The lead was separated and purified in laboratory clean rooms by an anodic deposition method (Arden and Gale 1974) and converted to the nitrate form. A small aliquot of the sample was then loaded onto an outgassed rhenium filament with phosphoric acid and silica gel. The lead isotope compositions were determined using a VG–38–54 thermal ionisation mass spectrometer. The analyses were corrected for mass fractionation by numerous measurements of the NBS 981 isotopic standard and the analytical uncertainties (2σ) were better than 0.05% for $^{207}Pb/^{206}Pb$ and 0.1% for $^{208}Pb/^{206}Pb$ and $^{206}Pb/^{204}Pb$. The application of the method in archaeology is described elsewhere (Gale and Stos-Gale 2000). The analyses are set out in Table 10.3; those isotope ratios marked with an asterisk are the mean of two analyses.

Metallographic examination of a socketed ferrous axehead from the Power Station

by Vanessa Fell and Chris Salter

The axehead

The object examined in this study was found in Area 1 of the Power Station (Fig 10.11, 269). The axehead was examined by metallography to investigate its metal structure and method of manufacture. A sample from the cutting edge was mounted and polished according to standard metallographic techniques. Etching with 1% nital revealed uniformly distributed ferrite and pearlite with some grain-boundary cementite. Carbon content was *c* 0.2%, hardness 157–61 HV (0.2). Grains were relatively small in size (5–6 ASTM). The specimen revealed abundant non-metallic inclusions. Minor and trace element analysis (Table 10.5) showed high levels of phosphorus coinciding with concentrations of non-metallic inclusions and forming bands (Fig 10.24) that were not visible in the macrostructure or carbon distribution. The cutting edge comprises low-carbon steel (essentially wrought iron with a small amount of carbon). The carbon was uniformly distributed across the specimen; there was no evidence of surface carburization although it is always possible that this had been removed through corrosion. The carbon is therefore likely to have arisen from the bloom (primary carburization), which is common in early iron produced by the bloomery process. The microstructure indicates that the axehead was air-cooled in the final heating cycle.

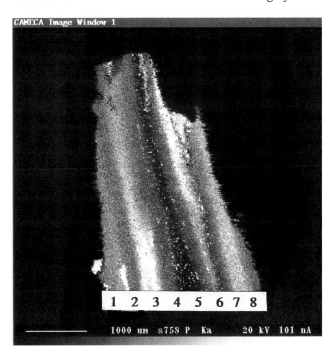

Fig 10.24 Phosphorus distribution map of sample from iron socketed axehead, 269 (actual size 4 × 2.5mm, with cutting edge at top). Points 1–8 refer to positions determined in Table 10.4

Table 10.5 Minor and trace element composition of axehead 269

point	P	Mo	S	Ni	Cu	Zn	As
1	0.355	0.000	0.013	0.025	0.016	0.009	0.000
2	0.278	0.005	0.014	0.026	0.001	0.000	0.028
3	0.496	0.001	0.015	0.022	0.003	0.017	0.015
4	0.268	0.002	0.012	0.019	0.029	0.002	0.009
5	0.199	0.000	0.010	0.027	0.028	0.000	0.005
6	0.287	0.000	0.012	0.027	0.017	0.002	0.000
7	0.470	0.007	0.017	0.022	0.000	0.000	0.033
8	0.272	0.000	0.014	0.029	0.010	0.011	0.011

Measured on electron probe microanalyser (Camera Semprobe) from Ka lines at 20kv accelerating voltage with target area 40 × 30mm (the following elements were below detection limit: Si, Co, Ti, Cr, Mn)

Two other Iron Age socketed axeheads from Britain have been examined and these are broadly similar in carbon composition, hardness and microstructure. One from Rahoy, Argyll, comprises 0–0.3% carbon (Desch 1938, 41–3), whereas one from Buscot, Oxfordshire (Barclay *et al* 1995), is carbon-free, though of similar hardness to the one from Flag Fen. None of these axeheads was deliberately hardened by carburization or by heat treatment. Five shaft-hole examples from England are similar, although two from Fiskerton, Lincolnshire, have enhanced carbon levels at their surfaces (Fell and Salter forthcoming). From Northern Ireland, however, two socketed and two shaft-hole axeheads all seem to be technologically more sophisticated, with evidence of deliberate carburization and, in some cases, the use of quenching to harden the cutting edge (Scott 1990).

Late Bronze Age Swords and Spears from the Power Station and Flag Fen

by S D Bridgeford

Examination of eight Late Bronze Age weapons from the Power Station/Flag Fen complex was performed as part of my ongoing research into weapons of the period from all over Britain, which concentrates on evidence for design, manufacture, use, and social context. This brief report will concentrate on those particular aspects of the weapons, which have already been placed in their broader archaeological contexts by Coombs (above, Discussion).

Discussion

The spearheads are fairly typical of the Late Bronze Age in general, although all differ in detail and in their proportions. The swords, which show characteristics of both the Wilburton and Ewart Park varieties, have been found in the geographic area where south-eastern and northern traditions are most likely to have met. Burgess and Colquhoun (1988, 70) term the development of Ewart Park swords in northern Britain a 'simplification' of the south-eastern Wilburton type, starting with the Wilburton 'G' variant. Since Wilburton sword types are, however, very rare in northern contexts, the argument that development from Middle Bronze Age traditions was much slower in the north is unconvincing (Needham 1990). The presence of swords with mixed characteristics does not necessarily confirm such a progression and it is tempting to see it as the result of a chronological and geographic overlap of two traditions, which were originally geographically separate. Such an overlap, if it existed, would require that the Ewart Park tradition in northern Britain spanned a much longer period than is currently accepted.

The results of a recent programme of dating organics associated directly with bronze objects, such as spear shaft remnants, show that the time span of the Wilburton tradition is rather earlier than previously believed, starting from 'at least the late twelfth century BC' (Needham 1996, 135). The southern Blackmoor hoard, which has both Wilburton and Ewart Park typological characteristics, gave a calibrated date range centred on the tenth century BC (Needham 1996, 136). This provides the probable transition period from Wilburton to Ewart Park traditions in southern Britain.

The preservation of wood at the Power Station and Flag Fen, including hafts and small wooden artefacts as well as large structural timbers, is generally good. This caused Coombs (1992) to query whether the lack of hilt plates on the swords resulted from their removal prior to deposition. There is an inclination to think that it did, but the possibility remains that the deposition of the weapons in shallow water (French 1992b) led to their subjection to alternating wet and dry conditions in the period immediately after deposition. This would have accelerated the removal of any wood not protected by, say, the socket of a spearhead. The survival of wooden shafts is further considered by Maisie Taylor in Chapter 7.

Given the almost total lack of decoration on the metal of Late Bronze Age swords, the only areas left to give a sword 'identity' would be those parts that were of organic material, such as the scabbard and hilt plates. Any deliberate 'killing' of such a weapon would therefore involve their removal or destruction. The survival of rivets attached to the weapons would depend on the heads being not only too large to pass through the original holes in the (now destroyed) organic material, but also too large to pass through the rivet holes or slots in the underlying metal.

It is also possible that in some at least of the weapons the organic parts were removed by burning, perhaps during some form of cremation rite. On the other hand, none of the weapons bears the incontrovertible signs of exposure to the higher range of temperatures that can occur in pyres (c 900° C — Peter Northover personal communication), exhibited by certain other weapon deposits (eg Duddingston Loch and Wilburton). The lower temperatures at the edge of a pyre, however, or the protection afforded by the pelvis and trunk of a body (J McKinley personal communication) could result in the burning of organic material without noticeable damage to the metal.

The current state of the metal is surprisingly poor, especially when compared with weapons deposited in rivers, such as the Thames and the Tyne. It resembles the state of many items in the Wilburton hoard, some elements of which were quite definitely exposed to fire, as well as deliberate breakage. Although some heat treatment would anneal the metal, thereby removing the strain lines along which electrochemical corrosion tends to penetrate, excessive heat could make the surface more susceptible to corrosion, without necessarily distorting the object.

Corrosion layers on ancient bronzes tend to stabilise relatively soon after burial (several dozen years at most — Robbiola and Fiaud 1992), unless a substantial change in conditions causes renewed attack. The different types of corrosion, that which respects the original surface and that which extends beyond it, indicate different conditions of burial context. The latter type of corrosion represents a more hostile environment, often including exposure to chlorine (Robbiola and Fiaud op cit). Both types of corrosion occur on the weapons, indicating that the microenvironment was indeed hostile in some places. A regime of changes between a wet and a dry environment in the initial period after deposition, postulated above as a possible explanation of the removal of organic components, could also have exacerbated the effects of corrosion. Such a fluctuation is more likely to have occurred at the Power Station than at Flag Fen.

The weapons

For details of measurements, see the respective entries in the catalogue by Coombs above.

Sword 6 (Fig 10.2)

This sword, a Ewart Park type (Fig 10.25), is unusual in having two elongated rivet holes and a slot in the tang (with two rivets in situ). Slotted tangs occur more often in swords of Wilburton type. Tangs with a combination of slots and holes are rare and elongated rivet holes are themselves far from common. The hilt is flanged and there are four rivet holes in the shoulders (with three rivets *in situ* and one loose). A ricasso is present and is blunt. The blade is leaf shaped with a ridge parallel to the edges, particularly noticeable at the tip. The cross-section of the blade is lenticular. The turning moment about the shoulders falls within the range 10,000–15,000cm gm, which feels reasonably well balanced and seems to be the norm for swords of the period.

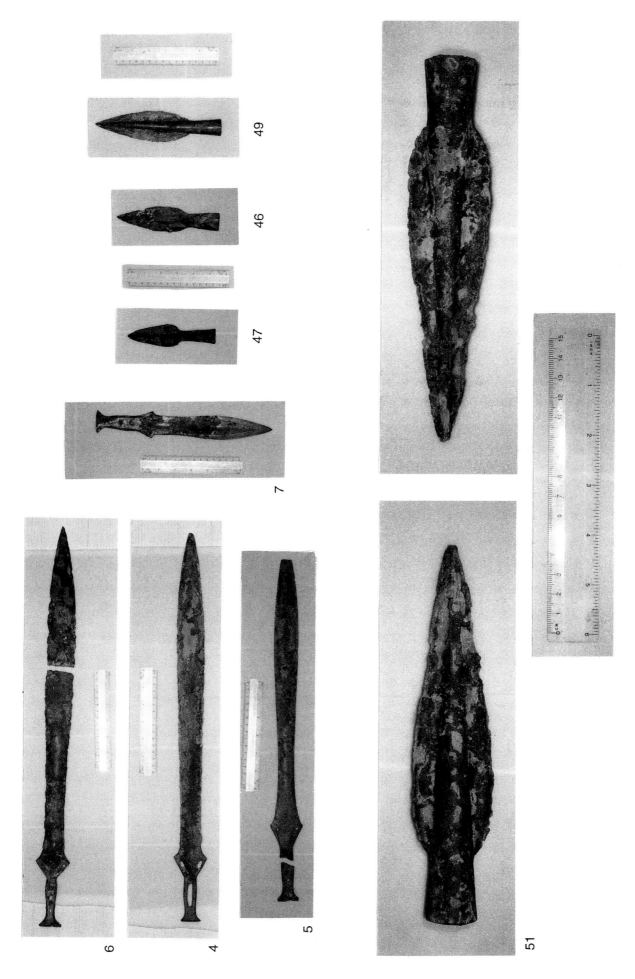

Fig 10.25 Late Bronze Age swords and spearheads from the Power Station and Flag Fen (showing surface condition)

Fig 10.26 Details of sword 6

The surface and edges are quite heavily corroded, although the hilt seems rather less badly affected. The cross-section at the break, which has been drilled to sample the composition, shows signs that there was sufficient porosity in the casting to cause the blade to fracture at that particular point if sufficiently strained (Fig 10.26, bottom row). The upper section is quite severely bowed, indicating bending of the sword, which might have resulted in the break. The break is not recent, nor is the bending, since, due to subsequent corrosion, the metal would now be too brittle for such distortion to be sustained without fracturing in the immediate area. Despite the heavy corrosion of the blade, it is clear from the few relatively undamaged sections that the edges were originally fine and sharp. It is also clear from distortion of the edges in places that they were severely damaged, in a manner unlikely to have been the result of 'normal' combat use (Fig 10.26, top right).

Sword 4 (Fig 10.2)

This Wilburton sword (Fig 10.25) is of the 'G' variant, which is the closest in typology to the Ewart Park swords (Burgess and Colquhoun 1988). The hilt might have been cast on (Coombs 1992) or had casting faults repaired with molten metal (visible on one side). This might well have been done before the sword was used.

The hilt is flanged with a slot in the tang and in each shoulder. A ricasso is present and blunt (Fig 10.27, bottom left). The blade is leaf shaped, with a ridge parallel to the edge and a lenticular cross-section. The turning moment about the shoulders falls within the normal range of 10,000–15,000cm gm. Corrosion damage to the surface and edges (Fig 10.27, bottom left) is severe but some distortions, probably remnants of edge damage, are visible. The tip is also damaged (Fig 10.27, top right) and there is deep surface marking in the area of the tip, which does not look recent (Fig 10.27, top left). There is also a very slight bow to the blade.

Sword 5 (Fig 10.2)

This sword is of Ewart Park type (Fig 10.25). The hilt is flanged (Fig 10.28, bottom right) with one rivet hole in the tang and one in each shoulder. The tang is broken at the point where, in many such swords, a second rivet hole or casting depression would be. A slight ricasso is present and is blunt. The blade is leaf shaped and fairly narrow relative to the shoulders. It has the usual ridge parallel to the edge and a lenticular cross-section (Fig 10.28, bottom left). Although the missing tip makes it impossible to calculate the turning moment accurately, it is clearly at the very low end of a sample of some 72 Late Bronze Age swords, for which data has been collected. The balance would

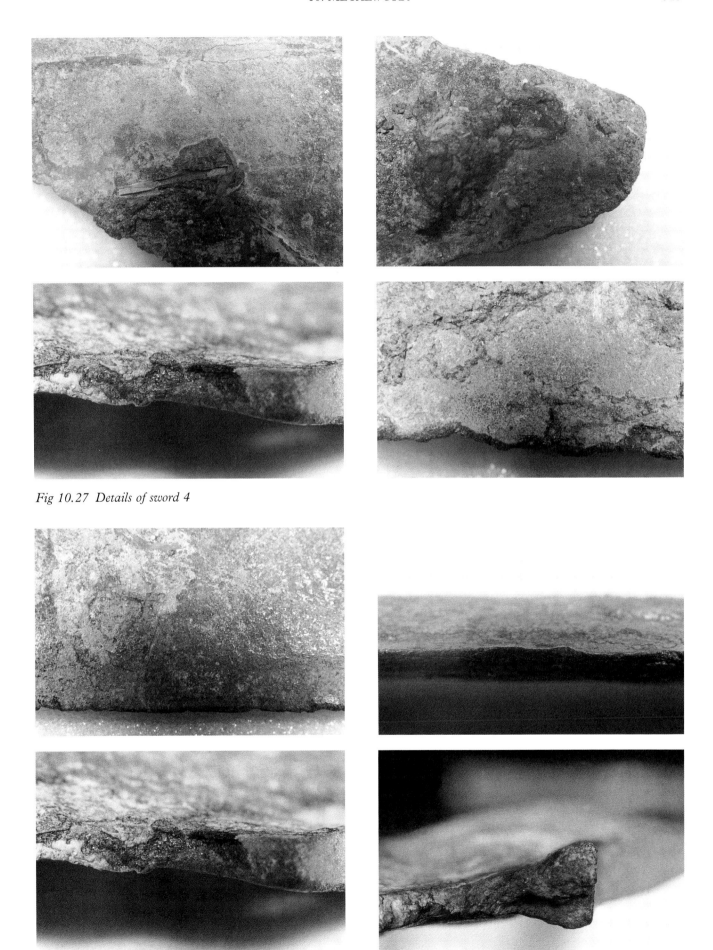

Fig 10.27 Details of sword 4

Fig 10.28 Details of sword 5

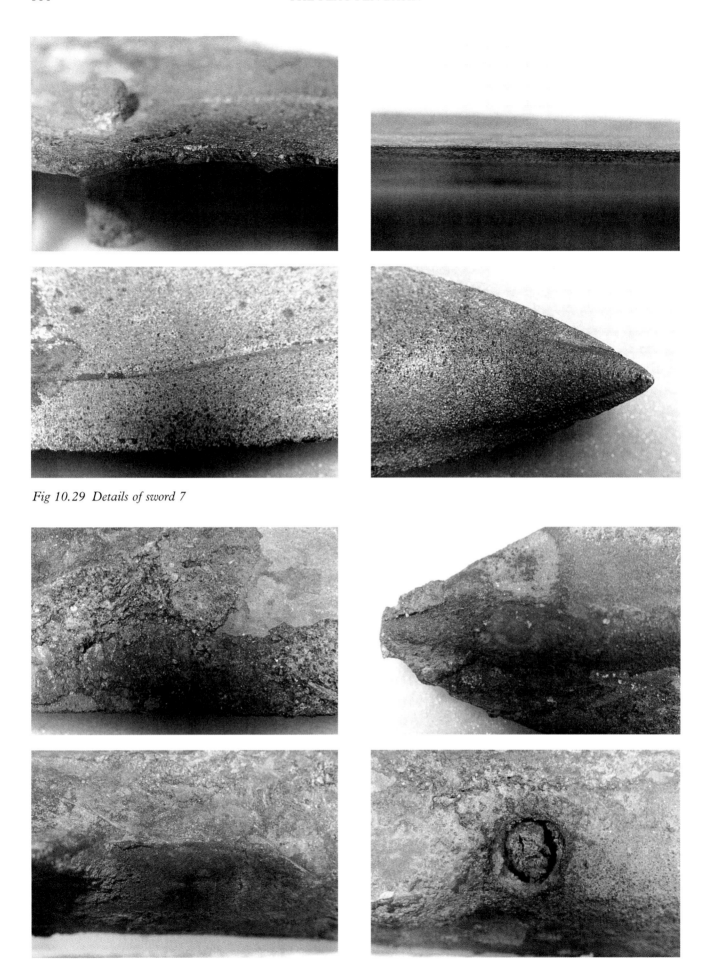

Fig 10.29 Details of sword 7

Fig 10.30 Details of spearhead 47

therefore feel very light by comparison with most Late Bronze Age swords. The surfaces and edges are corroded, as are the ancient breaks in tang and tip, the broken surfaces of which both show possible signs of casting flaws (Fig 10.28, bottom row). What is left of the edges shows that they were fairly sharp and some distortions remain visible (Fig 10.28, top row). These are not so severe as to rule out normal combat or accidental damage. The blade is bowed in a manner similar to, but much less severe than, sword 6.

Sword 7 (Fig 10.2)

This miniature sword (Fig 10.25) combines a hilt of Ewart Park type with the decorative features of an incised groove following the blade outline and punched decoration in the groove towards the hilt (Fig 10.29, bottom and top left). Decoration is generally seen on only a few Wilburton, St Nazaire, and much earlier sword types (Coombs 1992).

The hilt is flanged and the tang has three rivet holes with two rivets *in situ*. There are two rivet holes in each shoulder and all the shoulder rivets remain in place (Fig 10.29, top left).

The ricasso area is blunt but there is, at most, only a very slight ricasso (Fig 10.29, top left). The blade is very short, leaf shaped and of lenticular cross-section. There is a ridge, more pronounced towards the tip (Fig 10.29, bottom row), parallel to the edges, which were

thin and sharp (Fig 10.29, top right). Inside the ridge is the incised groove mentioned above, which stops at the lower pair of rivets. The extreme tip is bent although, apart from areas of surface corrosion, there is no visible damage to surface or edges.

This unique object was originally cast as a miniature. The length from shoulder to terminal falls well outside the range set by a sample of some 96 complete Late Bronze Age hilts from all over Britain and the maximum shoulder width also is smaller than the lowest in the range exhibited by 132 Late Bronze Age swords. The blade does not appear to have been broken and refashioned. The gradation in thickness towards the tip is even, unlike other 'sword' knives with somewhat bulbous tips (eg sword number 1911:170 from the Ulster Museum in Belfast; Bridgeford 1997). The surface shows no sign whatever of regrinding to achieve this effect.

Spearhead 47 (Fig 10.4)

This spearhead has a leaf-shaped blade with rounded midrib and there is no visible ridge parallel to the edges (Fig 10.25). The socket is very slightly flared and has two peg holes, one of which shows the remains of a wooden peg, approximately half way along (Fig 10.30, bottom left). There are slight marks along either side of the socket where the casting flash was removed (Fig 10.30, bottom left) and the socket walls are fairly thick.

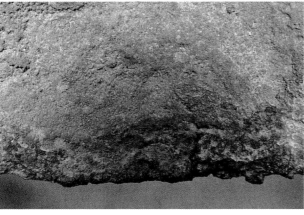

Fig 10.31 Details of spearhead 46

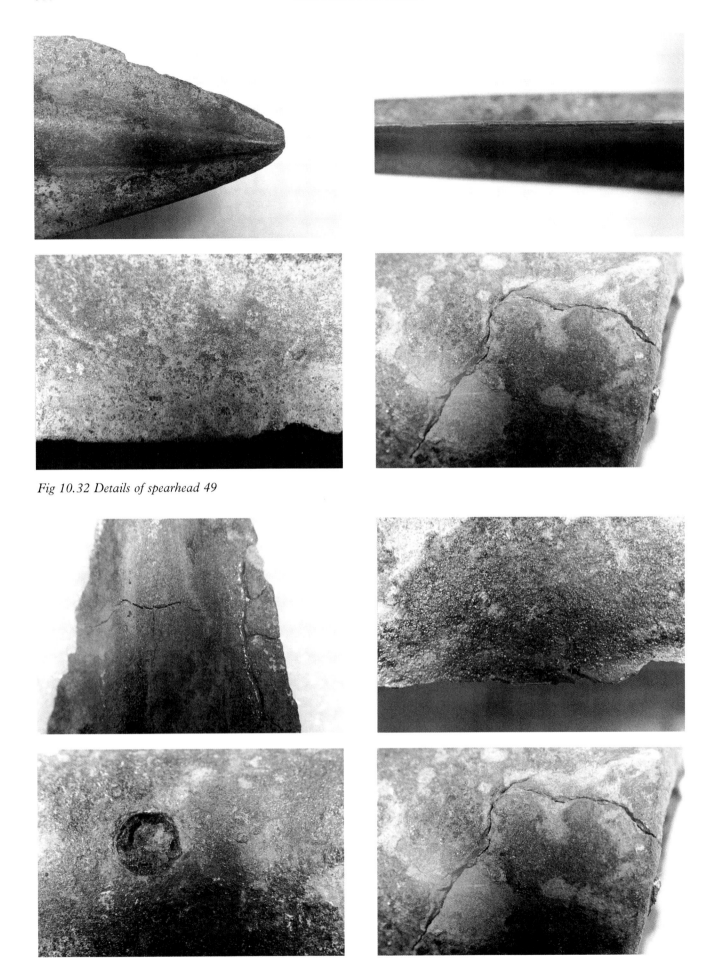

Fig 10.32 Details of spearhead 49

Fig 10.33 Details of spearhead 51

The tip is slightly damaged (Fig 10.30, top right) and the surface and edges quite corroded (Fig 10.30, top left). The edges were fairly sharp and all the visible damage appears to be due to corrosion.

Spearhead 46 (Fig 10.4)

This spearhead has a leaf-shaped blade with rounded midrib and there is a very slight ridge parallel to the edges (Fig 10.25). The tip was originally fairly sharp (Fig 10.31, top left). The socket has two peg holes approximately half way along (Fig 10.31, bottom right), and is slightly bulbous.

The original quality of the metal might have been quite poor and the surface and edges are very corroded (Fig 10.31 top right and bottom left) but show no other signs of damage.

Spearhead 49 (Fig 10.4)

This spearhead (Fig 10.25) has a leaf-shaped blade with rounded midrib (Fig 10.32, top left) and a ridge parallel to the edges, which were originally fairly sharp (Fig 10.32, top right). The socket has two peg holes somewhat below half way along (Fig 10.32, bottom right) and has fairly thin walls.

The surface and edges have some corrosion damage but, apart from some surface marks Fig 10.32, bottom left), show no obvious signs of any other type of damage. The entire spearhead is severely bowed in profile, however, and, since this cannot be a fault of manufacture, this damage must have occurred either before or during the early stages of deposition.

Spearhead 51 (Fig 10.4)

This spearhead has a leaf-shaped blade with rounded midrib and a slight ridge parallel to the edges, which appear, where they survive, to have been fairly sharp (Fig 10.25). The socket has two peg holes somewhat above half way along and has fairly thick walls. There are some remains of wood in the socket, visible through the peg hole (Fig 10.33, bottom left).

The surface and edges are very corroded (top right) and the tip region and socket end are both severely cracked (Fig 10.33, top left and bottom right). Although the cracking might have been exacerbated by the change in conditions since discovery, since the metal is now in a fragile condition, the corrosion pattern indicates that surface faults already existed in these areas.

11 Finds of flint, stone, and shale

Flint

Cat's Water Excavations 1990

The main significance of the five flints found in the Cat's Water excavations of 1990 (Table 11.1) is that the assemblage provides the only independent dating evidence for the hengiform monument. All are fresh and unabraded and were found within the fillings of features. The penannular ditch of the hengiform monument (Fig 3.9, F80) produced three flints, an unused blade-like flake, a utilised flake, and a large retouched and utilised primary (cortical) flake (Fig 11.1, 1). The latter had flat bifacial retouch at its distal end; its left side, viewed from the ventral aspect, carried diffuse silica lustre along some 60% of its length. All five flints were probably worked from local gravel pebbles. Although a very small sample, the assemblage is in fresh condition and should not be regarded as residual. All flints are blade based and of Neolithic type.

The Power Station

The Power Station excavations took place under rescue and salvage conditions and the damp, clayey nature of the subsoil made sieving difficult. It was, however, possible to distinguish the pre-alluvial palaeosol from the later deposits while the earthmoving was taking place. This material was dumped in separate spoil heaps, which were spread and allowed to weather. They were then searched. Many of the flints described below were found in this manner. Using stratigraphic evidence it is only possible to state that the flintwork from the Power Station most probably predates the Iron Age. Further dating must rely on typology alone. The assemblage will be treated together, as there were few finds from closed groups, the exception being a utilised flake from the large charcoal-filled pit, F87 (Fig 4.22).

Implements

The assemblage was small but diverse (Table 11.2). The two arrowheads illustrate this well. The transverse arrowhead (Fig 11.1, 2) carries fine, bifacial retouch and had broken close to its hafting point. The type is generally found in Late Neolithic contexts (eg Pryor 1978, fig 44). The tanged arrowhead (Fig 11.1, 3) shows less control in its secondary working, with uneven bifacial retouch. Arrowheads of this type are generally found in later Bronze Age contexts (Pryor 1980, fig 62, 5), but the present example is wider and rather more finely made than the general run of tanged arrowheads with vestigial barbs — all of which might suggest an earlier Bronze Age date. Six of the seven scrapers are large and recall the Late Neolithic assemblage of Storey's Bar Road; they are characterised by

oblique retouch, which is carried round onto the sides; one is illustrated (Fig 11.1, 4). One long end-scraper has steep retouch, which is confined to the distal end; this is probably an earlier Neolithic implement.

Both fabricators found are bifacially retouched and both are broadly consistent with later Neolithic practice (eg Pryor 1978, fig 49, 8–9). One is illustrated (Fig 11.1, 6). Of the two denticulates found, one was on irregular workshop waste (with three piercing points), the other was on a side-struck cortical flake (with 7 piercing points; Fig 11.1, 7). The type is characteristic of the later Bronze Age and was common in field boundary ditches of the Bronze Age system, especially

Table 11.1 Summary of flints from the Cat's Water excavations (1990), by category

implement	number	%
serrated flakes	1	20
retouched flakes (both faces)	1	20
complete utilised flakes	1	20
utilised irregular workshop waste	1	20
by-product		
waste flakes	1	20

Table 11.2 Summary of flints from the Power Station, by category

implement	number	%	% of total
arrowhead, transverse	1	2.86	1.16
arrowhead, tanged	1	2.86	1.16
fabricators	2	5.71	2.33
scraper, long-end	3	8.57	3.49
scraper, short-end	3	8.57	3.49
scraper, on broken flake	1	2.86	1.16
denticulate	2	5.71	2.33
serrated flakes	2	5.71	2.33
retouched flakes (one face)	2	5.71	2.33
complete utilised flakes	11	31.43	12.79
broken utilised flakes	6	17.14	6.98
utilised irregular workshop waste	1	2.86	1.16
sub-total	35	100.00	40.70
by-product			
core remnants	1	1.96	1.16
core rejuvenation flakes	1	1.96	1.16
broken waste flakes	10	19.61	11.63
complete waste flakes	28	54.90	32.56
irregular workshop waste	11	21.57	12.79
sub-total	51	100.00	59.30
total	86		100.00

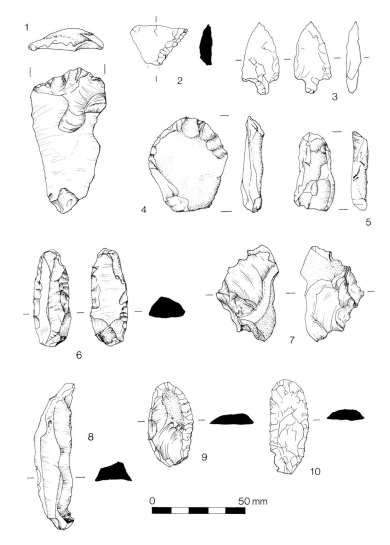

Fig 11.1 Flints from Cat's Water (1990), 1, and the Power Station (1989), 2–10

in the Newark Road subsite (Pryor 1980, figs 64–5). Both serrated flakes were on long ridged blades. One had been heavily utilised and had broken across the middle; the other was lightly serrated. The type is commonly found in earlier Neolithic assemblages (eg Pryor 1974, fig 7, 14, and 23).

The two retouched flakes (Fig 11.1, 9 and 10) closely resemble plano-convex knives, but they lack the bifacial retouch that is characteristic of the type. One (10) had been burnt. A later Neolithic/Early Bronze Age date is indicated.

The utilised flakes were only classed as such if the use-wear evidence was both obvious and tightly confined; even so a proportion of 'wear' must be attributed to natural causes, such as water action, although modern plough damage may be discounted. The dimensions of the utilised flakes are given in Tables 11.3–11.5.

By-products

The ratio of implements to by-products was approximately 2:3, a high proportion of implements (Table 11.2). The assemblage of by-products was dominated by waste flakes. The absence of complete cores is notable. The core remnant had been reused as a small hammerstone and was bashed beyond classification. The core striking platform rejuvenation flake was from a Neolithic blade core, in high quality black flint.

The breadth:length statistics (Fig 11.2) show a preference for short, squat flakes, which would indicate a later Neolithic or Early Bronze Age date, but there was also a substantial blade-based component. Many of these had been broken and do not appear in the histogram. Perhaps 10% of the entire flake assemblage consisted of blades, the vast majority of which were of earlier Neolithic type (two patinated and very narrow blades were probably Mesolithic).

The irregular workshop waste generally derived from smaller gravel pebbles, rather than the higher quality black flint. In general, it had been bashed about and no apparent attempt had been made to remove flakes or blades. This is characteristic of later Bronze Age practice, where the intention was probably to produce pieces with sharp points, such as the denticulates described above (Pryor 1980). These were used to score or pierce, rather than to cut.

Table 11.3 Quantities and dimensions (in mm) of flints from the Power Station: complete utilised flakes

length 0–10	10–20	20–30	30–40	40–50	50–60	60–70	70–80	80–90	total
–	–	4	4	3	–	–	–	–	11
		36.36%	36.36%	27.27%					100%
breadth 0–5	5–10	10–15	15–20	20–25	25–30	30–35	35–40	40–45	total
–	–	2	3	2	2	1	1	–	11
		18.18%	27.27%	18.18%	18.18%	9.09%	9.09%		100%
breadth:length ratio 0–1.5	1.5–2.5	2.5–3.5	3.5–4.5	4.5–5.5	5.5–6.5	6.5>			total
1	3	3	–	3	–	1			11
9.09%	27.27%	27.27%		27.27%		9.09%			100%

Table 11.4 Quantities and dimensions (in mm) of flints from the Power Station: complete waste flakes

length 0–10	10–20	20–30	30–40	40–50	50–60	60–70	70–80	80–90	total
–	8	10	5	4	1	–	–	–	28
	28.57%	35.71%	17.86%	14.29%	3.57%				100%
breadth 0–5	5–10	10–15	15–20	20–25	25–30	30–35	35–40	40–45	total
–	2	7	4	7	4	–	3	1	28
	7.14%	25.00%	14.29%	25.00%	14.29%		10.71%	3.57%	100.00%
breadth:length ratio 0–1.5	1.5–2.5	2.5–3.5	3.5–4.5	4.5–5.5	5.5–6.5	6.5>			total
1	4	5	10	2	1	5			28
3.57%	14.29%	17.86%	35.71%	7.14%	3.57%	17.86%			100%

Table 11.5 Quantities and dimensions (in mm) of complete flints from the Power Station: breadth:length ratios of all flakes

breadth:length ratios 0.0–1.5	5–2.5	2.5–3.5	3.5–4.5	4.5–5.5	5.5–6.5	6.5>	total
2	7	8	10	5	1	6	39
5.13%	17.95%	20.51%	25.64%	12.82%	2.56%	15.38%	100

Discussion

Typologically, the implements can be dated from the earlier Neolithic to the later Bronze Age. In general, however, there is a preponderance of Late Neolithic forms. The serrated flakes are of special interest, given the presence of the two polished stone axe fragments (described below), and would indicate a significant earlier Neolithic presence. The nature of this presence will be considered in Chapter 19. There were fewer of the irregular, 'bashed' pieces that were so characteristic of the nearby Newark Road assemblage. Instead, flakes and blades predominated. This would suggest that the Power Station subsite was occupied in later Neolithic and earlier Bronze Age times. At some time towards the end of the earlier Bronze Age, local ground

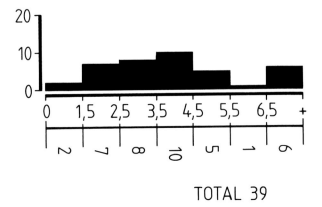

Fig 11.2 Histogram showing breadth:length ratios of all flint flakes from the Power Station

conditions became too wet for more than sporadic occupation and people retreated to the slightly higher ground of the Newark Road subsite to the west.

The by-products echo the implements. The breadth:length ratios of the combined waste and utilised flakes show a strong tendency for short, squat flakes, but there is also a significant blade component (Fig 11.2).

Finally, the proportion of implements to by-products does not suggest that the area was consistently used to knap flint. Most implements had been made from gravel pebbles, which were probably collected from local deposits on higher ground to the west.

Northey

The small assemblage of flintwork described here came from trial trenches excavated at Northey in 1994 (Fig 5.5). The filling of the probable barrow ditch (Trial Trench I) produced one arrowhead and four waste flakes. The arrowhead is bifacially retouched, of leaf type, and probably of Neolithic date (Fig 11.3, 1). It is not, however, as finely made as many of the examples from Etton and a somewhat later date in the Neolithic is always possible.

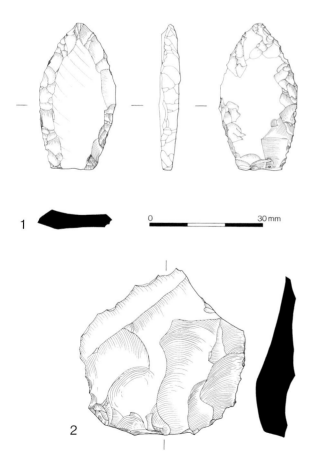

Fig 11.3 Selected flints from Trial Trench 1, barrow ditch, Layer 2, Northey (1994): 1, leaf arrowhead and 2, waste flake

Only one of the four waste flakes is at all distinctive (Fig 11.3, 2). It is in high quality black flint and probably of later Neolithic type. The filling of the southern droveway ditch (Trial Trench 2) produced a single cortical flake with light traces of possible use-wear.

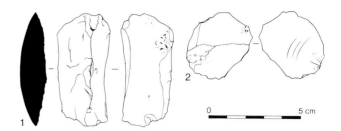

Fig 11.4 Polished stone axe fragments from the Power Station excavations

Stone

Polished stone axe fragments: context and description

Two polished stone axe fragments were found in the Power Station excavations of 1989. The larger fragment (Fig 11.4, 1) is polished across most of one surface. The length of one edge shows clear evidence for hinge fracture, suggesting the use of considerable force. It weighs 24.5g. This fragment originated from near the centre of a large axe. It was found in the palaeosol spoil heap search described above (see flints) near grid 1900 9040.

The second polished stone axe fragment (Fig 11.4, 2) was found in situ within the palaeosol some 10m away (grid 1882 9053). It weighs 6g. Efforts were made to position the spoil heaps that were to be systematically searched as close as possible to the area from which the soil originated. It is possible therefore that the two fragments were originally located quite close to each other. The smaller fragment is notably paler than the larger and might have derived from a different axe. Their depositional conditions were so similar that it seems improbable that the colour difference was a taphonomic effect. The second fragment was catalogued in the field as a flint flake, but its true identification became clear on cleaning. It has a bulb of percussion and a clear point of impact. The flake was detached just below the bevel along the axe's side. It could not have been removed from the cutting edge during normal use.

A note on the petrology of the Power Station stone axe fragments
by D F Williams

The fragments comprise two small, greenish-grey flakes of a fine-grained altered basic tuff. Both are polished on the outer curved surface and appear to have become detached from possible axes, with no signs of

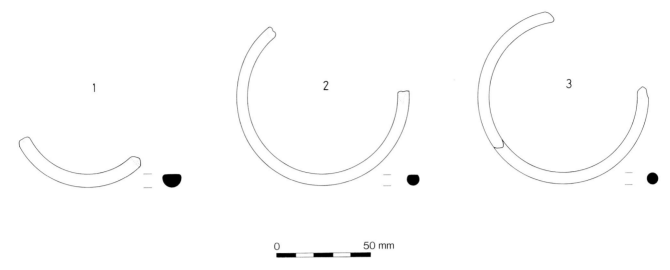

0 ____ 50 mm

Fig 11.5 Polished shale bracelets

retouching along the irregular edges. A close examination under a binocular microscope (×40) with comparative material, shows that the two fragments undoubtedly belong to the epidotized tuffs of the Great Langdale complex, Cumbria, the most prolific of the Neolithic stone axe factories in Britain, with a very wide distribution for its products (Bradley and Edmonds, 1993). They can be placed in Group VI of the Implement Petrology Committee's petrological classification (Clough and Cummins, 1979).

Shale

Fragments of four shale bracelets were found at Flag Fen, Area 6 (Fig 11.5, 1–3). Three are described below, the fourth was described in the first report (Pryor *et al* 1986, pl 11a). A shale armlet with lead inlay was found at the Power Station and is described with the metalwork (Fig 10.10, 257).

Catalogue

1   Small (*c* 25%) fragment of polished shale bracelet, D section, internal diameter 85mm, width 11mm, thickness 7.5mm. Area 6A. Other Find 02, Level 5 (0.22m OD); grid 2710 8893.
2   Large (*c* 33%) fragment of polished shale bracelet, D section, internal diameter 80mm, width 7.5mm, thickness 6mm. Area 6A. Other Find 03, Level 6 (0.18m OD); grid 2710 8893.
3   Two conjoining fragments of polished shale bracelet, round section, internal diameter 78mm, diameter 6.5mm. Area 6B. Other Find 22, Level 5 (0.17m OD); grid 2709 8886.

Discussion

Shale bracelets were a relatively common artefact of the later Bronze Age (Cunliffe and Phillipson 1968) and their manufacture flourished in the Iron Age (Cunliffe 1991, 463–5). A broken shale bracelet of

cruder manufacture and thicker section was found in ditch 1 of the Bronze Age field system, Padholme Road subsite (Pryor 1980, fig 13).

Bracelets 1 and 2 were found close to each other, but have very different cross-sections and diameters. The broken ends of bracelet 1 were straight, whereas those of bracelet 2 were jagged. The break between the two conjoining fragments of bracelet 3 was clean and jagged and the fit precise.

The evidence indicates that two of the bracelets were broken deliberately and in the case of 3, probably *in situ*. The practice of ritual breakage was also observed to be part of the depositional rites of Bronze and Iron Age metalwork (Chapter 10).

The saddle querns from Flag Fen
by D G Buckley and C J Ingle

The four saddle querns from the Flag Fen excavations form a close group found beneath timbers dated by dendrochronology to 1350 BC. All are lower stones, in good condition, that might never have been used. The geological identification of the stones from thin sections was made by Andrew Middleton of The British Museum (below).

Catalogue

Fig 11.6. A complete saddle quern, length 520mm, width *c* 311.5mm, maximum thickness 190mm. The grinding surface is pecked, the underside fairly roughly finished. Fine to medium grained silica-cemented sandstone ('quartzite'), possibly sarsen. Other Find 24.

Fig 11.7. A complete saddle quern, length 470mm, width 270mm, maximum thickness 100mm. Slightly concave pecked grinding surface. Underside more roughly finished. Fine to medium grained silica-cemented sandstone ('quartzite'), possibly sarsen. Other Find 26.

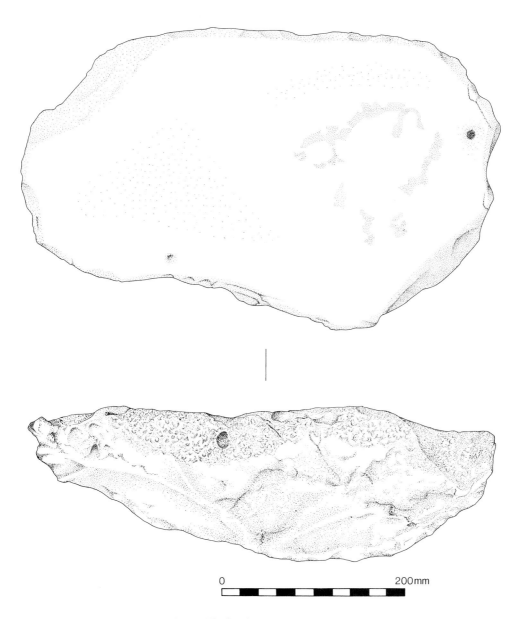

0   200mm

Fig 11.6 Quern from Flag Fen, Area 6B (Other Find 24)

Fig 11.8. Approximately 33% of a saddle quern, length 345mm, width 210mm, maximum thickness 100mm. Almost flat grinding surface with pecked striations parallel to the width of the stone. Calcite cemented glauconitic sandstone, possibly from the Lower Cretaceous Folkestone Beds at Folkestone. Other Find 27.

Fig 11.9. Complete saddle quern, of irregular shape, length 350mm, 242mm, maximum thickness 100mm. Coarsely pecked grinding surface. Underside roughly shaped and finished.

Gabbro, source unknown, possibly derived from a glacial erratic boulder. Other Find 28.

Discussion

The saddle querns from Flag Fen are of particular interest in that they add to the number and range of high quality objects carried to this unique site during the Bronze Age. These stones, like many of the other finds from the site, are considered by the excavator to have been 'ritually' deposited in the waters of the fen. Their discovery provides an opportunity to examine the nature and possible scale of ritual deposition of querns throughout the second and first millennia BC.

The form, use, and general background to saddle querns was considered by Curwen in his important article (1937). This and a subsequent article (1941) remain the standard references for quern studies. Despite the recognition that quernstones are a vital part of the evidence of human subsistence (Cunliffe 1991), they have received relatively little attention. There has recently been a marked increase in research, however, into the production, movement, and use of quernstones. Various regional surveys have been undertaken of existing museum collections, which give some indication of the quantity of stones that have been archived, often without much study. These studies have started to establish a framework for the patterns

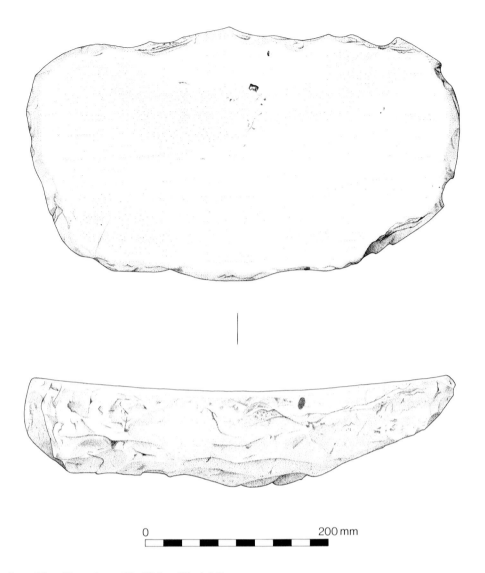

Fig 11.7 Quern from Flag Fen, Area 6B (Other Find 26)

of stone exploitation for both saddle and rotary quern forms. They include the survey by King (1982) of Bedfordshire, Buckinghamshire, Hertfordshire, and Middlesex; that by Hurcombe (1981) of Norfolk, Suffolk, Essex, and Hertfordshire, research by Ingle (1989) of beehive querns in eastern, central, and southern England and the first author's own records.

Date

Even when they occur within a dated context, fragments of saddle quern are difficult to date, since they are often residual in later features. Saddle querns were in use from the Neolithic period, are often found on Bronze Age and Iron Age sites, and even occur in Roman contexts. The Flag Fen querns are of particular value since they were sealed directly beneath timbers dated to 1350 BC.

The form of a saddle quern can give a very broad indication of its date. Earlier prehistoric saddle querns are generally quite large and are often roughly finished (as are the Flag Fen stones). This contrasts with later

examples, which are often smaller, better shaped, and generally well finished. These are more likely to have been derived from 'factory' sites such as that at Lodsworth, West Sussex. The earliest saddle querns identified from this source date to the Late Bronze Age/Early Iron Age and have been found at various sites across south-east England (Peacock 1987, 67). Although saddle querns were gradually superseded by rotary querns during the Middle to Late Iron Age, at sites such as Gussage All Saints, Dorset, saddle and rotary querns were found in direct association in pits (Buckley 1979).

Sources

In their report (below), Middleton and Bowman have suggested the possible sources of raw material for the Flag Fen querns, but also point out the difficulties in identifying specific geological sources for these stones. With this proviso in mind, the options can be considered in relation to the range of rock types known to have been utilised for querns in East Anglia. This region

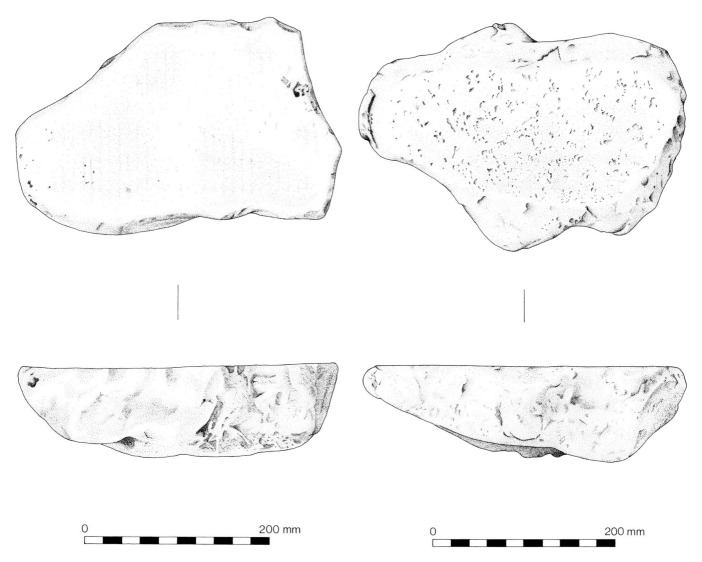

Fig 11.8 *Quern from Flag Fen, Area 6B (Other Find 27)*   Fig 11.9 *Quern from Flag Fen, Area 6B (Other Find 28)*

is notably lacking in hard rock sources. Puddingstone and sarsen, derived from eroded Eocene beds, were both used for saddle and rotary querns. Also available within the region and utilised for querns are erratics from the extensive drift deposits, which include a variety of sedimentary and igneous rock types. Various sandstones from further afield were also used for querns, notably greensand from both Lincolnshire and Kent, and Millstone Grit.

These have been found across East Anglia and the Midlands. It is clear that a diverse range of sources was exploited for querns found in the region, but the fact that three different stone types is represented within the small Flag Fen assemblage adds to their interest.

Sarsen: stones 24 (Fig 11.6) and 26 (Fig 11.7) can be added to an increasing corpus of sarsen saddle querns. The use of sarsen for querns was fairly common in southern England, more so for saddle than the later rotary querns. Sarsen is found as large boulders in a belt across England from Wessex to Norfolk and was readily available for collection and use. Examples of

sarsen saddle querns are recorded from Maiden Castle, Dorset (Wheeler 1943, 322, 1) and Bishopstone, Sussex (Bell 1977), of Neolithic date; Carshalton, Surrey (Adkins and Needham 1985, querns 409 and 410) of Late Bronze Age date; Danebury, Hants (Cunliffe 1984, microfiche), Pewsey, Wilts (Thompson 1971), Rucstalls Hill, Hants (Oliver and Applin 1978, quern nos 40 and 41), and Winnall Down, Hants (Fasham 1985, 80, 2), of Iron Age date; and Baldock, Herts (Stead and Rigby 1989, 179, 788), and Newhaven Sussex (Bell 1976) from Roman contexts.

Greensand: stone 27 (Fig 11.8) is representative of a smaller, but growing, list of greensand querns from the eastern region. The source for this is the greensand belt from Wessex to the Humber and around the Weald. It is only of sufficient hardness and readily available for exploitation at certain points, particularly in the eastern part of the country, in Lincolnshire, around Folkestone in Kent, and in the Weald in Sussex. Calcite-cemented varieties like stone 27 are found at both Folkestone and in the Lincolnshire Wolds, but the identification of a possible Kent source for the Flag Fen querns is especially interesting. There is extensive evidence that the Folkestone Beds were a source of stone for Late Iron Age/Romano-British querns (Keller 1988). The large collection of roughout rotary querns collected from the foreshore at Folkestone indicates large scale production by this time. Other finds of Folkestone Beds querns point, however, to an earlier date for first exploitation of this source. Keller (1988, 65) cites two examples from Kent, one from a Neolithic context at Wingham, the other from a Late Bronze Age/Early Iron Age pit at Dorsett Court, Upper Deal, while in Essex, a saddle quern from this source was recovered from a Late Bronze Age well at Heybridge, near Maldon (Major 1988). If the Kent provenance for the Flag Fen quern is correct, it is one of the earliest recorded and considerably extends the known range of distribution.

Gabbro: stone 28 (Fig 11.9), a large complete stone of igneous origin, raises several questions. The regional surveys in southern and eastern England indicate the relatively scarce use of igneous rocks for querns of either saddle or rotary type in these parts of the country. A logical explanation for the Flag Fen gabbro quern is that a glacial erratic of suitable size from the boulder clay was picked up and utilised. This has been the explanation for various other finds of saddle querns of igneous material, including those from Spong Hill, Norfolk (Buckley 1995a), Goldington, Beds (Williams 1992), Burghfield, Berks (Bradley *et al* 1980), Feltwell villa, Norfolk (Buckley 1986), and Spratton, Northants (Ingle 1989). Similarly, in her survey of eastern England Ingle (op cit) recorded rotary querns of igneous rock, albeit in only small numbers, from Northamptonshire, Lincolnshire, Leicestershire, and Norfolk. It should be borne in mind, however, that elsewhere in southern Britain, beyond the ice front where glacial erratics are not found, in several instances Iron Age sites have produced pieces of igneous rock, eg Dartmoor granite at Gussage All Saints, Dorset (Buckley 1979), and Balksbury, Hants (Buckley 1995b). Whether these derive from querns or not, they represent long distance trading of these rock types and it is quite possible that movement of igneous rock could have taken place into East Anglia at an earlier date.

Ritual deposition

The four saddle querns from Flag Fen were in very good condition. Three of them were complete and possibly even unused, although in this respect it is curious that only the lower stones, without their associated rubbers, were found. It is possible that the incomplete stone was deliberately broken prior to deposition, a practice documented for other classes of artefact from the Neolithic period (Grinsell 1961). Despite the fairly long length of post alignment excavated, these were the only querns recovered. This and the fact that they

were found close together suggests that they were deposited as a group. These factors together reflect the importance of these objects and point to deposition by an individual or group able to acquire high status objects. In addition, the diverse range of rock types, and the distance they were brought to the site indicate the scale of the exchange network of the group. The special nature of Flag Fen and its activities, which led to the accumulation of such a remarkable collection of Bronze Age finds, leaves little doubt that these saddle querns represent a ritual deposit. As such, they now provide an anchor point for much that was suspected, but not clearly defined, relating to the religious importance attached to quernstones throughout British prehistory.

The earliest evidence of the importance of querns as items for possible ritual deposition appears during the Neolithic, at Popudnia, in the western Ukraine. Here miniature clay mould shrines of the Late Cucuteni of about the mid fourth millennium BC have been discovered in some numbers. One of these is notable in that it comprises a room containing a large rectangular oven, the sculpture of a woman pounding grain, and near the quernstone, a small depression to accommodate the ground grain (Gimbutas 1982). In Britain, saddle querns have been found at a variety of types of Neolithic site. Two querns were found *in situ* on a house floor at Loch Olabhat (Armit 1988, 24), as was a large example at Knap of Howar (Ritchie 1983, 292 and fig 3). These could have been abandoned as inconvenient to move, particularly given the massive size of the Knap of Howar example. They might have been left as part of a process of abandonment, however, similar to that discussed by Barrett and Needham (1988, 134–6) for Middle Bronze Age settlements. As will be seen, the bulky nature of querns does not appear to have hampered their transport. A number of causewayed enclosure sites have produced saddle querns, notably Windmill Hill, where sarsen stones comprised a significant feature of the rubbish deposits in the ditches (Smith 1965). Pryor (1998a, 107 and personal communication) goes further and specifically identifies saddle querns as part of the religious activities occurring at the nearby Etton causewayed enclosure, where they are regarded as a component of the range of items ritually deposited both within the causewayed ditch and in isolated pits.

At the Springfield cursus, Essex, one of the eastern region's major Neolithic monuments, a pit within the east end of the enclosure is of particular interest. It contained 'sooty' soil with burnt flints suggesting *in situ* burning. Within the fill there was a small quantity of crushed cremated bone with cattle, sheep, and possibly pig represented. There was also a collection of stones, including a piece of Carstone from the Lower Greensand, almost certainly part of a saddle quern, a large sarsen pebble, and other small pebbles (Hedges and Buckley 1981, 5). This assemblage has all the characteristics of a deliberate 'ritual' deposit.

During excavation of a henge site at Barford, Warwicks, a pit of probable Neolithic date was found, dug some 500mm into the gravel to receive a large saddle quern or grinding stone of Coal Measures sandstone. The quern had been buried upside down in a hole, which had been filled in immediately with almost clean gravel. The edge of the pit cut part of the ditch of a henge monument, but the heavily burnt quern was buried below the level of the inner platform.

A second pit, outside the henge, contained a deposit of seven saddle querns, which the excavator concluded suggested deliberate rather than chance deposition (Oswald 1967, 11–13).

Saddle querns have been recovered from several long mound barrows, but as yet no detailed research into these has been carried out. It is difficult, subsequently, to tell to what extent they might represent deliberate rather than incidental deposits. Similarly, they have been found in round barrows, but in some cases in situations that appear to represent more than just casual association. These include a cist burial within a ploughed out double-ditched barrow at East Tilbury in Essex. This contained an urn inverted over a cremation burial with a faience bead, placed on a complete Lower Greensand (Wealden) ironstone saddle quern (Bannister 1961, 24–6). Also, at Carshalton, Surrey, a partially calcined infant skeleton was found lying on a saddle quern (Adkins and Needham 1985, 46).

Many Middle and Late Bronze Age settlement sites have produced saddle querns. In Essex, for example, these include fragments of greensand (from a source south of the Thames) from Middle Bronze Age contexts at North Shoebury (Buckley and Major 1995) and pieces of sarsen and other quartzitic sandstone recovered during excavation of a Late Bronze Age enclosure at Windmill Field, Broomfield (Major 1995). In Sussex, Drewett collated the evidence from 12 certain and probable settlement sites of the period *c* 1400–800 BC and demonstrated that seven had utilised greensand for querns and whetstones (Drewett 1982). In the main, these are simply scattered pieces from broken querns, but on occasion they are found complete in pits and postholes. At Winnall, near Winchester, the occurrence of a pair of complete sarsen saddle querns within a Middle Bronze Age pit caused some consternation for the excavator. In this instance, once the conclusion had been reached, somewhat reluctantly, that these stones had some ritual significance and were possibly a form of religious offering, she was able to cite several other Bronze Age sites at which complete and apparently serviceable querns had been found deposited in pits. These included Thorny Down and Martin Down in Hampshire, Junction Pit and Green Lane at Farnham, Wrecclesham in Surrey, and Itford Hill in Sussex (Hawkes 1969, 6–8). At the South Rings enclosure at Mucking, Essex, it is suggested that three fragments of saddle querns from the inner enclosure ditch represent specific ritual deposits within the butt ends of the inner enclosure ditch (Etté 1993; Buckley and Major forthcoming).

Saddle and rotary querns have occurred on a number of Iron Age sites. In the early Iron Age, the tradition of burying complete saddle querns appears to continue, as represented by Croft Ambrey. Here the excavator reported that 'it may be noted, however, that a complete unbroken saddle quern was found in Pit 14 as though it had been rejected as old fashioned' (Stanford 1974, 186). This tradition continues in the Late Iron Age with rotary querns, and in several cases it has been concluded that these were querns selected for special deposition. These include finds at Gussage All Saints, Dorset (Buckley 1979), Danebury, Hants (Cunliffe 1984), and more recently Sudden Farm, Nether Wallop, Hants (Brown 1991). Such deposits form part of a wide range of items interpreted as having been deliberately placed in storage pits.

The preceding preliminary review of sites from the Neolithic through to the Iron Age, which have produced saddle querns in contexts interpreted as representing ritual deposits, help to put the Flag Fen querns into context. The activities giving rise to these deposits are understandable, given the realisation that grain production and its processing were essential operations within society. As noted above, querns were deliberately deposited at a range of Bronze Age settlements (Barrett and Needham 1988). It is therefore natural that this importance should be reflected in religious activities and that these rites should find archaeological expression in the deliberate disposal of querns. It is now clear that querns were an important item in prehistoric trade or exchange in Britain. Further, despite the weight of a saddle quern, they could have been carried quite long distances, which would have been the case with stone 27. If the stone had indeed come from Kent, it is probable that this involved coastal trade. The distances that these items had travelled from their source suggests that this was not just routine trade, but quite likely that the querns were part of extensive and complex networks of gift exchange. They might have been considered as prestige objects suitable for exchange, or might possibly have related more specifically to marriage arrangements, for example, the stones forming part of a 'dowry'. A quern might indeed be seen as a symbol of family or domestic life (Pryor 1998a, 369). As such, they can be considered highly valued objects and it is to be expected that they should be included in the range of items prized as worthy of 'presentation' to the gods or the world of the ancestors (Bradley 1990, 164, 199). It is therefore not surprising, given the nature of Flag Fen, that saddle querns should be among the finds recovered from this unique site.

Future research

The evidence collectively demonstrates a requirement for excavators to give much greater thought to the location, recovery, and recording of querns on their sites. The thinking must extend far beyond the noting of complete querns in pits and encompass finds from a wide range of contexts including postholes, wells, and abandoned structures. These are all situations in which finds of other classes of object, especially pottery and bone, have often been interpreted as representing ritual activity. It is also necessary to go further and ask if all the many querns found in non-settlement locations can simply be explained as the result of movement at a later date, since, even for quernstones from isolated contexts, the explanation could be more complex. Hopefully, this short consideration of the subject of quern deposition will lead to new research involving both new sites and a closer scrutiny of earlier discoveries.

Report on the examination of four Bronze Age quernstones from Flag Fen

by A P Middleton and S G E Bowman

Four saddle querns excavated from the Bronze Age site at Flag Fen have been examined to determine the types of stones used. The querns were initially examined using a hand lens. Small fragments were removed from three of the stones (26, 27, and 28; laboratory nos 50384P, 50385Y, and 50386W/50387U (two samples from quern 28)). These fragments were prepared as polished thin sections for examination using a petrographic microscope.

More detailed descriptions of the thin sections are provided in Appendix 4.

Querns 24 and 26

Visual examinations suggested that these two querns are of the same type of stone. Only one (26) was, therefore, sampled for thin-section examination. Both are white, compact, fine-grained sandstones with a saccharoidal texture. There is clear evidence of 'pecking' on both stones. On quern 24 there are what appear to be spills of metal. It is suggested that these might be mineral sulphides, deposited during burial under anaerobic conditions (see eg Duncan and Ganiaris 1987), but analysis would be required to confirm this. In thin section it can be seen that the stone is a very pure, fine to medium grained silica-cemented sandstone ('quartzite').

Quern 27

Visual examination suggests that this quern was made from glauconitic sandstone. The natural bedding of the stone appears to be sub-parallel to the worked surface. The lower part of the stone seems to be more friable and shows some evidence of bioturbation (ie disturbance of the sediment by burrowing organisms at the time of its formation). Examination in thin section confirmed that this is a glauconitic sandstone and showed that it has a sparry calcite cement.

Quern 28

The stone of this quern is quite heavily weathered and has undergone some exfoliation. It appears to be a medium- to coarse-grained plutonic igneous rock of basic composition. Examination of the thin section supported these observations and showed that this is a gabbro.

Sources of the stones

The East Anglian region has extensive superficial geological deposits including glacial boulder clays. These might include 'erratic' boulders derived from distant geological sources. At various times, ice sheets brought material from areas to the west and north and also from Scandinavia. This complicating factor must be considered in any attempt to suggest geological sources for the quern stones.

Querns 24 and 26

These compact pure quartz sandstones are similar to so-called sarsen, which is reported to occur as scattered blocks across the southern part of Suffolk (Chatwin 1961, 39). This attribution is not certain, however, and other, more distant geological sources would seem to be possible, for example, the older strata to the west and northwest. Even if this should be the case, however, it is still quite possible that these stones were obtained fairly locally as erratic boulders from glacial drift, rather than from their more distant primary geological outcrops.

Quern 27

The most obvious source for a calcite-cemented, glauconitic sandstone would seem to be the Lower Cretaceous Spilsby Sandstone, which has a restricted outcrop around the Wash, and also occurs in the glacial drift (Bridgland *et al* 1995). Thin sections of several samples of Spilsby Sandstone (kindly supplied by Caroline Ingle) generally contained less glauconite, however, and did not include any of the 'silty glauconite' noted in Quern 27 (Appendix 4). Possible alternative sources were therefore investigated, by comparison with thin sections of other glauconitic sandstones. The closest match observed was with the Lower Cretaceous Folkestone Beds at Folkestone (samples kindly supplied by Peter Keller). There is extensive evidence that these beds were a source of stone for Late Iron Age/Romano-British querns (Keller 1988). Any suggestions that the Folkestone Beds were a source for this quern from Flag Fen must, however, remain tentative; it would certainly imply deliberate transportation of the stone from Kent.

There are no obvious primary geological sources for the gabbro rock of this quern and the most probable source would seem to be relatively local glacially derived drift. The possibility that it was obtained from a more distant, primary geological source can not, however, be totally excluded.

Conclusion

Petrographic examination, including thin section analysis, has shown that three distinct rock types were used for the four Bronze Age querns excavated at Flag Fen. One, a gabbro, was probably fashioned from an 'erratic' boulder, two, of fine white sandstone, might be of sarsen from southern Suffolk, and the fourth might be of Spilsby Sandstone, although a more distant source, the Folkestone beds at Folkestone, gives a closer match in thin section. These tentative attributions are discussed in the context of an area that has extensive deposits of glacial drift.

12 Non-human and human mammalian bone remains from the Flag Fen platform and Power Station post alignment

by Paul Halstead, Ellen Cameron, and Stephen Forbes

The bone material discussed here consists of two distinct samples, each of modest size, which were collected under rather different conditions of retrieval. Both samples were collected by hand, but that from the Flag Fen platform site derives from a meticulous, small-scale research excavation, while the Power Station post alignment sample was picked out during a mechanised, large-scale rescue excavation. In addition, while bone from the Flag Fen platform site is closely associated, stratigraphically, with the prehistoric deposition of wood, much of that from the Power Station post alignment site is more loosely linked with the linear wooden feature. Earlier attempts to distinguish different layers within the Flag Fen platform site have been abandoned here, because it is evident that groups of associated bones have penetrated the woody matrix to varying depths (Halstead and Cameron 1992, 499). Likewise, in the case of the Power Station post alignment site, a preliminary distinction between bone within and above the old ground surface has been blurred rather than refined by post-excavation work, and so this assemblage too is treated here as a single unit. Ceramic finds suggest that all the bone from the Flag Fen platform site and the bulk of that from the Power Station post alignment site is of Late Bronze Age date, with possible admixture of earlier and later material at the western or landward end of the Power Station post alignment (John Barrett personal communication). The concentration of pottery and other artefacts to the south of the alignment and of bone to the north (Halstead and Cameron 1992, 500, fig 1), however, weakens the value of the former as dating evidence for the latter. Because of the enigmatic nature of the Flag Fen complex, the analysis of the bone assemblage has been concerned principally with attempts to explore the manner of bone deposition. Identification of non-human mammal bones was carried out by Ellen Cameron (Power Station post alignment site only) and Paul Halstead, of human remains by Stephen Forbes (Power Station post alignment site) and Helen Bush (Flag Fen platform site), and of fish bones by Pippa Smith. This report has been compiled by Paul Halstead.

Methods of analysis

The assemblages were identified with the aid of the modern skeletal reference collections in the Department of Archaeology and Prehistory, University of Sheffield.

Domestic mammals securely identified were cow (*Bos taurus*), pig (*Sus domesticus*), sheep (*Ovis aries*), horse (*Equus caballus*) and dog (*Canis familiaris*). Distinction between sheep and goat (only sheep was

positively identified) was based on the criteria of Boessneck *et al* (1964), Kratochwil (1969), and Payne (1985). Identified wild mammals include red deer (*Cervus elaphus*), fox (*Vulpes vulpes*), badger (*Meles meles*), polecat (*Mustela putorius*), hare (*Lepus europaeus*), and beaver (*Castor fiber*). No bones of cow were large enough to suggest the presence of wild aurochs (*Bos primigenius*) but, on grounds of size, one loose mandibular canine of pig was suggestive of wild boar (*Sus scrofa*) and two mandibular fragments of dog could conceivably be assigned to wolf. A modest number of human skeletal remains was identified from both sites.

In addition, identifiable fish remains included two fragments of pike from the Flag Fen platform site and 25 fragments of pike and one of carp from the Power Station post alignment site. For non-human mammals, age at death was estimated from the state of eruption and wear of mandibular cheek teeth and from the development of postcranial bones. The recording and analysis of dental development follows Payne (1973 and 1987) for sheep, Grant (1982) and Silver (1969) for cattle and pigs, and Silver (1969) for dogs. The ageing of postcranial bones on the basis of epiphyseal fusion follows Silver (ibid). Postcranial bones classified as 'neonatal' on grounds of size, morphology, and surface texture (cf Prummel 1987a and 1987b) might represent late foetal or newborn animals (up to, say, one month after birth). Pelves and metacarpals of sheep and cattle have been sexed on morphological grounds (sheep: after Boessneck *et al* 1964; cattle: after Grigson 1982). Metrical data were recorded after von den Driesch (1976); measurements were taken to the nearest millimetre in the case of the overall length of long bones and otherwise to 0.1 mm. Shoulder heights have been calculated for dogs after Harcourt (1974). Also recorded were traces of gnawing and cut marks.

Cut marks were examined with a ×10 hand lens and, where possible, were classified as the result of skinning, dismembering, or filleting (after Binford 1981); a few examples of bone fragmentation were attributed to deliberate breakage for the extraction of marrow (also after Binford op cit).

For the few human remains, age at death has been estimated from dental eruption (after Ubelaker 1989) and wear (after Brothwell 1965), from epiphyseal fusion (after McKern 1970) and also from the closure of cranial sutures (after Meindl and Lovejoy 1985). Sex determinations are based on metrical criteria (following Bass 1987) and also on cranial morphology (following Bass op cit; Buikstra and Ubelaker 1994). Measurements follow the conventions of Bass (ibid) and Buikstra and Ubelaker (ibid), while stature has been estimated after Trotter (1970).

Systematic analysis is restricted to a selected set of anatomical units, which are durable, highly identifiable, informative, and relatively easy to quantify: horn/antler, maxilla (canine, premolar and molar tooth row), mandible (canine, premolar, and molar tooth row), scapula (articular area including 'neck'), proximal half of humerus, distal half of humerus, proximal half of radius, distal half of radius, proximal half of ulna, proximal half of metacarpal, distal half of metacarpal, pelvis (acetabular region), proximal half of femur, distal half of femur, proximal half of tibia, distal half of tibia, astragalus, calcaneum, proximal half of metatarsal, distal half of metatarsal, phalanx 1, phalanx 2, and phalanx 3; for 'long bones', the proximal and distal units include their respective halves of the shaft. Units from the left- and right-hand side of the skeleton are distinguished, where possible, but phalanges from the fore- and hind-limb are not. All specimens of these selected anatomical units identified to species (or to 'sheep/goat'), are listed in Tables 12.1–12.2, together with any information recorded on side of body (left/right), completeness (for long bones: proximal or distal or both), age, sex, size, butchery, gnawing, and so on. For simplicity, the provenance of specimens is indicated in Tables 12.1–12.2 not by their locational coordinates but by the 'lot' numbers assigned during excavation either to individual bones or to groups of bones found together. For analytical purposes, identifiable specimens are quantified in terms of both minimum numbers of anatomical units (MinAU–Halstead 1985) and minimum numbers of individuals (MNI; Tables 12.3–12.4). Where two or more fragments

might be derived from the same anatomical unit (eg left proximal tibia), only the most complete example contributes to MinAU. Notional 'joins' between fragments were sought within but not between the Flag Fen platform and Power Station post alignment sites. To simplify comparison between species with different numbers of foot bones, MinAU quantification of fragments of metapodial bones and phalanges has also been standardised, in terms of minimum numbers of feet: thus if two specimens of phalanx 2 of, say, sheep (or sheep/goat) could be derived from the same foot, only one contributes to MinAU. Identified specimens 'discounted' from MinAU are distinguished in Tables 12.1–12.2 by parentheses.

Estimates of MNI, which took account of size, age, and morphological details, were also conducted independently for the Flag Fen platform and Power Station post alignment sites. At both sites, some bone fragments were recovered singly, as 'loose' fragments, and others in apparently associated groups of more or less complete skeletons. The sample from each site was 'strewn', therefore, partly to facilitate the assessment of MinAU, partly to explore the possibility of articulation or pairing between bones not recovered in apparent association, and partly to improve the estimation of MNI. Tables 12.1–12.2 also list all recorded pairings and matches between articulating units, together with inferences as to MNI and suggested associations of (part-) skeletons. Tables 12.3–12.4 summarise the MinAU and MNI data for each site, in the case of MinAU distinguishing between 'loose' bones and associated '(part-) skeletons'.

Key to Tables 12.1 and 12.2

body part	age/sex			
H/A	horn/antler		*limb bones*	
MAX	maxilla		UF	unfused
MAN	mandible		FG	fusing
SCA	scapula		F	fused
HUM	humerus		*mandibles*	
RAD	radius		D4	deciduous premolar 4
ULN	ulna		P4	permanent premolar 4
MC	metacarpal		M1	molar 1
PEL	pelvis		M2	molar 2
FEM	femur		M3	molar 3
TIB	tibia		V	visible in crypt
AST	astragalus		E	erupting
CAL	calcaneum		H	half-way up
MT	metatarsal		U	erupted but unworn
PH1	phalanx 1		J	just in wear
PH2	phalanx 2		W	worn
PH3	phalanx 3		c-m	cow tooth wear stages after Grant (1982)
p	proximal		2a, 16L, etc	sheep tooth wear stages after Payne (1987)
d	distal		S	socket
( )	specimens discounted from MinAU		$	mandible broken
★	specimens identified to sheep rather than sheep/goat			
size				
Bp, Bd etc	standard measurements (mm) after von den Driesch (1976)			

Table 12.1 Catalogue of 'identified' mammalian bones from the platform site

cow (MNI=6)

lot no	body part	age/sex	size	butchery, etc	comments
probable single skeleton, age c *5–6 months (several paired and matching body parts) = 'individual 1'*					
189	H/A L				pair
189	H/A R				
190	MAX L				pair
190	MAX R				
190	MAN L	D4W(j) M1H$			pair
190	MAN R	D4W(j) M1H$			
038	SCA L	UF			prob pair
189	SCA R	UF			
038	HUM Lpd	pUF dUF			pair
189	HUM Rpd	pUF dUF			match
184	RAD Rpd	pUF dUF			pair
038	RAD Lpd	pUF dUF			match
038	ULN R	UF			prob pair
184	ULN L	UF			
038	MC Lpd	dUF			pair
038	MC Rpd	dUF			
038	PEL L	UF			pair
038	PEL R	UF			
038	FEM Lpd	pUF dUF			pair
038	FEM Rpd	pUF dUF			
038	TIB Lpd	pUF dUF			?pair
038	TIB Rpd	pUF dUF			
038	CAL L	UF			
038	AST R				
038	MT Lpd	dUF			
038	PH1	pUF			
038	PH2	pUF			
038	PH2	pUF			
038	PH3				
038	PH3				
parts of at least five further individuals					
168	H/A R				
001	MAX R				
081	MAX L				
081	MAX R				
077	MAN L	D4W(j/k) M1W(h) M2W(d) M3E			pair
093	MAN R	D4W(j/k) M1W(h) M2W(d) M3E			
172	MAN L	P4W(f) M1W(j) M2W(g)$			'individual 2'
204	MAN L	D4W(f)$			
079	SCA L				
140	SCA R				
199	SCA R	F	BG 37.5 GLP 54.6	dismembered	
071/78	HUM Lpd	dUF			prob pair
071/78	HUM Rpd	pUF dUF			
167	HUM Lpd				
152	HUM Rd	dUF			
048	RAD Lpd	pF dUF			prob pair
140/44	RAD Rpd	pF dUF			
073	ULN L				pair
074	ULN R	UF			
075	MC Rpd	dUF			
039	MC Rpd	newborn			'individual' 3
115	MC Lpd	dUF	> 'individual 1'		
182	MC Lpd	dF	Bp 48.6 Bd 53.6 GL 178	skinned	
133	PEL L	UF			
071/160	FEM Lpd	dUF			?pair
169	FEM Rd	dUF			
034	FEM Rpd		> FEM 071/160		
173	FEM Lpd		< 'individual 1'		'individual 4'
170/71	TIB Lpd	pUF dUF	>> 'individual 1'		'individual 5'

Table 12.1 *(Cont'd)*

220	TIB Lp	pUF	> TIB 170/71		'individual 6'
132	TIB Rpd	pUF dUF			
127	TIB Rpd	dUF			
208	TIB Ld	dF			
131	AST R				
070	CALC L	UF			pair
072	CALC R	UF			
088	MT Lpd				
030	MT Lpd	dF	GL 196		
029	MT Lpd				
069	MT Rpd	dUF			
160	MT Rpd				
035	MT Lpd				
139	PH2	newborn			
151	PH2	pUF			
009	PH3				

sheep/goat (MNI=12)

lot no	body part	age/sex	size	butchery, etc	comments
parts of at least 12 individuals (including some paired and matching body parts; also 050 = axis, fused, dismembered					
136	H/A L⋆				pair
136	H/A R⋆				
017	MAX L				
023	MAX R				
066	MAX L				pair
067	MAX R				
058	MAX R				
187	MAN R⋆	d4W(16L) M1W(9A) M2W(7A)			'individual 1'
018	MAN L	M2W(8A)$			pair
019	MAN R	M1W(9A) M2W(8A) M3W(6G)			'individual 3'
021/23/24	MANL	M1W(9A) M2W(6A)			pair
020	MAN R	M1W(9A) M2W(6A)			'individual 3'
036	MAN R	P4W(9A) M1W(11A) M2W(9A)$			
006	MAN L	P4W(9A) M1W(9A) M2W(9A) M3W(6G)			'individual 4'
010/11	MAN R	M1W(9A) M2W(7A?) M3H/E			'individual 5'
013	MAN R	M2W(9A) M3W(5A)			'individual 6'
040	MAN R	M2W(8A) M3W(2A)			'individual 7'
174	MAN L	P4U/J M1W(9A) M2W(8A) M3 H/E			'individual 8'
090	MAN L	P4W(2A) M1W(9A) M2W(7A) M3S			
015	MAN R	P4W(7A) M1W(9A)$			
015	MAN L	P4H M1W(9A) M2W(7A) M3U/J			'individual 9'
090	MAN L	P4W(2A) M1W(9A) M2W(7A) M3W(2A)			'individual 10'
125	MAN L	M1W(9A) M2W(8A) M3J/H			'individual 11'
108	SCA L⋆	F			?pair
112	SCA R⋆	F	BG 17.5 GLP 27.2		
055	SCA L⋆	F	GLP 26.2	dismembered	
060	SCA R⋆	F	BG 17.9 GLP 26.9		
031	HUM Lpd				
175	HUM Lpd⋆	dF			
065	HUM Lpd⋆	dF	Bd 26.9		
111	HUM Rpd⋆	dF	Bd 27.3		
109	RAD Rpd	pF dF	GL c145		
165	RAD Lpd⋆	pF dUF	Bp 23.9	gnawed	
046	RAD Rpd	pF			
098	RAD Rpd⋆	pF dF	Bp 26.8 GL 141	filleted	match
099	ULN R				
112	RAD Lpd⋆	pF dF	Bp 26.9 Bd 25.7 GL 140		prob match
080	ULN L				
026	MC Lpd⋆	?female	Bp 20.7		
012	MC Lpd⋆	female			
041	MC Rpd⋆	dF, ?male	Bd 23.0	?marrow	
045	MC Rpd⋆				
076	MC Lpd⋆	dUF, ?female			
062	MC Lpd⋆				

Table 12.1 *(Cont'd)*

134	PEL L★	?female			
100	PEL R★	F, ?female	LA 25.4		
112	FEM Lpd				
095	FEM Rpd				
078	FEM Ld	dF			
052	FEM Rp	pF			
052	FEM Rd				
050	TIB Lpd	dF		filleted, marrow	
097	TIB Rpd★	dF			
094	TIB Lp			worked	
043	AST R★		GLl 24.5		
007	MT pd	newborn			'individual 12'
052	MT Lpd★	dF	Bd 21.0	dismem, ?marrow	?pair
050	MT Rpd★	dF		prob marrow	
005	MT Lpd★	dF	Bp 17.4 Bd 20.0 GL 134		pair
004	MT Rpd★				
025	MT Lpd★				
032	MT Lpd★	dF	Bd 19.3		
027	MT Rpd★	dF	Bp 17.5 GL 133		
127	MT Rpd				
126	MT Lpd★		Bp 19.3		
197	MT Rpd★	dF	Bp 17.4 GL 129		
112	PH2★	pF			

horse (MNI=2)

lot no	body part	age/sex	size	butchery, etc	comments
probable part-skeleton of mature adult (including skull, L forelimb, R hindlimb = 'individual 1')					
206	MAX L	well-worn permanent teeth			pair
206	MAX R	well-worn permanent teeth			
202	SCA L	F	BG 38.1 GLP 79.2		
200	HUM Lpd				
203	RAD Lpd				
201	FEM Rd				
205	PH2	pF	Bp 42.7		
fragments including parts of at least one further individual (= 'individual 2')					
110	FEM Rpd	pUF dF			
002	AST L				
128	MT Rpd	dF	Bp 41.9 Bd 42.9 GL 236		
186	PH3				

pig (MNI=2)

lot no	body part	age/sex	size	butchery, etc	comments
parts of at least one juvenile and one newborn individual					
081	MAN L	male			
033	HUM Rpd	dUF			'individual 1'
047	FEM Lpd	pUF			
042	MT pd	newborn			'individual 2'

dog (MNI=4)

lot no	body part	age/sex	size	butchery etc	comments
one part-skeleton (including several paired or matching body parts) = 'individual 1'					
213	MAN L				
213	HUM Lp	pF			?pair
213	HUM Rp	pF			
213	RAD Lpd	pF dF	Bp 19.6 Bd 25.7 GL 177		pair
213	RAD Rpd	pF dF	Bp 19.7 Bd 25.6 GL 176		
213	MC2 Lpd	dF	Bd 9.1		
213	(MC3 Lpd)	dF	Bd 9.0		
213	(MC4 Lpd)	dF	Bd 8.8		?paired
213	(MC5 Lpd)	dF	Bd 9.4		feet
213	MC3 Rpd	dF	Bd 8.9		
213	(MC5 Rpd)	dF	Bd 9.9		
213	PEL L	F	LAR 23.9		pair
213	PEL R	F	LAR 23.7		

Table 12.1 *(Cont'd)*

213	FEM Ld				
213	TIB Lpd	pF dF	Bd 24.3		
213	CAL R	F	GL 47.8		
213	MT3 Lpd	dF	Bd 9.3		
213	MT3 Rpd	dF	Bd 9.5		?paired
213	(MT4 Rpd)	dF	Bd 9.0		feet
213	(MT5 Rpd)	dF	Bd 9.1		
213	PH1	pF	Bp 8.6		
213	PH2	pF	Bp 7.4		
213	PH3				

one part-skeleton (adult, including several paired or matching body parts = 'individual 2') + at least one foot of a second younger individual (= 'individual 3')

221	MAN R				
220	RAD Lpd	pF dF	Bp 21.3 Bd 26.5 GL 163		pair
220	RAD Rpd	pF dF	Bp 20.6 Bd 26.5 GL 165		match
220	ULN L	F			prob pair
220	ULN R	F			
220	MC5 Lpd	dF	Bd 10.0		
220	(MC3 Lpd)	dF	Bd 9.3		match
220	(MC4 Lpd)	dF	Bd 9.0		pair
220	MC4 Rpd	dF	Bd 9.1		
220	(MC2 Rpd)	dF	Bd 9.2		
220	AST R		GL 8.0		
220	MT3 Rpd	dF	Bd 9.4		
220	(MT4 Rpd)	dF	Bd 8.7		
220	MC5 Rpd	dUF			
220	(MC3 Rpd)	dUF			?match, 'indiv 3'
220	(MC4 Rpd)	dUF			
221	MC/MT d	dUF			
221	PH1	pF			
221	(PH1)				

one probable part-skeleton = 'individual 4'

183	MAN L	P4W M1W M2S M3S			pair
183	MAN R	M1W M2S M3S			
130	HUM Rpd	dF	Bd 35.0		
130	RAD Lpd	pF dF	Bd 25.0 GL c175		prob pair
183	RAD Rpd	pF dF	GL c174		match
183	ULN R	F			
183	TIB Rpd	pF dF	Bd 23.4		
130	MT5 Rpd	dF			

fragments (including paired and matching body parts) potentially from 'individuals 1–4'; at least one male indicated by baculum (lot 217)

159	MAX L				
181	(MAX L)				
089	HUM Lpd	dF	Bd 33.8		
157	ULN L	F			
137	PEL R	F	LAR 23.8		pair
137	PEL L	F	LAR 24.0		match
147	FEM Lpd	pF dF	Bd 33.6		pair
146	FEM Rpd	pF dF	Bp 43.3 GL 199 DC 21.1		
135	TIB Lpd				
138	CAL L	F	GL 46.4		

hare (MNI=1)

lot no	body part	age/sex	size	butchery, etc	comments
220	PEL R	F	LA 12.0		

red deer (MNI=1)

lot no	body part	age/sex	size	butchery, etc	comments
219	H/A	male		shed	

human (MNI=2)

lot no	body part	age/sex	size	butchery, etc	comments
000	MAN	loose (unshed) D1?U (c 1.5–2.5 yr)			MAN: MNI=1
189	TIB Lpd	very young			TIB: MNI=2
214	TIB Lpd				

Table 12.2 Catalogue of 'identified' mammalian bones from the post alignment site

cow (MNI=16)

lot no	body part	age/sex	size	butchery, etc	comments
parts of at least 16 skeletons (including some paired and matching body parts)					
417	H/A L				pair, H/A: MNI=2
417	H/A R				
508	H/A L				pair
508	H/A R				
499	MAX R				MAX: MNI=5
421/26	MAX R				
343	MAX L				
384	MAX L				
370	(MAX L)				
482	MAX L				
508	MAX L				
498	(MAX L)				
276	(MAX L)				
517	MAX L				
369	MAN L				'individual 1', MAN:MNI=16
078	MAN L				'individual 2'
245	MAN R	P4S M1S M2S M3S			'individual 3'
545	MAN R	P4W(g) M1W(l) M2W(k) M3W(k)			prob pair
545	MAN L	P4S M1S M2S M3S			'individual 4'
373	MAN R	D4W(e/f) M1W(g) M2W(d) M3V			'individual 5'
332	MAN R	M3W(m)			'individual 6'
341	MAN R	M3W(e)			'individual 7'
506	MAN R	M3W(j)			'individual 8'
590	MAN L	P4S M1W(l) M2W(k) M3W(g)			'individual 9'
506	MAN L	P4S M1S M2W(k) M3W(j)			'individual 10'
490	MAN L	P4S M1S M2S M3W(k)			'individual 11'
582	MAN L	D4W(j) M1W(d)$			'individual 12'
540	MAN L	M3W(j)			'individual 13'
468	MAN L	M3W(e)			'individual 14'
532	MAN L	P4S M1S M2S M3S			'individual 15'
049	MAN L	M1W(c)			'individual 16'
468	(MAN R)	M1/M2W(g)			
493	(MAN R)	M1W(k)			
468	(MAN R)	P4W			
083	(MAN R)				
504	(MAN R)	P4S$			
468	(MAN R)				
282	(MAN R)				
163	(MAN L)	P4S M1S M2S$			
468	(MAN L)				
481	(MAN L)				
468	(MAN L)	P4J			
149	(MAN L)	M1W(k)			
468	(MAN L)	M1W(k)			
458	(MAN L)	M1/M2W(g)			
545	(MAN L)	M2W(k)			
506	(MAN L)	M1/M2W(l)			
256	SCA R	F	BG c46 GLP c65		SCA: MNI=6
253	SCA R	young			
461	SCA R	F	BG c38 GLP c58	filleted	?pair
456/68	SCA L	F			
433	SCA L	F			
464	SCA L				
418	SCA R	young			
546	HUM Lpd				HUM: MNI 13
465	HUM Lpd	dF	BT c64		prob pair, ?match
344/454	HUM Rpd	dF	BT c64		RAD pair 457/475
035	(HUM Ld)			gnawed	
551	HUM Ld				

Table 12.2 *(Cont'd)*

lot no	body part	age/sex	size	butchery, etc	comments
469	(HUM Lp)				
381	HUM Ld				
481	HUM Lpd				
382	HUM Rpd			?filleted	
044	HUM Rpd				
036	HUM Rd				
557	HUM Rd				
482	HUM Rpd			gnawed	
183	HUM Rd				
505	HUM Rp	pUF			
471	HUM Lpd	dF	BT 72.0		
100	RAD Rp				RAD+ULN: MNI=13
475	RAD Rpd	pF dF	Bp 70.4 GL 242		prob pair, ?match
457	RAD Lpd	pF dF	Bp 70.1 GL 245		HUM pair, 344/465/454
033	RAD Rpd	pF	Bp 73.7	gnawed	match
033	ULN R				
038	RAD Rpd	pF		gnawed	
118	RAD Rpd	pF dUF	Bp 71.4		
539	RAD Rp				
145	ULN R			gnawed	
468	ULN L			gnawed	
428	RAD Lpd	pF			
559	RAD Lpd	pF	Bp 74.5		
372	RAD Lpd	pF		gnawed	
592	RAD Lpd	pF		gnawed	
128	RAD Lp	pF		gnawed	
102	RAD Ld				
253	RAD Lp	pF			
485	RAD Lpd	pF		gnawed	
577	MC Rpd	dF, female	Bp 46.6 Bd 50.1 GL 181		MC: MNI=12
583	MC Rpd		Bp 55.1	skinned	
037	MC Rpd	male		gnawed	
480	MC Rpd		Bp 46.4		
589	MC Rp				
123	MC Rd	dF, female	Bd 49.3	gnawed	
363	MC Lpd	dUF	Bp 45.8		
453	MC Lpd	dF, female	Bp 47.0 Bd 49.7 GL 177		
230	MC Lpd		Bp 49.0		
152	MC Lpd				
042	MC Lpd	?male			
028	MC Lpd				
107	MC pd			gnawed	
294	MC Lpd	male	Bp 54.9	gnawed	
056	PEL R	female			PEL: MNI=4
498	PEL R	female		gnawed	
432	PEL R	F, female		gnawed	
069	PEL R	F, ?female			
481	PEL L				
275	PEL L			gnawed	
480	(PEL L)				
482	(PEL L)				
032	(PEL L)			gnawed	
255	FEM Rpd			gnawed	FEM: MNI=11
501	FEM Rpd			gnawed	
565	FEM Rpd			gnawed	
058	FEM Rpd	young			
053	FEM Lpd	pF dF			
450	FEM Lpd				
473	FEM Ld	dF			
535	FEM Ld	dUF			

Table 12.2 *(Cont'd)*

lot no	body part	age/sex	size	butchery, etc	comments
054	FEM Ld	dUF			
104	(FEM Ld)				
596	FEM Ld				
520	FEM Lpd				
339	(FEM Lp)				
566	TIB Rpd	dF	Bd 58.2	gnawed	TIB: MNI=10
529	TIB Rp	pFG		gnawed	
600	TIB Rpd				
052	TIB Rd				
290	TIB Rpd			gnawed	
586	TIB Lpd			gnawed	
374	TIB Lpd	dF		gnawed	
457	TIB Lpd				
533	TIB Lpd	dF	Bd 56.5		
376	TIB Ld				
188	TIB Ld				
547	TIB Ld	dF	Bd 49.6		
188	TIB Lp				
503	(TIB Lp)				
325	(TIB Lp)				
088	TIB Lpd			?filleted	
174	AST R				AST: MNI=4
161	AST R		Bd 33.1 GLl 54.1		
518	AST R				
013	AST R				
319	CAL R				CAL: MNI=1
254	CAL L			gnawed	
048	MT Lpd			gnawed	MT: MNI=12
452	MT Rpd				?pair
463	MT Lpd			gnawed	
254	MT Lpd		Bp 46.1		
203	MT Lpd				
366	MT Lpd		Bp 40.5	gnawed, skinned	
474	MT Rpd	dUF	Bp 43.8		
597	MT Rpd	dF	Bp c40 Bd c46 GL 196	gnawed	
126	MT Rpd	dF	Bp 53.2 Bd 55.8 GL 215	gnawed	pathology (prox artic)
027	MT Rpd				
553	MT Rpd			gnawed	
225	MT Rp				
040	MT Rpd				
154	MT Rpd				
352	(MT d)				
046	MT Lpd			dismembered	
047	MT Rp				
549	(MT d)				
324	PH1	pF			PH1: MNI=2
576	PH1	pF			
166	PH1	pUF			
187	PH1	pF	Bp 25.8	?skinned	
328	PH2	pF			PH2: MNI=1
269	PH3				PH3: MNI=1

sheep/goat (MNI=10)

lot no	body part	age/sex	size	butchery, etc	comments
fragments (including a few paired and matching body parts) of several individuals					
085	H/A R*			attached	H/A: MNI=1
265	MAX L				MAX: MNI=2
077	MAX L				
019	(MAX L)				
009	MAX R				
099	(MAX R)				
201	MAX R				
072	(MAX R)				

Table 12.2 *(Cont'd)*

lot no	body part	age/sex	size	butchery, etc	comments
419	MAN L	D4S M1S$			MAN: MNI=10
104	MAN L	P4W(12S) M1W(12A) M2W(9A) M3W(11G)			'individual 1'
190	MAN L	P4W(9A) M1W(9A) M2W(9A) M3W(11G)			'individual 2'
441	MAN L	P4S M1S M2S M3W(5A)			'individual 3'
143	MAN L	M3W(11G)			'individual 4'
267	MAN L	M1W(7A)			'individual 5'
031	(MAN L)	M1W(9A)			
212	MAN L	M1W(9A)			
422	MAN L	M1W(9A)			
390	MAN L	M1W(9A)			
310	MAN R	M3W(5A)			'individual 6'
312	(MAN R)	M2W(9A)			
224	MAN R	M3W(11G)			'individual 7'
364	MAN R	M2W(2A)			'individual 8'
222	MAN R	M1W(5A)			'individual 9'
073	MAN R	M1W(5A)			'individual 10'
132	(MAN R)	M1/M2W(9A)			
248	(MAN R)	P4S$			
325	(MAN R)				
191	SCA L*	F	BG 21.5 GLP 31.9		SCA: MNI=3
209	SCA L*	F	BG c17		
037	SCA R*	F	BG 22.3 GLP 32.8		
281	SCA R*				
469	SCA R*				
480	HUM Lpd*	dF	Bd 26.2		HUM: MNI=4
239	HUM Lpd	dF			
466	HUM Lpd	young			
236	HUM Rpd*				
172	RAD Lpd*	pF dUF	Bp c24	dismembered	RAD+ULN: MNI=4
022	RAD Ld*	dUF			
221	RAD Rpd*	pF dF	Bp 30.2 Bd 27.4 GL 153		
231	RAD Rpd*	pF dUF	Bp 26.7		match
232	ULN R				
157	RAD Lpd				
074	RAD Lpd				
121	ULN L				
283	RAD Lp				
125	MC Rpd*				MC: MNI=6
126	MC Lpd*	dF, female	Bp 22.8 Bd 24.4 GL 128		prob pair
127	MC Rpd*	dF	Bp 22.7 GL c127		
383	MC Lpd*				
286	MC Lpd*				
460	MC Lpd*				
536	MC Lpd*				
525	MC d				
220	MC Rd				
197	PEL L*	F, female	LA c24		PEL: MNI=3
199/228	PEL L*	F, female			
556	PEL R*	F, male	LA c26	gnawed	
176	FEM Lpd*	pF			FEM: MNI=3
470	FEM Lpd	pF			
218	FEM Lp	pUF			
065	FEM Rd	dUF			
247	FEM Ld				
175	TIB Lpd*	pF dF	Bd 24.2 GL 214		TIB: MNI=7
000	TIB Lpd*	pUF dF	Bd 22.5		
124	TIB Lpd*	dF			?pair
425	TIB Rpd*	dF			
068	TIB Rpd*	dF	Bd 23.5		
262	TIB Rp			filleted	
237	TIB Rpd*				
362	TIB Lpd	dUF			

Table 12.2 *(Cont'd)*

lot no	body part	age/sex	size	butchery, etc	comments
160	TIB d	dF			
350	TIB Lp				
164	TIB Ld				
257	MT Lpd★		Bp 19.9	gnawed	MT: MNI=5
180	MT Lpd★	dF	Bd 22.8 GL 138	gnawed	
214	MT Lpd★	dUF			
043	MT Lpd★			gnawed, dismembered	
202	MT Rpd★				
596	MT Ld★				

horse (MNI=5)

lot no	body part	age/sex	size	butchery, etc	comments
parts of five individuals (including matching body parts)					
323	MAX R				MAX: MNI=5
554	MAX L				
554	MAX R				
042	MAX L				
042	MAX R				
550	(MAX R)				
000	(MAX R)				
579	MAX R				
581	(MAX R)				
578	MAX L				
550	MAX L				
024	MAX L				
029	MAN L	teeth worn			MAN: MNI=3
039	MAN R	teeth worn			
552	MAN R	teeth worn			
593	SCA L	F	BG c41 GLP c81	gnawed	SCA: MNI=1
041	HUM Lpd	dF	Bd c70		match HUM: MNI =1
520	RAD Lpd	pF dF	Bp 76.5 Bd 71.0 GL 321		RAD: MNI=4
530	RAD Rpd	pF dF	Bp 75.0 GL 317	gnawed	
520	RAD Rpd	pF	Bp 72.3	gnawed	
033	RAD Lpd	pF		gnawed	join
033	ULN L			gnawed	
541	MC d				MC: MNI=1
085	PEL L	F	LAR 54.3		join PEL: MNI=5
085	PEL R	F	LAR 54.3		
527	PEL L	F	LAR 55.1	gnawed	
601	PEL L	F			
599	PEL R	F	LAR 56.4	gnawed	
603	PEL R	F			
196	FEM Rpd				FEM: MNI=1
429	TIB Rpd	dF	Bd 70.7	gnawed	TIB: MNI=3
550	TIB Ld	dF	Bd 64.7		
097	TIB Ld	dF			
018	TIB Lp				
574	MT Lpd	dF	Bp 48.0 Bd c46 GL 263		MT: MNI=4
417	MT Lpd	dF	Bp 39.7 Bd 39.8 GL 237	skinned	
484	MT Lpd	dUF	Bp 43.9		
526	MT Rd	dF	Bd 45.2		
484	PH1	pFG	Bp 47.4		PH1: MNI=1

pig (MNI=5)

lot no	body part	age/sex	size	butchery, etc	comments
digested bones, ?of a single foot, perhaps representing last meal of one of associated dog skeletons; potentially derived from one of 5 'individuals' below					
519	CAL L			digested	possibly
519	MC/MT pd			digested	single
519	PH1	pF		digested	foot
519	PH3			digested	
parts of at least five individuals					
115	MAN R	female			MAN: MNI=4

Table 12.2 *(Cont'd)*

lot no	body part	age/sex	size	butchery, etc	comments
604	MAN L	male			join
604	MAN R	P4S M1S$, male			
482	MAN R	male			
298	MAN R	male	??wild boar (loose canine)		
253	HUM Ld	dF			HUM: MNI=2
107	HUM Rd				
244	RAD Lpd				RAD+ULN: MNI=3
241	RAD Rpd	pUF			
170	ULN R				
004	ULN R				
486	ULN L				
595	TIB Rpd				TIB: MNI=5
538	TIB Rpd	dUF		filleted	
151	TIB Rd				
111	TIB Rpd	young			
243	TIB Rpd	young		filleted	

dog (MNI=10)

lot no	body part	age/sex	size	butchery, etc	comments
two part-skeletons (probably one ± complete skeleton and parts of a second) of similar size, including at least 1 male (baculum), = 'individuals 1–2'					
519	MAX L				pair, MAX: MNI=1
519	MAX R				
519	MAN L	P4S M1S M2S M3S			prob pair, MAN: MNI=1
519	MAN R	P4W M1W M2W M3SM1L c22			
519	SCA L	F	BG 17.4 GLP 29.8		pair SCA: MNI=1
519	SCA R	F	BG 17.7 GLP 29.9		
519	HUM Lpd	pF dF	Bp 40.8 Bd 32.5 GL 168		pair, HUM: MNI=1
519	HUM Rpd	pF dF	Bp 41.1 Bd 32.8 GL 168		
519	RAD Lpd	pF dF	Bp 17.7 Bd 24.7 GL 169		RAD: MNI=1
519	RAD Rpd	pF dF	Bp 17.6 Bd 24.8 GL 169		matching
519	ULN L	F			pairs, ULN: MNI=2
519	ULN R	F			
519	ULN R	F			
519	MC4 Lpd	dF			pair, MC: MNI=1
519	MC4 Rpd	dF			
519	(MC2 Lpd)	dF			
519	PEL L	F	LAR 21.4		join, PEL: MNI:1
519	PEL R	F	LAR 22.1		
519	FEM Lpd	pF dF	Bp 37.7 Bd 31.8 GL 183 DC 18.3		pair, FEM: MNI=1
519	FEM Rpd	pF dF	Bp 37.7 Bd 31.9 GL 184 DC 18.0		
519	TIB Lpd	pF dF	Bp 35.6 GL 187		pair, TIB: MNI=2
519	TIB Rpd	pF dF	Bp 37.4 Bd 23.7 GL 188		
519	TIB Lpd	pF dF	Bp 34.8 Bd 23.5 GL 185		pair
519	TIB Rpd	pF dF	Bp 35.4 Bd 23.0 GL 186		
519	CAL R	F	GL 44.9		CAL: MNI=1
519	MT2 Rpd	dF			MT: MNI=2
519	MT2 Rpd	dF			pair
519	MT2 Lpd	dF			
519	(MT3 Rpd)	dF			
519	(MT4 Rpd)	dF			
519	(MT4 Rpd)	dF			
519	(MT5 Lpd)	dF			
519	PH1	pF	Bp 8.6 Bd 7.3 GL 24.9		PH1: MNI=1
part-skeleton = 'individual 3'					
084	MAX L				pair
084	MAX R				
084	MAN R	P4W M1W M2W M3SM1L c23			
084	SCA L	F	BG 18.9 GLP 31.9		
084	RAD Rpd	pF dF	Bp 19.1 Bd 24.9 GL 171		pair
084	RAD Lpd	pF dF	Bp 18.6 Bd 24.7 GL 170		?match

Table 12.2 *(Cont'd)*

lot no	body part	age/sex	size	butchery, etc	comments
084	ULN L	F			
084	MC2 Rpd	dF			
084	PEL R	F	LAR 21.9		
084	FEM Rpd	pF dF	Bp 37.3 Bd 34.9 GL 182 DC 19.2		pathology (dist artic)
084	CAL L	F	GL 47.1		

part-skeleton = 'individual 4'

023	MAN R	P4U M1–M2U M3S			?pair
023	MAN L				
023	HUM Lpd	pF dF	Bp 38.3 Bd 29.4 GL 154		pair
023	HUM Rpd	pF dF	Bp 38.0 Bd 29.7 GL 152		
023	RAD Rpd	pF dF	Bp 16.7 Bd 22.4 GL 150		match
023	ULN R	F			
023	FEM Rpd	pF dF	Bp 35.7 Bd 29.0 GL 165 DC 17.4		
023	TIB Rpd	pF dF	Bp 32.6 Bd 21.5 GL 172		

part-skeleton = 'individual 5'

189	MAX L				pair
189	MAX R				
189	MAN L	P4J M1J M2U M3S			prob pair
189	MAN R	M1J$			
189	HUM Ld	dF	Bd 30.9		?pair
189	HUM Rpd				
189	RAD Lp				
189	ULN L				
189	TIB Lpd				?pair
189	TIB Rpd	dF			
189	MC/MT p				
189	PH1	pF	Bp 8.3 Bd 6.7		

fragments including parts of at least five further individuals

387	MAX R				
078	MAN R		wolf-size		
020	MAN L	P4S M1–M2J M3S			'individual 6'
478	MAN L	P4S$	wolf-size		'individual 7'
249	MAN L				
550	HUM Lpd	pF dF	Bp 42.9 Bd 33.9 GL 181		'individual 8'
561	HUM Rpd	pF dF	Bp 43.5 Bd 35.2 GL 174		'individual 9'
561	RAD Lpd	dF	Bd 26.5		
307	RAD Rpd	pF dF	Bp 17.1 GL >157		'individual 10'
103	MC3 Rpd	dF			
387	MC3 Rp				
016	PEL L	F	LAR 19.2		
233	FEM Lpd				
034	TIB Lpd				
093	MT2 Rpd	dF			

red deer (MNI=2)

lot no	body part	age/sex	size	butchery, etc	comments
606	(H/A)			worked	H/A: MNI=2
598	(H/A)				
573	H/A			attached	?pair
572	H/A			attached	
026	H/A			shed	
598	(H/A)				
591	(H/A)				
562	MAN R	P4W M1W M2W M3W			MAN: MNI=1
015	HUM Lpd				HUM: MNI=1
571	FEM Rpd	dF		gnawed, dismembered	FEM: MNI=1
477	TIB Lpd	dF	Bd 54.0		TIB: MNI=2
351	TIB Rpd	dF			
352	CAL R	F			CAL: MNI=1
522	MT Rpd	dF	Bp 40.8 Bd 46.0 GL 315		MT: MNI=1
353	PH1	pF	Bp c19		PH1: MNI=1
095	PH2	pF			PH2: MNI=1

Table 12.2 (Cont'd)

fox (MNI=1)

lot no	body part	age/sex	size	butchery, etc	comments
064	MAN L	P4W M1W M2S M3S			
251	RAD Ld	dF			
061	MC2 Rpd	dF			
252	MT5 Rpd	dF			
066	(MT3 Rpd	dF)			

badger (MNI=1)

lot no	body part	age/sex	size	butchery, etc	comments
081	MAN R				

polecat (MNI=1)

lot no	body part	age/sex	size	butchery, etc	comments
193	FEM Rpd	pF dF	Bp 10.7		

beaver (MNI=1)

lot no	body part	age/sex	size	butchery, etc	comments
153	MAX				

human (MNI=7)

lot no	body part	age/sex	size	butchery, etc	comments

fragments from at least 7 adult individuals, including at least 1 male young adult and 1 probably male mature adult (cranial fragments indicate a young adult [no 258: sutures fused endocranially only] and a probably male mature adult [no 146: sutures partially closed and obliterated ectocranially])

lot no	body part	age/sex	size	butchery, etc	comments
305	MAN L	M3S (>18 yrs)			MAN: MNI=3
301	MAN R	M1W (25–35 yrs)			
147	MAN L				
147	MAN R				join
369	HUM Lpd				HUM: MNI=2
209	HUM Lpd				
302	HUM Rpd				
64	RAD Rp				RAD: MNI=1
354	ULN L				ULN: MNI=1
307	ULN R				
306	MC3 Lpd	dF			MC: MNI=1
143	PEL R	adult			PEL: MNI=1
139	FEM Lpd				FEM: MNI=7
F4	FEM Lpd	pF(just) dF (young adult), male/head diam 49.0 bicondylar W 82.2 L 475, pair			
F4	FEM Rpd	pF(just) dF (young adult), male/head diam 48.6 bicondylar W 81.2 L 474			
148	FEM Lpd				
148	FEM Lpd				
594	FEM Lp				
537	FEM Lp				
382	FEM Lpd				
299	FEM Rpd				
380	FEM Rp				
383	FEM Rp				
228	TIB Rd				TIB: MNI=2
531	TIB Rpd				

Tables 12.5–12.6 summarise the distribution of traces of gnawing and of cut marks among both associated groups of bone and loose material of each species. In this case, the frequency of gnawing and butchery is quantified in terms of absolute numbers of specimens, ie even if a complete long bone has recognisable cut marks (or gnawing) only at one end, it is evident that humans (or animals) have played a part in the depositional history of the whole bone.

Tables 12.7–12.10 summarise, for cattle and sheep respectively, the evidence on age at death, in each case presented in terms of MNI. Tables 12.11–12.12 list the estimates of shoulder height in dogs.

Formation of the assemblage: recovery, attrition, and discard

The bone assemblage is small, comprising *c* 300 MinAU from the Flag Fen platform site and *c* 500 MinAU from the Power Station post alignment site (Table 12.2); additional identified anatomical units, discounted from MinAU as described above, were 26 and 57 respectively (listed in Table 12.1). Differences in retrieval method at the two sites imply a more severe bias against small bone fragments at the Power Station post alignment site and so are likely to have affected the anatomical, taxonomic, and demographic composition of the two samples differentially: small body parts, small taxa, and small (ie young) individuals should be more strongly underrepresented at the Power Station post alignment site. The relative scarcity of small body parts (ulna, astragalus, calcaneum, phalanx 1–3) at the Power Station post alignment site (Table 12.2), therefore, is most parsimoniously attributed to biased retrieval. At the Flag Fen platform site, this effect is less clear (Table 12.1) and might anyway reflect a tendency for small bones to pass through the woody matrix of the Flag Fen platform rather than failure in recovery.

The standard of bone preservation ranged from excellent to poor, presumably reflecting variation in the degree and constancy of waterlogging. In particular, the examination of traces of gnawing and butchery was often impeded by the poor preservation of bone surfaces and, in some material from the Power Station post alignment site, by extensive superficial scoring, perhaps reflecting deposition in an abrasive environment. Nonetheless, traces of both gnawing and butchery are apparent in both samples.

Traces of gnawing (suggestive of both dogs and smaller animals), are extremely rare in the Flag Fen platform assemblage, but relatively common in that from the Power Station post alignment site (Table 12.3), presumably reflecting the greater accessibility of the latter, landward area to domestic dogs and also, perhaps, the admixture of bone from 'dryland' contexts predating the Power Station post alignment. Neither assemblage, however, displays a conspicuous lack of such body parts as proximal humerus, which tend to be severely underrepresented in assemblages subject to severe attrition from carnivores (Brain 1981). Traces of butchery or bone/antler working were recognised on c 4% of identified specimens from both sites. These traces, which included knife marks indicative of skinning, dismembering, filleting, and also fracturing suggestive of marrow extraction (Table 12.1) indicate a human role in the formation of both assemblages.

With varying degrees of confidence, (part-)skeletons have been identified of horse and cow at the Flag Fen platform site, of pig at the Power Station post

Table 12.3 Minimum numbers of body parts (MinAU) and individuals (MNI) for each mammalian species from the platform site

	cow		sheep	horse		pig	dog		red deer	hare	human	all spp.
	a	b	a	a	b	a	a	b	a	a	a	a+b
MinAU												
horn/antler	1	2	2	na	na	na	na	na	1	na	na	
maxilla	3	2	5	–	2	–	1	–	–	–	–	
mandible	4	2	16	–	–	1	–	4	–	–	1	
scapula	3	2	4	–	1	–	–	–	–	–	–	
humerus p	3	2	4	1	1	1	1	3	–	–	–	
humerus d	4	2	4	1	1	1	1	1	–	–	–	
radius p	2	2	5	–	1	–	–	6	–	–	–	
radius d	2	2	5	–	1	–	–	6	–	–	–	
ulna	2	2	2	–	–	–	1	3	–	–	–	
metacarpal p	4	2	6	–	–	–	–	5	–	–	–	
metacarpal d*	4	2	6	–	–	–	1	5	–	–	–	
pelvis	1	2	2	–	–	–	2	2	–	1	–	
femur p	3	2	3	1	–	1	2	–	–	–	–	
femur d	4	2	4	1	1	1	2	1	–	–	–	
tibia p	4	2	3	–	–	–	1	2	–	–	2	
tibia d	4	2	2	–	–	–	1	2	–	–	2	
astragalus	1	1	1	1	–	–	–	1	–	–	–	
calcaneum	2	1	–	–	–	–	1	1	–	–	–	
metatarsal p	6	1	11	1	–	1	–	4	–	–	–	
metatarsal d	6	1	11	1	–	1	–	4	–	–	–	
phalanx 1	–	1	–	–	–	–	–	2	–	–	–	
phalanx 2	2	2	1	–	1	–	–	1	–	–	–	
phalanx 3	1	2	–	1	–	–	–	1	–	–	–	
total	66	41	97	8	9	7	14	54	1	1	5	303
%		35.3	32.0		5.6	2.3		22.4	0.3	0.3	1.7	100
MNI	6		12	2		2	4		1	1	2	30

Key
na = not applicable, a = 'loose' bones, b = '(part-)skeletons'; p = proximal, d = distal; * includes rare specimens identified only to metacarpal/metatarsal. NB because phalanges of the fore- and hind-limb are not distinguished, MinAU figures for phalanx 1–3 are effectively inflated by a factor of 2 compared to other body parts.

Table 12.4 Minimum numbers of body parts (MinAU) and individuals (MNI) for each mammalian species from the post alignment site

	cow	sheep	horse	pig		dog		red deer	fox	badger	polecat	beaver	human	all spp.
	a	a	a	a	b	a	b	a	a	a	a	a	a	a+b
MinAU														
horn/antler	4	1	na	na	na	na	na	3	na	na	na	na	na	
maxilla	7	4	9	–	–	1	6	–	–	–	–	1	–	
mandible	17	14	3	–	–	4	7	1	1	1	–	–	4	
scapula	7	5	1	–	–	–	3	–	–	–	–	–	–	
humerus p	9	4	1	1	–	2	5	1	–	–	–	–	3	
humerus d	14	4	1	1	–	2	6	1	–	–	–	–	3	
radius p	14	6	4	–	–	2	6	–	–	–	–	–	1	
radius d	11	6	4	–	–	2	5	–	1	–	–	–	–	
ulna	3	2	1	–	–	–	6	–	–	–	–	–	2	
metacarpal p*	13	7	–	–	1	2	4	–	1	–	–	–	1	
metacarpal d*	13	9	1	–	1	1	3	–	1	–	–	–	1	
pelvis	6	3	6	–	–	1	3	–	–	–	–	–	1	
femur p	7	3	1	1	–	1	4	1	–	–	1	–	11	
femur d	11	4	1	1	–	1	4	1	–	–	1	–	7	
tibia p	10	9	2	–	–	1	7	2	–	–	–	–	1	
tibia d	12	9	3	–	–	1	7	2	–	–	–	–	2	
astragalus	4	–	–	1	–	–	–	–	–	–	–	–	–	
calcaneum	2	–	–	–	1	–	2	1	–	–	–	–	–	
metatarsal p	16	5	3	1	–	1	3	1	1	–	–	–	–	
metatarsal d	14	6	4	1	–	1	3	1	1	–	–	–	–	
phalanx 1	4	–	1	–	–	–	2	1	–	–	–	–	–	
phalanx 2	1	–	–	–	1	–	–	1	–	–	–	–	–	
phalanx 3	1	–	–	1	–	–	–	1	–	–	–	–	–	
total	200	101	46	8	4	23	86	17	6	1	2	1	37	532
%	37.6	19.0	8.6	2.3		20.5		3.2	1.1	0.2	0.4	0.2	7.0	100
MNI	16	10	5	5		10		2	1	1	1	1	7	59

Key
na = not applicable, a = 'loose' bones, b = '(part-)skeletons'; p = proximal, d = distal; * includes rare specimens identified only to metacarpal or metatarsal. NB because phalanges of the fore- and hind-limb are not distinguished, MinAU figures for phalanx 1–3 are effectively inflated by a factor of 2 compared to other body parts.

Table 12.5 Numbers of identified mammalian specimens with traces of gnawing and butchery from the platform site

	cow		sheep	horse		pig	dog		red deer	hare	all spp.	% all
	a	b	a	a	b	a	a	b	a	a	a+b	spp.
gnawed	–	–	1	–	–	–	–	–	–	–	1	0.5
butchered	2	–	7	–	–	–	–	–	–	–	9	4.1
total NISP	30	45	67	7	5	4	50	10	1	1	220	

* Human bones have been excluded because of the poor preservation of bone surfaces.

Table 12.6 Numbers of identified mammalian specimens with traces of gnawing and butchery from the post alignment site

	cow	sheep	horse	pig		dog		red deer	fox	badger	polecat	beaver	all spp.	% all
	a	a	a	a	b	a	b	a	a	a	a	a	a+b	spp.
gnawed	33	4	8	–	4	–	–	1	–	–	–	–	50	12.1
butchered	7	3	1	2	–	–	–	2	–	–	–	–	15	3.6
total NISP	170	79	39	17	4	15	64	16	5	1	1	1	412	

* Human bones have been excluded because of the poor preservation of bone surfaces.

Table 12.7 Age of death of cattle at the platform site (MNI)

individual (see Table 12.1)	evidence for age (see key to Tables 12.1 and 12.2)	suggested age
'individual 3'	MC newborn	0–1 mths
'individual 4'	FEM smaller than 'individual 1'	= 5–6 mths
'individual 1'	MAN M1H, postcranial bones UF	5–6 mths
'individual 5'	TIB pUF, much bigger than 'individual 1'	>>5–6 mths, <42 mths
'individual 6'	TIB pUF, much bigger than 'individual 5'	>>5–6 mths, <42 mths
'individual 2'	MAN M2W(g)	(?young) adult

Table 12.8 Age at death of cattle at the post alignment site (MNI)

individual (see Table 12.1)	evidence for age (see key to Tables 12.1 and 12.2)	suggested age
'individual 16'	MAN M1W(c)	>5–6 mths <24–30 mths
'individual 5'	MAN D4W(e/f) M1W(g) M2W(d) M3V	>15–18 mths <24–30 mths
'individual 12'	MAN D4W(j) M1W(d)$	>5–6 mths <28–36 mths
'individual 14'	MAN M3W(e)	young adult
'individual 7'	MAN M3W(e)	young adult
'individual 9'	MAN P4S M1W(l) M2W(k) M3W(g)	mature adult
'individual 10'	MAN P4S M1S M2W(k) M3W(j)	old adult
'individual 13'	MAN M3W(j)	old adult
'individual 8'	MAN M3W(j)	old adult
'individual 4'	MAN P4W(g) M1W(l) M2W(k) M3W(k)	old adult
'individual 11'	MAN P4S M1S M2S M3W(k)	old adult
'individual 6'	MAN M3W(m)	senile
'individual 3'	MAN P4S M1S M2S M3S	adult
'individual 15'	MAN P4S M1S M2S M3S	adult
'individual 1'	MAN	?
'individual 2'	MAN	?

Table 12.9 Age at death of cattle at the platform site (MNI)

individual (see Table 12.1)	evidence for age (see key to Tables 12.1 and 12.2)	suggested age
'individual 12'	MT newborn	?0–2 mths
'individual 3'	MAN M1W(9A) M2W(6A)	1–2 yrs
'individual 1'	MAN d4W(16L) M1W(9A) M2W(7A)	1–2 yrs
'individual 5'	MAN M1W(9A) M2W(7A?) M3H/E	1–2 yrs
'individual 9'	MAN P4H M1W(9A) M2W(7A) M3U/J	1–2 yrs
'individual 8'	MAN P4U/J M1W(9A) M2W(8A) M3 H/E	1–2 yrs
'individual 11'	MAN M1W(9A) M2W(8A) M3J/H	1–2 yrs
'individual 10'	MAN P4W(2A) M1W(9A) M2W(7A) M3W(2A)	2–3 yrs
'individual 7'	MAN M2W(8A) M3W(2A)	2–3 yrs
'individual 6'	MAN M2W(9A) M3W(5A)	2–3 yrs
'individual 4'	MAN P4W(9A) M1W(9A) M2W(9A) M3W(6G)	3–4 yrs
'individual 2'	MAN M1W(9A) M2W(8A) M3W(8G)	3–4 yrs

alignment site, and of dog at both sites (see Table 12.1 for details). Such associated groups of bones are particularly characteristic of dogs: most identifiable dog bones have been attributed to one of the nine recognised (part-) skeletons. Moreover, no bones of this species bore traces of either gnawing or butchery, suggesting the fairly rapid burial of relatively intact carcasses. On the other hand, the group of bones collected as lot number 220 at the Flag Fen platform site included at least one foot of an immature dog, as well as several parts plausibly attributable to a single older individual. Likewise, at the Power Station post alignment site, lot 519 includes parts of two dogs of similar size, but the presence of only one matching pair of most body parts perhaps suggests the presence of one more or less complete skeleton and of just odd parts of a second.

Table 12.10 Age at death of sheep at the post alignment site (MNI)

individual (see Table 12.1)	evidence for age (see key to Tables 12.1 and 12.2)	suggested age
'individual 9'	MAN M1W(5A)	6 mths–1 yr
'individual 10'	MAN M1W(5A)	6 mths–1 yr
'individual 5'	MAN M1W(7A)	6 mths–1 yr
'individual 8'	MAN M2W(2A)	1–2 yrs
'individual 3'	MAN P4S M1S M2S M3W(5A)	2–3 yrs
'individual 6'	MAN M3W(5A)	2–3 yrs
'individual 2'	MAN P4W(9A) M1W(9A) M2W(9A) M3W(11G)	4–6 yrs
'individual 1'	MAN P4W(12S) M1W(12A) M2W(9A) M3W(11G)	4–6 yrs
'individual 4'	MAN M3W(11G)	4–8 yrs
'individual 7'	MAN M3W(11G)	4–8 yrs

Table 12.11 Stature of dogs from the platform site

individual (see Table 12.1)	measurement (mm) after von den Driesch (1976)	shoulder height (mm) after Harcourt (1974)
'individual 1'	radius GL 176, 177	580
'individual 2'	radius GL 164	540
'individual 3'	–	–
'individual 4'	radius GL c 175 (humerus Bd 35.0)	c 580

Table 12.12 Stature of dogs from the post alignment site

individual (see Table 12.1)	measurement (mm) after von den Driesch (1976)	shoulder height (mm) after Harcourt (1974)
'individual 1–2'	humerus GL 168, 168 (Bd 32.5, 32.8)	550
	radius GL 169, 169	560
	femur GL 183, 184	560
	tibia GL 187, 188	560
	tibia GL 185, 186	550
'individual 3'	radius GL 170, 171	560
	femur GL 182	560
individual 4'	humerus Gl 152, 154 (Bd 29.4, 29.7)	500
	radius GL 150	500
	femur GL 165	510
	tibia GL 172	510
'individual 5'	(humerus Bd 30.9)	(>post alignment site 4, <post alignment site 1–2)
'individual 6'	–	–
'individual 7'	(mandible frags ≥ wolf-size)	>other individuals
'individual 8'	humerus GL 181 (Bd 33.9)	590
'individual 9'	humerus GL 174 (Bd 35.2)	570
'individual 10'	radius GL >157	>520

These two examples raise at least the possibility that dogs were deposited along the Power Station post alignment or on the Flag Fen platform after a prior period of exposure and decomposition, such that some mixing of carcases might occur.

In the case of pig, the only apparently associated group of bones, from lot 519 in the Power Station post alignment site, might all have been derived from a single foot. These bones, small enough to have been swallowed whole by a dog (cf Payne and Munson 1985), all showed clear surface signs of digestion (cf O'Connor 1991, pl 15a) and so might well represent the last meal of one of the dogs with which they were found. Other suggested associated groups are the largely complete skeleton of a calf of c 5–6 months, found in lots 038, 184, 189 and 190 at the Flag Fen platform site, and a possible part-skeleton of an adult horse, found in lots 200-203 and 205-206 at the same site. In addition, again at the Flag Fen platform site (lots 070-074, 078, 160 and 169), a series of pairs of compatible size, but without any demonstrable matches between articulating body parts, might represent another part-skeleton of a juvenile cow. None of these groups identified as (part-)skeletons revealed any recognisable butchery marks or (with the exception of the digested pig's foot) any clear traces of gnawing.

In addition to these suggested (part-)skeletons, paired or articulating (but not physically fused) body parts were identified among 'loose' bones of horse, cow, sheep and dog at the Flag Fen platform site and of horse, cow, sheep, red deer, and human at the Power Station post alignment site (Table 12.1). Such pairs and articulations tend to be rare in faunal assemblages, apart from 'special deposits', and so their strikingly high frequency in the 'loose' material from Flag Fen might suggest that much of this material represents disturbed (part-)skeletons. This interpretation is particularly plausible in the case of the paired human femora from the Power Station post alignment. These are derived from feature 4 cut into the underlying old ground surface, and so might well represent a disturbed burial. In the case of non-human remains, such disturbance might plausibly be attributed to dogs and other scavengers at the Power Station post alignment site, where traces of gnawing were fairly common on 'loose' material (including an articulating cow radius and ulna from lot 033 and a pair of cow metatarsals from lots 452 and 463). Virtually no traces of gnawing were recognised, however, on bone from the Flag Fen platform. Conversely, butchery marks were recognised on loose material from both sites: from the Flag Fen platform, including an articulating sheep radius and ulna with traces of filleting (from lots 098 and 099) and a pair of sheep metatarsals with indications of dismembering and fracturing for marrow (from 050 and 052); from the Power Station post alignment, including a pair of cow scapulae with traces of filleting (from 456, 468 and 461). This suggests that the difference between the associated (part-)skeletons and 'loose' bone was the product not only of disturbance by animals after deposition, but also of butchery by people before deposition. The high frequency of paired and articulating 'loose' bones thus arguably represents the deposition not of more or less complete carcases, which were subsequently disturbed by animals, but rather of paired body parts or articulated (part-)limbs, already stripped of meat and perhaps even broken open for marrow. Moreover, the prevalence of this pattern of deposition is almost certainly underestimated by the number of recognised pairs and articulations, given that the Power Station post alignment sample has been subjected to both post-depositional scavenging and to partial retrieval under rescue conditions, and that some bone from the Flag Fen platform sample has surely filtered through the underlying woody matrix.

In the case of the domesticates, all parts of the body seem to have been deposited at both sites, if allowance is made for small sample size and for partial retrieval; the remains of wild animals are too few to allow consideration of this issue. There is no evidence of preferential deposition of either left- or right-sided bones (Table 12.1), but there are possible indications of the preferential deposition of particular body parts (Table 12.2). At the Flag Fen platform site, MinAU for sheep includes 16 mandibles, 11 proximal metatarsals, and 11 distal metatarsals, compared with a range of nought to six for other body parts. It is possible, therefore, that the deposition of sheep bones at the Flag Fen platform site preferentially comprised the extremities — a practice clearly represented at the nearby Romano-British shrine of Haddenham (Beech 1987). At the Power Station post alignment, the issue of preferential deposition of body parts is less clear cut. There are at least 14 mandibles of sheep, compared with a MinAU of nought to nine for other body parts, but the metatarsal is not particularly well represented (proximal metatarsal MinAU five; distal metatarsal MinAU six) and, of course, the mandible is particularly resilient to attrition (Brain 1981).

At the Flag Fen platform site, cattle, sheep, and pig are each represented by fragments of at least one newborn individual, perhaps indicating some bone deposition in spring. Caution is advised, however, by the earlier, very tentative suggestion that dog (part-)carcases might have been exposed elsewhere for a period before final deposition on the Flag Fen platform or along the Power Station post alignment.

The nature of the animals discarded

In terms of MNI, the domesticates at the Flag Fen platform site are dominated by sheep (12 individuals), followed by cow (six), dog (four), horse and pig (two each). In terms of MinAU, sheep (32%) and cow (35%) are equally important, reflecting the frequent deposition of extremities in the case of sheep and the more even representation of body parts in the case of cow. At the Power Station post alignment site, cow predominates (16 MNI, 38% of MinAU), followed by dog (10 MNI, 21% of MinAU) and sheep (10 MNI, 19% of MinAU) and then by horse (five MNI, 9% of MinAU), and pig (five MNI, 2% of MinAU); poorer retrieval at the Power Station post alignment site has probably exaggerated the abundance of cattle. Human remains, which are very scarce at the Flag Fen platform site (two MNI, 2% of MinAU), are more abundant at the Power Station post alignment site (seven MNI, 7% of MinAU), possibly reflecting disturbance of burials predating the Power Station post alignment. The remains of sheep, cow, dog, and human are sufficiently numerous or informative to warrant further discussion.

The sheep from the Flag Fen platform site include one newborn individual, six immature individuals in their second year, and five young adults in their third or fourth year. The age range for sheep from the Power

Station post alignment site includes four immature animals in their second or late first year and two young adults in their third year, but also four mature or even elderly adults of four to six or four to eight years (Table 12.5). At both sites, a tiny sample of sexable bones suggests a predominance of female over male sheep (Tables 12.1 and 12.2). In the case of cattle, the Flag Fen platform sample includes one newborn individual, two calves of up to six months of age, two older immature individuals, and one (possibly young) adult. The Power Station post alignment sample includes three immature individuals of up to three years of age, two young adults, and at least nine older adults of varying age (Table 12.4); for this site, a tiny sample of sexed cow bones suggests a predominance of females over males (Table 12.2). One cow metatarsal from the Power Station post alignment site exhibits erosion of the proximal articulation, accompanied by remodelling of the articular surface and extension of this surface by new bone formation. This perhaps hints that one of the older cattle had been subjected to physical stress, for example through use as a draught animal (cf Baker and Brothwell 1980, 114–15). For both sheep and cattle, therefore, the Power Station post alignment site has yielded a wider age range, including more and older adults, than the Flag Fen platform site.

A possible interpretation of the contrasting mortality evidence from the two sites is that, while younger cattle and sheep (prime meat animals) were selected for deposition both on the Flag Fen platform and along the Power Station post alignment, the latter assemblage also includes older animals (perhaps culled breeding/working stock) derived from the features cut into the underlying old ground surface.

The dog remains from the Flag Fen platform represent at least four individuals, of which three were skeletally mature (>18 months; Silver 1969) and one immature; at least one of these dogs was male (on the evidence of a baculum perceptively labelled by the excavator as a 'bone tool'!). The Power Station post alignment site yielded parts of at least ten dogs, all skeletally mature and including both young adults (with permanent teeth unworn or just coming into wear) and older individuals (with worn permanent teeth). Again, at least one of these animals was a male (Table 12.1). Because most of these dogs were skeletally mature and many of their bones were complete, shoulder heights can be estimated for three of the four 'individuals' from the Flag Fen platform site and for six of those from the Power Station post alignment, yielding a range of between 500 and 590mm (Tables 12.11 and 12.12). Two further 'individuals' from the Power Station post alignment might fall within the same range, one on the basis of a minimum shoulder height estimate (>520mm) and a second, very tentatively, on the basis of a distal breadth measurement for humerus (31mm, intermediate between the values for two dogs of shoulder height 500 and 550mm); a third unmeasurable 'individual', on the basis of mandibular fragments

approaching wolf in size, might be rather larger than the remaining dogs. Overall, the Flag Fen dogs fall in the upper part of the ranges reported for a small sample of Bronze Age dogs from Britain (430–620mm; Harcourt 1974, 159, table 12.6) and for a larger sample of Iron Age dogs (280–600mm; Clark 1995, 26, fig 1). The large size of these animals perhaps hints that they were hunting dogs, deposited here because of their symbolic connotations (cf Hamilakis 1996), rather than 'lap dogs', buried for sentimental reasons.

The sparse human remains from the Flag Fen platform site represent at least one infant and one probable adult. Those from the Power Station post alignment include parts of at least seven adults, including one young adult (17–25 years old) and one middle adult (25–30 years old). The young adult was apparently male, with an estimated stature of 1.745m, and a mature adult was also probably male.

Conclusion

The value of the bone remains discussed here is plainly limited by the small size of the sample, particularly from the Flag Fen platform site, by partial retrieval at the Power Station post alignment site, and, above all, by the stratigraphic problems associated with the latter assemblage. Nonetheless, 'structured deposition' is apparent in a number of respects. First, both assemblages have yielded a large number of (part-)skeletons and of paired or articulating body parts, indicating less reworking of bone than is often encountered on settlement sites. Secondly, the nature of deposition varies between species. Whole or part-skeletons are particularly characteristic of dog, but have also been suggested for cow and horse. In each case, surviving evidence of butchery is lacking; in the case of dogs, there are hints that some mixing of individual skeletons might have occurred during deposition, perhaps implying a prior period of exposure and decomposition. Conversely, paired and articulating elements, which have been recognised among the 'loose' bone for cow, sheep, horse, dog, red deer, and human, have traces of dismembering, filleting, and marrow extraction, indicating deposition after consumption. All body parts are represented at both sites, but in the case of sheep, there is also evidence of the selective deposition of mandibles and hind feet, particularly at the Flag Fen platform site. Thirdly, the cattle and sheep deposited on the Flag Fen platform are mainly immature animals or young adults, while elderly animals were also found in the Power Station post alignment sample, possibly derived from earlier features. Conversely, the dogs deposited at both sites might have been selected for their large size. Fourthly, the concentration of bone within and to the north of the Power Station post alignment contrasts strongly with the deposition of artefacts to the south.

Interpretation of the meaning of these patterns is more difficult, but the sparse human remains on the Flag Fen platform site (where possible derivation from earlier underlying features is not an issue) indicate a funerary component to bone deposition. Apparently unbutchered (part-)skeletons might be interpreted as sacrifices, possibly associated with, or in place of, funerary activity, and it is tempting to see a connection between the deposition here of large hunting dogs and of metal weaponry (cf Hamilakis 1996).

Finally, much of the bone discarded on the Flag Fen platform or along the Power Station post alignment had been processed for consumption, implying that feasting, sacrifice, funerary activity, and bone discard all played a part in maintaining the evidently important boundary or barrier marked by this huge linear wooden feature.

13 Flag Fen: the vegetation and environment

by Robert G Scaife

Presented here are the results obtained from the study of pollen and plant macrofossil analysis, which was initiated at the outset of the discovery of the Flag Fen platform. Only preliminary data have so far been published (Scaife 1992). Pollen data are available from four 'long profiles' taken from the principal areas of archaeological activity–the platform itself and its immediate environs and from the Fengate excavations at the Power Station site. A number of radiocarbon dates have been obtained from peats associated with these sites. The results of this investigation provide information on the vegetative development of the Flag Fen Basin prior to the onset of peat formation, the development of the fen mire during the Bronze Age, and subsequent alluviation that resulted in the overlying silts and clays.

Aims and methodology

The discovery of the Bronze Age timber platform in the fen peat posed specific questions relating to:

- the local ecology and environment in which this platform was constructed
- the wider environment and palaeogeography of the Flag Fen Basin
- information relevant to the construction of the platform and its possible uses
- the effect on the local landscape of the deforestation that must have taken place

It was expected that plant pollen analysis would establish the character of the 'on' and 'near' site aquatic and mire vegetation communities. Consideration has been given to the depth of water and any changes in the local hydrology of the reed swamp fen that might have affected the environment and use of the platform. Since the development of the vegetation in the fen basin is a retrogressive hydrosere, that is, development from terrestrial/dryland to fully aquatic, it is considered that the initiation of peat in different areas and altitudes in the basin might be asynchronous. The initiation of peat formation dependent upon increased waterlogging is thus time transgressive. Radiocarbon dating has provided some degree of absolute chronology for the basin's filling and lithostratigraphy. Pollen analysis of the peat, sediment, and basal soil sequences also provides evidence for the vegetation prior to fen development and for land use of the interfluve areas to the west, and Whittlesey and Northey to the east. Consideration has also been given as to whether the landscape had been totally or partially cleared for agriculture and, whether this environment was the source of the very substantial quantity of timber used in the platform's construction. Samples taken on a grid square basis from sands, originally thought to have been floor covering, have also been analysed for evidence of botanical activities such as crop processing (flax, cereals, and so on) and use as floor and roof materials.

To achieve the above aims, sampling of the Flag Fen mire sequences was undertaken in close proximity to the platform excavations of Area 6A (Fig 6.21, Platform Pollen Profile), the mere (Fig 6.1, Mere Pollen Profile), in the deepest section of the basin close to Northey (Fig 6.1, Pollen C) and on the fen margin at the Fengate Power Station, Area 1, eastern edge (Fig 4.1, Pollen Profile B). Samples for pollen, seeds, and radiocarbon dating were taken directly from the open sections using box monolith tins. Stratigraphical positions and OD levels were accurately established. Pollen samples from the platform floor have been taken and defined in relation to spatial grid and stratigraphical depth of the different levels.

Pollen analytical methodology

Samples of 1–2ml were analysed at standard sampling intervals of 0.04m and 0.08m.

Standard procedures were used for the extraction of the sub-fossil pollen and spores (Moore and Webb 1978; Moore *et al* 1991) and are not discussed further. Pollen identification and counting was carried out using Zeiss and Olympus research microscopes with phase contrast facility at magnifications of ×400 and ×1000. The pollen diagrams are based on a pollen sum of generally 400 dry land pollen grains (dlp), although poor pollen preservation in some levels at Fengate necessitated lesser counts or even absence at some levels. Pollen calculations are based on each taxon as a percentage of the total dry land pollen sum (tdlp).

Aquatic/marsh and mire taxa have been calculated as a percentage of their total at each level (not as a percentage of the arboreal or total pollen plus aquatics). This has been done specifically because of the interest noted above in the fluctuating relationships of the aquatic/mire habitat in which the platform was constructed. Spores are as a percentage of the dry land sum plus spores. *Alnus* forms part of the aquatic/marsh sum although in 'general' diagrams it has been excluded from the pollen sum because of its high pollen production and statistically adverse effect on other taxa calculated as percentages within the sum (Janssen 1969). The taxonomy used follows that of Stace (1991), modified according to Bennett *et al* 1994. Data have been plotted using Tilia and Tilia Graph in the Quaternary Environmental Change Research Centre of the Department of Geography, University of Southampton.

Plant macrofossil analyses

Wood identification, technology and timber structures have been dealt with elsewhere (Chapters 7 and 8). A limited study of seeds was also undertaken to ascertain if cultivated plant were present in the peats. This proved not to be the case, with only fen/aquatic taxa present. Samples for the latter were obtained directly from the open section and taken in conjunction with samples for insect analyses (Robinson 1992; Chapter 15). Seeds were extracted from samples of *c* 100ml, using hydrogen peroxide for deflocculation, and passed through nested sieves at 1mm, 500μ and 300μ. Residues were examined/scanned under a low power binocular microscope (Wild M3c).

The pollen data

Because of the time transgressive character of the peat and sediment accumulation in the Flag Fen Basin, both spatially and stratigraphically, the pollen data are presented in two parts.

First, the three sequences from the deepest part of the basin, the Northey (Fig 6.1, Pollen C), mere (Fig 6.1, Mere Pollen Profile) and platform (Fig 6.21, Platform Pollen Profile) sections are discussed. These relate most clearly to the environment in which the platform was constructed. Second (section 5) is the site of Fengate on the fen edge (Fig 4.1, Pollen Profile B). This is intermediary between the dryland, interfluve zone on which prehistoric activity has been proven (Pryor 1974; 1980) and the fen basin proper with the Bronze Age platform structure. Furthermore, the site of Fengate is at a critical point because of the 'causeway' post alignment and the greater likelihood that such a 'marginal' zone would be more sensitive to the effects of local hydrological changes than the deeper fen basin, once the latter had become established. The principal characteristics of each site are discussed below and an attempt at integrating the vegetational history has been made.

The mere section

A second and smaller mere was excavated in 1989, using a mechanical digger. This lies 7m east of the platform and is designated the mere section (Fig 6.1). This profile contains the principal biostratigraphical and lithostratigraphical units occurring in this area down to the basal Devensian gravels. The pollen sequence thus provides one of the most complete diagrams (Fig 13.1) obtained from Flag Fen, the other being Northey, Section 4 (below, Fig 13.2).

Lithostratigraphy

Samples for pollen analysis were taken at 0.04m intervals from the base of the section at –0.16m OD in the underlying palaeosol to +0.85m OD in the upper alluvial deposit (1m–0m in pollen, Figs 13.1–13.3). The stratigraphy of the section comprises the following biostratigraphical and lithostratigraphical units:

depth

not sampled (1–1.32m OD) Alluvial clay, showing recent edogenic processes exhibiting gleying and surface disturbance. Not pollen analysed. Not pollen sampled.

0.36–0m   (+0.48–0m OD.) Alluvial sediments. Grey organic silt/clay. Evidence of drying out. Cracks and gleying. Pollen samples are from lower layers of sediment.

0.93–0.36m (–0.09–0.48m OD.) Fen peat. Dark brown to black, highly humified, generally structureless detrital peat. Some monocot. remains and small wood fragments, No visible division between lower compacted and upper peat (Pryor *et al* 1986 and Scaife 1992).

1–0.93m   (0.16–0.09m OD) Basal Devensian gravels. Rounded to sub-angular (30–40mm) in silt/sand matrix. Palaeosol (palaeoargillic brown earth) developed in upper surface.

The pollen biostratigraphy

Three local pollen assemblage zones (lpaz) and two sub-zones have been recognised. The principal pollen zones (FFM:1–FFM:3) relate directly to the primary stratigraphic units recognised above. These are described from the base of the sequence at 1m (–16m OD to +0.84m OD). Wetland/mire taxa are as percentages of their sum at each level.

Lpaz FFM:1, 1m–0.90m (–0.16 to +0.09m OD). The old land surface. This is the basal pollen zone that spans the old land surface, underlying the fen mire peats in which the platform was constructed. The pollen is characterised by relatively high values of *Tilia* (to 28% TP). *Alnus* (to 87% of the sum of wetland taxa) is also important. Other tree taxa present include *Quercus* (to 18% TP), with sporadic occurrences of *Betula*, *Pinus*, and *Ulmus*. *Pinus* (to 5%) is highest in the basal levels. Few dryland shrubs are present. The exception is *Corylus avellana* type, which attains highest values in the basal level. Examination of the best preserved pollen grains indicates that here, *Corylus avellana* rather than *Myrica* is present. Herb taxa are dominated by Poaceae (to 35% TP). There are sporadic occurrences of other herbs, which include small quantities of cereal and associated weed taxa (*Sinapis* type, *Chenopodium* type, *Spergula* type, *Plantago lanceolata*, *Rumex*, and Asteraceae taxa). Wetland taxa comprise Cyperaceae, *Sparganium* type (includes *Sparganium* and *Typha angustifolia*) and *Typha latifolia*. Spores of *Dryopteris* type are present in low values, increasing in the subsequent zone (FFM:2). Values of *Pteridium aquilinum* and *Polypodium vulgare* are higher than in subsequent zones.

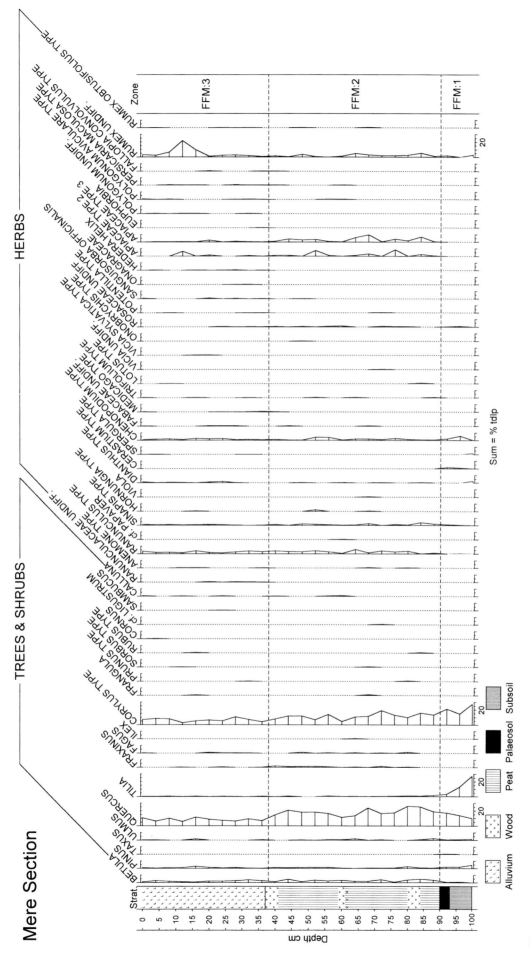

Fig 13.1 Pollen diagram of the mere section

354

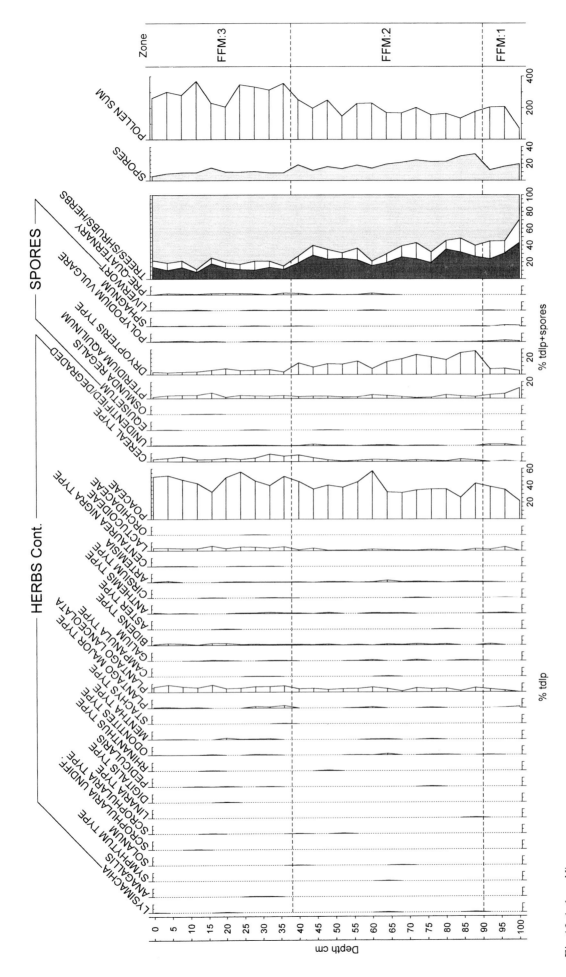

Fig 13.1 (cont'd)

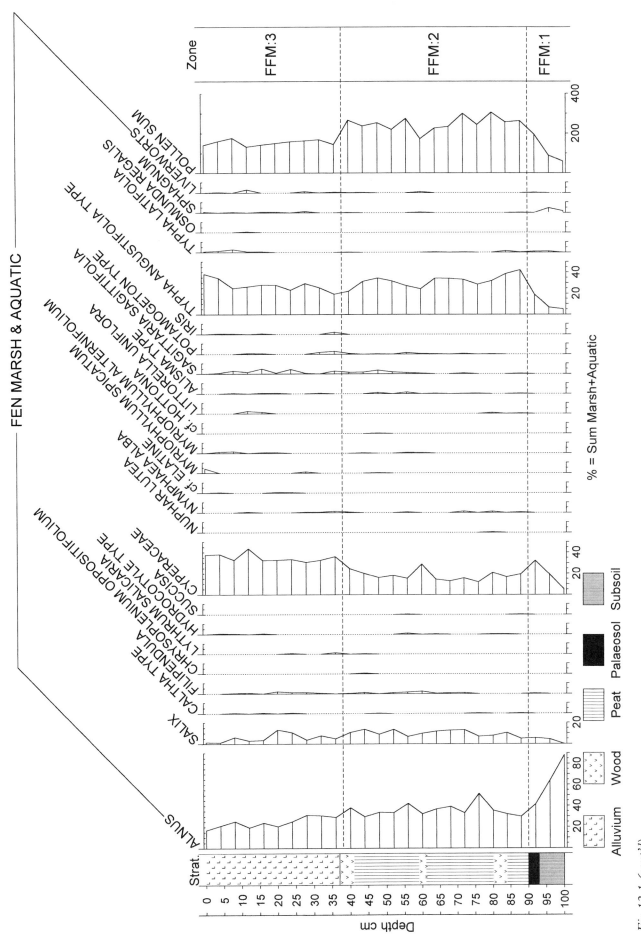

355

Fig 13.1 (cont'd)

Lpaz FFM:2, 0.9–0.38m (–0.08m to +0.48m OD). Fen peat deposits. Characterised by high values of autochthonous, aquatic, and fen taxa and a diverse assemblage of woodland and dryland herb taxa. *Tilia* declines from its relatively high values in FFM:1 to sporadic occurrence (<1%). The dominant arboreal taxon is *Quercus* to 26% but with fluctuating occurrence giving two pollen sub-assemblage zones. There are small but consistent values of *Betula* (to 5%), *Pinus* and sporadic *Ulmus*, *Fraxinus*, *Tilia* and *Fagus*. *Alnus* and *Salix* are important (30–50% sum and to 30% sum of wetland taxa respectively). Shrubs are dominated by *Corylus avellana* type (to 25%) and *Salix* (to 70%) but with few other pollen in this group.

Dryland herbs increase in number and diversity. Poaceae remain dominant (average 45%) being more or less consistent throughout the diagram. Other herb taxa include cereal pollen (expanding), segetal and ruderals: Cruciferae, Chenopodiaceae, Polygonaceae, Plantaginaceae (*P. lanceolata* and *P. major* type) and Asteraceae types. Wetland taxa are dominated by *Sparganium* type and Cyperaceae (35–45% and 10–20% respectively). Freshwater aquatic taxa include *Nuphar lutea*, *Nymphaea alba*, *Myriophyllum* (*M. spicatum*, *M. alterniflorum*), *Hottonia*, cf *Littorella*, *Alisma* type, *Sagittaria*, and *Potamogeton* type.

Spores become increasingly dominated by monolete, *Dryopteris* type, which are highest in this fen peat zone (to 30% TP+spores). *Pteridium* is consistent but in lower values than in the preceding zone (to 5%). *Polypodium* has similarly reduced values and occurs only sporadically. Pre-Quaternary (Jurassic) palynomorphs are intrusive and are synonymous with the presence of some fine silt in the peat fen.

Lpaz FFM:3, 0.38–0m (+0.48m to +0.84m OD). Grey alluvial fen clay and silt deposits. The biostratigraphy might be seen as a continuation of the preceding zone FFM:2, but with a major change occurring in the lithostratigraphy. The zone is characterised by dominant *Alnus*, *Sparganium* and Cyperaceae. There are also increases in percentages of some herb taxa; notably *Plantago lanceolata*, *Rumex*, and Asteraceae types. *Quercus* shows some reduction over the previous zone (to <10%). There are continued but sporadic occurrences of *Betula*, *Pinus*, *Tilia*, *Fraxinus*, and *Fagus*. Shrubs are dominated by *Corylus avellana* type (5–10%) with *Salix* (to 10%). *Frangula*, cf *Buxus*, *Prunus* type, *Sorbus/Crataegus* type, *Rubus* type, *Cornus*, *Ligustrum*, and *Sambucus* occur sporadically but represent a somewhat diverse range of shrubs. Herb pollen (dryland) are dominated by Poaceae (to 56%) with increased frequencies of other taxa, notably *Rumex*, which attains high values, peaking to 21% TP at 0.12m. *Plantago lanceolata* (to 9%) and Asteraceae taxa similarly show increases.

The highest values of cereal-type pollen are found at the base of this pollen zone, with an increase occurring across the junction between the fen peats (0.38m: +0.48m OD) and the alluvial silts. This is associated

with the occurrences of segetal taxa including *Polygonum aviculare*, *Fallopia convolvulus*, *Spergula* type, and possibly other taxa whose pollen morphology does not allow separation to a lower taxonomic level. Marginal aquatic and aquatic taxa are well represented. Cyperaceae and *Sparganium* type remain dominant (maximum 43% and 38% respectively). *Nymphaea*, *Elatine*, *Myriophyllum alterniflorum*, *M. spicatum*, cf *Littorella*, *Alisma* type, *Sagittaria*, *Potamogeton*, *Iris*, and spores of *Osmunda regalis* and *Sphagnum* are present. Derived Jurassic pollen and spores occur in greater numbers and consistently through this upper stratigraphic series.

Pollen assemblage sub-zones

The three pollen assemblage zones described relate to and define the principal lithostratigraphic and biostratigraphic characteristics. There are, however, a number of features that might relate to local variations in anthropogenic activity and land use. These are itemised briefly.

FFM:2 pasz:i, 0.88–0.6m. This is tentatively recognised by a reduction in *Quercus*, which is then followed by a peak, also recognised in the sequence obtained from the north-east corner of the platform (below, Fig 13.3). This reduction in *Quercus* is also accompanied by an increase in *Corylus avellana*, starting at a slightly higher stratigraphical level. These events might be important, since these levels might correlate with the period of platform construction. In this sub-zone, there is also some increase in the percentages of herb taxa, including Ranunculaceae, *Chenopodium* type, Apiaceae, *Rumex*, and cereal type. Overall, there is an increase in the diversity of herbs, with an increase in sporadic occurrences of dryland herbs.

FFM2/FFM:3 pasz:ii, 0.40–0.28m. This sub-zone spans the transition from the fen peat to alluvial sediments and is recognised by an increase in cereal pollen (to 7% TP) and herb diversity. In addition to sporadic occurrences of herbs such as *Polygonum* spp, increases of *Plantago lanceolata* (to 7% TP), *Plantago major* type, and Asteraceae occur.

The changing vegetational environment

The mere section provides an almost complete sequence of vegetation changes from the Flag Fen Basin. It differs only from Northey Section 4 (below), the deepest part of the fen basin, by having a 'shorter' basal stratigraphy of inorganic sediments and organic lake muds. Upper fen peats overlying the 'upper alluvial deposits', as in all other areas of the central basin, have been removed, but are found on the fringes at Fengate. The pollen sequence thus embraces the underlying Neolithic palaeosol (palaeoargillic brown earth) developed in Devensian gravel deposits. *Tilia* was clearly the dominant woodland type growing on this soil, prior to increasing water table and development fen peat (FFM:1). This period is postulated as

Neolithic since there is evidence of cereal cultivation and low values of *Ulmus*, which suggest a post-primary *Ulmus* decline age, ie later than *c* 5500–5000 BP.

Increasing water tables due to allogenic factors saw the demise of *Tilia* on site and the expansion of marginal aquatic and aquatic taxa at this locality (FFM:2). Taxa recorded represent a rich and diverse range of floating-leaved macrophytes (*Nuphar lutea*, *Nymphaea alba*, *Myriophyllum* spp, and *Potamogeton*) and associated peat formation in a rich fen. This retrogressive hydrosere culminated with the strongly fluvial conditions responsible for deposition of the upper alluvial deposits from 0.36–0m (+0.48m to +0.84m OD; zone FFM:3). Construction of the platform from the Middle to Late Bronze Age took place in the upper section of those peats that had accumulated in this fen-mire habitat.

Clearly, the increasing water table must have played a significant part in the development and upward building of the platform levels.

The 'extra-local' components of paz FFM:2 indicate that there was increasing human use of adjacent dryland both for timber and for arable and possibly pastoral agriculture. This is suggested by dominance of Poaceae (although some might have been from *Phragmites*), *Plantago lanceolata*, other meadow/grassland taxa, cereals, and associated segetals. Woodland comprising *Quercus*, *Ulmus*, *Tilia*, *Fraxinus*, and *Fagus* remained as constituents of the extra-local vegetation. *Fraxinus* and *Fagus* are present in this zone and might represent development of secondary woodland. *Tilia* might, however, have remained important but is less well represented as the dryland where it grew retreated progressively further away from the platform.

The uppermost pollen assemblage zone FFM:3 spans the alluvial clays and silts overlying the peats of the fen basin. There is no doubt that these alluvial sediments contain some fluvially derived pollen from extra-local sources. As this occurred during the Late Iron Age/Romano-British period, the pollen spectra of FFM:3 indicate an extension of agricultural activity in the region with many characteristic herbs noted. The allochthonous origin of the pollen through fluvial transport, however, makes interpretation of the pollen assemblages more difficult.

Northey section 4

In order to understand more clearly the lithological characteristics of the Flag Fen Basin and to obtain the longest possible pollen sequence, machine trenches were cut in the deepest part of the basin (Fig 6.1, Pollen A–C). This was carried out using a mechanical excavator and enabled larger sections to be examined than if hand-coring devices had been used. A stratigraphical profile 1.3m in depth was obtained, which spans the lower freshwater sediments, the main peat in which the platform was constructed, and the overlying alluvium.

Samples for pollen plant macrofossil analysis and radiocarbon dating were taken using monolith trays. These were sampled for pollen at an interval of 0.04m and the resulting pollen data are presented in diagram form (Fig 13.2).

Lithostratigraphy

The following summary of lithostratigraphy was recorded directly from the section and from the monolith samples from which pollen samples were subsampled (present surface +1.39m OD).

depth

0–0.09m	Alluvial deposits (French 1992b) containing modern rootlets (OD at base of the alluvial deposits = +0.55m).
0.09–0.64m	Brown/black humified detrital fen peat (in which platform constructed). Top dated 2180±60BP (GU-5616) and the base to 3500±60 BP (GU-5618). Noted within this peat were distinct horizons: 0.20–0.21m pale silt band; 0.26–0.27m wood.
0.64–0.82m	Brown organic mud — *Gyttja*.
0.82–0.84m	Transition. Lenses of grey clay (Basal OD height for this unit 0.2m).
0.84–1.1m	Largely grey mottled clay/silt with some yellow mottles; containing black rootlets.
1.1–1.28m	Darker, coarser, and more organic silt with rootlets.
1.28m	Stone horizon (to 0.15m).
1.3m	Yellow clay basement (Quaternary) with Fe staining/mottling (basal OD height –0.73m).

Pollen biostratigraphy and zonation

Five pollen assemblage zones (FFN:1–5) and four pollen assemblage sub-zones (lpasz:i–iv) have been recognised. These are characterised from the base of the profile at 1.3m (–0.73) upwards.

Lpaz FFN:1, 1.27–0.94m. Mineral sediments characterised by higher percentage of *Tilia* (to 6%) and *Quercus* (to 32%). *Corylus avellana* type (38%) and *Alnus* (22%) are dominant with other arboreal taxa including *Pinus*, *Ulmus* (see pasz:i), and *Fraxinus*. Herbs are dominated by Poaceae (to 31%) and *Chenopodium* type (to 10%). There is a moderately diverse range of herbs including *Plantago lanceolata*, Asteraceae types, and cereal type to the base of the zone/profile.

Aquatic/marsh taxa are dominated by *Alnus* and Cyperaceae. There are sporadic records of *Potamogeton* type.

Lpasz:i (1060–820mm). In the upper part of lpaz:1 and lower part of lpaz:2, there is an expansion of *Ulmus* and possibly *Fraxinus* (both <5). There are also expansions in percentages of Chenopodiaceae, *Artemisia*, and a peak of derived pre-Quaternary (Jurassic) palynomorphs.

Northey Section

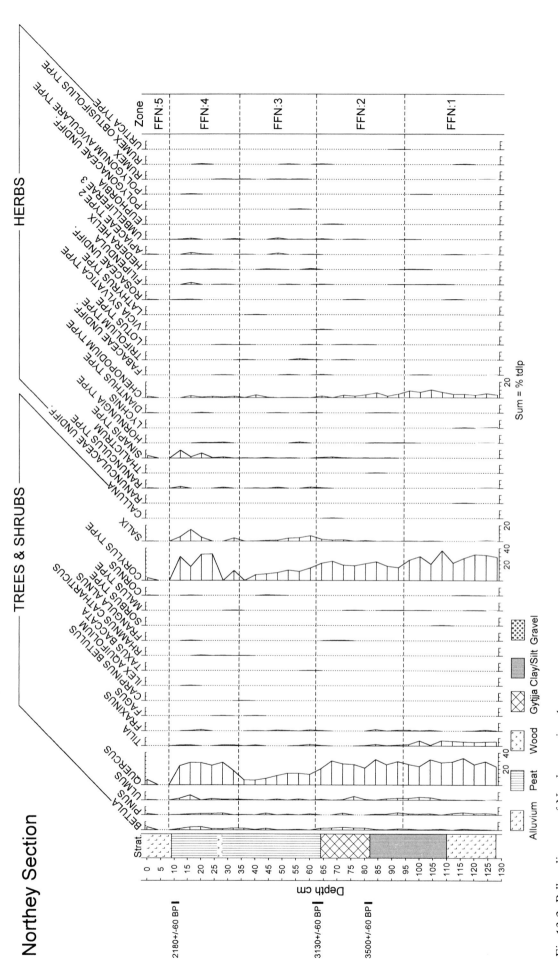

Fig 13.2 Pollen diagram of Northey section 4

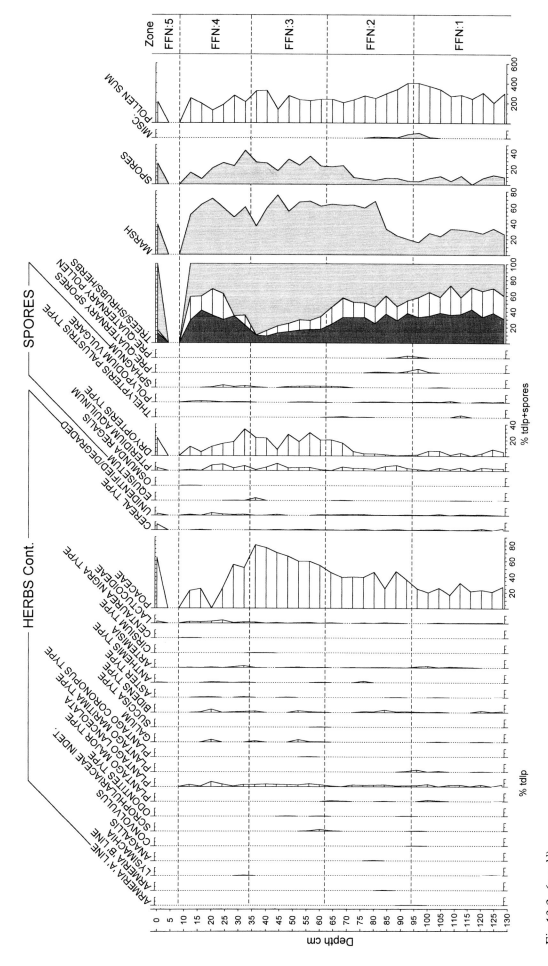

Fig 13.2 (cont'd)

360

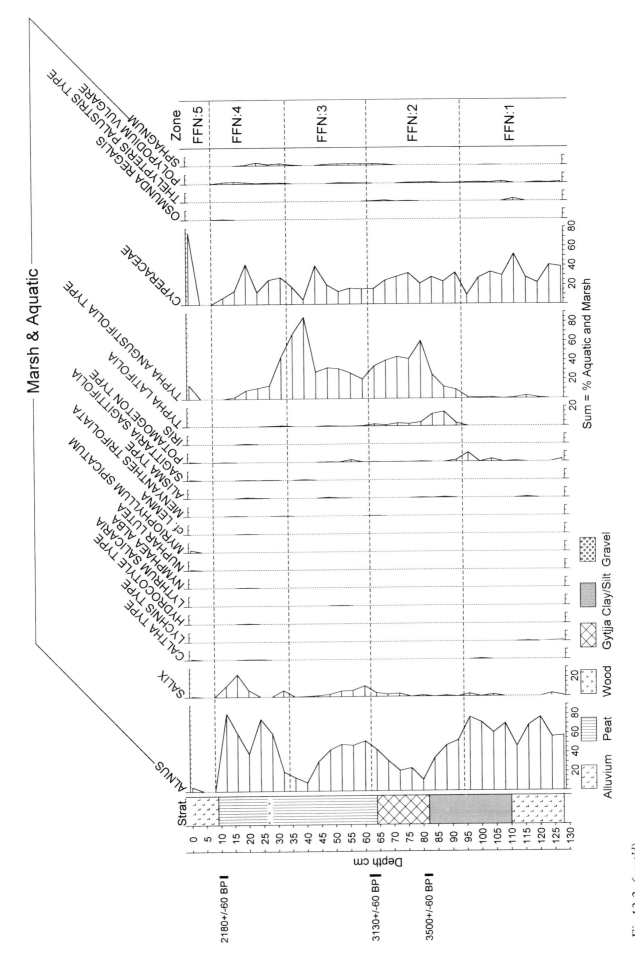

Fig 13.2 (cont'd)

Lpaz FFN:2, 0.94–0.62m. Organic muds (*gyttja*) with a basal radiocarbon date of cal BC 2030–1680 (GU-5618; 3500±60BP). This zone is characterised at its lower junction with lpaz:1 by a marked reduction in the values of *Tilia* and significant changes in the character of the mire component. Similarly, *Fraxinus*, which peaks in lpasz:i, also decreases throughout (into lpasz:ii). Overall, the values for tree pollen remain more or less constant with continued dominance of *Quercus* and *Corylus avellana* type plus the lesser arboreal taxa noted from lpaz:1. A small increase in *Betula* occurs (lpasz:ii.).

Herbs are also similar to the preceding zone but with reduction of Chenopodiaceae to low values. The mire/wetland component undergoes significant changes. While *Alnus* remains largely constant, there is a slight increase in *Salix* throughout the zone.

Typha angustifolia/*Sparganium* type (40%) and *Typha latifolia* (5%) increase. Spores of ferns increase with *Thelypteris palustris* type (<2%), *Pteridium aquilinum* (to 7%), and *Dryopteris* (to 20%). Pre-Quaternary palynomorphs decline.

Lpasz:ii, 0.82–0.62m. After a small increase of *Ulmus* and *Fraxinus* in lpasz:i, values decrease. *Betula* expands to the upper zone boundary of lpaz:2. This appears to correspond with a lithostratigraphical unit of organic mud.

Lpaz FFN:3, 0.62–0.34m. This zone occurs in the main peat of the basin. Radiocarbon dated to cal BC 400–90 (GU-5616; 2180±60BP) at the top and cal BC 1530–1260 (GU-5617; 3130±60BP) at the base. The zone has been delimited on the declining values of *Quercus* (to 7%) and *Alnus* (5%); the latter occurs in the upper part of the zone. *Corylus avellana* type also declines from 20% at the base to low values. *Salix*, in contrast, expands at the start of the zone (to 7%). Sporadic occurrences of *Betula*, *Pinus*, *Ulmus*, *Tilia*, *Fraxinus*, *Carpinus*, and *Fagus* remain. Herbs are dominated by Poaceae expanding throughout the zone to 80%. There is also an overall increase in the diversity of taxa present. Only *Chenopodium* type show some reduction. Aquatic/marsh taxa remain dominated by *Typha angustifolia*/*Sparganium* type although *Typha latifolia* declines.

Lpasz:iii, 0.62–0.46m. Delimited by *Alnus* and *Salix*, values expand to 32% and 7% respectively.

Lpasz:iv, 0.42–0.30m. Delimited by a decline in *Alnus* (to 5%) and *Quercus* (7%).

Lpaz FFN:4, 0.34–0.08m. In these upper peat levels there is an expansion in tree pollen (to 40%), and shrub pollen (to 33%). Conversely, herbs decline progressively. The zone is delimited by an expansion of *Quercus* (to 29%) and *Corylus avellana* type (32%).

Alnus (43%) and *Salix* expand sharply after lpasz:iv. There are expansions in some herb types, especially *Plantago lanceolata* type, Asteraceae taxa, Cyperaceae, and spores of *Polypodium* and *Sphagnum*. The dominance of *Typha angustifolia* type finishes as this taxon declines to low levels and absence at the top of the zone.

Lpaz FFN:5, 0.80–0m. This uppermost zone with poorly preserved pollen is in the upper mineral sediments of the 'upper alluvial deposit'. The single level presented shows a decline in percentages of arboreal and shrub taxa — *Quercus*, *Alnus*, *Corylus avellana* type, and *Salix*. Percentages of herb pollen increase to a maximum of 84% dominated by Poaceae and Cyperaceae. There is some reduction in herb diversity.

The changing vegetation and environment

Northey Section 4, sampled in 1993, has the most complete lithostratigraphic sequence recorded and comes from the central part of the basin. As with other central basin sites, however, the upper peat that overlay the upper alluvial deposits has been removed through drainage, desiccation, and agriculture.

The basal pollen assemblage zone FFN:1, as with the other sections examined, clearly illustrates a woodland dominated by *Tilia* with *Quercus* and *Corylus avellana* growing locally on this basal palaeoargillic brown earth. High percentages of *Alnus* indicate local presence. These values are not, however, high enough to indicate on-site dominance of Alnetum (alder-willow carr) although it is likely that *Alnus* formed a community peripheral to the progressively expanding fen. Cereal pollen and associated segetal taxa, as at the other basin sites, similarly suggest a Neolithic or Early Bronze Age date for this palaeosol. This is corroborated by low *Ulmus* values implying a post-elm-decline age. Some expansion of *Ulmus* and *Fraxinus* in lpasz:i is evidence of secondary woodland regeneration in the late Neolithic and is a phenomenon noted especially in sites in southern England (Scaife 1988). This lpasz is stratigraphically correlated with the lake *gyttja*, however, and it is possible that the taphonomic changes might be responsible for these expansions of *Ulmus* and *Fraxinus* with pollen input via alluvial rather than subaerial processes.

At 0.88m the significant stratigraphical change to detrital fen peat is mirrored by expansion of fen-mire and aquatic taxa (especially *Typha*/*Sparganium*, *T. latifolia*, and the presence of Cyperaceae and possibly Poaceae). This suggests a wet reed-swamp habitat.

Stratigraphically, this corresponds with lenses of grey clay and the underlying coarser silt containing rootlets provided an ideal rooting medium for *Sparganum*/*Typha* dominated reed swamps. The occurrence of sporadic rooting macrophytes and deposition of *gyttja* also attests to local standing water. Overall, this represents one stage of the retrogressive hydrosere. Subsequently, the change to typical detrital fen mire peat (FFN:3) at cal BC 1530–1260 (GU-5617; 3130±60 BP) is clear evidence of allogenically controlled increase in water tables, that is ponding from the eastern fens and the Ouse and Welland. *Alnus* became important (lpasz:iii, 0.62–0.46m) and was likely to have been growing peripherally to the fen mire. Contractions of *Alnus* and *Salix* in lpasz:iv might be interpreted in two ways.

First, the rising groundwater table might have 'pushed' this peripheral community further up the interfluve and away from the sample site. This is a strong possibility and is discussed in relation to the Fengate section lying to the west. Second, the peat sequence is broadly contemporaneous with the construction of the platform. The decline in *Alnus* and *Quercus* percentages might correspond with woodland clearance for its building (Chapters 8 and 16).

Characteristically, the peats (FFN:3/4) are sealed by the overlying alluvial sediment representing widespread alluviation of the basin during the Iron Age/Roman periods.

Radiocarbon dating suggests that this inundation occurred at cal BC 400–90 (GU-5616, 2180±60 BP).

The platform section

This was the first section examined for pollen and plant macrofossils, diatoms (Juggins nd), and insects (Robinson 1992 and Chapter 15). The site chosen for environmental sampling (1984) was located some 5m away from the north-east edge of the platform (Fig 6.21).

Lithostratigraphy

This sequence of 1.12m spans the stratigraphy from the basal Neolithic palaeoargillic brown earth/soil (Chapter 14), the primary peat of the fen basin, and the overlying silt sediments of the alluvial deposit. This is essentially similar to that described for the mere section and the Flag Fen Basin as a whole (below).

The pollen biostratigraphy and zonation

Pollen zonation of Figure 13.3 has been carried out on the inherent variation in the pollen spectra.

Lpaz FFP:1, 1.12–1m. This zone corresponds with the basal Neolithic palaeosol developed in Devensian sands/gravels and the transition into peat accumulation. The zone is characterised by *Quercus* (27%), *Corylus avellana* type (21%), and *Alnus* (increasing from 20% into the subsequent zone), with *Ulmus* (2%) and *Tilia* (3%). Herbs are dominated by Poaceae (to 30%) and Cyperaceae (marsh). Spores of *Dryopteris* type, *Pteridium aquilinum* and *Polypodium* are present. The latter is only important in this zone. A small number of marsh and aquatic taxa (and *lnus* and Cyperaceae noted) include *Typha latifolia*, *Iris*, and cf *Callitriche*.

Lpaz FFP:2, 1–0.52m. This is the basal peat series. *Ulmus* declines from low values to sporadic occurrences. *Quercus* declines throughout to 10% along with *Corylus avellana* type (from 30% to <5%) at the top of the zone. Small values of *Tilia* remain with *Pinus*, and *Betula*. There is a more constant record of *Fraxinus*.

Fagus occurs at the top. There is an increase in herb diversity with notable taxa including *Plantago lanceolata*,

P. media/major, *P. coronopus* type, Chenopodiaceae, and *Artemisia*. Cereal type shows a slight expansion. The change to peat lithology is characterised by high values (65%) of *Typha angustifolia/Sparganium* type (plant macrofossils show this to have been *Sparganium*). Spores remain constant except for *Polypodium*, which occurs only sporadically after pollen assemblage zone:1.

Lpaz FFP:3, 0.52–0.36m. This zone corresponds with the lower levels of the platform and is delimited by a reduction to their lowest percentage values of *Quercus* (5%), *Alnus* (5%), and *Corylus avellana* type (2%), with a peak of Poaceae (to 76%).

Tilia becomes absent in this zone. Marsh taxa remain dominated by *Typha angustifolia/Sparganium* type and Cyperaceae with some aquatic macrophytes (*Nuphar lutea* and *Potamogeton*).

Lpaz FFP:4, 0.36–0m. This zone corresponds with the upper transition from peat into the overlying silts/clays. It is characterised by renewed expansions of arboreal and shrub percentages including *Quercus* (26%), *Alnus* (to 35% in the upper level), and *Corylus avellana* type (10%). Of note are increases in *Betula* at 0.04m (to 20%), *Salix* (to 25%), and *Ilex*, *Fagus*, Frangula *Alnus*, and *Viburnum*. Poaceae remains the dominant herb but declines from the preceding zone. Apiaceae types 2 and 3 might correspond with wetland/marsh taxa. Marsh/aquatic taxa show an increase in diversity with occurrences of *Nuphar lutea*, *Nymphaea alba*, cf *Hottonia*, *Myriophyllum alterniflorum*, cf *Callitriche*, *Potamogeton*, and spores of *Osmunda regalis* and *Sphagnum*.

The mire zonation

Four pollen assemblage zones have been recognised in the wetland taxa. These have been calculated as a percentage of their total and are thus examined without relation to terrestrial communities. It must, however, be noted that, due to inability to separate mire pollen type to a lower taxonomic/greater specificity, some types in the dryland diagram might also pertain to the marsh habitat (eg Poaceae). In spite of these palynological inexactitudes, clear changes in the aquatic/mire habitat are seen. These zones are designated FFP a–d and are characterised as follows:

FFP:a (1.12–1m), two levels. *Alnus* (24%) and Cyperaceae are dominant.
FFP:b (1–0.84m). *Alnus*, Cyperaceae, and increasing *Typha angustifolia*.
FFP:c (0.84–0.34m). *Alnus* and *Salix*, increasing Cyperaceae, and especially *Typha angustifolia/Sparganium*. Sporadic aquatics also increase.
FFP:d (0.34–0m). Increasing *Alnus* and *Salix*, some decrease in *Typha angustifolia*. Cyperaceae remains constant. Increase in true aquatics especially in top half of the zone ('alluvial deposits').

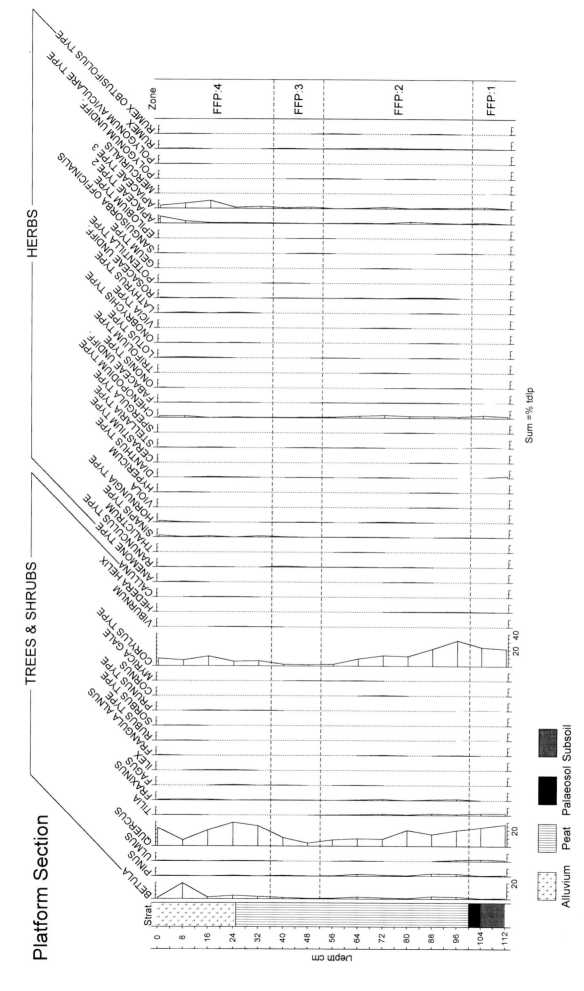

Fig 13.3 Pollen diagram of platform section

364

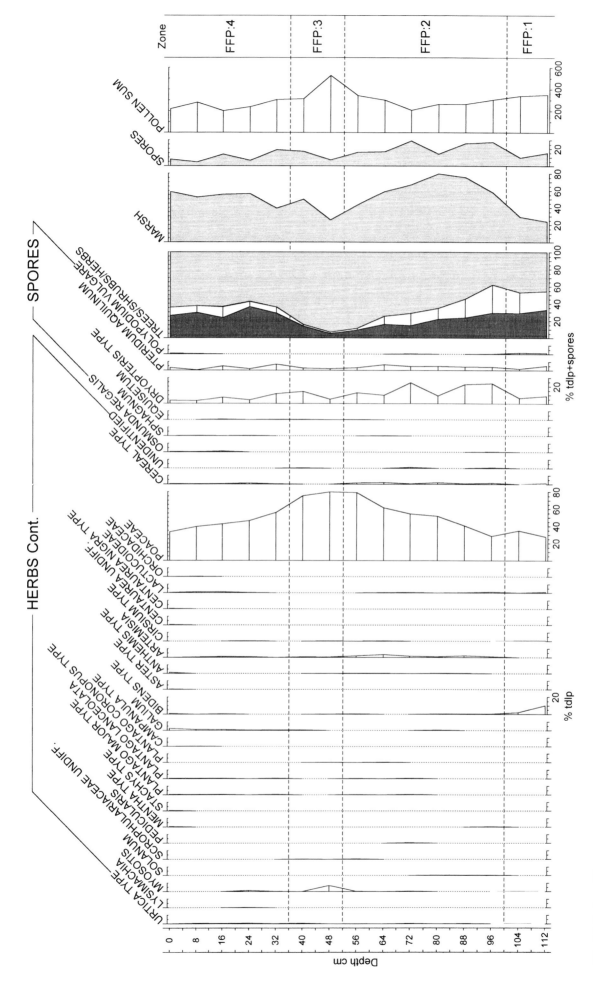

Fig 13.3 (cont'd)

365

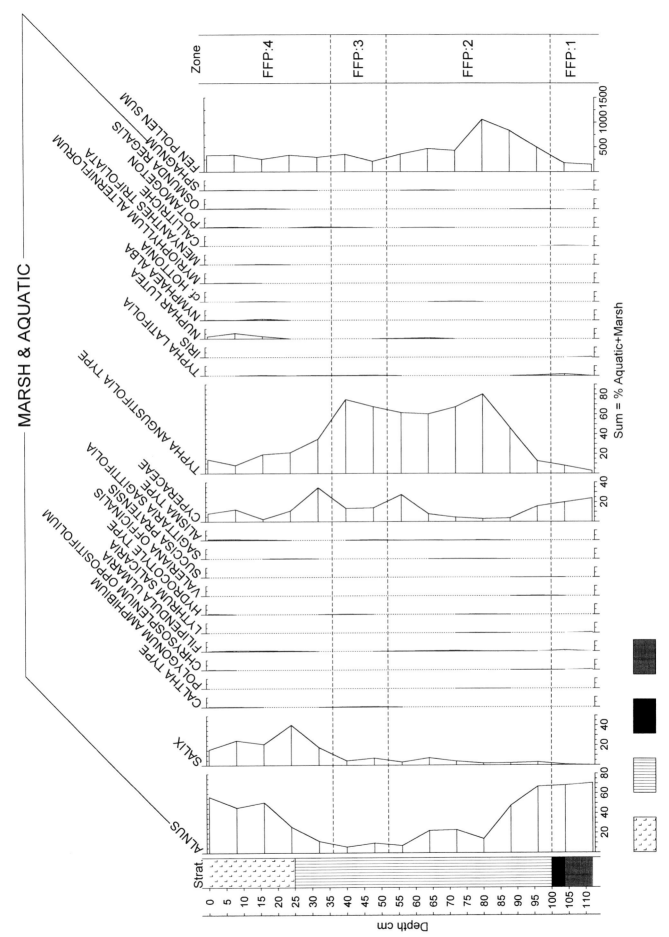

Fig 13.3 (cont'd)

The inferred vegetation

The lower levels of pollen zone FFP:1 relate to the basal palaeosol. The rather low percentage values of *Ulmus* here suggest a post-elm-decline date, Neolithic age. This is commensurate with the occurrence of cereal-type pollen and associated herbs in this zone.

The presence of *Alnus* in this soil, however, implies that carr woodland was present nearby, possibly in wetter, lower areas of the basin. Some reed swamp and aquatic taxa also occur sporadically. The expansion of these along with *Alnus* and *Salix* in zone FFP:b (ie 0.42–0.5m) is evidence of increasing water tables and wetness, as fen mire conditions started to impinge on the dryland soils, the start of the retrogressive hydrosere.

Proximity of this profile to the north-east corner of the structure and the allied study of insects and plant macrofossils provide a useful insight into the 'on-site' environment in which the platform was constructed. Pollen evidence shows a clear change in the vegetation of the fen basin. There is a retrogressive hydroseral succession from terrestrial, but possibly damp, soils (see French 1990, 1992a, b, c, and Chapter 14) of Neolithic or Early Bronze Age date, through wet fen during the Bronze Age, to full alluvial incursion in the Late Iron Age/Romano-British period.

Thus, the expansion of *Alnus* across the zone FFP:2/3 boundary might be seen as local colonisation by fringing carr woodland prior to the aquatic marsh/fen phase. This 'wave' of expanding vegetation is similarly seen (but later) at other sites along the fringes of the basin at the Power Station site (below section 5). In mire zone FFP:c reed swamp dominated by *Typha angustifolia/Sparganium* type, *Sagittaria sagittifolia*, *Alisma plantago-aquatica*, and aquatic macrophytes suggest that rich fen conditions prevailed. This resulted in the creation of the fen peat environment in which the platform was built.

In mire zone FFP:d, the further increase in water tables and periodic flooding with sediment inwash can be seen by the increased numbers of aquatic macrophytes — *Nuphar lutea* and *Nymphaea alba*. Radiocarbon measurements of the Northey section and Fengate suggest this occurred after 1400–900 BC. The expansion of *Alnus* and *Salix* attest to the regional importance of carr. Given the changes in pollen taphonomy, however, which undoubtedly occurred with transition from peat to peaty sediments, and ultimately the upper alluvial deposits, there is a strong likelihood that much of this pollen might be from extra-local sources, perhaps remaining as fringing vegetation to the Flag Fen Basin. Conversely, there is a decline in the numbers of dryland vegetation taxa such as *Tilia*, as their areas of growth became progressively diminished and also further away from the sampling site (Waller 1993 and 1994b).

Vegetation environment and environmental change in the Flag Fen Basin

Underlying the main fen peats of the Flag Fen Basin is a diagnostic palaeosol. This is a palaeoargillic brown earth developed in the basal silts, sands, and gravels of Devensian age. It is typical of the area, occurring widely under the later Flandrian/Holocene peats (French 1988a; 1988b; 1990; 1992b; French and Pryor 1993). Soil micromorphological analysis of Crowtree and Oakhurst Farm and associated pollen work (Scaife in French and Pryor 1993) have shown that these similar soils might have been truncated prior to the deposition of the overlying peats. Small values of *Ulmus* and presence of cereal pollen in these soils suggest a post-*Ulmus*-decline, Neolithic age, for this lime dominated woodland. The vegetation growing on this palaeosol is evidenced in pollen zones FFM:1, FFN:1, and FFP:1.

These are typical of soil sequences in which there has been mixing by faunal disturbances and translocation of pollen down the profile rather than a vertical stratigraphical accretion as takes place in peat. The pollen spectra are likely to be representative of the very near or 'on-site' vegetation (Dimbleby 1962 and 1985).

The pollen data clearly indicate that *Tilia* was the dominant tree on the drier soils with *Quercus* and *Corylus avellana* also important. *Fraxinus* might also have been growing but, as with *Tilia*, the poor pollen production and entomophily results in the limited representation in pollen spectra (Andersen 1970 and 1973). Where these occur in soil pollen spectra, values fluctuate markedly because of changing local dominance. Keatinge (1982) has shown this for southern England in the case of *Tilia*. The regional importance of lime in southern and eastern England as a whole is now well established (Birks *et al* 1975; Birks 1989; Baker *et al* 1978; Greig 1982a; Moore 1977; Scaife 1980, 1987, and 1988; Waller 1993). The dispersal bias noted can result in significant under-representation in peat sequences. This bias is evident in subsequent Flag Fen pollen zones (FFM:2/FFM:3) as paludification (Waller 1994b) caused *Tilia* to be progressively distanced from the middle basin sample sites. It is clear in East Anglia, however, that lime appears to have been of great importance in many areas, growing on better drained soils (Clark and Godwin 1962; Godwin 1940, 1975a, and 1975b; Godwin and Clifford 1936; Greig 1982b; Smith 1958; Vishnu-Mittre 1971; Waller 1993) and has continued to be used in coppice today (Rackham 1980). Whether *Quercus* and *Corylus* were also constituents of the *Tilia* dominated woodland is not ascertainable. It is possible that these taxa were growing on the heavier (Jurassic) clay soils or in drier fen carr woodland on the fringes of the mire.

Herb pollen taxa from these soil pollen zones (FFM:1, FFP:1, and FFN:1) are relatively few in comparison to subsequent zones. There are indications of cereal cultivation (cereal-type pollen) and some weed taxa including some Brassicaceae, Chenopodiaceae, *Rumex*, and *Plantago lanceolata*. The latter and the relatively higher values of Poaceae might, however, be indicative of grassland. Higher values of spores of *Pteridium aquilinum* are indicative of the dryland character of the basal zone. It is also possible that the grasses relate to the encroaching grass/sedge fen community.

The onset of freshwater conditions in the basin instigated a retrogressive hydrosere. Dry land became progressively waterlogged from the centre of the basin outwards towards the margins with the establishment of a fringing wet fen (reed-swamp) community. In marginal areas, peat accumulated directly on the now preserved land surface. Areas of open, shallow-water fen remained while these fringing communities became wetter and resultant peat accumulation occurred directly onto the Pleistocene gravels and palaeosol. Peat accumulation directly onto the basal lithology is seen in the mere section, the platform section, and at Fengate (below), although the latter, being on the upper margins of the basin as discussed, represents the final phases of the inundation.

Waterlogging of the deeper part of the basin (Northey section) occurred at cal BC 2030–1680 (GU-5618; 500±60 BP), depositing organic silts and *gyttja* (–0.49–0.84m OD). This was in response to regionally rising sea levels ponding back the major Fenland river systems (Welland and Ouse) and local tributary systems (eg the Cat's Water). To demonstrate this marine encroachment, Waller (1994a) has produced palaeogeographic maps of the limits of freshwater and marine conditions pertaining throughout the later Holocene.

The transitional phase of freshwater sedimentation is only seen in the base of the Fengate/Northey sequence (above, zone FFN:2), whereas at sites with the basal gravels at higher OD levels, the fen peat rests directly on the basal palaeosol developed in the basal gravels (ie. at the mere section, platform section, and on the basin fringes at Fengate). This lower transition appears to show a fluvially lain silt and organic mud horizon, perhaps the product of an expanding floodplain in the lower parts of the basin. Reed-swamp taxa start to make their expansion to a marked dominance in the Flag Fen Basin throughout the Bronze Age. *Typha angustifolia/Sparganium*, Cyperaceae, and *Alnus* suggest the expanding area of reed swamp was surrounded by a belt of alder/willow carr. Continued rise in base levels resulted in freshwater organic muds being deposited in a freshwater marsh in the deepest part of the basin (ie Northey, the upper part of FFN:2). This corresponds with the dominance 'on-site' of the reed-swamp taxa noted above. Subsequently, a rapid and stratigraphically marked change to fen-peat deposits occurred diachronously on the old land surface, consequent upon regionally increasing groundwater table. The earliest

date obtained for this peat growth was cal BC 1530–1260 (GU-5617; 3130±60BP) in the Northey section.

In zones FFM:2, and FFN:3 there is a marked reduction in the values of *Tilia* in these peat pollen spectra. In long pollen sequences from southern and eastern England, the 'lime decline' has been much discussed; initially this was regarded as a consequence of climatic change marking the transition from Godwin's pollen zones VIIb and VIII (sub-Boreal to sub-Atlantic) and latterly as a function of human deforestation (Turner 1962). The decline of *Tilia* here might thus be regarded as a function of:

A Fen encroachment pushing the nearest *Tilia* woodland communities relatively farther from the sampling site, with consequent reduction in pollen input. 'On-site' *Tilia* growth would have been destroyed by the rising water tables and waterlogging of the soils. Waller (1993) has also invoked this as a cause for the *Tilia* decline in Sussex and other East Anglian sites (Waller 1993 and 1994b). Thus, evidence for the 'dryland' vegetation might become skewed towards those taxa with greater pollen production and anemophilous dispersion.

B Due to increased land pressure, woodland clearance for agriculture might have resulted in declining *Tilia* in the Middle to Late Bronze Age. During the period represented by FFP:2–3, FFN:3–4, and FFM:2, there is, however, continued evidence of woodland, although the relative proportions change, *Quercus* becoming the dominant taxon. This might not represent a real increase in the importance in the landscape of oak, if factors noted above for *Tilia* are considered. Also recorded are *Betula* and *Pinus* in relatively small percentages. Given the high pollen production and anemophily of these latter taxa, they are not likely to have been important in the region of Flag Fen. In contrast, however, the sporadic/lesser records of *Tilia*, *Fraxinus*, *Fagus*, and *Ilex* (one occurrence) are all greatly underrepresented in pollen spectra (Andersen 1970 and 1973). It is likely that these trees remained locally on drier soils.

Continuous presence of cereal pollen and dry land herbs (including *Polygonum* spp, *Plantago lanceolata*, *P. major* type, *Chenopodium* type, and Asteraceae spp) are evidence of clearance and mixed agriculture on the dryland/interfluve areas. These are in evidence in zones FFM:2, FFN:3, and FFP:4, with increasing values upwards from the basal zones of all sequences examined. A period of increased arable cultivation, or continued activity, but in closer proximity to the sample sites (Bronze Age platform), occurs at the top of the mire sequence in zone FFM:2 (approximately 0.46–0.3m). This has been recognised as a pollen assemblage sub-zone (i). The dominance of Poaceae, plus the presence of *Plantago lanceolata* and other herb taxa, suggest that areas of grassland were also present.

It is likely that mixed arable and pastoral agriculture was being practised throughout the period represented by these peats, that is, the Bronze Age. This suggestion is, however, somewhat tentative since the interpretation of pastoral pollen spectra can be difficult: the Poaceae and other herbs often used as indicators of pastoral or even grassland environments might derive from a wide variety of habitats, such as field boundaries, wet meadows, or floodplain environments.

The Flag Fen platform was constructed on the detrital fen peats of paz FFM:2, FFN3–4, FFP:2–3, and FENG:1. Stratigraphically, the basal timbers of the platform occur at an estimated depth of 0.45–0.5m in FFM:2 and 0.4–0.5m in FFP:3. This is based on the recovery of some timbers marginal to the main platform structure in these pollen sections. Thus, these zones represent the palaeoenvironments in which the principal archaeological activity was taking place. The character and changes in the basin filling and mire ecology itself are discussed below (Chapter 17).

The terrestrial vegetation concurrent with the building of the platform probably consisted of areas of mixed deciduous woodland, possibly with some lime remaining. Some areas of certainly arable, but possibly also pastoral agriculture existed on the nearby, better drained soils. Clearance of some woodland must have taken place, by virtue of the vast numbers and large size of timbers used in the construction of the platform. These areas were perhaps subsequently used for agriculture. The tree taxa used in construction, although comprising predominantly alder in the lower levels and oak in the upper (Chapters 7 and 8), also include a variety of other shrub and tree taxa. The pollen sequence from the platform section is comparable with the mere and Northey sections, showing decline of *Quercus* pollen in zones FFM:2 (lpasz:i), FFP:3, and FFN:3. Coincident with this is a relative increase in *Corylus* and agricultural activity. Although these could be within-sum statistical effects, it is possible that the diminution of timber through felling for platform construction is being seen here. The increase of *Corylus* in the pollen record is significant, since light is needed for hazel to flower, although it flowers early in the year when deciduous trees are not in leaf. Its increase in lpasz:i possibly reflects woodland management for coppice, with a period of increased area of growth and flowering occurring on the removal of oak. Similarly, the expansion of herb pollen in some cases might be a function of an extended pollen catchment caused by removal of screening woodland communities (Tauber 1967).

After this forest clearance and/or management, there is some evidence for woodland regeneration with increased percentages of *Quercus* in the upper peat horizons of Late Bronze Age date (FFP:3/4 and FFN:4). It is not, however, seen in the mere or Fengate profile and might, thus, be a localised phenomenon. It is tentatively postulated that this represents a phase of woodland regeneration after the clearance for platform timber.

Culmination of rising base levels resulted in the widespread deposition of the 'upper alluvial deposits', which 'cap' the peat deposits of most of the Fenland basins (French 1992a; Waller 1994a). This is represented by pollen zones FFN:5, FFP:4, FFM:3, and FENG:2. Radiocarbon dates from Fengate and the Northey section show this occurred at, or shortly after cal BC 410–90 (GU-5619; 2290±50 BP; GU-5616, 2180±60BP). The aquatic vegetation represented in this lithological unit is discussed below (Chapter 15). The dryland pollen taxa show a broad continuation of the preceding upper peat pollen assemblage zones. There would have been changes in depositional circumstances, however, and thus, the taphonomy of the pollen and spores in these levels. It is likely that pollen input from a wider catchment is represented in these sediments, with an increase in fluvially transported grains (Burrin and Scaife 1984; Peck 1973; Scaife and Burrin 1992). There are increases in the number of herb taxa and in their relative percentages.

Increases in arable and possibly pastoral indicators might represent a local intensification of agricultural land use on the drier interfluve areas. Another interpretation might be that the rising water table and changing depositional environment caused an opening of the pollen catchment and increased pollen input from wider afield; that is, a taphonomic change rather than an actual increase in anthropogenic activity. Certainly, however, these data provide evidence for arable and possibly mixed agriculture in the region during the Late Bronze Age/Iron Age, to which the lower alluvial sediments are attributed. A pollen assemblage sub-zone has been recognised in the mere section between 0.4m and 0.28m (+0.44m and +0.56m OD) by such an increase in cereal pollen and associated segetal taxa indicating a period of increased arable agriculture. The fact that this sub-zone spans the transition from the fen peat to alluvial sediments suggests that this phase of activity was occurring locally to Flag Fen.

Also associated with this phase are increased values of taxa regarded as being pastoral indicators. Notable in this respect are Poaceae and many herbs, including *Plantago lanceolata*, *Rumex*, and Asteraceae types, especially between 0.16m and 0.08m (+0.68 and +0.76m OD in FFM:3).

The alluvial sediments are overlain by upper peats of medieval date, which have largely been removed from the major part of the basin. They do, however, remain in some fringing areas of fen and have been examined on the Fengate B site (below). As might be expected for peats of this relatively late date, there is a large representation of herbs dominated by Poaceae with strong indications for pastoral and arable agriculture on adjacent dry land. This is similar to pollen assemblages of similar age obtained from Deeping St Nicholas (Scaife in French 1994). *Quercus, Corylus avellana*, and sporadic *Fagus* and *Carpinus* pollen suggest at least some local woodland remained in these areas at this later date. The variations illustrated by the Fengate peat sequence perhaps reflect the 'sensitive' position of these deposits on the western and upper/higher altitude margins of the fen basin. As such, they represent the latter stages of peat formation and alluvial inundation. It seems likely that there is a substantial hiatus between the alluvial deposits described and the upper peat, which is emphasised by the palaeosol formed in the upper alluvial sequence. Thus, it is in the marginal zone that higher resolution pollen data might be expected to accrue, from both the dryland vegetation communities (including agriculture) and the changing character of the wetland fringing zone dependent on water table fluctuations. The Fengate 'B sequence' was accordingly examined and is discussed next.

The fen margins: Fengate B — the Power Station site

Excavation of the Fengate complex in 1989 produced sections of peat and sediments that were deposited along the fen edge to the west of the deeper peat profiles discussed above.

The pollen diagram from Fengate B spans the principal stratigraphical units recognised in this fen-edge zone and the pollen data provide evidence for the character of vegetation at the interface of the mire and dry land (Fig 4.1, Pollen Profile B).

Lithostratigraphy

A number of long sections were examined and analysis of the selected pollen sequence (Fengate B) spans the lower peat, which is broadly contemporary with the main basin fen peats and archaeological structures of Flag Fen, the post alignment, and upper medieval peats. The fen peats contain some fine sedimentary laminations indicating minerogenic input from phases of soil erosion consequent upon anthropogenic interference of the nearby dry land. The peats are of circumneutral pH and are highly humified. There is much evidence of drying out and some cracking has occurred, possibly through lowering of the local groundwater table in recent years (French and Taylor 1985).

Interleaved between the two peat accumulations is a sequence of alluvial silts that are also dehydrated. These correspond with the 'upper alluvial deposit', which overlies the main peats of Flag Fen lying 100m to the east. It appears that the upper horizons of these alluvial silts have been subject to pedogenic processes (French 1992b) and they might represent an old land surface. Thus, the stratigraphical sequence described here and the palynology are seen to be comparable with the deeper stratigraphical sequences described (above) for the Flag Fen platform basin and platform zone. Proximity to the dry land, however, has resulted in relatively thinner peat sequences.

Radiocarbon dating has shown that peat development was diachronous as the wetland extended over the dryland surface consequent upon the regionally rising groundwater table.

Subsequent drying out of this area has caused degradation of the peat and alluvial silts and of their contained pollen, which in some levels has caused marked differential preservation. This is especially the case in the fen clay alluvium of Late Iron Age to Romano-British date. The section examined (Fig 13.4) comprised the following lithostratigraphical units:

depth

0–0.11m	Dark/black, humified detrital fen peat, no visible vegetative structure remaining.
0.11–0.175m	Brown organic, loamy sand and silt.
0.175–0.21m	Dark, black humic (Ah) horizon. Top of buried soil/palaeosol.
0.21–0.24m	Subsoil transition zone.
0.24–0.37m	Dark grey silts of the upper alluvial horizon.
0.37–0.44m	Buff-coloured silts.
0.44–0.5m	Grey silts, Fe staining/gleying?
0.5–0.8m	Dark brown, well humified peat. Dry with little evidence of vegetative structure. Radiocarbon sample at top: cal BC 410–200 (GU-5619; 2290±50 BP)
0.8–0.85m	Wood peat: brushwood fragments.
0.85–0.92m	Black, humified detrital peat. Radiocarbon sample: cal BC 800–400 (GU-5620; 2840±50 BP)
0.92+m	Basal palaeosol developed in Quaternary/Devensian gravels.

Pollen stratigraphy and zonation

Three local pollen assemblage zones (FENG:1–3) can be recognised in the 0.92m profile whose base lies at +1.03m OD. A hiatus in the pollen sequence occurs between 0.5m and 0.35m in the alluvial sediments where only small numbers of badly degraded pollen was present. The pollen zones are characterised from the base of the profile upwards as follows:

Lpaz FENG:1, 0.92–0.5m. Lower fen peat, characterised by high values of wetland taxa including *Alnus*, Cyperaceae, *Typha angustifolia/Sparganium*, and some Poaceae. Trees and shrubs are dominated by *Quercus* (to 16%), *Corylus avellana* type (to 19%), and *Alnus* (10–15%). Also present are *Betula* (<5%), *Pinus*, *Tilia*, *Fraxinus*, *Fagus*, and *Viburnum*. Herbs are dominated by Poaceae (55%), Cyperaceae (declining from 40%–20%), Lactucae, (expanding to 10%), Chenopodiaceae, and Asteraceae. Some aquatic taxa are present (*Nymphaea*, *Myriophyllum* spp, *Potamogeton* type, and algal *Pediastrum*), largely in the upper levels.

Lpaz FENG:2, 0.34–0.18m. This zone has been delimited on the pollen contained in a palaeosol developed in the top of the alluvium. Pollen was sparse and thus, the pollen count/sum was small in these levels.

370

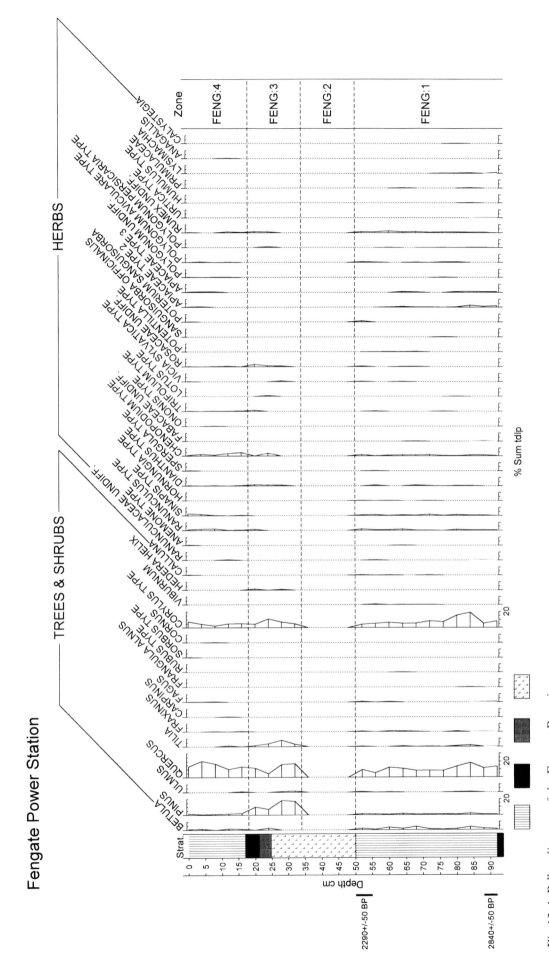

Fig 13.4 Pollen diagram of the Fengate B section

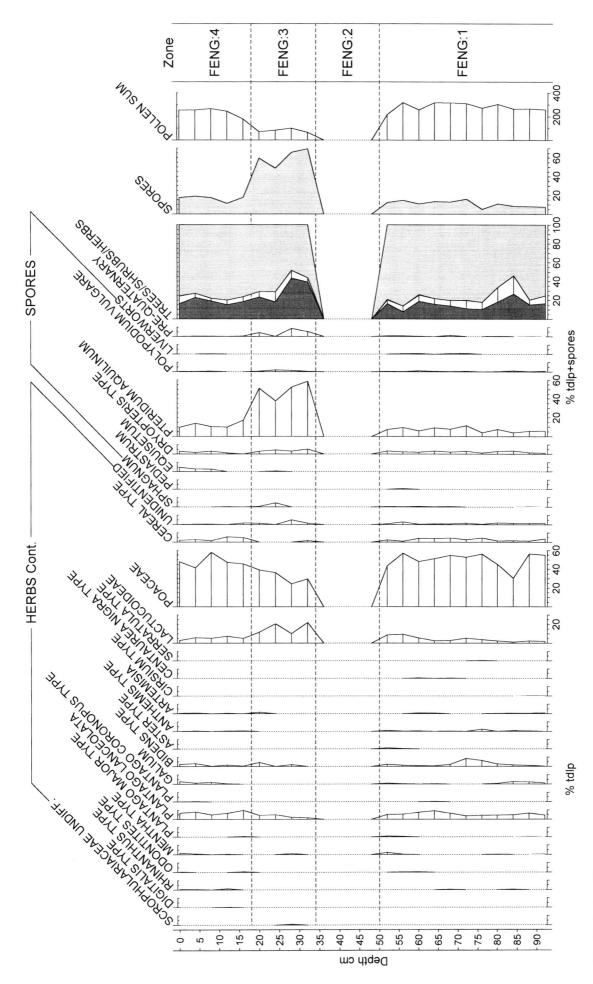

Fig 13.4 (cont'd)

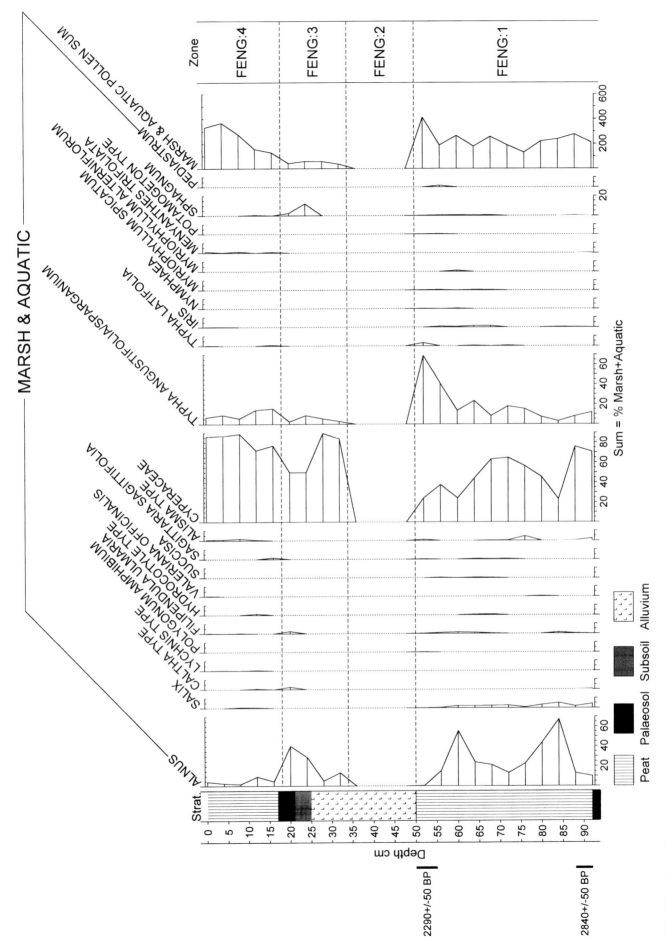

Fig 13.4 (cont'd)

Tree pollen are dominated by *Pinus* (15%), *Quercus* (15%), *Tilia* (8%), and *Corylus avellana* type (10%). Herb diversity is less than in FENG:1, with dominance of Poaceae (expanding to 45%), Lactucae (to 25%), and *Plantago lanceolata* (expanding from 5%–10% in FENG:3). Marsh taxa are dominated by Cyperaceae (37%), with some *Typha angustifolia/Sparganium*. There are substantial numbers of *Pteridium aquilinum* (60%), with *Dryopteris* type (5%), and *Polypodium vulgare* (<5%).

Lpaz FENG:3, 0.18–0m. Upper medieval fen peat, with high values of Poaceae (to 60%) and Cyperaceae (increasing to 50%). Tree pollen remain dominated by *Quercus* (to 20%), with sharp reductions of *Pinus* and *Tilia* from FENG:2. *Fraxinus*, *Carpinus*, and *Fagus* occur sporadically. Shrubs are dominated by *Corylus avellana* type (to 10%). Herbs are characterised by increasing diversity but with marked expansion of *Plantago lanceolata* (10%), *Chenopodium* type, and cereal type (6%). Lactucae are diminished. Marsh/aquatic types are dominated by Cyperaceae (to 5%), with *Typha angustifolia* type (6%) and a range of other fen taxa.

Discussion of vegetation change

A radiocarbon date of cal BC 1210–900 (GU-5620; 2840±50 BP) establishes that peat started to accumulate on the dry land at the fen-edge soil surface during the later Bronze Age/Iron Age transition — much later than in the deeper part of the basin (cal BC 1530–1260: GU-5617; 3130±60 BP).

A retrogressive hydrosere is evidenced by *Alnus* and *Salix* in the basal levels (0.92–0.8m) giving way to dominant reed swamp with *Typha angustifolia/Sparganium* type (bur reed and greater reedmace) and other herbs of shallow water and damp ground. It appears from the fluctuating values of *Salix* and *Alnus* and corresponding change to taxa of more open, wetter conditions (*Sparganium*, *Iris*, and Cyperaceae) that, either local hydrological conditions were fluctuating, or that *Alnus* and *Salix* were being used in the construction of the nearby platform and causeway, thus affecting the local ground water table, surface run-off, and the vegetation communities. In fact, the situation might be quite complex, since there is a trend towards a wetter environment regionally in the Fenland, culminating in the deposition of the upper alluvial deposits during the Late Iron Age to Romano-British period. Radiocarbon measurements at this site and in the Northey section (the basin centre above) establishes this phase at cal BC 410–200 (GU-5619; 2290±50 BP) and cal BC 400–90 (GU-5616; 2180±60 BP) respectively. Local fluctuation of the water table appears to have affected the mire community along the fringes of the dry land. A progressive overlap of fen conditions ensued, as the regional water table rose throughout the Fenlands as a whole during the Bronze Age (Waller 1994a). An alder and willow carr community fringing

the Whittlesey island was progressively inundated, giving rise to a shallow-water fen dominated by taxa typical of shallow-water muddy conditions.

The proximity of this peat site to drier and potentially suitable agricultural land provided an opportunity to ascertain what agriculture was being practised on the drier soils adjacent to the fen basin. Throughout the lower peats (FENG:1) there is a consistent presence of cereal pollen with percentages to 5% and a variety of other weed taxa (Brassicaceae, Polygonaceae, and Chenopodiaceae). There is also consistency of pastoral type herbs with Poaceae (although some might be attributed to the 'on-site' plant community) and typical indicators such as *Plantago lanceolata*, *Ranunculus* type, *Rumex* spp, and possibly types within the Asteraceae. It seems likely that mixed arable/pastoral agriculture was being practised nearby. This is more apparent in the upper part of the zone and is commensurate with suggestions made for the main basin profiles.

Overlying the basal peat deposits are the upper alluvial silts/clays, which mantle the larger part of the Fen area with varying degrees of thickness. Pollen was not present in sufficient quantity to allow valid counts to be made from the lower levels of this alluvium at Fengate. There is, however, evidence of pedogenesis in the upper part of this unit, indicating a period of dryness. Absolute pollen numbers increase upwards through these alluvial silts to the top, in which the buried soil developed. This enabled pollen counts to be made in these levels of the alluvium (pollen zone FENG:2). Pollen assemblages are dominated by taxa having robust exines such as, for example, *Pinus*, *Tilia*, Asteraceae, and the spores of *Pteridium aquilinum*. As the derivation of these taxa is problematic, the high pollen percentages can not be taken at face value, ie that they represent local dominance of these taxa.

The pollen is highly degraded and might be derived from the reworking of earlier deposits. These robust exine types survived transport and redeposition, or the result of differential preservation over long time periods in the soil (Havinga 1964). The fact that no pollen is present in the lower (bulk) of the alluvium suggests, however, that here, pollen in the upper/palaeosol is derived from that falling directly onto the old land surface.

The spectra can in fact be regarded as a typical soil pollen series, with an increase in pollen values to the top of an old land surface (Dimbleby 1961 and 1985), the contained pollen being deposited on the land surface and then subject to downward movement. The pollen taxa are likely to represent to a greater extent the flora growing on, or closely adjacent to the site, with the effects of mixing between soil levels (Dimbleby 1962).

Although a somewhat circular argument, the evidence from other pollen spectra in the region also shows that neither *Pinus* nor *Tilia* were of local or regional importance during this period of soil/sediment deposition (Late Iron Age–Romano-British period).

Some taxa are, however, of more fragile character and might represent the autochthonous component, which are present by virtue of their high pollen production and rapid incorporation into the sediments. These include notably *Alnus*, *Sparganium* type, Poaceae, and Cyperaceae.

It may thus be tentatively assumed that these indicate the existence of fen carr and sedge community in shallow water and/or muddy conditions during the period of fen clay deposition, or nearby if pollen was falling on the old land surface. Alder appears to have been important, perhaps becoming so as the fluvial conditions responsible for alluviation were changing to somewhat lower water levels, allowing the reestablishment of fen carr community with sedge and rooting aquatics along the fringes of the dry land. There is some evidence of woodland for this period with *Quercus* and *Corylus avellana* type, although the latter might also include *Myrica*, since pollen preservation did not allow differentiation between hazel and sweet gale. Pollen values are calculated as a percentage of total dryland pollen and also possibly include some residual (ie derived) *Quercus*, *Tilia*, and certainly *Pinus*. These elements might have had a suppressive effect on the contemporary pollen percentages of oak and hazel, which could result in the underestimation of the 'real' vegetational importance of these latter taxa. It is considered likely that some open woodland, comprising oak with hazel understorey, was growing on the drier, better drained soils of the near region. Furthermore, it is likely that this was managed woodland, although this can not be shown from these pollen data.

Other dryland communities present appear to have been grassland/pasture, evidenced by the high values of *Plantago lanceolata*, Poaceae, and other herbs. These taxa are consistent through all pollen assemblage zones in this sequence and might be indicative of the continuous presence of areas of grassland, perhaps pasture land. Evidence of arable activities is absent in the soil levels, although it is witnessed in the lower peats (FENG:1) and upper peats (FENG:3). From this, it is suggested that pasture was dominant on or near the sample site and that arable agriculture might have been going on slightly further afield.

The transition from the alluvium on which a drier land surface formed (FENG:2) to one of peat is a retrogressive, hydrosere transition. The change back to fen environment is manifest in the pollen zone FENG:3 with a decline in importance of *Alnus*. As suggested above, this formed a fringing carr community around the island, which changed to one of more open, species-rich sedge fen in shallow water. The change from telmatic alder carr to fen might reflect the post-Roman transgressive phase of the Fenland as a whole (see discussion in Waller 1994a). By the end of pollen zone FENG:3, this had resulted in shallow-water fen with rooting marginal aquatics including *Sparganium* (bur reeds and reed mace), *Menyanthes trifoliata*, *Alisma*, and *Sagittaria* in a sedge dominated environment.

The upper peats (lpaz FENG:3) provide a clearer representation of the vegetation of the medieval period, although it is unfortunately not possible to deduce the woodland structure from these pollen data. There is, however, evidence for the continuity of some woodland of mixed character. While *Quercus* and *Corylus avellana* (noted in the previous zone, FENG:2) remain important, there is evidence for other constituents in the woodland. It must be noted, however, that these elements, and also oak and hazel, might not have been growing in close association but as individual trees or stands in the environment. In addition to *Quercus* and *Corylus*, are *Fraxinus*, *Tilia*, and *Fagus* pollen.

These latter taxa are typically underrepresented in pollen spectra through low pollen production (*Tilia* and *Fraxinus* being entomophilous) and/or poor pollen (*Fagus*) dispersal characteristics (Andersen 1970 and 1973). Thus, the latter are likely to have been growing near the sample site. Conversely, the small percentages of *Betula* and *Pinus* are not considered as being of local importance because of their high pollen productivity and anemophilous characteristics.

The dryland flora represented in FENG:3, in addition to some woodland, also has evidence of both grassland and arable agriculture. The former is possibly grassland for pastoral agriculture, since the region was undoubtedly largely cleared of woodland at an earlier date (Neolithic/Early Bronze Age) for such purposes. This can only be conjectured, since pollen assemblages from grassland communities and managed pasture appear similar.

Ranunculus type, *Dianthus* type, *Ononis* type, *Trifolium* type, *Medicago* type, *Vicia* type, *Rumex*, Scrophulariaceae, *Plantago lanceolata*, Asteraceae types, and Poaceae might be referable to this habitat.

These are broad pollen categories, however, and the taxa might also include some genera growing in the fen mire community. Segetals and ruderals along with cereal pollen are evidence of arable/cereal cultivation taking place on drier soils surrounding the fen. Typical are Brassicaceae (*Sinapis* type), *Chenopodium* type, *Polygonum aviculare* type, *Persicaria maculosa* type, *Plantago coronopus* type, *P. major* type (although *P. media* is included and might be referable to pastoral habitats), and cereal type pollen (*Hordeum*/*Triticum* type). Of particular note is the occurrence of *Humulus* type. This pollen taxon includes *Cannabis sativa*, which, in good pollen preserving conditions, can be delimited from *Humulus*. Unfortunately, this was not possible here. It is possible that *Humulus* (hop) was a natural constituent of the flora of the region, typically growing in fen carr. Alternatively, it is possible that *Cannabis sativa* (hemp) was being cultivated locally for fibre. Godwin (1967) and Bradshaw (*et al* 1981) have previously discussed the subject, which would be in accord with the known agriculture of the medieval period in the Fenland. Apart from this and the undoubted arable cultivation, no other evidence of cultivated crops was forthcoming from this or other pollen sequences at this site.

Palaeobotanical evidence from the platform floor

Few archaeobotanical studies have been carried out on lake dwellings in Britain, but of note are the pollen and macrofossil analyses of Houseley for the Meare lake dwellings (Houseley 1987) and for Oakbank Crannog in Loch Tay, Scotland, of Bronze Age date (Clapham and Scaife 1988). Such analyses have, however, been commonplace in Europe since the earliest and classic works on European lake dwellings by Munro (1882 and 1890) and Keller (1866).

At Flag Fen, pollen samples have been taken spatially from the surface levels of the platform.

Floor coverings of sand have been found at a number of sites in Britain and Europe. At Oakbank Crannog in Loch Tay (Dixon 1982), such deposits have yielded pollen and seed assemblages (Clapham and Scaife 1988). It was considered that the sands at Flag Fen might also be remnants of floor covering and, therefore, worthy of investigation for introduced plant commodities.

A small number of samples have been analysed (Fig 13.5). The results show some differences between the pollen spectra from the long peat pollen sequences taken from near the platform and the samples obtained from these platform floor levels. Pollen analysis of the Oakbank Crannog samples proved interesting, showing that the floral elements were different to other organic horizons forming the occupational debris of this submerged site.

It was clear from the examination of these deposits (both sand and organic) that the taphonomy of the contained pollen and seeds might be complex. This is discussed in full and a tentative model of the sources of pollen and seeds has been outlined (Clapham and Scaife 1988). This is relevant to the interpretation and discussion of the pollen assemblages so far analysed from Flag Fen floor horizons. It was hoped that a plot of the spatial patterns of pollen variation would portray patterns of variation of a number of taxa growing on, or being used on the platform.

Certain problems became apparent, however, in attempting to study the pollen in such spatial contexts:

- Pollen contained in the sand mentioned above might have been derived from the sources of sand (dry land).
- Peat in the interstices of the platform was not satisfactory because of its compaction from above into the voids between timbers.
- Since the full scale of the site is now realised, such a project could take many years and would require much larger areas to be excavated before meaningful results could be obtained.
- The number of individual floor horizons now delimited increases the above problem considerably.

- The total number of pollen samples that would require analysis would run into many hundreds, or even thousands.
- From the samples investigated, there appears to be little inherent variation, although herb numbers seem to be greater than in the adjacent fen deposits.

Those samples examined from the platform floor (Level 1) have been shown in diagram form (Fig 13.5), although it should be noted that these have no vertical context but are all from one horizontal level/floor. In the pollen samples analysed, the diversity of herbs is substantially greater than noted in the contemporaneous fen peats (FFP:2). Cereal type pollen is present with values ranging from 1% to 9% of dryland taxa. This is substantially more than that recorded in the adjacent peat, which attains a maximum value of around 2% of dryland pollen.

Also possibly associated with this cereal pollen are a variety of segetal taxa. The taphonomy of these cereals and segetal taxa might be complex. Among a number of sources that could be postulated for the derivation of the pollen are: straw roofing materials, straw floor coverings and bedding (human/animal); cereal processing and/or storage (although no macroremains of cereals have yet been recovered); and finally, pollen derived from human and/or animal dung. With regard to the latter, cereal pollen is frequently recovered from faecal material since it is present in food/bread and passes readily through the gut (Greig 1981 and 1982c; Hall *et al* 1983; Scaife 1986 and 1993a, b). No evidence was found for any crop-processing activity in either the pollen or seed samples analysed.

Looking at other elements of the pollen component, *Urtica* type reaches values of up to 12% of dryland pollen. This taxon includes *Urtica* (nettle) and *Parietaria* (pellitory), both typical of growth in areas of waste ground and human disturbance. Either taxon could have typically been growing on the platform surface and/or walls. If the *Urtica/Parietaria* was of autochthonous origin this might imply that the platform had drier areas. In the case of *Urtica*, a nitrogen-rich environment might be in evidence, caused by enrichment from animal urine and dung.

On the other hand, it is clear that the aquatic conditions in which the platform was constructed are equally evidenced in the floor samples, which contain diverse ranges of aquatic types, such as *Callitriche*, *Elatine*, *Nuphar*, *Nymphaea*, *Typha latifolia*, *Sparganium* type, and the ferns *Osmunda regalis* and *Isoetes lacustris*. The presence of these may be interpreted as pollen from the adjacent fen raining on to the platform structure. It is also possible that the pollen derives from deposition during seasonally high water levels directly on to the platform. This is pertinent to the interpretations of Robinson (1992 and Chapter 15), who has suggested that at least part of the platform was continuously under water.

Flag Fen Platform

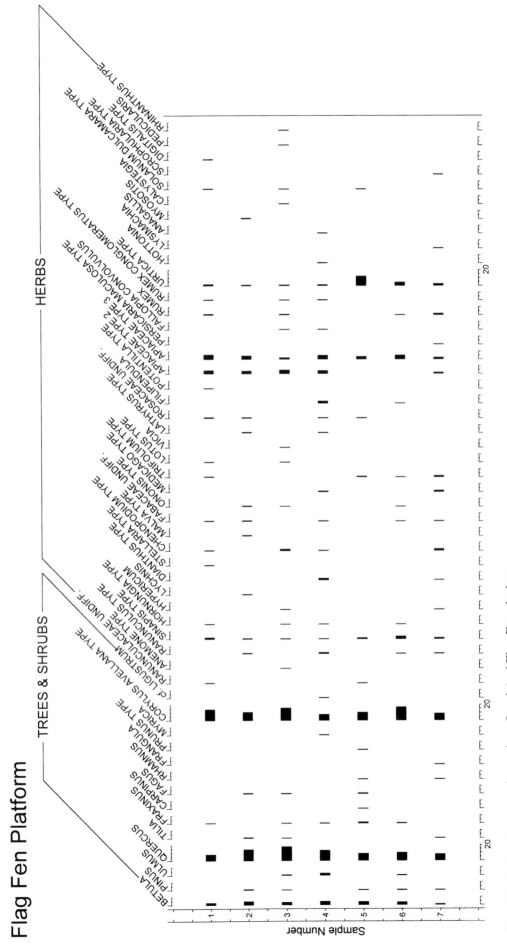

Fig 13.5 Pollen diagram of taxa from Level 1 of Flag Fen platform

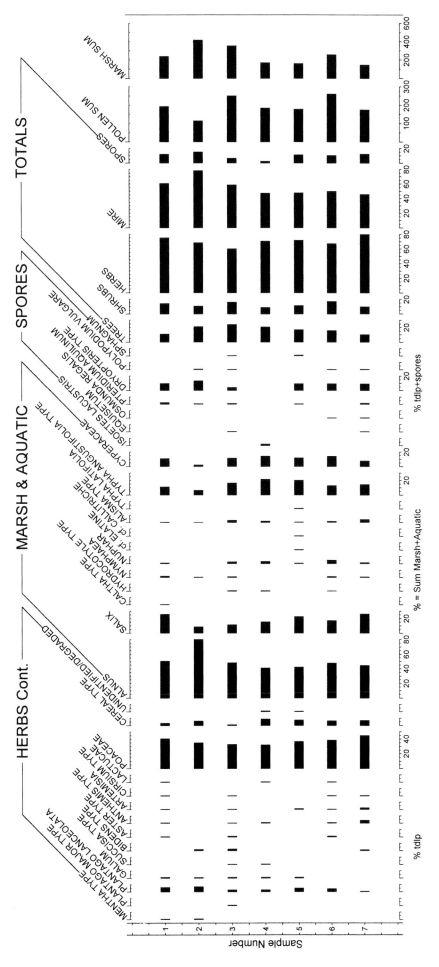

Fig 13.5 (cont'd)

Flag Fen: the changing environs

An attempt has been made here to correlate the pollen zones recognised and the environmental changes inferred from these pollen data. This is also summarised in Table 13.1.

The aquatic-fen environment

Subsequent to pollen analysis, radiocarbon dating has been carried out by Scottish Universities Research and Reactor Centre, East Kilbride, on critical transitions between the organic and inorganic units. Attempts to date small wood fragments from within the peat of the mere section were not successful due to small size and mineral content. Dating of the peat was not attempted because of possible contamination from slurry deposited on the adjacent fields. Valuable dates have been obtained from the deepset part of the basin (the Northey profile), however, and from the fen edge at Fengate (Fengate B). These have provided a tentative chronology for the development and filling of the Flag Fen Basin. These data might be relevant to the western Fens as a whole. This information is tabulated and further discussed below:

1 cal BC 2030–1680 (GU-5618; 3500±60 BP). Freshwater inundation of the Neolithic palaeosol in the deepest parts of the basin (Northey). Deposition of sediments and *gyttja* within reed swamp and open water.
2 cal BC 1530–1260 (GU-5617; 3130±60 BP). Hydroseral succession and development of fen peat from the centre of the basin upwards and outwards.

3 cal BC 1210–900 (GU-5620; 2840±50 BP). Continued lateral extension of peat growth to the present fen-edge margins (Fengate B). Diachroneity of peat developing at later time periods over soils at higher levels above OD.
4 cal BC 410–200 (GU-5619; 2290±50 BP) and cal BC 400–90 (GU-5616, 2180±60 BP). Continued peat accumulation in the fen basin produced a widespread surface that was inundated by alluvium during the Late Iron Age.
5 Rising water tables and flooding of the fens caused by allogenic processes (?woodland clearance or late Bronze Age/Iron Age eustatic change). Deposition of alluvium over wide areas.
6 Alluvium continuing to accumulate through overbank deposition, until a phase of drying out in the post-Roman period (undated) and pedogenesis on the fen margins (Fengate).
7 Reexpansion of wetland initiated by rising base levels. Peat formed over the alluvium and soils during the medieval period.

In the pollen sequences discussed here, there is evidence of change from dry land to freshwater reed swamp and subsequently into a rich fen, peat-forming community. This change probably resulted from regional base level changes initiated throughout the Fenland from *c* 6000 to *c* 3600 BP (Waller 1994a, 54). Waterlogging and freshwater conditions became prevalent in the deepest part of the basin (Northey section) at cal BC 2030–1680 (GU-5618; 3500±60 BP), that is, during the Early Bronze Age. Development and transition to rich sedge fen occurred diachronously across the basin from cal BC 1530–1260 (GU-5617;

Table 13.1 Suggested correlation of pollen assemblage zones and summary of environmental change

unit	pollen zones	vegetation
upper peat	FENG:3	Oak woodland with mixed agriculture. Reed swamp with less alder carr.
palaeosol	FENG:2	Oak and hazel woodland with some linden? Alder carr with sedges. Bracken scrub.
alluvial deposit	FFM:3 FFP:3 FFN:5	Oak and hazel dominant. Beech and other trees locally. Aquatic and marsh taxa important. Fringing alder willow carr. Mixed agriculture.
upper peat	FFM:2 FFN:4 FFP:3 FENG:1	Oak and hazel but reduced in lower part; building material? Recovery at top. Also alder reduced from felling? Alder/willow carr remains important, many aquatic/fen taxa.
lower peat	FFM:2 FFN:3 FFP:2 FENG:1	Oak, ash, hazel important. Lindens remain local but declining. Beech present. Evidence of pastoral agriculture. Freshwater aquatic macrophytes. Alder/willow carr fringing dry land.
gyttja lower silt	FFN:2 FFN:1	Oak and hazel dominant with linden woodland nearby. Centre of basin lake with reed swamp colonising. Evidence of agriculture.
basal palaeosol	FFM:1	Post-elm decline, oak, ash, linden woodland. Alder carr fringing wet basin. Basin reed swamp. Evidence of cereal cultivation.
Devensian gravels		No pollen in basal gravels. Presumed cold stage. Devensian outwash.

3130±60 BP) to cal BC 410–200 (GU-5619; 2840±50 BP). Construction of the platform and Fengate post sequence took place within this period of fen expansion and peat accumulation, from 1300–1250 BC, with major enlargement of the post alignment (and perhaps the platform too) throughout the eleventh century BC, and with final repairs at 955 BC. Subsequently, continued regional eustatic change (around 400–200 BC) produced waterlogging, causing alluviation during the Late Iron Age and Romano-British periods. A period of drying out occurred with soil formation on the alluvium. The Fengate upper peat levels appear to show a changing fluvial environment, again with higher base levels, which resulted in the reformation of fen peat during the medieval period.

An attempted correlation has been made between fen-margin and central-basin pollen sequences. The character of the Flag Fen vegetation itself (the autochthonous component) is important since it represents the environment in which the platform was constructed.

Palynologists have often disregarded the character of this component in pollen studies, simply regarding the pollen produced by on-site vegetation communities as masking the wider aspects of the regional terrestrial environments and human activity. The mire is here regarded as important to the study of the raft and the environment in which it was constructed. Such data must also be viewed in light of the evidence obtained from other environmental studies undertaken, including diatom, plant macrofossil, wood and coleopteran assemblages, and soil and sediments (see Chapters 7, 8, 14, and 15).

In the mere and platform sections, the underlying buried soil, apart from showing the importance of *Tilia* woodland, also shows *Alnus*, Cyperaceae, and *Typha angustifolia/Sparganium* type. *Alnus* pollen in palaeosols underlying the fen peats has also been noted by Waller (1993). This possibly relates to the local growth of alder fen carr communities fringing the edge of the encroaching sedge/reed fen community and in damp embayments peripheral to the fen. *Alnus* favours or can tolerate waterlogged and nutrient-rich conditions (Bennett and Birks 1990; Brown 1988; McVean 1953 and 1956). The growth of alder carr communities, which also contained *Salix* and other fen carr shrubs and herbs, was controlled in this region by both the long- and short-term hydrological fluctuations (water table) and the possible effects of the use of its timber in construction of the Flag Fen platform. The consistent occurrence of alder throughout all pollen sequences examined here might be largely due to its characteristics of high pollen production and wind dispersal. Thus, a spatially changing pattern of alder growth consequent upon transgressive sedge/reed swamp invasion over a relatively small basin area might not be evidenced in pollen profiles taken some hundreds of metres apart. It can, however, be noted that the mere and platform sequences and section 4 (Figs 13.1–13.3)

exhibit consistency of alder numbers throughout the profiles whereas the Fengate sequence (Fig 13.4) shows fluctuating values in both the lower and upper peat horizons. Considering that the Fengate sequence represents the fringing peats of the Flag Fen Basin (where *Alnus* was thought to be more important), it seems plausible that here, evidence of fluctuating water table is being seen and/or felling, causing the demise of some areas of alder. The latter idea is especially attractive, since the marked decline from 0.84m to 0.72m at Fengate B is stratigraphically correlated with the period of platform construction. The transgressive nature of the fen mire should also be considered in correlating these sequences. It can be noted that *Quercus* also shows some reduction at this time in both peat sequences and that these taxa were especially important in construction of the fen platform.

There is no question that the Fens to the east became progressively waterlogged from the middle Holocene (Waller 1993). Here, freshwater inundation occurred in the deepest part of the basin (Northey) at cal BC 2030–1680 (GU-5618; 3500±60 BP). There is evidence, especially in the deeper Northey Section, but also in the mere and platform profiles, that the environment in which the platform was constructed was one of shallow water. A range of pollen and plant macrofossils of shallow water rooting aquatics are growing during its period of construction. These include yellow water and white water lily (*Nuphar luteum* and *Nymphaea alba*), water milfoil (*Myriophyllum* spp), water plantain (*Alisma plantago-aquatica*), arrowhead (*Sagittaria*), pondweed (*Potamogeton*), *Typha latifolia* (common reed mace), and especially lesser reed mace/bur reed type (*Sparganium* type). Wet/damp ground plant taxa characteristic of muddy/shoreline environments occur, including particularly marsh marigold (*Caltha palustris*), meadowsweet (*Filipendula*), marsh pennywort (*Hydrocotyle vulgaris*), and possibly shoreweed (*Littorella uniflora*), which might have been growing on or along the platform or fringing the fen swamp. Cyperaceae (sedge) pollen also relates to the fen community although genus/species attribution has not been made. It is likely that these include sedges rooting in shallow water such as saw sedge (*Cladium mariscus*) although there is also the strong possibility that taxa from the alder fen carr are also represented (eg *Carex paniculata*, the tussock sedge). It is concluded that the platform was built in a shallow water/aquatic fen environment. It appears from the pollen data given in paz FFP:2 and FFM:2 that these conditions prevailed throughout the Bronze Age during which the peat accumulated.

There is no evidence for fluctuations in the water table, but rather a progression towards more aquatic conditions. The pollen data are not detailed enough to ascertain any seasonal fluctuations in the fen although it is probable that standing water was a permanent feature, enabling the continuity of growth of taxa noted above.

Comparing the pollen sequences from the central part of the basin with the fringing one represented by the Fengate section, a lesser preponderance of aquatic and fen taxa in the latter would be expected. In fact, this is only partially the case. It is apparent that in the lower peats, the numbers of aquatic macrophytes is small. In the soil at Fengate (lpaz FENG:1) there is, however, a strong representation of plants typically rooting in shallow water or muddy/sediment environments fringing aquatic habitats. There are, in consequence, high values of reed mace/bur reed (*Typha angustifolia*/*Sparganium* type), sedges (Cyperaceae) and also meadowsweet (*Filipendula*), water plantain (*Alisma* type; cf *Alisma plantago-aquatica*), arrowhead (*Sagittaria*), bog bean (*Menyanthes*), and flag (*Iris*). This suggests that the lateral, circumzonal vegetation of the fen immediately adjacent to or in association with the alder/willow carr discussed above is here apparent. In the mere section in particular, there is evidence of increasing water depth towards the transition from fen peat to alluvium. Correspondingly, in the upper peat levels of paz FENG:1 (Fengate B), there is evidence of this transgressive phase and indications of increasingly wetter conditions with white water lily (*Nymphaea alba*), water milfoil (*Myriophyllum* spp), and pond weed (*Potamogeton*). Also noted is a small peak of the algae *Pediastrum*, indicative of aquatic conditions. The marked peak in *Sparganium* type in the upper levels of FENG:1 attests to its strong 'on-site' importance and from this it is likely that this was a transgressive belt of fringing *Typha angustifolia*/*Sparganium*, which reached dominance at the sample site prior to inundation by true riverine/alluvial conditions during the Late Iron Age at cal BC 400–90 (GU-5616; 2180±60 BP, ie FENG:2). It is also possible that extensive clearance of local woodland resulted in changes in the local hydrology leading to a reduction in evapotranspiration rates, increased surface run-off, and/or higher groundwater table in the local area. Such changes might be manifest by changes in the local vegetation to taxa characteristic of a wetter environment. The now widespread evidence for regional inundation and perimarine sedimentation further east in the Fenland at this time, however, negates this argument, or at least such local anthropogenic effects might have been masked by more regional and natural changes in base level.

The alluvial deposits that cap the fen peats appear to do so conformably with no evidence, at least at Flag Fen, for truncation of the upper peat levels. It appears that regional inundation occurred with ponding back of the Fenland river systems (here the Ouse and Welland) during the Late Iron Age period. Deposition of alluvium took place over a large area. The aquatic character of these sediments has been studied from diatom assemblages, which provide evidence of its largely freshwater status but with some indications of brackish water taxa (Juggins nd). The pollen assemblages from the basin pollen sequences, however, illustrate a continuity of those aquatic and mire taxa

present in the peat, with no real evidence for an increase in percentages of these aquatic taxa in the overlying alluvium. This might be explained by the fact that pollen in these sediments could also contain a strong allochthonous component fluvially transported from farther afield. This is especially pertinent to *Alnus*, which occurs consistently. At Fengate B, pollen in the alluvium has been largely destroyed because of a period of dryness that resulted in pedogenesis in its upper levels. Only *Alnus* and some *Sparganium* type remain.

In the centre of the basin, the retrogressive hydrosere ended with a fall in base level, a period of soil formation and later, a return to peat-forming, fen-mire conditions in the post-Roman/medieval period. The 'Upper Peats', which accumulated over wide areas of the south-west fen, are absent in the centre of Flag Fen, where they have been destroyed through peat drainage and agriculture. At Fengate they do, however, survive, attaining a thickness of up to 0.2m. On the edges of the fen as represented at Fengate, a retrogressive phase is again shown in the pollen sequence, since it appears that the upper fen clay was subject to drying out, pedogenesis, and then progressive waterlogging to produce fen peat. Thus, the *Alnus* present in the buried soil might mark a transitionary phase from alder growth to one of reed swamp dominated by *Menyanthes trifoliata*, *Alisma* type, *Sagittaria*, *Iris*, *Sparganium* type, and Cyperaceae.

The Flag Fen Basin development: a summary

Dry land, which supported lime dominated woodland growing on an argillic brown earth in this area, was inundated by sedge fen/reed swamp during the Bronze Age. In the deepest parts of the basin, this occurred earlier at cal BC 2030–1680 (GU-5618; 3500±60 BP), while at the margins this was later at cal BC 1210–900 (GU-5620; 2840±50 BP). Species-rich aquatic fen and marginal reed swamp colonised the basin as the water table continued to rise. It was during this phase that the Flag Fen platform was constructed and although evidence is tentative, there are indications that locally growing alder and oak were utilised in its construction. Throughout the development of the main fen peat sequence (pollen zones FFP:2 and FENG:1), there is evidence of increasing wetness, with expansions in numbers of aquatic taxa in the mere sections and rooting marginal aquatics on the fringes of the fen as seen at Fengate. There is, however, continued representation of alder, which is likely to have formed a fen carr community along the fringes of the mire.

In the mere sequences, there is a consistent presence of alder throughout the pollen profiles.

In the marginal areas of the fen mire as illustrated by the Fengate sequence, the values show marked fluctuations. These changes are interpreted as changes in the 'on-site' vegetation community caused by natural and/or anthropogenic factors. Continued rise in water table through the Bronze Age was possibly responsible for the building and rebuilding of the higher floor levels of the Flag Fen platform.

Ultimately, during the Late Iron Age period, fen/reed swamp conditions with peat formation gave way to deposition of the 'upper alluvial deposits'. Subsequently in the Roman or post-Roman period, falling base level allowed drying out of the alluvium and soil formation. This was again superseded by rising base levels and reincursion of wetter conditions with fen and peat accumulation. These peats are now absent from the centre of the basin (due to peat wastage and agriculture), but remain isolated on the fen edge at Fengate. They are also undated but are of suspected medieval period.

Terrestrial vegetation of the environment around Flag Fen: a summary

Interpretation of the pollen data must take into account the changing character of the terrestrial vegetation caused by possible anthropogenic activity, and by the fact that the dryland vegetation (represented in the basal levels of the pollen diagram) became progressively further from the environs of the Flag Fen platform, as the peat-forming community progressively inundated the edges of the Flag Fen Basin. This is relevant, since the area of the pollen catchment will have become larger in the more open fen-mire environment than that of soil in a woodland environment. Other dispersal factors might also cause fluctuations in input from nearby terrestrial plant communities. For example, the growth and/or movement of fringing alder carr and other woodland might have a filtration effect, as suggested by Tauber (1965 and 1967), and any anthropogenic and/or natural changes in such communities will cause fluctuations in pollen rain into the fen. This might be especially pertinent here, in view of the very substantial numbers of alder and oak timbers used in the platform construction. It has also been noted above that there were fluctuating values for *Alnus*, which might be evidence of clearance and/or movement of an alder carr community fringing the expanding or contracting basin.

The vegetation of the fen basin prior to inundation by reed swamp comprised dominant *Tilia* woodland with a variety of other deciduous elements. The oldest pollen sequences analysed from the Flag Fen Basin are pollen assemblage zones FFP:1, FFM:1, and FFN:1 (the basal palaeosol underlying the Fen peats). This is attributed to the Late Neolithic/Early Bronze Age with

small percentages of *Ulmus* indicating a post-elm-decline date (ie c 5500–5000 BP) for pollen incorporated into this soil. Discussion of the elm-decline phenomenon is not included here (see Scaife 1988; Smith 1970 and 1981) but is important in illustrating that in these pollen sequences we are dealing with an environment where there has been potential for Neolithic agricultural activities. In these lower levels, there is some evidence of agriculture, with cereal pollen occurring in the basal palaeosol, although a few other herbs, including *Plantago lanceolata* and Chenopodiaceae are present. It is possible that this might correlate with the evidence for earlier phases of Fengate activity (Pryor 1974). If this is so, it would appear that the environment of the Late Neolithic/Early Bronze Age comprised a mosaic of woodland and mixed agricultural land. This would also be in accord with environmental data from Etton Neolithic enclosure and subsequent Beaker activity. There are marked contrasts between the pollen analysis of the buried soil under the peat and the pollen sequences obtained from the peat of the central basin. The high values of *Tilia* in the soil profile, representing 'on-site' growth, give way to more consistent occurrences of *Quercus* and *Corylus avellana* in the peat. There are, however, also sporadic occurrences of tree taxa that have much poorer pollen production and dispersal characteristics than oak and hazel. These taxa include *Tilia*, *Fraxinus*, and *Fagus*, all of which are underrepresented in pollen assemblages. Thus, it is concluded that the peat sequence, although showing the relative dominance of oak and hazel (perhaps managed woodland during the Bronze Age), also indicates that a diverse range of deciduous trees remained in the landscape surrounding the Flag Fen platform.

From the earliest cereal cultivation noted above, there is a progressive increase in the number and diversity of herb pollen taxa, which might be attributed to agricultural activity. These, as noted in relevant sections above, include taxa that are often used as indicators of pastoral and/or arable agriculture. Although it is difficult to define pastoralism in pollen spectra, it is suggested from the pollen data that a mixed arable and pastoral economy was practised during the Middle–later Bronze Age on the drier and better drained soils of the land surrounding Flag Fen Basin. This also provides evidence for the continuity of human activity on the fringes of Flag Fen from the Late Neolithic/Early Bronze Age through to the Late Iron Age activity noted in pollen assemblage zones FENG:3, FFM:3, and FFN:5. This is not unexpected, given the possibility that these soils were likely to have been fertile and well drained.

14 Soils and sediments: the Flag Fen environs survey
by C A I French

A series of three machine trenches was cut on the east side of Mustdyke and the eastern edge of the Flag Fen platform (Fig 6.1) in order to prospect for buried soils, well preserved peat deposits (for pollen analysis), and for further evidence of archaeological activity. Trench 2 was located on the extreme north-western edge of Northey 'island'. It revealed the following stratigraphic sequence:

0–0.3m	ploughsoil (1.96m OD)
0.3–0.72m	desiccated peat
0.72–1.05m	desiccated peat and alluvial silty clay
1.05–1.1m	gravel lens (probably dyke upcast)
1.1–1.24m	buried soil; a pale greyish brown silty (clay) loam with oxidation mottling
1.24m+	fen gravel subsoil (0.72m OD)

A sample block through the buried soil was taken for micromorphological analysis.

Trench 1 revealed a similar sequence, but without the presence of dyke upcast and a buried soil. This trench was located off the 'island' and in the basin. The top of the underlying subsoil now dipped to 0.22m OD.

Trench 3 was located beyond the northern extent of the platform in the narrow 'neck' of fen between the Fengate and Northey 'island' shores. Beneath about 1m of desiccated peat mixed with alluvial silty clays, there remained a substantial depth (c 1m+) of waterlogged peat and grey lacustrine silt. The lower part of this sequence was sampled for pollen analysis (Chapter 13).

The soil block taken from Trench 2 was made into a 'mammoth' thin section using the methodology of Murphy (1986) and described using the accepted conventions in Bullock et al (1985). Detailed micromorphological descriptions are given in Appendix 5.

Description

In the field, the buried soil appeared to be all one horizon of a poorly developed soil, much affected by subsequent root action and oxidation mottling. In thin section, the soil exhibited two distinct horizons, each approximately 70mm thick.

The upper horizon of the palaeosol consisted of a dense, homogeneous, pale yellowish brown, loamy sand. It is dominated by very fine quartz sand (50%), with only minor silt (10%) and clay (5%) components. It is devoid of structure and organic matter. The only minor inclusions of note were rare aggregates of silty clay and minute fragments of pure clay within the groundmass.

The lower horizon is similarly dense, homogeneous, inorganic, and apedal, but its greater oriented clay component gives it a sandy loam texture. The clay component (15%) is dominated by non-laminated dusty or impure clay coatings exhibiting greater or lesser concentrations within the groundmass and also within the voids, and to a lesser extent as coatings on sand grains. There were also rare to occasional non-laminated limpid or pure clays within the groundmass and rare laminated dusty clay coatings of voids.

Interpretation

This thin palaeosol contains evidence of some soil development, in terms of the presence of two horizons and clay illuviation features, but there has been little in the way of development of soil structure.

The depleted nature of the upper half of this palaeosol suggests that it is a lower A or Eb horizon of a brown earth (after Avery 1980). The distinct absence of organic matter, and to a lesser extent a fines component, indicates that this horizon has been subject to severe leaching. To a large extent, this is undoubtedly associated with subsequent freshwater flooding associated with peat fen development. On the other hand, the minor presence of fragments of pure clay and the rolled silty clay aggregates suggest that this soil occasionally received alluvially derived fine material prior to the advent of peat formation.

The lower horizon contains sufficient oriented clay pedofeatures to suggest that it was a lower B or Bw horizon of a moderately well developed brown earth (after Avery 1980). Nonetheless, the greater and lesser zones of intensity of oriented clay formation within this horizon suggests that this part of the profile also suffered considerable post-depositional leaching. The minor presence of pure or limpid clay within the groundmass points to some initial illuviation occurring under stable, perhaps wooded conditions (after Macphail et al 1987). The soil then suffered some disturbance, which caused the within-soil illuviation of impure or silty clay down-profile. Although it is impossible to directly ascribe this feature to human activities, it could be associated with clearance activities opening up the surface of the soil and making it more susceptible to illuviation. Finally, impure or silty clay coatings are acting as void and root channel infills, which might either be associated with the alluvial conditions noted to affect the upper horizon of this soil, and/or are indicative of recent leaching and the down-profile movement of fines.

Up to about one-third of the groundmass of both horizons is affected by amorphous sesquioxide impregnation, especially around the void space and root zones. This could well be a relatively recent feature associated with the general drying out of this fenland basin.

The presence of a rather poorly developed brown earth on the western edge of Northey 'island' is consistent with the results of other micromorphological investigations undertaken in this area. Micromorphological analysis by the writer of nine profiles on the Fengate terrace/fen-edge area to the west and south-west of the Flag Fen platform has indicated similar results (French 1992a and Chapter 3). On the higher and better drained ground, argillic brown earths formed under former woodland conditions, which become less well developed brown earths as the land dips fenward. These soils are gradually affected through time by human activities and freshwater flooding in the form of alluvial deposition and peat development.

To the south on the south-western edge of Northey island, an extensive buried soil was observed over long distances, exposed in freshly cleaned dykesides. This was examined micromorphologically in two places and indicated the presence of a well preserved brown earth that might have been subject to ploughing in the Bronze Age (French in French and Pryor 1993, 97–9).

Conclusions

The examination of the palaeosol immediately to the east and adjacent to the Flag Fen platform has revealed the presence of a brown earth soil developed on a fen gravel subsoil. This is complementary to the evidence recovered from another 11 profiles already examined on the Fengate first terrace and Northey 'island' shores. As the basin dips below about 0.5m OD, the buried soil, if present, tends to be thinner and less well developed. Immediately beneath the Flag Fen platform, no real soil development is evident. The main implication of this work is that it indicates the presence of well drained, relatively fertile and base-rich soils on the land immediately surrounding the Flag Fen Basin. As the peat fen gradually encroached upon this diminishing dryland soil resource during the later second and first millennia BC, these soils suffered increased leaching and eventual burial.

15 Late Bronze Age Coleoptera from Flag Fen

by Mark Robinson

A column of samples was taken at intervals of *c* 0.05m through the peat and buried soil for macroscopic plant and insect remains, immediately to the outside and south of the platform. The column was about 0.85m in length but the top 0.35m (Column B) was slightly off-set from the bottom 0.5m (Column A); the sample location is shown in Figure 6.40 (Pollen Sampling Trench). Bulk samples were also taken from well estab-lished contexts on the Late Bronze Age platform (both were from Area 6B, Level 2; Platform Sample 1 was from grid 2708 8884 and Platform Sample 2 from below timber B61 at grid 2709 8883).

From each sample, 250g was sieved over a stack of sieves down to 0.2mm and sorted for plant and inver-tebrate remains. Insect remains were absent from the buried soil and very sparse in the bottom 0.2m of the peat. Well preserved insect remains were present in the upper 0.6m of the column and in the bulk samples. The insects showed little faunal variation throughout the column. Therefore alternate samples only were examined in more detail from most of the column. A further subsample of each of these column samples, bringing them up to 1kg, was washed over a 0.2mm mesh, subjected to paraffin flotation, the flot washed with hot water and detergent, and sorted for insect remains. Further material was processed from the two bulk samples for insect remains, bringing each up to 4kg.

Results

The minimum number of individuals for each species of Coleoptera in each sample is given in Table 15.1. Nomenclature follows Kloet and Hincks 1977. The Coleoptera are broken down into habitat-related groups expressed as percentages of the total ter-restrial Coleoptera in Figure 15.1 and Table 15.2.

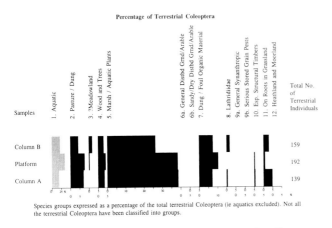

Fig 15.1 Species groups of Coleoptera from Flag Fen

Further details of the habitat groups are given in Robinson (1981, 1983, and 1991). The host plants of the phytophagous species are given in Table 15.3.

General environmental conditions

The assemblages of Coleoptera from all the samples, including those from the platform, showed a strong fenland character. The largest group of Coleoptera comprised species that feed on marsh or aquatic plants, followed by aquatic species. A very high proportion of the remaining beetles occur in other fenland habitats. There was, however, also an element from the back-ground landscape to the fen that included both pas-tureland and some woodland.

Surprisingly, there was little evidence for dead wood or human habitation from the insects.

The fen

The relatively high proportion of aquatic beetles sug-gests that the deposits sampled accumulated at least partly under water. The most numerous water beetle was *Ochthebius minimus* but various other species most-ly favouring well vegetated stagnant water, such as *Hydrochus* sp and *Dytiscus* sp, were also present. There was a strong amphibious element, including some Hydraenidae and *Dryops* sp. There were also numerous Scirtidae (cf *Cyphon* sp), which have larvae that live in shallow water and adults that occur on waterside vege-tation. The only flowing water beetle to be identified was a single specimen of *Oulimnius* sp, suggesting that the majority of the aquatic insects had their origins in the fen rather than that they were transported in the floodwaters of the river.

The most abundant of the phytophagous beetles was *Tanysphyrus lemnae*, which was present in almost all the samples. It is a weevil that feeds on species of *Lemna* (duckweed), a small free-floating plant that carpets standing water. There were also many chrysomelids, which feed on emergent reed-swamp vegetation. The main reed-swamp monocots seem to have been *Phragmites australis* (reed), as indicated by *Donacia clavipes* and *Plateumaris braccata*, and *Sparganium erectum* (bur-reed), the host of *Donacia marginata*. Aquatic Umbelliferae, probably *Oenanthe* sp (water dropwort) are suggested by *Prasocuris phellandrii* and *Carex* spp (sedges) by *Plateumaris affinis*. *Schoenoplectus lacustris* (bulrush) does not seem to have been a major component of the reed swamp, there being only a single individual of *Donacia impressa*. Other minor components of the aquatic vegetation included *Nymphaea* or *Nuphar* sp (water-lily), the hosts of *Donacia* cf *crassipes*, *Sagittaria* (arrow-head),

Table 15.1 Coleoptera from Flag Fen (depths in mm)

	platform		column A						column B					total
	S1	S2	450–400	400–350	350–300	250–200	150–100	50–00	350–300	300–250	250–200	150–100	50–00	
Blethisa multipunctata (L)	–	1	–	–	–	–	–	1	–	–	1	–	1	4
Elaphrus cupreus Duft	–	1	–	–	–	–	–	–	–	–	–	–	–	1
E. riparius (L)	–	–	–	–	–	–	–	–	–	–	1	–	–	1
Dyschirius globosus (Hbst)	–	1	–	–	1	2	–	–	–	–	1	–	–	5
Trechus micros (Hbst)	–	–	–	–	–	–	–	–	–	–	–	1	–	1
Bembidion properans Step	–	1	–	–	–	–	–	–	–	–	–	–	–	1
B. semipunctatum Don	1	–	–	–	–	1	–	–	–	–	–	–	–	2
B. assimile Gyl or clarki Daw	1	–	–	–	–	–	–	–	–	–	–	–	–	1
B. doris (Pz)	–	1	–	–	–	–	–	–	–	–	–	–	–	1
Bembidion sp.	–	–	–	–	–	–	1	1	–	–	–	1	–	3
Pterostichus anthracinus (Pz)	–	–	–	–	–	–	1	–	–	–	–	–	–	1
P. aterrimus (Hbst)	2	1	–	–	–	–	–	1	–	–	–	–	–	4
P. gracilis (Dej)	1	–	–	–	–	–	–	–	–	–	–	–	–	1
P. melanariu (Ill)	–	–	–	–	–	–	–	–	–	1	–	–	–	1
P. minor (Gyl)	2	–	–	–	–	–	1	2	–	–	1	1	2	9
P. nigrita (Pk)	–	–	–	–	–	–	–	–	–	–	–	1	1	2
P. cupreus (L) or versicolor (Sturm)	–	–	–	–	–	–	1	–	–	–	–	–	–	1
Synuchus nivalis (Pz)	–	–	–	–	–	1	–	–	–	–	–	–	–	1
Agonum fuliginosum (Pz)	–	1	–	–	–	–	–	–	–	–	–	–	–	1
A. obscurum (Hbst)	1	1	–	–	–	–	–	–	–	–	–	–	–	2
A. piceum (L)	–	1	–	–	–	–	–	–	–	–	–	–	–	1
A. thoreyi Dej	1	–	–	–	–	1	–	–	–	–	–	–	1	3
Agonum sp.	–	–	–	–	–	–	–	1	–	–	–	–	–	1
Amara sp.	–	1	–	–	–	–	–	–	–	–	1	1	–	3
Acupalpus flavicollis (Sturm)	–	1	–	–	–	–	–	–	–	–	–	1	–	2
Chlaenius tristis (Schal)	–	–	–	–	–	–	–	–	–	–	–	–	1	1
Odacantha melanura (L)	–	–	–	–	–	–	1	–	–	–	–	–	1	2
Haliplus sp.	1	1	–	–	–	–	–	–	–	–	–	–	–	2
Noterus clavicornis (Deg)	–	–	–	–	–	1	–	–	–	–	–	1	1	3
Hygrotus inaequalis (F)	2	6	–	–	–	–	–	–	–	–	–	–	–	8
Hydroporus sp.	1	1	–	–	–	–	–	–	–	–	1	–	–	3
Copelatus haemorrhoidalis (F)	–	1	–	–	–	–	–	–	–	–	–	–	–	1
Agabus bipustulatus (L)	–	–	–	–	–	–	1	–	–	–	1	–	1	3
Agabus sp. (not bipustulatus)	1	1	–	–	–	–	–	–	1	–	–	1	–	4
Rhantus sp.	1	–	–	–	–	–	–	–	–	–	–	–	1	2
Colymbetes fuscus (L)	1	1	–	–	–	–	–	1	–	–	–	–	1	4
Dytiscus sp.	1	2	–	–	–	–	1	–	–	–	–	–	–	4
Gyrinus sp.	1	–	–	1	1	–	–	–	–	–	–	–	–	3
Hydrochus sp.	2	1	–	–	1	–	–	1	1	–	–	–	1	7
Helophorus sp. (brevipalpis size)	–	–	–	–	–	1	2	–	–	–	1	–	–	4
Coelostoma orbiculare (F)	–	3	–	–	–	1	2	1	–	–	–	–	1	8
Cercyon haemorrhoidalis (F)	1	1	–	–	–	–	–	–	–	–	–	–	–	2
C. melanocephalus (L)	–	–	–	–	–	–	–	–	–	–	–	1	–	1
C. pygmaeus (Ill)	–	–	–	–	–	–	–	–	–	–	–	–	1	1
C. sternalis Sharp	4	2	–	–	–	1	2	1	–	–	–	–	1	11
Cercyon sp.	–	5	–	–	–	–	–	1	1	1	–	1	1	10
Megasternum obscurum (Marsh)	1	–	–	–	–	1	–	–	–	–	–	1	1	4
Hydrobius fuscipes (L)	1	2	–	–	–	–	1	1	–	–	1	1	–	7
Anacaena globulus (Pk)	–	–	–	–	–	–	–	–	–	–	2	–	–	2
A. bipustulata (Marsh) or limbata (F)	–	–	–	–	–	–	–	–	–	–	–	–	1	1
Helochares lividus (Forst) or obscurus (Müll)	1	–	–	–	–	–	–	–	–	–	–	–	–	1
Enochrus sp.	1	1	–	–	–	–	–	–	–	–	–	–	–	2
Hister bissexstriatus F	–	–	–	–	–	1	–	–	–	–	–	–	–	1
Ochthebius minimus (F)	3	9	–	–	–	–	1	–	–	–	1	1	–	15
O. cf. minimus (F)	6	7	–	–	2	1	1	3	–	–	2	3	5	30
Hydraena pulchella Germ	1	1	–	–	–	–	–	–	–	–	1	–	–	3
H. cf. riparia Ku	1	1	–	–	–	–	–	–	–	–	–	1	–	3

Table 15.1 (*Cont'd*)

	platform		column A						column B					total
	S1	S2	450–400	400–350	350–300	250–200	150–100	50–00	350–300	300–250	250–200	150–100	50–00	
H. testacea Cur	–	1	–	–	–	1	–	–	–	–	–	–	–	2
Limnebius aluata (Bed)	1	–	–	–	–	–	–	–	–	–	–	–	–	1
Ptiliidae indet. (not *Ptenidium*)	1	2	–	–	–	–	–	–	–	–	–	–	2	5
Silpha obscura L	–	–	–	–	–	1	–	–	–	–	–	–	–	1
Micropeplus caelatus Er	–	–	–	–	–	–	–	1	–	–	–	–	–	1
Olophrum fuscum (Grav) or *piceum* (Gyl)	2	1	–	–	–	–	2	–	–	–	–	–	–	5
Lesteva cf. *heeri* Fauv	–	1	–	–	–	–	–	–	–	–	–	–	–	1
Dropephylla ioptera (Step)	–	1	–	–	–	–	–	–	–	–	–	–	–	1
Carpelimus cf. *corticinus* (Grav)	–	–	–	–	–	–	–	–	–	–	1	2	–	3
C. cf. *rivularis* (Mots)	–	–	–	–	–	–	–	–	–	–	–	1	–	1
Platystethus cornutus gp	–	–	–	–	–	–	–	–	–	–	–	1	–	1
P. nitens (Sahl)	–	–	–	–	–	–	–	–	–	–	–	1	–	1
Anotylus rugosus (F)	1	1	–	–	–	–	–	–	–	–	1	–	1	4
A. sculpturatus gp	–	1	–	–	–	–	–	–	–	–	–	–	–	1
Stenus spp.	1	6	–	–	–	2	1	1	–	–	1	4	5	21
Paederus riparius (L)	–	1	–	–	–	–	–	–	–	–	–	–	–	1
Lathrobium spp.	1	2	–	–	–	–	–	1	–	–	1	3	2	10
Gyrohypnus fracticornis gp	–	1	–	–	–	–	–	–	–	–	–	–	–	1
Gyrohypnus sp.	–	–	–	–	–	–	1	–	–	–	–	–	–	1
Xantholinus longiventris Heer	1	–	–	–	–	–	–	–	–	–	–	–	–	1
X. linearis (Ol) or *longiventris* Heer	–	–	–	–	–	1	–	–	–	–	–	–	–	1
Philonthus spp.	1	1	–	–	–	–	–	–	–	–	–	1	1	4
Gabrius sp.	–	1	–	–	1	2	1	–	–	–	2	–	1	8
Staphylinus aeneocephalus Deg or *fortunatarum* (Woll)	–	–	–	–	–	–	–	–	–	–	1	–	–	1
Tachinus sp.	–	–	–	–	–	1	–	–	–	–	–	–	–	1
Aleocharinae indet.	1	4	–	–	–	1	1	–	–	1	–	2	1	11
Pselaphidae indet.	1	–	–	–	–	–	–	–	–	–	–	1	–	2
Geotrupes sp.	1	1	–	–	–	1	–	–	–	–	–	–	–	3
Aphodius contaminatus (Hbst)	–	–	–	–	–	–	–	–	–	–	–	1	–	1
A. cf. *foetidus* (Hbst)	1	–	–	–	–	–	–	–	–	–	–	–	–	1
A. granarius (L)	–	–	–	–	–	–	–	–	1	–	–	–	–	1
A. cf. *prodromus* (Brahm)	–	2	–	–	–	–	–	–	–	–	–	–	–	2
A. rufipes (L)	–	–	–	–	–	–	1	–	–	–	–	–	–	1
A. cf. *sphacelatus* (Pz)	4	5	–	–	–	1	2	–	–	–	–	1	2	15
Aphodius sp.	–	–	–	–	–	1	1	–	–	–	–	–	1	3
Onthophagus ovatus (L)	–	–	–	–	–	1	1	–	1	–	–	–	–	3
O. taurus (Schreb)	–	–	–	–	–	1	–	–	–	–	–	–	–	1
Onthophagus sp. (not *ovatus* or *taurus*)	1	–	–	–	–	–	–	–	–	–	–	–	–	1
Amphimallon solstitialis (L)	–	–	–	–	–	–	–	–	1	–	–	–	–	1
Phyllopertha horticola (L)	1	1	–	–	–	1	1	–	–	–	1	1	1	7
cf. *Cyphon* sp.	4	4	–	–	–	2	3	2	1	–	2	3	3	24
Dryops sp.	1	3	–	–	–	–	–	1	–	–	1	1	2	9
Oulimnius sp.	–	–	–	–	–	1	–	–	–	–	–	–	–	1
Agrypnus murinus (L)	–	–	–	–	–	1	1	–	–	–	–	–	–	2
Agriotes sputator (L)	–	–	–	–	–	–	–	–	1	–	–	–	–	1
Agriotes sp.	–	–	–	–	–	1	1	–	–	–	–	–	1	4
Silis ruficollis (F)	–	–	–	–	–	–	–	–	–	–	–	–	1	1
Grynobius planus (F)	–	1	–	–	–	1	1	–	1	1	–	1	–	6
Anobium punctatum (Deg)	–	1	–	–	–	–	1	–	–	–	–	–	–	2
Brachypterus urticae (F)	–	–	–	–	–	–	–	–	–	–	–	1	–	1
Meligethes sp.	–	–	–	–	–	1	–	–	–	–	–	–	–	1
Cryptophagidae indet. (not *Atomaria*)	–	–	–	–	–	–	–	–	1	–	–	–	–	1
Atomaria sp.	1	2	–	–	–	1	1	–	–	–	1	1	2	9
Phalacrus sp.	1	1	–	–	–	1	1	1	–	–	1	1	1	8
Corylophus cassidoides (Marsh)	–	1	–	–	1	1	1	–	–	–	–	1	1	6

Table 15.1 (*Cont'd*)

	platform		column A						column B					total
	S1	S2	450–400	400–350	350–300	250–200	150–100	50–00	350–300	300–250	250–200	150–100	50–00	
Coccidula rufa (Hbst)	–	–	–	–	–	1	–	–	–	–	–	–	–	1
Chilocorus renipustulatus (Scriba)	–	1	–	–	–	–	–	–	–	–	–	–	–	1
Coccinella sp.	–	1	–	–	–	–	–	–	–	–	–	–	–	1
Enicmus transversus (Ol)	–	–	–	–	–	–	1	–	–	–	–	–	–	1
Corticariinae indet.	–	–	–	–	–	–	–	–	–	–	–	2	1	3
Donacia cinerea Hbst	1	1	1	–	–	3	1	1	–	–	–	–	2	10
D. clavipes F	–	1	–	–	–	1	–	–	–	–	–	1	2	5
D. cf. *crassipes* F	1	–	–	–	–	–	–	–	–	1	–	–	–	2
D. dentata Hop	–	1	–	–	–	–	–	–	–	–	–	–	–	1
D. cf. *impressa* Pk	–	–	–	–	–	–	–	–	–	–	–	–	1	1
D. marginata Hop	3	2	–	–	–	1	–	2	–	–	1	–	1	10
D. cf. *marginata* Hop	–	2	–	–	–	–	–	–	–	–	–	–	1	3
Plateumaris affinis (Kun)	2	2	–	–	–	1	–	3	–	–	–	–	3	11
P. braccata (Scop)	1	1	–	–	1	3	7	1	–	–	1	–	2	17
P. sericea (L)	–	–	–	–	–	–	1	–	–	–	–	–	1	2
Lema cyanella (L)	–	1	–	–	–	–	–	–	–	–	–	–	–	1
Chrysolina polita (L)	–	–	–	–	–	–	–	1	–	–	–	–	–	1
C. varians (Schal)	–	–	–	–	–	–	1	–	–	–	–	–	–	1
Phaedon sp. (not *tumidulus*) (Germ)	1	–	–	–	–	–	–	–	–	–	–	–	–	1
Prasocuris phellandrii (L)	2	5	–	–	–	–	1	–	–	–	3	1	1	13
Agelastica alni (L)	1	1	–	–	1	–	–	–	–	1	–	–	–	4
Phyllodecta vulgatissima (L)	–	2	–	–	–	–	–	1	–	–	–	1	–	4
Phyllotreta atra (F)	–	–	–	–	–	–	–	–	–	–	1	–	–	1
Aphthona nonstriata (Gz)	–	1	–	–	–	–	–	–	–	–	–	–	–	1
Altica sp.	–	–	–	–	–	–	–	–	–	–	–	–	1	1
Crepidodera ferruginea (Scop)	–	–	–	–	–	–	–	–	–	–	–	–	1	1
Chalcoides sp.	–	1	–	–	–	–	–	1	–	–	–	–	–	2
Epitrix pubescens (Koch)	1	2	–	–	–	–	–	–	–	–	1	–	1	5
Chaetocnema concinna (Marsh)	–	–	–	–	–	–	–	–	–	–	–	–	1	1
Chaetocnema sp. (not *concinna*)	–	1	–	–	–	–	–	–	–	–	–	–	–	1
Apion spp.	–	1	–	–	–	–	–	–	–	1	1	–	1	4
Hypera punctata (F)	–	–	–	–	–	–	1	–	–	–	–	–	–	1
Alophus triguttatus (F)	–	1	–	–	–	–	–	–	–	–	–	–	–	1
Tanysphyrus lemnae (Pk)	14	20	–	–	1	5	1	7	2	1	2	–	3	56
Bagous spp.	4	4	–	–	–	3	1	3	1	1	–	2	1	20
Notaris acridulus (L)	–	–	–	–	–	–	1	1	1	–	3	2	1	9
N. cf. *scirpi* (F)	1	1	–	–	–	–	–	–	–	–	–	–	–	2
Thryogenes festucae (Hbst)	1	–	–	–	–	–	–	–	–	–	–	–	–	1
T. cf. *nereis* (Pk)	2	–	–	–	–	–	–	–	–	–	–	–	–	2
Limnobaris pilistriata (Step)	–	1	–	–	–	–	–	2	–	–	–	–	–	3
Anthonomus sp.	–	–	–	–	–	–	–	–	–	–	1	–	–	1
Curculio salicivorus Pk	1	–	–	–	–	–	–	–	–	–	–	–	–	1
Miccotrogus picirostris (F)	–	1	–	–	–	–	–	–	–	–	–	–	–	1
Scolytus scolytus (F)	1	–	–	–	–	–	–	–	–	–	–	–	–	1
totals	103	158	1	0	10	52	54	50	14	7	40	53	81	623

or *Alisma* sp (water plantain) as indicated by *Donacia dentata*, and *Iris pseudacorus* (yellow flag), the food plant of *Aphthona nonstriata*. An interesting potential member of the fen vegetation is *Solanum dulcamara* (woody nightshade). Several individuals of *Epitrix pubescens* were present. It feeds on members of the Solanaceae and *S. dulcamara* does on occasions grow in shallow water.

The majority of the Carabidae (ground beetles) are species that occur in waterside or fen habitats. Some, such as *Odacantha melanura*, live among *Phragmites* stems.

Agonum thoreyi occurs on damp soil near water with dense *Phragmites*. In contrast, *Elaphrus riparius* lives on open ground at the margin of freshwater habitats, usually with moss and *Carex* vegetation. There were several

Table 15.2 Species groups of Flag Fen Coleoptera

		percentage for A + B + platform
1	aquatic	27.1
2	pasture/dung	6.5
3	?meadowland	0.8
4	wood and trees	3.7
5	marsh/aquatic plants	34.3
6a	general disturbed ground/arable	0
6b	sandy/dry disturbed ground/arable	0
7	dung/foul organic material	8.6
8	Lathridiidae	0.8
9	synanthropic	0
10	esp structural timbers	0.4
11	on roots in grassland	2.9
12	unclassified	42.0
total number of terrestrial individuals		490

Table 15.3 Host plants of the phytophagous Coleoptera

food plant	*beetle*
Cruciferae	*Phyllotreta atra*
Hypericum spp.	*Chrysolina varians*
Leguminosae esp. *Trifolium* sp.	*Hypera punctata,*
	Miccotrogus picirostris
mostly Rosaceae	*Anthonomus* sp.
aquatic Umbelliferae	*Prasocuris phellandrii*
Polygonaceae	*Chaetocnema concinna*
Urtica spp.	*Brachypterus urticae*
mostly *Ulmus* spp.	*Scolytus scolytus*
Alnus glutinosa	*Agelastica alni*
Salix spp.	*Curculio salicivorus*
Populus and *Salix* spp.	*Phyllodecta vulgatissima,*
	Chalcoides sp.
Solanaceae	*Epitrix pubescens*
Labiatae	*Chrysolina polita*
Alisma and *Sagittaria* spp.	*Donacia dentate*
Iris pseudacorus	*Aphthona nonstriata*
Lemna spp.	*Tanysphyrus lemnae*
Sparganium erectum	*Donacia marginata*
Schoenoplectus lacustris	*Donacia* cf *impressa*
Carex spp.	*Plateumaris affinis*
mostly *Carex* spp.	*Plateumaris sericea*
Cyperaceae	*Thryogenes festucae,*
	Limnobaris pilistriata
Phragmites australis	*Donacia clavipes,*
	Plateumaris braccata

(based mainly on Freude *et al* 1966–83; Hoffmann 1950–58)

examples of the now very rare *Pterostichus aterrimus*, which is restricted in England to peaty soil in fens in Hampshire, Cambridgeshire, and Norfolk. There was also a single specimen of *Chlaenius tristis*, which is now extinct in Britain, but there are old records from the Cambridgeshire fens (Lindroth 1974, 71, 121).

The group of hydrophilid and staphylinid beetles that feed on various categories of decaying organic material including dung (Species Group 7) was, at 8.6% of the non-aquatic Coleoptera, quite well represented. The majority of these beetles seems, however, to have been associated with accumulations of decaying fen vegetation. The most numerous of this group, *Cercyon sternalis*, occurs in decaying vegetation on marshy ground rather than in dung. Other beetles of decaying vegetation included *Corylophus cassidoides*, which commonly occurs in reed-swamp debris, and the amphibious *Coelostoma orbiculare*.

The fen seems to have presented quite a varied habitat. The *Sparganium erectum* and water-lilies would have grown in permanent shallow water whereas the *Phragmites australis* could have extended from the reed-swamp zone onto exposed peat. The numerous Carabidae and Staphylinidae show that there was an extensive area of probably sedge-covered peat that was above water level for much of the year. The *Lemna* was probably growing both in pools on the peat surface and on the larger areas of open water.

The background landscape

The majority of the wood- and tree-dependent beetles (Species Group 4) were leaf-feeding chrysomelids of trees that could have been growing on the peat of the fen. There were several examples of *Agelastica alni*, the alder leaf beetle. This beetle is now extinct in Britain and seems to require large tracts of alder woodland for its survival. It was identified from Neolithic deposits at the Etton causewayed enclosure, which had more evidence of woodland than Flag Fen, and its presence suggests that some vestiges of the extensive alder woodland survived into the Late Bronze Age. The other potential fenland tree indicated by the insects was *Salix* (willow) or *Populus* (poplar) sp, the host plant of *Phyllodecta vulgatissima* and *Chalcoides* sp. There is little evidence for woodland on the drier ground beyond the fen edge. There was a single specimen of *Scolytus scolytus*, however, the elm bark beetle. Archaeological finds of this beetle have attracted undue attention because it is the vector of the fungus that causes Dutch elm disease. Given that most native British trees have scolytids associated with them, it would have been surprising for elm to have been present without its bark beetle. All that can be said about this beetle from Flag Fen is that an elm with moribund branches grew in the vicinity (or had been brought to the site with its bark on).

Scarabaeoid dung beetles (Species Group 2) comprised 6.5% of the non-aquatic Coleoptera. It is possible that limited grazing of the sedge fen took place during the drier months of the year. The elaterids and chafers with larvae that feed on roots in grassland (Species Group 11), such as *Phyllopertha horticola* and *Agrypnus murinus*, would mostly have been unable to develop in the wet peat, suggesting that there was grassland on the drier ground, with a mineral soil surrounding the fen. It is likely that many of the dung beetles were from pasture land beyond the edge of the fen. One species of note, *Onthophagus taurus*, which was represented by a single individual, is now extinct in Britain but is another species recorded from Neolithic deposits at the Etton causewayed camp. A Late Bronze Age example of this beetle was identified from Pilgrim Lock on the Warwickshire Avon (Osborne 1988). There was no evidence from the Coleoptera for the presence of arable or disturbed weedy ground beyond the edge of the fen. The species suggestive of these habitats (Species Groups 6a and 6b) do not have such good dispersive powers, however, as the various grassland indicators and their absence need not be significant.

Comparison between the column and the platform

There were only very minor differences between the lower part of the column (Column A) and the upper part of the column (Column B). They could not be related to any ecological changes.

The results from the platform were very similar to those of the column, indeed they gave no indication that the platform was a timber structure. The platform had a slightly higher proportion of dung beetles (Species Group 2) and beetles of dung/foul organic material (Species Group 7) (Fig 15.1), but this was not high enough to suggest human activity on the platform. There was a lower proportion of beetles with larvae that feed on roots in grassland, (Species Group 11),

perhaps because more of the beetles had a local origin. The beetle assemblages from the platform had a higher proportion of aquatic individuals than the column, suggesting that the platform was periodically flooded. There was also a higher concentration of the *Lemna*-feeding weevil, *Tanysphyrus lemnae*, perhaps reflecting stagnant pools of water between some of the timbers.

It has been argued that there was a settlement with houses on the Flag Fen platform. Perhaps the most similar site from which insects have been investigated was the Iron Age settlement of Meare Lake Village. This site also had timber structures on fen peat. The Meare samples contained very high numbers of *Anobium punctatum* (the woodworm beetle), however, particularly from samples from under fallen timbers, and also numerous Lathridiidae (compost beetles), mostly *Lathridius minutus* gp (Girling 1979). *Ptinus fur*, a synanthropic beetle that tends to be associated with human settlement was present. There was only a single specimen of *Anobium punctatum* (Species Group 10) and one other wood-boring beetle, *Grynobius planus*, from the platform samples. The Lathridiidae and the synanthropic group of beetles (Species Groups 8 and 9) were entirely absent. The insects therefore provide no indication of upstanding timber structures or settlement. Since the platform clearly incorporated much timber, an explanation is needed for the absence of wood-boring beetles. If all the timbers had rapidly become waterlogged, they would cease to be a suitable substrate for them. Wood-boring beetles were notably absent from the trackway timbers of the Somerset Levels, except where the infestation had taken place before the timbers had been laid.

16 Radiocarbon and absolute chronology

by Alex Bayliss and Francis Pryor

The principal aim of this chapter is to reconcile the radiocarbon measurements obtained from Fengate in the 1970s with tree-ring dates obtained from Flag Fen and the Power Station (see Chapter 8). In addition, we are able to report the results of three samples taken from handles or hafts of bronze implements from the Power Station assemblage, together with results from environmental samples (Chapter 13). The former samples were processed as part of a British Museum programme to obtain radiocarbon determinations on materials directly associated with bronze implements (Needham *et al* 1997).

Radiocarbon analysis

All the samples from the Fengate series (Table 16.1) were dated between 1972 and 1979. The 27 samples measured by AERE Harwell were processed using methods outlined in Otlet and Slade (1974), Otlet (1977), and Otlet and Warchal (1977). Measurement was by liquid scintillation counting (Noakes *et al* 1965). Quoted errors are estimates of total laboratory error, not just based on counting statistics (Otlet 1977). The three samples measured by Gakushuin University were processed using methods outlined in Kigoshi and Endo (1963), and measured by gas proportional counting (acetylene). Quoted errors are based on counting statistics only (Kigoshi *et al* 1973). The three samples measured by the Queen's University, Belfast, were processed using methods outlined in Smith *et al* (1970a, 1970b, and 1971), and measured by gas proportional counting (methane). It is not known whether the error terms include any allowance for factors other than counting statistics.

The three samples from the Power Station implement series (Table 16.2) were processed by the Oxford Radiocarbon Accelerator Unit in 1995 using methods outlined in Hedges *et al* (1989 and 1992) and measured by Accelerator Mass Spectrometry with a carbon dioxide gas ion source (Bronk and Hedges 1989, 1990, and 1997). Quoted errors are estimates of total laboratory error (Hedges *et al* 1992). The six samples taken for 'wiggle-matching' the tree-ring sequence from Flag Fen (Table 16.3) were measured at the Queen's University, Belfast, in 1991. They were processed using methods outlined in McCormac (1992) and McCormac *et al* (1993) and measured using liquid scintillation counting (Pearson 1984). Quoted errors are estimates of total laboratory error.

Five dates were produced by the Scottish Universities Research and Reactor Centre in 1996 from sediment samples relating to the environmental sequence of the Flag Fen Basin (Table 16.1). These samples were processed using methods outlined in Stenhouse and Baxter (1983) and measured by liquid scintillation spectrometry (Noakes *et al* 1965). The 'humic' fraction was selected for dating. A sixth sample was too small for measurement.

Quoted errors are estimates of total laboratory error.

Quality assurance

In the 1970s, the importance of quality assurance for radiocarbon dating was less widely appreciated, although laboratories did maintain internal programmes of quality assurance using a range of standard materials (eg Polach 1972). From the Fengate series only HAR-3196 and HAR-3204, measured in 1978, have published quality assurance. They were measured at the time when the first steps towards formal interlaboratory comparison were being taken within the United Kingdom. The results of these measurements were published in 1980 (Otlet *et al* 1980) and show that the British laboratories were in good agreement.

Full quality assurance data are available for the three series of samples that were processed in the 1990s. The laboratories concerned maintain continual programmes of quality assurance procedures, in addition to participation in international intercomparisons (Scott *et al* 1990; Rozanski *et al* 1992; Gulliksen and Scott 1996). These tests indicate no laboratory offsets and demonstrate the validity of the precision quoted.

Results

The results are given in Table 16.1, and are quoted in accordance with the international standard known as the Trondheim convention (Stuiver and Kra 1986). They are conventional radiocarbon ages (Stuiver and Polach 1977).

The concentration of charcoal from (ditch) 254 was subdivided and three replicate measurements taken (HAR-1970–72). These are statistically consistent (T'=0.5; T' (5%)=6.0; v=2; Ward and Wilson 1978), and so have been combined before calibration by taking a weighted mean in the analysis that follows. This is 2946±40 BP, which calibrates to cal BC 1310±1020.

Calibration

The calibrations of these results, which relate the radiocarbon measurements directly to the calendrical time scale, are given in Table 16.1 and Figures 16.1–16.4 (outline distributions).

All have been calculated using the datasets published by Stuiver and Pearson (1986), Pearson and Stuiver (1986), and Pearson *et al* (1986) and the computer program OxCal (v2.18); Bronk 1994 and 1995).

The calibrated date ranges cited in the text are those for 95% confidence. They are quoted in the form recommended by Mook (1986), with the end points rounded outwards to 10 years if the error term is greater than or equal to 25 radiocarbon years, or to 5 years if less than this. The ranges quoted in italics are ranges derived from mathematical modelling of archaeological problems (see below). The ranges in Table 16.1 have been calculated according to the maximum intercept method (Stuiver and Reimer 1986). All other ranges, and the distributions, are derived from the probability method (Stuiver and Reimer 1993; van der Plicht 1993; Dehling and van der Plicht 1993).

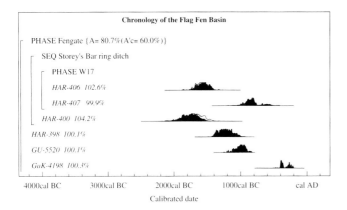

Fig 16.1 Probability distributions of dates from isolated features in the Fengate landscape: each distributions represents the relative probability that an event occurs at some particular time. For each of the radiocarbon dates two distributions have been plotted, one in outline, which is the result of simple radiocarbon calibration, and a solid one, which is based on the chronological model used. The large square brackets down the left-hand side, along with the OxCal keywords, define the overall model exactly

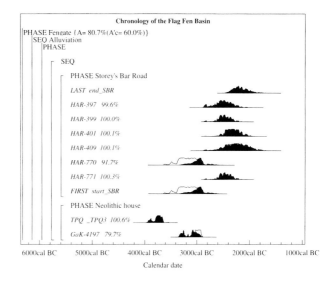

Fig 16.3 Probability distributions of dates from the Neolithic activity on the Storey's Bar Road site: the format is identical to that for Figure 16.1. The large square brackets down the left-hand side, along with the OxCal keywords, define the overall model exactly

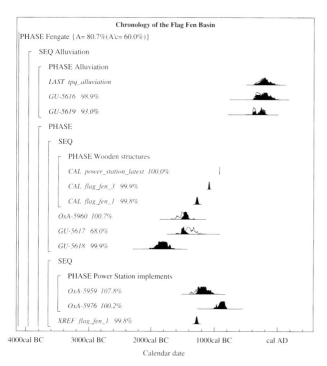

Fig 16.2 Probability distributions of dates from the sequence around the post alignment: the format is identical to that for Figure 16.1. The large square brackets down the left-hand side, along with the OxCal keywords, define the overall model exactly

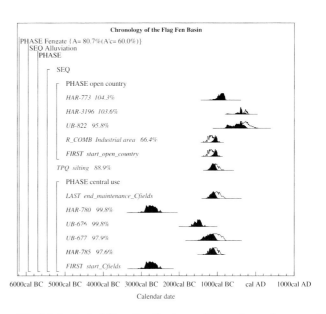

Fig 16.4 Probability distributions of dates from the central Bronze Age field system: the format is identical to that for Figure 16.1. The large square brackets down the left-hand side, along with the OxCal keywords, define the overall model exactly

Table 16.1 Summary table of radiocarbon dates

lab no	context	comment	radiocarbon age	d13C (‰)	calibrated date range (95% confidence)	reference
Fengate series						
pre-fields						
GaK-4196	charcoal from Neolithic house 'wall foundation trench'	Charcoal not identified, might be considerable age-at-death offset (Bowman 1990, 51). Possibly residual, as no functional relationship between context and sample can be demonstrated.	4906±64		3960–3630	Pryor 1980, 247
GaK-4197	charcoal from post (oak roundwood) of Neolithic 'house'	Roundwood was probably of <100 years growth. Structural timber probably not residual.	4395±50		3310–2910	Pryor 1980, 247
HAR-397	charcoal 'hearth sweepings' from small pit (B24)	Twigs and small roundwood, interpreted as secondary (redeposited) material from adjacent domestic activity. Pit probably backfilled.	3980±100	−25.4	2880–2200	Pryor 1980, 247; Otlet 1977
HAR-398	wattle from probable wattle lining of well	Short-lived wood forming a structural component of well, dates construction.	3000±70	−28.4	1430–1010	Pryor 1980, 247; Otlet 1977
HAR-399	charcoal 'hearth sweepings' from small pit (B61)	Twigs and small roundwood interpreted as secondary (redeposited) material from adjacent domestic activity.	3970±70	−24.4	2860–2290	Pryor 1980, 247; Otlet 1977
HAR-400	charcoal, contents of Collared Urn	Charcoal not identified, so might be a considerable age-at-death offset (Bowman 1990, 151), although probably dates use.	3410±120	−19.6	2040–1430	Pryor 1980, 247; Otlet 1977
HAR-401	charcoal 'hearth sweepings' from large pit (Y4)	Twigs and small roundwood, interpreted as secondary (redeposited) material from adjacent domestic activity. Pit probably backfilled.	3860±90	−21.9	2870–2200	Pryor 1980, 247; Otlet 1977
HAR-404	charcoal 'hearth sweepings' from large pit (Y12)	Mostly heartwood of *Quercus* sp., with some sapwood, *Corylus* sp., and Pomoideae (possibly hedgerow). Interpreted as secondary (redeposited) from adjacent domestic activity. Pit probably backfilled.	3880±80	−24.9	2580–2130	Pryor 1980, 247; Otlet 1977
HAR-406	stake (hazel/alder) (Maisie Taylor pers comm) at bottom of 'quarry'pit (W17)	Short-lived material forming stake *in situ* on bottom of pit. Dates last use or abandonment of pit.	3290±80	−21.3	1750–1410	Pryor 1980, 247; Otlet 1977
HAR-407	waterlogged twigs from primary fill of 'quarry' pit (W17)	Short-lived material; deposit accumulated on abandonment of pit as an active gravel quarry.	2670±90		1010–560	Pryor 1980, 247; Otlet 1977
HAR-409	charcoal 'hearth sweepings' from small pit (W32)	Twigs and small roundwood interpreted as secondary (redeposited) material. Pit probably backfilled.	3810±150	−24.6	2860–1820	Pryor 1980, 247; Otlet 1977
HAR-770	charcoal 'hearth sweepings' from small pit (P10)	Twigs and small roundwood interpreted as secondary (redeposited) material. By analogy with similar pits from Storey's Bar Road Pryor 1978), material represents domestic activity. Pit probably backfilled.	4460±130		3780–2940	Pryor 1980, 247; Otlet 1977

lab no	context	comment	radiocarbon age	$d^{13}C$ (‰)	calibrated date range (95% confidence)	reference
HAR-771	charcoal 'hearth sweepings' from small pit (P59)	Twigs and small roundwood interpreted as secondary (redeposited) material. By analogy with similar pits from Storey's Bar Road (Pryor 1978), material represents domestic activity Pit probably backfilled.	3960±70		2860–2280	Pryor 1980, 247; Otlet 1977
fields-in-use						
HAR-775	concentrated deposit of charcoal and burnt stones on north side of Bronze Age ditch (*n*)	Twigs and roundwood, interpreted as redeposited occupation material from settlement to north.	3120±70		1530–1220	Pryor 1980, 248
HAR-776	concentrated deposit of charcoal and burnt stones at butt end of Bronze Age ditch *b*	Twigs and roundwood, interpreted as redeposited occupation material from settlement to west.	3050±80		1520–1050	Pryor 1980, 248
HAR-777	concentrated deposit of charcoa 1 and burnt stones at butt end of Bronze Age ditch *b*	Twigs and roundwood, interpreted as redeposited occupation material from settlement to west.	3550±200		2470–1420	Pryor 1980, 248
HAR-779	charcoal from secondary and tertiary contexts, Bronze Age ditches *f* and *I*	Finely comminuted charcoal bulked from two slowly deposited ditch silts; probably represents material of widely differing dates.	4190±90		3030–2500	Pryor 1980, 248
HAR-780	charcoal and twigs from around inhumation in Bronze Age ditch *f*	Twiggy material, laid in base of grave (Pryor 1980, pl 12).	4190±90		3030–2500	Pryor 1980, 248
HAR-781	charcoal from secondary context, Bronze Age ditch 9	Finely comminuted charcoal bulked from two slowly deposited ditch silts; probably represents material of widely differing dates.	2940±90		1420–900	Pryor 1980, 248
HAR-782	charcoal from secondary context Bronze Age ditch 9	Finely comminuted charcoal bulked from two slowly deposited ditch silts; probably represents material of widely differing dates.	2930±80		1410–910	Pryor 1980, 248
HAR-783	charcoal from secondary context, Bronze Age ditch 9	Finely comminuted charcoal bulked from two slowly deposited ditch silts; probably represents material of widely differing dates.	2990±80		1430–990	Pryor 1980, 248
HAR-784	charcoal from upper primary fill, Bronze Age ditch 9	Finely comminuted charcoal bulked from two slowly deposited ditch silts; probably represents material of widely differing dates.	2990±70		1420–1000	Pryor 1980, 248
HAR-785	twigs from primary context of Bronze Age ditch 9	Short-lived material; deposit accumulated directly after the final recutting of the ditch (Pryor 1980, 202–6).	2890±60		1300–910	Pryor 1980, 248
UB-676	concentrated deposit of charcoal and burnt stones in Bronze Age ditch 3	Twigs and roundwood; interpreted as redeposited material from domestic or industrial site adjacent.	3230±70	−24.4	1690–1400	Pryor 1980, 249; Pearson and Pilcher 1975

Table 16.1 (cont'd)

lab no	context	comment	radiocarbon age	d13C (‰)	calibrated date range (95% confidence)	reference
UB-677	birch twigs from primary context of well-like enlargement of Bronze Age ditch 1	Short-lived material; deposit accumulated directly after the final recutting of ditch/well.	2885±135	−24.7	1430–800	Pryor 1980, 249; Pearson and Pilcher 1975
HAR-3204	oak from young tree, with roots intact, which had collapsed into Bronze Age ditch (F862)	Fairly short-lived material; deposit accumulated directly after the final recutting of ditch/well.	3140±80	−25.0	1610–1220	Pryor 1984; microfiche 307
late use of fields						
HAR-1970	charcoal from dense concentration in Bronze Age ditch	Twigs and roundwood; spread around ditch and derived from associated 'industrial' activity.	2910±70		1380–910	Pryor 1980, 248
HAR-1971	as HAR-1970	as HAR-1970	2980±70		1420–1000	Pryor 1980, 248
HAR-1972	as HAR-1970	as HAR-1970	2950±70		1410–930	Pryor 1980, 248
post-date use of fields						
HAR-773	charcoal from posthole of structure B cut into tertiary filling of Bronze Age ditch e	Twigs and roundwood; concentrated with freshly broken pottery and animal bone, suggesting a deposit of domestic refuse. Provides *terminus post quem* for ditch.	2740±80		1100–790	Pryor 1980, 247
HAR-3196	oak stake with dovetail joint from primary contexts at bottom of well 1551	The stake may be split down from a wheel (Maisie Taylor pers comm). Reused, but not from ancient timber, so age on deposition unlikely to be >100 years.	2310±60	−26.8	520–200	Pryor 1984, microfiche 307
UB-822	twigs from primary contexts of rock-cut well 6	Short-lived material related to use or early abandonment of well.	2290±125	−26.2	790–50	Pryor 1980, 249; Pearson and Pilcher 1975
Ga-4198	wood from probable wattle lining of well	Short-lived wood forming a structural component of well; dates construction.	2300±46		410–240	Pryor 1980, 247

lab no	context	comment	radiocarbon age	$d^{13}C$ (‰)	calibrated date range (95% confidence)	reference
Power Station implement series						
OxA-5959	shaft of conical ferrule (Other Find 24)	From old land surface. Probably contemporary with post alignment.	2965±45	−25.2	1390–1030	Needham et al 1997, 62
OXA-5960	shaft of socketed gouge (Other Find 33)	From upper primary contexts of droveway ditch 8. Pre-dates post alignment. Implement itself very worn.	3230±45	−27.0	1630–1420	Needham et al 1997, 65
OxA-5976	shaft of socketed axe (Other Find 93)	From a shallow scoop in the buried soil. Probably contemporary with post alignment.	2740±45	−25.4	1000–810	Needham et al 1997, 64
Flag Fen wiggle match						
UB-3422	timber B9, block 2 dated by dendrochronology to BC 1139–1120		3004±19	−27.5±0.2	1380–1170	
UB-3423	timber B9, block 3 dated by dendrochronology to BC 1119–1100		3061±21	−27.7±0.2	1420–1260	
UB-3424	timber B9, block 4 dated by dendrochronology to BC 1099–1080		2960±22	−28.5±0.2	1300–1100	
UB-3425	timber B9, block 5, and timber A1895, block 1, dated by dendrochronology to BC 1079–1060		2921±17	−28.5±0.2	1260–1040	
laUB-3426	timber B9, block 6, and timber A1895, block 2, dated by dendrochronology to BC 1059–1040		2935±17	−27.8±0.2	1260–1060	
UB-3427	timber B9, block 7, and timber A1895, block 3, dated by dendrochronology to BC 1039–1020		2918±17	−28.6±0.2	1260–1040	
Environmental series						
GU-5616	Northey 9–12 (peat)	Monocot fen peat; from the top of the peat immediately before alluviation.	2180±60	−28.6	400–90	
GU-5617	Northey 61–65 (peat)	Monocot fen peat; from the first development of sedge fen on which the platform wasa constructed.	3130±60	−29.2	1530–1260	
GU-5618	Northey 80–85 (peat)	Monocot fen peat/detritus; from the base of the peat in the deepest part of the Flag Fen Basin.	3500±60	−28.3	2030–1680	
GU-5619	Fengate B 46–55 (peat)	Detrital fen peat; from the top of the peat immediately before alluviation.	2290±50	−28.6	410–200	
GU-5620	Fengate B 85–95 (peat)	Detrital fen peat with fragments of alder; from the base of the peat at the fen edge.	2840±50	−29.4	1210–900	

Reliability

Before analysis can begin, it is necessary to assess the reliability of the radiocarbon samples and measurements. This has to be done from two points of view–one that examines the archaeological context of the material that was dated and one that looks at the composition and processing of that material.

In fact this dataset stands up remarkably well to critical examination. In our view it is reasonable to argue that most of the material dated is close in date to the context in which it was deposited (see Table 16.1).

However, five samples were composed of finely comminuted charcoal from slowly deposited ditch silts (HAR-779 and HAR-781–4). Much of this charcoal might be residual and the bulked sample probably contained fragments of widely differing dates. Indeed in some cases (eg HAR-779), material was bulked together from more than one context. Although these results do not relate directly to the time when the contexts were deposited, all the material that has been bulked together must date to the period of context formation or earlier. In consequence these results can be use as *termini post quem* for the date of deposition of their contexts.

Three samples taken from concentrations of charcoal and settlement material within secondary ditch infilling must also contain a proportion of residual material (HAR-775–7). If material from primary ditch filling is earlier than all material from secondary silting, then the model is inconsistent (overall A=30.7% [<A'c=60.0%]; eg HAR-777 A=4.0%). It is felt that this assumption is archaeologically valid, provided that the field system at a given level (OD) was abandoned at the same time. These samples were from contexts at approximately the same level, in the same subsite. Consequently, it is believed that a proportion of the material dated was probably derived from earlier contexts. For this reason, the three samples HAR-775–7 might not be later than material from primary contexts, but may still be used as reliable *termini post quem* for material (such as HAR-1970–72) above it.

Two further samples must be treated as *termini post quem* only. GaK-4196 and HAR-400 consisted of charcoal that was not identified as to age or species before dating. This means that there could be a considerable age-at-death offset between the tree-rings dated and the production of the charcoal (Bowman 1990, 51). In addition, the taphonomy of the charcoal that was discovered in the wall foundation trench (GaK-4196) is rather doubtful. It might have been structural, although there was no evidence of *in situ* burning. Again, however, as material from both contexts must be the same age or earlier than those contexts, these results may also be used as *termini post quem*.

In general, the charcoal submitted for dating was not identified to species, although it was scanned to determine the maturity of the wood. This was usually assessed as coming from twigs or roundwood of less than 100 years old. Although the recent identification

of HAR-404 from the residual material remaining after dating suggests that some heartwood might be represented, the presence of sapwood in this sample and the general age composition of woodland resources utilised in the Fengate landscape imply that any age-at-death offset for these samples is likely to be well under fifty years (see Chapter 8).

It is difficult to assess the scientific reliability of the 33 samples measured in the 1970s, as this preceded the first formal intercomparison exercises (Otlet *et al* 1980; International Study Group 1982). We know that some of the measurements have quoted error terms based only on counting statistics. These are therefore expressions of minimum error, although it is not now possible to evaluate how much larger the total error on the measurements would be.

In this study, these results have been included by choice, while noting the minimum error terms. In effect, because the estimates are relatively imprecise, any additional error is unlikely to make an archaeologically significant difference to the analysis.

Fortunately, all the material dated in the 1970s was charcoal or waterlogged wood. This was processed using the acid-alkali-acid method (Mook and Waterbolk 1985), which is used today in many laboratories to process these materials.

Analysis and interpretation

Although the simple calibrated date ranges of the radiocarbon measurements are accurate estimates of the dates of the samples, this is usually not what archaeologists really wish to know. It is the dates of the archaeological events represented by those samples that are of interest. Fortunately, explicit methodology is now available that enables the results of the radiocarbon analyses to be combined with other information, such as archaeological phasing, to produce realistic estimates of those dates of archaeological interest. It should be emphasised that these distributions and ranges are not absolute, they are interpretative *estimates*, which can and will change as further data become available, and as other researchers choose to model the existing data from different perspectives.

The technique we have used is known as 'Gibbs' sampling' (Gelfand and Smith 1990) and has been applied using the program OxCal v2.18 (http://units.ox.ac.uk/departments/rlaha/). Full details of the algorithms employed by this program are available from the on-line manual or in Bronk (1995), and fully worked examples are given in the series of papers by Buck *et al* (1991 and 1992, 1994a, and 1994b). The algorithms used in the models described below can be derived from the structure shown in Figures 16.1–16.4.

Here we concentrate on the archaeology — particularly on the reasoning behind the interpretative choices that we have made in producing the models presented. These archaeological decisions fundamentally underpin our choice of statistical model.

Aims of the analysis

The principal objective is simple to state — to correlate the events defined by dendrochronology at Flag Fen and the Power Station with the broader series of land management and environmental changes, which have been defined by radiocarbon assay in Fengate, Northey, and Flag Fen.

Building the model

The mathematical model that combines the radiocarbon evidence with the tree-ring dates and stratigraphic information from sites in the Flag Fen Basin is shown in Figures 16.1 to 16.4. It is important to understand the use of the terms *event* and *phase*. All radiocarbon determinations refer to events, which may be defined as short-lived episodes of activity, such as the construction of a building. A number of separate events may be grouped together on archaeological grounds to form a phase, such as the occupation of a building; for further discussion see Allen and Bayliss 1995, 528.

A summary of the main events and phases is given in Figure 16.5; these can be briefly described as follows:

1 Neolithic mortuary structure (Pryor 1974, 1988, and 1993). Although this probably represents a phase of activity, the only available result (GaK-4197) refers to its initial construction. It is, therefore (in terms of the model), an archaeological event.

2 Storey's Bar Road (Grooved Ware) settlement (Pryor 1978). The start and finish of this phase of activity can be estimated from a range of radiocarbon measurements of events (pit backfilling) included within the phase. Because we have relatively few measurements and these are imprecise, no attempt has been made to model the distribution of the events. This means that the statistical scatter on the measurements suggests that the settlement started earlier and finished later than was actually the case.

3 Use of central Bronze Age fields. This phase begins with the deposition of the Newark Road inhumation (an event, HAR-780; Pryor 1980, 39–40). The period during which the fields were in use cannot be directly dated, as the ditches were maintained clean and open; their final use can, however, be estimated from short-lived material in the surviving primary filling (HAR-785; UB-676 and UB-677).

4 Accumulation of short-lived and residual material in abandoned Bronze Age field ditches of central system. This phase does not consist of definable events, as each radiocarbon sample will include material derived from contexts of different age. For this reason, this phase can only be used as a *terminus post quem* for events that stratigraphically post-date it. It includes the following determinations: HAR-775-7, HAR-779, and HAR-781-4.

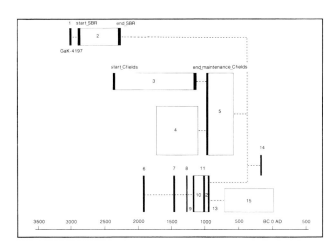

Fig 16.5 Summary of the chronological sequence of the principal phases and events. The solid blocks represent events, the open blocks phases

5 Phase of open country. By this phase the ditches of the central Bronze Age system had filled in. The model can be used to provide an estimate for the date when this started, based on the latest evidence for the abandonment of the Bronze Age fields and the earliest evidence for features that stratigraphically post-date them. The phase includes four events: the 'industrial area' of Newark Road (Pryor 1980, 70–73; HAR-1970-2), four-post structure A, from Newark Road (Pryor 1980, fig 44; HAR-773), Iron Age well F1551 (Pryor 1984a fig 89; HAR-3196), and the rock-cut well F6 (Pryor 1974, 19; UB-822).

6 First formation of peat in the lowest-lying part of Flag Fen investigated to date (Chapter 13; GU-5618).

7 Peat formation directly below the timber platform (Chapter 13; GU-5617).

8 Shaft of socketed gouge from the filling of Bronze Age droveway ditch 8 at the Power Station (OxA-5960).

9 Initial construction of the post alignment across Flag Fen. Archaeological evidence suggests that this was an event lasting at most a few seasons (cf post alignment, Phase 1).

10 Phase of use and desultory maintenance of the post alignment (cf post alignment, Phase 2).

11 Major reconstruction and enlargement of the post alignment. Probably an event lasting a few seasons, consequent on wetter conditions (cf post alignment, Phase 3).

12 Phase of intense maintenance and replacement of the post alignment, as conditions continue to grow wetter (cf post alignment, Phase 4).

13 Last maintenance of the post alignment timbers. An event.

14 Start of alluviation in the Flag Fen Basin. The two samples GU-5616 and GU-5619 provide *termini post quem* for the earliest phase of alluviation. The alluvium seals the Storey's Bar Road settlement, the open country phase and the posts of the alignment.

15 Iron Age use of post alignment. A phase during which material was deposited within and around the post alignment. This phase probably continued into the phase of alluviation.

Results of the analysis

A summary of the chronology of the Flag Fen Basin is given in Figure 16.6. The *estimated dates* of the events defined in the model are given as ranges in Table 16.2.

The Padholme Road mortuary structure is dated to the earlier Neolithic and is very likely to be earlier than the Storey's Bar Road (Grooved Ware) settlement (at more than 95% confidence). The latter settlement lasted for between 440 and 1170 years (at 95% confidence), although the scatter on the radiocarbon measurements means that this estimate is likely to be too large.

The start of the central Bronze Age field system is very likely to have occurred during the time in which the Storey's Bar Road settlement was in use (at 92% confidence). The onset of peat growth in Flag Fen is, however, likely to post-date the Storey's Bar Road settlement (at more than 95% confidence).

The initial construction (Phase 1) of the post alignment at the Power Station appears to take place in the first half of the thirteenth century BC. The clearest evidence of this date is provided by tree-ring samples Y1009 and Y0138, which have felling dates spanning this period (above, Fig 8.2). This slight evidence is, however, supported by the series of *termini post quem* consistent with this dating. The dating for this early phase at Flag Fen is based on stratigraphic criteria alone, as oak was not used in the earlier periods there.

Table 16.2 Estimated date ranges for the events defined in the model (see Figs 16.1–16.4)

Dates based on radiocarbon evidence are given as 'cal BC' and those based on dendrochronology as 'BC'

Neolithic mortuary structure	GaK-4197	cal BC 3330–3230 (at 32% confidence) or cal BC 3190–3150 (at 4% confidence) or cal BC 3140–2920 (at 59% confidence)
Storey's Bar Road Grooved Ware settlement	start of SBR	cal BC 3280–2820 (at 93% confidence) or cal BC 2810–2770 (at 2% confidence)
	end SBR	cal BC 2440–1890
use of central Bronze Age fields	start fields	cal BC 3030–2990 (at 3% confidence) or cal BC 2930–2560 (at 90% confidence) or cal BC 2540–2490 (at 3% confidence)
	end of maintenance of central fields	cal BC 1260–1020
phase of open country	start open country	cal BC 1170–990
first formation of peat	GU-5618	cal BC 2020–2000 (at 1% confidence) or cal BC 1980–1680 (at 94% confidence)
peat formation directly below timber platform	GU-5617	cal BC 1610–1550 (at 11% confidence) or cal BC 1540–1420 (at 84% confidence)
initial construction of the post alignment	Flag Fen 1	first half of thirteenth century BC
major reconstruction and enlargement of the post alignment	Flag Fen 3	first quarter of eleventh century BC
last-minute maintenance of the post alignment	Power Station latest	after 924 BC
start of alluviation	*terminus post quem* alluviation	cal BC 370–100

Table 16.3 Wiggle matching UB-3422 to UB-3427 against Pearson and Stuiver (1986)

Dates based on radiocarbon evidence are given as 'cal BC' and those based on dendrochronology as 'BC'

UB-3422	BC 1139–1120	cal BC 1310–1275, cal BC 1260–1240
UB-3423	BC 1119–1100	cal BC 1290–1255, cal BC 1240–1220
UB-3424	BC 1099–1080	cal BC 1270–1235, cal BC 1220–1200
UB-3425	BC 1079–1060	cal BC 1250–1215, cal BC 1200–1180
UB-3426	BC 1059–1040	cal BC 1230–1195, cal BC 1180–1160
UB-3427	BC 1039–1020	cal BC 1210–1175, cal BC 1160–1140

Following this initial phase, the tree-ring evidence suggests a period of stability (Phase 2), with only minor repairs. This lasted for approximately 150 years spanning the late thirteenth and twelfth centuries BC. It is very likely that the end of the maintenance of the central Bronze Age field system occurred during this phase (at 77% confidence). Radiocarbon results suggest that the central Bronze Age field system was in use for between 1340 to 1890 years (at 95% confidence).

There appears to have been a major episode of enlargement and renewal along the post alignment during the first quarter of the eleventh century BC (Phase 3). This is shown most clearly in Row 4 at Flag Fen. Here bark-edge felling dates of 1094 BC? (A0520) and 1083 BC winter (B1622) can closely be attributed to this episode. Many other tree-ring dates are consistent with major construction at this period (above, Fig 8.2). During this period the posts of Row 1 were replaced by those of Row 2 (at Flag Fen only). This period sees the continuation of Row 3 and the addition of Rows 4 and 5. It is just possible that the outer rows (1 and 5) were added to the alignment at the Power Station at this period (above, Fig 8.6).

Large-scale and extensive repairs were required frequently during the next two centuries (above, Figs 8.2 and 8.3). The last repairs were carried out at Flag Fen shortly after 955 BC and at the Power Station after 924 BC. The large number of tree-ring samples available for Phase 3 strongly suggest that repairs ceased during the second half of the tenth century BC.

Flag Fen 'wiggle-matching'

In 1990, six samples of waterlogged wood from the floating tree-ring sequence at Flag Fen were submitted to the Radiocarbon Dating Laboratory at Queen's University of Belfast for high-precision ^{14}C measurement. The samples came from two separate timbers (B9 consisting of 155 rings and A1895 consisting of 108 rings), which cross-matched with a *t* value of 6.02. During the radiocarbon analysis, the master chronology (FF88T), of which these samples form part, was dated by dendrochronology (Chapter 8).

Using the known number of years that separate each bi-decadal sample, the absolute date of the tree-rings can be estimated using the model shown in Figure 16.7. This has been calculated using the data of Pearson and Stuiver (1986). The model does not exhibit good agreement (n=6 A=31.8% [An=28.9%]). Nevertheless, the estimated dates of each block of wood are shown in Figure 16.7 and Table 16.3.

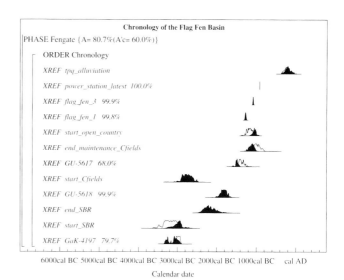

Fig 16.6 Probability distributions of the main dates from the Flag Fen Basin: the format is identical to that for Figure 16.1

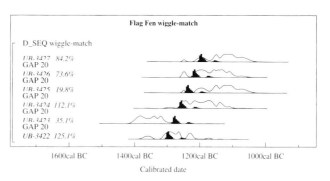

Fig 16.7 Probability distributions of dates from the dated tree-ring sequence at Flag Fen: the format is identical to that for Figure 16.1. The large square brackets down the left-hand side, along with the OxCal keywords, define the overall model exactly

The dates for the tree-rings estimated by the wiggle-matching do not correspond precisely to the dates provided by dendrochronology. The reasons for this difference are not fully understood at present, although some discussion of possible contributory factors is provided by Kromer *et al* (1996). Furthermore, recent work (McCormac *et al* 1995; Kromer *et al* 1996 and references therein) has high-lighted the need for refinements to the present calibration dataset. Here, the calibration data adopted internationally in 1986 have been used, although readers should be aware that this was revised in 1993 (Stuiver and Pearson 1993) and a new internationally accepted revision (Stuiver *et al*) was published in 1998.

17 The development of the prehistoric landscape in the Flag Fen Basin

by C A I French

Despite the past 25 years of intensive archaeological excavations, environmental analyses, and research that have been carried out in the lower reaches of the Nene valley at Fengate and in the adjacent fenland basin of Flag Fen, much is still based on inferential linkage and wider analogy. Nonetheless, few regions of lowland England have been the beneficiary of so much focussed attention as this river-terrace/fen-edge zone and contain such a wealth of associated archaeological and environmental data. What follows is a period-by-period attempt to draw together all of the available data that currently exists, presented as a landscape history of the Fengate/Flag Fen/Northey region from the third millennium BC to the medieval period.

Third millennium BC

Although the rectangular structure of the earlier third millennium BC, found at the Padholme Road subsite, Fengate, currently sits in isolation as the earliest archaeological evidence in the study area, by the end of this millennium considerably more human activity was evident. A series of relevant sites are all situated on first-terrace gravels on the northern side of the lower Nene valley at Fengate. These include the pre-Beaker enclosure north of Newark Road at c 6.1m (20') OD (Mahany 1969), the Grooved Ware settlement and associated field system north of Storey's Bar Road subsite at c 4.6m (15') OD (Pryor 1978), and the small hengiform monument discovered in 1990 just to the east of the Cat's Water Iron Age complex at c 2.75m (9' (OD (French 1992a and Chapter 3).

In addition, a length of Neolithic ditch was discovered immediately to the east of what was to become the easternmost extent of the subsequent second millennium BC field system at the Power Station site (Pryor 1992a, fig 8). This zone, at c 3.05m (10') OD, had always previously been considered to be the fen edge, but it might well have been dry land at this stage. This picture of a much wider zone of delimited dry land fringing the Flag Fen Basin was further corroborated by the watching brief at the Peterborough sewage treatment works in the south-western or most landward corner of the Flag Fen Basin. It revealed a swathe of thinly alluviated terrace gravel soils c 150m wide. These supported well drained brown-earth soils, which remained unburied to at least post-Bronze Age times.

Palynological and micromorphological studies would suggest that this Fengate fen edge had been a wooded environment. A mixed deciduous woodland dominated by lime with alder and to a lesser extent oak was developed on a stable and well drained argillic brown earth.

Obviously, by the time that these later Neolithic enclosures and field systems were constructed, some substantial clearance inroads had been made into this environment. What is noticeable in the soils is that there has been little truncation and no degradation in terms of soil developmental changes and/or the advent of poorer conditions of drainage. These soils were well structured, freely draining, and of loamy texture, all of which would have contributed to their ease of use and ready fertility. Unfortunately, there is no absolute evidence of the nature of the land-use on the fen edge itself, but certainly no tangible evidence of arable cultivation.

Similarly, in the adjacent fen basin, it is only possible to surmise from the pollen record contained in the old land surface from beneath the Flag Fen platform. Scaife (1992 and Chapter 13) suggests that there was a combination of woodland and mixed agricultural land by the beginning of the second millennium BC. In addition, there was strong evidence for nearby wetland, especially alder and willow in carr woodland, and the common occurrence of sedges, bur reed, and lesser reedmace.

Taking these fragments of evidence from the fen and Fengate terrace areas into account, it is possible to suggest that there was a gradual opening up of the deciduous woodland on the first terrace (above c 3.05m OD) throughout the third millennium, with very minor evidence of arable cultivation. The contemporary fen edge was anything up to 150–200m further to the east of the perceived fen edge as defined by the Cat's Water Drain, thus substantially extending the flood-free zone of dry land on the fen edge and effectively adding the land between 1.52m and 3.05m OD. The eastern and southern limit of this zone (at c <1.52m OD) was fringed by a wide zone (perhaps 200m across) of carr woodland dominated by alder and willow, with a shallow reed swamp occupying most, if not all, of the remainder of the then very small Flag Fen Basin (at c 0.61m (2') OD).

Earlier second millennium BC

This period was one in which major changes took place. The most extensive development was the large-scale division of the landscape by the establishment of the rectilinear, ditched field systems and east-west aligned droveways of the Newark Road, Cat's Water, and Fourth Drove subsites of Fengate between c 3.05m and c 6.01m OD (Pryor 1980). A similar and contemporary field system was discovered on the fen 'island' of Northey on the eastern side of the Flag Fen Basin (Gurney 1980), and is now known to extend over a much greater area to the north-east (Upex and Pryor personal communication and Chapter 5).

Until the excavations took place at the Power Station site (1989) and the Cat's Water site (1990), the eastern limit and nature of these field systems on the Fengate terrace was unknown. At the Power Station site, ditches 8 and 9 of the Newark Road system returned at right angles to themselves and parallel to the contour/fen edge of the day. Perhaps significantly, these enclosures ended just upslope from a seasonal stream channel that was situated along the break of slope (French 1992b; French *et al* 1992).

At the Cat's Water site (1990), some 100m further upstream to the north-west, the south-eastern/fen-edge aspect of the fields were completely different. The ditched enclosures that lay beneath the adjacent and later ROM/DoE Cat's Water site, changed to open-ended fields defined by fencelines. It is possible that this was a 'tacked on' extension to the enclosure system as originally laid out, or perhaps an even earlier system. Nonetheless, these fields might have opened up into the unenclosed fen-edge zone, effectively acting as common grazing areas of flood meadow, available on a seasonal basis depending upon local flooding conditions.

Micromorphological analysis of eight palaeosol profiles from the Coop and Power Station sites suggests that stable brown earth soils had developed on this lower half of the first-terrace gravels. These soils had once supported a woodland cover and allowed the development of argillic brown earths. Subsequent to clearance and the establishment of the field enclosure system, these soils remained flood-free and exhibited no indication of disturbance caused by cultivation. The sedimentary and molluscan analyses of the Newark Road Bronze Age ditch system (French 1980, 190–212) suggested that these enclosure ditches became infilled by natural weathering processes under ostensibly open conditions. No evidence of the influence of freshwater flooding was forthcoming, except at the extreme eastern edge of the system (ie at the Fourth Drove, Fengate, subsite; ibid, 210–12).

The palaeobotanical evidence from the ditches of the Newark Road Bronze Age enclosure system indicated similar open conditions, dominated by species of pasture, with some evidence of the presence of hedgerow species (Pryor 1980; Wilson 1984, microfiches 242–4). There was only a minor presence of cereals–it has been suggested that corn supplies might have been brought in from elsewhere, ready threshed.

The pollen record from the lowermost peat beneath the Flag Fen platform indicated a further expansion of wet fen associated with a rising water table (Scaife 1992 and Chapter 13). It was a diverse assemblage containing many aquatic species, which suggested that the water depth was increasing in the lowest part of the basin (and by implication spreading out over a much greater area of previously marginal land). A belt of alder carr woodland on the fringes effectively surrounded a gradually enlarging and encroaching fen.

Combining these strands of evidence, the earlier second millennium BC witnessed an extensive and long-lived opening up and management of large tracts of the lower part of the first-terrace gravels. Nonetheless, there was continued evidence of woodland in the immediate hinterland, in which oak was now more dominant than lime. The ditched enclosure system, with droveways aligned at right angles to the fen basin to the east, suggests that this system was intended as an integral part of a wider landscape. Pryor's (1980) original suggestion of the Newark Road field system being an area for overwintering livestock in enclosed pasture has been reinforced. The zone of lowermost terrace (c 1.52–3.05m OD) fringing the fen edge, more or less corresponding to the 50–100m upslope from the Cat's Water Drain, and perhaps 100–200m downslope into the fen basin beyond the Cat's Water Drain, was available for seasonal and unenclosed pasture. This zone would have been most ideal for late spring and summer grazing as the winter floodwaters receded south-eastwards, and acted as natural flood meadow. Over the millennium, this resource would have diminished very gradually, imperceptibly in terms of a human lifetime. A belt of alder carr fringed this flood meadow to the south-east, with sedge fen and shallow, open water beyond that in the lowest part of the Flag Fen Basin. Again, over the millennium, the zone of open water would have begun to deepen and widen, ultimately beginning to 'drown' the fringing carr vegetation.

The later second millennium BC

This is a period of marked change in environmental and landscape organisational terms.

By about 1300–1200 BC, the easternmost set of fields (ie those in the Fourth Drove subsite area) would have succumbed to seasonal flooding, as witnessed by the infilling of these ditches with silts containing a rich freshwater molluscan assemblage (French 1980, 204–12) and the overlying of the hengiform site and eastern field at the Coop site (French 1992b). The Fourth Drove subsite area of natural flood meadow became dominated by the post alignment (from 1363 to 967 BC; Neve 1992, 473), which was set in place on a similar alignment to ditches 8 and 9, overlying them and crossing the stream channel at c 3m OD. Furthermore, the remainder of the field system on the higher terrace to the north began to fall into disuse by the end of the second millennium BC (Pryor 1980).

During this period, the brown earth soils in the lower first-terrace zone became affected by the incorporation of considerable quantities of fines (or silt and clay), as well as minor amounts of eroded soil material derived from forest soils, presumably upstream and inland. These features suggest that this part of the terrace was subject to seasonal flooding carrying alluvial sediment. This evidence corroborates Scaife's (1992) pollen evidence for the development of a natural flood meadow environment fringing established pasture that was not subject to seasonal flood events. Furthermore, this environment was subject to a fluctuating water table and probably variable human exploitation.

Evaluation work of this same lower terrace zone further upstream between the modern Second Way and Third Way at the Depot (1992) site has provided further corroboration of this (Chapter 2; Evans 1992). This work has revealed an extensive area of Iron Age fields with upstanding banks. The buried soils sealed beneath these banks consistently show a brown earth soil that is receiving alluvial fine material prior to burial. These soils exhibit isolated signs of disturbance, which in one case has been caused by a narrow 'ridge and furrow' type of cultivation (compare with the Depot site; see also French 1992c).

To the east, Northey 'island', with its steeper and more abrupt fen edge, remained relatively drier and less affected by the encroachment of freshwater deposits than the Fengate 'shore' (French and Pryor 1993, 94–100). Nonetheless, there were indications that the brown earth soils were occasionally subjected to periods of peat encroachment, followed by drying, and perhaps occasional episodes of cultivation.

At the same time, the area of open water in which the Flag Fen platform was now under construction was deepening and enlarging, but still fringed by sedge fen. The post alignment crossed this entire landscape complex.

Analysis of the insect assemblages associated with the Flag Fen platform has provided evidence that corroborates that indicated by the palynological and micromorphological studies. It gives a uniform picture of well vegetated stagnant water or reed swamp, with permanent to near permanent water, and pools of water present on the platform and peat surfaces (Robinson 1992). In addition, a background element to the assemblage indicates the presence of a few trees, such as alder and willow, in a peat fen landscape, with grassland on drier ground and minerogenic soil surrounding the fen.

In summary, the end of the second millennium BC witnesses a substantial increase in the extent and influence of wetland in the Flag Fen Basin. The area of open water immediately around the platform has increased in extent and depth to a lesser amount, while the fringing sedge fen with associated peat development has encroached up to c 3.05m OD on the Fengate shore to the north-west, and begun to affect the edges of Northey 'island' to the east.

The alder carr fringing the fen remained despite the gradual progression to more aquatic conditions. In this context, as originally postulated in Pryor (1992b), the idea that the post alignment linked dry land to dry land across a narrow 'neck' of open fen takes on much greater significance. It might, perhaps, have formed a symbolic and human-made boundary against the rising water table of the encroaching deep fen to the east. In contrast, the dry hinterland continued to support a diverse assemblage of woodland and dryland herb taxa, with some evidence for a reduction in oak and an increase in alder, possibly associated with the construction of the Flag Fen platform and post alignment (Chapter 13).

The first millennium BC

A similar progression of events to those already set out for the later second millennium BC might be envisaged for the remainder of the later Bronze Age and throughout the Iron Age.

The first half of the millennium (spanning the later Bronze Age/Early Iron Age transition) sees base levels rising significantly in the Flag Fen Basin and the disuse and submergence of peat of the platform and the post alignment by the seventh century BC at the latest. All the known field systems on the adjacent first terrace and Northey 'island' are now out of use and substantially infilled. Despite this apparent 'abandonment', the pollen evidence suggests mixed agricultural land-use in the immediate region (Chapter 13). Perhaps associated with this are indications in the palaeobotanical record that hedgerow species reached a relative peak in the later Bronze Age (Wilson 1984, microfiches 242–4). Throughout this period it appears that alternating conditions of peat formation and minerogenic soil accumulation were associated with episodes of alluvial deposition over the fen-edge fringe zone between c 3.05m and c 4.57m OD. These stratigraphic features were best observed at the Power Station and Cat's Water (1990) sites. Further upstream at the Depot (1992) site, the landscape was solely dominated by the seasonal deposition of alluvium, with substantial periods of drying out in between.

This first half of the first millennium BC apparently witnessed a reversion to a relatively unordered and open landscape, in terms of settlement and ditched enclosure systems.

Instead, a largely open, pastoral landscape on the fen margins and lower first-terrace gravel was perhaps divided by a system of hedgerow boundaries. As no associated settlements have been found on the Fengate/Northey gravels, this might imply a shift in settlement somewhere, possibly to higher ground above c 6m (20')OD that has yet to be discovered. On the other hand, it might just imply a settlement pattern of dispersed small farmstead type of settlement. The large areas of common land between did not require enclosure. The gradually encroaching peat fen of the Flag Fen Basin would have begun to limit the available permanently dry land, but on the other hand, started to create more extensive zones of natural flood meadow on its margins. These would have been available on a seasonal basis for pastoral exploitation. Unfortunately, the distinct absence of relevant archaeological discoveries for this period, in both the fen and terrace landscape zones, makes these suggestions no more than surmises.

As early as the fifth century BC, there are the first archaeological signs of nucleation at the ROM/DoE Vicarage Farm subsite (Pryor 1974) and, with the development of the substantial 'hamlet' at the Cat's Water subsite by the third century BC, of occupation throughout the Middle and later Iron Age (Pryor 1984a, 210–27). Most of the archaeological features, namely pits and enclosure ditches, have semi-water-logged primary fills that suggest that there was a reasonably constant and high groundwater table over most of the first-terrace gravel zone between *c* 3m and *c* 6m OD. Palaeobotanical evidence for weed species associated with arable land and cultivation reach a peak in the Iron Age, as do species of cultivated plants, a feature that continued into the Roman period (Wilson 1984, microfiches 242–4). This is corroborated by the relative increase in the number and diversity of herb pollen (Chapter 13). Nonetheless, evidence for cereal cultivation remains minor, as does evidence for hedgerow and woodland species. There is, however, a distinct increase in the species of water and marsh plants. A wide range of species that inhabit wet mud, shallow water, and wet ditches is represented. The faunal remains indicate that cattle predominated slightly over sheep as the mainstay of the livestock component of the economy (Biddick 1984, microfiches 245–75). In addition, fish were represented by remains of pike, tench, bream, and carp, and birds by duck, swan, goose, heron, stork, cormorant, sea eagle, and goosander. Incidentally, along with another Iron Age site at Haddenham in the fens to the south, this is the best evidence recovered from the fenland for the exploitation of fish and fowl resources (Evans and Serjeantson 1988).

It would appear that, by the later part of the first millennium BC, the Fengate fen edge was being much more extensively settled and exploited. It was very much a mixed economy, utilising the best of the adjacent fenland resources as well as the fen margins and drier terrace hinterland. While there was an evident increase in the enclosure and division of the landscape by ditch systems on the terrace gravels, the fen edge was well defined at the southern edge of the Cat's Water settlement site at *c* 2.7m OD. The adjacent Flag Fen Basin was dominated by peat growth, with many semi-aquatic and marginal aquatic plants present. The remaining alder/willow carr fringing the higher ground around the basin became progressively inundated, giving rise to a shallow, muddy water fen community (Chapter 13). Finally, brief periods might have been influenced by brackish water within the basin in the later first millennium BC, as suggested by Juggins from his diatom analyses (discussed in Pryor *et al* 1986, 21), probably derived from the backing up of freshwater against high spring tide conditions further to the east.

The Roman and later periods

The landscape and environmental setting of the Fengate/Flag Fen Basin areas during the first two centuries AD probably continued that of the earlier conditions.

There might, however, have been a period of drying out of the surface of the peat fen when the gravel road or Fen Causeway was being constructed across the peat surface of the Flag Fen Basin in the later first century AD (Pryor 1984a; Chapter 13).

By the third century AD, most of the remaining open ditches at the Cat's Water site had been affected by the deposition of silty clays. These were undoubtedly derived from a renewal of freshwater flooding and the deposition of alluvially derived fines over a much larger and higher area of terrace for the first time, that is above *c* 3m OD. The greyish brown colour and silty clay composition of these infills, which is particularly distinctive, has been observed in similar situations in the lower Welland valley at Etton (French *et al* 1992) and at Barnack (Passmore and Macklin 1993). In terms of clearance and cultivation, it suggests that exploitation of the 'heavier' soils on the limestone higher ground to the west of present day Peterborough and Stamford had begun by this period. This led to increased hillwash erosion and alluvial transport of these silt/clay-rich sediments in floodwaters and their deposition downstream.

The remainder of the surviving stratigraphic sequence on the Fengate fen edge continues to be dominated by the deposition of silty clay alluvial deposits. This has been observed more or less continuously from the present day Second to Fourth Drove area on the terrace gravels up to above *c* 3.7m OD. Several major levels of alluvial deposition are also evident in the Flag Fen Basin sections. At least one phase is visible below and one phase above the Fen Causeway section (Pryor *et al* 1986, fig 3), while two phases are evident above the post alignment at the Power Station site (French in Pryor *et al* 1992, 458–61, fig 7).

Indeed the micromorphological analyses of these alluvial deposits (French, Chapter 3) confirms that these silty clay deposits are composed of eroded topsoils and fine material derived from elsewhere, presumably from upstream and inland, from the Nene valley. Similar and extensive post-Late Roman alluvial deposits have also been observed in the Nene floodplain, overlying the Orton Longueville barrow group on the western side of Peterborough (French 1983; O'Neill 1981), and overlying the post-Late Roman landscape of the lower Welland valley to Borough Fen area to the north of Peterborough (French 1990; French and Pryor 1993, 68–79, 105–7).

The Late Roman and medieval landscape of the Fengate fen edge was therefore dominated by freshwater flooding and the gradual accretion of fine sediments carried in these floodwaters. It would have provided natural flood meadows for grazing on an extensive scale.

Their lateral extent would have varied considerably on an annual basis, very much controlled by land-use and abuse upstream, as well as by peat growth and the influence of high tides acting as physical barriers in the

Table 17.1 Summary of the main landscape history events in the Flag Fen Basin

third millennium BC	earlier second	later second	earlier first	later first	Romano-British	later
Fengate						
mixed deciduous woodland	extensive and gradual deforestation and establishment of grassland					
argillic brown earths; well drained brown earths		becoming seasonally wet		drier	wetter	
	mixed land-use with extensive pasture; ditched field systems with droveways		abandonment of fields; hedgerow enclosed fields nucleation abandonment			
Fen edge						
wide zone of natural flood meadow encroaching to 3m contour; peat growth and alluvial aggradation					drier; then renewed alluvial aggradation	
Flag Fen Basin						
wide fringe of carr woodland — diminishes with time reed swamp and zone of shallow open water which becomes more extensive						
		Flag Fen platform and post alignment		peat surface drier		
				renewed peat growth and alluviation		
Northey 'island'						
wooded, becoming more open with field systems				abandoned; peat encroachment		

fens further to the east. The naming of the present day roads across this Fengate fen edge as First, Second, Third, and Fourth Droves must refer to this uninterrupted period of land-use.

The Flag Fen Basin continued to be subject to shallow-, muddy-water, sedge fen, and peat-growth conditions, with additions of alluvially derived sediments from time to time often captured in this basin. This period of peat growth with alluvial additions continued throughout the medieval period. Very little of this peat has survived the impact of post-seventeenth-century AD drainage, so that today it is very much confined to the central part of the basin.

This peat might have been up to 2m or more in thickness above the present day ground surface (R Evans personal communication). Today, the desiccated upper peat is largely incorporated within the (once) underlying alluvium.

Conclusions

The influence of gradually rising base water levels in the fens, as well as seasonal, lateral, and vertical variation in the influence of peat formation and alluvial deposition, were all intrinsically linked to the development of the landscape in the Flag Fen Basin and adjacent to the terrace gravel and 'island' margins. Although seasonal episodes of flooding, aggradation, and erosion might have been disruptive of this organised landscape, the layout of this landscape (as recovered in the archaeological record) throughout the second and first millennia BC took good advantage of and adapted to the dry and seasonally and permanently wet zones of this evolving landscape (Table 17.1). Moreover, the Fengate gravel terrace, Flag Fen Basin, and Northey 'island' landscapes must now be viewed as interdependent in terms of their use, exploitation, and development.

18 Discussion, part 1: patterns of settlement and land-use

This chapter will be devoted to the changing patterns of settlement and land-use around the fringes of the Flag Fen Basin. Special attention will be paid to the results of recent excavations, summarised in Chapters 2 to 5. The purpose of the chapter will be to provide an archaeological context and rationale for the Bronze Age timber structures of Flag Fen, which will be considered in Chapter 19.

Definitions

The Fens are a wetland — albeit a drained wetland — and Fenland sites are frequently cited in reports on wetland archaeology (eg Coles and Lawson 1987; Coles 1992). In reality, however, many ancient sites were located on dry ground close to but not in the wetland, as defined below. The use of the term 'wetland' in such circumstances can be justified by the wide scope of the studies cited. In the present instance, however, it is necessary to be more precise, as this is a study in the development and exploitation of the landscape at a microlevel. For the purposes of this discussion, five separate categories of land-use potential will be considered, which can be defined as follows:

Dry land. Not flooded and capable of crowing cereals and other crops on a regular basis.
Occasionally flooded land. Capable of growing crops in most years, but sometimes subject to flooding. This might be good hay and grazing land.
Regularly flooded land. The flooding in this instance was probably seasonal. This land would not have been suitable for cereal crops that will not tolerate flooding during their growing season (Groenman-van-Waateringe and Jansma 1969). This type of land would have been very suitable for grazing and even for hay (in drier years).
Wetland. Land that was under shallow water for most of the year. The vegetation when clear of trees (alder carr) was mainly of aquatic marginals and fen types, such as reed, reedmace, flag iris, sedge, rush, and water-loving grasses. Suitable for extensive summer grazing and browsing in dry seasons.
Open water. Land that was permanently flooded and that supported a true aquatic fauna and flora. Suitable for fishing and wildfowling.

The Flag Fen Basin consists of a very gently sloping plain of terrace gravel, which shelves eastwards from the eastern edge of modern Peterborough (Fig 1.7) and out into the low-lying land of Flag Fen for approximately a kilometre. The ground rises more steeply on the other side of the basin at Northey, a north-west extension of the large natural 'island' on which the

town of Whittlesey is located. The precise extent of the basin to the south is hard to estimate, as much of the area lies beneath the southern suburbs of Peterborough, but it undoubtedly amounted to up to half a dozen square kilometres. For present purposes, the discussion will be confined to the Fengate/Northey area, which was the point of access into the flood meadow of the enclosed embayment from the open fen to the north.

In the previous chapter, the processes of environmental change were described. These essentially amount to increasing wetness through time, first in the lower-lying parts of Flag Fen and later around the fringes of Fengate and Northey. The size of the Flag Fen wetland and regularly flooded land would therefore have depended on the period in question. In the later Neolithic it was restricted, but by the Iron Age it consisted of the entire area (Fig 1.3 — Area of Encroaching Fen).

The nature of prehistoric landscape change

It is now quite apparent that the demise of the Bronze Age ditched fields was far more gradual and complex than had been thought (eg Pryor 1980, 186–9). In the discussion that follows it will be seen how that field system (Landscape 3) appears to have been abandoned progressively, starting with the wettest land. Indeed, it is perfectly possible that the lowest-lying enclosed areas were being abandoned at the same time that new fields were being established on higher ground. Rising water levels must have played an important part in these changes, but they would also have accommodated the wider social changes that ultimately led to the inception of nucleated and, later on, to defended settlements in the region (Cunliffe 1991, 213–46). Given this newly extended timetable of events, it is becoming possible to understand how local communities could have adapted to the significant changes of culture and environment that were taking place over the millennium between, say, 1300 and 300 BC. A changing landscape can be shaped to accommodate the needs of a changing society. It is an interactive or reciprocal process in which the requirements of society are constrained by the nature of the natural environment. By the end of the Bronze Age, for example, the higher ground around Tower Works had become the focus of settlement. This area suited the emerging regional polities better than the equally flood-free land around Newark Road or Vicarage Farm. At present, it can only be guessed why the focus shifted to the south-west, but it was almost certainly not due to water alone. Perhaps the historical knowledge of what the post alignment and its landfall represented, to which the presence of so much Iron Age metalwork so vividly attests, exerted a constraining influence on later developments.

Recent research has provided opportunities to examine both the pace and process of landscape change. It is now apparent that the sharp breaks that were once so evident between the different landscape regimes were a product of a foreshortened archaeological perspective — itself the result of evaluating only partial data and an inadequate appreciation of chronology. The complexity of the transition between the landscapes of the Bronze and Iron Ages might well also have been reflected in antiquity. By the same token, it is doubtful whether there really were such abrupt changes between the landscapes of the earlier and late Neolithic. At present, however, the means to appreciate such detail are lacking.

After more than twenty-five years of continuous research into the prehistory of landscape development to the east of Peterborough, it is becoming increasingly apparent that the story is very complex. More is known about the Bronze Age landscapes than any others. Evidence for the earlier Neolithic landscape is still slight. The Iron Age landscape remains the most difficult to elucidate: clearly there was more than one landscape, both in time and space, but more information is required to clarify the picture. Recent work by the Cambridge and Birmingham University Units at the Depot site and at Area 1 of Site O has revealed that the preservation of Iron Age levels is outstanding and that settlements can be closely associated with field systems. In the future, this is probably the area in which most progress will be made.

Although the discussion that follows will concentrate on the Bronze Age landscape, which was particularly relevant to events in Flag Fen, it will first be necessary to provide short accounts of the less well understood landscapes that went before and after.

Landscape 1: the earlier Neolithic

Available evidence suggests that the Flag Fen Basin was partially cleared of tree cover from the earlier Neolithic period (Chapter 17). At that time all but the very lowest parts of the basin were still essentially dry; no direct evidence (ie bones or grain) for the nature of the local economy is known, but a possible Neolithic droveway at Vicarage Farm (Pryor 1974, fig 12, F14 and F17) would indicate that livestock were significant, and might already have been kept in some numbers.

The earlier Neolithic landscape is so far only known at Fengate and the evidence for it is very slight. On the other hand, it is also consistent and involves a number of different sites and monuments (Pryor 1988). The orientation of the earlier Neolithic landscape was significantly different to that of the Bronze Age landscape (Fig 18.1). At this point, it is appropriate to note that in a recent discussion it was stated that the orientation of the earlier Neolithic landscape, when compared with the

Fig 18.1 Map showing location and orientation of the earlier Neolithic landscape: 1, Vicarage Farm droveway; 2, Site 11 mortuary enclosure; 3, Padholme Road funerary 'house'; 4, Cat's Water multiple burial; 5, Cat's Water (1997) mortuary structure. Diverging arrows show the orientations of the earlier Neolithic landscape (EN) and Bronze Age landscapes (BA)

Bronze Age landscape, did not respect the edge of the nearby fen (Pryor 1988). Since that was written, however, it has emerged that the edge of the fen south of the Storey's Bar Road subsite actually swings significantly 'inland', towards the south-west, in part following the line of the now canalised Cat's Water Drain. Very recently (January 1998) a commercial evaluation at Site Q has demonstrated that the 'inland' tendency of the buried fen edge resembled more a true 'inlet' or embayment (Fig 2.10; the 'inlet' is defined by the 2m contour).

The orientation of the earlier Neolithic landscape can now be seen to have been at right angles to the fen edge in the 'inlet' upon which it was aligned. In other words, as a small-scale layout it makes perfect sense, since it respected the fen to the south-west. It seems unlikely that it ever covered an area as large the Bronze Age landscape, as it would have had to change its orientation quite abruptly at several points in order to do so. Its orientation can only make sense if it was limited in area. It is possible that the surviving archaeological evidence–essentially a linear arrangement of sites and features extending back from the edge of the fen–might be a direct reflection of the shape of the ancient landscape, which was, in other words, both small and linear.

A confined linear cleared landscape might well have evolved if livestock were regularly driven from higher ground to the developing fen and fen-edge pastures along a particular route.

Indeed, some animals might have been left to graze within this landscape, specifically to clear trees and browse off secondary regrowth of trees killed in previous years. It is quite conceivable that the earliest cleared landscapes could have been both linear and open spaces.

It is, of course, possible that the land immediately north of the earlier Neolithic landscape was still uncleared. This would accord well with French's interpretation of the contemporary natural landscape (Chapter 17). If this was indeed the case, then it can be suggested that the earlier Neolithic clearings of the wooded countryside around the edge of the Flag Fen Basin were somewhat larger than the hypothetical clearance of a few trees around settlements and waterholes as has been suggested, for example, in Denmark (Madsen and Jensen 1982). In the Danish model, livestock obtained their forage by browsing in the woods or woodland edge around the settlements. Whatever its origins, the size of the Fengate earlier Neolithic landscape suggests that woodland had been cleared specifically to encourage the growth of grassland. The evidence for the existence of a landscape cleared of tree cover by the end of the third millennium BC has been discussed by French in the previous chapter. It was suggested that by the time the fields of the later Bronze Age landscape were laid out, some 'substantial clearance inroads' had been made. Micromorphological analysis of these soils clearly demonstrated that they had not been subject to disturbance brought about by tillage. It must be supposed, therefore, that the clearance was brought about to assist the development of pasture.

The dating of the first landscape is problematical and is based on the Padholme Road subsite 'house' or funerary structure. The original excavations produced two radiocarbon dates that were widely separated. In the present report we have selected the date from a possible cornerpost of the structure (GaK-4197; 4395±50 BP); this sample gave a result of cal BC 3310±2910 (Table 16.1). The rectilinear mortuary enclosure, the Cat's Water multiple pit burial, and other elements of the earlier Neolithic landscape would fit the evidence best if they were placed in the earlier Neolithic period. Such a date would also accord quite well with the Cat's Water (1997) Neolithic mortuary structure in its earlier (plainware) phase. The analysis of absolute chronology in Chapter 16 suggests that the Neolithic mortuary structure is very likely to be earlier than the Storey's Bar Road (Grooved Ware) settlement.

So far we have discussed a single, elongated, earlier Neolithic landscape. The Boongate Roundabout excavations (Chapter 2) have recently provided indications of another possible Neolithic settlement some 350m south-west of the 'main' linear landscape. It is tempting to suggest that this site might represent a possible southern edge to the 'main' landscape.

Alternatively, it might form part of an altogether separate landscape. Much will depend on the dating of this site, for it is difficult to determine, at present,

whether it is earlier or later Neolithic. If it were later Neolithic, then its presence so close to the Storey's Bar Road settlement could be explained in terms, perhaps, of 'settlement drift'.

Landscape 2: the later Neolithic

The nature of the transition from the earlier Neolithic to the Bronze Age landscape is still unclear, but the suggested change in landscape orientation argues strongly for a period when the countryside was not parcelled up in a rigidly axial or coaxial fashion, but neither was it abandoned. There is good evidence that the landscape was open and clearance probably continued, but whether at an increased or decreased pace is unknown. Late Neolithic settlements included the Storey's Bar Road subsite (Pryor 1978) and the well known pit groups of the pre-war Gravel Pits sites (Fig 1.5; Abbott 1910; Leeds 1922). Excavations at the Depot in 1992 established beyond any doubt that the field boundary ditches and the Grooved Ware settlement at Storey's Bar Road (Pryor 1978) were not connected, either chronologically or functionally (Evans and Pollard, Chapter 2).

Fresh evidence for further Late Neolithic settlement was provided recently by excavations in Area 1 of Site O (Chapter 2). Here, numerous small pits and postholes of later Neolithic and earlier Bronze Age date were found to the east of the Storey's Bar Road subsite. Although the evidence from trial trenches can, of course, give a misleading impression, the distribution of features across Site Q showed little or no evidence for discontinuity. In early 1999 came the discovery of a large backfilled pit containing fresh sherds of Grooved Ware, some 150m south-west of the 'inlet' defined by the 2m contour (Fig 2.10). It is interesting to note that the large pit contained a possible aurochs skull, very reminiscent of pit Y4 at Storey's Bar Road. Smaller pits containing Neolithic flintwork were found close by the large backfilled pit (Pryor and Trimble 1999). Taken together, the evidence suggests that the Storey's Bar Road settlement area was very much larger than once thought. Indeed, it would now appear to be one of the larger Grooved Ware settlements in England.

In landscape terms, the later Neolithic in the Flag Fen Basin can perhaps be seen as a phase of retrenchment between periods of expansion and of more intensive exploitation. It was also a time when the 'liturgical movements' of people and flocks between the gradually developing fen pastures and the dry land at the margins, must have had their origins (Bradley 1978, 107).

In essence, however, the landscape appears to have been open, without permanent field boundary features. Barrows or ring-ditches regularly spaced along the marginal plain of the developing fen might have been used as markers to divide the landscape into blocks very roughly 200m wide. Three monuments of this type are known from the southern parts of Fengate, at the Depot (1992) site, the Storey's Bar Road sub-site (Pryor 1978, 35), and the Cat's Water (1990) site.

It is of some interest that the best preserved and most archaeologically investigated part of the Bronze Age ditched field system, around the Fengate landfall of the Flag Fen post alignment, has not yet produced evidence of such a marker. Since the 'Area of Encroaching Fen' shelves very gently at this point, it is possible, if there was a marker, that it pre-dates the Bronze Age fields and might still lie hidden beneath the superficial deposits of Flag Fen. Having said this, it is unlikely that a barrow mound could be concealed below less than 2m of covering deposit. A monument with a lower physical profile, such as a henge, or even a causewayed enclosure, perhaps remains to be found. The presence of reworked Group VI axe fragments and serrated flint flakes within the buried soil of the Power Station (Chapter 11) hint at a possible earlier Neolithic site of some importance somewhere in the immediate vicinity. If, however, an early site of this type lies hidden in Flag Fen, why no marker was constructed on the dry land (unless, of course none was required) is without explanation. The clue to the problem appears to be that, if there was a possible linear landscape in earlier Neolithic times, why was there not something similar, but on a different alignment, in the later Neolithic? If the landfall and route of the post alignment was also the path of an ancient, but unbounded droveway, there would be no need to mark the route with a permanent monument, such as a barrow. The droveway itself would do the job perfectly well.

In the city of Peterborough's Sites and Monuments Record, three barrows or possible barrows are noted, north of the post alignment. One was located east of Storey's Bar Road on the alignment of ditches 10 and 11 (it has been destroyed by a reservoir). Another lay east of Newark Road, just north of the Paving Factory site and the third is recorded some 200m to the north, but closer to the fen margins. Whatever the accuracy of the original reports, the point to note is that the monuments in question are widely, if not evenly spaced. They are certainly not clumped together. There is no suggestion that barrows in Fengate were arranged in tightly grouped, or linear 'cemeteries', as at Borough Fen, just 7km to the north-west (Hall 1987, 24), or around Haddenham and Over in the southern Fens (Hall and Coles 1994, 83). The conclusion is hard to avoid that the widely spaced barrows in Fengate served a rather different territorial role to those of the Fenland 'cemetery' sites.

Landscape 3: the Bronze Age

The Bronze Age landscape will be considered in three parts: first, the central and northern elements of the Fengate system; then the more recently revealed southern element, and finally Northey. It will shortly be seen that the droveway defined by ditches 1 and 2 of the ROM/DoE Bronze Age system (Fig 1.4) was an important division in the landscape; this drove, and the fields springing off it to the north, will form the boundary between the centre/north and the southern elements of the Bronze Age field system.

The full extent of the Fengate Bronze Age landscape will take many years to reveal, as large areas still lie hidden beneath alluvium. Enough has been exposed over the past twenty-five years, however, to assess how it might originally have developed and operated. Recent commercial excavations, considered in Chapters 2 and 3, have shown that the system is still surprisingly well preserved, both north and south of the original extent of the fields, as revealed by the ROM/DoE project. The principal features of the Bronze Age landscape have been fully described in the third and fourth Fengate reports (Pryor 1980 and 1984); results from more recent excavations have been added to the original ROM/DoE plans to produce a more comprehensive general map (Fig 1.4). No attempt will be made here to describe the ROM/DoE fields in other than the broadest outline. Instead, the discussion will concentrate on new information provided by the many excavations that have taken place since the last ROM/DoE season of 1978.

The Bronze Age fields: centre and north

The central elements of the Bronze Age fields were located at the following sites and subsites: Padholme Road, Cat's Water, Site Q, Power Station, Fourth Drove, Site 11, and Newark Road (Fig 1.4, ditch 1 to ditch 11). The northern element comprised ditches north of ditch 11 at Newark Road, ditches at Global Doors, and those at the Paving Factory.

Character and layout

The fields of the central and northern parts of the Bronze Age system are best described as axial, rather than coaxial. The system is divided up by double-ditched droveways, which run across the fen-margin gravel plain, towards the edge of the regularly flooded land, at right angles (Fig 1.4). There is a droveway at intervals of approximately 100m, or slightly less — roughly half the distance between the barrows and ring-ditches that might have formed the original sight-lines or 'markers' for the initial laying-out of the system. Patterns and intervals of partitioning between the main east–west droveways seem to have been more haphazard. These might reflect the individual management requirements of different farms or landholders. The arrangement of the landscape would still accord with the original suggestion that flood-free land at Fengate was a 'home base' for people and flocks that made extensive use of seasonally available fenland pasture (Pryor 1978, 157–63). In the autumn, flocks would be driven to higher ground around the fringes of the Flag Fen Basin where they would be sorted, exchanged, and culled.

Domestic settlement within the central and north part of the Bronze Age landscape was extensive and dispersed. It usually consisted of a house and one or two outbuildings that have left insubstantial archaeological traces. Rather remarkably, none of the houses found to date have shown evidence for rebuilding or for the replacement of more than one or two individual posts. A use life of perhaps a generation is indicated for most of these buildings.

This would suggest that the human settlements were relatively short-lived, in contrast to the livestock-handling features of the landscape.

Origins

The most significant step in the evolution of the ancient landscape of the Flag Fen Basin undoubtedly took place in the early centuries of the second millennium BC. This period saw the laying-out of an extensive axial ditched enclosure system on dry and occasionally flooded land. The system was arranged at right angles to the gradually encroaching margins of the regularly flooded land.

The origins of the ditched fields, droves, and paddocks are difficult to pin down with precision.

Most of the ditches were both drains and boundaries. In the Fenland, field drains were cleaned out (ie recut) on a regular basis. This usually involved slight enlargement of the ditch.

In effect, this meant that objects found within the ditch fillings were either residual or were contemporary with the final recutting. In archaeological terms, this pattern of regular maintenance inevitably gives rise to a foreshortened chronology.

The chronological analysis of Chapter 16 has demonstrated that the central component of the Bronze Age fields overlaps with the Storey's Bar Road Grooved Ware settlement of the previous landscape. This would support the idea that the Bronze Age droveway that led up to the (later) post alignment might well have been an important landscape feature by the start of the Bronze Age. There are no absolute dates for the northern element of the Bronze Age fields, but Evans and Pollard (Chapter 2) have clearly demonstrated that the southern fields postdate Storey's Bar Road. It would seem likely, therefore, that the southern Bronze Age fields came into use somewhat later than the central Bronze Age fields. Since both follow the same alignment, there must have been a broad period of overlap.

Development and extent

It will be suggested that the ditched enclosures on either side of the 'main' droveway defined by ditches 8 and 9 formed a system of communal stockyards, akin in some respects to a marketplace (Fig 18.2). As this central part of the field system was closely linked to the post alignment, it seems reasonable to suppose that it

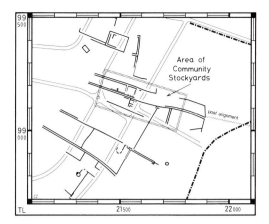

Fig 18.2 Map showing the principal features of the Bronze Age landscape in the vicinity of the post alignment

was also a place of special significance. As just noted, the evidence would suggest that the central area (between ditches 1 and 11, Fig 1.4) was perhaps also the longest-lived part of the field system. Certainly the ditches were on the whole more substantial than those of the southern and northern elements, suggesting perhaps that they had been subject to a longer period of regular and repeated recutting.

Even in flat country, landscapes might share common points of orientation, and it is of interest to note that both the earlier Neolithic landscape and the most southerly droveway of the central Bronze Age landscape (defined by ditches 1 and 2 of the ROM/DoE system) were aligned on the 'inlet' of wet fen revealed by the recent evaluation excavation of Site Q (Fig 2.10). Clearly this small and seemingly unremarkable 'inlet' had been an important feature of the prehistoric countryside for a very long time.

Excavation at the Depot (1992) site (Chapter 2) and Barleycroft Farm in southern Cambridgeshire (Fig 1.2) have suggested that certain arrangements of double ditches might have been used to drain, mark out, or define a hedge line (Evans and Knight 1997). The suggestion by Chris Evans (personal communication and Chapter 2) that many of the Newark Road smaller, subsidiary droveways could in fact have been hedge lines (Fig 18.3) has much to commend it.

The double ditches around enclosure C could well have enclosed a hedge, as could the double ditches along the north side of enclosure B and part of enclosure A (Fig 18.3). It could be argued, however, that if the double ditches around enclosure C were for a hedge, then the entranceway between C and B might have been squared off, like the more probable hedge lines on the north sides of enclosures A, B, 1, and 3. The round-house eaves-drip gully drains into a very substantial ditch. This shows repeated evidence of recutting along its entire length, as if the land around it was regularly disturbed by the passage of livestock (Pryor 1980, pl 14).

The paired ditches around the south side of enclosure C were also entered at two points (Fig 18.3, i and ii), in a manner that suggests access was being sought to the space between the two ditches. If the ditches around the southern sides of enclosure C were droves, then those around the northern side were also probably droves. The parallel ditches on the east side of enclosure B also make more sense as short droves, perhaps for sorting stock, but the short triple ditches at the south-east corner hint at an unditched hedge line along the enclosure's southern side.

The double ditches parallel to and south of ditch 8 would certainly make sense as hedges. Evans' suggestion has added an important new dimension to the complexities of interpreting ancient ditch systems. In future, it will be important to prove possible droveways or hedge lines on a case-by-case basis, either by means of soil science (phosphates, soil micromorphology, and so forth) or through general considerations of livestock management. The northern element of the system has been less fully investigated than other parts. There was a clear, ditch-free void some 40m wide north of ditch 11 (Pryor 1988, 27), which would indicate that the two elements of the system were functionally separated. The droveway running north-south in Area VII of Newark Road shows much evidence for recutting, although the ditches themselves are slight. While it is hard to be certain, the pattern of modification and recutting, together with the general layout, suggest that these were indeed droveways subject to damage by trample and traffic.

Some 50m east of the Newark Road open area excavations, aerial photographs have revealed a double- (perhaps even triple-) ditched rectangular enclosure clearly aligned on east–west droveways of the main system that might, in turn, have joined the recut and modified droveways just described (Fig 1.4). This enclosure finds a close parallel in size and layout at Welland Bank Quarry, some 10km north of Fengate (Pryor 1998c). The Welland Bank enclosure was of Late Bronze/Early Iron Age date and was completely excavated. It produced very few finds and no evidence for internal houses. There was, however, a substantially built timber corral or stockade at one corner, and the entire enclosure seems to have been used for the containment and management of livestock. Like its Fengate counterpart, it formed an integral part of a ditched field system, served by droveways and corner entranceways. Since the Welland Bank enclosure was located near a settlement, it was probably used to house the animals belonging to that small community. A recent planning pre-determination excavation about 300m east of ditch 18 revealed a peat-filled 'inlet', of comparable size to that found further south (illustrated in Pryor 1998b, fig 61; Fig 2.10). Close to the north side of this 'inlet' was a Beaker period settlement of small pits, filled with flintwork and pottery (Vaughan and Trevarthen 1998). An association between the settlement and the northern fields can not be proven, but it seems most probable. Again, it would perhaps suggest an early date for the Bronze Age fields in this part of Fengate.

The cropmarks west of Newark Road are slight, suggesting that the ditches themselves might be shallow; certainly the ditches revealed in the most northerly parts of the system, as it is presently known at Global Doors and the Paving Factory, are also insubstantial (Fig 3.2).

Demise

It is difficult to provide a sound *terminus ante quem* for ditches of the central and northern element. We have seen that the lowest-lying parts of the system had gone out of use in the Middle Bronze Age and we know that the yards of the Cat's Water Iron Age settlement were laid out on an entirely different alignment. The only reliable *terminus ante quem* is provided by a four-post structure on the Newark Road site that was cut into a completely filled-in Bronze Age field boundary ditch. Charcoal from a posthole of the structure, which also yielded Late Bronze Age pottery, gave a radiocarbon result (HAR-773; 2740±80 BP) of cal BC 1100±790 (Table 16.1).

The chronological analysis of Chapter 16 showed that the main period of abandonment of the central fields was between cal BC 1260 and 1020 (Table 16.2). This was the time when regular maintenance ceased. It coincides remarkably closely with a period of some 150 years (Phase 2) when building activity ceased at the post alignment. This was probably a period when water levels (and perhaps storms and gales) in Flag Fen were relatively stable, so that constant maintenance and new building was not required.

The Bronze Age fields: south

The droveway defined by ditches 1 and 2 of the ROM/DoE system (Fig 1.4) was the most southerly feature of the central element of the Bronze Age ditched field system. Ditches of the southern element were found at Storey's Bar Road, Sites O and Q, the Depot (1992 and 1997), and Tower Works sites.

Recent commercial development in the southern part of Fengate has given rise to an important series of excavations, which have been summarised in Chapters 2 and 3. Hitherto, knowledge of the southern Bronze Age fields was provided by the ROM/DoE excavations of 1973 in the Storey's Bar Road subsite (Pryor 1978). Recent work has, however, transformed understanding of this area, where archaeological deposits are particularly well preserved. The three most important excavations were at the Depot (1992), Sites O and Q, and the Tower Works; all were evaluations, and so more work still remains to be done.

Character and layout

The fields of the southern parts of the Bronze Age system, in contrast to those just described, can best be defined as truly coaxial. This at least can be shown to apply to the Depot and Storey's Bar Road sites. Elsewhere the evidence is less clear cut. In general the ditches of the southern element are slighter than those further north and there is evidence to suggest that the system might have been in use for a shorter, or perhaps later, period of time. It has been suggested that the droveway defined by ditches 1 and 2 of the ROM/DoE fields formed the southern boundary of the central element of the system. However, two right-angled or L-shaped ditches are shown on aerial photographs to run south of ditch 1 (Fig 1.4). These were exposed and excavated in 1974 at the Storey's Bar Road subsite (Pryor 1984a, 13–15). The two ditches concerned (ibid fig 9, N1 and P18) were larger than others of the southern system and shared the characteristic filling and U profile of ditches belonging to the central system, as excavated at Padholme Road (eg Pryor 1980, 15). They are best considered as 'outliers' of that system.

The clearance of a large open area north of the Grooved Ware settlement site at Storey's Bar Road demonstrated clearly that there was an open, ditch-free 'void' between the southern and central elements of the system, just as there was between the central and northern parts. Excluding the two 'outlying' L-shaped ditches, the void between ditch 1 of the central system and the northernmost ditch of the Storey's Bar Road system (Pryor 1978, fig 6, W23 and R2) was approximately 105m wide (Pryor 1984a, fig 8).

Origins

The excavation of the Depot site in 1992 led to a reappraisal of the Storey's Bar Road ditched fields, which Evans and Pollard (Chapter 2) have convincingly shown belong within the Bronze Age and not the later Neolithic (contra Pryor 1978). The only secure relative dating is still Storey's Bar Road, where a *terminus post quem* is provided by the relationship of a field boundary ditch to the ring-ditch, which it cuts. The ring-ditch yielded sherds of Collared Urn. At the Depot Site (1992), Bronze Age field ditches 1 and 2 clearly bend to respect another ring-ditch of probable Late Neolithic or Early Bronze Age date (Fig 2.4; Evans 1992, fig 4).

Development and extent

The ditched Bronze Age fields of the Depot site most probably represent an extension of the nearby Site O and Storey's Bar Road fields. At each site, the ditches were relatively slight and followed the same alignment. It has been suggested above and in Chapter 2 that the paired ditches of the Depot Bronze Age system probably ran alongside a central bank on which a hedge was planted. Certainly it is hard to see them as droveways: the corners are too sharp and entranceways into or out of the hypothetical 'drove' are rare in the extreme. It is perhaps best to see these fields as hedged paddocks.

Although it shared a common axis or alignment, the southern system was not homogeneous.

The Depot site was characterised by small hedged paddocks, whereas the Bronze Age fields of Site O seem to have been laid out on a somewhat larger scale, complete with at least one convincing double-ditched droveway running at right angles to the edge of the regularly flooded land. Storey's Bar Road might be seen as a compromise between the two. The important excavations at the Tower Works have enlarged the known extent of the Fengate Bronze Age system into the heart of the original Gravel Pits settlement area of G Wyman Abbott (1910). Although concrete hardstanding and other modern disturbance caused the archaeologists from the Cambridge University Unit practical problems, they were able to reveal ditches of the Bronze Age system, and more importantly, to plot their approximate orientation (Fig 1.4). This work showed that the ditches of the southern system 'slavishly' followed the orientation of the central system, which was aligned on the edge of the fen as known between Site Q and the Power Station. This orientation ignored the fact that the fen edge swings quite sharply south and west, south of the Cat's Water subsite, a course that is followed by the Cat's Water Drain. The network of modern roads follows the curve, but the ditches of the Tower Works system clearly ignore the westward sweep of the fen edge and the natural rise and fall of the gravel terrace on which they sit. This rather peculiar layout would suggest that the southern element of the Bronze Age system was laid out later than the central and that, for practical or cultural reasons, it was decided that the two should closely adhere to the same alignment, despite local topography.

Demise

The Bronze Age ditches of the Depot site (1992) appear to have been abandoned by the time that the rectangular 'settlement compound' enclosing a round building (Structure II) was constructed (Figs 2.4 and 2.5). The dating of the compound is uncertain, but on present evidence it would appear to be more Iron Age than Bronze Age. Also at the Depot site, the ditches of a 'late' (Iron Age) field system clearly cut those of the Bronze Age system. It is possible that the Bronze Age fields close to the fen edge, at the Depot Site, were abandoned very much earlier than those on higher ground, as can be demonstrated at the Power Station.

So far the Tower Works has revealed the Bronze Age ditched fields at by far the highest point yet examined in Fengate, no less than 5m OD. The ditched fields here appear to be associated with a remarkable post-built rectangular building and deposits of 'dark earth'.

Features associated with this settlement produced pottery that lacked the finer wares and decoration usually associated with the Gravel Pits material (Hawkes and Fell 1945). Pottery from the ROM/DoE project at Vicarage Farm and Cat's Water was found in features that gave late radiocarbon dates, suggesting that the style continued in use at Fengate well into the full Iron Age (Table 16.1: cal BC 520–200; HAR-3196, 2310±60BP: cal BC 790–50; UB-822, 2290±125 BP). The plain coarseware pottery is accordingly dated by Hill (1997) to the Late Bronze Age — in rough terms a period centred on the eighth century, approximately 900–700 BC.

The Tower Works also revealed an area of 'dark earth'. This was associated with filled-in quarry pits, which contained pottery akin to that published by Hawkes and Fell (1945), and which would normally be considered perhaps two or three centuries later (eg Cunliffe 1991, 566). Does this later 'pits' settlement represent continuity with the earlier (Bronze Age) landscape? Although It is hard to see why it should not, the case will need to be demonstrated either way.

The Northey Bronze Age landscape

The Northey landscape on the eastern side of the Flag Fen Basin was discussed in Chapter 5 (Fig 5.1). So far only very limited work has been undertaken, but there is already evidence that Bronze Age linear ditches extend under the superficial peats, down to and possibly below the 2m contour.

Recent aerial photographs indicate that the Northey Bronze Age landscape was laid out on much the same lines as the central element at Fengate. The double-ditched droveways are less apparent on the aerial photographs, but this is most probably a function of the thick alluvial cover (Fig 5.4). The principal linear ditches ran down to the frequently flooded land at right angles. The two droveways excavated so far have both proved to be similar in size and general layout to those found at Fengate (Gurney 1980; Fig 5.7). Excavations in 1994 also revealed part of a barrow of probable Neolithic date. This site lay at the edge of the wettest ground and might well have been used as a sightline or 'marker'. It is doubtful whether the Bronze Age ditched fields ever extended quite so far into the fen.

In the Bronze Age, salt extraction took place at Northey and Fengate (Gurney 1980; Pryor 1980, 21). At both sites, briquetage was found in contexts that were set well back from the immediate edge of the regularly flooded land. The quantity of burnt soil, charcoal, and briquetage found at Fengate/Northey was very much smaller than the vast mounds of burnt material found, for example at the contemporary north-east Lincolnshire saltern at Tetney (Palmer-Brown 1993). This might suggest that Fengate and Northey were secondary processing sites, where brine that had already been concentrated at lower-lying extraction sites was solidified and placed in ceramic containers.

The inception of nucleated settlement

The settlement pattern associated with the Bronze Age fields at Fengate, and probably at Northey too, consisted of single small round buildings, sometimes associated with an outbuilding of some sort. Single-family settlements of this general type were spaced throughout the field system, seemingly at random, but probably at the centre of the various individual holdings. To date these small farmsteads are known at Site 11, Newark Road, Fourth Drove, Cat's Water (ROM/DoE), and the Depot site (1992). The house at the Depot site (structure I) was slightly larger than the usual run of such buildings at Fengate. No certain eaves-drip gullies were found in Bronze Age contexts at Site O, but on present evidence it seems most probable that a settlement will one day be found there.

This pattern of settlement is best described as extensive. It contrasts very much with the earliest evidence for nucleated settlement. There are two known early nucleated settlements in the region. At Welland Bank (already mentioned; Pryor 1998b, 109–23; 1998c), the settlement consisted of round and rectangular houses that were associated with a 'dark earth'. The site was remarkable for the quantities of material it produced — thousands of potsherds, animal bones, pieces of daub, burnt stones, and general domestic refuse. In all important respects, the Tower Works settlement appears to be identical to that at Welland Bank. On current ceramic evidence, the area that produced the rectangular house might predate Welland Bank by a century or two, but no more. The Welland Bank post-Deverel-Rimbury pottery assemblage is dominated by plain forms and coarse wares, but there are a very few fine wares and decorated pieces. This would indicate a date slightly later than the Tower Works Late Bronze Age group (David Knight personal communication; Barrett 1980).

Both sites provide a striking contrast with the extensive settlement pattern at Fengate, where 'dark earth' was never found, and where domestic refuse rarely amounted to more than a handful of abraded potsherds.

Since the Welland Bank nucleated settlement was closely associated with a ditched field system, there are no *a priori* reasons why Tower Works might not go with a late use of the Bronze Age fields. By the fifth and sixth centuries BC, however, ground conditions were becoming very wet indeed. This might well explain why the earliest evidence for nucleated settlement is located above the 5m contour.

Before moving on to later periods, it should be noted that rectangular structures within defined settlement areas are not unique to the Peterborough region. In the southern Fenland, research by the Cambridge University Unit at Barleycroft Farm has revealed ditched Bronze Age field systems along a flat, gravel valley bottom. These appear to follow on from an earlier, probably later Neolithic/Early Bronze Age open landscape. The earlier landscape was broadly partitioned by ring-ditches and barrows (Evans and Knight 1997). While the general pattern of landscape development might appear similar, the layout and perhaps the use of the Barleycroft Farm fields appears to differ from Fengate in a number of important aspects, not least the rarity of droveways, the integration of settlement, and even funerary areas within the fields. Barleycroft Farm, like Welland Bank and Tower Works, has produced good evidence for post-built rectangular buildings.

Landscape 4: the earliest Iron Age

It was noted at the outset of this discussion of landscapes that the periods of change and transition were prolonged. This is particularly true of the fourth landscape at Fengate (and possibly of Northey, too). The earliest Iron Age landscape might well be defined as a landscape of transition, similar in certain respects to the second, Late Neolithic landscape.

It would appear that when the ditched fields of the Bronze Age landscape were abandoned, they were not replaced by another system of land partition for several centuries (if at all). It is also possible, indeed most probable, that the relict hedges of the Bronze Age system survived for a long time after their abandonment. Certain hedge species, such as elm, sucker freely and would prove both long-lived and very difficult to fell or grub out (eg Rackham 1976, pl xiii).

Although we must view this post-Bronze Age landscape as essentially open, it would not have been bereft of all form. There is no environmental evidence to suggest that forest or woodland cover regenerated over the recently abandoned fields but some scrub development is probable (Charles French personal communication).

Open, scrubby landscapes are not abandoned landscapes, however. Scrub provides browse and shade and, should land be required for arable, can be readily cleared. As a means of land management, scrub or rough grazing (Kerridge 1973, 24) can be less intensively productive, as regards livestock, than a 'properly' maintained field system; but it is also less labour intensive and provides an excellent support or back up in a mixed farming economy. It might almost be seen as a functionally similar, prehistoric version of the medieval outfield, in an infield/outfield system (Pryor 1998b, 145). Alternatively, the land could have been used in a more mobile pattern, perhaps in the manner of the long-fallow system of Boserup (1965, 28–34), although it might be doubted whether pre-existing patterns of land tenure would have allowed such wholesale change. Certainly by medieval times, as a category of semi-woodland, scrub had become highly productive of woodland products. Its characteristics were clearly defined as 'tracts of young woodland within plains' (Rackham 1989, 234–6).

The open countryside of Landscape 4 was the scene of several settlements. The later 'pit' settlement at Tower Works might belong within this landscape, but further work is awaited to resolve this important issue. The Early Iron Age settlement at Vicarage Farm undoubtedly belongs here, however, as does the rectangular 'settlement compound' of the Depot (1992) site (Fig 2.5).

Another recent development of some interest is the discovery of a possible ditched and gravelled road at the Depot site in 1997 (Fig 3.2). This road appeared to be running along the fen edge and it might have provided a dry link between the Tower Works and the Gravel Pits settlement area and the post alignment at Flag Fen. It should be recalled that a surprisingly high proportion of the metal finds from Flag Fen were of Iron Age date (Chapter 10). An important new element within the farming economy was undoubtedly cereals.

Previously, since the evidence for the growing of cereals had been slight, it had been

concluded that the communities who used the Bronze Age fields obtained their supplies of grain from higher land nearby, or from outside the Fengate area altogether (Pryor 1980, 180–1). There is, however, some evidence for the use of cereals in the Bronze Age at Fengate.

Caryopses of hulled barley and spelt were found in pits at Site O, for example, but such finds are the exception rather than the rule (Scaife 1998b, 28). Put another way, the ingredients of change were available, but the conditions were not yet right. It is perhaps ironic that it took a gradual change in the local environment towards wetter ground (Chapter 17) to help create a regime of farming, which is normally associated with drier ground. Nonetheless, that is what happened.

Open landscapes are often equated with 'retrenchment' and indeed, such an explanation has been advanced here for Landscape 2. In the present case this seems less plausible.

Landscape 4 was a landscape of change, it is true, but it might also have witnessed a degree of agricultural intensification and population growth. It was a time when mixed farming was gaining a foothold in the area and the previous system of intensive livestock farming was gradually being replaced by something altogether different. Rather than write off the period as one of 'retrenchment' or 'decline', perhaps the persistence of people who managed to adapt their ways of life to new circumstances so effectively should be admired.

Landscape 5: Middle Iron Age to Roman

By the later Iron Age the gradually encroaching fen to the east had inundated large areas of seasonally available pasture. Although the ditched fields of the Bronze Age landscape had been abandoned for several centuries, elements of past landscapes still survived, perhaps in the form of overgrown, relict hedges. Archaeologically, the best known (but not necessarily the main) settlement of this period was at Cat's Water, where the ditches of the later Iron Age farm run parallel to, but do not cross a boundary ditch of the earlier (Bronze Age) landscape (Pryor 1984a, fig 18, ditch 5). The successive landscapes of Fengate might have

marked major new developments in land-use, but there
were always threads of continuity running through the
patterns of change.

Although we still possess only a partial picture of
the later Iron Age landscape, it is clear that large areas
remained open and unenclosed. Increasingly, however,
there are signs of prehistoric 'assarting', as new fields
and paddocks, usually close by the settlements they
served, were imposed on the open countryside.

Fengate

Vicarage Farm shows the clearest continuity from earlier to later Iron Age settlement and land-use (Pryor
1974, 15–22 and 1984, 7–10). Since field or paddock
boundary ditches do not appear there until Middle or
later Iron Age times, it would seem that the earliest
Iron Age settlement was entirely open and unenclosed.

The Cat's Water settlement was a major local focus
of activity in this period (Pryor 1984a).

Despite the fact that the site produced evidence for
over 50 buildings, it was concluded that no more than
perhaps half a dozen houses were occupied at any one
time. The settlement was therefore little more than a
hamlet or large farmstead. It is also important to note
that the main Iron Age and Roman droveway into the
farm and stockyards ran away from the wetland edge in
a south-west direction for at least 1350m, towards the
higher land around Tower Works. It was surprising that
the main farmyards, where the principal houses and
outbuildings were located, did not have entrances or
gateways that gave onto the fen to the east. The animal
handling area of the enclosed farmyard was to the
north-west and consisted of five rectilinear yards measuring some 10–15m square. In terms of practical livestock management, these yards were not intended to
handle more than a few dozen cattle and perhaps
100–200 sheep. The long droveway was breached by
two entranceways very close to, and perhaps actually
into, the farmyard (Pryor 1984a, fig 18); further down
its length, it appeared on excavation to be continuous
(Pryor 1984a, figs 8–12). This dearth of entranceways
surely indicates that the drove was intended to conduct
livestock through (perhaps) arable and garden areas
and out to pastures on the higher ground. Nothing
could illustrate the change in economy from Bronze
Age to Iron Age times more effectively than this, for in
the Bronze Age the drove would have run directly
down to the fen pastures.

The Depot (1992) site has provided the first comprehensive evidence for Middle Iron
Age/Romano-British fields, which were laid out
without regard for the earlier, Bronze Age enclosures
(Fig 2.6). They consisted of a series of small ditched
paddocks that were positioned very close to (and
respecting) the edge of the regularly flooded land. The
clear evidence for ard marks on palaeosols associated
with the fields was remarkable, given the site's low-
lying position. These 'late' fields postdate the settle-

ment compound. Evans has suggested that they had
their origins in later (maybe even Middle?) Iron Age
times (Chapter 2; Evans 1992, 32). They are associated with settlement material that included quantities of
charcoal, burnt cobbles, animal bone, and so on, and
that would appear to extend along the fen edge into the
south part of Area 1, in Site O. Although no saltern
briquetage was found, it is difficult to think of an alternative explanation for a settlement so very close to the
fen margins, and moreover, at a wet period of fen prehistory. It is perhaps worth noting that briquetage
found among the pottery assemblage suggests that
much of the charcoal staining of the 'dark earth' at
Welland Bank might be associated with salt extraction
(Pryor 1998c).

The Depot excavations confirmed that arable farming was practised in this period. The positioning of
livestock (or more probably mixed livestock/arable)
fields nearby suggests that animals might have been
folded on straw or other crop residues to clear the land
and enrich it with dung or manure. The contemporary
fields/paddocks of the Depot site were small and it
would seem probable that the main flocks were grazed
on higher land elsewhere, just as at Cat's Water.

Evaluation excavations have revealed that the Iron
Age settlement and field system of the Depot site
extends along the fen edge into Site O, where it is even
better preserved.

Intercalating deposits of alluvium make it possible
to distinguish at least four stratified episodes of settlement, which in turn ought to be linked to changes in
the developing field system. Evans has suggested that
the Depot/Site O settlement might have been linked to
Cat's Water, but this remains to be proved (Evans
1992, 32).

Finally, the 'late' fields at the Depot continued in
use until the third century AD, by which time, increasing alluviation would have become a serious practical
problem (Chapter 17).

Romano-British features are, however, known from
the Gravel Pits settlement area (RCHM 1969, fig 1)
and others were found on the alignment of the Cat's
Water farm droveway during the Tower Works evaluation (Lucas 1997b, 20–1). Towards the end of
Landscape 5, it would seem that settlement in Fengate
moved onto higher ground to the south-west, and
doubtless too, to ground that now lies beneath the
modern city.

Northey

No excavation of Iron Age features has yet been possible at Northey, but aerial photographs show two small
yard-like enclosures immediately east of Northey Road
(Fig 5.2, C and D). A few pits and linear ditches might
possibly be associated with the small enclosures. In
Roman times Northey was the eastern landfall for the
Fen Causeway after it had crossed the Flag Fen wetland.

The Fengate fields and archaeological approaches to pastoral farming

Mainstream literature on prehistoric farming in Britain has, until quite recently, focused on arable (Fowler 1983; Mercer 1981). Britain has a climate and landscape, however, that is traditionally much better suited to livestock. Sites such as Fengate have, moreover, turned archaeological attention towards the practical aspects of prehistoric animal husbandry (Pryor 1996 and 1998b). Different approaches to the landscape are, of course, possible–the closely comparable lowland Iron Age landscape at Maxey (Pryor and French 1985) has recently benefitted from the stimulating insights provided by a post-structuralist study (Taylor 1997).

The intentions of the present analysis are rather more modest. While ever-mindful of symbolic and social factors, an attempt will be made to examine the Fengate Bronze Age landscape from a livestock farmer's perspective, and to ask — what was the scale of animal husbandry and how did ancient landscapes such as Fengate, in which livestock movement and exchange were prime considerations, function as integrated systems?

The management of pastoral landscapes

Individual landscapes might or might not have possessed a communal area in which livestock were gathered together for purposes of exchange. In upland regions, such as the Dartmoor Reaves, it is possible that these areas would have been situated on lower ground. The large 'pastoral enclosures', at Shaugh Moor (Wainwright and Smith 1980) and Dean Moor (Fleming 1988, fig 67) could also have served such a purpose, especially during their known period of use after the main episode of domestic settlement (Fleming 1988, 103). It will be argued that, at Fengate, the elaborately laid-out stockyards of the Newark Road and Fourth Drove subsites could have been used for such purposes.

There is as yet no systematic study of stock management systems in prehistoric Britain. Much of the evidence for such a study, however, still lies within the countryside, in numerous working farms and fields, especially in the Highland Zone. Any practising farmer knows that the key to running a successful livestock unit lies in the size and layout of the stockyard or stockyards (Goodwin 1979, 158–72). Although it is, of course, very unwise to draw direct parallels between modern (or indeed medieval) stock management methods and those of a more remote period, certain basic rules will still apply and must have been known by pre-Roman stock farmers too. Sheep will behave more placidly when confined within a restricted area. Most stock can be inspected and sorted when restrained within the confines of a narrow path, or 'race'. Large numbers of sheep, for example, can be controlled within a very small space. Goodwin (1979, fig 71)

illustrates a foot bath, dipping, and dosing system designed to accommodate 400 ewes, which has overall dimensions of 15 × 49m. Some modern compact systems use space even more economically.

The technology of livestock handling systems on most British farms is still very basic. Until the recent introduction of organo-phosphorus dips, which require all-metal handling equipment and concrete floors, most sheep farms used wooden hurdles, gates, and fences within the stockyard. Woven wattle hurdles can still be bought from certain farmers' suppliers, as they make excellent, draughtproof, lambing pens. So there is no *a priori* reason why general comparisons cannot be drawn between modern and ancient handling systems.

The Newark Road community stockyards

The Fengate landscape was probably divided up into droves, enclosures, and paddocks to accommodate large flocks of animals on their return to the flood-free grazing of the fen edge during the wetter months of the year. At first glance, the landscape looks straightforward (Fig 1.4). Droves ran to the wetter land at right-angles and the land between them was parcelled up into small, rectilinear fields. On closer inspection, however, evidence for hierarchy can be discerned within this landscape. Indeed, it is now possible to suggest that the extremely elaborate arrangement of enclosures and droveways of the Newark Road and Fourth Drove subsites (Pryor 1980, figs 18 and 78) were a socially important focus within the contemporary domestic landscape of the second millennium BC (Fig 18.3). Regular social gatherings attended by large numbers of people will include a significant ritual or ceremonial component (Thomas 1991; Bradley 1990). The complex of ditched yards, droves, and enclosures revealed at Newark Road and Fourth Drove was linked directly, via the post alignment, to the liminal and ritually important site at Flag Fen. The area of yards was a key focus within an already intensively managed landscape. It was the centre of redistribution, a stockyard system that served the local community and outside communities, too (Pryor 1996).

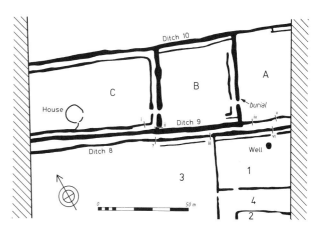

Fig 18.3 Plan of the Newark Road 'community stockyards'

Certain observations are essential to the 'community stockyards' interpretation. First, ditch 10 was continuous and never appeared to have been broached by an entranceway. Second, there were six entranceways (and one possible entranceway) that had been blocked at some time during the active life of the yard system (Fig 18.3, i–vi). Third, away from the area of complex stockyards, the droveway formed by ditches 8 and 9 doubled in width (Pryor 1992a, fig 8). Fourth, the roundhouse was not distinguished by high phosphate levels, nor an increase in the density of finds, either around the circumference of its ring-ditch or within the nearby enclosure ditches (Pryor 1980, fig 111).

It is possible to make suggestions as to how the Newark Road community stockyards might have functioned (Fig 18.3). In the third report (Pryor 1980) and subsequently, it was stated that the droveway formed by ditches 8 and 9 was a local boundary, as the 'fields' on either side of it were laid out quite differently (suggesting, perhaps, that ownership/control rested with different kin-groups). This impression was enhanced by the fact that none of the entranceways off the droveway lined up transversely to allow a simple, direct crossing to be made. Ditch 10 marked a clearly defined edge to the community stockyards, with a large area of open pasture between it and the next, northerly, element of the field system (Pryor 1980, fig 18). The supposed 'house' was remarkably free of ordinary settlement debris. Its door faced directly onto the two main entranceways into enclosure B. Whatever happened in the enclosure could have been seen from the round building. Enclosures A–C were surrounded by large ditches with accompanying banks. By any standards, these were very labour-intensive measures just to demarcate three small paddocks. It is suggested that these yards were the 'core area' of the community stockyard system, where the main transfer transactions took place. This was where people met other people and where livestock was bartered or exchanged. In the terms of a modern livestock market, yards A–C were the main 'auction rings'.

It is suggested that the contrasting layout of enclosures on either side of the main droveway formed by ditches 8 and 9 was a reflection of use or function, rather than of land tenure alone.

Livestock was held in the enclosures south of the main droveway prior to and after the sorting/exchange ceremonies that took place in the enclosures, A–C. South of the enclosures, the layout was altogether less elaborate and the ditches are far shallower. Enclosure 3 might have been subdivided, but as ground conditions were poor in this area, it is difficult to be more precise. Enclosure 4 was a droveway, but far wider than the 'main' drove. The southerly enclosures were served by the well in enclosure 1.

The southerly enclosures were probably short-term holding areas for livestock before and after the process of sorting and exchange. The narrowness of the main drove in this area suggests that it too was used to inspect, rather than drive stock on their way to and from yards A–C. 'Enclosure' 4 was in fact a droveway intended for large numbers of animals, but the positioning of the entranceways from it into enclosures 1 and 3 suggests that traffic was from the drove into the enclosures, and not the other way about. It might be supposed, therefore, that unsorted livestock from other parts of the Fengate field system found its way into the community stockyards by this route. The main droveway was the principal access to and from the regularly flooded pastures of Flag Fen; as noted above, however, it became much wider in the Power Station subsite (ie away from the community stockyards) as the wetter land was approached.

If the community stockyards of the Newark Road subsite were the scene of regular gatherings of livestock and people, they might also have provided an important social focus. When animals are culled or exchanged in non-industrial societies, it is rarely a simple economic process, as in modern livestock markets. The exchange of livestock would probably have been closely bound up with wider social ties and obligations (Pryor 1996). If the Newark Road enclosures were the scene of regular large social gatherings, it is not surprising that they produced a broken bronze spearhead (Pryor 1980, fig 75, 7), nor that the Flag Fen post alignment, with its strong ritual element, had its western landfall at the point where the main droveway from the community stockyards reached the edge of the regularly flooded land. The two sites might well have been in use concurrently when the regular gatherings — important events — were taking place. In the next chapter, it will be seen that the rituals at Flag Fen, a liminal site deliberately removed from settlement, were probably associated with rites of passage and death (Pryor 1992b). Social gatherings at the Fengate community stockyards would have added the wider, collective, or social dimension to the individual and kin-group ceremonies that took place at Flag Fen.

The Newark Road community stockyards were both elaborate and functional. Apart from the broken spearhead already referred to, 'direct' evidence for ritual is rare, although a crouched inhumation was found close to the butt end of a droveway ditch in enclosure A (Fig 18.3; Pryor 1980, fig 27).

The elaborate community stockyards of the Newark Road subsite were plainly intended to pass livestock through a number of quite separate processes. The individual yards intercommunicated to a remarkable extent, but it is notable that there was only one well. This would suggest that none of the yards north of the main droveway (Fig 18.3, yards A–C) were intended for the long-term housing of livestock. Yard B, which measured approximately 40m square, could comfortably have accommodated between 500 and 1000 primitive sheep (using a formula to be discussed below) and still leave room for a large attendance of people. As will be seen when individual stockyards are examined more closely, the community stockyard system as a whole could readily have processed many thousands of sheep at any one time.

The Storey's Bar Road stock-handling system

As was noted in the second report (Pryor 1978, 157) the fields or paddocks of the Storey's Bar Road fields were all entered via corners, which strongly suggests that they were intended for the use of livestock. All the corner entranceways, moreover, provided evidence for diversion or narrowing, which again suggests they were used for handling stock. The deliberate narrowing of entranceways (eg Pryor 1978, figs 12 and 13) might indicate, perhaps, a possible move from cattle or mixed flocks to a system that was intended to handle sheep alone.

Individual stock-handling systems, such as that proposed for Storey's Bar Road, allow very approximate estimates of flock sizes to be made. The discussion that follows makes use of certain terms that are specific to the handling of livestock. They can be defined as follows:

Crush. Sheep might be reluctant to enter a confined space, even if a decoy sheep is visible. The funnel-shape of the crush aids the process.
Decoy. Sheep are flock animals and will enter an unknown space more readily if other sheep can be seen (or heard) to be already there.

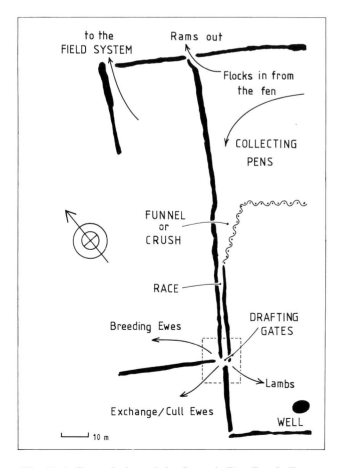

Fig 18.4 General plan of the Storey's Bar Road (Bronze Age) farm stockyards

Race. An essential part of any stock handling system. It allows the animals to calm down and enables them to be inspected for teeth (ageing), worms, fly-strike, and so on. Long races are used for inspection, shorter races for sorting or *drafting*.
Drafting gate. Usually two- or three-way. Enables animals to be sorted by category (ewe, cull ewe, shearling ewe, lamb, and so on) by the shepherd or flockmaster.

The original plan of the livestock-handling system at Storey's Bar Road (Pryor 1974, fig 12) shows clear indications that the alignment of ditches B21 and B38 had been slightly kinked, doubtless to accommodate the hurdles and decoy pen of the drafting gates (Fig 18.4). On paper the drafting gates' arrangement could have involved from five to six wattle hurdles (an economical use of resources), although the same results could be achieved by two people with three hurdles (Fig 18.5).

The Storey's Bar Road handling system was undoubtedly intended to process large numbers of animals, probably thousands rather than hundreds. The length of the race (25m) was notable and there is a direct link between the length of race and the numbers of animals to be handled. The author's own race is 7m long and the system is designed to handle up to about 250 modern sheep; a professional shepherd uses a race 35m long to inspect, inject, and worm upwards of 2000 sheep (Mike McCoy personal communication). Small numbers of sheep would not be managed easily using systems intended for larger flocks, as the fundamental principle behind a stockyard system is that compaction aids handling.

The space recommended for retaining modern sheep within a collecting yard or pen is one mature animal per $0.47m^2$ (Goodwin 1979, 159). Using this figure (probably an underestimate, given the small size of primitive sheep), Newark Road yard B could have handled approximately 3400 sheep at one time. Using the same figure, the excavated extent of the hypothetical collecting yard (Fig 18.4) at Storey's Bar Road could have held some 2500 animals. This estimate would agree well with the length of race employed there. Possible ways in which the system could have been used are shown in Figure 18.5. In the reconstruction, it has been assumed that animals entered the system from the direction of the fen pastures to the south-east, outside the limit of the excavation. Hurdles and hurdle fencelines have been added where appropriate (there was no archaeological evidence for these).

The livestock handling system at Storey's Bar Road is located away from settlement, just like many modern equivalents. Since animals will often need to be sorted at several places around the farm, it is not always convenient to drive them to a single, central location. Today, many farmers avoid this problem by using lightweight transportable equipment. Another, although rather more substantial, livestock-handling area has been identified in the northern element of the Bronze Age

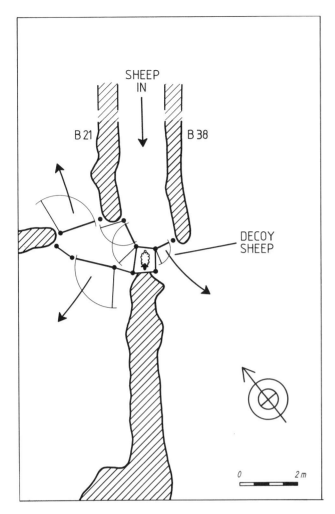

Fig 18.5 Hypothetical reconstruction of the drafting gate arrangements, Storey's Bar Road (Bronze Age) farm stockyards (see Fig 18.4)

ditch system, just west of the main Newark Road open area excavation, near ditches 12 and 13 (Fig 1.4). This enclosure has not been excavated, but as we have noted above, it bears a superficially striking resemblance to a Late Bronze Age or Early Iron Age livestock yard at Welland Bank Quarry (Pryor 1998c). The Welland Bank yard was outside the contemporary settlement.

The Fengate and Northey landscapes were parcelled up by droveways that ran down to the edge of the regularly flooded land. It is probable that these droveways formed the boundaries between different holdings of land: for example, the Bronze Age house and partly encircling ditch found at Cat's Water is linked to the droveway immediately north of it (Pryor 1980, fig 94). This would suggest that the droveway 'belonged to' or went with the house. If that was the case, the 'territory' of the farm would be defined to the north and south by ditches 2 and 4 of the ROM/DoE system, while the southerly drove, formed by ditches 1 and 2, would have been 'farmed' by a group resident immediately south of ditch 1. A broadly similar pattern of farm buildings south of a main drove was also observed in the Fourth Drove subsite (Pryor 1980, fig 80). In this case, the entrance from the house into the

drove had been blocked in at least two places and, as if to emphasise the contemporaneity of all the features involved, the southerly drove ditch had been kinked to skirt around the building. A similar pattern of farm or settlement features closely associated with droveways can be seen at the broadly contemporary site at West Deeping, in the Welland valley (Figs 1.2 and 18.6; Hunn 1993).

Other examples of lowland pastoral landscapes

It is becoming increasingly apparent that the fen edge and certain Fen 'islands' were parcelled up in a way that indicates that stock were kept in numbers comparable with Fengate (Evans 1993a and b; Pryor forthcoming). Sites with Bronze Age and Early Iron Age ditched droves and enclosures include Block Fen, Mepal (Hunn 1993). One extraordinarily dense area of droves and linear ditches might well be a candidate for another 'community stockyard' (Palmer 1993, fig 1).

Rescue excavations at West Deeping, Lincs, some 14km north-west of Fengate, have provided evidence for a large-scale coaxial field system along the fen-edge valley of the river Welland. This remarkable system includes axial droveways that run down to the flood-plain.

It is currently dated to the later Bronze Age and earlier Iron Age (Fig 18.6). Only a small sample of the ditches has been excavated so far, but the provisional dating still holds (Hunn personal communication and 1994). Pollen samples taken from the ditches almost exclusively contained herb pollen, indicative of open pasture (James Rackham personal communication).

Although several large stockyards are clearly visible on aerial photographs of West Deeping, only excavation will be able to indicate whether focal 'community stockyards' comparable with Newark Road are present. The even spacing of the possible stockyards within each major parcel of land suggests, however, that they served that parcel alone (Fig 18.6). It should be noted that each possible stockyard was located at the edge of the 'territory' or parcel of land it served. As at Fengate, this position gave it access to the droveway that led down to the floodplain. There was no evidence for paired stockyards that straddled a drove; moreover, each yard was located on the west side of its drove. This would suggest that individual droveways 'belonged' to individual stockyards. For these reasons alone, the West Deeping potential stockyards are best interpreted as farm rather than community stockyards.

The aerial photographs of West Deeping show that the possible farm stockyards are approximately the same size, *c* 50–100m square or slightly larger. Since none have yet been completely exposed, speculation about flock size handled must be treated with caution.

There are certain indications that can, nonetheless, be followed up with some confidence. It might be assumed that at least half the area of the stockyards was

Fig 18.6 Cropmarks of a later Bronze Age to Iron Age field system at West Deeping in the Welland valley. The broken lines indicate areas of possible stockyards (after Hunn 1994)

for handling pens and the like and that the actual stock management area might have been perhaps 20m square. Even so, that approximate (and most conservative) size of yard would be appropriate for handling individual flocks of a thousand or two. The known extent of the West Deeping landscape revealed on aerial photographs (Fig 18.6) covers some 255ha (630 acres). If a stocking rate in the region of 5–10 primitive sheep per acre is assumed, this gives a range of 3150 to 6300 for the whole landscape. This overall figure appears entirely consistent with the size of the stockyards.

Slightly further afield, the recent publication of the Mucking Site Atlas (Clark 1993) has revealed plans of at least two regular (60 × 110m), rectangular ditched fields or paddocks served by a narrow central droveway just 2m wide. These fields are dated to the Middle Bronze Age and can be linked to the two well known Bronze Age circular enclosures, the North and South Rings (Jones and Bond 1980, 472; Bond 1988). As at West Deeping and Fengate, the barrows at Mucking might have played a significant role in the original parcelling up of the landscape.

A similar landscape, also flat but lower-lying than Mucking, might be found around the rivers Stour and

Colne, also in Essex (McMaster 1975; Erith and Longworth 1960). McMaster published plans of cropmark droveways and paddock boundary ditches that undoubtedly respect ring-ditches. Superficially, this large-scale landscape appears closely to resemble those at Fengate and West Deeping.

Further afield, in the Thames valley west of London, using information from recent, PPG16-based, commercial excavations, David Yates has demonstrated that there were extensive systems of Bronze Age ditched fields (Pryor 1998b, 140–4). These fields generally resemble those at Fengate and were undoubtedly laid out to manage livestock. Features such as droveways running at right angles to the river floodplain occur frequently. Yates was able to show that there were four main areas of fields. Each was separated from the next by areas of open or unenclosed country, which were by no means devoid of settlement, but merely lacked the intensive pattern of livestock management that led to the construction of ditched fields.

The important multi-period prehistoric site at Yarnton is located in one of these tracts of open countryside (Hey 1997; Allen *et al* 1997). The four areas of fields also coincided with significant concentrations of Bronze Age metalwork from the river itself. Yates was also able to offer contenders for 'community stockyards' in the Thames valley; an example from Dorchester-on-Thames (Benson and Miles 1974, 92) bears a particular resemblance to Newark Road. Originally considered to be of Roman date, that suggestion has been questioned and a Bronze Age date now seems just as probable (David Yates personal communication). Extensive excavations by the Oxford Archaeological Unit in the Kennet valley, at Reading Business Park, revealed an evolving ditched field system and associated settlement of Late Bronze Age date (Moore and Jennings 1992). Although only a relatively small part of this system was excavated, it was characterised by corner entranceways, much as at Storey's Bar Road. There were also instances of very close parallel double ditches, which the excavators regarded as part of a hedge arrangement, the hedge planted on the bank between the two ditches (Moore and Jennings 1992, 46). This recalls parts of the central Fengate Bronze Age fields once again and, most particularly, the Depot Site of the southern Bronze Age system.

Livestock numbers and 'wealth'

A case has been made for the landscapes around the edge of the Flag Fen Basin supporting large numbers of animals, in what might be considered a climax pastoral farming economy.

Taken at face value, this suggests that the communities who maintained the flocks and herds were both prosperous and able to produce and distribute a surplus. This surplus of wealth could have been used both to construct the massive timber structure at Flag Fen and to obtain the exotic items that were deposited there. A simple and attractive idea, it still needs to be demonstrated. For example, did the hypothetical flocks actually produce a 'surplus', or were their numbers maintained at a high level for other reasons, perhaps as symbols of social prestige? The evidence as a whole suggests that the Bronze Age communities of the region, like those in the Thames valley, were prosperous enough, but that prosperity might also have derived from the control of other key resources, such as salt, timber, or prestige goods, some of which were deposited in the waters of Flag Fen. Further research will be required to answer such complex but nonetheless important questions.

19 Discussion, part 2: the Flag Fen timber structures

The previous chapter provided an archaeological context for the Bronze Age timber structures of Flag Fen, which will form the principal subject of the present chapter. The discussion that follows is largely based on the detailed stratigraphic analysis of excavations in Area 6 (Chapter 6).

The analysis showed that the post alignment comprised five rows of posts: Row 1 was exclusively made of alder wood and was probably the earliest; Row 2 was mainly of oak and, like Row 1, was used as the basis for a double wattle wall or revetment; the central row, 3, was the most densely packed, narrowly confined, and species rich (mainly oak, alder, and ash) of the five; Row 4 was a wider, less linear, band of posts that resembled a *chevaux de frise*; the north (outer) side of Row 4 was strengthened and defined by a straight line of oak posts, Row 5, which included a double wattle revetment.

It is suggested that the post alignment was subdivided axially and transversely. The central posts of Row 3 formed a wall or axial division, which probably ran along its entire length. North of the wall (ie Rows 4 and 5) the posts formed a defensive palisade. South of the wall was a pathway (between Rows 2 and 3) and (between Rows 1 and 3) partitioned areas given over to ritual.

The transverse division of the alignment was into segments 5–6m in length, separated by partitions. This arrangement has so far only been observed in Area 6. Partitions were numbered 1 to 4 from east to west as. In addition to the main pathway of Rows 2–3, there were also narrow walkways between Rows 5–4, and 4–3, and along Rows 1 and 2 at lower levels.

Horizontal timbers occurred in at least five separate levels. The lowest two (Levels 4 and 5) were mainly of wet-loving species (alder and willow), and the highest included many oaks. In between was Level 3, which was comprised of mixed oak and fen species. The development of the post alignment and platform fell into three structural and dendrochronological phases, which have been fully discussed in Chapters 6 and 8. The overall chronology was reviewed in Chapter 16.

Dates and phasing

The chronological position of the post alignment

Dendrochronology has shown that the post alignment was constructed and maintained for almost four centuries, from the first half of the thirteenth century until shortly after 924 BC. In relative terms the four centuries would span Hawkes' (1960) Middle Bronze Age 2, Middle Bronze Age 3 and Late Bronze Age 1 periods; in Burgess' system (Burgess 1979; Cunliffe 1991)

the span covers the Taunton, Penard (1 and 2) and Wilburton Phases. The most recent, and perhaps most satisfactory, scheme is that of Stuart Needham (1996; Needham *et al* 1997). In this scheme, Flag Fen would centre on Period 6 (cal BC 1150–950). In terms of the continental (Müller Karpe) system the periods represented are Bronze D, Hallstatt A1, A2, and B1 (Coles and Harding 1979, 342; Cunliffe 1991, 26). In the second half of the tenth century BC, the last timbers were felled and placed in position. Thereafter, the use of the site can only be dated by the artefacts deposited there.

David Coombs' study of the metalwork (Chapter 10) shows that objects of all periods from Wilburton to La Tène II (and even later) were being deposited both at Flag Fen proper, and around the post alignment at the Power Station; using Cunliffe's (1991, 26–7) simplified system for the British Iron Age, this later use of the site would centre on his Earliest, Early, and Middle Iron Age periods. There is also a possibility that use of the site for ritual purposes continued sporadically into the Late and Latest Iron Age (ie La Tène III), and perhaps even the Early Roman period, but it is difficult to be certain that the few objects of very late date found at the Power Station had not been derived from the nearby Cat's Water settlement, nor indeed from the Roman Fen Causeway that traversed diagonally the north-west part of the Power Station subsite (Fig 5.1).

Structural phases

The dendrochronological study was bedevilled by a lack of sapwood and bark at the Power Station and the rarity of oak in primary levels (4 and 5) at Flag Fen. These problems have made it difficult to exact precise dates for the various structural developments that were clearly visible in the excavations. A more detailed discussion of the problems of dating is to be found in Chapters 8 and 16. The intention here is to provide a general overview of the principal developments.

Phase 1 (Fig 19.1)

Tree-ring evidence for this phase was present only at the Power Station, where initial construction appears to have taken place in the first half of the thirteenth century BC. At Flag Fen, it is assumed that non-oak (mainly alder) posts of Rows 1 and 3, the lower foundation timbers of Levels 4 and 5, together with certain pathway surfaces belong to this initial phase. It is entirely possible that one or more of the wooden wearing surfaces was lost to wet rot or erosion in the following phase.

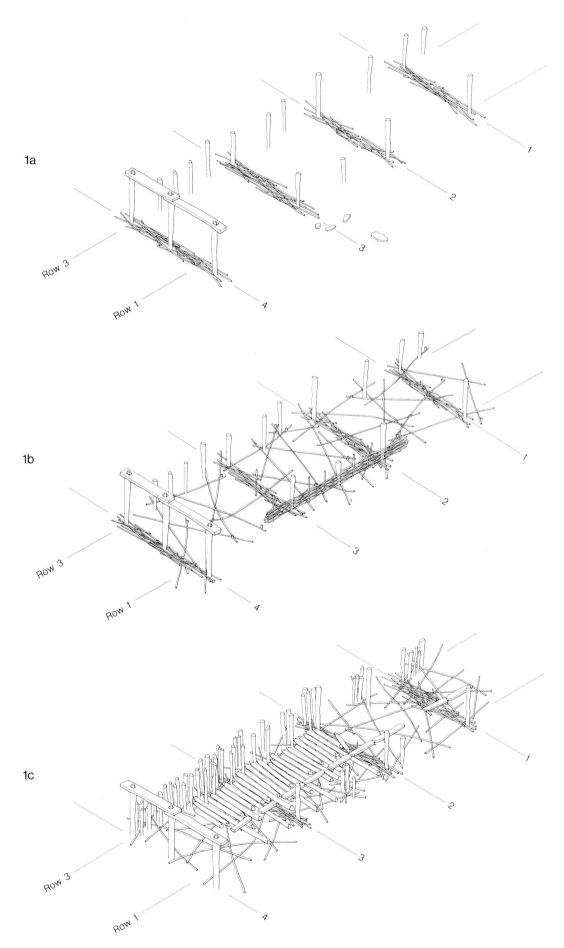

Fig 19.1 The Flag Fen post alignment, Area 6: isometric reconstruction of Phase 1 by Colin Irons. Not to scale

Phase 2

A period of seeming stability, lasting about 150 years, spanned the late twelfth and thirteenth centuries BC. Water levels in the surrounding fen were constant and repair was not required.

There is no evidence, however, that the site was abandoned. On the contrary, it would seem probable that ritual and other activity continued unabated.

Phase 3 (Figs 19.2 and 19.3)

A major episode of enlargement and renewal along the entire length of the post alignment took place during the first quarter of the eleventh century BC. The posts of Row 1 went out of use early in this phase (or indeed, during Phase 2) and Row 2 was constructed to replace them. The two rows (4 and 5) north of the central row (3) were constructed and maintained in good order. The last repairs were carried out at Flag Fen shortly after 955 BC and at the Power Station after 924 BC. The sequence of alterations, modifications and enlargements was probably complex, and difficult, therefore, to disentangle the individual components. A general trend of the more detailed developments has been suggested above (Chapter 6, Discussion).

Structure and function of the post alignment

Both the wood technology and tree-ring studies (Chapters 7 and 8) suggested that reused timber played no major role at Flag Fen. The tree ring research demonstrated that, in fact, several timbers derived from the same trees (Table 8.1). In one instance, single samples from widely separated locations (Area 6B, the lake lining exposure, and the Power Station) were probably from the same tree. This would suggest that timber was felled specifically for use within the post alignment. It would also suggest that the *structure* of the alignment and platform (including maintenance) was under the control of a single authority. If that was the case, the structural stages observed in Area 6 might also have applied to other parts of the monument.

As the central post row (3) was very tightly packed, it most probably formed a near-solid wall from shortly after its first construction. It was this row that provided the spine and axis of the alignment. In Phase 1, the wall formed by Row 3 most probably provided a barrier across the access into the Flag Fen embayment. It is not entirely clear what happened to the south of the wall at this stage, but there is evidence for a revetment or walkway around Row 1, and later along the north edge of Row 2 (from early in Phase 3).

Phase 3 saw the construction of the irregular palisade (Row 4) north of the central (Row 3) wall. The northernmost row (5) was a slightly later revetment to the outward-leaning posts of Row 4. Small walkways (perhaps to service the palisade) were constructed to the south and north of Rows 5 and 3 respectively.

There were very few gaps through the posts of Rows 3–5; only one (in Row 5) was assuredly an entranceway. In this report, it is discussed under Level 2 of Area 6A (Fig 6.41). It was interpreted as a doorway in the first Flag Fen report (Pryor *et al* 1986, pl 6b). It would presumably have been accessed from the narrow pathway immediately south of Row 5. It was marked by a large threshold plank, which had been pegged in place. The restriction of the gap to some 600mm surely suggests that it was not intended to be used regularly or by large numbers of people.

If Row 3 and the posts to the north could be considered as defensive in the broadest sense, the posts and horizontal timbers to the south served a dual role–as a major path across Flag Fen and as a focus for ritual activities. At the Power Station, the distribution of metalwork was almost entirely to the south. At Flag Fen, the same was probably true (although only a small area has so far been excavated north of the alignment). The south half of the alignment contained ritual deposits, including dog bones and a group of quernstones (Fig 6.90).

The main walkway across Flag Fen was that between the posts of Rows 2 and 3. The walkway surface had been built up in several episodes (which, sadly, it was not possible to cross-correlate). Its foundations had been constructed in two layers, a basal 'log layer' of mainly alder tree trunks (which were placed in position during Phase 1) below a higher, load-spreading layer consisting mainly of roundwood poles, which had been wedged between the posts on either side of the walkway early in Phase 3. A low wattle revetment wall ran along the walkway on its southern side. The walkway surface was mainly composed of oak planks, oak woodchips, sand, and fine gravel.

The gaps in the post rows south of Row 3 were much wider than that through Row 5. The widest (some 5m) was in Row 1 and it was matched by another, much narrower, in Row 2.

The so-called 'poolside area' of Area 6D was most probably an area of special ritual importance marked off from the rest of the post alignment by a timber portal. The portal was probably constructed in Phase 1, after which the area continued in use as a ritual focus throughout Phases 2 and 3. The final deposit, which was placed almost directly beneath the site of the former portal, was a deliberately broken and finely decorated La Tène II sword scabbard plate.

Segmentation

The detailed evidence for segmentation was considered in the description of Levels 4–6 in Chapter 6. The main evidence consisted of large posts in Rows 1 and 3, which were combined with prominent horizontal timbers that ran transversely across the alignment. The segments were also marked by hypothetical 'boundary' deposits placed at their limits. Possible examples

Phase 3 Early

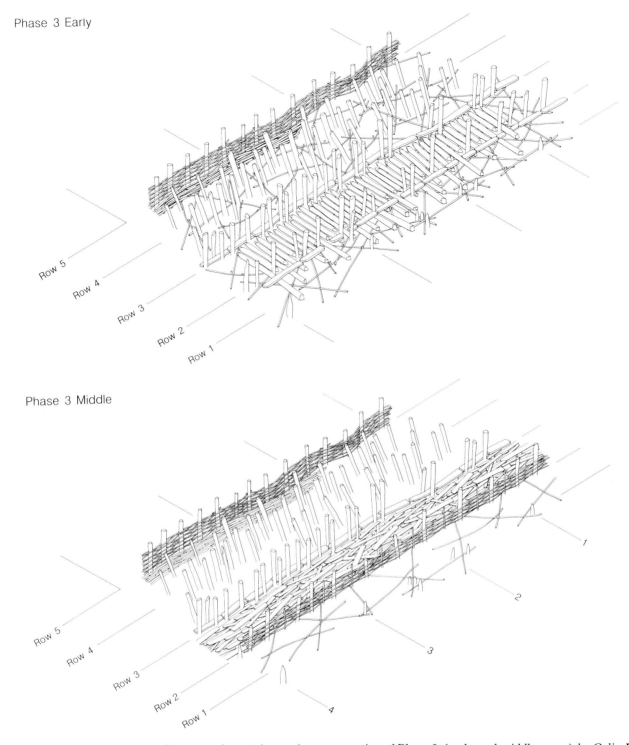

Row 5
Row 4
Row 3
Row 2
Row 1

Phase 3 Middle

Row 5
Row 4
Row 3
Row 2
Row 1

Fig 19.2 The Flag Fen post alignment, Area 6: isometric reconstruction of Phase 3 (early and middle stages) by Colin Irons. Not to scale

included a complete ceramic jar in Level 2, the group of four quernstones in Level 5 (Fig 6.90) or the broken scabbard plate from slightly above Level 1. If the scabbard plate and dog bones of Area 6D, Levels 1 and 2, were indeed 'boundary' deposits, this might suggest that the system of segmentation continued throughout the time that the monument was in use.

Where they could be identified in Areas 6 A–D, the suggested segments were 5–6m in length. There was no evidence for them in Area 8 (Fig 6.1), but it should

be recalled that work in this area only exposed the uppermost timbers. The Power Station excavations showed no obvious signs of segmentation, but as preservation was much poorer, very little horizontal timber of any sort had survived. It is very difficult, as a result, to draw any firm conclusions as to the original extent of segmentation. There are two probable explanations: first, that there was segmentation along the entire length of the post alignment, for which evidence has either been lost or awaits discovery; or that

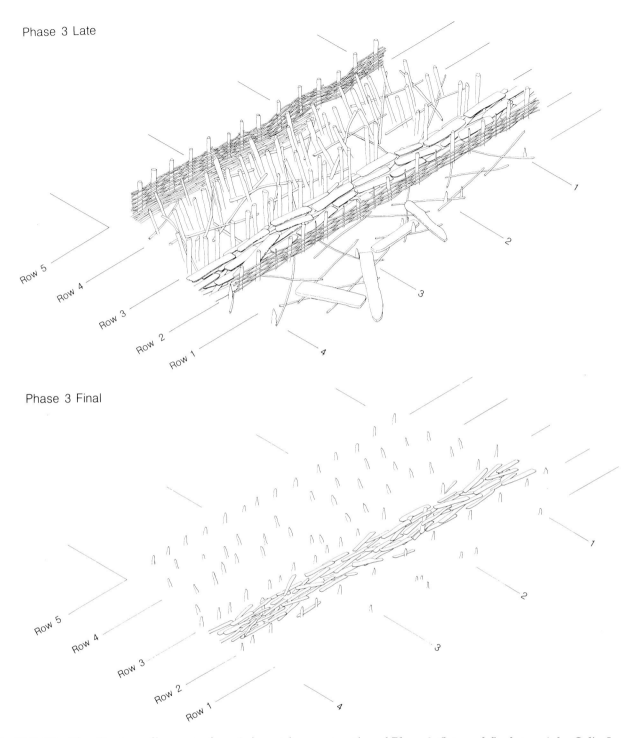

Phase 3 Late

Row 5
Row 4
Row 3
Row 2
Row 1

1
2
3
4

Phase 3 Final

Row 5
Row 4
Row 3
Row 2
Row 1

1
2
3
4

Fig 19.3 The Flag Fen post alignment, Area 6: isometric reconstruction of Phase 3 (late and final stages) by Colin Irons. Not to scale

segmentation was confined to the 'core' of the monument in the deepest, wettest part of Flag Fen, in and around the platform, and was never employed elsewhere.

On the whole the second hypothesis appears the most attractive and would concur with the slight evidence revealed in the lake lining exposure. It also suggests that parts of the monument had more than one level of importance, significance, or status. This accords with our knowledge of prehistoric ritual sites:

Neolithic long barrows had forecourts; Early Bronze Age round barrows had primary burials; causewayed enclosures had entranceways, and so forth. So far, wetland ritual sites have generally lacked such a range or hierarchy of ritual significance, which is to deny them an essential component of any working place of worship or ritual. If the post alignment was segmented in its more remote or 'deep fen' areas, it might also follow that the platform itself was also segmented, whatever its actual form.

The significance of segmentation

The possible segmentation of the Flag Fen structure finds close parallels in certain hillforts where sufficiently large areas of rampart have been excavated to view longitudinal structure.

The best known example of segmented rampart construction is Moel y Gaer (Guilbert 1975).

The revetment at the foot of the rear of the Breiddin rampart was also clearly constructed in short segments (Musson 1991, fig 21).

So called 'unfinished' hillforts show striking evidence for segmentary structure. The ditch and rampart at Ladle Hill, Hampshire, for example, resembles a causewayed enclosure more than an Iron Age hillfort (Feacham 1971). Unfinished Iron Age hillfort ditch or quarry pit segments were also a prominent feature at Crickley Hill, Gloucestershire (Dixon 1994, 195).

The undulation of the ditch bottom at Maiden Castle, Dorset, is also of interest in this regard.

Throughout the circuit of the defences, the bases of the ditches are irregular, consisting of shallow hollows separated by slight causeways. At many points, these hollows correspond to 'peaks' or steps on the tops of the adjacent ramparts. Such features have been taken to suggest the work of different gangs during the construction or refurbishment of the defences (Sharples 1991, 38).

It is inappropriate here to attempt a comprehensive review of hillfort constructional practices, but common sense would suggest that, if they so wished, the builders of monuments as magnificent as Maiden Castle were perfectly capable of constructing ramparts with smoothly shaped banks or ditches. Were the undulations that we see as mere evidence of 'gang labour' in fact part of the monument's structure, in turn closely related to its use? The gentle undulations we see today were surely originally sharper and better defined–the communities who used the sites would have been aware of the significance of each hump and bump. Could it be that the 'unfinished' hillforts were nothing of the sort and that they represent a regional variation in which the concept of segmentation has been given special physical expression?

Hillforts were not built by individuals or small groups of individuals; their sheer size would have demanded a larger cooperative effort. The drawing together of people might well have been one of their social roles (Bradley 1984). It is the nature of the hypothetical 'gang labour' that holds the clue to the possible significance of segmentation, both in the upland zone and at Flag Fen.

It is suggested that segmentation served to divide up a large monument into manageable pieces. This was not just a practical measure to do with construction and maintenance, it also had to do with the monument's function, in that the construction and the subsequent 'use' of many monuments need not have been seen as separate processes (Pryor 1984b).

The same could also be said of hillforts. It seems, however, that the 'gangs' had to work to a grander plan. At Flag Fen, there were rows of posts that had to run in a straight line, with appropriately sized gaps. In the upland zone, the hillfort builders had also to follow the agreed layout of ramparts and complex entrances. The overall design or layout of the monuments would have been agreed by everyone who took part. This process would doubtless have played an important part in reinforcing various intracommunal social roles and intercommunal links (Bradley 1990, 202).

If, as the same-tree evidence suggests, the maintenance of the post alignment was the responsibility of a single authority, there can be no fundamental reason why that authority could not also have supervised and undertaken its construction. A single authority need not have divided the monument into segments. There are indications, moreover, that, away from the platform, the post alignment was not segmented. If that was the case, it could be argued that segmentation had nothing to do with 'gang labour' at all. It could be further suggested that, given indications that partitions were significant throughout the use life of the monument, segmentation had more to do with use than with the structure's initial construction.

The platform

It has been possible to assess the approximate extent of the platform through a combination of trial trenches, hand-augered borehole surveys, and watching briefs (Fig 6.1). Its area is approximately 22,100m² (2.21ha or 5.46 acres). The largest single area of platform timbers revealed to date was the initial, dykeside exposure of 1982, which produced some 500 timbers along its length of 72m (Fig 6.9). This exposure is of interest as there were no significant gaps in the distribution of wood. In addition, the thickest accumulation of horizontal timbers, complete with its own substantial basal 'log layer', like that in Area 6B, was some distance north of the post alignment.

It was originally considered that the platform was a single structure, sufficiently solid to support the buildings of a 'lake village' (Pryor et al 1986). Further investigation has caused this simple view to be modified (Pryor 1992a). The 'pool' or relict watercourse in Areas 6A, 6C, and 6D showed that the platform was not solid and that areas of open water might have formed a component of the site's ritual use. There was also evidence for post-built structures at some distance from the post alignment and these have been tentatively interpreted as partitions.

Evidence concerning the role played by the platform is very enigmatic. Permanent domestic settlement can be ruled out for two reasons — wetness and a lack of environmental (particularly Coleoptera) evidence for human habitation. If the platform was not a home for the living, could it not have been a resting place for the dead? Slight evidence in support of this hypohesis was provided by fragments of adult human bone, which were found in upcast on the south side of the Mustdyke about 10m east of the small footbridge immediately south of Areas 7 and 8 (Fig 6.1). Although the bone fragments could have derived from Bronze Age levels, they could equally have come from earlier features cut into the surface of the basal gravels. A few loose human bones were also found in the faunal bone assemblage and these must be both *in situ* and non-residual (Chapter 12).

It seems most appropriate to regard the platform as an 'island' of diverse ritual importance, which might, for example, have held bodies for excarnation or for submersion in water. It might also have been intercalated with small watercourses and pools, which could have provided settings for smaller-scale rituals, perhaps to do with rites of passage. Together with the small pools, there might have been paths and walls or screens, and in all likelihood, there were areas of greater and lesser importance or of differing significance.

The finds from Flag Fen

In the discussion that follows, items of all types, whether artefacts and ecofacts, will be considered together. Special emphasis will be placed on taphonomy, distribution, and details of context or burial. It is hoped that these detailed observations will throw light on the circumstances surrounding the various objects' original deposition.

The deposition of artefacts and ecofacts

The tree-ring study (Chapter 8) has shown that at least a proportion of the oak timber used in the post alignment had been split from the same trees. Such splitting can only be carried out when the wood is still green — perhaps within the first six months after felling (Richard Darrah personal communication; Pryor 1991, 81). This would suggest that the said trees were designated for use at Flag Fen either before or shortly after felling. The wood technology study showed that, by and large, the timber had not been worn through prior use and that secondary damage (such as woodworm attack) was extremely rare. These studies would suggest that a proportion — perhaps the majority — of the wood had been felled and selected specifically for use at Flag Fen.

The evidence for reuse is surprisingly rare and is largely confined to specific artefacts, such as the possible axle fragment (B1751) or the wheel fragment, both of which carried clear signs of wear–they are the exceptions that might prove the rule. Although it is difficult to extend the argument to other types of artefact or ecofact, it should not be assumed that all bones, potsherds, shale bracelets, and metalwork were necessarily removed from domestic contexts. Some items, such as certain swords, were faulty and could never have

been used. Others, such as the querns, showed little or no evidence for wear. There is a strong argument for concluding that these objects were destined for Flag Fen almost from the outset.

The rich and diverse assemblage of metalwork provides a few clues as to its previous history.

Some of the swords, as just mentioned, had broken along casting flaws, which indicates that their previous use life had been neither stressful or prolonged. The bronze shears still had straight cutting edges, again suggesting a short use life with minimal sharpening. Bridgeford has convincingly shown that some of the cutting edges of the leaf-shaped swords showed signs of damage. This appears to have been caused by deliberate bashing against something hard, rather than by battle damage or wear during regular ceremonial use (Fig 10.26, top right).

Ritual destruction of items such as swords, or the smashing to tiny fragments of a metal shield(s) and a possible helmet(s) fall into a familiar pattern of status-related ceremonial rites, for which there is now a wealth of evidence (Bradley 1990). But the picture of Bronze Age ritual at Flag Fen encompasses far more than just competition for social status.

The distribution plans of metalwork at the Power Station have been discussed in Chapter 10, but certain trends can be summarised. The earliest metalwork (Fig 10.12) is mainly concentrated towards drier ground. By contrast, Iron Age metalwork is mainly found in wetter contexts (Fig 10.16). Certain artefact categories, for example tanged awls (Fig 10.19), show a clear separation into 'wet' and 'dry' distributions. Does this mean that different types of ritual deposition are being witnessed, in which wet finds represent a final rite of passage and those from drier ground something more transitory, such as the completion of apprenticeship?

Some of the most prestigious ('valuable' in modern terms) metalwork was also small in size and was by no means ostentatious. The miniature tin wheels, for example, were probably Alpine products; the tiny gold ring (possibly part of a composite earring) was also of possible central European manufacture (Chapter 10). It is difficult to view the destruction of objects as tiny as these in terms of, say, the contexts of a large-scale potlatch-style ceremony of competitive destruction (Dalton 1977, 204–7).

The four quernstones provided unequivocal evidence for non-use, or at best very light use, within domestic contexts. Whether the gabbro querns came from far afield or from local glacial erratics still remains to be decided, but the quern from Kent must surely have been transported to Flag Fen by sea. It might, on the one hand, have been just one of a batch that were used in the normal way, or it could have been a one-off, destined for ritual deposition from the outset. The fact remains, however, that four freshly made querns were deposited directly beneath the lowest and earliest timbers of the post alignment.

The study of quern ritual deposition by Buckley and Ingle is of particular importance (Chapter 11). Not only does it call into question the assumed domestic contexts of many quern finds, but it demonstrates an extraordinarily long-lived tradition of ritual deposition from Neolithic to Iron Age times. If this tradition is what it seems, the drawing of broad parallels between sites such as Etton and Flag Fen might not be so far-fetched.

The taphonomy of the animal bone suggests that many of the dog bones derived from complete skeletons that had been buried (presumably beneath timbers) and thereby protected from erosion. The other bone material had more in common with domestic assemblages. This would suggest that the dogs represent deliberate deposition (in effect sacrifice) whereas the sheep, cattle, and other bones probably represent food residue.

The animal bone distribution mirrors to an extent that of the metalwork. It is also reasonable to assume that the Power Station dog bodies probably dated to the main (Late Bronze Age) phase of metalwork deposition. In Flag Fen, animal bone also occurred within and around the timbers of the post alignment and platform and frequently in close association with the metalwork. The distribution of pottery, on the other hand, had a different, but nonetheless distinctive pattern (Chapter 9).

At the Power Station site, the variety of fabrics in the distribution pattern suggested longevity (Fig 9.1). There was evidence for Beaker, Grooved Ware, and Iron Age fabrics, but material of the Middle and Late Bronze Ages was rare or absent. At Flag Fen, on the other hand, later Bronze Age pottery occurred in far greater quantities. In seven cases, single vessels were represented (usually jars or cups). These had broken, or been broken at specific locations, mainly in the higher levels (1 and 2), whereas animal bone and metalwork were found in both higher and lower levels. This would suggest that pottery did not form an important element of the ritual deposition throughout the sequence at Flag Fen. The appearance of pottery in the higher levels might indicate a shift of ritual emphasis during the life of the monument.

The hypothesis that the pottery at Flag Fen represented activities that were not central to the original ritual purpose of the site is supported by the vessels themselves, which were very plain in shape, fabric, and decoration (which was extremely rare). The very 'ordinariness' of the pottery was a main contributory reason why the Flag Fen posts were originally interpreted as domestic dwellings (Barrett in Pryor *et al* 1986).

There was evidence among the finds for several rites of deposition, but most had deliberate smashing or breaking in common; some instances of this practice have already been mentioned. Many of the pins and brooches, for example, had been bent, twisted, or damaged — not a single sword, rapier, or dirk has a straight blade. Where present, all the shafts of spearheads or ferrules had been snapped off within the socket.

All the shale fragments had jagged breaks. Two of these joined together, suggesting that the breakage had taken place *in situ*.

The subsequent treatment of broken objects was by no means uniform. A number of loose sword/rapier rivets and fragments of sword hilt and pommel suggest that the other parts of the weapons might lie scattered outside the area of the Power Station metal-detector survey.

These loose fragments would indicate 'high-energy' depositional rites, involving throwing or transport of some sort.

Other 'low-energy' rites took place on a smaller scale and were perhaps more intimate. The bronze socketed axe and its haft from the Power Station, for example, were found together (Fig 10.6, 60; Taylor 1992, fig 20). They had probably been placed in a shallow scoop in the mud, because the small wooden fragments would otherwise have floated away. Similarly, the tanged dagger and red deer antler hilt were found together, the hilt resting on top of the blade (Fig 10.5, 54 and 54a). The two Ewart Park swords were each found in two pieces within respective square metres of ground (Fig 10.2, 5 and 6). The complete Middle Bronze Age jar decorated with fingertip impressions had been placed on its side, directly below an alder log that had been pegged into position by four wooden pegs (Fig 9.2 add cat number).

It was not always possible to decide which of the two styles of rite just discussed had been used to deposit a particular find. The context usually provides the clue: some objects, such as the flesh hook (Fig 10.5, 58) or the socketed spearhead from Area 6B (Fig 10.4, 49) were concealed beneath a large timber. This would suggest a 'low-energy' rite. The group of querns (Figs 11.6–9) provided an example of yet a third type of rite, perhaps best described as a 'foundation deposit'. Most unusually, no breakage seems to have been involved in this instance, although, as Buckley and Ingle note, the absence of top-stones is remarkable. It could be argued that to separate a top-stone from a bottom-stone is to render the latter 'broken' and useless.

The two commonest styles of rite appear at first glance to be very different, in that one is essentially public, the other more intimate. The quality of the artefacts themselves offer no evidence to suggest which type of rite was of greater or lesser prestige. If so high a proportion of the objects from Flag Fen were selected for deposition, it must be asked to what extent they were representative of contemporary domestic usage. Fortunately, as Flag Fen does not sit in isolation and is surrounded by a domestic landscape, many of the stone and ceramic objects found in the ritual wetland context would be perfectly at home there. The metalwork was, however, different.

Finds of Bronze Age metal objects are notoriously rare in domestic contexts and usually consist of small items, such as the tanged awl from Newark Road (Pryor 1980, fig 77). This would suggest that larger domestic items, such as axes, were retained for scrap at the end of their useful lives; indeed, this is the explanation given by Northover (Chapter 10) for the uniformity of much of the copper-alloy composition. In view of these considerations, it would probably be wise to treat the typological development of later Bronze Age metalwork with more caution than is customary. It should not be forgotten that many metal objects destined for ritual deposition need not be representative of those that were in use at the time.

It was noted in the previous chapter that the Bronze Age dryland landscape around Flag Fen was given over to intensive (perhaps 'climax') pastoral farming. High status artefacts, such as flesh hooks (eg Fig 10.5, 58) and cauldrons that might be associated with meat eating occur in later Bronze Age times at Flag Fen and at other Fenland locations, such as Feltwell Fen and Eriswell (Chapter 10). If by the later Bronze Age meat eating had become a prestigious activity in its own right, this might help to explain the scale of livestock keeping in and around the Fens. A broadly similar phenomenon can also be observed at the contemporary site at Runnymede Bridge, Egham, but in this instance the meat in question was probably beef (Stuart Needham personal communication).

Possible precursors to Flag Fen

It would seem inherently improbable that the Flag Fen structure was built from scratch at the centre of an ancient landscape at the end of the Middle Bronze Age, without precursors of any sort. The Fengate Bronze Age and Neolithic landscape, as it is presently understood, lacks a major early monument, in the way, for example, that the Etton causewayed enclosure figured in the Maxey area (Pryor 1998a).

Etton was located in a marginal situation, at the very edge of a floodplain. If there was ever such a monument at Fengate, it is most likely to be found beneath the alluvium, somewhere between the wettest, lowest-lying part of Flag Fen (which would probably have been too wet, even in Middle Neolithic times) and the Fengate fen edge. Possible indications of the presence of such a site in the vicinity were provided by finds at the Power Station. The flint assemblage included two serrated blades and, perhaps more significantly, two fragments of Group VI polished stone axes (Chapter 11; Fig 11.4). Serrated blades seem to occur with greater frequency at causewayed enclosures than elsewhere, added to which, the deliberate smashing of stone axes was a notable feature of the Etton enclosure (Edmonds 1998). Both the axe fragments from the Power Station had been smashed in a way that strongly recalled Etton and that could not possibly be explained by ordinary use.

A less chronologically distant precursor to Flag Fen might well have been a simple drove or route across the wetter ground. We have noted in the previous chapter that the Fengate landfall of the post alignment was not marked by a barrow or ring-ditch, nor was that at Northey.

Does this suggest that the course of the post alignment and its associated dryland routes has origins extending back to Neolithic, or even earlier times? Certainly the fragmentary and very shallow Neolithic ditch found below the posts at the Power Station would not contradict such a view (Fig 4.4).

Social roles of Flag Fen

Continuity

One remarkable aspect of the Bronze Age landcape of the Fengate/Flag Fen Basin is its longevity. The chronological study of Chapter 16 has demonstrated that the central Bronze Age field system was in use for between 1340 to 1890 years (at 95% confidence). It is also probable that parts of the system, especially around the Tower Works, might have continued in use until the very dawn of the Iron Age. During that extended period of time, the area of regularly flooded land was growing progressively larger. At first the process was slow, but it gained in pace towards the latter part of the second millennium BC. During the 'heyday' of the Bronze Age landscape, large flocks of animals were kept and local communities appear to have been prosperous. As far as can be determined, it was also a time of social stability.

There is no evidence for fortification or nucleation within or between the settlements around the edges of the Flag Fen Basin. Furthermore, an open, but parcelled-up, landscape could not have operated as a farming system, had the various elements within it been hostile to each other. Such systems depend on mutual cooperation if they are to operate successfully (Pryor 1998b, 82–5).

The Flag Fen timber structure was built in the second half of the life of the Bronze Age landscape, at a time of increasing wetness and perhaps of emerging social tensions. The central part of the system was actively being abandoned. The stability of the preceding centuries was beginning to break down: pressures of all sorts were building up.

It has been seen above (Chapter 6 and this chapter) that segmentation might have been an essential element in the monument's design, and one that had a direct bearing on its eventual function. It has also been argued that it was not merely a practical adjunct to successful, 'cost effective' construction. To find the closest prehistoric parallel for the proposed segmentation at Flag Fen, besides reviewing the partitioning of hillfort ramparts, a feature within a site nearer to hand, namely the segmented (or causewayed) ditch at Etton, should also be considered (Pryor 1998a). There was much evidence to suggest that the ditch at Etton was dug in segments, not only to divide up the ditch itself, but also perhaps the periphery of the interior. Ritual deposits were repeatedly placed, recut after recut, at the butt end of ditch segments, as if to emphasise the fact that the ditch ended.

The parallels between Etton and Bronze Age Flag Fen doubtless result from 'convergent evolution', rather than continuity of practice over so long a period (approximately 2500 years).

Both sites were positioned in topographically marginal areas removed from settlements. Both exhibit clear evidence for spatial segmentation, for the deliberate destruction of valued objects, and for the careful deposition of both artefacts and animal bone. Both can be considered as ritually specialised, liminal places of perceived danger, where the world of the living came close to the world of the ancestors (Bradley 1990; Thomas 1991). Etton played a dual role: it provided a focus for regular (perhaps seasonal) gatherings of many people in which feasting played an important part. There were also, however, indications of more private, perhaps single-person or kin-group-related ceremonies in which specific rites of passage were commemorated. The 'small filled pits' could be seen as deposits commemorating individual people, whereas the nearby ditch segments and the deposits within them were about kin-group cohesion and the perceived identity of the kin-groups to which the individuals belonged.

The Etton enclosure was divided into two distinct halves, separated by a north–south ditch and linear posthole settings (Pryor 1998a, fig 10)). It has been suggested that the east half was largely given over to rites of passage and most particularly to those of death and subsequent transformation; this was the area of smaller-scale, kin-group-related activities.

The western half, on the other hand, served a different function. Since the ditch deposits produced much evidence for feasting, in the form of animal bone heaps, it has been suggested that this part of the enclosure was used for more public, communal gatherings.

Flag Fen was a linear site and, by its very layout, was unsuited for large gatherings. On the other hand, it was very well adapted to serve the needs of smaller, more intimate groups of people. At Flag Fen, the two levels of social interaction seen at Etton, public and kin-group, had become separated. The regular communal gatherings would have taken place in and around the community stockyards on the nearby higher ground at Fengate. The exchange of livestock must have played a key role in the regular communal gatherings. While the larger assemblies of people and livestock took place in and around the communal stockyards, smaller, perhaps more intimate, kin-group and individual ceremonies would have taken place in and among the segmented parts of the post alignment, deep in Flag Fen.

It is possible that the post alignment segments were identified with individual kin-groups. As people travelled along the main pathway between Rows 2 and 3 they would have been aware of the symbolic social and ideological 'landscape' they were passing through. Perhaps, as at Etton, particularly important or high-status areas were screened off from the common gaze.

Doubtless the deposits expressed social competition, as well as identity. At all events, the numerous 'offerings' of broken metalwork and other items can be seen as the later equivalent of the Neolithic 'small filled pits'— the individual expressions of major events in life, of which death itself was probably the most significant.

One characteristic of very shallow, seasonally flooded fen-margin land is the extent to which the appearance of the vegetation cover changes with the seasons. In winter and early spring, the reeds and marginal vegetation die down and water levels rise; the look of the fen at this time of year is of open water or sheets of ice. In summer and autumn, on the other hand, tall leaves of plants such as great reed-mace, flag iris, reeds, and sedge grow up rapidly and soon cover large areas of all but the deepest waters. At Flag Fen today, great reed-mace (*Typha angustifolia*) regularly grows 2.5m tall. The lush vegetation of the summer/autumn fen would thus have provided a secluded setting for private ceremonies. If ceremonies took place in the autumn, at the time communities and their livestock were gathering at Fengate, the vegetation in the regularly flooded parts of Flag Fen would be close to its tallest. The small areas of open water within the platform would be cut off and secluded. The pathway between Rows 2 and 3 was undoubtedly a route across Flag Fen, but it need not necessarily have been an ordinary day-to-day causeway. It showed signs of regular use, but it might also have been a 'ceremonial way' for many people at significant times in their lives.

The waters of Flag Fen might have been seen as a boundary between the world of the living and the world of the ancestors. It was a place of communication and transition. The physical defences provided by the posts might have marked the edge of the embayment, but they were more than a physical barrier, just as the pathway was more than a trackway alone. They were both powerful symbols. The posts divided the world of the living from that of the dead.

Symbolic acts of the living (and most particularly their last rites) took place to the south of the posts, on the physically and symbolically 'safe', defended side of the barrier. This side was also where the Power Station metalwork was found (Figs 10.12–16). On the other side lay the next world. At the Power Station, this was where the Iron Age skeleton and the Bronze Age dog bodies were found.

Display and competition

Much stress has been placed in this report on the small-scale, almost intimate, nature of the rituals that were performed at Flag Fen. The distribution of metalwork at the Power Station indicates, however, that the picture was by no means as straightforward towards the edge of the fen. There might have been a gradual shift in emphasis over time, with more deposition on dry land towards the Middle Bronze Age (Fig 10.12) and in the wetter fen in the Iron Age (Fig 10.16).

A wet/dry distinction was also evident in the intervening period, which might indicate, as already noted, a variety of rituals with their own, quite distinct, aims and objectives. It might just be possible to discern a shift towards bigger gestures or more grandiose depositions in the Iron Age. Items such as the elaborate plate brooch (Fig 10.8, 146), the short-sword scabbard plate (Fig 10.11, 273), the two iron swords (Fig 10.10, 259 and 260), and the shears in their wooden box (Fig 10.11, 276) must, however, be set against the humbler swan's-neck and other pins and brooches (Fig 10.9, 200–14). All in all, it is a case that can not be made with much conviction at Flag Fen, but it is possible that other sites, such as Fiskerton, might provide the supporting evidence for gradual diachronic changes of this nature (Michael Parker-Pearson personal communication).

It is possible to state that while the rituals might have been small in scale, there is ample evidence in the objects themselves for display and competition within society as a whole. The direct evidence for display comes from the items placed in the water — the swords, possible helmet rivets, the shield tab, spearheads, and ferrules. The many pins and brooches might well have been attached to clothing. Had conditions of preservation been different, pieces of textile would doubtless have been found. Sheep were important to the economy, suggested by the many cylindrical loomweights found at Fengate. Weaving was, therefore, a significant local industry, dating from perhaps as early as the Early Bronze Age — if the recently discovered fired clay object from Site O is indeed a loomweight (Fig 2.11). The production of woven textiles from the Early Bronze Age offered a most important new opportunity for personal display, in which patterns could indicate an individual's kin-group, status, and a variety of more subtle 'messages' (Timothy Champion personal communication and 1975; Champion et al 1984, 207–9, 290).

Change

Whether Flag Fen was constructed de novo or was an enlargement or embellishment of an already existing ritual focus, the principal local stimulus for its construction can be seen in the steadily rising waters of the Fens to the north-east. The posts can, indeed, be seen as a symbolic weir or dam against their inexorable rise. There is, however, a very great danger of being too deterministic: human societies have their own dynamics and do not respond to outside stimuli in ways that are necessarily predictable. In other words, local environmental factors on their own would probably have been insufficient to stimulate such a major development. Other forces would also have been involved. It should also be recalled that the initial centuries of the first millennium BC were times of widespread 'fragmentation and social change' (Bradley 1984, 129). The changes that were perhaps initially brought on by the gradual loss of summer grazing and the shrinking

size of winter flood-free lands had a serious local effect when they were combined with these other, more general, processes of social fragmentation and change.

The latter centuries of the second millennium BC were also times of change, albeit somewhat less turbulent. Cunliffe has characterised the period as one of 'transition from the simple agricultural regimes of the Neolithic/Early Bronze Age, to the settled and intensive exploitation that typified the Iron Age and Roman periods' (Cunliffe, 1991, 59). The inhabitants of the Flag Fen Basin were unaware that the Bronze Age formed but a step along the stairway that led inexorably towards the settled, intensive exploitation of later prehistoric and Roman times.

On the western fen edge, and elsewhere in lowland Britain, it would appear that 'simple agricultural regimes' actually followed the 'intensive exploitation' of the Bronze Age. Which is not to deny the underlying processes involved, since the period was undoubtedly one of major social and economic change.

Setting broader social factors aside, it would appear that the combined effects of two apparently unrelated processes, the increasing intensification of livestock farming and the gradually encroaching fen, appear to have produced near catastrophic results on the land, where it mattered. The Bronze Age fields were abandoned and Flag Fen ceased to be maintained as a 'working' timber structure, although, to judge from the large number of Iron Age artefacts found there, it continued to be visited. Recent commercial excavation has produced important new evidence on the nature of the Bronze/Iron Age transition, reviewed in the previous chapter. The important point that arises from this new evidence is that the changes in question, and the subsequent developments they gave rise to, were both unpredictable and far from straightforward.

It is, surely, more than mere coincidence that the abandonment of the central Bronze Age fields at Fengate coincides almost exactly with the Phase 2 period of stability at Flag Fen (Chapter 18). In this regard the word 'stability' is crucial. Flag Fen must have provided the social and ideological stability to allow people to cope with the wholesale change that was taking place around them. It is a functional explanation, certainly, but it is also a simple one, which helps to explain the observation that at Flag Fen the rituals of the Middle Bronze Age continued, seemingly unchanged, until the latter part of the Iron Age. The classes of objects deposited (mainly weapons and ornaments) remained much the same, as did the manner of their deposition (mainly single offerings, involving breakage). It is the very obstinacy of the ritual continuity that might provide an explanation of itself: the rites that took place around the rotten stumps of the once-great posts provided a firm link with more stable times. Put another way, the conservatism of the rites harked back to times when life was more stable; in this way the regular visits to the abandoned site at Flag Fen helped Iron Age communities find some equanimity in a world turned upside down (Bradley 1991).

By Late Iron Age times, the deposition of metal-work in the ever-deeper waters of Flag Fen had begun to tail off, as the regional settlement pattern was becoming more stable. From about 200 BC, the nucle-ated farmstead at Cat's Water was established. By con-trast with earlier periods, its focus of activity was away from the wetland. By the third century AD, the once lush pastures of Flag Fen had been largely abandoned.

Sometime during the Middle Iron Age, the centre of influence shifted westwards away from Fengate, towards the river Nene at Orton Meadows, on the far side of modern Peterborough. Here currency bars, finely decorated swords, and other objects were deposited in the Nene waters, starting in La Tène I times (Stead 1984). It is, perhaps, instructive to note that an area such as this was able to support two important ritual foci in the Iron Age. Whether more remain to be discovered is a matter of conjecture.

Comparative sites in Britain and Continental Europe

As our knowledge of Flag Fen is still partial, this factor alone impeded the search for convincing parallels else-where. It should be stated from the outset that there are, or have been, in reality, very few good *comparanda* for the site and none that can be placed within their landscape contexts.

Richard Bradley's recent analysis of prehistoric hoards and votive deposits has drawn together most of the significant European wet-site ritual finds. This most important study has placed Flag Fen, and partic-ularly the Power Station site, within wider contexts (Bradley 1990). To attempt an overview of comparable quality would be impossible. This review will, there-fore, concentrate on seeking parallels for aspects of Flag Fen that were not available or fully understood when Bradley wrote his synthesis. The discussion will begin with the British evidence.

Britain

The Fenland of East Anglia has long been well known as an area rich in Bronze Age metalwork (Rowlands 1976). Even the contiguous Fens of south Lincolnshire, where Bronze Age levels are buried below Iron Age and later silts, have also produced large quantities of metalwork, especially around the edges of regularly flooded land (Davey 1973). It would be tempting, in the light of Flag Fen, to suggest that most of these 'chance' finds were the result of deliberate, rit-ual deposition. The prehistoric Fens were, however, a complex environment of small islands and meandering watercourses. Consequently, great care must be exer-cised and no single find or hoard should be pro-nounced 'ritual' until it can be established that the findspot is both precisely located ('the Ely district', for example, is of little use) and that the site in question was wet at the time of deposition.

Some of the peculiar features of the metalwork from Flag Fen, for example, bashed sword blades, deliberate breakage, and so on, might be of some assistance when seeking parallels, but they are of little use when removed from their all-important landscape context. Nothing short of a detailed, well researched study will be able to quantify the actual extent of ritual deposi-tion within the Fens. For these reasons we will not seek parallels for Flag Fen from concentrations of metal-work alone.

The closest local parallel for Flag Fen was undoubt-edly the possible timber 'causeway' between Fordey and Little Thetford, near Ely (Fig 1.2). The site was found by the local farmer and was investigated by T C Lethbridge and Sir Harry Godwin. The site consisted of an 'alignment of posts' and horizontal timbers inter-mixed with brushwood. There was also a sandy layer associated with the horizontal timbers. The report (Lethbridge 1935) makes it clear that this sand was brought from some distance away. The main site report is very informative. The section shows that the posts protruded well above the horizontal timbers of the walkway, in a manner that is not characteristic, for example, of the majority of trackways in both the Somerset Levels and Ireland (Coles and Coles 1989; Raftery 1990). Many of the posts were truly massive (every bit as large as those at Flag Fen) and the major-ity were of oak (Godwin 1978, pl 20).

As far as can be ascertained from the report, the hand-cut trial trenches, although small, produced a surprising number of finds, including a patch of small handmade potsherds, a Late Bronze Age bronze bracelet and, perhaps most significantly, a large sherd of coarse pottery (possibly Middle Bronze Age?) from a bucket-shaped vessel. This sherd had been concealed within the brushwood of the walkway. Lethbridge clearly realised that these two finds were not the casu-al losses of people using a track.

While it is certain that the sand was brought from some little distance away and might have contained fragments of early pottery, it is difficult to account for anyone putting the sherds of a small handmade pot into a faggot of brushwood, which he was laying for a foundation in a bog.

The same argument applies to the bronze ring, which is probably an armlet (Lethbridge 1935, 88). Lethbridge's second report is less detailed, but it does contain several significant new developments (Lethbridge and O'Reilly 1936, 161–2). A cache of red deer and ox bones was found alongside the post alignment, sealed beneath the sand layer. There were sufficient bones for Lethbridge to conclude that they had been put in the ground to consolidate the causeway; pieces of Deverel-Rimbury and Iron Age pottery were also found in the sand layer above (and around?) the bones. Given the quantities of timber that were freely available, it would seem improbable that the cache of bones represented 'hardcore' for consolidation. It is also difficult to see it as simple domestic refuse, so far from dry land.

Lethbridge and O'Reilly describe the causeway as being perfectly straight and ten yards (9.14m) wide in places. This width is very much greater than most prehistoric trackways. The distance of the causeway from dry land to dry land was about half a mile (800m). In size, straightness, and width it closely resembled Flag Fen. Lethbridge ends the second report with an urgent plea for further research — would that someone had listened at the time!

A similar, but undated, causeway to Fordey/Little Thetford was reported by Lethbridge as being straight, about a mile (1.6km) long, and also ten yards (9.14m) wide (Lethbridge and O'Reilly 1936, 162). It ran between dry land at Ely and Stuntney. The modern Ely–Soham road (A142) follows its alignment and has probably destroyed any prehistoric evidence. The well known Stuntney hoard of 80 bronze objects, packed into a wooden tub or bucket, was found immediately alongside the causeway (Clark and Godwin 1940; Godwin 1978, 74–5; Hall and Coles 1994, 80–4).

More recently, salvage excavation has revealed yet another possible post alignment or causeway, in the extreme southern Fens in the Cam (or Rhee) floodplain, at Lingey Fen, Haslingfield (Pullinger 1981). The site consisted of two exposures of posts, probably from different causeways, within a peat-filled basin. It was thought to date to the Late Bronze Age.

Many of the posts were of oak and had pencil-like axed tips. The site was observed during its destruction by dragline and the archaeologists did well to acquire the data they managed to retrieve. The axe marks (Pullinger 1981, pl 1a) resemble those at Flag Fen and the wood specialist drew parallels with timber from the Bronze Age Somerset Levels trackway at Meare Heath (Heal 1981, 27). The circumstances of the salvage excavation made it difficult to assign context with any accuracy, but a large number of animal bones were found around the timbers. Significantly perhaps, the bones included dog and a very high proportion of red deer; there were also many shed and unshed antlers, recalling Fordey/Little Thetford (Legge 1981).

In conclusion, it seems possible that all three sites just described could have been more than mere trackways. Ritual, it would seem, played an important role in their original use. Of the three, Fordey/Little Thetford would appear to resemble Flag Fen in so many respects that further work to determine its nature, preservation, and extent is urgently required. At the very least, metal-detector surveys should be carried out by responsible authorities, before others conduct an unofficial survey to less demanding standards.

Linked to the Fens in terms of river catchment, but just outside the main sedimentary basin, the floodplain of the river Witham, south of Lincoln, revealed a remarkable Iron Age post-built structure at Fiskerton (Field 1983 and 1986). The structure has been provisionally interpreted as a bridge, pier, or causeway across or into the river, although a final report is still awaited.

The posts were in two close rows and could be shown through tree-ring studies to have been arranged in pairs at intervals of 3–4m (Hillam 1985b, fig. 2). Dendrochronology also revealed that the structure was rebuilt every 16 to 18 years. Unlike Flag Fen, the posts of the two rows were grouped together, with narrow gaps of a metre or so between each group. What made the site extraordinary, however, was the discovery of quantities of military material, including swords and spearheads, within and around the posts. Large amounts of pottery and possible net-mending pins were also found. One sword hilt was richly decorated with inlay and one of the finest yet found in Britain (Ian Stead personal communication). Since it seems hard to believe that this assemblage was either derived from elsewhere or was lost by travellers, an *in situ* ritual role has surely to be considered.

An instructive illustration of emerging complexity is provided by the important Thameside Neolithic and later Bronze Age site at Runnymede Bridge (Longley and Needham 1980; Needham 1991). The interpretation of Runnymede Bridge, like that at Flag Fen, is continuing as the post-excavation research evolves. While the main thrust of the interpretation would still favour an essentially settlement/domestic role for the site, it is increasingly being recognised that the deposits also include a substantial ritual component (Stuart Needham personal communication). Needham has kindly drawn attention to the 4–6m undulations in the plan of the riverside revetment posts. They do not appear to have a simple functional explanation and might possibly recall the suggested segmentary structure of the Flag Fen post alignment (Needham 1991, fig 14).

A recent discovery of great importance was made in the course of development at Shinewater Park, Eastbourne, East Sussex. Here, the parallels with Flag Fen are numerous and very close. On visiting the site shortly after its discovery in 1995, Maisie Taylor and the author were quite struck by its superficial resemblance to Flag Fen. A 'trackway' or alignment of posts traversed a strait that gave access to a small, almost landlocked, fenny embayment, which was subject to marine influence (Greatorix 1998). The alignment of posts was just over 500m long and led to at least one platform towards the middle of the strait (Greatorix 1995). The posts seemed to traverse the platform, as at Flag Fen. The landscape around the embayment was more steeply shelving than at Flag Fen, but there is evidence for a substantial livestock-based field system on the downland hills roundabout (Andrew Woodcock personal communication). The post alignment, which consisted of at least three rows of posts, included deposits of sand and fine gravel and had undoubtedly been used as a trackway. There were many horizontal timbers, some of which contained joints. Finds from the alignment and platform have been remarkable and include a handled socketed sickle, a bronze curved knife, three socketed axes, an end-winged axe, a bracelet,

a probable tanged chisel, amber beads, and large quantities of animal bone and Late Bronze Age pottery. The
assemblage from the platform seems to comprise
domestic material, but the number of metal and other
special finds is most unusual.

Shinewater Park is located in a different environment from Flag Fen, in an area with a very different
subsequent (ie Iron Age) prehistory. It is essential that
it continues to be seen as a monument in its own right.
Only in that way will it provide a truly independent
comparison with sites in other regions.

Further afield, the Late Bronze Age site at Caldicot
Castle Lake, Monmouthshire, in the Severn estuary,
was also characterised by an irregular alignment of
substantial oak piles (Nayling 1993). At least one of
these piles has been dated dendrochronologically to
the early first millennium BC. The site has been provisionally described as a causeway/trackway, but it has
produced one 'military' bronze of Late Bronze Age
type, a diminutive stub chape. The site also revealed a
boat and a near-complete, and partially articulated,
male dog skeleton. Again, as at Fiskerton, the evidence
is both tantalising and far from simple. All that can be
said with any confidence is that, in the light of Flag
Fen, the site could have had considerable ritual significance. One practical lesson arises from this brief
review of the British evidence. It is now widely accepted that settlements are best understood by means of
open-area excavation. Curatorial authorities and others should take note, however, that ritual and ceremonial sites also require large areas to be examined in
detail, if the complex diversity of prehistoric symbolic
behaviour in lowland Britain is ever to be appreciated.

The Continent: La Tène

It was noted above that Bradley has recently (1990)
discussed the continental evidence in detail and the
same ground will not be covered again here. Much
Iron Age ritual deposition in wet sites, especially in
France, has also been described by the several authors
of *The Celts* (Moscati *et al* 1991). Very few of the sites
discussed in either book have been excavated as extensively or in the same detail as Flag Fen. The notable
exception to this is La Tène. This discussion of the
Continental evidence will therefore be largely confined
to a brief reassessment of the type site of the European
later Iron Age.

Ritual deposition of bronzes and other items in the
waters or muds of fens, bogs, lakes, and rivers is a well
known and widespread phenomenon of the Bronze
and Iron Ages across most of north-western and central Europe (Piggott 1965; Coles and Harding 1979;
Champion *et al* 1984). The majority of the depositions
are thought to have been single items or isolated
hoards, but this need not necessarily be so: without a
detailed metal-detector survey, it is impossible to be
certain one way or the other. It is also unusual to find
evidence for structures that can be linked reliably to

depositions (eg Hvass and Storgaard 1993); the so-
called 'temple' at Bargeroosterveld was a Bronze Age
ritual structure in a wetland in north-west Holland, but
there were no accompanying ritual deposits of metalwork (Bloemers and Louwe-Kooijmans 1981).

En route to the Swiss Lakes and closer to the
English Channel, the enclosed site at Gournay sur
Aronde, which dates to the third century BC, was situated in marshy ground of the Aronde floodplain.
Within the ditches of this defended sanctuary were
found bones of sacrificed animals and swords, many of
which had been bent or folded into S- or Z-shaped patterns; one batch of iron sword scabbards had been bent
into a neat parcel, shaped like a bow-tie. Both edges of
a sword blade had been struck against something sharp
(perhaps another sword) to produce an irregular, serrated effect (Bruneaux 1991).

If ritual deposition in wet places can not be used of
itself to draw regional parallels with Flag Fen and the
small group of similar sites from contemporary Britain,
it becomes necessary to seek other points of coincidence. The well known site at La Tène had many
points in common with Flag Fen and a study tour of
(and subsequent visits to) the French and Swiss alpine
lakes has focused the author's attention on the area.
The region and the finds from it are also well served by
English language publications, both old (Keller 1878;
Munro 1890 and 1912), and new (De Navarro 1972;
Jacobsthal 1944; Harding 1980; Hodson 1990).

La Tène in the light of Flag Fen

The early history of archaeological research at La Tène
is most charitably described as chequered. The situation was eventually brought under a measure of control
by Paul Vouga whose excavations and other researches
were published (1923). Vouga's report includes an
invaluable general plan, which, while it does not plot
the numerous finds from the haphazard *anciennes
fouilles*, is at least a representative distribution pattern
in its own right (Fig 19.4). The finds from La Tène
have recently been described by Egloff (1992).

The layout of the site was straightforward. It was
located within the natural bed of the now canalised
river Thiele, at the point where it debouched into Lake
Neuchâtel. Its limits were defined, more or less, by two
post-built 'bridges', the Pont Vouga (to the south-west
close to the lakeside) and the Pont Desor, upstream to
the north-east. Between the two bridges, the riverbed
was both shallower and narrower and might have
formed a passable ford in wintertime or when the
water was not frozen solid.

The two 'bridges' aside, the edges of the channel
were lined in many places by piles that were thought to
have supported the platform foundations of domestic
buildings. The bed of the river was also littered with
numerous horizontal timbers, mainly planks and
beams. There were fewer horizontal timbers around
the Pont Desor than the Pont Vouga, but this might

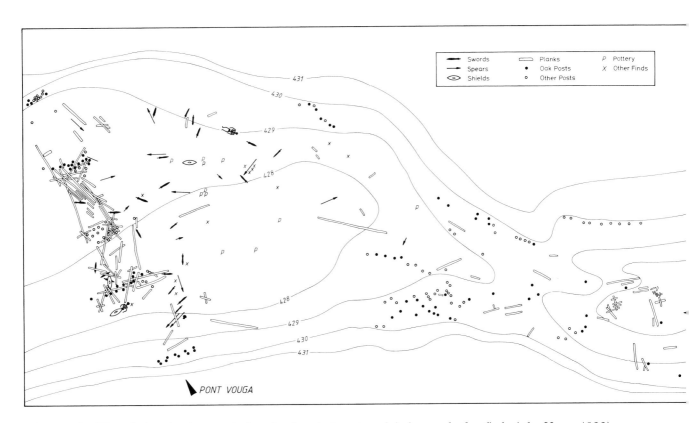

Fig 19.4 La Tène, Switzerland: general plan showing the location of timbers and other finds (after Vouga 1923)

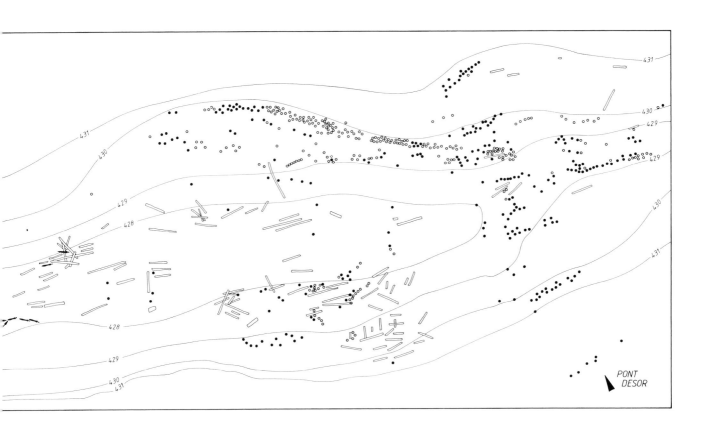

PONT
DESOR

have been due to water action. Apart from timbers, the stream-bed produced large numbers of swords, spears, and apparently domestic artefacts. A corpus of swords has been published by De Navarro (1972).

The history of archaeological investigation and interpretation of La Tène has recently been summarised by Cynthia Dunning (1992). Although a ritual explanation has been advanced by certain scholars (De Navarro 1972; Bradley 1991), it is by no means universally accepted. The purpose of the present reconsideration is to point out general parallels with Flag Fen and to question whether the two 'bridges' were anything of the sort.

The illustrations of finds in Vouga (1923) reveal numerous similarities with Flag Fen, but mostly of a later period. Shears feature prominently and there are miniature and full-sized wheels and so on. Damage is less evident, but, as was the practice of the time, many fragments were probably not illustrated. It is hard to imagine how so large an assemblage of fine artefacts could have found its way into a small riverbed by any means other than deliberate deposition. Bradley (1991, 159) considered the available options and concluded that La Tène was a ritual site. It could, however, be argued that Bradley's conclusion was inevitable, given the overall thrust of his study. On the other hand, as will shortly be seen, the close parallels provided by Flag Fen offer independent support for his hypothesis.

The discussion will begin with the two 'bridges'. First, it can quite reasonably be asked why they were not located at the narrow 'straight' or ford between them. This would have provided a far shorter and simpler crossing place. Second, it seems strange to have constructed two contemporary bridges so close to each other. One would surely have been sufficient merely to cross a small river. Third, the 'bridges' lack structural conviction: the largest spans between the groups of uprights were at the sides of the channel and not, as might be expected, at its deepest point, where it would have been important to avoid restricting the flow. Furthermore, some of the spans were quite large — some 9m (Pont Vouga) and 11m (Pont Desor) — and yet there is no evidence for abutment bracing, piers, angled piles, or other engineering measures needed to support so tall a bridge and so long a span.

When the river was in spate, moreover, any superstructure would surely have been at risk and required substantial reinforcement. In addition, given what is known about ancient timber bridge construction, especially in an area where lake levels fluctuated so much, the piles must be considered very flimsy supports for even a small bridge. The vertical piles at La Tène do not compare, for example, with the massive early medieval timber bridge foundations found recently at Hemington, Leicestershire (Cooper et al 1994), or the eighth-century AD Mercian bridge pier at Cromwell, near Newark, Notts (Salisbury, 1995). The paired posts at Fiskerton, which were comparable in size to those at La Tène spanned 3 to 4m, not 10 or 11m (Field 1986).

Many of the piles of the Pont Vouga were of 'white wood' (bois blanc, probably pine), which was a weaker load-bearing timber than oak and more readily subject to decay. Further, if it was a bridge, the most structurally important central group of piles of the 'Pont' Vouga were exclusively of bois blanc.

An alternative hypothesis to possibly explain the La Tène phenomenon is that the site owed its location and origin to the central shallow crossing or ford. This would have been the nearest place where the river could have been crossed by traffic that was skirting around the edge of Lake Neuchâtel. For whatever reason(s), the site then gained in importance and expanded both upstream and downstream. The piles around the edge of the stream-bed and those of the two 'bridges' demarcated the limits of the ritually significant area and were also used to mark internal divisions.

The piles around the edge of the stream-bed have been interpreted as the foundations for house platforms (references in Dunning 1992). It is remarkable, however, that these piles were generally arranged in single rows or narrow linear bands (Fig 19.4). It could be argued that only a part of the platform projected over the water and that the remainder was supported on piles that were driven into dry land, and have not therefore survived. This explanation, however, ignores the gap on the bank (or shoreward side) of the piles, which in most instances amounted to several metres. It also ignores the usual Alpine pattern of piling, which was frequently dense, often clustered, but rarely so narrowly linear and lacking reinforced corners (eg Perini 1984). The discontinuous piles around the edges of the stream-bed at La Tène resemble most the palisades that surrounded individual settlement areas at Cortaillod-Est, also on Lake Neuchâtel (Arnold 1986).

The bunching of posts at each 'bridge' could have been a form of segmentation or partitioning, whereby different depths of water were marked out in a manner that would have been visible from the surface. Being segmented, the gaps in either boundary would have permitted access to the ritual area by boat–albeit deliberately restricted access. The gaps would also have allowed water to pass through when the river was in spate. If not a result of 'anciennes fouilles', the cluster of finds on one side only of the Pont Vouga recalls Flag Fen and supports the view that the 'bridge' was in fact a boundary and served little or no practical purpose.

While too much should not be read into Vouga's schematic plan, the structures can also, very tentatively, be seen to be composed of longitudinal segments of approximately equal length (20–25m). Starting at the Pont Vouga and working upstream, the first zone was largely free of piles; on either side of the 'ford', the piles reappeared and many seem to have been arranged in rows that respected the contours of the stream-bed. There was then another zone where piles were largely absent. The next zone was characterised by numerous piles on either side of the stream. This zone could perhaps be divided into two parts of equal size on the basis of the southerly posts and horizontal timbers. Upstream of the Pont Desor, the posts change location sharply from the edges of the stream to its centre. Finally, it should be noted that the sections published by Vouga show extensive disturbance caused by earlier excavation or looting and it is always possible that much of the apparent horizontal patterning was caused by these later activities.

The layout of La Tène was potentially complex and exhibited tantalising hints at internal structure and possible segmentation, both axially and transversely. Sadly, so much has been destroyed by the *anciennes fouilles* that it will never be possible to offer more than very tentative attempts at reconstruction. If Flag Fen is anything to go by, however, simple functional explanations will not provide satisfactory answers to the many questions posed by this most remarkable of sites.

Appendix 1 Detailed soil micromorphological descriptions of samples from the Depot (1992) and Cat's Water (1990) sites, Fengate (Chapters 2 and 3)

by C A I French

Introduction

The following detailed descriptions refer to discussions of soil micromorphological analyses in the Depot (1992) and Cat's Water (1990) excavation descriptions of Chapters 2 and 3 respectively.

Throughout, c:f = coarse:fine.

The Depot site (1992)

Profile A: sample 1 (11cm)

Structure: irregular blocky (upper 1–2cm) to poorly developed irregular blocky, becoming apedal vughy with depth. *Porosity*: 20% upper — 10% with depth. Frequent vughs (250–500μm, occasionally 500–1000μm), and occasional channels (fewer with depth), 250–500μm wide, up to 5mm long, irregular, partially accommodated, curved ends. *Mineral components*: c:f ratio — 45:55: upper part — coarse; very coarse sand <5%, coarse sand 10%, medium sand 15–20%, fine sand 15%; fine; very fine sand 15%, silt 20%, clay 15–20%; lower part — coarse; very coarse and coarse sand 5%, medium sand 15–20%, fine sand 20%; fine: very fine sand 20%, silt 25%, clay 10–15%. Sandy loam. Coarse/fine fraction — variably well to poorly mixed throughout. Grains are mostly quartz (sub-rounded to sub-angular, mono- and poly-crystalline). Rock fragments are mostly sandstone (sub-rounded/sub-angular), mica and limestone. *Organic components*: 10% throughout. Mostly <50μm, integrally mixed with groundmass, but also rounded/subrounded particles from 50–250μm, occasionally larger. Very occasional root casts (dark reddish brown, *c* 500μm in size), rare charcoal (oblong and subrounded, with cell structure). *Groundmass*: coarse: open porphyric related distribution; fine: stipple-speckled, weakly to moderately birefringent, reddish to golden brown (CPL), reddish brown (PPL), orange (RL). Occasionally granular and reticulate striated, especially in upper part of thin section. Occasional linear zones *c* 25–50μm wide and *c* 100μm long monostriated in the groundmass. *Pedofeatures*: *textural*, non-laminated dusty clay and silt infillings (coatings and bands) integral with the groundmass; dusty yellow-gold (CPL) discontinuous clay coatings of void space (especially in upper 1–2cm — alluvium/B transition), <10μm to *c* 50μm thick, with moderate birefringence; dusty/dirty orange to reddish-orange (CPL) clay coatings up to 40μm thick, sometimes laminated, becoming thinner deeper in the profile, occasionally associated with silt coatings/infillings. In general, clay coatings decrease in thickness and clarity with depth, but clay is still present in most pores. *Amorphous*, sesquioxide impregnation (25–50%, increasing with depth), occasional small root pseudomorphs, rare amorphous iron/phosphate concretions; rare bone fragment.

Profile A: sample 2 (10.5cm)

Structure: apedal vughy. *Porosity*: 10–20%, mostly irregular medium and small vughs. *Mineral components*: c:f ratio — 45:55: coarse: very coarse and coarse sand 5%, medium sand 15–20%, fine sand 20%; fine: very fine sand 25%, silt 20%, clay 10–15%. Sandy loam. Components as in A1. *Organic components*: 5–10%, as in A1. *Groundmass*: as in A1. *Pedofeatures*: *textural*, thin dusty yellow-gold (CPL) clay coatings in groundmass and as granostriations; dusty/dirty orange and yellow-orange (CPL) clay coatings 20–30μm thick, occasionally with iron staining (very dark brown) — all as described above (A1); rare yellow (CPL) clean non-laminated clay coatings in void space. In general, very little clay in void space. *Amorphous*, some sesquioxide impregnation (20–30%), sesquioxide nodules.

Profile B: sample 1 (9cm)

Structure: (1) upper 1cm — alluvium. Moderately developed sub-angular blocky. *Porosity*: 10%: mostly channels, occasional vughs and vesicles; (2) 4cm of poorly developed sub-angular blocky to irregular peds, 1–2mm size or larger. Less well developed with depth. Porosity: 20%: frequent vughs of all size classes, undulating, subrounded. Occasional chambers; (3) lower 4cm — becoming a mixture of weak irregular blocky and apedal vughy, with structure weakening with depth. Porosity: 10%: mostly medium-sized vughs, rare channels. *Mineral components*: c:f ratio — (1) 40:60: coarse: very coarse and coarse sand <5–10%, medium sand 10–20%, fine sand 10%; fine: very fine sand 10%, silt 25%, clay 25%. Clay loam. Well sorted; (2) 40:60: coarse: very coarse and coarse sand 5%, medium sand 20%, fine sand 15%; fine: very fine sand 20%, silt 20%, clay 20%. Sandy clay loam; (3) 35:65: coarse: very coarse and coarse sand <5%, medium sand 15%, fine sand 15%; fine: very fine sand 20%, silt 25–30%, clay 15–20%. Sandy (clay) loam. Components as in A1. *Organic components*: (1) 10%, mostly 'punctuations', some larger charcoal. (2) and (3) 5% throughout. As described in A1. *Groundmass*: (1) coarse: open porphyric related distribution; fine: stipple-speckled, with areas of reticulate and granostriated, high birefringence. Golden brown (CPL), medium brown (PPL), yellow (RL), moderate to strong birefringence. (2) coarse: open porphyric related distribution; fine: stipple-speckled with moderate to high birefringence. (3) coarse — as in (2); fine: stipple speckled and some granostriation (5–10μm thick, up to *c* 200μm long — most 100μm). Overall, poorly sorted. Colours (2) and (3) as in A1. *Pedofeatures*: *textural*, (1) and (2) — very fine yellow (CPL) dusty clay coatings in groundmass, and occasionally in pores/channels; (3) occasional zones of clay — red (CPL) dusty laminated; very thin clay coatings, frequent, but not strong; yellow (CPL) and reddish brown (PPL) <10μm up to *c* 40μm thick, dusty to slightly dirty clay in voids. *Amorphous*, (1) occasional fine root pseudomorph; (2) root pseudomorphs, occasional sesquioxide staining (<10%), rare sesquioxide nodules; (3) sesquioxide staining (<10%). *Fabric*: (1), (2) and (3) — <200μm silt/clay aggregates; (2) and (3) — zones of apparent mixing of the 3 fabrics.

Profile B: sample 2 (7–8cm)

Structure: very poorly developed irregular blocky to apedal vughy. *Porosity*: 10–20%: mostly medium and small, subrounded, undulating vughs, occasional channels. *Mineral components*: see B1 (2) and (3) — B2 consists of a mixture of the same fabrics, but mainly (3). Clay content decreases with depth in groundmass and in pores. Quartz and rock fragments as previously described. *Organic components*: 5%, mostly punctuations and small black rounded particles. *Groundmass*: coarse: open porphyric related distribution; fine: stipple-speckled, low birefringence, reddish-gold (CPL), reddish-brown (PPL), orange (RL). *Pedofeatures*: *textural*, very thin yellow (CPL) dusty non-laminated clay coatings in void space; orange dusty/dirty clay coatings 20–60μm thick (as previously described), occasionally mixed with silt. >50% of pores have no clay. Occasional occurrence of reddish (CPL) alluvium (Fabric 1) infilling old channels. *Amorphous*, sesquioxide staining (10–20%, increasing with depth). Excrement: porous microaggregates 50–100μm in size. Fabric: an area of sesquioxide-stained angular blocky peds (500–1000μm) in upper 0.5cm, apparently organic (turf) material.

Profile C: sample 1 (9.7cm)

Structure: Very poorly developed sub-angular blocky, especially in lower 2–3cm, to apedal vughy. *Porosity*: 10–20%: 15% vughs of various sizes (1–2cm to <100μm). Most are 300–500μm, with undulating sides, and are sub-rounded and sub-angular; 5% channels *c* 1–2mm long and 250μm wide (occasionally longer and wider), straight and curved, with rounded ends, and nonaccommodated, irregular sides. *Mineral components*: c:f ratio — 45:55: coarse: very coarse and coarse sand 5%, medium sand 20%, fine sand 20%;

fine: very fine sand 20%, silt 25%, clay 10%. Sandy loam. 90% quartz — monocrystalline, rounded and subrounded, occasionally polycrystalline and sutured; occasionally sheared; occasionally micaceous. Rare feldspar. Rock fragments: sandstones — mostly quartz arenite, fine and medium grained, sometimes micaceous; ironstone, chert, and occasional limestone/dolomite fragment — packed oomicrite (silicified?). *Organic components*: 10–20%: very frequent 'punctuations' and occasional black, rounded/subrounded particles. *Groundmass*: coarse: open porphyric related distribution; fine: stipple-speckled, with moderate to low birefringence, colour as in B2. *Pedofeatures*: *textural*, very thin yellow (CPL) dusty clay coatings (as previously described); 10–40μm thick orange-yellow (CPL) dusty/dirty non-laminated (possibly laminated occasionally) clay infilling/coatings in groundmass and voids (as previously described), occasionally forming link cappings on particles, rarely associated with a discontinuous silt layer; orange (CPL) slightly dusty clay coatings 20–60μm thick in voids; rare infilling of laminated reddish (CPL) clay — slightly dusty — and linear bands of reddish clay. Clay coatings less prominent with depth. *Amorphous*, irregular sesquioxide staining (10–50%), occasional root pseudomorphs. *Fabric*: mixing — inclusion of Fabric 2, iron-stained.

Profile C: sample 2 (10cm)

Structure: (1) 1–1.5cm of Fabric 2 — irregular blocky to apedal vughy. Porosity: 15%: 10% ped-related channels and connecting vughs (three size categories: 50–100μm wide, partially accommodated; 250μm wide partially accommodated vertical cracks; 500μm wide, curved, made of interconnected vughs. (2) apedal vughy. Porosity: *c* 15%, mostly vughs — subrounded, with undulating sides or smooth where clay-coated. Size: 50–100μm, often 250–400μm, occasionally larger. Occasional channels. *Mineral components*: c:f ratio — 40:60: coarse: very coarse sand 5%, coarse sand 5%, medium sand 15%, fine sand 15%; fines: very fine sand 20%, silt 25%, clay 25%. Sandy (clay) loam. Clay increasing with depth. Quartz and rock fragments as described in C1. *Organic components*: 10–20%: frequent silt-size rounded and sub-angular black particles, well integrated into the groundmass. Occasional charcoal (up to 1cm size) with some cell structure. Frequent 100–250μm and smaller subrounded black and brownish particles. Some root pseudomorphs. *Groundmass*: poorly sorted — zones of fines/coarse and mixed zones. Coarse: random, but with some zoning. Open porphyric related distribution; fine: stipple-speckled, but with some grano- and porostriation. Moderate bifringence. Colour as in A1. *Pedofeatures*: *textural*, very fine yellow (CPL) dusty clay coatings (as previously described); orange (CPL) dusty clay coatings, sometimes mixed with silt and very fine sand, up to 40–50μm thick, in pores and in the groundmass. With depth coatings are dirtier and often have silt coatings on them. Clay coatings more frequent and substantial with depth (70% of pores have clay coatings/infillings). *Amorphous*, sesquioxide staining (10–30%), root pseudomorphs, iron quasicoatings.

Profile D: sample 1 (8cm)

Structure: apedal vughy, occasional irregular blocky, with some pellety areas (fine sand-sized aggregates). *Porosity:* 10–20%, mostly vughs 200–500μm and smaller, subrounded, with undulating sides. Occasional channels with rounded ends, partially accommodated, undulating sides, 2mm long and 300–400μm wide. *Mineral components*: Upper: c:f ratio — 50:50: coarse: very coarse sand 5%, coarse sand 5%, medium sand 20%, fine sand 20%; fine: very fine sand 20%, silt 20%, clay 10%. Loamy sand. Lower: c:f ratio — 45:55: coarse: very coarse sand 5%, coarse sand 5%, medium sand 15%, fine sand 20%; fine: very fine sand 20%, silt 20%, clay 15%. Sandy loam. Components as described in D2. *Organic components*: 20–30%. Punctuations and small particles as previously described, with some semi-rotted plant tissues and frequent small and occasionally larger iron-stained plant fragments. *Groundmass*: poorly sorted. Coarse: greyish, with an open porphyric related distribution; fine: stipple-speckled, moderately birefringent, reddish (CPL), reddish brown (XPL), orange (RL). Some linear zones of reddish gold (CPL) clay, up to 1mm long and 50μm wide. *Pedofeatures*: *textural*, very thin yellow dusty clay coatings (as described previously), also some orange-red dusty/dirty coatings <10 up to 50μm thick. At base — linear zones *c* 1cm × 0.5cm of dusty orange-red clay. *Amorphous*, strong sesquioxide staining (30–60%). Excrement: porous microaggregates, 50μm in size. Fabric: inclusion of reddish (CPL) alluvium.

Profile D: sample 2 (10cm)

Structure: (1) upper 3cm — irregular blocky. Porosity: 20%, mostly channels and vughs; (2) irregular blocky to apedal vughy. Occasional pellety structure. Porosity: 10–15%, mostly small and medium sized vughs. With depth, porosity is *c* 20%, of which 15% is vughs, mostly 100μm or less in size, with undulating and rough sides; and 5% is channels up to 1mm long, with widths from 250μm to 50μm, These are straight and curved, with undulating sides, and are unaccommodated or partially accommodated, with rounded or squared ends. *Mineral components*: (1) c:f ratio — 35:65: coarse: very coarse sand 2%, coarse sand 5%, medium sand 15%, fine sand 15%; fine: very fine sand 25%, silt 25%, clay 13%. Sandy (clay) loam; (2) c:f ratio — 45:55: coarse: very coarse sand 5%, coarse sand 5%, medium sand 15–20%, fine sand 15%; fine: very fine sand 15–20%, silt 15–20%, clay <10–15% (increasing with depth). Sandy loam. Mineral components include quartz (>90% of grains), with micaceous sandstone and ironstone rock fragments. *Organic components*: 20%:

moderate occurrence of black sub-angular and sub-rounded fragments, 100–300μm in size, and frequent 50μm and 'punctuations'. Also root pseudomorphs and semi-rotted plant fragments. Also some areas of organic staining. Organic content decreases with depth. *Groundmass*: poorly sorted; coarse: open porphyric related distribution; fine: (1) stipple-speckled with moderate to high birefringence (colour as in A1); (2) stipple-speckled, with moderate birefringence. *Pedofeatures*: *textural*, (1) thin dusty yellow (CPL) highly birefringent clay coatings, mostly lining ped faces, also in fabric — some linear zones 50–200μm thick and of varying lengths; occasional thin orange-yellow (CPL) dusty clay coatings; (2) not much clay in pores, but where present it is as dusty orange-yellow and reddish-orange (both in CPL) dirty/dusty clay coatings *c* 40μm thick. Some zones of (1) (Fabric 2) as infillings in old channels. *Amorphous*, (2) sesquioxide staining (30–80%), root pseudomorphs.

Profile E: sample 1 (10cm)

Structure: (1) 2–3cm alluvium remains on top. This has a sub-angular blocky structure, with peds from 500μm to *c* 1cm in size. Porosity: as in B1 (1); (2) mixed weakly developed sub-angular blocky and apedal vughy. Porosity: 20%: 10% interped channels, 250–750μm, occasionally 200μm, long, accommodated to partially accommodated, with relatively smooth, but slightly undulating sides; 10% vughs ranging from 10μm to 600μm in size, most 50–200μm, with smooth undulating sides, occasionally rougher sides. Sometimes these are very round. *Mineral components*: (1) c:f ratio — 10:90: coarse–coarse sand 5%, medium sand and fine sand 5%; fine: very fine sand 5%, silt 45%, clay 40%. Clay loam. (2) c:f ratio — 55:45: coarse–very coarse sand 2%, coarse sand 3%, medium sand 30%, fine sand 20%; fine–very fine sand 20%, silt 15%, clay 10%. Loamy sand. Also areas of sandy clay loam. Minerals: mostly quartz grains — sub-angular, mono- (occasional poly-)crystalline (sutured). Rock fragments — micaceous sandstone, red (oolitic) ironstone (limestone), chert. *Organic components*: (1) 5–10%, mostly less than 50μm, subrounded and sub-angular black fragments and 'punctuations'. Occasional 250–500μm subrounded particles. *Groundmass*: poorly sorted. (1) as in B1 (1); (2) coarse: open porphyric related distribution; fine: stipple-speckled, occasionally grano- and porostriated, moderate to low birefringence. Colour as in A1. *Pedofeatures*: *textural*, dusty, bright golden yellow (CPL) clay coatings in voids, 50–250μm thick, mixed with fine and very fine sand. Also seen as coatings/cappings on grains. Also dusty/dirty coatings as described previously. *Amorphous*, sesquioxide staining (10–20%, increasing with depth), occasional root pseudomorphs. Fabric: rounded orange (CPL) clay and silt aggregates from <50 to 300μm in size; areas of alluvium (Fabric 1) lower in profile.

Profile E: sample 2 (13cm)

Structure: (1) upper 1cm (<5% of thin section) — irregular blocky; (2) apedal with vughy microstructure. *Porosity:* 10%, decreasing with depth: mostly vughs 50–100μm, occasionally larger. These are often elongated, but are also rounded, with undulating sides. *Mineral components*: (1) clay 20–25%, decreasing with depth. The rest is the same as D2 (1) — Fabric 2. (2) c:f ratio — 45:55: coarse: very coarse sand 5%, coarse sand 2%, medium sand 20%, fine sand 20%; fine: very fine sand 20%, silt 20%, clay 10–15%. Sandy loam. *Organic components*: 10%, as in E1. *Groundmass*: coarse: open porphyric related distribution; fine: (1) stipple-speckled, reddish, moderately to highly birefringent; (2) stipple-speckled with low birefringence. *Pedofeatures*: *textural*, (1) clay coatings: orange (CPL), dusty-dirty, and yellow (CPL) dusty, up to 50μm thick, sometimes with silt. Some linear in groundmass. (2) clay coatings: in voids and groundmass — composite very thin dusty yellow and dusty/dirty orange (all as previously described), up to 15μm thick. Also zones of slightly dusty limpid clay and zones of very dirty clay. Clay features decrease in frequency with depth. *Amorphous*, (2) root pseudomorphs, some sesquioxide staining in lower part of profile (20–30%, increasing with depth). Fabric: (2) ovoid and rounded clay/silt aggregates, dark orange (CPL) speckled, 200μm in size.

Profile F: sample 1/A (12cm)

Two horizons/fabrics with discrete boundary.

Structure: (1) weak irregular to sub-angular blocky, poorly sorted. Porosity: 20–25%, possibly decreasing slightly with depth, mostly vughs of all sizes, rounded and subrounded, undulating. Some channels/chambers, ranging from fine (1000μm long and 100μm wide) to large, up to 2000μm long and 700μm wide. These are curved with tapering, rounded or pointed ends. One very long discontinuous straight channel 3mm long and 100–200μm wide; (2) lower 1–1.5cm. Poorly developed irregular blocky to apedal vughy. Porosity 10–20%, mostly vughs — rounded and ovoid, 50μm up to 200μm, occasionally up to 1mm. Some channels from 1mm to 1cm size and 250, and 500–700μm wide. Curved, rounded or squared-off ends, non- to partially-accommodated. *Mineral components*: (1) c:f ratio — 40–45:55–60: coarse: very coarse sand <1%, coarse sand 5–10%, medium sand 20%, fine sand 15%; fine: very fine sand 20–25%, silt 25%, clay 10%. Sandy loam; (2) c:f ratio — 45–55: coarse: very coarse and coarse sand <10%, medium sand 15%, fine sand 20%; fine: very fine sand 20%, silt 20%, clay 15%. Sandy loam. Components as described in F2/A below. *Organic components*: (1) 15–20%: frequent 'punctuations' and small (10–20μm) sub-angular and subrounded black particles; 5% sub-rounded black and dark brownish particles, 50 to 500μm;

5% carbonised remains. Occasional fragments of rotting plant remains. These are larger and reddish brown, and show cell structure (including some vascular), but are quite broken up, and can be up to 1cm in size. More larger organic particles and organic staining with depth. (2) 20–30%: mostly punctuations, and 50–100μm size black subrounded/sub-angular fragments; iron-replaced cell tissue; organic staining; 5% carbonised remains. *Groundmass*: (1) poorly sorted, with some clustering of coarser and finer components. Coarse: open porphyric related distribution; fine: stipple-speckled, low birefringent fabric. Fines sometimes concentrated in patches c 1000–2000μm. (2) coarse: open porphyric related distribution; fine: stipple-speckled, low birefringence. *Pedofeatures*: *textural*. (1) c 10μm thick dusty yellow (CPL) clay coatings — poro- and granostriated; 500μm thick very dusty clay coatings with occasional sand inclusions around grains; some silt coatings around rock fragments. These are c 100–200μm thick, with relatively random orientation, but with some silt and clay aligned parallel to surface; dusty/dirty orange (CPL) clay in pores, some well incorporated into surrounding groundmass. Very little clay in pores. (2) Thin yellow dusty clay coatings (as previously described). *Amorphous*, (2) Hypocoatings of iron in some channels. General sesquioxide staining ((1) 40–80%, increasing with depth; (2) 30–50%). Fabric: some Fabric 2 (transition horizon material) inclusions.

Profile F: sample 1/B (10cm)

Two horizons identified: (1) upper 1–2cm (2) lower 8–9cm. Boundary marked by sudden change in porosity — line of elongated (vertically) vughs 250–500μm in size, leading to more open structure of (2). Also there is a sudden line of root pseudomorphs (iron oxidation).

Structure: (1) As (2) in F1/A. Porosity: 20%: 16% vughs, 4% channels; (2) irregular, becoming mixed with apedal with depth. Porosity: 10–15%, mostly vughs; occasional channels/chambers 500–1000μm long and 100–200μm wide, rounded ends, unaccommodated to partially accommodated, undulating sides. *Mineral components*: (1) as in F1/A (2); (2) c:f ratio — 40:60: coarse: very coarse sand 5%, coarse sand 5%, medium sand 15%, fine sand 15%; fine: very fine sand 20%, silt 30%, clay 10%. Sandy loam. Components as in F2/A (below). *Organic components*: (1) As in F1/A, Fabric 2. (2) 20–30%. As described in D2, but with lots of charcoal. *Groundmass*: (1) As in F1/A (2); (2) low to moderate birefringence, stipple speckled. Coarse — open porphyric. *Pedofeatures*: (1) as in F1/A (2); (2) *textural*, (as previously described) dirty orange-yellow (CPL) clay coatings 50–150μm thick. Also some infilling of voids with silty material. *Amorphous*, amorphous sesquioxides throughout ((1) 30–50%; (2) 40–70%), root pseudomorphs; occasional shell fragment. Fabric — zones of alluvium present, especially in porous areas (faunal). As alluvium described previously, but redder in colour; clay/silt aggregates, red (as found in alluvium). Excrement — excrements as seen in B2.

Profile F: sample 2/A (9.5cm)

Structure: apedal vughy with some poorly developed sub-angular blocky. *Porosity*: 10%, mostly vughs of various sizes. Becoming 10–15% with depth — mostly vughs of all sizes, occasional channels (straight, 150–250μm wide, varying lengths, partial to non accommodated, occasionally infilled with fines). *Mineral components*: c:f ratio — 40:60: coarse: very coarse sand <2%, coarse sand <5%, medium sand 20%, fine sand 15%; fine: very fine sand 15%, silt 35%, clay <10%. Sandy silt loam. Mostly quartz. Rock fragments: sandstone, ironstone, brown flint. *Organic components*: as in F1/B (2), with frequent charcoal particles <100μm in size. A slight decrease in percentage organics with depth (to 15%). *Groundmass*: coarse: open porphyric related distribution; fine: stipple-speckled with moderate to low birefringence. *Pedofeatures*: *textural*, occasional complete clay infilling *c* 250μm, quite clean, orange-red (CPL). Thin dusty yellow and thicker orange clay coatings (as previously described) occasionally occur. Occasional discontinuous channel infilling with silt and clay. *Amorphous*, sesquioxide impregnation (30–80%, increasing with depth), root pseudomorphs; microsparite.

Profile F: sample 2/B (9–10cm)

Structure: apedal vughy. *Porosity*: 20%: mostly medium and small vughs and channels up to 2cm long and 300μm wide. *Mineral components*: c:f ratio — 40:60: coarse: very coarse sand 2%, coarse sand 5%, medium sand 20%, fine sand 15%; fine: very fine sand 15–20%, silt 30%, clay 10–15%. Sandy loam. Components as in F2/A. *Organic components*: 15–20%. As in F2/A, but increase in charcoal in the lower part of thin section. *Groundmass*: coarse: open porphyric related distribution; fine: stipple-speckled, occasionally granostriated, with moderate birefringence. Poorly sorted. *Pedofeatures*: *textural*, thin yellow dusty clay coatings in voids; orange dusty/dirty clay coatings in voids and groundmass (all as previously described). Occasional old channel infill of silt and dusty clay, some apparently of alluvium — these are not 'pure' as described elsewhere, but quite sandy — *c* 30% sand, 30% silt and 30% clay — and are orange-red in colour (CPL). Most pores are empty or have only very fine dusty component as coatings. *Amorphous*, sesquioxide staining (30–80%, increasing with depth); root pseudomorphs frequent; microsparite. Fabric: rounded clay silt aggregates 250μm in size.

Profile G: sample 1 (13–14cm)

Structure: irregular blocky to apedal vughy. *Porosity*: 20%: mostly vughs of all sizes, often *c* 500μm, subrounded, undulating, with rough sides. Fabric 3, but much more gravelly.

Mineral components: c:f ratio — 45:55: coarse: very coarse sand 10%, coarse sand 5%, medium sand 20%, fine sand 10%; fine: very fine sand 20%, silt 20%, clay 15%. Sandy loam. Components as in G2. *Organic components:* 10%, mostly 'punctuations' and small black particles, as previously described. *Groundmass:* coarse: open porphyric related distribution; fine: stipple-speckled, with moderate to low birefringence. Colour as in A1. *Pedofeatures: textural*, fine yellow dusty clay coatings in voids (as previously described); slightly dusty yellow-orange (CPL) clay coatings up to *c* 40μm thick, becoming dirtier and thinner with depth, but still frequent — associated with some silt. By the middle of the section, only some pores have clay. Most are empty. *Amorphous*, sesquioxide staining (10–30%), root pseudomorphs. Excrement: occasional excrements *c* 50μm in size — square. Fabric: zones of reddish (CPL) alluvium/sand mixture seen. Occasional silt aggregates.

Profile G: sample 2 (13cm)

Structure: apedal vughy, occasionally pellety. *Porosity*: 20%: 18% vughs (most <100μm, occasionally larger. Irregular, undulate); <2% channels (straight and curved, *c* 300μm wide and 1–2mm long (occasionally 4mm), often discontinuous, with rounded or rough ends, unaccommodated, with undulating/rough sides). Porosity increases near base to 20–30%. As above, but more frequent rounded vughs <50μm in size. *Mineral components*: c:f ratio — 40:60: coarse: coarse sand <5%, medium sand 10%, fine sand 20%; fine: very fine sand 20%, silt 25%, clay 10–15% (clay increases with depth). Sandy loam. Almost all grains are quartz, mostly monocrystalline and subrounded, but occasionally polycrystalline and sutured. Rare mixed quartz/feldspar. Rock fragments: chert, mica, sandstone. *Organic components*: 10–15%: as in G1. *Groundmass*: coarse: open porphyric related distribution; fine: stipple-speckled with moderate birefringence. Dirty clay integrated into groundmass. With depth (especially lower 2–3cm), reticulate striated and granulometric organisation. Apparently more clay in central 2–3cm vs upper/lower. Colour as in A1. *Pedofeatures*: *textural*, frequently vughs have a thin coating of dusty yellow clay (as previously described), and these are also seen around some grains. All are <5μm thick. These are somewhat less frequent with depth, and are dirtier and better integrated with the groundmass. Silt coatings are occasionally associated where these clay coatings occur in void space. There are also clay coatings up to *c* 50μm thick, quite dusty and yellow-orange (CPL). *Amorphous*, sesquioxide impregnation (10–40%), and root pseudomorphs, especially in lower 2–3cm.

Profile H: sample 1 (10cm)

Structure: poorly developed irregular blocky to apedal vughy, occasionally pellety. *Porosity*: >20% upper, 10–20% at base, mainly elongate medium vughs, occasional channels (irregular, partially accommodated). *Mineral components*: c:f ratio — 40:60: coarse: very coarse and coarse sand 5%, medium sand 20%, fine sand 15%; fine: very fine sand 20–25%, silt 25%, clay 10–20%. Sandy loam. Clay decreases with depth in groundmass and pores, but regular coatings still occur. Components as in H2 (below). *Organic components*: 10–20%, increasing with depth. As described in D2. Moderate charcoal. *Groundmass*: poorly sorted; coarse: open porphyric related distribution; fine: stipple speckled, low to moderate birefringence. *Pedofeatures*: textural, thin dusty yellow clay coatings/infillings; *c* 20–30μm thick yellow-orange (occasionally reddish) dusty clay in pores (all as described previously). *Amorphous*, sesquioxide staining (30–70%). Fabric: zones of alluvium mixed into the groundmass.

Profile H: sample 2 (13cm)

Structure: irregular blocky to apedal with vughy structure, occasionally pellety. *Porosity*: 10–20%, less porous with depth: mostly 250–500μm undulating, rounded vughs, occasionally larger (up to 2mm). Occasional fine channels 100μm to 250μm wide and up to 2mm long. These run vertically and occasionally horizontally, with partially accommodated rough sides. *Mineral components*: c:f ratio — 35:65: coarse: very coarse sand <2%, coarse sand 5% (slightly more with depth), medium sand 10%, fine sand 20%; fine: very fine sand 25%, silt 30%, clay 10% (<10% with depth). Sandy loam. Components: quartz, sandstone, chert. *Organic components*: 10–20%, increasing with depth: 'punctuations' and fine black particles. Moderate charcoal. *Groundmass*: poorly sorted; coarse: open porphyric related distribution; fine: stipple-speckled with low birefringence. *Pedofeatures*: textural, rare fine silty coatings in root channels; occasional very fine dusty yellow coatings in pores (as previously described). *Amorphous*, root pseudomorphs and very strong sesquioxide staining (30–70%); rare yellow (PPL) mottling. Fabric: occasional rolled clay/silt aggregates up to *c* 250μm size. Alluvial peds mixed in with main fabric.

Cat's Water (1990)

Profile 1: Sample 1: Lower buried soil (Grid 992/1008)

Structure: apedal to very weakly sub-angular blocky; 3 fabrics in heterogeneous mixture; *Porosity*: fabrics 1) and 2): <10% intra-aggregate vughs, sub-rounded to irregular, <250μm, smooth to weakly serrated; <5% inter-aggregate channels, weakly serrated, walls partially accommodated, 75–300μm; fabric 3): 15% intra-aggregate vughs, sub-rounded, smooth to weakly serrated, <400μm; 5% inter-aggregate channels, weakly serrated, partially accommodated, <100μm wide, 2mm in length. *Organic components*: in fabrics 1–3): very few (<2%) fragments of plant tissue with cell

structure evident; very few (<2%) fragments of charcoal, sub-angular to sub-rounded, <75μm; very few (<1%) carbonised seeds, <75μm; in fabric 2): few (10%) amorphous, fine, black organic matter, <50μm. *Mineral components*: fabric 1): limit 100μm; c:f ratio: 40:60; coarse fraction: 20% medium and 20% fine quartz, sub-rounded to sub-angular, 100–250μm; fine fraction: 20% very fine quartz, sub-rounded to sub-angular, 50–100μm; 20% silt and 20% clay; moderately speckled; reddish brown to golden brown (XPL), reddish brown (PPL), orangey brown (RL); 90% of middle 4cm of slide; fabric 2): limit 100μm; c:f ratio: 15:85; coarse fraction: 15% medium quartz, 200–250μm; fine fraction: 10% very fine quartz, sub-angular to sub-rounded, 50–100μm; 40% silt and 35% clay; weakly to moderately speckled; golden brown (XPL), pale golden brown to brown (PPL), pale greyish brown (RL); 10% of groundmass of middle 4cm and 100% of upper 2cm; fabric 3) limit 100μm; c:f ratio: 45:55; coarse fraction: 5% coarse, 20% medium and 20% fine quartz, sub-rounded to sub-angular, 100–400μm; fine fraction: 35% very fine quartz, sub-angular to sub-rounded, 50–100μm; very weakly speckled; greyish brown (XPL), very light brown (PPL), light orangey-brown (RL); 100% of groundmass of lower 4cm. *Groundmass*: fabric 1): fine: random to weakly reticulate striated; coarse: undifferentiated; related: close porphyric; fabric 2): fine: weakly mosaic speckled; coarse: undifferentiated; related: close porphyric; fabric 3): fine: very weakly speckled; coarse: undifferentiated; related: porphyric. *Pedofeatures: textural*, in fabric 1): occasional (2–5%) non-laminated limpid clay in groundmass, yellowish-gold (XPL), strongly birefringent; abundant (15%) non-laminated dusty clay in groundmass, moderate birefringence, yellowish gold to reddish orange (XPL); in fabric 2): very abundant (up to 35%) of non-laminated dusty clay in groundmass, moderate birefringence, orange (XPL); in fabric 3): rare to occasional (2–5%) non-laminated dusty clay as void/channel coatings and groundmass, yellow to light orange (XPL), moderate to strong birefringence. *Amorphous*, very few (<2%) rolled aggregates of silt, sub-rounded, orangey-brown (XPL), in fabric 3); amorphous sesquioxide impregnation in fabrics 1) (up to 50%) and fabrics 3) (up to 25%); few (<10%) sesquioxide nodules in fabrics 1) and 2), sub-rounded, <250μm.

Profile 1: Sample 2: Upper buried soil (1000/995)

Structure: apedal; homogeneous, but very porous in zones. *Porosity*: 20–50%; few (10–15%) vughs: irregular to sub-rounded, smooth to weakly serrated, <200μm; few to frequent (10–30%) channels, irregular, weakly serrated, walls partially accommodated, 50–100μm wide, <1.5cm long, weakly serrated; simple packing voids between soil aggregates, up to 50% of total slide. *Organic components*: very rare (<2%) black amorphous organic matter in groundmass, <50μm; very rare (<1%) fragments of cell tissue. *Mineral components*: fabric 1): limit 100μm; c:f ratio: <5/:95; coarse fraction: <5% fine quartz, sub-rounded to sub-angular, 100–150μm; fine fraction: 5% very fine quartz, sub-rounded to sub-angular, 50–100μm; 45% silt and 45% clay; weakly striated, moderate birefringence; light yellow to yellowish-orange (XPL), light to medium brown (PPL), greyish/orangey brown (RL); >95% of the total groundmass; fabric 2): limit 100μm; c:f ratio: 35:65; coarse fraction: 30% medium and 5% fine quartz, sub-rounded to sub-angular, 100–250μm; fine fraction: 10% very fine quartz, sub-rounded to sub-angular, 50–100μm; 30% silt and 25% clay; weakly speckled, moderate birefringence; orangey-brown (XPL), reddish brown (PPL), light reddish brown (RL); <5% of total groundmass in the upper three-quarters of the slide, with up to 30% of the groundmass in the lower quarter of the slide. *Groundmass*: fine: monic; coarse: undifferentiated; related: monic to open porphyric. *Pedofeatures: textural*, occasional to many (5–10%) non-laminated dusty clay coatings of grains and of channels, moderate birefringence, sometimes acts as discontinuous infills of channels. *Amorphous*, up to 30% of the total groundmass is impregnated with amorphous sesquioxides, especially lining channels and vughs.

Profile 2: Sample 1: Lower buried soil (1000/995)

Structure: apedal; heterogeneous mixture of two fabrics; *Porosity*: fabric 1): 10% vughs, sub-rounded, smooth to weakly serrated, <200μm; fabric 2): 5% vughs; 10% simple packing voids, irregular, <1cm; *Organic Component*: very few (5%) fine flecks of black amorphous organic matter in fabric 1), <25μm; few (10%) in fabric 2), <50μm. *Mineral components*: in upper half: fabric 1): limit 100μm; c:f ratio: 40:60; coarse fraction: 5% coarse, 20% medium and 15% fine quartz, sub-rounded to sub-angular, 100–500μm; fine fraction: 30% very fine quartz, 50–100μm, sub-angular to sub-rounded; 15% silt and 15% clay; weakly speckled; golden brown (XPL), yellowish brown (PPL), orangey-brown (RL); >90% of total groundmass; fabric 2): limit 100μm; c:f ratio: 20:80; coarse fraction: 10% medium and 10% fine quartz, 100–250μm, sub-rounded to sub-angular; fine fraction: 20% very fine quartz, 50–100μm, sub-rounded to sub-angular; 30% silt and 30% clay; speckled; golden brown (XPL), brown (PPL), orangey-brown (RL); 10% of groundmass; lower half of profile: similar to fabric 1) above. *Groundmass*: fabric 1): weakly mosaic speckled to weakly reticulate striated; coarse: undifferentiated; related: close porphyric; fabric 2): fine: weakly mosaic speckled to random striated; coarse: undifferentiated; related: close porphyric. *Pedofeatures: textural*, in fabric 1): abundant (10%) non-laminated dusty clay in groundmass and of voids, moderate to strong birefringence,

yellow to yellowish gold (XPL); in fabric 2): very abundant (<30%) non-laminated dusty clay in groundmass and voids, moderate birefringence, orangey-red to golden brown (XPL). *Amorphous*, very few (<5%) sesquioxide nodules, sub-rounded, <200μm; <30% of fabric 1) exhibits amorphous sesquioxide impregnation; very few (<5%) sub-rounded aggregates of birefringent, limpid clay, silt and silty clay, <250μm.

Profile 3: Sample 1: Upper buried soil (992/1008)

Structure: apedal; partially heterogeneous mixture of two fabrics. *Porosity*: 15% vughs, sub-rounded to irregular to elongate, smooth to weakly serrated, <400μm; 15% channels, irregular and elongate, weakly serrated, walls partially accommodated, <1mm wide, <15mm long. *Organic component*: very few (<1%) fragments of carbonised wood; very few (<2%) fine, black amorphous organic matter. *Mineral components*: fabric 1): limit 100μm; c:f ratio: 40:60; coarse fraction: 30% medium and 10% fine quartz, sub-rounded to sub-angular, 100–300μm; fine fraction: 30% very fine quartz, 50–100μm; 20% silt and 10% clay; speckled; golden brown (XPL), golden brown (PPL), light orangey-brown (RL); fabric 2): limit 100μm; c:f ratio: 40:60; coarse fraction: 30% medium and 10% fine quartz, 100–300μm, sub-angular to sub-rounded; fine fraction: 15% very fine quartz, 50–100μm; 20% silt and 25% clay; speckled; gold (XPL), golden brown (PPL), light yellow (RL); 50% of groundmass in upper half and <25% in lower half of sample. *Groundmass*: fabric 1): fine: weakly speckled; coarse: undifferentiated; related: open porphyric; fabric 2): fine: weakly reticulate striated; coarse: undifferentiated; related: porphyric. *Pedofeatures: textural*, in fabric 1): very rare (<1%) fragments of limpid clay in groundmass, <50μm, golden orange (XPL), moderate birefringence; many (10%) non-laminated dusty clay in groundmass, grains and voids, moderate to strong birefringence, gold (XPL); in fabric 2): very abundant (25%) non-laminated dusty clay in groundmass and grains, moderately birefringent, gold (XPL). *Amorphous*, very few (<5%) sesquioxide nodules, sub-rounded; very few (<5%) silty clay aggregates, sub-rounded, <200μm; <25% of groundmass impregnated with sesquioxides.

Profile 3: Sample 2: Lower buried soil

Structure: apedal, homogeneous. *Porosity*: 10% simple packing voids, irregular; 20% vughs, sub-rounded to irregular, smooth to weakly serrated, <300μm. *Organic components*: very few (<2%) fine flecks of amorphous organic matter throughout groundmass, <50μm. *Mineral components*: fabric 1): limit 100μm; c:f ratio: 50:50; coarse fraction: 30% medium and 20% fine quartz, 100–300μm, sub-rounded to sub-angular; fine fraction: 30% very fine quartz, 50–100μm; 10% silt and 10% clay; weakly speckled; gold/grey (XPL); light golden brown (PPL); light yellowish brown (RL). *Groundmass*: fine: weakly mosaic speckled; coarse: undifferentiated; related: porphyric; *Pedofeatures: textural*, many (8%) non-laminated dusty clay coatings in groundmass, both evenly distributed and in zones, and of grains, gold (XPL), moderately birefringent; very rare (<2%) laminated limpid clay coatings of grains, moderate to strong birefringence, orangey-red (XPL). *Amorphous*, very rare (<1%) sub-rounded aggregates of organic silt, <200μm, orange (XPL); amorphous sesquioxide impregnation of 10% of groundmass, of voids, and as pseudomorphs of organic matter.

Profile 4

Structure: apedal; homogeneous; very dense, massive microstructure. *Porosity*: <10% vughs, sub-rounded, weakly serrated, <250μm. *Organic components*: very few (<2%) ferruginised plant remains; very few (<2%) fine, black amorphous organic matter, <75μm. *Mineral components*: fabric 1): limit 100μm; c:f ratio: 60/40; coarse fraction: 30% medium and 30% fine, 100–250μm, sub-rounded to sub-angular; fine fraction: 30% very fine quartz, 50–100μm; 8% silt and <2% clay; very weakly speckled; grey (XPL), light grey brown (PPL), light greyish yellow (RL). *Groundmass*: fine, undifferentiated to very weakly speckled; coarse, undifferentiated; related, close porphyric. *Pedofeatures: textural*, very rare (<2%) non-laminated clay in groundmass, moderate birefringence, orangey-gold (XPL). *Amorphous*, very few (<5%) sesquioxide nodules, <200μm; very few (<2%) sub-rounded aggregates of silt, <200μm; few zones of amorphous sesquioxide impregnation, <10% of groundmass.

Appendix 2 Detailed soil micromorphological descriptions of samples from the Power Station site (Chapter 14)

by C A I French

Introduction

The sample locations are described in the soil micromorphological report of the Power Station excavations in Chapter 4.

Sample 1: 'Reddened' soil in uppermost alluvium, Trench II

Structure: apedal; heterogeneous mixture of three fabrics; massive structure for fabrics 1 a/b'. *Porosity*: fabric 1: <10%; few vughs (5%), sub-rounded to irregular, smooth to very weakly serrated, <200μm; very few (<5%) channels, elongate and irregular, walls mainly accommodated, smooth to very weakly serrated, unoriented, random, <20μm long, 25–200μm and 0.5–1mm wide; fabric 2: 20% vughs, 50–100μm, sub-rounded to irregular, smooth to weakly serrated; fabric 3: <1% vughs, <150μm. *Organic components*: fabric 1 a: very few (<1%) very fine flecks of black amorphous organic matter; fabric 1b: few (<10%) very fine flecks of black amorphous organic matter throughout groundmass, <25μm; fabric 2: very few (<5%) very fine flecks of black amorphous organic matter; fabric 3: frequent (20%) very fine flecks of black amorphous organic matter; general: rare (<1%) sub-rounded fragments of peat, <200μm, very dark brown to black (XPL/PPL). *Mineral components*: fabric 1); limit: 100μm; c:f ratio: <5:>95; coarse fraction: 2% medium and 3% fine quartz, 100–250μm, sub-rounded to sub-angular; fine fraction: 5% very fine quartz, 50–100μm, sub-rounded to sub-angular; 45% silt and 40% clay; very weakly speckled; grey/gold and yellowish-orange (XPL), greyish-yellow and orangey-red (PPL); *c* 85% of total groundmass, of which 50% burnt (fabric 1b) and 50% unburnt (fabric 1a); fabric 2): limit: 50μm; c:f ratio: 5:95; coarse fraction: <5% very fine quartz, 50–100μm, sub-rounded to sub-angular; fine fraction: 75% silt and 20% clay; speckled; golden brown (XPL), yellowish-brown (PPL); *c* 10% of total groundmass; fabric 3: limit: 100um; c:f ratio: <5:>95; coarse fraction: <2% medium and <3% fine quartz, 100–250μm, sub-rounded to sub-angular; fine fraction: <2% very fine quartz, 50–100μm, sub-rounded to sub-angular; >3% silt and <30% clay; very weakly speckled; yellowish brown (XPL), tan to brown (PPL); <5% of total groundmass. *Groundmass*: fabric 1a — fine: random to weakly reticulate striated; coarse: undifferentiated; related: monic; fabric 1b — fine: undifferentiated; coarse: undifferentiated; related: monic; fabric 2 — fine: weakly random striated; coarse: undifferentiated; related: close porphyric to monic; fabric 3 — fine:

weakly random speckled; coarse: undifferentiated; related — close porphyric. *Pedofeatures: textural*, fabric 1a: very abundant (40%) non-laminated limpid clay, moderate to strong birefringence, yellow to light yellow (XPL); fabrics 1a and 1b: rare to occasional (2–3%) non-laminated dusty clay, as discontinuous void/channel infills, moderate birefringence, reddish yellow (XPL); fabric 2: many (10%) non-laminated limpid clay in groundmass, moderate birefringence, yellow (XPL); many (10%) non-laminated dusty clay in groundmass, moderate birefringence, yellowish-orange to amber (XPL); fabric 3: many (15%) non-laminated limpid clay within groundmass, moderate birefringence, yellow (XPL); many (15%) non-laminated dusty clay in groundmass, moderate birefringence, yellow to yellowish-orange (XPL); miscellaneous: non-laminated dusty clay coatings occur around the edges of the sub-rounded aggregates of fabrics 2 and 3, <75μm thick, moderate birefringence, orangey-red (XPL); non-laminated dusty clay coatings of channels in fabric 1, <25μm thick, moderate birefringence, yellow to gold (XPL); Fabric: few (<10%) irregular aggregates of eroded soil, composed of 10% medium, 20% fine and 10% very fine quartz, 30% silt and 30% clay, strongly speckled and birefringent, yellow to orange (XPL) and amber to reddish amber (PPL) for clay fraction, grey/black (XPL) and light greenish-grey (PPL) for silt/very fine sand fraction. *Amorphous*, very rare (<2%) sub-rounded aggregates of silty clay, <300μm, orangey-brown (XPL); few (<10%) sesquioxide nodules in all fabrics, but mainly in fabrics 1a and b, sub-rounded, <75μm; up to 50% of fabric 1 is impregnated with amorphous sesquioxides.

Sample 2: Sand bank on western side of timber avenue, Trench I

Structure: apedal; bridged to pellicular grain structure to single grain; dense to loose, poorly sorted; *Porosity*: 15–25%; 10–15% simple packing voids, irregular, much interconnected, 150–300μm; 10% vughs, irregular to sub-rounded, <300μm. *Organic components*: frequent (20–30%); frequent (15%) fragments of plant tissue with cell structure evident, sub-rounded, <500μm, often ferruginised; frequent (15%) wood fragments, with well preserved cell structure, ferruginised, 3–10cm long, 2–4cm wide. *Mineral components*: limit: 100μm; c:f ratio: 85:15; coarse fraction: 75% medium and 10% fine quartz, sub-rounded to sub-angular, 100–250μm; rare mica grains present; fine fraction: 10% silt and <5% clay; black to dark orange (XPL), reddish brown to brown (PPL). *Groundmass*:

fine: undifferentiated; coarse: undifferentiated; related: gefuric to chitonic. *Pedofeatures: textural*, rare (<2%) non-laminated limpid clay as coatings of grains, moderate to strong birefringence, dark gold to reddish-orange (XPL); very rare (<2%) fragments of non-laminated limpid clay in groundmass, sub-angular, strong birefringence, yellowish gold (XPL); very rare (<1%) laminated dusty clay in groundmass, strong birefringence, yellow to reddish orange (XPL); Fabric: very rare (<1%) fragment of silty clay (dominated by very fine quartz and non-laminated dusty clay), moderate birefringence, sub-rounded, <200μm, yellowish orange (XPL); very rare (<1%) sub-rounded fragment of silt, very fine quartz and very fine amorphous organic matter, 200–300μm, grey (XPL), light greyish brown (PPL); one sub-rounded zone (2mm in diameter) of another fabric composed of fine quartz, silt, non-laminated limpid clay and very fine amorphous organic matter, with strong birefringence, yellow (XPL); Crystalline: very few (<1%) of calcite crystals, pseudomorphic subhedral, platy to columnar, in the form of a compound, irregular star shape, <150μm, silver grey and dark brown (XPL). *Amorphous*, few (5%) phosphatic-iron compounds in groundmass, orange (PPL); few (5%) fragments of shell, <5mm long; very rare (<1%) sesquioxide impregnated fragments of fine fabric, <200μm, reddish brown (XPL); one amorphous zone of sesquioxide impregnated groundmass, 2–10mm; very few (<5%) discontinuous infills of organic matter with silt, fine quartz and phosphatic-iron compounds.

Sample 3: Sand bank on eastern side of timber avenue, Trench I

Structure: apedal; dense; poorly sorted; bridged to pellicular grain structure. *Porosity*: <15%; few (<10%) simple packing voids, irregular, much interconnected, <350μm; very few (<5%) vughs, irregular to sub-rounded, smooth to weakly serrated, <200μm. *Organic components*: frequent (20–30%); few (10%) wood fragments, sub-rounded, 2–12mm × 2–8mm; few (10–15%) ferruginised plant material as irregular fragments, <2mm; very few (<5%) amorphous organic matter in groundmass, <25μm, dark reddish brown to black (PPL). *Mineral components*: limit: 100μm; c:f ratio: 85:15; coarse fraction: 5% coarse, 70% medium and 10% fine quartz, 100–350μm, sub-rounded to sub-angular; fine fraction: 5% very fine quartz, 50–100μm, sub-rounded to sub-angular; 10% silt and <5% clay; black to dark orange (XPL), reddish brown to brown (PPL). *Groundmass*: fine: undifferentiated; coarse: undifferentiated; related: gefuric to chitonic. *Pedofeatures: textural*, limpid clay rarely acts as near continuous infill of root channel; one discontinuous/crescentic infill of void composed of successive layers of limpid clay, non-laminated, strong birefringence, parallel extinction, inner layer yellow (XPL) and outer layer yellowish orange (XPL); Fabric: very rare (<15)

fragment of silt, sub-angular to sub-rounded, 150–200μm, greyish yellow (XPL); very rare (<1%) sub-rounded aggregates of non-laminated dusty clay within groundmass, 100–150μm, yellowish orange (XPL); Crystalline: very rare (<1%) sub-rounded clusters of microsparite crystals (<25μm) in groundmass. *Amorphous*, most of fine fraction and organic matter is impregnated with amorphous sesquioxides.

Sample 4: Basal peat and buried soil, soil sample profile 3, Trench II

Structure: apedal; homogeneous; two fabrics separated stratigraphically; fabric 1): massive microstructure; fabric 2): vughy to intergrain micro-aggregate microstructure; *Porosity*: dense; <5% in fabric 1); <10% in fabric 2); very few (5–8%) vughs, irregular to sub-rounded, <150μm, smooth to weakly serrated, random; very few (<2%) channels associated with plant tissue fragments, irregular, <75μm wide, <2cm long, weakly serrated, walls partially accommodated. *Organic components*: fabric 1): frequent (30%); few (5%) irregular fragments of peat, sub-rounded, <250μm, black (XPL), dark brown (PPL); few (5%) sub-angular fragments of wood, <150μm, brown (PPL); few (10%) fragments of plant tissue with cell structure evident, often replaced by sesquioxides, black (XPL), dark brown (PPL); few (10%) pseudomorphs of plant tissue and roots, replaced by sesquioxides; fabric 2): 25%; few (10%) pseudomorphs of plant tissue, especially within channels, black (XPL), brown/black (PPL);· few to frequent (15%) plant tissue fragments with cell structure, <300μm, brown (PPL), black (XPL). *Mineral components*: 2 fabrics; fabric 1): limit: 100μm; c:f ratio: 15:85; coarse fraction: 10% medium and 5% fine quartz, sub-rounded to sub-angular, 100–250μm; fine fraction: 10% very fine quartz, sub-rounded to sub-angular, 50–100μm; 15% silt and 60% amorphous calcite; amber/greyish white (XPL), pale yellowish-brown (PPL); fabric 2: limit: 100μm; c:f ratio: 30:70; coarse fraction: 20% medium and 10% fine quartz, sub-rounded to sub-angular, 100–300μm; 20% silt and 20% clay; weakly speckled; amber/dark brown (XPL), light to medium brown (PPL). *Groundmass*: fabric 1): fine: undifferentiated; coarse: undifferentiated; related: close porphyric; fabric 2): fine: weakly mosaic speckled to weakly reticulate striated; coarse: undifferentiated; related: close porphyric. *Pedofeatures: textural*, in fabric 2): rare to occasional (2–5%) laminated dusty clay in groundmass, strong birefringence, yellowish-orange to dark red (XPL); very rare (<2%) non-laminated limpid clay in groundmass, moderate birefringence, dark gold (XPL); abundant (10–13%) non-laminated dusty clay in groundmass, weak to moderate birefringence, dark gold to yellowish gold (XPL); Crystalline: *c* 60% of fabric 1) is amorphous calcite, probably microsparite and sparite, <25μm, greyish white (XPL).

Sample 5: Basal peat and buried soil, soil sample profile 2, Trench I

Similar to Sample 4 (above), except for:
Fabric 1) = upper 5.5cm of lower slide and 7cm of upper slide; Fabric 2) = lower 1cm of lower slide.

Organic components: in upper slide: much rooting, replaced as ferruginised pseudomorphs; one peaty zone in fabric 1), 12 × 15mm; few sub-rounded fragments of peat, 3–5mm in diameter. *Pedofeatures: amorphous*, in lower slide: few (5%) lenticular gypsum in void space, <200μm, greyish white to white (XPL).

Sample 6: Buried soil, soil sample profile 1, Trench I

Structure: apedal; homogeneous, very poorly sorted; *Porosity*: 20%; 15% vughs, irregular to sub-rounded, weakly serrated, <500μm; 5% simple packing voids. *Organic components*: frequent (30%) of fabric 1); 10% fragments of wood, 2–12mm; 10% plant tissue with cell structure evident; <500μm; 10% peat, <75μm. *Mineral components*: fabric 1); limit: 100μm; c:f ratio: 40:60; coarse fraction: 205 medium and 20% fine quartz, sub-rounded to sub-angular, 100–250μm; fine fraction: 10% very fine quartz, sub-rounded to sub-angular, 50–100μm; 25% silt and 25% clay; weakly speckled; gold to dark brown (XPL), reddish brown (PPL); fabric 2): limit: 100μm; c:f ratio: 90:10; coarse fraction: 50% medium and 40% fine quartz, sub-rounded to sub-angular, 100–250μm; fine fraction: 5% very fine quartz, sub-rounded to sub-angular, 50–100μm; 3% silt and 2% clay; grey (XPL), brown/white (PPL). *Groundmass*: fine: random striated; coarse: undifferentiated; related: close porphyric to monic. *Pedofeatures: textural*, in fabric 1): very rare (<1%) laminated limpid clay in groundmass, strong birefringence, yellow/black (XPL); very rare (<1%) non-laminated limpid clay in groundmass, moderate to strong birefringence, yellowish orange (XPL); very abundant (>20%) non-laminated in groundmass and occasionally of grains, moderate to strong birefringence, yellow to yellowish-orange (XPL); Fabric: in fabric 1): very few (<2% of groundmass) aggregates of organic silt, sub-rounded, 2–4mm, greyish brown (XPL), light brown to brown (PPL), composed of very fine quartz (5%), 75% silt and 25% clay; clay mainly non-laminated dusty and limpid, moderate birefringence, with weakly random striated groundmass.

Appendix 3 Concordance list of published and archive trench designations (Chapter 6)

As published	*As in archive*
Area 1	Trial trench 8 (1987)
Area 2	Trial trench 6 (1987/1988)
Area 3	Trial trench 7 (1987)
Area 4	Trial trench 3 (1987)
Area 5	Trial trench 5 (1988)
Area 6A	Areas 1–10 (1984–1986)
Area 6B	Area 11 (1987–1992)
Area 6C	Area 12 (1989, continuing)
Area 6D	Area 14 (1993, continuing)
Area 7	Area 13 (1990)
Area 8	Area 15 (1993–1994)

Appendix 4 Thin section descriptions of the quernstone samples (Chapter 11)

by A P Middleton and S G E Bowman

Quern 26

In thin section the stone is seen to be composed of a well sorted fine sand, cemented by interstitial silica, which has grown epitaxially on the quartz grains. The individual grains are typically <0.25mm diameter, although there are a few grains up to *c* 0.75mm. Original grain shapes are difficult to discern because of the overgrowth of silica cement. The sand grains are mainly monocrystalline quartz, although there are a few cherty grains and some more cloudy grains might be feldspar. The rock is a silicified quartz arenite.

Quern 27

Abundant, well rounded, sub-spherical and well sorted sand grains are contained in a continuous sparry calcite (sparite) cement. The sand grains are typically *c* 0.5mm diameter but range from 0.25mm to *c* 1mm. They are predominantly monocrystalline quartz, together with a few grains of chert and also some more cloudy grains (?feldspar). Glauconite is quite common and occurs as bright green grains of similar grade to the sand; it occurs as well rounded pellets, 'dissected' pellets and as more irregular, sub-rectangular grains. Some of the glauconite contains sparse sub-angular quartz silt. Yellow-brown, isotropic grains, which might be phosphatic material are rare. Sparse to common well rounded pellets and more elongate grains of micritic to sparry calcite are probably fragments of fossil shell. The rock is a calcite-cemented, glauconitic sandstone.

Quern 28

The thin section from this quern was, of necessity, from rather weathered stone. Nevertheless it can be seen to be comprised essentially of colourless chinopyroxene and a calcic plagioclase feldspar, together with minor opaque minerals. The rock is extensively altered: some of the feldspars are sericitised and additional, highly altered (chloritised) green/brown grains might represent relict orthopyroxene. The rock is a gabbro.

Appendix 5 Detailed soil micromorphological descriptions of the Flag Fen environs (Chapter 14)

by C A I French

Introduction

The detailed soil micromorphological descriptions given below relate to the discussion of the Flag Fen environs project, of Chapter 14.

Trench 2

Structure: apedal, homogeneous, massive; severe root disturbance in the centre zone of the slide. *Porosity*: dense (<7%); very few (<2%) channels, <1mm wide and <2mm and <38mm long, smooth to weakly serrated, walls partially accommodated; few (<5%) vughs, sub-rounded, 100–750μm. *Organic components*: none. *Mineral components*: rare (<2%) small gravel pebbles, <12mm; limit 100μm; two fabrics, fabric 1) in upper half (7cm) of slide and fabric 2) in lower half (7.5cm) of slide; fabric 1): c:f ratio: 35:65; coarse fraction: 15% medium and 20% fine quartz, sub-rounded to sub-angular, 100–300μm; fine fraction: 50% very fine quartz, sub-rounded to sub-angular, 50–100μm; 10% silt; 5% clay; weakly speckled; yellowish grey (CPL), yellowish brown (PPL), pale yellow (RL); fabric 2): c:f ratio = 15–25:75; coarse fraction: 10–20% medium and 5% fine quartz, sub-rounded to sub-angular, 100–300μm; fine fraction: 40–50% very fine quartz, sub-rounded to sub-angular, 50–100μm;

10% silt; 10–15% clay, in greater or lesser zones of concentration; weakly speckled; grey/reddish gold (CPL), pale to dark orangey brown (PPL), pale yellow to orange (RL). *Groundmass*: fine and related: close porphyric, weakly striated; coarse: undifferentiated. *Pedofeatures*: *textural*, in fabric 1): occasional (<5%) oriented clays; occasional (3%) non-laminated dusty clay in groundmass, weak birefringence, yellow to gold (CPL); rare (<2%) fragments of limpid clay in groundmass, moderate birefringence, yellow (CPL); in fabric 2): many to abundant oriented clays (10–15%); rare (2%) non-laminated limpid clay in groundmass, moderate to strong birefringence, orange to reddish orange (CPL); very rare (<1%) laminated dusty clay in voids, moderate birefringence, orangey red (CPL); many (5–10% non-laminated dusty clay in groundmass and as coatings of grains, moderate birefringence, gold to reddish orange (CPL); occasional (3–5%) non-laminated dusty clay in voids, moderate birefringence, reddish orange (CPL). *Amorphous*, in both fabrics; few zones of amorphous sesquioxide impregnation, especially around voids and root channels, and of silt/clay fraction of groundmass, <10% of groundmass in fabric 1) and <30% of groundmass in fabric 2); very few (<2%) sesquioxide nodules in groundmass, sub-rounded, <250μm; rare (<1%) aggregate of silty clay in fabric 1), sub-rounded, reddish orange (CPL).

Bibliography

Abbreviations

BAR   British Archaeological Reports
CBA   Council for British Archaeology
EH   English Heritage

Abbott, G W, 1910 The discovery of prehistoric pits at Peterborough, *Archaeologia*, **62**, 332–52

Adkins, L, and Needham, S, 1985 New research on a late Bronze Age enclosure at Queen Mary's Hospital, Carshalton, *Surrey Archaeol Collect*, **76**, 11–50

Allen, M J, and Bayliss, A, 1995 Appendix 2: the radiocarbon dating programme, in *Stonehenge in its landscape: twentieth-century excavations* (R M J Cleal, K E Walker, and R Montague), EH Archaeol Rep, **10**, 511–35

Allen, T, Hey, G, and Miles, D, 1997 A line of time: approaches to archaeology in the upper and middle Thames valley, England, *World Archaeol*, **29**, 114–29

Andersen, S T, 1970 The relative pollen productivity and pollen representation of north European trees, and correction factors for tree pollen spectra, *Danmarks Geologiske Undersogelse*, 2 ser **96**, 1-99

——, 1973 The differential pollen productivity of trees and its significance for the interpretation of a pollen diagram from a forested region, in *Quat Plant Ecol* (eds H J B Birks and R G West), 109–15, Oxford

Anon 1976, Miscellanea, *J Roy Soc Antiq Jr*, **46**, 146–7

Arden, J W, and Gale, N H, 1974 New electrochemical technique for the separation of lead at trace levels from natural silicates, *Analytical Chemistry*, **46**, 2–9

Armit, I, 1988 *Excavations at Loch Olabhat, North Uist, 1988: 3rd interim report* Dept Archaeol Univ Edinburgh Project Paper, **10**

Armstrong, E, 1924 The Early Iron Age or Hallstatt period in Ireland, *J Roy Soc Antiq Ir*, **54**, 109–27

Arnold, B, 1986 *Cortaillod-Est, un village du Bronze final, 1: fouille subaquatique et photographie aerienne, Archéologie neuchâteloise* **1**, Saint Blaise: Editions du Ruau

Atkinson, R J C, 1951 The henge monuments of Great Britain, in *Excavations at Dorchester, Oxon* (R J C Atkinson, C M Piggott, and N K Sandars), 81–107, Oxford

Avery, B W, 1980 *Soil Classification for England and Wales*, Soil Survey Technical Monogr, **14**, Harpenden

Baillie, M G L, 1982 Tree-ring dating and archaeology, London

Baillie, M G L, and Pilcher, J R, 1973 A simple cross-dating program for tree-ring research, *Tree Ring Bull*, **33**, 7–14

Baker, C A, Moxey, P A, and Oxford, P M, 1978 Woodland continuity and change in Epping Forest, *Field Studies* **4**, 645–69

Baker, J, and Brothwell, D, 1980 *Animal diseases in archaeology*, London

Bannister, K, 1961 Barrow at East Tilbury, Essex, *Thurrock Local Hist Soc J*, **6**, 19–27

Barclay, A, Fell, V, and Wallis, J, 1995 An iron socketed axehead from the River Thames, Buscot, Oxfordshire, *Oxoniensia*, **60**, 417–19

Barrett, J C, 1980 The pottery of the later Bronze Age in lowland England, *Proc Prehist Soc*, **46**, 297–319

Barrett, J C, Bradley, R J, and Hall, M, 1991 *Papers on the Prehistoric Archaeology of Cranborne Chase*, Oxbow Monogr, **11**, Oxford

Barrett, J C, and Needham, S, 1988 Production, circulation and exchange: problems of the interpretation of Bronze Age bronzework in *The archaeology of context in the Neolithic and Bronze Age: recent trends* (eds J Barrett and I A Kinnes), 127–41, Sheffield

Bass, W M, 1987 *Human osteology: a laboratory and field manual*, 3 edn, Columbia, Missouri

Becker, B, Kromer, B, and Trimborn, P, 1991 A stable-isotope tree-ring timescale of the Late Glacial/Holocene boundary, *Nature*, **353**, 647–9

Beech, M, 1987 A study of the animal bones from the Romano-Celtic shrine at Haddenham, unpubl MA dissertation, Dept Archaeol Prehist, Univ Sheffield

Bell, M, 1976 The excavation of an early Romano-British site and Pleistocene landforms at Newhaven, Sussex, *Sussex Archaeol Collect*, **114**, 218–305

——, 1977 Excavations at Bishopstone, *Sussex Archaeol Collect*, **115**

Bennett, K D, and Birks, H J B, 1990 Postglacial history of Alder (*Alnus glutinosa* (L. Gaertn.)) in the British Isles, *J Quat Sci*, **5**, 123–33

Bennett, K D, Wittington, G, and Edwards, K J, 1994 Recent plant nomenclatural changes and pollen morphology in the British Isles, *Quat Newslett*, **73**, 1–6

Benson, D, and Miles, D 1974 *The Upper Thames valley: an archaeological survey of the river gravels*, Oxford Archaeol Unit survey, **2**

Benton, S, 1930–31 The Excavation of the Sculptors Cave, Covesea, Morayshire, *Proc Soc Antiq Scotl*, **65**, 177–216

Biddick, K, 1980 Appendix 7: animal bones from the second millennium ditches, Newark Road subsite, Fengate, in Pryor 1980, 217–34

——, 1984 Animal bones from the Cat's Water subsite, in Pryor 1984a, microfiche 245–75

Binford, L R, 1981 *Bones: ancient men and modern myths*, New York

Birks, H J B, 1989 Holocene isochrome maps and patterns of tree spreading in the British Isles, *J Biogeogr*, **16**, 503–40

Birks, H J B, Deacon, J, and Peglar, S, 1975 Pollen maps for the British Isles 5000 years ago, *Proc Roy Soc*, B, **189**, 87–105

Blanchet, J-P, 1984 Les Premiers Métalurgistes en Picardie et dans le Nord de la France, *Mem Soc Préhist Française*, **17**, 1–608

Bloemers, J H, and Louwe-Kooijmans, L P, 1981 *Verleden Land*, Amsterdam

Boddy, L, and Ainsworth, A M, 1984 Decomposition of Neolithic wood from the Sweet Track, *Somerset Levels Papers*, **10**, 92–6

Boessneck, J, Müller, H-H, and Teichert, M, 1964 Osteologische Unterscheidungsmerkmale zwischen Schaf (*Ovis aries* Linné) und Ziege (*Capra hircus* Linné), *Kühn-Archiv*, **78**, 1–29

Bond, D, 1988 *Excavation at the North Ring, Mucking, Essex: a Late Bronze Age enclosure*, E Anglian Archaeol Rep, **43**, Chelmsford

Booth, B K W, Brough, R C, and Pryor, F M M, 1984 The flexible storage of site data: a microcomputer application, *J Archaeol Sci*, **10**, 81–9

Boserup, E, 1965 *The conditions of agricultural growth*, Chicago

Bowman, S, 1990 *Radiocarbon dating*, London

Bradley, R J, 1978 *The prehistoric settlement of Britain*, London

——, 1984 *The social foundations of prehistoric Britain*, London

——, 1990 *The passage of arms*, Cambridge

——, 1991 Monuments and places, in *Sacred and profane: proceedings of a conference on archaeology, ritual and religion, Oxford, 1989* (eds P. Garwood, D. Jennings, R Skeats and J Thoms), Oxford Univ Committee for Archaeol Monogr **32**, 135–40

Bradley, R J, and Edmonds, M, 1993 *Interpreting the axe trade: production and exchange in Neolithic Britain*, Cambridge

Bradley, R J, Entwistle, R, and Raymond, F, 1994 *Prehistoric land divisions on Salisbury Plain*, EH Archaeol Rep, **2**, London

Bradley, R, Lobb, S, Richards, J, and Robinson, M, 1980 Two Late Bronze Age settlements on the Kennet Gravels: excavations at Aldermaston Wharf and Knights Farm, Burghfield, Berkshire, *Proc Prehist Soc*, **46**, 217–95

Bradshaw, R H W, Coxon P, Greig, J R G, and Hall, A R, 1981 Fossil evidence of Cannabis (*Cannabis sativa* L) in Eastern England, *New Phytol*, **89**, 503–10

Brain, C K, 1981 *The hunters or the hunted?*, Chicago

Briard, J, 1965 *Les dépôts Bretons et L'Age du Bronze Atlantique*, Rennes

——, 1972 *Le dépôt de Bronze final de Saint Brieuc des Iffs (I et V)*, Travaux du Laboratoire d'Anthropologie Préhistorique, **41**

Briard, J, Goultequer, P, and Onnee, D 1966 *La Prairie de Mauves à Nantes*, Dépôt Travaux, Rennes

Bridgeford, S D, 1997 Mightier than the pen – an edgewise look at Irish Bronze Age swords, in *Material harm: studies in the archaeology of war and violence* (ed J Carman), 95–115, Worldwide Archaeology Series, Glasgow

Bridgland, D R, Lewis, S G, and Wymer, J J, 1995 Middle Pleistocene stratigraphy and archaeology around Mildenhall and Icklingham, Suffolk: report on the Geologists Association field meeting, 27 June 1992, *Proc Geol Ass*, **106**, 57–69

Briggs, S, 1991 Some processes and problems in later Prehistoric Wales and beyond, in *L'Age du Bronze Atlantique* (eds C Chevillot and A Coffyn), 59–76, Beynac-et-Cazenac, Dordogne

Briscoe, G, and Furness, A, 1955 A hoard of Bronze Age weapons from Eriswell near Mildenhall, *Antiq J*, **35**, 218–19

British Museum, 1920 *A guide to the Antiquities of the Bronze Age in the Department of British and Mediaeval Antiquities*, London

British Museum, 1953 *Later Prehistoric Antiquities of the British Isles in the British Museum*, London

Britnell, W J, and Earwood, C, 1991 Wooden artefacts and other worked wood from Buckbean Pond, in Musson 1991, 161–72

Britton, D, 1960 The Isleham hoard, Cambridgeshire, *Antiquity*, **34**, 279–82

Bronk, C R, 1994 *Oxcal (v2 0): A radiocarbon calibration and analysis program*, Oxford Radiocarbon Accelerator Unit

——, 1995 Radiocarbon calibration and analysis of stratigraphy, *Radiocarbon*, **36**, 425–30

Bronk, C R, and Hedges, R E M, 1989 Use of the CO_2 sources in radiocarbon dating by AMS, *Radiocarbon*, **31**, 298–304

——, 1990 A gaseous ion source for routine AMS radiocarbon dating, *Nuclear instruments and methods in physics research B*, **52**, 322–6

——, 1997 A gas ion source for radiocarbon dating, *Nuclear instruments and methods in physics research B*, **29**, 45–9

Brothwell, D, 1965 *Digging up bones*, Ithaca, NY

Brown, A G, 1988 The palaeoecology of *Alnus* (alder) and the postglacial history of floodplain vegetation: pollen percentages and influx data from the West Midlands, United Kingdom, *New Phytol*, **110**, 425–36

Brown, D M, Munro, M A R, Baillie, M G L, and Pilcher, J R, 1986 Dendrochronology — the absolute Irish standard, *Radiocarbon*, **28** (2A), 279–83

Brown, L, 1991 Quernstones from Sudden Farm, Nether Wallop, Hants, *Quern Study Group Newsletter*, **2**

Brown, M A, and Blin-Stoyle, A E, 1959: A sample analysis of British Middle and Late Bronze Age metalwork using optical spectrometry, *Archaeometry*, **2**, Supplement

Bruneaux, J-L, 1991 The Celtic Sanctuary at Gournay-sur-Aronde, in Kruta, V, Frey, OH, Raftery, B, and Szabó, M, (eds) *The Celts*, 364–5, London

Bruneaux, J-L, 1992 The celtic sanctuary at Gournay-sur-Aronde, in Moscati *et al* 1992, 364–5

Bruneaux, J-L, and Rapin, A, 1988 *Bouclier at lances, dépôts et trophées, Gournay II*, Paris

BS 565, 1972 *Glossary of terms relating to timber and woodwork*, British Standards Institution, London

Buck, C E, Christen, J A, Kenworthy, J B, and Litton, C D, 1994a Estimating the duration of archaeological activity using ^{14}C determinations, *Oxford J Archaeol*, **13**, 229–40

Buck, C E, Kenworthy, J B, Litton, C D, and Smith, A F M, 1991 Combining archaeological and radiocarbon information: a Bayesian approach to calibration, *Antiquity*, **65**, 808–21

Buck, C E, Litton, C D, and Scott, E M, 1994b Making the most of radiocarbon dating: some statistical considerations, *Antiquity*, **68**, 252–63

Buck, C E, Litton, C D, and Smith, A F M, 1992 Calibration of radiocarbon results pertaining to related archaeological events, *J Archaeol Sci*, **19**, 497–512

Buckley, D G, 1979 The Stone, in *Gussage All Saints* (G J Wainwright), Dept Environment Archaeol Rep, **10**, 89–97, London

——, 1986 The quern, in D. Gurney, *Settlement, religion and industry on the Roman fen-edge, Norfolk*, E Anglian Archaeol Rep, **31**, 37

——, 1995a Quernstones and quern rubbers, in *The Anglo-Saxon cemetery at Spong Hill, North Elmham Part VII: the Iron Age, Roman and Early Saxon settlement* (R Rickett), E Anglian Archaeol Rep, **73**, 86–7

——, 1995b, Stone, in *Balksbury Camp: excavations 1973 and 1981* (G J Wainwright and S M Davies), EH Archaeol Rep, **4**, 40–49, London

Buckley, D G, and Major, H, 1995 Querns, in *Excavation at North Shoebury: settlement and economy in south-east Essex 1500 BC–AD 1500* (J J Wymer and N Brown), E Anglian Archaeol Rep, **75**, 72–3, Chelmsford

——, forthcoming The quernstones, in *Mucking South Rings* (J P A Etté)

Buikstra, J E, and Ubelaker, D H (eds) 1994 *Standards for data collection from human skeletal remains*, Arkansas Archaeol Survey Res Ser, **44**, Fayetteville

Bulleid, A, and Gray, H St G, 1911, *The Glastonbury lake village*, **1**, Glastonbury Antiq Soc, Glastonbury

Bulleid, A, and Gray, H St G, 1917 *The Glastonbury lake village*, **2**, Glastonbury Antiq Soc

Bullock, P, Federoff, N, Jongerius, A, Stoops, G, and Tursina, T, 1985 *Handbook for soil thin section description*, Wolverhampton

Bullock, P and Murphy, C P, 1979 Evolution of a Palaeo-Argillic Brown Earth (Palendalf) from Oxfordshire, England, *Geoderma*, **22**, 225–52

Burgess, C B, 1968a The Later Bronze Age in the British Isles and north-western France, *Archaeol J*, **125**, 1–45

——, 1968b *Bronze Age metalwork in northern England* c *1000 to 700 BC*, Newcastle upon Tyne

——, 1969 Some decorated socketed axes in Canon Greenwell's collection, *Yorkshire Archaeol J*, **42**, 267–72

——, 1979 A find from Boynton, Suffolk and the end of the Bronze Age in Britain and Ireland, in *Bronze Age hoards: some finds old and new* (eds C B Burgess and D G Coombs), BAR, **67**, 269–82, Oxford

——, 1982 The Cartington knife and the double edged knives of the late Bronze Age, *Bull Northumberland Archaeol Group*, **3**, 32–45

Burgess, C B, and Colquhoun, I 1988 *The swords of Britain, Prähistorische Bronzefund*, **4**(5), Munich

Burgess, C B, Coombs, D G, and Davies, D G, 1972 The Broadward Complex and barbed spearheads, in *Prehistoric Man in Wales and the West* (eds F Lynch and C B Burgess), 11–284, Somerset

Burgess, C B, and Gerloff, S, 1981 *The dirks and rapiers of Great Britain and Ireland, Prähistorische Bronzefunde*, **4** (7), Munich

Burley, E, 1955–6 A catalogue and survey of the metalwork from Traprain Law, *Proc Soc Antiq Scotl*, **89**, 118–26

Burns, B, Cunliffe, B, and Sebire, H 1996 *Guernsey — an island community of the Atlantic Iron Age*, Oxford Univ Comm Archaeol Monogr, **43**, Oxford

Burrin, P J, and Scaife, R G, 1984 Aspects of Holocene valley sedimentation and floodplain development in southern England, *Proc Geol Ass*, **95**, 81–96

Butler, J J, 1963 *Bronze Age connections across the North Sea, Palaeohistoria*, **9**, Groningen

Buurman, J, 1979, Cereals in circles — crop processing activities in Bronze Age Bovenkarspel, in *Festchrift [for] Maria Hopf* (ed U Körber-Grohne), 21–37, Cologne

Cameselle, G M, 1988 *Las Espadas de Bronce Final en la Peninsula Iberica, Arqueohistorica*, **1**, Santiago

Caple, C, and Dungworth, D, 1998 *Waterlogged anoxic archaeological burial environments*, Ancient Monuments Laboratory Report, **22/98**, London

Champion, T, 1975 Britain in the European Iron Age, *Archaeol Atlantica*, **1**, 127–45

Champion, T, Gamble, C, Shennan, S, and Whittle, A, 1984 *Prehistoric Europe*, London

Chatwin, C P, 1961 *British regional geology: East Anglia and adjoining areas*, HMSO, London

Chevillot, C, and Gomez de Soto, J, 1979 Roues de char et statuettes en terre cuite de Chalucet (Saint-Jean-Ligoure, Haute-Vienne), Leur signification culturelle, *Bull Soc Préhist Française*, **76**, 10–12, 434–44

Clapham, A, and Scaife, R G, 1988 A pollen and plant macrofossil investigation of Oakbank Crannog, Loch Tay, Scotland, in *The exploitation of wetlands* (eds P Murphy and C A I French), BAR, **186**, 293–325, Oxford

Clark, A, 1993 *Excavations at Mucking, 1: the site atlas* EH Archaeol Rep, **20**, London

Clark, J G D, and Godwin, H A 1940 Late Bronze Age find near Stuntney, Isle of Ely, *Antiq J*, **20**, 52–71

——, 1962 The Neolithic in the Cambridgeshire Fens, *Antiquity* **36**, 10–23

Clark, J G D, Higgs, E, and Longworth, I H, 1960 Excavations at the Neolithic site at Hurst Fen, Mildenhall, Suffolk (1954, 1957, and 1958), *Proc Prehist Soc*, **26**, 202–45

Clark, K M, 1995 The later prehistoric and protohistoric dog: the emergence of canine diversity, *Archaeozoologia*, **7**, 9–32

Clarke, D L, 1970 *Beaker pottery of Great Britain and Ireland*, Cambridge

Clarke, R R, 1951 A hoard of metalwork of the Early Iron Age from Ringstead, Norfolk, *Proc Prehist Soc*, **17**, 214–25

Cleal, R M J, 1982 A re-analysis of the ring-ditch site at Playden, East Sussex, *Sussex Archaeol Collect*, **120**, 1–17

Clough, T H McK, and Cummins, W A (eds), 1979 *Stone axe studies: archaeological, petrological, experimental and ethnographic*, CBA Res Rep, **23**, London

Coffyn, A, 1971 Le Bronze Final et le début du Premier Age du Fer autour de l'estuaire Girondin, unpubl PhD thesis, Univ Bordeaux

Coffyn, A, 1985 *Le Bronze Final Atlantique dans la Peninsule Iberique*, Paris

Coffyn, A, Gomez, J, and Mohen, J-P, 1981 *L'Apogée du Bronze Atlantique Le Dépôt de Vénat L'Age du Bronze en France I*, Paris

Coghlan, H H, and Case, H J, 1957 Early metallurgy of copper in Ireland and Britain, *Proc Prehist Soc*, **23**, 91–123

Coles, B, 1992 (ed) *The wetland revolution in prehistory*, Prehist Soc/WARP, Exeter

Coles, B, 1995 *Wetland management: a survey for English Heritage*, Exeter: Wetland Archaeology Research Project

Coles, J M, 1959–60 Scottish Late Bronze Age Metalwork typology, distributions and chronology, *Proc Soc Antiq Scotl*, **93**, 16–134

——, 1962 European Bronze Age shields, *Proc Prehist Soc*, **28**, 156–90

——, 1973 *Archaeology by experiment*, London

——, 1987 *Meare Village East: the excavations of A Bulleid and H St George Gray 1932–56, Somerset Levels Papers*, **13**

Coles, J M, and Coles, B J, 1989 *People of the wetlands*, London

Coles, J M, and Harding, A F, 1979 *The Bronze Age in Europe*, London

Coles, J M, and Hibbert, F W, 1972 A Neolithic wooden mallet from the Somerset Levels, *Antiquity*, **46**, 52–4

Coles, J M, and Lawson, A J, 1987 *European wetlands in pre-history*, Oxford

Coles, J M, and Orme, B J, 1982 Beaver in the Somerset Levels: some new evidence, in *Somerset Levels Papers*, **8**, 67–72

Colquhoun, I, 1979 The Late Bronze Age hoard from Blackmoor, Hampshire, in *Bronze Age Hoards, some finds old and new* (eds C B Burgess and D G Coombs), BAR, **67**, 90–116, Oxford

Coombs, D G, 1975 Bronze Age weapon hoards in Britain, *Archaeol Atlantica*, **11**, 49–82

——, 1979 A late Bronze Age hoard from Cassiobridge Farm, Watford, Hertfordshire, in *Bronze Age Hoards, some finds old and new* (eds C B Burgess and D G Coombs), BAR, **67**, 90–116, Oxford

——, 1988 The Wilburton Complex and BF II in Atlantic Europe, in *Le groupe Rhin-Suisse-France orientale et la notion de civilisation des Champs d'Urnes* (eds P Brun and C Mordant), Nemours

——, 1992: Flag Fen platform and Fengate Power Station post alignment — the metalwork, *Antiquity*, **66**, 504–17

Coombs, D G, and Pryor, F M M, 1994 An Early Iron Age bronze scabbard mount from Flag Fen, *Antiq J*, **74**, 337–40

Cooper, L, Ripper, S, and Clay, P, 1994 The Hemington bridges, *Current Archaeol*, **140**, 316–21

Corbet, G, and Ovenden, D, 1980 *The mammals of Britain and Europe*, London

Corkhill, T, 1979 *A glossary of wood*, London

Courty, M-A and Federoff, N, 1982 Micromorphology of a Holocene dwelling, *Nordic Archaeometry*, **2**, 257–77

Cunliffe, B W, 1984 *Danebury: an Iron Age hillfort in Hampshire, 2, The excavations 1969–1978: the finds*, CBA Res Rep, **52**, London

——, 1988 *Mount Batten, Plymouth: a prehistoric and Roman port*, Oxford University Committee for Archaeol Monograph, **26**

——, 1991 *Iron Age communities in Britain*, 3 edn, London

Cunliffe, B W, and Phillipson, D W, 1968 Excavations at Eldon's Seat, Encombe, Dorset, England, *Proc Prehist Soc*, **34**, 191–237

Cunliffe, B W, and Poole, C, 1991 *Danebury, an Iron Age hillfort in Hampshire, 5, the excavations of 1979–1988: the finds*, CBA Res Rep, **73**, London

Curwen, E C, 1937 Querns, *Antiquity* **11**, 133–51

——, 1941 More about querns, *Antiquity* **15**, 15–32

Cuttler, R, 1995 *Marshall's Garage, Boongate, Peterborough: an archaeological evaluation, 1995*, Birmingham University Field Archaeology Unit Report, **341**

——, 1998 *Land off Third Drove, Fengate, Peterborough: an archaeological evaluation, 1998*, Birmingham Univ Field Archaeol Unit Rep, **515**

Dalton, G, 1977 Aboriginal economies in stateless societies, in *Exchange systems in prehistory* (eds T K Earl and J E Ericson), 191–212, London

Davey, P J, 1973 Bronze Age metalwork from Lincolnshire, *Archaeologia*, **104**, 51–127

Dehling, H, and van der Plicht, J, 1993 Statistical problems in calibrating radiocarbon dates, *Radiocarbon*, **35**, 239–44

De Navarro, J M, 1972 *The finds from the site of La Tène, 1: scabbards and the swords found in them*, Oxford

Dent, J, 1996, A distinctive form of inlaid brooch from Iron Age Britain, in *Sites and sights of the Iron Age* (B Raftery, V Megaw, and V Rigby), Oxbow Monogr, **56**, 41–8, Oxford

Desch, C H, 1938 Report on the axe, in The vitrified fort at Rahoy, Morvern, Argyll (V G Childe and W Thorneycroft), *Proc Soc Antiq Scotl*, **72** (1937–8), 23–43

Desch, H E, 1973 *Timber and its structure and properties*, London

Dimbleby, G W, 1961 Transported material in soil profile, *J Soil Sci*, **12**, 12–22

Dimbleby, G W, 1962 Soil pollen analysis, *J Soil Sci* **12**, 1–11

——, 1985 *The palynology of archaeological sites*, London

Dixon, P W, 1994 *Crickley Hill, 1: the hillfort defences*, Nottingham

Dixon, T N, 1982 A survey of crannogs in Loch Tay, *Proc Soc Antiq Scotl*, **112**, 17–38

DoE, 1990 *Planning Policy Guidance: archaeology and planning*, PPG16, London

Drewett, P L, 1982 Later Bronze Age downland economy and excavations at Black Patch, East Sussex, *Proc Prehist Soc*, **48**, 321–400

Duncan, S J, and Ganiaris, H, 1987 Some sulphide corrosion products on copper alloys and lead alloys from London waterfront sites, in *Recent advances in the conservation and analysis of artefacts*, 109–18, Inst Archaeol, UCL, London

Dunning, C, 1992 *La Tène*, in Moscati *et al* 1992, 366–8

Dunning, G, 1934 The swan's neck and ring headed pins of the Early Iron Age in Britain, *Archaeol J*, **91**, 269–95

Duval, P-M, 1975 La décoration des fourreaux d'épée lateniens en Europe de centre-est et en Europe occidentale, *Albia Regia*, **14**, 9–13

Earwood, C, 1988 Wooden containers and other wooden artefacts from the Glastonbury Lake Village, *Somerset Levels Papers*, **14**, 83–90

——, 1993 *Domestic wooden artefacts*, Exeter

Edlin, H L, 1973 *Woodland crafts in Britain*, Newton Abbot

Edmonds, M, 1998 Polished stone axes and associated artefacts, in Pryor 1998a, 260–8

Egloff, M, 1992 Celtic craftwork at La Tène, in Moscati *et al* 1992, 369–71

Eluère, C, 1989 A 'gold connection' between the Etruscans and Early Celts? *Gold Bull*, **22**, 48–55

——, in press *Les Objets en or de Chaffois (Doubs)*

Eluère, C, Raub, C, and Weiss, H, 1988 Eine moderne Anwendung des Probierteines bei der Analyse antiker Edelmettalfunde, *Archäologisches Korrespondenzblatt*, **18**, 275–7

Eogan, G, 1964 The Later Bronze Age in Ireland in the light of recent research, *Proc Prehist Soc*, **30**, 268–351

——, 1965 *Catalogue of Irish Bronze swords*, Dublin

——, 1966 Some notes on the origin and diffusion of the bronze socketed gouge, *Ulster J Archaeol*, **29**, 97–102

——, 1974 Pins of the Irish Late Bronze Age, *J Roy Soc Antiq Ir*, **104**, 74–119

Erith, F H, and Longworth, I H, 1960 A Bronze Age urnfield on Vinces Farm, Ardleigh, Essex, *Proc Prehist Soc*, **26**, 178–92

Etté, J P A, 1993 The Late Bronze Age, in *Excavations at Mucking, 1: the site atlas* (A Clark), EH Archaeol Rep, **20**, London

Evans, C, 1992, *Archaeological investigations at Fengate, Peterborough: the Depot site*, Cambridge Univ Archaeol Unit Rep

——, 1993a The Fengate Depot site, *Fenland Res*, **8**, 2–9

——, 1993b Sampling settlements: investigations at Lingwood Farm, Cottenham and Eye Hill farm, Soham, *Fenland Res*, **8**, 26–30

——, 1997 Hydraulic communities: Iron Age enclosure in the East Anglian fenlands, in *Re-constructing the Iron Age* (eds A Gwilt and C Haselgrove), Oxbow Monogr, **71**, 216–27, Oxford

Evans, C, and Knight M, 1997 *The Barleycroft Paddocks*, Cambridge Univ Archaeol Unit Rep, **218**

Evans, C, and Serjeantson, D, 1988, The backwater economy of a fen-edge community in the Iron Age: the upper Delphs, Haddenham, *Antiquity*, **62**, 381–400

Evans, J, 1881 *Ancient bronze implements, weapons and ornaments of Great Britain and Ireland*, London

Fasham, P, 1985 *The prehistoric settlement at Winnall Down, Winchester*, Hampshire Fld Club Archaeol Soc Monogr, 2/ M3 Archaeol Rescue Comm Rep, **8**

Feacham, R W, 1971 Unfinished hillforts, in *The Iron Age and its hillforts* (ed M Jesson and D Hill), 19–39, Southampton

Federoff, N and Goldberg, P, 1982 Comparative micromorphology of two late Pleistocene palaeosols (in the Paris basin), *Catena*, **9**, 227–51

Fell, V, and Salter, C J, forthcoming Metallographic examination of seven Iron Age ferrous axeheads from England, *Hist Metall*

Field, N, 1983 Fiskerton, Lincolnshire, *Proc Prehist Soc*, **49**, 392

——, 1986 An Iron Age timber causeway at Fiskerton, Lincolnshire, *Fenland Res*, **3**, 49–53

Fitzpatrick, A, 1984 The deposition of La Tène Iron Age metalwork in watery contexts in Southern England, in *Aspects of the Iron Age in central southern England* (eds B W Cunliffe and D Miles), Univ Oxford Comm Archaeol Monogr, **2**, 178–90, Oxford

——, 1994 Objects of copper alloy, in Thorpe *et al* 1994, 47–9

——, 1996 Night and day: the symbolism of Astral Signs on Late Iron Age Anthropomorphic Short Swords, *Proc Prehist Soc*, **62**, 373–98

Fleming, A, 1988 *The Dartmoor Reaves — investigating prehistoric land divisions*, London

Fowler, P, 1983 *The farming of prehistoric Britain*, Cambridge

Fox, C, 1923 *Archaeology of the Cambridge region*, Cambridge

——, 1958 *Pattern and purpose: a survey of Early Celtic Art in Britain*, Cardiff

French, C A I, 1980 Appendix 4: an analysis of molluscs from two second millennium BC ditches at the Newark Road subsite, Fengate, Peterborough, in Pryor 1980, 204–12

——, 1983 An environmental study of the soils, sediments and molluscan evidence associated with prehistoric monuments on river terrace gravels in north-west Cambridgeshire, unpubl PhD thesis, Univ London

——, 1984 A sediment analysis of the Late Iron Age ditches at Fengate, Peterborough, in Pryor 1984a, 259 and microfiche 223–33

——, 1988a Aspects of buried soils in the lower Welland valley and the fen margin north of Peterborough, Cambridgeshire, in *Man made soils: Symposia of the Association for Environmental Archaeology No 6* (eds Groenman-van Waateringe and M Robinson), BAR, **S410**, 115–27, Oxford

——, 1988b Further aspects of the buried prehistoric soils in the fen margin northeast of Peterborough, Cambridgeshire, in *The exploitation of wetlands: Symposia of the Association for Environmental Archaeology No 7* (eds P Murphy and C A I French), BAR, **S186**, 193–211, Oxford

——, 1990, Neolithic soils, middens and alluvium in the lower Welland valley, *Oxford J Archaeol*, **9**, 305–11

——, 1992a, Alluviated fen-edge prehistoric landscapes in Cambridgeshire, England, in *Archaeologia Del Paesaggio* (ed M Bernardi), 709–31, Firenze

——, 1992b, Fengate to Flag Fen: summary of the soil and sediment analyses, *Antiquity*, **66**, 458–61

——, 1992c, *Fengate 1992: soils assessment*, Cambridge Univ Archaeol Unit, internal report

——, 1994 *Excavation of the Deeping St Nicholas Barrow Complex, South Lincolnshire*, Lincolnshire Archaeol and Heritage Rep Ser, **1**, Heckington

——, 1997 Murden's former depot site Fengate, Peterborough (1997): soils assessment, in Pryor 1997a, 16

French, C A I, Macklin, M G, and Passmore, D G, 1992, Archaeology and palaeochannels in the Lower Welland and Nene valleys: alluvial archaeology at the fen-edge, Eastern England, in *Alluvial archaeology in Britain* (eds S Needham and M G Macklin), Oxbow Monogr, **27**, 169–76, Oxford

French, C A I, and Pryor, F M M, 1993 *The South-West Fen dyke survey project 1982-86*, E Anglian Archaeol Rep, **59**

French, C A I, and Scaife, R G, 1988 Flag Fen and its environment, *WARP Newsletter*, **5**, 25–9

French, C A I, and Taylor, M 1985 Desiccation and destruction: the immediate effects of de-watering at Etton, Cambridgeshire, *Oxford J Archaeol*, **4**, 139–57

Freude, H, Harde, K W, and Lohse, G A, 1964–83 *Die Käfer Mitteleuropas*, **1–11**, Krefeld

Gale, N H, and Stos-Gale, Z A, 2000 Lead isotope analyses applied to provenance studies, in *Modern analytical methods in art and archaeology* (eds E Ciliberto and G Spoto), New York, 503–84

Gdaniec, K, 1998 *Archaeological investigations at Third Drove, Fengate, Peterborough, Cambridgeshire*, Cambridge Univ Archaeol Unit, interim report

Gelfand, A E, and Smith, A F M, 1990 Sampling approaches to calculating marginal densities, *J Amer Stat Assoc*, **85**, 398–409

Gerloff, S, 1975 The early Bronze Age daggers in Great Britain, *Prähistorische Bronzefunde*, **6** (2), Munich

——, 1986 Bronze Age Class A cauldrons: typology, origins and chronology, *J Roy Soc Antiq Ir*, **116**, 84–115

Gibson, A, and Kinnes, I A, 1997 On the urns of a dilemma: radiocarbon and Peterborough chronology, *Oxford J Archaeol*, **16**, 65–72

Gibson, D, 1998 *Archaeological excavations at the Co-op Site, Fengate*, Cambridge Univ Archaeol Unit Rep, **264**

Gibson, D, and Pollard, J, forthcoming *The Neolithic of Fengate: recent work and re-interpretation*

Gimbutas, M, 1982 *The goddesses and gods of old Europe: 6500–3500 BC: myths and cult images*, Berkeley and Los Angeles

Ginoux, N, 1994 Les fourreaux ornés de France du Ve au IIe Siècle avant J-C, *Etudes Celtiques*, **30**, 7–86

Girling, M, 1979 The fossil insect assemblages from the Meare Lake Village, *Somerset Levels Papers*, **5**, 25–32

Godwin, H, 1940 Pollen analysis and forest history of England and Wales, *New Phytol*, **39**, 370–400

——, 1967 The ancient cultivation of hemp, *Antiquity*, **41**, 42–9

——, 1975a *The history of the British flora*, 2 edn, Cambridge

——, 1975b History of the natural forests of Britain: establishment, dominance and destruction, *Phil Trans Roy Soc London*, B, **271**, 47–67

——, 1978 *Fenland: its ancient past and uncertain future*, Cambridge

Godwin, M E, and H Clifford, M H, 1936 Plant remains in peat, in Report on a Late Bronze Age site in Mildenhall Fen, West Suffolk (J G D Clark), 34–6, *Antiq J*, **16**, 29–50

Gomez de Soto, J, 1980 *Les Cultures de l'Age du Bronze dans le Bassin de la Charente*, Périgueux

——, 1991 Le fondeur, le trifiquant et les cuisiniers. La broche d'Amathante de Chypre et la chronologie absolue du bronze final atlantique, in *L'Age du Bronze Atlantique, Actes du Premier Colloque de Beynac* (eds C Chevillot and A Coffyn), 369–73, Association des Musee de Sarladais

——, 1993 Cooking for the elite: feasting equipment in the Late Bronze Age, in *Trade and Exchange in Prehistoric Europe* (eds C Scarre and F Healy), Oxbow Monogr, **33**, 191–8

Gomez de Soto, J, and Pautreau, 1988 J-P Le crichet protohistorique en bronze de Thorigné à Coulon (Deaux-Sevres), *Archäologisches Korrespondenzblatt*, **18**, 31–42

Goodwin, D H, 1979 *Sheep management and production*, 2 edn, London

Grant, A, 1982 The use of tooth wear as a guide to the age of domestic ungulates, in *Ageing and sexing animal bones from archaeological sites* (eds B Wilson, C Grigson, and S Payne), BAR, **109**, 91–108, Oxford

Gray, H St G, and Bulleid, A, 1953 *The Meare Lake village*, **2**, Taunton

Greatorix, C, 1995 *An archaeological evaluation at Shinewater Park, Eastbourne, East Sussex, Report on Project Number 409*, Inst Archaeol Field Archaeol Unit, UCL, London

——, 1998 *The Shinewater track: an excavation of a Late Bronze Age waterlogged structure on the Willingdon Levels, near Eastbourne, East Sussex, Report on Project Number 408*, Archaeology South-East, Hassocks, West Sussex

Green, H S, 1976 The excavation of a late Neolithic settlement at Stacey Bushes, Milton Keynes, and its significance, in *Settlement and economy in the third and second millennia BC* (eds C Burgess and R Miket), BAR, **33**, 11–28, Oxford

——, 1978 Late Bronze Age wooden hafts from Llyn Fawr and Penwyllt, *Bull Board Celtic Stud*, **28**, 136–41

Green, M, 1984 *The wheel as a cult symbol in the Romano-Celtic world*, Brussels

Greig, J R A, 1981 The investigation of a medieval barrel-latrine from Worcester, *J Archaeol Sci*, **8**, 265–82

——, 1982a Past and present lime woods of Europe in *Archaeological aspects of woodland ecology* (eds M Bell and S Limbrey), Assoc Environ Archaeol Symposia, 2, BAR, **S146**, 23–55

——, 1982b Forest clearance and the barrow builders of Butterbump, Lincolnshire, *Lincolnshire Hist Archaeol*, **17**, 11–14

——, 1982c The interpretation of pollen spectra from urban archaeological deposits in *Environmental archaeology in the urban context* (eds A R Hall and H Kenwood), CBA Res Rep, **43**, London, 47–65

Grigson, C, 1982 Sex and age determination of some bones and teeth of domestic cattle: a review of the literature, in *Ageing and sexing animal bones from archaeological sites* (eds B Wilson, C Grigson, and S Payne), BAR, **109**, 7–23, Oxford

Grinsell, L V, 1961 The breaking of objects as a funerary rite, *Folklore*, **72**, 475–91

Groenman-van-Waateringe, W, and Jansma, M J, 1969 Diatom and pollen analysis of the Vlaardingen Creek: a revised interpretation, *Helinium*, **9**, 105–17

Gulliksen, S, and Scott, M, 1996 Report of the TIRI workshop, Saturday 13th August 1994, *Radiocarbon*, **37**, 820–21

Guilbert, G, 1975 Moel-y-Gaer, 1973: an area excavation on the defences, *Antiquity*, **49**, 109–17

Gurney, D A, 1980 Evidence of Bronze Age salt-production at Northey, Peterborough, *Northamptonshire Archaeol*, **15**, 1–11

Haffner, A, 1989 *Graber-Spiegel des Liebens zum Totensbruchtum der Kelten und Romer am Beispiel des Treverer-Gräberfeldes Wederath-Belginum*, Mainz

Hall, A R, Jones, A K G, and Kenward, H K, 1983 Cereal bran and human faecal remains from archaeological deposits, in *Site, environment, and economy* (ed B Proudfoot), BAR, **S173**, 85–104

Hall, D N, 1987 *The Fenland Project, no 2: Cambridgeshire survey, Peterborough to March*, E Anglian Archaeol Rep, **35**

Hall, D N, and Coles, J M, 1994 *Fenland Survey: an essay in landscape and persistence*, EH Archaeol Rep, **1**, London

Hall, M, and Gingell, C, 1974 Nottingham Hill 1972, *Antiquity*, **48**, 306–9

Halliday, T M, 1986 A note on the Flag Fen site and its recent history, in Pryor *et al* 1986, 2

Halstead, P, 1985 A study of mandibular teeth from Romano-British contexts at Maxey, in *Archaeology and environment in the Lower Welland Valley* (F M M Pryor and C A I French), E Anglian Archaeol Rep, **27**, 219–24

Halstead, P, and Cameron, E, 1992 Bone remains from Flag Fen platform and Fengate Station post alignment, *Antiquity*, **66**, 499–501

Hamilakis, Y, 1996 A footnote on the archaeology of power: animal bones from a Mycenaean chamber tomb at Galatas, North East Peloponnese, *Annu Brit Sch Athens*, **91**, 153–66

Harcourt, R A, 1974 The dog in prehistoric and early historic Britain, *J Archaeol Sci*, **1**, 151–75

Harding, A F, 1980 *The lake dwellings of Switzerland — retrospect and prospect*, Edinburgh

Harding, A F, and Lee, G E, 1987, *Henge monuments and related sites of Great Britain*, BAR, **175**, Oxford

Harman, M, 1978 Appendix 7: the animal bones, in Pryor 1978, 177–88

Hattatt, R, 1982 *Ancient and Romano-British Brooches*, Oxford

Hattatt, R, 1985 *Iron Age and Roman brooches*, Oxford

Havinga, A J, 1964 Investigation into differential corrosion susceptibility of pollen and spores, *Pollen et Spores*, **6**, 621–35

Hawkes, C F C, 1960 A scheme for the British Bronze Age (unpublished address to the Council for British Archaeology Conference, London, December 1960, quoted in Burgess, 1979, 280)

Hawkes, C F C, and Clarke, R R, 1963 Gahlstorf and Caistor on Sea; two finds of Late Bronze Age Irish gold, in *Culture and environment* (eds J Foster and L Alcock), 193–250, London

Hawkes, C F C, and Fell, C I, 1945 The early Iron Age settlement at Fengate, Peterborough, *Archaeol J*, **100**, 188–223

Hawkes, S, 1969 Finds from two Middle Bronze Age pits at Winnall, Winchester, Hampshire, *Proc Hampshire Fld Club and Archaeol Soc*, **26**, 5–18

Heal, S V E, 1981 Report on the timbers from Lingey Fen, Cambs, in Pullinger 1981, 25–7

Hedeager, L, 1992 *Iron Age societies*, Oxford

Hedges, J D, and Buckley, D G, 1981 *Springfield Cursus and the cursus problem*, Essex County Council Occas Pap, **1**, Chelmsford

Hedges, R E M, Bronk, C R, and Housley, R A, 1989 The Oxford accelerator mass spectrometry facility: technical developments in routine dating, *Archaeometry*, **31**, 99–113

Hedges, R E M, Humm, M J, Foreman, J, van Klinken, G J, and Bronk, C R, 1992 Developments in sample combustion to carbon dioxide, and the Oxford AMS carbon dioxide ion source system, *Radiocarbon*, **34**, 306–11

Hencken, H O'N, 1971 *The earliest European helmets*, American School of Prehist Res Bull, **28,** Cambridge, Mass

Herne, A, 1988 A time and a place for the Grimston bowl, in *The archaeology of context in the Neolithic and Bronze Age: recent trends* (eds J C Barrett and I A Kinnes), 9–29, Dept Prehist Archaeol, Univ Sheffield

Hey, G, 1997 Neolithic settlement at Yarnton, Oxfordshire, in *Neolithic landscapes* (ed P Topping), Oxbow Monogr, **86**, 99–112, Oxford

Hill, J D, 1997 The later prehistoric pottery, in Lucas 1997b, 35–8

Hillam, J, 1985a Theoretical and applied dendrochronology — how to make a date with a tree, in *The archaeologist and the laboratory* (ed P Phillips), CBA Res Rep, **58**, London, 17–23

——, 1985b, Recent tree-ring work in Sheffield, *Current Archaeol*, **96**, 21–6

Hillam, J, Morgan, R A, and Tyers, I, 1987 Sapwood estimates and the dating of short ring sequences, in *Applications of tree-ring studies: current research in dendrochronology and related areas* (ed R G W Ward), BAR, **S333**, 165–85, Oxford

Hodges, H, 1956 Studies in the Late Bronze Age in Ireland 2: the typology and distribution of bronze implements, *Ulster J Archaeol*, **19**, 29–56

Hodson, F R, 1990 *Hallstatt: the Ramsauer graves*, London

Hoffmann, A, 1950 *Coléoptères curculionides: 1*, Fauna de France, **52**, Paris

——, 1954 *Coléoptères curculionides: 2*, Fauna de France, **59**, Paris

——, 1958 *Coléoptères curculionides: 3*, Fauna de France, **62**, Paris

Horton, A, Lake, R D, Bisson, G, and Coppack, B C, 1974, *The geology of Peterborough*, Inst Geol Sci Rep, **73/12**, London

Houseley, R A, 1987 The carbonised plant remains from Meare 1984, in Coles 1987, 226–30

Hull, M R, and Hawkes, C F C, 1987 *Corpus of ancient brooches in Britain*, BAR, **168**, Oxford

Hunn, J R 1993, The Block Fen field system: 1992 investigations, *Fenland Res*, **8**, 10–13

——, 1994 *An interim report on the archaeology of Rectory Farm, West Deeping*, MS prepared for Lincolnshire County Council by Tempvs Reperatvm

Hurcombe, L, 1981 Iron Age and Roman rotary querns in Norfolk, Suffolk, Essex, and Hertfordshire, unpubl undergraduate dissertation, Univ Southampton

Hussen, C-M, 1983 *A rich La Tène burial at Hertford Heath, Herts*, Brit Mus Occas Pap, **44**, London

Hvass, S, and Storgaard, B, 1993 *Digging into the past — 25 years of archaeology in Denmark*, Copenhagen

Ingle, C J, 1989 Characterisation and distribution of beehive querns in eastern England, unpubl DPhil thesis, Univ Southampton

International Study Group, 1982 An inter-laboratory comparison of radiocarbon measurements in tree-rings, *Nature*, **298**, 619–23

Jackson, R, 1985 Cosmetic sets from Late Iron Age and Roman Britain, *Britannia*, **16**, 165–92

——, 1993 The function and manufacture of Romano-British cosmetic grinders: two important new finds from London, *Antiq J*, **73**, 165–9

Janssen, C R, 1969 *Alnus* as a disturbing factor in pollen diagrams, *Acta Bot Neere*, **8**, 55–8

Jacobsthal, P, 1944 *Early Celtic art*, Oxford

Jockenhövel, A, 1974 Fleischaken von den Britischen Inseln, *Archäologisches Korrespondenzblatt*, **4**, 329–38

——, 1980 Die Raisermesser in Westeuropa, *Prähistorische Bronzefunde*, **8**(3), Munich

Jones, M, 1981 The development of crop husbandry, in *The environment of man: the Iron Age to the Anglo-Saxon period* (eds M Jones and G Dimbleby), BAR, **87**, 95–127 (Oxford)

Jones, M U, and Bond, D, 1980 Later Bronze Age settlement at Mucking, Essex, in *Settlement and Society in the British Later Bronze Age* (eds J Barrett and R J Bradley), BAR, **83**, 471–82, Oxford

Jope, E M, 1961 Daggers of the Early Iron Age in Britain, *Proc Prehist Soc*, **27**, 307–44

Jørgensen, S, 1985 *Tree-Felling with original Neolithic flint axes in Draved Wood*, National Museum of Denmark

Juggins, S, n d Diatom analysis of Flag Fen, unpubl MSc thesis, Univ London

Kaye, B, and Cole-Hamilton, D, 1993 Novel approaches to the conservation of wet wood, in *A celebration of wood* (ed J Spriggs), WARP Occas Pap, **8**, 15–20

Keatinge, T, 1982 Influence of stemflow on the representation of pollen of *Tilia* in soils, *Grana*, **21**, 171–4

Keller, F, 1866 *The lake dwellings of Switzerland and other parts of Europe*, London

——, 1878 *The Lake Dwellings of Switzerland and other parts of Europe*, **1** and **2**, London

Keller, P, 1988 The evidence for ancient quern production at Folkestone: an interim note, *Kent Archaeol Rev*, **93**, 59–68

Kenny, E J A, 1933, A Roman bridge in the Fens, *Geographical J*, **52**, 434–41

Kerridge, E, 1973 *The farmers of old England*, London

Kigoshi, K, and Endo, K, 1963 Gakushuin natural radiocarbon measurements II, *Radiocarbon*, **5**, 109–17

Kigoshi, K, Suzuki, N, and Fukatsu, H, 1973 Gakushuin natural radiocarbon measurements VIII, *Radiocarbon*, **15**, 42–67

King, D, 1982 Petrology, dating, and distribution of querns and millstones: the results of research in Bedfordshire, Buckinghamshire, Hertfordshire, and Middlesex, unpubl undergraduate dissertation, Univ London)

Kloet, G S, and Hincks, W D, 1977 *A check list of British insects (revised): coleoptera and strepsiptera*, 11, pt 3, Roy Entomological Soc, London

Kratochwil, Z, 1969 Species criteria on the distal section of the tibia in *Ovis ammon f aries* L and *Capra aegagrus f hircus* L, *Acta Veterinaria (Brno)*, **38**, 483–90

Krausse, D, 1996 *Hochdorf III*, Stuttgart

Kromer, B, Ambers, J, Baillie, M G L, Damon, P E, Hesshaimer, V, Hofman, J, Jöris, O, Levin, I, Manning, S W, McCormac, F G, van der Plicht, J, Spurk, M, Stuiver, M, and Weninger, B, 1996 Report: summary of the workshop 'Aspects of high-precision radiocarbon calibration', *Radiocarbon*, **38**, 607–10

Lambrick, G H, and Robinson, M A, 1979 *Iron Age and Roman river-side settlements at Farmoor, Oxfordshire*, CBA Res Rep, **32**, London

Lane, T, 1992 Excavation and evaluation of an Iron Age and Romano-British waterlogged site at Market Deeping, *Fenland Res*, **7**, 43–7

Lawson, A, 1989 A Late Bronze Age Hoard from West Caistor, Norfolk, in *Bronze Age Hoards, some finds old and new* (eds C B Burgess and D G Coombs), BAR, **67**, 173–80, Oxford

Leeds, E T, 1922 Further discoveries of the Neolithic and Bronze Ages at Peterborough, *Antiq J*, **2**, 220–37

Legge, A J, 1981 Lingey Fen: the fauna, in Pullinger 1981, 27–33

Lejars, T, 1994 *Les fourreaux d'Epee le sanctuaire du Gournay-sur-Aronde et l'armament des Celtes de La Tène moyenne, Gournay III*, Paris

Lethbridge, T C, 1935 Investigation of the ancient causeway in the fen between Fordy and Little Thetford, Cambridgeshire, *Proc Cambridge Antiq Soc*, **35**, 8–89

Lethbridge, T C, and O Reilly, M, 1936 Archaeological Notes, *Proc Cambridge Antiq Soc*, **36**, 161–2

Lindroth, C H, 1974 *Coleoptera Carabidae*, 4, pt 2, Roy Entomological Soc, London

Longley, D, and Needham, S P, 1980 *Runnymede Bridge 1976: excavations on the site of a Late Bronze Age settlement*, Surrey Archaeol Soc Res, **6**, Guildford

Longworth, I H, 1984 *Collared urns of the Bronze Age*, Cambridge

Louwe-Kooijmans, L P, 1974 *The Rhine/Meuse delta: four studies on its prehistoric occupation and Holocene geology*, Leiden

——, 1980 Archaeology and coastal change in the Netherlands, in *Archaeology and coastal change* (ed F H Thompson), 106–33, Soc Antiqs Occ Pap (new series), **1**

——, 1993 Wetland exploitation and upland relations of prehistoric communities in the Netherlands, in *Flatlands and wetlands: current themes in East Anglian archaeology* (ed J Gardiner), E Anglian Archaeol Rep, **50**, 71–116

Lucas, A T, 1972 Prehistoric Block-Wheels from Doogarymore, Co Roscommon, and Timahoe, East Co Kildare, *J Roy Soc Antiq Ir*, **102**, 19–48

Lucas, G, 1997a *Tower Works, Fengate, Peterborough: a desktop assessment*, Cambridge Univ Archaeol Unit Rep, **197**

——, 1997b *An archaeological evaluation at the Tower Works, Fengate, Peterborough*, Cambridge Univ Archaeol Unit Rep, **206**

Lynch, F, 1970 *Prehistoric Anglesey*, 1 edn, Denbigh

——, 1991: *Prehistoric Anglesey*, 2 edn, Llangefni

MacGregor, M, 1976 *Early Celtic art in Northern Britain*, Leicester

Macphail, R I, Romans, J C C, and Robertson, L, 1987 The application of micromorphology to the understanding of Holocene soil development in the British Isles, with special reference to early cultivation, in *Soil Micromorphology* (eds N Federoff, L M Bresson, and M-A Courty), 647–56

Madsen, T, and Jensen, H J, 1982 Settlement and land use in Early Neolithic Denmark, *Analecta Praehistorica Leidensia*, **15**, 63–86

Mahany, C, 1969, Fengate, *Current Archaeol*, **17**, 156–7

Major, H, 1988 Stone, in N Brown and P Adkins (eds), Heybridge, Blackwater Sailing Club, *Trans Essex Archaeol Hist*, **19**, 243–8

——, 1995 Miscellaneous finds, in A Late Bronze Age enclosure at Broomfield, Chelmsford (M Atkinson), *Trans Essex Archaeol Hist*, **26**, 1–23

Manning, W, and Saunders, C, 197? A socketed iron axe from Maids Moreton, Buckinghamshire and a note on the type, *Antiq J*, **52**, 276–92

Margary, I D, 1973 *Roman roads in Britain*, 3 edn, London

McAlister, R A S, 1949 *The archaeology of Ireland*, London

McCormac, F G, 1992 Liquid scintillation counter characterisation, optimisation, and benzene purity correction, *Radiocarbon*, **34**, 37–45

McCormac, F G, Baillie, M G L, and Pilcher, J R, 1995 Location-dependent differences in the ^{14}C content of wood, *Radiocarbon*, **37**, 943–53

McCormac, F G, Kalin, R M, and Long, Austin, 1993 Radiocarbon dating beyond 50,000 years by liquid scintillation counting, in *Liquid scintillation spectrometry* (eds J E Noakes, F Schonhofer, and H A Polach), Tucson, 125–33

McInnes, I J, 1971 Settlements in later Neolithic Britain, in *Economy and settlement in Neolithic and Early Bronze Age Britain and Europe* (ed D D A Simpson), 113–30, Leicester

McKern, T W, 1970 Estimation of skeletal age: from puberty to about 30 years of age, in *Personal identification in mass disasters* (ed T D Stewar), 41–56, National Museum of Natural History, Washington, DC

McMaster, I, 1975 A further four years aerial survey, 1970–74, *Colchester Archaeol Group Quarterly Bull*, **18**, 12–27

McVean, D N, 1953 Biological flora of the British Isles *Alnus glutinosa* (L) Gaertn, *J Ecol*, **51**, 447–66

——, 1956 Ecology of *Alnus glutinosa* (L) Gaertn VI, postglacial history, *J Ecology*, **44**, 331–3

Meindl, R S, and Lovejoy, C O, 1985 Ectocranial suture closure: a revised method for the determination of skeletal age at death based on the lateral-anterior sutures, *American J Phys Anthrop*, **68**, 57–66

Megaw, J, and Megaw, M R, 1990 *Semper Aliquid Novum*: Celtic Dragon Pairs Reviewed, *Acta Archaeol Hungaricae*, **42**, 55–72

Mercer, R J (ed) 1981 *Farming practice in British prehistory*, Edinburgh

Miller, S H, and Skertchly, S B J, 1878 *The Fenland past and present*, London

Mohen, J-P, 1977a Broches à rôtir articulées de l'Age du Bronze, *Antiquités Nationales*, **10**, 23–32

——, 1977b *L'Age du Bronze dans la région de Paris*, Paris

Mohen, J-P, and Bailloud, G 1987 *La Vie Quotidienne: Les Fouilles du Fort Harrouard, L'Age du Bronze en France*, **4**, Paris

Monteguado, L, 1977 *Die Beile auf der Iberischen Halbinsel, Prähistorische Bronzefunde*, **9** (6), Munich

Mook, W G, 1986 Business meeting: recommendations/resolutions adopted by the Twelfth International Radiocarbon Conference, *Radiocarbon*, **28**, 799

Mook, W G, and Waterbolk, H T, 1985 *Radiocarbon dating*, European Science Foundation handbook for archaeologists, **3**, Strasbourg

Moore, J, and Jennings, D, 1992 *Reading Business Park: a Bronze Age landscape*, Oxford Archaeological Unit

Moore, P D, 1977 Ancient distribution of lime trees in Britain, *Nature*, **268**, 13–14

Moore, P D, and Webb, J A, 1978 *An illustrated guide to pollen analysis*, 1 edn, London

Moore, P D, Webb, J A, and Collinson, M E, 1991 *Pollen analysis*, 2 edn, Oxford

Morgan, RPC, 1979 *Soil Erosion* (New York)

Morrison, I, 1985 *Landscape with Lake Dwellings: the crannogs of Scotland*, Edinburgh

Moscati, S, Frey, O H, Kruta, V, Raftery, B, and Szabo, M, (eds) 1991 *The Celts*, London

Müller, F 1991 The votive deposit at Tiefenau near Berne, in Moscati *et al*, 1991

Munro, M A R, 1984 An improved algorithm for cross-dating tree-ring series, *Tree Ring Bull*, **44**, 17–27

Munro, R, 1882 *The lake-dwellings of Europe*, London

——, 1890 *Ancient Scottish lake dwellings or crannogs*, Edinburgh

——, 1912 *Palaeolithic man and the terramara settlements in Europe*, Edinburgh

Murphy, C P, 1986, *Thin section preparation of soils and sediments*, Berkhamstead

Musson, C R, 1991 *The Breiddin hillfort*, CBA Res Rep, **76**, London

Nayling, N, 1993 Caldicot Castle Lake, in *Archaeology in the Severn Estuary 1993* (ed M Bell), 77–80, Lampeter

Needham, S P, 1979 Two recent shield finds and their Continental parallels, *Proc Prehist Soc*, **45**, 111–34

——, 1980 An assemblage of Late Bronze Age metalworking debris from Dainton, Devon, *Proc Prehist Soc*, **46**, 177–216

——, 1982 *The Ambleside hoard*, British Museum Occ Pap, **39**, London

——, 1990 The Penard-Wilburton Succession: new metalwork finds from Croxton (Norfolk) and Thirsk (Yorkshire), *Antiq J*, **70**, 239–52

——, 1991 *Excavation and Salvage at Runnymede Bridge, 1978: the Late Bronze Age waterfront site*, London

——, 1996 Chronology and periodisation in the British Bronze Age, in Absolute Chronology: Archaeological Europe 2500–500 BC (ed K Randsborg), *Acta Archaeol*, **67**, 121–40

Needham, S, Bronk CR, Coombs, D, Cartwright, C, and Pettitt, P, 1997 An independent chronology for British Bronze Age metalwork: the results of the Oxford Radiocarbon Accelerator programme, *Archaeol J*, **154**, 55–107

Needham, S, and Hook, D, 1988 Lead and lead alloys in the Bronze Age — recent finds from Runnymede Bridge, in *Science and Archaeology Glasgow 1987* (eds E Slater and J Tate), BAR, **196**, 259–74, Oxford

Neve, J, 1992, An interim report on the dendrochronology of Flag Fen and Fengate, *Antiquity*, **66**, 470–75

——, 1999 *Dendrochronology of the Flag Fen Basin*, Ancient Monuments Lab Rep 58/1999, London

Noakes, J E, Kim, S M, and Stipp, J J, 1965 Chemical and counting advances in liquid scintillation age dating, in *Proceedings of the 6th international conference on radiocarbon and tritium dating* (eds E A Olsson and R M Chatters), 68–92

Northover, J P, 1980 The analysis of Welsh Bronze Age metalwork, in *A guide catalogue to the Bronze Age collections* (H N Savory), Cardiff

——, 1982 The metallurgy of the Wilburton hoards, *Oxford J Archaeol*, **1**, 69–109

——, 1983 The exploration of the long distance movement of bronze in Bronze Age and early Iron Age Europe, *Bull Inst Archaeol*, **19**, 45–72

——, 1991 Non-ferrous metalwork and metallurgy, in Sharples 1991, 156–65, London

——, forthcoming The metalwork from Caldicot Castle, in *Excavations at Caldicot Castle, Gwent 1991–3* (N Nayling)

——, 1997 The metalwork, in *Excavations at Caldicot, Gwent: Bronze Age palaeochannels in the lower Nedern valley* (N Nayling and A Caseldine), CBA Res Rep, **108**, York, 249–53

Northover, J P, and Gale, N H, 1983 The use of lead isotopes in the study of Bronze Age metallurgy, in *The Proceedings of the 22nd International Symposium on Archaeometry, Bradford, 1982* (eds A Aspinall and S E Warren), 262–72, Bradford

Northover, J P and Gillies, C 1999 Questions in the analysis of ancient tin, in *Metals in Antiquity* (eds S M M Young, A M Pollard, P Budd and R A Ixer), 78–85, BAR, **792**, Oxford

Oakeshott, E R, 1960 *The archaeology of weapons*, London

O'Connor, B, 1980 *Cross channel relations in the Later Bronze Age*, BAR, **S91**, Oxford

O'Connor, T P, 1991 Bones from 46–54 Fishergate, The Archaeology of York, **15/4**, CBA, London

Olausson, D S, 1983 *Lithic technological analysis of the thin butted axe*, Institute of Archaeology, Lund

Oliver, M, and Applin, B 1978 Excavation of an Iron Age and Romano-British settlement at Rucstalls Hill, Basingstoke, Hampshire 1972–5, *Proc Hampshire Fld Club Archaeol Soc*, **35**, 41–92

O' Neill, F E, 1981 A Neolithic and Bronze Age barrow site at Orton Longueville, Cambs, unpubl rep, Nene Valley Res Comm

Osborne, P J, 1988 A late Bronze Age insect fauna from the River Avon, Warwickshire, England: its implications for the terrestrial and fluvial environments and for climate, *J Archaeol Sci*, **15**, 715–27

Oswald, A, 1967 Excavations for the Avon/Severn Research Committee at Barford, Warwickshire, *Trans Proc Birmingham Archaeol Soc*, **83**, 1–64

Otlet, R L, 1977 Harwell radiocarbon measurements II, *Radiocarbon*, **16**, 400–23

Otlet, R L, and Slade, B S, 1974 Harwell radiocarbon measurements I, *Radiocarbon*, **16**, 178–91

Otlet, R L, and Warchal, R M, 1977 Liquid scintillation counting of low-level ^{14}C, in *Liquid Scintillation counting* (eds M A Crook and P Johnson), **5**, 210–17, London

Otlet, R L, Walker, A J, Hewson, A D, and Burleigh, R, 1980 ^{14}C interlaboratory comparison in the UK: experiment, design, preparation, and preliminary results, *Radiocarbon*, **22**, 936–46

Palmer-Brown, C, 1993 Bronze Age salt production at Tetney, *Current Archaeol* **136**, 143–5

Passmore, D G and Macklin, M, 1993, Geochemical analysis of fine-grained late Holocene alluvial deposits at Barnack Quarry, Cambridgeshire, unpubl rep, Cambridgeshire County Council Archaeol Unit

Passmore, D G and Macklin, M, in preparation

Payne, S, 1973 Kill-off patterns in sheep and goats: the mandibles from Asvan Kalé, *Anatolian Stud*, **23**, 281–303

——, 1985 Morphological distinctions between the mandibular teeth of young sheep, Ovis, and goats, Capra, *J Archaeol Sci*, **12**, 139–47

——, 1987 Reference codes for wear states in the mandibular cheek teeth of sheep and goats, *J Archaeol Sci*, **14**, 609–14

Payne, S, and Munson, P J, 1985 Ruby and how many squirrels?: the destruction of bones by dogs, in *Palaeobiological investigations: research design, methods, and data analysis* (eds N R J Fieller, D D Gilbertson, and N G A Ralph), BAR, **S266**, 31–40, Oxford

Peacock, D P S, 1987 Iron Age and Roman Quern Production at Lodsworth, West Sussex, *Antiq J*, **67**, 61–85

Pearson, G W, 1984 The development of high-precision ^{14}C measurements and its application to archaeological timescale problems, unpubl PhD thesis, Queen's Univ, Belfast

Pearson, G W, and Pilcher, J R, 1975 Belfast radiocarbon dates VIII, *Radiocarbon*, **17**, 226–38

Pearson, G W, Pilcher, J R, Baillie, M G L, Corbett, D M, and Qua, F, 1986 High-precision ^{14}C measurement of Irish oaks to show the natural ^{14}C variations from AD 1840–5210 BC, *Radiocarbon*, **28**, 911–34

Pearson, G W, and Stuiver, M, 1986 High-precision calibration of the radiocarbon time scale, 500–2500 BC, *Radiocarbon*, **28**, 839–62

Peck, R M, 1973 Pollen budget studies in a small Yorkshire catchment, in *Quat Plant Ecol* (eds H J B Birks and R G West), 43–60, Oxford

Perini, R, 1984 *Scavi archeologici nella zona palafitticola di Fiave-Carera*, Trento

Phillips, C W 1970, *The Fenland in Roman times*, Roy Geograph Soc Res Ser, **5**, London

Piggott, S, 1965 *Ancient Europe*, Edinburgh

——, 1983 *The earliest wheeled transport*, London

Polach, H A, 1972 Cross checking of the NBS oxalic acid and secondary laboratory radiocarbon dating standards, in Proceedings of the 8th international conference on radiocarbon dating (eds T A Rafter and T Grant-Taylor), 688–717, Wellington

Pollard, J, 1998a Prehistoric pottery, in Gibson 1998, 20–2.

——, 1998b *Excavations at Over — Late Neolithic occupation (sites 3 and 4)*, Cambridge Univ Archaeol Unit Rep, **281**

Powell, T G E, 1948 Late Bronze Age hoard from Welby, Leicestershire, *Archaeol J*, **105**, 27–40

Primas, M, 1984 Bronzezeitlicher Schmuck au Zinn, *Helvetia Archaeol* **57–60**, 33–42

——, 1985: Tin objects in Bronze Age Europe, in *Studi di Paletnologia in onore di Salvatore M Puglisi*, Roma, 554–62

Proudfoot, V, 1955 The Downpatrick gold find, *Archaeological research publication (Northern Ireland)*, **3**, Belfast

Prummel, W, 1987a Atlas for identification of foetal skeletal elements of cattle, horse, sheep, and pig, 1, *Archaeozoologia*, **1** (1), 23–30

——, 1987b Atlas for identification of foetal skeletal elements of cattle, horse, sheep and pig, 2, *Archaeozoologia*, **1** (2), 11–42

Pryor, F M M, 1974 *Excavation at Fengate, Peterborough, England: the first report*, Royal Ontario Mus Archaeol Monogr, **3**, Toronto

——, 1978 *Excavation at Fengate, Peterbrough, England: the second report*, Roy Ontario Mus Archaeol Monogr, **5**, Toronto

—— 1980 *Excavation at Fengate, Peterbrough, England: the third report*, Northants Archaeol Soc Archaeol Monogr, **1**, Royal Ontario Museum Archaeol Monogr, **6**, Northampton and Toronto

——, 1982 *Fengate*, Shire Archaeology, Princes Risborough

——, 1983 Gone, but still respected: some evidence for Iron Age house platforms in eastern England, *Oxford J Archaeol*, **2**, 189–98

——, 1984a *Excavation at Fengate, Peterborough, England: the fourth report*, Northants Archaeol Soc Archaeol Monogr 2, Royal Ontario Mus Archaeol Monogr, 7, Northampton and Toronto

——, 1984b Personalities of Britain: two examples of long-term regional contrast, *Scott Archaeol Rev*, **3**, 8–15

——, 1986 Etton 1986: Neolithic metamorphoses, *Antiquity*, **61**, 78–80

——, 1988 Earlier Neolithic organised landscapes and ceremonial in lowland Britain, in *The Archaeology of context in the Neolithic and Bronze Age: recent trends* (eds J Barrett and I A Kinnes), 63–72, Sheffield

——, 1989 Look what we've found — a case-study in public archaeology, *Antiquity*, **63**, 51–6

——, 1990 The many faces of Flag Fen, *Scott Archaeol Rev*, 7, 114–24

——, 1991 *The English Heritage book of Flag Fen: prehistoric Fenland centre*, London

——, 1992a Introduction to current research at Flag Fen, Peterborough, *Antiquity*, **66**, 439–57

——, 1992b Discussion: the Fengate/Northey landscape, *Antiquity*, **66**, 519–31

——, 1993 Excavations at Site 11, Fengate, Peterborough, 1969, in Simpson *et al* 1993, 127–40

——, 1996 Sheep, stockyards, and field systems: Bronze Age livestock populations in the Fenlands of eastern England, *Antiquity*, **70**, 313–24

——, 1997a, *Archaeological evaluation at Murden's former depot, Fengate, Peterborough, Cambridgeshire*, Fenland Archaeol Trust Rep, **97/1**, Peterborough

——, 1997b *Peterborough East: a guide to curation in an area of outstanding archaeological importance*, Fenland Archaeol Trust, Peterborough

——, 1998a *Etton: excavations at a Neolithic causewayed enclosure near Maxey Cambridgeshire, 1982–87*, EH Archaeol Rep, **18**, London

——, 1998b *Farmers in prehistoric Britain*, Chalford

——, 1998c Welland Bank Quarry, South Lincolnshire — a tale of a sausage sandwich, *Current Archaeol*, **160**, 139–45

Pryor, F M M, and French, C A I, 1985 *The Fenland Project, number 1: archaeology and environment in the Lower Welland Valley*, E Anglian Archaeol Rep, **27**

Pryor, F M M, French, C A I, and Taylor, M, 1986 Flag Fen, Fengate, Peterborough I: discovery, reconnaissance, and initial excavation, *Proc Prehist Soc*, **52**, 1–24

Pryor, F M M, and Taylor, M, 1990 Bronze Age building techniques at Flag Fen, Peterborough, England, *World Archaeol*, **21**, 425–34

Pryor, F M M, and Taylor, M, 1992 Flag Fen, Fengate, Peterborough II: further definition, techniques and assessment, in *The wetland revolution in prehistory* (ed B Coles), 37–46, WARP/Prehist Soc, Exeter

——, 1993 Use, re-use or pre-use?: aspects of the interpretation of ancient wood, in *A spirit of enquiry — essays for Ted Wright* (eds J Coles, V Fenwick, and G Hutchinson), 81–6, WARP, Exeter

Pryor, F M M, and Trimble, D, 1999 *Archaeological investigations at the premises of T K Packaging Ltd, Fengate*, Soke Archaeol Services Rep, **99/3**, Peterborough

Pullinger, J, 1981 The M11 by-pass: three sites near Cambridge Part 2, Lingey Fen, Haslingfield, *Proc Cambridge Antiq Soc*, **71**, 25–40

Rackham, O, 1976 *Trees and woodland in the British landscape*, London

——, 1980 *Ancient woodland: its history, vegetation, and uses in England*, London

——, 1989 *The last forest*, London

Raftery, B, 1982 Two recently discovered shields from the Shannon Basin, *J Roy Soc Antiq Ir*, **112**, 5–17

——, 1983 *A catalogue of Irish Iron Age antiquities*, Verroffentlichung des Vorgeschichten Seminars Marburg Sonderband, **1**, Marburg

——, 1990 *Trackways through time*, Dublin

——, 1992 Recent developments in Irish wetland research, in *The wetland revolution in prehistory* (ed B Coles), WARP Occas Pap, **6**, 37–46, Exeter

——, 1994 *Pagan Celtic Ireland*, London

Rainbow, H, 1928 Socketed and looped iron axes of the British Isles, *Archaeol J*, **85**, 170–75

R C H M, 1969 *Peterborough New Town: a survey of the antiquities in the areas of development*, Roy Comm Hist Monuments Engl, London

Ritchie, A, 1983 Excavation of a Neolithic farmstead at Knap Howar, Papa Westray Orkney, *Proc Soc Antiq Scotl*, **113**, 40–121

Robbiola, L, and Fiaud, C, 1992 Apport de l'analyse statistique des produits de corrosion à la comprehension des processus de degradation des bronzes archéologiques, *Revue d'Archaeométrie*, **16**, 109–19

Robinson, M A, 1981 The Iron Age to early Saxon environment of the Upper Thames Terraces, in *The environment of man: the Iron Age to the Anglo-Saxon period* (eds M Jones and G Dimbleby), BAR, **87**, 251–86, Oxford

——, 1983 Arable/pastoral ratios from insects?, in *Integrating the subsistence economy* (ed M Jones), BAR, **S181**, 19–55, Oxford

——, 1991 The Neolithic and late Bronze Age insect assemblages, in Needham 1991, 277–326, London

——, 1992 The Coleoptera from Flag Fen, *Antiquity*, **66**, 467–9

Rohl, B M, 1995 Application of lead isotope analysis to Bronze Age metalwork from England and Wales, unpubl DPhil thesis, Univ Oxford

Rohl, B M, and Needham, S P, 1998 The circulation of metal in the British Bronze Age: the application of lead isotope analysis, Brit Mus Occas Pap, **102**, London

Ross, A, 1967 *Pagan Celtic Britain*, London

Rowlands, M J, 1976 *The organisation of Middle Bronze Age metalworking*, **1** and **2**, BAR, **31**, Oxford

Rozanski, K, Stichler, W, Gonfiantini, R, Scott, E M, Beukens, R P, Kromer, B, and van der Plicht, J, 1992 The IAEA ¹⁴C intercomparison exercise 1990, *Radiocarbon*, **34**, 506–19

Ruiz-Galvez Priego, M, 1984 La peninsula Iberica y sus relaciones con el circulo cultural Atlantico, unpubl PhD thesis, Univ Compultense de Madrid

——, 1995 *Rites de paso y puntos de paso: la Rio de Huelva en al mundo del Bronce Final Europeo*, Madrid

Rychner, V, 1979 L'âge du bronze final à Auvernier: typologie et chronologie des anciennes collections conservées en Suisse, 1–2, *Bibliothèque Historique Vaudoise, Cahiers d'Archéol Romande*, **15–16**, Lausanne

——, 1987 Auvernier 1968–75: le mobilier métallique du Bronze final: formes et techniques, *Bibliothèque Historique Vaudoise, Cahiers d'Archéol Romande*, **37**, *Auvernier*, **6**, Lausanne

——, 1990 Recherches sur les cuivres et les alliages du l'âge du Bronze moyen et final Suisse, *Prähistorische Zeitschrift*, **65** (2), 204–17

Rychner, V and Kläntschi, N, 1995 Arsenic, antimoine et nickel, *Bibliothèque Historique Vaudois, Cahiers d'Archéol Romande*, **63**

Rychner-Faraggi, A M, 1993 Hauterive-Champréveyres, **9**, métal et parure au Bronze Final, *Archéol Neuchâteloise*, **17**, Musée Cantonal de Neuchâtel, **45**, Neuchâtel

Ryder, M, 1983 *Sheep and man*, London

Salisbury, C, 1995 An 8th-century Mercian bridge over the Trent at Cromwell, Nottinghamshire, England, *Antiquity*, **69**, 1015–18

Sands, R, 1994 The recording and archaeological potential of toolmarks on prehistoric worked wood, unpubl PhD thesis, Edinburgh Univ

——, 1997 *Prehistoric woodworking*, Wood in Archaeology, **1**, London

Savory, H, 1958 The Late Bronze Age in Wales, *Archaeol Cambrensis*, **107**, 3–63

——, 1980 *Guide catalogue of the Bronze Age collections*, National Museum of Wales, Cardiff

Scaife, R G, 1980 Late-Devensian and Flandrian palaeoecological studies in the Isle of Wight, unpubl PhD thesis, Univ London

——, 1986 Pollen in human palaeofaeces, and a preliminary investigation of the stomach and gut contents of Lindow man, in Stead *et al* 1986, 126–35

——, 1987 The Late-Devensian and Flandrian vegetation of the Isle of Wight, in *Wessex and the Isle of Wight, Field Guide*, (ed K E Barbe), 156–80, Cambridge

——, 1988 The elm decline in the pollen record of south-east England and its relationship to early agriculture, in *Archaeology and the flora of the British Isles* (ed M Jones), Oxford Univ Comm Archaeol Monogr, **14**

——, 1992 Flag Fen: the vegetation environment, *Antiquity*, **66**, 462–6

——, 1993a Pollen analysis at Crowtree Farm, in Franch and Pryor 1993, 48–51

——, 1993b Pollen analysis at Oakhurst Farm, in French and Pryor 1993, 54–7

——, 1994 The pollen analysis, in French 1994, 81–8

——, 1998a Assessment of soil pollen, in *An archaeological investigation at the proposed materials reprocessing facility, Third Drove, Fengate, Peterborough, Cambridgeshire* (K Gdaniec), Cambridge Univ Archaeol Unit, interim rep, 5–8

——, 1998b Charred plant remains, in *Land off Third Drove, Fengate, Peterborough — an archaeological evaluation* (R Cuttler), Birmingham Univ Field Archaeol Unit Rep, **515**, 27–8

Scaife, R G, and Burrin, P J, 1992 Archaeological inferences from alluvial sediments: some findings from southern England, in *Alluvial archaeology in Britain* (eds S Needham and M Macklin), Oxbow Monogr, **27**, 75–91, Oxford

Scott, E M, Long, A, and Kra, R S (eds), 1990 Proceedings of the international workshop on intercomparison of radiocarbon laboratories, *Radiocarbon*, **32**, 253–397

Scott, B G, 1990 *Early Irish ironworking*, Belfast

Schlichtherle, H, and Wahlster, B 1986 *Archäologie in Seen und Mooren*, Stuttgart

Schmidt, P, and Burgess, C B, 1981 *The axes of Scotland and northern England, Prähistorische Bronzefunde*, **9** (7), Munich

Sharples, N M, 1991 *Maiden Castle: excavation and field survey 1985-6*, EH Archaeol Rep, **19**, London

Shennan, I, 1982 Problems of correlating Flandrian sea-level changes and climate, in *Climate change in later prehistory* (ed A F Harding), 52–67, Edinburgh

Silver, I, 1969 The ageing of domestic animals: a survey of progress and research, in *Science in archaeology* (eds D Brothwell and E Higgs), 2 edn, 283–302, London

Silvester, R J, 1991 *The Fenland Project, Number 4: Norfolk Survey, the Wissey Embayment and Fen Causeway*, E Anglian Archaeol Rep, **52**, Dereham

Simpson, W G, 1981 Excavations at Field OS 124, Maxey, Cambridgeshire, *Northants Archaeol*, **16**, 34–64

Simpson, W G, Gurney, D A, Neve, J, and Pryor, F M M, 1993 *The Fenland Project No 7: excavations in Peterborough and the lower Welland Valley, 1960–69*, E Anglian Archaeol Rep, **61**, Norwich

Smith, A G, 1958 The context of some Late Bronze Age and Early Iron Age remains from Lincolnshire, *Proc Prehist Soc* **24**, 78–84

——, 1970 The influence of Mesolithic and Neolithic man on British vegetation: a discussion, in *Studies in the vegetational history of the British Isles*, (eds D Walker and R G West), 81–96, Cambridge

——, 1981 The Neolithic, in *The environment in British prehistory* (I G Simmons and M Tooley), 125–209, London

Smith, A G, Pearson, G W, and Pilcher, J R, 1970a Belfast radiocarbon dates I, *Radiocarbon*, **12**, 285–90

——, 1970b Belfast radiocarbon dates II, *Radiocarbon*, **12**, 291–7

——, 1971 Belfast radiocarbon dates III, *Radiocarbon*, **13**, 103–25

Smith I F, 1956 The decorative art of Neolithic ceramics in south east England and its relations, unpubl PhD thesis, Univ London

Smith, I F, 1965 *Windmill Hill and Avebury: excavations by Alexander Keiller 1925–1939*, Oxford

Smith, M, 1959 Some Somerset hoards and their place in the Bronze Age of southern Britain, *Proc Prehist Soc*, **25**, 144–87

Smith, R A, 1911 Lake dwellings in Holderness, Yorks, *Archaeologia*, **62**, 593–610

Stace, C, 1991 *New flora of the British Isles*, Cambridge

Stanford, S C, 1974 *Croft Ambrey*, Leominster

Stead, I, 1984a Celtic Dragon Pairs from the River Thames, *Antiq J*, **64**, 269–79

——, 1984b Iron Age metalwork from Orton Meadows, *Durobrivae*, **9**, 6–7

——, 1991 *Iron Age cemeteries in Eastern Yorkshire*, EH Archaeol Rep, **22**, London

Stead, I, Bourke, J, and Brothwell, D, 1986 *Lindow Man: the body in the bog*, London

Stead, I M, and Rigby, V, 1989 *Baldock: the excavation of a Roman and pre-Roman settlement: 1968–72*, Britannia Monogr Ser, 7

——, 1989 *Verulamium, The King Harry Lane site*, EH Archaeol Rep, **12**, London

Stenhouse, M J, and Baxter, M S, 1983 ¹⁴C dating reproducibility: evidence from routine dating of archaeological samples, *PACT*, **8**, 147–61

Stuiver, M, and Kra, R S, 1986 Editorial comment, *Radiocarbon*, **28** (2B), ii

Stuiver, M, and Pearson, G W, 1986 High-precision calibration of the radiocarbon time scale, AD 1950–500 BC, *Radiocarbon*, **28**, 805–38

——, 1993 Calibration 1993, *Radiocarbon*, **35**, 1–244

Stuiver, M, and Polach, H A, 1977 Discussion: reporting of ¹⁴C data, *Radiocarbon*, **19**, 355–63

Stuiver, M, and Reimer, P J, 1986 A computer program for radiocarbon age calculation, *Radiocarbon*, **28**, 1022–30

——, 1993 Extended ¹⁴C data base and revised CALIB 3 0 ¹⁴C age calibration program, *Radiocarbon*, **35**, 215–30

Stuiver, M, Reimer, P J, Bard, E, Burr, G S, Hughen, K A, Kromer, B, McCormac, G, van der Plicht, J, and Spurk, M, 1998 INTCAL98 radiocarbon age calibration, 24000–0 cal BP, *Radiocarbon*, **40**, 1041–84

Tauber, H, 1965 Differential pollen dispersion and the interpretation of pollen diagrams, *Danmarks Geologiske Undersogelse*, 2 ser, **89**, 1–69

——, 1967 Differential pollen dispersion and filtration, *Proc Congr Int Ass Quat Res*, **7**, 131–4

Taylor, J, 1997 Space and place: some thoughts on Iron Age and Romano-British landscapes, in *Reconstructing Iron Age societies* (eds A Gwilt and C Haselgrove), Oxbow Monogr, **71**, 193–204, Oxford

Taylor, M, 1984 An Early Iron Age stake with dovetail housing joint from F1551, Cat's Water subsite, Fengate, in Pryor 1984a, 175–6

——, 1988 Some preliminary thoughts on coppicing and pollarding at Etton, in *The exploitation of Wetlands* (eds P Murphy and C A I French), BAR, **186**, 93–100, Oxford

——, 1992 Flag Fen: the wood, *Antiquity*, **66**, 476–98

——, 1998 Wood and bark from the enclosure ditch, in Pryor 1998a, 115–59

Thomas, J, 1991 *Rethinking the Neolithic*, Cambridge

Thompson, N, 1971 Archaeological research in the Pewsey Vale, *Wiltshire Archaeol Natur Hist Mag*, **66**, 58–75

Thorpe, R, Sharman, J, and Clay, P, 1994 An Iron Age and Romano-British enclosure system at Normanton-le-Heath, Leicestershire, *Leicestershire Archaeol and Hist Soc/Trans*, **68**, 45–63

Trotter, M, 1970 Estimation of stature from intact long limb bones, in *Personal identification in mass disasters* (ed T D Stewart), 71–83, National Museum of Natural History, Washington DC

Turner, J, 1962 The *Tilia* decline: an anthropogenic interpretation, *New Phytol*, **61**, 328–41

Ubelaker, D H, 1989 *Human skeletal remains: excavation, analysis, interpretation*, Manuals on Archaeology, **2**, Taraxacum, Washington DC

van der Plicht, J, 1993 The Gröningen radiocarbon calibration program, *Radiocarbon*, **35**, 231–7

Vaughan, T, and Trevarthen, M, 1998 *Land off Vicarage Farm Road Peterborough, Cambridgeshire*, Hertfordshire Archaeol Trust Rep, **322**, Hertford

Vishnu-Mittre, 1971 Fossil pollen of *Tilia* from East Anglian Fenland, *New Phytol*, **70**, 693–7

von den Driesch, A, 1976 *A guide to the measurement of animal bones from archaeological sites*, Peabody Mus Bull, **1**, Harvard

Vouga, P, 1923 *La Tène: monographie de la station publiée au nom de la Commission des fouilles de La Tène*, Leipzig

Wainwright, G J, and Davies, S, 1995 *Balksbury Camp, Hampshire Excavations 1973 and 1981*, EH Archaeol Rep, **4**, London

Wainwright, G J, and Longworth, I H, 1971 *Durrington Walls: excavations 1966–68*, Rep Res Comm Soc Antiq, **29**, London

Wainwright, G J, and Smith, K, 1980 The Shaugh Moor project: second report – the enclosure, *Proc Prehist Soc*, **46**, 65–122

Wait, G 1985 *Ritual and Religion in Iron Age Britain*, BAR, **149**, Oxford

Waller, M, 1993 Flandrian vegetational history of south-eastern England pollen data from Pannel Bridge, East Sussex, *New Phytol*, **124**, 345–69

——, 1994a *The Fenland Project, number 9: Flandrian environmental change in Fenland*, E Anglian Archaeol Rep, **70**, Cambridge

——, 1994b The *Tilia* decline and paludification in southern England, *The Holocene* **4**, 430–34

Ward, G K, and Wilson, S R, 1978 Procedures for comparing and combining radiocarbon age determinations: a critique, *Archaeometry*, **20**, 19–31

Wheeler, R E M, 1943 *Maiden Castle, Dorset*, Rep Res Comm Soc Antiq, **12**, London

Wheeler, R E M, and Wheeler, T, 1932 *Report on the excavation of the prehistoric, Roman, and post-Roman site in Lydney, Gloucestershire*, Rep Res Comm Soc Antiq, **9**, London

Whimster, R, 1977 Harlyn Bay reconsidered: the excavations of 1900–05 in the light of recent work, *Cornish Archaeol*, **16**, 16–88

White, D A, 1982 *The Bronze Age cremation cemeteries at Simons Ground, Dorset*, Dorset Nat Hist Archaeol Soc Monogr, **3**

Wild, J P, 1974 Roman settlement in the lower Nene valley, *Archaeol J*, **131**, 140–70

Williams, D F, 1980 Second millennium BC pottery from the Newark Road subsite, Fengate, Peterborough, in Pryor 1980, 87–106

——, 1992 *Neolithic and Bronze Age saddle querns and rubbers from Goldington, Bedford, Bedfordshire*, Ancient Monuments Laboratory Rep, **35/92** (Interim Specialist Rep)

Wilson, G, 1984, A report on the plant macrosossils from Fengate, in Pryor 1984a, microfiche 242–4

Wood-Martin, W G, 1886 *The lake dwellings of Ireland* (facsimile reprint 1983), Dublin

Index

Note: Page numbers in *italics* refer to illustrations. Page numbers in **bold** indicate a main reference to the subject. Numbers in square brackets denote catalogue numbers. There is no entry for 'Bronze Age' as this is taken to be the main subject of the report. The fold-out figures have not been included in the index.

EIA   Early Iron Age
EN   Early Neolithic
LBA   Late Bronze Age
LIA   Late Iron Age
PS   Power Station

Abbott, George Wyman 6, 7–9, 10, 36, 411
Acer campestre (field maple) 158, *159*
aerial photography 9, 37
    Depot (1992) 18–19, *18*, 22
    Northey 6, 7, 75, 80
agriculture (pastoralism, arable farming) 378, 400, 402, 415–20, 429
    Flag Fen 351, 357, 367, 368, 369, 373, 374, 381
    Neolithic 400
    Late Bronze Age/Iron Age 368, 403, 429
    Iron Age 42, 50, 413, 414
    medieval 374
    see also animal bone; cereals; droveways; field systems; livestock; stockyards
alder (*Alnus*) 351, 352, 356, 357, *360*, 361–2, *365*, 366, 367, 369, *372*, 373, 374, *376*, 378, **379**, 380, 381, 388, 400, 402, 421
    beavers 202, 203
    drying out 169, *169*
    felling? 378, 379, 380
    joints 204, 209–10, 211, 212
    posts 88, **96**, 157, 158, 160
    rafters(?) 211
    tree-ring study 248
    wheel 213
    see also portal; Row 1; Row 2; Row 3; Row 4; Rows 2/3 pathway
alder (willow) carr woodland 361, 373, 378, 380, 401, 402, 403
alluviation
    Iron Age 30, 38, 398, 402
    Late Iron Age/Romano-British 357, *357*, 362, 366, 368, 369, 373, 378, 379, 380, 381
    Roman 30, 41, 42, 43, 403
    Northey 357, 361, 367
    Power Station *53*, 56, 57, 58, 369, 373, 374, 402, 403
    radiocarbon dating 395, 397, 398
    see also flooding
Alnus see alder
ancestors 430
animal bone **330–50**
    badger 330, 343, 345
    beaver 202, 330, 343, 345
    cattle (cow) 26, 330, 332–3, 336–8, 343, 344–5, 346, 347–8, 349, 403, 428
    dog and skeletons 111, 112, 162, 237, 330, 334–5, 341–2, 344–50 *passim*, 423, 424, 433, 434
      round post 70, *70*, 428

fox 330, 343, 345
hare 330, 335, 344, 345
horse 330, 334, 340, 344–5, 348, 349
pig 26, 330, 334, 340–1, 344–5, 347
polecat 330, 343, 345
red deer 330, 335, 342, 344–5, 348, 349, 432, 433
sheep 26, 330, 331, 333–4, 338–40, 343, 344–5, 347, 348, 349, 403, 428, 431
wild boar 330
wolf(?) 330, 349
and ritual 428, 430
sites
    Cat's Water (1997) 49
    Depot site (1997) 29
    Flag Fen platform 139, 149, 330, 331, 332–5, 343–50, 428
    Fordey/Little Thetford 'causeway' 432
    Lingey Fen 433
    Northey 77
    Power Station post alignment 254, 330, 331, 336–50, 428
    Storey's Bar Road 26
    Tower Works 34, 35
animal dung 375
animals, burrowing damage by 95, 168
animal trampling 45, 61, 240
antler
    hilt fixings *see* daggers [54/54a]
    picks or hooks 91
aquatic macrophytes 366, 378, 380
ard marks, Iron Age 24, 414
Area 1: 81, *83*, 157, 165, 240
Area 2: **81**, *83*, *84*, **85**, 165, 253
    tree-ring study 240, 243
Area 3: *84*, **85–6**, 240, 253
Area 4: 85, 86, *86*, 165
    tree-rings 240, 243
Area 5: **87**, *87*, 88, 165
    revetment 87, *87*
    tree-rings 240
Area 6: **95–166**
    excavation of post rows 152–4
    general excavation procedures 93
    grid references 9
    isometric reconstruction of post alignment *422*
    levels 93–4, **96–152**
    methods and areas excavated 91
    post-depositional effects 154–5
    vertical section 157
Area 6A: 81, *91*, 93, **95**, 96
    entranceway *see* Row 5
    hardstanding(?) 121
    hollowed log vessel 226–7, *228*
    knife/dagger [52] 263, *264*, 287, 301
    Level 1: 97–100
    Level 2: 95, 112
    Level 3: 95, 121–2
    Levels 4–5: 95, 135
    Levels 5–7: 95, 140, 142
    perimeter revetment 97–100, 165
    post alignment 97
    pottery 250, *251*
    relict stream 69, 121

toolmarks 194–202, *194–5*
    blade widths 197–8, *198–9*
tree-ring study 165, 241, 243, 246, 247
wattle 'cavity wall' revetment 97, 112, 122, **247**
wood 167, 171–5
    joints 204, 206, 208, 210, 211
wood-free zones 112, 162
yoke 218
see also bracelets, shale; scoop
Area 6B: 93, **95**, 96
    box-like structure 112, 121
    chape, wooden 228
    fibula, Iron Age 271, *273*, 293–4
    Level 1: *98*, *99*, 100–4
    Level 2: 112–21
    Level 3: 122–31, 254
    Level 4/5: 135–40
    Level 5/6: 142–52
    north-east quadrant 100–1, *102*, 113, 116, *117*, 122, *127*, 135–6, *136*, 144–5, *148*, 149
    north-west quadrant 104, *108*, *120*, 121, *121*, 126, *130*, 131, 139–40, *141*, 152, *156*
    pins 274, *275*, 276, 289, 293
    plans 93
    pool 112
    pottery 101, 103, 104, 139, 149, 162, 250, *251*, 254
      complete jar [6] below timber 123, 250, *251*, 254
    south-east quadrant 100–1, *104*, 116–17, *118*, 120–1, 122–3, 125, *128*, 136, *137*, 139, 149, *150*
    south-west quadrant 101, 103–4, *103*, *105*, *106*, *119*, 121, 125–6, *129*, *138*, 139, *139*, 149, *151*, 152
    spearheads and shafts 225, 226, *262*, 263, 286
    toolmarks 194–202, *195–7*
    trample 121
    tree-ring study 241, 243
    wattlework structure 167
    wood 167
      beaver-chewed 202, *202*
      blade widths 197–8, *198–9*
      joints 203–4, *205*, 206, 208, 209–10, 211–12
    wooden artefacts 214, 216, 218, 222, 228
    see also axe hafts; bracelets, shale; chapes [38], [42]; flesh hook
Area 6C: 93, **95**, 167
    tree-rings 241, 245
    wheel 213
    wood-free zone 112, 162
Area 6D: 93, **95**, 103, 424
    dog bones 111, 112, 162
    entranceway and portal 96, 104, 111, 112
    handle 225
    Level 2: 95, *110*
    'poolside area' (Level 1) 95, 96, **104**, *109*, 111–12, **162**, 164
    sand and gravel 111
    snail shells 104, 111
    tree-rings 241, 245
    walkways and pathways 111–12, 164

wood 167, 204, 206, 210, 211
wood-free zone 112, 162
see also scabbard plate [273]
Area 7: **88**, *89*, 240
Area 8: **88**, **90–1**, *90*, 96, 97, 157, 165,
   240, 424
   antler pick or hook 91
   relict stream with timbers over 91, 162
   spearhead and wood [51] 90, *262*, 263
Areas 9 and 10: 91
Areas 11 and 12: 91
armlet, shale with lead inlay 322
arrowheads, flint 318, *319*, 321, *321*
   Storey's Bar Road 25
artefacts, deposition 427–9
artificial lakes *see* lakes
ash (*Fraxinus*) 158, 212, *353*, 356, 357,
   358, 361, 362, *363*, 366, 367, 369,
   370, 373, 374, *376*, 378, 381, 421
   dowels (wheel) 213
   drying out 169
   ferrule shafts 225–6
   reduction of 203
   shears box 227–8
aurochs skulls 32, 407
awls 265, *266*, 267, 287–8, 297, *299*, 301,
   427
   bone-handled iron [272] *281*, 282, 295
   Newark Road 428
axe hafts, wooden 219–22
   (B2737) below quern [24] 149, 152,
      155, 220, 221
   Power Station 219–20, *220*, *224*
   see also axes [60]
axe marks *see under* axes
axes 182
   Neolithic, stone (PS) 321–2, *321*, 408,
      429
   Bronze Age *264*, 265, *266*, 287, *296*,
      428–9
   Iron Age, socketed iron [269] 29, *281*,
      282, 292, 309, *309*, 428
   Roman 292
   dimensions and blade curvatures
      194–202
   North British, profiles 194
   petrology 321–2
   socketed axe and haft [60] (PS) 219–20,
      220, 265, *266*, 428
      radiocarbon dating 265, 390, 395
   stone 169, 182–4, 186, 320, 321, *321*
      smashing of 429
   toolmarks/axe marks 53, 154, **194–202**,
      433
   for woodworking 203, 206
      bronze 169, 182, 184, 186
      stone 169, 182–4, 186
   see also axe hafts
axle, wooden, for wheel 216, *217*, 218,
   218, 427

Barford (Warwicks), querns 327
Bargeroosterveld (Holland) 434
Barleycroft Farm (Cambs) *2*, 36, 409,
   412–13
Barnack 403
barrows 407–8, 412
   Mucking 419
   Northey, Neolithic 76, 77, *78*, *79*, 80,
      321, *321*, 412
   querns from 327

ritual (Neolithic and Bronze Age) 425
Storey's Bar Road 23, 25, 26, 408
   see also ring-ditches
bars, tin 272, *273*, 291
beads 301, 306
   tin 270–1, *270*, 291
   white metal 269, *270*, 291
Beaker period 381
   awls 287
   fire-cracked stones (PS) 71, 72
   flints (PS) 70
   pits as boundary (PS) 72
   pits (PS Area 1) *54*, 70–2, *71*, *73*
   roundhouse/settlement (Site 11) 9, 71
   settlement 410
   see also pottery
beavers 202–3; *see also* animal bone
bedding, human/animal 375
beech (*Fagus*) *353*, 356, 357, *358*, 361,
   362, *363*, 367, 368, 369, *370*, 373,
   374, *376*, 378, 381
beetles *see* Coleoptera
Betula see birch
Billingborough *2*
binding strip (copper-alloy ring), Late
   Iron Age/Romano-British 269, *270*,
   294, 301
birch (*Betula*) 352, *353*, 356, *358*, 361, 362,
   363, 367, 369, *370*, 374, *376*, 394
bird bone 403
Birmingham University Field Archaeology
   Unit 6, 30, 32, 50
Blackmoor hoard (Hants) 283, 288, 291, 310
blades
   flint, Neolithic 23, 429
   metal, widths and curvature of axe
      blades 197–202
Block Fen, Mepal 418
blocking posts 101
bone *see* animal bone; bird bone; bone
   (unspecified); fish bone; human
   remains
bone and antler working 344
bone (unspecified), Beaker period 70
Boongate Roundabout *5*, 6, **32–3**
   buried soil 33
   flint (inc blade) 33
   Neolithic settlement (postholes and pits)
      33, *33*, 49, 407
   palaeosol 33
   pottery, pre-Iron Age(?) 33
Borough Fen
   barrows 408
   droveway 72
   ring-fort, Iron Age 9
boundaries
   Beaker pits as(?) 72
   ditch (17) 50
   droveways and ditches as 1, 47, 60, 72,
      409, 416, 418
   'boundary' deposits 423–5; *see also* querns
      [26–8]
box *see* shears and box
box-like structure (Level 2, Area 6B) 112,
   114, 121, 133, *159*
bracelets
   bronze *270*, 271, 290
   Covesea 290
   shale *279*, 280, 322, *322*, 427, 428
bracket fungus 167
brackish water diatoms 403

The Breiddin, mallets 222
'bridge', over Row 1 gap 126; *see also*
   brushwood
briquetage 412, 414
brooches 431
   from shrines 295
   plate, Late Iron Age/Romano British 29,
      271, *273*, 294, 301, 306, 428, 431
brushwood 121, 160, 369
   bridge/ford over ditch 69–70, *69*, *70*
buildings and structures
   Neolithic 'house' (Padholme Road) *see*
      mortuary structures
   post-built rectangular, LBA/EIA, Tower
      Works 18, 33, 35, *35*, 36, 411
   rectangular structures 412–13
   see Cat's Water (1990); clamp; Depot
      (1992); farmsteads; mortuary struc-
      tures; Newark Road; roundhouses;
      stackstands
burials, Earlier Neolithic, multiple 50, *406*,
   407; *see also* cremations; inhumations
buried soils 382, 383
   Boongate Roundabout 33
   Cat's Water (1990) 39–43
   Global Doors site 37
   Newark Road 37
   Power Station 53–6, 57–8, 70, 446–7
   Third Drove 50
   Tower Works site 33, 34–5, 36
Burwell (Cambs), beaver tooth 202
buttons *266*, 268, 290–1

Caldicot Castle Lake (Monmouthshire)
   causeway/trackway 434
   ladles 226
Cambridge University Archaeological
   Unit 6, 33, 47, 411, 412
Cannabis sativa see hemp
Carp's Tongue 255, 258, 260, 261, 263,
   265, 267, 268, 271, 276, 278, 287,
   288, 289, 290, 291, 301, 306
Cat's Water *5*, 6, 20, 27
   flint 318, *319*
   Early Iron Age stake with dovetail joint
      213–14
   Iron Age settlement (farmstead) 46, 72,
      403, 410, 413, 414, 421, 432
      droveway to (Iron Age and Roman) 414
      pottery 251, 252, 253, 254, 411–12
      wattle bundles as ford(?) 70
      radiocarbon dating 411–12
   ROM/DoE 1976 excavation 38–9, 43,
      47, 401, 403, 408, 411
Cat's Water (1990) 6, *8*, **38–47**, 401
   Neolithic *39*
      flint 47, 318, *319*
      pottery 250, *250*
   Early Neolithic multiple burial *406*,
      407
   pre-Bronze Age clearance for agriculture
      42, 43
   Iron Age stackstands 47
   Roman alluvium 41, 42, 43
   Area 1: 38–9, *39*, *40*, 43, 45
   Area 2: 39, *39*, *44*, 45–6, *45*, 47 (*see also*
      below)
   buried soils 39–43
   curving gully (F75, Area 2) *44*, *45*, 46, 47
   farmstead (roundhouse settlement), BA
      46, 412, 418

fenceline (Area 2) *44*, 45, 47, 401
field system (ditches 3 and 4), BA 38–9,
    39, 43, *43*, 45, 46–7, 59, 401, 418
flooding (freshwater) and flood meadow
    41, 42, 43, 401
'floor or yard' surface 41, 42
'mini-henge' (small penannular ditch
    F73, Area 2) 38, *44*, 46, 47
pit or posthole (F91) 46, 47
ploughed soil 41, 42
pottery 46, 47
ring-ditch/hengiform monument (penan-
    nular ditch F80, Area 2) (Neolithic?)
    10, 26, 38, 41, 42, 45–6, *45*, *46*,
    47, 49–50, 318, 400, 401
roundhouse settlement, BA 46
soil micromorphology 39–43, 442–4
wooded conditions 41, 42, 43
Cat's Water (1997) 6, **47–50**, 401
animal bone absent 49
flints 48
Neolithic mortuary (post-built structure)
    11, 18, 33, 48, 49, *49*, 50, *406*, 407
palaeosol 48
plant remains 49
pottery 48–9
trenches 47–8, *48*
Cat's Water drainage ditch *4*, 81, *82*, 86,
    400, 401, *406*, 411
causewayed enclosures 425
at Flag Fen? 8, 429
    see also Etton
causeways
Caldicot Castle Lake 434
Fordey/Little Thetford 432–3
Lingey Fen 433
'cavity walls' (revetments) *see* wattle walls
cereals 49, 351, 352, 356, 357, 361, 362,
    366, 367, 368, 373, 374, 375, 378,
    381, 403, 413
Newark Road 401
roots 168
Site O 32, 413
chains *275*, *276*, 293
chapes (tongue chapes)
bronze [42] 164, *259*, 261, 283
copper alloy [38], French-style 144, *259*,
    260–1, 283, 301, 305
    with wood in socket *224*, 228
Ewart Park [41] *259*, 261, 301
Wilburton, copper alloy [39] *259*, 261,
    300
charcoal, radiocarbon dating 392–4, 396
ditch (254) 390, 394
Newark Road 394, 397, 410
chevaux de frise (Row 4) 96, 122, 158,
    164, 421
clamp(?), turf-built (Structure III, Depot
    1992) 20, *20*, 24
cloth manufacture, Bronze Age 31
Coleoptera, Late Bronze Age 384–9, 426
Collared Urn *see* pottery
Colne river 419
communal stockyards *see* stockyards
comparative sites 432–6
Continental comparisons, for Flag Fen
    434–6
Coop site *see* Cat's Water (1997)
coppice 202, 203, 368
coppice products 171, 182
Corylus avellana see hazel

cosmetic sets *see* mortar; pestle
Cottenham (Cambs), wheel, Iron Age
    213, *216*
Covesea bracelets 290
cremations
at East Tilbury 327
Bronze Age Collared Urn 25, 26
Bronze Age Deverel-Rimbury ('little skin
    bag') 7–8, 10
cropmarks, Northey
Neolithic or Bronze Age *74*, 76, *76*, *77*,
    78, 80
Iron Age and Roman 78–80
crop-processing 351, 375
Iron Age 32
    see also cereals
cross-ties 116, 131
Crowtree Farm 366
cruciform construction, post alignment 144
crush (stock-handling) 417
currency bars 432

daggers (knives/daggers) 263, *264*, 287,
    296, 301
with antler handle [54/54a] and wooden
    fixings 224, 263, *264*, 287, 428
'dark earth'
Tower Works site 33, 34–5, 411, 412
Welland Bank 36, 412, 414
daub 31
decoy (stock-handling) 417
deforestation *see* woodland (tree) clearance
dendrochronology *see* tree-ring studies
Denmark, livestock 407
Depot (1992) 5, 6, 8, *17*, 18–27
Neolithic
    flint blades 23
    macehead (LN/EBA) 23
late Neolithic/Early Bronze Age ring-ditch
    17, 19, *20*, 22–3, 25, 26, 408, 411
barrow mound 20, 21
bone 23
soils 20
Bronze Age 19, *20*, 22, 23, *23*, 26, 411
droveways 19, 21
field system (ditches) 18–19, 20, *20*,
    23, *23*, 24, **26–7**, 29, 407, 409, 411
paddocks 411
Structure I, farmstead *20*, 23, 27, 412
Structure II, round building 19, *20*,
    23–4, 27, 411
Late Bronze Age/Early Iron Age 'settle-
    ment compound' *17*, 19, *21*, 23–4,
    411, 413
pit oven and oven plate 23–4
Iron Age 19, 22, *22*, 27, 28, 32
ard marks 24, 414
burnt stone spread 21, 24, *24*
'late' field system and paddocks (ditches
    16, 17, 20) *17*, 19, 20, *22*, *23*,
    24–5, 27, 29, 32, 402, 411, 414
pottery 24, 25
soils 21
Structure III, turf-built clamp? 20, *20*,
    24
Roman 19, 22, *22*, 25, 27
ditch/bank and enclosure ditch 19, 21,
    22, 25, 27, 28
pottery 25
aerial photography 18–19, *18*, 22
flint assemblage 23

palaeosols 18, 20, 24
soil micromorphology 17–18, 20–2,
    437–42
Depot (1997) 6, **27–30**
Neolithic
    flint 28
    pits 27, 28, 29
Bronze Age ditches 27, 28, 29
Early Iron Age 27, 28, 29
    roadway 27, 28, 29, 413
Late Iron Age ring-gully for round
    building 27, 28, 29
Late Iron Age/Early Roman settlement
    (linear ditches) 28, 29
Roman 27, 28, 29, 30
animal bone 29
palaeosol 27
pottery 27, 28, 29, 30
dessication 11
Devensian gravels 352, 356, 366, 369,
    378
diatoms 380, 403
dirks 255, *256*, 282–3, 300, 304
discs *266*, 268, 269, *270*
bronze, Iron Age *266*, 268, 269, *270*,
    294
lead 272, *273*, 291
white metal *270*, 271
display and competition 430–1
ditches 1 and 2 *see* droveways
ditches 3 and 4 *see* Cat's Water (1990);
    droveways
ditches 8 and 9 *see* droveways; Power
    Station
ditches 16 and 20 *see* Depot (1992), Iron
    Age
ditch 17, Iron Age *17*, 23, 24, 27, 32, 50;
    see also Depot (1992)
ditches/ditch systems *see* droveways; field
    systems
dogs, Bronze and Iron Ages 349; *see also*
    animal bone
Doogarymore (Co Roscommon), wheels
    213, 218
Dorchester-on-Thames, stockyard 420
drafting gates (stock-handling) 417, *417*,
    418
driftwood 100, 112, 121, 160
Draved Wood, Denmark 186
droveways 19, *20*, 21, 23, *23*, 26, 411
ditches 1 and 2: 26, 50, 408, 409, 410,
    411, 418
Depot *20*, 26
extension (Site Q) 50
radiocarbon dating 394
ditches 3 and 4: 26, 36, 38–9, *39*, 43,
    43, 45, 46–7, 59, 401, 418
radiocarbon dating 393
ditches 5 and 6: 26
ditches 8 and 9 (main) 409, 410, *415*,
    416
abandonment 61
Depot (1992) 19, *20*, 21, 23, *23*, 26,
    411
Fourth Drove 60, 61
Newark Road 60, 61
and the post alignment 1, 62, 233,
    401, 408, 409, 416
Power Station 1, 52, 53, *54*, **60–2**, 72,
    254, 401, 416
radiocarbon dating (ditch 9) 393, 397

Borough Fen 72, 408
  as boundary 1, 47, 60
  Cat's Water (1990) see ditches 3 and 4
  Depot (1992) 19, 21, 411
  Fengate 26, 36, 50, 72, 418
  Fourth Drove 36, 60, 415
  Newark Road 32, 36, 60, 400, 409, 410,
    415–16
  Northey, Bronze Age 76, 77–8, 79, 80,
    321, 412, 418
    Iron Age(?) 79–80
  Site O 31, 32, 411
  Site Q 50
  Tower Works, Romano-British 34, 414
  Vicarage Farm, Neolithic 406, 406
  see also field systems
dung 375, 414
dung beetles 388–9
Dyke Survey 9
dykeside exposure (1982) 82, 86, 87, 91,
  135, 165, 426

Early Iron Age see under Iron Age
East Tilbury (Essex), cist burial and
  quern 327
electron probe microanalysis, metalwork
  308
elm bark beetles 388
elm (Ulmus) 352, 353, 356, 357, 358, 361,
  362, 363, 366, 370, 376, 381, 413
English Heritage Fenland Project 10
Etton 2, 72, 403, 428, 429
  animal bone 430
  arrowhead 321
  axe marks 182–4
  beetles 388, 389
  causewayed ditch 8, 10, 429–30
  causewayed enclosure 8, 10
  Fengate Ware 8
  Neolithic wood 169, 171, 172, 175, 181,
    192
  pollen 381
  querns 326
  'small filled pits' 29, 77, 430
  woodchips 185
Ewart Park metalwork 255–6, 258, 260,
  261, 263, 265, 267, 268, 271, 276,
  278, 283, 287, 288, 290, 291, 300,
  301, 303, 305, 306, 309–15, 428
  swords 255–6, 257, 283, 301, 310, 311,
    312, 312, 313, 315, 428

Fagus see beech
farmsteads 412
  Fourth Drove 412, 418
  Iron Age 413
  see also Depot (1992), Structure I
feasting 430
Federsee (Germany), wheel 213
Feltwell Fen hoard (Norfolk) 289, 301, 429
Fen Causeway Roman Road 421
  gravel makeup and surface (PS) 52, 53,
    59, 74, 80, 403, 414
  rectilinear soil mark associated with(?)
    74, 80
fen edge 50, 400, 401, 402, 404, 431
  Neolithic 50, 406
  Bronze Age 50, 431
  Iron Age 50, 403
  and droveways 60, 72
  Fengate 4

Northey 50
  Power Station 50, 56, 57, 58, 60, 72
  Third Drove 50–1
fenceline, Bronze Age, Cat's Water (1990)
  44, 45, 47, 401
Fengate 1, 1, 2, 4, 5, 6, 9, 10
  Iron Age landscape 413, 414
  radiocarbon dating 366, 368, 392–4
  recent research in central and north
    Fengate 37–51
  recent research in south Fengate 17–36
  salt extraction 412
  see also droveways; field systems
Fengate Gravel Pits 36
Fengate series, radiocarbon dating 392–4
Fenlake Business Centre 50
Fenland Archaeological Trust 6, 10, 27, 38,
  81, 171
Fenland Survey 3, 6, 75
ferrules 286–7, 300, 301, 428, 431
  with wooden shaft [44] 224, 226, 261, 262
  with wooden shaft [45] 224, 225–6, 261,
    262
  radiocarbon dating 261, 286, 395
fibulae 269, 270, 272
  Iron Age 271, 272, 273, 293–4, 300,
    301
field boundary ditches 37; see also field
  systems
field drains 409
field systems (double ditches etc), Bronze
  Age 400–1, 406, 408–12
  abandonment and demise 396, 397,
    398, 399, 402, 405–6, 410,
    411–12, 413, 431
  Barleycroft Farm 409, 412
  Cat's Water (1990) ditches (3 and 4)
    38–9, 39, 43, 43, 46–7, 401
  dating for use 399
  Depot (1992) 18, 19, 20, 20, 22, 23, 24,
    26–7, 29, 409, 410, 411
  Depot (1997) ditches 27, 28, 29, 410
  development and extent 409–10, 411
  Fengate (main) system 1, 26–7, 36, 47,
    429
  Fourth Drove ditches 52, 233
  Global Doors site (linear ditches) 37,
    38, 38
  Newark Road ditches 36, 37, 400, 401,
    409
  non-local 418–20
  Northey, linear ditches (fields or pad-
    docks) 75, 76, 80, 402, 412
  origins 409, 411
  Padholme Road 411
  Paving Factory site ditches 37–8
  radiocarbon dating 391, 393–4, 396,
    397, 398
  Site O field ditches 30, 31, 32
  Site Q, extension to ditches 1 or 2 50
  Storey's Bar Road, field boundary 18,
    25–6, 27, 410, 411
  Tower Works site 18, 33, 35, 36, 429
  West Deeping 418–19, 419
  see also droveways
field systems, Iron Age, 'late' (Depot
  1992) 17, 19, 20, 23, 24–5, 27, 29,
  32, 402, 411, 414
fire-cracked stones, Beaker 71, 72
First Drove 36, 404
fish bones 330, 403

Fiskerton (Lincs) 2, 246, 431
  Iron Age structure 433, 435
Flag Fen 1, 2, 5, 6, 81–166
  animal bone see under platform
  bracelets, shale 322, 322
  Fenland setting 3–6
  human remains 335, 344, 348, 349–50
  insects 402
  metalwork 59, 282, 291, 292, 298, 300,
    301, 302–4
    listed 284–6
  palaeosol 356, 361, 362, 366, 367, 369,
    373, 378, 379, 381
  peat growth 398
  platform see separate entry
  post alignment see separate entry
  post rows 1–5 see Row 1 to Rows 4/5
  pottery 249–54, 251, 428
  radiocarbon dating 397, 398
  tree-ring study 229, 230, 231–2, 231,
    238–9, 240–2, 243–5, 246–8, 390,
    397, 398, 399
  'wiggle-matching' 390, 395, 398, 399
  wood 167–71, 171–86
    beaver-chewed 202–3
    joints and mortises 203–12
    toolmarks 194–202
    wooden artefacts 212–28 passim
    woodland clearance 367, 368, 374, 378,
      380, 381
    see also Area 1 to Areas 11 and 12; lake
      lining exposure; querns
Flag Fen Basin 1–16
  dendrochronology 232–48
  development of the prehistoric landscape
    400–4
Flag Fen environs, soils and sediments
  382–3, 450
flail, wooden 218–19, 219
Flakerton 2
Flandrian
  peats 366
  watercourses 50
flax 351
flesh hook [58] 149, 155, 263, 264, 265,
  288–9, 301, 428, 429
  wooden handle 224, 225
flint 318–21
  Mesolithic 319
  Neolithic 23, 25, 28, 47, 77, 318, 319,
    320, 321, 407, 408, 429
  Bronze Age 318, 319, 320–1
  Beaker period 70
  Boongate Roundabout (inc. blade) 33
  Cat's Water (1990), Neolithic 47, 318,
    319
  Cat's Water (1997) 48
  Depot site (1992) 23
  Depot site (1997), Neolithic 28
  Newark Road 319, 320
  Northey 74, 77, 321, 321
  Power Station 318–21, 319, 408, 429
  Site O 32
  Storey's Bar Road, Neolithic 25, 318
flint knapping 169, 172
flood meadows 401, 402, 405
  Cat's Water (1990) 41, 42, 43, 401
  Late Bronze Age 402
  Roman and later 403
flooding 382, 383, 401–2, 429
  Neolithic 405

Iron Age 405
Roman 403
medieval 403
Cat's Water (1990) 41, 42, 43, 401
land-use definition 405
Northey 379
Power Station 53, 55, 56, 58, 59, 71
flooring materials, sand and straw 160,
    351, 375
foil, white metal 273, *273*, 291
Folkestone Beds, querns 323, 325–6, 328
Fordey/Little Thetford causeway 432–3
'foundation deposit' *see* querns [24]
Fourth Drove 27, 36, 81, 400, 401, 404
alluvial deposits 403
ditch system, Bronze Age 36, 52, 233
drove 60, 61, 415
farmstead, Bronze Age 412, 418
flooding 401
molluscs 401
ROM/DoE subsite 52
France
chapes 300, 301, 305, 308
flesh hook 288, 289
Iron Age ritual deposition 434
knives/daggers 287
pins 289, 290, 301
rings 294
rivets 290
tools 301
Fraxinus see ash

gabbro querns *325*, 326, 328, 329, 427,
    449
'gang labour' 426
Glastonbury (Somerset)
gouges 224, 225
ladles 226
mallets 222
vessels 227
Global Doors site 6, *8*, 37, *37*
Bronze Age linear ditch 37, *37*, 38, *38*,
    410
buried soil 37
palaeosol 38
pottery 37
gold object *see* rings
gouge [57] 263, *264*, 288, *296*
radiocarbon dating of shaft 225, 263,
    288, 395, 397
wooden handle *224*, 224–5
Gournay sur Aronde (France) 434
grain
production 327
supplies 413
see also cereals
grassland 389, 402, 407
platform 367, 368
Power Station 56, 374
Site O 32
gravel pits 7, 253
Tower Works 18
Gravel Pits 6, 7, 33, 407
pottery 411
road to 413
settlement area 29, 411, 414
gravel platform (?hardstanding), Iron Age
    (PS) *9*, 59, 60, 61, 73
greensand (sandstone) querns 325–6, *325*,
    328, 329, 449
grid references 7

Grooved Ware enclosed settlement,
    Storey's Bar Road 25, 26, 32, 49, 50,
    398, 400, 407, 409, 411
Gussage All Saints (Dorset), querns 324,
    326, 327
Gussage St Michael (Dorset), awls 287

Haddenham 403
barrows 408
Romano-British shrine 348
Halfpenny Toll House *75*, 76, *78*, 80
hammer, wooden 222–4, *222*
handles and hafts
radiocarbon dating 390, 395
wooden 225, *225*
see also axe hafts; gouge
hardstandings
Area 6A 121
edge of poolside 164
Iron Age gravel platform (PS) *9*, 59, 60,
    61, 73
Hauterive-Champreveyres 307, 308
hazel (*Corylus avellana*) 352, *353*, 356,
    357, 361, 362, *363*, 366, 368, 369,
    370, 373, 374, *376*, 378, 381
drying out 169
hedges and hedgerows 402, 403, 404,
    409, 410, 411, 413, 420
Depot site 26
helmet fragment *266*, 268, 291, 301, 427
helmet rivets 258, 296, 431
hemp (*Cannabis sativa*) 374
henges and hengiform monuments *9*, 408;
    see also Cat's Water (1990), ring-ditch/
    hengiform monument *and* 'mini-henge'
herbs 352, *353–4*, 356, 357, *358–9*, 361,
    362, *363–4*, 366, 367, 368, 369,
    370–1, 373, 374, 375, *376–7*, 379,
    381, 402, 403, 418
hillforts 426
hilt fixings 428; *and see* daggers [54/54a]
Hio hoard, Pontvedra (Spain) 289
Holland
estuary environment 50
wattle bundles 70
holly (*Ilex*) *353*, *358*, 362, *363*, 367
Holocene 366, 367, 379
hook, iron *279*, 280, 295
hop (*Humulus* type) 374
horizontal timbers *see* post alignment
horse gear fittings 291, 295
'house' (funerary structure) *see* Padholme
    Road
hub roughout, for wheel 214
human dung 375
human remains 330, 349, 427
Flag Fen 335, 344, 348, 349–50
skeleton, Iron Age (PS) 59, 73, 343,
    345, 348, 349, 430
Hunsbury (Northants), scabbard 292

Ilex see holly
inhumations
Early Bronze Age 7
Newark Road 393, 397, *415*, 416
inlet
Site Q *30*, 50, 406, 409
Welland Bank 410
insects 352, 362, 366, 384, 402
Ireland
boxes 228

pins 290, 293
rings 306
trackways 432
Iron Age *4*, 381, 421
alder 403
cropmarks at Northey 78–80
crop-processing 32
Depot (1997) 27, 28, 29
dogs 349
Early Iron Age landscape 413
fen edge 50, 403
field system 429 (*see also* Depot (1992))
flooding 405
gravel platform (?hardstanding) (PS) *9*,
    59, 60, 61, 73
hedgerows 403
human skeleton (PS) 59, 73, 430
landscape 406, 413–20, 431
metalwork 59, *266*, 267, 268, 269, *270*,
    271, 272, *273*, *275*, 276, 278, *279*,
    280, *281*, 282, 292–8, 406, 413,
    430–1
analysis *299*, 300, 301, 302, 303–4, 306
distribution 295–6, 297–8, 427
ritual deposition of 158, 295, 427,
    430–1, 432, 434
in wetter contexts 427
see also axes; binding strip; bracelets;
    brooches; discs; fibulae; knives;
    pestle; pins; rings; rods; scabbard
    plate; shears and box; swords
peat 403
post-built rectangular building
    (LBA/EIA), Tower Works 18, 33,
    35, *35*, 36, 411
Power Station **59–60**, 73
rectilinear enclosures 75
ring-gully, LIA 27, 28, 29
roadway (Depot 1997) 27, 28, 29
Site O 30, 32
Site Q 32
stackstands 47
temple(?) at Northey *74*, 75, 80
turf-built house/clamp (Structure III,
    Depot 1992) 20, *20*, 24
wheel symbol 291
woodchips 192
woodland 403
see also agriculture; alluviation; ard marks;
    Depot (1992); Depot (1997); hill-
    forts; La Tène; post alignment;
    pottery; querns; ritual; settlements
iron objects 269, *270*, 280, 282, 295; *see
    also* nail; rings; rods; swords
Isleham hoard (Cambs) 283, 287, 288,
    289, 290, 291
isometric reconstructions, post alignment
    422, *424*, *425*
Italy, metalwork 291

joints *see under* wood

Knap of Howar, quern 326
knives (knives/daggers) 263, *264*, 287,
    296, 301
Early Iron Age [52] 263, *264*, 287, 301

La Tène
metalwork *279*, 280, 292, 295, 300, 301,
    304, 305, 421
sites 434–6

lake lining exposure *82*, 87–8, 165, 425
  tree-ring study 241, 243, 423
lake size 91
lakes
  artificial lakes as 'water conditioners' 11
  construction of artificial lakes 11, *12*, 13–14, 86
land-use patterns 405–20
landholdings 60, 72
landscapes
  prehistoric 1, 400–4
  Neolithic 3, 72, 406–8, 409, 412
  Bronze Age 3, 405–6, 408–13, 429
  Iron Age 3, 406, 413–20, 431
  Roman 1, 3, 403, 413–20
Late Bronze Age/Early Iron Age *see* agriculture; buildings and structures; peat; settlements
lead isotope analysis 301–6, 308
lead objects 269, *270*, 272, *273*, 291, 296, *297*; *see also* discs; lead rolls
lead rolls (sinkers?) 272, *273*, 294–5
Leeds, E T 7
Levels 1–7, post alignment (in Area 6) 93–4, **96–152**
Level 1: 81, *83*, *84*, 87, *87*, 88, 90, *92*, 94, 95, 96, **97–112**, 121, 126, 159, 162
  'boundary' deposits 424
  'bridge' (Row 1 gap) 126
  dog bones 112
  flooring 160
  horizontal timber 159
  perimeter revetment 97–100, *97*
  pollen from floor 375
  pottery 101, 103, 104, 162, 250, *251*, 254, 428
  Rows 2/3 pathway 97, 100, 101, 111–12, 135, 160, 164
  Rows 3/4 walkway 101, 160
  Rows 4/5 walkway 160
  wattle revetments 97
  wood (PS) *63*, *65*, *67*, *68*, *69*
  see also Area 6D; portal; scabbard plate
Level 2: 81, *83*, 87, *87*, 90, 95, *97*, **112–21**
  axle, wood 216
  boundary deposits 424
  box-like structure (Area 6B) 112, *114*, 121, 133
  dog bones 162
  entranceway *see* Row 5
  flooring material 160
  horizontal timber 116, 159
  pottery 250, *251*, 253, 424, 428
  revetments *64*, 87, 112, 113, 116
  Rows 1 and 2 walkway 117
  Rows 2/3 pathway 112, 117, 121, 135, 159, 160
  Rows 3/4 walkway 112, 116–17, 121, 136, 160
  Rows 4/5 walkway 116, 160
  stream channel infilled 69
  trample 121, 159
  wood (PS) *64*, *66*, 67
  wood-free zone 112
  yoke, wood 218
Level 3: *83*, 87, *88*, **121–31**, 135, 159, 160, 163, 421
  axle roughout 218
  'blocking posts' 101
  'bridge' (Row 1) 126
  hardstanding 121, 122

horizontal (oak) timber 159
  Phase 3: 163
  pottery 250, 253, 254
    complete jar [6] below timber 123, 250, *251*, 254
  Rows 1 and 2 access 125, 126, 131
  Rows 2/3 pathway 125, 126, 131
  Rows 3/4 walkway 122, 123, 126, 136, 159, 160
  Rows 4/5 walkway 122, 126
  stream 69, 121
  wattle revetments 122, 126
  wood-free zone 112, 121, 162
Level 4: 93, 94, 95, 103, **131**, 135, 159, 163, 421
  animal bone 139
  box-like structure 133, *159*
  horizontal (oak) timber 159, 160, *161*
  partitioning 111, 131, *131–4*, 133, 135, *141*, 142, 160, 162, 421
  Phase 1: 163, 421
  Phase 3: 163
  post outside alignment 135
  pottery 139, 250, 253
  quern [24] 135, 139, 149, 152
  Rows 2/3 pathway, basal log layer 131, 135, 139, 140, 159, 160
  Rows 3/4 walkway 136, 139, 140, 158, 160
  spear shaft 224, 225
  three uprights 136
  wattle revetments 139, 158
  wood-free zone 135, 140, 162
  see also chapes [42]
Levels 5 and 6: *88*, 93, 94, 95, 96, 103, 139, **140–52**, *156*, 159, 421
  animal bone 149
  axe haft, with quern [24] 149, 152, *155*, 220
  cruciform construction 144
  horizontal (oak) timber 159, *161*
  partitioning 111, 131, 135, 145, 149, 152, 160, 162, 163, 421
  Phase 1: 163, 421
  pottery 149, 250
  querns [26–8] 135, 140, 149, *152*, *154*, *155*, 162, 163, 424
  revetments 139, 140, 142, 149, 152, *155*, 158, 160, 162
  Rows 2/3 pathway, log layer 131, 139, 140, 142, 149, 152, 160
  Rows 3/4 walkway 149
  Rows 4/5 walkway 144
  wheel 213
  wooden artefacts 214, 218, 220, 222, 226, 228
  see also chapes [38]; flesh hook
Level 7: 95, 142, *144*
  partitions 142
lime (*Tilia*) 352, *353*, 356, 357, *358*, 361, 362, *363*, 366, 367, 369, *370*, 373, 374, *376*, 379, 380, 381, 400, 401
Lincoln City Unit 52
Lincolnshire
  Bronze Age metalwork (axes and palstaves) 197, 198, *200*, *201*
  Fens 432
Lingey Fen, Haslingfield, causeway 433
Little Thetford *2*, 432
livestock 410, 429, 430, 431
  Cat's Water, Iron Age 45, 414
  Neolithic 406–7

  overwintering on Newark Road site 401
  on scrub land, Iron Age 413
  stockhandling 415–20
  and 'wealth' 420
  see also agriculture; animal bone; stockyards
Llangwyllog hoard, Anglesey 306
Llyn Fawr Phase 263, 277, 287, 300, 301
Lodsworth (West Sussex), quern 'factory' site 324
'log layer' *see* Rows 2/3 pathway
log vessel, hollowed 226–7, *228*
loomweights 431; *see also* weight

macehead (Depot site 1992) 23
Maiden Castle (Dorset) 426
maple, beaver marks 202, *202*
Market Deeping, woodchips, Iron Age 192
Maxey
  Iron Age 415
  oval barrow 23, 47
  small henges 47
  stackstands 47
Meare Heath (Somerset)
  hammer 222
  trackway 432
Meare Lake village (Somerset) 294–5, 308, 375, 389
medieval
  agriculture 374
  flooding 403
  landscape 403–4
  peats 57, 368–9, 373, 374, 378, 379, 380, 381, 404
  roads 36
  scrub 413
mere section, pollen 351, 352–7, 367, 368, 379, 380
Mesolithic
  flint 319
  sites 3
metal-detector survey 52, 53, 59–60
metalwork (Flag Fen and Power Station) 60, 142, 164, **255–317**, 421, 423, 427, 430
  Bronze Age 255–91
    domestic 428–9
  analysis 298–308
  electron probe microanalysis 308
  lead isotope analysis 301–6, 308
  ritual breakage of 111, 322, 427, 428, 430
  ritual deposition, Iron Age 295, 427, 430–1, 432
  see also Iron Age; Power Station; *and object name*
metalworking 297
  engraving tools 301
  lead objects 296–7
'mini-henge', Cat's Water (1990) 38, *44*, 46, 47
molluscs
  Fourth Drove 401
  Newark Road 401
  post alignment, snail shells 104, 111, 112, 121
mortar (medicinal), bronze *281*, 282, 294, 301
mortises *see under* wood
mortuary structures, Neolithic
  Cat's Water (1997) 11, 18, 33, 48, 49, *49*, 50, *406*, 407

Padholme Road 'house' 11, 398, *406*, 407
radiocarbon dating 392, 397, 398
Site 11, mortuary enclosure 9, *406*, 407
Third Drove (EN), and ditched enclosure 50
tree-ring dating 398
Mucking
barrows 419
fields or paddocks 419
Mustdyke (drain) 11, *82*, 86, 87, 88, 91, 97, 144, 165, 168, 241, 427
enlargement 52
root damage 168
trench for soils and sediments 382

nail, iron *281*, 282
needle or bodkin, wooden 228, *228*
Nene river (valley) 1, 74, 403, 432
Nene Valley Research Committee 6, 9, 10
Neolithic 249
agriculture 381
animal bone 49
barrows 425
Northey 76, 77, *78*, *79*, 80, 321, *321*, 412
Boongate Roundabout settlement, post-holes and pits 33, *33*, 49
cropmarks at Northey *74*, 76, *76*, *77*, *78*, 80
ditch (PS) *55*, *56*, **72**, 400, 429
droveway 406, *406*
fen edge 50
field systems 400
flooding 405
landscape 72, 406–8, 409, 412, 429
macehead, flint (LN/EBA) 23
multiple burial 50, *406*, 407
Northey 75–7
pits ('small filled pits') 27, 28, 29, 430
pits and Grooved Ware (Cat's Water 1997) 47, 48, 49–50
pollen 356–7, 361, 362, 366, 374, 381
Power Station *55*, *56*, 72, 320, 408, 429
querns 325, 326–7
radiocarbon dating *391*, 392, 393, 397
ring-ditch, Neolithic/Early Bronze Age *17*, 19, *20*, 22–3, 25, 26
ritual, narrow entranceways 47
Site O 30, 31, 32
Site Q 50
sites 3, *4*
stone axe fragments 321–2, *321*
wood 169, 171
woodland (tree) clearance 400, 406, 407
see also flint; mortuary structures; pottery; ring-ditches; Storey's Bar Road
Netherlands, stackstands 47
Newark Road *5*, 20, 27, 321, 405
awl 428
barrow east of 408
buried soil 37
cereals 401
Collared Urn 31, 32
community stockyards 415–16
droveways 32, 36, 60, 61, 400, 409, 410, 415–16
enclosure 400, 410
farmstead, Bronze Age 412
field ditches, Bronze Age 36, 37, 400, 401
flints 319, 320
inhumation 393, 397, 416

molluscs 401
overwintering livestock 401
pick or hook, antler 91
pollen 401
radiocarbon dating 393, 394, 397, 410
'industrial area' 394, 397
rock-cut well (F6) 394, 397
roundhouse (structure) 394, 397, 410, *415*, 416
spearhead 416
stockyards 415–16
well (F1551), Iron Age 394, 397, 416
Nipperweise shields 287, 304
Northey ('island') 1, *1*, *3*, *4*, *5*, 6, 7, 10, 72, **74–80**, 400, 402, 404, 405
Neolithic 75–7
Bronze Age 75–7
Iron Age 75, *75*, 78–80, 414
droveway(?) 79–80
temple *74*, 75, 80
Roman 75, 414
animal bone 77
barrows 76, 77, *78*, *79*, 80, 321, *321*
cropmarks
Neolithic or Bronze Age *74*, 76, *76*, *77*, *78*, 80
Iron Age and Roman *75*, 78–80
disuse of fields 402
droveway 74, 76, 77–8, *79*, 80, 321, 418
felled timber 247
fen edge 50
flint 74, 77, 321, *321*
landscape, Bronze Age 412–13
linear ditches (fields or paddocks) 75, 76, 80
palaeosol 75, 77, 361, 378
peat 361, 362
pollen 351, 352, 356, 357–62, 378
post alignment landfall 1, 10, 62, 80, 91, 95, 232, 233, 240, 429
pottery 74
radiocarbon dating 357, 361, 362, 366, 367, 368, 373, 378, 395, 397
rectilinear enclosures, Roman or Iron Age 75
ring, bronze 10
ring-ditch 76, *78*
salt extraction (salterns) 74
soils 382–3
Trial Trench 1 *see above* barrows
Trial Trench 2 *see above* droveway
Nottingham Hill hoard (Glos) 290
nucleated settlement, Northey 405, 412–13

oak (*Quercus*) 70, 81, 85, 86, 87, 88, 90, 91, 96, 100, 103–4, 121, 352, *353*, 356, 357, *358*, 361, 362, *363*, 366, 367, 368, 369, *370*, 373, 374, *376*, 378, 379, 380, 381
axe hafts 219–20
axles 216, 218
braces (wheel) 213
drying out 168–9, *169*
horizontal timbers **159**, *159*, *161*
joints 203–4, 206, 208, 210, 211–12
radiocarbon dating 392, 394, 398
reduction of 203
same-tree use 427
tree-ring study 230, 233, 240, 242, 246, 247, 248
see also flail; yoke
Oakbank Crannog 194, 375

Oakhurst Farm 366
off-terrace investigations 32
open country phase 402
radiocarbon dating 397, 398
open water 405
organic muds (*gyttja*) 154–5, 163, 361, 367, 378
Orton Meadows 432
oven plate, clay 23–4
Over (Cambs)
barrows 408
Grooved Ware settlement 49
Oxford Archaeological Unit 420

paddocks 409, 419
corner entranceways 417, 420
Depot (1992) 411, 414
Iron Age 414
Newark Road 415
Northey 75, 80
Power Station 61
Storey's Bar Road 417
Padholme Road *5*
bracelet 322
ditches 411
Neolithic 'house' (mortuary structure) 11, 33, 49, 398, 400, *406*, 407
pottery 253
Roman road 80
palaeochannels, Third Drove 50
palaeosols 382, 383
Boongate Roundabout 33
Cat's Water (1997) 48
Depot site (1992) 18, 20, 24
Depot site (1997) 27
Flag Fen 154, *353–5*, 356, 361, 362, 366, 367, 369, 373, 378, 379, 381
Global Doors site 38
Northey 75, 77, 361, 378
Paving Factory site 38
Power Station 53, 401
palisade, post alignment (post Row 4) 122, 164, 421, 423; *see also* Row 4
Parish Drain *8*, 24, 30, *30*, 32, 38, *39*, 50
partitions (segments) *see under* post alignment
pathways, post alignment **160**; *see also* Rows 2/3 pathway
Paving Factory site *5*, 6, **37–8**, *37*
Bronze Age
ditch 37–8, 410
settlement(?) 38
Iron Age alluvium 38
palaeosol 38
peat 356, 362, 366, 367, 368, 369, 378, 379, 381, 382, 383, 402
Late Bronze Age/Iron Age 373
Iron Age 58, 403
medieval 368–9, 373, 374, 378, 379, 380, 381, 404
Cat's Water (1990), LBA/EIA 41, 42, 43
first formation 397, 398
Power Station 53, 57, 58, 59, 369, 373, 374
radiocarbon dating 351, 395, 397, 398
pedogenesis 19, 373, 378, 380
pegs
bronze 260
Flag Fen post alignment 81, 85, 91, 94, 95, 101, 112, 116, 117, 123, 125, 135, 149, 152
wooden 212
for wheel 218

Penard Phase 255, 258, 260, 261, 263, 265, 268, 274, 276, 277, 278, 283, 286, 289, **300–1**, 302, 304, *304*, 305, 421

perimeter revetment (walkway), of platform 87, *87*, 97–100, 165, 246

Perkins Diesel Engines factory 38

pestle, bronze, Late Iron Age/Romano-British *281*, 282, 294

Peterborough 1, *1*, 9, 18, 74
  sewage treatment works 400

petrology 321–2

pewter *see* shoe buckle; strapends

Phases (Structural), post alignment **421–3**
  Phase 1: 163, 247, 248, 397, 421, *422*, 423
  Phase 2: 163, 247, 248, 397, 410, 423
  Phase 3: 163, 247, 248, 397, 423, *424*, *425*
  Phase 4: 164, 397

photomontages 93, 95, 97, *99*, 100, 112, *114*, *124*, 131, *134*, 139, 144, *146*

Pilgrim Lock (Warwicks), beetle 389

pine (*Pinus*) 352, *353*, 356, 357, *358*, 361, 362, *363*, 367, 369, *370*, 373, 374, *376*

pins 274, *275*, 276–7, 280, 289–90, 293, 297, *298*, 299, 301, 304, 306, 428, 431
  Iron Age, with chain *275*, 276, 293, 301
  Iron Age, swan's-neck ring-headed 29, *275*, 276, 289, 293, 301, *275*, 276, 293, 301, 431

Pinus see pine

pit-oven, sunken 23

plant remains 351, 352, 366, 375
  Cat's Water (1997), wheat 49
  as hosts of Coleoptera 384, 387, 388
  see also pollen

plant roots 168

platform 1, 3, *4*, 7, 9, *9*, 11, 58, *82*, 402, 423, **426–7**
  animal bone 139, 149, 330, 331, 332–5, 343–50, 428
  beaver-chewed wood 202–3
  Coleoptera (Area 6B) 384–9
  construction and use 165, 351, 352, 357, 362–6, 367, 368, 373, 379, 380, 381
  dating 245–6, 248
  disuse and submerged 58, 402
  extent 165, 426
  floor, palaeobotanical evidence 375–7, 381
  horizontal timbers 426
  human bone 427
  'log layer' 426
  open water ('pool') 426, 427, 430
  peat below 357, 363, 366, 367, 368, 395, 397, 398
  perimeter revetment (walkway) 87, *87*, 97–100, 165, 246
  pollen 362–6, 379, 380–1, 401
  pottery 249–54
  relationship to post alignment 165–6
  resting place for the dead? 426–7, 430
  schematic section *9*
  soil near 382–3
  timber reused in 242
  tree-ring study 232–48 *passim*
  wood 172

Playden, hengiform monument 25

Pleistocene
  stream channel/watercourses 50
  terrace gravels 53, 74, 367

ploughing 41, 42, 168, 383

pollen *82*, 351, 352–81 *passim*, 382, 400, 401
  Early Bronze Age 361, 366, 378, 381
  Roman 403
  mere section 351, 352–7, 367, 368, 379, 380
  Northey 351, 352, 356, 357–62, 378
  Site O 32
  Power Station 72
  see also by name (not all of the individual species have been indexed)

pommels
  Bronze Age (or terminal) *259*, 260, 292, 306, 428
  tin *259*, 260, 283

Pomoideae (apple, pear, hawthorn) 158, 224

pond *12*, 14

pools 423, 426, 427

'poolside area' *see* Area 6D

poplar (*Populus*) 158, 169, 202, 388

portal (alder posts), to 'poolside area' 111, 112, 160, 162, 163, *422*, 423

post alignment 1, 3, *4*, 7, 9, 11, 405–6, 421–36
  abandonment, disuse and submergence 58, 233, 248, 402
  alder posts 248
  animal bone 254, 330, 331, 336–50, 428, 430
  Beaker pits near 72
  'boundary' deposits 423–4
  British comparisons 432–4
  'cavity walls' (PS) 67
  construction 58, 163–4, 229, 248, 397, 398, 421, 429
  Continental comparisons 434–6
  crossed stream/relict river (PS) 56–7, 58, 69, 401
  dating/chronology 163, 245–6, 247, 248, 421, 423
  dog bones 423, 424, 428, 430
    skeleton round post 70, *70*, 237
  and the droveway (ditches 8 and 9) 1, 62, 233, 401, 408, 409, 416
  enlargement 379, 397, 398, 399, 423
  extent 165
  'foundation deposit' *see* querns [24]
  from stockyards 415
  horizontal timbers 67, 81, 88, *89*, 90, 104, 131, 144, **159–60**, 163, 421, 423, 424, 426
  isometric reconstructions *422*, *424*, *425*
  last repairs 162, 163, 245, 248, 397, 398, 399, 423
  layout and structure 157–62
  lifting of 62, 144
  'log layer' *see* Rows 2/3 pathway
  maintenance and repairs of 157, 163, 245–6, 248, 397, 399, 426
  metalwork 58, 295–8, 421, 423, 427, 428–9, 430, 431, 432
  Neolithic origins? 429
  Northey 'island' landfall 1, 10, 62, 80, 91, 95, 232, 233, 240, 429
  numbered timbers (PS) 62

partitions (1–4)/segmentation (transverse segment boundary) 103, 111, 131–40, 142, 145, 149, 152, **160**, **162**, 163, 165, 421, *422*, *424*, *425*, **423–6**, 429–30

pathway **160**, 421 (*see also* Rows 2/3)

pattern and purpose 164

post rows **158** (*see* Row 1 *to* Rows 4/5)

pottery 249–54, *254*, 424, 428
  complete jar [6] below timber 123, 250, *251*, 254

Power Station ('causeway') 52, *54*, 55, 56, *56*, 58, **62–70**, 73, 157, 158, 163, 229–32, 233–40, 242, 402, 421, 423, 427, 428

precursors 429

querns 423, 424, 427–8

radiocarbon dating *391*, 397, 398, 399

relationship to platform 165–6

ritual 421, 430–1
  areas between Row 1 and Row 3: 164, 165, 421, 423, 430
  'poolside' area *see* Area 6D; portal and segments 423–6

same-tree timbers 229, 230–1, 234–6, 238–9, 240, 241, 242, 246, 247, 248

sand and gravel surfaces 90, 97, 100, 112, 126, 140, 157, 158, 160

single authority control 423, 426

Structural Phases *see* Phases

structure and function 423

trampled areas 111, 121, 122, 159, **160**

tree-ring study 229–48 *passim*, 398, 399, 421

trenches 5

uprights removed in antiquity 65, 66, 67, 69

wear **160**, 421

walkways **160**, 172, 421 (*see also* Rows 1/2; Rows 3/4; Rows 4/5)

wood 62–60, *63–6*, 172

Iron Age
  platform/hardstanding at landfall (PS) 59, 73
  posts removed 69
  ritual 112, 157, 158, 164, 421
  road to 413
  use of 73, 112, 398, 421, 430, 431–2
    (*see also* metalwork)
  see also Level 1 *to* Level 7; Phases; revetments; Row 1 *to* Rows 4/5; scabbard plate

post rows (Area 6), excavation of 152–4; *see* Row 1 *to* Rows 4/5

pottery **249–54**, 428
  Neolithic 7, 25–6, 47, 48–9, 250, *250*, 251, 252–3
    Ebbsfleet Ware 49
    Fengate Ware 8, 48, 49
    Grooved Ware 25, 26, 32, 47, 48, 49–50, 407, 428
    Mildenhall 46
    Mortlake 48, 49
    Peterborough Ware 7, 46, 49, 72
    plainware bowl 48, 49
  Late Neolithic/Early Bronze Age 30
  Early Bronze Age 250, *250*, 251, *251*, 252, 253
  Bronze Age 23, 25, 32, 37, 252, 253, 254, 428
    Beaker 7, 25, 70, 71, 250, *250*, 253, 254, 428
    Collared Urn 25, 26, 31, *31*, 32, 250, 392, 411

Late Bronze Age 30, 34, 35, 36, 410,
    412
pre-Iron Age(?) 33
Early Iron Age *251*
Iron Age 7, 24, 27, 29, 61, 251, 252,
    252, 253, 254, 412, 428
    'scored ware' 24, 25, 253
    shell-tempered 28
Roman/Romano-British 25, 28, 30, 254
    Nene Valley Colour-Coated Ware 28
fabrics (1–7) 249–50
flint tempered 250, 251, 253
post alignment
    Level 1: 101, 103, 104, 162, 250, *251*,
        254, 428
    Level 2: 250, *251*, 253, 424, 428
    Level 3: complete jar [6] below timber
        (Area 6B) 123, 250, *251*, 254
    Level 4: 139, 250, 253
    Level 5/6: 149, 250
saltglazed 254
sand (quartz) tempered 250, 251, 253
shell tempered 28, 249, 250, 251, 252,
    253, 254
sites
    Cat's Water 251, 252, 253, 254,
        411–12
    Cat's Water (1990) 46, 47, 250, *250*
    Cat's Water (1997) 48–9
    Flag Fen 249–54, *251*, 424, 428
    Global Doors 37
    Power Station 61, 72, **249–54**, *250*,
        252, *254*, 428
    Site O 30, 31, *31*, 32
    Site Q 407
    Storey's Bar Road 253
    Tower Works 34, 35, 36, 411–12
    Vicarage Farm 411–12
    Welland Bank 412
Power Station (1989) 5, 6, 7, 8, *8*, **52–73**,
    401
Pleistocene terrace gravels 50, 53, *53*
Neolithic 408
    ditch (Area 1) *55*, *56*, **72**, 400, 429
    Late Neolithic landscape 72, 429
    occupation 320
    pottery 72
    stone axes 408, 429
Bronze Age 60–2, 320–1
Iron Age **59–60**, 73
    gravel platform (?hardstanding) *9*, **59**,
        60, 61, 73
    human remains **59**, 73, 343, 345, 348,
        349, 430
    metalwork 59, 60, *266*, 267, 268, 269,
        270, 271, 272, *273*, 275, 276,
        278, *279*
    peat growth *53*, 57, 58
Early Roman finds 421
Roman road (Fen Causeway), gravel
    makeup and surface 52, *53*, **59**, 421
Roman/post-Roman alluvium 57, 58,
    403
medieval, peat 57
alluviation *53*, 56, 57, 58, 369, 373,
    374, 402
animal bone (post alignment) 254, 330,
    331, 336–50, 428
areas excavated (1–4) 52–3
Beaker period pits and finds *54*, **70–2**,
    71, *73*

boundary/marker 72
buried soil 53, **53–6**, 57–8, 70, 446–7
Collared Urn 31
dog skeleton around post **70**, *70*, 428
droveways (ditches 8 and 9) 1, 52, 53,
    54, **60–2**, *60–2*, 72, 254, 401, 416
fen edge 50, 56, 57
ferrule shafts *224*, 225–6, 261, *262*
fields 52, 60, 72
flint 318–21, *319*, 408, 429
flooding 53, 55, 56, 57, 58, 59, 71
horizontal timbers 424
human remains *see* Iron Age *above*
metalwork (Bronze Age–Iron Age) 58,
    59, 60, **255–317**, 421
    distribution 142, 164, **295–8**, 421,
        423, 427, 428, 430
palaeosol 53, 401
peat 53, *53*, 57, 58, 59, 369, 373, 374
post alignment (causeway) 11, 52, *54*,
    55, 56, *56*, 58, 59, **62–70**, 73, 421,
    423
    last repairs 245, 248, 397, 398, 399, 423
pottery 61, 72, 249–54, *250*, *252*, *254*, 428
radiocarbon dating 261, 265, 369, 373
'reddened area' 53, **57**, 445
revetment wall(?) *64*, 67
Rows 1 and 5 229, 399
sand banks (seasonal stream?) 53, **56–7**,
    58, 445–6
site grids 52–3
soil micromorphology **53–8**, 401, 445–7
spear shaft *224*, 225, 226
streams and relict river channel 57, 58,
    69, 73
toolmarks on wood 53, 194, *197*
tree-ring study 62, 163, 192, 229–48
    passim, *230*, *232*, *233*, 390, 397,
    398, 399, 421
trenches (A–H), hand-excavated 53,
    62–72
vegetation and environment (Fengate B)
    351, 368, 369–74, 378, 379, 380
wattle bundles 69–70, *70*
well-like pit (F27) 60–1
wood 53, *54*, *55*, *63–6*, *68*, 167, 168,
    169, *185*, **186–93**, 310
woodchips 188–9, 190–3
wooden artefacts 310
woodland (tree) clearance 57, 58
woodworking 190, 191, 192
see also axes [60]; brooches; daggers [54];
    fibulae; gouge; shears and box
prehistoric landscapes 1, 400–4
Prunus/Pomoideae, gouge handle 224–5

quadrants *see under* Area 6B
querns [24–28] **322–9**, 449
    Neolithic 325, 326–7, 428
    Iron Age 324, 325, 326, 327, 428
    Roman 325, 326
    post alignment 423, 427–8
    as boundary deposit(?) [26–8] (Level 5)
        135, 140, 149, *152*, *154*, *155*, 162,
        163, 322–3, *324*, 325–6, *325*,
        328–9, 424
    as 'foundation deposit' [24] (Level 4) 139,
        149, 152, 322, *323*, 325, 328, 428
    with axe haft 149, 152, *155*, 162, 220
    ritually deposited 152, 163, 323, 326–7,
        427–8

race (stock-handling) 415, 417
radiocarbon dating 230, 240, 351, 378,
    380, **390–9**
    Cat's Water 411–12
    Fengate 366, 368
    Flag Fen 397, 398
    Newark Road 393, 394, 397, 410
    Northey 357, 361, 362, 366, 367, 368,
        373, 378, 395, 397
    Padholme Road 'house' 407
    Power Station 261, 265, 369, 373
    Storey's Bar Road pits 26, 397, 398
    Vicarage Farm 411–12
    see also axes; ferrules; gouge; peat
rapiers 255, *256*, 282–3, 300, 428
razors, copper alloy and bronze 265, *266*,
    288, 289, *296*
Reading Business Park, field system 420
Recycling Facility *see* Third Drove
reeds 168, 400
reed-mace 379, 380, 400, 430
reed swamp fen 351, 361, 366, 367, 373,
    378, 379, 380, 381, 400, 402, 404
relict stream/river *see* streams
retrogressive hydrosere 351, 357, 361,
    366, 367, 373, 374, 380
revetments, post alignment 97, 122, 126,
    139, 140, 142, 149, 152, *152*, *155*,
    158, 163, 164, 175, 421
    distribution plan *153*
    with jar beneath 122–3
    log-pile 98
    perimeter walkway (revetment) for plat-
        form (Area 5) 87, *87*, 97–100, 165,
        246
    Power Station *64*, 67
    tree-ring study 247
    wattle 'cavity walls' 112, 113, 116, 122,
        133, 135, 162, 164
'ridge and furrow' 402
ring-ditches 408, 412
    Neolithic/Early Bronze Age *17*, 19, *20*,
        22–3, 25, 26, 408, 411
    barrow mound 20, 21
    Northey 76, *78*
    soils 20
    Storey's Bar Road 23, 25–6, 411
ring-ditch/hengiform monument, Cat's
    Water (1990) (penannular ditch
    F80) 10, 26, 38, 41, 42, 45–6, *45*,
    46, 47, 49–50, 318, 408
ring-gully, Late Iron Age (Depot site
    1997) 27, 28, 29
rings
    bronze 10, 269, *270*, 271, 277–8, *279*,
        280, 291, 294, *298*, 301, 306
    copper alloy 269, *270*, 277, 278, *279*, 280
    gold 269, *270*, 294, 427
    iron *279*, 280, *281*, 295
    Iron Age 269, *270*, 278, *279*
    tin *279*, 280, 291
    white metal *279*, 280
ritual 10–11, 164, 421, 423, 427–8, 432
    boundary deposits 423–5
    breakage/destruction of objects 322,
        424, 427, 428, 429, 430, 431, 432
    the dead 430
    dog bones 70, 111, 112, 428
    human skeleton 73
    Iron Age 158, 295, 427, 430–1, 432,
        434

metalwork 149, 162, 295, 322 (*see also* flesh hook; scabbard plate)
platform 165, 426–7
pools 423, 426, 427
quern deposition 152, 163, 323, 326–7, 427–8
repeated visits at Etton 72
at social gatherings 415
water 165
wet/dry environments 430–1
see also Area 6D, 'poolside area'; post alignment; querns
rivets 258, *259*, 260, 290, *297*, 301, 310, 428
roads
Early Iron Age (Depot site 1997) 27, 28, 29, 413
Roman 52, *53*, 59, 80, 299
rods, iron *281*, 282
Iron Age (bar) *266*, 267, 294
ROM/DoE 6, 7, **9–10**, 29, 50, 411, 418
Bronze Age ditch system 52, 60, 408, 409, 410, 411
Fourth Drove subsite 52, 60
Iron Age settlement *see* Cat's Water
Newark Road drove 60
Roman/Romano-British period
Cat's Water (1990), alluviation 41, 42, 43
cropmarks at Northey 78–80
Depot (1992), ditch/bank and enclosure 19, 21, 22, *22*, 25, 27, 28
Depot (1997) 27, 28, 29, 30
droveway 34, 414
flood meadow/flooding 403
Gravel Pits, Romano-British features 414
landscape 1, 3, 403, 413–20
metalwork 300, 301, 304
Northey, rectilinear enclosures 75, 414
pollen 403
post alignment 421
querns 325, 326
Tower Works site, linear ditches 34
see also alluviation; axes; brooches; Fen Causeway; mortar; pottery; roads; shears and box; strapends
roofing materials 351, 375
roundhouses (round structures), Bronze Age
Cat's Water (1990) settlement 46
Depot (1992), Bronze Age/Iron Age 19, *21*
Depot (1992), Structure I, farmstead 19, *20*, 23, 27
Depot (1992), Structure II 19, *20*, *21*, 23–4, 27, 411
Newark Road 397, 410, *415*, 416
Site 11, Beaker 71
Rows (post rows), of the post alignment **158**
spacing 158
tree-ring study 229–32, 233
Row 1: 90, *90*, **96**, 101, 104, *107*, 111, 112, *126*, 139, *140*, **158**, 159, 163, 399, 421
abandoned 163, 423
alder posts 88, **96**, 111, 157, 158, 421
distance apart 111
gap/entranceway 96, 104, 111, 112, 125, 126, 158, 162, 164, 166, 423
wattle across 126
isometric reconstructions (Phases 1 and 3) *422*, *424*, *425*
lean/angle 158

metalwork 288
partitions (segments) and large posts 133, 135, 142, 149, 160, 162, 163, *422*, 423
portal (alder post) 111, 112, 160, 162
Power Station 229, 399
rotted 88, 104, 121
tree-ring study **152**, 229, *230*, *232*, 248
walkway round 423
wattle revetment/barrier 139, 149, *152*, 158, 160, 162, 164, 421, 423
see also Rows 1/2 walkway
Row 2: 90, *90*, **96**, 100, 101, *107*, 111–12, *115*, 120, 121, 122, *122*, 139, 140, *140*, 157, **158**, 163, 399, 421
alder posts (portal) 111, 112, 160, 162
cross-ties 131
gap 96, 111, 112, 125, 158, 423
hooked-shaped plank 121, *121*
isometric reconstruction (Phase 3) 423, *424*, *425*
lean/angle 158
partition 135, 142
tree-ring study 229, *231*
wattle 'cavity wall' (revetment) 122, 139, 158, 163, 164, 421, 423
wood-free zone 112
see also Rows 1/2 walkway; Rows 2/3 pathway
Row 3: *86*, 90, *90*, **96**, 100, 101, *101*, 104, *107*, 111–12, *115*, 116–17, *116*, 121, 122–3, *124*, 126, *147*, **158**, 159, 163, 164, 165, 399, 421, 423
alder posts (logs) 133, 139, 157, 158, 160, 163, 421
angle 158
horizontal timbers 104
isometric reconstructions (Phases 1 and 3) *422*, *424*, *425*
log layer 131, 139
partitions (segments) 133, 135, 136, 142, 152, 163, 165, *422*, 423
pegs 123, 125
portal (alder posts) 111, 112, 160, 162
pottery 123
revetment 122–3
structure and function 423
tree-ring study 229, *231*
walkways 100, 101, 121, 123, *125*, 164
wood species 96, 158, 421
see also Rows 2/3 pathway
Row 4: *86*, 90, *90*, **96**, 101, *107*, 112, *115*, 116–17, 121, 122, 126, *147*, 149, 152, 157, **158**, 163, 399, 421
alder logs 140, 158
chevaux de frise or palisade 96, 122, 158, 164, 421, 423
cross-ties 116
felling dates 399
horizontal timbers 159, 164
isometric reconstruction (Phase 3) 423, *424*, *425*
lacing of posts 122
lean/angle 96, 104, 122, 158, 423, *424*
partitions 135, 142, 159
structure and function 423
tree-ring study 229, *231*
Row 5: 90, *90*, 91, **96**, 97, 113, 116, 142, 144, 149, 157, **158**, 159, 163, 399, 421, 423
angle 158

cross-ties 116
entranceway to platform 112, 122, 158, 164, 423
split oak post at 'threshold' 112, 135, 145, 158, 164, 423
isometric reconstruction (Phase 3) *424*, *425*
partition 135
Power Station 229, 399
sill plate 114, 116
tree-ring study 229, *230*, *232*
walkway 164, 423 (*see also* Rows 4/5)
wattle 'cavity wall' (revetment) 90, 97, 112, 114, 122, 158, 163, 164, 421, 423
Rows 1/2 walkway 117, 120, 126, 131, 139, 163, 164, 421
Rows 2/3 pathway 100, *100*, 101, *101*, 111, 112, 117, 121, 122, 125, *125*, 126, 131, 139, 142, 149, 152, 159, 160, 163, 164, 165, 421, 423
blocking posts 101
as 'ceremonial way' 430
'log layer' (alder logs) 131, 133, 135, 139, 140, 145, 149, 152, 159, 160, 164, 423
sand and gravel 90, 97, 111, 112, 121
Rows 3/4 narrow walkway 96, 101, *101*, 112, 116–17, 121, 122, 123, *125*, 126, 136, 139, 140, 142, 149, 152, 157, 158, 159, 160, 163, 164, 421, 423
Rows 4/5 narrow walkway 122, 126, 144, 160, 163, 421, 423
Runnymede Bridge (Surrey) 283, 290, 291, 429, 433

sacrifices, of skeletons 350, 428
Salix see willow
salt extraction (salterns) 412
Northey 74, 412
Welland Bank 414
same-tree timbers *see under* post alignment
sand, as flooring 375
sand and gravel surfaces *see under* post alignment
sarsen stone, querns *323*, *324*, 325, 326, 327, 329
scabbard plate [273], copper alloy, Iron Age 111, 112, 162, 164, *281*, 282, 292, 423, *424*, 431
scoop, wooden 226, *227*
scrapers, flint 318
scrub land 378, 413
sea level rise 3, 367
Second Drove 36, 403, 404
sedges and sedge fen 367, 380, 395, 400, 401, 402, 404
segmentation 423–6, 429–30
at La Tène 435, 436
see also post alignment, partitions
settlements **405–20**, 429
Neolithic 407
Grooved Ware 25, 26, 32, 49, 50, 398, 400, 407, 409, 411
Bronze Age
Paving Factory site 38
Site O 30, 31, 32
Late Bronze Age/Early Iron Age
Depot (1992) 'settlement compound' *17*, 19, *21*, 23–4, 411, 413
Tower Works 'pit settlement' 18, 29, 33, 34–5, 36, 405, 412, 413, 414

Iron Age 406, 413
  Site O 30, 32
  Vicarage Farm 29, 253, 405, 413, 414
  see also Cat's Water
Late Iron Age/Early Roman, Depot site
    (1997), linear ditches 28, 29
  nucleated 405, 412–13
  see also Gravel Pits
shale see armlet; bracelets
shears, Roman 292, 293
shears and box, Iron Age 281, 282, 292–3,
    297, 301, 306, 427, 431
  wooden box 227–8
sheep, stock management 415, 416, 417;
    see also animal bone
shell see molluscs
Shepperton, axe haft 220, 223–4, 224
shield tab 259, 261, 287, 300, 304, 427, 431
Shinewater Park, Eastbourne (East
    Sussex), post alignment 433–4
shoe buckle, pewter 279, 280
shrines
  brooches from 295
  Romano-British, at Haddenham 348
Site 11: 6, 9, 10–11
  Neolithic mortuary (rectangular) enclo-
    sure 9, 49, 406
  Beaker period roundhouse 9, 71
  Bronze Age farmstead 412
Site O 5, 6, 8, 30–2, 30
  Neolithic/Bronze Age 30, 31, 32, 33, 407
  Iron Age 32
    cereals 413
    ditch 24
    settlement 30, 32, 414
  clay weight 31, 31, 431
  Collared Urn 31, 31
  droveway 31, 32, 411
  field ditches 30, 31, 32, 410, 411
  flint 32
  'late' fields 414
  pottery 30, 31, 32
  settlement, Bronze Age 18, 30, 31, 32,
    412
  trenches 3, 30, 30
Site Q 3, 5, 6, 8, 30, 50–1, 407, 410
  Bronze Age ditches (extension of ditch 1
    or 2) 50
  Neolithic
    'inlet', 50, 406, 409
    mortuary structure and enclosure 50
    multiple burial 50
  Iron Age 32
Smith, R A 7
snails see molluscs
social roles 426, 429–32
  livestock exchange 415, 416
soil micromorphology
  Cat's Water (1990) 39–43, 442–4
  Depot (1992) 17–18, 20–2, 437–42
  Power Station 53–8, 401, 445–7
soils and sediments 382–3, 450
  argillic brown earth 19, 356, 361, 362,
    366, 383
    Cat's Water 41, 42, 43
    Power Station 58
  brown earth 19, 382, 383, 400, 401
    Cat's Water 41, 42
    Power Station 56, 58
  see also buried soils; palaeosols
Soke Metal Detector Club 60

Somerset Levels
  beetles 389
  trackways 432
Sompting axes 287
South-West Fen Dyke Survey 74–5
Spain
  Bronze Age weapons 283
  flesh hook 288, 289
  rivets 290
  spike/punch 290
spear shafts, wooden 224, 225
spearheads, bronze [46–51] 261, 262,
    263, 286–7, 296, 300, 301, 309–10,
    311, 314, 315–17, 428, 431
  Flag Fen [49, 51] 90, 262, 263
    wooden shaft [49] 224, 225
  Newark Road 416
  see also ferrules
spikes 258, 259, 290
  socketed spikes/punches 266, 268, 290,
    297
Springfield cursus (Essex), querns 326
stackstands, Iron Age 47
stock-handling system, Storey's Bar Road
    417–18
stockyards (communal) 72, 409–10,
    415–16, 430
stone objects 321–9; see also axes
Storey's Bar Road 5, 25–6, 27, 406
  Neolithic
    flint 25, 318, 407
    Grooved Ware enclosed settlement 25,
      26, 32, 49, 50, 398, 400, 407,
      409, 411
    pottery 25–6
    radiocarbon dating 391, 392, 393, 397
  alluvium sealing 397
  animal bone 26
  arrowhead 25
  aurochs skull 32, 407
  barrow 23, 25, 26, 408
  Beaker pottery 25
  corner entranceways 417, 420
  cremation 25, 26
  field boundary ditch 411
  fields and ditches 18, 25–6, 27, 410, 411
  paddocks 417
  pottery 253
  radiocarbon dating of pits 26, 391, 392,
    393, 397, 398
  ring-ditch 23, 25–6, 411
  stock-handling system 417–18
  well (W17) 26
Stour river 419
strapends
  pewter (bag-shaped) 272, 273, 291, 295,
    306
  Roman 295
  tin or lead alloy(?) 272, 273, 291, 295
straw
  for animals 414
  as flooring 375
  as roofing 375
streams (relict streams, watercourses) 135,
    162, 165
  Area 8 stream channel 162
  Pleistocene (pre-Flandrian) relict channel
    and Bronze Age use (PS) 50, 57,
    58, 69, 73, 401, 426
  brushwood bundles for crossing 69–70,
    69, 70

sand banks (seasonal?) (PS) 53, 56–7,
    58, 445–6
Site O, natural channels 32
Structural Phases, of post alignment see
    Phases
studs 266, 267–8, 274, 290–1
Stuntney hoard 432
  bucket 227
Switzerland
  axe hafts 223
  metalwork 291, 306, 308
  swords 255–8, 257, 282, 283, 296, 296,
    300–1, 309–15, 427
    blade tip 259, 260
    breaking ('killing') of 310, 427, 428, 432
    Ewart Park 255–6, 257, 283, 301, 310,
      311, 312, 312, 313, 315, 428
    at Fiskerton 433
    hilts [37, 40] 259, 260, 261
    Iron Age iron hilts 279, 280, 292, 297,
      431
    miniature [7] 257, 258, 283, 314, 315
    Wilburton type 60, 255, 257, 283, 300,
      301, 311, 312, 313
    see also chapes; pommels; scabbard plate

tab, tin 272, 273, 291
Taunton Phase 255, 258, 260, 261, 263,
    265, 268, 274, 276, 277, 278, 283,
    300, 302, 304, 304, 305–6, 421
temple, Iron Age, Northey 74, 75, 80
Tetney (Lincs), saltern 412
textiles 431
Thames valley, field systems 419–20
Third Drove 5, 6, 17, 18, 36, 404
  buried soil 50
  fen edge 50–1
  Recycling Facility excavation 6, 30
  Neolithic 30–1, 32, 50
  Iron Age 30, 32, 414
  see also Site O; Site Q
Thorney Site 46 (1977 Northey excava-
    tion) 74
Tilia see lime
tin alloy 268, 270, 291, 300, 302, 306–8
tin objects 269, 270, 271, 272, 273, 291,
    300, 302, 305, 306–8; see also bars;
    beads; pommels; rings; strapends; tab
tongue chapes see chapes
toolmarks see under axes
Tower Works 5, 6, 7, 8, 33–6
  animal bones 34, 35
  buried soil 33, 34–5, 36
  'dark earth' 33, 34–5, 411, 412
  field system (boundary ditches), Bronze
    Age 18, 33, 35, 36, 410, 411, 429
  gravel pits, Bronze Age 18, 33
  'pit settlement' (LBA/EIA) 18, 29, 33,
    34–5, 36, 405, 412, 413, 414
  post-built rectangular building
    (LBA/EIA) 18, 33, 35, 35, 36, 411
  pottery 34, 35, 36, 411–12
  road to, Iron Age 413
  Roman linear ditches 34, 414
trampled areas, post alignment 111, 121,
    122, 159, 160
transverse segment boundary see post
    alignment, partitions
tree clearance see woodland (tree) clearance
tree-ring studies 229–48, 390, 396, 397, 398–9
  chronology 421

Flag Fen 157, 158, 163, 390, 397, 398, 399
Power Station 62, 163, 192, 390, 397, 398, 399
see also same-tree timber *under* post alignment
tweezers, bronze *266*, 267, 291

Ulmus see elm

vegetation and environment 351–81, 430; *see also* pollen
vessels
 hollowed log 226–7, *228*
 metal fragments *266*, 268, 291
Vicarage Farm
 Neolithic droveway 406, *406*
 Iron Age settlement 29, 253, 403, 405, 413, 414
 pottery 253, 411–12
visitor centre *12*, 14–16, *82*

walkways *see* post alignment; Rows 1/2; Rows 3/4; Rows 4/5
WANABE Project 11
watercourses *see* streams
watery deposits
 metalwork 295, 310, 431
 shields 287
wattle bundles, Power Station 69–70, *70*
wattle walls (revetments) 97, 112, 113, 116, 122, 126, 133, 135, 139, 140, 142, 149, 152, *152*, *153*, *155*, 157, **158**, 160, 163, 175, 421
 'cavity walls' 112, 113, 116, 122, 133, 135, 162, 164
 distribution plan *153*
wattlework structure (Area 6B) 167
weeds 32, 352, 367, 403
weevil 389
weight (?loomweight), clay 31, *31*, 431
Welland Bank *2*
 Bronze Age(?) roadway 29
 'dark earth' 36
 enclosure (building), Late Bronze Age/ Early Iron Age 36, 410, 412, 418

field system 412
'inlet' 40
pottery 412
wheeled vehicle ruts 214
wells
 Newark Road, rock-cut (F6) and Iron Age (F1551) 392, 394, 397, *415*, 416
 Storey's Bar Road 26
West Caistor hoard (Norfolk) 291
West Deeping (Lincs) *2*
 stackstands 47
 stockyards and field system 418–19, *419*
West Furze Lake Dwelling 225
wet/dry environments, for finds 427, 430–1
wetland 405
wheat 49
wheel symbol 291
wheels
 tin 272, 273–4, *273*, 291, 306, 308, 427
 wooden 213–14, *214–16*, 427
  associated items (peg, axle, hub) 214–18
white metal objects *270*, 271, 273, *273*, 291, *297*, 300; *see also* beads; discs; foil
Whittlesey 'island' 1, *1*, *3*, 74, 373, 405
wiggle-matching 390, 395, 398, 399
Wilburton *2*
Wilburton Phase 255, 256, 258, 260, 261, 267, 268, 274, 283, 286, 287, 288, 289, **300, 301**, 302–3, 304–5, 306, *306*, 309–10, *311*, 312, *313*, 421
 axe blades 197, 198
 bracelet 88
 swords 60, 255, 257, 283, 300, 301, *311*, 312, *313*
willow (*Salix*) 158, *355*, 356, *358*, *360*, 361, 362, *365*, 366, 367, *372*, 373, *377*, 379, 388, 400, 402, 403, 421
 beaver-chewed 202
 drying out 169
 joints 204, 206
 scoop 226
wood **167–228**

beaver-modified 202–3
dovetails 211, 213–14, *215*
drying out effects 168–9
housing joints 210, *210*
joints 94, 203–4, 211–12
lap joints 209–10, *209*, *210*
mortises 67, 69, 81, 86, 94, 100, 103, *104*, *106*, *107*, 203, 204–8
reduction of timber (splitting) 203, *203*
sampling 167
slots 208, *209*
tenons 208
wear, rot and breakage 167–8
woodchips **175–86**, 188–9, 190–3
 Flag Fen 167–71, **171–86**
 Power Station 53, *54*, *55*, *63–6*, *68*, 167, 168, 169, *185*, **186–93**
wood-free zones 112, 121, 135, **162**
wooden artefacts 212–28, 310
woodland 230, 246, 247, 248, 356, 357, 366, 367, 368–9, 374, 380, 381, 382, 383, 400, 401, 402, 404
 beetles 388
 Cat's Water (1990) 41, 42, 43
 Iron Age 413
 Power Station 57
woodland (tree) clearance 362, 367, 368, 382
 Neolithic 400, 406, 407
 pre-Bronze Age, Cat's Water (1990) 42, 43
 Bronze Age 367, 368, 374, 378, 380, 381
 Power Station 57, 58
woodworking 87, 169, 171, 182–6, 190, 191, 192
 using axes 203, 206
 using bronze axes/tools 169, 182, 184, 186
 using stone axes 169, 182, 183, 184, 186
woodworm 167, 427

Yarnton, fields 419–20
yokes, wooden 218
Yorkshire, axe blades 197, 198, 201

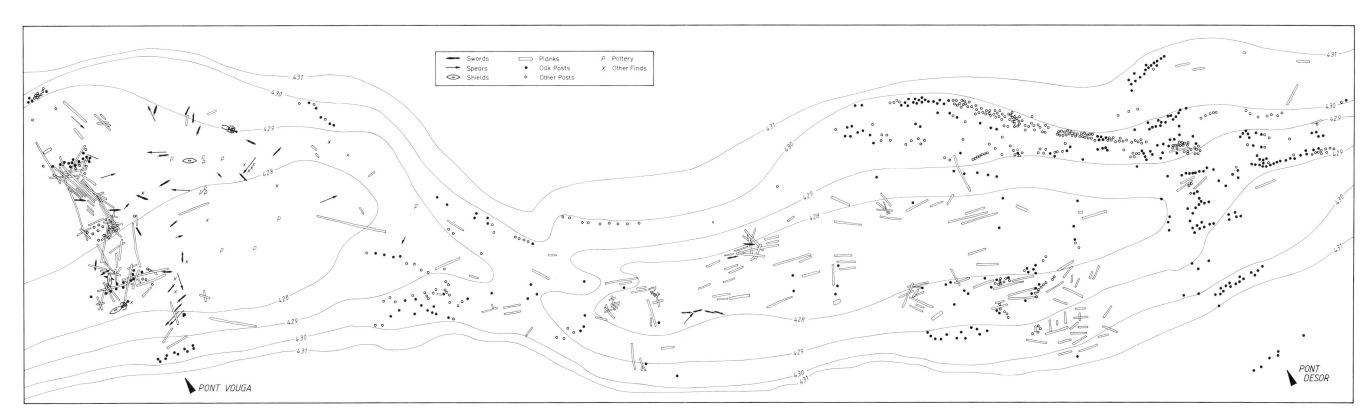

Fig 19.4 La Tène, Switzerland: general plan showing the location of timbers and other finds (after Vouga 1923)

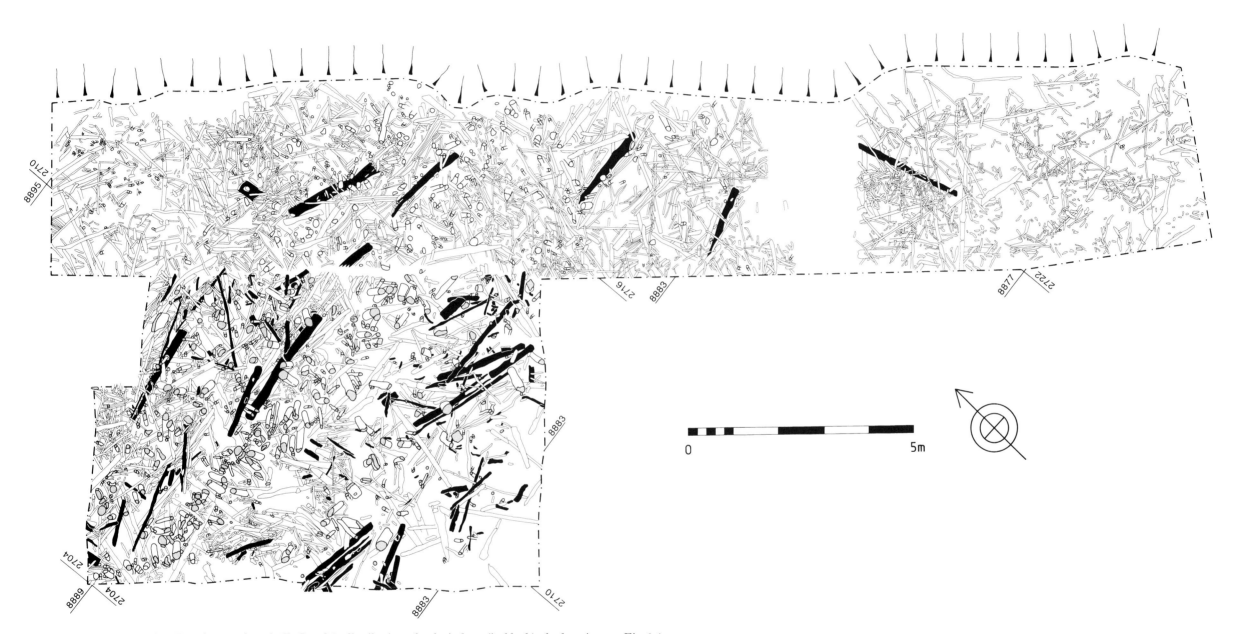

Fig 6.100 Flag Fen, Areas 6A and 6B, Level 3: distribution of oak timbers (in black); for location see Fig 6.1

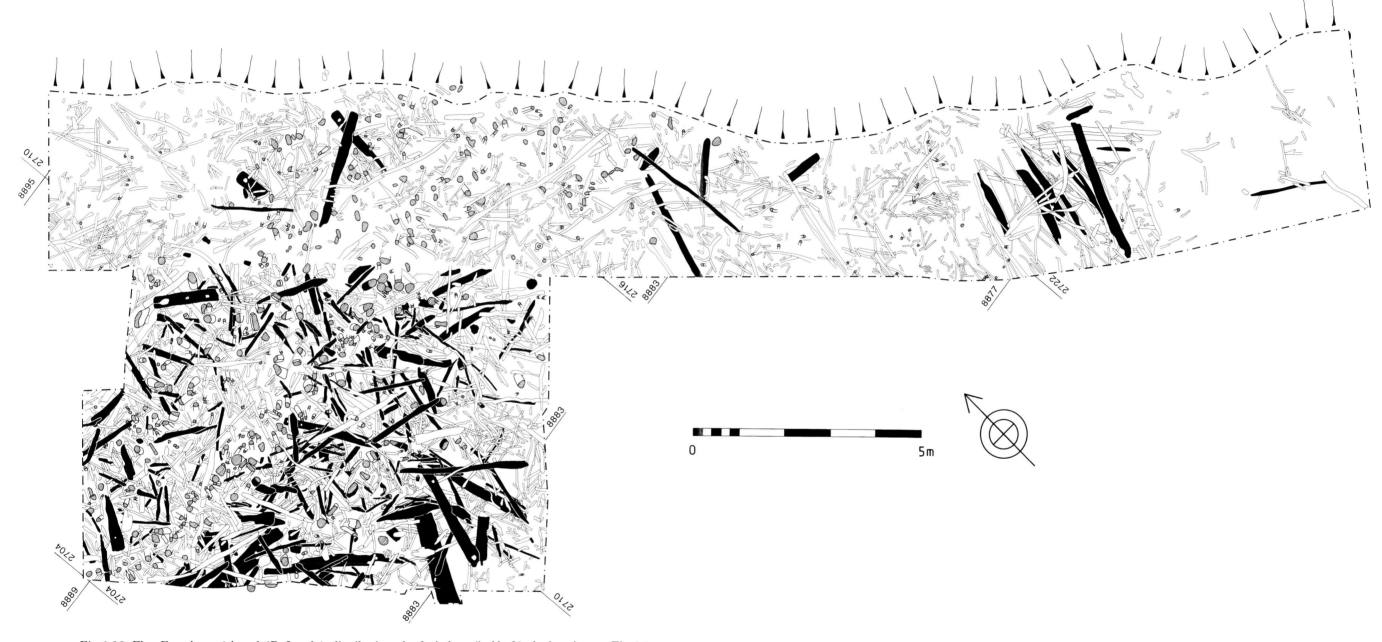

Fig 6.98 Flag Fen, Areas 6A and 6B, Level 1: distribution of oak timbers (in black); for location see Fig 6.1

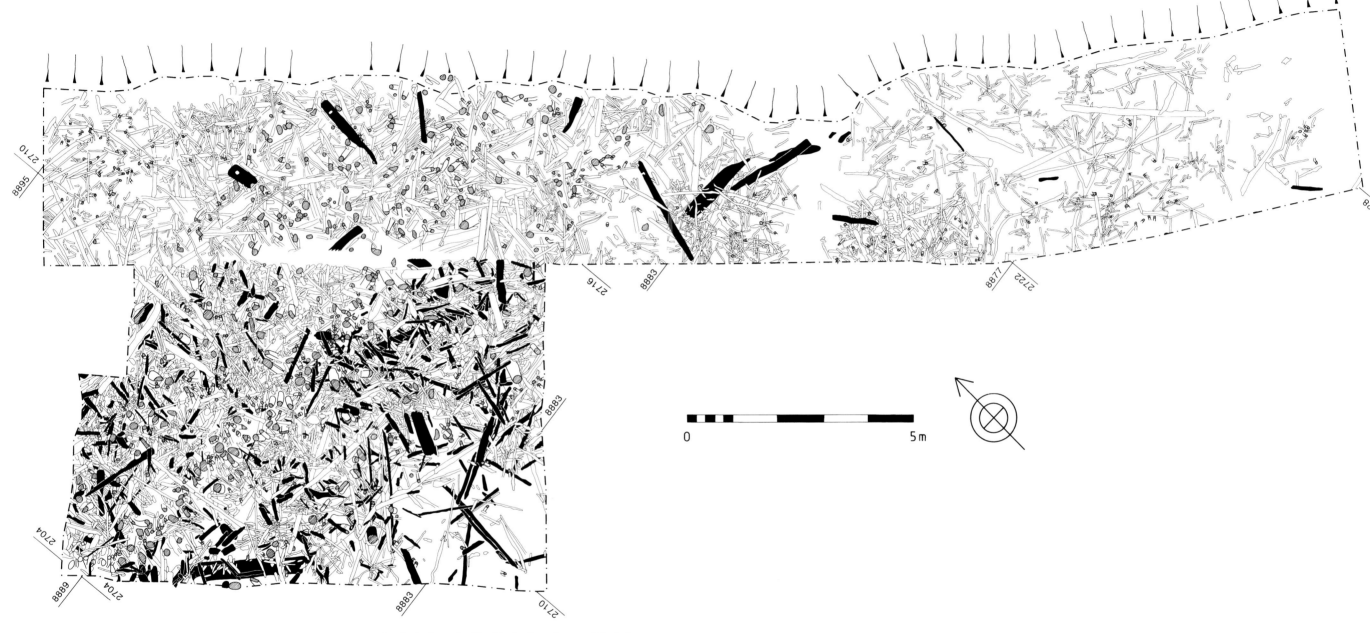

Fig 6.99 Flag Fen, Areas 6A and 6B, Level 2: distribution of oak timbers (in black); for location see Fig 6.1

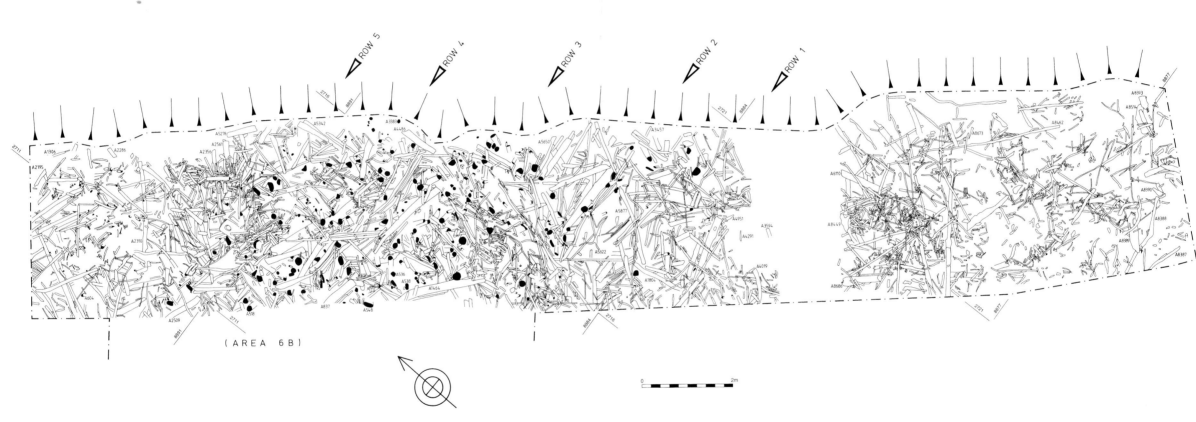

ROW 5　ROW 4　ROW 3　ROW 2　ROW 1

(AREA 6B)

0　　　　　　2m

Fig 6.53 Flag Fen, Area 6A, Level 3: general plan of wood, with principal pieces numbered (for location see Fig 6.52)

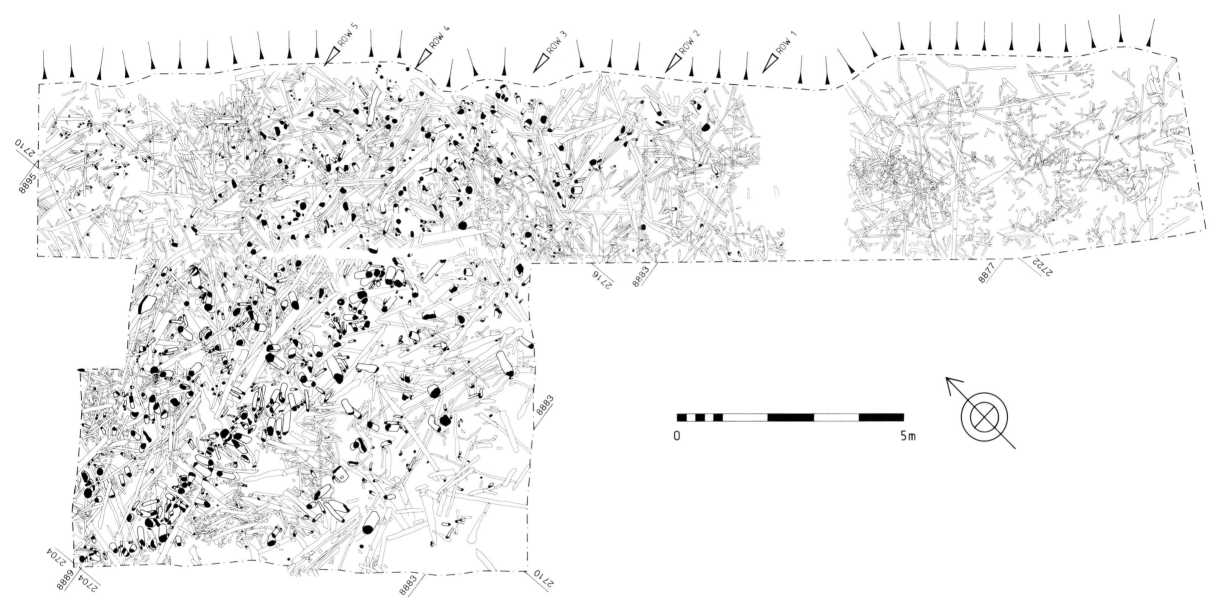

ROW 5
ROW 4
ROW 3
ROW 2
ROW 1

2710
5688
2716
8883
8877
2722
8883
2704
6888
2704
8883
2710

0   5m

Fig 6.52 Flag Fen, Areas 6A and 6B: general plan of wood exposed in level 3 (for location see Fig 6.1)

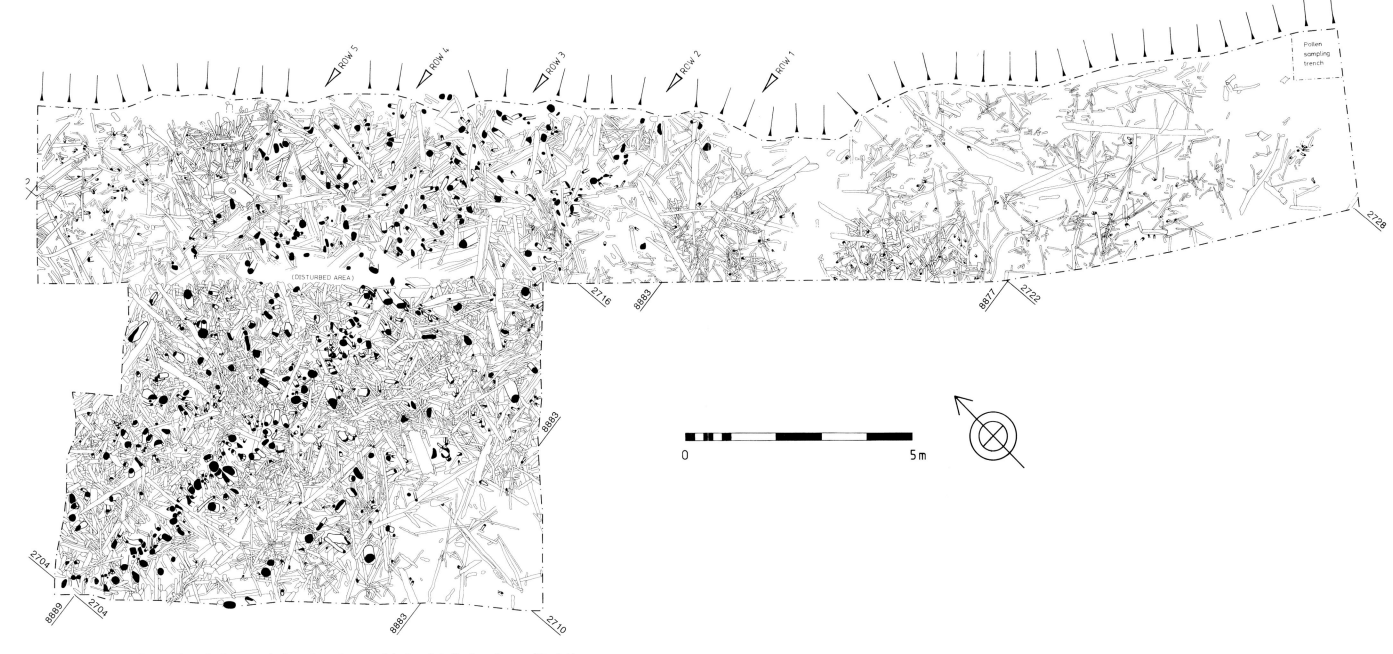

Fig 6.40 Flag Fen, Areas 6A and 6B: general plan of wood exposed in Level 2 (for location see Fig 6.1)

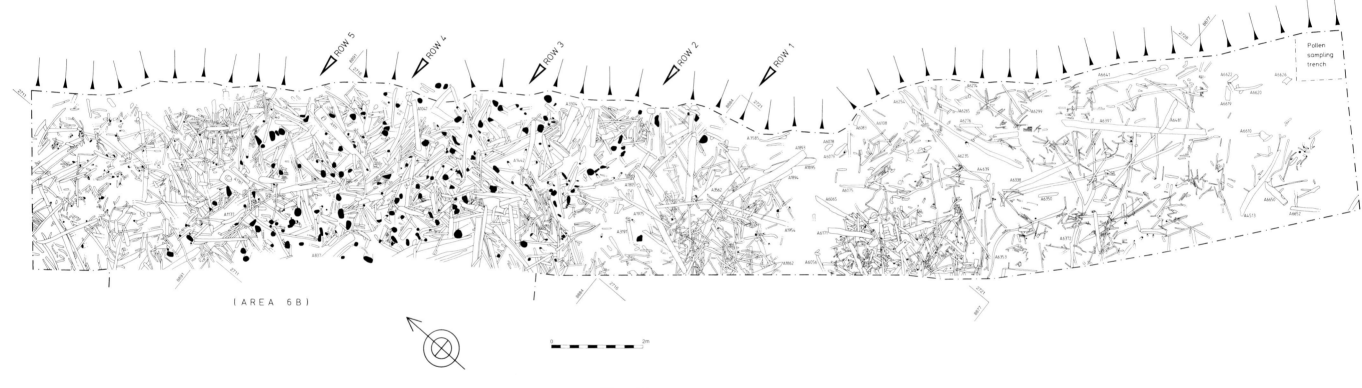

ROW 5 ROW 4 ROW 3 ROW 2 ROW 1

Pollen
sampling
trench

(AREA 6B)

0   2m

Fig 6.41 Flag Fen, Area 6A, Level 2: general plan of wood, with principal pieces numbered (for location see Fig 6.40)